Jim,

With
Admiration
+ Best
Wishes,

Vera

THE
STRANGE SURVIVAL
OF
LIBERAL BRITAIN

VERNON BOGDANOR

THE
STRANGE SURVIVAL
OF
LIBERAL BRITAIN

POLITICS AND POWER BEFORE
THE FIRST WORLD WAR

Biteback Publishing

First published in Great Britain in 2022 by
Biteback Publishing Ltd, London
Copyright © Vernon Bogdanor 2022

ISBN 978-1-78590-762-3

10 9 8 7 6 5 4 3 2 1

A CIP catalogue record for this book is available from the British Library.

Set in Adobe Garamond Pro and Futura

Printed and bound in Great Britain by
CPI Group (UK) Ltd, Croydon CR0 4YY

MIX
Paper from
responsible sources
FSC
www.fsc.org
FSC® C013604

For Sonia with thanks

CONTENTS

Europe, 1895

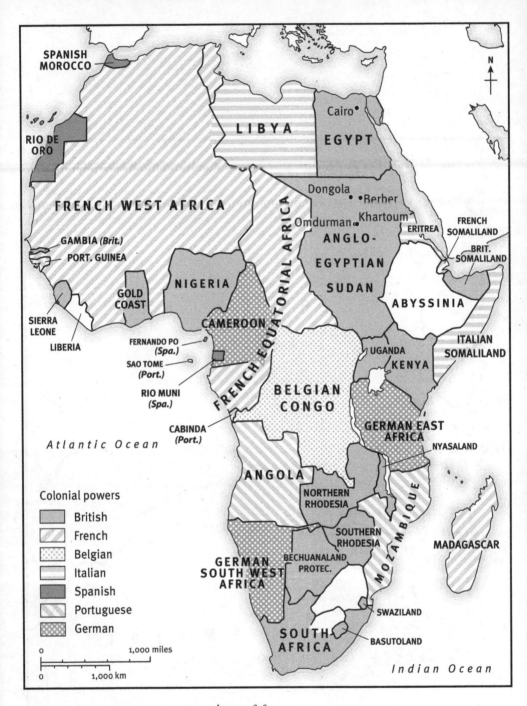

SPANISH
MOROCCO

RIO DE
ORO

FRENCH WEST AFRICA

GAMBIA *(Brit.)*
PORT. GUINEA

GOLD
COAST

NIGERIA

SIERRA
LEONE
LIBERIA

CAMEROON

FERNANDO PO
(Spa.)

SAO TOME
(Port.)

RIO MUNI
(Spa.)

CABINDA
(Port.)

Atlantic Ocean

LIBYA

EGYPT

Cairo

Dongola •Berber

Omdurman Khartoum

ANGLO-
EGYPTIAN
SUDAN

ERITREA

FRENCH
SOMALILAND

BRIT.
SOMALILAND

ABYSSINIA

ITALIAN
SOMALILAND

FRENCH EQUATORIAL AFRICA

UGANDA

KENYA

BELGIAN
CONGO

GERMAN EAST
AFRICA

NYASALAND

ANGOLA

NORTHERN
RHODESIA

SOUTHERN
RHODESIA

MOZAMBIQUE

MADAGASCAR

GERMAN
SOUTH WEST
AFRICA

BECHUANALAND
PROTEC.

SWAZILAND

SOUTH
AFRICA

BASUTOLAND

Indian Ocean

N

Colonial powers

British
French
Belgian
Italian
Spanish
Portuguese
German

0   1,000 miles

0   1,000 km

AFRICA, 1898

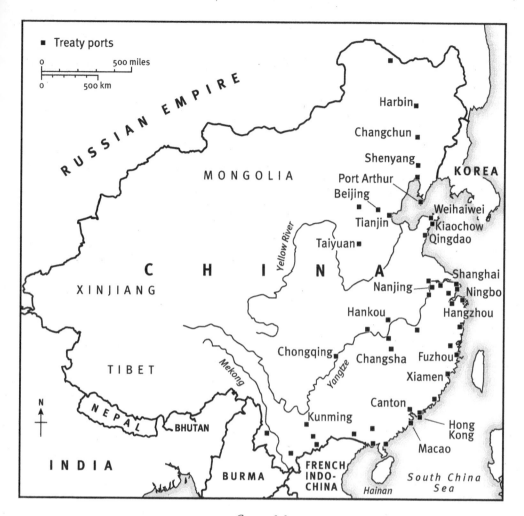

■ Treaty ports

0   500 miles

0   500 km

RUSSIAN EMPIRE

MONGOLIA

Harbin

Changchun

Shenyang

Port Arthur

KOREA

Beijing

Weihaiwei

Tianjin

Kiaochow

Qingdao

Taiyuan

CHINA

Shanghai

XINJIANG

Nanjing

Ningbo

Yellow River

Hankou

Hangzhou

Chongqing

Changsha

Fuzhou

TIBET

Xiamen

Mekong

Yangtze

Canton

Kunming

Hong Kong

NEPAL

Macao

BHUTAN

INDIA

BURMA

FRENCH INDO-CHINA

South China Sea

Hainan

China, 1898

SOUTH AFRICA, 1899

Border of the nine
counties of Ulster

*Atlantic
Ocean*

DONEGAL

LONDONDERRY

ANTRIM   •Larne

THE SIX COUNTIES

U   L   S   T   E   R

TYRONE   L. Neagh   •Belfast

FERMANAGH   ARMAGH   DOWN

MONAGHAN

CAVAN

•Howth
The Curragh •   •Dublin

I R E L A N D

N

0   50 miles

0   50 km

IRELAND

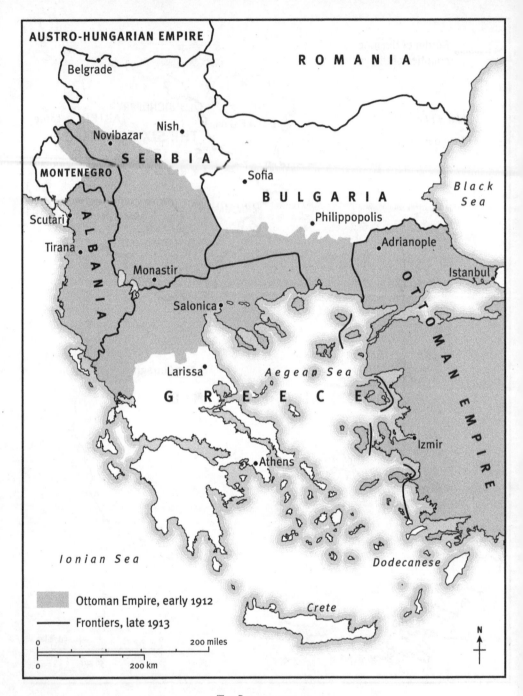

AUSTRO-HUNGARIAN EMPIRE

Belgrade

ROMANIA

Nish

Novibazar

S E R B I A

MONTENEGRO

Sofia

Scutari

A L B A N I A

Tirana

BULGARIA

Philippopolis

Monastir

Adrianople

Black
Sea

Istanbul

Salonica

O T T O M A N   E M P I R E

Larissa

Aegean Sea

G   R   E   E   C   E

Izmir

Athens

Ionian Sea

Dodecanese

Crete

Ottoman Empire, early 1912

Frontiers, late 1913

0   200 miles

0   200 km

N

THE BALKANS, 1912–13

TIMELINE OF MAIN EVENTS

1895

JUNE Liberal government led by Lord Rosebery resigns. Replaced by Unionist coalition comprising Conservatives and Liberal Unionists led by Lord Salisbury.

JULY General election. Unionists win overall majority.

DECEMBER United States President Grover Cleveland threatens war with Britain.
Jameson Raid in South Africa.

1896

MARCH Reconquest of Sudan begins under Sir Herbert Kitchener.

OCTOBER Rosebery resigns Liberal leadership. Sir William Harcourt remains as Liberal leader in the Commons.

1897

Workmen's Compensation Act.

FEBRUARY Sir Alfred Milner appointed British High Commissioner in South Africa.

NOVEMBER National Union of Women's Suffrage Societies (NUWSS) founded.

1898

Irish Local Government Act.

JULY Britain secures 25-year lease of Weihaiwei in China.

SEPTEMBER Reconquest of Sudan completed in Battle of Omdurman.

NOVEMBER France withdraws from Sudan following Fashoda crisis.

DECEMBER Harcourt resigns Liberal leadership in Commons.

1899

	London Government Act.
FEBRUARY	Sir Henry Campbell-Bannerman becomes Liberal leader in the Commons.
MAY	Milner sends despatch to London complaining that Uitlanders in Transvaal are treated like 'helots'.
MAY–JUNE	Bloemfontein conference between Milner and Kruger.
SEPTEMBER	Trades Union Congress (TUC) resolution calls for special congress of labour organisations to secure greater representation of labour in Parliament.
OCTOBER	Boer ultimatum followed by invasion of Cape Colony and Natal. Boer War begins.

1900

| FEBRUARY | Labour Representation Committee formed – renamed Labour Party in 1906. |
| OCTOBER | General election. Unionists returned with overall majority. |

1901

JANUARY	Death of Queen Victoria. Succeeded by Edward VII.
JUNE	Campbell-Bannerman's 'methods of barbarism' speech.
JULY	*Taff Vale* judgment.

1902

	Education Act.
JANUARY	Treaty with Japan. Further treaties in 1905 and 1911.
MAY	Boer War ends with Treaty of Vereeniging.
JULY	Salisbury resigns. Succeeded as Prime Minister by Arthur Balfour.

1903

	Irish Land Purchase Act.
MAY	Edward VII visits Paris.
MAY	Chamberlain's speech in Birmingham calling for inquiry into tariff reform.
SEPTEMBER	Electoral pact agreed between Liberals and LRC (Labour Party).

SEPTEMBER Chamberlain and four free trade ministers resign
–OCTOBER from government.

1904

APRIL Entente with France.

1905

Aliens Act.
Unemployed Workmen Act.
MARCH First Moroccan crisis.
DECEMBER Balfour resigns. Campbell-Bannerman appointed Prime Minister.

1906

Education (Provision of Meals) Act.
Trade Disputes Act.
JANUARY General election. Liberal landslide.
JANUARY–APRIL Conference to resolve Moroccan crisis at Algeciras.

1907

Education (Administrative Provisions) Act, providing for
medical inspection in schools.
AUGUST Convention with Russia.

1908

Old-Age Pensions Act.
APRIL Campbell-Bannerman resigns, dying shortly after. Asquith
appointed Prime Minister.
OCTOBER Austria–Hungary annexes Bosnia–Herzegovina.

1909

Labour Exchanges Act.
Trade Boards Act.
APRIL Lloyd George's People's Budget.
NOVEMBER House of Lords reject Budget.

DECEMBER   *Osborne* judgment – trade union funding to political parties declared unlawful.

1910

JANUARY   General election. Liberals lose overall majority, but they remain in government with support of Irish Party and Labour.

MAY   Death of Edward VII. Succeeded by George V.

JUNE–NOVEMBER Constitutional Conference.

AUGUST   Lloyd George's Criccieth memorandum proposing coalition.

NOVEMBER   George V promises to create peers if necessary to pass Parliament Bill limiting powers of Lords, providing that Liberals win adequate majority in general election.

DECEMBER   General election. Outcome similar to that of January election.

1911

            National Insurance Act.

APRIL   Irish Home Rule Bill introduced into Commons.

JULY   Second Moroccan crisis.

AUGUST   Lords pass Parliament Bill.

AUGUST   Commons resolution providing for payment for MPs.

NOVEMBER   Balfour resigns Conservative leadership. Andrew Bonar Law becomes Conservative leader in Commons.

1912

JULY   Bonar Law's speech at Blenheim Palace supporting Ulster resistance to Home Rule.

SEPTEMBER   Solemn League and Covenant signed in Belfast pledging to establish a provisional government in Ulster after introduction of Home Rule.

1913

            Trade Union Act restoring right of trade unions, under conditions, to contribute funds to political parties.

JANUARY   Paramilitary Ulster Volunteer Force formed.

MAY   Treaty of London ends First Balkan War.

AUGUST   Treaty of Bucharest ends Second Balkan War.

OCTOBER–DECEMBER Asquith and Bonar Law fail to agree compromise solution for Ireland.

NOVEMBER Irish Volunteer Force formed in Dublin.

1914

MARCH Asquith proposes temporary exclusion for Ulster.

MARCH Curragh 'mutiny'.

APRIL Unionist gun-running at Larne.

JUNE Amending Bill introduced providing for temporary exclusion of Ulster from Home Rule.

JULY Buckingham Palace Conference fails to achieve agreement on Ulster.

JULY Nationalist gun-running at Howth. Police shoot demonstrators, killing three and wounding thirty-eight.

JULY Death of Chamberlain.

AUGUST Britain declares war on Germany.

SEPTEMBER Bills to disestablish Welsh Church and provide for Home Rule for Ireland enacted but suspended for duration of war.

PREFACE

In 1895, a young army officer was told by one of the leaders of the Liberal Party, Sir William Harcourt, that 'the experiences of a long life have convinced me that nothing ever happens'.[1] The young officer was Winston Churchill. But since 1895, so Churchill went on, 'nothing has ever ceased happening'. By 1930, Churchill could ask:

> whether any other generation has seen such astounding revolutions of data and values as those through which we have lived. Scarcely anything material or established which I was brought up to believe was permanent and vital, has lasted. Everything I was sure or taught to be sure was impossible, has happened.[2]

Much of this revolution occurred between 1895 and 1914.

These years were formative. The tectonic plates were beginning to shift. The years from 1895 to 1914 saw a transition from one political system to another, from aristocratic rule to mass politics. What had seemed a stable political system was buffeted by new and often unexpected forces.

> Whole classes or strata of society were, in some degree, tasting power for the first time ... In religion, in social relations, in politics, in business, men grown contemptuous of the old ideals were stridently asserting new ones. The former clear objectives were gone, and as yet nothing took their place.[3]

Those hitherto outside the system – trade unionists and women – were clamouring to get in. Hence the revolt of labour and of the suffragettes.

The structure of politics was changing. Traditional conflicts – middle classes versus landowners, Anglican Church versus Nonconformists – receded into the background, to be replaced by new conflicts: between workers and employers and between the sexes. There was also a new ideological conflict. The old liberalism, based on the struggle for the franchise and religious

---

1   Winston Churchill, *The World Crisis: 1911–1918* [1923], Odhams, 1938, vol. 1, p. 14.
2   Ibid.; Winston Churchill, *My Early Life 1874–1908* [1930], Fontana, 1959, pp. 74–5.
3   R. C. K. Ensor, *England 1870–1914*, Clarendon Press, 1936, p. 304.

freedom, was giving way to a new liberalism involving a greater role for the state. As early as 1887, Harcourt, speaking on a Bill introduced by a Conservative government providing for the compulsory acquisition of land for allotments, declared, 'We are all socialists now.'[4]

The years 1895 to 1914 saw a decline of authority: primarily the authority of the aristocracy, dominant politically in 1895 but no longer so in 1914, having been superseded by the new democracy; the authority of employers, challenged by trade unions, was no longer absolute; the authority of men, challenged by suffragettes and a wider feminist revolt, was no longer absolute either. In the nineteenth century, liberals had sought a rational basis for authority to replace one based on precedent or prescription. So, from one point of view, the years 1895 to 1914 may be seen as marking the completion of the liberal programme. But the challenge to authority seemed also to be undermining liberalism itself when it took an extra-parliamentary form, as with militant trade unionists and suffragettes. And it was by no means only radicals of the left who were confronting parliamentary authority. The challenge came also from the right when the House of Lords disputed the legitimacy of the 1906 Liberal government and when Ulster Unionists questioned the legitimacy of Parliament itself. Would liberalism prove tough enough to survive these attacks?

During the years 1895 to 1914, liberalism also faced a global challenge from rising powers with different philosophies. Before 1895, Britain appeared both secure and supreme, the world's only global power. Now her supremacy seemed under threat, and she was to find herself engulfed in foreign complications. The global challenge was not only diplomatic but also military, from the autocracies of the Continent, and difficult for a liberal polity to combat. It was a challenge that was to culminate in war in 1914, a war which would destroy many of the certainties of the Victorian and Edwardian years.

In addition to these political and international problems, Britain, the first industrial nation, faced an economic problem, having lost her industrial leadership to the United States and Germany. In 1896, Germany overtook her in steel production. In 1899, the United States was to surpass her in coal output. 'The old country must wake up', the Prince of Wales, later George V, would declare in December 1901, 'if she intends to maintain her competitive pre-eminence in her colonial trade against foreign competition.'[5] Britain's institutions and industry, so it appeared, needed modernisation. Many asked

---

4 House of Commons Debates, 11 August 1887, vol. 319, col. 140. All references in this book to Hansard debates are to the 3rd series (up to 9 February 1892), the 4th series (up to 10 February 1909) and then the 5th series.
5 *The Times*, 6 December 1901.

whether her aristocratic and seemingly remote and amateurish elite was capable of providing the leadership needed to undertake that transformation.

The years after 1895 saw a reaction against Gladstonian liberalism – the liberalism of the small state at home and non-intervention abroad. The answer to the new challenges, many believed, could be summed up in one word: organisation. There was an emphasis on pushing society in a more collectivist direction and organising the empire into a more united force. Policies designed to achieve this could be summarised in the slogan 'national efficiency'. In 1903, Joseph Chamberlain was to propose that Britain abandon her long tradition of free trade, so initiating a debate on Britain's economic future which resonates even today. The economy came to the forefront of political debate, where it still remains. The political agenda was being transformed. In the nineteenth century, it had seemed that what happened at Westminster and what happened in the economy were in two separate compartments, neither influencing the other. Westminster then had been dominated by constitutional, political and religious issues. In the twentieth century, by contrast, politics and the economy came to be intertwined. And Westminster today remains dominated by socio-economic issues – economic management and social welfare.

The years 1895 to 1914 saw the introduction of 'the social question' into British politics. In 1892, Arthur Balfour, Conservative leader in the House of Commons, observed:

> We all of us see, the blindest of us must see – that a change has come over the character of political controversy, political speculation, and political aspiration during the last generation, which some people describe as Socialism, but ... which ought more properly to be described as a desire for the amelioration of the lot of the great classes of the community ... It is an interesting question to see how far the democratic constitution now firmly established in these islands is going to deal successfully with the social problem with which we are brought face to face.[6]

The next year, the economist Alfred Marshall told the Royal Commission on the Aged Poor that 'the problem of 1834 was the problem of pauperism, the problem of 1893 is the problem of poverty ... that extreme poverty ought to be regarded, not indeed as a crime, but as a thing so detrimental to the State that it should not be endured'.[7] At the turn of the century, William Beveridge

---

6   Blanche E. C. Dugdale, *Arthur James Balfour, First Earl of Balfour, 1848–1905*, Hutchinson, 1936, vol. 1, p. 157.
7   Quoted in Bentley B. Gilbert, *The Evolution of National Insurance in Great Britain: The Origins of the Welfare State*, Michael Joseph, 1966, p. 27fn.

was told by the head of his Oxford college, 'When you have learned all that Oxford can teach you, then one thing that needs doing is to go and discover why, with so much wealth in Britain, there continues to be so much poverty and how poverty can be cured.'[8] Inequalities of income and wealth, so it seemed, were not divinely ordained but could be altered by political action.

In the new century, empirical investigation came to replace the theorising of the philosophers. By 1913, the economic historian R. H. Tawney believed that the social scientists had shown that 'whatever may be true of more primitive communities, the characteristic note of modern poverty is its association, not with the personal misfortunes peculiar to individuals, but with the economic status of particular classes and occupations'.[9] This intellectual shift was given concrete expression in the work of social investigators such as Charles Booth (1840–1916) and Seebohm Rowntree (1871–1954), who for the first time showed, instead of merely asserting, that there were huge disparities of wealth in Britain. Prior to this, so Beatrice Webb believed, 'neither the individualist nor the socialist could state with an approach to accuracy what exactly was the condition of the people of England. Hence the unreality of their controversy.'[10] The social question gave rise to new and disturbing problems for a new generation of politicians – problems which the Liberal government, elected in 1906, began to confront.

These years, then, 1895 to 1914, heralded a new political agenda which still dominates our politics. The problems of the period – economic modernisation, social welfare and inequality, secondary and technical education, a new role for Britain in the world – were complex and difficult and the late Victorians and Edwardians did not succeed in resolving them. But they are also to a large extent the problems of today, and we have not succeeded in resolving them either. We too face dramatic and hitherto unforeseen problems – the long-term consequences of the financial crisis, migration, terrorism, Covid. Will we prove any more successful at dealing with them than the Edwardians were? Will our political system prove as adaptive as it was then? The answers are by no means obvious.

*　　*　　*

When I began to write, I did not do so with the intention of proving any particular thesis, and I did my best to clear my mind of prejudice, but gradually an interpretation began to force itself upon me. It is that the robustness

---

8　Quoted in Asa Briggs, 'Liberal Economics', *The Listener*, 14 June 1956.

9　John Cooper, *The British Welfare Revolution, 1906–14*, Bloomsbury, 2017, p. 25.

10　Beatrice Webb, *My Apprenticeship* [1926], Cambridge University Press, 1979, p. 216.

of Britain's parliamentary and political institutions, with the commitment to rational debate and argument, were powerful enough to carry the country through one of the most turbulent periods of her history; and so make possible the remarkable survival of liberal Britain. My interpretation, therefore, is the direct opposite of that put forward in a classic work by George Dangerfield, published as long ago as 1935, *The Strange Death of Liberal England* – by England, of course, he meant Britain, as was common in that era. The great French historian Élie Halévy also saw the period as one of decadence in the two-volume epilogue to his *History of the English People in the Nineteenth Century*, the first volume of which was published in 1926. A similar view has been put forward more recently by Simon Heffer in his book *The Age of Decadence*, published in 2017. It is for the reader to judge which interpretation best fits the facts.

I have sought to justify my interpretation by analysing how Britain was governed during the years 1895 to 1914, and how the men of government sought to resolve the massive problems which they faced. I have tried to approach their proposed solutions with sympathy for their difficulties. I have often found, upon detailed investigation, that the policies of governments, whether Unionist or Liberal, had more to be said for them than either contemporary critics or modern historians have been willing to concede. I have tried to do justice to the complexity of the problems, and to all sides, especially to points of view that may appear unfashionable today. I have tried, in particular, not to use the advantage of hindsight. Historians must always remember that what for them lies in the past lay, for those they are writing about, in the future. So I have tried to write from the perspective of the past.

Looking at the past in this light, there are many myths about the period, judgements that have become common currency but are almost entirely mistaken. They include:

- That the Boer War was instigated by Britain against a small nation struggling for freedom.
- That in the concentration camps set up during the Boer War, all of the deaths were a result of deliberate cruelty by a regime and better only by degrees than the cruelties inflicted by the Nazis in the 1930s and 1940s.
- That the Aliens Act of 1905 was inherently antisemitic and that political, as opposed to social, discrimination against Jews was widespread.
- That the delay in giving women the vote was almost entirely due to male misogyny.
- That the Labour Party was in a position to overtake the Liberals in 1914.
- That Britain was near to civil war in 1914.

- That, in 1914, the powers, including Britain, sleepwalked into war as suggested by Christopher Clark in his influential book *The Sleepwalkers*.[11]
- That, had Britain kept out of the war, she could have secured an honoured place in the kaiser's European Union, as suggested by Niall Ferguson in his book *The Pity of War*.[12]

These commonly accepted views are, I believe, based on misconceptions – misconceptions which become clear when the evidence is examined dispassionately.

The book falls naturally into two parts. The first deals with the years of Conservative or Unionist dominance from 1895 to 1905. This period saw a diplomatic revolution when Britain hesitantly abandoned isolation, signed a treaty with Japan and came to terms with her hereditary enemy, France. In domestic affairs, the period seemed one of quiescence, but subterranean new forces were seething, and they came to the surface after the Liberal election victory in 1906. That election heralded not just a change of government but a change of regime – the theme of the second part of the book. For, in the years after 1906, the foundations of the modern welfare state were laid. If, therefore, the first period seemed in domestic affairs a continuation of the past, the second appears as a pointer to the future, indeed to much of the twentieth century.

My theme, then, is large but also limited. Total history may be possible, though I have my doubts. But, in any case, I have not attempted it. To have done so would have made the book, already long, quite unmanageable. The decision to restrict the book to just one central theme – the resilience and effectiveness of the British political system in the face of unprecedented challenges – explains, I hope, the omissions. The empire and Ireland are discussed only insofar as they affected the political history of Britain. There is nothing on the intellectual or cultural developments of the period. There is nothing either on social or economic history, and far too little on electoral behaviour and military and naval developments. More important, the British people hardly appear in this book, which is primarily a history of the key decisions determining Britain's future and those who made them – a small and often close-knit political elite. But I hope my readers will bear in mind a warning often given by Aneurin Bevan, founder of the National Health Service, that a country appears very different looking at it from the bottom up than looking at it, as this book does, from the top down.

In his book *Eminent Victorians*, published in 1918, Lytton Strachey wrote

---

11   Christopher Clark, *The Sleepwalkers: How Europe Went to War in 1914*, Allen Lane, 2012.
12   Niall Ferguson, *The Pity of War*, Allen Lane, 1998.

that 'the history of the Victorian Age will never be written: we know too much about it'. That is even more true of the years 1895 to 1914. The monographic literature is vast, and I cannot claim to have consulted more than a fraction of it, nor more than a small number of the numerous private archives dealing with this period. Strachey went on to say that 'ignorance is the first requisite of the historian – ignorance, which simplifies and clarifies, which selects and omits'.[13] If ignorance is a qualification, it is certainly one that I possess. But I doubt if anyone could claim to have read all of the voluminous material on this period. So the picture I have drawn is inevitably incomplete and no doubt over-simplified, but I hope that it is not distorted. Specialists will be appalled at my over-simplifications and superficialities. But it seemed to me worth risking their strictures in order to attempt an overall interpretation of the period.

---

13   Lytton Strachey, *Eminent Victorians*, Chatto & Windus, 1918, p. vii.

HOW BRITAIN WAS GOVERNED

Britain in 1895 seemed at the height of her power. She was the centre of the largest empire the world had ever seen, to which around one-fifth of the world's population belonged and with territories in every continent except Antarctica. 'How many millions of years has the sun stood in heaven?' asked the *Daily Mail* at Queen Victoria's Diamond Jubilee in 1897. 'But the sun never looked down until yesterday upon the embodiment of so much energy and power.'[1] In the same year, the French newspaper *Le Figaro* declared that the Roman Empire had been 'equalled, if not surpassed, by the Power which in Canada, Australia, India, in the China Seas, in Egypt, Central and Southern Africa, in the Atlantic and Mediterranean rules the people and governs their interests'. The Berlin *Kreuzzeitung* regarded the empire as 'practically unassailable'.[2]

But British pride was not directed primarily towards the empire. For the British people believed they had found the solution to the long-standing problem of devising a form of rule which combined both stability and progress. In the years before 1914, they prided themselves on their system of government which they believed was superior to that of other nations. In 1908, an American professor of government at Harvard University, A. Lawrence Lowell, published a two-volume work entitled *The Government of England*. In the preface, he declared:

> The typical Englishman believes that his government is incomparably the best in the world. It is the thing above all others that he is proud of. He does not, of course, always agree with the course of policy pursued ... but he is certain that the general form of government is well-nigh perfect.

Lowell endorsed the verdict of 'the typical Englishman'.

> Measured by the standards of duration, absence of violent commotions, maintenance of law and order, general prosperity and contentment of the people, and by the extent of its influence on the institutions and political

---

1   Quoted in Jeremy Paxman, *Empire: What Ruling the World did to the British*, Viking, 2011, p. 170.
2   Karl E. Meyer, 'An Edwardian Warning: The Unravelling of a Colossus', *World Policy Journal*, Winter 2000/2001, p. 48.

thought of other lands, the English government has been one of the most remarkable the world has ever known.[3]

In Europe, only Britain and Sweden had, in modern times, avoided revolution, invasion, foreign occupation, national liberation, civil war or a coup d'état. 'It is well', Disraeli had declared at Manchester in April 1872,

> to comprehend what is meant by a country not having a revolution for two centuries. It means, for that space, the unbroken exercise and enjoyment of the ingenuity of man. It means, for that space, the continuous application of the discoveries of science to his comfort and convenience. It means the accumulation of capital, the elevation of labour, the establishment of those admirable factories which cover your district, the unwearied improvement of the cultivation of the land, which has extracted from a somewhat churlish soil harvests more exuberant than those furnished by lands nearer to the sun. It means the continuous order which is the only parent of personal liberty and political right.[4]

During the latter half of the nineteenth century, which had seen a wide expansion of the franchise, it had seemed that the middle classes, despite having won the vote, were content to leave government to the traditional rulers, the aristocracy. But that was changing. At the end of the nineteenth century, government was in transition from an aristocratic system to a plutocratic and then a democratic one, a transformation being brought about more smoothly than many had anticipated, and one that was, in one sense, 'a radical venture into new ground, but in another it was profoundly conservative, a continuation of what was good in aristocracy by other means. No other country has made such a transition at such low a price.'[5]

The secret, so it appeared, lay in parliamentary and responsible government. 'For a quarter of a century,' one commentator had written in 1858,

> parliamentary government has been established in this country with greater purity and efficiency than it ever possessed before ... innumerable measures of unequalled public importance have been adopted in rapid succession by the legislature; and while discord has shaken, and despotism subdued, almost every other great nation in Europe, the people of

---

3   A. L. Lowell, *The Government of England*, Macmillan, 1908, vol. 2, p. 507, vol. 1, p. v.
4   *The Times*, 4 April 1872.
5   Simon Peaple and John Vincent, 'Gladstone and the Working Man', in Peter J. Jagger, ed., *Gladstone*, Hambledon Press, 1998, p. 83,

England have never been more heartily attached to their institutions, or more happy at peace among themselves.[6]

'Our system', the Colonial Secretary Joseph Chamberlain told the German Chancellor in 1898, 'was entirely different from that of other nations. It was Parliamentary in a fuller sense.'[7] Parliamentary government, according to A. V. Dicey, one of the first to analyse constitutional conventions, depended upon Parliament's ability 'to appoint or dismiss the executive'.[8] That was what distinguished parliamentary government from other forms.

Britain in 1895 certainly enjoyed parliamentary government in this sense. Parliament was both the legislature of the United Kingdom but it was also the Imperial Parliament, the supreme authority in the empire. The term 'Imperial Parliament' indicated that Britain was undertaking a new experiment, combining imperial rule with a representative system. The Imperial Parliament ruled over peoples such as Australians and Canadians who were represented in their own subordinate Parliaments. But it also ruled over many peoples in Africa and Asia who were not represented at all.

Parliament was composed, as today, of three elements – the queen, the House of Commons and the House of Lords. But their role and functioning were somewhat different from what they were later to become.

THE FRANCHISE AND ELECTORAL SYSTEM

While Britain enjoyed responsible as well as representative government, she did not enjoy democratic government in the sense even of universal male suffrage. Indeed, the suffrage was narrower than in the major Continental states, except for Russia, and narrower than in what were regarded as authoritarian states.

The House of Commons was then, as today, the most influential of the three components, but its predominance in relation to the monarchy and the Lords was not as great as it would become later in the twentieth century. It was elected, not by universal suffrage, but on a restricted franchise which entirely excluded women. This was coming to be perceived as an injustice, and female suffrage had been on the parliamentary agenda ever since the philosopher John Stuart Mill had first advocated it, unsuccessfully, as Liberal MP for Westminster in 1865 in an amendment to the 1867 Reform Bill.

---

6   *Edinburgh Review*, July 1858, p. 219, quoted in Angus Hawkins, '"Parliamentary Government" and Victorian Political Parties, c. 1830–c. 1890', *English Historical Review*, 1989, p. xx.

7   J. L. Garvin, *The Life of Joseph Chamberlain*, Macmillan, 1934–69, vol. 3, p. 263.

8   A. V. Dicey, 'Divisions of Constitutions' [1900], in Dicey, *Comparative Constitutionalism*, vol. 2, ed. J. W. F. Allison, Oxford University Press, 2013, p. 239.

Indeed, the Commons had voted in favour of the principle as early as 1870; and during the following thirty years, there were a number of Commons debates on it. But since neither Conservative nor Liberal governments were prepared to enact it, the issue languished. The new century, however, was to see renewed agitation for female suffrage, but its supporters were divided as to how best to achieve it.

The vote, then, was restricted to men. But Britain was far from enjoying even universal male suffrage. 'I can remember', Harold Macmillan, Prime Minister from 1957 to 1963, reminisced in 1975, 'attending public meetings before the First War, when it was a common practice for the chairman, before calling upon a candidate to answer a question or in reproving a heckler, to use the phrase, "Are you a voter, sir?"'[9] Often the answer was no.

At the end of the nineteenth century, the franchise was regarded not as a right but as a privilege, for which a man qualified by having a stake in the country, symbolised primarily by the ownership or occupation of property. 'You will find', declared the constitutional historian F. W. Maitland in 1888, 'that all through our history the qualification of the voter has depended in some manner or another on his relation to what, loosely speaking, we may call real property.'[10] A man enjoyed the vote not as an individual but as an owner, occupier, lodger, resident or university graduate. The 1867 and 1884 Reform Acts had sought to enfranchise what Gladstone had called the 'capable citizen', 'that is, an employed adult male, with a regular domicile, of some substance, the head of a household with the initiative to get himself registered'.[11] At the end of the nineteenth century, the best indicator of civic competence was believed to be economic competence. So, until 1918, a man was disqualified from the vote if he was in receipt of relief, other than medical relief, from the Poor Law Guardians.

The rules regulating the franchise were extraordinarily complex. The scope of the franchise had been determined by the Reform Acts of 1832, 1867 and 1884. But instead of repealing earlier qualifications, these statutes had incorporated them, so as not to disenfranchise those already enjoying the vote. The result was an untidy patchwork.

The basic qualification for the franchise was the household franchise, but there were various other qualifications, some quite archaic. In consequence, so a Liberal minister claimed, introducing an abortive Reform Bill in 1912, 'the intricacy of our franchise laws is without parallel in the history of the civilised world'.[12]

9   Harold Macmillan, *The Past Masters: Politics and Politicians, 1906–1939*, Macmillan, 1975, p. 28.
10 F. W. Maitland, *The Constitutional History of England* [1888], Cambridge University Press, 1919, p. 352.
11 H. C. G. Matthew, 'Gladstone, Rhetoric and Politics', Jagger, ed., *Gladstone*, p. 214.
12 House of Commons Debates, 17 June 1912, vol. 39, col. 1326.

There were seven ways in which a man could qualify for the vote. The first was the household franchise, provided for by the 1867 and 1884 Reform Acts, granted to adult males occupying a dwelling, as owners or tenants, and contributing towards the rates.

The second qualification was the occupational franchise granted to those owning property or tenants of property valued at £10 per annum or more – equivalent to a little over £1,000 in 2022 – with a residential requirement of at least eighteen months. Around 84 per cent of those qualifying for the vote did so as either householders or occupiers.

The third qualification was ownership of property or land with an annual rent of at least forty shillings a year, after charges had been met. Around 8 per cent of voters qualified under this head, mainly in county constituencies.

The fourth qualification was the lodger franchise for occupiers of lodgings valued at over £10 per annum unfurnished, which tended to exclude poorer voters outside London, where property prices were lower. Around 5 per cent qualified under this head.

The fifth qualification was the service franchise, for which only a small number qualified, giving the vote to those living in or occupying a separate dwelling by virtue of an office, service or employment – for example, bank managers, schoolmasters, railwaymen and caretakers. As Chancellor of the Exchequer in 1902, Charles Ritchie would obtain a service vote thanks to his occupying 11 Downing Street![13] But this qualification was only of importance in the City of London.

The sixth qualification was the university franchise, enjoyed by around 0.6 per cent of men who were university graduates.

The seventh qualification applied to an even smaller percentage – around 0.3 per cent of the electorate – who were freemen in boroughs where this qualification had existed before 1832.[14]

Even so, a man qualified for the vote would not necessarily be able to exercise it. That depended upon being on the electoral register. Not all those who qualified could necessarily achieve this. Indeed, 'the proper keeping of the register', according to one authority writing in 1902, 'which is of such paramount importance for the exercise of the vote, is really a most complicated piece of business. The legislative provisions on the subject are contained in more than a hundred statutes, to which must be added a vast and obscure mass of judicial decisions.'[15] The process of registration was indeed 'so replete with technicalities, complications and anomalies that every obstacle is put

13   Duncan Tanner, *Political Change and the Labour Party 1900–1918*, Cambridge University Press, 1990, p. 100.
14   The various qualifications and numbers of voters qualifying under each head are listed in Neal Blewett, 'The Franchise in the United Kingdom, 1885–1918', *Past and Present*, 1965, p. 32.
15   M. Ostrogorski, *Democracy and the Organisation of Political Parties*, Macmillan, 1902, vol. 1, p. 372.

in the way of getting on, and every facility exists for getting struck off the register'.[16] The British electoral system was, so one MP declared in 1892, a system of 'democracy tempered by registration'.[17]

Electors qualifying under the household, lodger and service franchises required twelve months' possession of this qualification before being eligible for the register. This was compiled every July, but it did not become effective in England and Wales until the January of the following year – in Scotland, in the November of the year in which it was compiled. There could, therefore, be a delay of eighteen months between qualifying for the vote and being on the register. But even when on the register, continued inclusion was by no means automatic. With the lodger franchise, an annual application was necessary, and a lodger would lose his place if he moved residence, even within the same constituency – even if he moved next door. Occupiers, on the other hand, could move from one house to another within the same constituency without losing their vote.

The complexities of registration made it difficult for the citizen to understand how to ensure that he remained registered. Some men were registered to vote in one election only to be excluded from the next or vice versa.[18] Moreover, the intricacies yielded considerable influence to party agents, experts on electoral law, who sought to secure the inclusion of those they believed politically sympathetic, while objecting to those they believed hostile. The process of adjudicating claims for inclusion on the register was often adversarial, dependent on perceived prospects of party advantage. The litigants were the political parties, not the would-be electors themselves.

In consequence of the restricted franchise and complex registration process, it has been estimated that in 1895, only around 63 per cent of adult males were actually on the register, and the proportion varied considerably in different parts of the country. Moreover, the complexities are estimated to have disenfranchised at least 1 million people, particularly from the poorer classes and especially in London.[19] In 1911, just 20.5 per cent of the adult male population of Whitechapel were registered voters, compared with 75.3 per cent in Birmingham.[20]

Those excluded from the franchise included those receiving poor relief (around 5 per cent of the adult male population in 1910 in England and Wales), male domestic servants (around 2.5 per cent), soldiers living in barracks (just over 1 per cent), bachelors living with their parents and those

16 *Rogers on Elections*, cited in Blewett, 'Franchise', p. 28.
17 Charles Parker MP, House of Commons Debates, 25 May 1892, col. 1814, cited in ibid., p. 43.
18 Martin Pugh, *Electoral Reform in War and Peace, 1906–18*, Routledge & Kegan Paul, 1978, p. 4.
19 Blewett, 'Franchise', p. 36.
20 Paul Thompson, *Socialists, Liberals and Labour, The Struggle for London 1885–1914*, Routledge & Kegan Paul, 1967, p. 131.

whose occupation required frequent movement from one constituency to another, which was almost certainly the largest group of the excluded – probably just under 10 per cent of those excluded belonged to this category.[21] Others not on the register would include lodgers failing to meet the registration requirements and those who had not bothered to seek registration. For it was the duty of the elector, not of the state, to ensure that his name was on the register.

The various excluded groups had little in common, and by no means comprised only those of a lower social class. On 30 August 1902, a school teacher wrote to *The Times*, complaining that, though a graduate, he had never been able to vote in a constituency election, since his very success as a teacher involved regular changes of residence. 'It is a common saying that many respectable people are disenfranchised from this cause, although the slums, which move little, are not.' One estimate suggests that before 1914, working-class voters comprised up to 76 per cent of the electorate.[22]

But even those qualified and on the register might not be able to exercise their right to vote, since before 1914 many constituencies were uncontested. 'It was almost thought rather bad form', Harold Macmillan reminisced, 'to contest a constituency where the result was obvious and the Member had been long installed.'[23] The norm until 1922 was for over 100 seats to remain uncontested.[24] In 1895, 189 out of 670 constituencies were unopposed (28 per cent) and in 1900, 243 (36 per cent).

But if many men were unable to vote, there were some who enjoyed more than one vote. For there was extensive plural voting. There were three types of plural voters.

Male university graduates and, in universities other than Oxford and Cambridge, university teachers as well – in total around 44,000 – enjoyed, in addition to a constituency vote, a vote for university constituencies, provided they had paid the fees needed to keep their names on the books. But electoral registers in the universities seem to have been somewhat inefficient. At Oxford, in default of other information, 'it was customary to leave names on the register for eighty years after matriculation before assuming the death of the elector'.[25] In 1895, the universities returned nine MPs to the Commons – Oxford, Cambridge and Dublin two each, London one, Edinburgh & St Andrews one and Glasgow & Aberdeen one. These university constituencies

21 S. Rosenbaum, 'The General Election of January 1910, and the Bearing of the Results on Some Problems of Representation', *Journal of the Royal Statistical Society*, May 1910, pp. 476–7.
22 Tanner, *Political Change and the Labour Party*, p. 119fn.
23 Blewett, 'Franchise', p. 30.
24 H. J. Hanham, *Elections and Party Management: Politics in the Time of Disraeli and Gladstone*, Longmans, 1959, p. 197.
25 D. E. Butler, *The Electoral System in Britain since 1918*, 2nd edition, Clarendon Press, 1963, p. 152fn.

were much smaller than territorial ones. Oxford had around 6,000 gradu-ates, Cambridge nearly 7,000 and Dublin just 4,500. In these constituencies, the ballot was not secret, most votes were given by a proxy, but graduates could also vote by post or by word of mouth.[26] MPs sitting for university constituencies had to be graduates of the university they were representing. Between 1885 and 1914, the universities returned Unionists – that is, Con-servatives or Liberal Unionists allied to the Conservatives – in every general election except for 1885, when a Liberal had been returned for London Uni-versity. Many elections in university constituencies were uncontested. There was no contest at Oxford or Trinity College Dublin between 1885 and 1914. At Cambridge, there was just one contest in 1906, but all the candidates were Unionists.

The second type of plural voter was the borough freeholder in England and Wales who enjoyed a second vote in the county constituency embracing the borough where he lived.[27]

The third type was the man owning a house in more than one county constituency, or a business with a rateable value of over £10 in a constituency other than that in which he lived. But no one could vote more than once in the same constituency. A well-to-do occupier could give his sons a £10 occupational vote by claiming that they were joint occupiers; he could also make sure that his lodgers voted. A labourer whose house would probably not be worth £10, let alone the £20 needed to make one of his sons a joint occupier qualifying for the franchise, could not do the same. 'We give one vote', Lloyd George told the National Liberal Federation at Leicester in 1898, with typical exaggeration,

> or probably no vote at all, to the man who handles the plough, and ten to the man who handles the hunting-whip ... one vote to the busy bee, and ten to the devouring locust ... It is not the soil of the country, but the soul, which we want represented in the House of Commons.[28]

Until 1918, voting took place not in a single day but over a period of around a month. Thus, property owners could, if they wished, travel to a number of constituencies to exercise their plural vote; the development of motor transport in the early twentieth century greatly helped the plural voter. It was alleged that in one of the elections of 1910, a septuagenarian voter sped by

---

26 Lowell, *Government of England*, vol. 1, p. 221. See also T. Lloyd Humberstone, *University Representation*, Hutchinson, 1951.

27 Except in Bristol, Exeter, Norwich and Nottingham – which were regarded as counties in their own right.

28 John Grigg, *Lloyd George: The Young Lloyd George* [1973], HarperCollins, 1997, p. 215.

car to six widely separated constituencies in one day.[29] Conservative Central Office estimated that around 2,000 men had four or more votes. Joseph Chamberlain, it appears, enjoyed six votes, and claimed to know someone who enjoyed twenty-three. In a debate in the Commons on 14 May 1906, one man was alleged to enjoy thirty-seven votes, while in January 1910, two brothers between them apparently cast forty-five votes.

It is impossible to determine the total number of plural voters, but the probability is that there were between 450,000 and 475,000 – roughly 6 per cent of the electorate.[30] In Campbell-Bannerman's papers, in notes for a speech on electoral reform, it is stated:

> There are about 600,000 electors in London of whom from ⅓ to ⅙ are probably disenfranchised on account of the registration and residential qualifications ... While the poor man is handicapped at every point in the registration system, the property voter – the burgher – is made to count for anything from one vote up to a dozen.[31]

Plural voting helped primarily the Unionists. In the January 1910 election, in sixty-nine English county divisions, the plural vote was larger than the Unionist majority. Forty-one of these constituencies were Unionist gains. In them, the total Unionist vote was just under 80,000, but there were nearly twice as many plural voters – at least 156,000. In the City of London constituency, there were 3,865 inhabited houses but 23,500 plural voters.[32] After the January 1910 general election, resulting in a hung parliament, Prime Minister H. H. Asquith estimated that the number of plural voters was greater than the Unionist majority in seventy-eight county constituencies.[33]

In a speech at Bath in November 1911, after the Liberals had promised to introduce a Bill providing for adult male suffrage and the abolition of plural voting, Lloyd George lashed out at the unfairness of the system, declaring:

> Liberalism ... is getting tired of appealing for justice to packed juries, whether at the polling booths or at the courts ... If in a commercial enterprise anybody reckons his assets three times over – well, he is guilty of a fraud, and I say that if a man votes three times over by this process, he is a fraud on the democracy.

29 Neal Blewett, *The Peers, the Parties and the People: The General Elections of 1910*, Macmillan, 1972, p. 476.
30 Tanner, *Political Change and the Labour Party*, p. 100. Chapter 5 of this book gives an excellent account of the complexities of the electoral framework at the beginning of the twentieth century.
31 David Morgan, *Suffragists and Liberals: The Politics of Woman Suffrage in England*, Basil Blackwell, 1975, p. 45.
32 House of Commons Debates, 1 April 1901, vol. 15, cols 1600–1601.
33 In a speech at Oxford, 18 March 1910, cited in Edward Porritt, 'Barriers Against Democracy in the British Electoral System', *Political Science Quarterly*, 1911, p. 8.

As for the university seats, 'no constituency in the land turns out narrower, more bigoted or more fierce partisans'. The other anomalies were equally unfair. 'All these dodges', Lloyd George concluded, 'have just one basis, and that is a fundamental distrust of the people.'[34]

The electoral system, then, was undoubtedly biased against the less well off and against the Liberals. Property qualifications and plural voting gave the wealthy more votes than their numerical strength would have entitled them to. Even so, the Liberals probably exaggerated their effect. Of constituencies where the property vote was over 40 per cent, the Liberals won nearly half of the seats between 1886 and 1910.[35] And, although some of the very poor were excluded, no major class or section of the community was completely excluded, except for women. Amongst the working classes, the better off, and in particular trade unionists, were more likely to have the vote than poorer sections, since they would be more likely to enjoy job security and a settled residence. There was also a generational effect. Those aged twenty-one to thirty in working-class constituencies were more likely to be disenfranchised than their elders, since they were more likely to be living with their parents or in lodgings. This was perhaps the age group in the working class most likely to identify with the new Labour Party.[36]

In 1908, Professor Lowell of Harvard summed up 'the present condition of the franchise' as 'historical, rather than rational'.

> It is complicated, uncertain, expensive in the machinery required, and excludes a certain number of people whom there is no reason for excluding, while it admits many people who ought not to be admitted if anyone is to be debarred. But the hardship or injustice affects individuals alone. No considerable class in the community is aggrieved.[37]

For this reason, there was no mass pressure for reform as there had been before 1832, 1867 and 1884; and for all its weaknesses, it is not unreasonable to conclude with one commentator that it was 'roughly representative' – though only of men.[38] The electoral system needed tidying up rather than radical reform and the impetus to tidy up was much weaker than that behind the great reform movements of the nineteenth century. In 1909, Philip Snowden, one of the leaders of the Labour Party, declared that he had never

---

34 *The Times*, 25 November 1911.
35 Charles Seymour, *Electoral Reform in England and Wales: The Development and Operation of the Parliamentary Franchise, 1832–1885*, Yale University Press, 1915, p. 481.
36 Michael Childs, 'Labour Grows Up: The Electoral System, Political Generations and British Politics, 1890–1929', *Twentieth Century British History*, 1995.
37 Lowell, *Government of England*, vol. 1, pp. 213–14.
38 Pugh, *Electoral Reform*, p. 4.

been questioned about male suffrage in fifteen years of addressing public meetings. 'By the early twentieth century the franchise seems to have become a politician's issue rather than one that stirred the population at large.'[39]

If the franchise was biased towards the well-to-do, candidatures were even more so. Indeed, without wealth it was hardly possible to entertain parliamentary ambitions. When Anthony Trollope's Phineas Finn first thought of standing for the Commons, his father countered that such a 'proposition, coming from so poor a man, was a monstrosity'. And his political career was to be ruined by lack of money. Yet Phineas had an allowance of £150 a year, three times the income of the average worker. Before 1918, a candidate had to cover not only his own but also the electoral expenses of the returning officer for his constituency. In 1908, the cost of a contested election was estimated at being between £500 and £1,000, and the annual outlay for purposes of registration and nursing a constituency at between £400 and £500.[40] Some MPs were also asked to pay for an election agent to relieve the constituency association of financial burdens. In addition, candidates were expected to contribute to constituency party expenses, as well as entertaining and contributing to various good causes. The novelist Rider Haggard, Unionist candidate for Norfolk East in 1895, declared:

> From the moment a candidate appears in the field he is fair game and every man's hand is in his pocket. Demands for 'your patronage and support' fall on him, thick as leaves in Vallombrosa. I remember that I was even pestered to supply voters with wooden legs! Why should an election in a county cost, as this one did, something over £2,000 in all?[41]

James Bigwood, Conservative MP for Brentford from 1886 to 1906 and unopposed from 1892, claimed to have spent £50,000 on his constituency.[42] So a rich man was worth more to a constituency than someone less well-to-do.

An ex-Liberal MP declared that 'we no longer bribe, we subscribe'. One unsuccessful Conservative candidate wrote of a 'cheque book system' of election and a Conservative commentator complained in 1909 of the idea which 'pervades the upper regions of the Tory Party that politics always have been, and always ought to be, a career reserved for the amusement of the well-born

39 House of Commons Debates, 19 March 1909, vol. 2, col. 1384; Pugh, *Electoral Reform*, p. 29.
40 Lowell, *Government of England*, vol. 2, pp. 48–9.
41 H. Rider Haggard, *The Days of My Life*, Longmans, Green & Co., 1926, vol. 2, p. 115.
42 John Vincent, ed., *The Crawford Papers: The Journals of David Lindsay, Twenty-Seventh Earl of Crawford and Tenth Earl of Balcarres, 1871–1940, during the years 1892 to 1940*, Manchester University Press, 1984, pp. 40, 59. These papers present an unrivalled picture of Conservative high politics during the period.

and the wealthy'.[43] But the Liberal Party appeared more willing than the Conservatives to finance impecunious candidates, and, between 1910 and 1912, 'many unknown men without a big balance got their first chance in political life' through the Liberal Chief Whip.[44] Once elected, an MP would have to provide for his maintenance, since payment for MPs was not instituted until 1911; while a minister would need to spend even more money than a backbencher to entertain and preserve his social position.

The Irish Parliamentary Party had sought to resolve these problems by paying a salary, essential if the small traders and farmers on whom the party relied could stand for election and sit in the Commons, and it used payment of members to enforce discipline. For, in return for the salary, candidates had to sign a letter pledging themselves not publicly to oppose, either inside or outside Parliament, any party decision, even if it went against his constituency's interests, and to resign if a majority of MPs thought the pledge had been broken. 'The sovereign rights of the constituencies', declared John Dillon, one of the party's leaders in December 1900, 'is a doctrine that strikes at the root of discipline and unity in the Irish party.'[45] The pledge was in the following form:

> I pledge myself that in the event of my election to parliament, I will sit, act and vote with the Irish parliamentary party and if, at a meeting of the party convened upon due notice specially to consider the question, it be determined by resolution ... supported by a majority of the Irish party, that I have not fulfilled the above pledges, I hereby undertake to resign my seat.[46]

Working men too sought representation in the Commons. After the 1867 Reform Act, giving the vote to many working men in towns, some trade unions began to sponsor MPs. In 1874, two such MPs were returned, both miners (it was easier for miners than for most other trade unionists to secure such representation, owing to their geographical concentration). In 1900, the Miners' Federation of Great Britain set up a centralised fund, to which all members contributed, to sponsor candidates supporting the Liberals, known as the 'Lib-Labs'. And, in 1893, the Scottish socialist James Keir Hardie had played a leading role in helping to form a new party with a socialist constitution, the Independent Labour Party (ILP), whose candidates were eligible for

---

43 Arthur A. Baumann, 'Money and Brains in Politics', *Fortnightly Review*, October 1909, p. 600; G. W. E. Russell, *Social Silhouettes*, Smith, Elder & Co., 1906, p. 127.
44 Blewett, *Peers, Parties and People*, pp. 280, 273, 281.
45 F. S. L. Lyons, *The Irish Parliamentary Party, 1890–1910*, Faber & Faber, 1951, p. 42fn.
46 Ibid., p. 143fn.

party funding if they, like the Irish, committed themselves in writing to supporting the party programme and acting in accordance with party decisions.

But otherwise, entry into the Commons was restricted to those with means.

*   *   *

The 1884 Reform Act had been accompanied by a Redistribution Act in 1885, which, for the first time, established numbers of electors rather than communities as the basis for representation. The basic principle was one constituency for every 54,000 people. More important, the single-member constituency became the norm, whereas, before 1884, the two-member constituency had been predominant. Between 1867 and 1884, just 200 of the 658 MPs had been elected in single-member constituencies. But after 1884, only twenty-seven two-member constituencies remained – twenty-three boroughs, the City of London and three university constituencies (Oxford, Cambridge and Dublin). All other MPs were elected in single-member constituencies.

There were many debates in Victorian and Edwardian times on the proper qualification for the vote. But, arguably, the electoral system – first past the post in mainly single-member constituencies – was of greater importance in determining the character of governments. The system was often thought to be of great antiquity. But, in reality, it had been agreed in inter-party meetings as recently as 1884. It reinforced a two-bloc system and was a disincentive to party fragmentation. It militated, in particular, against a centre party such as might have been constructed through an alliance between Liberal Imperialists and Unionist free traders at the beginning of the twentieth century. Only the Labour Party managed to establish itself as a new party during this period, and that was because it enjoyed concentrated support in some working-class constituencies; but Labour, as we shall see, was to depend for its survival on an electoral agreement with the Liberals.

In Ireland, the electoral system sustained one-party dominance, giving the Nationalists almost every seat outside Ulster and the Unionists a monopoly of seats in the Protestant areas of Ulster. Sizeable minorities were excluded from representation – Unionists outside Ulster and Liberals in the whole of Ireland. After the 1885 election in which no Liberals were returned in Ireland, the O'Conor Don, a leading Liberal, wrote:

> This is the result of the single-seat constituencies without provision for minority representation. No one that knows anything about Ireland can maintain that this is a true representation of the feelings of the country.

One necessary consequence of the present representation is that every Catholic who wishes to have any voice or influence in the Legislature or government of the country must join the Nationalists, and it seems to me that it will be next to impossible to govern Ireland constitutionally against the will of 86 per cent of the representation.[47]

This was to prove an all too accurate prophecy.

In 1884, it had been widely believed that single-member constituencies of roughly equal size would produce accurate representation both of majorities and minorities, and there was little interest in alternative systems such as proportional representation. In 1885, Beatrice Webb, after attending a meeting of the Proportional Representation Society, established in the previous year, declared that 'the subject ... is at present a dead one'.[48] Gradually, however, it came to be seen that the system did not in fact yield accurate representation, and that it generated landslides for the major parties on very small swings of the vote. In 1895, for example, the Unionists – the Conservative and Liberal Unionist coalition – won 411 out of 670 seats in the Commons on 49 per cent of the vote, and in 1900, they won 402 seats with just over 50 per cent of the vote. By 1906, the pendulum had swung, and the Liberals benefited disproportionately, winning 399 seats on just over 49 per cent of the vote. The Unionists with 44 per cent of the vote won just 157 seats.

In 1908, the Liberals, though sceptical of electoral reform, appointed a Royal Commission on Electoral Systems. It concluded on the working of the electoral system established in 1885:

Whether the authors of the Bill of that year did or did not believe that the single-member constituency would secure a general correspondence between the support in votes and the representation of the two great parties, such a belief was no doubt widely held at the time. It has proved to be unfounded. Majorities in the House have since shown a very great, and at the same time variable, disproportion to majorities in votes, and there is nothing in the system to warrant the belief that such exaggerations will not recur.[49]

47 G. P. Gooch, *Life of Lord Courtney*, Macmillan, 1920, p. 245.
48 Norman MacKenzie, ed., *Letters of Sidney and Beatrice Webb*, Cambridge University Press, 1978, vol. I, p. 33. The school boards, however, established by the 1870 Education Act, were elected under the cumulative vote system, whereby each elector had as many votes as there were seats in multi-member constituencies, and could cumulate votes on a single candidate if they wished. Voters could 'plump' all of their votes for one candidate. This method was generally believed to encourage sectarian divisions and 'faddists'. The experiment ended in 1902 when local authorities replaced the school boards as education authorities in England and Wales. See Vernon Bogdanor, *The People and the Party System: The Referendum and Electoral Reform in British Politics*, Cambridge University Press, 1981, pp. 99–101.
49 Report of Royal Commission Appointed to Enquire into Electoral Systems, Cd 5163, 1910, para. 125.

In evidence to the Commission, James Parker Smith argued that it was not fortuitous that small shifts in votes led to large shifts in seats, and he put forward a 'cube law'. This law stated that, if the ratio of votes between two parties is A:B, the ratio of seats would be A cubed: B cubed. In its report in 1910, the Commission recommended the alternative vote system.[50] But it appeared at an unpropitious time, three days after the death of Edward VII and in the midst of the crisis over the House of Lords, and was generally ignored. Asquith was unsympathetic to reform, as Gladstone had been, and as were most of the radicals in the Liberal Party. In 1906, one Liberal had written to the secretary of the Proportional Representation Society to confess:

> I find no zeal for PR even among the Members who consented to back our Bill [for reform] and a large amount of deliberate opposition among Liberals. Many Liberals also avow that they want the system of large majorities whichever way the balance may go. They hold that small majorities would make weak ministries.

That opinion did not seem much altered even with the hung parliaments of 1910. Asquith was prepared, in 1912, to accept proportional representation for the proposed Irish Parliament, but he insisted that he was 'not an adherent of or even a convert to the principle of proportional representation as applied to popular elections in this country'.[51]

The alternative vote would have prevented the Labour/Liberal progressive vote from being split, but most Liberals clearly did not believe that Labour posed enough of a challenge to make it a priority. Unionists were also generally unsympathetic. They sought a majority of their own, not coalition with any other group. Such pressure as there was for reform came from minority groups, for example, the Unionist free traders. For such groups, *The Times* complained on 16 May 1910, 'There is the guillotine inside the House if they speak their minds. There is outside the House another guillotine in our electoral system to prevent them entering.' The Labour Party was divided, but Ramsay MacDonald was opposed, believing that Labour would eventually become a majority party and would then benefit from the system. The Fabians were against reform as militating against effective government. Indeed, Clifford Sharp, shortly to become the first editor of the *New Statesman*, wrote in 1912 that the British electoral system was 'on the whole, the most perfect piece of representative machinery which has yet been created anywhere in the world'.[52]

---

50 One member of the Commission recommended the single transferable vote method of proportional representation.
51 House of Commons Debates, 30 October 1912, vol. 43, col. 507.
52 Quoted in Andrew Chadwick, *Augmenting Democracy: Political Movements and Constitutional Reform During the Rise of Labour, 1900–1924*, Ashgate, 1999, p. 176.

Until 1944, there was no permanent machinery to redistribute constituencies in accordance with population movements. After 1885, with population movement from the inner cities to the suburbs and the countryside, the inner cities came to be over-represented. Ireland, whose population was almost halved, due to famine and emigration, from a peak in 1845 of around 8,295,000 to around 4,750,000 in 1891, was also grossly over-represented. Redistribution in 1885 had taken insufficient account of this decline in population, and politicians were chary of intervening, fearing to add to Irish grievances. A Committee on Redistribution of Seats, reporting in 1906, proposed various schemes, each of which would have cost Ireland at least twenty seats.[53] With redistribution in strict proportion to population, Ireland would have lost thirty seats, England would have gained around twenty, Scotland would have gained one, while Wales would have lost three.[54] Near the end of their term of office in 1905, the Unionists were intending to propose redistribution, but the Irish complained that this would violate Article 4 of the 1800 Act of Union, allotting 100 constituencies to Ireland, which they alleged was in the nature of a compact or treaty for all time and could not be reduced without the consent of Irish MPs. So the over-representation of Ireland continued.

In the United Kingdom as a whole, by 1910, there was one MP for every 62,703 inhabitants; but, while in England there was one MP for every 66,971, in Ireland, an MP represented on average 44,147.[55] There were gross discrepancies in constituency size. By 1910, a vote in Kilkenny was worth twenty times the value of a vote in Romford.[56] In 1911, the smallest constituency in the country, Newry, in Ireland, contained a population of 12,841, whereas the population of Romford was 312,804, while Durham, the smallest constituency in England, had a population of just 15,986.[57]

*　　*　　*

The system in 1895 now appears as a halfway house between the pre-1867 aristocratic system and the democratic system that was to come with universal suffrage in the Reform Acts of 1918 and 1928. During the twentieth century, the vote came to be conceived of as a basic right of citizenship, rather than requiring a property qualification. Britain has moved during the twentieth century from a diversified franchise, with various different ways of qualifying for the vote, to a simple franchise, with just one way of qualifying.

---

53 Henry Pelling, *Social Geography of British Elections, 1885–1910*, Macmillan, 1967, p. 9.
54 Lowell, *Government of England*, vol. 1, p. 201.
55 Ibid.
56 Ramsay Muir, *Peers and Bureaucrats: Two Problems of English Government*, Constable, 1910, pp. 22–3.
57 H. L. Morris, *Parliamentary Franchise Reform in England from 1885–1918*, Columbia University Press, 1921, pp. 11–12.

But with the electoral system, Britain has moved in the opposite direction, from a broadly uniform electoral system, based upon first past the post, to a more diverse set of arrangements. By 2020, the first-past-the-post system was used only to elect the House of Commons and local authorities in England and Wales. Local authorities in Scotland and Northern Ireland were elected by proportional representation, as were devolved bodies in the non-English parts of the United Kingdom and the London Assembly.

Britain, then, in 1895 was far from being a democracy. Nevertheless, as Joseph Chamberlain and A. V. Dicey noticed, she had what the major Continental states, with the exception of France, lacked – namely, a genuine system of parliamentary government with an executive responsible to the elected chamber of the legislature. This, as we shall see, when describing the coming of war in 1914, had important consequences. By contrast, the absence of responsible government in Germany, Austria and Russia meant that the army and navy were not wholly under civilian control.

Responsible government required a 'non-fluid' party system – that is, a system of two parties or blocs, one representing the government, the other the opposition. The defeat of the government either in a general election or in the Commons on a confidence vote would then mean its replacement by the opposition. Britain was the only major European power to enjoy such a system. That was because the evolution of Parliament in Britain had been quite different from that of legislatures on the Continent. For, in Britain, Parliament was regarded not only as a body mirroring the opinion of the nation but more fundamentally as an executive-choosing body. Conflict between a government and an opposition had begun in effect in the seventeenth century between ancestors of the Conservative and Liberal parties, and had spread outwards from Parliament to meet the demands of a new mass electorate. The Labour Party, created in 1900 as a party outside Parliament, rapidly adapted itself to the conventions of the system such as collective Cabinet responsibility and party discipline – the preconditions of responsible government.

These conventions were buttressed by an electorate broadly divided into two opposing tribes, a picture memorably captured by W. S. Gilbert when he marvelled in *Iolanthe*:

> How Nature always does contrive – Fal, lal, la!
> That every boy and every gal
> That's born into the world alive
> Is either a little Liberal
> Or else a little Conservative.

17

France also seemed to enjoy responsible government but only in theory since she had a multi-party and 'fluid' party system. In France, by contrast with Britain, if the government was defeated in the legislature, there was no dissolution and the next government would often include ministers from the previous one, and be supported from the ranks of the previous government. There was no equivalent in the French multi-party system to Her Majesty's Opposition. And since there was no fear that a hostile majority might come to power, there was far less incentive for party discipline for those in the governing party or parties. In consequence, the parties – particularly the ruling Radical Party – were in reality loosely organised federations with little cohesion on matters of policy. While in Britain real power lay with the government, in France it lay with the parties in Parliament, or even the individual member. As a result, there was often a vacuum of responsibility.

Germany seemed to enjoy a system of responsible government, but this was deceptive. The powers of the Reichstag appeared on paper considerable. It could initiate legislation and all laws required its consent, as did the annual Budget. But the German system was based in reality upon a separation of powers in which, although the Reichstag represented the people, it did not choose the government which served the kaiser. The government was not responsible to the Reichstag; nor did a hostile vote in the Reichstag entail the resignation of the Chancellor, who was not a party leader, or the government. In 1913, for example, Chancellor Bethmann Hollweg was twice defeated in votes of confidence in the Reichstag but, retaining the confidence of the kaiser, he did not resign. So the people through the legislature could neither remove the government nor replace it with an alternative. The government was not a party government, it was chosen by the Chancellor and designed to produce the goals laid out by the kaiser. The government was an agglomeration of fiefdoms, not a unified executive. Moreover, the heads of the army and navy were not responsible to the Chancellor or the Reichstag but to the kaiser, and had access to him without the Chancellor being present. If the Chancellor were to act against the military contrary to the kaiser's wishes, he might be dismissed, as was to happen to Bethmann's predecessor, Bülow, in 1909. When Bethmann was appointed, the kaiser had told him, 'Foreign policy you can leave to me!'[58] Opposition to the kaiser or the military was seen as unpatriotic. On 8 December 1912, the kaiser called a conference to consider military and naval matters. Neither the Chancellor nor the foreign minister were invited. Indeed, the Chancellor did not learn about it until a week later, when he was informed of its decisions.[59] The con-

58   Gordon Craig, *Germany 1866–1945*, Clarendon Press, 1978, p. 287.
59   John C. G. Röhl, 'Admiral von Müller and the Approach of War, 1911–1914', *Historical Journal*, 1969, p. 672.

sequences of this system were to prove momentous. It would mean that the German war plan of 1914, which envisaged violating Belgian neutrality, was never systematically scrutinised by the Reichstag since ministers were not responsible to it. In February 1913, the German foreign minister had warned the Chief of the General Staff that the invasion of Belgium would mean Britain entering the war, but he was brushed aside. The foreign minister then insisted that the Chief of the General Staff tell the kaiser of his plans, but when this occurred, neither the Chancellor nor the foreign minister were present. By 1914, the plan to invade Belgium was not 'subject to political interference'.[60] The ultimatum to Belgium was in fact drafted by the Chief of the General Staff not the Foreign Office.[61] The German government not only accepted decisions made by the military which had diplomatic implications but took no initiative itself to discover the precise military plan of action. For example, the decision by the General Staff in April 1913 to start wartime operations by attacking Liege was not made known to Bethmann until 31 July 1914, the very eve of war.

The British system of responsible and representative government, while by no means wholly democratic, did at least enable public opinion to be felt through Parliament. Government policy needed parliamentary sanction, and had to avoid antagonising public opinion too strongly. The Commons could remove governments, as it was to do in 1895 and had done in 1892 and, in effect, twice in 1886, and voters could at general elections replace a government they disliked with an alternative.

THE HOUSE OF COMMONS

For mid-Victorians, Parliament was the centre of the political universe. But by 1895, it seemed that the House of Commons no longer enjoyed as much prestige as it once did. Indeed, it displayed to contemporary commentators many features often assumed to be modern developments – subordination to the executive, overcrowding of the parliamentary timetable, excessive burden of legislation, control by party whips and decline of the private member. Perhaps every generation regards previous generations as a golden age of parliamentary government. The historian Robert Rhodes James once told me that, as a young Clerk of the Commons in 1955, a very elderly parliamentary official told him, 'This place has never been the same since Mr Gladstone died,' which had been in 1898.

---

60 Craig, *Germany*, p. 317.
61 Isabel V. Hull, *A Scrap of Paper: Breaking and Making International Law During the Great War*, Cornell University Press, 2014, pp. 25, 31.

In 1894, the constitutional writer Sidney Low wrote an article entitled 'If the House of Commons were Abolished?', insisting that abolition would make little difference. It would 'not necessarily bring the Constitution to a standstill ... The main difference would be that we should then recognise the real character of our system of government as it has developed itself in comparatively recent years.' It was not the House of Commons but 'the Cabinet and the Caucus' that were 'the real, efficient working parts of the political machine. So far as law-making goes, there is no room for the House of Commons between those upper and nether millstones.'[62] By 1904, Low had come to believe that the Commons had become a mere electoral college, 'a kind of preparatory school for the polls'.[63]

The great mid-Victorian writer on the constitution, Walter Bagehot, writing in *The Economist* in 1874, had believed that the literary, scientific and philosophical worlds were hardly comparable, in dignity, to the political. 'I wrote books ... and I was nobody. I got into Parliament, and before I had taken my seat I had become somebody.'[64] But by 1901, Sir Almeric Fitzroy, Clerk of the Privy Council, could say:

> Members of Parliament are slow to realise how rapidly the credit of the House of Commons as an institution is declining ... The power of the Press and the creation ... of a public opinion independent of and indifferent to the claims of the popular Chamber, have relegated Parliament as a political mouthpiece to a subordinate position where, if it so wills, it can still play a useful though less authoritative part.[65]

By 1895, the government's control over the parliamentary timetable was well established. In the 1880s, the Commons had adopted measures restricting debate to overcome obstruction by Irish members. In 1882, the closure, allowing the Speaker to terminate debate if 200 MPs supported him, was first enshrined in standing order, to be applied in standing committees, as well as the floor of the House. In its new and more effective form, after 1887, the closure was moved by the government 651 times before 1905, failing to secure the consent of 200 MPs just seventy-five times.[66] The guillotine, first introduced in 1881, allowed the Commons to timetable Bills to limit debate, and was first used on the Irish Crimes Bill of 1887. Timetabling had, by the beginning of the twentieth century, become 'a regular, because a necessary,

62 Sidney Low, 'If the House of Commons were Abolished?', *Nineteenth Century*, December 1894, pp. 847, 850–51.
63 Sidney Low, *The Governance of England*, T. Fisher Unwin, 1904, p. 104.
64 Norman St John-Stevas, ed., *The Collected Works of Walter Bagehot*, *The Economist*, 1974, vol. 6, p. 55.
65 Sir Almeric Fitzroy, *Memoirs*, 6th edition, Hutchinson, no date, vol. 1, p. 49.
66 Lowell, *Government of England*, vol. 1, p. 296fn.

practice in the case of difficult and hotly contested measures' and was frequently applied to supply.[67] In 1902, Leader of the House Arthur Balfour was to introduce further reforms strengthening government dominance to meet renewed obstruction by Irish members; but even before then, government business was taking up around 85 per cent of the time of the Commons, and private members' business was being squeezed out entirely. In 1896, Augustine Birrell, a Liberal MP and future minister, complained that, while

> at one time the private Member had an opportunity of making some reputation by legislative effort ... now he had hardly any chance. His occupation was well nigh gone, and there was nothing for him to do but to stroll listlessly about the Lobbies, and to come in and out when a Division is threatened.[68]

Private members' influence was exercised mainly at Question Time and on comparatively insignificant Early Day Motions.

The late Victorian period had seen a considerable decline in the independence of backbench MPs and an increase in whipping. In 1860, only 67 per cent of divisions in the session were subject to a Whig/Liberal government whip; by 1894, the figure was 90 per cent. In 1899, the Conservatives put on the whips in 86 per cent of divisions. The growth of party cohesion was also striking. The table below shows the percentage of MPs voting with their party in divisions in 1860 and 1894.

	Liberals	Conservatives
1860 all divisions	60 per cent	57 per cent
1860 whipped divisions	59 per cent	63 per cent
1894 all divisions	87 per cent	94 per cent
1894 whipped divisions	90 per cent	98 per cent[69]

The closure undermined the centrality of the House of Commons, while party caucuses and party discipline undermined the independent-minded MP. The House of Commons had lost its supremacy over the government, and was losing to the electorate its control over policy. Lowell, writing in 1908, noted that the whips could pressurise an MP through his constituency, provided this was done with some subtlety.

---

67 Ibid., vol. 1, p. 299.
68 House of Commons Debates, 27 February 1896, vol. 37, col. 1278.
69 Samuel H. Beer, *Modern British Politics: A Study of Parties and Pressure Groups*, Faber, 1965, pp. 263, 257.

Any direct attempt by the whips to bring pressure upon a Member through his constituents would be likely to irritate, and do more harm than good. But it is easy enough, in various ways, to let the constituents know that the Member is not thoroughly supporting his party; and unless his vote against the government is cast in the interest of the constituents themselves, they are not likely to have much sympathy with his independence.[70]

MPs were coming to be squeezed between the Cabinet and the constituencies. Normally, they could be relied upon as voting fodder. It was rare for amendments to be carried against the government. From 1895 to 1900, only one amendment was carried against the government, and from 1900 to 1905, just seven.[71]

The great danger for governments of the period came when they were internally divided or when their backbench support melted away. Then they would fall before a general election as had happened to the Liberals in 1885 and in 1895, while internal division was similarly to destroy the Unionist government in 1905.

Far-sighted conservatives were becoming concerned at the dangers arising from executive dominance, 'strong government'. An acute foreign observer noted in 1902 that the 'extrinsic independence' which Bagehot had thought essential to parliamentary government had become compromised. The equilibrium between government and Parliament had been 'destroyed in favour of the leaders'. The party leader, once *primus inter pares*, was now

a general in command of an army. He barely consults his staff, the front bench, and practically confines his confidences to an inner circle of a few lieutenants. All the rest of the army simply receives marching orders. He no longer takes the advice, as formerly, of this or that leading Member, who served as an intermediary between the leaders and the main body of their adherents. These intermediate ranks have disappeared.[72]

By 1910, Lord Robert Cecil could tell the Select Committee on Public Business:

I should say that if you really looked into the real principle of our constitution now, it is purely plebiscitical, that you have really a plebiscite by

---

70 Lowell, *Government of England*, vol. 1, p. 453. For a detailed picture of whipping in a slightly earlier era, see Viscount Chilston, *Chief Whip: The Political Life and Times of Aretas Akers-Douglas, 1st Viscount Chilston*, Routledge & Kegan Paul, 1961. Akers-Douglas had been the Conservative government's Chief Whip in 1885 and from 1886 to 1892.
71 Lowell, *Government of England*, vol. 1, p. 317fn.
72 Ostrogorski, *Democracy and the Organisation of Political Parties*, vol. 1, p. 607.

which a particular man is selected as Prime Minister, he then selects his Ministry himself, and it is pretty much what he likes.[73]

The growth of disciplined parties meant that what happened in the Commons was becoming less important than in the mid-Victorian era. 'Parliament was ceasing to be the sounding-board of the nation.'[74] Increasingly, what happened outside Parliament was more important than what happened on the floor of the Commons. The process had begun with Gladstone's Midlothian campaign in 1879, when he had called upon 'the people' to remove from office an iniquitous government. 'We have only to imagine, if we can,' *The Times* commented on the first Midlothian campaign, 'a Pitt or a Castlereagh stumping the provinces, and taking into his confidence, not merely a handful of electors, but any crowd he could collect in any part of this island.' Before Gladstone, the platform had been largely confined to agitators and outsiders – such as Richard Cobden and John Bright – not party leaders. The arena for debate, it was assumed, was Parliament, not the country. Gladstone had altered all that. 'The duty of making political speeches', Lord Salisbury had told the queen in 1887, 'is an aggravation of the labours of your Majesty's servants which we owe entirely to Mr Gladstone.'[75] This was recognised by Lord Hartington, the nominal leader of the Liberals, who, after the 1880 election, in which Disraeli's Conservatives were defeated, was called upon by the queen to form a government but had to give way to Gladstone. Hartington had already declared in December 1879 that 'there is not room for argument about the proposition that the man who leads the Liberal Party out of doors ought to lead it in parliament. It is only fair to the Queen, to the country, to the party, that this should be acknowledged at once.'[76] In 1880, Gladstone had told Rosebery that 'what is outside Parliament seems to me to be fast mounting, nay to have already mounted, to an importance much exceeding what is inside. Parliament deals with laws, and branches of the social tree, not with the root.' Gladstone's example was to be followed by Joseph Chamberlain in his 'Unauthorised Programme' of 1885, and later in his tariff reform campaign; and, on the Conservative side, by Lord Randolph Churchill. In 1885, Lord Argyll, a Whig peer who had resigned from Gladstone's second government in 1881 in protest at its Irish policy, complained to Gladstone that

---

73 Quoted in Jane Ridley, 'The Unionist Opposition and the House of Lords, 1906–1910', *Parliamentary History*, 1992, p. 253.
74 A. J. P. Taylor, *The Trouble Makers: Dissent over Foreign Policy, 1782–1939*, Hamish Hamilton, 1957, p. 95.
75 Martin Pugh, *The Making of Modern British Politics, 1867–1945*, 3rd edition, Blackwell, 2002, pp. 3, 4–5.
76 Bernard Holland, *The Life of Spencer Compton, Eighth Duke of Devonshire*, Longmans, Green & Co., 1911, vol. 1, p. 260.

from the moment our government was fairly under way, I saw and felt that speeches *outside* were allowed to affect opinion, and politically to commit the cabinet in a direction which was not determined by you deliberately, or by the government as a whole, but by the audacity ... of our new associates.[77]

The Commons was becoming a secondary institution. 'The Platform has, in some ways, usurped the place of or supplanted Parliament,' one commentator thought in 1892. 'The really great and vital discussions are now carried on outside Parliament.'[78] In this, as in other matters, Gladstone had been a bridge between the nineteenth and twentieth centuries, between the golden age of parliamentary government of the mid-nineteenth century and the modern world of mass parties and professional politicians dependent for their position on popular approval.

THE HOUSE OF LORDS

If Britain was not yet a democracy, that was not solely because of the limited franchise. For the Commons was subject to the check of the unelected House of Lords, whose legislative powers, undefined in statute in 1895, were, in theory at least, co-equal with the Commons.

In 1895, the House of Lords comprised around 600 hereditary peers, together with twenty-eight Irish representative peers, elected from their number for life, and sixteen Scottish representative peers, elected from their number at each general election. These elections were rarely contested. Unelected Irish peers, but not unelected Scottish peers, were eligible for membership of the House of Commons. The House also contained in 1895 four law lords, together with retired law lords, as well as the two archbishops and twenty-four senior bishops of the Anglican Church. In 1896, eleven of these clerics took the Conservative or Liberal Unionist whip, nine the Liberal whip while six were cross-benchers. But they rarely attended except when the rights of the established church were under discussion.[79] The archbishops, bishops and the law lords were the only non-hereditary peers. Women could hold peerages but were not allowed to sit in the House.

In the late nineteenth century, the Lords still exerted great social as well as political influence. Lowell believed that extension of the franchise had 'rather increased than diminished the influence of the nobility'; and, as an

---

77 John Morley, *The Life of William Ewart Gladstone*, Macmillan, 1906, vol. 2, p. 243.

78 Henry Jephson, *The Platform: Its Rise and Progress*, Macmillan, 1892, vol. 2, p. 606.

79 Andrew Adonis, *Making Aristocracy Work: The Peerage and the Political System in Britain, 1884–1914*, Clarendon Press, 1993, pp. 40, 46, 48. This book contains a most valuable account of the workings of the House of Lords before 1914.

American, he was 'impressed by the popular confidence in those peers who have attained a position in the forefront of politics. There seems to be a feeling that they ... are beyond the reach of the temptations that beset the ordinary man.'[80] In Gladstone's Liberal government of 1892, six out of the nineteen members had been peers, and in Lord Salisbury's 1895 Unionist government, eight out of twenty. Since the fall of Robert Peel in 1846, every Prime Minister except Gladstone and Lord Palmerston (an Irish peer who had not been elected to the Lords, and in consequence sat in the Commons) had governed for at least part of his term from the Lords not the Commons, although Salisbury was to be the last Prime Minister from the Lords. Between 1851 and 1905, every Foreign Secretary had been a peer, though Lords Derby and Russell had begun in the Commons but been translated to the Lords while Foreign Secretary. Paradoxically, the advent of mass politics was leading to a greater emphasis on the constitutional importance of the Lords.

Although there were no statutory limits on the powers of the Lords, there seemed, until 1909, a convention that the Lords should not alter or reject Money Bills, a convention expressed in resolutions of the House of Commons of 1671 and 1678. The Lords had never explicitly accepted this restriction, but they had in practice submitted to it until 1860, when they rejected Gladstone's Bill to repeal the paper duties. The Commons had then passed three resolutions insisting that supply was the sole concern of the Lower House, and in 1861, Gladstone had circumvented the Lords by combining all revenue-raising measures for the year in an annual Budget, so that, were the Lords to reject it, they would be denying the government supply. In 1894, Chancellor of the Exchequer Sir William Harcourt repeated Gladstone's ploy to secure the passage of higher and graduated death duties through the Conservative-dominated House of Lords. Conservatives argued that it was illegitimate to put social reform measures into the annual Budget, a process they labelled 'tacking'. They insisted that the Upper House retained the power to reject a Budget if it contained measures beyond the strict requirements of supply. As late as 1908, one year before Lloyd George's 'People's Budget', Lowell could refer to the Lords as 'a co-ordinate branch of the legislature', so that 'every Act of Parliament requires its assent, and although in practice it is far less powerful than the House of Commons, the only subject on which the limitations of its authority can be stated with precision is that of finance'.[81]

Except when major issues came before them, such as Home Rule or the 1909 Budget, the Lords were rather somnolent, and composed largely of absentees. Until 1906, few beside ministers and opposition aspirants attended

---

80 Lowell, *Government of England*, vol. 1, p. 413.
81 Ibid., vol. 1, p. 400.

with any regularity. In 1897, for example, of 580 peers on the roll, the mean attendance was just eighty-six – 15 per cent. On few occasions did as many as 100 peers attend, and, when they did, that was largely due to pressure from the whips. That year, just 21 per cent of the peers on the roll made speeches. Sittings also tended to be short – around ninety minutes to two hours. In 1897, the mean length of sittings was sixty-eight minutes, and just eleven sittings lasted after 7 p.m. 'The first principle of debate in the House of Lords', declared the parliamentary journalist Sir Henry Lucy, 'is that, except under direct pressure, discussion shall be concluded in time to dress for dinner.' In its obituary of Salisbury on 24 August 1903, the *Manchester Guardian* likened the Upper House to 'a family meeting of hereditary councillors'. One reason for the shortness of debates was that Bills generally reached the Lords at the end of the session when standing orders were suspended for the Glorious Twelfth, the beginning of the grouse-shooting season. 'Some peers tell me', Lord Salisbury told the Duke of Devonshire in August 1894, 'that from the grouse point of view, it is desirable that the division should be taken on a Friday, as that will interfere least with country house parties, bent on slaughter.' There were hardly any real debates.

One peer compared speaking in the Lords to 'speaking by torchlight to corpses in a charnel house'. 'We have no debates', Lord Salisbury told Lord Selborne in 1896, 'because we have no debaters.'[82] After the Parliament Act of 1911, limiting the Lords' powers, matters became even worse. 'The atmosphere', declared the Earl of Crawford in 1913, 'is so soporific, spreading its atrophy with so potent an influence, that it is hopeless to arouse interest in its component members.'[83] In his classic text *The English Constitution*, published in 1867, Walter Bagehot had stressed the need for a revising chamber. 'While the House of Commons is what it is, a good revising, regulating and retarding House would be a benefit of great magnitude.' He then went on to ask, 'But is the House of Lords such a chamber? Does it do this work? This is almost an undiscussed question.' By 1895, it would have been difficult to answer in the affirmative. 'The *cure* for admiring the Lords', Bagehot had continued, 'was to go and look at it.'[84] He believed the danger facing the Upper House was not abolition but atrophy.

Yet this somnolent chamber had been given an important constitutional role by Lord Salisbury. In 1869, he had put forward the doctrine of the mandate, according to which it was for peers to test whether a particular government measure genuinely enjoyed electoral approval. 'There is', he believed,

82 Adonis, *Making Aristocracy Work*, pp. 55, 59, 57, 50.
83 Vincent, ed., *Crawford Papers*, p. 320.
84 St John Stevas, *Collected Works of Bagehot*, vol. 5, p. 277.

a class of cases small in number, and varying in kind, in which the nation must be called into council and must decide the policy of the Government. It may be that the House of Commons in determining the opinion of the nation is wrong; and if there are grounds for entertaining that belief, it is always open to this House, and indeed it is the duty of this House, to insist that the nation shall be consulted ... We must decide ... whether the House of Commons does or does not represent the full, the deliberate, the sustained convictions of the body of the nation.[85]

The Lords, therefore, enjoyed a referendal function. 'We have', declared Dicey in 1890, 'introduced into our constitution the spirit, though not as yet the form, of the referendum.'[86] In consequence, it was held that the Lords had the right to force a dissolution, a right they exercised when they rejected the People's Budget in 1909. It was, however, by no means clear how a partisan and hereditary chamber such as the House of Lords could determine whether a Bill passed by the Commons represented or did not represent the real 'opinion of the nation'.

The referendal function had supposedly been exercised in 1893 when the Lords had rejected Home Rule. The Duke of Devonshire, leader of the Liberal Unionists in the Lords, declared that the Lords must 'prevent changes' touching the fundamental institutions of the state, 'without the absolute certainty that they are in accordance with the will of the majority of the people'. 'No human being', he insisted,

> can tell on what question the majority which put the present Government in power was returned. No doubt some electors voted for Home Rule, but it is quite certain that a larger number voted for disestablishment, or local option, or for parish councils, or for changes in the incidence of taxation in towns, or for changes in the labour laws ... I deny that the House of Commons received any mandate upon Home Rule at all in the last election.[87]

The justification for rejecting a Bill approved by the Commons was, then, that there might not be an electoral majority for Home Rule. But Salisbury added a gloss to the doctrine. In addition to an overall mandate, he argued, the consent of all four nations – Scotland, England, Wales and Ireland – was needed if Home Rule was to achieve legitimacy; and, since the Liberals lacked

---

85 House of Lords Debates, 17 June 1869, vol. 197, col. 84.
86 A. V. Dicey, 'Democracy in Switzerland', *Edinburgh Review*, 1890, p. 141.
87 House of Lords Debates, 5 September 1893, vol. 17, col. 31.

a majority in England, the 'predominant partner', whose electors were believed to be opposed to Home Rule, the English were actually better represented in the Lords than in the Commons. The Upper House, Salisbury declared:

> represents an overwhelming majority of England in its objections to [the government's] measures, and it is only by a very scanty majority, swept up from various other places – especially from the south and west of Ireland – that [the Prime Minister] is able to carry his measures through the House of Commons.[88]

In accordance with the mandate doctrine, Lord Salisbury challenged the Liberals to dissolve the Commons after the defeat of Home Rule in the Lords in 1893. Gladstone wanted to accept the challenge, but his colleagues would not allow him to. But even if the Liberals had dissolved, and won the ensuing election, the peers could still say that they had won in spite of, not because of, Home Rule. 'When the great oracle speaks,' Lord Salisbury declared, 'we are never quite certain what the great oracle said.'[89] A general election can hardly ever be interpreted as yielding a verdict on a distinct policy issue. A policy proposal would have had to be the only major issue at stake between the parties in the election, and the verdict of the voters would have had to be quite unambiguous. It was not enough, the Duke of Devonshire had insisted in 1893, merely for the principle of Irish Home Rule to have been put to the voters; in addition, 'the form in which it is to be conceded, and the provisions by which this principle is to be carried into effect should also undoubtedly receive the popular approval'.[90] The duke was making the hurdle even higher, indeed almost insurmountable. It would be difficult ever to prove that voters had unequivocally endorsed a specific item of legislation. For Salisbury, this was part of the charm of the doctrine. 'The plan which I prefer is frankly to acknowledge', Salisbury had written cynically to a colleague in 1872,

> that the nation is Master, though the House of Commons is not, and to yield our own opinion only when the judgement of the nation has been challenged at the polls and decidedly expressed. This Doctrine, it seems to me, has the advantage of being: (1) Theoretically sound, (2) popular, (3) safe against agitation, and (4) so rarely applicable as practically to place little fetter upon our independence.[91]

---

88 Ibid., 5 February 1895, vol. 30, col. 32.
89 Ibid., 15 August 1895, vol. 36, col. 51.
90 Ibid., 5 September 1893, vol. 17, col. 30.
91 Salisbury to Carnarvon, 20 February 1872, cited in Lady Gwendolen Cecil, *Life of Robert, Marquess of Salisbury,* Hodder & Stoughton, 1921, vol. 2, p. 26.

In failing to dissolve in 1893, the Liberals seemed to be confirming the constitutional propriety of what the Lords had done. Instead of dissolving, the Liberals followed a policy labelled 'filling up the cup', putting forward reforming measures and challenging the Lords to reject them. This was, as Churchill was to say in 1907, foolish: a policy 'of bowling lobs for the House of Lords to sky in the hope that the spectators will take pity on the bowler'.[92] The Lords tended to restrict their blocking activities to Bills for which electors seemed to have little enthusiasm. If the Liberals were to fight an election on a Bill of this sort and were beaten, the Upper House would end up stronger, not weaker. 'The plain truth', the Gladstonian minister John Morley had told Sir William Harcourt in 1894, 'is that we can do nothing with the House of Lords unless they really resist the will of the British constituencies – and this they are not now doing.'[93]

Since the Lords was heavily dominated by Unionists – the 1893 Home Rule Bill had been defeated there by 419 votes to forty-one – the mandate doctrine seemed only to apply when a government of the left, a Liberal government, was in power. By 1906, the year of the Liberal election victory, there were 461 Unionist peers, ninety-eight Liberals and forty-four who sat as independents.[94] The seventy-five peers who voted for Lloyd George's People's Budget in 1909 'constituted the largest pro-Liberal vote in the Lords on a major issue for twenty-five years'.[95] And, unlike the Commons, the Lords could not be dissolved.

The Lords never took the view that legislation proposed by a Unionist government lacked a mandate. The doctrine was used only against Liberal governments. In the words of the Radical Sir Charles Dilke, 'The claim of Lord Salisbury to force us to "consult the country" is a claim for annual Parliaments when we are in office, and septennial Parliaments when they are in office.'[96] (Before the 1911 Parliament Act, the maximum duration of a parliament was seven years, not five.) In the 1890s, the Liberal Prime Minister Lord Rosebery had told the queen that the House of Lords was 'a permanent barrier raised against the Liberal Party', since it 'controls a Liberal but not a Conservative Government', something he believed 'obnoxious to the conscience of the country as well as to its best interests'.[97] He was to fight the 1895 election largely on the platform of Lords reform. While that campaign failed, when, in 1909, the Lords rejected the Budget, they would test the referendal theory to destruction.

92 Randolph Churchill, *Young Statesman: Winston S. Churchill 1901–1914* [1967], Minerva, 1991, vol. 2, p. 320.
93 Adonis, *Making Aristocracy Work*, p. 123.
94 Giles St Aubyn, *Edward VII: Prince and King* [1979], Faber, 2010, p. 401.
95 Adonis, *Making Aristocracy Work*, pp. 20–21.
96 S. Gwynn and G. Tuckwell, *Life of the Right Hon. Charles Dilke*, John Murray, 1917, vol. 1, p. 371.
97 G. E. Buckle, ed., *Letters of Queen Victoria*, 3rd series, John Murray, 1930–32, vol. 1, p. 76, vol. 2, p. 439.

THE MONARCHY

The era of mass politics, then, seemed to be regenerating the Lords. It also seemed to be regenerating the monarchy. Balfour indeed believed at the end of Queen Victoria's reign that 'the importance of the Crown in our Constitution is not a diminishing, but an increasing factor'.[98] Queen Victoria (1819 1901) was the first modern sovereign to gain popular enthusiasm and affection, especially in her last years. She had altered the image of the monarchy from that of her dissolute predecessors, William IV and George IV, whom she called her 'wicked uncles'. The queen's reign, in Lord Salisbury's words:

> bridged over that great interval which separates old England from new England. Other nations may have had to pass through similar trials, but have seldom passed through them so peaceably, so easily, and with so much prosperity and success as we have. I think that future historians will look to the Queen's reign as the boundary which separates the two states of England.

To a writer on the Victorian age in 1936, the changes which that period had seen appeared greater than anything that had been witnessed before or since. 'I am speaking of changes in men's minds, and I cannot in my own time observe anything of greater consequence than the dethronement of ancient faith by natural science and historical criticism, and the transition from oligarchic to democratic representation.'[99] The queen was quite out of sympathy with these changes, deprecating anything which appeared to threaten revealed religion and insisting that she could never be queen of a democratic country. She '*cannot*', she had written to the Liberal minister W. E. Forster in 1880, 'and will not be the Queen of a *democratic monarchy*'.[100] In 1892, after the electoral defeat of the Unionists, she wrote to her daughter, the Empress Frederick of Prussia, that 'it seems to me a defect in our famed Constitution to have to part with an admirable Government like Lord Salisbury's for no question of any importance, or any particular reason, merely on account of the number of votes'.[101] Nevertheless, Lord Salisbury believed that she had

> an extraordinary knowledge of what her people would think – extraordinary because it could not have come from any personal intercourse. I have

98 House of Commons Debates, 25 January 1901, vol. 89, col. 20.
99 G. M. Young, *Victorian England: Portrait of An Age* [1936], Oxford University Press, 1960, p. 149.
100 Buckle, ed., *Letters of Queen Victoria*, 2nd series, vol. 3, p. 166.
101 Frank Hardie, *The Political Influence of Queen Victoria, 1861–1901*, Oxford University Press, 1935, p. 13.

said for years that I always thought that when I knew what the Queen thought I knew pretty certainly what view her subjects would take, and especially the middle classes of her subjects.[102]

But her popularity spread wider than 'the middle classes'. In 1897, the year of the Diamond Jubilee, Lady Ampthill, a Lady of the Bedchamber to the queen, travelling in the royal train from Scotland to Windsor, pulled up the blind at 4 a.m. She saw people who had tramped across the country lining the way, 'in the more populous counties sometimes thirty, forty deep – all this on a dark threatening grey morning'. When the queen heard about this, she was 'more moved' by it 'than by any of the numerous stirring moments which have hitherto marked the celebrations'.[103] Even members of the ruling elite were overawed by her. In 1899, Sir Edward Carson, the former Solicitor General for Ireland, declared that he had first met the queen at the time of the Diamond Jubilee. 'He broke down – could not help crying: and what a tribute from the man who is the most pitiless prosecutor in the kingdom.'[104] The queen had become the symbol of British pride and prosperity. She had come to be associated, however erroneously, with the beneficent changes of the era. She was also, by contrast with her predecessors, an exemplar of the domestic virtues with a close and affectionate family life.

The prestige and affection in which the monarchy was to be held would have appeared highly unlikely when Victoria came to the throne in 1837. The three previous sovereigns had been, in the words of Sir Sidney Lee in his biography of the queen in the *Dictionary of National Biography*, 'an imbecile' (George III), 'a profligate' (George IV) and 'a buffoon' (William IV). In 1830, Peel had thought the monarchy so unpopular that only a miracle could save it. During the agitation over the 1832 Reform Bill, William IV had felt the crown 'tottering' on his head. At that time, the sovereign was regarded as being personally responsible for the measures of the government, and it was believed that a government needed the sovereign's confidence to survive. But the 1832 Reform Act had constrained royal power, and Victoria had no room for manoeuvre against a representative majority in the Commons. Since 1832, it has only been on exceptional occasions – the Aberdeen coalition of 1852 and Ramsay MacDonald's national government of 1931 – that royal influence could determine the political colour of the government. The second Reform Act of 1867 had led to the growth of political organisation outside Parliament, and this further limited the scope for royal intervention.

---

102 House of Lords Debates, 25 January 1901, vol. 89, col. 15.
103 Vincent, ed., *Crawford Papers*, p. 40.
104 Ibid., p. 55.

It was only when party lines were fluid, as with the Home Rule crisis in 1885–86, or when the sovereign was required to choose a new Prime Minister in the absence of agreement by the party in power – as in 1894 when Victoria appointed Lord Rosebery – that the queen could exercise decisive influence.

The queen was sceptical of, if not downright hostile towards, the new political ideas of the Victorian era – liberalism and popular government. Indeed, she never wholly discarded the earlier view that government was the servant of the sovereign rather than the people. Yet the prestige of the monarchy at the end of her reign owed much to its association with parliamentary and responsible government in which the sovereign was required to act on the advice of her ministers. It is a paradox that constitutional monarchy arose as a result of political forces of which the queen disapproved. Nevertheless, she was a sovereign of a new type – as Balfour was to tell the House of Commons, in moving an address on the accession of Edward VII in 1901, 'the first of all constitutional Monarchs whom the world has yet seen'.[105] 'If we look at history', Bagehot had declared in *The English Constitution*, 'we shall find that it is only during the period of the present reign that in England the duties of a constitutional sovereign have ever been well performed.'[106] Victoria's reign had coincided with a fundamental change in the nature of monarchy. Its power was declining, but its influence increased, and its symbolic role in both Britain and the empire grew in importance. The power of the queen as head of state was in decline; her influence as head of the nation, a symbolic figure representing the whole of Britain, had grown.

The development of responsible government in the empire increased the importance of the monarchy since the empire was, in Balfour's words, 'constitutionally linked to us through the person of the Sovereign, the living symbol of Imperial unity'.[107] Victoria's popularity increased with the Golden Jubilee of 1887 and the Diamond Jubilee of 1897, to both of which the self-governing colonies sent their Prime Ministers. In 1876, Disraeli had added 'Empress of India' to the queen's title, implicitly recognising that India was a separate part of the empire. Liberal opposition to this change annoyed the queen and no doubt strengthened her Conservative sympathies. The role of the sovereign in the empire was to be recognised in an amendment to the Royal Titles Act, passed in 1901, after the death of Victoria. After the words 'of the United Kingdom of Great Britain and Ireland', there was added 'and of the British Dominions beyond the Seas'. In 1909, Balfour told a royal confidant, Lord Esher, that 'during the latter half of Queen Victoria's reign, and more than

105 House of Commons Debates, 25 January 1901, vol. 89, col. 20.
106 St John-Stevas, *Collected Works of Bagehot*, vol. 5, p. 258.
107 House of Commons Debates, 25 January 1901, vol. 89, col. 20.

ever now, Great Britain means the British Empire. Our people overseas do not care a rush for Asquith or me. They hardly know our names. For them the symbol of the Empire is the King.'[108] The sovereign – not Parliament or the Cabinet – was the institutional link holding the empire together at a time when the self-governing colonies were intent on confirming their independence from the Imperial Parliament and the British government. Britain was embarking on a great experiment, that of combining an empire with a system of representative government, and in that experiment, the monarchy was crucial.

Many had believed that the growth of parliamentary government would render the sovereign a mere cipher, that she would become, in the words of Baron Stockmar, an adviser to the prince consort, 'nothing but a mandarin figure which has to nod its head in assent, or shake it in denial, as his minister pleases'.[109] But Victoria showed that the power of the monarchy could be replaced by influence. Bagehot had laid down three constitutional rights which a sovereign enjoyed – the right to be consulted, the right to encourage and the right to warn. There was, however, no easy road to monarchical influence. The details of political affairs were, in Bagehot's words, 'vast, disagreeable, complicated and miscellaneous. A king, to be the equal of his ministers in discussion, must work as they work; he must be a man of business as they are men of business.'[110] Victoria was the first sovereign prepared to master the endless boxes of state papers sent to her with monotonous regularity by her private secretary. It had been her 'great aim to follow' the prince consort's plan, 'which was to sign nothing until he had read it and made notes upon what he signed'.[111] Balfour referred to her life of 'continuous labour'. Noticing during the queen's final illness the accumulating mass of untouched documents which awaited her attention, he

> marvelled at the unostentatious patience which for sixty-three years, through sorrow, through suffering, in moments of weariness, in moments of despondency, had enabled her to carry on without break or pause her share in the government of this great Empire. For her there was no holiday, to her there was no intermission of toil. Domestic sorrow, domestic sickness, made no difference in her labours, and they were continued from

108 Maurice V. Brett and Oliver, Viscount Esher, *Journals and Letters of Reginald, Viscount Esher*, Nicholson & Watson, 1934–8, vol. 2, p. 421.
109 Baron Stockmar to the prince consort, 1854, cited by Robert Blake, 'The Crown and Politics in the Twentieth Century', in Jeremy Murray-Brown, ed., *The Monarchy and the Future*, Allen & Unwin, 1969, p. 11.
110 St John-Stevas, *Collected Works of Bagehot*, vol. 5, pp. 253, 259.
111 W. L. Arnstein, 'Queen Victoria Opens Parliament: The Disinvention of Tradition', *Historical Research*, 1990, p. 192.

the hour at which she became our Sovereign to within a few days – I had almost said a few hours – of her death.[112]

When Bagehot described the monarchy in the 1860s, he wrote as if he were describing accepted constitutional conventions. But, of course, the idea of constitutional monarchy was comparatively recent and there were no authoritative guidelines as to what the queen could or could not do. Bagehot's three rights were more prescriptive than descriptive, and he implied that a sovereign ought not to use them in a partisan manner. It is not clear whether the queen had read *The English Constitution*, but she deplored Bagehot as an 'irreverent' writer, and was much displeased when she found her grandson, the future George V, studying his works.[113] When Victoria's letters were published, after her death, it became clear that Bagehot had seriously underestimated the extent of the queen's influence and indeed partisanship. Disraeli had been more perceptive. 'I know it will be said', he declared in 1872,

> that, however beautiful the theory, the personal influence of the Sovereign is now merged in the responsibility of the minister. I think you will find there is a great fallacy in this view. The principles of the English Constitution do not contemplate the absence of personal influence on the part of the Sovereign; and if they did, the principles of human nature would prevent the fulfilment of such a theory.[114]

This influence was to become blatantly partisan in the last twenty-five years of the queen's life, exerted in favour of the Conservative and Liberal Unionist cause and against the Liberals. She wrote incessantly to Gladstone and Rosebery complaining about policies she disliked and speeches of Liberal ministers which she believed were too 'extreme'. A commentator in 1926 stated:

> If, as some have held, it is the duty of the English monarch to be passive and impartial, the Queen was certainly the least constitutional of sovereigns. That she retained the reputation of a model monarch was due to the fact that, though she strained the constitution almost to breaking point, her prejudices and her conventions were so exactly those dominant in her age that she seemed to embody its very nature within herself. Her influence, moreover, was almost always in the direction on which middle class sentiment would have approved.[115]

---

112 House of Commons Debates, 25 January 1901, vol. 89, col. 25.
113 Kenneth Rose, *King George V*, Weidenfeld & Nicolson, 1983, p. 35.
114 Hardie, *Political Influence of Queen Victoria*, pp. 10, 245.
115 Kingsley Martin, 'The Victorian Monarchy', *Edinburgh Review*, 1926, pp. 382–3.

The queen's partisanship is often explained by her antipathy to Gladstone; but, while undoubtedly a major factor, it extended also to Gladstone's successor, Lord Rosebery, whom she had personally chosen upon the Grand Old Man's retirement in 1894, and who 'was almost as chivalrous, as gallant, as flattering in his method of approach to the Queen as had been Disraeli'.[116] The queen's hostility to the Liberals was as much political as personal. She was opposed to policies which she believed encouraged democratic and populist forces and to what she perceived as Liberal weakness in imperial and foreign affairs. She was opposed, above all, to Irish Home Rule, which she believed would lead to the disintegration of her kingdom. After Gladstone's conversion to that policy in 1886, she sought to bring together a coalition of Conservatives and 'moderate' Unionist Liberals, and communicated with the Conservative opposition as to how this might best be achieved. In 1886, she pressed the Liberal Unionist Lord Hartington to support Lord Salisbury's Conservative government.

The queen was criticised in 1894 for using her prerogative of appointing a Prime Minister by choosing as Gladstone's successor a Liberal of the right, the Liberal Imperialist Lord Rosebery, rather than Sir William Harcourt, who would probably have been the choice of Liberal MPs, or Lord Spencer, who would have been Gladstone's own choice. She did not consult Gladstone before appointing Rosebery. But, in the queen's defence, it could be argued that she was under no obligation to consult Gladstone, who was resigning because he had been repudiated by the Cabinet on the issue of naval expenditure, and who had, therefore, lost the authority which gave him the right to be consulted. Spencer was later to declare that he would not have accepted appointment as Prime Minister. As for Harcourt, other members of the Cabinet regarded him as an impossible colleague and his biographer admits that 'Lord Rosebery was already emerging as the choice of the Cabinet'.[117] Ministers could, had they chosen to do so, refused to serve under Rosebery and the queen would then have been compelled to appoint someone else. It is therefore reasonable to conclude that 'the Queen was working with the grain of politics when she sent for Rosebery. She was exercising a casting vote rather than expressing a purely personal preference.'[118]

Rosebery had sought to reform the Lords, widening its composition, so as to dilute the hereditary element. To this the queen was vehemently opposed, seeing it as tantamount to abolition. Lord Salisbury, then Leader of the Opposition in the Lords, gave her a novel constitutional doctrine to use

116 Hardie, *Political Influence of Queen Victoria*, p. 117.
117 Gardiner, *The Life of Sir William Harcourt*, Constable, 1923, vol. 2, p. 262.
118 G. H. L. Le May, *The Victorian Constitution*, Duckworth, 1979, p. 89.

against Rosebery. 'On a matter of this vital importance', Salisbury told her, the Prime Minister 'has no constitutional right to announce a totally new policy without first ascertaining your Majesty's pleasure on the subject, and if he is unable to convince your Majesty, it is his duty to tender his resignation'. The queen then told Rosebery that Lords reform was '*not* a mere question of policy, but as he himself said, "*a question of enormous importance*", a "*question of the revision of the entire Constitution*", and, as such, she maintains her sanction for its public declaration should have been obtained'. The implication was that, on 'constitutional' matters, the Prime Minister needed the confidence of the queen, as well as the Commons. As Rosebery told the queen, this 'would tend to make the Sovereign a party in all controversies of the hour, and would hazardously compromise the neutrality of the Sovereign'.

The Rosebery government, dependent on the Irish Party for its majority, and beset by fissiparous tendencies within the Liberal Party, could, so it seemed, be forced to go to the country at any time. The queen asked Lord Salisbury what would be the most suitable time for a dissolution from the Unionist point of view, and Salisbury told her that she would be within her rights in insisting upon a dissolution.[119] Through her private secretary, in November 1894, the queen asked Sir Henry James, a Liberal Unionist, and therefore in opposition, and a former Attorney General, 'whether she was constitutionally entitled to order a Dissolution, and failing consent of Rosebery, to dismiss the Government'. James tactfully replied that, while the queen undoubtedly had such a right in theory, it would be inexpedient to exercise that right, at least at the present time, since, if Rosebery dissolved, he would say that he was dissolving at the queen's insistence. If, on the other hand, as was more likely, he refused to dissolve, the queen would have to dismiss him. 'I could scarcely express myself as strongly as I felt,' James later wrote, 'for my view was that it would be a most dangerous act of folly if any premature interference of the Crown took place.'[120] Even so, the queen never abandoned the claim that she was entitled to dismiss ministers, or indeed the whole Cabinet, a claim which George V, supported by leading constitutional lawyers such as Dicey and Sir William Anson, was to maintain as late as 1913 during the Home Rule crisis.

During the last part of her reign, the queen, like the House of Lords, was a source of difficulty to every Liberal government and encouragement to every Conservative one. But her partisanship was not known to the public, since neither Gladstone nor Rosebery, nor indeed any Liberal leader, publicly revealed it. Liberal reticence, therefore, was as important a factor in

---

119 Hardie, *Political Influence of Queen Victoria*, pp. 109, 110, 43, 44.
120 Garvin, *Chamberlain*, vol. 2, p. 613; Lord Askwith, *Lord James of Hereford*, Benn, 1930, p. 232.

maintaining the prestige of the monarchy as Conservative celebration of it, and because the queen appeared little in public after the death of the prince consort, it was generally assumed that she played little part in politics. It is a paradox that the queen 'was regarded by the vast mass of her subjects as a divine institution, without flaw ... at the very moment when she was behaving more unconstitutionally than ever before'.[121] But when the government controlled a united party enjoying a comfortable majority in the Commons, she had little real scope for altering its policy or personnel. So Victoria was, perforce and despite herself, more of a constitutional monarch than her predecessors had been; and by the end of her reign, it had come to be generally accepted that the sovereign should be impartial between the parties.

THE CABINET

The executive in Britain in 1895 was, as today, the Cabinet, in which the Prime Minister was generally the dominant figure. But, remarkably, until 1905, that office had no existence in law; and, as Balfour told his constituents shortly after entering Downing Street, the post was

> not recognised by any statute, and ... does not form part of the British Constitution, as understood by lawyers. The Prime Minister of the day has no salary as Prime Minister. He has no statutory duties as Prime Minister, his name occurs in no act of Parliament, and though holding the most important place in the Constitutional hierarchy, he has yet no place which is recognised by the laws of his country.[122]

In 1889, a leading Liberal, John Morley, wrote a biography of the first Prime Minister, Sir Robert Walpole, containing a chapter on the Cabinet said to have been scrutinised by Gladstone. Morley believed that the great virtue of the Cabinet system was its 'flexibility', which allowed 'the Prime Minister in an emergency to take upon himself a power not inferior to that of a dictator, provided always that the House of Commons will stand by him'. The Prime Minister was, in any case, 'the keystone of the Cabinet arch' and occupied 'a position which, so long as it lasts, is one of exceptional and peculiar authority'.[123] Sidney Low went even further in 1904, claiming that if a Prime Minister 'is a Pitt, a Peel, a Palmerston, a Disraeli or a Gladstone, he may come near to being a dictator'.[124] In the previous year, Balfour, not normally

---

121 Laurence Housman, cited in Hardie, *Political Influence of Queen Victoria*, p. 219.
122 R. J. Q. Adams, *Balfour: The Last Grandee*, John Murray, 2007, p. 172.
123 John Morley, *Walpole*, Macmillan, 1889.
124 Low, *Governance of England*, p. 158.

thought of as a strong Prime Minister, had confirmed this judgement by in effect peremptorily dismissing three Cabinet ministers without prior warning because they insisted on sticking to the doctrine of free trade, which he was determined to modify.

In foreign and imperial affairs, in particular, the power of the Prime Minister was considerable, and not easily checked by the Cabinet. Under Lord Rosebery's Liberal government of 1894–95, only an inner ring of ministers – sometimes just the Prime Minister and the Foreign Secretary – saw the boxes of foreign despatches. This practice was continued under Lord Salisbury's Unionist administration in 1895. Until 1900, Salisbury combined the premiership with the Foreign Office, and it was not always easy for the Cabinet to discover what was happening in foreign affairs, although after 1895, as Salisbury's strength declined, other ministers were able to exert more influence.

By contrast with today, the Cabinet in 1895 had no regular time of assembly or fixed place of meeting. It was summoned at the behest of the Prime Minister, or, more rarely, when a senior minister insisted. The date of meeting was fixed by the Prime Minister, often at short notice. In January 1898, Lord Salisbury's private secretary omitted to inform Lord James of a Cabinet meeting, and he was told by letter what had transpired.[125] Under Salisbury, the Cabinet met relatively infrequently. It did not, for example, meet between 5 November 1895 and 8 January 1896, despite serious foreign and imperial problems – insurrection in the Turkish Empire and the Jameson Raid.[126] In 1900, despite the outbreak of the Boer War in September, the Cabinet did not meet between the beginning of August and the middle of November.[127] In 1901, in the middle of the war, the Cabinet did not meet between the end of August and the beginning of November. Speaking in Oldham in October 1901, Sir Michael Hicks Beach, the Chancellor of the Exchequer, said that this did not matter since 'there are such things as interviews between ministers ... There are official messengers who carry communications between different departments.' One commentator interpreted this as 'a rather plain-spoken admission that the formal Council, the pledge of solidarity and collective responsibility has been virtually superseded by informal interviews and communications between certain selected members of the Cabinet'.[128] Some believed the Cabinet was already becoming, in Bagehot's sense, a 'dignified' part of the constitution, a conclusion to be resurrected sixty years later

125 T. G. Otte, *The China Question: Great Power Rivalry and British Isolation, 1894–1905*, Oxford University Press, 2007, p. 104fn.
126 Keith M. Wilson, *Empire and Continent: Studies in British Foreign Policy from the 1880s to the First World War*, Mansell, 1987, p. 17.
127 Anthony Seldon, 'The Cabinet System', in Vernon Bogdanor, ed., *The British Constitution in the Twentieth Century*, Oxford University Press, 2003, p. 100.
128 Low, *Governance of England*, p. 169fn

as a new discovery by the Labour MP and intellectual Richard Crossman, in his introduction to a new edition of Bagehot's *English Constitution*, published in 1963.

The Cabinet had no written agenda, nor any record or minutes of what was decided. A minister requiring an issue to be considered had to seek the consent of the Prime Minister. Frequently, other ministers were not warned in advance that a particular issue was to be considered. No officials were present, the post of the Cabinet Secretary not coming into existence until 1916. The prime source of information until then for what happened in Cabinet are the letters sent to the sovereign by the Prime Minister, the contents of which were not normally seen by other ministers.

Indeed, the Cabinet seems not to have been mentioned in any official document until 1900. In 1895, there was just one permanent Cabinet committee, on defence, established by Lord Salisbury, which, so the Duke of Devonshire complained in 1900, 'has met rarely, and generally without any definite agenda. No minutes have been kept.'[129] Other Cabinet committees were occasionally established on an informal and ad hoc basis. But in 1903, the defence committee was to become an advisory council and renamed the Committee of Imperial Defence, which did have a secretary and minutes.

Morley believed that one of the fundamental principles of Cabinet government was 'the doctrine of collective responsibility'. But at the end of the nineteenth century, there was some willingness to suspend it when a government was faced with a contentious issue by allowing it to remain an 'open question'. Female suffrage was to be one such 'open question' for the Liberal government after 1905. But it was in any case somewhat difficult to enforce the convention since, in the absence of a secretariat or minutes, it was not always easy for ministers to agree or remember precisely what had been decided. In 1900, Balfour agreed with his uncle, the Prime Minister, that 'a brief record of Cabinet discussion would be a convenience. My own memory in such matters is very untrustworthy and I sometimes find it difficult after our confused discussions to recollect even the instructions I have received on matters which I have myself brought before it.'[130]

This difficulty was to have serious consequences in the crisis over tariff reform in 1902–03. Joseph Chamberlain, the Colonial Secretary, had believed, before visiting South Africa in late 1902, that the Cabinet had agreed to retain a duty on imported corn introduced in the Budget of 1902. But he was to find that at least one minister was quite unaware that there had been

---

129 TNA CAB 37/53/71, cited by Anthony Seldon, 'The Cabinet System', in Bogdanor, ed., *The British Constitution in the Twentieth Century*, p. 101.

130 Cited in W. H. Greenleaf, *The British Political Tradition*, Methuen, 1987, vol. 3, part 1, p. 698.

such a commitment. In the 1903 Budget, the duty was removed. Chamberlain wrote in anger to his colleague, the Liberal Unionist leader in the Lords, the Duke of Devonshire:

> What did I ask of you before I went to South Africa? That you should retain the shilling corn duty and give a drawback to Canada. I thought you had all, except Ritchie [the Chancellor of the Exchequer], accepted this policy. While I was slaving my life out you threw it over as of no importance, and it is to this indifference to a great policy, which you had accepted, that you owe the present situation.

Devonshire replied:

> We must go back to the Cabinets immediately before and after your visit to South Africa, the proceedings at which are still extremely obscure to me. As you know, I am rather deaf, and I am afraid sometimes inattentive. I certainly failed to understand that at the first of these a decision was even provisionally taken of such importance as that to which you refer, and it must have been taken after very little discussion.[131]

The crisis led to the resignation of five Cabinet ministers, including both Chamberlain and the duke, and the eventual disintegration of the Balfour government. It was perhaps this episode to which Austen Chamberlain, Joe's son, was referring when he told the Commons in 1922 that, under the old system, 'I have known Cabinets break up under the impression that they had settled something, and every Minister going away asking his neighbour what was the decision to which they had come.'[132] Indeed, according to Lord Curzon, who, admittedly, did not himself enter the Cabinet until 1916, 'the experience of every Cabinet Minister' was 'that cases frequently arose when the matter was left so much in doubt that a Minister went away and acted upon what he thought was a decision which subsequently turned out to be no decision at all, or was repudiated by his colleagues'.[133]

LOCAL GOVERNMENT

At the turn of the century, many were proud not only of the parliamentary system but of Britain's local government, which was rooted, it was often

---

131 Holland, *Life of Devonshire*, vol. 2, pp. 356–7.
132 House of Commons Debates, 13 June 1922, vol. 155, col. 224.
133 House of Lords Debates, 19 June 1918, vol. 30, col. 265.

alleged, in historic communities. Observers contrasted localism in Britain with centralisation in France. Indeed, an Austrian constitutional authority believed, with perhaps more romance than realism, that 'the English idea of the state' was that of 'an association or federation of self-governing communities'.[134] 'England', one textbook writer suggested in 1894, again with some romantic exaggeration, 'is pre-eminently the country of local government',[135] though at the time the remark was made, it seemed, apparently, a 'commonplace'.[136]

Representative local government in the towns had been instituted in 1835 in the Municipal Corporations Act. But the term 'local government' was not used before 1858, and until the 1880s, local government was 'chaotic, rudimentary, corrupt – altogether behind the needs of the community'. The only nationwide coverage was in the hands of the somewhat unwieldy boards of guardians administering the 1834 Poor Law, of which there were 648. These boards were elected, but turnout in elections for them was very low. Other services were provided by ad hoc school boards in England and Wales established under the provisions of the 1870 Education Act, to ensure that there were sufficient primary schools in every part of the country – by the 1890s there were well over 2,000 of these boards – and by various other ad hoc authorities and improvement commissioners.[137]

Despite the rhetoric of localism, turnout in local elections tended to be much lower than in general elections. In 1906, turnout in the general election was 82.6 per cent, in the county council elections 55.5 per cent, in borough elections 48.2 per cent but in elections for the guardians just 28.1 per cent.[138] But turnout in local elections could on occasion be high. Fred Jowett, a Bradford Labour MP, wrote in 1907 that 'it is by no means uncommon in the North of England towns where the Labour and Socialist movement is strong, for 75 to 85 per cent of the number of persons entitled to vote to exercise that right at a municipal election'. In 1908, there was a 90 per cent poll in Nelson and in 1909 a 82 per cent poll in Northampton. When turnout fell to 77 per cent in Rochdale in 1912, there were complaints of 'apathy'.[139] Today, turnout in local government elections is generally between 30 per cent and 40 per cent.

The boards of guardians and school boards had been established before

134 Josef Redlich and Francis Hirst, *Local Government in England*, Macmillan, 1903, vol. 1, p. 9.
135 Edward Jenks, *An Outline of English Local Government* [1894], 5th edition, Methuen, 1921, p. 9.
136 Martin Loughlin, 'The Demise of Local Government', in Bogdanor, ed., *The British Constitution in the Twentieth Century*, p. 523.
137 Ensor, *England*, pp. 124–5.
138 Lord George Hamilton, *Journal of the Royal Statistical Society*, 1910, p. 31. He gives, however, a turnout figure for the general election of 78 per cent which seems to me inaccurate.
139 Duncan Tanner, 'Elections, Statistics and the Rise of the Labour Party, 1906–1931', *Historical Journal*, 1991, p. 894fn.

the introduction of a system of representative local government and were somewhat makeshift. But the extension of the franchise for parliamentary elections in 1867 and 1884 prompted the creation of representative local government institutions. It would have been anomalous if those allowed to elect their Parliament could not also elect local authorities. The Local Government Act of 1888 had extended representative government into the counties, including London, with the establishment of county councils. The Act had also provided that boroughs with a population of over 50,000 would become all-purpose authorities, outside the jurisdiction of the counties; and in the Technical Instruction Act of 1889, county boroughs and county councils were given powers to establish 'higher intermediate schools' for technical education.

The franchise qualification for borough and county councils in 1895 for men was for ratepayers residing in the borough or owning a shop in the borough and occupying property worth at least £10. But the vote was not restricted to men in local government or in elections for Poor Law Guardians or school boards. Duly qualified unmarried women and widows were also able to vote and even, in the case of some of these bodies, to be elected. The electorate for borough councils was on average around one-eighth larger than for the Commons. But there were wide variations between different boroughs and the percentage registered in London was much lower than the average due to the large number of lodgers in the capital.[140]

Although the 1888 Act had rationalised the local government system, there remained a tangle of different authorities and ad hoc bodies with different boundaries and different qualifications for voting. The President of the Local Government Board H. H. Fowler told the House of Commons in 1893 that England and Wales had sixty-two county councils, 302 municipal boroughs, thirty-one Improvement Act districts, 688 Local Government Act districts, 574 rural sanitary districts, fifty-eight port sanitary districts, 2,302 school board districts, 362 highway districts, 6,477 highway parishes, 1,052 burial board districts, 648 Poor Law unions, 13,755 ecclesiastical parishes and nearly 15,000 civil parishes.[141]

The system had been improved by Fowler's Local Government Act in 1894. This created urban and rural district councils below county level. The Act also provided for qualified married women to vote in local government elections, though few were able to do so since married women could not qualify on the basis of their husband's residence. The Act also provided that women could become candidates for election to the new councils, and

140 Lowell, *Government of England*, vol. 2, pp. 146–8, 269, 278.
141 House of Commons Debates, 21 March 1893, vol. 10, col. 681.

abolished the property qualification for candidates, which was also abolished for urban Poor Law boards of guardians, the rural guardians being absorbed by the new rural district councils.

The 1894 Act also created elective parish councils for villages with over 300 inhabitants, to be responsible for such matters as footpaths, allotments, parish charities and street lighting; and made provision for the direct democracy of parish meetings for villages with under 300 inhabitants. Liberals placed high hopes in these new councils, which they believed would erode the vestiges of feudal power in rural areas, removing influence from the squire and parson, the *ex officio* chairman of the local vestry, and take control of parochial charities from the clergy; the parish councils would also provide village halls, which, unlike church halls, would be open to those of all denominations. The parish council would, so the leader of the agricultural workers' trade union, Joseph Arch, hoped, 'revolutionise our villages; it will give England back her vanished peasantry'. The Liberal Party's 'Parish Councillor's Handbook' claimed that the parish council 'will abolish patronage and banish privilege. For the rule of the few it will substitute the responsibility and cooperation of the many. It is the Charter of the peasant's liberty.' One local newspaper declared that parish councils would be 'the People's Magna Carta', while another considered the first election day for these councils as 'Emancipation Day in Rural England … The democratic curfew will ring out the vestiges of feudal power and ring in the new era of equal self-government.'[142] Liberals hoped indeed that the parish councils would bring village democracy to Britain, but the councils were to fall far short of Liberal aspirations. Their powers were very limited, and they were hampered by their spending being restricted by an opposition amendment to a threepenny rate – or sixpence with the consent of the parish meeting. The first elections to parish councils showed little alteration in the village hierarchy, although a wider cross-section of the community was represented on them than on county councils, with labourers and other unskilled workers comprising around 9 per cent of the total number of councillors. But few women were returned – no more than around 200 out of 57,000 parish councillors.[143] The forces of deference were greater in rural areas than many Liberals had appreciated, and in 1951, one commentator concluded that the 1894 Act had done 'little to alter the basic form of local government at parish level; it merely provided the squire and the parson with a more useful means of carrying on as before'.[144] Parish meetings, which Liberals hoped would illustrate the virtues of direct democracy, did not prove effective, and many members held meetings

142 K. P. Poole and Bryan Keith-Lucas, *Parish Government 1894–1994*, National Association of Local Councils, 1984, pp. 59, 44, 48. This book provides an admirably concise account of the development of parish councils.
143 Patricia Hollis, *Ladies Elect: Women in English Local Government, 1865–1914*, Clarendon Press, 1987, p. 361.
144 G. D. Mitchell, 'The Parish Council and the Rural Community', *Public Administration*, 1951.

only on rare occasions. They tended to be lobbyists to rural district councils and county councils rather than active authorities in their own right. Even so, in 1972, when local government was being radically reformed in England and Wales, Lord Redcliffe-Maud, who had chaired a Royal Commission on Local Government, declared:

> The parish provides some of the best examples of genuine British self-government that one could find anywhere in this country, and as fine an example of local self-government as one would find anywhere in the world. In the parish community there are people who at least know each other by sight. It is that grass-roots community which I think should continue to be the basis of the whole structure of local self-government.[145]

The 1894 Act put the coping stone on a structure of local government which was not altered in any fundamental respect until the 1970s. An Austrian admirer of British institutions observed that, in consequence of the Act:

> The grand principle of representative democracy has now been fully applied to local government – England has created for herself 'self-government' in the true sense of the word. She has secured self-government – that is to say, the right of her people to legislate, to deliberate and to administer through councils or parliaments elected on the basis of popular suffrage – and this is the root of the incomparable strength of the English Body Politic.[146]

That was an over-romanticised view. Admittedly, central government played a much smaller role in local affairs than it was to do in the twentieth century. But this was less because of a deep-seated belief in local autonomy than because the functions of local councils were so very minimal that they did not impinge upon the concerns of central government. County council functions, for example, were in 1888 a curious hotch-potch. The county

> repairs all main roads and county bridges ... It prevents the pollution of rivers ... It regulates all Local Government elections. It pays the salary of the clerks to the justices ... It grants licences for music and dancing and racecourses; it insists on the proper use of weights and measures; it protects the purchaser of coal and bread.[147]

---

145 Poole and Keith-Lucas, *Parish Government*, pp. 204–5.
146 Cited in Bryan Keith-Lucas, *Parish Councils: The Way Ahead*, The Fourth Mary Brockenhurst Lecture, Devon Association of Parish Councils, 1985, p. 1.
147 W. B. Odgers and E. J. Naldrett, *Local Government*, 2nd edition, Macmillan, 1909, pp. 210–11.

Most of these matters did not require central intervention and could happily be left to local representatives. There was a sharp division between the 'high politics' of foreign and colonial policy, the politics of diplomacy and management of the empire, and the 'low politics' of highways and sanitation. No true statesman would concern himself with the latter.[148]

Local authorities had minimal powers, most of which were permissive, on many of the matters later to become cornerstones of the welfare state. For example, public health was from 1894 a function of urban district and rural district councils, but there were few statutory duties. Aid to the poor and, in England, Scotland and Ireland, education – with the exception of 'technical education' after 1889 – lay outside local government entirely, being, until 1902, the responsibility of directly elected ad hoc boards. It was not until after the Liberal election victory in 1906 that local authorities were to expand their welfare functions, although aid to the poor, except in rural areas, did not become a local government responsibility until 1929.

Local authorities were also limited by their narrow financial base. Their main sources of revenue were a rate on property, together with a small though growing grant from the central Exchequer. In 1898, of approximately £69 million local authority revenues, around £38 million was derived from the rates and £11 million from central government. The rest came from receipts and fees, sales of property and revenue-raising undertakings such as waterworks and gasworks.[149] In addition, local authorities tended to be dominated by the well-to-do and the propertied, who sought not to extend local services but to economise and hold down the level of rates.

There was one area of municipal government, however, where there had been considerable expansion in the last thirty years of the nineteenth century: the municipalisation of utilities. By 1882, 148 local authorities owned municipal gas undertakings, and Joseph Chamberlain, as Mayor of Birmingham between 1873 and 1876, had made the city a byword for effective local government with its municipal water supply, sanitary arrangements and gas supply. Birmingham was not in fact the pioneer of municipalisation, but Chamberlain was its most effective publicist. 'I am so parochially minded', he declared in 1880 – paradoxically in the light of his later career – 'that I look with greater satisfaction to the annexation of the gas and water' than to the annexation of new colonies.[150] Chamberlain's approach was sometimes labelled 'municipal socialism', and indeed it influenced the early Fabians, but its prime purpose was to apply business principles to local government

148 J. G. Bulpitt, *Territory and Power in the United Kingdom: An Interpretation*, Manchester University Press, 1983, *passim*.
149 Sir Henry Hartley Fowler, 'Municipal Finance and Municipal Enterprise', *Journal of the Royal Statistical Society*, 1900, p. 384.
150 Quoted in Richard Jay, *Joseph Chamberlain: A Political Study*, Clarendon Press, 1981, p. 27.

by using profits from municipal enterprise to finance slum clearance, sanitation and house-building. As President of the Board of Trade from 1880 to 1885, Chamberlain had promoted legislation enabling local authorities to buy private electricity companies – the Electric Lighting Act of 1882. By 1900, most large city authorities owned their gasworks, electricity supply and tramways.[151] Until the nationalisation of the major public utilities by the Attlee government of 1945–51, most public ownership of utilities was under local not central government. But in areas such as the economy, education, health, transport, housing, welfare and the environment, the late nineteenth century state had a very limited role. It is a paradox that, although the British may have believed their form of government the best in the world, they did not expect it to do very much.

SCOTLAND, WALES AND IRELAND

The United Kingdom is and has been since 1707 a composite state. Despite the rejection of Home Rule in 1886 and 1893, it would be a mistake to describe it as unitary, if that implies a Jacobin state, built around an unambiguous political centre and following a policy of administration standardisation. The political elite has always resisted the integration of the non-English parts of the kingdom, preferring indirect rule, which offered scope for the indigenous institutions of the non-English parts to be preserved. The Britain of this period is best described not as a unitary state but as a union state.[152] Such union states had been common in Europe before the nineteenth century but had been swept away on the Continent in the process of nation-building after the French Revolution, under the influence of the doctrine of popular sovereignty, which implied that there was a single unified will which was to be represented at the centre. But that doctrine had never taken hold in Britain, since the nation had been created with the Anglo-Scottish Union in 1707, nearly a century before the French Revolution; and Britain did not, until her first national referendum, on Europe, in 1975, recognise popular sovereignty as the basis of legitimacy. Paradoxically, it was the historic foundations of the British state and the absence of administrative standardisation that facilitated the sense of Britishness in the nineteenth century and much of the twentieth.

Of the 38 million inhabitants living in Britain at the end of the nineteenth century, some 28 million – around 70 per cent – lived in England, by far the

---

151 J. A. Chandler, *Explaining Local Government: Local Government in Britain since 1800*, Manchester University Press, 2013, pp. 76–80.

152 A term used by Stein Rokkan and Derek Urwin in 'Introduction: Centres and Peripheries in Western Europe', in Rokkan and Urwin, *The Politics of Territorial Identity: Studies in European Regionalism*, Sage, 1982, p. 11.

dominant part of the kingdom, though not as dominant as it would become in the twenty-first century, when England was to contain 85 per cent of those living in Britain. Part of the reason for this was, of course, that, until 1921, the whole of the island of Ireland was part of the United Kingdom. In the late nineteenth century, the majority of English MPs rejected Home Rule for Ireland, but they nevertheless accepted that the non-English parts of the kingdom required separate institutions. They did not seek to integrate the non-English parts of the kingdom into a uniform system of government. Separate institutional arrangements for Scotland and Wales proved far less contentious than Home Rule for Ireland.

The office of Secretary of State for Scotland, which had a population of around 4 million, had been created in 1885, as a result of the efforts of Lord Rosebery, the future Liberal Prime Minister. But the first holder, the Duke of Richmond and Gordon, was to be appointed by Lord Salisbury's Conservative government later that year. The post was seen as a sinecure. 'The work is not heavy,' Lord Salisbury assured the duke, 'it really is a matter where the effulgence of two Dukedoms and the best salmon river in Scotland will go a long way.'[153] In February 1898, the Secretary, Lord Balfour of Burleigh, 'illustrating the good government of Scotland and the satisfaction of the people with their parliamentary ministers' declared:

> that on the opening day of the session his work at the Scots Office was concluded in twenty minutes. He received no letter and only two visits from MPs, one Radical and one Conservative, who in each case called in order to thank the Secretary for what he had done during the recess.[154]

Nevertheless, the secretary was responsible for home office, local government, education and some trade functions in Scotland, and during the twentieth century his responsibilities steadily increased. From 1892, the secretary was in peacetime always a member of the Cabinet. And since debates on the Scottish Vote in the Commons were, by convention, confined to Scottish MPs, Scotland, by the end of the nineteenth century, had obtained 'some of the substance, without the form, of home rule'.[155] Between 1895 and 1914, Scotland was to produce two of the four Prime Ministers (Balfour and Campbell-Bannerman), while a third (Asquith) sat for a Scottish constituency (East Fife), as did two post-1918 Prime Ministers (Andrew Bonar Law and Ramsay MacDonald). One third of Campbell-Bannerman's 1905 Cabinet

153 H. J. Hanham, 'The Creation of the Scottish Office, 1881–87', *Juridical Review*, 1965, p. 229.
154 Vincent, ed., *Crawford Papers*, p. 46.
155 Ensor, *England*, p. 130.

were Scots. Scotland, then, seemed fully integrated into British politics in comparison with Ireland and Wales.

In Wales, the population was around 2 million. There, by contrast with England and Scotland, the first county council elections in 1889 saw not the election of the well-to-do – former justices of the peace and landowners – but a radical triumph, with the Liberals winning every county except Brecknock. This was largely the result of Welsh national feeling, hostile to the landed interest and the gentry. But Welsh national feeling took a different form from that in Ireland. In Wales, there was not 'that self-generating demand for an ever-increasing degree of exclusion from the British political system that stamped the nationalist movement in Ireland'.[156] Liberals regarded the essence of Welshness as lying in its Nonconformity and sought religious equality and recognition of their status rather than separation. Welsh Liberals were divided on Home Rule for Wales, but they were united in seeking recognition for their religious distinctiveness and cultural aspirations. There was no equivalent in Wales of Irish conditions – memories of famine, forced emigration and absentee landlords. 'It is not the Irish case over again,' Gladstone had told his friend Stuart Rendel, MP for Montgomery, in November 1892.[157] Industrialisation in south Wales was tying her economy more closely to that of England, weakening nationalism by relieving pressure on the land and so providing an alternative to migration that was not so easily available to the Irish peasant. Welshness, then, was to be achieved not through separation but recognition by the English of Welsh claims. In 1896, the Cymru Fydd movement – calling for Home Rule – collapsed, largely due to conflict between north Wales, which was sympathetic to Home Rule, and the South Wales Liberal Federation, which was not. An alderman from south Wales declared that 'a cosmopolitan population from Swansea to Newport' would 'never bow to the domination of Welsh ideas'.[158] Tom Ellis, leader of Cymru Fydd, came to perceive 'that it was the nonconformity of Wales that created the unity of Wales, rather than any spontaneous national demand for home rule'.[159] So the focus was less on a Welsh Parliament than on national educational institutions and the disestablishment of the Anglican Church in Wales. The former proved easier to achieve than the latter.

In 1889, the Intermediate Education Act had made Welsh county councils the first local education authorities in Britain, empowered to raise a

---

156 Kenneth O. Morgan, *Wales in British Politics, 1868–1922*, 3rd edition, University of Wales Press, 1991, p. 164. This book remains the most comprehensive account of Welsh politics during this period.
157 J. Graham Jones, 'Michael Davitt, David Lloyd George and T. E. Ellis: The Welsh Experience, 1886', *Welsh History Review*, 1997, p. 481.
158 Quoted in Neville Masterman, *The Forerunner: The Dilemmas of Tom Ellis, 1859–1899*, C. Davies, 1972, p. 256.
159 Morgan, *Wales in British Politics*, p. 164.

halfpenny rate for secondary education, with an Exchequer grant being made available equivalent to the sum raised by rates, the system later to be adopted in England in Balfour's Education Act of 1902. In 1893, a charter had been granted to the University of Wales, and in 1896 a Central Welsh Board had been established to administer examinations. The Welsh educational system was becoming 'a national system, the first and most striking expression in institutional terms of the reawakened consciousness of nationhood'.[160] The disestablishment of the Welsh Church, however, was far more contentious and was not enacted until 1914.

By 1914, Scotland and Wales were well integrated into the United Kingdom. A Scottish humorist, Ian Hay, wrote a book in 1917 in which he declared how sorry he felt for the English.

> Today a Scot is leading the British army in France [Haig], another is commanding the British grand fleet at sea [Beatty], while a third directs the Imperial General Staff at home [Robertson]. The Lord Chancellor is a Scot [Lord Finlay]; so are the Chancellor of the Exchequer and the Foreign Secretary [Bonar Law and Arthur Balfour]. The Prime Minister is a Welshman [Lloyd George], and the first Lord of the Admiralty is an Irishman [Carson]. Yet no one has ever brought in a bill to give home rule to England.[161]

But Ireland was not so well integrated. Indeed, in 1886, in preparing the First Home Rule Bill, Gladstone had believed that 'the long, vexed and troubled relations between Great Britain and Ireland exhibit to us the one and only conspicuous failure of the political genius of our race to confront and master difficulty, and to obtain in a reasonable degree the main ends of civilised life'.[162] The question which Ireland posed at the end of the nineteenth century was, as with Scotland in the twenty-first, whether she could be reconciled to the Union. The Act of Union of 1800, uniting Ireland with Britain, had been carried in the Irish Parliament by corrupt means, and by virtue of a promise of Catholic emancipation – a promise not honoured until 1829. By contrast with the Union with Scotland, this Union never achieved general acceptance in Ireland.

In 1895, the population of Ireland was just under 5 million. It had been falling in every decade since the great famine of the 1840s, widely blamed on English cruelty and insensitivity. The Catholic population of Ireland

---

160 R. Coupland, *Welsh and Scottish Nationalism: A Study*, Collins, 1954, p. 199.
161 Ian Hay, *The Oppressed English*, Doubleday, Page & Co., 1917, p. 30.
162 Gladstone Papers, May 1886, BL Add. MS 44772, f. 82.

regarded itself as belonging to a conquered and stigmatised people ruled by coercion. When, in the debates on the Commonwealth of Australia Bill, federating the Australian colonies, a Liberal spokesman, R. B. Haldane, declared, 'Parliament does not coerce her children,' an Irish MP interjected. 'We do not accept that statement.'[163] So it was far more difficult to create institutions reconciling Ireland to the Union than to create institutions recognising Scottish and Welsh distinctiveness; and it was a problem which Victorian and Edwardian politicians failed to solve.

From 1886, when Gladstone introduced the First Home Rule Bill, Ireland was to remain central to British politics. Introducing his Bill, Gladstone declared, 'We have arrived at a stage in our political transactions with Ireland, where two roads part one from the other, not soon probably to meet again.'[164] The rejection of the Bill on Second Reading by 343 votes to 313 was to determine the future not only of Irish but of British politics for many years. It was to have the effect in the long run of turning Irish Nationalists away from constitutionalism. By contrast, the passage of Home Rule might well have set both Ireland and Britain on an alternative constitutional path, marked by a recasting of relationships between the centre and the periphery. Perhaps it might have led to the kind of quasi-federal system which Tony Blair sought to construct after 1997; and perhaps even a written or codified constitution charting the relationships between the nations and regions of the United Kingdom. But it was not to be.

Many otherwise liberally minded people refused to support Home Rule since they believed that, even though tainted by corruption, the Union with Ireland was the consummation of a long historical process uniting the British Isles under one Parliament. To undo this process would be, in the words of the great constitutional lawyer Dicey, a Liberal Unionist, to 'undo the work not only of Pitt, but of Somers, of Henry VII and of Edward I'.[165] It would, many believed, lead not only to the disintegration of the United Kingdom but also of the empire. 'If Ireland goes,' Lord Salisbury believed, 'India will go fifty years later.'[166] In fact, India 'went' in 1947, just twenty-five years after Ireland became independent in 1922. Both were to be partitioned, and had, perhaps, only been held together by British rule. In 1895, however, fears that Ireland would 'go' appeared quite misplaced. An observer noticed in 1896 greater enthusiasm at the opera in Dublin for 'God Save the Queen' than 'God Save Ireland'.[167] The queen, admittedly, did little to encourage

163 House of Commons Debates, 14 May 1900, vol. 83, col. 102.
164 Ibid., 8 April 1886, vol. 304, col. 1036.
165 A. V. Dicey, *England's Case Against Home Rule* [1886], Richmond Publishing Co., 1973, p. 191.
166 Quoted in Algernon Cecil, *Queen Victoria and Her Ministers*, Eyre & Spottiswood, 1953, p. 324.
167 Vincent, ed., *Crawford Papers*, p. 37.

this feeling. When, in November 1897, the Cabinet declared that it would be desirable to establish a royal residence in Ireland, she flatly refused.

With the rejection of Home Rule, the British government was faced with the problem of how Ireland was to be governed under a Union to which she seemed no longer to consent. The government of Ireland was quite different from that of any other part of the kingdom. Although she sent MPs to Westminster, her executive and administration were in Dublin, headed by the Lord Lieutenant, representing the sovereign, and the Chief Secretary, normally a member of the British Cabinet, and in effect Secretary of State for Ireland. The Chief Secretary was in charge of some twenty-nine Irish departments as well as the Irish police force, prisons and legal offices, and was 'effectively an interior or justice minister'.[168] There was a separate Irish Privy Council and separate judiciary and law officers. Ireland, therefore, had a separate executive and judiciary but no separate legislature, and the Chief Secretary, the political head of the Irish government, normally spent nine months of every year in London. Between 1855 and 1905, there had been twenty-seven Chief Secretaries, with an average tenure of just under two years. Since 1871, no Irishman by birth had been appointed, and some were total strangers to the country.

The Lord Lieutenant was supposed to exercise the functions of the queen in Ireland. Until 1918, he was always a hereditary peer, although by convention he did not speak in the Lords, and was not responsible to Parliament for the exercise of his functions.[169] He was, nevertheless, a political appointee, and, from 1895 to 1902, and in 1918, he was a member of the Cabinet. The existence of such a post was in itself contentious, since it underlined Ireland's lack of integration with the rest of the United Kingdom. In 1902, George Wyndham, the Irish Secretary, a Unionist, declared that the post should be abolished since it was 'an anachronism which serves only to confirm memories of a constitutional division between Great Britain and Ireland which has long since been abolished and ought never to revive'.[170] But the constitutional division depended upon more than the post of Lord Lieutenant.

From 1885, when the vote had been extended to the Irish agricultural labourer, giving Ireland for the first time a popular franchise, nearly every Irish constituency outside Ulster returned a member of the Irish Parliamentary Party, a party whose *raison d'être* was Home Rule. After 1885, Irish Nationalists never won fewer than eighty-one of the 103 Irish constituencies. So Ireland could only be governed by those opposed to the majority of her

168 Eunan O'Halpin, *The Decline of the Union: British Government in Ireland, 1892–1920*, Gill & Macmillan, 1987, p. 6.
169 Adonis, *Making Aristocracy Work*, pp. 69–70fn.
170 O'Halpin, *Decline of the Union*, p. 6.

representatives. Whether Liberals or Conservatives were in power in London, the Chief Secretary and the Irish administration were in the hands of a party which had only minority support in Ireland. Irish representatives, unless they belonged to the minority Unionists, could play no part in the government of their country. The constitutional implication of the Anglo-Irish Union of 1800 had been the legal equality of Ireland with the rest of the kingdom; but to most in Ireland, the relationship seemed one of subordination. Ireland appeared, by contrast with Scotland, a dependency not a partner.

When, in 1884, Gladstone was preparing to expand the franchise, his Home Secretary, Sir William Harcourt, feared that

> there will be declared to the world in larger print what we all know to be the case, that we hold Ireland by force and by force alone, as in the days of Cromwell, only that we are obliged to hold it by a force ten times larger than he found necessary ... We have never governed and we never shall govern Ireland by the good of its people.[171]

In 1908, Lowell was to conclude that while 'Scotland is governed by Scotchmen in accordance with Scottish ideas ... Ireland has been governed by Englishmen, and until recently, in accordance with English ideas'.[172]

Harcourt's fellow Liberal John Morley, who had been Chief Secretary from 1892 to 1895, told an audience in Manchester in 1902 that the government of Ireland was 'a very good machine for governing a country against its own consent'.[173] The administration of Ireland was primarily by Protestants and men committed to the Union. An Irish magistrate reminiscing in 1951 gave a not unfair verdict when he declared, 'We were governed from London by people who knew little about our country, but who ruled it fairly though in the English interest, through an oligarchy in Dublin.'[174] In 1893, Chamberlain had asked, 'Does anybody doubt that if Ireland were a thousand miles away from England she would not have been, long before this, a self-governing colony?'[175] But Ireland, unlike the self-governing colonies, was ruled not through popular consent but paternalistically, to which was added an admixture of coercion.

Ireland was administered quite differently from the rest of the country by boards with members nominated by the Chief Secretary, almost always belonging to the Unionist ascendancy. They could not be called to account

171 Gardiner, *Harcourt*, vol. 1, p. 497.
172 Lowell, *Government of England*, vol. 1, p. 139.
173 *The Times*, 13 March 1902.
174 O'Halpin, *Decline of the Union*, p. 8.
175 Trevor West, *Horace Plunkett: Co-operation and Politics: An Irish Biography*, Colin Smythe, 1986, p. 120.

by Irish MPs. Arrangements for preserving law and order were also quite different from those in the rest of the country. The Royal Irish Constabulary, by contrast with police forces elsewhere, was a national and centralised force, used for internal security and characterised as a paramilitary organisation operating as an agent of government.[176] The constabulary was seen by many Catholics as in effect an army of occupation, since most of its officers belonged to the Protestant minority. For almost the whole of the nineteenth century, Ireland was governed by special coercive legislation which had no counterpart in the rest of Britain. In 1912, Augustine Birrell, the Irish Secretary, declared that there had been eighty-six coercion acts in the century following the Act of Union, including a Peace Preservation Act (Ireland) by which any person possessing or suspected of possessing arms or ammunition could be arrested without a warrant, an Act which had been repealed by the Liberals in 1906.[177] Ironically, had it remained on the statute book, it would have prevented the Unionists from arming in 1914. The Crimes Act of 1887 allowed the Lord Lieutenant to prohibit organisations he thought 'dangerous' and to allow offences of agrarian violence to be tried by a magistrate without a jury. It remained on the statute book until Irish independence in 1922. In 1886, Sir William Harcourt, Gladstone's Chancellor of the Exchequer, had predicted that, if Home Rule were to be rejected, 'its ghost will ever haunt your festivals of coercion'.[178] This was to prove an all too true prediction.

Gladstone had believed that repressive legislation in Ireland was 'morally worn out', since it was imposed by a foreign authority. In consequence, the success of coercive legislation depended upon two 'essential conditions' – 'the autocracy of government and the secrecy of public transactions'. Neither of these conditions could be met in a liberal state. Further, the breakdown of law and order in Ireland served, in the rest of Britain, to produce 'not only disparaging and hostile judgment but estrangement of feeling from Ireland'. It thus served 'to widen the breach between the countries'. Home Rulers had hoped that by making the Irish police responsible to an elected Parliament, respect for the law would increase. Law and order, Gladstone believed, could be preserved only if 'as in England the law is felt to be indigenous'.[179]

'The administration of Ireland', Lowell noted in 1908,

has been the conspicuous failure of the English government. Its history for a century has been a long tale of expedients, palliations and concessions,

176 Richard Hawkins, 'The "Irish" model and the Empire: A Case for Reassessment', in David M. Anderson and David Killingray, *Policing the Empire: Government, Authority and Control, 1830–1940*, Manchester University Press, 1991, p. 18.
177 House of Commons Debates, 16 April 1912, vol. 11, col. 302.
178 Ibid., 13 April 1886, vol. 304, col. 1458.
179 Gladstone Papers, BL Add. MS 44772, ff. 58–60; House of Commons Debates, 8 April 1886, vol. 304, col. 1043.

which have never availed to secure either permanent good order or the contentment and loyalty of the inhabitants. Each step has been taken, not of foresight, but under pressure.[180]

Government in Ireland was in form free but in reality autocratic. The problem of how to govern an Ireland which did not consent to rule from Westminster was to vex both Liberal and Unionist governments until, in 1918, Ireland outside Ulster returned a majority of MPs from Sinn Féin, which had almost entirely replaced the Irish Parliamentary Party. Sinn Féin MPs refused to take their seats at Westminster and established their own Parliament in Dublin. After an abortive attempt to put down a guerrilla uprising, Westminster was forced to concede independence in the Anglo-Irish Treaty of 1921.

THE EMPIRE

Westminster was the Parliament not only of the United Kingdom. It was also the Imperial Parliament at the centre of the largest land empire the world had ever seen, containing in 1895, in addition to the 38 million living in Britain, around 360 million people, and covering around one-fifth of the globe, around 12 million square miles out of a habitable total of 60 million square miles. The 400 million living in the empire comprised over a quarter of the world's population of around 1,500 million, and a larger area and population than either Russia or the United States.

In addition to the formal empire, under the authority of the crown, there was also an informal empire. This included territories such as the Indian native states, whose rulers were 'advised' by Britain, and Egypt, formally a part of the Ottoman Empire but 'temporarily' occupied by Britain from 1882 to 1936. In Afghanistan, by agreement with the emir, Britain controlled her foreign relations, guaranteed her against external aggression and paid the state a subsidy. In other parts of the world such as China, not subject to formal control, Britain enjoyed extra-territorial privileges such as bases, treaty ports and trade concessions; while in parts of Latin America, trade arrangements were supported when necessary by financial control, or, in the last resort, by diplomatic or even military intervention.

The empire was not a product of design. It had been unsystematically acquired, in part by conquest – 'If our ancestors had cared for the rights of other people,' Lord Salisbury had said in the 1870s, 'the British Empire would not have been made' – but also by colonisation and settlement.[181] It

---

180 Lowell, *Government of England*, vol. 1, p. 140.
181 Andrew Roberts, *Salisbury: Victorian Titan*, Weidenfeld & Nicolson, 1999, p. 169.

was organised on a ramshackle basis. At its zenith in 1913, it contained over 100 separate political units.[182] It is hardly possible to explain the empire in terms of any single theory. Nor was there ever a single vision of empire but different and opposed visions – 'humanitarian, authoritarian, democratic, protectionist, free-trading, religious-minded and militaristic'.[183] Because its internal diversity was so great, no single pattern of rule was possible, and it was hardly feasible to impose a uniform imperial policy from London. The empire rested, the Boer General Smuts believed, 'more upon prestige and moral intimidation than upon true military strength'.[184] Perhaps it rested on a large-scale confidence trick, but when challenged in wars, from the time of the Indian rebellion or 'mutiny' in 1857 to the attempt by Boers in South Africa to undermine it in the 1890s, the British fought tenaciously to maintain it.

The strength of the empire during the 'imperial century', which lasted from 1815 to 1914, was based on contingent factors, control of the sea and the absence of hegemonic competitors on the Continent able to challenge British rule, as well as the inability or unwillingness of Asians and Africans to resist British domination.

There were three British empires in 1895, divided largely on grounds of race and colour.[185] They were governed in quite different ways.

The first empire comprised in 1895 colonies of white settlement in temperate climes – Canada, Newfoundland and Labrador (not joined to Canada until 1949), the Australian colonies (to be federated in 1900), New Zealand and the two British colonies in South Africa (Cape Colony and Natal). These had begun as in large part the British nation spreading itself across the world rather than ruling over foreign peoples, although admittedly Canada and the South African colonies contained large white populations – French and Dutch – not of British origin. In the self-governing colonies, native populations – Māoris, Aboriginal Australians, Bantu peoples, Bushmen and the Khoekhoe in South Africa – had not been able to resist the domination of white immigrant settlers. They had been subdued and dispossessed, often by violence, and sometimes by what approached genocide. 'In spite of their human likeness, the Tasmanians', H. G. Wells writes at the beginning of his novel *The War of the Worlds*, published in 1898, 'were entirely swept out of

---

182 John Darwin, *Unfinished Empire: The Global Expansion of Britain*, Allen Lane, 2012, p. 7. This book provides a most impressive overview of the British imperial experience.
183 Ibid., p. 293.
184 Ibid., p. xx.
185 A standard account from the early twentieth century, C. P. Lucas, *Greater Rome and Greater Britain*, Clarendon Press, 1912, states on p. 44 that there were two empires. But India was governed in a quite different manner from the rest of the dependent empire and is best treated as a separate unit.

existence in a war of extermination waged by European immigrants in the space of fifty years.'[186]

The colonies of settlement comprised a population of around 11 million and in them the settlers provided a popular foundation for self-government. The revolt of the American colonies had shown that remote colonies could not be ruled from London, while distance made it impracticable for them to send representatives to Westminster. The only logical solution, therefore, was seen to be responsible government, first implemented in Nova Scotia in 1848, following recommendations of the Durham report in 1839. Since Britain, unlike the major Continental powers, had a system of responsible government, an executive responsible to a directly elected legislature, the settlers could adapt it to the colonies. In addition, free trade destroyed the rationale of a centralised empire with a single tariff policy, something which Chamberlain was later to attempt to institute. But for the mid-Victorians, there had been an intimate connection between free trade and responsible government, and so the self-governing part of the empire was quite different in this regard from the colonies of other powers, few of which were colonies of settlement. In them, mercantilism remained the norm.

The growth of responsible government meant that, as Rosebery told his audience at Adelaide in 1884, the self-governing colonies were in reality 'no longer colonies in the ordinary sense of the term'. For, although constitutionally subordinate to Westminster, they were not politically subordinate. Indeed, as early as 1859, Britain had gone so far as to recognise their right to tariff autonomy, which included the right to levy tariffs against British goods. Australia, Rosebery went on, had become 'a nation – a nation not in aspiration or in the future, but in performance and fact'. He then asked, 'Does this fact of your being a nation ... imply separation from the Empire?', and answered, 'God forbid! There is no need for any nation, however great, leaving the Empire, because the Empire is a commonwealth of nations.'[187] This was, apparently, the first use of the term 'commonwealth' into which the empire was to be transformed in the twentieth century. Empire designates a relationship of superior and subordinate, but commonwealth designates a quite different relationship, one of equals.

In 1775, Edmund Burke had predicted that the ties linking the colonies with the mother country, though 'light as air', would be 'strong as links of iron'. By 1895, that was certainly so with the self-governing colonies. As Chamberlain noted in his first major public speech as Colonial Secretary in

---

186 H. G. Wells, *The War of the Worlds* [1898], Penguin, 1946, p. 3.
187 Quoted in G. Bennett, ed., *The Concept of Empire: Burke to Attlee, 1774–1947*, Adam & Charles Black, 1953, p. 283; S. R. Mehrotra, 'On the Use of the Term "Commonwealth"', *Journal of Commonwealth Political Studies*, 1963, p. 1.

November 1895, it was a paradox of self-government that, as freedom spread, so did attachment to the mother country. 'As the possibility of separation has become greater, the desire for separation has become less.'[188] That attachment was symbolised by allegiance to the queen. Legislation on domestic affairs, as well as tariffs and defence, was, by convention, for the colonial government alone; and at some international conferences, they would be represented by their own delegations and not by Britain. Westminster, by convention, would legislate for these colonies only on imperial matters, except with the consent of the colony. The very limited power of disallowance, or veto, which Westminster in theory retained was employed only when a self-governing colony proposed to legislate in a manner prejudicial to other parts of the empire or foreign countries. But even this very limited degree of subordination was voluntary, since if a colony had sought to sever the connection, it was hardly likely that Britain would seek to restrain it by force. On almost all legislation in the self-governing colonies, therefore, the queen acted in practice on the advice of her colonial and not her British ministers. The relationship had become one of states coexisting with the mother country on a basis of near equality. The 'mid-Victorian disengagement from the settlement colonies was', it has been argued, 'a major development in British colonial policy and an unprecedented transfer of power by an imperial state, comparable in its way with the decolonisation of Africa a century later ... a recognition of reality as much as a failure of will'.[189] At the 1907 Imperial Conference, the special position of the self-governing colonies was to be recognised by calling them 'dominions'. In these colonies, Britain had been, so Lord Salisbury believed in 1897, engaging in 'a great experiment', 'trying to sustain an Empire entirely upon the basis of mutual goodwill, sympathy and affection'.[190]

But the colonies of settlement represented only part of the empire. For there was, secondly, a dependent empire of territories where there had been little white settlement. In the novel *The Gay-Dombeys*, published in 1919, but referring to a visit to Salisbury's Hatfield home in 1888, the explorer Sir Harry Johnston wrote, 'It is a curious anomaly that the future weal or woe of millions of black or brown people ... is being determined in a Hertfordshire beech avenue ... where there hasn't been the shade of a palm for two million years.'[191] The self-governing colonies were held together by ethnicity, religion and language, but there were no such ties in the dependent empire or in India.

---

188 Garvin, *Chamberlain*, vol. 3, p. 26.

189 Peter Burroughs, 'Colonial Self-government', in C. C. Eldridge, ed., *British Imperialism in the Nineteenth Century*, Macmillan, 1984, pp. 62–3.

190 Donald Read, *The Age of Urban Democracy: England 1868–1914*, revised edition, Longman, 1994, p. 363.

191 Roberts, *Salisbury*, p. 520.

The colonies of the dependent empire were ruled by a governor appointed by the queen on the advice of the Colonial Secretary. The dependent empire and India tended to be ignored by those such as the Cambridge historian Sir John Seeley, who had sought to foster a consciousness of empire in his book *The Expansion of England*, first published in 1883, when he wrote that the empire consisted primarily of the British peoples transplanting themselves overseas.

In the dependent empire as well as India, self-government was seen as a distant goal unlikely to be achieved for many years, if at all. The justification of imperial rule there was less as a preparation for self-government than as a civilising mission to less advanced races. Much of the dependent empire had the constitutional status of crown colonies, so-called because in them the crown retained full control of the executive. Some – for example, Bermuda, Jamaica, Ceylon (now Sri Lanka) and Fiji – enjoyed a partial degree of self-government with a legislature comprising nominated or locally elected members; but the governor was not responsible to that legislature. Other crown colonies had no representative body at all, although in some, the governor was advised by nominated members. Crown colony government, therefore, was a flexible form of government giving the British authorities and the governor wide discretion.

In addition to the formal dependent empire, there were various protectorates and other possessions, not formally annexed, in which the inhabitants were not British subjects and not part of the British dominions but in which the crown had authority, either through treaty or by other means. Protectorates were in a loose and often ill-defined and indefinite relationship with the crown. They were generally subject to indirect rule, with the local ruler being under the authority of a Commissioner or High Commissioner appointed by the queen on the advice, generally, of the Colonial Office; although, in some cases, by the Foreign Office. The majority of such protectorates were in Africa, Asia or the Arab world. They included Aden (now part of Yemen), Bahrain and, from 1899, Kuwait; many of the territories now comprising Malaysia and various islands in the Western Pacific; and in Africa, the Anglo-Egyptian Sudan, ruled in condominium with Egypt from 1899, and most of the territories for which Britain was responsible other than the white-ruled colonies, Cape Colony and Natal. There were also various protectorates on the frontiers of India to protect the Indian empire.[192] Protectorates were generally in territories where there had been no previous organised or stable system of government. A protectorate, like a crown colony, was a flexible

---

192 A contemporary list of the various colonies and their constitutional status can be found in E. J. Payne, *Colonies and Colonial Federations*, Macmillan, 1904.

form of government which could be adjusted to the needs of the moment. This flexibility was needed both to protect indigenous peoples from other powers but also to protect them 'from the grosser forms of ill-treatment and oppression by their rulers, and from raids of slave dealers and marauders'.[193] Joseph Chamberlain, Colonial Secretary from 1895 to 1903, argued that Britain ought to assume much greater responsibility for such territories, which he regarded 'as being in the condition of undeveloped estates, and estates which can never be developed without Imperial assistance'.[194] 'What is wanted for Uganda', Chamberlain had declared in 1894, 'is what Birmingham has got – an improvement scheme.'[195] But while Birmingham could accept a large increase in its indebtedness, the Treasury would not, so Chamberlain could not do as much for the colonies as he had been able to do for Birmingham.

The third element in the empire was India, an empire in itself. The Indian subcontinent contained nearly 300 million people – three-quarters of the total population of the empire – but was ruled by around 300,000 British civil and military officials. It was around eight times the size of Britain and five times the size of the whole French colonial empire, while in territory it was equal to the whole of Europe minus Russia, and was larger than the Roman Empire.[196] Bengal alone with 66 million people had a larger population than any European state except Russia, and a larger population than the United States.

The Indian empire had been acquired by conquest and cession, not by settlement, nor by what Sir John Seeley was to characterise as a 'fit of absence of mind'. By contrast with the colonies of settlement, the peoples of India had no natural ties or affinities with the population of Britain, being different in ethnicity, religion and language. Constitutionally, the Indian empire was a strange anomaly, being ruled autocratically by foreigners who lived beyond the seas, a feature which distinguished it from, for example, the Russian Empire. Since the rebellion or 'mutiny' of 1857, India had been for the first time in her history under one supreme authority: the Imperial Parliament. By contrast with the rest of the dependent empire, it was represented in the Cabinet by a Secretary of State, responsible, not to Indians in whose interests he was expected to govern, but to the House of Commons. He was assisted by a Council of India, a primarily consultative body with no power to initiate legislation and only a very limited power of veto, and generally

---

193 John Branston, an official of the Colonial Office, in October 1895, quoted in Peter Burroughs, 'Imperial institutions and the Government of Empire', in Andrew Porter, ed., *The Oxford History of the British Empire, vol. 3: The Nineteenth Century*, Oxford University Press, 2001, p. 195.

194 House of Commons Debates, 22 August 1895, vol. 36, col. 641.

195 Bennett, ed., *Concept of Empire*, p. 21.

196 William Roger Louis, 'Introduction', in Judith M. Brown and William Roger Louis, eds, *The Oxford History of the British Empire, vol. 4: The Twentieth Century*, Oxford University Press, 2001, p. 5.

recruited from retired officials who had worked in India. The first two Indian members were not to be appointed until 1907.

As with the dependent empire, government in India was autocratic, contradicting the liberal premises on which Britain and the self-governing empire were based. Indian participation in government was almost non-existent. The government in India was headed by a viceroy, representing the queen-empress, assisted by an executive council whose members he nominated; in 1897, just five of its twenty-four members were Indians. The viceroy had the power to overrule the council on matters that he regarded as of particular importance. The purpose of the council was to protect the viceroy from political interference, although 'a far better protection was parliamentary boredom, artfully maintained by the avalanche of reports – a printed mass of impenetrable detail – supplied by the Indian government'.[197]

For the purposes of legislation, the Indian executive council was enlarged into a legislative council with additional members, comprising officials from the Indian provinces, and others either chosen from provincial legislatures or appointed through recommendations by various bodies to the viceroy to give it a representative aspect. The viceroy was free to reject recommendations from the legislative council, although he hardly ever did so. But the official element was always in the majority and the legislative council had very limited powers. Many measures could not be introduced without the viceroy's sanction, and no Bill could be put before the council without the approval of the Secretary of State for India. The legislative council was for most practical purposes an instrument of the viceroy; it could discuss the Budget but not vote on it, and its functions were primarily deliberative and interrogative. It existed not to control but to assist the viceroy. As viceroy Curzon wrote to the India Secretary in June 1901, 'As you and I know, though perhaps it is desirable that the world should not, India is really governed by confidential correspondence between the Secretary of State and the Viceroy.' Curzon declared himself 'surprised that such a form of rule was permitted by the British Constitution'.[198]

Nor was there much control of Indian affairs at Westminster. The Secretary of State's salary was paid from Indian revenues and this made him less accountable to Parliament than other ministers. In any case, he initiated little, and most of his answers to parliamentary questions merely referred to actions of the government in India. The Indian Budget was regularly submitted to Parliament, but the financial statement was generally debated in a perfunctory way on one of the last days of the parliamentary session. There were few real opportunities for MPs to scrutinise the Indian administration,

197 John Darwin, 'Britain's Empires', in Sarah Stockwell, ed., *The British Empire: Themes and Perspectives*, Blackwell, 2008, p. 11.
198 David Gilmour, *Curzon: Imperial Statesman, 1859–1925*, John Murray, 1994, pp. 149, 151.

and when they sought to do so, the government was perfectly prepared to ignore parliamentary motions, as with, for example, a motion in April 1891 condemning the opium revenue, and one in June 1893 requesting that examinations for the Indian civil service be held in India as well as in Britain. In consequence, 'few British MPs took more than an occasional interest in Indian affairs and a debate about India was sure to empty the Commons'.[199] That was, Lowell believed, 'highly fortunate, for there is probably no body of men less fitted to rule a people than a representative assembly elected in another land by a different race'.[200] Curzon was worried at this indifference, complaining that an Indian famine received 'no more attention at home than a squall on the Serpentine'.[201] No Prime Minister visited India between Wellington in the 1820s and Ramsay MacDonald in the twentieth century.

There was also in India a separate military system, and a separate commander-in-chief of the army. India, by contrast with the rest of the empire, was required to maintain an army and paid through taxes around two-thirds of its cost. Indian troops composed around half of this army and were to be despatched to help maintain order in Sudan and East Africa.

The Indian Councils Act of 1892 had marked the beginning of representative government on the subcontinent, empowering various bodies, such as universities and chambers of commerce, to nominate members to legislative councils. But these councils were purely advisory and could do little more than debate. Still, the Act, though unsatisfactory to Indian nationalists, can be seen in hindsight as the beginning of a long process of constitutional development leading eventually to independence within the Commonwealth. But that was far from the thoughts of statesmen at the turn of the century. In his book *Considerations on Representative Government*, the liberal philosopher John Stuart Mill had thought the Indians unsuited to parliamentary rule. Curzon thought India would never be ready for self-government. Instead, she needed 'beneficent rule, a Roman proconsulship or an enlightened despotism, not sympathetic guiding towards constitutional development'.[202] The otherwise enlightened Liberal, John Morley, disciple of Gladstone, ardent Home Ruler and India Secretary in the reforming 1905 Liberal government, thought that self-government would not come for a very long time. When introducing reforms to Indian government in 1908, providing for a more representative system at the centre, and Indian majorities in the provincial councils, he told the Lords, 'If I were attempting to set up a Parliamentary system in India, or if it could be said that this chapter of reforms led directly

199 Darwin, 'Britain's Empires', p. 11.
200 Lowell, *Government of England*, vol. 1, p. 90.
201 Gilmour, *Curzon*, p. 285.
202 Ibid., p. 344.

or necessarily up to the establishment of a Parliamentary system in India, I, for one, would have nothing at all to do with it.'[293]

Even Ramsay MacDonald, the Labour leader, believed that 'the warring elements' in Indian life needed 'a unifying and controlling power'. Britain, he believed, was 'the nurse of India. Deserted by her guardian, India would be the prey of disruptive elements within herself as well as the victim of her own too enthusiastic worshippers to say nothing of what would happen to her from incursions from the outside.'[204] Many believed that the British model of parliamentary government was unsuitable for Asian people or people of colour, and India in particular was seen 'as a colossal honeycomb of conflicting communities and interests, not a nation to be enfranchised by territorial constituencies and on the principle of "representation by population"'.[205] As late as 1943, a Labour Party statement on colonial policy was to declare that, 'for a considerable time to come, most colonial peoples will not be ready for self-government'.[206] In the same year, Labour's Herbert Morrison stated that some colonies were not yet 'mature' enough for self-government. It would be like giving 'latch-keys, bank accounts and shotguns' to 'a child of ten', while Ernest Bevin, the former trade union leader and future Foreign Secretary, believed that Britain could 'sidetrack the small, politically-minded minority ... if we could guarantee security from external attack to, and raise the standard of living of, the Indian people as a whole, the vast majority of them would not trouble their heads about political development'.[207]

At the end of the nineteenth century, few in Britain doubted that the British presence in India was beneficial. Even so radical a critic of imperialism as J. A. Hobson believed that Britain had contributed much to India. Admitting that Britain had undermined Indian culture and done too little to alleviate poverty, he nevertheless waxed eloquent on the benefits.

We have established a wider and more permanent internal peace than India had ever known from the days of Alexander the Great. We have raised the standard of justice by fair and equal administration of laws; we have regulated and probably reduced the burden of taxation, checking the corruption and tyranny of native princes and their publicans. For the instruction of the people we have introduced a public system of schools and colleges ... Roads, railways and a network of canals have facilitated

203 House of Lords Debates, 17 December 1908, vol. 198, col. 1985.
204 David Marquand, *Ramsay MacDonald*, Jonathan Cape, 1977, p. 118.
205 Darwin, 'Britain's Empires', p. 13; John Darwin, 'Durham in the East? India and the Idea of Responsible Government, 1858–1939', *Journal of Canadian Studies*, 1990, p. 147.
206 Quoted in Sneh Mahajan, *British Foreign Policy 1874–1914: The Role of India*, Routledge, 2002, p. 4.
207 Bernard Porter, 'Trying to Make Decolonisation Look Good', *London Review of Books*, 2 August 2007; Duff Hart-Davis, ed., *King's Counsellor: Abdication and War: The Diaries of Sir Alan Lascelles*, Weidenfeld & Nicolson, 2006, p. 154.

communication and transport ... In Bombay and elsewhere cotton mills with modern machinery have been set up ... We are gradually breaking down many of the religious and social superstitions which sin against humanity and retard progress, and even the deeply rooted caste system is modified wherever British influence is felt. There can be no question that much of the work of England in India is well done.[208]

That estimate was shared even by some Indian nationalists, with the Indian National Congress, founded in 1885, proclaiming its 'unswerving loyalty' to the crown and calling British rule a 'divine dispensation'.[209] Satyendra Sinha, the first Indian to become a member of the viceroy's executive council, and later Lord Sinha, was no doubt being flattering when he told Lady Minto, the viceroy's wife, 'If the English left India today ... we should have to telegraph to Aden, and get them to return as fast as they could, for in a couple of days India would be in chaos.' The nationalist leader Gokhale apparently said something similar, and one authority has insisted that 'for many years' the empire 'was regarded by most educated and politically-minded Indians as a necessary and even beneficent phenomenon'.[210] But while the motives may have seemed beneficent to many in Britain, and administration was generally constructive and not corrupt, it was impossible to ignore the fact that Indians were second-class citizens in their own country, and looked upon as subject races. 'The Imperialist', according to Sir Charles Eliot, a former lieutenant governor of Bengal, in 1906,

> thinks of 'our dependencies', of the white man's burden, and the glories of the island race. He puts himself and his countrymen in the place of an Imperial monarch ... but that is exactly the type of sentiment that is not wanted in India ... The many well-authenticated tales of provocation, rudeness and injustice which I heard ... would fill a volume all by themselves.

In many areas of Indian life – clubs and in many libraries – there was a colour bar. There were even two separate official parties to mark the birthday of the queen-empress. Keir Hardie on a visit to India in 1909 was shocked to find that 'travelling on a Government railway line in their own country', Indians 'are treated by the governing white caste much as they themselves treat the

---

208 J. A. Hobson, *Imperialism: A Study*, James Nisbet & Co., 1902, p. 307.
209 Gilmour, *Curzon*, p. 169.
210 Sir Penderel Moon, *The British Conquest and Dominion of India*, Duckworth, 1989, pp. 956, 765. This book, by a British administrator, sympathetic to Indian nationalism, provides a magisterial account of the history of the Raj.

poor outcast pariahs'. Some carriages were labelled 'Europeans Only'.[211] Even so, Hardie regarded the empire as 'the one great power that would mould the affairs of the world' and thought that it 'was right that this should be so'.[212] Ramsay MacDonald, visiting India in 1910, found that the civil servant there was 'an Englishman first and foremost ... He is always complaining of India. He is like a philanthropic slum-dweller at best.' MacDonald concluded, 'The Pax Britannica has produced insolence amongst the governors.'[213] 'I cannot help thinking,' the Prince of Wales, later George V, declared at the Guildhall in 1906, 'from all I have heard and seen, that the task of governing India will be made all the easier if, on our part, we infuse into it a wider element of sympathy.'[214] The tragedy of British rule was, in the words of the great Indian writer Rabindranath Tagore, that what was 'truly best' in British civilisation, 'the upholding of dignity of human relationships, has no place in the British administration of this country'.[215]

In his novel *Kim*, published in 1901, Rudyard Kipling highlights the ignorance of Indian culture and traditions of most of the British sahibs living in India. Few knew any of the Indian languages and many remained alienated from the country they were ruling, believing themselves to be superior, a privileged caste. A similar picture was to be painted many years later by E. M. Forster in his novel *A Passage to India*, published in 1924. And Forster, unlike Kipling, realised that paternalism by a foreign race could never yield satisfactory relationships. The first Prime Minister of India, Jawaharlal Nehru, wrote in his autobiography published in 1936 that India was treated as an enormous country house with Indians located in the servants' hall, pantry and kitchen, although, 'sometimes we were treated to a rare honour – we were given a cup of tea in the drawing-room'.[216] What most upset him, Mahatma Gandhi declared in later life, was 'the hardness of heart of the educated'.[217] The British saw themselves as trustees, but in this, there was a large element of hypocrisy.

Of India's population of around 300 million, 230 million lived in British India. The rest lived in the princely states, of which there were nearly 700, the largest of which, Hyderabad, was the size of Italy, although some were of minuscule size. The princely states were not strictly part of the empire and were not ruled from the India Office in Whitehall but governed by native rulers, princes and maharajahs. The laws of British India did not apply, and

211 J. Keir Hardie, *India: Impressions and Suggestions*, Independent Labour Party, 1909, pp. 97–8.
212 Robert J. Finlay, *A Partnership for Good? Scottish Politics and the Union since 1880*, John Donald, 1997, p. 32.
213 Quoted in J. Ramsay MacDonald, *The Awakening of India*, Hodder & Stoughton, 1910, pp. 150, 152, 164, 153.
214 A. G. Gardiner, *Pillars of Society*, James Nisbet & Co., 1913, p. 6.
215 Amartya Sen, *Home in the World: A Memoir*, Allen Lane, 2021, p. x; 'Illusions of Empire', *The Guardian*, 29 June 2021.
216 Quoted in A. P. Thornton, *The Imperial Idea and its Enemies: A Study in British Power* [1959], Macmillan, 1966, p. 228.
217 Quoted in Sankar Ghose, *Mahatma Gandhi*, Allied Publishers, 1991, p. 156.

sovereignty was divided between the British government and the ruler in different proportions, regulated by treaties, charters and customary practices. The vast majority of the princely states enjoyed substantial self-government in domestic affairs under the 'suzerainty' of Britain, the paramount power, but they were forbidden to enter into alliances with other powers or conduct an independent foreign policy; and British residents, responsible for the safety and welfare of British subjects, were assigned to them as 'advisers' to prevent misgovernment and ensure internal peace. In the early 1880s, the princely states were regarded as 'a wilderness of oppression and misrule', but in the last resort, a ruler could be removed for misgovernment, as with the Gaekwad of Baroda in 1875.[218] British advisers had ensured that barbaric customs, for example, infanticide and suttee – the burning of widows – had been abolished in the princely states. For Britain, these states were of value in inhibiting the growth of Indian nationalism, and indeed the princes had shown little sympathy for the 'mutiny' in 1857. Further, as Lord Salisbury, when Secretary of State for India, had argued in 1867, they offered careers to 'clever and pushing natives ... energetic spirits ... [who] will fret under our rule, as not merely an alien domination, but a personal injury to themselves'.[219]

The government of India revealed in stark form the conflict between two principles: parliamentary and responsible government as practised in Britain and the self-governing colonies, and autocracy as practised in India. But such a system was hardly new to India, which had been ruled autocratically both under the Mogul Empire and under the Hindu rulers who had preceded it. The British system was, however, different since, although autocratic, it was neither despotic nor arbitrary but constitutional, basing itself, in theory at least, on the rule of law. It sought to fuse what seemed to be conflicting principles in a constitutional autocracy. It was not, for the moment, rejected by the vast majority of Indians.[220]

*   *   *

In 1887, at the first Colonial Conference – predecessor to Imperial Conferences and modern Commonwealth Heads of Government Meetings – the Prime Minister, Lord Salisbury, noted the sprawling character of the empire and its 'want of continuity'. He declared that the empire 'has this peculiarity which distinguishes it; it is separated into parts by large stretches of ocean'.

218 Moon, *British Conquest and Dominion of India*, p. 872.
219 E. D. Steele, 'Salisbury at the India Office', in Lord Blake and Hugh Cecil, eds, *Salisbury: The Man and his Policies*, Macmillan, 1987, p. 130.
220 Moon, *British Conquest and Dominion of India*, p. 955.

'We could not', he continued, 'emulate the German Empire in conducting all our Imperial affairs from one centre.'[221] Nor, he might have added, did it wish to emulate the Roman Empire by making it unitary, with its members subordinate to the centre. The empire, by contrast with the Roman, and the compact empires of Russia and Germany, was not ring-fenced but maritime, distributed along the world's sea lanes.

The maritime and insular nature of the empire had profound implications for foreign policy, defence and the constitution. It meant that, by contrast with many other empires, rival powers were interposed between the mother country, its various dominions and possessions, and India. So Britain required a strong navy. 'What really determines the Foreign Policy of this country', Foreign Secretary Sir Edward Grey was to tell the imperial defence conference in May 1911, 'is the question of sea power. It is the Naval question which underlies the whole of our European Foreign policy.'[222] But as an insular and maritime nation, it seemed that Britain did not need conscription or a large army. Britain's army was in fact smaller than Switzerland's. Bismarck had once declared that if the British Army ever invaded Germany, he would send a police force to arrest it.[223] In 1914, Kitchener was to say that Britain had a 'town clerk's army'.[224] The army had a very limited purpose – not so much to defend the home territory (which was achieved by the navy) or to conduct operations on the Continent (since, until the early twentieth century, British participation in a Continental war was deemed unlikely) but to hold British India – not so much against internal disaffection (which was not seen at the end of the nineteenth century as a serious threat) but against foreign powers and in particular Russia. In 1897, there were seventy-seven battalions in India and various colonial outposts, and just sixty-four in Britain.[225] 'Our Regular Army', Balfour had told Lord Kitchener, commander-in-chief of the army in India,

> does not exist primarily for the defence of Great Britain, but almost en-
> tirely (1) for the defence of India, (2) the retention of South Africa, (3)
> conceivably (but only barely conceivably) for the defence of Canada, and
> (4) for the purpose of small expeditions against the Naval stations and
> Colonies of other Powers ... The defence of India is undoubtedly the most

---

221 Quoted in Maurice Ollivier, ed., *The Colonial and Imperial Conferences from 1887 to 1937*, vol. 1, Ottawa, Queen's Printer, 1954, p. 15.

222 G. P. Gooch and Harold Temperley, eds, *British Documents on the Origins of the War, 1898–1914*, HMSO, 1928, vol. 6, Appendix V; Doreen Collins, *Aspects of British Politics, 1904–1919*, Pergamon, 1965, p. 15.

223 Philip Murphy, 'Britain as a Global Power in the Twentieth Century', in Andrew Thompson, ed., *Britain's Experience of Empire in the Twentieth Century*, Oxford University Press, 2012, pp. 39–40.

224 Edward Grey, *Twenty-Five Years, 1892–1916*, vol. 2, Hodder & Stoughton, 1925, p. 68.

225 Aaron Friedberg, *The Weary Titan: Britain and the Experience of Relative Decline, 1895–1905*, Princeton University Press, 1988, p. 231.

formidable and the one which throws the greatest strain upon the Mother Country.[226]

For only India was vulnerable to the land forces of another nation – Russia, whose programme of railway development was bringing her nearer to the Indian frontier.

It was indeed because Britain had a small army that her naval supremacy was acceptable to other powers. For without a large army, the navy could not be used for aggressive purposes. But were a power with a large army, such as Germany, to seek also to establish naval supremacy, that would be seen both by other powers and also by Britain as a threat.

The empire made British foreign and defence policy highly complex. Other powers had a more focused perception of where danger might arise – France primarily from Germany, and Germany from her eastern and western frontiers. But Britain with worldwide responsibilities faced global dangers – dangers more difficult to confront when the development of railway communications allowed large armies to be swiftly transferred over land, rendering naval supremacy a wasting asset. The geographer Halford Mackinder, in a lecture to the Royal Geographical Society, published in the *Geographical Journal* in 1904, entitled 'The Geographical Pivot of History', noticed a changing balance between land and sea power, so that the era in which naval power was dominant was coming to an end. The pre-eminent nations would in the future be those in command of large armies, not large navies. The implication was that Britain would be threatened by rivals which naval forces could not reach and that her global pre-eminence could not last.

The empire also gave rise to two constitutional problems. Its maritime nature raised the conundrum of how peoples distant from the centre should be ruled. Either they would be ruled as dependencies from London or be given self-government. There was no middle way. Self-government, as we have seen, had been implemented by the end of the nineteenth century in the colonies of settlement, but it was far from being accepted for crown colonies, protectorates and India. Yet foreign rule was incompatible with a liberal polity. Burgeoning liberal ideas of democracy and freedom in Britain awakened in subject peoples liberal demands which logically a liberal polity could not in the end resist.

Colonial self-government gave rise to a second constitutional question. How could the various dispersed and apparently disconnected territories become sufficiently cohesive to act together? How could colonial

---

226 John McDermott, 'The Revolution in British Military Thinking from the Boer War to the Moroccan Crisis', *Canadian Journal of History*, 1974, p. 167.

self-government be reconciled with the imperial connection? One answer had been imperial federation. But by 1895, this seemed outside the range of practical politics, as it would unacceptably limit colonial autonomy. Instead, the imperial connection was to be strengthened by evolutionary methods through the development of the Colonial Conference, renamed the Imperial Council in 1905, as a real consultative body. But there was an alternative, more radical answer. It was to link the disparate parts of the self-governing empire through a new commercial policy, tariff reform and imperial pref-erence. That answer, challenging the principle of free trade, would in due course shatter the Unionist coalition which governed Britain from 1895 to 1905.

* * *

At the beginning of the twentieth century, the empire was widely believed to be a bulwark of Britain's international position. A mere offshore island had been transformed into a global power. 'England without an empire?' Chamberlain was to enquire in 1906,

> Can you conceive it? England in that case would not be the England we love … This England of ours … would no longer be a power, if not su-preme, at all events of the greatest influence, generally well exercised on the civilisation and the peace of the world. It would be a fifth-rate nation, existing on the sufferance of its more powerful neighbours.[227]

Nevertheless, it is doubtful if for much of the period the empire attracted great enthusiasm or even interest amongst the British people. Indeed, until the late 1890s, the public seemed little concerned with imperial matters. In 1883, Sir John Seeley, Regius Professor of History at Cambridge, had written, in much quoted words, that he had found 'something very characteristic in the indifference which we show towards this mighty phenomenon of the diffusion of our race and the expansion of our state. We seem, as it were, to have conquered and peopled half the world in a fit of absence of mind.'[228]

Imperialists sought to make the British public enthusiastic towards empire. But, except perhaps for bursts of popular excitement in the late 1890s, such enthusiasm remained largely confined to the elites. On the day after his Commons speech on the colonies as 'undeveloped estates', Cham-berlain addressed a deputation on West African Railways, appealing to them

---

227 Julian Amery, *The Life of Joseph Chamberlain*, Macmillan, 1932–69, vol. 6, p. 905.
228 J. R. Seeley, *The Expansion of England: Two Courses of Lectures*, Macmillan, 1883, p. 8.

to support 'what is in a certain sense a new policy' that 'the people of this country' should 'invest some of their superfluous wealth in the development of their great estate ... I shall appeal to the opinion of this country, which is gradually ripening'. The implication was that there was little spontaneous feeling for empire. Indeed, even Chamberlain's Cabinet colleagues, though calling themselves imperialists, objected to policies involving greater public expenditure and therefore higher taxation. Imperial feeling was something which had to be evoked. It did not appear to be natural or spontaneous.[229]

Perhaps attitudes to empire were changing in the late 1890s, but they came to the surface only sporadically on occasions of heightened emotion such as the Diamond Jubilee, the victory in Sudan in 1898 (avenging the murder of General Gordon in 1885) or the Relief of Mafeking in 1900. But Mafeking occurred after a long line of unexpected defeats in the Boer War towards which the public had seemed on the whole indifferent. One contemporary commentator noted that Mafeking 'cannot be judged except by contrast with the long months of painful self-suppression which had preceded it'.[230] And the outburst was 'as sudden as it proved to be short-lived', apparently felt most strongly amongst those previously politically inarticulate. Even this sporadic enthusiasm, moreover, appeared stronger in some regions than in others. Wales, Scotland and Yorkshire and a number of rural areas seemed largely resistant to it. Ideological support for imperialism appeared 'more manifestly literary and emotional than political', and, 'in practice, policy devoted itself rather to development and consolidation than to expansion'.[231] In his novel *Mr Britling Sees It Through*, published in 1916, H. G. Wells wrote that 'nineteen people out of twenty in the middle class and most of the lower class know no more of the Empire than they did of the Argentine Republic or the Italian renaissance'.[232] In 1942, George Orwell, with his usual penetrating insight, was to write that 'the mass of the people in the nineties as now, were anti-militarist, bored by the Empire, and only unconsciously patriotic'.[233] The Unionist government of 1895 was continually worried that popular enthusiasm for empire was too weak, especially when it sought to awaken public opinion to the iniquities visited on British citizens in the Transvaal. On 11 July 1899, just three months before the outbreak of the Boer War, Salisbury told the queen that the majority of the Cabinet 'were

229 Ronald Robinson and John Gallagher with Alice Denny, *Africa and the Victorians: The Official Mind of Imperialism*, Macmillan, 1961, p. 399.
230 'Calchas' [J. L. Garvin], 'Will England Last the Century?', *Fortnightly Review*, January 1901, p. 24.
231 A. F. Madden, 'Changing Attitudes and Widening Responsibilities, 1895–1914', in E. A. Benians, Sir James Butler and C. E. Carrington, eds, *The Cambridge History of the British Empire*, Cambridge University Press, 1959, vol. 3, pp. 339, 341.
232 H. G. Wells, *Mr Britling Sees It Through*, Macmillan, 1916, p. 212.
233 George Orwell, 'Rudyard Kipling' [1942], in Sonia Orwell and Ian Angus, eds, *The Collected Essays, Journalism and Letters of George Orwell*, Secker and Warburg, 1968, vol. 2, p. 18.

impressed with the want of support such a war would seem likely to command with public opinion in this country; and were in favour of very circumspect action'.[234] When voters were offered, in the 1906 election, tariff reform, which might mean higher food prices, to unite the empire, they rejected it. In the twenty-first century, voters were to prove equally unwilling to accept higher food prices for the sake of the European Union. In December 1906, Lord Milner, just returned from South Africa as governor of the Transvaal, complained to his fellow imperialist Leo Amery, 'One must unfortunately explain to these d——d fools [i.e. the voters] why we want ... an Empire'.[235] As late as 1951, a Colonial Office survey discovered that 49 per cent of a sample were unable to name a single UK colony, although one respondent suggested Lincolnshire![236] The lack of popular enthusiasm or even interest in the empire no doubt helps to explain how decolonisation from the 1940s onwards could be undertaken without the internal traumas that scarred, for example, Belgium, France and Portugal, enabling Britain to be transformed from a global power to a small island off the continent of Europe with little psychological dislocation. 'I think that I can save the British Empire from anything,' Winston Churchill told his private secretary in the 1940s, 'except the British.'[237]

Admittedly, attitudes were changing amongst the governing class in the 1890s. The struggle against Home Rule had served to release what Lord Salisbury called the 'slumbering genius' of imperialism.[238] Chamberlain in particular was striking 'a new chord in his political rhetoric', an imperialist chord.[239] Chamberlain's politics of social reform seemed to be meeting an imperialist cross-current. What both had in common was a reaction against Gladstonianism, the politics of the limited state at home and non-intervention abroad. The new chord struck by Chamberlain was a response to a perceived threat to Britain's global and industrial supremacy. British imperial dominance had depended largely upon the absence of rivals, and upon factors which were coming to appear transitory – industrial prowess and naval supremacy. It could no longer be taken for granted in the face of jealous rivals. The assertive, sometimes strident, imperialism of the 1890s was in large part a response to a lost feeling of security. And it cast doubt on whether Britain's policy of avoiding alliances was any longer the right one. Queen Victoria herself appreciated the alteration in Britain's international position,

234 J. S. Marais, *The Fall of Kruger's Republic*, Clarendon Press, 1961, p. 288.
235 John Darwin, *The Empire Project: The Rise and Fall of the British World-System, 1830–1970*, Cambridge University Press, 2009. This book provides a wonderful overview of the history of the British Empire.
236 Cited in Paxman, *Empire*, p. 257.
237 Anthony Montague Browne, *Long Sunset: Memoirs of Winston Churchill's Last Private Secretary*, Cassell, 1995, p. 41.
238 Winston Churchill, *Lord Randolph Churchill*, Macmillan, 1906, vol. 2, p. 117.
239 Peter T. Marsh, *Joseph Chamberlain: Entrepreneur in Politics*, Yale University Press, 1994, p. 233.

telling Lord Salisbury in 1896, 'Affairs now are so different from what they used to be, that the Queen cannot help feeling that our isolation is danger-ous.'[240] In imperial affairs, the 1890s saw a more 'forward' policy, in foreign policy, the beginnings of the so-called new course, the search for alliances.

Many imperial problems which the Unionist government had to confront occurred in Africa, where there were challenges both from other powers and from local nationalisms. In 1878, at the time of the Treaty of Berlin, less than 10 per cent of Africa was ruled by a European power. By the end of the century, after the 'scramble for Africa', the whole of Africa except Ethiopia and Liberia had been gobbled up by European powers. Britain had played a large part in the scramble. Between 1882 and 1898, over 70 million Africans were incorporated into the empire, and in 1897, Lord Rosebery boasted to an Edinburgh audience that in the previous twelve years, 2.6 million square miles of territory had been added to it, predominantly in Africa. Facing com-petition from powers which did not adhere to free trade and were closing markets to British commerce, older informal methods of control appeared no longer sufficient. Speaking in Bradford in 1895, shortly before the general election, Salisbury blamed 'the dreary period of general depression and dif-ficulty and distress through which we have passed for the last few years' on hostile tariffs. So we must 'make our way not only in the civilised, but in the uncivilised markets of the world'. He went on to criticise those who

> have dreamt that it would be a pleasant thing, so to speak, to close the capital account of the Empire and to add no further to its responsibilities … If we mean to hold our own against the efforts of the civilised Powers of the world to strangle our commerce by their prohibitive finance we must be prepared to take the requisite measures to open new markets for ourselves among the half-civilised nations of the globe, and we must not be afraid if that effort, which is vital to our industries, should bring with it a new responsibility of empire and government. (Cheers.)[241]

In West and East Africa, the trade motive was predominant in the scramble for colonies. We had not gone to equatorial Africa, the *Pall Mall Gazette* declared, in an excess of frankness in an article in July 1899 entitled 'Why We Seek Tropical Colonies',

> from religious or humanitarian motives. Missionaries and philanthropists, indeed, complain sometimes that their work is hampered by Downing

---

240 Buckle, ed., *Letters of Queen Victoria*, 3rd series, vol. 3, p. 22. The queen to Lord Salisbury, 14 January 1896.
241 *The Times*, 25 May 1895.

Street regulations. Still less have we sought out the African in order to endow him with the vices (and virtues) of western civilisation. The fact is that when what has been done through pure love of adventure and the pride of power has been eliminated, the dominating force which has taken us to Equatorial Africa is the desire for trade. We are in the tropical countries for our own advantage, and only incidentally for the good of the Africans.[242]

At the end of the century, trade with the tropical empire was greater than that with Canada, Cape, Natal, New Zealand and the Australian states, with the exception of Queensland, combined. It was difficult for the Liberal opposition to oppose the scramble since there was a broad consensus that trade should be protected, but by the end of the century, there was a growing belief that expansion had come to an end and that consolidation was now needed. Most Liberals did not want to abandon the empire, but they believed that it was now large enough and that further acquisitions were no longer needed. The irony is that the flag-waving imperialism of the late 1890s came well after the bulk of colonial acquisitions had already been made. Popular imperialism, such as it was, appeared more a consequence of the expansion of empire than a cause.

The more self-conscious imperialists amongst the elite comprised not only Conservatives but also Liberals or ex-Liberals – Chamberlain, Rosebery, Milner – together with Rosebery's disciples amongst the Liberal Imperialists, Asquith, Haldane and Grey. And imperialism also struck a chord with Fabians such as the Webbs and Bernard Shaw. But it was to split both parties. In the 1890s, the Liberal split was often described as between imperialists and anti-imperialists. Yet, Campbell-Bannerman, Liberal leader from 1899, and often thought of as an anti-imperialist, insisted in an election speech in September 1900 that he was 'as proud of the Empire as any man' and indeed that 'the Empire was largely created by Liberal enterprise and has been consolidated by Liberal policy'.[243] Hardly anyone was anti-imperialist in the sense of wanting to abandon the empire, while after the 1890s few wanted to annex more territories. The differences were largely concentrated on British policy in Africa, and particularly South Africa. They concerned how best the empire was to be preserved. The Unionists proved beneficiaries of the imperial spirit and of the Liberal split in the 1895 and 1900 elections. But when tariff reform came to split the Unionists, the Liberals would be the

---

242 G. N. Uzoigwe, *Britain and the Conquest of Africa: The Age of Salisbury*, University of Michigan Press, 1974, pp. 27–8.
243 *The Times*, 22 September 1900.

beneficiaries, winning a landslide victory in 1906. Voters were not prepared to support the empire if that meant a rise in the price of food.

* * *

In Joseph Conrad's novel *Heart of Darkness*, the narrator, Marlow, declares:

> The conquest of the earth ... is not a pretty thing when you look into it too much. What redeems it is the idea only. An idea at the back of it; not a sentimental presence but an idea; and an unselfish belief in the idea – something you can set up, and bow down before, and offer a sacrifice to.

Imperialists believed that the British Empire was redeemed by an idea or rather ideas – the rule of law; freedom of religion; honest public administration; the development of public services such as schools and medical facilities; the removal of traditional superstitions such as human sacrifice in India; the ending of tribal warfare; and the abolition of the slave trade organised by Arabs in East Africa. Yet, in India, when empire ended, life expectancy was just thirty-two, and the adult literacy rate was around 15 per cent.[244] In theory, the colonial empire and India were based on religious and racial equality, and after the Indian 'mutiny' Queen Victoria had prohibited racial discrimination on the subcontinent. In Africa, similarly, racial discrimination was in theory outlawed. Yet all too often fine ideals were not realised in practice. There was widespread racial and social discrimination in India and Africa, as well as economic exploitation. In Sierra Leone, Fiji and self-governing Natal, there was discrimination in taxation levels, and in some colonies there was forced labour.[245] While British administration was rarely corrupt, it was often insensitive and cruel. Attitudes to non-white people were frequently insulting, and there was some brutality. As late as the 1940s, the travel writer Jan Morris was shocked when, travelling from Port Said to Palestine with a commanding officer, 'a young lieutenant-colonel of particularly sweet temperament, very gentle, a very nice man, as popular with his soldiers as he was with his officers', Morris found the train corridor blocked by an Egyptian leaning into a compartment and talking to someone inside. The officer simply kicked the Egyptian out of the way. The empire allowed the British to 'wander the world like the children of rich parents'.[246] But the official rationale for empire was not based on permanent racial or

---

244 Sen, *Home in the World*, p. xx.
245 Madden, 'Changing Attitudes', p. 352.
246 Jan Morris, 'Kipling and the British Empire', *Kipling Journal*, September 2001, pp. 12–13.

fundamental biological differences. The eugenics movement which developed in Britain in the early twentieth century did, it is true, emphasise such differences, but it never became a powerful force amongst government or people. The rationale for empire was instead based on a perversion of Darwinism which suggested that certain groups were less 'advanced' than others. And the evils of empire could at least be scrutinised by a parliamentary system and a free press, something less true in the authoritarian states. The imperial system had, it has been suggested, 'a built-in capacity for self-criticism', and so historians can 'draw on the material accumulated by ... commissions of inquiry, parliamentary debates, metropolitan blue books, and similar records which formed part of a self-corrective mechanism of a type ... They played an important part in putting a stop to imperial abuses.'[247]

British defenders of empire hoped that it would spread free trade and what would now be called globalisation to the benefit of all. But the economic balance sheet of empire is unclear and economists have not reached a consensus on it. Economic factors were probably not, however, decisive in political decision-making, except where other powers sought to shut off access to trade by means of tariffs. But Britain felt a responsibility for developing Chamberlain's 'undeveloped estate', and that involved an economic cost. So did defending the empire. The profit and loss account, therefore, is uncertain. Indeed, any calculation of profit and loss is complicated, as the Indian economist Amartya Sen has pointed out, because it is impossible to answer the counterfactual question of what India and the colonies would have been like had the British Empire not existed. But, of course, the fundamental fact about the dependent empire is that it involved the rule of one people by another and was therefore incompatible with liberal norms.

'God forgive us', one native administrator declared, 'for our sorry deeds and our generous intentions – for the fact is that no race can govern another quite justly.'[248] It is difficult to find a more appropriate epitaph.

The empire has cast its shadow over much of the world and also over Britain herself. Around one-quarter of today's sovereign states have been 'hewn from its fabric'.[249] And there is evidence that it was not seen as an unmitigated evil by all its non-white colonial subjects. In 1914, 1.5 million Indians volunteered to fight with Britain, and, every subject nation, with the solitary exception of Burma – now Myanmar – chose voluntarily on achieving independence to remain in the Commonwealth, an institution based on sovereign equality replacing an empire based on domination.

247 L. H. Gann and P. Duignan, *Burden of Empire: An Appraisal of Western Colonialism in Africa South of the Sahara*, Pall Mall Press, 1968, p. 372. I owe this reference to Nigel Biggar.
248 Quoted in MacDonald, *Awakening of India*, p. 134.
249 Darwin, *Unfinished Empire*, p. 1.

CONCLUSION: A LIBERAL POLITY

In the novel *Our Mutual Friend*, published in 1865, Charles Dickens's Mr Podsnap declared, 'We Englishmen are Very Proud of our Constitution ... It was Bestowed Upon Us By providence. No other Country is so Favoured as This Country.' What Dickens had intended as satire had seemed to many, in the Victorian era, sober realism. Bagehot in the second edition of *The English Constitution*, published in 1872, had little doubt that the British system of government was a model and exemplar for all civilised peoples. 'As I write for Englishmen,' he declared in 1874, 'I need not draw out a formal proof that England is a country successful in politics.'[250] But in the early twentieth century, doubts were beginning to creep in. In 1908, Lowell found some 'discontent with some of the results of democracy, a feeling which finds vent in widespread criticism of representative institutions'.[251] British critics shared this worry. In 1896, the historian W. E. H. Lecky had discerned a 'declining respect of parliamentary government' due to 'the tendency of democracy to impair the stability of government and the working of parliamentary institutions'.[252] 'Under the present condition of things,' Dicey wrote, in private correspondence in 1894, 'sham Parliamentary government means a very vicious form of government by party.'[253] Criticism of the British system of government became louder during the Boer War, when military reverses during its early phases together with the poor physical condition of many army recruits led some to conclude that it was inimical to efficiency, and that government needed to be run on more businesslike lines. A state, Lord Rosebery declared in 1900, was 'in essence a great joint stock company with unlimited liability on the part of its shareholders'. The editor of the influential periodical *The Nineteenth Century* insisted that 'the business of the country, as administered by all the various Departments of State', needed to be based on 'ordinary business principles and methods'.[254] Similar criticisms were to be heard throughout the twentieth century and are by no means entirely absent today. The British people were to listen politely to these sermons but took little notice of them.

British commentators and foreign observers had, nevertheless, not been wholly wrong to praise British institutions. Although, as we have seen, Britain was far from being a democracy, the rule of law prevailed, impartially administered, even though much of the criminal law remained barbarous and access

250 St John-Stevas, *Collected Works of Bagehot*, vol. 7, p. 226.
251 Lowell, *Government of England*, vol. 1, p. 195.
252 W. E. H. Lecky, *Democracy and Liberty* [1896], Longmans, Green & Co., 1899, pp. v, xi.
253 A. V. Dicey to Leo Maxse, 2 February 1894, cited in Richard A. Cosgrove, *The Rule of Law: Albert Venn Dicey, Victorian Jurist*, Macmillan, 1980, p. 207.
254 Rosebery, *Miscellanies* [1921], vol. 2, quoted in G. R. Searle, *The Quest for National Efficiency: A Study in British Politics and Political Thought, 1899–1914*, Blackwell, 1971, pp. 87, 88.

to the courts was prohibitively expensive. The labour movement agreed with leaders of the 'capitalist' parties that the state, despite gross inequalities, far from being an instrument of the ruling class, could be captured by representatives of the working class who would then be able to transform society. The trade unions had confidence in the justice system, only temporarily interrupted by a series of legal judgments at the turn of the century restricting their hitherto accepted status. In public administration, standards of integrity were high with comparatively little corruption. Outside Ireland, there was an atmosphere of ideological and religious tolerance. Civil liberties, and in particular freedom of speech, were widely respected. And even though Britain was some way from being a democracy, it was a country in which public opinion could make itself felt. It was a liberal society in which the police were unarmed, with a lively and free press in which no one need fear the hand of the authorities if they expressed unpopular opinions or opinions opposed to those of the government. It was the same country in which years ago Karl Marx had been able to research and preach his subversive doctrines, doctrines which wreaked havoc elsewhere but found no more than minuscule support in the country in which he had taken refuge. Compared to most of the Continent, the British people could breathe the freer air of a tolerant society within a profoundly liberal culture.

There were, admittedly, gross – some would argue obscene – social and economic inequalities. Around 1 per cent of the population over twenty-five owned 67 per cent of the national capital, while 87 per cent owned 8 per cent.[255] Britain was a paradise for the rich, a country in which 'five dukes spent on themselves more than was spent on university education throughout Great Britain'.[256] In Edwardian Britain, the plutocracy was less shy of displaying its wealth than its predecessors had been. Socially, Britain was even further from being a democracy than it was politically. There remained much deference towards the landed classes, and some social ostracism directed towards Non-conformists, Catholics and Jews. Writing in 1941, Orwell was to point out that Britain was 'certainly two nations, if not three or four'. Nevertheless, 'at the same time the vast majority of the people feel themselves to be a single nation and are conscious of resembling one another more than they resemble foreigners. Patriotism is usually stronger than class-hatred, and always stronger than any kind of internationalism.' Britain was, Orwell believed, 'a family. It has its private language and its common memories, and at the approach of an enemy it closes its ranks.' But it was 'a family with the wrong members in control'.[257] The same was true of Britain during the years 1895 to 1914.

---

255 Paul Thompson, *The Edwardians: The Remaking of British Society*, Weidenfeld & Nicolson, 1975.
256 Chris Wrigley, ed., *Struggles for Supremacy: Diplomatic Essays by A. J. P. Taylor*, Ashgate, 2000, p. 102.
257 George Orwell, 'The Lion and the Unicorn: Socialism and the English Genius', in Orwell and Angus, eds, *Essays, Journals and Letters of George Orwell*, vol. 2, pp. 64, 68.

CHAPTER 1

THE POLITICS OF UNIONISM, 1895–1900

UNIONISM

The rejection of Gladstone's first Irish Home Rule Bill in 1886 was to determine the future of British politics for many years. It had been achieved by a combination of Conservatives and dissident Liberals, to be known as Liberal Unionists, led by Lord Hartington who, in 1891 became the Duke of Devonshire, and Joseph Chamberlain. Liberal Unionists had been assisted by an electoral pact, so that they would not face opposition in their constituencies from Conservatives. The two parties gradually grew closer together, until in 1912 they fused. But even before that they were sometimes referred to as the 'Unionist Party' rather than the Unionists.

The general election of 1895 saw the defeat of a Liberal government led by Gladstone's successor, Lord Rosebery, and its replacement by the Unionists. It signified a new era, a post-Gladstonian era. Gladstone – the Grand Old Man of British politics – had retired as Prime Minister and Liberal leader in 1894, at the age of eighty-four, having been Prime Minister four times during his political career of over sixty years. Rosebery had then led an undistinguished and quarrelsome administration for fifteen months before resigning in June 1895 after being defeated in a snap Commons vote. The Rosebery government was replaced not by a single-party government but by a coalition of Conservatives and Liberal Unionists.

The rejection of Home Rule shattered the Victorian party system, replacing it with one more closely mirroring class divisions. The secession of the Whigs, led by Hartington, was accompanied by, in Gladstone's words, 'the permanent severance of its aristocratic and landowning section from the Liberal Party … Probably nine out of every ten acres in the United Kingdom were now in Tory hands.'[1] The secession of the Radicals, led by Chamberlain, took with it a section of the employing class. Chamberlain claimed to be the main influence behind the rejection of Home Rule, a claim accepted by Irish Nationalist MPs, who labelled him Judas. But, in fact, the majority of the defectors had been Whigs. In July 1895, Beatrice Webb wrote in her

---

1 The Personal Papers of Lord Rendel, diary entry for 19 January 1891, cited in Grigg, *Young Lloyd George*, pp. 120–21.

diary that 'the majority of the Liberal Unionists in the House of Commons have been anti-Chamberlainites – more hostile in their hearts to Joe than the bigoted Tories'.[2] But Chamberlain was more important electorally since he had far more support in the country. Indeed, the large Unionist majority in the khaki election of 1900, fought during the Boer War, was due less to the Conservative leaders than to Chamberlain, a dissident Liberal. Later in the twentieth century, similarly large Conservative majorities were twice to be secured with the aid of non-Conservatives – in 1918 with another dissident Liberal, Lloyd George, and in 1931 with a dissident socialist, Ramsay Mac-Donald. The politics of Chamberlain, Lloyd George and MacDonald have been variously described, but they were never thought of as Conservatives. Yet they helped secure landslide majorities for the Conservatives in three general elections. The Conservatives in the twentieth century were to prove far more flexible and adaptive in attracting dissident elements than parties of the left; and this was one of the reasons for their success. 'The last purely Conservative government', Harold Macmillan claimed, with mischievous exaggeration, 'was formed by Mr Disraeli in 1874 – it is the fact that we have attracted moderate people of Liberal tradition and thought into our ranks which makes it possible to maintain a Conservative government today.'[3] That process of attracting 'moderate people of Liberal tradition' began in 1886; and it prefigures Conservative electoral success in the twentieth century.

The Whig secession was perhaps inevitable in the long run, even without Home Rule, for the Whigs were Liberals of the right who believed that the liberal programme had been largely completed. They had little sympathy for further radical reforms. But the secession of the radicals was by no means inevitable and accentuated a trend already occurring – the loss of industrial seats from Liberals to Conservatives. Increasingly, the two parties came to be divided both socially and geographically. Between 1895 and 1914, Unionist strength lay primarily in the south-east and the West Midlands, where around two-thirds of the seats were normally safe for them. The strength of the Liberals lay in the north-west, Wales and to a lesser extent Scotland, where around two-thirds of the seats were normally safe for them.

Of the two parties comprising the Unionist alliance, the Conservatives were long established. Traditionally, they had been the party of the landed interest – the aristocracy and the squirearchy – and the Anglican Church. But since the 1870s, they had become increasingly attractive to business and financial interests and those living in the newly growing suburbs, which Lord Salisbury had labelled with some disdain, 'villa Conservatism'. The Liberal

---

2   Norman and Jeanne MacKenzie, eds, *The Diary of Beatrice Webb*, Harvard University Press, 1983, vol. 2, p. 77.
3   Macmillan, *Past Masters*, pp. 18–19.

Unionists, a new party, formed in 1886, had at first maintained some degree of distance from the Conservatives, believing that Home Rule might prove a temporary aberration, and that, after Gladstone's retirement, their old party might be reunited. During the years of Conservative rule after the 1886 election, the Liberal Unionists had sustained the Conservatives from outside but had continued to sit with the Gladstonian Liberals on the opposition benches. Chamberlain was later to insist that if the Liberals, 'acting in a true democratic spirit, had accepted the overwhelming voice of the people' in 1886 by abandoning Home Rule, 'I think it would have been inevitable we should have rejoined our old friends and colleagues.'[4] Gradually, however, it became clear that Home Rule was to be the new dividing line in politics and that there would not be Liberal reunion. In January 1894, Chamberlain marked the final breach with his old colleagues by declaring, 'I am, and shall be in the future, proud to call myself a Unionist, and be satisfied with that title alone, believing that it is a wider and nobler title than that either of Conservative or Liberal, since it includes them both.'[5]

The Liberal Unionists were geographically concentrated, their main strength lying in the West Midlands, the west of Scotland and Cornwall, where they were the senior rather than, as elsewhere, the junior partner in the coalition. Ideologically, the party was highly diverse, containing both reformers and conservatives. There was, Lord Hartington had said in a speech at Ipswich in March 1888, 'room within the Liberal Unionist party ... for the extremest radical as well as for the most moderate whig'.[6] The party was in fact highly fragmented, with a number of overlapping factions. In Oscar Wilde's *Importance of Being Earnest*, first performed in 1895, Lady Bracknell asks Jack Worthing, 'What are your politics?' He replies, 'Well, I am afraid I really have none. I am a Liberal Unionist.' Lady Bracknell finds that satisfactory. 'Oh, they count as Tories. They dine with us. Or come in the evening, at any rate.' But there was some degree of ideological coherence. The historian of the party finds the 'desire to preserve the independence of MPs' to be 'perhaps the single most common motivating factor in the decision of most of the 1886 rebels to join the breakaway Liberal Unionist Association'. Jack Worthing may have been right to suggest that the Liberal Unionists had no politics, but they did have principles – primarily civil and religious liberty, which they believed to be threatened by the Catholic hierarchy in Ireland, and the rule of law, threatened by terrorism in Ireland. These had been the Liberal principles of 1885 before Gladstone's conversion

---

4 *The Times*, 15 June 1895.
5 Quoted in Enoch Powell, *Joseph Chamberlain*, Thames & Hudson, 1977, p. 94.
6 Ian Cawood, *The Liberal Unionist Party: A History*, I. B. Tauris, 2012, pp. 84–5. This book offers a fine account of the history of the Liberal Unionist Party until 1895.

to Home Rule. The Liberal Unionists argued that it was they who had stood their ground in 1886, and that it was the Gladstonians who had instigated a radical departure from traditional Liberal policy and values. And, while the Liberal Unionists may, as Lady Bracknell suggested, have counted as Tories, they were not in fact Tories. They were still distinct from the Conservatives in 1895, although they were to move closer towards them until fusion in 1912. But with their large Nonconformist element, they remained socially distinct from the Conservatives. In 1895, they believed it vital to retain their separate identity if Home Rule was to be defeated, since they could attract a distinct electoral constituency of their own. 'No one', Chamberlain told his son Austen in January 1895, 'who has not worked among the electors can be aware how strong are old prejudices in connection with party names and colours and badges. A man may be a good Unionist at heart and yet nothing can persuade him to vote "Blue" or give support to a Tory candidate.'[7]

The secession of Chamberlain and his followers in 1886 made the Liberals appear less relevant to the burgeoning issues of the day, while the Conservatives, strengthened by their Liberal Unionist allies, appeared more in tune with new demands; or perhaps, simply by being in office, the Unionists were forced to confront them. But whatever the cause, the Liberals came to appear less modern, the Unionists more modern. The rejection of Home Rule weakened, divided, distracted and discredited the forces of the left, blunting the radicalism of which Chamberlain had been so powerful a representative. The Liberals remained preoccupied, until Gladstone's retirement in 1894, with Home Rule, and then turned in on themselves. During the 1890s, they seemed out of touch with the concerns of many voters, particularly working-class voters and trade unionists. That no doubt was one of the reasons for the formation of the Labour Party in 1900.

The rejection of Home Rule was to herald twenty years of Unionist dominance, interrupted for just three years by the weak Gladstone/Rosebery government, dependent for its majority on the Irish Nationalists. The rejection of Home Rule ended a period of Liberal hegemony and inaugurated Conservative hegemony such that the twentieth century has been aptly called 'the Conservative Century'.[8] Between the first Reform Act in 1832 and 1886, there had been just two majority Conservative governments – Peel's in 1841 and Disraeli's in 1874. After 1886, there was to be just one further majority Liberal government – the Campbell-Bannerman government, elected in

---

7   M. C. Hurst, *Joseph Chamberlain and West Midlands Politics 1886–1895*, Dugdale Society Occasional Papers, no. 15, 1962, p. 69.
8   The title of an edited volume on the history of the Conservative Party in the twentieth century, edited by Stuart Ball and Anthony Seldon, and published by Oxford University Press in 1994.

1906; and just one other majority government of the left in the next sixty years – the Attlee government, elected in 1945.

Conservative hegemony would have surprised many at the time when the franchise was being extended in the nineteenth century. For, after 1884, there was, amongst the electorate, a working-class majority which could in theory have been united in supporting a radical government of the left, something which many nineteenth-century conservatives feared. But to the extent that the working class was united, it was united by patriotism, often subconscious, as much as or perhaps more than by class. 'Of all men, I think,' Disraeli had declared in 1878, 'working men should be most Conservative. It is no light thing to belong to a nation where liberty and order co-exist in the greatest degree. That must benefit all classes and most particularly it must benefit the working man'.[9] On the second anniversary of Disraeli's death, on 18 April 1883, *The Times* declared that 'in the inarticulate mass of the English population', he had 'discerned the Conservative workingman as the sculptor perceives the angel prisoned in a block of marble'. In Britain, as in many countries on the Continent, popular feeling was to display many conservative tendencies. Indeed, in 1910, a number of Conservatives were to toy with bringing the people into the constitution through the referendum to curb the radical instincts of the Liberal government of Asquith and Lloyd George.

Many in the working class held culturally conservative attitudes, in particular, a hostility to Irish and Jewish immigration. In the late nineteenth century, in Lancashire and Glasgow, where there was heavy Irish immigration, working-class Conservatism was strong. In the years between 1885 and 1910, the average Conservative vote in Wales was 39 per cent while in inner London it was 53 per cent. No one would suggest that Wales, much of which is rural, had a higher percentage of working-class voters than London. But London was subject to pressure from Irish and Jewish immigrants while Wales was not. And there was a further important factor – religion. For if the working class was united by patriotism, it was divided by religion. Wales was predominantly Nonconformist, and religion and nationalism combined to help the left, while London was primarily Anglican or secular. Until 1910, the division between church and chapel was at least as important as class in determining voting behaviour. Finally, the working class was also divided by the nature of its employment, and sensitivity to foreign competition. Employment in large-scale industry tended to be associated with membership of a trade union, leading to support for the Liberals or in due course the Labour Party. But in small-scale industry, as in Chamberlain's Birmingham, in agriculture, or in personal services, trade unionism was weak, and

9   Robert McKenzie and Allan Silver, *Angels in Marble: Working Class Conservatives in Urban England*, Heinemann, 1968, p. 43.

working people might be in closer contact with their employer than with other members of their class. In small-scale industry, there was less sense of working-class solidarity, and therefore a smaller propensity to vote for a party of the left. Where industries were in danger from foreign competition, tariff reform had an appeal to the working class which it lacked in industries such as cotton which were dependent upon free trade.

But as well as bringing about Conservative hegemony, the Home Rule crisis of 1886 prefigured a long period of party realignment and flux. Between 1886 and Attlee's Labour administration in 1945, there were to be just three 'normal' single-party majority governments – the Liberal government of 1906–10 and the Conservative governments of 1922–23 and 1924–29. Every other administration was either a minority government or coalition.

The decision in 1886 of the Commons, supported by voters in the ensuing general election, to reject Home Rule had important effects on the way in which Britain was governed, as well as on the party system. The eighty or so Irish Nationalist MPs in the Commons were a permanent irritant, and after 1886, Irish issues continued to absorb a disproportionate amount of parliamentary time. Between 1892 and 1895, and after the January 1910 election, Liberal governments were dependent on Irish MPs, distracted by the problem of governing Ireland, and compelled to continue with Home Rule, even though some Liberals were becoming sceptical of it. Nor were Unionist governments free of Irish pressures. The Unionist policy after 1895 of 'killing Home Rule with kindness' meant reform – reform of Irish land, Irish local government, and perhaps even some degree of devolution. But such measures were anathema to Unionist landowners and were to divide the 1895 Unionist administration. Governments of both parties were to pay for the mismanagement of Ireland, which was making it more difficult to govern the rest of Britain.

The Unionist alliance was based on an electoral pact first negotiated for the 1886 general election when the Conservatives had agreed not to contest the constituencies of the ninety-three Liberals who had voted against Home Rule to avoid splitting the Unionist vote. In 1889, the electoral pact was formalised in a 'compact', the terms of which were:

1. That no Conservative or Liberal Unionist seat would be attacked by the other partner to the alliance.
2. That seats contested by Conservatives or Liberal Unionists in 1886 would not be contested by the other partner without the consent of the whips of both parties.
3. That seats held by Gladstonian Liberals and uncontested by Conservatives

or Liberal Unionists should be contested in future elections 'as may seem most advisable having regard to local circumstances'.[10]

This compact worked so well that by 1901, Lord Salisbury could claim that the two parties were like 'two men in one pair of trousers'.[11]

In June 1895, shortly before the general election, Liberal Unionist leaders attended a Conservative dinner for the first time, with one Conservative MP remarking that this 'marked an epoch in their political history'. The Duke of Devonshire, formerly Lord Hartington, Liberal Unionist leader in the Lords, declared that closer relations were made possible by an 'enormous change in the character and policy' of the Conservatives, who, influenced by Lord Randolph Churchill and Balfour, now enjoyed a 'closer contact … with the people, with the democracy'.[12] A month later, on 10 July, Chamberlain called for the formation of 'a national party to which every patriotic man may be proud to belong … pledged … to maintain the greatness and integrity of the Empire. And … to a policy of constructive social reform'.[13]

It had been agreed before Rosebery's resignation that the new government would be a coalition, and not a single-party government as in 1886. The Unionist coalition would have the advantage, denied to both the Conservative minority government of 1886 and the Liberal minority government of 1892, of a comfortable majority in the Commons. From the time of Gladstone's retirement from the office of Prime Minister in March 1894, Unionist leaders had been negotiating 'for a common policy and a joint administration'.[14] They had come to broad agreement on policy and on distribution of government posts. So, even though the 1895 election would give the Conservatives an overall majority, they would not be governing alone.

But Lord Salisbury did not find it easy to form a coalition, complaining to a colleague of the 'odious tiresomeness of … forming a Government from two camps'.[15] The government was to be, in the phrase of one former minister, an 'omnium gatherum', formed primarily to conciliate the various elements of the Unionist coalition.[16] In a Cabinet of nineteen members, there were to be five Liberal Unionists – Chamberlain (Colonial Secretary), Devonshire (Lord President), Goschen (at the Admiralty), Lord James (Chancellor of the Duchy of Lancaster) and Lord Lansdowne (Secretary for War). The size

---

10 This 'compact' is printed in Appendix 1 of Cawood, *Liberal Unionist Party*, pp. 253–4.
11 Roberts, *Salisbury*, p. 783.
12 *The Times*, 15 June 1895.
13 Ibid., 11 July 1895.
14 Garvin, *Chamberlain*, vol. 3, p. 611.
15 Quoted in J. R. Holding, 'An Examination of the Third Salisbury Cabinet, 1895–1902', MLitt thesis, Oxford University, 1978, p. 15.
16 Andrew Gailey, *Ireland and the Death of Kindness: The experience of constructive unionism 1890–1905*, Cork University Press, 1987, p. 91.

of the Cabinet – large for those days – was due to the need to accommodate the various elements in the coalition. It had in fact been formed before the election, when it could not be foreseen that the Conservatives would secure an overall majority on their own so that, from a strictly arithmetical point of view, they would have no real need of the Liberal Unionists. Perhaps if the government had been formed after the election, the Liberal Unionists would have secured less Cabinet representation. In 1892, *The Spectator* had complained that, though the 1886–92 government had been purely Conservative, Lord Salisbury had been a mere 'figure-head, but the screw that imparts motion to the vessel is Mr Chamberlain' – a reference perhaps to the fact that Chamberlain's social origins, in 'trade' as a screw manufacturer, were so remote from those of leading Conservatives who tended to be either owners of great estates or members of the squirearchy.[17] Of the 1895 government, a contemporary wrote:

> Among the rank and file of the Conservatives there was audible grumbling at the number and importance of the offices that had fallen to Liberal Unionists. It was felt that Mr Chamberlain had driven too hard a bargain with Lord Salisbury, that the Prime Minister had too easily yielded to importunity.[18]

The Conservatives needed to accommodate Liberal Unionists not so much to conciliate its leaders but to retain the loyalty of its rank and file. For, although the Liberal Unionist leaders might have little alternative but to maintain the Conservatives in office, that was not true of the rank and file. To carry their supporters, especially in Birmingham, the Liberal Unionist leaders had to point to reforming measures from a Unionist government. Otherwise the Liberal Unionists would become a party of leaders without followers.

THE UNIONIST GOVERNMENT

The Prime Minister of the Unionist government, following Rosebery's resignation, was Lord Salisbury (1830–1903), now entering his third term of office as premier. Until 1900, he combined the premiership with the Foreign Office, the last Prime Minister to do so apart from Ramsay MacDonald during the first Labour government in 1924.

---

17 'The Tory Complaints of Lord Salisbury', *The Spectator*, 30 July 1892, p. 7.
18 H. R. Whates, *The Third Salisbury Administration, 1895–1900*, Vacher, 1900, p. 8.

'Who has been my greatest Prime Minister?' Queen Victoria asked one of her courtiers.

'Lord Beaconsfield – Disraeli,' the courtier suggested.

'No! Lord Salisbury,' replied Queen Victoria.

Even more remarkably, the Labour Prime Minister Clement Attlee was to believe that Salisbury had been the best Prime Minister during his lifetime, which extended from 1883 to 1967.[19] Salisbury was Queen Victoria's longest-serving Prime Minister. Indeed, only Walpole, Pitt the Younger and Lord Liverpool have enjoyed a longer tenure in 10 Downing Street. Salisbury was also Foreign Secretary for longer than anyone in British history other than Palmerston. He was, before anything else, a man of government.

Born in 1830 in Hatfield House, Salisbury was a scion of one of the oldest aristocratic families in the land, a descendant of Lord Burghley, minister to Queen Elizabeth I. A third son, he became the heir after the second son had died in infancy, and the eldest, who suffered from a debilitating illness, had died, unmarried, at the age of fifty. The family had not been noted in the recent past for intellectual or indeed any other kind of distinction. 'During more than a century and a half,' Salisbury's daughter wrote, in the official biography of her father, 'the general mediocrity of intelligence which the family displayed was only varied by instances of quite exceptional stupidity.'[20] An awkward and sickly child, Salisbury had, while at Eton, from which he was withdrawn at the age of fifteen, been 'bullied from morning to night without ceasing'. He had hated his time there so much that during the holidays he would never venture into a main street for fear of meeting a schoolfellow there.[21] He had also been starved of affection by his domineering father, his mother having died when he was nine. At Oxford, he was too ill to take his degree, and was awarded an honorary fourth class, but in 1853, he won the chief academic prize that the university had to offer, a fellowship by examination at All Souls College, the only Prime Minister so far to have achieved this accolade. He was an unlikely figure to enter politics – stooping, short-sighted and intellectual, shy, introverted and somewhat neurotic. Nor did he share the leisure interests of his class – field sports and hunting.

Having been brought face to face with the less amiable features of human nature at an early age, Salisbury developed a permanent scepticism towards schemes of human improvement. His ardent Christianity, like Gladstone's, with whom he otherwise had little in common, was based on the belief that only Christianity could account for man's inherent sinfulness. Men were as

19 Lord David Cecil, *The Cecils of Hatfield House*, Constable, 1973, pp. 221, 231. This book, written by his son, contains a fine character sketch of Salisbury. Roberts, *Salisbury*, p. 836.

20 Quoted in Lord Blake, 'Introduction', in Blake and Cecil, eds, *Salisbury*, p. 2.

21 Lady Gwendolen Cecil, *Life of Robert, Marquis of Salisbury*, Hodder & Stoughton, 1921, vol. 1, pp. 13, 15.

they were, he believed, and little could be done about it. He 'simply does not believe in the possibility of improvement in human affairs', Sidney Webb was to complain in 1901, 'a view which is rather the philosophy of an independent income and a peerage than of the mass of electors existing in obviously improvable circumstances'.[22] His dislike of any form of enthusiasm, of ideology, indeed of political doctrine of any sort made him particularly congenial to most Conservatives, more congenial than Disraeli, whom Conservatives had found difficult to comprehend. 'When great men get drunk with a theory,' Salisbury wrote, 'it is the little men who have a headache.'

Salisbury's early experiences also gave him a strong concern for human individuality, 'a passionate belief in a man's right to do and think as he wishes, however much the majority of his fellows disagreed with him, and a contempt for those who surrender that right to please the majority'. Little concerned with the impression he made on others, he was indifferent to his appearance, and was once refused admission to a casino at Monte Carlo because he was thought to be homeless. The Irish Party MP, T. P. O'Connor, by no means an unprejudiced witness, found that he had a

not very attractive personality for he is lumbering, uncouth, ponderous beyond the ordinary, bleak in visage, pale in cheek, heavy and awkward in frame; he strikes one as a very rough piece of Nature's carving – not in the least like the delicate and more refined material out of which we suppose aristocrats to be composed.[23]

But Salisbury was a man of wide intellectual interests and a practising scientist, establishing a laboratory at his family seat at Hatfield, one of the first houses in the country to install a telephone. Salisbury was an intellectual also in his approach to politics. Indeed, he has been regarded as 'the most formidable intellectual figure that the Conservative Party has ever produced'. He was that rare phenomenon, a philosophical Conservative. His defence of Conservatism, by contrast with that of Disraeli, his predecessor as Conservative Prime Minister, was in no way romantic or sentimental but hard-headed and, in his view, empirical and utilitarian. If the Conservatives were ever to abandon 'the principles for which I joined them', he declared in his early years, 'I should walk for the last time down the steps of the Carlton Club without casting a glance of regret behind me'.[24]

At the age of twenty-three, he had been returned as Conservative MP

---

22 Sidney Webb, 'Lord Rosebery's Escape From Houndsditch', *Nineteenth Century*, 1901, p. 373.
23 Roberts, *Salisbury*, pp. 838, 636–7.
24 Cecil, *Cecils of Hatfield House*, pp. 221, 231; Roberts, *Salisbury*, p. 851.

for the pocket borough of Stamford, thanks to the influence of his cousin, the Marquess of Exeter. He sat for Stamford until succeeding to the peerage in 1868, without ever having to fight a contested election – the last Prime Minister to have enjoyed this privilege. No one ever voted for him, and he labelled importuning constituents 'vermin of that kind'. 'Educated men', he was accustomed to say, 'do not like going round, hat in hand, begging for votes of a mob [that] requires him to swallow the most claptrap pledges as a condition for their support.'[25] He rapidly established a reputation as a reactionary opponent of democratic advance through his Commons speeches and voluminous journalism. He became Secretary of State for India in Lord Derby's Conservative government in 1866, at the age of thirty-six, but resigned after just nine months, being opposed to what he regarded as Disraeli's reckless concessions in the direction of household suffrage. Even so Disraeli admired him, telling his daughter and biographer, Lady Gwendolen Cecil, 'courage is the rarest of all qualities to be found in public men. Your father is the only man of real courage that it has been my lot to work with.'[26] When Disraeli came to form his Conservative majority government in 1874, Salisbury again became India Secretary, and then in 1878 Foreign Secretary. He became Prime Minister of a short-lived minority government in 1885–86, and then of a longer-lasting minority government, sustained by the Liberal Unionists, from 1886 to 1892. He was sixty-five when he became Prime Minister for the third time in 1895.

For Salisbury, the essence of Conservatism was the preservation of aristocratic rule. Disraeli had told him in 1880 that 'during a long parliamentary life, and long before I was in Parliament, I have been profoundly convinced that the greatness and character of this country depended on our landed tenure. All the rest I look upon, and have ever looked upon, as leather and prunella.'[27] Salisbury would have agreed with this sentiment. He did not, however, any more than other Conservatives, view the aristocracy as a caste apart. During the First World War, the American ambassador was to declare that 'English history is aristocracy with the doors open. Who has courage and faculty let him enter?'[28] In 1862, Salisbury had insisted in an article in the *Quarterly Review* that every community had natural leaders – 'Always wealth, in some countries birth, in all intellectual power and culture, mark out the men to whom ... a community looks to undertake its government. They are the aristocracy of a country in the original and best sense of the word.'[29]

25 Eric Midwinter, *Salisbury*, Haus, 2006, pp. 12, 99.
26 Quoted in Cecil, *Cecils of Hatfield House*, p. 234.
27 Richard Faber, *Beaconsfield and Bolingbroke*, Faber, 1961, p. 19.
28 B. J. Hendrick, *The Life and Letters of Walter H. Page*, Heinemann, 1922, vol. 3, p. 28.
29 Cecil, *Life of Salisbury*, vol. 1, p. 159.

Birth, wealth and talent, then, were the basis of the British aristocracy. 'To survive in London society,' Disraeli had declared, 'you require birth, genius or a million.'[30] Outsiders not born into the aristocracy could enter the ruling group through wealth or talent. Gladstone was the son of a rich merchant, Campbell-Bannerman the son of a wealthy manufacturer and large landowner, Asquith and Haldane were talented barristers and Morley a journalist.

Salisbury, however, did not share Disraeli's view, which formed the basis of Lord Randolph Churchill's 'Tory democracy', that preservation of aristocratic rule might on occasion require radical reform. Less imaginative than Disraeli but more realistic and attuned to concrete realities, the leitmotif of his Conservatism was resistance to change. He was indeed the last Tory of the old school for whom the essence of Toryism lay in defence of the church and landed interest. But by 1895, he had come to appreciate that the best way of defending them was not by resisting democracy but by accepting it and guiding it towards conservative ends. He had come to realise, as Bismarck had done in Germany, that a mass electorate could prove an ally of conservatism, not its opponent. That involved adding new elements to the Conservative cause – the growing managerial and professional class and the patriotic portion of the working class. 'If Gladstone and Disraeli won the people's hearts, Salisbury won their votes.'[31] Lacking the glamour and charisma of Disraeli, Rosebery or Chamberlain, Salisbury was more electorally successful than any of them, indeed the most electorally successful Conservative leader until Margaret Thatcher.

Like Bismarck, Salisbury understood that it was better to tame democracy, to resist it with its own weapons, than seek to thwart it. 'The best form of government', he had written in his first long essay in 1858, 'is one where the masses have little power and seem to have a great deal.'[32] By temperament and conviction alike, Salisbury was a man of caution. By contrast with Disraeli, his policies at home and abroad were marked by an unwillingness to take risks, so that 'though he adopted the Disraelian tradition, his methods were the very opposite of Mr Disraeli's.'[33] The Conservative Party, Salisbury told the imperial proconsul, Sir Alfred Milner, was 'shackled by tradition. All the cautious people, all the timid, all the unimaginative, belong to it. It stumbles slowly and painfully from precedent to precedent with its eyes fixed on the ground.'[34] Salisbury was not averse to cautious social reform,

---

30 Quoted in Low, *Governance of England*, p. 187.
31 Roberts, *Salisbury*, p. 850.
32 'The Theories of Parliamentary Reform', quoted in Elie Kedourie, 'Tory Ideologue: Salisbury as a Conservative Intellectual', *Encounter*, June 1972, p. 50.
33 E. T. Raymond, *Portraits of the Nineties*, T. Fisher Unwin, 1921, p. 60.
34 Roberts, *Salisbury*, p. 800; J. P. D. Dunbabin, 'The Politics of the Establishment of County Councils', *Historical Journal*, 1963, p. 252fn.

but it was obvious to him that the Conservatives would have to legislate at a slower pace than their opponents. 'We have so to conduct our legislation that we shall give some satisfaction to both classes and masses,' he had warned Lord Randolph Churchill in 1886. But this was 'especially difficult with the classes – because all legislation is rather unwelcome to them, as tending to disturb a state of things with which they are satisfied. It is evident, therefore, that we must work at less speed and at a lower temperature than our opponents.'[35] Salisbury was in tune with the fundamental instincts of the late nineteenth-century Conservative Party. Sir Michael Hicks Beach, Chancellor of the Exchequer in the 1895 government, believed that 'on the leading questions of Home politics of the time, such as the constitution of Parliament, local government or Irish land, he was more Tory than his colleagues'. The 1895 Queen's Speech contained no proposals for social reform and, speaking in Brighton in November of that year, Salisbury declared that 'our legislation should be careful and tentative ... However much you may desire to benefit your neighbour, do not benefit him by taking money out of the pockets of another man.'[36] He was out of sympathy with many currents of the new age, and in particular with the pressure for social reform and 'efficiency'. Under a Unionist administration, the crown, the church and the constitution were now safe. Why, then, disturb the status quo? So his last government, from 1895 to 1902, was devoid of any major legislative initiatives and was marked by quiescence in domestic affairs.

Salisbury was kindly and thoughtful towards his colleagues, when he recognised them and remembered who they were – something that could not be taken for granted in his later years. But he was reserved, distant and enigmatic. He did not cultivate close personal relations with his ministers, to most of whom he appeared remote. By 1895, 'few of the rank and file of his party in the House of Commons had ever exchanged a word with him, nor was he better known to the majority of the Peers. Two members of his Cabinet were not always sure that he knew them.'[37] He spent much of his time at Hatfield and ministers found it difficult to contact him. In 1896, a newly elected MP stayed at Hatfield for 'four or five days', dining with him every night. 'I have met him several times', he wrote in his diary, 'and now have stayed four or five days in his house – yet I have never spoken to him, neither has he done so to me.' But he added:

it is rather attractive this distant attitude towards those around him: it

35 Churchill, *Lord Randolph Churchill*, vol. 2, pp. 223–4.
36 Cawood, *Liberal Unionist Party*, p. 102.
37 Garvin, *Chamberlain*, vol. 3, p. 8.

impresses one with a halo of mystery circling about the man whose words are heeded in the remotest parts of the world. Were he more talkative – in fact if he had spoken to even one of his guests whom he does not know by sight – our curiosity would have been gratified but our admiration could not have been increased.[38]

Unlike Gladstone, Disraeli or Chamberlain, Salisbury lacked popular appeal. Nor could he summon the moral uplift which characterised Gladstone's speeches. Indeed, he would not have wished to do so. Unlike Disraeli, who founded a political doctrine or Gladstone whose moral fervour inspired Liberals, Salisbury left no distinctive political legacy. Instead, he administered a creed; and in doing so, he helped to make the Conservatives what they had not been in the nineteenth century: the natural party of government in the twentieth.

As Prime Minister, Salisbury left his colleagues very much to themselves on domestic affairs. He did not 'exercise the control over his colleagues, either in or out of Cabinet that Lord Beaconsfield [Disraeli] did ... Lord Salisbury frequently allowed important matters to be decided by a small majority of votes, even against his own opinion.' On foreign policy, though dominant, he could no longer be sure of getting his own way. In 1895, he was to favour coercing Turkey over her treatment of her Armenian subjects, but he was overruled by Goschen, First Lord of the Admiralty. Salisbury was not what in modern parlance would be called a 'strong' Prime Minister. In the opinion of Hicks Beach, his achievement would have been greater 'if his nature had been harder and more self-assertive, but this might possibly have detracted from his personal charm, which is no small asset in the conduct of affairs'.[39] Salisbury was in fact ageing rapidly, and it gradually became clear that he was past his best. In his later years,

he was walking in a street near his London house accompanied by his soldier son, when an elderly, well-dressed man raises his hat to them. 'Who is your guardsman friend?' asked Lord Salisbury, to the amusement (though not to the surprise) of his son, for the polite passer-by was his father's butler.[40]

In March 1898, Jack Sandars, Balfour's private secretary, told Balfour's niece that Salisbury 'no longer had the power of going to the depth of subjects

38 Vincent, ed., *Crawford Papers*, p. 32.
39 Hicks Beach, 'Memorandum on Salisbury written at the request of Lady Gwendolen Cecil', January 1914, in Hicks Beach, *Life of Hicks Beach*, pp. 360, 362, 363.
40 A. L. Kennedy, *Salisbury, 1830–1903: Portrait of a Statesman*, John Murray, 1953, p. 310.

coming before him'.[41] In July, Curzon, the viceroy of India, wrote to the India Secretary of the difficulty of working under 'that strange, powerful, inscrutable, brilliant, obstructive deadweight at the top'.[42]

After 1899, when his wife died following a long illness, he became even more of a fading force. 'In the latter years of his premiership,' according to Hicks Beach, 'Lord Salisbury was obviously weary and ill, and shrank from any new departure.' 'He looked in his middle sixties', one of his sons has said, 'more like eighty: bowed, dim-sighted, enormously heavy. He felt permanently tired, so that he was liable to go to sleep in inopportune moments, dictating a dispatch, or presiding over a Cabinet meeting.'[43] After the death of his wife, he wanted to resign, but the queen begged him to stay.

The main focus of Salisbury's energies and indeed his consuming interest lay in foreign affairs. His foreign policy was marked by the twin motifs of conciliation and avoidance of commitment but also a show of strength when that was needed. But by 1895, his mastery of foreign affairs was no longer unquestioned. He suffered from an ever growing inability to handle the large amount of work required, and did not appear wholly aware of what was needed in a new international environment in a new age. Nevertheless, he continued to regard the Foreign Office as his own bailiwick, and complained when colleagues sought to interfere. But the more active ministers in the government were coming to question the assumptions on which Salisbury had based his foreign policy; and his retirement from the Foreign Office in 1900 was to herald a new course.

Salisbury's genius was of the negative kind. He used to maintain:

> Mr Gladstone's existence was the greatest source of strength which the Conservative Party possessed ... He did not shrink from facing the fact that according to his view the success of his own party was dependent on the existence of the other: 'I would rank myself no higher in the scheme of things than a policeman – whose utility would disappear if there were no criminals.'[44]

The Conservatives won elections when the voters were frightened, as they were in 1895 by the threat of Home Rule. On domestic affairs, Salisbury tended to postpone problems rather than resolve them. As Prime Minister, he 'originated little; he delayed much that was good as well as much that was ill; he belonged emphatically to that class of men who must be praised

---

41 Otte, *The China Question*, p. 130.
42 Earl of Ronaldshay, *Life of Lord Curzon*, Ernest Benn, 1928, vol. 1, pp. 282–3.
43 Cecil, *Cecils of Hatfield House*, p. 264.
44 Blake, 'Introduction', in Blake and Cecil, eds, *Salisbury*, pp. 4–5.

rather for what they avoided than for what they accomplished'.[45] Although Prime Minister for a total of nearly fourteen years, there is, by contrast with most occupants of No. 10, no great legislative measure standing to his name. 'There is no evidence', his daughter wrote, 'upon which he can be credited with the paternity of any measure introduced while he was Prime Minister.'[46] In foreign policy, he sought to preserve rather than extend the empire and maintain Britain's strong position in the world, which meant, he believed, avoiding entangling alliances. But by postponing change, Salisbury ensured that pent-up forces, when they eventually came to the surface, proved even more disruptive than they might otherwise have been.

*   *   *

Salisbury was leader of the Conservative Party in the House of Lords. The leader of the Liberal Unionists in the Lords was the Duke of Devonshire (1833–1908), formerly Lord Hartington. He had benefited from a privileged start in politics, first elected to the Commons in 1857 at the age of twenty-four as a supporter of Palmerston, whose patriotic foreign policy and sceptical attitude towards domestic reform he shared. Just two years after entering the Commons, in 1859, Hartington had been asked to move the successful vote of no confidence in Lord Derby's Conservative government, which led to Palmerston's return to power. He made just three speeches in his first four years in Parliament, and is said to have yawned in the middle of his maiden speech. Disraeli predicted accurately that 'to any man who can betray such extreme languor under such circumstances the highest post in the gift of the Commons should be open'.[47] He was indeed to serve in six of the ten ministries between 1859 and 1905. He first gained junior office in 1863, and entered the Cabinet in 1866 at the age of thirty-three in Lord Russell's brief Liberal government. By the end of Gladstone's first ministry in 1874, Hartington was recognised as a leading figure in the Liberal Party. From 1875 to 1880, he led the party in the Commons during Gladstone's temporary retirement. He served in Gladstone's second ministry but declined office in the third, being opposed to Home Rule. He had been Chief Secretary for Ireland between 1870 and 1874, in which capacity he had not hesitated to urge suspension of habeas corpus in response to agrarian outrages. One of the richest landlords in Britain and an absentee landlord in Ireland, owning 60,000 acres in Cork and Waterford, Hartington believed that Home Rule would

---

45 Raymond, *Portraits of the Nineties*, p. 68.
46 Roberts, *Salisbury*, p. 848.
47 Patrick Jackson, *The Last of the Whigs: A Political Biography of Lord Hartington, later Eighth Duke of Devonshire (1833–1908)*, Associated University Presses, 1994, p. 31.

undermine respect for law and the rights of property and establish in Dublin a clerical regime threatening the civil and religious rights of the Protestant minority. His brother, Lord Frederick Cavendish, had been assassinated in Phoenix Park, Dublin, in 1882, shortly after being appointed Chief Secretary for Ireland, after which Hartington always carried a loaded revolver with him. He had moved the rejection of both Home Rule Bills in 1886 and 1893. His rejection of Home Rule was at least as important as Chamberlain's in defeating it, since he carried greater weight with moderate, centrist opinion. On breaking with Gladstone, he became leader of the Liberal Unionist Party in the Commons until his father's death in 1891, upon which he became the 8th Duke of Devonshire. He was to serve in the Salisbury and Balfour governments until 1903 when he resigned in protest at Balfour's government policy of departing from free trade.

Devonshire bore some resemblance to Trollope's Duke of Omnium, in his somewhat rackety private life as well as his politics, and was said to be the model for St Aldegonde in Disraeli's novel *Lothair*, published in 1870.[48] He owned, as well as Irish estates and Chatsworth, the family seat in Derbyshire, properties in Piccadilly, Lancashire, Yorkshire, Chiswick, Eastbourne and Newmarket. He had managed to achieve a second in mathematics at Cambridge, even though 'academic work was not to his taste', and he was not what was known as a 'reading man'.[49] By contrast with Salisbury, he had no intellectual interests. His main spare-time interests were cards and horse-racing. Largely for this reason, the two men, though politically in broad agreement, were never personally close. In October 1891, Salisbury had written despairingly to Balfour that 'Hartington is at Newmarket and all political arrangements have to be hung up till some quadruped has run faster than some other quadruped'.[50] In the 1895 government, when the time of the next Cabinet meeting was to be decided, Salisbury 'would sometimes suggest a date, and then turn to the Duke and say with a smile, "Does that happen to be a sacred day, Duke?" in case it should coincide with the Derby or Ascot'.[51]

Politically, the duke was the last of the Whigs, the group of aristocratic families who had engineered the Glorious Revolution of 1688–89, to establish a limited monarchy, a balanced constitution and civil and religious liberty. The Whigs had been reformers so long as reform could be contained within the framework of aristocratic leadership. But by 1895, they were a distinctly conservative force; their great achievements lay in the past, and,

48 Holland, *Life of Devonshire*, vol. 2, p. 167.
49 Ibid., vol. 1, pp. 14, 17.
50 Jackson, *Last of the Whigs*, p. 262.
51 From a memorandum written around 1900 by Lord James of Hereford, quoted in Askwith, *Lord James of Hereford*, pp. 255–6.

even if Gladstone had not taken up Home Rule, they would, in time, have drifted towards the Conservatives. Indeed, Hartington refused to join Gladstone's Home Rule government in 1886 for conservative reasons. Gladstone had changed his mind. Hartington had not. He had not, he declared in his election address of 1886, 'seceded from the principles or traditions of the Liberal party. I contend, on the contrary, that I am maintaining them.'[52] Later in 1903, he was similarly to resign from Balfour's government, not because his views on free trade had changed but because they remained the same, while Balfour and the majority of the Cabinet had become converts to 'fiscal freedom', i.e. tariffs. Hartington, even more than Lord Salisbury, was a man of deeply conservative instincts. Indeed, his only worry in working with Salisbury from 1886 was 'an occasional nervousness on his part lest the Government should not prove sufficiently Conservative'![53] In 1896, Rosebery declared that the government was using him as 'a universal refrigerator'. When a new idea was produced, 'the noble Duke's icy cold spray has been turned on, and no political plant with which I am acquainted has survived that mortifying process'.[54] He was later to be described by Chamberlain as 'a drag on the wheel', and characteristically welcomed this description, declaring that 'a drag is a not unimportant part of the mechanism ... [especially when someone is] running the locomotive at full speed down the line and against all the signals'.[55] Wide differences of policy and temperament meant that his relationship with Chamberlain was always uneasy.

Salisbury's resistance to change was based in large part upon belief, Devonshire's on instinct. His adherence to the Union ensured rejection of Home Rule in 1886; his adherence to free trade would help ensure rejection of tariff reform in 1903. He broke both Home Rule and protection.

It is difficult at first sight to account for Devonshire's huge influence. Uncharismatic and dull, he was a poor orator who loathed public speaking. 'No man was more completely without colour or atmosphere ... the simplest speech caused him torment.' Devonshire's biographer emphasises

> his determination to be dull. No other political figure in recent times has so successfully created a personal image of worthy mediocrity. He endlessly apologised for his own limitations ... He claimed to be bored by his own speeches, and by the duties of ministerial office. Repeatedly he would

52 Holland, *Life of Devonshire*, vol. 2, p. 161.
53 Cecil, *Life of Salisbury*, vol. 3, p. 313.
54 House of Lords Debates, 11 February 1896, vol. 37, col. 31.
55 Speech by Devonshire in the Queen's Hall, 24 November 1903, in Jackson, *Last of the Whigs*, p. 354.

claim that the racecourses interested him more than the cabinet room, and too many people, then and since, have taken him at his word.[56]

In April 1902, the Cabinet was discussing Manchuria, as it had been for some weeks previously. Gerald Balfour 'got up and went to a map of China, and was joined by the Duke who asked innocently, "Where *is* Manchuria?"'[57] But all this was deceptive. He appeared lazier than he was. In Chamberlain's words, he 'shammed stupid'.[58] As Balfour told his uncle, 'in spite of his blunt manner and ungrammatical sentences there's no man who weighs his words more carefully than Hartington or has more "intention" in what he says'.[59] When he wanted to master an issue, as with the 1902 Education Act, he did; and indeed the Act owes more to him than to any other minister. He had a shrewd common sense which stood him well against more glamorous figures such as Gladstone and Chamberlain. 'The very slowness of the Duke's mental processes', Sir Almeric Fitzroy believed, 'makes him invaluable in discussion, because he is never convinced until he has traced to his own satisfaction the ultimate developments of a line of policy, and is not content, like most men, with a general perception of it. The Duke's rugged candour makes self-deception impossible.' On the Education Act of 1902, his 'talent for probing to the bottom the objections to any given course has the advantage of enabling him to write State Papers of convincing power', and he was to surprise 'his colleagues by displaying a complete mastery over the issues involved and unfolded his views in a speech of great cogency'.[60] And he was a more effective speaker than at first appeared. Indeed, the American radical William Jennings Bryan named the duke the most effective of all the leading English speakers that he had heard in Britain, finding his method of developing an argument to be like 'the driving in of piles'.[61]

The duke was seen as a man without vulgar ambition. That was quite misleading. His private secretary in 1878 had written of 'the mythical Hartington ... the man who loves pleasure to the exclusion of work, who is *altogether* without personal ambition, whose mind turns away from long and serious contemplation of dull subjects. All this is fiction.' Indeed, 'apart from politics, he has no *real* interest in life and cut off from them he would be in reality as bored as he appears to be by them'.[62]

He enjoyed enormous public confidence and trust – in private matters

56 Ibid., p. 10.
57 Vincent, ed., *Crawford Papers*, p. 66.
58 Jackson, *Last of the Whigs*, p. 10.
59 Blake and Cecil, eds, *Salisbury*, p. 29.
60 Fitzroy, *Memoirs*, vol. 1, pp. 50–51, 67, 7.
61 Ibid., vol. 1, p. 315.
62 Brett, *Esher*, vol. 1, pp. 125–6.

also. He once said, 'I don't know why it is, but whenever a man is caught cheating at cards the case is referred to me.'[63] This was partly because he seemed to epitomise common sense but even more because he was seen as a man of integrity, disinterested, with no axe to grind and someone who genuinely sought the public good. There was indeed some justification for this view. His refusal to support Gladstone on Home Rule In 1886 may well have cost him the Liberal leadership. He was felt to be 'a safe man, who would not go far, but therefore could not go far wrong ... His character, however prosaic, was based on a foundation of granite firmness. If not a great man he was at least a true and honest one.'[64] It was for this reason that, although not in any way an eloquent speaker, 'few speakers either in the House of Commons or in the country have been more telling than him'.[65]

On his death, Asquith, a political opponent, declared that 'in the closing years of his life he commanded in a greater degree than perhaps any other public man the respect and confidence of every shade and section of opinion in this kingdom'.[66] The duke's influence was exerted primarily on moderate or centrist opinion, the floating vote which generally swings elections. In 1886, rejecting Home Rule, and in 1903, rejecting tariff reform, he seemed the epitome of that moderate or centrist opinion. He was, as Lord Rosebery declared in the House of Lords when news came of his death, 'one of the great reserve forces of this country'. His first biographer sums him up, not unjustly, by saying that he

> had in a high degree the character produced by the ordinary breeding and training of an English gentleman, with its merits and defects. If all statesmen were of this kind no great or rapid domestic changes would be effected; if none were, the far more important foreign and imperial affairs of the nation would be badly administered.[67]

It is hardly surprising that he had found the solid and reliable Salisbury a more congenial colleague than the volatile Gladstone. In 1895, he was offered the Foreign Office, but he declined in favour of a non-departmental post, Lord Presidency of the Council, with special responsibility for imperial defence and education. But he had far wider influence than his departmental responsibilities would indicate, an influence, so Jack Sandars declared, that 'was always enormous, with a class which is mainly conservative ... viz. the

---

63 Holland, *Life of Devonshire*, vol. 2, p. 211fn.
64 Raymond, *Portraits of the Nineties*, pp. 86–7.
65 Review of *Life of Devonshire* by Holland, *The Spectator*, 21 October 1911, p. 642.
66 Holland, *Life of Devonshire*, vol. 2, p. 418.
67 Ibid., vol. 1, p. 290.

well-to-do middle and upper classes. They are politically timorous and suspicious; their ideal leader is a "safe" man preferably belonging to the "aristocracy" with a "stake in the country".[68] That safe man was the duke. Such was his influence that in 1906, Sandars told Balfour that one of twelve key factors in the Liberal landslide had been the departure from the government in 1903 of the Duke of Devonshire.

*   *   *

Salisbury and Devonshire were the negative elements in the Unionist coalition, formed to prevent Home Rule and resist 'radicalism'. The more active elements in 1895 were Arthur Balfour, Lord Salisbury's nephew, who became Leader of the Commons, a crucial position when the Prime Minister was in the Lords; and Joseph Chamberlain, who became, to the surprise of many, Colonial Secretary.

By 1895, Balfour (1848–1930) enjoyed enormous prestige amongst the politically aware, such that his appointment as Leader of the Commons did not appear as nepotism. He was the scion of a wealthy family whose father owned large estates in Scotland. His mother was Lord Salisbury's sister, and one of his godfathers had been the Duke of Wellington. Upon coming of age in 1869, he inherited £4 million in land and equities – worth perhaps around £250 million today. But he was far from being a moneyed idler. He had thought in his early years of becoming a professional philosopher, and by 1895 had published two books on philosophy which received respectful notices in academic journals. But his early political apprenticeship was anything but arduous. He had appeared to drift into politics, entering the Commons in 1874, unopposed, for Hertford, virtually a pocket borough controlled by Salisbury. He spoke little in the Commons, although in 1878 he opposed a Liberal attempt to extend the household franchise to the counties. In the 1880 election, he was opposed by the Liberals but secured a majority of 164 votes – almost exactly the same number, one observer noted, as the number of houses owned in the borough by Salisbury, some of which were slums.[69] After redistribution in 1885, Balfour represented, until 1906, the working-class constituency of East Manchester, but he enjoyed little rapport with the public at large or indeed much popular appeal. His languid appearance, mannered way of speaking and love of social life, made many think that he was 'little more than an eminent trifler'.[70] He did not make

---

68 Sandars Papers, cited in Adonis, *Making Aristocracy Work*, p. 181.
69 Adams, *Balfour*, p. 44.
70 Ibid., p. 123.

his maiden speech until 1876, on the highly technical subject of the Indian currency, to an almost empty House. His nickname was 'Pretty Fanny'. He seemed languid, lackadaisical and cynical. He cultivated an image of political dilettantism, sprawling supinely on the Treasury bench and often arriving late for debates. As Prime Minister, he was to be criticised for attending the Commons too infrequently and failing to keep in touch with backbench opinion. He sometimes arrived in evening dress, implying that his duties in the Commons were but a tiresome interruption to an important dinner engagement. He claimed not to be prone to over-exertion. In 1898, just before a crucial Cabinet on the Fashoda crisis in Sudan, 'the most critical held for some years', he was 'in bed, till midday: then two hours golfing on the lawn. Biggish luncheon and two hour's walk – tea and long talk: earlyish dinner and soon after nine we drove together to Dunbar.' Balfour declared of himself, 'I have one faculty of statesmanship, namely the power of taking a perfect holiday ... In this matter I am quite perfect! It is the first requirement of the public man.'[71] Every September, he took a month's golfing holiday, usually in Scotland. In 1920, a French critic described him as 'a Tory preaching democracy, a sceptic with a mania for theology, a politician profoundly disgusted with politics ... If he were sincere, what a riddle ... if he were not, what a comedy!'[72] But much of this was a pose. The journalist Henry Lucy saw through it and regarded him as 'the most perfect living example of the mailed hand under the silken glove'.[73] Balfour worked hard and thought more carefully than most of his colleagues about political problems. He was widely read and once told an audience of working men that Karl Marx was infinitely superior to the land reformer, Henry George.[74] He was better equipped to examine free trade and tariff reform than Chamberlain, having studied economics for some years, indeed since he had been an undergraduate at Cambridge. Those who took Balfour to be a mere dilettante were to pay heavily for their mistake. His charm and courtesy meant that he was liked by leading politicians from all parties, Campbell-Bannerman being a notable exception.[75] But they hid a ruthlessness which, as the tariff reform crisis of 1903 was to show, enabled him to dispose of long-serving colleagues without a qualm. Margot Asquith once asked him whether he would mind if his three best friends died. 'I would mind', Balfour responded, 'if you all died on the same day'.[76] Julian Amery, the biographer of Chamberlain,

71 Ibid., p. 52.
72 E. T. Raymond, *Mr Balfour*, Collins, 1920, p. 221.
73 Henry W. Lucy, *A Diary of the Salisbury Parliament, 1886–1892*, Cassell, 1892, p. x.
74 Edward R. Pease, *The History of the Fabian Society*, A. C. Fifield, 1916, p. 45.
75 Fitzroy, *Memoirs*, vol. 1, p. 261.
76 Jane Ridley and Clayre Percy, eds, *The Letters of Arthur Balfour and Lady Elcho, 1885–1917*, Hamish Hamilton, 1992, pp. 17–18.

once told me that Harold Macmillan had consciously modelled himself on Balfour – the languid air, the hooded eyes, the impression of detachment. And Macmillan, like Balfour, was charming but ruthless when challenged.

In 1887, Balfour had been appointed Chief Secretary for Ireland,

> the tenth man in a decade to take his place in what must have seemed the graveyard of ambitions. One had been murdered and several had retired with damaged health; the Liberal G. O. Trevelyan broke down under the strain, and his hair was said to have turned white in his year in the post.

A Nationalist journal declared that Balfour had only three qualifications for the job. 'He was the Prime Minister's nephew, had no statesman-like reputation to injure, and he was totally ignorant of Ireland.'[77] Another journal called him a 'silk-skinned sybarite, whose rest a crumpled rose leaf would disturb'.[78] Few believed he could cope. Yet he proved more than a match for the Irish Party in the Commons and for agitators in Ireland. He acquired a new nickname, 'Bloody Balfour', for the energetic steps that he took to put down Irish agitation, which included imprisoning over twenty Irish MPs for contravening the provisions of the 1887 Crimes Act. 'You cannot', he characteristically confided to a friend, 'sit opposite to people who accuse you of murder every night without getting rather to like them!' But he sought to combine 'repression as stern as Cromwell' with 'reform as thorough as Mr Parnell or anyone else can desire', through measures of economic development, providing public money to fund land purchase by tenants. He accepted in Ireland the principle of state responsibility for social conditions by establishing in 1891 a Congested Districts Board to relieve poverty in the west.[79] One Irish priest and ardent Home Ruler declared that while he felt he ought to hate Balfour, 'as a mere man, I can't deny that he has done more for Ireland than any of his predecessors, Saxon or otherwise'.[80] Balfour remains one of the very few ministers to have enhanced his reputation by serving in Ireland. But he remained a determined opponent of Home Rule.

Balfour was to be Leader of the Commons for a longer continuous period than anyone since Pitt in the eighteenth century. His air of detachment did not exclude strong political views. Like Salisbury, he believed that a healthy society required government by a traditional ruling class which had a wisdom born of long experience, and an instinctive understanding of how Britain's empire and great power status could be preserved. In domestic

---

77 Adams, *Balfour*, p. 76.
78 Raymond, *Mr Balfour*, p. 39.
79 Adams, *Balfour*, pp. 95, 82.
80 Ibid., p. 99.

affairs, Balfour did not believe that extensive mobility from one social class to another was possible. He regarded social differences as largely determined by heredity and in 1913 was to become vice-president of the Eugenics Society. He detested all forms of radicalism and socialism and had little understanding or indeed interest in the habits or mode of living of his countrymen. He claimed, admittedly, not to be opposed to social reform, declaring in 1895:

> Social legislation, as I conceive it, is not merely to be distinguished from Socialist legislation, but is its most effective antidote. Socialism will never get possession of the great body of public opinion ... among the working classes or any other class if those who wield the collective force of the community show themselves desirous ... to ameliorate every legitimate grievance and to put society upon a proper and more solid basis.[81]

But in practice he was sceptical. 'I am not one of those', he insisted, also in 1895, 'who suppose that legislation can cure all the ills to which flesh is heir. I am not one of those who think that, if ministers are clever enough, and Parliament only industrious enough, we can so remodel this world of ours that it shall blossom as the rose.'[82] His attitude to the unfortunate was hostile. As Prime Minister, having been invited to address a meeting of the unemployed in Tower Hamlets, he wrote flippantly to a colleague, '*Entre nous* I hate the poor – when they struggle! I like 'em best in workhouses; my sister tells me that in *Prisons* they are too *Delicious* – but in Poplar I am sure they are odious. Therefore be merciful to a sinner and let me off.'[83] He was once heard asking, 'What is a trade union?'[84]

'The bulk of men bore him,' Beatrice Webb was to write in July 1905, near the end of his premiership, 'whether regarded as individuals or as an electorate, or a Parliament and all the common thoughts and feelings of common folk seem to him ineffably banal, fit only for the subject matter of Bernard Shaw's derisive wit.'[85] His successor in the Conservative leadership, Andrew Bonar Law, complained after the electoral defeat of 1906 that Balfour 'does not understand the man in the street – not to speak of the working man'. His niece and biographer Blanche Dugdale was to conclude that he lacked any 'instinct for gauging the popular mind' since he had concluded early in life that, even if such a phenomenon existed, it was 'essentially unknowable

81 Sydney Zebel, *Balfour: A Political Biography*, Cambridge University Press, 1973, p. 122.
82 Adams, *Balfour*, pp. 76, 82, 95, 99, 144.
83 José Harris, *Unemployment and Politics: A Study in English Social Policy, 1886–1914*, Clarendon Press, 1972, p. 153.
84 Lucy Masterman, *C. F. G. Masterman: A Biography* [1939], Frank Cass, 1968, p. 61.
85 MacKenzie, *Diary of Beatrice Webb*, vol. 2, p. 351.

and so not worth bothering about'.[86] His 'ideas of leadership out of the House of Commons', Lord Selborne, his cousin, and a sympathetic critic, was to tell his wife in 1911, 'are as scanty as his power of leadership in the House is wonderful.'[87] His lack of sympathy with the labour movement and remoteness from the public were to prove serious hindrances when he came to enter 10 Downing Street. He was to be the only Prime Minister to lose all three general elections which he fought.

Because of his close relationship to Salisbury, who was losing such interest as he had in domestic affairs, more was devolved to Balfour as Leader of the Commons than had been customary. It was Balfour who was entrusted with the detailed preparation and management of most legislation of importance, even when it fell nominally under the responsibility of another minister. The 1899 London Government Bill, for example, establishing borough councils in London, would normally have been the responsibility of the President of the Local Government Board, Henry Chaplin; but as Chaplin was 'quite unequal to the difficult manipulation of this problem', it was drafted by Balfour, together with the parliamentary draftsmen, 'and neither Chaplin or his officials had any share in the production and management' of it.[88] Balfour was somewhat more clubbable in Cabinet than Salisbury, not perhaps something difficult to achieve, and he was able to establish good relationships with a number of ministers and, in particular, with Chamberlain. He was to prove the lynchpin of the 1895 government, and would become de facto Prime Minister some time before Salisbury resigned. But he tended to be cliquey, relying too much on a close circle of aristocratic friends and advisers, whom one of his colleagues was to characterise as 'the family'.[89] When he finally became Prime Minister in 1902, he was to prove a better chairman of the Cabinet than Salisbury. But he did not sit on the front bench often enough to take the pulse of the Commons, so when problems arose, he lacked sufficient understanding of the feeling of the House. He was remote from Conservative backbenchers. In August 1895, one MP was astonished that

Arthur Balfour spoke to me this evening. The rank and file of our party generally consider themselves to be merely voting automata regulated by the orders of their political leaders – this is an outcome of the singular rarity of any personal acquaintance between a conservative member and a conservative

---

86 Adams, *Balfour*, p. 161.
87 E. H. H. Green, 'Radical Conservatism: The Electoral Genesis of Tariff Reform', *Historical Journal*, 1985, p. 672.
88 Sandars Papers, Bodleian Library, MSS. Bodl. MS Eng. Hist. c. 771, 'As First Lord of the Treasury', f. 323, undated. I am indebted to Professor T. G. Otte for showing me this document.
89 Gailey, *Ireland and the Death of Kindness*, p. 269. 'The family' was the term used by Arnold-Forster, who was to become War Secretary in Balfour's Cabinet in 1903.

minister. It is a great contrast with the attitude of the Liberal leaders towards their supporters. Mr Gladstone for instance always made a point of knowing every member of his party – this perhaps sounds pleasant and nothing more, but it is really the secret of that astounding cohesion which (in spite of many differences of opinion) has animated the whole Liberal party.[90]

Balfour was perhaps too intellectually sophisticated to lead a modern political party. Edward VII found him 'rather more argumentative on paper than he liked'.[91] Trained as a philosopher, he was prone to considering all sides of a political issue, and clothed his statements with so many qualifications that it was sometimes difficult to discover precisely what he meant. He was aware of this defect, saying that his qualifications were intended to ensure that he did not give unnecessary hostages to fortune. But the qualifications made him appear indecisive. 'I am not sure', he was to write to Bonar Law, his successor as Conservative leader, in 1913, 'that I made my own point of view quite clear to His Majesty; nor, indeed, with regard to some aspects of the question, am I quite sure what my point of view is.'[92] That was not a problem faced by other political leaders. Balfour's deficiencies were to be starkly revealed when he became Leader of the Opposition in 1905. He was to prove ineffective as an attacking leader both in the Commons and in the country, and incapable of arousing enthusiasm either at Westminster or in the constituencies. He was ill-suited to the new age of representative democracy and mass politics.

* * *

In the general election campaign of 1895, 'the Man of the Moment' was Chamberlain. It was a 'testimony to the marvellous force of Chamberlain's personality', Beatrice Webb wrote in her diary that year, 'that he pervades this election'.[93] Chamberlain (1836–1914) was a new phenomenon in British politics. Unlike the other leaders of the Unionist coalition, he was a self-made man, rather than a product of the leading public schools and universities. His father's family had been shoemakers in the City of London and belonged to the Unitarian branch of Nonconformity. An ancestor had been burnt at the stake in 1556 for his religious beliefs. On leaving University College school, Chamberlain had been sent to Birmingham to work in a factory making screws, where he prospered and began to show the executive ability which was to characterise his political career. In 1873, he became a

90 Vincent, ed., *Crawford Papers*, p. 31.
91 Sir Sidney Lee, *King Edward VII: A Biography*, Macmillan, 1927, vol. 2, p. 160.
92 Quoted in Peter Rowland, *The Last Liberal Governments: Unfinished Business, 1911–1914*, Barrie & Rockliff, 1971, p. 217.
93 MacKenzie, *Diary of Beatrice Webb*, vol. 2, p. 77, entry for 8 July 1895.

Radical mayor of Birmingham, and in 1876 entered Parliament as a Liberal, becoming a Liberal Unionist in 1886. He was the first industrialist and the first dissenter to conquer the inner citadels of power. Lacking advantages of birth, landed property or an Oxbridge education, the main paths of entry to a political career at the end of the nineteenth century, it had taken him far longer to get into Parliament than Salisbury, an MP at the age of twenty-three, Devonshire, an MP at the age of twenty-four, and Balfour, an MP at the age of twenty-six. Their paths had been smoothed by hereditary connections and influence. Chamberlain did not enter the Commons until he was forty, and did not become a Cabinet minister until he was forty-four. 'You might as well start training for ballet at forty-five', it has been written, 'as start training for Cabinet.'[94] Not having risen by the conventional route, he did not, according to Gladstone, 'know the rules of the game'.[95]

Chamberlain, by contrast with Devonshire, had been a radical, not a conservative Whig. He remained a radical in the sense of being impatient with the status quo all his life, and his interest in social reform was not to be blunted by his Unionism. He remained true to the spirit of a speech that he had made, as a Liberal, at Warrington in September 1885, in which he foreshadowed much twentieth-century legislation. 'The great problem of our civilisation', he had declared,

> is unsolved. We have to account for and grapple with the mass of misery and destitution in our midst, contrasted as it is with evidences of abundant wealth and teeming prosperity. It is a problem which some men would put aside by reference to the eternal laws of supply and demand, to the necessity for freedom of contract, and to the sanctity of every private right in property. These phrases are the convenient cant of selfish wealth. They are not answers to our questions.

He did not believe that the Unionists could retain power by mere negation or by ignoring social issues. 'In my opinion,' he wrote to his fellow Unionist Sir Henry James, shortly to become Lord James, in December 1894, 'a good unionist government should, from the outset, declare its settled intention to leave all questions of Constitutional reform and change of machinery alone for the present, and to devote itself entirely to the study and prosecution of social legislation.' 'Unfortunately,' he went on, 'the Conservative Party is weak in constructive statesmanship, but the Government must contain men capable of giving practical application to the principles on which such

---

94 G. M. Young, *Mr Gladstone*, Clarendon Press, 1944, p. 29.
95 J. A. Spender, *The Public Life*, Cassell, 1925, vol. 1, p. 87.

legislation is to be based ... There must be a considerable infusion of new blood.'[96] He wanted the Unionists to assist with home purchase for the working classes, control 'alien', i.e. Jewish, immigration, introduce old-age pensions, provide employers liability in the case of industrial accidents, legislate for shorter hours for shopworkers and an experimental eight-hour day in the mining industry.[97] In the event, however, only a Workmen's Compensation Bill was to reach the statute book. Most of his colleagues were little interested in social reform while Salisbury believed that social issues would prove divisive. Salisbury, Balfour and Devonshire did not share Chamberlain's view that Unionists should be primarily a party of social reform. So, while Chamberlain could be an ally with the more conservative Unionists, he could never be their partner.

In 1892, Salisbury had told Balfour that, if the Conservatives took up Chamberlain's policies, 'we must in so doing alarm a good many people who have always been with us'. He added presciently, 'I fear these social questions are destined to break up our party' – as they were indeed to do with the 1902 Education Act and Chamberlain's tariff reform campaign. If the coalition broke, the Union with Ireland, the very *raison d'être* of the alliance would be threatened. Therefore, Salisbury argued, 'why incur the danger, before the necessity has arrived – and while the party may still be useful to avert Home Rule?'[98] Later, heavy expenditure on the Boer War was to preclude spending on social reform unless direct taxation were raised to levels which Unionists regarded as prohibitive. It was because he was sceptical whether a Salisbury administration would make social reform a priority that Chamberlain claimed, perhaps not wholly sincerely, that his personal inclination would have led him to remain outside the government. 'Why', he asked his wife in February 1895, 'should I ruin myself, incur all this abuse and misrepresentation only to be a subordinate member of a Cabinet with whose general policy I am not in hearty sympathy?'[99]

Chamberlain was to prove the dominant figure of the years from 1895 to 1906, when a severe stroke incapacitated him. As Winston Churchill was to put it in 1937, he it was who 'made the weather'. He was indeed the only Unionist leader with mass popular appeal. 'At the time when I looked out of my regimental cradle and was thrilled by politics,' Churchill wrote, 'Mr Chamberlain was incomparably the most live, sparkling, insurgent, compulsive figure in British affairs. Above him in the House of Lords reigned

---

96 Askwith, *Lord James of Hereford*, p. 232.
97 A poster outlining Chamberlain's social programme in 1895 is reprinted in Cawood, *Liberal Unionist Party*, p. 206.
98 Ibid., p. 98.
99 Garvin, *Chamberlain*, vol. 2, pp. 618, 625.

venerable, august Lord Salisbury ... Beside him on the Government Bench ... Arthur Balfour led the House of Commons.' But Chamberlain

> was the man the masses knew. He it was who had solutions for social problems; who was ready to advance, sword in hand if need be, upon the foes of Britain; and whose accents rang in the ears of all the young peoples of the Empire and of lots of young people at its heart ... He lighted beacon-fires which are still burning; he sounded trumpet-calls whose echoes still call stubborn soldiers to the field.[100]

At the time of the Queen's Speech in February 1896, a contemporary journalist wrote:

> There are nineteen members of the Cabinet. Public attention within the House and outside is concentrated upon one. Liberal Conservative, Home Ruler, Coercionist, Churchman, Dissenter, whatever we be, we are each all one in our admiration of the policy and conduct of Mr Chamberlain since trouble began in the Transvaal. It is this unanimity of applause that makes the case unique. When Lord Beaconsfield and Lord Salisbury came home from Berlin bringing Peace with Honour, town and country rang with acclamation. But the applause was after all the clamour of a political party. It is Mr Chamberlain's rare privilege to find himself extolled not only by his party but by his political opponents.

Indeed, 'the applause which rings in the Colonial Secretary's ears comes with fuller force from the Liberal side'.[101] Chamberlain was particularly skilful, until the 1902 Education Act, in mobilising the Nonconformists, traditionally suspicious of the Conservatives, in support of Unionism. His role, he told the Duke of Devonshire in 1895, was 'to keep a number of strong Liberals and Radicals staunch to the nation. To do this I have to give evidence that I remain a liberal at heart although I am loyally working with the Tories'.[102] Because he did this so successfully until 1902, he was so largely responsible for the landslide victories of the Unionist coalition at the polls in 1895 and in the khaki election of 1900.

Chamberlain, the only politician to have split both major parties, was a symbolic figure. He was the originator of modern politics, pioneer of the changes in politics which were to distinguish the twentieth century from

---

100 Winston S. Churchill, *Great Contemporaries* [1937], Fontana, 1959, pp. 66–7, 51.
101 Henry W. Lucy, *A Diary of the Unionist Parliament, 1895–1900*, Simpkin, Marshall, Hamilton, 1901, pp. 21, 19. Lucy dedicated this book to Chamberlain.
102 Devonshire MSS. 340/2608, quoted on p. 10 of Holding, 'Third Salisbury Cabinet'.

the nineteenth – the extension of democracy, the development of mass parties, the idea that elections should be decided by party programmes, that decisions should be taken by majority rule, that there should be tight party discipline, that local government should be developed on a popular basis, that there should be what was called gas-and-water socialism involving the municipalisation of public utilities, that there should be a national system of education, that the state had a responsibility for social welfare and that Britain was entering an age of power politics and imperial rivalry, He was the first to sense the decline in Britain's international position and appreciate that rapid and bold action was needed to avert it, the first to notice that Britain was entering a new era of international rivalry in which traditional shibboleths were irrelevant. Unlike other late Victorian radicals, such as Harcourt and Morley, his was a radicalism geared to constructive purposes. Unlike Salisbury and Devonshire, he sought to mould the opinion of the newly enfranchised voters, not to keep them at bay.

Chamberlain had entered politics to destroy the last vestiges of aristocratic rule and the political power of the Anglican Church which, so he believed, sustained it. He helped to build, first, the Liberal Party and then the Unionist coalition, transforming both Liberals and Unionists in the process, but he then proceeded to shatter both of them – the Liberals by rejecting Home Rule, the Conservatives by rejecting free trade. Having in the 1870s and the early 1880s pioneered education reform, local government reform, gas and water socialism and remedies for unemployment, he was, after 1886, to pioneer Unionism, imperialism and protection.

When Chamberlain entered the Commons in 1876, both parties were dominated by the landed aristocracy. As a businessman, he was the first major intruder into a parliament and political system dominated by the landed interest – Liberals, as well as the Conservatives. Under Gladstone's leadership, the Liberal Party had been 'like a people's crusade at the bottom and like a gentleman's club at the top'.[103] Chamberlain was as opposed to the Whigs in his own party, led, ironically, by Lord Hartington, later to be his Unionist ally, as he was to the Conservatives. Whigs, Gladstonians and Tories all believed in limited government and a parsimonious state. The older generation of Liberals had been suspicious of the state and had sought to limit its power. So had the Conservatives. Salisbury had told Balfour that 'the feebleness of our government is our security – the only one we have against revolutionary changes of our law'.[104] Chamberlain, by contrast, favoured a strong executive. He saw the state as a constructive instrument to

---

103 Peter Clarke, *A Question of Leadership: Gladstone to Thatcher*, Hamish Hamilton, 1991, p. 67.
104 Salisbury to Balfour, 29 March 1886, quoted in Dugdale, *Balfour*, vol. I, p. 79.

be used for radical purposes, at home for social reform, and, in the interests of the empire, for tariff reform. In 1886, Chamberlain had told Balfour:

> A democratic government should be the strongest government from a military and imperial point of view in the world, for it has the people behind it. Our misfortune is that we live under a system of government originally contrived to check the action of Kings and Ministers, and which meddles far too much with the Executive of the country. The problem is to give the democracy the whole power, but to induce them to do no more in the way of using it than to decide on the general principles which they wish to see carried out, and the men by whom they are to be carried out. My Radicalism at all events desires to see established a strong government and an Imperial government.[105]

In his last public speech at the Bingley Hall, Birmingham, on 9 July 1906, celebrating his seventieth birthday and thirty years as a Birmingham MP, Chamberlain remembered that his

> bitterest opponents were the so-called Liberals, the descendants and representatives of the old Whig Party, the Duke of Devonshire, Lord Goschen, Lord James ... These gentlemen, Free Traders as they are, were quite right in opposing the proposals of social reform, as they are right now in opposing proposals for fiscal reform.[106]

Chamberlain sought power for a purpose, a purpose different from that of Salisbury or Devonshire, whose main concern often seemed to be to postpone change for as long as possible. Chamberlain's opponents feared abuse of power. He, by contrast, feared the neglect of vital problems.

As a pioneer of the active state and an outsider in politics, Chamberlain's methods were bound to be different from those of politicians whose power base lay in closed circles in the Cabinet, Parliament and large country houses. He had to work outside the system. In business, his success had been based on amalgamation, on building a company large enough to outdo its competitors. Similarly, in politics, both domestic and imperial, Chamberlain believed in the power of organisation. He was the pioneer of large-scale organisation in government and in his conception of a more unified and tightly organised empire. He was the pioneer also of party organisation outside Parliament – the Birmingham caucus, the National Liberal Federation, the Liberal Unionist organisation and the Tariff Reform League, organisations

---

105 A. J. Balfour, *Chapters of Autobiography*, Cassell, 1930, pp. 230–31.
106 Amery, *Chamberlain*, vol. 6, pp. 903–4.

which threatened the ruling elites. Whigs and Tories were both content with loosely organised parliamentary parties. Chamberlain, by contrast, sought tight party discipline, buttressed by a powerful extra-parliamentary organisation, the caucus, so that the party could use public opinion as a battering ram to secure change. Both in 1885 with his radical 'Unauthorised Programme' and after 1903 with the Tariff Reform League, he used agitation in the constituencies to subvert parliamentary leaders – Gladstone in the 1880s, Balfour after 1903. And, to prevent the leadership ignoring the extra-parliamentary organisation, Chamberlain sought after 1903 to control Unionist policy by ensuring that his opponents in the party, Unionist free traders, were deselected, and that the parliamentary party was bound by a tightly drawn manifesto from which dissent would not be tolerated. His methods were in many respects similar to those of the Bennites on the left of the Labour Party in the 1980s who also sought to subvert the parliamentary leadership through pressure from extra-parliamentary organisations.

An outsider in politics by social origin, Chamberlain was also an outsider by temperament, a combative extremist who saw many of his colleagues – Whig and Tory alike – as weak and feeble. His opponents saw him as a vulgar upstart. 'Almost every Englishman', St Loe Strachey, editor of *The Spectator*, was to write to Rosebery in April 1910, 'has a touch of the essential Whig in him and a liking for moderation and the *via media*. Joe has none. Once a Jacobin always a Jacobin.'[107] Outsiders could be accepted, as Disraeli had shown, if they were prepared to assimilate the ethos of the governing class, but not if they broke the code. As in business, where it was vital to act rapidly once a decision had been made, so also in politics, rapid action was needed to secure change. But a stance which was successful in business might have less success in politics. Chamberlain, however, was prepared to wreck parties if they did not submit to him. For him, as later for Lloyd George with whom he had much in common, party was an instrument, not an end in itself. But unlike Lloyd George, Chamberlain is remembered more for destructive achievements than constructive ones, although his destructive career transformed both political parties in a more representative and democratic direction. His destructive tactics can in part be explained by his desperate impatience to transform an old order, but they attracted widespread resentment. The inner citadels, he believed, could be conquered only by radical methods, methods which made him widely distrusted. When Chamberlain was to resign from the government over tariff reform in 1903, none of his colleagues resigned with him. He lacked the first quality of a constructive

107 David Dutton, 'Unionist Politics and the Aftermath of the General Election of 1906: A Reassessment', *Historical Journal*, 1979, p. 862.

politician: the ability to win the support of colleagues. His extremism and ruthlessness alienated not only his colleagues but, after 1903, the Edwardian floating voter. So it was that, despite being a statesman with a greater under-standing of future trends than almost all his contemporaries, and a career as a successful administrator in business, local government and the Cabinet, he achieved less than other politicians far less gifted. He alienated those whose habits of thought were slower, split parties and in consequence his political career is relatively barren of achievement. There are no major social reforms to his credit except the Workmen's Compensation Act of 1897, while his external policy of imperial federation and protection was to be decisively rejected by the voters in 1906 and even by the colonies whom it was intended to benefit. A supremely constructive statesman, Chamberlain's legacy was primarily destructive.

But all this lay in the future. In 1895, he was the centre of political attention. 'No one trusts him,' Beatrice Webb wrote in her diary, 'no one likes him, no one really believes him, yet everyone accepts him as the leader of the natural Union-ists.'[108] Salisbury offered Chamberlain the choice of any post in the government apart from the Foreign Office, which Salisbury was himself to hold after the Duke of Devonshire had refused it. To the surprise of many, Chamberlain chose the Colonial Office 'in the hope of furthering closer union between them [the colonies] and the United Kingdom'.[109] He was the only front-rank politician ever to hold that office with the exception of Iain Macleod from 1959 to 1961. But his choice was by no means a sudden impulse. A South African politician had predicted it as early as 1884, and Chamberlain had unsuccessfully sought it from Gladstone in 1886.[110] In 1888, he had written to his future wife, Mary En-dicott, an American, 'I mean some day to be Colonial Minister.'[111] He had been awakened to the significance of empire on a visit to Canada and the United States in 1888–89, and hoped to rouse the British people to an awareness of their imperial responsibilities. Admittedly, the great age of territorial expansion was over by the time he became Colonial Secretary. But the preservation and strengthening of the empire was to prove a central concern for the Unionist government. And empire now lay at the centre of Chamberlain's political creed. Faced with the growth of competing empires – Russia, Germany, the United States – Britain could only hold her own by tightening links with the self-gov-erning empire. 'It seems to me', he said in 1897,

that the tendency of the time is to throw all power into the hands of the

---

108 MacKenzie, *Diary of Beatrice Webb*, vol. 2, p. 77, entry for 8 July 1895.
109 Garvin, *Chamberlain*, vol. 3, p. 5.
110 Ibid., p. 9.
111 Ibid., vol. 2, p. 347.

greater empires, and the minor kingdoms – those which are non-progressive – seem to be destined to fall into a secondary and subordinate place. But, if Greater Britain remains united, no empire in the world can ever surpass it in area, in population, in wealth or in the diversity of its resources.[112]

Chamberlain's powerful position in the country and the constituencies was not matched by support in the Cabinet. The Conservative leaders were well aware of his importance and treated him with more consideration than Gladstone had done. But they distrusted him, in part because of his social origins but more because of his methods and his disruptive tendencies. In 1892, Balfour had written that 'Joe, although we all love him, somehow does not absolutely and completely mix, does not form a chemical combination with us. Why? I cannot tell; but so I think it is.'[113] The Conservatives instinctively and rightly sensed that he was a fissiparous element in the Unionist coalition. They always remembered that, in the words of Balfour's sister-in-law, he was 'a Birmingham Radical, hampered by what he said when he was ... not a Unionist ... I own his speaking gifts, but he belongs not to the true heaven'.[114] For all his populist acclaim, he was to remain a perpetual outsider.

* * *

The Chancellorship of the Exchequer had first been offered to the Liberal Unionists, Chamberlain and Goschen, both of whom refused. It was then accepted by a Conservative, Sir Michael Hicks Beach (1837–1916), who had held it once before in 1885–86. A Gloucestershire baronet and member of the squirearchy, he had been returned unopposed in a by-election in 1864 for East Gloucestershire, his father's seat. He had first entered the Cabinet in 1874 as Chief Secretary for Ireland in Disraeli's government, returning to that office in 1886, but in 1887 had been compelled to resign because of fears for his eyesight, though he was able to return to office the next year as President of the Board of Trade. In 1895, he indicated that he would have preferred to return as the Irish Chief Secretary rather than the Exchequer since he doubted whether he had 'a turn for finance', but he was pressed, both by Salisbury and by Goschen, to become Chancellor. A fine speaker, regarded by Austen Chamberlain as the best of his generation, he was little known to the general public. He was to remain at the Exchequer until 1902, and is indeed the only Chancellor, apart from Gladstone, Gordon Brown

---

112 Quoted in Bennett, ed., *Concept of Empire*, p. 320.
113 Ridley and Percy, eds, *Letters of Balfour and Lady Elcho*, p. 88.
114 Lady Frances Balfour, *Ne Obliviscaris*, Hodder & Stoughton, 1925, p. 231.

and George Osborne, to have introduced seven successive Budgets; and, despite his doubts as to his fitness for the post, by the time he retired, he was regarded by his Permanent Secretary as 'one of the ablest men I have ever served'. He distrusted Chamberlain, 'as one who has tainted the Tory party with demagogue intrigues and fiscal hearsay', and was to be the only Cabinet member 'who contested Chamberlain's strongly pronounced opinions'. But 'this opposition was weakened by the tendency Hicks Beach had to oppose most of the views of his colleagues'.[115] His Permanent Secretary believed that Hicks Beach 'would have had more influence with his colleagues had he managed them with a little more tact – had there been more of the *suaviter in modo* weighed with the *fortiter in re*'. He was, Goschen believed, 'the only man I know who habitually thinks angrily'.[116] He was known as Black Michael – after the villain in *The Prisoner of Zenda* – 'because he was never happier than when refusing a favour to a friend'.[117] 'It is rare', Salisbury declared, 'to get a letter from Beach without a "No, I will not," on the first page.'[118] Balfour thought of him as obstructive, dropping 'little grains of sand into the wheels of every department in turn', but perhaps that was exactly what a Victorian Chancellor needed to do.[119] He alienated other ministers by his manner, speaking gruffly to them and, on occasion, snubbing them – he was once summed up as 'a bad horse to go up to in the stable'. This, however, made him useful to the Whips Office who used him to rid themselves 'of importunate place-holders or grievance-mongers'.[120] He would, Lord Salisbury believed, 'make a very good Home Secretary and would hang everybody'.[121] By 1900, other ministers were 'filled with dismay' that Hicks Beach decided not to retire but to remain at the Treasury.[122]

Hicks Beach's ideas on finance were those of a traditional Conservative Chancellor. In his Budget Speech of April 1899, he declared that he looked

> with alarm on the tendency of the present day ... a tendency which is, perhaps, more rife on this side of the House than on that, to look on the Exchequer and the central Government for superintendence, for assistance, for inspection, and for control in all kinds of departments of life,

---

115 Askwith, *Lord James of Hereford*, p. 256; Fitzroy, *Memoirs*, vol. 1, p. 246.

116 Roy Jenkins, *The Chancellors*, Macmillan, 1998, pp. 90, 94.

117 Vincent, ed., *Crawford Papers*, p. 64.

118 Zara Steiner, *The Foreign Office and Foreign Policy 1898–1914*, Cambridge University Press, 1969, pp. 51–2.

119 Letter to Salisbury, 20 October 1900, cited in Neil Daglish, *Education Policy-Making in England and Wales: The Crucible Years, 1895–1911*, Woburn Press, 1996, p. 158.

120 Hicks Beach, *Life of Hicks Beach*, vol. 2, pp. 14–15, 16fn, 17.

121 T. G. Otte, *Black Michael: Sir Michael Hicks Beach and the Problems of Late Victorian Conservatism*, Conservative History Group, 2006, p. 5.

122 Gailey, *Ireland and the Death of Kindness*, p. 174.

in all kinds of relations between individuals in which, in the old days, the government of the country was never deemed capable of acting at all.[123]

He saw the Budget in terms of balancing the books, and not, as Asquith and Lloyd George were later to do, as an instrument of social policy. He was traditional also in being a strong free trader and would prove a thorn in the side of Chamberlain and his tariff reformers. He had little interest in the new social questions which were to animate politics in the twentieth century, nor in the foreign policy problems which led Britain to seek new alliances and new commitments, the cost of which would unbalance his Budget. He was, in short, a figure from the past.

Goschen (1831–1907) became First Lord of the Admiralty. He had first held that post under Gladstone in 1871, even though it had then been alleged that 'Goschen has no notion of the motion of the ocean'. He had been the model for the First Lord, Sir Joseph Porter, in the Gilbert and Sullivan opera *HMS Pinafore*. But his real interest lay in economics and he was a vigorous exponent of non-interference with the market, whether that interference took the form of Chamberlainite radicalism or protection. He had broken with the Liberals well before Home Rule, refusing to join Gladstone's second administration in 1880 because of his opposition to the extension of household suffrage to the counties, which he believed would lead to the doctrines of political economy being discarded and treated with contempt. Goschen had been the only Liberal to vote against the Second Reading of the 1884 Reform Bill when even the Conservatives had been unwilling to oppose the extension of the franchise to the counties. A skilled financier, and less tied to the Liberals than other opponents of Home Rule, he had been the first Liberal Unionist to join a Conservative government, becoming Chancellor of the Exchequer in 1887, following the quixotic resignation of Lord Randolph Churchill. Goschen was also the first Liberal Unionist actually to join the Conservative Party, signalling his change of allegiance by joining the Carlton Club in 1893. Florence Nightingale had regarded him as a man 'with no practical insight. It is an awkward mind – like pudding in lumps', and it has been suggested that he was less suited to the Admiralty than the Exchequer since 'the counting house rather than the quarter-deck was his natural habitat'.[124] Although he had no popular constituency of his own, he was regarded, both in 1887 and in 1895, as a safe pair of hands, and therefore a valuable addition to Unionist governments. He was, like Devonshire, even more opposed to change than his Prime Minister. After offering him the

---

123 House of Commons Debates, 13 April 1899, vol. 69, col. 1006.
124 Jenkins, *The Chancellors*, p. 74.

Exchequer in 1887, Salisbury had been 'struck with his "timidity"' which, as Salisbury's niece remarked, merely means that Goschen is more Tory than Uncle Robert [i.e. Salisbury]!'[125] By 1895, he had become an obstructive element in the government, a dead weight, leaning heavily on his advisers, and maintaining a tenacious resistance to new ideas of all kinds, including inter-service coordination.

The Lord Chancellor was the 72-year-old Lord Halsbury (1823–1921), who had held the same position in Salisbury's earlier Conservative Cabinets, in 1885–86 and 1886–92. He was to be Lord Chancellor for a total of seventeen years, longer than any other holder of that office except for Lord Eldon in the nineteenth century and Lord Hardwicke in the eighteenth. Born in 1823 and blind in one eye, he had secured a fourth-class degree at Oxford and was called to the Bar in 1850. A dyed-in-the-wool reactionary, he had, as a parliamentary candidate, opposed free education as 'the thin end of the wedge' and a 'means of raising up a race of clever devils'. In 1875, he had become Solicitor General, and in 1877 had been elected MP for Launceston. His maiden speech, in which he opposed a resolution calling for the closer supervision of the funds of city companies, was greeted with the comment that it 'would have done him honour to the days of Lord Eldon and Lord Lyndhurst'. His third tenure of the Woolsack in 1895 hardly met with universal acclaim, 'Woolsack a great difficulty', Moberly Bell, manager of *The Times*, wrote to a correspondent. 'Everybody wants to get [rid of] Halsbury except himself and Salisbury.' The Prime Minister, who shared many of the Lord Chancellor's reactionary views, was the only member of the Cabinet to whom Halsbury was at all close. In Cabinet, he said little. On his death in 1921, at the age of ninety-eight, *The Times* declared that he had 'lacked the legal restraint and balance that distinguish the legal mind at its best'.[126]

'Promotion' to the bench, one commentator was to write in 1903, 'is often – perhaps too often – the reward for political services'.[127] Of the thirty High Court judges Halsbury appointed, six were Conservative MPs, one an ex-Conservative MP, three others were Conservative candidates and one was a Liberal Unionist MP; just four were Liberals. One of his worst appointments, a Conservative MP, was the brother of the Home Secretary, and was to be criticised by the *Law Journal* as one which 'can be defended on no ground whatever. It would be easy to name fifty members of the Bar with a better claim'.[128] Many of Halsbury's appointments were of men with little legal learning, and hardly added to the lustre of the bench. When told that

125 Lady Frances Balfour, Salisbury's niece, to Gerald Balfour, 5 January 1887, quoted in Dugdale, *Balfour*, vol. 1, p. 92.
126 A. Wilson Fox, *The Earl of Halsbury, Lord High Chancellor (1823–1921)*, Chapman and Hall, 1929, pp. 153–4.
127 Redlich and Hirst, *Local Government in England*, vol. 2, p. 370.
128 R. F. V. Heuston, *Lives of the Lord Chancellors, 1885–1940*, Clarendon Press, 1964, p. 50.

appointments ought to be based, *ceteris paribus*, on merit, he is said to have replied, '*Ceteris paribus* be damned. I'm going to appoint my nephew.'[129] In 1897, there was a petition to the Bar Council against the appointment of a Conservative MP to the High Court, alleging that in making the appointment, 'Lord Halsbury has shown his contempt for the opinion of the profession – and, we will add, of the Bench'. The *Solicitors' Journal* declared:

> The way to the High Court Bench is once more shown to be through contested elections and general service as a political hack. When those claims are present, learning, experience in practice, and the moral qualities which go to make an efficient and trusted judge are altogether unnecessary. We do not remember a more unanimous or sweeping condemnation than that with which the new appointment has been met by professional opinion.[130]

Political appointments to the bench were, however, by no means unusual at this time, and it was never clear whether disreputable appointments owed more to Halsbury or to his Prime Minister. When the editor of *The Times* called on Salisbury

> for the express purpose of impressing upon the Prime Minister the disrepute which the Lord Chancellor was bringing upon the Government by certain partisan legal appointments … Lord Salisbury observed with meditative detachment that it was hard on his colleague that he should be so much abused for what was in fact his own responsibility. 'I believe it was I who pressed most strongly on him the claims of those who are considered the worst.'

In 1908, a Liberal commentator was to write that Halsbury had 'reduced the Bench to a lower level than it had touched for a century. Any party hack, any necessitous relative of a Tory magnate might look for office from the Lord Chancellor.'[131]

Lord Salisbury was to tell Halsbury in September 1897 that it was

> the unwritten law of our party system, and there is no clearer statute in that unwritten law than the rule that party claims should weigh very heavily in the disposal of the highest legal appointments. In dealing with them you cannot ignore the party system as you do in the choice of a general or an archbishop. It would be a breach of the tacit convention on which politicians and lawyers have worked the British Constitution together for

the last two hundred years. Perhaps it is not an ideal system – some day no doubt the Master of the Rolls will be appointed by competitive examination in law reports, but it is our system for the present and we should give our party arrangements a wrench if we threw it aside.[132]

Salisbury also thought, if his daughter and biographer Lady Gwendolen Cecil is to be believed, that it would in general be best if the judges were Conservatives since 'within certain limits of intelligence, honesty and knowledge of the law, one man would make as good a judge as another, and a Tory mentality was ipso facto more trustworthy than a Liberal one'.[133]

Halsbury's claims on the Woolsack meant disappointment for the obvious candidate, the Liberal Unionist Sir Henry James, raised to the peerage as Lord James of Hereford. He had been offered the Lord Chancellorship by Gladstone in 1886, but he declined, because of his opposition to Home Rule. In 1895, he became Chancellor of the Duchy of Lancaster. The Lord Privy Seal was Lord Cross who, as Richard Cross, had been a notable reforming Home Secretary in Disraeli's 1874 government. But by 1895, he was long past his best, had begun to drink heavily and counted for little in Cabinet.[134]

The 1895 Cabinet proved a highly cohesive and united body. Lord James recorded in 1900:

> There is no cleavage whatever between the two sections of the Cabinet [i.e. Conservatives and Liberal Unionists]. Chamberlain has once or twice expressed his personal view as being of a more liberal character than the policy of the Cabinet represented, but he has always yielded his opinion to the others. Especially he seems desirous to show his accord with Arthur Balfour, his leader in the House of Commons.[135]

Remarkably, there were no resignations on matters of policy or any changes of personnel between 1895 and the khaki election of October 1900.

The Cabinet was the last aristocratic government in British history, led by a marquess and containing a duke, an earl, two viscounts, three barons, two baronets, another marquess, the son of a duke, the brother-in-law of a duke and just six commoners, one of whom was the Prime Minister's nephew.[136] Ministers outside the Cabinet included a duke and five other peers, two eldest sons of peers and another nephew of the Prime Minister. The

---

132 Heuston, *Lives of the Lord Chancellors*, pp. 52–3.
133 Cecil, *Life of Salisbury*, vol. 3, pp. 192–3.
134 Dennis J. Mitchell, *Cross and Tory Democracy: A Political Biography of Richard Assheton Cross*, Garland, 1991, p. 231.
135 Askwith, *Lord James of Hereford*, p. 255.
136 A. J. Davies, *We, the Nation: The Conservative Party and the Pursuit of Power*, Little, Brown, 1995, p. 9.

government's composition reflected the Conservative view that its prime purpose was to defend the landed interest. Professional men or businessmen such as Chamberlain were acceptable, but they were essentially appendages and subordinates, not to be admitted to the inner citadel of power. Political authority was derived from social position more than professional competence or popularity in the country. Until the early twentieth century, it was widely held that those not belonging to the landed interest might be suitable for the less important offices – the Board of Trade for Chamberlain in 1880 and the Local Government Board in 1886, and in 1892 for Fowler, the first solicitor and also the first Methodist to enter a Cabinet – but not the major offices of state. When, in 1886, Chamberlain had sought the Colonial Office from Gladstone, the Prime Minister had replied, 'What, a Secretary of State!' Gladstone had believed that Fowler, a member of his last Cabinet, could not be trusted 'in the sense that the ideas of cabinet loyalty of a Wolverhampton solicitor were not the same as those of a highly cultivated statesman of an older stamp'. Of W. L. Jackson, a Leeds businessman who had been appointed Irish Secretary in 1891, Balfour told Salisbury:

> He has great tact and judgment – middle class tact and judgment, I admit, but good of their kind. He justly inspires great confidence in businessmen: and he is that *rara avis*, a successful manufacturer who is fit for something besides manufacturing. A Cabinet of Jacksons would be rather a serious order, no doubt; but one or even two would be a considerable addition to any Cabinet.[137]

The Cabinet of 1895 was composed of very rich men. Most of its members had been born rich; others, such as Chamberlain, had become rich. 'Our political leaders', one commentator noted,

> have not often been forced to undergo that routine of unrelaxed toil pursued for the greater part of the day during the great part of the year, which falls to the lot of the majority of adult human beings on the face of this earth. Many of them, indeed, would speedily break down under such continuous and sustained exertion.[138]

The Cabinet was one of veterans, with an average age of just under sixty. The youngest member, Balfour, was forty-eight. The ministers were also political veterans. Five had first entered the Cabinet before 1880. Salisbury and

---

137 Adonis, *Making Aristocracy Work*, p. 176.
138 Low, *Governance of England*, p. 196.

Devonshire had entered politics before 1860. Half of the Cabinet had held office before 1880, and only three – Balfour, Lansdowne and Walter Long – were to play a major part in politics after the fall of the Unionists in 1905. Britain was to be governed by an oligarchy, public-spirited and on the whole honest and moderately able, but it was a highly unrepresentative administration. It was a nineteenth-century Cabinet forced to confront twentieth-century problems.

THE 1895 GENERAL ELECTION

Defeated in the Commons in June 1895, the Rosebery Cabinet had chosen to resign rather than dissolve. It hoped that the Unionists would have to put forward a programme of their own which the Liberals could then attack. Chamberlain had hoped that the Unionists would put forward the common programme which he had outlined and sent to Salisbury in October 1894 as a 'Memorandum of a Programme of Social Reform'. But Salisbury was evasive and committed himself to little.[139] The Unionists were no doubt wise, from a purely electoral point of view, in making no major domestic policy commitments since it allowed them to concentrate on unpopular Liberal policies – Home Rule, the disestablishment of the Welsh Church and the local veto on the opening of public houses. Remarkably little was said in the election on foreign and imperial affairs, even though they were to prove the key issues for the new government.

The great strength of the Unionists lay in their appeal to the fears of moderate and uncommitted voters that Home Rule would lead to the disintegration of the United Kingdom, if not also the empire. As long as that fear remained powerful, the Unionist coalition would hold together and the Liberals would be kept out of government. It was only when that fear faded and the Liberals decided that Home Rule was no longer a priority that they would be able to recover.

In the 1895 general election, the Liberals suffered the greatest defeat of any party since 1832. The outcome was as follows:

Government	Seats won	Percentage of vote
Conservatives	340	40.6
Liberal Unionists	71	8.5
Total government	411	49.1

---

139 Garvin, *Chamberlain*, vol. 2, p. 616.

Opposition	Seats won	Percentage of vote
Liberals	177	45.7
Irish Parliamentary Party	82	4.0
Total opposition	259	49.7[140]

The total opposition percentage of the vote was slightly higher than that of the government. But that is a misleading statistic, since, of the 189 uncontested constituencies, 132 were Unionist, forty-six were held by the Irish Parliamentary Party and just eleven were held by the Liberals. Even so, the first-past-the-post electoral system exaggerated the strength of the leading parties, as it was to do in almost every general election in the twentieth century. The swing in votes since 1892, when the Liberals and Irish Party had enjoyed an overall majority of forty seats, was comparatively small, around 4.5 per cent.

What were the reasons for the defeat of the Liberals? Liberalism as a political creed had been formed during the period of solid Victorian prosperity – between repeal of the Corn Laws in 1846 and the agricultural depression of the late 1870s. Did it retain its relevance? Winston Churchill believed that the end of the 1880s had seen 'the end of an epoch ... Authority everywhere was broken. Slaves were free. Conscience was free. Trade was free. But hunger and squalor and cold were also free and people demanded something more than liberty.'[141] Even before his retirement in 1894, Gladstone had seemed a figure from the past, from another age. The classical Liberal programme had been to extend the franchise, abolish the rights and privileges of the landed aristocracy and the Anglican Church, remove Nonconformist grievances, open careers to the talents, ensure free and compulsory education and abolish legal and traditional barriers to free competition. These aims had largely been achieved by 1895. Did Liberalism still have a role in the changed conditions of the end of the nineteenth century? Did it have answers to new problems?

For the mid-Victorians, Liberalism was a philosophy of security, the security of an era in which British global and economic dominance seemed assured. It seemed less appropriate to the dawning age of great power rivalry. Gladstone had seemed unaware of the problems of a new age and out of sympathy with new currents of thought. He disliked in particular the new radicalism. 'Its pet idea', he declared 'is what they call construction – that is to say, taking into the hands of the state, the business of the individual man',

---

140 Minor parties and independents secured the remaining 1.2 per cent of the vote.
141 Quoted in H. M. Lynd, *England in the Eighteen-Eighties: Toward a Social Basis for Freedom*, Oxford University Press, 1945, p. 3.

and he deplored 'the leaning of both parties to socialism of which I radically disapprove'. During the period of Gladstonian rule, his lieutenant, John Morley, had declared that the Liberals had 'three corps d'armée – Scottish Presbyterians, English and Welsh Nonconformists and Irish Roman Catholics'.[142] But this was to prove a fragile alliance. Most Irish Roman Catholics now supported the Irish Party, which was prepared to sustain a Liberal government only on condition that it gave a priority to Home Rule, while many Scottish Presbyterians and English, though not Welsh, Nonconformists were opposed to Home Rule and had become Liberal Unionists, providing Chamberlain with his electoral base. But for as long as Gladstone remained leader, the Liberals had been, perforce, committed to Home Rule. On his retirement in 1894, it became clear that the Liberal Party had lost its sense of direction, the old battles having seemingly been won. But Gladstone's leading lieutenants were too absorbed in personal quarrels to restore a sense of direction to the party.

The Liberals had fought the 1895 general election on a rag-bag of policies united only by two inter-related ideas. The first idea was social, though not economic, equality. Nonconformists resented the social power of the landowner, the squire and the Anglican Church and felt, in consequence, second-class citizens. They sought independence, self-respect, the right to be treated as equals. The second idea was the extension of democracy. Liberals believed that the achievement of household suffrage in 1867 and 1884 was by no means the end of constitutional reform, and that further reforms were needed for government to become more accountable to the people. But they found it difficult to agree on what these further reforms might be, or to weave them together into a coherent whole. Gladstone had provided both a policy and an inspiration. The Liberals in 1895 had neither. They seemed leaderless and without a policy – or rather they appeared to have a multiplicity both of leaders and of policies. They were becoming known as a party of faddists, with each section of the party having a different cure for the nation's ills. In the 1895 election campaign, John Morley, who had been Irish Secretary, remained true to the Gladstonian faith by emphasising Irish Home Rule as the one transcendent issue which had to be confronted before other items on the Liberal programme could be implemented. But by 1895, so one Liberal MP, reminiscing about the past in 1909, thought, 'Home Rule had ceased to be a bugbear and had become a bore.'[143] Sir William Harcourt, the former Chancellor and leader of the party in the Commons, emphasised the local veto, the idea that local communities be given power to decide by

---

142 Morley, *Gladstone*, vol. 1, p. 669.
143 'Over the Hedge', *Manchester Guardian*, 11 September 1909.

a two-thirds majority in a referendum whether their community should be 'wet' – open for the sale of alcoholic drinks – or 'dry'. The effect of such a provision would be to transfer the power to issue licences from unelected magistrates to the people, and the policy was defended not only on grounds of temperance but also local democracy. The Liberal candidate for South East Essex, for example, declared that he desired 'to see local self-government carried out to its full extent and therefore advocate local control of the Drink Traffic by the people themselves'.[144] But the policy was open to easy attack by the Unionists, who claimed that the Liberals were seeking to deprive the working man of his alcoholic recreation. When a Bill providing for local option had been presented to Parliament in 1895, it had been denounced by a leading brewer, Lord Burton, as 'a Bill to enable a small clique of fanatical ratepayers in any parish to interfere with the habits and social enjoyments of the working classes, and to dictate to them their mode of living'.[145] The Bill had exempted restaurants, hotels, wine merchants, clubs and railway station working rooms, patronised by the well-to-do, from its provisions, and this laid it open to devastating criticism from Balfour,

> The poor man, the man of moderate means, who gets his glass of beer – and surely he has a perfect right to get his glass of beer – at the public house will be prevented from doing so, while the rich man who supplies his consumption from the wholesale dealers, the member of the club, the person who has access to the railway station, will all be outside [the provisions of the Bill].[146]

Temperance, therefore, was hardly a popular cause. Indeed, it has been calculated that, in Lancashire, if every set of premises allowing for the sale of alcohol caused the transfer of two votes from the Liberals to the Conservatives, it would have cost the Liberals twenty-two seats in that county alone.[147]

The Liberals also proposed to extend the powers of parish councils, abolish plural voting and institute payment of MPs, and vest control of denominational schools in ratepayers rather than the Church of England. But for Lord Rosebery, the 'permanent and primary' issue of the 1895 election was Lords reform, since all other Liberal reforms – Home Rule, the local veto and the disestablishment of the Welsh Church – depended upon removing the veto of the Upper House. These reforms could 'only pass the portals of the constitution

---

144 Paul A. Readman, 'The 1895 General Election and Political Change in Late Victorian Britain', *Historical Journal*, 1999, p. 472.
145 Peter Stansky, *Ambitions and Strategies: The Struggle for the Leadership of the Liberal Party in the 1890s*, Clarendon Press, 1964, p. 177.
146 Readman, 'The 1895 General Election', p. 479.
147 Joseph Rowntree and Arthur Sherwell, *The Temperance Problem and Social Reform* [1899], 7th edition, Hodder & Stoughton, 1900, pp. 681–7.

over the body of the House of Lords'.[148] Speaking in Bradford in October 1894, Rosebery had claimed that the Lords was 'the greatest issue since your fathers resisted the tyranny of Charles I and of James II'. But the Liberals offered no precise proposals on how the veto of the Lords was to be removed.

With three leaders putting forward three different priorities, none of them overwhelming priorities for most voters, it is hardly surprising that the Liberals failed to enthuse the electorate. Rosebery summed up the causes of the defeat in a letter to a Cabinet colleague: 'We have offended every interest … Three leaders proclaimed three different policies.' He then added, 'but there was a more general & deeply rooted cause – Mr G's [Gladstone's] general policy since 1880.'[149]

The third party in the Commons in 1895 was the Irish Parliamentary Party, with eighty-two MPs. After 1885, it generally won every seat outside Ulster, with the exception of the Trinity College Dublin university seat and, on occasion, two other constituencies in Dublin in which the English community – consisting primarily of administrators – was congregated. The party's seats were so safe that most constituencies outside Ulster were not contested by Unionist or Liberal candidates, and in December 1910, 80 per cent of the Irish Party's MPs were returned without opposition.

In 1885, the leader of the party, Charles Stuart Parnell, had declared that there was just one plank in the party's platform, Home Rule. Until that was achieved, the party was, in the words of John Redmond, its leader from 1900, being brought 'forcibly' to Westminster, instead of being allowed 'to remain at home, and in their own humble way attend to their own humdrum Irish matters'. The party's only interest in Westminster was to advance the case for self-government for Ireland, rather than 'interfere in British matters about which they know nothing'.[150] In 1890, however, the party had been split over the issue of whether Parnell should remain as leader following a divorce case in which he was cited as co-respondent, Gladstone having declared that he could have no further dealings with it for as long as Parnell remained leader. The split, with the anti-Parnellites in the majority, remained after Parnell's death in 1891, and dissipated the party's strength at Westminster.

The Irish Party faced a problem similar to that which would soon face the Labour Party: should it cooperate with the Liberals or insist on its independence? The former strategy offered more hope of securing Home Rule through parliamentary methods, but at the cost of compromises which might make the party more remote from those it represented. The Parnellite wing of

148 Readman, 'The 1895 General Election', p. 467.
149 Keith Robbins, *Sir Edward Grey: A Biography of Lord Grey of Fallodon*, Cassell, 1971, p. 57.
150 House of Commons Debates, 21 February 1910, vol. 14, col. 64.

the party repudiated alliance with the Liberals, and proposed that it act as an independent opposition, seeking to put pressure on both major parties. But Parnell had no successor as a leader of stature, and, for some time after 1895, both wings of the party appeared leaderless. 'One-man power', William O'Brien declared, 'was replaced by eighty-man powerlessness ... There was not one leader but a dozen.'[151] Nevertheless, the Irish Party remained disciplined, enforcing a kind of democratic centralism upon its MPs through the salary which it paid them. But this discipline muffled genuine differences, tending to stifle debate and deprive the party of its vitality. It was partly for this reason that it was to prove unable to absorb the more radical and Nationalist elements in Irish society which were to form Sinn Féin in 1905. The Irish Party remained a parliamentary party adhering on the whole to constitutional methods and was coming gradually to be absorbed into Britain's liberal culture. Both wings of the party accepted that Parliament was the institution through which redress of Irish grievances was to be obtained. That influence was to remain even after the party's collapse, and was to be seen in the liberal and parliamentary character of the independent Irish state. But from the time of Parnell's death in 1891, there was a growing gap between its MPs and its supporters in Ireland. The majority of its MPs had a main residence in England, and many had been educated in England.[152] By 1912, the party 'no longer consisted of young men, and had acquired some of the weaknesses of a vested interest'.[153]

In 1895, however, Ireland seemed quiescent and some in the Irish Party appeared ready to discuss with the new Unionist government reforms falling far short of Home Rule, which was for the moment a dead issue. 'The commonplace in English politics upon which nearly everybody at present agrees', declared Professor Mahaffy of Trinity College Dublin in 1895, 'is that Home Rule is dead. You seldom hear it mentioned in political circles in any other connections. One party [i.e. the Unionists] proclaims it aloud, the other [the Liberals] sotto voce.'[154] By 1901, a contemporary journalist could write with some justice that 'the disappearance of Home Rule is not less remarkable a feature of the lifetime of the Third Salisbury Administration than the ruin – though it may not yet be irretrievable – which has overtaken its advocates. Even in Ireland the separatist agitation has died down.'[155]

In 1895, there was, besides the Unionists, the Liberals and the Irish Party, a fourth party, a new party, though hardly noticed. That fourth party was

---

151 Lyons, *The Irish Parliamentary Party*, p. 40.
152 Alan O'Day, *The English Face of Irish Nationalism*, Gill and Macmillan, 1973.
153 Ensor, *England*, p. 451.
154 *The Times*, 20 November 1895.
155 Whates, *Third Salisbury Administration*, p. 430.

the Independent Labour Party (ILP), formed in 1893, which, in 1900, was to play a large part in the formation of the Labour Party. The ILP was a socialist party and at its 1895 conference it was decided that only socialists should be endorsed as candidates.[156] At this conference, the party required its members, like the MPs of the Irish Party, to sign a pledge, which read as follows:

> I hereby pledge myself a Socialist, pledge myself to sever all connexion with any other political party, and to vote in the case of local elections as my branch of the ILP may determine, and in the case of Parliamentary general elections as the Conference specially convened for that purpose may determine.

In 1895, the ILP put up twenty-eight candidates, all of whom were defeated, including Keir Hardie, who had been returned as an independent MP for West Ham South in 1892, and had been instrumental in the formation of the party.[157] ILP candidates secured in total fewer than 40,000 votes. Socialism, like Home Rule, indeed like all radical causes, seemed irrelevant in the face of a triumphant Unionism.

*   *   *

The 1895 election involved more than the replacement of one group of politicians who were Liberals by another who were Unionists. It heralded the gradual replacement of one political mindset by another. The Unionist victory of 1895 seemed at first sight a reversion to the past, a decision by the voters to choose a government whose primary appeal was negative, and a government defensive in character. 'It cannot be altogether bad', the Duke of Devonshire declared, characteristically, at Sheffield on 7 November 1895,

> for a nation to have an occasional interval of repose, and it is to such an interval of repose that at present we are looking forward with some confidence. On their own declaration the government, at first at any rate, are pledged to abstain from raising, if they can avoid it, issues of a political character.[158]

But the new government was not to be allowed the luxury of an 'interval of repose'. It found itself confronting a new and dangerous world in almost

---

156 *The Times*, 18 April 1895.
157 David Howell, *British Workers and the Independent Labour Party, 1888–1906*, Manchester University Press, 1983, pp. 129–282.
158 *Liberal Magazine*, 1895, p. 486.

every quarter of the globe, a world in which Salisbury's negativism and aristocratic leadership were barely relevant. Far from proving a reversion to the past, 1895 opened a new era, an era in which, both at home and abroad, Britain's liberal political culture would find itself under challenge.

CHAPTER 2

LORD SALISBURY'S FOREIGN POLICY: RESERVE BUT PROUD RESERVE

THE CONCERT OF EUROPE

In 1895, with the growing power of the United States but dimly perceived, Europe was still the centre of the world, and the great powers of the world were concentrated there.[1] There were, apart from Britain, four major European powers – France, Germany, Austria–Hungary and Russia. After the Franco-Prussian war in 1871, a unified Germany had become the leading power on the Continent, facing to her west a defeated France, embittered by the cession of Alsace-Lorraine; and to the east Russia, which, from the 1890s, Germany believed to have aggressive designs upon her. Germany was allied to Austria–Hungary, a multinational empire dominated by German-speakers but including speakers of eleven different languages.

The dominance of the five powers yielded stability in the international system between 1871 and 1914. Since 1815, an informal but generally effective international system, the Concert of Europe, had regulated conflict between the powers. Unlike its successor, the League of Nations, the Concert was not an institution but existed as an idea in the minds of leaders of the great powers until it broke down in 1914. Its effectiveness depended 'upon a self-denying ordinance from each of the great powers', which 'usually consulted each other, although not the small states, on major issues. They saw themselves as guardians of peace in Europe, and assumed responsibility for maintaining order in neighbouring states.'[2] The smaller states sought protection from the great powers and generally accepted their pre-eminence. The Concert was made concrete through conference diplomacy, and between 1822 and 1913, there were twenty-six conferences between the great powers. It was tacitly accepted that territorial changes required the consent of these powers, and that international treaties could not be altered unilaterally. The last such conference was to be in London in 1913, one year before Sarajevo, brokering

---

1   See pp. xii–xiii for a map of Europe in 1895.
2   F. R. Bridge and Roger Bullen, *The Great Powers and the European States System, 1814–1914*, 2nd edition, Pearson Longman, 2005, pp. 2, 4. This paragraph is based on Bridge and Bullen.

a peace settlement after the First Balkan War. But the Concert dealt only with European affairs, and its writ did not run elsewhere.

France, Germany and Austria–Hungary were primarily European powers, although France, and to a lesser extent Germany, had also become colonial powers with extra European interests. But otherwise, apart from Britain, only Russia amongst European powers had extensive interests outside Europe, and these were confined to Asia. Britain, however, was the only global power, with possessions and economic interests in all five continents. There was, literally, no part of the world in which she was or could be disinterested.

Uniquely a global and imperial power, Britain faced a twofold strategic problem. The first was to ensure that no other power could establish such dominance over the Continent as to be able to invade or threaten her independence, as Napoleon had sought to do. So Britain had a strong interest in the maintenance of the balance of power on the Continent. Provided that balance held, there seemed no reason for Britain to enter into alliances or other entangling commitments. As long as what happened there did not threaten her, Britain had little interest in Continental affairs, seeking only the freedom to pursue her imperial and global interests. That, however, did not preclude Britain working with other powers to secure collective solutions to international disputes.

Britain's second problem was to ensure that no other power could interrupt her communications with the rest of the world and, in particular, her colonial possessions. By 1895, that was becoming more difficult as other powers began to seek outlets for expansion. As early as 1885, the *Pall Mall Gazette* had noticed this. 'In times past ... we did what we pleased, where we pleased and as we pleased. The whole of heathendom ... was our inheritance, and the salt sea our peculiar possession. All that has changed. Europe has overflowed into Africa, Asia, America, Australasia and the Pacific.'[3] In 1914, Churchill was to remind his Cabinet colleagues:

We are not a young people with an innocent record and a scanty inheritance. We have engrossed to ourselves an altogether disproportionate share of the wealth and traffic of the world. We have got all we want in territory, and our claim to be left in the unmolested enjoyment of vast and splendid possessions, mainly acquired by violence, largely maintained by force, often seems less reasonable to others than to us.[4]

To retain her predominance, Britain had to remain impregnable, not only

---

3   Quoted in Bernard Porter, *The Lion's Share: A Short History of British Imperialism, 1850–1970*, Longman, 1976, p. 117.
4   Darwin, *Empire Project*, p. 268.

in the waters surrounding her shores, the Channel, the North Sea and the Eastern Atlantic, but also in other oceanic waters, particularly routes to India through the Mediterranean, Suez and the Cape. This required a strong navy, and it was naval supremacy which secured the empire. But with such a navy, Britain's island status would protect her from convulsions on the Continent. One of Asquith's favourite quotations – from an ode on the coronation of Edward VII – was:

> Time and the ocean and some fostering star
> In high cabal have made us what we are.

But towards the end of the nineteenth century, Britain began to fear naval competition from other powers, and, in 1889, the Naval Defence Act provided that the Royal Navy must be at least as strong as the next two largest navies of other powers. In 1894, the First Lord of the Admiralty in Gladstone's Liberal government, Lord Spencer, had sought naval expansion. He had the support of the Cabinet but not of his aged Prime Minister, who, outvoted in Cabinet, used it as an excuse for resignation. The battleships built under the Spencer programme were to prove a major factor deterring intervention against Britain by Continental powers during the Boer War. Salisbury believed that the two-power standard enabled Britain to counter the growth of the French and Russian navies, so that Britain would not be dependent on Germany to counter these powers.

But the navy was not needed only for home but also imperial defence. Since the end of the Napoleonic Wars, Britain had become detached from the Continent, concentrating her energies upon the empire, particularly her empire in the east based on India. Britain had come to believe that her strength depended upon her being an imperial power, and the key to that strength lay with India. 'As long as we rule India,' Lord Curzon, the viceroy, told Balfour in 1901, 'we are the greatest power in the world. If we lose it we shall drop straight away to a third-rate power.'[5] Disraeli had perhaps been the first to recognise that India gave Britain her strength as a world power when, in 1877, he had proposed that Queen Victoria become Empress of India. In 1866, he had gone so far as to say that Britain was 'more an Asiatic power than a European'.[6] India made British foreign policy infinitely more complicated than it would otherwise have been. Protecting her against incursions by other powers and especially Russia was a key principle

---

5   Quoted in Evgeny Sergeev, *The Great Game 1856–1907: Russo-British Relations in Central and East Asia*, Johns Hopkins University Press, 2013, p. 230.
6   Cited in Mahajan, *British Foreign Policy*, p. 7.

of foreign policy, and it gave rise to responsibilities in territories lying on the route to India, for example in the Nile valley and also South Africa to ensure security of the Cape route. And the empire included various ports and coaling stations, such as Gibraltar, Malta, Aden, Ceylon and Hong Kong on the trade routes linking imperial possessions, a necessity for a trans-oceanic empire. The Mediterranean and the Middle East had to be kept free from hostile powers. Therefore, Britain had to control the Mediterranean from both ends – from Gibraltar in the west to the Dardanelles in the east. So, to ensure the security of her Indian empire, Britain had also to become, perforce, a Mediterranean and a Middle Eastern power. But she was also, in addition, a power on the American continent, thanks not only to Canada and imperial possessions in the Caribbean but also to trading interests there, in particular in South America; and she was also a Far Eastern power thanks to extensive commercial interests in China. In both India and China, Britain was in danger of conflict with Russia, whose expanding railway network was believed to threaten India's north-west frontier and commercial interests in China. And in the Far East, naval supremacy was of much less value against a land power with a common border with China. Nor could the navy alone secure the defence of India, as the Military Intelligence Division was to tell the government in 1901.

> As long as the Navy fulfils its mission, the British Empire is impervious to the great land forces of continental nations except in one point – India. Here alone can a fatal blow be dealt us. The loss of India by conquest would be a death blow to our prosperity, prestige and power ... Next in importance, then, and second only to the security of the United Kingdom itself, comes the question of the defence of India.[7]

Defence policy, the dispositions of the army and the navy and colonial policy were undertaken with the defence of India in mind. So a maritime and insular nation on the periphery of Europe came to play a major role in the eastern hemisphere from the Persian Gulf in the west to Singapore and China in the east.

Towards the end of the nineteenth century, Britain's global interests came to be threatened by other European powers seeking empires of their own in Asia and Africa, largely unexplored by Europeans until the middle of the century and often labelled 'the dark continent'. The last quarter of the century had been the age of imperialism with a competitive scramble between the powers not in Europe but in Asia and Africa. To avoid this leading to

7   Ibid, pp. vii–viii.

conflict, the Berlin conference of 1884 had established the principle, for African colonisation, of 'effective occupation' as a basis for territorial claims. But by the end of the century, territorial aggrandisement appeared to have come to an end, and consolidation was needed. Africa seemed to most Europeans as an empty continent with room for all, but regulation of disputes proved more difficult where there seemed to be decaying empires whose central authorities were unable to maintain order. In May 1898, Lord Salisbury made a prescient speech to the Primrose League, a social organisation dedicated to spreading Conservative principles, pointing to a conflict between the 'living' and the 'dying' nations. The 'living' nations were the great powers,

> growing in power every year, growing in wealth, gaining in dominion, growing in the perfection of their organisation. Railways have given them the power to concentrate upon any one point the whole military force of their population and to assemble armies of a magnitude and power never dreamt of in the generations that have gone by. Science has placed in the hands of these armies weapons ever growing in their efficiency of destruction, and therefore, adding the power fearfully to the power of those who have the opportunity of using them.

To these 'living' nations were counterposed 'dying' nations in which

> disorganisation and decay are advancing almost as fast as concentration and increasing powers are advancing in the living nations that stand beside them. Decade after decade they are weaker, poorer, and less provided with leading men or institutions in which they can trust, apparently drawing nearer and nearer to their fate and yet clinging with strange tenacity to the life which they have. In them misgovernment is not only not cured but is continually on the increase.

It needed no particular prescience, Salisbury concluded, to appreciate that 'from the necessities of politics or under the pretence of philanthropy – the living nations will gradually encroach on the territory of the dying, and the seeds and cause of conflict amongst civilised nations will speedily appear'. The 'dying' nations or empires were the Ottoman or Turkish Empire, the Chinese Empire and later the Austro-Hungarian Empire. The conflict between 'living' and 'dying' nations would, as Salisbury anticipated, cause new conflicts between the powers. And, indeed, in 1914, it was the fears of Austro-Hungary that her 'dying' empire would decay unless it took a firm stand against Serb nationalism that proved the trigger for world war. But in

1898, Salisbury believed that Britain could cope with the new international conditions. She could, he thought, 'look forward without disquietude' to 'our colonies and our possessions and our growing enormous trade', since 'we know that we shall maintain against all comers that which we possess, and we know ... that we are amply competent to do so'. 'But', he concluded ominously, 'that will not secure the peace of the world.'[8]

At the end of the nineteenth century, competition from other powers triggered a debate on whether freedom from alliances was still a tenable policy. On 13 May 1898, Chamberlain, speaking in Birmingham, declared:

> Since the Crimean War nearly fifty years ago, the policy of this country has been a policy of strict isolation. We have had no allies. I am afraid we have had no friends ... We are liable to be confronted at any moment with a combination of Great Powers ... We stand alone.[9]

The Boer War would confirm Chamberlain's fears. In November 1899, Lord George Hamilton, the India Secretary, was to tell Curzon, the viceroy, 'We have not a friend in Europe, and ... the main cause of the dislike is ... that we are like an octopus with gigantic feelers stretching out over the habitable world, constantly interrupting and preventing foreign nations doing that which we in the past have done ourselves.'[10]

The debate on foreign policy was in large part generational. Those, such as Salisbury, who had reached maturity in the Victorian heyday of empire, were slow to recognise the need for readjustment if they did so at all. A later generation and more dynamic members of the older generation such as Chamberlain were coming to believe that this was dangerously complacent. The change of government in 1902 with the retirement of Salisbury and Hicks Beach shifted the balance in favour of the new generation, which sought to abandon the policy of avoiding commitments in favour of alliances to minimise dangers from Britain's competitors.

NEW CHALLENGES IN FOREIGN POLICY

Before the opening of the Suez Canal in 1869, the route to India had lain through seas adjacent to the Ottoman or Turkish Empire – the Dardanelles, the Bosporus and the Persian Gulf. The security and integrity of the Ottoman Empire seemed therefore of great importance for Britain. In Europe,

8   *The Times*, 5 May 1898.
9   Garvin, *Chamberlain*, vol. 3, pp. 282–3.
10 Darwin, *Empire Project*, p. 66.

the Ottoman Empire comprised what are now Albania, Kosovo, Macedonia, parts of modern-day Bulgaria and Greece, as well as various islands in the Aegean, the most important of which was Crete, which would achieve, in effect, independence in 1898. In addition, Turkey enjoyed a nominal suzerainty over Bosnia–Herzegovina which, since 1878 had, by the terms of the Treaty of Berlin, been ruled by Austria–Hungary. Of Turkey's European population, around two-thirds were Christian and one-third Muslim. Until 1908, the sultan ruled his empire as a theocratic absolute monarch, claiming to be the spiritual leader of all Muslims as well as a temporal ruler. He was indeed recognised as a caliph – a successor to the Prophet – in much of the Muslim world. The sultan's Christians were treated as second-class citizens, and subject, from time to time, to oppression and even massacre. Throughout the nineteenth century, the sultan promised reform and, by Article 62 of the Treaty of Berlin, he had promised to respect the principles of religious liberty and freedom of worship and avoid discrimination on grounds of religion. These promises had not been kept.

The powers, while espousing humanitarian concerns for the sultan's Christians had nevertheless wanted to preserve his ramshackle empire, widely thought of as the sick man of Europe. Its disintegration would, it was believed, cause instability, and could encourage Russia, as protector of the Slavs, in a forward policy in Europe, so upsetting the balance of power. But British governments had sought to protect not only Turkey in Europe but also Turkey in Asia, though it was never clear whether Parliament would sanction such protection if ever it involved military or naval action. Nevertheless, Salisbury warned at the Guildhall on 9 November 1895 that 'the danger, if the Ottoman Empire fell, would not merely be the danger that would threaten the territories of which that Empire consists; it would be the danger that the fire there lit should spread to other nations and should involve all that is most powerful and civilised'[11] – not a bad prediction perhaps of the effects of the collapse of the Turkish Empire, both in Europe and in the Middle East. Indeed, in the third decade of the twenty-first century, the repercussions of its collapse are still being felt – in Israel, the Palestinian territories, Iraq, Syria, as well as the Balkans.

By the end of the nineteenth century, however, Salisbury was coming to believe that it might no longer be possible to prevent the disintegration of the Ottoman Empire in Europe. In 1898, he went so far as to suggest to the British ambassador to Russia that, in the two seemingly unstable empires of Turkey and China, there might be a 'partition of preponderance' between

---

11   Quoted in *Liberal Magazine*, 1895, p. 486.

Britain and Russia.[12] Few appreciated that both empires were more resilient than they appeared and that it would take a world war to destroy the Ottoman Empire.

British strategists believed that she must contain Turkey's enemy, Russia, which had sought, throughout the nineteenth century, to penetrate the Dardanelles with her warships to control the Black Sea. This, it was believed, would enable her to threaten the British route to India, and cut off Britain's communications with the Indian empire. For the Black Sea was the only area from which the British Navy could invade Russia, as she had done during the Crimean War, to prevent her moving through the north-west frontier into India. 'The interests of the empire, India, and all Britain's eastern possessions', the Director of Naval Intelligence wrote in November 1895, 'required that as long as Britain can keep it so, Russia should be vulnerable through the Black Sea – to secure this, the Dardanelles and Bosphorus must either be kept unarmed, or in the hands of Russia's foes'. The Cabinet were told that 'once the Black Sea is a Russian lake with the Dardanelles as her safe outlet, Russian influence and power will extend through Asia Minor and Syria, and England will be separated from India by the distance of the Cape route'.[13] In a memorandum in 1892, Lord Salisbury had declared that 'the protection of Constantinople from Russian conquest had been the turning point of the policy of this country for at least forty years, and to a certain extent for forty years before that'.[14]

Russia was also believed to be a threat to Britain's overland routes to India. In the Crimean War, Britain had sought to counter this threat by forcing the straits and landing troops in southern Russia. But this strategy had become less viable since, during the last decade of the century, Russia had begun to expand her railway network into central Asia, linking it with European Russia. The Trans-Caspian Railway, begun in 1879, reached Bokhara in 1888 and the Afghan frontier in 1899. As a land power, Russia could send troops much more rapidly to the area than Britain, a maritime power. Curzon, the viceroy, constantly warned the government in London of dangers on the north-west frontier, where good relationships had to be maintained with precariously friendly tribes and with buffer states separating India from the Russian Empire – Afghanistan, Persia and Tibet. The conflict between Britain and Russia on the north-west frontier was known as the Great Game, a term immortalised by Rudyard Kipling in his novel *Kim*, published in 1901.[15]

---

12   Lillian M. Penson, 'The Principles and Methods of Lord Salisbury's Foreign Policy', *Cambridge Historical Journal*, 1935, p. 94.

13   Mahajan, *British Foreign Policy*, pp. 26, 115.

14   Ibid., p. 18.

15   The phrase 'the Great Game' was apparently first used by Captain Arthur Conolly of the Sixth Bengal Native Light Cavalry Regiment in 1840 in a message to his military officer: 'You have a great game, a noble one, before you.' Sergeev, *The Great Game*, p. 3. But it was Kipling who gave it wider currency.

But Britain, with her small army, could hardly counter the Russian threat on her own. Therefore, so it increasingly appeared, she needed the help of an ally.

As an imperial power, then, Britain's interests in Europe seemed secondary to those of the empire for much of the nineteenth century. She had therefore remained aloof from alliances, not perhaps in isolation but in detachment from the Continent. Her policy towards the Continent was, as Disraeli had declared in 1872, one of 'reserve, but proud reserve'.[16] Britain had hardly any commitments on the Continent, and no troops there. The other powers, however, were bound by alliances. Germany, Austria–Hungary and Italy formed one, first negotiated in 1882 and periodically renewed, the so-called Triple Alliance, while in 1894, France and Russia formed a competing alliance sometimes called the Dual Alliance.

By 1895, it was not only Russia that seemed to be challenging the empire but also her ally France in the Nile valley and West Africa. The Franco-Russian Alliance increased the dangers. 'The weakest spot in the Empire', Balfour told Lord Lansdowne in December 1901, 'is probably the Indian frontier ... A quarrel with Russia anywhere, about anything, means the invasion of India and, if England were without allies, I doubt whether it would be possible for the French to resist joining in the fray. Our position would then be perilous.'[17]

Outside Europe, the growing power of the United States and Japan was a further source of worry. The United States, seeking to become the dominant power in the hemisphere, was coming to interpret the Monroe Doctrine more aggressively so as to secure hegemony over the whole continent. This created fears for Canada and for Britain's possessions in Latin America and the West Indies, while Japan, by her victory over China in the war of 1894–95, had shown that she too was a power with which to be reckoned. These were early signs that European predominance in world affairs would come to an end in the twentieth century.

There were, Lord Selborne, First Lord of the Admiralty, was to tell Curzon in January 1903, 'three exceptions to our naval & insular character'.[18] The first was the need to defend Canada against the United States, a problem being resolved through diplomacy and appeasement. The second was the hostility of the Boers in South Africa. That had been resolved by war. The third was Russia in central Asia. That was to be resolved by alliance with Japan.

The history of British foreign policy from 1895 to 1905 is largely the story

---

16 Mahajan, *British Foreign Policy*, p. 33.
17 Ibid., p. viii.
18 Keith Neilson, *Britain and the Last Tsar: British Policy and Russia, 1894–1917*, Oxford University Press, 1995, pp. 125-6.

of how Britain came to meet these new challenges while maintaining her detachment from the Continent. After 1905, that detachment was, slowly and gradually, to come to an end.

Lord Salisbury, Foreign Secretary for the fourth time, was to leave as great a mark on foreign policy as Palmerston. But he was a very different sort of Foreign Secretary from Palmerston, who had sought, so Salisbury believed, to spread Britain's liberal values abroad. Palmerston appeared to Salisbury a crusader, seeking friendship with liberal regimes, while keeping his distance from illiberal ones. He had based his policy on the character of foreign regimes. This, Salisbury believed, was a mistake. For him, the essence of foreign policy was defence of the national interest. Success depended on a careful definition of British interests and then finding the best means to protect them. That might well require association with illiberal and despotic regimes. Ideology was irrelevant, and could only cloud the attempt to achieve a clear perception of British interests. The prime such interest was peace, and that was best secured pragmatically, through a careful balancing of British interests in different parts of the world, distinguishing what was fundamental from what was less important, using strength to preserve what was fundamental, while relying upon diplomacy to balance competing claims where less fundamental interests were at stake. But Salisbury did not fully appreciate the new problems facing Britain. Isolation, he continued to believe as late as 1901, was 'a danger in whose existence we have no historical reason for believing'.[19] Many of his colleagues did not agree. For them, Britain was coming to be overextended. Britain, Chamberlain was to tell the 1902 Colonial Conference, was a 'weary Titan', which 'staggers under the too vast orb of its fate. We have borne the burden long enough.'[20] Alliances would enable Britain to deter hostile powers and concentrate her forces more effectively, so the new men such as Chamberlain and Balfour believed, and they were becoming increasingly influential as Salisbury aged.

Nevertheless, there seemed on the Continent a balance of power, if not deadlock. For, after the Franco-Russian Alliance of 1894, the two alliance systems seemed roughly equal, balancing each other out. Outside the Balkans, a perpetual source of flux and upheaval, the European state system appeared fixed and unalterable. It seemed, in the words of one commentator, that 'two defensive systems stood opposed to each other. Nothing could be done, excepting at the cost of a great conflagration.'[21] Great power conflict, therefore, was diverted outside Europe, to Africa and the Far East. Britain

---

19   Gooch and Temperley, eds, *British Documents*, vol. 2, no. 86.
20   The epigraph and central theme of Friedberg, *Weary Titan*.
21   William L. Langer, *The Diplomacy of Imperialism 1890–1902*, 2nd edition, Knopf, 1951, p. 190.

was to meet new challenges to her global predominance largely through a policy of accommodation – rapprochement with the United States, alliance with Japan, entente with France and a convention with Russia. Her agreements with France and Russia, however, were not intended to yield a Continental commitment. They were envisioned as strengthening British detachment from the Continent rather than subverting it. If imperial conflicts could be resolved through agreement, British statesmen believed, the causes of friction with European powers would also be lessened and that would actually diminish the need for a Continental commitment. Indeed, war, when it came in 1914, was to be the outcome not of imperial conflict but of developments on the Continent.

THE CHALLENGE FROM AMERICA

The years from 1895, then, saw Britain seeking to reduce the threats from her competitors. The first such challenge came from the United States. During much of the nineteenth century, and especially during the American Civil War from 1861 to 1865, diplomatic relations between Britain and the United States had often been uneasy, but there had been no real danger of armed conflict since the War of 1812. In 1895, however, suddenly and seemingly without warning, the two countries appeared on the verge of war over a boundary dispute in which the Latin American republic of Venezuela was claiming almost two-thirds of British Guiana, a colony on which British subjects had long been settled. On 20 July 1895, the American Secretary of State Richard Olney sent a peremptory note to Britain demanding that she put the dispute to arbitration and claiming that it was of fundamental concern to the United States, since, Olney claimed, the Monroe Doctrine entailed that 'the United States is practically sovereign on this continent and its fiat is law upon the subjects to which it confines its interposition'.

The Monroe Doctrine, first promulgated in 1823, had declared that European powers were not to be allowed to use the American continent for colonisation or territorial aggrandisement. Olney now seemed to be extending its scope by insisting that the United States had the right to determine how disputes between a European power and an independent republic in the western hemisphere should be settled, to arbitrate between them, and indeed to veto any transfer of territory to a non-American power. In truth, it was an assertion of American power, although critics of British imperialism could allege that she too had her Monroe Doctrine in India and in much of Africa. Olney's note contained a veiled threat of war with Britain if she did not put the dispute to arbitration. 'While the measures necessary or proper to the vindication of that policy [the Monroe Doctrine]', Olney declared, 'are to be determined by another branch of the Government [i.e. Congress], it is clearly for the Executive to leave nothing undone which may tend to render such determination necessary.'

Olney's interpretation of the Monroe Doctrine was strongly contested by South American international lawyers and by Chamberlain, who sent Salisbury a memorandum pointing out that 'Great Britain is an American Power with a territorial area greater than the United States themselves, and with a title acquired prior to the independence of the United States'.[22] Salisbury did not reply to Olney's note for four months, until 26 November. He declared that the Monroe Doctrine was irrelevant, since the issue was 'simply the determination of the frontier of a British possession which belonged to the Throne of England long before the republic of Venezuela came into existence'. Olney's interpretation of the Monroe Doctrine was, Salisbury argued, illegitimate, since international law was 'founded on the general consent of nations; and no statesman, however eminent, and no nation, however powerful, are competent to insert into the code of international law a novel principle which was never recognised before, and which has not since been accepted by the Government of any other country.' 'The Government of the United States', Salisbury went on, 'is not entitled to affirm as a universal proposition, with reference to a number of independent States for whose conduct it assumes no responsibility, that its interests are necessarily concerned in whatever may befall those States simply because they are situated in the Western Hemisphere.' The reply was sent by the ordinary mail, not by cable, and it had not arrived in Washington by the time the new congressional session began.

The American President, Grover Cleveland, a Democrat, was unsympathetic to imperialism, and believed that European powers had designs on the continent. He was, unsurprisingly perhaps, furious when he received Salisbury's reply. On 17 December, just three weeks after getting it, he sent a message to Congress reaffirming Olney's interpretation of the Monroe Doctrine and calling for an investigatory commission to examine the border dispute. He renewed the threat of war with Britain, declaring that, when the report of the commission had been completed, it would be

the duty of the United States to resist by every means in its power, as a wilful aggression upon its rights and interests, the appropriation by Great Britain of any lands or the exercise of governmental jurisdiction over any territory which after investigation we have determined of right belongs to Venezuela.

---

22 See the letter by Emil Reich in *The Times*, 9 January 1896; and, for Chamberlain, Ernest R. May, *Imperial Democracy: The Emergence of America as a Great Power*, Harper and Row, 1973, pp. 44–5.

There was a spontaneous demonstration of support for Cleveland in the Senate, while, in the House of Representatives, the Bill providing for the investigatory commission was passed without a single dissenting vote. In Britain, the fleet was put in readiness, and, for a few days, it seemed as if the two countries could soon be at war. 'A war with America,' Salisbury told Hicks Beach in January 1896, 'not this year but in the not distant future ... has become something more than a possibility.'[23]

But wiser counsels rapidly prevailed. In both countries, public opinion was shocked at the mere possibility of war between the two great English-speaking nations. The Prince of Wales, later Edward VII, and his son, the Duke of York, later George V, cabled to America expressing the hope that the crisis could be resolved and be 'succeeded by the same warm feeling of friendship which has existed between them for many years'. Balfour declared that 'the idea of war with the United States carries with it some of the unnatural horror of a civil war' and looked forward to the time when 'some statesman of authority ... will lay down the doctrine that between English-speaking peoples war is impossible'.[24] Salisbury predicted, correctly, that the warlike feeling in the United States would soon 'frizzle away'. He also came to realise that his brusque reply to Olney's note had been a mistake. He assured Americans that Britain had no imperialistic designs in Latin America, and reiterated that he would accept arbitration, provided that the long-standing rights of British settlers were recognised. 'The real difference between the Governments was on the limits, not on the principle, of arbitration.'[25] The outcome was to give Britain most of what she sought, but a small strip of land controlling the Orinoco river was ceded to Venezuela.

Britain was clearly in no position to combat America. She was facing the aftermath of the Jameson Raid in South Africa, shortly to be followed by the kaiser's Kruger telegram, while in China, she was facing threats to her trading position from France and Germany as well as Russia. Salisbury soon came to appreciate that Britain could in fact benefit from Olney's interpretation of the Monroe Doctrine. For, if friendly relations could be restored, Britain could then rely upon the Americans to police the western hemisphere on her behalf. The United States would prevent other powers from encroaching on the Continent and defend Britain's colonial and economic interests in the Americas. Indeed, a later President, Theodore Roosevelt, who entered the White House in 1901, accepted that the Olney extension of the Monroe Doctrine entailed the exercise of a police power by the United States in the

---

23 Roberts, *Salisbury*, p. 617.
24 Dugdale, *Balfour*, vol. I, p. 171.
25 Ibid., p. 173.

western hemisphere. In February 1903, Roosevelt was to tell the British ambassador that he was opposed to European powers using force to collect debts incurred towards them by Latin American states. The ambassador then asked him whether he was prepared to police the whole American continent. Roosevelt did not demur, and indeed the so-called Roosevelt Corollary of the Monroe Doctrine in 1904 insisted that the United States bore responsibility for order in the whole American continent.

Britain's acquiescence to American demands, and tacit acceptance of the extension of the Monroe Doctrine, was not solely a result of realpolitik. For the crisis brought to the surface in Britain sentiments of Anglo-American solidarity, helped by the fact that two leading politicians, Chamberlain and Harcourt, both had American wives.

The rapprochement was sealed by Britain's friendly attitude towards the United States in the Spanish–American War. In 1898, the United States imposed a naval blockade on Cuba, seeking independence from Spanish colonial rule, and sent a battleship, the USS *Maine*, to protect American interests in Cuba. The battleship was blown up and sunk, with the loss of three-quarters of the American crew. It was not clear who was responsible for the explosion, but the American public blamed Spain and called for military retaliation. President McKinley, Grover Cleveland's Republican successor, demanded that Spain declare Cuba independent. Spain refused and declared war on the United States, which rapidly emerged victorious and succeeded in expelling Spain from Cuba. But in Europe, there had been sympathy for Spain and the kaiser had at one point sought to form a Continental league to press the United States to compromise. From this attempt, Britain ostentatiously stood aside, making plain that, alone amongst the European powers, her sympathies lay with the United States.

The war with Spain occurred before the Panama Canal had been constructed, and so American warships seeking to reach the Atlantic from the Pacific had to travel round Cape Horn. This was clearly a considerable inconvenience which, some Americans believed, could have led to their defeat. The United States government determined, therefore, to build a canal linking the Pacific and the Atlantic across the isthmus in what was then Colombia but is now part of Panama, a country created when, under American guidance, it seceded from Colombia in 1903. The Americans wanted the canal to be under their control. But by the terms of the Clayton–Bulwer Treaty of 1850 between Britain and the United States, a canal connecting the two oceans had to be neutral, available to all nations and unfortified. This treaty now seemed to Americans a violation of the Monroe Doctrine, and the American government demanded that it be revised since it wanted to both control the canal and fortify it. Britain at first sought a quid pro quo, but in February 1901, the Foreign Secretary, Lord Lansdowne, who had succeeded Salisbury at the Foreign Office the previous year, wrote to Sir Julian Pauncefote, British ambassador to Washington, that Britain would abandon her claims under the Clayton–Bulwer Treaty, 'as a signal proof of their friendly disposition and of their desire not to impede the execution of a project declared to be of national importance to the people of the United States'.[26] Britain did, however, secure agreement to her demand that there be no differential tolls or discrimination amongst users of the canal. A new treaty was drawn up, the Hay–Pauncefote Treaty, named after the American Secretary of State John Hay, and Pauncefote, broadly granting the demands of the United States. Settlements were also achieved on two other disputes with the United States – over fishing rights in Newfoundland and over a disputed border between Alaska and Canada. In response to these sentiments of British goodwill, the American government refused to support the Boers in the war in South Africa, while in 1901 Britain removed the United States from the list of countries whose navies it needed to match in terms of the two-power standard.

It was, nevertheless, becoming clear that, in the new and closer relationship between the two countries, the wishes of the United States would prevail whenever they clashed with those of Britain. 'All that I have ever done with England', wrote John Hay to a friend, with no more than a little exaggeration, 'is to have wrung great concessions out of her with no compensation.'[27] In 1902, Britain was to cooperate with Germany in a debt-collecting expedition in Venezuela. But Britain ended that cooperation when the United States objected. Britain had accepted that the United States could enlarge the Monroe Doctrine and intervene in determining the borders of British Guiana, that the United States could insist on conditions for the control of the Panama Canal and that she could intervene in determining the boundary of Canada. Appeasement of the United States was a conscious choice made by the British elite, supported by the sentiment of Anglo-Saxonism, so as to lessen the number of Britain's opponents.

The crisis of 1895, therefore, had momentous consequences, marking as it did the beginnings of Anglo-American amity, which was to turn in due course into what many in Britain perceived as a special relationship. 'America', a future British ambassador to Washington, James Bryce, wrote in 1898, 'is looked upon as the champion of popular government against the great military monarchies of continental Europe.'[28] The crisis was, in the words

---

26 R. B. Mowat, *The Life of Lord Pauncefote: First Ambassador to the United States*, Houghton Mifflin, 1929, p. 285.
27 Ibid. p. 248.
28 Quoted in Kori Schake, *Safe Passage: The Transition from British to American Hegemony*, Harvard University Press, 2017, p. 195.

of the great French historian of nineteenth-century Britain, Élie Halévy, 'a turning-point in British foreign policy'. For the British government, Halévy wrote in 1926, 'has never since departed from the attitude, now definitely adopted, of deliberately courting the friendship of the American Government and people'.[29] American friendship, Lord Selborne, First Lord of the Admiralty, declared in 1904, was the 'principal aim' of British foreign policy. There were many rhetorical flourishes around the idea of the racial unity of the Anglo-Saxons, and its civilising mission, particularly by Chamberlain, whose wife was the daughter of a minister in the Cleveland Cabinet. This idea had few obvious consequences except to act as ideological cover for British accommodation to the United States. But in the longer run, the Salisbury and Balfour governments were right to believe that the growth of American power would have beneficial consequences for Britain. In an earlier generation, Bismarck had presciently remarked that the key to the twentieth century would be that the Americans spoke English, while the kaiser feared that 'the United States with Monroeism is nearly as much in the way of Powers desiring to expand as Great Britain'.[30] Sir Edward Grey, the Liberals' foreign affairs spokesman, agreed with the government on relations with America, declaring in the Commons in July 1903 that 'it ought to be an object of British policy ... to make an understanding with the United States our first object, and, if possible, an understanding with the United States alone'.[31] As Foreign Secretary in the new Liberal government in December 1905, Grey expressed hope to the ambassador in Washington that 'a bond of union between ourselves and the United States will be found ... in our tendency to take the same view of events in the world generally'. And a year later, in December 1906, Grey came to reflect on the basis of the relationship to the American President Theodore Roosevelt, with whom he was developing a close friendship. 'People call it race, but I doubt if it can be that.' He mentioned common language and similarity of religious views,

> but more than all of this I should say that some generations of freedom on both sides has [sic] evolved a type of men & mind which looks at things from a kindred point of view & a majority which has a hatred for what is not just or free.[32]

The American historian Brooks Adams presciently declared in 1898:

29 Élie Halévy, *History of the English People in the Nineteenth Century, vol. 5: Imperialism and the Rise of Labour (1895–1905)* [1951], 2nd edition, Ernest Benn, 1961, p. 45.
30 Schake, *Safe Passage*, pp. 208, 199.
31 House of Commons Debates, 23 July 1903, vol. 126, cols 126–7.
32 T. G. Otte, *Statesman of Europe: A Life of Sir Edward Grey*, Allen Lane, 2020, ch. 9.

The support of the United States may ... be said to be vital to England, since, without it, if attacked by a Continental coalition, she would have to capitulate. Great Britain may ... be not inaptly described as a fortified outpost of the Anglo-Saxon race, over looking the eastern continent and resting upon America.[33]

And so it proved to be.

The years from the end of the nineteenth century to the mid-1950s were years in which it seemed that an even closer relationship between Britain and America might be possible. In the Sherlock Holmes story 'The Adventure of the Noble Bachelor', published in 1892, the great detective declares:

It is always a joy to me to meet an American, Mr Moulton, for I am one of those who believe that the folly of a monarch and the blundering of a minister in far-gone years will not prevent our children from being some day citizens of the same world-wide country under a flag which shall be a quartering of the Union Jack with the Stars and Stripes.

In 1958, Churchill was to conclude the fourth and final volume of his *History of the English-Speaking Peoples* with the hope that there would be 'ultimate union' between the two countries. He was the last British statesman so to hope.

THE CHALLENGE IN THE MIDDLE EAST

The new Unionist government was rapidly faced with a foreign policy problem which starkly indicated the limitations on British power.[34] By Article 61 of the Treaty of Berlin, the sultan had undertaken 'to carry out, without further delay', 'reforms ... in the provinces inhabited by the Armenians'. The powers would 'superintend their application'. But when the new Parliament assembled in August 1895, the public were horrified by reports of the massacre of Armenian Christians in Turkey, some of whom had taken part in armed rebellion against the sultan. There had been 'horrors to the like of which', Salisbury told the Nonconformist Unionist Association, 'Europe has not listened since the days of Genghis Khan and Tamerlane'.[35] While there is no evidence that the massacres were ordered by the sultan, he had done little, if anything, to prevent them. Indeed, he had seemed to countenance them by

---

33 Quoted in Charles S. Campbell, *Anglo-American Understanding*, Johns Hopkins Press, 1957, p. 24.
34 See p. xiv for a map of Africa in 1898.
35 Roberts, *Salisbury*, p. 610.

decorating the mufti who had incited troops against the Armenians and had been one of the commanders involved in the massacres.[36] Atrocities against a Christian people living in a Muslim state shocked the British conscience, and led to the retired Gladstone's last public speech, in Liverpool, to an audience of 6,000, in September 1896, three months before his eighty-seventh birthday. He condemned the massacres, declaring that the Concert of Europe 'has failed', that 'the Powers collectively have undergone miserable disgrace' and that the sultan seemed to enjoy 'an assurance of impunity'. Britain, he insisted, should break diplomatic relations and enforce reform on the sultan. But suppose this led to war? 'Coercion', Gladstone insisted unconvincingly, 'does not of itself mean war.' If war was threatened, the aged statesman declared, with what some regarded as typical Gladstonian legerdemain, 'it might be necessary to recede ... without loss either of honour or power', a policy which *The Times* regarded as both 'dangerous' and 'cowardly'.[37] It is difficult to see how, if Britain 'receded', humiliation could be avoided. 'If there is one rule of diplomacy which I regard as sacred,' Lord Rosebery declared, 'it is this – you should never put your foot farther than you can keep it down.'[38]

The Unionist government had to decide how to respond to the public clamour and assist the Armenians. Salisbury, although often seen as a realist by contrast with Gladstone's idealism, in fact shared Gladstone's view that Britain should intervene, alone if need be; and after failing to secure agreement with the other powers, he proposed exactly that. For once Salisbury was more bellicose than his colleagues. But he was overborne in Cabinet. Goschen, First Lord of the Admiralty, spoke of professional advice that the navy could not force the Dardanelles against hostile powers, which now included Russia. For the Russians were modifying their traditional hostility to the Turkish Empire, for fear that Armenians living in the Russian Empire would join with their brethren in Turkey to seek independence; and the Russian Navy, with the navy of her ally, France, was likely to prove stronger than the Royal Navy. It was, in any case, not clear what the navy could achieve. Britain did not have the military resources to occupy Armenia against the wishes of the powers and against an Ottoman army of around 300,000. The Cabinet would not allow Salisbury to intervene unilaterally and risk a European war, and for the first time he was overruled on a foreign policy issue. Armenia cast a sudden shaft of light on the limits to British policy; and, as Salisbury sadly told Queen Victoria, 'if our ships are always to be kept

---

36 Whates, *Third Salisbury Administration*, pp. 23–4.
37 *The Times*, 25 September 1896.
38 Robert Rhodes James, *Rosebery: A Biography of Archibald Philip, Fifth Earl of Rosebery*, Weidenfeld & Nicolson, 1963, p. 395.

wrapped in silver paper for fear of their paint getting scratched', it would be difficult to defend the naval estimates in Parliament.[39]

Salisbury was certainly not prepared to follow Gladstone's policy of denouncing the atrocities and then 'receding' if, as was likely, war were threatened. He saw this as a policy of bluff for the sake of a moral gesture. He was therefore compelled to continue with Rosebery's policy of relying on collective intervention to press reforms on the sultan. In a speech at the Guildhall on 9 November 1896, he proposed a Mixed Commission to secure reforms in Turkey, composed of the governments of Britain, France and Russia. He also suggested that more Christians be appointed in the administration of provinces largely inhabited by Armenians. The sultan, as so often in the past, appeared to agree, but in practice, as Salisbury had feared, little was to change. Indeed, there were further massacres and ill-treatment of Armenians and the other powers refused to act. Salisbury came under much criticism from liberal opinion for not following the policy of intervention which he had himself sought, and was denounced for his supposed realism and cynicism. But the Armenian crisis had a greater effect on the Liberal opposition. It provided the occasion, though perhaps not the cause, of Rosebery's resignation from the Liberal leadership. Rosebery had supported the Unionist government's policy of opposition to unilateral British intervention, believing that intervention could lead to war. This outraged his Nonconformist followers, and their opposition, strengthened by Gladstone's Liverpool speech, proved the last straw for the touchy and over-sensitive ex-Prime Minister.

The massacres in Armenia had important long-term consequences for foreign policy. In the past, the powers had, under one formula or another, assisted the Ottoman Empire's Christian subjects in Romania, Serbia, Greece, Bulgaria and Bosnia, to escape Ottoman rule. But now, they seemed feeble and impotent and unable to prevent atrocities. Europe's ineffectiveness seemed confirmed in 1897 when it failed to enforce reforms upon the Turkish administration in Crete, and failed to prevent Greece from aiding her ethnic brothers and sisters by declaring war on Turkey. Salisbury had wanted to blockade Crete to prevent war, but he was again overruled by his Cabinet.[40] Yet the powers did manage at least to ensure that the war was localised, and that Turkish gains after her victory were limited. Nevertheless, it was coming to seem that the Concert of Europe could be preserved only for negative purposes – to prevent change – rather than to enforce reform or prevent local wars. Perhaps, then, the Concert could no longer be the basis of British foreign policy. That left two alternatives: the first was to align

---

39 Roberts, *Salisbury*, p. 608.
40 Ibid., p. 649.

Britain with a Continental alliance system, as advocated by Chamberlain; the second, embraced by Salisbury, was a policy of appeasement, reducing risks by making, where necessary, graceful concessions, and coming to terms with adversaries and potential adversaries while preserving fundamental British interests.

The Armenian fiasco confirmed Salisbury's thoughts that support for the Turkish Empire should no longer be the keynote of Britain's foreign policy. 'It is impossible', Salisbury told the French ambassador in July 1895, 'to keep things as they are ... Turkey is dying slowly.' In the Lords in January 1897, Salisbury declared that in propping up the Ottoman Empire at the Berlin conference, 'we put all our money on the wrong horse', sustaining the empire in return for promises of reform which had not materialised.[41] He was now prepared to accept partition of the Ottoman Empire so long as it did not lead to conflict with other powers. But in any case, Turkey was losing her strategic importance. The opening of the Suez Canal in 1869 meant that there was now an alternative route to India, and one more securely under British control. In 1875, Disraeli's government had purchased the shares of the Khedive, the nominal ruler of Egypt, and since then Britain had enjoyed a controlling interest in the company which administered the canal. Disraeli declared that his purchase had not been a 'financial investment' but a 'political transaction', since it 'secures to us a highway to our Indian Empire and other dependencies'.[42] Security of the Suez Canal, Egypt and the Nile valley became fundamental to British policy, and if Britain no longer needed to fear control of Constantinople by a hostile Russia, the assumptions of the settlement embodied in the Treaty of Berlin of 1878 were no longer valid.

Egypt had been ruled by Britain and France under a system of dual control in 1876. But in 1882, following a nationalist revolt, Britain assumed effective control, after France had refused to take part in a joint military operation to put down the revolt, in effect ending dual control. Gladstone instituted what he insisted would be a 'temporary' occupation. Between 1882 and 1922, Britain promised sixty-six times to leave Egypt once order had been restored.[43] But the 'temporary' occupation in fact lasted until 1936. 'No one', George Wyndham, the Under-Secretary for War, told the Commons in March 1900, 'has ever been able to find the time or the occasion for withdrawing – and no one ever will.'[44] But British rule took place behind the scenes, with Egypt

41 House of Lords Debates, 19 January 1897, vol. 45, col. 29; A. J. P. Taylor, *The Struggle for Mastery in Europe, 1848–1918*, Clarendon Press, 1954, p. 359.
42 Mahajan, *British Foreign Policy*, p. 36.
43 Taylor, *Struggle for Mastery*, p. 289.
44 House of Commons Debates, 16 March 1900, vol. 80, col. 620.

becoming part of the informal empire. Legal forms masked the realities of power. In theory, Egypt remained an autonomous part of the Ottoman Empire, ruled by a Khedive or viceroy. But from 1882, the Khedive was 'advised' by a British agent and Consul General. In 1955, when British Foreign Secretary Anthony Eden entertained his nemesis, Egypt's President Nasser, to dinner in the British embassy in Cairo, the President is alleged to have said how glad he was to be dining in the house from which Egypt had been ruled for so long. 'Not ruled,' Eden responded, 'advised perhaps.'[45] From 1883 to 1907, the British agent was Sir Evelyn Baring, created Lord Cromer in 1892, and in effect Egypt's ruler. In theory, he was preparing Egypt for self-government, but Baring took the view, as he had of the Indians, having served in India before moving to Cairo, that the Egyptians were not sufficiently 'civilised' for self-government and would not be so for many years to come. 'We need not', Cromer believed, 'always inquire too closely what these people, who are all, nationally speaking, more or less *in statu pupillari*, themselves, think is best for their own interests.'[46] His approach to the problems of Egyptian government was paternalistic and authoritarian, so much so that he came to be nicknamed 'Over-Baring'.

The occupation of Egypt damaged Britain's relations with France, which came to regret that she had not joined with Britain in 1882. French influence continued through the Public Debt Commission, formed in 1876 to supervise the repayment of loans made to Egypt, on which Britain and France together held the majority of votes. France was coming to threaten the Upper Nile, expanding eastwards from the French Congo and French Equatorial Africa, covering the territory of what is today the Republic of the Congo, Gabon and the Central African Republic. But Britain's position in Egypt was also threatened by nationalism in the south, in what is now Sudan. In 1881, a sheikh calling himself the Mahdi, an Arabic term for the Redeemer prefigured in the Koran, and claiming to be a descendant of the Prophet, had led a revolt against Egypt and Britain, and had established a despotic Islamic regime based on slave-ownership and committed to jihad towards unbelievers who included Christians.[47] In 1885, the Mahdi had defeated and destroyed a British relief force in Khartoum led by General Gordon. Gladstone's Liberal government then withdrew from Sudan. But in March 1896, the Salisbury government decided to move south from Egypt into Sudan. The immediate cause of this decision was the failure of the Italians, who possessed colonies in Eritrea and Italian Somalia, in their campaign to conquer

45 Keith Kyle, *Suez*, Weidenfeld & Nicolson, 1991, p. 60.
46 David Levering Lewis, *The Race to Fashoda*, Bloomsbury, 1988, p. 10.
47 P. M. Holt, *The Mahdist State in the Sudan 1881–1898*, Clarendon Press, 1970, gives the details.

Ethiopia. Italian forces had been decisively defeated at the Battle of Adwa, ensuring that Ethiopia would remain, with Liberia, one of just two African states to avoid colonisation. The Italian defeat was the first occasion since the European powers had begun to expand in Africa, except for the defeat of Gordon in 1885, that an African territory had overcome a European power, and it gave a fillip to African and Arab nationalism. After Adwa, the Italians sought help from the powers. Britain responded, fearing that the victorious Ethiopians would join with the French to threaten Britain in the Nile valley, or alternatively join those of the Mahdi's successor, the Khalifa, to threaten Egypt, as the Khalifa had tried to do in 1889. The Khalifa was a 'capricious tyrant', who had terrorised the population of Sudan. An Anglo-Austrian explorer, Sir Rudolf Slatin, who had administered part of Sudan when Gordon had been governor general, had been captured in 1885 by the Mahdists and imprisoned for eleven years. Of his captivity, it has been said that 'for a parallel to the constant stress and fear and degradation he had to go through and the daily horrors he had to witness ... we can look only to the plight of his fellow-Jews in Hitler's concentration camps'. After escaping from the Khalifa, Slatin joined Kitchener's army in the recapture of Khartoum.[48]

But British motives were by no means wholly humanitarian. There was a powerful strategic motive. For if Britain did not intervene, the French might, threatening Britain's position in Egypt. As Lord Lansdowne, the War Secretary, told the Cabinet, 'the ulterior object' of the expedition, ostensibly to aid the Italians, was in fact 'to restore a portion of her lost territory to Egypt'.[49] The Khedive and his ministers – in theory the government of Egypt – were informed of the British decision only after it was made. 'By far the best arrangement plan', Cromer wrote to Salisbury in December 1896, 'will be not to consult them [the Egyptian government] but to communicate to them [the] decision of Her Majesty's government. I am sure this is what they would prefer.'[50] The sultan of Turkey, in theory the suzerain authority, was not consulted at all, the British government's argument being that disturbances in Sudan were in areas that had been entrusted by the sultan to the Khedive so therefore the sultan's consent was not needed. The military expedition was led by the Sirdar – commander-in-chief of the Egyptian Army – Sir Herbert Kitchener, who had no hesitation in seizing and forcing Egyptians to serve for very low pay. When these Egyptians were 'past work', they were, in the words of one diarist, 'pitilessly cast adrift without pension

---

48 Richard Hill, *Slatin Pasha*, Oxford University Press, 1965, p. 24; Gordon Brook-Shepherd, *Between Two Flags: The Life of Baron Sir Rudolf von Slatin Pasha, GCVO, KCMG, CB*, Weidenfeld & Nicolson, 1972, p. 81.
49 Cabinet Memo, 'Proposed Advance up the Nile Valley', 24 March 1896, quoted in Robinson, Gallagher and Denny, *Africa and the Victorians*, p. 349.
50 Mekki Shibeika, *British Policy in the Sudan, 1882–1902*, Oxford University Press, 1952, p. 375.

or provision of any kind. Yet we English pretend that our mission in Africa is to put down slave-raiding and slavery.'[51]

The advance into Sudan was cautious and at first tentative, taking the Anglo-Egyptian army only as far as Dongola, which fell in September 1896. After that, authorisation was given to take Berber, which fell in August 1897, and then in January 1898, to advance to Khartoum, which fell after the Battle of Omdurman in September 1898. It was here that the young Winston Churchill led a cavalry charge of British Lancers. Around 10,000 of the Khalifa's Dervish troops were killed, compared to around 500 British and Egyptian troops. Many of the wounded Dervishes were left to die, while other followers of the Khalifa were later found in Khartoum and killed in cold blood. Mahmoud, one of the Khalifa's generals, was dragged in chains and lashed by Sudanese guards while Kitchener rode by on a white horse. The Mahdi's tomb was desecrated, and his skeleton minus the skull was thrown into the Nile. The skull was used by Kitchener as an ash tray, which elicited a protest by Queen Victoria who regarded it as cruel and savouring of the Middle Ages. Kitchener had to be reminded by Cromer that he was dealing with human beings and not blocks of wood.[52] But Gordon had finally been avenged and the British and Egyptian flags were raised over the former governor general's palace. Kitchener then proceeded southwards along the Nile to Fashoda (now Kodok in South Sudan), which he reached in September 1898.

Fashoda was a hot, unhealthy and remote mud-flat fortress, surrounded by swamp where Kitchener encountered a small French presence led by Captain Marchand, who had arrived three months earlier with six other French officers and around 120 Sudanese soldiers. Kitchener and Marchand greeted each other cordially, toasting in whisky and soda, though Marchand declared that drinking 'that ghastly smoky liquid' was one of the greatest sacrifices he had ever been called on to make for France.[53] However, the cordiality was misleading. The meeting at Fashoda led to a diplomatic crisis between Britain and France which nearly brought the two countries to war.

'Any European power established on the Upper Nile', Lord Salisbury had declared in 1889, 'would have Egypt in its grip.'[54] France could not challenge Britain frontally in Egypt but now seemed to be challenging her from the rear in Sudan. But for Britain, control of the Upper Nile was essential to ensure that its waters were not diverted or used by another power. Germany in 1890

---

51 Wilfrid Scawen Blunt, *My Diaries: Being a Personal Narrative of Events, 1888–1914*, Martin Secker, 1920, vol. 1, pp. 224–5, entry for 10 April 1896.
52 Roger Owen, *Lord Cromer, Victorian Imperialist, Edwardian Proconsul*, Oxford University Press, 2004, pp. 301–2, 303.
53 Darrell Bates, *The Fashoda Incident of 1898: Encounter on the Nile*, Oxford University Press, 1984, p. 133.
54 Ibid., p. 12.

and Italy in 1891 had recognised that the Upper Nile lay within the British sphere of influence, and Britain had sought to exclude Belgium, whose king, Leopold, had colonised part of the Congo. In March 1895, Edward Grey, Under-Secretary of State for Foreign Affairs in the Rosebery government, had told the Commons that 'the Egyptian and British spheres together cover the whole course of the Nile'.[55] He had warned that any French penetration into the Nile valley would be regarded as an 'unfriendly act' – that is, an act that could lead to war – and 'would be so viewed by England'.[56] The radical element in the Cabinet had been strongly opposed to Grey's declaration. But it remained, nevertheless, a fundamental statement of policy.

Imperialists such as Cecil Rhodes had dreamt of British control of Africa from south to north, Cape to Cairo. The French dream had been to control territory from west to east, from the Niger to the Nile. The lines from Cape to Cairo and from Dakar to Djibouti, formerly French Somaliland, intersected in eastern South Sudan in the area of Fashoda. Marchand's presence was intended to turn the dream of Niger to Nile into reality. But Britain now demanded his unconditional withdrawal. The Berlin conference of 1884 had provided that the title to a new colony in a coastal region would depend upon 'effective occupation', and both sides sought to use this concept to justify their position. Britain argued that Sudan belonged to Egypt and that Egypt's title could not be lost simply because Sudan had been conquered by the Mahdi. Anglo-Egyptian troops had now recovered this lost province, and Marchand's handful of men could not be regarded as an 'effective occupation'. France counterargued that the British occupation of Egypt in 1882 had not been recognised by the powers but was based on a fait accompli, and that, in any case, Britain had claimed that her occupation was temporary and that she intended in due course to withdraw. The French had arrived before the British at Fashoda and had found the territory unoccupied. The British had, admittedly, captured Khartoum, but there was, the French argued, no basis in international law to justify a right to the whole of the territory of which it was the capital. The British, however, replied that the French would not have been able, with so few men, to make their occupation effective, and would have been driven out in short order by Sudanese rebels.

The British legal title to Sudan was by no means watertight, but she had the naval strength to enforce her claims and France did not. The British government, accused of weakness and appeasement in failing to stand up to the Russians in China, was not prepared to compromise; nor probably

---

55 House of Commons Debates, 11 March 1895, vol. 31, cols 781–2.
56 Ibid., 28 March 1895, vol. 32, cols 405–6.

would the public have supported it if it had. 'There is no need to argue the point', the *London Evening News* declared,

> if a householder finds a man in his back garden, he does not go to arbitration about the matter or enter into elaborate arguments to show that he, the householder, is the owner of that garden. He simply orders the trespasser out, and if he will not go out of his own accord, he has to go in another fashion.[57]

Punch was more concise – 'Marchez! Marchand!' it declared on 8 October.[58] Salisbury sent the fleet to sail past Cherbourg as a warning.

Leading Liberal Imperialists, such as Rosebery and Asquith, supported the government, declaring that Salisbury was following the policy of the last Liberal government and would be supported by a united public opinion. 'If the nations of the world are under the impression that the ancient spirit of Great Britain is dead,' Rosebery thundered, 'or that her resources are weakened, or her population less determined than ever it was to maintain the rights and the honour of its flag, they make a mistake which can only end in a disastrous conflagration.'[59] Indeed, after the crisis had been resolved in Britain's favour, Chamberlain was to declare that this was due 'as much to the spectacle of a united nation ... as it was to those military and naval armaments about which the foreign press talks so much and knows so little'.[60] The nation was not, however, quite as united as Rosebery and Chamberlain suggested. One element in the Liberal Party, albeit a minority, argued that Fashoda was not worth a war. Sir Wilfrid Lawson, a radical Liberal MP, speaking in Workington on 26 October, attacked the 'false glamour of glory', declaring that 'the British ... were slaughtering people wholesale in the Sudan', and that 'now the newspapers were talking about war with France in an offhand way as if talking of a football match'. But

> what was all this talk of war about? It was simply because a half starved Frenchman was sitting in a swamp on the banks of the Nile with two flags floating over him, and a few hundred wretched soldiers with him and no ammunition ... The Frenchman might sit there for all eternity as far as he was concerned.[61]

---

57 Quoted in T. W. Riker, 'A Survey of British Policy in the Fashoda Crisis', *Political Science Quarterly*, 1929, p. 66.
58 Bates, *Fashoda Incident*, p. 109.
59 Rhodes James, *Rosebery*, p. 406.
60 *The Times*, 16 November 1898.
61 *Manchester Guardian*, 27 October 1898.

Even Queen Victoria had told Salisbury of her surprise that a war might be fought 'for so miserable and small an object', while Cromer had declared that Sudan comprised 'large tracts of useless territory which it would be difficult and costly to administer properly'.[62]

The crisis exposed, once again, divisions in the opposition between Liberal Imperialists and radicals. Sir William Harcourt, the party leader, was in a difficult position. He opposed the government's policy in Sudan, feeling there was no reason why Britain should be there at all. He feared that Liberals were chasing after 'strange gods, and that we shall see at least as powerful a contingent of Liberal jingoism as of Liberal Unionism – Khartum [sic] and Fashoda will rally the popular sentiment as much as Trafalgar and Salamanca'.[63] But constrained by the Grey declaration, he adopted a policy of embarrassed silence which did nothing to assist his leadership against more glamorous figures like Rosebery and Asquith, and led him, shortly afterwards, to resign as Liberal leader.

But the problems of a distracted and divided opposition could not sway the government from its firm purpose; and facts on the ground favoured Britain. For Marchand was effectively isolated and imprisoned by a large Anglo-Egyptian force which could, in the last resort, deny him food and provisions. The French government, in the throes of the Dreyfus affair and suffering from the ministerial instability which seems to have been endemic in the Third Republic, had no means of resisting the British demand. The Royal Navy was far stronger than the French, and could intercept the transport of French supplies to Africa. France's Russian ally was unwilling to assist her. France, however, went so far as to hint to Germany at the possibility of an alliance if only Germany would agree to autonomy for Alsace-Lorraine. This was, according to A. J. P. Taylor, 'the last and greatest opportunity at which the Germans might have established a peaceful hegemony of Europe'.[64] But Germany rejected the French offer. In consequence, as the French foreign minister Théophile Delcassé told his wife, 'All we have is argument, and they have soldiers on the spot.'[65] In November 1898, the French government ordered Marchand to withdraw, and in March 1899, France withdrew all claims to the Nile valley.

Once the Fashoda crisis was over, Britain was prepared to follow a policy of appeasement in West Africa, where the French had been pressing their claims of effective occupation in the hinterland of British colonies, areas

62 G. N. Sanderson, *England, Europe and the Upper Nile, 1882–99: A Study in the Partition of Africa*, Edinburgh University Press, 1965, p. 1.
63 Harcourt to Morley, 10 October 1898, quoted in Stansky, *Ambitions and Strategies*, p. 260.
64 A. J. P. Taylor, 'Fashoda: A Turning-Point in Diplomacy', *Manchester Guardian*, 18 September 1948.
65 Bates, *Fashoda Incident*, p. 152.

which Britain held to be within her own sphere of influence. But West Africa did not have the same strategic importance for Britain as Egypt or South Africa, and by the time Africa had been partitioned by the powers, Britain was in occupation of just four enclaves – the Gambia, Sierra Leone, the Gold Coast (now Ghana) and Lagos Colony (now part of Nigeria). Salisbury was prepared to make generous concessions to the French and, in March 1899, an agreement between the two countries delimited the respective possessions and spheres of influence of the two powers west and east of the Niger.[66] Frontiers were agreed separating the British colonies of the Gold Coast and Lagos from the French colonies of Ivory Coast, Niger and Dahomey. In compensation for excluding France from Sudan, which would henceforth be ruled in theory by an Anglo-Egyptian condominium but in reality by Britain, Salisbury agreed not to expand further along the Niger, thereby allowing the French to consolidate their West African possessions into one solid bloc. In a further move to conciliate the French, Lord Cromer substituted for 'Fashoda' the ancient name 'Kodok' in 1901. It is still called by that name.[67] Fashoda had raised the spectre of a France subordinated to Germany in Europe. The outcome, however, helped to ensure that France would remain a power in her own right; but it also implied that French power might need to be sustained by Britain. It pointed, therefore, to the entente of 1904 and the commitments which Britain was to make in the years following.

Salisbury had shown great skill. The Upper Nile as well as the Cape and its interior were, he believed, essential in securing the route to India. So there could be no compromise with other powers in these areas, nor with the Boers who were threatening British supremacy in South Africa. In other areas, however – British Guiana, for example, China or West Africa – British interests were not quite so fundamental. There, compromise and adjustment, through normal diplomatic procedures, would be possible. Salisbury showed skill also in isolating his opponents, both in South Africa and in Sudan. In South Africa, the Boers might hope for intervention from other powers, but they were to be deterred by the strength of the Royal Navy; while Salisbury would ensure, through agreements with other powers, that the Boer republics were isolated and denied access to the sea. In Sudan, Salisbury had ascertained that Russia, preoccupied with events in the Far East, would not help her ally, France. In such crises, he showed his realism, concentrating on what was fundamental and compromising on what was not.

Fashoda was a great imperialist triumph; but it was also, though few realised it at the time, almost the last. Britain's diplomatic victory seemed

66 C. 9334, 1899.
67 See the letter from Clara Boyle, widow of Cromer's secretary, in the *Manchester Guardian*, 27 September 1948.

to some to show that lack of allies on the Continent was not so much of an impediment as some had supposed. Perhaps her relative isolation could be splendid after all. France too had been shown to be isolated, but her isolation seemed anything but splendid. Defeat at Fashoda rankled, but it did remove a major cause of dispute between the two powers. Henceforth, it was clear that France could not maintain her claims on the Nile and must seek colonies elsewhere. She turned, therefore, to West and North Africa, and, in particular, to Morocco. So it was that the agreement which resolved the Fashoda crisis proved the precursor, though few foresaw it, to the entente cordiale of 1904, by which France acknowledged Egypt, including Sudan, as a British sphere of influence in return for British acceptance of Morocco as a French sphere of interest. Since Britain and France were, amongst the major European powers, the only parliamentary powers, what could be more natural than that they should resolve their differences peacefully and discover that, behind the façade of conflict, they had important interests in common? But in addition, with Britain now secure in Egypt and in control of the Suez Canal, there was no longer any reason to fear Russian control of Constantinople or the straits. So a huge obstacle to better relations between Britain and Russia had been removed. Since the days of Disraeli and Bismarck and the 1878 Treaty of Berlin, Britain had seemed to need the support of the central powers – Germany and Austria–Hungary – to protect her against Russia. But the first half of the twentieth century would be devoted instead to containing a powerful Germany rather than a predatory Russia. So Fashoda laid the groundwork not only for the entente with France but also for the convention with Russia in 1907, although it required Russia's profound weakening following her defeat by Japan in 1905 for her to accept this.

THE CHALLENGE IN THE FAR EAST

There was another 'dying' empire which seemed ripe for partition just as Africa had been: China.[68] British concerns with China were based on her very extensive commercial and trading interests rather than strategic interests as in parts of Africa. Around half of all commerce going to and coming from China was with Britain, as was around 60 per cent of China's shipping. Indeed, as late as 1900, Britain's preponderance of trade with China was larger than that of all the other powers put together.[69] These interests appeared to give rise to almost limitless British obligations in China. The

---

68 See p. xv for a map of China in 1898.
69 Shih-tsung Wang, *Lord Salisbury and Nationality in the East: Viewing Imperialism in its Proper Perspective*, Routledge, 2019, p. 166.

decaying Chinese Empire appeared a buffer state, and, like the Ottoman Empire, Persia and Afghanistan, a barrier to Russian expansion. The fear was that, as with the Ottoman Empire, China, the 'sick man of Asia', would, in its decay, become an arena for conflict between the powers. That is why this seemingly 'dying' empire became a focus for great power politics between 1895 and 1905. Britain hoped to prevent the division of China into spheres of influence which could have led to her partition and dismemberment, and to preserve an open door for all trading nations in accordance with free-trade principles. But it was clear even by 1895 that it would be impossible to maintain these principles, and if Britain was to keep her commercial position in China intact, she would need to expand her influence there.

The Far East was a greater problem for Britain than the Middle East since naval power could not be so effective in resisting other powers there. Some would compare China with Africa, which had been partitioned. But in much of Africa, there had appeared to be a power vacuum and an absence of effective government. China, by contrast, was governed by various warlords loosely grouped together in a confederation. So occupation would be more difficult and more painful than in Africa. The Chinese could make life challenging for the occupier. 'People forget the passive resistance of the Chinese,' declared the British minister to Japan, Sir Ernest Satow, in February 1898, 'who are like India rubber. You can make an impression with your finger, but as soon as you move it, the effect disappears.'[70] In consequence, as Salisbury declared in 1898, 'we cannot possibly have over the internal government and military administration of China the same influence which we have over India, that we conquered by the sword, or over Egypt, of which the government by the sword has been placed at our command'.[71] China was quite different from Africa also in that the European powers had more extensive financial and trading interests there, interests protected by various unequal treaties giving foreigners extra-territorial rights and providing that Chinese law would not apply to them in certain parts of Chinese territory. In 1843, for example, China had signed a most-favoured-nation treaty with Britain, and Britain had secured by means of unequal treaties leases of Hong Kong in 1841 and Kowloon in 1858. She had also secured trading privileges in five treaty ports at the mouth of the Yangtze river. At the end of the nineteenth century, other powers were also encroaching on Chinese sovereignty, without formal occupation, while paying lip service to Chinese integrity and independence – a further example of informal empire, but an informal empire in which Britain was not the only participant. Still, so long as trading and commercial

70 Otte, *The China Question*, p. 178.
71 Wang, *Lord Salisbury and Nationality*, p. 169.

interests could be protected, informal empire did not need to be superseded by occupation, which would have imposed unnecessary costs. There was, therefore, in the words of one authority, a 'tacit understanding' between the powers that China should not be formally partitioned, since their interests could be preserved without it. 'The preservation of China was in the logic of financial imperialism.'[72] Instead of occupying China as they had done in Africa, the powers 'leased' and isolated parts of it, and Chinese independence became to a considerable degree purely theoretical. China was not partitioned but divided into spheres of influence. In each sphere, the dominant power would 'advise' the nominal rulers, and secure the 'lease' of strategic areas – 'lease' being a euphemism for occupation. Indeed, some areas were 'leased' without bothering to secure the consent of the Chinese at all. In China, by contrast with Africa, there was to be 'no partition of territory, but only a partition of preponderance'.[73]

China had come to be drawn into European rivalries after the war between her and Japan in 1894–95, which had resulted in a victory for Japan, and showed in the words of a future Japanese minister in London that 'a new Power had arisen in the East'. Before the war, China had been 'regarded as the sleeping lion of Asia'. But it was now clear that, 'far from being a lion, China was only a sleeping badger'.[74] By the Treaty of Shimonoseki in April 1895, Japan imposed onerous terms on her defeated enemy. China was required to recognise the 'independence' of Korea, which had, until then, been 'advised' by a Chinese resident, and had paid tribute to China. Korean 'independence' was to prove as theoretical as the 'integrity' of China, since she fell rapidly under Japanese influence and was to be formally annexed in 1910. China was also forced to surrender Formosa (Taiwan), the eastern portion of the bay of the Liaodong Peninsula and the southern part of Manchuria, which included Port Arthur (Lüshunkou), together with other ice-free ports. In addition, China was required to pay a war indemnity, open her ports to Japan and grant her most-favoured-nation status.

Many feared that these harsh terms heralded the establishment of a Japanese protectorate over China. For this reason, immediately after signature of the treaty, France, Germany and Russia presented a collective note to Japan demanding its revision. Japan would be required, in particular, to retrocede the Liaodong Peninsula, which Russia sought so as to use Port Arthur as an ice-free port. France supported her Russian ally, as did Germany. The three powers invited Britain to join them in pressuring Japan to revise the treaty.

72 Otte, *The China Question*, p. 2.
73 Gooch and Temperley, eds, *British Documents*, vol. 1, no. 9.
74 A. M. Pooley, ed., *The Secret Memoirs of Count Tadasu Hayashi*, E. Nash, 1915, pp. 62, 296.

Rosebery, together with his Foreign Secretary Lord Kimberley, as well as the queen, had wished to do so, but the Cabinet decided not to join with the other powers.[75] This decision proved fortunate since Russia was in the short term at least a greater threat to Britain in China than Japan; and it would be easier for Japan to deter Russia than it would be for Britain. In consequence of the refusal to join with the other powers, Britain won much goodwill from the Japanese. Nevertheless, Japan was compelled, under threat of war, to surrender her claims to the Liaodong Peninsula in return for an increased war indemnity from China. The increased indemnity meant that China had to borrow more from abroad, and this made her even more subject to the claims of the three powers. They were not slow to demand something in return.

Russia was the first to act. In 1891, she had begun construction of the Trans-Siberian Railway, linking Moscow with the Russian Far East. In the spring of 1896, she negotiated a secret treaty with China for a link from the railway to Port Arthur, in return for helping with the loan needed to pay the war indemnity. Russia was also granted use of harbours in north China, and began to fortify the Liaodong Peninsula, recently evacuated by the Japanese.

In November 1897, the murder of two German Christian missionaries in Shantung gave Germany the excuse to unilaterally occupy the port of Kiaochow, a large inlet in the maritime province of Shantung, 300 miles north of Shanghai. In March 1898, the Chinese, in a secret agreement not revealed until 1906, agreed to 'lease' Kiaochow to Germany for ninety-nine years – a 'lease' which surrendered Chinese sovereign rights in the area. Kiaochow became in effect a German protectorate administered by the German Navy. The British Inspector-General of the Imperial Chinese Maritime Custom Service declared that the 'German action simply drives me wild – it is so high-handed and opposed to all that's right'.[76] But the threat to British interests was limited since Kiaochow became a free port. It is possible that Germany had secured Russian consent for the occupation of Kiaochow in exchange for not opposing a Russian 'lease' of Port Arthur. The powers which had in 1895 rebuked Japan for grabbing Chinese territory were now joining in the scramble themselves. In mid-December 1897, Russia sent a naval squadron to Port Arthur, a fortress at the southern end of the Liaodong Peninsula, and in March 1898, secured a 'lease' there and in the neighbouring port of Talienwan (Dalian Bay) for twenty-five years, which she proceeded to fortify as a naval base for her fleet and to protect her commerce. This seemed but a prelude to occupation, and gave Russia in effect a large degree

---

75   Rhodes James, *Rosebery*, p. 377.
76   Otte, *The China Question*, p. 102.

of control of Manchuria, to be consolidated in 1900 after the Boxer Uprising when Manchuria became a de facto Russian protectorate. Russia was becoming the preponderant power in northern China, and a threat to British trading and commercial rights there. The motto of Count Witte, Russia's finance minister, was 'trade and industry always in the front, the army always in the rear'.[77] Not to be outdone, France, in April 1898, obtained a 99-year 'lease' of Kwangchow Bay (Guangzhouwan), a small enclave in southern China. Between 1895 and 1901, eight countries were to secure concessions from China between Hankow and Tientsin.

The outcome of the Sino-Japanese War, therefore, not only heralded the rise of Japan as a power in Asia. It also showed that Britain's position in China was under pressure. She seemed no longer to have the strength to maintain her pre-eminent position there. Her weakened position led to parliamentary and public criticism that her diplomacy was ineffective and that it was time she secured her own share. Her main sphere of influence lay in the Yangtze valley. But how was she to make it secure? In 1895, speaking in the Guildhall, Salisbury had quoted 'the great words of Lord Beaconsfield [Disraeli]' that 'in Asia there is room for us all', but his critics accused him of weakness, and alleged that his speech had been interpreted by the Russians as an open invitation to occupy Port Arthur. Salisbury, however, maintained a sceptical attitude towards further British intervention. 'The public', he told Chamberlain in December 1897, 'will require some territorial or cartographic consolation in China – as a matter of pure sentiment we shall have to do it.' Chamberlain responded that 'if we make no move it will be a great encouragement to further tail-twisting on the part of our dear friends & allies of the Concert of Europe'. The Japanese, Chamberlain suggested, would be 'valuable allies', and Britain should draw closer to them.[78] But Salisbury had no intention of doing so since he needed, for the time being at least, to appease Russia so that she would not support her ally, France, in the Nile valley. 'I can't afford to quarrel with Russia now,' he told his daughter and biographer, Lady Gwendolen Cecil.[79] But in February 1898, to prevent further Russian encroachment into her territory, China made an unsolicited offer to Britain of a 25-year lease of Weihaiwei, a small naval and coaling station with a population of around 2,000, just over 100 miles from Port Arthur, and a possible naval base, occupied since 1895 by Japan, as surety for payment of the Chinese indemnity after the Sino-Japanese War. After much discussion in Cabinet, this offer was accepted in July, with Chamberlain

---

77 Taylor, *Struggle for Mastery*, p. 373.
78 Otte, *The China Question*, p. 100.
79 Roberts, *Salisbury*, p. 761.

dissenting, though it was agreed that the lease would be surrendered before twenty-five years if Russia were to leave Port Arthur. British occupation was to prove more symbolic than real. To turn Weihaiwei into a naval base could only be achieved, the Cabinet believed, at prohibitive cost, and, by contrast with Port Arthur, which was linked to the Trans-Siberian Railway, it had no obvious railway links. In the event, it became little more than a naval rest centre. Nevertheless, the occupation gave Britain in effect a protectorate in the Yangtze valley, which contained nearly half of China's total population. This showed that Britain was, together with the other powers, coming tacitly to abandon the principles of preserving the territorial integrity of China and the open door. In 1899, by the terms of the Scott–Muravyev agreement, Britain agreed not to seek railway concessions north of the Great Wall of China, nor obstruct Russian applications for such concessions in return for Russian abstention in the British sphere on the Yangtze. But Britain, primarily a naval power, seemed to have little leverage to enforce this agreement, since enforcement might require the army as well as the navy, and the agreement did not succeed in blocking Russian expansion between Manchuria and the Yangtze.

Perhaps, then, the Japanese could be enlisted to assist Britain. Goodwill had been won when Britain had refused to join the powers in abrogating the Treaty of Shimonoseki in 1895. It was strengthened when they cooperated in 1900 to suppress the Boxer Uprising in China. That rising was a popular movement dedicated to combating those foreign powers which had benefited from the unequal treaties, dedicated also to combating the activities of Christian missionaries in China. The name 'Boxer' derived from a literal translation of the Chinese designation 'the fist of the righteous'. The Boxers' slogan was 'Exterminate the foreigners'. They succeeded in cutting off Beijing from the rest of the country and setting siege to foreign legations there in June 1900. They were suppressed with considerable brutality by an international army, led by Germany, the only occasion before 1914 in which troops of the major powers served under a single commander, the German Field-Marshal Count Waldersee. Suppression of the Boxer Uprising seemed to show that this same concert of powers might be able to maintain peace in the Far East and that the Chinese Question would fizzle out as rapidly as it had arisen in 1895. In May 1898, Salisbury had told the Primrose League that China was 'a sort of diplomatic cracker that has produced a great many detonations, but ... the smoke ... has now floated into the distance'.[80] But the problem of how to preserve British interests in China remained unsolved,

---

80 *The Times*, 5 May 1898.

and it called into question fundamental assumptions lying behind the policy of 'isolation'.

For Britain would find it difficult to maintain her interests in China without an ally. Japan was an obvious candidate for that role. Acting for the first time with the other powers, she had helped suppress the Boxer Uprising. Her role in protecting British citizens under siege in Beijing was much appreciated in Britain and Queen Victoria asked Count Hayashi, the Japanese minister in London, to convey her thanks to the Emperor. The seeds of an alliance with Japan were being sown.

CHAPTER 3

THE WAR IN SOUTH AFRICA

THE CHALLENGE FROM THE BOERS

The most immediate challenge to British supremacy, however, came not in America, the Middle East or the Far East, but from a small, farming community in South Africa: the Boers.[1] Britain proved unable to combat this challenge peacefully. The Boer War was to expose the weakness of her army, the poor physical condition of many of her recruits and the dangers of a foreign policy which sought to remain aloof from alliances.

The Boers were primarily of Dutch origin, but there was a minority who were of French and German descent. They had arrived before the British, from the second half of the seventeenth century, and had conquered the African population. In 1795, however, the British occupied the Cape, and later the whole of Cape Colony. In response to the abolition of slavery in British colonies in 1833, a large section of the Dutch population of the Cape migrated in the Great Trek to the interior, where, after dominating the native population, they established the Orange Free State and the Transvaal.

British control of the Cape, confirmed by treaty in 1814, was regarded as the key to South Africa, which, so Lord Kimberley, Foreign Secretary in the Rosebery government, believed, was 'perhaps the most vital interest of Great Britain because by the possession of it communication with India was assured'. Indeed, it was 'of even greater importance to England than Malta or Gibraltar'.[2] The route to India via the Suez Canal and Egypt could not, many thought, necessarily be relied upon in time of war. But the Cape, it was believed, could be held only if Britain also controlled the interior, since, in the words of a War Office memorandum in October 1884, 'it is impossible for political reasons to create a Gibraltar out of the Cape Town peninsula, and … the permanent retention of this peninsula … is dependent upon the maintenance of British ascendancy in all South African colonies'.[3] There was

---

1 See p. xvi for a map of South Africa in 1899.
2 Mahajan, *British Foreign Policy*, p. 26.
3 Quoted in D. M. Schreuder, *Gladstone and Kruger: Liberal Government and Colonial 'Home Rule', 1880–85*, Routledge & Kegan Paul, 1969, p. 15. This book provides an authoritative account of the settlement between Britain and the Transvaal in the 1880s.

a further incentive for Britain to be drawn into the interior after the discovery of diamonds in the Northern Cape in 1870. In addition, humanitarians were concerned to protect the African peoples against the oppressive attitudes of the Boers in the two Boer states. In 1881, when the Transvaal gained autonomy, African chiefs had asked Gladstone not to place them under Boer rule. Queen Victoria had supported them, telling Gladstone in August 1881, 'we shall be guilty of *great* injustice and *cruelty* if we do not assist and support them ... the Queen *must* ask that ... we shall not abandon them to the tender mercies of a most merciless and cruel neighbour, and in fact oppressor'.[4] There were, then, both strategic and humanitarian arguments for British supremacy in South Africa. But there was a conflict between the humanitarian impulse and the maintenance of good relations with the Boer states. When, in 1897, Asquith was to declare that British policy in South Africa should be based on maintaining good relations between the Dutch and the English but also protecting the African population, Sir Alfred Milner, British High Commissioner in South Africa, responded:

> What I am so anxious that you and other English statesmen, especially Liberal statesmen, should understand is that object No. 1 is, and always has been the principal obstacle to the attainment of object No. 2. I should feel quite confident of being able to get over the Dutch-English difficulty, if it were not so horribly complicated by the native question ... You have therefore this singular situation, that you might indeed unite Dutch and English by protecting the black man, but you would unite them against yourself and your policy of protection. There is the whole crux of the South African position.[5]

The 'natives' had been British subjects before the Transvaal had secured autonomy in the Convention of Pretoria in 1881, after the Boers had defeated British troops at the Battle of Majuba. That convention was revised by the London Convention of 1884, which prohibited slavery, but under Boer rule, the African population was reduced to a condition not too far removed from it.

In South Africa as a whole, whites constituted around one-fifth of the total population – around 1 million out of 5 – but held all the powers of government in their hands. In 1895, South Africa was divided between two British self-governing colonies of settlement – Cape Colony and Natal – and two landlocked Boer republics: the Orange Free State and the Transvaal. In the early 1890s, Africans in Natal outnumbered whites by around ten to

4   Quoted in ibid., p. 217.
5   Quoted in Lord Brand, 'Lord Milner and General Smuts', *The Listener*, 15 October 1953, p. 632.

one, and in Cape Colony by around three to one. In Cape Colony, 60 per cent of the white population were Boers. Indeed, there were more Boers in Cape Colony, the only self-governing colony in the empire in which the British were not in a majority, than in the two Boer republics combined. In the Orange Free State, the white population was around 100,000 and the African population around twice as large, while in the Transvaal in 1897, the white population, according to the state almanac, was 245,397 and the black population over two and a half times as large – 622,544.[6]

The Boers had sought to preserve their Afrikaner identity and follow their own distinctive religious and fundamentalist view of non-white peoples. The Transvaal, Salisbury had written in 1860, was 'their last retreat', where they could 'maltreat the natives to the utmost of their heart's content'.[7] Many Boers believed that whites were the chosen of the Lord, while Africans were descendants of the biblical Ham, son of Noah, and as such doomed to be menials serving the whites. At the time of the creation of the Union of South Africa in 1909, the Boer general, de Wet, was to declare that 'providence had drawn the line between black and white and we must make that clear to the Natives and not instil into their minds false ideas of equality'.[8] In the Boer republics, non-whites were excluded from the franchise as a matter of doctrine. Colour bars had been written into the constitutions of the Orange Free State in 1854 and the Transvaal in 1858. In addition, in the Transvaal, no Catholic or Jew was allowed to hold office. Every Boer was required to own a rifle; no non-Boer was allowed to own one. English was banned in official proceedings; judges were appointed by the President and dismissed when their decisions were not to the government's liking.[9] In Cape Colony, by contrast, though not in Natal, the constitution was colour-blind. Africans had been granted the vote in 1853, seventeen years before the 15th Amendment in the United States prohibiting denial of the vote on grounds of race. The franchise was granted to males over twenty-one who owned property to the capital value of £75 or were earning an annual wage of £50. But land under tribal tenure was excluded and Africans living in the tribal areas were not enfranchised. In 1903, out of 135,168 voters in the Cape, 19,505 were non-white. Ramsay MacDonald believed that 'the native vote is the deciding quantity in seven constituencies returning two members each, and in several others it is of the greatest importance to candidates'.[10] But in no constituency

6   Printed in *The Mining Industry: Evidence and Report of the Industrial Committee of Enquiry*, Witwatersrand Chamber of Mines, 1897, pp. 574–5.
7   Roberts, *Salisbury*, p. 716.
8   F. A. van Jaarsveld, *The Afrikaner's Interpretation of South African History*, Simondium, 1964, pp. 7–8.
9   Roberts, *Salisbury*, p. 717.
10 James Ramsay MacDonald, *Labour and the Empire*, Associated University Presses, 1907, p. 56fn.

were Africans in the majority. The financial qualification for candidates, as distinct from voters, was more stringent, and no non-European was ever elected to the Cape Parliament during the period of its existence from 1853 to 1910. Non-Europeans were, however, occasionally returned in local elections.

In Natal, conditions were far worse for non-whites, even though in the British proclamation of 1843 annexing it, discrimination on grounds of race had been prohibited. Hardly any non-whites had the vote. The franchise was based on possession of £50 in property or payment of £20 annual rent – effectively excluding nearly all Indians and Africans. In 1896, Natal enacted legislation specifically disenfranchising all Indians not already on the voting rolls. Indians and Africans in Natal were also generally denied access to public educational facilities and their right to alcohol was restricted; workers were required to register when in a town and Indians could be arrested for not being in possession of a pass.[11] Chamberlain could have used the imperial power of disallowance to veto legislation enacting such measures, but he did not do so, on the grounds that he should not interfere with responsible government in a self-governing colony. That, however, seemed a lame excuse since Britain, as the suzerain power, had vetoed a law of the Transvaal in 1885 providing that all Indians be moved to special locations.[12]

The Transvaal had been forcibly annexed by Disraeli's government in 1877, a step towards creating a federation of South Africa. But the Boers took up arms against the annexation following Gladstone's return to power in 1880, and after the Boer victory at Majuba in 1881, Gladstone decided to come to terms with Afrikaner nationalism. Otherwise, he feared, the Transvaal would become another Ireland, held to the empire only by force. In the 1881 Pretoria Convention, the Transvaal was given a large degree of autonomy subject to British 'suzerainty', an ill-defined term, used in connection with the government of the Indian princely states. The London Convention of 1884, which superseded the Pretoria Convention, made no mention of suzerainty, but it did not explicitly renounce it. The Colonial Secretary Lord Derby had told the Lords on 17 March 1884 that the word had been avoided because it was not capable of precise legal definition but that nevertheless Britain maintained the 'right to veto any negotiations into which the dependent State may enter with foreign Powers'. The London Convention did, however, remove the previous royal veto on enactments specifically affecting Africans, much to the detriment of the African population. Most legal experts advised

---

11 H. R. Hahlo and Ellison Kahn, *The Union of South Africa: The Development of its Laws and Constitution*, Stevens, 1960, pp. 54fn, 71. I am grateful to Professor Christopher Forsyth of Cambridge University for this reference. Robert A. Huttenback, 'No strangers within the gates: Attitudes and policies towards the non-white residents of the British empire of settlement', *Journal of Imperial and Commonwealth History*, 1973, *passim*.

12 Huttenback, 'No strangers within the gates', p. 277.

that the effect of the London Convention was to revoke the preamble of the Pretoria Convention referring to suzerainty. Upon returning from London, the Boer delegates told their Parliament, the Volksraad, that they had secured the abolition of suzerainty, and the British did not revive the claim until 1897. But in a sense the argument over suzerainty was irrelevant. For it was not true, as was often to be alleged, that the Transvaal was made independent even in its internal affairs. The London Convention provided for internal independence only under certain conditions. Article 4 prohibited her from signing treaties with any foreign power with the exception of the Orange Free State, while Article 8 prohibited slavery; Article 9 provided for freedom of religion, a principle which the Transvaal government transgressed by prohibiting Catholics and Jews from holding office; Article 14 provided for equal rights for future non-African immigrants. All such persons 'conforming themselves to the laws of the South African Republic [as the Transvaal had been renamed] would have full freedom to enter, travel or reside within any part of the Transvaal, and would have rights relating to housing and commerce'. They would not be subject to any taxes other than those imposed on the burgher population. Kruger had promised in 1881 at the time of the Pretoria Convention that 'there will be equal protection for everybody ... We make no difference so far as burgher rights are concerned. There may perhaps be some slight difference in the case of a young person who has just come into the country.'[13] This promise too was flagrantly broken, especially in regard to taxation. British immigrants – the so-called Uitlanders – paid £16 to £20 for every £4 paid by the burghers. The Queen's Speech in August 1899 declared that 'the position of my subjects in the South African Republic is inconsistent with the promises of equal treatment on which my grant of internal independence in that Republic was founded'. Article 19 gave assurances to the African population, which was given the right to buy land, to access the courts and freedom of movement within the state. This too was ignored by the Transvaal.

The London Convention had been intended to maintain Britain's position as the paramount power in South Africa, whether or not that position was well described by the term 'suzerainty'. It was clear that the Transvaal was not a sovereign or independent state. Neither of the conventions had been between two equal powers. Both were grants from the queen, laying down the conditions under which Britain was prepared to tolerate Boer autonomy. The Boers, however, did not see the conventions in this light, and regarded the Transvaal as a sovereign independent state, the limitations in the London Convention being regarded as tiresome irritations soon to be removed. They

13   Whates, *Third Salisbury Administration*, p. 315.

hoped to erode them as they had eroded the Pretoria Convention; indeed, some wanted to drive the British out of South Africa entirely. Salisbury, by contrast, believed that the policy embodied in the conventions was appeasement of the worst sort and contained 'the most dangerous fault a policy can have ... It was an undue belief in the effect of amiable acts not supported by requisite strength'.[14] Since Britain had agreed the conventions after defeat in war, the Boers regarded them as a product of fear and believed that they could gradually whittle away the restrictions embodied in them. So the settlement of 1884 left ambiguous the key question of who was to be supreme in South Africa – the Boers or the British – and it was not clear how British interests could be protected against a recalcitrant Transvaal except by force.

The conventions of 1881 and 1884 were what Salisbury called an 'attempt at the Quakerisation of Mankind'.[15] Gladstone had hoped that by displaying goodwill, friendly relations could be achieved between the British and the Boers, so that the issue of supremacy need not be confronted. But his hope was not to be fulfilled. For the Boers were not susceptible to Quakerisation. They drew instead two lessons from the settlement of the 1880s. The first was that they had more to hope for from a Liberal rather than a Conservative government, and that hostile measures by the Conservatives might be undone by the Liberals. The second was that the British, once defeated in the field, would make concessions rather than continue the fight. But while the Boers thought that the settlement of the 1880s imposed too many constraints, the British were coming to believe that they imposed too few. 'Some day or other', Salisbury had told the Lord Mayor of London in 1885, 'that terrible blunder [the concession of Boer autonomy] would have to be repaired.'[16] Hardly anyone in Britain, even on the left, favoured the complete independence of the Transvaal, fearful of the consequences not only for British prestige but for the African population. Most were prepared to accept Boer autonomy provided that it could be reconciled with imperial interests.

A modus vivendi might have been achieved had it not been for the discovery of gold on the Rand in 1885. This brought wealth to the Transvaal, making it the economic centre of the region and a magnet for the rest of South Africa. By 1899, the Transvaal had been converted from the poorest part of South Africa to the richest and was the source of one-quarter of the world's gold supply. This made it easier for the Transvaal to remain free of the British orbit, indeed to draw the rest of South Africa into her own orbit. With her new wealth, the fear in Britain was that she would lead a movement

---

14 House of Lords Debates, 27 July 1899, vol. 75, col. 662.
15 Roberts, *Salisbury*, p. 716.
16 Uzoigwe, *Britain and the Conquest of Africa*, p. 40.

towards a republican federation in South Africa, threatening Britain's naval base at the Cape. In 1896, Lord Selborne, Under-Secretary for the Colonies, asked his colleagues in the government whether South Africa would develop into another Canada, united as part of the empire, or whether the British colonies would secede as the United States had done.[17]

The discovery of gold had led to a large immigration of so-called Uitlanders – largely English speaking – into the Transvaal, the white population doubling between 1880 and 1890, and settling primarily in the new town of Johannesburg. There was no census in the Transvaal until 1904, and so there are no precise statistics on the proportion of Uitlanders in the white population. It is probable that the Boers outnumbered them, though not greatly, but it may be that, amongst adult males, Uitlanders outnumbered the Boers since adult males comprised a larger percentage of the Uitlanders than of the Boer population.[18] In Johannesburg itself, the Uitlanders almost certainly outnumbered the Boers. By the time of the first census in 1904, the Uitlanders had come to be in the majority amongst the white population, but that was after around 10 per cent of the Boer population had been killed in the Boer War, and after heavy Uitlander immigration following the conflict.

The Uitlanders were, in the eyes of the Boers, of alien culture, and they spoke a different language. They were urban, whereas the Boers were predominantly agrarian. The 'veldt' remained Dutch while the Rand became British. But the Uitlanders made the Transvaal rich, her revenue rising from £177,876 in 1885 to £3,983,560 by 1898.[19] The Uitlanders contributed the bulk of this revenue – Johannesburg paid around nineteen-twentieths of the total taxation – and were liable for military service, but they were granted neither citizenship nor voting rights, and the official language of the Volksraad remained Dutch. So there was a divide between those who governed and those who provided the revenue. Kruger, one contemporary writer declared, had 'his right hand on the throat of the British Uitlander and his left hand in the latter's pocket'.[20]

The Boers feared that the Uitlanders would threaten their autonomy and quiet, agrarian way of life. Critics of British policy were apt to dismiss the Uitlanders as mainly millionaires, and some used the racialist argument that there were many Jews amongst them, as if millionaires and Jews were not as deserving of protection as everyone else. In fact, as was to be shown in a petition of protest, signed by 40,000, the Uitlanders comprised people from many classes – workmen as well as merchants, traders and professional people,

17 Iain R. Smith, 'A century of controversy over origins', in Donal Lowry, ed., *The South African War Reappraised*, Manchester University Press, 2000.
18 Iain R. Smith, *The Origins of the South African War, 1899–1902*, Longman, 1996, p. 47.
19 C. 9345, p. 226.
20 H. Whates, 'Mr Chamberlain', *Fortnightly Review*, 1900, p. 741.

there were not 40,000 capitalists or 40,000 Jews in the Transvaal – and the conventions gave them an absolute right to immigrate. The Boers believed that, if they gave the Uitlanders voting rights, they would be swamped, and then incorporated into a British-dominated South Africa. That indeed was the aim of Cecil Rhodes, Prime Minister of Cape Colony from 1890 to 1896. He hoped to achieve a federal union in South Africa as the prelude to a larger union of the empire, by means of a customs union with the Boer republics. The Orange Free State did in fact enter into such a customs union, but the Transvaal, under President Kruger's intransigent leadership refused. Rhodes was infuriated. All that stood in the way of a federal South Africa, so Dr Jameson, his close associate, told an audience at the Imperial Institute in 1894, was 'a handful of Transvaal Boers'.[21] Kruger, for his part, feared that the Uitlanders would try to achieve by stealth what Disraeli in 1877 had sought to achieve by force. To protect herself, the Transvaal began to form closer relations with Germany, which had established colonies in south-west Africa, in what is now Namibia, and in East Africa, in what is now Tanzania. In response, Lord Ripon, Colonial Secretary in the Rosebery government, had in 1894 annexed a strip of land between Swaziland and the sea, closing Boer access to the ocean and making it more difficult for the Transvaal to form links with Continental powers or to import arms. But in January 1895, on the kaiser's birthday, Kruger greeted him, declaring that he would 'ever promote the interests of Germany, though it be but with the resources of a child, such as my land is considered'. 'This child,' Kruger went on to say, 'is now being trodden on by one Great Power, and the natural consequence is that it seeks protection from another. The time has come to knot ties of the closest friendship between Germany and the South African Republic – ties such as are natural between father and child.'[22] Kruger wanted Germany to be the protector of the Transvaal. But the introduction of a foreign power into South Africa would clearly threaten British supremacy. Rhodes was to claim that it was Kruger's greeting on the kaiser's birthday that had convinced him of the need for intervention in the Transvaal, intervention which was to come about in the form of the Jameson Raid.[23]

THE JAMESON RAID

Seeing no possibility of redressing their grievances by peaceful means, some of the Uitlanders began to plan a rising against the Transvaal government.

---

21 Jean van der Poel, *The Jameson Raid*, Oxford University Press, 1951, p. 24. The Prince of Wales was in the audience.
22 Excerpt from speech of 27 January 1895, reported in *The Times*, 14 February 1896.
23 House of Commons, Second Report of the Select Committee on British South Africa, HC 311, 1897, 15 February 1897, Q 19.

Rhodes encouraged them. He was not only Prime Minister of Cape Colony but also managing director of the British South Africa Company. He assisted the Uitlanders in two ways. First, he paid for arms and ammunition to be smuggled into the Transvaal to aid the rising, using for this purpose the De Beers Company of which he was a principal director.[24] Second, he planned to assist the rising through armed intervention from outside in support of it. Then Sir Hercules Robinson, High Commissioner for South Africa who was stationed in Cape Town, would go to Pretoria, the Boer capital, together with Rhodes, to 'restore order' and act as arbitrator. A provisional government for the Transvaal would be established, elected by the votes of all adult white males, i.e. including the Uitlanders. That government would decide whether the Transvaal should be directly ruled from London or be given responsible government as part of a federal South Africa. Either way, the autonomy of the Transvaal would come to an end.

For a raid from outside to be possible, it was necessary for Rhodes to acquire the Pitsani Strip in the Bechuanaland Protectorate as a jumping-off point, Pitsani being the nearest place from outside the Transvaal to Johannesburg. Rhodes would station an armed police force from the British South Africa Company in the strip to invade the Transvaal once the rising had begun. He accordingly sought from the British government permission to annex the protectorate, a crown colony, to the British South Africa Company. That would deny Germany control of Bechuanaland, also denying her a land link with the Transvaal. In 1895, the Rosebery government had taken Tongaland – now called Maputaland – under British rule, cutting off one possible outlet to the sea for the Transvaal. Rhodes wanted to build a railway linking the Cape with Rhodesia – now Zambia and Zimbabwe – to the north of the Transvaal, strengthening the British hold on the interior and further enclosing the Boer republics within British territory. The railway was given as the reason for requesting the transfer of territory; but it was as much a pretext as a reason. The request had first been made to the Rosebery government, which may, so it seems, have agreed to it in principle, though the evidence is conflicting. But permission was not in fact given until the Unionists had returned to power. Three African chiefs appealed to London against the transfer, not wishing to live under Rhodes's South Africa Company. 'There is no government that we can trust other than that of the Great Queen,' they said.[25] In response, Chamberlain ensured that African reserves were excluded from the transfer. So the northern part of the protectorate was not transferred, much to

---

24 Ibid., p. vii.
25 Christopher Saunders, 'African Attitudes to Britain and the Empire Before and After the South African War', in Lowry, ed., *The South African War Reappraised*, p. 142.

Rhodes's annoyance, and was to remain under imperial control, as the chiefs had desired, until becoming the independent country of Botswana in 1966. The southern part, however, was transferred to the company, becoming part of Cape Colony, and it included the Pitsani Strip.

In November 1895, Chamberlain authorised Sir Hercules Robinson to release the Bechuanaland Border Police from imperial control and allow it to transfer its services to the British South Africa Company. The British government knew that there would probably be a rising – that indeed was hardly a secret in Johannesburg – but wanted to ensure the armed force which would come to the aid of the rising was neither under imperial control nor operating from imperial territory. This meant, however, that the nature and timing of the intervention would be determined by Rhodes and his chartered company. Chamberlain had conceded these powers to a body over which neither he nor the British government had any control. There was, admittedly, nothing illegal in stationing a force on the border of the Transvaal, with instructions to move after a spontaneous uprising so as to ensure its success. But although there was spontaneous pressure for a rising, it was being financed and armed by Rhodes and by his partner, Alfred Beit; and the force on the border was subject to the orders of the company, not the British government. That was where the illegality arose, and Chamberlain was complicit in it. He transferred the Pitsani Strip to the company, knowing its purpose, and was almost certainly aware of the activities of Rhodes and Beit.[26]

The raid was to be led by Dr Leander Starr Jameson, an associate of Rhodes, who had been made administrator of the territories in Bechuanaland that had been transferred to the company. In November 1895, Jameson travelled to Johannesburg and secured an undated letter from the leaders of the reform movement there calling upon him for assistance in the event of a rising. The letter declared that 'the position of thousands of Englishmen and others is rapidly becoming intolerable', and drew attention to a franchise petition signed by nearly 40,000, ending by saying that 'we feel constrained to call upon you [Jameson] to come to our aid should disturbance arise here'. This became known as the 'women and children' letter, since it referred to the danger that 'thousands of unarmed men, women, and children of our race ... will be at the mercy of well-armed Boers'. Despite the invitation to intervene, the letter was composed 'at a time when there was no apparent indication of any serious outbreak in Johannesburg'.[27]

26 Robert Blake, 'The Jameson Raid and "The Missing Telegrams"', in Hugh Lloyd-Jones, Valerie Pearl and Blair Worden, *History and Imagination: Essays in Honour of H. R. Trevor-Roper*, Duckworth, 1981, pp. 327–8. This essay provides the best short account of the Jameson Raid.
27 Report of Select Committee of the Cape of Good Hope House of Assembly on the Jameson Raid into the Territory of the South African Republic, C. 8380, 1897, para. 18.

But the plan went wrong. The rising in Johannesburg did not occur, whether because the Uitlanders got cold feet or for some other reason is unclear. Rhodes told Jameson to wait. But Jameson did not wait. On 29 December 1895, he made an impulsive incursion into the Transvaal with around 500 armed men and a strong force of artillery, saying, 'Clive would have done it.' *The Times* in London then published the 'women and children' letter. The hope was that the raid would instigate the rising in Johannesburg. But there was still no rising. Perhaps, as has been suggested in another context, it was 'as sensible to rely upon millionaires to stage a successful revolt as it is to enter a carthorse to win a Derby'.[28] Johannesburg remained quiet and the raid was a fiasco. After four days, Jameson and his men surrendered to Boer troops. Kruger treated the leaders of the raid with leniency, commuting death sentences, and releasing all but two of the conspirators on payment of a large fine. He embarrassed the British government by releasing Jameson for trial in Britain rather than prosecuting him in Pretoria. Jameson was sentenced in London to fifteen months' imprisonment for violating the Foreign Enlistment Act, but his health seemingly broke down in prison and he was released after four months. He was, however, to prove remarkably resilient and his health recovered rapidly, as did his political position. Indeed, Jameson was to become Prime Minister of Cape Colony from 1904 to 1908. Kipling's famous poem 'If' was composed in 1895 as a tribute to him. The light sentences imposed on the raiders did nothing for Britain's international reputation.

The British government disavowed the raid, which appeared as an act of aggression against a friendly territory, disclaiming responsibility for it. But the kaiser added fuel to the flames by sending Kruger a telegram congratulating him for 'defending the independence of the country against attacks from without', and without needing to summon the aid of any friendly power, the implications being, first, that the Transvaal was in fact an independent state and, second, that Germany would have assisted her if asked to do so. Germany had in fact wanted to send a naval detachment to Pretoria as a demonstration of support, but the Portuguese had refused landing facilities. Kruger, replying to the kaiser, told him that he relied on God, not the great powers! The German ambassador in London asked if the British government had approved of the raid – if it had answered in the affirmative, the ambassador had been instructed to send for his passports.[29] Britain moved rapidly to deprive the Transvaal of hopes of German support, concluding, in 1898, a secret treaty with Germany providing for the division of the Portuguese

---

28 Nicholas Mansergh, *Nationalism and Independence: Selected Irish Papers*, Cork University Press, 1997, p. 245.
29 Garvin, *Chamberlain*, vol. 4, p. 94.

colonies in the event that these proved economically unsustainable in return for Germany agreeing not to challenge British supremacy in South Africa.

There were of course suspicions that Chamberlain and Sir Hercules Robinson, the High Commissioner, were complicit in the raid. It would seem surprising if Sir Hercules could remain unaware that a group of armed men were gathering on the frontier of the Transvaal when it was an open secret in Johannesburg that a rising was being prepared. Writing in 1897, James Bryce, the former Liberal Cabinet minister, who had visited the city in 1895, reported:

> Never before was there except on the stage so open a conspiracy ... The visitor had hardly installed himself in a hotel at Pretoria before people began to tell him that an insurrection was imminent, that arms were being imported, that Maxim guns were hidden ... The knowledge that an insurrection was impending was not confined to the Transvaal. All over South Africa one heard the same story; all over South Africa men waited for news from Johannesburg, though few expected the explosion to come so soon. One thing alone was not even guessed at. In November it did not seem to have crossed any one's mind that the British South Africa Company would have any hand in the matter.[30]

Sir Hercules seemed guilty of, at the very least, culpable ignorance. Had he in fact known, it would have been his duty to tell Chamberlain and prevent the illegal conspiracy; and, if he had foreknowledge and was implicated, Robinson would not, as an accomplice, have been a plausible arbitrator, a role that needed the confidence of both parties to the conflict. It became apparent when his private secretary's papers were made available in 1946 that Robinson had in fact been told of the conspiracy by Rhodes, and had planned his arbitration with Rhodes, the leading conspirator. After talking to Rhodes, Robinson significantly told his private secretary, 'the less you and I have to do with these damned conspiracies of Rhodes and Chamberlain the better'. Nevertheless, Robinson ordered his secretary to allow troops of the chartered company to go to Pitsani. When the private secretary expressed his worries to Rhodes, the latter retorted, 'Then you are disloyal to your chief, Chamberlain, who is hurrying me up.'[31] This was not revealed to the various inquiries.

There were, then, suspicions as to Chamberlain's involvement. When he heard of the raid, on 30 December, the Colonial Secretary was at Highbury,

---

30 James Bryce, *Impressions of South Africa*, Macmillan, 1897, p. 425.
31 Van der Poel, *Jameson Raid*, p. 76.

his Birmingham home, preparing for an end-of-year ball. His immediate response was, 'If this succeeds it will ruin me. I am going up to London to crush it,' and he took a late train to London to condemn the raid, instructing Sir Hercules to denounce it as 'an act of war or rather filibustering'. This, it was said, proved his innocence. For he condemned the raid before he knew that it would fail – when, indeed, it might appear that it could succeed.

That, however, did not prove lack of involvement or complicity. Chamberlain could legitimately deny that he had been aware of a raid and then a rising. For no one except Jameson could have known that there would be a raid before the rising, since the plan was for the raid to occur *after* the rising, not before. And not even Jameson knew that there would be a raid but no rising. So Chamberlain could, with seeming plausibility, deny foreknowledge. The key questions, which the Select Committee into the raid was hardly to consider, were quite different. They were whether Chamberlain had helped encourage the rising by being aware of, and doing nothing to prevent, illegal smuggling of arms into the Transvaal, and whether he helped encourage the raid by agreeing to the cession of part of the Bechuanaland Protectorate, knowing that Rhodes wanted it for the purpose of making an armed incursion into the Transvaal. The evidence strongly suggests that Chamberlain was 'guilty' on both counts. In 1897, Chamberlain wrote to a correspondent:

> You put me on my honour ... The fact is I can hardly say what I knew and what I did not. I did not want to know too much. Of course I knew of the precautions, the preparations, if you like, in view of the expected trouble in Johannesburg, but I never would have imagined that Jameson would take the bit between his teeth.[32]

The conspiracy was almost certainly known both to Chamberlain and also the Colonial Office. The Permanent Secretary, Sir Edward Fairfield, told Robinson's private secretary that 'he had written to Mr Chamberlain at Birmingham suggesting that the revolution should be damped down. Chamberlain had replied telling him to hurry it up on account of the Venezuela dispute.'[33] A telegram to this effect was sent to Rhodes and shown to Robinson on 20 December. This telegram was not produced at any of the inquiries and appeared to be 'missing'. But when it seemed that there might not be a rising after all, Chamberlain did warn both Rhodes and Robinson against forcing the pace, threatening revocation of the British South Africa

32 Garvin, *Chamberlain*, vol. 3, p. 83.
33 Van der Poel, *Jameson Raid*, pp. 71–2.

Company's charter. Unfortunately, this warning reached them after Jameson had already set out.

The Commons Select Committee inquiry into the raid found Rhodes guilty but exonerated Chamberlain. However, many were sceptical and the report came to be dubbed 'The Lying in State at Westminster'. The eccentric Radical Henry Labouchère dissented and issued a minority report. But the official Liberal opposition concurred with the Unionists in the report, content perhaps to secure a verdict against Rhodes and not appreciating the weight of evidence against Chamberlain. However, the Rosebery government did not have entirely clean hands either. Indeed, Rosebery appeared himself to have been privy to the raid, warning Rhodes 'that the police must not move till after the rising'.[34] In addition, the combined effect of the Kruger telegram and crisis with the United States over Venezuela made Britain appear isolated and under threat from foreign powers, and this was not the time to sow dissension. But there may have been a deeper reason for Liberal ambivalence. The aim of the rising in Johannesburg, after all, was to secure the vote for British subjects. Ironically, had the Uitlanders been granted citizenship by the Transvaal, they would no longer have been British subjects, and Britain would no longer have been under a duty to protect them. Balfour declared that while the raid was 'inexcusable', 'difficulties must arise with a State whose inhabitants are so arbitrarily divided between those who pay and those who govern'.[35] The Liberals had, historically, been the party of voting rights and civil liberties, supporting Greeks in Crete and Armenians in Turkey who were rebelling against Ottoman domination, while Garibaldi had been a Liberal hero. Were Liberals to be in favour of all those seeking the vote except British subjects in South Africa? The response might have been that the evils of the Transvaal were not on the same scale as those in Italy under Austrian rule or Crete under Ottoman rule, and that a policy of peaceful persuasion made more sense than an attempt at a violent overthrow. But such an argument, which could be portrayed as anti-patriotic, was difficult to present to the British public. The Liberals could easily be characterised as friends of every country but their own. So they were bound to be circumspect in condemning the raid.

At the time, the consequences of the raid seemed profound both in Britain and in South Africa. Asquith, the former Home Secretary and a rising star in the Liberal Party, declared at Trowbridge in May 1896 that it 'had cast a moral stain upon the moral title of Great Britain to be the paramount

---

34 Leo McKinstry, *Rosebery: Statesman in Turmoil*, John Murray, 2005, p. 405.
35 Dugdale, *Balfour*, vol. 1, p. 170.

power in South Africa'.[36] Significantly, he did not doubt that Britain had the right to be the paramount power, only that this right must be secured by moral means. That presumably meant using friendly persuasion to convince the Transvaal to alter her ways. But the obloquy attaching to Britain after the raid made it more difficult for such persuasion to be exerted with any hope of success.

In South Africa, the raid confirmed Kruger's view that the demand for Uitlander voting rights was but a cover for the destruction of Boer self-government, and he was strengthened against his more moderate opponents. In 1897, he signed a treaty of alliance with the Orange Free State, and in 1898 was triumphantly re-elected to the presidency by a large majority – in 1893, by contrast, he had only narrowly won re-election against a more liberal opponent. After the raid, he began rapidly to rearm. The raid, therefore, seemed to make it more difficult to achieve a satisfactory settlement of the conflict.

But perhaps, even without the raid, conflict could not have been avoided. Kruger was hardly likely to consent to British supremacy, while Britain would not have consented to the Uitlanders remaining second-class citizens. Perhaps indeed the raid was as much a consequence as a cause of conflict between the Boers and the British; and perhaps the realities were much less affected by it than was commonly believed at the time.

SIR ALFRED MILNER AND THE UITLANDERS

After a hiatus following the raid, Britain renewed pressure on Kruger to grant political rights to the Uitlanders, claiming both that she had a general right to protect her subjects and also that Article 14 of the London Convention (providing that immigrants should not be taxed more heavily than the indigenous population) gave her a specific right. It was, moreover, customary for most civilised states to grant full citizenship rights to those willing to accept naturalisation after a short probationary period. In the Orange Free State, by contrast with the Transvaal, those of British origin enjoyed voting rights and English was recognised as an official language.

In 1890, under the impact of what it regarded as an Uitlander invasion, the Volksraad had enacted a law requiring fourteen years' residence before a foreigner could acquire voting rights. In 1894, a further measure was passed making it virtually impossible for Uitlanders to obtain the vote. In the Commons in October 1899, Haldane was to compare their position to

---

36   *The Times*, 11 May 1896.

that of Irish Catholics before the Union.[37] In May 1894, 13,000 Uitlanders petitioned the Transvaal government for the franchise; and in April 1895, 32,500 signed a second petition. Both were ignored. Some Afrikaners shared Britain's view that Kruger was breaching the spirit if not also the letter of the terms on which peace had been granted after Majuba. Sir Henry de Villiers, Afrikaner Chief Justice of the Cape, told President Steyn of the Orange Free State in May 1899:

> I am quite certain that if in 1881 [i.e. at the time of the Pretoria Conven-
> tion] it had been known to my fellow-Commissioners that the President
> would adopt his retrogressive policy, neither President Brand [the then
> President of the Orange Free State], nor I would ever have induced them
> to consent to sign the Convention.

They would have advised Britain to let matters revert to the condition before peace was concluded; in other words to recommence the war. De Villiers went on that it had been

> suggested to me by Sir Evelyn Wood [second in command of the British
> Army at Majuba], that the Transvaal might show its hatred of the Britisher
> by subsequently making the franchise almost prohibitive, but I indignant-
> ly scouted the idea. He reminded me of the remark the year before last and
> I felt that I had been in the wrong.[38]

In February 1896, Chamberlain invited Kruger to London for talks, and suggested that if he would not extend the franchise to the Uitlanders, Home Rule for the Rand would be acceptable as an alternative to provide some measure of self-government for the Uitlanders. Kruger rejected this, declaring that it would amount to creating a state within a state. He said that he would come to London provided he could discuss the removal of Article 4 of the Convention of London, prohibiting the Transvaal from signing treaties with any other state except the Orange Free State, a restriction which Kruger regarded as having 'no more cause for existence' and being 'injurious to the dignity of an independent Republic'.[39] Chamberlain, however, refused to consider this, and Kruger responded that he would not then come to London. The exchange between the two men crystallised the opposed positions of the two sides. Kruger was prepared to reform the franchise provided the Transvaal

---

37 House of Commons Debates, 19 October 1899, vol. 77, col. 316.
38 Evelyn Wrench, *Alfred Milner: The Man of No Illusions, 1854–1925*, Eyre & Spottiswoode, 1958, p. 173; Cd 369, p. 1; Garvin, *Chamberlain*, vol. 3, p. 401.
39 Garvin, *Chamberlain*, vol. 3, p. 130.

became independent. Britain would never concede this and insisted that the rights of the Uitlanders could not be part of a bargain. It proved impossible to reconcile these two positions.

In February 1897, Sir Hercules Robinson, a dying man, was replaced as High Commissioner by Sir Alfred Milner (1854–1925). Robinson had been sceptical of Rhodes's militant policy, though too feeble to combat it with any effect. He had been a force for moderation. Milner, by contrast, was in full sympathy with Chamberlain's policy and indeed came to believe that the Colonial Secretary was too restrained in his approach.

Sir Alfred had enjoyed a remarkable career. Born in Germany of a German father and English mother, he had opted for British nationality, which was granted by virtue of a statute of 1773, repealed in 1914, allowing naturalisation for someone whose grandfather was British. But his temperament, according to one critic writing in 1936, 'conformed far more to a German than an English type'.[40] Brought up in comparatively modest circumstances – he often claimed that he was born with a copper spoon in his mouth – he had won a scholarship from a London day school to Balliol, academically the pre-eminent Oxford college at the end of the nineteenth century, where he had befriended Asquith.[41] At Oxford, he had a brilliant career, gaining a double first and becoming president of the union. After brief sojourns at the Bar and journalism, he was appointed in 1884 private secretary to Goschen, who became his patron. In 1885, he fought Harrow unsuccessfully as a Liberal but, like Goschen, became a Liberal Unionist. Between 1889 and 1892, he worked as a financial administrator in Egypt, on which he wrote a well-received book, *England in Egypt*. He then served, between 1892 and 1897, as chairman of the Board of Inland Revenue, where he won the admiration of Sir William Harcourt, the Chancellor of the Exchequer. He played a major role in preparing Harcourt's 1894 Budget, radically increasing death duties and establishing them on a graduated basis, so that larger estates were to pay a greater proportion than smaller ones. Having shown that he could work with both Unionists and Liberals, Milner was offered the posts of Permanent Secretary of the Home Office and the Colonial Office. But he declined both, believing that his destiny lay in South Africa.

At Oxford, Milner had been taught by the idealist philosopher T. H. Green and had fallen under the influence of the Master of Balliol, Benjamin Jowett, and the economic historian Arnold Toynbee. These thinkers taught him that the old liberal doctrine of non-interference was inadequate, and

---

40 Ensor, *England*, p. 217fn.
41 J. Lee Thompson, *Forgotten Patriot: A Life of Alfred, Viscount Milner of St James's and Cape Town, 1854–1925*, Fairleigh Dickinson University Press, 2007, p. 27.

that those in positions of leadership had an obligation of public service. He developed a creed of imperial socialism. Although he had studied Marx and Lassalle, Milner's socialism was not that of the Labour Party, with its commitment to public ownership and equality, but a belief in social responsibility, in trusteeship. In 1883, he had been a founder of Toynbee Hall, an institution in which volunteers sought to combat poverty. But the duty of trusteeship was owed not only to those in Britain but also to those in the empire. Milner indeed was an imperial visionary, declaring that he had 'the fatal habit of seeing that there is a great deal to be said on both sides, and I am cursed with what is called a cross-bench mind'. But he then added, ominously, 'On one question, however, I have never been able to see the other side, and that is precisely this question of Imperial union.'[42] When he came to reconstruct South Africa after the Boer War, he would attract the devoted support of idealistic young men in what came to be called 'Lord Milner's Kindergarten'. But he had one fatal weakness. He lacked political sensitivity, what Lloyd George called 'a political nostril'.[43] Able and philanthropic, Milner saw himself as a philosopher king, knowing what was better for other people than they did themselves. Greatly admired by those who shared his beliefs, he had little popular support and seemed ill at ease in the world of democratic pressures and unruly party politics, believing that the empire should be above party and what he called 'that mob at Westminster'.[44] Indeed, he had contempt for most party politicians, if not for the very processes of representative government. Morley, a critic of imperialism, called him an 'imitation Bismarck'.[45] Sir Alfred found it particularly difficult to empathise with those from different backgrounds. In South Africa, he travelled widely and learnt Afrikaans; but he hardly mixed with Boers and had no Boer friends. Outside his close circle of friends and admirers, he was regarded as remote and unsympathetic. It is doubtful if, after the Jameson Raid, anyone could have conciliated an increasingly suspicious Kruger. But Milner was hardly the most suitable choice as a conciliator. He had been sent to South Africa, he believed, to ensure British supremacy, and did not undertake that task with much tact. Some have labelled the Boer War as 'Joe's war' and some have labelled it as 'Milner's war', something which Milner would himself not have disputed, since he told Lord Roberts, commander-in-chief of the British Army, in June 1900, 'I precipitated the crisis, which was inevitable, before it was too late. It is a not very agreeable, and in many eyes, not very creditable piece of business to have been largely instrumental

---

42 Garvin, *Chamberlain*, vol. 3, p. 144.
43 A. M. Gollin, *Proconsul in Politics: A Study of Lord Milner in Opposition and in Power*, Anthony Blond, 1964, p. 363.
44 Brand, 'Lord Milner and General Smuts', p. 651.
45 Searle, *Quest for National Efficiency*, p. 116.

in bringing about a big war.'[46] But perhaps the causes of war were such that no individual could have prevented it. And policy was made not by Milner alone, nor even by Chamberlain alone, but by the Cabinet, which broadly shared Salisbury's view that the fundamental issue was not only the rights of the Uitlanders but also British supremacy in South Africa.

Milner did not at first believe the conflict would lead to war. He hoped that, provided Britain did not repeat the weakness of Majuba, Kruger would meet Uitlander grievances. But he also sought to improve the position of the African population. In November 1897, he wrote to Asquith:

> In spite of Majuba, in spite of Jameson, I remain firmly of the opinion that, if it were not for my having some conscience about the treatment of the blacks, I personally could win over the Dutch ... You have only to sacrifice the n***** absolutely and the game is easy ... Deep down in the heart of every Dutchman in South Africa is the ideal of a white land-owning aristocracy resting on slave labour (of course the word 'slave' is carefully eschewed, nor do they exactly want slaves, but simply the cheap labour of the black proletariat without any rights of any sort or kind).[47]

Milner hoped to avoid armed conflict. 'While we meant to be masters,' he said,

> and to exclude foreign interference, we have not the least wish to take away their local independence ... We have put our foot down and we must keep it there ... We should be very patient with them, very conciliatory, remembering how much excuse they have for regarding us with suspicion ... And from war with England I believe even the most violent of the reactionaries will shrink, as they have shrunk already, if such a contingency stares them in the face.[48]

But his hopes of a peaceful settlement soon evaporated. Writing to Bryce in May 1898, he declared that his

> opinions have been somewhat modified by a year of South Africa. While I still, by personal temperament, sympathise with, and fully appreciate the arguments for a policy of patience, and while, such being my orders, I shall loyally carry it out, I am less hopeful than I was of an ultimate

---

46 Quoted in Thomas Pakenham, *The Boer War* [1979], Abacus, 1997, p. 113.
47 John Wilson, *CB: The Life of Sir Henry Campbell-Bannerman*, Constable, 1973, p. 300.
48 Despatches to Chamberlain, 5 May 1897, 2 August 1897, quoted in Garvin, *Chamberlain*, vol. 3, pp. 349, 350.

solution on these lines ... Two wholly antagonistic systems – a mediaeval race oligarchy, and a modern industrial state, recognising no difference of status between various white races – cannot permanently live side by side in what is after all one country. The race-oligarchy has got to go, and I see no sign of its removing itself.

In July 1898, he told Chamberlain that he had come to doubt that Britain could be 'masters' without war.[49] But British supremacy did not mean that the British would be 'masters' in the sense of denying the Boers rights in a Transvaal which was part of the empire, any more than the French were denied rights in Canada. In Cape Colony, the Dutch majority had equal rights with the British. The difference between Boer and British supremacy would be that, with Boer supremacy, the British would be second-class citizens, while with British supremacy, the Dutch would be equal citizens and the Africans, though remaining very much second-class citizens, would have greater rights than under the Boers, living under the protection of the law and enjoying voting rights, albeit very limited. But, as we shall see, the Africans were to be betrayed as British governments, both Unionist and Liberal, became desperate to conciliate the Boers after the war.

Kruger and many other Boers did not understand the evolution of British opinion under Milner, believing that the British having once accepted defeat, after Majuba, would do so again. The Boers did not appreciate the strong sentiment amongst Unionists to avenge Majuba.

In April 1897, Chamberlain asked Kruger to repeal recent Transvaal legislation, the Aliens Immigration and Aliens Expulsion Acts, which he declared were contrary to Article 14 of the London Convention. Chamberlain backed up his demand with a naval demonstration in Delagoa Bay and strengthened the British garrison in South Africa. Harcourt, the Liberal leader, denounced this as a 'war policy', declaring that the greatest breach of the London Convention had come from those preparing the rising and the raid. This seemed to put an end to bipartisanship, and confirmed Kruger's view that, playing a waiting game, he would get better terms from Liberals than from Unionists. Kruger, however, agreed to repeal one of the Acts and revise the other, so confirming Chamberlain and Milner in their view that the Boers would back down under pressure. But Kruger continued to rearm and took steps which made Uitlanders believe that their rights were being further eroded. In 1897, it was enacted that future resolutions of the Volksraad would have the force of law and would not be subject to review by the High Court. The Chief Justice protested but was dismissed in February 1898, appealing unsuccessfully

---

49 Quoted in Smith, *Origins of the South African War*, pp. 191, 207

to Britain as 'the Suzerain Power' against dismissal. He was later to say, 'If you want anything out of the old man [Kruger], you must take him by the throat and then you'll get it; he's just a wily old Kaffir chief.'[50] That was also coming to be the opinion of Chamberlain and Milner. The Volksraad also prepared a new municipal law for Johannesburg with voting qualifications favouring the Boers, and wide discretionary powers for the burgomaster, appointed by the government, who could be dismissed by the President and had to be a Boer. Half the members of the council were to be Boers, although there were apparently just 1,039 male adult Boers in Johannesburg and 23,503 Uitlanders. In addition, the government would be able to veto resolutions of the council, and its minutes would be in Dutch only.

The Uitlanders had further long-standing grievances. The police and jurors were drawn entirely from the Boer population. By contrast with both the Orange Free State and Cape Colony, where English and Dutch were on a basis of equality, lessons in most schools in the Transvaal, towards which Uitlanders paid taxes, were taught in Dutch after the fourth school year. So English speakers were obliged to provide schools at their own expense.[51] Government consent was needed for open-air meetings, which could be limited 'in the interest of public order'. In practice, Boers were given full rights to hold public meetings, Uitlanders were not.

Milner believed that the best approach to Uitlander grievances was not to search 'for causes of complaint', nor to 'fuss about trifles', but instead to work 'steadily and inflexibly ... for the redress of substantial wrongs and injustices'. It would then 'not be difficult to work up an extremely strong cumulative case'. The difficulty, however, was that, as Chamberlain had declared in February 1896, 'since the Convention of 1884 Her Majesty's Government have recognised the South African Republic as a free and independent Government as regards all its internal affairs not touched by the Convention', and the franchise was not specifically mentioned in the convention. But equal rights for future immigrants was prescribed in Article 9 and Milner believed that Britain could appeal to 'the inherent right of every nation to protect its subjects against injury by foreigners'.[52] He feared that the Boers would not fulfil their obligations 'unless they are forced to it'. But Chamberlain replied that there should be no pressure until the 'irritation' caused by the raid had passed, and that, consequently, a 'waiting game' was best, since

time must be on our side. The mis-government in the Transvaal will in the

50 Ibid., pp. 187, 271.
51 C. 9345. Papers Relating to the Complaints of British Subjects in the South African Republic, June 1899, pp. 66–71, 184ff.
52 Garvin, Chamberlain, vol. 3, p. 128.

long run produce opposition within its borders, and when the present rule of President Kruger comes to an end, as it must do before many years are over, we might confidently look for an improvement in the position.

There were also foreign policy difficulties with France, Russia and Germany, not to mention complications following the recapture of Sudan, and on the north-west frontier of India. In a despatch to Milner on 19 March 1898, Chamberlain insisted that 'the principal object of Her Majesty's Government in Africa at present is peace. Nothing but a most flagrant offence would justify the use of force.' Milner replied, three days later, insisting that it was not possible to 'acquiesce permanently in the situation of having a strong and bitter enemy for ever seated on our flank, only waiting for the occasion of our being definitely involved elsewhere in order to fly at our throats'.[53]

In late 1898, the Uitlanders petitioned the queen. Uitlander leaders who had called a meeting at which the petition was presented for signature were arrested for unlawful assembly and released only after heavy bail was paid. Milner was absent in London when the petition was received in Cape Town, and the commanding officer of the British forces in South Africa refused to transmit it to London. In March 1899, however, a second petition was signed by around 22,000 Uitlanders. Milner believed that if he failed to transmit this, he would seem indifferent to their fate. Shortly before the petition reached London in mid-April 1899, Milner sent a despatch declaring that 'the spectacle of thousands of British subjects kept permanently in the position of helots, constantly chafing under undoubted grievances and call-ing vainly to Her Majesty's government for redress, does steadily undermine the influence and reputation of Great Britain and the respect for the British Government within the Queen's Dominions'. Britain, he declared, had, for too long, adopted a policy of non-intervention in the hope that the injustices of the Uitlanders would be remedied. But that had not happened, and their position had worsened. Milner disclaimed any intention of seeking to absorb the Transvaal. 'It could be made perfectly clear', he wrote, 'that our action was not directed against the existence of the Republic. We should only be demanding the re-establishment of rights which now exist in the Orange Free State, and which existed in the Transvaal itself at the time of and long after the withdrawal of British sovereignty.'[54]

The second petition, together with the 'helots' despatch, posed a dilem-ma for the British government. To reject the petition would be to disclaim concern for British subjects. To accept it and press for reform would raise the

---

53 Ibid., pp. 364–70.
54 C. 9345, p. 212.

possibility of war. Chamberlain believed the petition impossible to ignore but sought 'to avoid anything in the nature of a definite threat which would commit us to ulterior action'. Britain, therefore, should be content with a friendly remonstrance. Milner should put to Kruger the arguments for reform and disclaim any intention of having designs upon the autonomy of the Transvaal.[55] Chamberlain told Milner to confer with Kruger at Pretoria, but President Steyn of the Orange Free State invited them both to Bloemfontein, and from 31 May to 5 June 1899, Milner and Kruger met there in conference. Chamberlain did not publish the 'helot' despatch until the conference had ended.

Milner believed, and Chamberlain accepted, that the best way to deal with Uitlander complaints was not to emphasise specific instances of discrimination but to concentrate on securing the vote, so that the Uitlanders could themselves remedy their grievances. The franchise would obviate the need for further British remonstrances concerning, for example, public meetings, the police, the courts or the schools. It would therefore avoid irritating interference on detailed matters. The aim, then, was to secure immediate and substantial Uitlander representation. And it was believed that a request for the franchise was less of an interference in the affairs of the Transvaal than requests in relation to, for example, the police, the courts or the schools. But Kruger saw no reason why he should accept a British remonstrance. To him, and to most Boers, conceding the franchise would lead to the Transvaal being swamped by Uitlanders. Britain could only back up her remonstrance by threatening force; but then it would no longer be a friendly one. Kruger, for his part, was prepared to make real concessions on the franchise only if Britain would recognise the Transvaal as a sovereign independent state.

At Bloemfontein, Milner proposed a five-year retrospective franchise with a property qualification, together with extra seats for the Rand in the Volksraad, so that Uitlanders would be admitted immediately to full citizenship and voting rights. He stressed that Uitlanders were not asking for proportionate representation, since the Rand, with the extra seats, would still have only one-quarter of the total number, far less than they were entitled to proportionally. Kruger responded by proposing naturalisation for newcomers after two years and the franchise after a further seven. Those resident for two years or more would be immediately naturalised and would gain the franchise in five years. In addition, Kruger proposed that future disputes be settled by arbitration.

Milner responded that the principle of two stages towards citizenship was unacceptable, since Uitlanders would have to surrender their British

---

55 Garvin, *Chamberlain*, vol. 3, p. 393. Chamberlain memorandum for the Cabinet, 28 April 1899.

nationality and remain in stateless limbo for five years before being enfranchised. They would have obligations but no rights. Chamberlain agreed with Milner, telling him after the end of the conference, 'No Franchise Reform will be accepted which does not give the Uitlanders some genuine representation in the First Volksraad [the main legislative chamber] at once. Reforms that are postponed are of no value.'[56] Moreover, the proposed grant of the franchise was so hedged with administrative complications that Milner doubted whether in practice more than a small handful of Uitlanders would actually be enfranchised, for the executive would be able to veto the grant of a franchise to any individual, without right of appeal. Milner believed that the Kruger proposals were 'expressly designed to exclude rather than admit the newcomer. Practically speaking, the proposed law leaves the granting of the franchise almost entirely in the hands of either the officials or of the Government.'[57] Milner also rejected arbitration by foreign countries which a paramount power could not accept. He was, however, prepared to accept arbitration by the Judicial Committee of the Privy Council in London with the addition of Afrikaner judges. Too late to affect the outcome of the conference, Britain promised to guarantee the autonomy of the Transvaal once the franchise issue had been settled.

But the conference appeared deadlocked, and Milner ended it, which he later regretted. Chamberlain telegrammed, urging that the conference continue, but his telegram reached Milner after he had ended the conference. The truth was, however, that neither side trusted the other, and they were not as close to agreement as they seemed. While Kruger regarded his concessions as a final offer, the Cabinet, and not least Salisbury, saw them as a starting point for further negotiations. Salisbury was more hawkish than Chamberlain, who was prepared to settle – or at least to abandon the threat of force – on the Bloemfontein terms, although he would have preferred a five-year qualification. Kruger, for his part, was becoming convinced that, as he told Milner at Bloemfontein with tears in his eyes, 'It is our country you want.'[58] That, however, was not the case. Even under the most liberal scheme of franchise reform, the Boers would have remained in the majority in the Volksraad, since the Uitlanders were largely confined to the Rand. Not even the most liberal scheme of redistribution could have given the Uitlanders majority representation. Even so, it seemed that the dispute would be settled peacefully. The Assistant Under-Secretary at the War Office told Milner:

---

56 Chamberlain to Milner, 31 June 1899, C. 9415. Further Correspondence Relating to Proposed Political Reforms in the South African Republic, July 1899.
57 C. 9415, p. 54. The administrative problems are discussed in C. 9415, pp. 14ff.
58 Garvin, *Chamberlain*, vol. 3, p. 407.

The marvellous feature is the icy indifference, not only to Transvaal questions, but to *all* matters, in the House of Commons and in the Country
generally ... One feature is marked & that is a decided disinclination to
embark in war about anything ... You will know Chamberlain's mind. I
do not, but he is freely credited with an absolute resolve not to fight ...
He knows that a Government which goes to war loses the next election as
a matter of course.[59]

Nevertheless, Chamberlain raised the temperature in a speech on 26 June
1899, given to the Birmingham Liberal Unionist Association, declaring that,
in 1881, when the Pretoria Convention was being prepared, Kruger had
been asked 'by our representatives what treatment would be given to British
subjects in the Transvaal. He said, "All strangers have now and will always
have equal rights and privileges with the burghers of the Transvaal."' That
pledge had of course been made before the discovery of gold and the arrival
of the Uitlanders. Chamberlain insisted that the franchise issue had to be
resolved and that 'having undertaken this business we will see it through'.[60]
On 18 July, the Volksraad enacted a measure seemingly implementing Kruger's Bloemfontein proposals, granting Uitlanders a seven-year retrospective
franchise and five seats in the Volksraad (out of a total of thirty). Although
Milner had rejected these terms, Chamberlain now seemed prepared to
accept them, writing to Milner, 'I congratulate you on great victory. No one
would dream of fighting over two years in qualification period, and President
of South African Republic will have been driven by successive steps to almost
exact position taken by you.' But the proposals appeared, on examination,
less favourable than they had seemed at first sight. Only those who had been
naturalised for nine years would get the franchise immediately. They would
be joined by a small number in five years, and perhaps more in seven years.
But to secure the vote, Uitlanders would have to surrender their British
nationality for no immediate benefit. In addition, the proposals required a
certificate from local officials for citizenship to be granted, and it seemed that
the officials were not to be given any precise criteria for judging applications,
nor required to give reasons for rejection. Since the Boer administration
was not independent of the executive, this hardly appeared satisfactory. *The
Times* on 14 July dismissed the proposals as 'a mockery'. The British in South
Africa, both in the Cape and the Transvaal, agreed, some saying that acceptance would amount to a second Majuba. Milner soon appreciated that the
proposed reform was accompanied by unacceptable conditions, involving

59 Eric Stokes, 'Milnerism', *Historical Journal*, 1962, pp. 55–6.
60 Garvin, *Chamberlain*, vol. 3, pp. 415–16.

not only administrative restrictions on granting the vote but also foreign arbitration. Chamberlain proposed a joint inquiry to consider the Boer proposals, which Kruger rejected as infringing on his country's autonomy. In the Commons, Campbell-Bannerman, who had become Liberal leader in 1899, declared that there was no cause for war on the difference between seven and five years – an over-simplification of the causes of the conflict – and that Britain should not go to war in order to hurry British citizens into another citizenship. Nevertheless, when the parliamentary session ended in July 1899, war did not appear likely, since the British government continued to believe that the Transvaal would back down under pressure. In addition, the patrician element in the Cabinet – Salisbury, Balfour and Hicks Beach – were fearful of the expense and additional taxation needed to finance a war. The government, far from being aggressively imperialist and bent on expansion, sought to avoid war, not only because it did not believe that it would be supported by public opinion but also because the British public did not appear interested in the plight of the Uitlanders.

Seemingly to avoid pressure for a joint inquiry as proposed by the British, J. C. Smuts, the 29-year-old Transvaal state attorney who was in the following century to play a large a role both in South African history and in the history of the British Empire and Commonwealth, presented on 13 August a new and startling set of proposals. Smuts proposed broadly what Milner had sought at Bloemfontein – a five-year retrospective franchise with a quarter of the seats in the Volksraad for the Uitlanders and equal rights in electing the President. Once more there was hope that the crisis was over. Chamberlain, when he first heard of the offer, wrote to Milner telling him that the Smuts proposals constituted

> an immense concession and even a considerable advance on your Bloemfontein proposals. I think it will be a great advantage to get this offer formally made in writing ... You must avoid any language which would lead the South African Republic to think that we are determined to pick a quarrel.

But then on 22 August, it appeared that conditions had been added. These were that the current intervention of Britain was not to be regarded as a precedent, that there would be no further mention of suzerainty and that there would be arbitration for future disputes. There were also concerns that administrative conditions attached to the proposals for naturalisation and franchise would nullify their effect. In the Commons on 19 October, shortly after the war had begun, Chamberlain quoted the Liberal MP for South

Shields, William Robson QC, who was to become Solicitor General in the 1905 government, that the Act passed by the Volksraad embodying the Smuts proposals was 'a grotesque and palpable sham. I doubt whether 200 or 300 Uitlanders could be found who could honestly fulfil its conditions.'[61]

Chamberlain replied to the Smuts proposals by letter on 28 August. He insisted that they be examined to ensure that they would in fact provide for immediate and substantial representation for the Uitlanders, declaring that if a joint inquiry was unacceptable, the British agent in Pretoria should examine them before they were presented to the Volksraad. In addition, assurances were needed that the English language could be used in the Volksraad. On the question of further intervention, Chamberlain, while hoping that none would be necessary, declared that Britain could not divest herself of rights under the Pretoria Convention. Nor what Chamberlain called 'the ordinary obligations of a civilised Power to protect its subjects in a foreign country from injustice'.[62] On some other matters in contention, Britain was prepared to accept arbitration so long as this did not involve any foreign element other than that of the Orange Free State. There were also, admittedly, some matters that were not suitable for arbitration, but these, hopefully, could be resolved at a further conference. Chamberlain later told the Commons that what he had in mind were the rights of Indian and black British citizens in the Transvaal, who would almost certainly choose to remain British citizens, as well as certain boundary issues. The fact that these matters were not specified either at Bloemfontein or in Chamberlain's reply to the Smuts proposals might well have made the Boers believe that, despite Chamberlain's assurances, Britain was in fact contemplating further intervention even after Uitlander grievances had been resolved. In addition, Britain was suspected of hypocrisy in her concern for African rights. For the rights of non-white British citizens in Natal, the only part of South Africa with a British majority amongst the white population, had been raised in the Commons in 1896, when the Natal government had proposed legislation discriminating against Indians. The British government had then said that it could not intervene in a self-governing colony. The Transvaal, however, was more than a self-governing colony but autonomous and not part of the British Empire. Largely for this reason, Chamberlain did not press the African question on the Transvaal, though it was used to help persuade humanitarian opinion in Britain that the Boer War was justified.

Chamberlain added fuel to the flames in a provocative speech at a Unionist

---

61 House of Commons Debates, 19 October 1899, vol. 77, col. 292.
62 Chamberlain to Milner, 28 August 1899, C. 9521, Further Correspondence Relating to Political Affairs in the South African Republic, September 1899, p. 50.

rally in Birmingham on 26 August, two days before he was to reply to the Smuts proposals. 'Mr Kruger', Chamberlain declared,

> procrastinates in his replies. He dribbles out reforms like water from a squeezed sponge; and he either accompanies his offers with conditions which he knows to be impossible, or he refuses to allow us to make a satisfactory investigation of the nature and character of these reforms ... The issues of peace and war are in the hands of President Kruger and of his advisers ... Will he speak the necessary words? The sands were running down in the glass ... The knot must be loosened ... or else we shall have to find other ways of untying it.

A way had to be found to secure conditions 'which once for all shall establish which is the Paramount Power in South Africa'. Chamberlain insisted that he had no designs on the autonomy of the Transvaal but declared that if Britain had to go to war, her proposals would be withdrawn, and he implied that the republic would then be annexed. He made this speech because he and others in the government were coming to believe that Kruger was procrastinating while building up arms supplies and seeking foreign support for a conflict with Britain. His purpose was to tell Kruger that the questions at issue needed to be settled rapidly.

Despite his provocative tone and his reservations listed in the despatch of 28 August replying to the Smuts proposals, it is probable that Chamberlain still expected a constructive response. And he was not, as many assumed at the time and have continued to assume since, carrying out a policy of his own. His policy was at all times that of the Cabinet and indeed on occasion Salisbury was more hawkish than his Colonial Secretary.[63] Chamberlain's letter of 28 August was in fact more conciliatory than others in the Cabinet had wished.[64] He no doubt assumed that the Transvaal would climb down from conditions that he regarded as unacceptable, just as it had climbed down on the Aliens Immigration and Aliens Expulsion Acts. But that legislation had not been thought to endanger the autonomy of the Transvaal. Kruger believed that he had made a substantial concession, the only result of which had been to encourage further British demands. On 2 September, the Transvaal declared that the Smuts proposals had lapsed, claiming that the response to them showed that the British government would not be satisfied with a settlement of the franchise question along the lines which her government

---

63 This is clearly established in A. N. Porter, 'Lord Salisbury, Mr Chamberlain and South Africa, 1895–9', *Journal of Imperial and Commonwealth History*, 1972.

64 A. N. Porter, *The Origins of the South African War: Joseph Chamberlain and the Diplomacy of Imperialism 1895–1899*, Manchester University Press, 1980, p. 228.

had herself proposed at Bloemfontein. This confirmed the British view that the Smuts proposals were insincere, setting conditions which it had been well aware that London would not accept and a mere device to gain time.

Events now moved rapidly. The Cabinet formulated its own proposals for settlement in the form of an ultimatum. This required the repeal of all Transvaal legislation since 1881 that had prejudiced the position of Uitlanders, who, until then, had enjoyed: equal citizenship after one year's residence; representation in reasonable proportion to numbers but with safeguards for the Boers against being swamped; full rights in municipal elections; guarantees for judicial independence; the removal of religious discrimination against, for example, Catholics and Jews; a tribunal of arbitration for points of difference, excluding any foreign element; most-favoured-nation rights for British subjects; the limitation of excessive arms imports; and an end to the free passage of arms through Portuguese territory. Salisbury had wanted to go further and insist upon unilateral disarmament by the Transvaal, but Chamberlain was prepared to accept limitation of arms, another indication that Salisbury was more hawkish than his Colonial Secretary. In return, Britain would guarantee the Transvaal against attack from any part of the British Empire and from any foreign power.

But the British ultimatum was never sent. The Boers, anticipating it, sent their own, demanding, within forty-eight hours, agreement to the withdrawal of all British troops from her borders as well as all troop reinforcements that had arrived since 1 June 'within a reasonable time', and agreement that British troops now on the high seas should not be landed in any port in South Africa. The Boers knew of course that such demands could never be accepted, since no government could agree to restrict the movement of its own troops on its own territory. With the expiration of the Boer ultimatum on 11 October, Transvaal together with the Orange Free State, against whom Britain had no cause for conflict, declared war on Britain and invaded Natal. Significantly, most of the Boers in Cape Colony did not support their co-nationals in the Transvaal.

Contrary to what is often suggested, there is no evidence that the government was divided in its policy, nor that it was pushed into war by popular opinion. In November 1899, following a speech by Salisbury at the Guildhall, a friend of Sir Almeric Fitzroy, Clerk of the Privy Council, 'seemed surprised at what he called the absence of war enthusiasm in the vast audience'. Fitzroy himself commented:

To my thinking, the note struck by all the speakers, and responded to by the company, was not that of the exultation that goes with a light-hearted effervescence of feeling, often mistaken for enthusiasm, but rather the deep conviction of a solitary necessity expressing itself in unflinching resolution and unswerving purpose, a determination all the more emphatic because so sternly repressed.[65]

Fitzroy had been familiar with the course of the negotiations and could 'say with certainty that the hopes of a pacific solution of the difficulty were almost to the last moment as strong with the Government as their determination to work for it'.[66]

In Britain, there was a general belief that the war would be brief and that Britain would be rapidly victorious. Milner did not share this view, writing to the Colonial Office that 'the Empire is about to support the greatest strain put upon it since the [Indian] Mutiny'.[67] He was right.

THE CAUSES OF THE WAR

Why did it prove impossible to resolve the dispute by peaceful means, when it had seemed as recently as three months before that a settlement was within reach? After war had broken out, it was said that nine different answers had been given to the question of why Britain was at war. The grievances of the Uitlanders were undoubtedly real and genuine, and constituted an injustice, but were perhaps not as desperate as some of their supporters suggested. They were not such as to inhibit immigration to the Transvaal. Nor did they prevent most Uitlanders from living peaceful and stable lives while profiting from the goldfields. They could not be said to be in any real or immediate danger. Their plight was hardly to be compared with that of Greeks in Crete or Armenians in Turkey. Chamberlain himself was more worried in private concerning the strength of the Uitlanders' position than he was prepared to admit in public. On 2 September 1899, one month before the war, he told Milner:

Our clients the Uitlanders and the British in the Colonies [i.e. Cape Colony and Natal] are not wholly without reproach. The former are unfortunately identified with money-making – with the Raid – and are not supposed to be capable of much self-sacrifice even for a holy cause – and the latter are quite too ready to take all the profits of a war in the shape of Imperial expenditure, while doing nothing themselves but shouting on

65 Fitzroy, *Memoirs*, vol. 1, p. 24.
66 Ibid., p. 29.
67 Lowry, ed., *The South African War Reappraised*, p. 1.

every occasion that they will cut the painter if the Imperial Government does not do everything they want and do it as quickly as they consider possible and desirable.[68]

The Conservative Campaign Guide for the 1900 election declared that 'the moral rights of the question were with the Uitlanders; but legally and technically they and their allies were hopelessly in the wrong'.[69]

In a minute dated 8 April 1896, Chamberlain had declared, 'I am not at all anxious for war, and do not believe that it will come.' One month later, he told the Commons, in prescient words, that a war in South Africa

> would be one of the most serious wars that could possibly be waged. It would be in the nature of a Civil War. It would be a long war, a bitter war, and a costly war, and … it would leave behind the embers of a strife which I believe generations would hardly be long enough to extinguish … to go to war with President Kruger in order to force reforms in the internal affairs of his State, with which successive Secretaries of State, standing in this place, have repudiated all right of interference, that would have been a course of action as immoral as it would have been unwise.

In an undated memorandum written between June and October 1896, he wrote, 'I shall never go into such a war with a light heart, and at the present time we have no reason either of right or interest which would justify the enterprise … I do not believe there will be war.'[70] But Chamberlain 'was sure', as he told the queen in May 1897, 'that the Transvaal would ultimately come back to us, it could not help doing so, whatever we might wish. It was to be hoped this would happen peacefully and not by a war.'[71]

Milner, however, believed that time was not on Britain's side. He saw the Transvaal strengthening its defences and seeking alliances with foreign powers, particularly Germany. He also believed that there was growing disaffection amongst the Dutch in Cape Colony, fed by a sense that Britain was weakening, and that Kruger would exploit this to undermine the British position in South Africa.

But other observers took the contrary view that time was in fact on Britain's side. Kruger was, after all, an old man (seventy-four in 1899) and would not be in charge of the Transvaal for much longer – he was in fact to die in 1904. The younger Boers, who would have replaced him, and in particular

---

68 Garvin, *Chamberlain*, vol. 3, p. 458; Chamberlain to Milner, 2 September 1899.
69 Quoted in Roberts, *Salisbury*, pp. 639–40.
70 Garvin, *Chamberlain*, vol. 3, p. 138.
71 Buckle, ed., *Letters of Queen Victoria*, 3rd series, vol. 3, p. 157, extract from the queen's journal.

Smuts, seemed less intransigent. 'Impatience', Hicks Beach had told Milner in March 1897, shortly before he left for South Africa, 'has been at the root of our difficulties – the premature annexation of the Transvaal – the Zulu war – the abandonment of the Transvaal – the Jameson Raid – all were due to it.'[72]

Once war had broken out, Chamberlain told the House of Commons that he had come to believe that armed conflict was inevitable. For the issue was not just the rights of the Uitlanders. There was a larger problem. In a memorandum for the Cabinet on 6 September 1899, he declared:

> What is now at stake is the position of Great Britain in South Africa – and with it the estimate formed of our power and influence in the Colonies and throughout the world … it depends upon the action of the British Government now whether the supremacy, which we have claimed so long, and so seldom exerted, is to be finally established and recognised or for ever abandoned.

To Milner, he wrote:

> The majority of the people here, as I believe, recognised that there is a greater issue than the franchise or the grievances of the Uitlanders at stake, and that our supremacy in South Africa and our existence as a great Power in the world are involved in the result of our present controversy.[73]

The war, therefore, was fought not only or even primarily to secure Uitlander rights but to ensure British supremacy in South Africa. But the difficulty with the doctrine of supremacy, of the paramount power, a doctrine which Chamberlain was wont to compare to the Monroe Doctrine, was its vagueness. It could, seemingly, be used to justify quite wide-ranging intervention in the internal affairs of the Transvaal. That no doubt was what Kruger and his supporters feared. Indeed, Britain seemed to be seeking the equivalent of a Monroe Doctrine in South Africa.

In 1904, the head of the South Africa Department of the Colonial Office was to write a minute on the Uitlanders. They

> seem to think that we went to war solely on their behalf, and that they are therefore entitled to get everything they ask. The fact is that we were driven to war by the consistently hostile attitude of the South African Republic on almost every point of controversy, only one of which was the treatment

---

72 Quoted in Smith, *Origins of the South African War*, p. 157.
73 Garvin, *Chamberlain*, vol. 3, pp. 458, 459.

of the Uitlanders. It is true that the question of the franchise for the Uitlanders was put in the forefront during the latest round of our disputes,
but it was as a means to an end – not the end itself.[74]

A conflict over Uitlander grievances could in theory have been settled by
a bargain, giving the Uitlanders voting rights, but limited so as not to undermine the Boer character of the Transvaal. That indeed was what Milner
and Chamberlain had proposed at Bloemfontein. Instead, the conflict had
become one about supremacy, and a conflict between two contending nationalisms could not be resolved by bargaining. Chamberlain had come to
believe – no doubt correctly – that the Boers were not prepared to recognise
British supremacy. Kruger, for his part, had come to believe – no doubt
equally correctly – that the British government was not prepared to recognise
the internal autonomy of the Transvaal, something he believed had been
secured at the London Convention. So, while agreement might have been
reached on the franchise, it could not be reached on supremacy. Kruger,
like Chamberlain, had come to believe, according to Smuts, that war had
become 'unavoidable' – 'not because there is any cause, but because the
enemy is brazen enough not to wait for a cause'. Smuts told Hofmeyr, a
Cape Dutch leader:

> Our people throughout South Africa must be baptized with the baptism
> of blood and fire before they can be admitted among the other great peo-
> ples of the world … Of the outcome I have no doubt. Either we shall be
> exterminated or we shall fight our way out and when I think of the great
> fighting qualities that our people possess, I cannot see why we should be
> exterminated.[75]

The Boers, of course, were in no danger of being 'exterminated'.

The war divided the Liberals from the beginning. Indeed, it would almost
break up the party, and led in the country to a resurgence of support for
Rosebery. On 19 October 1899, a Liberal backbencher Philip Stanhope proposed an amendment criticising the conduct of the negotiations. Ninety-four
Liberals voted for it, but Campbell-Bannerman and forty-one other Liberals
abstained while fifteen voted with the government. In July 1900, an amendment by Sir Wilfrid Lawson denouncing the government's policy secured
the support of thirty-one Liberals; thirty-eight, including Grey, voted with
the government, while Campbell-Bannerman and Asquith, seeking to act as

---

74   Quoted in Ronald Hyam, 'The Partition of Africa', *Historical Journal*, 1964, p. 169.
75   Smith, *Origins of the South African War*, pp. 274–5.

unifiers, abstained, together with thirty-four other Liberals. Campbell-Bannerman in fact sympathised with critics of the government but felt it prudent as leader to suppress his private views so as to hold his party together.

Liberal divisions on the war were well described by the executive committee of the National Liberal Federation: 'There are some who hold that the war is just and necessary. Some that it is just but unnecessary, some that it is unjust but necessary, some that it is not unjust but unnecessary, some that it is both unjust and unnecessary.'[76] The first group of Liberals came to be known as Liberal Imperialists and comprised a number of the ablest younger leaders in the Commons – such as Asquith, Grey and Haldane. They argued that war had been forced upon Britain and that no lover of freedom need regret the absorption of the Boer republics into the empire. They criticised the Unionists for lack of preparation and mismanagement. They looked for leadership not to Campbell-Bannerman but to Rosebery, who had indeed coined the term 'Liberal Imperialism', declaring that Chatham had been the first Liberal Imperialist. But although comprising some of the party's most talented MPs, they were weak in the constituency parties, where the Nonconformist conscience remained strong. The second and third groups represented the centre of the party. The fourth group were the so-called pro-Boers. Campbell-Bannerman seemed to belong to the third group but gradually veered to the pro-Boer position. This position was powerfully expressed by John Morley in a speech on 15 September 1899, three weeks before the Boer ultimatum:

> Such a war will bring you no glory. It will bring you no profit but mischief, and it will be wrong. You may make thousands of women widows and thousands of children fatherless. It will be wrong. You may add a new province to your empire. It will still be wrong. You may give greater buoyancy to the South African stock and share market. You may create South African booms. You may send the price of Mr Rhodes's Chartereds up to a point beyond the dreams of avarice. Yes, even then it will be wrong.

The most prominent of the pro-Boers was to be Lloyd George. But they had little support in the country.

The term 'pro-Boer' was in a sense misleading. If the war was both unjust and unnecessary, it might seem to follow that the Boers were in the right and should be encouraged towards victory. That was the position of the Irish Party, which favoured Boer independence even though British troops in South Africa included many Irish soldiers, and even though the Irish

---

76 *Manchester Guardian*, 12 March 1900, quoted in John W. Auld, 'The Liberal Pro-Boers', *Journal of British Studies*, 1975, p. 82.

seemed so enthusiastic in their support for the war that Queen Victoria visited Dublin in April 1900 to express her appreciation. The attitude of the Irish Nationalists had an important political consequence. It confirmed the Unionist view that a Home Rule Ireland would be disloyal and therefore a danger to Britain and the empire. The Liberal pro-Boers were, however, more circumspect than the Irish Nationalists, not wishing to identify with a fundamentalist and racist regime in Pretoria, and avoided arguing for Boer independence. Morley avoided the dilemma by retiring from politics to write the biography of his hero, Gladstone.[77]

The pro-Boers could not easily 'oppose' the war, since it had been started by a Boer attack on British territory, and hardly any voted against supplies for the war. Campbell-Bannerman had accepted in a speech at Ilford in June 1899 that 'many of the complaints of the Uitlanders are well founded. They have not the municipal government, the police protection, the organised maintenance of order, the even-handed administration of justice, which in all civilised communities are regarded as the very elements of civil right and civil freedom.'[78] He told Harcourt on 10 October, the day after the Boer ultimatum, that he thought the franchise issue 'the biggest hypocrisy in the whole fraud', but he added

> as to the general power or responsibility of this country, it is no doubt vague, but I think it is substantial ... we have a stronger inducement or title to intervene than if it was merely the ill-treatment of some Englishmen at Calais. It is analogous, surely, to the right of the Powers of Europe to try and stop misgovernment in Turkey, which endangers general peace.[79]

In other words, he too accepted that the Uitlanders had serious grievances and that Britain had a duty to intervene. He did not deny that Britain needed to assert her supremacy. His argument was that it could have been achieved without war, through diplomacy and negotiation, but that was hardly plausible. Campbell-Bannerman believed that the government had made the mistake of mingling diplomacy with military preparations. There was nothing, so he had said in his Ilford speech just three months before the war, to justify warlike action or military preparations.[80] When Balfour asserted in the Commons that the Liberal leader believed the war to be 'a just war', Campbell-Bannerman replied, 'I did not say so,' leading to Balfour's riposte,

77 Taylor, *Trouble Makers*, p. 108.
78 *The Times*, 19 June 1899.
79 Porter, *Origins of the South African War*, pp. 261–2.
80 *The Times*, 19 June 1899.

'I never quite know where I have got the right honourable Gentleman.'[81] But Campbell-Bannerman did not say that the war was unjust either, and from the outbreak of the war he supported annexation of the Boer republics with self-government. So he did not in the early stages of the war ally himself with the pro-Boers. His position, even more than that of the pro-Boers, seemed equivocal, in part because he was so desperate to maintain party unity.

The critique of the Liberal Imperialists was the opposite to that of Campbell-Bannerman. They argued that diplomacy should have been backed up by a greater show of force, and that troops should have been sent out earlier to South Africa. Lord Wolseley, the commander-in-chief of the army, had also urged in June 1899 that more troops should be made ready for mobilisation. Lansdowne, who had been War Secretary, replied that he had not taken this advice, given 'on purely military grounds', because of 'the political circumstances of the moment'. The government had hoped that the concessions made by Kruger in regard to the franchise 'might be found the basis of a satisfactory settlement; and desiring, as we most earnestly did, that peace should not be broken, we determined that we would take at that time no steps which were of a distinctively provocative character'. Wolseley's policy, he said, 'if not a policy of provocation' was 'a policy of intimidation'.[82] This is clear evidence that the government sought to avoid war, not to precipitate it. The government had not in fact sent out reinforcements to South Africa until September, not wishing to make ostentatious military preparations so long as there was hope for a diplomatic solution, which it clearly wanted to achieve, even though Milner now believed that it was beyond reach.

The self-governing colonies outside South Africa – Canada, Newfoundland, the Australian states and New Zealand – supported Britain, and, in a striking display of imperial solidarity, sent troops to South Africa to assist. The Indian princes also offered help. But non-white troops were rejected as likely to offend Boer sensibilities. So were Catholics for the same reason.[83] The United States supported Britain. But on the Continent, criticism of Britain, portrayed as a bully seeking to crush the independence of two small states whose only offence was to lie in the way of an imperial juggernaut, was almost unanimous. The war revealed Britain's isolation in Europe, an isolation that no longer appeared particularly splendid.

Because British supremacy was not re-established in South Africa on a permanent basis, history has generally been kinder to opponents of the war than to supporters. It seems today that the Boer War was entered for motives

---

81 House of Commons Debates, 6 December 1900, vol. 88, col. 137.
82 House of Lords Debates, 15 March 1901, vol. 91, cols 10, 18,
83 Keith Jeffery, 'Kruger's farmers, Smuthcona's horse, Sir George Clarke's camels and the Kaiser's battleship: the impact of the South African War on imperial defence', in Lowry, ed., *The South African War Reappraised*, pp. 188–9.

later to be repudiated and conducted so inefficiently as to damage British prestige. It was fought for local gains which could not, in the long run, be preserved. 'The empire', it has been argued, 'went to war in 1899 for a concept that was finished, for a cause that was lost, for a grand illusion.'[84] But of course the government could not appreciate how transient the imperial experience would prove to be. The war would prove a crucial turning point in the evolution of the empire, and in the end it undermined the moral case for imperialism. Morley's verdict has resonated with later generations; Chamberlain's has not.

*   *   *

It would seem, at first sight, that the 30,000 burghers of the Transvaal would have little chance of success against the might of the British Empire. Kruger had hoped for an uprising by the Dutch against the British in Cape Colony. But only around 6,000 joined the Boers, the rest remaining loyal to Britain.[85] And, by the end of the war, 'perhaps one in four Boers still in the field was serving in the imperial forces'.[86] Kruger had also hoped that, if the Boers could make use of their initiative before British reinforcements could arrive, Britain might lose heart, as seemed to have happened after Majuba, or, alternatively, a Liberal government might come to power yielding a more generous settlement than was obtainable under the Unionists. Smuts believed:

> For six or seven years we shall be able to hold out in the mountains ... and long before that there will be a change of opinion in England. Other things will crop up, they will become tired and lose interest; there will be another general election and the Liberals will come into power.[87]

The Boers also hoped for help from friendly European powers. But by skilful diplomacy, Salisbury had isolated the Boers as he had isolated France during the Fashoda crisis. The Boer leaders had made a serious misjudgement, and their hopes were to prove illusory. Kruger in particular was wrong to believe that Britain's Bloemfontein proposals would have destroyed the autonomy of the Transvaal. For him, too, discretion would have been the better part of valour. He could have saved his people much misery by showing more goodwill and being contented with the limited but still substantial degree of autonomy that had been won after Majuba and which the British were still

---

84 Robinson, Gallagher and Denny, *Africa and the Victorians*, p. 461.
85 Hermann Giliomee, *The Afrikaners: Biography of a People*, Hurst, 2003, p. 249.
86 Donal Lowry, 'Introduction: Not Just a "Teatime War"', in Lowry, ed., *The South African War Reappraised*, p. 3.
87 Smith, *Origins of the South African War*, p. 204.

prepared to acknowledge. The alternative, as duly occurred, could only be a second annexation of the Transvaal and its incorporation into the British Empire. For Rosebery was expressing the general opinion when he wrote to *The Times* on 12 October 1899 that 'without attempting to judge the policy which concluded peace after the reverse of Majuba Hill ... there is no conceivable Government in this country which could repeat it'.

While Britain was entangled in South Africa, the world was changing and posing new challenges for British foreign policy. But for the time being, these new challenges did not disturb the Unionist government, which seemed supremely confident both in its foreign and in its domestic policies.

CHAPTER 4

UNIONISM CONFIDENT
AND TRIUMPHANT

In his election address in 1895, Balfour had proposed various reforms – Poor Law reform and old-age pensions, improved housing for the working classes, the exclusion of 'pauper aliens', reform of the registration system, redistribution and even the referendum.[1] None were to be implemented by the 1895 government. Contrary to what Chamberlain had hoped, the Unionists achieved little in the way of social reform. Amidst the mass ranks of Conservatives uninterested in it, he had little leverage. As Salisbury had perceived, social reform would divide Unionists while resistance to Home Rule united them. Remarkably, the most enlightened reforms occurred in Ireland, with a generous land purchase measure and the establishment of a democratic system of local government. But for the rest of the United Kingdom, there were only two reforms of note: the Workmen's Compensation Act of 1897 and the London Government Act of 1899. There was a Bill providing for much-needed reforms in education, but it fell foul of sectarian squabbles and had to be withdrawn, although aid to the extent of five shillings per pupil was provided for the financially hard-pressed voluntary denominational schools, primarily Anglican. The government also gave the Anglican clergy partial relief from rates levied on the tithe rent-charge. The Liberals and their Nonconformist supporters protested vigorously at what they claimed was aid to the clerical friends of the government. 'The squire and the parson', declared Lloyd George, somewhat rhetorically, 'have broken into the poor box and divided its contents among them.'[2]

The Unionists also helped the agricultural interest to combat the agricultural depression and consequent fall in prices by enacting in 1896 an Agricultural Rates Act, reducing by half the rates paid on agricultural land and buildings and providing for a grant of £1.1 million for five years to areas supplementing the rates. Liberals denounced this as 'a dole to the landed interest', even though it had been recommended by a majority in a Royal Commission established by the last Gladstone government. But Liberals now complained that it benefited rich farmers as well as poor. Rosebery said

---

1   Anon., 'The paralysis of Parliament', *Quarterly Review*, October 1901, p. 608.
2   Grigg, *Young Lloyd George*, p. 216.

that it would have been better simply to lower agricultural rents, but a House of Lords heavily dominated by the landed interest would hardly be likely to accept such a proposal. The Act was explicitly intended to be temporary and was followed by the establishment of a Royal Commission on local taxation. Liberals argued that the Royal Commission should have come before not after the legislation.

THE WORKMEN'S COMPENSATION ACT

The legislation on education and agricultural rating benefited Conservative supporters and was denounced by Liberals as class legislation. That accusation could not be levelled against the Workmen's Compensation Act of 1897. It was introduced into the Commons by the Home Secretary, Sir Matthew White Ridley, but it also bore the names of the Attorney General and of Chamberlain. It was in fact Chamberlain's Bill and indeed his last major legislative achievement. It offered, Chamberlain believed, 'a great opportunity'. So far the Unionists had, in his view, 'thrown sops to sections, but we have established no principle, and above all, we have not justified the claims made for the Conservative Party that it has always been the first in social reform'.[3] During the 1895 election campaign, Chamberlain had called for 'a Compensation Act for workmen, irrespective of cause of accident', and in 1894 he had said that the victims of industrial accidents should be regarded as 'the wounded soldiers of industry'. On this, Salisbury agreed. He endorsed the principle of compulsory insurance, first put forward by Lord Randolph Churchill in 1880, and declared in the Lords on 8 December 1893:

> If I could have my way I should like to see insurance made universal on the principle ... that it should apply to all accidents to whatever cause they are due – whether they are due to the negligence of the men or not – and I would gladly see the State giving its aid in order to provide the machinery for carrying such into effect.[4]

The Act provided for compensation for *all* accidents, however caused, on a basis of mutual and compulsory insurance. But employers could contract out, so long as they offered an alternative compensation scheme certified by a friendly society as offering benefits at least as favourable as those provided for in the legislation. The Act was to apply to the railways, the factories, the mines and the

---

3   Chamberlain to Matthew White Ridley, 11 February 1897, Chamberlain Papers 6/3/3/13, quoted in Holding, 'Third Salisbury Cabinet', p. 68.
4   David G. Hanes, *The First British Workmen's Compensation Act, 1897*, Yale University Press, 1968, pp. 90–91; W. C. Mallalieu, 'Joseph Chamberlain and Workmen's Compensation', *Journal of Economic History*, 1950, p. 46.

quarrying and engineering industries – agriculture was added in 1900. It excluded industries in which little machinery was used such as shipping and domestic service. But in 1906, Campbell-Bannerman's Liberal government extended the insurance principle to all trades. The 1906 Act was also to provide compensation for diseases in dangerous occupations and for less serious accidents.

The Workmen's Compensation Act of 1897 provided for liability without fault, so-called strict liability. Previous legislation, such as the 1880 Employers Liability Act, had provided compensation only when negligence by the employer could be proved. The 1897 Act, by contrast, broke the link between personal moral culpability and legal liability on the basis that many serious accidents at work were not attributable to negligence but were, as Chamberlain put it, 'inherent in the work itself'. It was for this reason that, in 90 per cent of cases of injury, there had been no right of compensation, since negligence, never easy to define, could not be proved. Chamberlain therefore believed that there should be a 'recognition of the universality of the right to compensation' as 'the only equitable and indeed the only logical principle'.[5] Absence of fault on the part of the employer would no longer absolve him from legal liability. He would therefore have to purchase insurance, and so, in future, the cost of accidents would be treated as a cost of production after the fashion of, for example, the depreciation of capital assets. The ultimate cost, no doubt, would be borne by the consumer.

The Act remained the main basis for compensating injured workers and their dependants for fifty years, and its principles were to be adopted in many other countries. Indeed, one commentator has claimed that the 'adoption of similar laws in all English-speaking countries is a tribute to the originality and political genius of Joseph Chamberlain'.[6] A Liberal coal owner and MP, Sir James Joicey, declared of the legislation:

> No more important Bill had been introduced during the last fifty years, and if he had been told some time ago that a Conservative Government would introduce a measure of such a character he would have been staggered by the information. There was more Socialism pure and simple in the Bill than in any Bill which had been submitted for the last half-century.[7]

It was this 'socialism' that annoyed Conservative peers such as Lord Wemyss, founder and leader of the Liberty and Property Defence League. But an irritated Balfour responded by saying, 'If you perpetually cry out "socialistic"

5 Joseph Chamberlain, 'The Labour Question', *Nineteenth Century*, 1892, quoted in Mallalieu, 'Joseph Chamberlain', p. 51; Garvin, *Chamberlain*, vol. 3, pp. 155–6.
6 Mallalieu, 'Joseph Chamberlain', p. 57.
7 Garvin, *Chamberlain*, vol. 3, p. 158.

whenever an Act for the benefit of the people is introduced, you do not weaken the socialist propaganda ... you destroy the arguments which will be used against it.'[8] The Conservative Party was in fact more statist at the end of the nineteenth century than it was to be at the end of the twentieth.

The Act seemed open to criticism not as being 'socialistic' but because of the provisions for contracting out enabling employers to establish private insurance funds towards which both employers and employees would contribute. Such arrangements gave employers greater control over their workforce, since an employee would be unwilling to seek alternative employment if it meant losing benefits from an accumulated insurance scheme to which he had contributed. For this reason, the trade unions were suspicious of contracting out, fearing that it could lead to intimidation of the workforce; and the Webbs regarded this provision as 'in many ways inimical to Trade Unionism'.[9] But contracting out gradually disappeared after 1897.

The Act was acceptable to employers, precisely because it did not impose heavy obligations upon them. But it did much less than was hoped to improve safety in the workplace. The Liberals argued that the Act was insufficient since compensation for accidents was of secondary importance. The priority should be the *prevention* of accidents, whereas the Act was concerned solely with compensation *after* they had occurred. By allowing employers to escape liability for negligence through insurance, the Act gave them no incentive to take extra care to prevent accidents. Increasing safety in the workplace would have meant supplementing the Act by drawing a statutory distinction between negligent and non-negligent employers, and making negligent employers legally liable. That would have forced employers to improve workplace safety. It would, of course, have imposed a greater cost on employers. As the Webbs wrote in their book *Industrial Democracy*, 'the setting aside of a few hundred pounds a year to form a fund out of which to pay compensation for occasional workmen's accidents, is a flea-bite compared with the cost and trouble of adopting elaborate precautions that might totally prevent their occurrence'.[10] A departmental committee appointed to inquire into the effects of the Act reported in 1904 that 'no evidence has been brought before us which enables us to find any great improvement in the direction of safety is to be placed to the credit of this Act'. It went on to state that 'some of the evidence rather points in the opposite direction'.[11]

---

8 House of Commons Debates, 29 July 1897, vol. 51, col. 1436.
9 Quoted in V. Markham Lester, 'The Employers' Liability/Workmen's Compensation Debate of the 1890s Revisited', *Historical Journal*, 2001, pp. 474, 481. This paragraph and the following are based on this article.
10 Quoted in ibid., p. 474.
11 Report of the Departmental Committee Appointed to Inquire into the Law Relating to Compensation for Injuries to Workmen, Cd 2208, 1904, p. 764.

It is indeed possible that the Act led to an actual reduction in workplace safety, since some employers, having paid an insurance premium, felt no sense of responsibility towards their employees.[12] Injuries to the workforce had become little more than a small extra cost on production. Even so, the Act did constitute a recognition, however minimal, of the duties of an employer towards his workforce. George Barnes, a leading member of the newly formed Labour Party, was to declare in 1906 that, even with its 'defects and blemishes', the Act had proved 'one of the best bits of social legislation that had been put on the Statute Book in recent years'.[13]

THE LONDON GOVERNMENT ACT

The other major reform of the Unionists, with the exception of reform in Ireland, was the 1899 London Government Act, providing for a system of local government in the capital broadly similar to that established as long ago as 1835 in municipal boroughs through the Municipal Corporations Act.

London was an anomaly in terms of local government. Remarkably, until 1855, there had been no organised local government in London at all. The only London-wide body was the Commissioners of Sewers. Otherwise, the government of London was carried on by vestries, haphazardly established by local Acts of Parliament as if London were a country parish. Then, in 1855, the Metropolis Management Act established directly elected administrative vestries and indirectly elected groupings of parishes, together with a Metropolitan Board of Works, to be elected from these vestries and parishes. In the 1888 Local Government Act, creating directly elected counties, the metropolitan board was replaced by the London County Council, a central authority capable of dealing with matters common to the whole of the metropolis. In 1894, a further Local Government Act had subdivided the counties into urban and rural districts but had not subdivided London.

London was the largest city in Europe, with a population greater than most of the smaller states – greater than Belgium, Bulgaria, Denmark, the Netherlands, Norway, Serbia and Switzerland. It was absurd to regard a county council representing a population of around 6 million people as genuinely *local* government, and indeed Ritchie, the President of the Local Government Board in 1888, had explicitly declared that the establishment of the London County Council was not a 'complete settlement' but that he would propose 'at some future date' districts in London with 'large and important

---

12 Markham Lester, 'The Employers' Liability/Workmen's Compensation Debate', p. 492.
13 House of Commons Debates, 26 March 1906, vol. 154, col. 901.

administrative functions'.[14] A lower tier of government was of particular importance in London, which, unlike other large cities, was a collection of separable towns and villages each with its own sense of local identity and patriotism. In a speech on 16 November 1897, Lord Salisbury insisted that London was not a single municipality but an aggregate of municipalities. So there was a strong case for creating a lower tier of local government, analogous to that in the English and Welsh counties. But there was also a political motive. The Unionists were unsympathetic to the London County Council, which had been controlled since its foundation by the progressives, a London-specific combination of Liberal and Labour supporters, whom Salisbury dismissed, somewhat disingenuously, as mere 'professional politicians'. The progressives were pioneering radical policies of municipal enterprise and social reform which sparked Salisbury's ire. The London County Council, he believed, was the place 'where Collectivist and Socialistic experiments are tried. It is the place where a new revolutionary spirit finds its instruments and collects its arms.'[15] The Liberals, for their part, feared that subdividing London would also mean transferring powers from the county council to the boroughs, and lead to what one critic labelled 'the vivisection of London'. But the vestries and district boards which the London boroughs were to replace were acknowledged to be corrupt and inefficient. A Royal Commission appointed by the Liberals recommended in 1894 that they be abolished, and the Liberals had themselves introduced a Bill in 1895 to create urban districts in London. So Liberal criticism of the government was little more than the small change of party politics; and in the event, the 1899 Act transferred only minor powers to the boroughs whose powers were not only less than those of county boroughs but less even than those of non-county boroughs.[16] J. Renwick Seager, secretary of the London Liberal and Radical Union, admitted that there was 'every prospect of the Act being a beneficial one to London'.[17]

The Act created the world's first two-tier metropolitan system. In addition to the London County Council, there would be twenty-eight metropolitan boroughs, subdividing the government of the capital, as the 1894 Act had done for the other counties. In its original form, a clause in the Bill provided for the election of women as councillors, but this was struck out by the Lords, and the Commons did not restore it. The boroughs, contrary to Conservative hopes, enjoyed little power, and were satirised by G. K. Chesterton in his novel *The Napoleon of Notting Hill*, published in 1904. The London County Council remained the dominant authority in London. Nor

14 House of Commons Debates, 19 March 1888, vol. 323, cols 1664–5,
15 *The Times*, 8 November 1894.
16 A. G. Gardiner, *John Benn and the Progressive Movement*, Ernest Benn, 1925, pp. 251–2,
17 Ken Young, 'The Politics of London Government 1880–1899', *Public Administration*, 1973, p. 106.

did the 1899 Act affect the Corporation of the City of London, dismissed by Mill in his book *Representative Government* in 1860 as a 'union of modern jobbing and antiquated foppery', which continued to be elected on a severely restricted franchise. Nevertheless, the Act genuinely improved London government, and it completed an edifice for the capital city which was to remain unchanged until the 1960s.

CONSTRUCTIVE UNIONISM IN IRELAND

Unionist reform was not confined to the British side of the Irish Sea. Remarkably, and perhaps unexpectedly, the Unionists proved to be a reforming government in Ireland, enacting measures that were both beneficial and long-lasting. The new Irish Secretary, Gerald Balfour (1853–1945), brother of Arthur, had been Salisbury's third choice for the post and was not in the Cabinet. Instead, and unusually, the Lord Lieutenant, Lord Cadogan, was a member of the Cabinet – despite the fact that, as a ceremonial figure rather than a responsible minister, he was not expected to take part in parliamentary debates; and the Chief Secretary was nominally subordinate to him. Cadogan, apparently, was not very bright. In November 1897, an MP commented that the most difficult part of local government reform in Ireland consisted 'in the process of installing the principles of the measure into the turgid brain of His Excellency, the Lord-Lieutenant of Ireland'.[18] One colleague said of him that 'you never can tell what he won't understand'.[19] He 'does not understand the elements of government, local or imperial, and he is very slow to learn'. The Chief Secretary had to spend 'hours and hours in coaching him: and after a morning of this wearing work, Lord Cadogan will blandly ask some question which will show that all the labour has been in vain'.[20]

But policy was made not by Cadogan but by Gerald Balfour. Arthur thought him cleverer than himself, though less diplomatic. Gerald had indeed achieved a better degree at Cambridge and had been a Fellow of Trinity College, Cambridge from 1878 to 1881. But at that time, an American visitor had thought him 'really the most conservative man that I have yet met. Believed the higher set of people, the Lords etc., set a good example, to the lower set of people – and ever so much more stuff that I had read of but never met anyone that believed it.'[21] Gerald had told the radical Wilfrid

---

18 Vincent, ed., *Crawford Papers*, p. 44.
19 Quoted in Gailey, *Ireland and the Death of Kindness*, p. 77. This fine book gives the best detailed account of the reforms of the Unionist government, perhaps a shade too critical of what were, after all, honourable and honest attempts at reform.
20 Vincent, ed., *Crawford Papers*, p. 44.
21 Gwen Raverat, *Period Piece: A Cambridge Childhood*, Faber, 1952, pp. 7–8.

Scawen Blunt in 1892 that, on the basis of Darwin's theory of the survival of the fittest, the Irish 'ought to have been exterminated long ago ,. but it is too late now'.[22] Perhaps Gerald had changed his mind by 1895. But whether so or not, he proved an active and reforming Irish Secretary. Indeed, Tim Healy, the first governor general of the Irish Free State, was to tell Arthur that Gerald was 'the best chief secretary that Ireland ever had'.[23]

Gerald detected a change of atmosphere in Ireland. Her people no doubt still sought Home Rule, but he believed they were tiring of agitation, and turning their energies to more immediate, practical matters. The time seemed ripe for a policy of amelioration. This new atmosphere, Gerald believed, somewhat over-optimistically, was enveloping Nationalist leaders as well as the people. The circumstances were propitious, therefore, for continuing with the Unionist alternative to Home Rule, first put forward by Arthur Balfour in his period as Irish Secretary from 1887 to 1891. That alternative was twofold – first, resolute government to enforce law and order, and second, constructive Unionism designed to remove the social and economic griev-ances which, it was believed, lay behind the demand for Home Rule. 'The government would, of course,' Gerald Balfour declared in 1895, 'be very glad if they were able by kindness to kill home rule', a statement that came to be abbreviated as 'killing home rule by kindness'.[24] There were three elements to constructive Unionism: land reform, reform of the rural economy and reform of local government.

In the debate on the Queen's Speech in 1895, Gerald had declared that 'the transference of the land from the landlord to the tenant must be ultimately the only effective solution of the land question in Ireland ... Our desire is to establish an industrious peasantry in the ownership of the land which they at present cultivate.'[25] Most Irish landlords were Protestants and many, outside Ulster, were absentees, differing from their tenants not only in social class but also religion. Land reform by creating a class of peasant proprietors, attached to the land, would, it was hoped, create a conservative class resistant to Nationalist agitation. Land reform had begun with two Land Acts in 1885 and 1891 and would culminate in an Act of 1903 which sought to complete a revolution in Irish landholding by buying out the landlord class.

The second element of constructive Unionism was development of the rural economy. That, too, had been initiated by an earlier Unionist govern-ment through the Congested Districts Board in 1891, designed to improve conditions in the rural west of Ireland through state-sponsored aid. Under

22 Gailey, *Ireland and the Death of Kindness*, p. 30.
23 Ibid., p. 131.
24 *The Spectator*, 19 October 1895.
25 House of Commons Debates, 15 August 1895, vol. 36, cols 132, 135.

Gerald Balfour, further reform was initiated, not by the government, but by Sir Horace Plunkett, who had been elected Unionist MP for South County Dublin in 1892. Plunkett was a close friend of Arthur Balfour, and also of Gerald, who had been his contemporary at Eton. He asked a question first put by the Irish philosopher Bishop Berkeley in the eighteenth century: 'Whether it would not be more reasonable to mend our state than complain of it?' At the turn of the century, Plunkett sought to detach Unionism from its close association with the landlord class. Hitherto, Unionists had sought 'to uphold the union by force rather than by a reconciliation of the people to it. It has held aloof from the masses.' Plunkett argued that Unionism should become a positive, not a merely negative force. But he was also critical of the Nationalists who had sought upheaval at Westminster and had made 'allies of every kind of foreign potentate, from President Cleveland to the Mahdi, from Mr Kruger to the Akhoom of Swat ... masters of the language of hate and scorn, yet mocked by inevitable and eternal failure'. By emphasising Home Rule to the exclusion of other reforms, the Nationalists had, Plunkett believed, missed the chance of securing beneficial economic and social change. Plunkett hoped that Unionists, in contrast,

> without abating one jot of our unionism, and nationalists without abating one jot of their nationalism, can each show our faith in the cause for which we have fought so bitterly and for so long, by sinking our party differences for our country's good and leaving our respective policies to the justification of time.[26]

Plunkett believed that the Irish question was 'fundamentally economic rather than political'.[27] He hoped to transcend the Unionist–Nationalist controversy, and create a new social order based on rural cooperation.

Collective self-help in Ireland could be encouraged through government support for agricultural cooperatives. Farmers could then pool their resources, improving their skills and standard of living. The first such cooperative was established in 1891, and in 1894 Plunkett founded an Irish Agricultural Society to coordinate their work. Some cooperatives were successful, others attracted the disapproval of Nationalists. When R. A. Anderson, a colleague of Plunkett's, sought to establish a cooperative in Rathkeale, a solicitor, having discovered that the cooperative movement was apolitical and non-denominational, declared that 'Rathkeale is a nationalist town – and every

---

26 Horace Plunkett, *Ireland in the New Century*, John Murray, 1904, Preface, p. 44.
27 Letter to Arthur Balfour, 9 February 1900, quoted in Gailey, 'Horace Plunkett and the Politics of the Non-Political, 1892–1908', Society for Co-operative Studies in Ireland: Papers and Proceedings, vol. 1, no. 1, April 1985, p. 60. I am indebted to Dr Gailey for sending me a copy of this paper, which contains a powerful critique of Plunkett's vision.

pound of butter must be made on nationalist principles or It shan't be made at all'.[28] But Plunkett continued to seek improvements through cross-party consent. In 1895, he established a parliamentary committee, known as the Recess Committee, since it met during the parliamentary recess, an ad hoc cross-party grouping of Irish parliamentarians. The Irish Party was divided on whether it should participate. Justin McCarthy, leader of the anti-Parnellite faction, refused to have anything to do with it, since, were it to be successful, Ireland would, as Plunkett had admitted, 'cease to desire Home Rule'; but John Redmond, leader of the Parnellite faction agreed to join. The leader of the Ulster Unionists, Colonel Saunderson, then declared that he could not join any committee on which Redmond sat; but other prominent Unionists did join. The Recess Committee reported unanimously to Gerald Balfour, recommending state assistance to supplement voluntary effort and a Department of Agriculture and Technical Instruction in Ireland, headed by a minister responsible to Parliament, a recommendation that was duly adopted. The Chief Secretary was to be *ex officio* head of the department, but its effective head until 1907 was its vice-president, Plunkett.

In Plunkett's view, the new department would need a connection with local opinion in Ireland if it was to be effective. Yet, until 1898, when a system of directly elected local government was established, there were no representative institutions in Ireland at all. The new department, therefore, needed to be supplemented with an elective structure of local government. This was achieved in 1898 as the third element of constructive Unionism.

The 1888 Local Government Act, creating representative local government in the counties, had no counterpart in Ireland, where local administration was by grand juries, appointed by the assizes judge of the county. These grand juries were largely composed of landowners, overwhelmingly Unionist and Protestant, and therefore, outside Ulster, unrepresentative. The Unionists were at first hesitant in creating representative local government lest it provide a platform for the Nationalists. In 1883, Lord Salisbury had opposed such proposals which he believed 'must lead to Home Rule'. But by 1898, he had come to believe that local government reform might instead prove a barrier to Home Rule. There was also a practical reason. The Unionists had introduced a measure of rate relief for landowners in Great Britain, but this had not been extended to Ireland since there was no effective local machinery to administer it. The money had instead been given to Dublin Castle, which had used it to fund Poor Law reform and the new Agriculture Board.

The 1898 Local Government Bill provided for a system of county boroughs

28   John L. Campbell, John A. Hall and Ove Pedersen, eds, *National Identity and the Varieties of Capitalism: The Danish Experience*, McGill-Queen's University Press, 2006, p. 188.

in the large towns, and, elsewhere, a two-tier system, as in England, of counties as well as a lower tier, both to be elected on a wide franchise which included women. This reform proved of great help to the Nationalists, rejuvenating the Irish Party which had been in a dispirited state since the fall of Parnell. In the first county elections in 1899, they took nearly 75 per cent of the seats. Outside Ulster, the Unionists took just thirty-nine of 465 seats, and local government reform helped end the long dominance of the Protestant Ascendancy. It also weakened opposition to Nationalism in another sense. For, hitherto, some Unionists had argued that the Irish were, by temperament, unsuited for self-government. That argument was undermined when the bulk of local administration in Ireland came to be undertaken by Home Rulers. Instead of undermining Home Rule, therefore, local government reform proved a stimulus. It provided a new platform for the Nationalists and showed that the Irish people were perfectly capable of running their own affairs. Redmond, the Nationalist leader, who had welcomed the reform, declared, 'If this Bill is worked successfully, I believe it will constitute an unanswerable argument for Home Rule.'[29]

Plunkett's new Department of Agriculture and Technical Instruction was to be advised by a representative council, two-thirds of whose members would be chosen from the new county councils, and it would have the power to veto departmental spending. Local councils would contribute from the rates to help finance the department.

Apart from local government reform, the various Unionist reforms – land purchase (to be completed by Wyndham's Act of 1903), the Congested Districts Board and the Department of Agriculture and Technical Instruction – had, as Balfour pointed out to a correspondent in 1900, 'no parallel in legislation for England, and are justified only by an anxiety to give exceptional aid to the sister kingdom'.[30] But Plunkett was absurdly over-optimistic about what the reforms could achieve. Writing to Lady Betty Balfour, sister-in-law of the two ministers, he declared his belief that Arthur, Gerald 'and my associates ought to settle the Irish Question between us'. The Irish people, 'seeing that the State does its part in promoting the real welfare of the people and were encouraging the people themselves to do their part' would forget about Home Rule. 'You seem to think', one Nationalist told him, 'the entire Irish question is contained within the sphere of your own Department.'[31]

As might have been predicted, Plunkett provoked the antagonism both of Nationalists, fearful that he would succeed in diverting Irish energies from

---

29 House of Commons Debates, 21 March 1898, vol. 55, col. 449; 21 February 1898, vol. 52, col. 1261.
30 Gailey, *Ireland and the Death of Kindness*, p. 64fn.
31 Gailey, 'Horace Plunkett and the Politics of the Non-Political', p. 59.

Home Rule, and of Unionists, fearful that concessions were being made to rebels. The new department was itself a constitutional anomaly, since it had a dual responsibility, to the Irish Secretary responsible to Parliament, and to Irish public opinion through the county councils. The success of the department would depend upon consensus between politicians at Westminster, predominantly Unionist, and politicians in Ireland, predominantly Nationalist. But on Irish matters, consensus was in short supply. Plunkett's reforms presumed an incipient spirit of political harmony which hardly existed, and a spirit of rural harmony which had never existed. He was ideologically challenging both Unionism and Nationalism. He sought to take agricultural cooperation out of politics and protested that he was not a party politician. 'The more business you introduce into politics and the less politics you introduce into business, the better for both,'[32] Plunkett had insisted at the inaugural meeting of the Irish Agricultural Organisation Society in 1894. Yet Plunkett was a Unionist MP, and became, in effect, a minister in a Unionist government. Admittedly, he tended to take an independent line in the Commons, and was often prepared to vote against his party. In Ireland, he supported distinctly non-Unionist causes such as the Gaelic Athletic Association, the Gaelic League and the campaign for a Catholic university. But Nationalists believed that Plunkett's success would weaken their cause. So did Plunkett, telling Lady Betty Balfour in August 1896 that the Nationalist MP John Dillon opposed the Recess Committee, since 'he sees in it the greatest danger Home Rule has yet to face. So do I.'

But ironically, Plunkett garnered even more hostility amongst the Unionists who accused him of appeasement. The reforms alienated vested interests who disputed the very notion that the Union needed reform. A retired Ascendancy grandee, the Marquess of Dufferin and Ava, received an anonymous letter in October 1899, characterising the government's policy as: 'victimize the unionist, bleed the loyalist, bribe the tenant ... to conciliate the disloyal and rebellious had been the essence of the "Balfourian millennium"'. 'God help the loyalist in Ireland under Mr G. Balfour's rule,' another correspondent wrote to Lecky, the Unionist historian, in May 1900.[33] This standpoint was supported by some in the Cabinet, who did not share the view of the Balfours and Chamberlain that Ireland needed reform. Unionism was united only in resisting Home Rule. Once positive policies came to be introduced, it was in danger of falling apart. Reform, therefore, had the paradoxical effect of rejuvenating Nationalism and weakening Unionism.

---

32 Ibid., p. 42.
33 Gailey, *Ireland and the Death of Kindness*, pp. 23, 136.

Rather than killing Home Rule by kindness, the reforms of Gerald Balfour and Horace Plunkett helped to kill Irish Unionism.[34]

It was the Unionists who brought Plunkett's career as an MP to an end. At the 1900 general election, to Arthur Balfour's fury, they put up a candidate in South Dublin against Plunkett. 'Irish unionists', Balfour declared, 'were often trying enough but their opposition to the one Irishman of their party who had ever worked for Ireland without some selfish motive was beyond all bounds of political decency.' Plunkett had hoped to gain Nationalist support to compensate for the loss of Unionist support, but he failed to do so. The Irish Nationalist and socialist Michael Davitt declared, 'A vote for Mr Plunkett would mean a vote for Mr Chamberlain and Lord Salisbury, a vote for Dublin Castle and a vote for Irish landlordism with all its bloody records in the process of the extermination of the Irish nation.'[35] With the Unionist vote split, Plunkett was defeated by the Nationalist. He was again defeated in a by-election for Galway City in 1901 by a Nationalist, who had fought for the Boers in South Africa. Later, Plunkett himself was to become a Home Ruler. But in his former constituency of South Dublin, the Unionists were to choose as their candidate in 1906 the rubicund squire and ex-Cabinet minister Walter Long, who could be relied upon not to challenge traditional shibboleths. Plunkett's electoral defeat was a sign that there was no middle ground in Irish politics and that ideological attitudes were too strongly entrenched for a consensual approach to succeed. Plunkett had some cause to reflect on another question posed by Bishop Berkeley: 'whether our parties are not a burlesque upon politics'. The 'kindness' of constructive unionism did not kill Home Rule, but it did kill Plunkett's political career. His creameries were to be burnt down after 1918 by British irregulars, the Black and Tans, and his house was to be burnt down by Republican irregulars in the Irish Civil War.

And, contrary to Unionist hopes, their reforms seemed to do little to quell anti-British feeling in Ireland, which erupted with renewed force during the Boer War. Hostility to Britain 'recurs like malarial fever', Horace Plunkett wrote sadly to Cadogan in November 1899.[36]

The problems which Plunkett encountered showed how difficult it was in Ireland to find a genuine middle way between Unionism and Irish Nationalism. The centre ground seemed an unstable quicksand, dragging down all who came into contact with it.

---

34 Ibid., pp. 132, 137.
35 West, *Horace Plunkett*, p. 56.
36 Richard Shannon, *The Age of Salisbury, 1881-1902: Unionism and Empire*, Longman, 1996, p. 459.

THE PARTIES IN 1900

Many had assumed that the Boer War would end with a rapid British victory. But the Boers had the advantage of first strike and knowledge of the terrain. They had in the immediately preceding years built up their armaments, enjoying a superiority of two to one in men and an even greater superiority in artillery. Had they been able to reach Durban and the Cape before British reinforcements could arrive, they might possibly have sapped the British will to resist and persuaded Boers in the British colonies to join them. Instead, their main effort was directed towards besieging British troops at Kimberley, Mafeking and Ladysmith, sieges which caused considerable loss of life and were setbacks for the British campaign but which could not in the long run affect the outcome. Nevertheless, in December 1899, Britain suffered 'Black Week' defeats at Stormberg, Magersfontein and Colenso, which, it was said, 'made the blood run cold in the veins of every patriotic Englishman'.[37] British casualties were 1,119, Boer casualties just fifty.[38] When Balfour told the queen about these disasters, she responded, 'Please understand that there is no one depressed in *this* house: We are not interested in the possibilities of defeat; they do not exist.'[39] The government appointed Field Marshal Lord Roberts, the most successful British military leader of the day, as commander-in-chief, and Kitchener, fresh from his success at Omdurman, as his chief of staff. After the Battle of Paardeberg in February 1900, the tide turned in Britain's favour. In June, Pretoria, the capital of the Transvaal, fell and the Transvaal and Orange Free State were annexed to the empire. In October, Kruger fled via Portuguese territory to Europe, and it appeared that organised Boer resistance was over. It remained, so it seemed, only to mop up the remnants of a defeated army. The government decided to take advantage of these successes to dissolve Parliament on 25 September for an election to be held between 28 September and 24 October. Salisbury argued that the existing Parliament, which would have to come to an end by July 1902, did not have a long enough life before it to settle post-war issues.

The precedents did not suggest that the Unionists would find it easy to secure a second term. As Salisbury pointed out to Lansdowne in September 1900, 'During the Queen's reign every Minister who ... has dissolved Parliament has been turned out within a year.'[40] But the Liberals were in no position to mount an effective campaign, remaining divided on both policy and personalities, seeming, in Chamberlain's words, a party 'of shreds

37 Jean de Bloch, 'Some Lessons of the Transvaal War', *Contemporary Review*, January 1902, p. 461.
38 Roberts, *Salisbury*, p. 749.
39 Stanley Weintraub, *Victoria*, John Murray, 1996, p. 611.
40 Holding, 'Third Salisbury Cabinet', p. 108.

and patches', with no realistic prospect of victory. Indeed, the Liberal Chief Whip, Herbert Gladstone, admitted in a speech at Leeds that 'the Opposition were not in a position to furnish a strong Government'.[41] Liberal weakness was graphically shown by the fact that Gladstone, in charge of electoral preparations, found himself unable to find candidates for many seats. The Liberals contested just 406 of the 670 constituencies – in Berkshire and Hertfordshire and in the nine university seats there were no Liberal candidates at all – while the Unionists contested 579. There were 163 Unionists returned unopposed, the largest number since the 1867 Reform Act, and there were also fifty-eight unopposed Irish Nationalists but just twenty-two unopposed Liberals. To gain a majority, the Liberals would have had to win 314 of the 427 contested seats.

The Liberals in opposition had not been able to develop policies on which they could unite. Rosebery had sought to relegate Home Rule from its central position on the party's agenda, believing, probably with justification, that it was a vote loser. In his first speech as Prime Minister in 1894, he had insisted that Home Rule required the consent of the 'predominant partner' in the United Kingdom, namely England. This declaration had annoyed not only the Irish Nationalists upon whom the Liberals had been dependent for their majority but also the Gladstonians. In a personal memorandum in July 1898, Rosebery annoyed them even more by putting forward three reasons why Home Rule should no longer be Liberal policy at all: that the constituencies outside Ireland had continually shown their hostility to it; that the Irish were disloyal; and that local government reform should be given time to work.[42] The party was also divided on foreign and imperial policy and on the war. On the central imperial issues that had faced the Unionist government – South Africa and the conquest of Sudan – the party seemed to be speaking with two voices. The Gladstonians clung to the Grand Old Man's policy, or what they regarded as his policy, of non-intervention, while the Liberal Imperialists pressed for a more activist stance. In domestic policy, the Liberals still lacked a clear sense of direction. Despite their defeat in 1895, they had not yet adjusted to new post-Gladstonian conditions. 'Poor Liberal Party!' Rosebery told a friend in March 1898.

> What a plight it is in! No policy and nobody to expound it. But it was itself greatly to blame. For the last thirty years it has leaned absolutely on Mr G [Gladstone]. It has been like a man who has become accustomed to get

41 *The Times*, 24 September 1900.
42 McKinstry, *Rosebery*, p. 415.

about with a crutch only, and when that crutch is withdrawn, helplessness and hopelessness ensued.[43]

Some Liberals were coming to believe that there was little public interest in further instalments of constitutional or political reform, and that the party should take a greater interest in social matters. They were developing a 'New Liberalism', but it was not to reach fruition for some years.

Policy differences continued to be compounded by personal squabbles. Rosebery and Harcourt, his Leader of the House of Commons and Chancellor of the Exchequer, had been barely on speaking terms, and were at cross purposes on policy – Rosebery being an imperialist and devotee of efficiency while Harcourt was opposed to imperialism and sympathetic to Home Rule. Both were prima donnas, not team players. Rosebery was touchy, petulant, brittle and self-obsessed. Never having undergone the experience of a parliamentary election or life in the Commons, he was too sensitive for the rough and tumble of political life. Harcourt, though a more capable administrator and lawyer of some repute, was gruff and rude to colleagues as well as opponents. He was 'a man who could never spot a problem without wanting to kick someone in the ankles'.[44] He had a talent for arousing hostility and antagonism. Indeed, the resentment of his colleagues at his hectoring manner was a main factor in his failure to secure the premiership after Gladstone's retirement. He was, one Conservative thought, 'a fine blustering humbug of an English gentleman: his defects ensure unstinted popularity on our side of the House'.[45]

Rosebery was too remote from ordinary Liberals to be an effective opposition leader. 'If you are going to carry on the fight,' Lord Esher advised him, 'it can only be by conquering first the sympathies and hopes of the rank and file of our party.'[46] That he never succeeded in doing. He lacked the enthusiasm for Liberal causes of Gladstone and Campbell-Bannerman, to many of which he was unsympathetic – unsympathetic not only to Home Rule but also to the disestablishment of the Anglican Church in Wales and local option. He was, in consequence, in the words of Raymond Asquith, son of the Liberal statesman, 'abhorred by the nonconformist conscience'.[47] Rosebery was continually urging Liberals to develop a fresh outlook and novel policies more appropriate to the new age, but it was never wholly clear what these policies should be. He had remained as party leader for a

---

43 Rhodes James, *Rosebery*, p. 405.
44 K. Theodore Hoppen, *Governing Hibernia: British Politicians and Ireland 1800–1921*, Oxford University Press, 2016, p. 242.
45 Vincent, ed., *Crawford Papers*, p. 74.
46 McKinstry, *Rosebery*, p. 383.
47 Ibid., p. 410.

further year after the end of his premiership in 1895. But in October 1896, he interpreted Gladstone's speech on Armenia as a criticism of himself, and petulantly resigned the leadership without consulting his colleagues or even informing them until after the event. 'You have handed us over to Harcourt without escape,' Lord Ripon complained to him, 'and you are not ignorant of all which that means.'[48] To avoid further squabbles, the president of the National Liberal Federation, Robert Spence Watson, stressed that there was no such position as leader of the whole party when the Liberals were in opposition. Harcourt, therefore, would be leader of the party only in the Commons, while Lord Kimberley, Foreign Secretary in Rosebery's government, would be leader in the Lords.[49] Nevertheless, the Liberals would not be anxious to have another Prime Minister in the Lords, and Harcourt was generally regarded as leader of the party, 'by default, if not by merit', as Balfour cattily remarked.[50] But Rosebery, with all his weaknesses, had a charisma which both Harcourt and Kimberley lacked, and remained a brooding presence overshadowing both of them. Many Liberal Imperialists hoped that Rosebery's retirement was not final and that he could be induced to return. But Rosebery never made it clear whether he wanted to return, form a new party or retire. He was, in Morley's words, 'a dark horse in a loose box'.[51]

Harcourt, ill-tempered, rude and prone to personal vendettas, was hardly an improvement on Rosebery. 'In all my experience,' Gladstone told Rosebery in August 1895, 'I have never known anything even approaching his power of self-deception.'[52] He proved as petulant and difficult as Rosebery, and fostered little enthusiasm either amongst his colleagues or the public. In January 1898, Asquith wrote to Milner in South Africa:

> The new birth has not yet come, nor is there anything in the heavens above or in the earth beneath to portend the event. Harcourt's leadership excites no enthusiasm, and, in view of his age [he was nearly seventy] is probably regarded by the bulk of the people as a merely provisional arrangement ... And for the moment there is no one else whose name is even generally acceptable, let alone a rallying cry for a broken army.[53]

Harcourt never acquired the confidence of his colleagues and had little support from them. In December 1898, without, according to Asquith, 'the

48   Rhodes James, *Rosebery*, pp. 392, 393.
49   Stansky, *Ambitions and Strategies*, p. 225.
50   Ridley and Percy, eds, *Letters of Arthur Balfour and Lady Elcho*, p. 150.
51   Patrick Jackson, *Harcourt and Son: A Political Biography of Sir William Harcourt, 1827–1904*, Fairleigh Dickinson University Press, 2004, p. 303.
52   Stansky, *Ambitions and Strategies*, p. 190.
53   Rhodes James, *Rosebery*, p. 402.

slightest tincture of a sense of public duty', he followed Rosebery's example in suddenly resigning the Liberal leadership. He resigned partly because he was out of sympathy with the new current of imperialism and wanted 'a stand against a Jingo invasion of the Liberal Party', but also out of pique. 'A party rent by sectional disputes and personal interests', he said in his resignation letter, 'is one which no man can consent to lead either with credit to himself or advantage to the country.'[54] Responding to a letter of appreciation from Grey, Harcourt perceptively declared that he was a man of the nineteenth century, while 'the twentieth century belongs to you'.[55] Morley resigned with Harcourt from the front bench, in order, as he said later, to be 'able to act with a freedom that was impossible so long as we were forced to keep in step with the jingoes in our camp'.[56] 'What a pity it is', Asquith wrote to Campbell-Bannerman, 'when big causes and interests get in the hands of grown-up children who will not play in the same nursery!'[57] But it was clear that, as told by one Liberal MP to Herbert Samuel, a young Liberal Imperialist, in October 1898, 'neither Harcourtian iconoclastic crusades nor Roseberian grand panjandrum secretiveness will do any good'.[58]

The Liberal whips pressed Asquith to take the leadership, although acknowledging that the post must first be offered to Campbell-Bannerman who was Asquith's senior, and therefore deemed to have a natural right to the succession.[59] But Asquith was widely perceived as the coming man, one observer noting that Asquith was the man for 'real business' while Campbell-Bannerman would be a mere '*locum tenens*'.[60] Asquith, however, declined to be considered, declaring that he had no private income and was dependent upon his earnings at the Bar. He was, therefore, he said, too poor to assume the leadership.[61] But perhaps the real reason was his perception that Liberal prospects were not bright, and that it would not be a happy task to lead the squabbling party. The leadership went instead to the veteran Campbell-Bannerman (1836–1908), who had been an MP since 1868, without making any particular impact. He was widely regarded as an uninspiring stopgap, chosen, in Snowden's words, 'as a makeshift because he was believed to be so harmless and guileless as to be incapable of doing any harm to any of the rival factions'.[62]

---

54 Ibid., pp. 234, 259, 273, 266; H. C. G. Matthew, *The Liberal Imperialists: The Ideas and Politics of a Post-Gladstonian Elite*, Oxford University Press, 1973, p. 31.
55 Otte, *Statesman of Europe*, pp. 141–2.
56 D. A. Hamer, *John Morley: Liberal Intellectual in Politics*, Clarendon Press, 1968, p. 329.
57 Rhodes James, *Rosebery*, p. 407.
58 Martin Pugh, 'The Triumph of the New Liberalism, 1899–1914', in Robert Ingham and Duncan Brack, eds, *Peace, Reform and Liberation: A History of Liberal Politics in Britain, 1679–2011*, Biteback, 2011, p. 147.
59 The whips did not, as Raymond, Asquith's son, told Ensor, actually offer Asquith the leadership. See Ensor, *England*, p. 239.
60 Stansky, *Ambitions and Strategies*, p. 278.
61 Ensor, *England*, p. 239fn.
62 Philip Snowden, *An Autobiography: Vol. 1, 1864–1919*, Ivor Nicholson & Watson, 1934, p. 176.

Balfour was prone to patronising Campbell-Bannerman, and was not alone in failing to detect the essential qualities that he could bring to the Liberals: shrewdness, tenacity, dedication to the party, Liberal ideals and a good-humoured affability. He was a man whom it was difficult to dislike and was to show great skill in holding together opposed wings of his party and creating good feeling amongst his colleagues. Indeed, Curzon said that he was the only member of the Rosebery government who had been on speaking terms with all of his colleagues![63] His emollient qualities were a great relief following the three prima donnas who had led the party for the past thirty years – Gladstone, Rosebery and Harcourt. Nevertheless, the Liberal leader in the Commons, unless an ex-Prime Minister, had no assured claim to the premiership when the party regained power. The sovereign could appoint the Liberal leader of the Lords as Prime Minister, or perhaps another leading Liberal. For much of Campbell-Bannerman's period as Liberal leader in the Commons, he was harassed by Rosebery, who seemed to want to supplant him. But Campbell-Bannerman's equable and friendly manner concealed a basic toughness. 'His bite', one historian has noted 'was worse than his bark.'[64] Balfour was not the only politician to discover that he had underestimated him. But Sir Henry did not have sufficient time by 1900 to make an electoral impact, and his leadership during the campaign was lacklustre. Indeed, in the summer of 1900, he had taken a long holiday to the annoyance of his Chief Whip, who declared ruefully that nothing could be done if the leader would not lead.[65] Campbell-Bannerman's time was not to come until 1906. The Liberal journalist A. G. Gardiner was justified, therefore, in writing in the introduction to a collection of speeches by Lloyd George in 1909 on 'the New Liberalism', that 'between 1886 and 1906 the Liberal Party in this country was dead. It was torn by civil war and miserable personal feuds.'[66]

So the Unionists, looking at opposition disarray, had good reasons for confidence, and were able to capitalise on patriotic feeling. Lord Salisbury's message to the electors implied that victory over the Boers had been achieved. It insisted that 'the Imperial Power over the territories of the two South African Republics which, as events have proved, was unwisely relinquished, must be rebuilt upon durable foundations'. It also promised eventual colonial self-government. The address declared that a strong Unionist majority was essential so that the Boers could not profit from domestic political weakness

63 Gilmour, *Curzon*, p. 94.
64 Alfred Gollin, *Balfour's Burden: Arthur Balfour and Imperial Preference*, Anthony Blond, 1965, p. 213.
65 T. O. Lloyd, 'The Whip as Paymaster; Herbert Gladstone and Party Organisation', *English Historical Review*, 1974, p. 803.
66 A. G. Gardiner, *What is the New Liberalism? Introduction to The New Liberalism: Speeches of Lloyd George, Daily News,* 1909, p. 5.

and parliamentary division. 'All the recent troubles of South Africa', it declared, 'have come from a shift of parliamentary opinion at a crucial moment.' The address was singularly bereft of policy commitments. And, indeed, the Unionists had hardly any record of social reform to put before the voters. But they could point to successes in foreign and imperial affairs. In the Nile valley, the African empire had been extended. Difficulties with the United States and with France had been peacefully resolved. Britain's position in China seemed to have been maintained against competing powers. And while the Boer War had isolated Britain on the Continent, she seemed beyond challenge thanks to her mastery of the seas. But the war was, so Unionists insisted, the first and foremost issue facing the nation beside which all other questions sank into insignificance. Chamberlain, who had championed old-age pensions in 1895, now declared that pensions and other social questions were no longer central. Pensions had featured in around 50 per cent of Unionist addresses in 1895, but they were mentioned in only around 20 per cent in 1900. Proposals for improvements to working-class housing and labour conciliation boards were dropped. Positive Unionism seemed in abeyance. The Liberals appeared tacitly to accept Unionist priorities, since 80 per cent of Liberal addresses had as their main subject the war. In no recent election had so few domestic issues been raised.

The election caught the Liberals at a huge disadvantage. It was fought on a stale register which, so Campbell-Bannerman believed, disenfranchised those whose qualifications were less than two years old – in his view around one-fifth of the electorate.[67] Those disenfranchised included soldiers whose occupancy of property had been interrupted by their military service. It was estimated that around 220,000 electors were fighting in South Africa. Chamberlain assumed in an election speech in Birmingham on 23 September that all of them would have voted Unionist. That assumption is by no means as watertight as it seems, since many soldiers were coming to be disillusioned with the methods used to fight the war, and coming to admire the Boers as brave antagonists.[68] In the past, Parliament had passed special Acts to accelerate the new register. But Unionists believed that most of those who moved their residence were likely to prove Liberal supporters. Harcourt claimed that those disenfranchised were 'Mr Chamberlain's Uitlanders'. And there were, he insisted, ten times more of them than in the Transvaal. Unionist doctrine, he declared, was: 'if you cannot get votes, get rid of the voters'.[69]

The stale register might not have mattered had the Liberals been able

---

67 *The Times*, 22 September 1900.
68 Keith Surridge, '"All you soldiers are what we call pro-Boer": The Military Critique of the South African War, 1899–1902', *History*, 1997.
69 *The Times*, 26 September 1900.

to maintain an agreed and consistent policy on the war. But they could not. Campbell-Bannerman and Harcourt, having claimed that Chamberlain and Milner had been provocative, now argued that annexation of the Boer republics was 'the only practical way of securing the unquestioned predominance of British authority in South Africa', thereby accepting the Unionist contention that Britain must remain the predominant power.[70] The Liberal criticism was that the Unionists had mismanaged negotiations with the Boers and had failed to prepare for the war with sufficient men and equipment. But since the Liberal Imperialists had argued that more reinforcements should have been sent, while the Gladstonians argued that the troops sent had been a provocation, they could make little headway. The cause was further damaged by letters to Kruger from three admittedly untypical radical Liberal MPs discovered at Bloemfontein after its capture by British troops, advising the Boers on what policies to follow; the radical Henry Labouchère had called on Kruger to give 'Joe a fall'.[71] In addition, a Liberal government might well have been dependent upon the support of the Irish Nationalists who were, to a man, pro-Boer. Indeed, one of the Irish Party's leaders, Michael Davitt, had hoped that God would 'strengthen the arm of every Boer who shoulders a gun'.[72] In 1900, the opposition seemed divided into fragments – Liberal Imperialists, Radicals, pro-Boers, Labour and the Irish – with nothing in common except that they did not like the Unionists. Amongst the 406 Liberal candidates, there were probably around sixty pro-Boer Liberals, compared with around 140 Liberal Imperialists. But the party as a whole was characterised by the Unionists as pro-Boer and wanting in patriotism.

In September 1900, the mayor of Mafeking had declared that 'every seat lost by the Government is a seat gained to the Boers'. Chamberlain quoted this slogan in a speech at Tunstall, Staffordshire, on 27 September.[73] It did not, as is often thought, originate with him. But he used the same words in a message of encouragement to the Liberal Unionist candidate in the Heywood division in Lancashire, a Unionist fighting not a 'pro-Boer' but a Liberal Imperialist. An unfortunate error on the part of a post office clerk turned the last part of the sentence into a seat *sold* to the Boers. The slogan became notorious. What the mayor of Mafeking and Chamberlain meant was that the Boers were holding out and resorting to guerrilla warfare in the hope of a change of government in Britain; and they had indeed secured better

70 Ibid., 22 September 1900.
71 Garvin, *Chamberlain*, vol. 3, p. 589.
72 Paul Readman, 'The Conservative Party, Patriotism and British Politics: The Case of the General Election of 1900', *Journal of British Studies*, 2001, p. 119.
73 *The Times*, 28 September 1900.

terms from Liberals after the Battle of Majuba in 1881 than they would have obtained from Conservatives. A Unionist victory in 1900, therefore, would deprive the Boers of their last hope, and rapidly end the war. But, of course, the implication was that the Liberals were unpatriotic allies of a foreign enemy, and Chamberlain's message was much resented by the Liberals and, in particular, by the Liberal Imperialists Lloyd George, though not a Liberal Imperialist, declared at his adoption meeting on 19 September that 'the man who tries to make the flag an object of a single party is a greater traitor to that flag than any man who fires at it'.[74] Beatrice Webb believed that '"the strong man" of the government [Chamberlain] has played it down low to the man in the street: the street has answered back with emphatic approval'. But she then added, 'And in doing so the electors have shown common sense.' That was because of the divisions and incoherence in the Liberal opposition.

> Who would trust a party with ... as the real leaders of the sections men who hate each other and each other's ideas, more than they do the persons or the views of the enemy ... In Imperialism they cannot outbid the Tories: in all social questions they lack knowledge or conviction and fear to lose their remaining rich men.[75]

This was not an unfair verdict.

The Liberal manifesto in the form of Campbell-Bannerman's election address was more detailed than Lord Salisbury's and attempted to strike some sort of a balance between the two wings of the party. The Unionists, the manifesto claimed, had done nothing to prevent the slaughter of Armenian Christians, while elsewhere British interests had been 'gratuitously sacrificed by a series of what were called "graceful concessions"'. In the Far East, Britain had been humiliated by entering into 'a futile and unnecessary contest with Russia', on which they had been defeated at every point. But they had also 'neglected golden opportunities' to protect British interests, and had been forced 'to console themselves and the country with Wei-hai-Wei, the possession of which has imposed an additional burden to our already over-taxed military resources, and is a source of naval weakness rather than strength'.

By contrast with the Unionists, the Liberals waxed eloquent on domestic affairs, where 'the lavish and grandiloquent promises with which the confidence of the country' had been wooed in 1895 had 'issued in a singularly bare and exiguous performance. The great social programme has evaporated into air.' Old-age pensions had 'disappeared in a vanishing vista of Committees

74 Grigg, *Young Lloyd George*, p. 270.
75 MacKenzie, *Diary of Beatrice Webb*, vol. 2, p. 185, entry for 7 October 1900.

of Inquiry'. The Workmen's Compensation Act was inadequate. There was, however, 'one section of their policy to which the Government have devoted themselves with zeal and persistence – that of administering doles from the public exchequer to the classes on whose support they rely', namely aid to the voluntary schools and to agricultural landowners. Meanwhile, what it called 'the Condition of the People Question' had been neglected. Social progress, the manifesto insisted, depended on a Liberal government, and for that reason 'every seat won from the Tories is a gain to the cause of the people'.

Until the Boer War, despite Liberal difficulties, it had seemed that the Unionists might face electoral challenges. Between 1895 and July 1899, in forty by-elections, the Liberals made a net gain of nine seats and the average swing to them was:

- 1896: 3.2 per cent
- 1897: 2.8 per cent
- 1898: 4.0 per cent

The Liberals needed a swing of just 2.5 per cent to win more seats than the Unionists, and 3.5 per cent for an overall majority. The Unionist journalist J. L. Garvin had written in August 1899 'that the question now is, not so much whether Unionism can avert defeat at the General Election, but how far it can minimise disaster ... The enthusiasm for Unionism which carried Lord Salisbury's Ministry into power in 1895 no longer exists.' The government's record was 'sluggish, to say the least, in foreign policy ... slovenly, if no worse in domestic legislation'.[76] The war, however, transformed Unionist prospects. There were eight contested by-elections between its outbreak and the 1900 general election in constituencies which both Unionists and Liberals had fought in 1895. In all except one, where there was no swing at all, there was a swing to the Unionists of between 0.3 per cent and 11 per cent, despite the early reverses sustained by British troops for which the government's lack of preparation could be blamed.

The Liberals claimed that the early dissolution restricted the number of electors who could vote and was an illegitimate attempt to restrict the issues needing to be considered to just one – the war. But it was to no avail. The Liberals faced the retort that if, as they believed, the conflict had been mismanaged, and the Unionist record was so lamentable, why did they not welcome the election? In fact, the election did indeed turn out to be a plebiscite on the fighting, a plebiscite which showed that the voters approved of it and wanted it carried to a victorious conclusion. Voters seemed to discriminate

---

76   J. L. Garvin, 'Why is Unionism Unpopular', *Fortnightly Review*, August 1899, p. 282.

amongst Liberal candidates according to their views on the war. The average swing against pro-Boer candidates was 2.4 per cent, against Liberal Imperialist candidates it was just 0.3 per cent. In the English boroughs, the difference was especially marked – the swing against pro-Boer candidates was 4 per cent, but there was no swing at all against Liberal Imperialist candidates. Only in Wales, where there was a swing of 8.6 per cent *against* the Unionists, were the Liberals able to resist the patriotic tide, although in East Anglia, Yorkshire, Devon and Cornwall, rural voters seemed unmoved either way by the conflict. There is evidence that the war and the patriotic feelings associated with it made a particular appeal to working-class voters. Labour and trade union leaders tended to be against the fighting, but Labour commanded the support of only a small portion of the working class, and the majority of the working class did not at that time belong to trade unions. Hyndman, the leader of the idiosyncratic Social Democratic Federation, and supporter of the war, wrote after the election:

> At this moment ... it is by no means the workers who are the least 'jingo' in their voting. Although the leaders of the organised trades have recently all declared against this war, the working class vote in London and the great industrial centres has in the majority gone for it ... we Social-Democrats have found ... that the poorest districts are generally the most reactionary and chauvinist.[77]

It appears indeed that the Unionists gained a larger working-class vote in the 1900 election than at any other election between 1885 and 1910.[78]

The outcome of the election was very similar to that of 1895.

Party	Total seats	Percentage of vote
Conservatives and Liberal Unionists	402, a net loss of 9 seats (of which Conservatives had 335 seats and Liberal Unionists 67)	50.3
Liberals	183, a net gain of 6 seats	44.8
Irish Parliamentary Party	77	1.6
Independent Nationalists	5	1.5
Labour Representation Committee	2	1.8
Others	1	1.0

77 Readman, 'The Conservative Party, Patriotism and British Politics', pp. 110, 112, 114, 117–18, 134, 137. This paragraph is based on Readman's article, whose conclusions I find more convincing than the arguments of Henry Pelling in *Popular Politics and Society in Late Victorian Britain*, Macmillan, 1968, and Richard Price in *An Imperial War and the British Working Class*, Routledge & Kegan Paul, 1972, that support for the war was primarily a middle-class phenomenon.

78 Blewett, *Peers, Parties and People*, p. 496.

Only around 75 per cent voted, the lowest in any election between 1886 and 1914, indicating that the war had not tapped any new source of massive enthusiasm. But of course the stale register had depressed turnout.

The conflict had, so Arthur Griffith-Boscawen, a Conservative MP and future Cabinet minister, was to write in 1907, given the Unionists 'a very much larger majority than we should have secured had there been no war'.[79] The triumphant Unionists were the first to be re-elected with a large majority since the Great Reform Act of 1832, and the first incumbent government to be returned since 1865. Even in Scotland, the Unionists had a majority of seats – for the first time. Only in Wales did the Liberals retain their ascendancy. The electoral pendulum had ceased to swing. 'The phenomenon is without example', Lord Salisbury commented,

> that a party should twice dissolve at an interval of five years and in each case bring back a majority of more than one hundred and thirty. What does it mean? ... Of course I recognise the justice of the verdict the country has just given: that the love of justice should have overborne the great law of the pendulum I confess puzzles and bewilders me.[80]

But the Unionists faced the danger that, to the extent that their victory resulted from the war, once it was over, their support could crumble. Admittedly, the Liberals would need to gain at least 150 seats to win an overall majority and would otherwise be dependent on the Irish as in 1892. But they had won nearly 45 per cent of the vote, and a swing of 5 per cent would give them an overall majority. And indeed there would soon be a swing towards them in by-elections in 1901. Winston Churchill, elected as a Unionist, wrote to Rosebery on 4 October, 'I think this election fought by the Liberals as a soldiers' battle, without plan or enthusiasm, has shown so far the strength, not the weakness, of Liberalism in the country.'[81] It was a shrewd verdict.

In the general election of 1900, both parties were living in the past. The Conservatives assumed that the war would be rapidly concluded, that the empire would remain as it had been and that the country could remain free from Continental entanglements. At home, it appeared, negativism would continue to suffice. The *Fortnightly Review* declared that the election 'has given Lord Salisbury and his colleagues an act of indemnity for all their previous errors and inefficiencies ... There is a strong sentiment that Ministers must give some emphatic and exceptional evidence of their extraordinary

---

79 A. Griffith-Boscawen, *Fourteen Years in Parliament*, John Murray, 1907, p. 128.
80 Roberts, *Salisbury*, p. 779.
81 Ibid., p. 418.

good fortune, or must expect to be critically judged.'[82] The Liberals, for their part, also took it for granted that Britain's global pre-eminence was assured and that society would remain broadly stable. They seemed unaware of the changes which the new century would bring, both at home and abroad. They were to have a rude awakening in the 1900 parliament. 'Not a single issue is being discussed at this election that will be remembered two years hence,' was Haldane's prediction.[83] He was right.

---

82 Ibid., p. 821.
83 MacKenzie, *Diary of Beatrice Webb*, vol. 2, p. 184, entry for 20 August 1900.

CHAPTER 5

THE LABOUR PARTY

REPRESENTING THE WORKING CLASS

Domestically, Britain was facing a problem which many countries would fail to resolve peacefully: that of incorporating the organised working class into the political system. Some believed that this could be achieved only by a new party representing that class. In 1892, Lord Randolph Churchill had written:

> The Labour community is carrying on at the present day a very significant and instructive struggle ... It realises that it now possesses political power to such an extent as to make it independent of either party in the State; and the struggle which it is now carrying on is less against capital, less one of wages or division of profits, but rather one for the practical utilisation in its own interest of the great political power which it has acquired.

He concluded, 'Personally I can discern no cause for alarm in this prospect.'[1] In the 1900 election, there was a new party seeking representation: the Labour Representation Committee (LRC), to be renamed the Labour Party in 1906. The LRC had been formed in February 1900, just a few months before the general election, and that is generally regarded as the date of the birth of the Labour Party.

The origins of the Labour Party were quite different from those of the two older parties. The Liberals and Conservatives had begun as parliamentary combinations and, with the growth of mass suffrage, had spread outwards into the constituencies, developing extra-parliamentary organisations. The Labour Party, by contrast, began as an extra-parliamentary organisation in the constituencies seeking representation in Parliament. The Conservative and Liberal parties moved outwards from Westminster to the country. The Labour Party moved inwards from the country into Westminster.

The idea that labour should be specifically represented in Parliament was by no means new. It had first been put forward by John Stuart Mill, although

---

1 Churchill, *Lord Randolph Churchill*, vol. 2, pp. 458–9.

he had not supported a separate party, having been a Liberal MP from 1865 to 1868. In 1871, Gladstone had accepted that 'the great blot on their representative system was that they had not been able to bring working men within those walls',[2] while in 1881 Engels had argued for a labour party independent of the 'ruling class parties'. The idea of the specific representation of labour was of course anathema to most Liberals, for whom Liberalism was a creed transcending social classes. But some thought that a division of parties on the basis of class rather than creed would be an inevitable consequence of expanding the franchise. In 1894, Harcourt had told Rosebery, 'You desire to avoid the "cleavage of classes". The hope on your part is natural, but you are too late. The horizontal division of parties was certain to come as a consequence of household suffrage ... The cleavage is increasing day by day.'[3] Early attempts at independent labour representation had, however, been ineffective, and, of course, the first-past-the-post electoral system meant that an independent labour candidate would, by splitting the left-wing vote, help the Conservatives.

The notion of labour representation was, however, ambiguous. It could mean, rather than the creation of a separate political party, simply securing the election of more working-class MPs; or, alternatively, the election of working-class MPs attached to a particular party, the Liberals – the so-called Lib-Labs sent by their unions to look after their members' interests. The Lib-Lab MPs were concentrated predominantly in close-knit mining constituencies. In 1900, the Miners' Federation of Great Britain had established a centralised fund to which all members would contribute. Other unions, however, whose members were less concentrated in particular constituencies, were unable to emulate the miners. There were, for example, no railwaymen's constituencies.

Labour representation could, however, alternatively mean electing MPs of a party specifically dedicated to securing the representation of the working class as a whole – the Labour Party. Finally, it could mean the election of MPs of a specifically socialist party which, socialists believed, would represent the working class better than any 'capitalist' party could.

The Liberal leadership was sympathetic to working-class representation, but all too many Liberal constituency parties were unwilling to adopt working-class candidates who, rather than contributing to constituency funds, would, in an era before MPs were paid, prove a drain on them. Three of the early leaders of the Labour Party – Keir Hardie, Ramsay MacDonald and Arthur Henderson – had begun as Liberals but had failed to be nominated

2   A. W. Humphrey, *History of Labour Representation*, Constable, 1912, p. 44fn.
3   Ensor, *England*, p. 333.

by Liberal constituency associations, and in consequence had sought to create a party whose *raison d'être* was to secure working-class representation. In joining the Independent Labour Party (ILP) in 1894, MacDonald wrote to Hardie:

> There never was any dispute as to objects. What I could not quite accept was your methods. I have changed my opinion. Liberals, and more particularly local Liberal Associations, have definitely declared against Labour, and so I must accept the facts of the situation and cordially admit that the prophecies of the ILP relating to Liberalism have been amply justified.[4]

'We didn't leave the Liberals,' MacDonald told the Liberal Herbert Samuel shortly after the 1895 election,

> they kicked us out and slammed the door in our faces. A little generosity on their part at the Election would have gone a long way in building a bridge of understanding between the parties. The Liberals chose to stick to their purses and official votes. There can be no going back now.[5]

Henderson, who was to be returned as LRC MP for the Barnard Castle constituency in a by-election in 1903, had actually been election agent for the Liberal MP Sir Joseph Pease, whose death precipitated the by-election. Becoming an LRC MP in 1903 did not for Henderson involve any alteration in his beliefs, which remained those of a Liberal/Radical. The breach between the LRC and the Liberals came not over ideology but over representation, and few of the early Labour MPs held views which could not have been accommodated within the Liberal Party. What united them was not ideology but experience. 'When workers' questions come up for discussion,' David Shackleton, an LRC MP from 1902, was to write, Labour MPs 'have to do little more than open the book of their own lives' and 'consider what they have themselves in most instances gone through'.[6]

In his last novel, *Endymion*, published in 1880, Disraeli had predicted that a movement of revolt would originate in the west of Scotland. Keir Hardie (1856–1915), the inspiration behind a party to represent the working class, came from Lanarkshire, adjacent to the west of Scotland if not precisely part of it. He had left school at the age of seven to begin paid employment and had become a miner at the age of ten, teaching himself to read from books

---

4   Quoted in L. MacNeill Weir, *The Tragedy of Ramsay MacDonald: A Political Biography*, Secker and Warburg, 1938, p. 21.
5   Herbert Samuel, *Memoirs*, Cresset Press, 1945, p. 27.
6   David Martin, 'Ideology and Composition', in K. D. Brown, *The First Labour Party 1906–1914*, Croom Helm, 1985, p. 18.

in the windows of stationers shops, and to write shorthand while working in the pit. Hardie then became a trade union organiser. He had been the first to stand as a working-class candidate entirely independent of the two main parties in a by-election in Mid-Lanarkshire in 1888; and in that same year, he formed a Scottish Labour Party. In 1892, standing as an independent but without Liberal opposition, he was elected MP for West Ham South. He was to light the spark that was eventually to destroy the Liberals as a party of government. But for the moment, he was careful not to alienate Liberal voters. 'Generally speaking,' his manifesto had declared,

> I am in agreement with the present programme of the Liberal Party so far as it goes, but I reserve to myself the absolute and unconditional right to take such action irrespective of the exigencies of party welfare, as may to me seem needful in the interest of the workers.[7]

His supporters hired a horse-drawn waggonette to take him to the Commons, accompanied by a cornet-player. Hardie contributed to this stage management since, instead of the customary outfit of the times, he arrived in a tweed jacket and deerstalker hat – not a cloth cap as is sometimes suggested. He was mistaken by a policeman on duty for a workman and was asked if he was working on the roof of the Commons. 'No,' he replied, 'on the floor.'[8]

Hardie was to be the inspiration behind both the Independent Labour Party, formed in 1893, and the Labour Party. His central insight was that it was not sufficient just to elect working-class candidates. They had to be independent of the other parties since otherwise they would be absorbed by parties which did not have the interests of the working classes at heart. Such a party, he believed, would eventually become a socialist party, since only a socialist society could emancipate the working class. Hardie therefore repudiated Lib-Labbery, which, he believed, might have been appropriate when the trade unions were composed mainly of skilled workers, but was no longer so for the new unionism of the unskilled. But he also repudiated a party excluding the trade unions. Since the majority of trade union members were not socialist, this meant that the socialist commitment of the new party would have to be diluted. In 1904, Hardie was to write that 'wherever free parliamentary institutions exist, and where socialism has attained the status of being a recognised party, dogmatic absolutism is giving way before the advent of a more practical set of working principles. The schoolman is being

---

7 Henry Pelling, *The Origins of the Labour Party, 1880–1900*, 2nd edition, Clarendon Press, 1965, p. 106.
8 Quoted in R. Cosss, *The Management of British Foreign Policy Before the First World War*, A. W. Sijthoff, 1948, p. 38.

displaced by the statesman.'[9] There was no other way in which working-class representation could be made effective. And if the new party was to wean members of the working class from the Liberals, it would have to retain much of the Liberal ethos, in particular the Nonconformist culture which animated many trade unionists, and which had hitherto linked them to the Liberals. A party based on such an ethos could have no truck with ideas of class war. 'Socialism', Hardie was to write in 1903, 'makes war upon a system, not upon a class.'[10] The appeal of a working-class party had to be fundamentally ethical, based upon the need for social justice. Hardie's ideas were to leave a deep imprint on the early years of the Labour Party, an imprint which has by no means totally disappeared today. Although in one respect, Labour was to depart from Hardie's vision. For Hardie, although he favoured such measures as school meals and a minimum wage, was not primarily a state socialist. Instead, he believed that socialism should be achieved by the mutual institutions of civic society – trade unions, cooperatives, friendly societies and Nonconformist chapels. He would have criticised even Tony Blair's New Labour as putting too much emphasis on the state.

THE INDEPENDENT LABOUR PARTY

In 1893, an event occurred which was, so Philip Snowden believed, 'the most important political event of the nineteenth century', when various socialist and radical organisations combined to form an Independent Labour Party (ILP), with Hardie presiding at its foundation conference.[11] The party was founded in Bradford, following a prolonged strike at Manningham Mills lasting from December 1890 to April 1891 which ended with textile workers being forced to accept a reduction in wages amounting in some cases to 35 per cent while the owner of the mill was elevated to the House of Lords. Strikers in need were refused relief under the Poor Law, since they were seen as having voluntarily refused work. The collapse of the strike led to widespread suffering. The American social reformer and philanthropist Margaret McMillan, visiting Bradford in November 1893, noticed

> how many of the children had been sewn into their clothing perhaps with pads of cotton wool underneath, for the whole of the winter months; the number deprived of their birthright of sleep by the nightly attention of bedbugs; the barefooted urchins turning cartwheels in the snow to attract

---

9   Quoted by Margaret Cole, 'Keir Hardie', in Michael Katanka, ed., *Radicals, Reformers and Socialists*, Charles Knight, 1973, p. 160.
10 Philip P. Poirier, *The Advent of the Labour Party*, George Allen & Unwin, 1958, p. 47.
11 Snowden, *Autobiography*, p. 53.

pennies of the carriage gentry; the bags of sulphur sewn round the hems of the teacher's trailing skirt to prevent the vermin climbing, sidling or leaping up.[12]

Some Liberals had supported the strikers, but others had taken the side of the owner. The Liberals clearly could not be relied on to ensure the interests of working people, and the strike reinforced the need for independent labour representation.

But the ILP did not seek labour representation as an end in itself but as a means to an end: socialism. Its aim was 'to secure the collective and communal ownership of the means of production, distribution and exchange'. But it had no sympathy with Marxism. 'No doubt', its newspaper declared in September 1894, 'not every ILP member would pass an examination in "Das Capital" [sic] but at least they knew that "Liberty, Equality, Fraternity" were the true laws of life.'[13] However, a motion to include the word 'Socialist' in the title of the party was heavily defeated, since, so Hardie believed, it would antagonise trade unionists who were not socialists. Admittedly, some of the leaders of the newer trade unions such as the dockers and gas workers were in fact socialist; but most of their members were not. So the party's name had to be 'Labour', to represent the working class, not 'Socialist'. The emphasis of the new party was, as also with the early Labour Party, not so much socialism but independence from the other parties. Socialism had to be achieved gradually through the education and persuasion of trade unionists and other non-socialists. Given that there were so few socialists in Britain at that time and that most of them belonged to the middle class, it would hardly have been possible to adopt any other strategy. So the new party had to downplay socialism, relegating it to a distant future. It was for this reason that Lenin dubbed the Independent Labour Party the 'Independent (of socialism) Labour Party', but that was unfair.[14] Hardie appreciated the real difficulty of securing socialism in a democratic society in which the vast majority regarded it with suspicion. He tried to persuade trade unions to support and affiliate to the ILP, a party which, like the Labour Party, to which it helped give birth, combined organisational independence with doctrinal tolerance. The ILP, Hardie wrote in 1894:

is avowedly a Socialistic organisation, and has been so from the first. But a great merit it possesses is that of enlisting to its aid at election times men

---

12 G. A. N. Lowndes, *Margaret McMillan, The Children's Champion*, Museum Press, 1960, p. 119.
13 Howell, *British Workers and the Independent Labour Party*, p. 354. This book provides a masterly account of the origins and significance of the ILP, and indeed of the origins of the Labour Party.
14 V. I. Lenin, *Collected Works*, Progress Publishers, 1975, vol. 18, p. 468.

who, though not yet Socialists themselves, agree with the Independent political action of the ILP, on Labour questions. These men once committed never return to political bondage.[15]

The ILP was in addition the first political party to accept women and men as equal members. One female activist declared that she joined after visiting a party function in Colne Valley where men had given a tea party for women, pouring out the tea, cutting the bread and butter and doing the washing up without any accidents. In 1895, the ILP came out in support of female suffrage.

But the ILP, unlike the Labour Party, never became a mass party. During the 1890s, its total paid-up membership exceeded 10,000 only in 1894–95; and in only two other years was it higher than 8,000.[16] And its membership seems mainly to have been middle class.[17] It was also very much a regional party, concentrated in areas where Nonconformity was strong, such as the north of England and, in particular, the West Riding of Yorkshire, where the ILP shared with the Liberals 'a multitude of common sentiments and prejudices that occasioned a remarkable similarity in their practical application of different principles to actual issues of public policy'.[18] In areas where the Anglican Church was strong, and in more secular areas such as London, its appeal was more limited. In London, moreover, where there were few large employers, cooperation between Liberals and Labour was possible in the London County Council under the progressive umbrella. In the provinces, such cooperation was more difficult. Engels noticed that the 'weight' of the new party 'lies in the provinces and not in London'.[19] But when it fought the general election of 1895, the ILP was routed and all of its twenty-eight candidates were defeated.

THE SOCIAL DEMOCRATIC FEDERATION AND THE FABIAN SOCIETY

There were a number of other socialist organisations besides the ILP – the most prominent being the Social Democratic Federation (SDF), formed as the Democratic Federation in 1881 but renamed in 1884; and the Fabian Society, founded in 1884. They adopted different tactics towards achieving

15   Colin Cross, *Philip Snowden*, Barrie & Rockliff, 1966, pp. 19–20.
16   Howell, *British Workers and the Independent Labour Party*, p. 328.
17   Pelling, *Popular Politics and Society*, p. 126.
18   Frank Bealey and Henry Pelling, *Labour and Politics, 1900–1906: A History of the Labour Representation Committee*, Macmillan, 1958, p. 9.
19   Pelling, *Origins of the Labour Party*, p. 123.

socialism from the ILP, but neither succeeded in creating mass support for it. The SDF, the first socialist party in Britain, claimed to be Marxist, but its Marxism was somewhat unorthodox. Marx had been on the whole ignored in Britain and his death in London in 1883 would have passed unnoticed had not the Paris correspondent of *The Times* written a paragraph on his European reputation. *Das Kapital*, published in 1867, was not translated into English until 1887, and its ideas were first popularised by the SDF leader, H. M. Hyndman, in 1881, in a book entitled *England for All*, anathematised by Marx for alleged plagiarism and inaccuracy. The SDF was somewhat reluctant to publish membership statistics, since these would reveal how small its support actually was. It used to be thought that its membership had reached around 10,000 in the mid-1890s, but it seems that this was a gross overestimate. By 1901, it appears that its fee-paying membership was just 2,380.[20] Although some leading members of the Labour Party such as George Lansbury and, surprisingly perhaps, Ernest Bevin, began with the SDF, it never succeeded in acquiring mass support. Nor, of course, did the ILP, but the ILP at least had the support of some trade unions. The leaders of the SDF were, however, sceptical of the role which trade unions could play under socialism, declaring in 1884 that 'trade unions as they now are cannot hope to participate' in the class struggle, even though some of its members such as Will Thorne, leader of the gas workers, and Ben Tillett, leader of the dockers, were prominent trade unionists.[21] Interestingly, Marx's daughter Eleanor disagreed with Hyndman on this point, and helped the gas workers' new union – an indication, perhaps, that Marx believed that in Britain the transition to socialism could be achieved peacefully. Indeed, Engels was to be a supporter of the ILP.

The SDF was also detached from the radical and Nonconformist roots of the labour movement – Keir Hardie complained that, while ILP members drank tea, there was too much beer at SDF meetings! It was strongest in London and Lancashire, where Nonconformity was relatively weak.[22] The SDF affiliated to the Labour Representation Committee in 1900, but withdrew the year afterwards, since it doubted the new party's socialist commitment. It became the main representative of Marxist ideas in Britain and was eventually to form a component of the Communist Party of Great Britain, formed in 1920. But the SDF would never play an important part in Labour politics.

---

20 P. A. Watmough, 'The Membership of the Social Democratic Federation, 1885–1902', *Bulletin of the Society for the Study of Labour History*, 1977, p. 37; and see, in general, Chushichi Tsuzuki, *H. M. Hyndman and British Socialism*, Oxford University Press, 1961.

21 Pelling, *Origins of the Labour Party*, p. 57.

22 Taylor, *Trouble Makers*, p. 106.

* * *

The Fabian Society was a think tank, not a political party, and did not put up candidates for Parliament. It was named after the Roman general Fabius Maximus who had defeated a numerically superior Carthaginian Army under Hannibal by adopting slow and persistent tactics of wearing down the opposition, rather than engaging in frontal attack. The Fabian Society would achieve this wearing-down strategy by research highlighting social inadequacies and making a rational and irresistible case for socialism. But the novelist H. G. Wells mischievously pointed to Plutarch's *Lives*, which showed that Fabius never did strike when the moment came.

The Fabians developed a distinctive doctrine of how socialism was to be achieved based, oddly enough, on the teachings of classical economics. They adapted the doctrine of rent to moveable capital, arguing that, like the landowner, the capitalist who was a mere receiver of dividends had outlived his usefulness and was being replaced by skilled managers and administrators. Like landlords, capitalists were no longer performing a useful social function. They should therefore be eliminated by a process which the Fabians called the socialisation of rent, involving the transfer of private property to the state, the functions of the capitalist being taken over by trained managers. Land, capital and the organisation of industry, which under capitalism were left to the irresponsibility of private individuals, would then be managed for the public good. The Fabians developed a form of socialism which, by contrast with Marxism, was, so they believed, suitable for a country evolving into a democracy and an industrial society characterised by joint-stock companies, salaried managers and some degree of public control. They were 'equally far from Marx and Morris', but 'they left the New Jerusalem alone, and sought to impregnate the existing forces of society with collectivist ideas'.[23] Fabianism was, it has been said, 'the first group in the field with a Socialism suitable for a nation so prosperous, so constitutional and so respectful of suave and confident authority as England'.[24]

The Fabians believed that the trends which they had noticed were already leading society in a collectivist direction. Writing on 'The Latest Age' in the *Cambridge Modern History* of 1910, Sidney Webb detected four main elements of collective advance: first, collective ownership of such services as railways, canals, telephones, postal communications; second, local municipal ownership of such services as water, gas, electricity, tramways, housing,

---

23   G. M. Trevelyan, *British History in the Nineteenth Century and After, 1782–1919*, 2nd edition, Longmans, Green & Co., 1937, p. 405.
24   A. M. McBriar, *Fabian Socialism and English Politics, 1884–1918*, Cambridge University Press, 1962, p. 348.

baths and washhouses and parks; third, community control of private property through such legislation as the Factory Acts, Merchant Shipping Acts and provisions for minimum wages; and, finally, collective provision for the dependent section of the community – in particular children and the elderly – all amounting to acceptance of the idea of state responsibility for a national minimum below which no one should be allowed to fall.[25]

The Fabians believed that Marx had underestimated the importance of democratic and electoral pressures which were pushing both major parties in the direction of state intervention. There was, the Webbs thought, 'far more Socialism than there are Socialists'.[26] The task of Fabians, therefore, was to encourage and speed up the process of democratic collectivism. But how was this to be done? There were two possibilities, according to Beatrice Webb: 'Do we want to organise the *unthinking* persons into socialist societies, or to make the *thinking* persons socialistic?' To this question she answered, 'We believe in the latter policy.' 'The organised working class' would have to be 'served and guided ... by an elite of unassuming experts who would make no claim to superior status, but would content themselves with exercising the power inherent in superior knowledge'.[27] The 'elite of unassuming experts' would be the educated minority. The Webbs believed that the Fabians should act *for* the working class rather than *with* them and were therefore not particularly enthusiastic about the creation of an independent labour or socialist party. By making socialism a matter of party politics, so they believed, progress would be hindered not helped, since socialism would become divisive, polarising opinion between socialists and anti-socialists and driving well-meaning radicals into the anti-socialist camp, the camp of reaction. It was better to encourage the trends towards collectivism which were influencing both major parties in the state. Whereas other socialists sought to differentiate themselves from the capitalist parties, the Webbs wanted to permeate them with socialist ideas. They sought to be instigators rather than leaders. They were 'intelligence offices without an army – there was no Fabian party in parliament'.[28] But there was a crucial weakness in their philosophy from the socialist point of view. For, as the social theorist L. T. Hobhouse wrote in 1898, they were tempted 'to hail any and every extension of State authority, whatever its principle or its object as a triumph for Socialism'. There was, Hobhouse wrote in a leader in the *Manchester Guardian* in 1899, 'all the

25 Sidney Webb, 'The Latest Age', in A. W. Ward, G. W. Prothero and Stanley Leathes, eds, *Cambridge Modern History*, vol. 12, Cambridge University Press, 1910, pp. 759–60.
26 MacKenzie, *Diary of Beatrice Webb*, vol. 2, p. 94, entry for 18 April 1896; Sidney and Beatrice Webb, 'What is Socialism?', *New Statesman*, 12 April 1913, p. 13.
27 José Harris, 'Political Thought and the Welfare State 1870–1940: An Intellectual Framework for British Social Policy', in David Gladstone, ed., *Before Beveridge: Welfare Before the Welfare State*, Institute of Economic Affairs, 1999, p. 84.
28 Trevelyan, *British History in the Nineteenth Century*, p. 401.

difference between benevolent officialdom setting the world in order from above, and the democratic Collectivism which seeks not to restrict liberty but to fulfil it'. 'As the "expert" comes to the front, and "efficiency" becomes the watchword of administration, all that was human in Socialism vanishes out of it.' What the Fabians were doing, Hobhouse was to argue in 1907, was seeking 'to force progress by packing and managing committees instead of winning the popular assent'.[29] Fabianism, the historian A. J. P. Taylor declared, was 'the socialism of snobs'.[30] These criticisms were echoed by the novelist H. G. Wells in a paper read to the society in February 1905, entitled *The Faults of the Fabians*. 'I find in our society,' Wells declared,

> something like a belief that the world may be manoeuvred into socialism without knowing it: that ... we shall presently be able to confront the world with a delighted, 'But you are Socialists! We chalked it on your backs when you weren't looking.' We in this society ... have tended more and more to become the exponents of a masked socialism that I fear and dread, that in the end may, quite conceivably, not leave one shred of the true socialist spirit alive in us ... No doubt it is quite possible to achieve all sorts of good purposes through existing organisations and institutions, only – it isn't the way to socialism. Make socialists and you will achieve socialism. There is no other way ... Even were it possible to achieve really socialist institutions in our insidious way, what would it all amount to? We should have the body of socialism without its spirit, we should have won our Utopia with labour and stress – and behold it would be stillborn.[31]

The Webbs had only limited success with permeation. They were to persuade Asquith that the Poor Law should be broken up, and the Liberal solution was to be quite different; and they influenced Churchill's Trade Boards Act of 1909, establishing criteria for minimum wages in sweated trades. But otherwise they had, before 1914, few achievements. They concentrated their attention primarily upon advocates of national efficiency, social imperialists – and particularly Rosebery and Haldane. But Rosebery was not to become a member of the Liberal government in 1905, while Haldane, who became War Secretary, was removed from domestic matters. The Fabians were in fact so far removed from the mainstream of the labour movement that the great French historian Élie Halévy regarded them as a British version of Prussian

---

29 Quoted in Peter Clarke, 'The Progressive Movement in England', *Transactions of the Royal Historical Society*, 1974, pp. 165, 167.
30 *New Statesman*, 22 June 1962, p. 908.
31 Quoted in Samuel Hynes, *The Edwardian Turn of Mind*, Princeton University Press, 1968, pp. 400–401. The whole paper is reprinted on pp. 390–409.

state socialism. But they were to make a massive contribution later in the century to the left by insisting that reform be based on painstaking social research rather than idealistic moralism or theories divorced from practical realities. One journalist writing in 1913 believed that they had 'done more than any one else to redeem politics from guess-work and to give it an exact and scientific basis'. And, he added, 'though their labours have been confined to the material fabric of society, I am not sure that they have not done as much as the poets to cleanse its soul as well'.[32] William Beveridge, author of the 1942 report which heralded the modern welfare state, was to acknowledge that he had been 'deeply impressed by the Fabian movement. Sidney Webb and his associates gave me the sense that by taking sufficient thought one could remedy all the evils in the world'.[33] Denis Healey, Labour Defence Secretary in the 1960s and Chancellor in the 1970s, declared that the Fabians had 'found socialists wandering aimlessly in Cloud Cuckoo land and set [them] working on the gas and water problems of the nearest town or village. The modern Welfare State is their monument.'[34]

Although leading Fabians were sceptical of the value of an independent labour party, the Fabian Society nevertheless affiliated to the LRC in 1900 and, unlike the SDF, maintained its affiliation. Their tactics nevertheless remained not the mass meeting or electoral canvassing but the policy document, of which they had published 175 by 1914 with an average circulation of around 100,000, and the dinner party to influence political leaders. Before 1914, the society probably never had more than around 1,000 members, mostly London-based, and until around 1909, its leaders devoted more attention to 'permeating' the Liberal and Conservative parties than Labour. But after 1909, largely because of the Liberals' lack of sympathy for the minority report of the Poor Law Commission, primarily written by Beatrice Webb, they began to believe that permeation was ceasing to bear fruit, that Liberals or Conservatives would not be persuaded to advance socialism by stealth. In 1912, the Webbs joined the ILP.

*　*　*

There were very few socialists in late nineteenth-century Britain – perhaps not more than around 10,000 in the 1890s. The more perceptive were under no illusions as to their lack of mass support. In 1890, one SDF member had said, 'We claim adult suffrage but we know if it were established tomorrow

32 Gardiner, *Pillars of Society*, p. 210.
33 Quoted in John Cooper, *The British Welfare Revolution*, p. 24.
34 Denis Healey, 'Power Politics and the Labour Party', in R. H. S. Crossman, ed., *New Fabian Essays*, Turnstile Press, 1952, p. 161.

and a vote taken whether all prominent socialists should be hanged, a majority might send us to the gallows.'[35] The socialists' inability to win mass support may be contrasted with the membership of the Primrose League, a social organisation founded in 1883 to spread Conservative principles. Its total membership in 1891, according to the eleventh edition of *Encyclopedia Britannica*, published in 1911, was just over 1 million; and by 1901, its membership had risen to nearly 1.5 million. There were more members of the Primrose League in Bolton alone in 1895 – around 6,000 – than of the ILP in the whole of Britain for much of the 1890s.

LABOUR AND THE TRADE UNIONS

The ILP, then, was the main parliamentary vehicle for socialists. Its economic ideas derived from the radical tradition, owing more to Mill than Marx. In his later works, Mill had argued that the problem of production had been broadly solved and that the key problem would now be that of distribution. Productive power, Mill believed, was increasing and would continue to increase so that it would soon be possible to provide the necessities of life for all. All that stood in the way was the maldistribution of income which allowed the rich to purchase socially useless goods. Most British socialists accepted mid-century doctrines of progress. For many, socialism was a doctrine of continuity as much as conflict. In foreign policy also, the ideas of socialists derived mainly from the radical tradition. But they devoted comparatively little attention to foreign policy and seemed oblivious of the extent to which Britain's economy depended on international conditions, and in particular upon her overseas trade. Labour's 1906 election manifesto had just one brief reference to foreign policy: 'Wars are fought to make the rich richer.' The sentence continued 'and schoolchildren are still neglected'. *Fabian Essays*, first published in 1889, had nothing on overseas trade or foreign policy, and in the 1920 edition, Sidney Webb admitted that there had been a failure to 'think internationally'. The philosophy of most socialists reflected an era in which Britain remained the predominant power in the world.

The key to the formation of the Labour Party, however, is not to be found in the beliefs or faith of the socialists but must be sought instead in the evolution of trade union opinion. At the end of the nineteenth century, the trade unions, having flourished in a capitalist society, seemed a constraint on socialism. There was an important contrast in this respect between Britain and the Continent. In France, Italy and Germany, the trade union movement began at the same time as the development of a working-class political party,

35 Pat Thane, 'The working class and State "welfare" in Britain, 1890–1914', in Gladstone, ed., *Before Beveridge*, p. 84.

while in Sweden, the social democrat party had preceded the growth of trade unions. In Britain, by contrast, a strong trade union movement had achieved legal recognition in the 1870s and was accustomed to collective bargaining with employers. Indeed, trade unions had been legitimised in the 1820s, with the repeal of the Combination Acts, well before a separate working-class party had been contemplated. Trade unions had, for the most part, avoided identification with political parties, though most trade unionists no doubt voted Liberal. In 1885, the president of the Trades Union Congress (TUC) declared that 'it had been the boast of trade unionists that they belong to no political party. I hope they never will as it is now understood.'[36] They saw themselves as being concerned with industrial not political matters. During the 1890s, despite the economic depression, trade unions grew in confidence and strength. They also became more sympathetic to labour representation.

Until the late 1880s, trade unions had been primarily organisations either for skilled workers in, for example, engineering, or processing workers in coal and cotton. Such unions used their often-extensive funds to provide benefits for their members – insurance against sickness and unemployment and funeral costs. They tended to be conservative in their approach. To take one example, the main railway union, the Amalgamated Society of Railway Servants (ASRS), founded in 1861, began as little more than a friendly society, distinctly hostile to strike action. It regarded its members as part of an industrial elite. Porters, paid comparatively well, were forbidden to take tips. These old-established unions had a quasi-monopoly power in the labour market which they used to restrict entry, preserving the privileges of their members by means of strict rules of demarcation. This often put them in conflict with members of other unions deemed to be encroaching upon these privileges and, particularly, with the unskilled. Such unions felt they could look after themselves and did not need a separate Labour Party. If other unions wanted representation, they should finance it as the miners, for example, had done. 'I should like to ask', Ben Pickard of the Miners' Federation of Great Britain enquired in 1899, 'why we as a Federation should be called upon to join an Association to find money, time or intellect to focus the weaknesses of other Trade Unionists to do what you are doing for yourselves.'[37]

But the structure of the trade union movement was changing. The New Unionism sought to organise previously unorganised, unskilled and semi-skilled workers. While older unions had been able to offer benefits to members, the low level of subscriptions to the new unions limited what they

---

36 Robert Currie, *Industrial Politics*, Clarendon Press, 1979, p. 41.
37 Hugh Clegg, Alan Fox and A. F. Thompson, *A History of British Trade Unions since 1889*, vol. 1, Clarendon Press, 1964, p. 376.

could offer. Instead, they emphasised collective action to improve the position of their members. They were fighting organisations but found it difficult to retain membership and enthusiasm amongst those working in unskilled, casual and low-paid trades. Part of the difficulty was that in trades such as the docks, there was a surplus of available labour, so that 'free' or non-union labour was available during a strike. It was of course easier to import non-union labour in trades for the unskilled than in trades represented by older unions such as engineering. A skilled engineer could not be replaced as easily as a docker. The new unions, unlike their older counterparts, were generally open to women as well as men, and Eleanor Marx, daughter of the great revolutionary, played an important part in their development. In the late 1880s, the economic environment, with unemployment falling, was favourable to the new unions and they had three notable successes: a strike by Bryant and May match girls in 1888 against atrocious factory conditions; a gas workers' strike in 1889 for an eight-hour day; and a dockers' strike for 6d an hour – the so-called dockers' tanner – also in 1889.

The leaders of the new unions were men of a very different stamp from those of the older unions. Of the leaders of the older unions at the 1890 TUC, John Burns, Liberal MP for Battersea and former trade union leader, noticed that 'a great number of them looked like respectable city gentlemen; wore very good coats, large watch-chains and high hats – and in many cases were of such splendid build and proportion that they presented an aldermanic, not to say a magisterial dignity'. In contrast, 'amongst the "new" delegates not a single one wore a tall hat. They looked [like] workmen. They were workmen.'[38] Some of the new union leaders, such as Will Thorne, leader of the National Union of Gas Workers and General Labourers, had been nearly illiterate. Some, such as Tom Mann, president of the dockers' union, had worked underground from the age of ten.[39] They were far more sympathetic than the older leaders to legislation such as the eight-hour day. They were also more sympathetic to socialism and separate labour representation. In 1889, the National Union of Gas Workers and General Labourers was to be the first to state in its constitution that amongst its aims was the return to Parliament of Socialist MPs. The ILP was to be founded largely by the new unions, and in 1893, the TUC was persuaded to establish a fund to be used only in support of socialist candidates. But the TUC was by no means fully committed to labour representation, and in 1895, it established a new method of voting at its annual conference designed to limit the role of

---

38   Quoted in Standish Meacham, '"The Sense of an Impending Crisis": English Working-Class Unrest before the First World War', *American Historical Review*, 1972, pp. 1,355–6.

39   Yvonne Kapp, *The Air of Freedom: The Birth of the New Unionism*, Lawrence and Wishart, 1989, p. 83; Joseph White, *Tom Mann*, Manchester University Press, 1991, pp. 1–4.

socialists, the so-called block or card vote by which each trade union voted as a single bloc in proportion to its membership. This gave great weight to the two largest unions – miners and cotton workers – both of which were opposed to socialism and to independent representation.

By 1899, however, more unions were coming to favour independent labour representation. This was primarily a result of judgments by the courts which threatened the unions' legal position, a position that unions believed had been secured through legislation in the 1870s – the Trade Union Act of 1871 and the Conspiracy and Protection of Property Act and the Employers and Workmen Act, both in 1875, passed by the governments of Gladstone and Disraeli. This legislation was seen by the unions as acts of emancipation. Unions were deemed to be unincorporated associations, and in consequence, so trade unionists believed, they would not be legally liable for actions taken during industrial disputes. The case of *Allen v. Flood* in 1898 appeared to confirm that view, since the House of Lords, acting in its judicial capacity, had held that a union could not be sued by a non-union member for pressing an employer not to hire him, whether or not the union's motive was malicious.[40] But a previous case, *Lyons v. Wilkins*, had cast doubt on the legality of peaceful picketing, and the judges had declared that even calling a man a 'blackleg' was intimidation and unlawful.[41]

In 1899, James Holmes of the railwaymen's union and a Liberal proposed at the annual TUC conference a resolution, probably drafted by MacDonald or Hardie, calling for a joint conference with socialist and cooperative bodies to discuss labour representation.[42] In 1897 and 1898, such resolutions had been rejected. But in 1899, it was passed by 546,000 votes to 434,000, with around one-sixth of the delegates absent or abstaining. Clearly, many trade unionists remained sceptical of labour representation; and the terms of the ASRS motion were ambiguous. The motion proposed that a 'special congress of representatives' of labour organisations be convened 'to devise ways and means for securing the return of an increased number of labour members in the next Parliament'. There was no mention of a separate party, and it was by no means clear that the resolution did in fact entail a separate party.

In February 1900, the conference proposed in the ASRS motion was held. There were just 129 delegates representing a total membership of 570,000, less than half of those represented at the TUC. The chair, W. C. Steadman, Lib-Lab MP for Stepney and, for many years, general secretary of the River Thames Barge Builders Trade Union, declared:

---

40 *Allen v. Flood* [1898] A.C. 1.
41 *Lyons v. Wilkins* [1896] 1 Ch. 811 [1899] 1 Ch. 255.
42 Poirier, *Advent of the Labour Party*, p. 74.

He was one of those Trade Unionists who believed, until the last ten years, that the workers of this country could attain their object in securing better conditions by voluntary efforts of trade organisations. But the dispute which occurred in his own trade ten years ago for a reduction in the hours of labour had convinced him that the leaders of the advanced movement who believed in political action were right and he was wrong (Cheers.) ... He had been a member of the House of Commons but a short time, but he had been there sufficiently long to know that every interest was represented and protected in that House (especially when privilege and monopoly were attacked) but the interest of labour. The great industrial army of the country, the men who were endeavouring to raise mankind not by the shedding of human blood, but by the peaceful conquest of the ballot-box were the only class who were insufficiently represented in the House of Commons ... For the first time in the history of the labour movement all sections of that movement were drawn together.[43]

The conference agreed to establish a Labour Representation Committee (LRC), a body which one could only join indirectly by joining one of the affiliated bodies, and it was not wholly clear whether it would become a party. The LRC was in fact a federation of national organisations – trades unions, socialist societies, cooperative societies and other local affiliated labour organisations such as trades councils which were local groups of trade unionists. In 1905, it was agreed that local constituency parties could be affiliated to the LRC in areas where there were no trades councils. But there was no national organisation of constituency parties and local propaganda was generally carried out not by constituency Labour parties but by the ILP, a national organisation.

The total affiliated membership at the inauguration of the LRC was 568,177 members, of which 542,316 were the members of affiliated trade unions, while the other 25,861 represented the ILP, the Fabians and the SDF. A trade union could affiliate upon payment of an affiliation fee of 10/- (50p) and would be entitled to one delegate for every 2,000 members affiliated. Voting at the annual conference would be on the basis of one vote for every 1,000 members affiliated. The LRC established an executive comprising members of affiliated organisations – seven trade unionists, including the chair; two from the ILP, of which Keir Hardie was one; two from the SDF (although the SDF was to disaffiliate in 1901); and one Fabian. The trade unionists had a majority, but the socialists were over-represented with five seats

---

43   Labour Party Foundation Conference, Hammersmith Reprints of Scarce Documents, no. 3, Hammersmith Bookshop, 1967, p. 10.

out of twelve, even though comprising just 8 per cent of the membership. But some of the trade union representatives were also socialists.

The conference adopted the ILP viewpoint on the main issues, rejecting an attempt by the SDF to commit the new organisation to 'a recognition of the class war' and also rejecting a proposal that Labour candidates should come exclusively from the working class.[44] The labour movement, Mac-Donald insisted, was not 'a Movement of trades' but 'of opinions'.[45] But the conference also rejected the Lib-Lab view that the LRC should remain uncommitted on all issues not relating to labour representation. The ILP believed that the LRC should have a distinctive view on all the questions that came before Parliament, not just those specifically affecting the labour interest, and successfully proposed a motion providing for the establishment of

a distinct Labour group in parliament, who shall have their own whips, and agree upon their policy, which must embrace a readiness to cooperate with any party which for the time being may be engaged in promoting legislation in the direct interests of labour, and be equally ready to associate themselves with any party in opposing measures having an opposite tendency.

It was agreed that this 'distinct Labour group' should be supported financially by means of affiliation fees from the component organisations represented at the conference. But this motion, like the TUC resolution of 1899, was also ambiguous. It did not, after all, specifically prescribe a new party, only a new group with its own whips. Some of the trade union members may have believed that the LRC would be a mere extension of Lib-Labbery and would work only for specific reforms, such as the legal rights of trade unions. But the implication was, to many participants and observers, clear. One socialist newspaper celebrated the occasion by declaring that 'at last there is a United Labour Party, or perhaps it would be safer to say, a little cloud, no bigger than a man's hand which may grow into a United Labour Party'.[46] But until 1918, it could hardly be described as a party at all. It had no programme, no agreement on whether it was socialist and no agreement on how socialism could be achieved. It was a somewhat ramshackle group with little effective organisation at constituency level. Indeed, the title Labour Representation Committee was little more than 'an accurate description of what already existed, without prejudice to the use of a more ambitious title if expansion

---

44 Marquand, *Ramsay MacDonald*, p. 51.
45 Ibid., p. 68.
46 Quoted in Pelling, *Origins of the Labour Party*, pp. 210–11.

were effected'.[47] Even the concept of independence was ambiguous. As late as 1918, Arthur Henderson was to tell the party conference that Labour 'had never in the proper sense claimed to be a national political party'.[48] Not was it clear precisely what independence meant. In a joint article written in January 1899 before the LRC was formed, Keir Hardie and Ramsay MacDonald insisted that 'independence is not isolation, and in so far as cooperation with kindred sections is possible, while retaining our freedom, there is no barrier to it in our methods or tradition'.[49] It certainly did not exclude an electoral pact with the Liberals, nor even a coalition with the Liberals, which Mac-Donald was to hanker after in 1914. MacDonald indeed believed that there was no profound gulf between Liberals and Labour but that Labour would eventually succeed the Liberals through an evolutionary process. Hardie felt that this would happen rapidly, but MacDonald was more realistic and thought that it would take time. However, the process would, MacDonald believed, be hastened, not hindered, by cooperation between the two parties.

The LRC offered a striking contrast not only to the older parties but also to Continental socialists and social democratic parties, which were doctrinal. The prime purpose of the LRC and later the Labour Party in its early years was not doctrinal – for it would not have been easy to discover a programme which could unite the socialist societies and the trade unions – but organisational, to represent the labour interest. Perhaps solidarity would have been a good watchword for the party, since it sought to create the solidarity of a united working class.[50] In Continental socialist parties, there were numerous doctrinal crises between Marxists, non-Marxists and social democrats. In the Labour Party, early crises were in relation to tactics, not doctrines.[51]

The secretary of the LRC was Ramsay MacDonald, appointed as the only person prepared to take the post without payment, something he could do since he was earning fees as a freelance journalist and his wife enjoyed a private income. No one anticipated that appointing MacDonald as secretary would be the first step that would take him to Downing Street as Labour's first Prime Minister in just twenty-three years. MacDonald, however, was at least as important as Hardie in Labour's formation and survival. If Hardie was a founder of the party, MacDonald ensured that it would survive into adulthood.

Two LRC MPs were elected in 1900 – Keir Hardie for Merthyr Tydfil, a

---

47 Bealey and Pelling, *Labour and Politics*, p. 36.
48 Quoted in Robert McKenzie, *British Political Parties: The Distribution of Power within the Conservative and Labour Parties*, 2nd edition, Heinemann, 1963, p. 475.
49 *Nineteenth Century*, January 1899, quoted in Bealey and Pelling, *Labour and Politics*, p. 129.
50 Bealey and Pelling, *Labour and Politics*, p. 188.
51 Egon Wertheimer, *Portrait of the Labour Party*, G. P. Putnam's Sons, 1929, p. 134.

two-member seat, defeated one of the two Liberal candidates, and Richard
Bell, general secretary of the railwaymen's union, in the two-member constituency of Derby. Bell's views, unlike Hardie's, were in fact indistinguishable
from those of Liberals, and he was never happy in the LRC. Indeed, he sat
in the Commons with the Liberals, regularly voting with them while Hardie
sat with the Irish members.

The foundation conference of the LRC attracted hardly any public attention. Just nine spectators watched from the gallery and *The Times* devoted
less than a quarter of a column to it.[52] Whether the LRC would be more
successful than previous attempts at labour representation would depend
on whether it could secure mass union support. At its foundation, only a
minority of unions – around 400 out of over 11,000 – were affiliated. The
larger unions, and in particular the coal and cotton unions, remained aloof.
Commenting on the first annual conference in 1901, Philip Snowden wrote,
'It looked as if this new effort was going to share the fate of previous attempts
to secure the direct representation of labour.'[53] The TUC might sympathise
in some of its resolutions with independent labour representation, but many
of its members were sceptical. It was to take the *Taff Vale* case in 1901 to make
the larger unions reconsider their aloofness from the Labour Representation
Committee.[54]

The case resulted from a strike which had begun in August 1900 on the
Taff Vale railway in south Wales, which linked the ports with collieries sup-
plying fuel for the navy during the Boer War. The national emergency, so
the strikers believed, put them in a strong bargaining position. But many
families in south Wales had men fighting in the war, and this deprived the
activists of much public support. The occasion of the strike was the demand
by railway workers to reinstate a signalman who, they claimed, had been
victimised for not following instructions to transfer to another signal box
'without his consent and in breach of earlier conventions'.[55] Since the union
was not recognised and there was no machinery for joint consultation, the
grievance festered. But the basic cause of the strike was the refusal of the
general manager of the company, Ammon Beasley, to grant more than a very
modest increase in wages during a period of rapidly rising prices. The men
had, however, gone on strike without handing in notice, breaching their
contracts of employment. The secretary of the railway union, Richard Bell,
the LRC MP, had been against the strike, but the union executive overrode
him and endorsed it. Bell tried to settle the dispute but was told by Beasley,

52 Pelling, *Origins of the Labour Party*, p. 208.
53 Snowden, *Autobiography*, p. 94.
54 *Taff Vale Railway Co. Ltd v. Amalgamated Society of Railway Servants* [1901] A.C. 426.
55 Norman McCord, 'Taff Vale Revisited', *History*, 1993, p. 245.

in effect, to mind his own business. Beasley then imported non-union 'free labour' to break the strike, which lasted for just one month, ending in early September in defeat for the union. The aggrieved signalman left the railway to become a miner.[56] During the conflict, the strikers put pressure on the strike-breakers not to work on the railway and damaged the tracks to prevent the railway operating. There were also attacks on the strike-breakers. While these had not been authorised by the union, it appeared that Bell and official representatives of the union in south Wales had agreed to methods of repelling strike-breakers which went beyond what was legally allowed. Beasley had sought an injunction to prevent what he regarded as unlawful picketing and sued the union for damages caused to the railway. The union believed that it had played a constructive role in helping to settle the strike. It argued that it was unfair for it to be held liable for the actions of individuals over whom it had no control. Nevertheless, in the High Court, Mr Justice Farwell asked whether the legislation of the 1870s defining the role of trade unions had 'authorized the creation of numerous bodies of men capable of owning great wealth and of acting by agents, with absolutely no responsibility for the wrongs they may do to other persons by the use of that wealth and the employment of those agents?' He answered, 'I do not think so.' 'It would', he declared, 'require very clear and express words of enactment to induce me to hold that the legislature had in fact legalised the existence of such irresponsible bodies with such wide capacity for evil.'[57] Trade unions, he argued, possessed the attributes of corporate bodies and should be treated as such. They should therefore be held liable for tortious acts committed on their behalf. But when the union took its case to the Appeal Court, it won since it was held that the legislation would have been explicit that a trade union could be sued if that had been Parliament's intention. But the House of Lords, acting in its judicial capacity, reaffirmed the judgment of the High Court in July 1901, with Lord Halsbury declaring:

> If the legislature has created a thing which can own property, which can employ servants, and which can inflict injury, it must be taken, I think, to have impliedly given the power to make it suable in a Court of Law for injuries purposely done by its authority and procurement.[58]

This was a blow to the trade unions since a Royal Commission on Labour in 1891–94 had accepted that they could not sue or be sued except in cases

---

56 Ibid., p. 246.
57 Quoted in Philip S. Bagwell, *The Railwaymen: The History of the National Union of Railwaymen*, George Allen & Unwin, 1963, p. 222.
58 *Taff Vale Railway Co. Ltd v. Amalgamated Society of Railway Servants* [1901] A.C. 426, 67.

involving the management of their own property. The majority had, admittedly, condemned this situation, which it regarded as one of 'collective action without legal collective responsibility', but the minority argued that 'the present freedom of Trade unions from any interference by the courts of law ... should be sustained'.[59] In *Taff Vale*, the House of Lords held that a trade union could be sued for damages for the acts of its members and that an injunction could be issued restraining a union not only from criminal acts but also from unlawful civil acts. Trade union funds, therefore, were not, as had hitherto been thought, immune from such actions. The union was fined £23,000 and required to pay costs, the total amounting to around £42,000. Following *Taff Vale*, other unions also came to be sued and were required to pay damages. So the judgment was a threat not just to the railwaymen but to the whole trade union movement. A union could not, it seemed, know in advance what powers it had during an industrial dispute nor whether actions it took or authorised might be regarded as lawful or unlawful by the courts. The right to strike seemed to have been gravely weakened. One modern historian has declared that 'later opinion has generally concluded that it [the judgment] was a sound interpretation of the law as it stood' and that it 'has in general been vindicated by subsequent legal assessments'. But that was certainly not the view of the trade unions or the labour movement at the time.[60]

The *Taff Vale* case seemed to many trade unionists just one of a series of judgments threatening what seemed a long-established and recognised legal position. A fortnight after the ruling, the law lords acting in their judicial capacity were to hold in *Quinn v. Leathem* that a trade union boycotting a butcher's business to enforce a closed shop was unlawful as a 'conspiracy to injure'.[61] Trade unions contrasted the decision in *Quinn v. Leathem* with that in the *Mogul Steamship* case when the law lords had decided that a cartel formed to drive competitors out of business was not unlawful.[62] *Quinn*, when considered in conjunction with *Lyons v. Wilkins*, seemed to call in doubt peaceful picketing, since that judgment had held that persuasion by more than one person generally involved annoyance and coercion.[63] So a trade union would find it difficult to resist the importation of non-union labour, so-called free labour. The unions feared an employer's counteroffensive against the unions, though such an offensive did not in the event materialise. Beasley was untypical of employers, most of whom continued to prefer

59 McCord, 'Taff Vale Revisited', pp. 250–51.
60 Ibid., pp. 251–2. The article provides the detail to sustain these judgments.
61 *Quinn v. Leathem* [1901] A.C. 495.
62 *Mogul Steamship* [1892] A.C. 25.
63 J. *Lyons & Sons v. Wilkins* [1899] 1 Ch. 255; *Quinn v. Leathem* [1901] A.C. 495.

negotiation to confrontation. Nevertheless, *Taff Vale* seemed to threaten all union funds and gave the whole movement a motive for seeking reform of the law and a motive also for supporting the LRC. When Keir Hardie asked Balfour in the Commons whether he would introduce legislation 'to give trade union funds the protection they have enjoyed for thirty years, but which the decision in question has taken away', the reply was, 'No, sir.'[64] So the trade unions were moved to parliamentary action to support their legal rights. The unions would in the future provide ballast for the Labour Party, holding it together in difficult times and ensuring that, when there was a split in the party, as in 1914, 1931 and 1981, it could survive relatively unscathed. But the trade unions could only be mobilised for radical action when collectively threatened, as with *Taff Vale* and later the 1926 General Strike, and on both occasions their activism was dedicated to restoring the status quo, not subverting it.

It was fortunate that the LRC had been formed in 1900, a year before *Taff Vale*. Within a fortnight of the judgment, Ramsay MacDonald sent a Circular to the unions on behalf of the LRC declaring that 'the recent decision of the House of Lords ... should convince the unions that a Labour Party in Parliament is an immediate necessity'.[65] Trade union membership of the LRC, which had been around 350,000 in the summer of 1900, increased to nearly 850,000 by February 1903. Attending the TUC conference in September 1902, Beatrice Webb noticed that the

> dominant note of the Congress is determination to run Labour candidates on a large scale and faith in the efficiency of this device for gaining all they require ... a certain unanimity of opinion among the delegates; less cleavage between trade and trade, or between old and new unionists than in any congress I have before attended. Practically the Congress has been captured – by the ILP.[66]

In 1904, the TUC conference was for the first time to welcome fraternal delegates from the LRC, with MacDonald declaring that 'the LRC is neither sister nor brother to Congress, but its child. We come therefore to offer our filial respects.' A fundamental alteration had taken place in the attitude of the unions towards labour representation. As the sociologist L. T. Hobhouse was to comment ironically, 'That which no Socialist writer or platform orator could achieve was effected by the judges.'[67] In 1903, the LRC was to take an

---

64 House of Commons Debates, 1 August 1901, vol. 98, col. 878.
65 Bealey and Pelling, *Labour and Politics*, p. 77.
66 MacKenzie, *Diary of Beatrice Webb*, vol. 2, p. 256.
67 L. T. Hobhouse, *The Labour Movement*, 3rd edition, Fisher Unwin, 1906, p. 12.

important step towards independence when at its Newcastle conference it passed a resolution declaring that its candidates and MPs were not to identify themselves with or promote the interests of 'any section of the Liberal or Conservative parties', but they would in future be required to abide by the LRC constitution and decisions of the LRC group in Parliament. Ironically, W. C. Steadman, chair of the LRC's 1900 foundation conference, left the committee at this point, since he would not desert the Liberal Party. Richard Bell also refused to accept the Newcastle decision, declaring that 'he was not going to have a collar put round his neck'.[68] His view was that the role of the LRC was to act as a subcommittee of the TUC. In 1906, he would not be included in the list of LRC candidates and stood as a Lib-Lab.

The difference of opinion between Bell and the LRC was one between two principles. Bell argued that he represented a trade union and that it was in his union's interest to support the Liberals, not the LRC. One union, the National Union of Teachers, went so far as to maintain two MPs in the Commons, one Liberal and one Conservative, to mirror the diversity of views of its members. The LRC, by contrast, believed that the interest of the working class could only be represented by a party separate from both Liberals and Conservatives.

At its Newcastle conference, the LRC also decided to follow the Irish example by establishing a central party fund, to be funded by a voluntary levy of one penny per member per year. From this fund, the LRC would pay its candidates one-quarter of the expenses of returning officers and £200 a year to its MPs. Local expenses would be largely met by constituency organisations such as trades councils, or whichever body was sponsoring the candidate, often a trade union. In 1904, payment to the parliamentary fund was made a condition of affiliation. Previously, LRC candidates had been dependent on their own organisation for electoral support – socialist societies or the richer trade unions. But by virtue of the LRC decision, candidates who were not sponsored by these bodies could not stand for election with LRC finance. This would strengthen the LRC's independence against trade union sectionalism and against those of a Lib-Lab tendency who thought that the LRC should hold a distinctive view only on labour issues. The fund would also strengthen the ties of party discipline against backsliders such as Bell, although the LRC never went as far as the Irish Party by requiring its candidates to sign undated letters of resignation.

The decisions of the Newcastle conference were a crucial step and, arguably, even more important than the formation of the LRC in 1900 in establishing a separate party. The Newcastle conference also showed that the

68   Bealey and Pelling, *Labour and Politics*, p. 196.

test for the Labour Party was political, not one of class. A rich capitalist could become a Labour MP, but a trade unionist such as Bell could not, since he would not vote with the party. Nor could a trade unionist such as Walter Osborne, who believed, as his case against his union would show in 1911, that trade unionists should be free to vote as they chose on political or religious issues.

The Labour Party rested on two stools: the trade unions and the socialists – one geared to securing practical improvements, the other to a doctrine, one seemingly sectional, the other dedicated to a new type of society. The problem for the Labour leadership was to fuse the two. On frequent occasions – the General Strike in 1926, the economic crisis of 1931, arguments about trade union reform in 1968–69 and the 'winter of discontent' in 1978–79 – the alliance seemed to be coming apart, but it always held. And, in addition to compromises required to secure the allegiance of non-socialist trade unionists, there were further compromises dictated by Labour's parliamentary position. For a minority party could only secure its legislation if prepared to cooperate with other parties, primarily the Liberals. But that meant further dilution of socialism, laying the leadership open to accusations of opportunism and compromising the party's separate identity. That dilemma was not to be resolved until after the 1914 war.

From their beginnings, the LRC and the Labour Party were far more than electoral machines. The new party saw itself as being quite different from the older parties, thanks to the commitment of the socialists. Admittedly, the socialists were far from united on the meaning of socialism and on how it might be achieved, and they appreciated that they were a distinct minority in the party. As Ramsay MacDonald wrote in 1911:

> The Labour Party is not socialist. It is a union of socialist and trade-union bodies for immediate political work … But it is the only political form which evolutionary Socialism can take in a country with the political traditions and methods of Great Britain. Under British conditions, a socialist party is the last, not the first, form of the socialist movement in politics.[69]

The Labour Party was from its formation a pluralist coalition and the concessions and compromises which many on the left were later to complain of were already, in a sense, built into the structure of the party at its birth. It would never prove easy to hold so ramshackle an organisation together. That is why the party, while perfectly willing to accommodate diversity of thought, was so insistent on firm discipline in Parliament.

---

69 J. Ramsay MacDonald, *The Socialist Movement*, Thornton Butterworth, 1911, p. 235.

Many trade unionists were to believe that the Labour Party had been formed to do their bidding. As late as November 1931, the general secretary of the TUC, Walter Citrine, told the party's National Executive:

> The TUC did not seek in any shape or form to say what the Labour Party was to do, but they did ask that the primary purpose of the creation of the Labour Party should not be forgotten. It was created by the Trade Union Movement to do those things in Parliament which the Trade Unions found ineffectively performed by the two-Party system.[70]

But the Labour Party was more than a mere instrument for the unions. Its dual character was inherited from the ILP, and sustained by its early leaders, in particular by Keir Hardie, Ramsay MacDonald and Philip Snowden. It sought not only to represent labour and secure practical improvements but also, as the ILP had done, to transform society. So Labour represented more than an interest, the interest of organised labour. It stood for an idea and the socialists had a faith. 'The early Socialist propaganda', in the words of an early pioneer,

> had a quality of ecstasy which few churches, and no other political party, could arouse. No purely selfish movement could have aroused and sustained an enthusiasm of the kind which then existed. The men and women who were its members were not moved by envy of those who were richer than themselves; they were in the grip of a new, a compelling faith. It appealed to the emotional side of their natures, and they became, in imagination, citizens of a new and better world.[71]

Because of their faith, the socialists enjoyed an influence out of all proportion to their numbers, believing as they did that socialism was the wave of the future. Like the early Christians, to whom they sometimes compared themselves, they had an emotional commitment and crusading zeal which kept them going through many difficulties. Their fundamental belief was ethical, that a society based on competition and individual self-interest could be transformed into a quite different kind of society, based on fellowship. 'Fellowship is life', William Morris had said in his novel *A Dream of John Ball*, 'and lack of fellowship is death.' Bruce Glasier, one of Keir Hardie's most loyal colleagues in the ILP, was to write a tract in 1919, called *The Meaning of Socialism*, in which he insisted that 'socialism means not only

---

70 R. I. McKibbin, 'Arthur Henderson as Labour Leader', *International Review of Social History*, 1978, p. 100.
71 Lord Snell, *Men, Movements and Myself*, Dent, 1936, p. 148.

the socialisation of wealth, but of our lives, our hearts – ourselves'. Socialism
consisted

> not in getting at all, but in giving ... that fundamentally Socialism is a
> question of right human relationship and is essentially a spiritual principle
> ... Socialism therefore is religion ... that part, the all-essential practical
> part of it that concerns the right state of our present lives, the right state of
> our relation to our fellows, the right moral health of our souls.[72]

Hardie was the symbol of this appeal. Hopeless as an administrator and party
leader, he was nevertheless fundamental in the formation of both the ILP
and the Labour Party. It was the ethical, quasi-religious appeal which Hardie
symbolised that gave the early Labour Party its dynamic and sustained its
leaders in what must at times have seemed a hopeless task. Labour's critique
of capitalism was moral even more than it was economic. The party sought
not only a new political and economic system but a new human order. Once
that had been achieved, men and women would not be regarded merely as
workers or factors of production but as fully rounded human beings. It was a
vision which derived as much from Victorian sages such as Dickens, Carlyle
and Ruskin as from socialist thought.

---

72 Quoted in Henry Pelling, ed., *The Challenge of Socialism*, Adam & Charles Black, 1954, pp. 363, 367.

CHAPTER 6

THE END OF THE VICTORIAN AGE

THE NEW CABINET

After the 1900 election, the Cabinet was reconstructed. Lord Salisbury's age and health no longer allowed him to combine the Foreign Office and the premiership. He had been failing for some time and lacked the energy to counter Chamberlain and the Cabinet's other more assertive members. He relinquished the Foreign Office to Lord Lansdowne (1845–1927) but continued to exercise a supervisory role over his old department. Indeed, the Cabinet continued on occasion to meet in the Foreign Office.

Lansdowne was summed up by Balfour in 1929 when asked by his niece and biographer Blanche Dugdale to describe him. Balfour's reply sums up the flavour of the administration.

'I shouldn't call him very clever. He was – I don't quite know how to put it – better than competent.'

His niece enquired, 'Sort of typical "governing classes" kind of ability, do you mean?'

Balfour responded, 'Yes, that's what I do mean, I think. Lansdowne had the mentality of the great Whigs – remember he was descended from a great line of them. But one must qualify even that a little, he wasn't quite an Englishman. His mother was French – she was a Flahault. I always felt a sort of Continental quality of mind in Lansdowne. I was always very fond of him. I was his fag at Eton, you know.'[1]

Walter Long (1854–1924), who had been President of the Board of Agriculture, was promoted to the Local Government Board. He was to play an important part in Tory politics in the years to come. He hailed from a family of Wiltshire landowners. His father, also a Conservative MP, had married into the Irish landed elite, his mother being a strong Irish Unionist and daughter of the 9th Earl of Cork and Orrery. Long's two grandfathers had also been Conservative MPs, one for a Wiltshire constituency, the other for a constituency in Wicklow. Both had been silent members. He himself was to marry into a southern Irish landed family. He had distinguished himself

---

1 Dugdale, *Balfour*, vol. 1, pp. 252–3.

at Oxford not by academic achievement but prowess at sport, especially fox hunting, and had left the university without taking a degree. Marrying into a southern Irish landed family served only to emphasise his already staunch Unionism. To many of his contemporaries, Long seemed the epitome of the rubicund, choleric country squire, not over-endowed with brains, but his family background and instincts made him an even more tenacious Unionist than his colleagues. He entered the Commons in 1880 and was to represent, in consequence of electoral vicissitudes, seven different constituencies until ennobled in 1921. He attracted much unfavourable comment. One critic alleged that he combined 'bone headedness with hypersensitivity', while Beatrice Webb dismissed him as 'a loud-voiced persistent creature, who talks his colleagues down at Cabinet and committee meetings and is in touch with the commoner kind of obscurantist Tory.'[2] But she was hardly an objective observer. He was in fact to prove a solid and capable administrator at the Local Government Board, where he was the first minister since Chamberlain in 1886 to devise measures to combat unemployment; and then briefly as Chief Secretary for Ireland. A moderate tariff reformer, he became the candidate of the middle-of-the-road country Conservatives for the leadership when Balfour resigned in 1911.

Gerald Balfour's position as Chief Secretary of Ireland was filled by George Wyndham (1863–1913), but the post remained outside the Cabinet until 1902. Wyndham seemed to have all the gifts needed for success in politics. He was athletic and handsome – he was, it has been said, 'the kind of handsome man who looks at himself in the mirror each morning with considerable approval'.[3] He had married into the family of the Duke of Westminster and had been mentioned in despatches after seeing action in Egypt. He had venerated Balfour from boyhood, becoming his private secretary at the age of twenty-one and then his parliamentary private secretary after being elected as MP for Dover in a by-election in 1889. In 1900, aged just thirty-seven, he was widely thought to be the coming man. He seemed eminently suitable for the post of Chief Secretary, having ancestral connections both with the Irish gentry and with the rebels of the 1798 uprising. His concern with reform in Ireland led him to spurn promotion to the Colonies, the Exchequer and the War Office in 1903 when the government was reconstructed following the resignation of Chamberlain and the free traders. But Wyndham was to fall foul of the Irish Unionists and proved to be a supremely unlucky politician, dying suddenly of a blood clot in 1913 when not yet fifty.

Amongst the new Cabinet ministers were two relatives of the Prime

---

2 MacKenzie, *Diary of Beatrice Webb*, vol. 2, p. 265.
3 Hoppen, *Governing Hibernia*, p. 268.

Minister: Gerald Balfour was promoted from Chief Secretary of Ireland to President of the Board of Trade to replace Ritchie, promoted to the Home Office; and Lord Selborne, a Liberal Unionist and son-in-law of the Prime Minister, was appointed First Lord of the Admiralty, in place of Goschen who also retired. The junior appointments included the Prime Minister's eldest son, Lord Cranborne, as Under-Secretary at the Foreign Office, and his nephew, Evelyn Cecil, as parliamentary secretary to the premier.

The new government inspired little confidence, and was nicknamed the 'Hotel Cecil', because of the large number of the Prime Minister's relations which it contained. Rosebery congratulated Lord Salisbury with some irony 'on being the head of a family with the most remarkable genius for administration that has ever been known'.[4] The Liberals criticised the new Cabinet for its nepotism, the Conservatives because it continued to give too many places to Liberal Unionists, while the country as a whole was disappointed since the reconstruction did nothing to rejuvenate the government. In his Chesterfield speech of December 1901, Rosebery was to declare that while the country needed new blood, it had instead been given merely an injection of blue blood. The reconstruction confirmed to many voters that the Conservatives were a class party, something Disraeli had warned would be fatal to its electoral chances. In addition, the new government seemed not to understand the new spirit of the times, summed up in the slogan 'national efficiency'. 'An assemblage of sexagenarians, most of whom have little knowledge or conception of the problems to be solved, who are bound by the shibboleths of a bygone era ... who are blind to the salient tendencies of modern life' was not, according to the *National Review*, 'the kind of body to reorganise the nation'. Milner was later to be more succinct, writing to a friend in April 1902, 'All these post-60 politicians, *bar Joe* ... must go ... The worn-out old gang.'[5]

The reconstruction had a further consequence. It confirmed Chamberlain's isolation in the Cabinet. The khaki election had been, to a large extent, his victory. But the new Cabinet was most definitely Salisbury's, not Chamberlain's. 'No English statesmen since the Midlothian campaign', one Liberal Unionist wrote,

has more conspicuously 'presided over' an appeal to the constituencies, and no politician at any time has won a more sweeping personal triumph. His little finger has become thicker than the loins of his colleagues, but

---

4   Roberts, *Salisbury*, p. 789.
5   Searle, *Quest for National Efficiency*, p. 53.

there is to be no official recognition by the Unionist party that any increase in Mr Chamberlain's importance has occurred.[6]

The Unionist leaders did not doubt that Chamberlain was firmly under control. Gladstone had thought the same in 1885 before the Home Rule crisis erupted. He too had failed to acknowledge Chamberlain's position outside the closed world of Westminster.

THE NEW REIGN

Not long after the election, on 22 January 1901, Queen Victoria died after a reign of nearly sixty-four years, the second longest in British history. She had outlived the end of the century by just three weeks, and had made herself by the end of her reign, 'in a degree unapproached by any of her predecessors, save Queen Elizabeth ... a national talisman'.[7] But she had outlived her age, and her presence was coming to seem oppressive to those in the innermost circles of public life. Attending the accession of Edward VII (1841–1910), the radical baronet Sir Charles Dilke found it 'a meeting of men with a load off them'.[8]

As heir to the throne, the new king had been widely regarded as the prince of pleasure, and there were fears that he would not devote himself to his red boxes with the same assiduity as the late queen. Some said he would not be the king his mother had been! *The Times* declared on his accession, 'We shall not pretend that there is nothing in his long career which those who respect and admire him could not wish otherwise.'[9] But the fears proved misplaced, and Edward VII was to work hard at his papers and at mastering the details of government. He had seen Foreign Office despatches since 1886 and the Prime Minister's reports to the sovereign since 1892.[10] As Prince of Wales, he had in fact interested himself in public affairs and had a far wider acquaintance with different classes in society than his mother. Uniquely for a member of the royal family, he had served on two Royal Commissions, the first on housing for the working classes, the second on the aged poor. He had familiarised himself with housing conditions by touring incognito the slums of Holborn and St Pancras and spoke in the Lords on what he had seen. He did not, however, sign the part of the housing commission's report on leasehold enfranchisement, which was politically controversial. In the case

6 W. L. Courtney, 'The Vindication of Democracy', *Fortnightly Review*, November 1900, p. 822.
7 Ensor, *England*, p. 268.
8 Young, *Victorian England*, p. 184.
9 Quoted in Jane Ridley, *Bertie: A Life of Edward VII*, Chatto & Windus, 2012, p. 349.
10 Steiner, *Foreign Office and Foreign Policy*, p. 202.

of the Royal Commission on the Aged Poor, he signed neither the minority report advocating non-contributory state pensions nor the majority report opposing them, on the grounds that these proposals too were politically controversial.

Although far from being a radical, Edward VII held political views less conservative than those of Queen Victoria or George V, and he was never to display Queen Victoria's partisanship. Neither he nor any future sovereign would consult with the opposition, as Queen Victoria had done in her later years when the Liberals were in power. Edward was more friendly to the Liberals than Queen Victoria in her later years – not perhaps very difficult to achieve. Unlike her, he tended to judge politicians as individuals rather than by their party allegiance. By contrast with his mother, he had remained on good terms with Gladstone, who said of him in 1896, 'No royalty I have ever met had such charm and tact as the Prince of Wales.'[11] After Gladstone's death, the prince became president of his memorial committee. Edward disliked politicians whom he thought of as bounders, such as Lloyd George and Churchill, but maintained good relations with the Liberal government which was to come to power in 1905. He particularly liked Campbell-Bannerman, whom he regarded as a straightforward, uncomplicated elderly gentleman like himself, and whom he often met on holiday in Marienbad. One newspaper published a photo of the two talking with a caption 'Is it Peace or War?' But Campbell-Bannerman told his private secretary, 'Would you like to know what the King was saying to me? He wanted to have my opinion whether halibut is better baked or boiled.'[12] In fact, Campbell-Bannerman was the only one of his four Prime Ministers whom the king really liked. He felt he had little in common with the ruminative Salisbury and did not care either for Balfour or Asquith, both of whom, he believed, patronised him. His relationship with the Liberals was helped by the fact that he was a free trader, being opposed to increases in the price of food which, he believed, would be brought about by Chamberlain's policy of colonial preference. In the summer of 1903, when the tariff reform debate was raging, he was to tell Ritchie, the free trade Chancellor, that he believed taxes should fall mainly on the rich, and when Ritchie asked, 'Your Majesty does not approve of taxing the food of the poor?' the king replied, 'No, and I do not care who knows it!' The Duke of Devonshire, like Ritchie a free trader, declared, 'We really must get this man on the stump.'[13] But that was the only occasion on

---

11   Hardie, *Political Influence of Queen Victoria*, p. 190.
12   Ridley, *Bertie*, p. 397fn.
13   Fitzroy, *Memoirs*, vol. 1, p. 146.

which the king expressed his political views outside his own immediate circle of friends.

The new king sought to forge a new relationship between monarchy and people, and that perhaps was his most important achievement. He had been upset when Queen Victoria withdrew from public life following the death of the prince consort and believed that the people had to see the sovereign if monarchy was to survive. He exuded goodwill and affability and showed an obvious delight in meeting people from all groups in society. 'He had', the women's suffrage leader Millicent Garrett Fawcett declared, 'the *joie de vivre* and the art of imparting it to others.'[14] He had considerable personal mag netism and reached out to groups in society who might hitherto have felt ignored. He objected to the form of the Protestant declaration in his accession oath, which he thought would give offence to Catholics, and made an informal visit to the Pope in 1904. He also did much to create an atmosphere of tolerance toward Jews, numbering several amongst his friends. On a state visit to Russia in 1908, meeting the Prime Minister, Stolypin, he criticised, against the advice of his ministers, officially inspired antisemitism. Stolypin promised to alleviate the condition of Jews, though little in fact was done.

The new king understood the human side of monarchy, opening stuffy windows which had been closed during the queen's reign. Liberal journalist A. G. Gardiner declared that 'there is an avuncular benevolence about the king which is irresistible. He likes to be happy himself, and he likes to see the world happy.'[15] Beatrice Webb, seeing him handing out certificates to London county scholars in 1897, condescendingly described him as having 'a simple kindly amoral temperament which makes a good fellow ... an almost perfect constitutional sovereign', noting 'his complete detachment from all party prejudice and class interests and his genius for political *discretion*'.[16] Margot Asquith, wife of the Prime Minister, wrote that 'a kinder, more considerate and courteous man than King Edward never lived'.[17]

The most immediate symbol of the new reign was the new king's attitude to ceremonial. During the last forty years of her reign, following the death of the prince consort, Victoria had appeared little in public and had been dubbed 'The Widow of Windsor'. She had not opened Parliament since 1886. Edward, by contrast, was to open Parliament in every year of his reign and he read the Speech from the Throne himself, something Queen Victoria had not done since 1861. The new king had a special talent for the ceremonial

14 Millicent Garrett Fawcett, *What I Remember*, G. P. Putnam's Sons, 1925, p. 108.
15 Quoted in Roger Fulford 'The King', in Simon Nowell-Smith, ed., *Edwardian England: 1901–1914*, Oxford University Press, 1964, p. 45.
16 MacKenzie, *Diary of Beatrice Webb*, vol. 2, p. 108, entry for 6 February 1897.
17 Margot Asquith, *More Memories*, Cassell, 1933, p. 223.

and public aspects of monarchy, but his love of ceremonial did not interfere with his ability to make contact with ordinary people – 'he loved ceremony', it was said, 'but he seldom stood on it'.[18]

His talents were to be shown to particular advantage during his 1903 visit to France, which helped to create the atmosphere that made the 1904 entente cordiale possible. He enjoyed foreign travel and had acquired the important skill of extracting valuable information from those with whom he came into contact on his visits. In 1860, he had been the first heir to the throne to cross the Atlantic, visiting Canada and the United States where he had met President Buchanan. He would eventually meet every crowned head in Europe except the kings of Serbia and Romania. He was adept at foreign languages and spoke fluent French and German; indeed, he spoke English with a German accent. On his visit to Paris in 1903, he gave two speeches in fluent French – one, impromptu, at the Hotel de Ville and another delivered without notes at a banquet in his honour. By contrast with Queen Victoria, he was more interested in Europe than the empire and had a particular affection for France. In August 1909, Wickham Steed, the correspondent of *The Times* in Vienna and a future editor of the paper, was to have a conversation with him, which

> made upon me an abiding impression ... His care for Europe was almost paternal. It sprang from knowledge acquired chiefly by personal experience and observation and from an ever-present sense that, though England was the heart and head of the British Empire, she was and must increasingly be, an essential part of Europe.

He had an 'essential quality, the sympathetic insight that is born of goodwill'.[19]

The death of Queen Victoria seemed to mark the end of an epoch, coinciding as it did with the new century. 'Grief affects us', Balfour told the Commons, 'not merely because we have lost a great personality ... but because we feel that the end of a great epoch has come upon us.'[20] Churchill believed that 'the Wonderful century was over'.[21]

To the mid-Victorians, change had been 'improvement'.[22] Their late Victorian and Edwardian successors were more apprehensive of what the future might bring. 'I was a child of the Victorian age', Winston Churchill, born in 1874, was to write in 1930,

---

18   Donald Read, ed., *Edwardian England, 1901–1915: Society and Politics*, Harrop, 1972, p. 68.
19   Wickham Steed, *Through Thirty Years*, Heinemann, 1924, p. 322.
20   House of Commons Debates, 25 January 1901, vol. 89, col. 20.
21   Quoted in Read, ed., *Edwardian England*, p. 14.
22   Asa Briggs, *The Age of Improvement*, Longmans, Green & Co., 1959.

when the structure of our country seemed firmly set, when its position in trade and on the seas were unrivalled, and when the realisation of the greatness of our Empire and of our duty to preserve it was ever growing stronger. In those days, the dominant forces in Great Britain were very sure of themselves and of their doctrines. They thought they could teach the world the art of government, and the science of economics. They were sure they were supreme at sea, and consequently safe at home. They rested therefore sedately under the convictions of power and security.[23]

But in January 1901, one commentator feared that 'we are a nation in jeopardy, but we are not a nation in decadence'.[24] The cry of national efficiency came to be raised, and there were calls for a critical examination of traditional British institutions and practices. One catalyst for these new concerns was the Boer War with its revelations of physical deterioration and military incompetence. Another catalyst was the concern about Britain's economic competitiveness since other countries, such as Germany and Japan, seemed to be more effective in applying modern methods of science and education to industrial and military organisation. Some were coming to believe that the British party and political systems were too antiquated to confront modern problems. These anxieties were to be expressed by Liberal Imperialists such as Rosebery and Haldane, as well as Fabians such as Sidney Webb and men above party such as Milner. But none produced a plausible effective concrete programme to remedy the ills that they had diagnosed.

During the new century, issues were opened which the mid-Victorians had regarded as settled and closed. There came, above all, to be a growing awareness of the problem of poverty. Since the 1880s, the intellectual atmosphere had shifted from the mid-Victorian idea of the minimal state. When Milner went to Oxford in the early 1870s, he had found that 'the *laissez-faire* theory still held the field. All the recognised authorities were "orthodox" economists of the old school. But within ten years the few men who still held the old doctrines in their extreme rigidity had come to be regarded as curiosities.'[25] In her autobiography, Beatrice Webb wrote:

The origin of the ferment is to be discovered in a new consciousness of sin among men of intellect and men of property ... The consciousness of sin was a collective or class consciousness; a growing uneasiness, amounting to conviction, that the industrial organisation, which had yielded rent,

---

23 Winston S. Churchill, Preface to the original edition of *My Early Life*, Thornton Butterworth, 1930, pp. 6–7.
24 'Calchas' [Garvin], 'Will England Last the Century?', p. 22.
25 Asa Briggs, *Social Thought and Social Action: A Study of the Work of Seebohm Rowntree, 1871–1954*, Longmans, 1961, pp. 58–9.

interest and profits on a stupendous scale, had failed to provide a decent livelihood and tolerable conditions for a majority of the inhabitants of Great Britain.[26]

Social concerns were intensified by the flagrant inequalities in wealth observable in the Edwardian era when the rich appeared to be showing less restraint than in the past. The value of unearned income was to increase in that era by around half while wages remained nearly stagnant. In his *Radical Programme* of 1885, Chamberlain had predicted that 'ideas and wants and claims which have been hitherto ignored in legislation will find a voice in parliament and will compel the attention of statesmen'.[27] In 1901, the Fabian Sidney Webb wrote that 'during the last twenty or thirty years, we have become a new people'. The country was living through 'an epoch of transformation':

> We have become aware, almost in a flash, that we are not merely individuals, but members of a community, nay citizens of the world ... The labourer in the slum tenement, competing for employment at the factory gate, has become conscious that his comfort and his progress depend, not wholly or mainly on himself ... but upon the proper organisation of his Trade Union and the activity of the factory inspector. The shopkeeper or the manufacturer sees his prosperity wax or wane ... according to the good government of his city, the efficiency with which his nation is organised, and the influence which his Empire is able to exercise ... The freedom that he now wants is not individual but corporate freedom – freedom for his Trade Union to bargain collectively, freedom for his co-operative society to buy and sell and manufacture, freedom for his municipality to supply all the common needs of the town, freedom, above all, from the narrow insularity which keeps his nation backing 'on principle' out of its proper place in the comity of the world. In short, the opening of the twentieth century finds us all, to the dismay of the old-fashioned Individualist, 'thinking in communities'.[28]

Britain was facing a new world with new problems in which past certainties were no longer a safe guide to the future. Many in the Unionist government seemed insensitive to this new mood. But some Liberals were equally insensitive.

---

26 Webb, *My Apprenticeship*, pp. 179–80.
27 Briggs, *Social Thought and Social Action*, p. 59.
28 Sidney, 'Lord Rosebery's Escape from Houndsditch', *Nineteenth Century*, 1901, pp. 368–9.

THE CONCENTRATION CAMPS IN SOUTH AFRICA

From the beginning of the new administration in 1900, everything seemed to go wrong. At the time of the election, it had seemed that the British were on the verge of victory in South Africa. The Transvaal and the Orange Free State had been annexed and were ruled from London. But the war proved to be far from over. The Boers continued their resistance longer than anyone had expected by guerrilla tactics, hoping that if they could prolong the fight, they would be helped by a Boer revolt in Cape Colony or assistance by friendly European powers; or, alternatively, that the British would tire of fighting and accept a compromise peace. From February 1901, peace talks were held, but they broke down over two Boer demands. The first was for an amnesty, not only for those in the Transvaal and Orange Free State, which the government was prepared to accept, but also for those fighting for the Boers in the British colonies, the Cape and Natal, which the government would not accept. The second demand was that there be no statutory recognition of native voting rights in the peace agreement. Kitchener was prepared to accept these terms, but Milner, Chamberlain and the Cabinet were not. So the war went on. Kitchener believed that Milner was 'vindictive, and I do not know of a case in history where, under similar circumstances, an amnesty has not been granted. We are now carrying on the war to be able to put two or 300 Dutchmen in prison at the end of it.'[29] But it also seemed that the Boers were not at that stage prepared to surrender their autonomy. Five months later in June 1901, the governments of the Transvaal and Orange Free State resolved that 'no peace conditions will be accepted by which our independence ... shall be the price paid'.[30]

Britain had not previously faced such guerrilla tactics whereby small numbers of Boer commandos, many not in uniform, were able to hold a much larger army at bay, and the army was ill-equipped to counter them. In response to guerrilla attacks on railway lines, Roberts, the commander-in-chief, inaugurated in June 1900 a policy of burning the closest homestead to the railway. Then, from September, he ordered that all homesteads within a radius of sixteen kilometres of an attack would be burnt, livestock killed or taken away and crops destroyed. In November 1900, Kitchener intensified the policy by burning homesteads and indeed whole towns indiscriminately. Around 30,000 farms were burnt down with the purpose of preventing guerrillas from having access to food supplies. On occasion, civilians were held as hostages. Collective fines were levied on communities. All this was in breach

---

29 Philip Magnus, *Kitchener: Portrait of an Imperialist* [1958], Penguin, 1968, p. 225.
30 Peter Warwick, 'Introduction: Not Just a Teatime War', in Peter Warwick, ed., *The South African War: The Anglo-Boer War 1899–1902*, Longman, 1980, p. 64.

of The Hague Convention of 1899, to which Britain was a signatory, forbidding the requisitioning of property not being used for military purposes. The British response might have been that the farm of every combatant was potentially of use for military purposes since it could supply food and shelter to fighting men. Kitchener proposed to the Boer leader, General Botha, that the British would leave the women and children in the farm and ensure that they were fed if Botha would promise their neutrality. Botha refused.[31] 'Every farm', Kitchener told the War Secretary in December 1900, 'is an intelligence agency and a supply depot', and the women, he declared in March 1901, gave 'complete intelligence to the Boers of all our movements and feed the commandos in their neighbourhood'.[32] This contention was never tested in a judicial tribunal and would probably not have been accepted. In any case, the farm-burning seemed ineffective. Its purpose was to end the war as rapidly as possible by persuading commandos to surrender and making as much of the veldt as possible a hostile environment. But it might well have had the opposite effect of stiffening Boer resistance, since many commandos remained on the veldt precisely because they no longer had homes to return to, and they resented the enemy's use of women and children to force them into submission. 'What fool in his folly', one observer commented, 'taught us we could prevent men from brigandage by making them homeless?'[33] Kitchener was prepared to go even further and contemplated permanently deporting large numbers of Boers to Fiji and Madagascar, but that was rejected by Brodrick at the War Office. Kitchener had a purely military mind and few human sympathies. In November 1900, Milner wrote to Chamberlain expressing his qualms at Kitchener's policy.

> There has been a great deal too much burning of farms. As a *punishment* I feel that the destruction of a homestead is fully justified ... But such a *discriminating* destruction which really has a deterrent effect is one thing. The indiscriminate burning of all houses in a particular district simply to make it untenable by the enemy is quite another. To that I object thinking it (1) barbarous and (2) ineffectual. By making a large number of people homeless, you increase the army of desperadoes roaming the country which it is our object to reduce. For my part, I am going as soon as I take over the civil administration, to set my face against wholesale destruction.[34]

31 House of Commons Debates, 4 March 1902, vol. 104, col. 436.
32 Bill Nasson, *The Boer War: The Struggle for South Africa*, Spellmount, 2011, p. 243.
33 Lionel Curtis, quoted in Nicholas Mansergh, *The Commonwealth Experience*, Weidenfeld & Nicolson, 1969, p. 82.
34 Isabel V. Hull, *Absolute Destruction: Military Culture and the Practice of War in Imperial Germany*, Cornell University Press, 2005, p. 186. This book compares the treatment of civilians in war by Britain and imperial Germany to the advantage of Britain.

Indiscriminate farm-burning would be rescinded in November 1901 largely as a result of intervention by Chamberlain and Milner.

The farm-burning created a vast humanitarian problem. What was to be done with the refugee women and children deprived as a result of food and shelter? At first they were left to drift through the countryside, but from December 1900, Kitchener decided to intern them in camps which came to be known as concentration camps. The term 'concentration camps', taken from the Spanish who had used them to suppress Cuban guerrillas, was apparently first used by a Liberal MP, John Ellis, in the Commons on 1 March 1901.[35] The camps were eventually to house around 150,000 Boers, mainly women and children.

The camps had first been established to protect those cooperating with Britain or those who had surrendered, together with their families – around 13,000 people, called by the Boers 'hands-uppers' – so that they should not be subjected to Boer vengeance or brought back into the war by guerrillas. Many of the male inmates who had surrendered worked in the camps for regular wages. Indeed, around one-fifth of the Boers still fighting at the end of the war were fighting on the British side, and some became British citizens.[36] It was intended that, with victory, the two Boer republics would become part of the empire, the Boers becoming British subjects, just as, for example, the French in Quebec had become. But the camps were now being used to accommodate those displaced and left homeless by the British Army's attempt to clear the countryside, involving, as we have seen, the mass burning or confiscation of farms to undermine 'possible civilian support for an evasive enemy who had resorted to guerrilla warfare'. Those so accommodated included the families of Boers still fighting, and they were being forcibly interned. The ratio between those forcibly interned and the 'hands-uppers' was around seven to three. The camps were causing 'a blurring of the distinction between combatant and non-combatant civilians'.[37]

There were also camps for black South African refugees and homeless people, where conditions were worse than in the white Boer camps. Black South Africans, with just a few exceptions and unlike the Boers, had to pay for their food, which was meagre and of poor quality.[38] Black South Africans particularly resented the fact that the Boers, whom they regarded as mainly responsible for the war, received free food, while they did not. And while, as we shall see, the British government did its best when conditions in the Boer

35 House of Commons Debates, 1 March 1901, vol. 900, col. 180; Pakenham, *The Boer War*, p. 505.
36 Smith, *Origins of the South African War*, p. 7.
37 Iain R. Smith and Andreas Stucki, 'The Colonial Development of Concentration Camps (1868–1902)', *Journal of Imperial and Commonwealth History*, 2011, pp. 417–9, 430.
38 Ibid., pp. 430, 427–8.

camps were made public, to improve them, they were grossly insensitive to conditions in the black camps.

One intended purpose of the camps was humanitarian, to provide food and shelter following Britain's mass destruction of property. Most Boer inmates were given free rations of meal, meat, coffee, sugar, salt and condensed milk, and in Natal potatoes also and on occasion fresh vegetables, but the rations were often inadequate; and, more important, did not constitute a sufficiently balanced diet to enable inmates to resist disease. Moreover, families of Boers still fighting were given fewer rations than others in the camps. Boer inmates were, however, given free clothing, medical and nursing care while the children were given educational facilities. Their education was designed to turn Boer children into patriotic British imperialists. Inevitably, it failed to do so. Nevertheless, pupil numbers in the camp schools were considerably higher than in the Boer republics. In the mid-1890s, for example, just one in five children in the Transvaal were attending school, while 'many farm children had previously had no education at all'.[39]

The camps were not intended as penal institutions. Nor were those in charge of them animated, with but a few exceptions, with a deliberately cruel purpose in mind. But poor conditions in the camps led to a high death rate. Of around 150,000 Boer inmates, the British estimate was that at least 14,000 and possibly as many as 20,000 died as a result. But the true figure for Boer deaths is probably nearer 25,000, of which around three-quarters were children under sixteen. Precise statistics were not kept of the camps for black South Africans, but at their peak they probably housed around 115,000 inmates of whom around 20,000 died, 80 per cent of them under sixteen. One cause of death in the camps was measles, but a more important cause was that the camps had been hastily improvised, were overcrowded and suffered from inadequate sanitation and medical arrangements. On occasion, soap was unavailable and no attempt was made to boil infected water. There was gross administrative incompetence and mismanagement. The organisation of the camps gave rise to huge administrative problems and the military authorities were unable to cope with them. They were also unable to cope with disease amongst British troops: typhoid and other diseases accounted for around 14,000 out of around 22,000 British fatalities.

In January 1901, Emily Hobhouse, a philanthropist and sister of the Liberal political philosopher and journalist L. T. Hobhouse, visited the Boer camps. On returning, she saw Campbell-Bannerman. In 1923, she gave her recollection of the meeting:

---

39 Eliza Riedi, 'Teaching Empire: British and Dominions Women Teachers in the South African War Concentration Camps', *English Historical Review*, 2005, pp. 1,321, 1,338.

Of all whom I saw ... he alone ... seemed to have the leisure and the determination to hear and understand everything ... For nearly two hours he listened with rapt attention now and then putting a question to elucidate a point. I dwelt upon the wholesale burnings of farms and villages ... the fever-stricken children lying sick unto death upon the bare earth, the disease-laden atmosphere, the appalling mortality, the attitude of sub-officials and the disastrous effect of all upon the colonial mind – he was deeply moved – and now and again murmured *sotto voce* 'methods of barbarism, methods of barbarism' ... He left the abiding impression of a man who spared no time or pains to arrive at truth and in whom wisdom and humanity were paramount.[40]

Speaking at a dinner of the National Reform Union on 14 June 1901, Campbell-Bannerman asked, 'What is the Government's policy?' and replied:

It is this – that now that we have got the men we have been fighting against down, we should punish them as severely as possible. It is that we should devastate their country, that we should burn their homes – that we should break up the very instruments of agriculture and destroy the machinery by which food is produced ... sweep the women and children into camps in which they are destitute of all the decencies and comforts and of many of the necessities of life ... When is a war not a war? When it is carried on by methods of barbarism in South Africa.

From this point, Campbell-Bannerman allied himself with the radical pro-Boer faction in the Liberal Party. His sympathies had in fact always been with that group, but in public he had taken a centrist position so as to maintain party unity. The immediate effect of the speech was to reignite the split in the Liberal Party. On a censure motion on the camps moved by Lloyd George on 18 June, Campbell-Bannerman voted for it together with seventy other Liberals. But around fifty other Liberals, including Asquith, Grey and Haldane, abstained. However, the longer-term effect of the speech, and of the revelations concerning conditions in the camps, was to discredit annexationist imperialism.

It was easy to misinterpret the 'methods of barbarism' speech as an imputation on the troops. But Campbell-Bannerman had made it clear that he did not think conditions in the camps were 'the deliberate and intentional policy of His Majesty's government'. He had, however, unfairly implied that the camps were administered with deliberate cruelty. Three days after the

40 Wilson, *CB*, p. 348.

speech, he partially retracted his comment, declaring that he had not meant to 'imply cruelty or even indifference on the part of officers or men in the British Army' and that the 'cruelty' involved was 'unintentional'. He also accepted that 'every effort has been made by the commandants of these camps in most cases to alleviate the sufferings of the unfortunate people entrusted to their care under difficulties of perfectly overwhelming character'. It was the system that he blamed.[41] In 1938, Hermann Göring, the Luftwaffe commander and in effect Hitler's deputy, declared that Britain had pioneered concentration camps. But the British camps bore little resemblance to the Nazi forced labour and extermination camps, in which criminal atrocities took place, whose purpose was to torture and kill racial undesirables and enemies of the regime.

If, however, there was little deliberate cruelty, there was, apart from gross incompetence, much harsh treatment and an almost criminal negligence.

Following the revelations by Emily Hobhouse, the government sent out an all-female Commission of Inquiry under the leadership of Millicent Garrett Fawcett, the suffragist leader. The Commission confirmed what Emily Hobhouse had found, although it also blamed the Boers' lack of understanding of hygiene, declaring that many Boer women had 'a horror of ventilation … It is not easy to describe the pestilential atmosphere of the tents.' The Commission was abused by some Boer women but responded by reminding them of how they themselves had treated native women. The Commission proposed reforms in the administration of the camps, which 'were promptly enacted', and administration of the white camps was transferred in November 1901 from the military to civilian authorities. Milner was told to expedite reforms. 'The accommodation, funding, food rations and sanitation in the camps were improved. Doctors, teachers and nurses were hastily recruited in Britain and dispatched to the camps.'[42] The government began to produce regular reports, and the death rate in the camps was rapidly reduced to under 2 per cent.[43] By mid-December, Kitchener ordered that women and children were no longer to be brought to the camps, though whether their condition improved as a result is not clear.

At the end of the war, General Botha, the Boer leader, admitted that 'one is only too thankful nowadays to know that our wives are under English protection'.[44] At the Rand Club in Johannesburg, there is a framed testimonial signed by many of the Boers in the Brandfort Camp to the military

41   House of Commons Debates, 17 June 1901, vol. 95, col. 599. I owe this reference to Nigel Biggar.
42   Wilson, CB, p. 428.
43   Roberts, Salisbury, p. 807.
44   Pakenham, The Boer War, p. 569.

commander, one on his birthday, one on his retirement, thanking him for his kindness and care.

Even so, nothing can detract from the deaths in the camps. And the Fawcett Commission investigated only the white camps, not the camps for black South Africans.

Whatever the mitigating circumstances, the camps were widely condemned on the Continent, though not, significantly, in the United States, where more volunteered to fight with the British than with the Boers and where African American sympathies were with Britain.[45] In late 1901, Milner admitted to Haldane that putting women and children into the camps had been a 'military mistake'.[46] Many thinking people in Britain believed that it had been a humanitarian and moral mistake also. It led to a humanitarian catastrophe, a result in large part of the probably illegal policy of the burning of farms. The camps discredited not only the Unionists but also the wider imperialist cause.

LORD ROSEBERY'S RETURN

The Unionist government, then, was beginning to find itself on the defensive. But the Liberals remained divided. Far from uniting them, Campbell-Bannerman's 'methods of barbarism' speech had widened the division. Liberal Imperialists regarded it as a slur on British troops and resented the fact that Campbell-Bannerman was moving into the pro-Boer camp, Grey declaring that he believed 'that this war has not only been carried on by civilised and legitimate methods, but that it has, on the whole, been conducted by more humane and more civilised methods than previous wars'.[47] Immediately after the dinner at which Campbell-Bannerman had denounced the methods of barbarism, Asquith and Grey responded in their own after-dinner speeches. There was now what the parliamentary journalist Henry Lucy christened 'war to the knife and fork'.[48] It appeared as if the Liberals might split. They seemed in no condition to provide an effective opposition, let alone an alternative government. With both government and opposition having seemingly lost their way, Rosebery now returned to the political arena. The Liberals appeared to be looking for a leader. Campbell-Bannerman was the nominal leader, but he seemed ineffective and also divisive. Rosebery seemed the obvious alternative.

45 Kathleen Burk, *The Lion and the Eagle: The Interaction of the British and American Empires 1783–1972*, Bloomsbury, 2018, p. 356.
46 Searle, *Quest for National Efficiency*, p. 117fn.
47 *The Times*, 18 July 1901.
48 Stephen Koss, *Asquith*, Allen Lane, 1976, p. 55.

Despite his failure in government and impulsive surrender of the Liberal leadership in 1896, Rosebery (1847–1929) retained an aura of glamour second, if at all, only to that which surrounded Chamberlain. At the beginning of his political career, he had seemed to many the natural successor to Gladstone, even though his views on both foreign and domestic policy had little in common with those of the Grand Old Man. His speeches had a dramatic power entirely absent from those of the more pedestrian Campbell-Bannerman. In April 1899, one newspaper declared that Rosebery 'was the most popular of all the Queen's subjects and attained the prestige of Royalty itself'. At his daughter's wedding, the Prince of Wales was, according to Margot Asquith, 'a nobody compared to Rosebery'.[49] The military historian Spenser Wilkinson had written in February 1900, 'There is no other public man who commands such general confidence ... Lord Rosebery could make a Government tomorrow if he would ignore parties and pick out the competent men wherever they are to be found.'[50] Remarkably, Ben Tillett, the trade union leader, was to write in his autobiography in 1931 that Rosebery was the only Prime Minister he had known except for Ramsay MacDonald who had really entered into the life of the poor.[51] Gladstone had declared that Rosebery 'is one of the very ablest men I have known', that 'he is of the highest honour and probity', but that 'I do not know whether he really has common sense'.[52] In his Rectorial Address at Glasgow University in November 1900, Rosebery had declared that national efficiency required the abandonment of Home Rule, some form of conscription and greater freedom for the military and naval chiefs from parliamentary control. This seemed more like Prussianism than liberalism. Even so, Liberal Imperialists still looked to Rosebery. In July 1901, he ended his political isolation by accepting an invitation to yet another dinner, organised by the City Liberal Club. This club significantly was open to both Liberals and Liberal Unionists. In his letter of acceptance, Rosebery denied that there was anything 'mysterious' about his resignation from the Liberal leadership in 1896. He had resigned, he wrote, 'with the hope rather than the expectation of promoting its unity'. That hope had not been realised. Since 1896, he had made no political pronouncements, and, even now, he did not wish 'to reenter the arena of party politics', adding, 'I shall never voluntarily return to it.' He went on to say that while the Liberals could unite around domestic policy, the party could not again become a force in the land until 'it has made up its mind on Imperial questions, which are at this moment embodied in the war'. Imperial questions were, he

---

49 McKinstry, *Rosebery*, p. 414.
50 Spenser Wilkinson, *Lessons of the War* [1900], quoted in Searle, *Quest for National Efficiency*, pp. 110–11.
51 Ben Tillett, *Memories and Reflections*, John Lane, 1931, p. 170.
52 Marquis of Crewe, *Lord Rosebery*, John Murray, 1931, vol. 2, p. 661.

believed, 'supreme issues; none greater ever divided two hostile parties'. The Liberals could not be reunited so long as Little Englanders and imperialists were rowing in different directions. Britain faced a national crisis, and it was for this reason that he was ending his silence. In his speech to the City Liberals, Rosebery insisted that he did

> not despair of seeing the Liberal party, or some such party, because if the Liberal party will not undertake it [the task of confronting 'in a new spirit the new problems of the age'] the matter is of such necessity that some party will create itself (loud cheers) ... I do not despair of seeing the Liberal party, purged from all anti-national elements ... proceeding in the work of domestic reform.

He then made an appeal for Liberal Unionist support: 'Is it too much to hope that in such a party there might be comprised those Liberal Unionists, who are more Liberal than some of their representatives? (Hear, hear.)' He reiterated that, since the Liberals were even more divided than in 1896, he would not return to the party leadership. 'For the present at any rate, I must proceed alone ... but before I get to the end of that furrow it is possible that I may find myself, not alone. (Loud cheers.)'[53] In addition to his prestige as a former premier, he seemed above party and therefore avoided the unpopularity of both the government and the opposition. But the primary reason for his resurgence from early 1900 after the initial disasters of the Boer War was that he seemed an ideal representative of the cult of national efficiency.[54]

In an article entitled 'Lord Rosebery's Escape from Houndsditch', written in September 1901, Sidney Webb drew out the ideological significance of Rosebery's position. Houndsditch was a tailoring district of London where, metaphorically, 'Gladstonian rags and remnants' had helped the old-fashioned Gladstonian Liberals to make 'patched-up suits'. Rosebery needed, Webb believed, to escape from Houndsditch and create an entirely 'new outfit'. For the Gladstonians were 'axiomatically hostile to the State'. That was why an unpopular government was able to remain in office, 'lest a worse thing befall us – to wit, a Government of Gladstonian ghosts'. But there was a new mood in the country, more sympathetic to state intervention, and that had been a factor in the advent of socialism. But the socialists, like the Liberals, had been undermined by the Boer War, since they were so out of touch with the imperial spirit. Rosebery, therefore, alone free of old shibboleths, could be the leader of the future. But he needed a programme. What

53 *The Times*, 17, 20 July 1901.
54 Searle, *Quest for National Efficiency*, pp. 110–11.

was that programme to be – a programme of 'National Efficiency', Webb believed. That required a national minimum standard of living guaranteed for all, a policy that was to be put into effect over forty years later by the 1945 Labour government led by Clement Attlee. National efficiency also required factory reform, sanitary reform, Poor Law reform and a 'great development of public education'.[55] It was now up to Rosebery to set out his stall. This he was to do when he came to address a large Liberal rally in Chesterfield on 16 December 1901.

There was enormous anticipation in political quarters of what Rosebery might say at Chesterfield. He seemed the one untainted figure able to provide the leadership the country needed. 'I doubt if the prospect of any speech', Spenser Wilkinson was to write of the Chesterfield meeting, 'ever created more excitement. It is striking testimony to the immense interest taken in the man. There is no one else on whom people hang in the same way.'[56] Beatrice Webb, who had many reservations about Rosebery, nevertheless wrote in her diary, 'Notwithstanding this absurd self-consciousness, he has a peculiar personal charm, the secret, I imagine, of his hold on a section of the Liberal Party and the public.'[57] Rosebery seemed to have the ability to inspire younger Liberals and indeed the wider public with his vision of Britain's imperial future. But Campbell-Bannerman wrote to James Bryce seeking to puncture the balloon in advance.

Outside Potentate – says he must save the country – urgent and critical – hang the plough; can no longer stand aside; will in six weeks be ready to utter the words which will save us from ruin. Takes some time, naturally, to think what will be most popular. Dec. 13. Six weeks not yet up; still thinking. General fuss: importance of position greatly relished by potentate.[58]

At Chesterfield, Rosebery spoke for two hours in a railway-carriage shed, packed to capacity with 4,000 people, to cries outside of 'the future Premier'. He spoke of the Liberals as a party in 'convalescence', being free of 'the Irish alliance' and its consequences. The Irish alliance could not be renewed since the Irish Party had 'ranged themselves openly with the enemies that we are fighting in the field'. He called for 'a clean slate' in regard to policy but told his audience 'a great secret. There are a great many Tory Liberals in

---

55   Webb, 'Lord Rosebery's Escape', pp. 366, 370, 373, 376, 382.
56   Spenser Wilkinson, *Lessons of the War*, quoted in Searle, *Quest for National Efficiency*, pp. 110–11.
57   MacKenzie, *Diary of Beatrice Webb*, vol. 2, p. 173.
58   Wilson, *CB*, p. 368.

the Liberal party.' He called for 'a policy adapted to 1901 or 1902, and not a policy adapted to 1892 or 1885'. But unfortunately, there were

> men who sit still with the fly-blown phylacteries bound round their obsolete policy, who do not remember that, while they have been mumbling their incantations to themselves the world has been marching and revolving, and if they have any hope of leading or guiding it, they must march and move with it too.

Above all, the party 'should not disassociate itself, even indirectly, from the new sentiment of Empire which occupies the nation'.

In his Chesterfield speech, Rosebery declared that a programme of national efficiency meant reform of the War Office, improvement in the navy, an extension of education (where there was 'nothing like a national system, but a great chaos of almost haphazard arrangement'), housing reform and temperance reform. But unlike Sidney Webb, he spoke in generalities and offered nothing specific. He concluded by reiterating:

> I am quite aware that my policy does not run on party lines (hear, hear), but it is not to party that I appeal (hear, hear). Party in this matter can avail little or nothing. I appeal unto Caesar from a parliament with its half-hearted but overwhelming Government supporters and a distracted and disunited Opposition. I appeal to the silent but supreme tribunal which shapes and controls, in the long run, the destinies of our people, I mean the tribunal of public opinion, that of common sense.[59]

The speech reinforced the view of Liberal Imperialists that Rosebery was their natural leader. Grey believed that all that remained was 'the faint hope that the genius of Rosebery may succeed in redeeming a party which seems past redemption'.[60] Even Lloyd George on the left wing of the party apparently expressed willingness to serve under Rosebery.[61] Campbell-Bannerman sought to appease Rosebery by offering him the Liberal leadership in the Lords, but he declined, saying that he could not accept Home Rule.

Once the applause had died down, it became apparent that Rosebery had actually said very little new. His gnomic speeches had not resolved the question of what precise policies were needed to secure national efficiency and they left his supporters little wiser as to what steps they should take if they

59 *The Times*, 17 December 1901.
60 Grey to J. A. Spender, 21 December 1901, Spender Papers, Add. MSS. 46,389, f. 7.
61 Rhodes James, *Rosebery*, p. 440.

wished to follow him or to put his prescriptions into action. The main thrust appeared to many Liberals as negative, demanding that the party repudiate everything it had been taught to believe for many years, including Home Rule. Such advice was hardly likely to endear Rosebery to Liberals in the constituencies. 'All the traditions, the pledges, and the faiths of the Liberal Party are to be wiped out,' Harcourt wrote to his son. 'The whole language is an insult to the whole past of the Liberal Party and a betrayal of its growth in the future.'[62] Indeed, many of Rosebery's political utterances seemed to be directed at his own party. When, in 1903, Chamberlain was to proclaim the need for tariff reform, Rosebery's first response was not to counterpose the Liberal ideal of free trade but to declare that free trade was not in the Sermon on the Mount. Then, however, he announced that he remained a free trader.

It was not wholly clear what Rosebery believed should be written on the clean slate. What precisely did efficiency mean? It was, so Campbell-Bannerman wrote to his Chief Whip, 'pure claptrap ... Who is against it?'[63] Speaking in Leicester in February 1902, the Liberal leader asked, 'Suppose every article of the Liberal creed was sponged off, who was to write on "the clean slate"? Who was to choose what was to be written?' And he declared that 'the inevitable accompaniment' to the clean slate was 'the practice and penance of the white sheet'.[64] The Chesterfield speech offended Liberals in the constituencies since it did not mention the 'methods of barbarism' in South Africa or endorse the demand of Campbell-Bannerman and his supporters for the recall of Milner. In a letter to *The Times* on 20 February 1902, Rosebery confirmed that not only on domestic matters but also on the Boer conflict, 'our views on the war and its methods are not less discordant'. He went on to declare that he therefore remained outside Campbell-Bannerman's 'tabernacle, but not, I think, in solitude'.

Rosebery's speeches caused a sensation in political circles, but they were widely misunderstood. His allies, Asquith and Grey, saw the speeches, despite Rosebery's explicit denial, as a new bid for the Liberal leadership. They hoped that he would throw himself into the struggle to assure the triumph of their wing of the party. He should, they believed, take active steps to return to the leadership. He could not just await the call. 'There is no such thing as a political conscript,' Grey had declared at Peterborough on 18 July.[65] But Rosebery's position was distinct from that of his supporters. Unlike them, he did not believe that differences within the party could be reconciled. Instead, either the Liberal Party could become effective by purging the 'anti-national'

62 Gardiner, *Harcourt*, vol. 2, pp. 536–7.
63 J. A. Spender, *The Life of the Right Hon. Sir Henry Campbell-Bannerman, GCB*, Hodder & Stoughton, 1923, vol. 2, p. 14.
64 *The Times*, 20 February 1902.
65 Ibid., 18 July 1901.

elements from its ranks; or else a new party must arise, one dedicated to empire and social reform. In either case, the Liberal Unionists would have a strong incentive to desert their coalition allies. But to attract Liberal Unionists, it would be necessary to discard Home Rule and make clear that the Liberals would not again govern with the aid of the Irish. Most Liberal Imperialists, and in particular Asquith, were not prepared to go so far. They were certainly unwilling to put Home Rule in the forefront of their programme as Gladstone had done, but they were not prepared to drop it entirely, with the consequence of causing a party split. Rosebery would have welcomed such a split. Asquith and Grey would not.

Rosebery's chances of success, therefore, did not appear good. Liberal Unionists, having entered into a coalition with the Conservatives, were hardly likely to desert it without a radical change in political circumstances. Perhaps Rosebery was hoping for an accretion of strength from Liberal Unionists at the constituency level. But the Liberal Imperialists appeared too weak to tempt Liberal Unionists. They were an elite group, far stronger at Westminster than in the constituencies. And the Liberals would be unlikely to purge themselves of their 'anti-national' element, since that element was almost certainly in the majority amongst their members in the constituencies.

Nevertheless, the Liberal Imperialists continued to organise under Rosebery's leadership. In early 1900, a Liberal Imperial Council had been formed by his allies. In February 1902, this was transformed into a Liberal League whose president was Rosebery and vice-presidents were Haldane, Grey and Fowler. The League was widely believed to be an organisation designed to secure the removal of Home Rule from the party's programme and then to challenge Campbell-Bannerman's leadership. Some feared it might herald a breakaway movement. But whatever the intentions of its founders, the League failed to attract mass support. Campbell-Bannerman mocked it by saying that 'the staff officers have already been gazetted ... although the troops are not yet in sight'.[66] And Rosebery would disappoint those who looked to him for leadership. Following his Chesterfield speech, he again withdrew into his tent, leaving his colleagues puzzled and leaderless. The speeches were not followed up by action. After the Chesterfield speech, *The Spectator* had suggested on 21 December that Rosebery call a meeting of Liberal MPs and peers to ask if they would accept his leadership. The overwhelming likelihood, however, is that they would not. When political parties are in difficulties, they do not like to be told that much of what they had hitherto believed was mistaken. They want instead a clarion call, a renewal of faith, not the undermining of it. In addition, Rosebery's petulant

---

66 *Manchester Guardian*, 6 March 1902.

and over-sensitive nature made it difficult for him to work with others, to lead a team. These temperamental difficulties had rendered his government a failure and had also prevented him from leading an effective opposition. Ambitious men such as Asquith and Haldane sought to rise in the Liberal Party, not, like Rosebery, to separate themselves from it. They sought not party realignment but a reunited party. From this point of view, Rosebery was not an alternative leader but an embarrassment. So the Liberal League proved ineffective. Indeed, its formation was itself a sign of the failure of Liberal Imperialists to win mass support in the constituencies; and, while Rosebery might have considerable support amongst the Liberal elite and in the country as a whole, he had little amongst Liberal MPs or constituency members. The Liberal Imperialists, who were nicknamed Limps, were in fact to prove themselves indeed limp as a political force.

PEACE IN SOUTH AFRICA

At last, in May 1902, the Boer War came to an end, with the signing of the Treaty of Vereeniging. Although the Boer republics were annexed to the British Empire, the terms were generous to the defeated. Indeed, in a speech in Pretoria in January 1903, Chamberlain called them 'the charter of the Boer people'. They provided for a near universal amnesty, legal protection for the Dutch language and Dutch education in the Transvaal and Orange Free State. Moreover, £3 million would be provided to help reconstruct the Boer colonies – around £10 million was in fact eventually provided – and there would be interest-free loans for two years. 'I say that never in the history of the world', Chamberlain asserted, 'has a conquering nation done so much for those who were so recently their opponents.'[67] The Boer republics would be administered for the time being by the military authorities, but they were promised a rapid reversion to civil government and then representative institutions 'leading up to self-Government ... as soon as circumstances permit'. The Uitlanders would of course be given the franchise. The key issue, however, was whether the franchise should be extended to Africans. Lord Salisbury had assured Parliament that, after a British victory, 'there must be no doubt ... that due precaution will be taken for the kindly and improved treatment of those countless indigenous races of whose destiny I fear we have been too forgetful'. Chamberlain had told Milner in March 1901 that Britain 'cannot consent to purchase peace by leaving the coloured population in the position in which they were before the war, with not even the ordinary civil rights

---

67   Charles W. Boyd, ed., *Mr Chamberlain's Speeches*, Constable, 1914, vol. 2, p. 73, 91-2.

which the Government of the Cape Colony has long conceded to them'.[68] In the original draft of the treaty, drawn up by Kitchener, it was provided that there would definitely be an African franchise after the introduction of self-government. But this was rewritten by Smuts to the effect that 'the question of granting the franchise to natives will not be decided until after the introduction of Self-Government', giving power to the Boers who would certainly not grant it.[69] Milner was later to regret this concession, saying that it was 'the greatest mistake he had ever made'.[70] When he became responsible for the Transvaal, he had improved the slave-like conditions Africans faced by abolishing flogging and the pass laws, though these laws were later to be reinstated. But he could make no headway on the franchise. In 1906, Smuts made it clear that he was unalterably opposed to giving non-whites the vote. 'I do not believe in politics for them … certainly so far as the natives are concerned politics will to my mind only have an unsettling influence. I would therefore not give them the franchise.'[71] With self-government, then, it was clear that there would be no native franchise. 'We got off the right lines', Milner later stated, 'when we threw over Mr Rhodes's principle of "equal rights for every civilized man".'[72] British 'throwing over' of this principle was to determine the future of South Africa for ninety years.

Milner believed that the fundamental post-war problem for the Transvaal was economic, restoring the prosperity of the mines. The mine owners claimed that the supply of African unskilled labour was insufficient and that whites were not prepared to work at the low wages which, the owners insisted, were necessary for the mines to become profitable. A further reason, however, why it was difficult to recruit labour was that conditions in the Rand mines and mine compounds were notoriously poor and the mortality rate was high. Brodrick, the India Secretary, had sought to secure more cheap labour by importing 20,000 Indians to work on the railways in the Transvaal, but Curzon, the viceroy, had refused to allow this.[73] Milner, by contrast, agreed to allow the import of indentured Chinese labourers in 1903 to supplement the deficiency and help restore the mines after the ravages of the war. Chamberlain was opposed to this policy, but he was overborne by Milner who told him that the policy was overwhelmingly desired by local opinion. Chamberlain felt unable to overrule local opinion on an issue which did not seem to involve imperial interests, even though the Transvaal

68 J. S. Mohlamme, 'Blacks in the ex-Boer Republics of the Transvaal and Orange Free State in the Aftermath of the South African War of 1899–1902', *Southern Journal of Contemporary History*, 2000, p. 279.
69 W. K. Hancock, *Smuts: The Sanguine Years 1870–1919*, Cambridge University Press, 1962, vol. 1, p. 159.
70 Mohlamme, 'Blacks in the ex-Boer Republics', pp. 280, 279.
71 Mansergh, *Commonwealth Experience*, p. 92.
72 Ibid., p. 90.
73 Gilmour, *Curzon*, p. 261.

was a crown colony, having not yet been granted self-government. By the time the crisis over Chinese labour came to a head in the spring of 1904, Chamberlain was out of office. Milner had appreciated the issue's political sensitivity and had obtained the approval not only of the government but also of his Liberal Imperialist friends, Asquith, Grey and Haldane, before committing himself to the policy. They promised Milner their support and, 'on that understanding, and that understanding alone, he decided to go on with … [the] project'.[74] Haldane, however, was the only one of the three not to oppose the policy when it came under criticism. Asquith and Grey were to desert their mentor and in 1904 Asquith condemned the policy in the Commons.

By February 1905, there were 27,000 Chinese labourers on the Rand, the vast majority without their wives or families. They were kept in closely guarded compounds under conditions which amounted almost to imprisonment. They needed permits to leave their compound, and permits were only issued for periods of up to forty-eight hours. They were also forbidden to own property. There was a stringent code of offences and penalties. Milner unwisely sanctioned corporal punishment of the Chinese workers for criminal offences. Sir Gilbert Parker, a Conservative MP, argued that 'flogging in itself' was 'not slavery, else what had been pursued in the British Navy and public schools was slavery'.[75] After four years, the Chinese labourers were to be compulsorily repatriated.

When the conditions under which the Chinese workers were living became known in Britain, there was an outcry from liberal opinion and flogging was abolished in June 1905 when it was admitted that it had been abused. Chinese labour symbolised the impatience which Milner and other imperialists could display when faced with what they regarded as humanitarian shibboleths hindering what to their minds was a great end, the reconstruction of South Africa, a reconstruction which would benefit everyone including the African population. 'Chinese slavery' was to become a Liberal cry in the 1906 general election, but it was not in the strict sense of the term slavery. The Chinese labourers in South Africa had a free choice whether to work or not, and were able to earn much more than they could in China for similar work.[76] The labourers were made aware of the conditions before they signed their contracts of employment, and they enlisted for a specific period. Therefore, as Churchill admitted, 'it cannot in the opinion of His Majesty's Government be classified as slavery in the extreme acceptance of the word

---

74 Cecil Headlam, *The Milner Papers, South Africa 1899–1905*, Cassell, 1933, vol. 2, p. 477 and note 1.
75 House of Commons Debates, 22 February 1906, vol. 152, col. 550.
76 Ibid., col. 536.

without some risk of terminological inexactitude'.[77] Nevertheless, the contract which the Chinese workers voluntarily signed was, in his view, neither 'desirable' nor 'proper' and constituted 'a notable and melancholy derogation from any standard of Labour Ordinance, even the lowest ... tolerated within the British Empire'. So, while not strictly slavery, Chinese indentured labour was regarded by many as being very close to it.

The Boer War has been called the last of the gentleman's wars.[78] It was nothing of the sort, being fought with great cruelty on both sides. Britain, as we have seen, burnt farms and on occasion shot prisoners. But Boer cruelty was far worse. On occasion, they used explosive bullets – dumdum bullets – against British troops, banned by the 1899 Hague Convention. They used women and children as cover for troops, also banned by the convention. Nor was the war, as used to be thought, solely a 'white man's war'. Probably around 30,000 armed Africans fought on the British side together with many more in non-combatant roles. A small number fought for the Boers, but the Africans on the Boer side were in non-combatant roles.[79] The Boers were merciless towards Africans. In July 1901, a Boer leader, General Kritzinger, told Kitchener that all Africans in the British Army should be shot, whether armed or not.[80] Canon Farmer, a British missionary in the Transvaal, wrote in 1901:

> Of all who have suffered by the war, those who have endured most & will receive least sympathy are the Natives in the country places of the Transvaal ... They have welcomed British columns & when these columns have marched on they have been compelled to flee from the Boers, abandon most of their cattle & stuff & take refuge in the towns or fortified places, or be killed.

In one village 'the Boers under Smuts' captured a post and, 'when afterwards a column visited the place, they found the bodies of all the Kaffirs murdered and unburied'. The canon concluded, 'I should be sorry to say anything that is unfair about the Boers. They look upon the Kaffirs as dogs & the killing of them as hardly a crime.'[81]

Although the Boers had in fact surrendered, the Treaty of Vereeniging provided what was in effect a negotiated settlement. The Boers sacrificed their independence, but that was soon restored. In 1906, the Liberal government

77 Ibid., cols 555–6.
78 Nasson, *The Boer War*, p. 15.
79 Ibid., p. 215.
80 Francis John Pretorius, 'Boer attitudes to Africans in wartime', in Lowry, ed., *The South African War Reappraised*, pp. 105–6.
81 Pakenham, *The Boer War*, p 573,

enacted self-government for the Transvaal and in 1907 for the Orange Free State. In 1909, Parliament passed a Union of South Africa Act providing for dominion self-government and a new constitution framed by the four British and Dutch colonies, now brought together in a unified single state. The aim of both Unionist and Liberal governments was to reconcile the British and the Boers. While the defeated Boers could not be expected to give allegiance to a British colony any more than the British could give allegiance to a Boer republic, perhaps both could give a common loyalty to a new Union of South Africa, just as British and French Canadians both gave allegiance to the Canadian Confederation. But in reconciling the Boers, the rights of the African population were sacrificed. The government seemed impotent in the face of the overwhelming view of the white population in South Africa that political rights not be given to Africans. Smuts wrote to Chamberlain in 1903 insisting on a 'just administration of the law to make it plain to the Natives that the war altered the relations between the two white races but not between the white and coloured population of the country'.[82] The outcome, however, was, as the veteran radical Sir Charles Dilke pointed out, that in the constitutions of the Boer colonies and the new Union of South Africa, the British government and Parliament instituted, for the first time in its history, 'a colour bar in the British Empire'. The constitutions of the Transvaal and the Orange Free State 'contained an absolute colour bar in the sharpest form in which it had ever appeared in the English language'. The vote there was to remain restricted to whites. In the 1909 Act, the African franchise was retained in the Cape but was made subject to removal by a two-thirds majority in both chambers of the Union of South Africa Parliament sitting together, although this was better protection than existed before. But the franchise for the Union of South Africa Parliament would be restricted to whites. During the war, Keir Hardie, a pro-Boer, had railed against the employment of African troops to fight the Boers, declaring in January 1902, 'We are breaking faith with every nation in Europe by arming the blacks to fight against white men.'[83] But he now waxed eloquent on the betrayal of African voting rights.

> For the first time, we are asked to write over the portals of the British Empire, 'Abandon hope, all ye who enter here'. So far as colour is concerned, this Bill lays it down that no native or person of other than European descent can ever hope to aspire to membership of the Parliament of South Africa.[84]

---

82 Lowry, *South African War Reappraised*, p. 7.
83 Roberts, *Salisbury*, p. 750.
84 House of Commons Debates, 17 December 1906, vol. 167, cols 1090, 1093; 16 August 1909, vol. 9, col. 994.

The Boer War had resulted in a British military victory in that the Boer colonies became part of the British Empire. It had secured the two main aims of the government: securing the franchise for the Uitlanders, although, admittedly, only the white Uitlanders, and securing British supremacy in South Africa. But British victory was the prelude to a moral defeat. The Africans had hoped that it would lead to improvement in their conditions, encouraged by Chamberlain who had told the Commons at the outbreak of war that 'the treatment of natives [in the Transvaal] has been disgraceful, it has been brutal; it has been unworthy of a civilised Power'.[85] In a general election speech in 1900, he had referred to 'the vast native population ... who depend upon British justice in order that their lives may be secure'.[86] A petition to Edward VII signed by over 25,000 Africans in the Transvaal calling for the abolition of discriminatory legislation was ignored.[87] The 1909 Act, though passed by a Liberal government, marked the triumph of the Boer principle that the Africans were not entitled to citizenship rather than the British principle that the empire should not distinguish on the basis of colour, religion or race, the principle Chamberlain and Milner had defended before the war but which had been conceded at Vereeniging. 'South Africa', Dilke quoted Smuts as saying, 'is to be a white man's country, whatever ill-informed people in England might say to the contrary.'[88] Smuts was supported by the Labour Party in the Boer republics which was not only against the native franchise but against the employment of African labour in the mines.

In debates on the 1909 Bill, MPs showed themselves uneasy with the colour bar and no speaker was prepared to justify it. Instead, it was defended as a regrettable necessity for reconciliation between Briton and Boer. Even Keir Hardie suggested no more than that the African franchise be guaranteed in the Cape and Natal. He did not advocate its introduction in the two Boer colonies, quoting Smuts as saying that 'there was a vast majority of people in South Africa opposed to the native franchise. The Transvaal was very largely opposed to it, and so were the Free States and Natal.'[89] Indeed, it was all that the more moderate Boer leaders could do to prevent resolutions being passed for removal of the African franchise in the Cape. MPs believed that South Africa could not be governed against the wishes of the Boers. More fundamentally they believed, even if subconsciously, that South Africa was a white man's country. There was no division on the Second Reading of the Bill. MPs were no doubt delighted to be free of the problems

---

85 Ibid., 19 October 1899, vol. 77, col. 271.
86 *The Times*, 24 September 1900.
87 Mohlamme, 'Blacks in the ex-Boer Republics', pp. 278, 270.
88 House of Commons Debates, 16 August 1909, vol. 9, col. 980.
89 Ibid., col. 990.

of South Africa. The hope perhaps was that, with independence, attitudes towards the African population would become more generous. That did not happen. When the Boers attained power under the Transvaal leaders, Botha and Smuts, they adopted policies of racial segregation and in 1948, when Smuts's Nationalist opponents under Dr Daniel Malan came to power, they introduced apartheid. Chief Albert Luthuli, the future president of the African National Congress and Nobel Prize winner, declared that by then 'it did not seem to us of much importance whether the whites gave us more of Smuts or switched to Malan'.[90] From 1936, the non-white franchise in the Cape was gradually removed in part by circumventing the South African constitution. A constitution providing for majority rule in South Africa was not achieved until 1996. 'You say and say truly', Milner had written in 1897 to Asquith, who was to be the Prime Minister of the government which was to legislate for union in 1909, 'that self-government is the basis of our colonial policy and the keystone of colonial loyalty. That principle, fearlessly and unflinchingly applied, would make South Africa as loyal as Canada – but what would be the price? The abandonment of the black races, to whom you have promised protection.' That, Milner believed, was 'the whole crux of the South African position'. The National Liberal Federation had demanded in 1901 'equal rights for both white races, an honourable measure of self-government, and a just and humane treatment for the natives'. With the Union of South Africa Act, the first and second aims were achieved but not the third.[91] Instead, a discrimination was being introduced into the Union of South Africa which had not been present in Cape Colony. The Indian nationalist Gandhi, working as a lawyer in South Africa, told the Colonial Secretary, 'Our lot today is infinitely worse than under the Boer regime.'[92] One writer has summed up the effect of the Boer War in the following way. 'The Boers said the war was for liberty. The British said it was for equality. The majority of the inhabitants, who were not white at all, gained neither liberty nor equality.'[93]

The betrayal of the Africans has been accompanied by some historical amnesia. In 1961, there was an anti-apartheid protest meeting in London with placards 'Down with Verwoerd', the South African racialist Prime Minister. An elderly activist turned to the chairman and said, 'Oddly enough the last time I spoke in this hall Lloyd George was in the chair and the theme was "Hands off the gallant little Boers".'[94]

---

90 Mansergh, *Commonwealth Experience*, p. 376.
91 Ibid., p. 94.
92 Peter Warwick, 'Black People and the War', in Warwick, ed., *The South African War*.
93 Rayne Kruger, *Goodbye Dolly Gray: The Story of the Boer War*, Cassell, 1959, p. 507.
94 Lowry, 'Introduction', in Lowry, ed., *The South African War Reappraised*, p. 19.

*   *   *

In his poem 'The Lesson', published in *The Times* on 29 July 1901, Rudyard Kipling, the poet of imperialism, wrote:

> Let us admit it fairly, as a business people should,
> We have had no end of a lesson: it will do us no end of good.
> Not on a single issue, or in one direction or twain,
> But conclusively, comprehensively, and several times and again,
> Were all our most holy illusions knocked higher than Gilderoy's kite.
> We have had a jolly good lesson, and it serves us jolly well right!
>
> ...
>
> It was our fault, and our very great fault – and now we must turn it to use.
> We have forty million reasons for failure, but not a single excuse.
> So the more we work and the less we talk the better results we shall get –
> We have had an Imperial lesson; it may make us an Empire yet!

In H. G. Wells's novel *The New Machiavelli*, the hero remembers how at the turn of the century, 'the prevailing force in my undergraduate days was not Socialism, but Kiplingism ... We were all ... very distinctly Imperialists.' But it had taken around 450,000 British and empire troops two and half years to subdue Boer forces of at most 87,000, primarily unorganised farmers. Around 22,000 British and colonial lives had been lost and the war had cost £223 million. It had not been the short, nearly costless war that so many had envisaged, and it had shown that Britain's military capabilities were far from being equal to her global responsibilities. Hugh Arnold-Forster, War Secretary from 1903 to 1905, told a friend that 'the British Army is a social institution prepared for every emergency except that of war, and governed by any and every consideration except that of professional necessity'.[95]

As early as January 1900, Beatrice Webb confided to her diary that the war had instilled

> the horrible consciousness that we have, as a nation, shown ourselves to be unscrupulous in methods, vulgar in manners as well as inefficient ... The Boers are, man for man, our superiors in dignity, devotion and capacity – yes *in capacity*. That, to a ruling race, is the hardest hit of all.

The trouble was that the

---

95   Nicholas d'Ombrain, *War Machinery and High Policy: Defence Administration in Peacetime Britain, 1902–1914*, Oxford University Press, 1973. p. 142fn.

Government of the country is firmly in the hands of little cliques of land-lords and great capitalists and their hangers-on. The social enthusiasm that inspired the intellectual proletariat of ten years ago has died down and given place to a wave of scepticism about the desirability, or the possibility of substantial change in society as we know it.[96]

By the time of the peace, the war had come to appear dubious in motive, inefficiently waged and damaging in its effect on British prestige, while the local gains for which it had been fought proved to be only temporary. Inefficient conduct of the war caused a change in sentiment which was to prove highly damaging to the Unionists. The country, the *Manchester Guardian* declared in April 1901, was passing through a 'great crisis' which 'will leave a profound mark upon the history of opinion ... It has rudely shaken the easy optimism so common a couple of years ago ... a time of Lenten penance follows the carnival.'[97] The war destroyed popular support for imperialism and led to great soul-searching. Another poem of Kipling's, 'The Islanders', written in 1902, summed up the feelings of many.

> Then was your shame revealed.
> At the hands of a little people, few but apt in the field.

Imperialism came to seem a fever which had run its course and had lost its moral and idealistic coating. In 1933, Lord Eustace Percy, a Conservative minister between the wars, reminisced:

> The world that went into ... the Boer War was a world completely satisfied that it had solved the secret of political well-being and progress; the world that came out of [it] was a doubtful and rather anxious world, wondering whether after all the political philosophy of the Victorian era was the last word in human wisdom.[98]

New men were, so it appeared, needed to confront new problems. 'The world of politics was passing through one of those periodic changes which separate one political generation from another. The Conservative regime of Lord Salisbury ceased to look inevitable and began to look merely old.'[99]

---

96 MacKenzie, *Diary of Beatrice Webb*, vol. 2, pp. 168–9.

97 *Manchester Guardian*, editorial, 10 April 1901.

98 Quoted in Morton Keller, 'Anglo-American Politics, 1900–1930, in Anglo-American Perspective: A Case Study in Comparative History', *Comparative Studies in Society and History*, 1980, p. 462. This article offers some fascinating comparisons between Britain and America at the turn of the century.

99 Vincent, ed., *Crawford Papers*, p. 57.

CHAPTER 7

THE EDUCATION ACT

THE PROBLEM OF EDUCATION

The South African war had dominated public debate in Parliament and the country. But from 1902, domestic matters came to the fore, a result of social forces that had been held in check for too long. The Unionist government had appeared not to appreciate the full strength of these forces. It had, as we have seen, made no constructive response to trade union pressure to restore their legal position which had, after all, been granted to them by Disraeli's Conservative government. Instead, the government appeared content to continue with Salisbury's negativism. But there was to be one major domestic reform. On the day the Boer War ended, the parliamentary debate on a new Education Bill began. The 1902 Education Act is now generally regarded as an imaginative reconstruction of an outdated education system. But it began the process of destroying the Unionists and left Chamberlain desperate for a new cry. He was to find it in tariff reform. 'If we had had no Education Bill of 1902,' his colleague Lord George Hamilton was later to write, 'we should have had no Tariff Reform in 1903.' That was an exaggeration. For imperial union lay at the very core of Chamberlain's beliefs. But the timing of the campaign was to be influenced by the feeling that a new issue would be needed to regenerate the Unionists.

Writing in 1936, the historian of Victorian England G. M. Young declared that the absence of substantial educational provision in England and Wales for much of the nineteenth century was 'the great Victorian omission'.[1] But in their attempt to reform education, the Unionists were not faced with a *tabula rasa*. The problem they faced in 1902 had deep roots in recent history and religious attitudes and can only be understand in that context.

Education in Britain had long been entangled with religion. In England, and in Wales until 1920, the Anglican Church was the established church. Before 1870, elementary education in England and Wales for those lacking means had been provided by religious societies, primarily Anglican

---

1 Lord George Hamilton, *Parliamentary Reminiscences and Reflections, 1886–1906*, Murray, 1922, p. 315; Young, *Victorian England*, p. 165.

and Nonconformist, but also by Catholic and other denominations, and funded by the generosity of subscribers. But the schools provided by these societies had reached very few children and had provided only rudimentary instruction. In 1833, the Whig government had made provision for a grant to aid schools, and a system of inspection had been instituted. But education remained dependent upon private generosity. The only way to obtain a state education without payment was 'by being a cadet, a felon or pauper, since the army, prison and workhouse did provide some schooling'.[2] There was no national system of education at all.

In 1870, an 'Act to Provide for Public Elementary Education in England and Wales' was passed. It was the outcome, *The Times* in 1901 believed,

> of agitation on the part of two classes – the intellectual classes, who saw that we were very nearly the worst educated nation in Christendom, and the commercial class, which saw that our markets were threatened by competition unless we took up in earnest the task of providing our children with the key of knowledge.[3]

The motivation in 1902 was not dissimilar.

The 1870 Act had not sought to establish a totally new system but rather to fill gaps by providing elementary education in areas where there were no denominational or, as they were generally called, voluntary schools. It sought to supplement these schools to ensure that every child received a primary education. It provided for the establishment of directly elected school boards to maintain and finance schools, known as board schools, in areas where voluntary provision was insufficient. But the state assumed no overall responsibility for elementary education and none at all for secondary education, which was provided almost wholly by endowed and mainly fee-paying grammar schools and public schools. H. G. Wells regarded the Act as one 'to educate the lower classes for employment on lower class lines, and with specially trained, inferior, teachers'.[4]

The main problem which governments faced in reforming the system was in relation to religion. Political and ecclesiastical leaders believed that moral teaching was an important part of education and that meant religious teaching. For few in Victorian Britain believed, or were willing to proclaim that they believed, that morality could be separated from religion. But what kind of religious teaching should be provided in the maintained board schools,

2   Derek Fraser, *Evolution of the British Welfare State*, Harper Row, 1973, p. 384.
3   *The Times*, 13 April 1901.
4   Quoted in David V. Glass, 'Education', in Morris Ginsberg, ed., *Law and Opinion in England in the Twentieth Century*, Stevens, 1959, p. 325.

and should the state financially support denominational schools? These questions were of great importance to the elite but of much less importance, one suspects, for those outside the elite. Most members of the working class, no doubt, were 'too preoccupied with the needs of day-to-day living to spend much time on the niceties of religious doctrine'.[5] Indeed, amongst the working class, religious apathy and non-attendance at church and chapel services were widespread. A census carried out in London by the *Daily News* in 1902–03 discovered that 'the poorer the district the less inclination is there to attend a place of worship'. In his survey of London in the 1890s, Booth had found that 'the bulk of the wage-earning class' was 'untouched' by religion, with the significant qualification that, nevertheless, 'their children attended Sunday School'. But church attendance and religious worship in England were 'primarily a middle-class affair' and sectarian loyalties were of greater importance to politicians, ministers and clergy than to the laity.[6]

But sectarian loyalties were intimately associated with political allegiances. The Anglican community was slightly larger than the Nonconformist, but Nonconformist attendance at Sunday schools was larger than Anglican and there were more Nonconformist Sunday school teachers. The chapel seemed a stronger instrument of social cohesion than the church, and Nonconformity tended to be strongest in industrial areas where the Anglican Church had failed to adapt. Nonconformists tended to vote predominantly for Liberals, Anglicans for Conservatives. Indeed, during this period, religion was at least as important as class in determining voting behaviour. Admittedly, civil society was becoming more secularised and religious belief more concerned with social ethics than preparing for the afterlife. But perhaps for this very reason, extremism amongst the denominational leaders seems to have become stronger.

Most Anglicans and Catholics, it was believed, sought a denominational education for their children. So did some Nonconformists, though the majority of Nonconformists wanted non-denominational religious education without sectarian tests, restricted largely to Bible teaching. In theory, no doubt the sectarian problem could have been resolved through the provision of Anglican schools in predominantly Anglican areas and Nonconformist schools in predominantly Nonconformist areas. But in around 8,000 parishes, there were several religious denominations but sufficient children only for one school. Often that school was an Anglican one in which teaching posts were reserved to Anglicans. Further, in many parts of the country, and particularly in Wales, the religious divide was associated with a social divide, the Church of England being seen as the church of the gentry and

---

5   Pelling, 'Popular Attitudes to Religion', *Popular Politics*, pp. 19, 28.
6   Ibid., pp. 19, 28, 22–25, 30–31, 36.

the squirearchy, and it was alleged that Anglican schools were run in their interests rather than for the people as a whole. The chapel, by contrast, was regarded as 'the poor man's church', the church not so much of the working classes but of the lower middle class and, in Wales, the peasants.[7] 'The little chapel', Lloyd George was to say on 16 December 1909, 'is the only place in the village that will stand up to that Castle. All the men in that village that would decline to cringe, they are there.'[8] The sectarian conflict, then, was a social conflict as well as a political one. It posed a particularly acute problem for a Unionist government. For the Conservatives were predominantly Anglican, while many Liberal Unionists were, like Chamberlain, Nonconformists. So the sectarian problem had the potential to undermine the Unionist coalition.

The 1870 Act had sought a compromise between conflicting religious views. The original intention had been to provide a link between the board schools and the voluntary schools by allowing the locally elected boards to aid voluntary schools from the rates. However, the so-called Cowper-Temple clause provided that there was to be no sectarian religious education in any rate-aided school but only non-denominational Bible teaching. The purpose was to ensure that the state would not subsidise those belonging to a particular denomination in rate-aided schools. *Punch* declared that the clause 'had reduced the fractions to the lowest common denomination'![9] The Anglicans would not have Cowper-Temple teaching in their schools which they regarded as indistinguishable from Nonconformist religious instruction, indeed almost too amorphous to be called religious education at all. Some Anglican clerics believed that a non-denominational education was not entitled to be called Christian at all, and some professed to regard the board schools as hotbeds of irreligion. The dean of St Paul's believed that 'School Boards have been a great misfortune all over the country; they have lowered the tone of morality and have increased the amount of crime'.[10] Even worse, some regarded them as being 'likely to favour socialism'. 'What do you mean by socialism?' the chair of a School Attendance Committee in Essex had been asked by the Royal Commission on Education in 1887. 'I mean', came the reply, 'the state of things in which there is not the respect for the classes above the children that I think there ought to be.'[11] In any case, the trust deeds of many voluntary schools prohibited them from employing anyone other than a member of the denomination as a teacher. So the Cowper-Temple clause

7   Quoted in Lynd, *England in the Eighteen-Eighties*, p. 331.
8   Quoted in O. F. Christie, *The Transition to Democracy, 1867–1914*, Routledge, 1934, p. 124.
9   Quoted in Read, *Age of Urban Democracy*, p. 99.
10 Quoted by James Bryce, House of Commons Debates, 5 May 1902, vol. 107, col. 656.
11 Quoted in Lynd, *England in the Eighteen-Eighties*, pp. 96–7.

meant that rate aid could not be given to any voluntary school – except that Section 25 of the 1870 Act allowed a payment from the rates towards the fees of needy children. But otherwise, the voluntary schools could be assisted only by grants from central government, not from the rates.

In 1880, elementary education was to be made compulsory for children in England and Wales between five and twelve – in Scotland it was compulsory between five and thirteen – but in Ireland it was not made compulsory until 1892 and then only for children in urban areas. Pupils in England and Wales could, if their parents so wished, stay at school until they were thirteen. Until 1889, however, there was no state provision of education beyond that age. It followed that, if the state was putting parents under a duty to send their children to school, it should also pay for the performance of that duty in cases where parents could not afford to do so. In 1891, fees were abolished in board schools, though around 10 per cent of voluntary schools still charged them.[12] In the early twentieth century, the argument was to go further. A child's education could hardly be of value if they went to school hungry or ill – and the 1905 Liberal government was to provide free school meals for necessitous children and free medical inspections.

The 1870 Act, then, had created a dual educational system in England and Wales. By 1902, there were around 14,500 voluntary schools, approximately 12,000 of which were Church of England schools, attended by around 60 per cent of primary schoolchildren. There were also around 5,750 board schools, financed from the rates and required to be non-sectarian. There were, paradoxically, voluntary or free schools supported by the state church, and state schools supported by the free Nonconformist churches. By 1902, the voluntary schools had a monopoly of primary education in around one-third of England and Wales, where there were no board schools. In Nottinghamshire, for example, there were 117 villages where the only school was Anglican, in Lincolnshire 313 and in Yorkshire 549.[13] So in these areas, Nonconformists were required to send their children to a school contravening their religious principles, schools which would not employ Nonconformists or indeed non-Anglicans as teachers. In addition, Nonconformists were contributing through taxes to the payment of grants to voluntary schools. There was admittedly a conscience clause in the voluntary schools allowing the children of Nonconformists and other dissenters to avoid religious education, but it seems that there was some stigma attached to children whose parents took advantage of this option.[14] Anglicans and Catholics, as well as

12   J. E. B. Munson, 'The Unionist Coalition and Education 1895–1902', *Historical Journal*, 1977, p. 610.
13   Alan Rogers, 'Churches and Children in the Controversy Over the 1902 Education Act', *British Journal of Educational Studies*, 1959, p. 43.
14   D. W. Bebbington, *The Nonconformist Conscience: Chapel and Politics, 1870–1914*, George Allen & Unwin, 1982, p. 139.

Nonconformists, were also contributing twice, through subscriptions and taxes to pay grants to the voluntary schools and through the rates to the board schools to which they did not send their children, although in areas where there were no voluntary schools, they had no alternative but to do so. So both Nonconformists and Anglicans had grounds for complaint.

The school boards were directly elected. The elections were in theory fought on educational issues but were in practice an arena for sectarian squabbles, the battlefield on which the ecclesiastical war was fought. 'It is your business', Lord Salisbury had told an Anglican audience at Westminster on 12 June 1895, 'to capture the Board Schools.'[15] The belief that school board elections were determined by educational matters was, so Sir John Gorst, vice-president of the Committee on Education (in effect the education minister in the Commons), declared in July 1901, tactlessly but not inaccurately, a 'farce'.

> Everybody knows that educational purposes are the very last ideas in the minds of the members of school boards. (Opposition cries of 'Oh'.) I have heard that they are elected, some on religious grounds, some on party grounds but I have never heard of anyone being elected on educational grounds.[16]

One authority writes of

> the cab-stall proprietor whose knowledge of education was nil, but who was elected to the local school board by the local cabbies because he sold good coffee; of farmers who put up the fees to children as soon as they reached the age of exemption in order to force them out into the fields; of the candidate who was disallowed election expenses of £60 spent on oyster parties; and, strangest of all to modern notions, of the notice posted in a school to the effect that double fees would be charged in future in respect of any children whose parents had joined the labourers' union.[17]

Turnout for school board elections seems to have been generally low – around 20 per cent – and to have been confined to the enthusiasts of one sect or another.[18]

The 1870 Act, therefore, had accentuated the division between Anglicans

---

15 *Liberal Magazine*, 1895, p. 503.
16 House of Commons Debates, 8 July 1901, vol. 97, col. 1180.
17 G. A. N. Lowndes, *The Silent Social Revolution: An Account of the Expansion of Public Education in England and Wales, 1895–1935*, Oxford University Press, 1937, p. 69.
18 Sidney Webb, *The Education Muddle and the Way Out*, Fabian Tract No. 106, 1901, p. 7.

and Nonconformists. Despite the decline of religious enthusiasm from its mid-Victorian level, 'by an interesting but not unnatural process, the growing popular indifference to religion had strengthened the hands of the extremists in Church and Chapel'.[19] Certainly, the Nonconformist conscience remained a powerful factor in British politics.[20] In 1886, it had ruined Sir Charles Dilke, the radical leader, and in 1890, Parnell, the Irish leader, both of whom had been involved in unsavoury divorce cases. In 1910, Edwin Montagu, Financial Secretary to the Treasury, expressed disquiet at the presence of Maud Allan, a Canadian dancer, notorious for performing the dance of the seven veils, at one of Asquith's garden parties, telling the Prime Minister, 'There is no getting away from the fact that ours is a Nonconformist Party with Nonconformist susceptibilities and Nonconformist prejudices.' But he added that it was 'equally characteristic of our Party that so many Members who object to meeting the lady were able apparently to recognise her'.[21] At the beginning of the twentieth century, Nonconformists had become a powerful pressure group calling for temperance, control of the liquor trade and disestablishment. That, in turn, roused Anglicans to a defence of the established church. These squabbles may have had little popular resonance, but politicians felt that the cries of activists could not be ignored.

The 1870 Act had applied only to England and Wales. Ireland was not thought suitable for directly elected school boards, while Scotland had a quite different and more effective system of education with wider provision. In Scotland, there had been a school in every parish since the seventeenth century as the sectarian difficulties bedevilling education in England and Wales were not present there. The Education (Scotland) Act of 1872 went further than its English and Welsh counterpart of 1870, providing not that school boards should merely fill gaps in provision but that they should be responsible for all of the schools in a district. The religious difficulty was resolved by a provision that in a Presbyterian school, the head should be Presbyterian but his assistant Catholic; and vice versa in the Catholic schools. In Scotland, therefore, legislation enabled the boards to supplant and take over the voluntary schools, rather than merely supplement them as in England and Wales. And education became compulsory in Scotland in 1872, eight years before it did in England and Wales. Further, the boards in Scotland were not limited as English and Welsh school boards were to providing elementary education but were empowered to provide secondary education

---

19 Amery, *Chamberlain*, vol. 5, p. 84.
20 Bebbington, *Nonconformist Conscience*, p. 2.
21 Blewett, *Peers, Parties and People*, p. 231.

as well. The 1902 Education Act was not to apply to Scotland, and school boards were to remain there until 1918.

In England and Wales, the 1870 Act had two unforeseen consequences. The first was that it gave rise to serious financial problems for the voluntary schools. As we have seen, these schools could not be aided by the rates. It was suggested that some church schools were in fact supported not by those of religious inclination but by companies anxious to avoid their collapse which would mean the introduction of board schools and a charge on the rates. 'In Eastbourne a limited liability company was formed, with the approval of the Duke of Devonshire, a large landowner in the town, to avoid a Board.'[22] Even so, by 1902, the average income of a voluntary school in England and Wales per child was around fourteen shillings lower than the average income of a board school. In rural areas, the voluntary schools had been particularly badly hit by the agricultural depression, which lowered rents and tithes and led to a fall in voluntary subscriptions. In addition, the introduction of free education in 1891 undermined the finances of the 90 per cent of the voluntary schools which no longer charged fees. In March 1902, Dr Macnamara, Liberal MP for North Camberwell, and a former president of the National Union of Teachers, told the Commons that, in relation to the voluntary schools, 'the time has come when we should no longer maintain in operation the educational work of working class children out of money collected at jumble sales and ping pong tournaments'.[23] Declining subscriptions meant that expenditure on voluntary schools needed increasing supplementation from state grants. The 1870 Act had provided for grants of up to £250,000, and this was raised by the Unionist government of 1895 so that they were now receiving over £2 million in grants. Between 1870 and 1896, the government share in the finance of these schools rose from 38 per cent to 74 per cent. Even so, by 1902, many voluntary schools were struggling. But in addition, the constitutional position of the voluntary schools was unsatisfactory. For, although they received public money in the form of a government grant, they were largely free from public control and the state had no say in their management, their governors being chosen by the ecclesiastical authorities.

The second unforeseen consequence of the 1870 Act was that the arrangements for the public sector of education, the board schools, had come to be confused. The boards had responsibility for financing the non-denominational schools, but after local government reform in 1888, the rating authorities were the new local authorities, counties and the county boroughs. They raised the revenue while the boards spent the money. The boards were not,

---

22 Munson, 'Unionist Coalition and Education 1895–1902', p. 610.
23 House of Commons Debates, 24 March 1902, vol. 105, col. 882.

therefore, accountable to those who had to raise the rates to finance board schools. Many Unionists accused the boards of wasteful expenditure. There were, moreover, a vast number of boards – 2,567 in England and Wales in 1902, of which 2,085 governed areas with a population of under 5,000.[24] In Northamptonshire, there were forty school boards, twenty-three exercising jurisdiction over fewer than 1,000 people, and one over a population of just 250. That hardly made for a coordinated or effective education system.[25]

The status of board schools was not high. Indeed, one educational authority has written:

'Board school' was a term of contempt in my 'middle-class' suburban milieu; and one said 'board school boy' much as Swift's Houyhnhnms used the term 'yahoo'. The products of these establishments were looked down upon as being shabby and dirty urchins, who shouted in the street and could not speak the Queen's English.[26]

On 19 November 1895, a Mr Malthouse asked the London Commissioner of Sewers whether the London School Board was entitled to give what he referred to as a 'classical education'. The 1870 Act, he declared, 'was passed in the interests of waifs and strays and gutter children, and that all that the ratepayers were called upon to pay for was the teaching of reading, writing and arithmetic'. Instead, 'they had now a curriculum fit for a university'.[27] In fact, the Whitehall Code provided for the teaching, in addition to the three Rs, of geography, history, algebra, English, elementary French and German and animal physiology, though not Latin or Greek. Even so, of around 500,000 pupils attending London board schools in 1895, under 1 per cent – around 3,000 – were learning French and just thirteen German. The social investigator Charles Booth, commenting on the London board schools in 1903, declared:

A whole generation has been through the schools, but in scholarship there is not much to show for it. Almost all can, indeed, read, though with some effort; and write, after a fashion; but those who can do either the one or the other with the facility that comes of constant practice are comparatively few.[28]

24 Munson, 'Unionist Coalition and Education', p. 607.
25 Lowndes, *Silent Social Revolution*, pp. 69–70.
26 H. C. Barnard, 'Were Those the Days?', cited in Daglish, *Education Policy-Making*, p. 7. This book provides the most thorough account available of the 1902 Act.
27 *Liberal Magazine*, 1895, p. 492.
28 Charles Booth, *Labour and Life of the People in London, Final Volume: Notes on Social Influence and Conclusion*, Macmillan, 1903, p. 203.

But at least basic literacy was being achieved. By 1900, just 3 per cent of men could not sign the wedding register; by 1914, the figure for both men and women was just 1 per cent.[29] The school boards, however, were not education authorities in the wider sense of having a general responsibility for elementary education in their areas. They were merely bodies with the duty of supplementing inadequate provision and enforcing attendance.

The outcome, then, by the twentieth century was that in the rural areas, the voluntary schools were inefficient because of a shortage of funds; while in the urban areas, the board schools were inefficient because there were too many of them and they had no responsibility for raising the money that they were spending. Both central and local government could apply funds for education, but only the school boards and the denominational authorities could actually provide schools; and there was no authority with overall responsibility for education.

The situation was well summed up by Chamberlain in a speech at Birmingham in May 1902.

> We have a system, which is no system at all, which is a state of anarchy and confusion ... The authorities which collect the taxes or the rates are not the authorities which spend the taxes or the rates. There is no efficient control over the secular education ... You have the secular education of the country in a vast number of schools starved and inefficient owing to the inability of the managers or persons in charge to provide the necessary funds. Who suffers by that? Not the managers but the children of the people ... All these things constitute a national weakness and a national danger in view of the competition to which we are subjected.[30]

But there was an even further unforeseen consequence of the 1870 Act. It had provided some sort of a system of elementary education but not of secondary education. Indeed, there was no national system of secondary education at all. In 1889, a Technical Instruction Act empowered county boroughs and urban sanitary authorities as well as the new counties created in 1888 to finance technical education beyond the elementary stage by a rate not exceeding 1d in the pound; and in 1890, this was supplemented by provision from customs and excise duties, the so-called whisky money. Technical education was defined widely so as to include every subject except 'theology, Greek and Shakespeare'.[31] By the end of the nineteenth century,

29 Roderick Floud, Jane Humphries and Paul Johnson, eds, *The Cambridge Economic History of Modern Britain, vol. 2: 1870 to the Present*, Cambridge University Press, 2014, pp. 398, 111.

30 Amery, *Chamberlain*, vol. 5, p. 64.

31 Webb, *The Education Muddle*, p. 4.

therefore, local authorities had become in effect authorities for secondary education. The rate for technical education was supplemented by a central government grant administered by a Department of Science and Art, which also financed further education and evening classes attended by adults as well as youngsters. That seemed to many a step towards making education as a whole not only a local government responsibility but also a responsibility of the national government. In Wales, an Intermediate Education Act of 1889 had put education into the hands of Welsh local authorities. This was proving a successful experiment, and it seemed to point to a similar reform in England. But in England, local authorities were statutorily forbidden to provide elementary education, which was the responsibility of the school boards. So, in secondary education as in primary, there was a lack of coordination and lack of system. There were, by the end of the nineteenth century, two elective authorities responsible for education – school boards providing elementary education and local authorities providing technical secondary education, with no links between them, while the voluntary schools were not linked to either.

But the system was even more complex, since the 1870 Act had not defined what was to count as 'elementary education'. So some school boards had taken it upon themselves to provide what was in effect secondary education and had indeed been encouraged to do so by the government minister responsible for education. Some boards had established classes on top of the elementary ones. Others, including the London School Board, the largest of all, established higher grade secondary schools – by 1899, there were forty-four such schools in London – and evening continuation schools for those, whether adults or youngsters, whose school education had been completed or who wanted to continue their studies. By 1898, in London alone, no fewer than 109,121 students were attending such schools.[32] This, of course, meant rivalry with the local authorities administering the Technical Instruction Act. There was, then, even further confusion and overlapping with a consequential waste of resources; and while in some areas two public authorities were spending rates and taxes on providing what was in effect secondary education, in others there was none at all, for it was only in the larger cities that the school boards had the resources to provide post-elementary education. Small school boards were unable to make such provision. Secondary education, therefore, was even more uncoordinated and unsystematic than primary. And if the counties could be trusted with secondary education through the Technical Instruction Act, why not also elementary education?

32 Tony Taylor, 'The Cockerton Case Revised: London Politics and Education 1898–1901', *British Journal of Educational Studies*, 1982, pp. 330–31.

A national system of secondary education was urgently needed if Britain was to be able to compete with other industrial societies. Michael Sadler, a senior official at the Board of Education, believed that 'the very existence of the Empire ... depends upon sea power and school power'.[33] English education, however, was, in Balfour's words, 'chaotic, ineffectual, utterly behind the age, the laughing-stock of every advanced nation in Europe and America'.[34]

THE *COCKERTON* JUDGMENT AND AFTER

In 1901, following a decision by the High Court, the Appeal Court ruled in the *Cockerton* judgment that the school boards lacked statutory authority under the 1870 Act to provide secondary education for children beyond compulsory school age. The London School Board, so the court ruled, was statutorily prohibited from spending money from the rates on such education since it was not elementary education as defined in the 1870 Act. Such spending, therefore, was outside the board's legal competence. Nor could the boards charge fees or use endowments for the purpose of providing such education.[35] If, therefore, a school board wished to exercise such powers, it would have to seek new legislation. In consequence of the *Cockerton* decision, reform could no longer be delayed.

Before 1902, so as to avoid the sectarian question, the Unionists had reformed education in a piecemeal fashion. In 1897, they had increased the grant to voluntary schools by an additional 5s per pupil and relieved them from rates on the same basis as places of worship. Then, in 1899, they had established a Board of Education, presided over by a senior Cabinet minister; while a Private Member's Bill in the same year provided for the raising of the school-leaving age from eleven to twelve. In 1900, school boards were empowered but not required to raise the leaving age to fourteen, which did not become the compulsory leaving age until 1918. But the *Cockerton* judgment made it impossible to postpone radical restructuring of a system which was clearly no longer fit for purpose.

Lord Salisbury was unsympathetic to reform. His main concerns were to preserve the position of the Anglican Church and Anglican schools and to ensure that education in the board schools did not absorb too much of the Budget. He told Balfour in November 1896 that the demands of the educationalists for more money were 'practically unlimited' and that he believed that 'the educationist is one of the daughters of the horse leech'.[36] He

---

33 Lowndes, *Silent Social Revolution*, pp. 4, 51, iv.
34 Dugdale, *Balfour*, vol. 1, p. 184.
35 *R. v. Cockerton*, C.A. 1901.
36 Daglish, *Education Policy-Making*, p. 62.

regarded the school boards as extravagant and wanted the education rate cut to reduce the burden of the rates. The Duke of Devonshire had to remind him that no sector of education had ever been self-supporting. But Salisbury, who was by this time prone to falling asleep in Cabinet, was not able to exert leadership on educational issues, nor indeed on much else.

The 1902 Act is sometimes referred to as the Balfour Act, but although Balfour steered the legislation skilfully through the House of Commons, he too was sceptical of the value of reform. To one correspondent he declared, no doubt facetiously, that he 'did not believe in education'.[37] He told the Bishop of Coventry in June 1901 that he would never have 'permitted any bill to be introduced had it not been for the Cockerton judgment. It was quite evident with the war going on in South Africa [that] ... a less convenient season for original legislation could not be imagined.'[38] A month later, Balfour reminded the Duke of Devonshire that he had 'as you know, been dragged (much against my will) into questions connected with education'.[39] He found the education issue 'worse than any metaphysics';[40] and in June 1901, the classical scholar Sir Richard Jebb, Regius Professor of Greek at Cambridge and MP for Cambridge University, was struck by 'the singular indifference to the subject of education which Arthur Balfour showed: he does not seem to realise that the question is of urgent national importance, and that the country is now keenly interested in it'.

The vacuum in leadership was filled, oddly enough, by the Duke of Devonshire. He was the leading reformer in the Cabinet and it was his conception of reform which was finally enacted. He then steered the Bill through the Lords. He was dismissed by his head official, who later became a Liberal MP and had an axe to grind, as being 'profoundly ignorant of the system the Department had to administer, of its routine, and of its duties' and as being 'a living wet blanket'.[41] But that was unfair. As president of the National Association for the Promotion of Technical Instruction, the duke had acquired considerable knowledge of educational problems and had assisted in the creation of new universities in the north of England.[42] His sympathy lay with the educationalists rather than the sectarians. In January 1901, Balfour lamented that, visiting Chatsworth, the duke's seat, the duke was 'sure to talk to me at length upon his educational schemes. I confess they alarm me.

37 Max Egremont, *Balfour: A Life of Arthur James Balfour*, Collins, 1980, p. 150.
38 Tony Taylor, 'Arthur Balfour and Educational Change: The Myth Revisited', *British Journal of Educational Studies*, 1994, p. 143.
39 Munson, 'Unionist Coalition and Education', pp. 625, 624.
40 Adams, *Balfour*, p. 168.
41 Sir G. W. Kekewich, *The Education Department and After*, Constable, 1910, pp. 92, 93.
42 Holland, *Life of Devonshire*, vol. 2, p. 274.

Not because they are defective but because they are too complete.'[43] The duke had authority not only from his ducal status but, more important, from careful consideration of the issues, and he was able to carry a sceptical Cabinet with him. His Cabinet colleague Lord Selborne wrote in his diary that the duke's

> mind acted slowly, whereas Balfour's and Chamberlain's acted like lightning, but his considered judgment was on the whole sounder than theirs in this sense: when once he had really worked out his position he never had to change it. They on the contrary often had to modify their first judgments.[44]

Chamberlain, his opponent on tariff reform, insisted that despite the Duke of Devonshire's dilatory manner, 'he was a very clever man'.[45] The duke told the Cabinet that they must either accept comprehensive reform or drop the measure altogether, the option favoured by the party whips.[46] The Clerk of the Privy Council, Sir Almeric Fitzroy, wrote in his diaries that the duke's 'delivery of his views to the Cabinet was so powerful and his resolution so unexpected that not even Chamberlain's interruption disturbed him. Salisbury did not call for a formal conclusion on the proposals believing that a negative outcome might have produced Devonshire's resignation.'[47] A modern commentator has concluded that 'he had a far sounder and more constant understanding of the problem than Morant [his official adviser] or even, perhaps, Mrs Webb'.[48]

The government responded to the *Cockerton* judgment first by an enabling Bill, allowing the school boards to continue with their activities for a further year; and then by a radical reform of the whole structure, designed to create a genuine national system of both primary and secondary education. But what was the shape of this national system to be? The legislation had to deal with three inter-related questions:

- What was to be the controlling and supervising authority for the schools?
- Who was to pay for them?
- What should be the nature of religious education in the schools – in particular, how were sectarian differences to be accommodated?

---

43 Taylor, 'Arthur Balfour and Educational Change', p. 142.
44 Quoted in Munson, 'Unionist Coalition and Education', p. 615.
45 Ibid., p. 644.
46 Ibid., p. 633.
47 Fitzroy, *Memoirs*, pp. 72–4.
48 Munson, 'Unionist Coalition and Education', p. 644.

This last question threatened the cohesion of the Unionist coalition and the allegiance of its Nonconformist supporters.

Chamberlain regarded the 1870 settlement as too favourable to the Anglican Church, and in 1869, he had co-founded a National Education League which had proposed a totally unsectarian system, with religious education being the responsibility not of public authorities but of parents and the churches. 'Our choice', he had declared in 1869, 'is between the education of the people and the interests of the Church. Education to be national must be unsectarian.'[49] He no doubt continued to hanker for such a system. But when he had tried to establish it in Birmingham as mayor, his Nonconformist supporters would not accept it. They sought not secularism but a national system of schools with non-denominational religious teaching. A Unionist government, predominantly Anglican, was hardly likely to favour such an option; and in any case it was quite impractical. By 1902, as we have seen, the majority of pupils in England and Wales were being educated in voluntary schools. The cost of abolishing them and establishing a national system of non-denominational schools was estimated by Balfour to be around £26 million, 18 per cent of total central government spending, and clearly prohibitive. The voluntary schools as the largest element in the elementary school system were therefore indispensable, and yet their position, owing to insufficiency of funds, was precarious. Moreover, if parents wanted a denominational education for their children, they were entitled in a free society to have their choices respected. This meant that, as in the 1870s, reform had to build on the existing system, rather than supplanting it and creating a wholly new structure. The trouble was that the voluntary schools lay largely outside a public system of education, placing in the hands of religious authorities duties which in a national system ought to be exercised by public authorities. So reform would require greater public control over the voluntary schools as well as financial aid to rescue them. But that would attract the ire of the Nonconformists, who would object to local subsidies of Anglicans and Catholics – 'Rome on the rates'. In November 1901, Chamberlain told Selborne, 'The question of Education is a very delicate one in the case of the Radical Unionists. If you were to promote a Bill giving Rate aid to denominational schools, I think you would lose Birmingham and the Birmingham influence.'[50] It was for this reason that Chamberlain, usually the most powerful advocate for reform in the Cabinet, was, with regard to education, a brake not an accelerator.

Chamberlain at first hoped to avoid the dilemma through a Bill dealing

---

49 Quoted in G. T. I. Machin, *Politics and the Churches in Great Britain, 1869–1921*, Clarendon Press, 1987, p. 32.
50 Amery, *Chamberlain*, vol. 5, p. 85.

only with secondary education; and on 13 December 1901, the Cabinet voted by ten votes to eight to do just that. But it was implausible to believe that proposals for secondary education could be enacted without reforming elementary education, and the Duke of Devonshire and Balfour persuaded the Cabinet to reverse its decision, so resurrecting the dilemma which Chamberlain had hoped to avoid.

If the voluntary schools were to be made financially viable, they would need more financial aid. How should this aid be given? In theory, it could have been provided by further increasing the state grant, and that was Chamberlain's preferred solution. He asked Robert Morant, the official primarily responsible for the legislation, 'Why not do as was done in 1870, and promise additional grants to Voluntary Schools out of State funds, thus avoiding recourse to the rates?' Nonconformists would then not be required to contribute through the rates towards supporting such schools; and since national revenues were not hypothecated, they might be less hostile to financial aid. But Morant replied, 'Your War [i.e. the Boer War] has made further recourse to State grants impossible,' as the war had converted the Budget surplus bequeathed by Harcourt, the Liberal Chancellor in 1895, into a deficit.[51] And a Unionist government was certainly not prepared to tax its wealthy supporters by raising income tax to pay for education. But even more important, if counties and county boroughs were to be genuine local education authorities, they had to be given the power to set the standard of efficiency in *all* the schools in their area, not just the board schools. They could only do so if they held the power of the purse over voluntary as well as board schools. Therefore, voluntary schools could only be helped through rate aid. The Duke of Devonshire had no worries about that since, despite cries of 'Rome on the rates', he appreciated that there was no difference in principle between rate aid and the state grant previously given to such schools. And in the denominational schools, religious teaching would be paid for by the managers, and so at least the rates would not be spent on sectarian teaching, while religious instruction in the board schools would continue to be non-denominational under the provisions of the Cowper-Temple clause.

This approach, however logical, was difficult for Chamberlain to accept. To secure his acquiescence, the Bill as first announced provided that the abolition of school boards together with rate aid to voluntary schools would be optional, dependent on the wishes of particular local authorities. So, with a local authority controlled by Nonconformists, the existing position would remain unchanged. But the danger with this solution would be that local authority elections would be dominated by the question of whether

51   B. M. Allen, *Sir Robert Morant: A Great Public Servant*, Macmillan, 1936, p. 168.

education should or should not be transferred to it from the school board. Further, if rate aid to voluntary schools were to remain optional, ratepayers of local authorities which chose not to give it would obtain financial relief at the expense of provision in the voluntary schools; and no doubt some local authorities might seek to advantage their ratepayers by not seeking to take over the school boards, while a local authority hostile to the Anglican Church might deny rate aid entirely. There would, therefore, be radically unequal provision in different parts of the country, and the patchwork would remain. Therefore, there had to be compulsory rate maintenance. On 9 July 1902, at a time when Chamberlain was absent from the Commons due to illness, Henry Hobhouse, Liberal Unionist MP for East Somerset, successfully moved an amendment *requiring* local authorities to provide rate aid. On a free vote, the amendment was passed by 271 votes to 102. Balfour supported it although Austen Chamberlain, Joe's son, voted against. Haldane and a few other Liberals also voted for the amendment. 'They did not want a mere patchwork plan,' Hobhouse insisted. 'Above all they did not wish to see continued a kind of chaos of different authorities with agitation proceeding and discontent prevailing in educational circles even where it did not exist at present.'[52] But however beneficial the Hobhouse amendment was to prove for education, it was a heavy blow to Chamberlain and to Nonconformists.

REFORMING EDUCATION

The 1902 Act provided for counties and county boroughs to be education authorities, thereby creating a unified system at local level, in place of the school boards which were abolished. Rather than around 2,500 school boards, there would now be just 328 local education authorities. Voluntary schools were placed under these authorities and their direct access to Whitehall by which they received a Treasury grant was ended. In return for rate aid, these schools would also lose the power to charge fees.

Local authorities would have powers to provide for all levels of education below university level and were given statutory powers to ensure standards of effectiveness in primary education as a whole, including voluntary schools. And, in addition to acquiring responsibility for primary education, local authorities would be given powers to provide secondary education and non-university higher education – in the words of the Act, 'to take such steps as seem to them desirable, after consultation with the Board of Education, to supply or aid the supply of education other than elementary'. These powers, by contrast with those over primary education, were permissive,

52   House of Commons Debates, 9 July 1902, vol. 110, col. 1234.

not compulsory. The 1870 Act had placed a *duty* on the state to ensure that primary education was provided. The 1902 Act did not place a similar duty on the state to ensure that secondary education was offered; and, where it was provided, it would not necessarily be free. Local authorities were given powers to offer scholarships for secondary education and to remit fees if they so wished. But councils were to be restricted in the provision of secondary education by a rate of 2d in the pound, unless the Local Government Board agreed that it could be exceeded.

The Act weakened clerical control in the voluntary schools, but it did not remove it entirely. In return for rate aid, voluntary schools would be required to accept that one-third of their managers would be appointed by the local authority, empowered to sanction the appointment and dismissal of teachers and inspect the schools. Nonconformists complained that this was taxation – through the rates – without adequate representation. To meet Nonconformist grievances, Balfour asked an orthodox Conservative backbencher, Colonel Kenyon-Slaney, MP for the Newport division of Shropshire and not hitherto noted for any particular interest in educational matters, to propose an amendment in committee in November 1902, giving the control of religious instruction in the voluntary schools to the managers rather than the clergy, so as to guard against abuse of clerical power. This seemingly innocuous amendment was passed by 294 votes to thirty-five. Some High Church Anglicans were furious. One clergyman declared it to be 'the greatest betrayal since the Crucifixion', adding that 'he would have preferred the Colonel should have seduced his wife rather than come to Parliament with such a proposal'.[53] But Chamberlain, worried about his Liberal Unionist supporters, did not believe the Kenyon-Slaney amendment went far enough. He wanted a *majority* of the managers to be from the local authority and was supported by Lloyd George, who had in private initially welcomed the Bill but now declared that it was an attempt 'to rivet the clerical chain around the necks of the people'.[54] 'The clergyman', Lloyd George told the Commons, 'would come down to the school like a roaring lion seeking what little Nonconformists he could devour at the expense of the ratepayers.' 'For the sake of teaching dogmas to children who cannot understand them, we, in the midst of our difficulties and the rocks that surround us, propose to put the chaplain on the bridge.'[55] Those who thought the Kenyon-Slaney clause did not go far enough complained that, if ratepayer representatives were only a minority of the managers, the denominational schools would not be genuine

53 Fitzroy, *Memoirs*, vol. 1, p. 112.
54 Allen, *Morant*, p. 183.
55 House of Commons Debates, 7 August 1902, vol. 112, cols 1022, 1025.

public institutions at all. But the argument against this was that a majority of ratepayer representatives would entirely destroy the denominational character of the voluntary schools, and Chamberlain was defeated on the issue in Cabinet. All the same, it was clear that in return for accepting rate aid, the denominationalists would lose that complete control of their schools which they had previously enjoyed, and the Kenyon-Slaney amendment could be regarded as a reasonable compromise.

Largely as a result of the ecclesiastical controversy, the Bill occupied more parliamentary time and took longer in committee than any other measure hitherto submitted to Parliament. It was introduced on 24 March but did not receive royal assent until December. The 1870 Bill had taken twenty-two days in the Commons, the 1893 Home Rule Bill forty-six days in the Commons, but the 1902 Bill took fifty-six days, with the closure being employed after thirty-nine days in committee. The sectarian issue swamped educational matters. Haldane told the Commons that education was 'a question far beyond sects and priests, whether of conformity or nonconformity; it is a question which affects the national life in a manner which is fraught with urgency'.[56] But he was almost a lone voice and spoke in vain. Nor did he actually vote for the Bill. Most of the protagonists in the debate seemed more concerned with their sectarian principles than the needs of children or requirements of a modern educational system. Little attention was given to the key issue of the future – the creation of a mass system of secondary education – which was drowned in sectarian squabbles. One Welsh Liberal attacked Lloyd George for fanning sectarian prejudices, claiming:

> Having had no literary education himself he is unable to realise the needs of the education system. He regards it simply as a political scaffolding and so long as he can see his way to set up the scaffolding he does not trouble himself with the character of the edifice.[57]

The absurdity of much opposition to the Bill was pointed out in 1911 by a former Liberal MP, the writer Hilaire Belloc, and Cecil Chesterton, brother of the novelist G. K. Chesterton, in their book *The Party System*, in which they declared that those agitating on the Bill were 'men who would as soon think of sending their children to be educated in Nigeria as at a public elementary school'.[58]

Summing up before the vote on Second Reading, Balfour said, 'I would

---

56 Ibid., 5 May 1902, vol. 107, col. 703.
57 Morgan, *Wales in British Politics*, p. 197.
58 Hilaire Belloc and Cecil Chesterton, *The Party System*, Stephen Swift, 1911, p. 137.

ask anyone whether, if the educational objections to the Bill had been the only objections present, there would have been a division on the Second Reading.' 'The Bill,' he went on to say, 'is opposed principally on account of the religious difficulty.'[59] He had become increasingly irritated with the sectarians. 'It is now equally clear', he minuted on one Anglican memorandum, 'that the Clergy, of whatever school, are equally stupid. I had thought the range of stupidity more limited.' He wrote to Wyndham that he wished he was 'with you fighting Irish Nationalists instead of English Nonconformists. The former is a much more congenial employment.'[60]

The protests of the Nonconformists were more important politically than those of the Anglicans. Campbell-Bannerman believed that 'the Nonconformist feeling (+ Protestant feeling) is roused as it never was before, and we shall come to eternal grief if we do not play up to it'.[61] Rosebery predicted in May 1902 that the 'operative effect' of the Bill 'would or should be to re-unite the Liberal Party'.[62] Leading Liberals, whether imperialist or pro-Boer, could agree to oppose the Bill. But two Liberal MPs associated with the teaching profession, T. J. Macnamara and James Yoxall, who had been respectively president and general secretary of the National Union of Teachers, found much to support in the legislation, and the Liberals seemed to lack any realistic alternative. The Act, however, was politically a godsend to a party disunited on so many other issues. It was, therefore, welcomed 'as a shipwrecked boat's crew would welcome the sight of land'.[63] It also brought the labour movement into line with the Liberals, the Labour Representation Committee joining with them in opposition. The Fabians were the only prominent group on the left to support the reform. They were out of touch with Nonconformist opinion.

The Free Churches established a National Passive Resistance Committee, under the leadership of Dr Clifford, a Baptist divine, declaring that they would refuse to pay rates in aid of denominational schools. Many protest meetings were held and, by November 1905, there had been 65,481 prosecutions for non-payment of rates, including MPs, the mayor of Sheffield, judges and rate collectors. A total of 170 individuals went to prison. Dr Clifford did not himself go to prison but appeared in court on forty-one different occasions in the ten years after 1902.[64] But it was difficult to understand how it could be a serious breach of moral principle to give rate

59 House of Commons Debates, 8 May 1902, vol. 107, col. 1211.
60 Adams, *Balfour*, p. 169.
61 Daglish, *Education Policy-Making*, p. 174.
62 Spender, *Campbell-Bannerman*, vol. 2, p. 38.
63 Lowndes, *Silent Social Revolution*, p. 67.
64 Bebbington, *Nonconformist Conscience*, p. 144.

aid to church schools, when grants from central government between 1870 and 1902 had been morally acceptable. Balfour adopted a sceptical attitude towards Nonconformist protests. 'Are we to suppose', he asked ironically, 'that the immutable principles of morality are thus inextricably involved in the technical peculiarities of educational finance?'[65]

The Act did not apply to London, but separate legislation applying the same principles to the capital and making not the boroughs but the London County Council the education authority was passed in 1903. The 1902 Act applied to Wales as well as England, but the changes in Wales were less radical than in England, since school boards had already been abolished through the Welsh Intermediate Education Act of 1889, with their powers given to joint authorities of counties and boroughs. But it was in Wales, where nearly all the schools were church schools, that the protests of Nonconformists, a majority of the population, had the most resonance. In 8,000 parishes in Wales, church schools were the only ones available.[66] In 1903, Welsh local authorities declared they would refuse to levy that part of the rate which went to supporting church schools. Their action was endorsed in local elections in 1904. The Liberals won control of every single county, largely on the education issue. There was something in the nature of a national rebellion, led by Lloyd George. In response, Parliament enacted an Education (Local Authority Default) Act in August 1904, giving the Board of Education power to force local authorities to administer the Act. Were they still to resist, the board was given power to step in and itself administer it. This legislation was labelled by one newspaper the 'Coercion of Wales Bill'. Four local authorities were found to be in default and had their funds withheld by the board. The government threatened to issue a writ of mandamus to compel them to fulfil their legal duties; but, as Haldane told the Commons, 'They could not mandamus a nation.'[67] The 1904 Act did not quench the revolt. In October of that year, a national convention of Nonconformists passed a resolution declaring that local authorities should not maintain church schools and encouraging Nonconformist parents to withdraw their children from them. The children would then be educated by the Nonconformists themselves out of their own pocket in chapels. But the revolt petered out after the election of the Liberal government in January 1906, when the new President of the Education Board, Augustine Birrell, declared that he would not administer the 'Coercion of Wales Act'.

Agitation against the Education Act did much to strengthen the reputation

---

65 Daglish, *Education Policy-Making*, pp. 253–4.
66 Morgan, *Wales in British Politics*, p. 185.
67 House of Commons Debates, 14 March 1904, vol. 131, col. 1017.

of Lloyd George, who was to become the first native Welsh member of a Cabinet when the Liberals came to power. The Act both reunited the Liberals and also resurrected the Nonconformist conscience, a term which had come into common currency in the 1890s. In 1906, the Nonconformist churches were to become recruiting agents for the Liberals. But resistance to the Education Act was to prove the Nonconformists' last stand. The religious fervour which the Act seemed to engender was largely confined to elites and seemed not to be matched by widespread popular concern, except in Wales. Most were more concerned with the prospects for educational progress which the Act held out. 'The religious difficulty', Gorst believed, 'exists not in the schools themselves but on the platform and in Parliament.'[68] The Liberalism of the past, based so heavily on Nonconformist grievances, seemed irrelevant to the needs of a developing industrial society. 'Believe me, gentlemen,' Chamberlain told the largely Nonconformist Birmingham Liberal Unionists in October 1902, 'if in this discussion we could hear a little more about the children and a little less about the sects, we should make greater progress.'[69]

If the Act reunited the Liberals, it undermined the Unionist coalition, drastically weakening Chamberlain's West Midlands base. He had predicted this in 1895, telling Devonshire that if the 1870 compromise were to be shattered, it would do more 'to reunite a solid Liberal opposition and also shatter the Unionist coalition than could be accomplished by any other means'. In August 1902, he told Balfour that the Bill had

> brought all the fighting Nonconformists into the field and made of them active instead of merely passive opponents. Their representations and appeals to the old war cries have impressed large numbers of the middle and upper working classes who have hitherto supported the Unionist party without joining the Conservative organisation. The transfer of their votes will undoubtedly have immense importance at a general election, and ... I do not think that any seat where there is a strong Nonconformist electorate can be considered as absolutely safe.[70]

His prediction was to come true. 'I told you', he wrote to Devonshire in September 1902,

> that your Education bill would destroy your own Party [i.e. the Liberal Unionist Party]. It has done so. Our best friends are leaving us by scores

68 Ibid., 5 May 1902, vol. 107, col. 678.
69 Amery, Chamberlain, vol. 5, p. 105.
70 Ibid., p. 97.

and hundreds and they will not come back. I do not think that the Tories like the situation, but I suppose they will follow the Flag. The Liberal Unionists will not.[71]

Chamberlain needed a new cause to rouse his followers. Hence tariff reform. Balfour was to tell the Duke of Devonshire that Chamberlain's tariff reform campaign arose in part from 'the notion that his [Chamberlain's] counsels had not all the weight which his public opinion justified'.[72]

The religious controversy had a further effect on high politics, imprisoning the Unionist free traders, such as Lord Hugh Cecil, and Conservative Anglicans within the Unionist coalition. A few would, admittedly, join the Liberals after being ousted in their constituencies by Chamberlain's campaign, while some contemplated a new centre party comprising Unionist free traders and Liberal Imperialists. But Anglican Tory free traders would not work with what they regarded as godless Nonconformists in the Liberal Party, while High Church Tories would never be acceptable to Liberal Nonconformists. Reunion of the Liberal Party also destroyed the chances of Rosebery, who had been relying on a split in which, with the 'anti-national' elements of the Liberal Party excluded, Liberal Imperialists could reunite with Liberal Unionists. So the Act ruined not only Chamberlain but also Rosebery. By March 1904, Beatrice Webb noticed that Rosebery was now 'at a discount – a heavier discount than he has been since he came back to speech-making politics'.[73] His day was over.

The religious controversy obscured the fact that, educationally, the Act of 1902 was a landmark. 'For the first time,' declared the Fabian Sidney Webb, 'we have made education a public function, simply as education without definition or limit, and without restriction of age, or sex, or class, or subject, or grade.'[74] This had been admitted privately, even by those who were later, for political purposes, to oppose it. Lloyd George, for example, who had come to public prominence through his vehement defence of Nonconformist grievances, told his wife when the Bill was published, that it

sweeps away School Boards. Creates the County the education authority and puts the Board schools and the voluntary Schools under it ... Up to the present I rather like the bill. It is quite as much as one would expect from a Tory Government – in fact, more than anyone could anticipate.[75]

71 Holland, *Life of Devonshire*, vol. 2, p. 284.
72 Munson, 'Unionist Coalition and Education', p. 644.
73 MacKenzie, *Diary of Beatrice Webb*, vol. 2, pp. 316–17.
74 Searle, *Quest for National Efficiency*, p. 208.
75 Kenneth O. Morgan, ed., *Lloyd George Family Letters, 1885–1936*, University of Wales Press. 1973, p. 131.

The Archbishop of Canterbury had found the Bill 'an honest endeavour to deal fairly with a problem of singular complexity'.[76] Macnamara, the representative of the teachers and a Liberal, gave the truest summing-up of what he hoped the significance of the Act would be.

> Whatever might be said of the merits of the Bill, I would like to say that it has worked something in the nature of a modern miracle ... It has created on the part of the English people something in the nature of an interest in the education question. The English people up to the present time have had little or no belief in intellectualism as a factor of national defence. They have won their way to superiority by physical superiority almost entirely in the past, but they will not do it in the future ... This Bill, with all its defects on its head, and there are many, has awakened [John Bull] to the importance of national education ... So long as we can keep John Bull awake we have a priceless stimulus.[77]

The 1902 Act remained the basis of the educational system in England and Wales until 1944; and in 1936, one historian described it as 'among the two or three greatest constructive measures of the twentieth century'.[78] That was a just estimate.

The main weakness of the Act lay not in its solution to the sectarian issue but in the inadequacy of the provision for secondary education, which was still seen as being for the few. 'It is not', declared Sir John Gorst, the minister in charge of the Bill in the Commons,

> the business and it is not the interest of the country to give everybody secondary education; not even everybody who asks for it. It is only the interest of the country to see that everybody who is fit to receive secondary education, and in the secondary education of whom the State has an interest, so that it will get out of it, by the improvement of the child's faculties, a return for the money expended – it is only in these cases that it is the duty of the state to give any secondary education at all.[79]

Free secondary education would be available only for those who could win scholarships. The situation improved with regulations passed in 1907 by the Liberal government which required secondary schools in receipt of public money to open at least 25 per cent of their places for scholarships to children

---

76 The Times, 15 December 1903.
77 House of Commons Debates, 2 December 1902, vol. 115, col. 1043.
78 Ensor, England, p. 255.
79 House of Commons Debates, 5 May 1902, vol. 107, col. 673.

in elementary schools. By 1911, secondary education had become available to around 60 per cent of those in elementary schools. But middle-class children were four times as likely as those from the working class to receive secondary education.[80] Until 1944, there was no effective nationally supervised system of secondary education, and secondary schools were still charging fees. In addition, quite insufficient provision was made for technical or vocational education, conceived of as being primarily the responsibility of industry, not the state. The Act did not do enough to equip Britain for her future as an industrial nation. In 1938, a Consultative Committee on Secondary Education was to declare that the Board of Education had done little or nothing to foster the development of secondary schools of a quasi-vocational type, designed to meet the needs of boys and girls who sought to enter industry and commerce at the age of sixteen. Secondary education was being shaped by the needs of ambitious students hoping to move on to higher education rather than by the needs of industry or society. So, while the 1902 Act helped a small number of academically gifted children, it did little for the vast majority. As early as 1897, the Webbs in their book *Industrial Democracy* had advocated a system of half-time working so that, until they reached the age of eighteen, pupils would be required to attend technical school and continuation classes. This, they believed, was essential in the training of future citizens.[81] But as one MP commented in 1956 on educational reform, 'The real trouble that the Minister is up against is the spiritual one that technical education is "non-U" whereas academic education is "U". Technical education is "servants' hall" whereas academic education is "drawing-room", or "upstairs".'[82] So little was done to follow the Webbs' prescription. The problem of a lack of technical skills in the workforce remains to plague Britain even in the twenty-first century.

More generally, the 1902 Education Act was not followed up by the great reforming Liberal government which succeeded the Unionists in 1905. Amidst its massive reform programme, little was done for education. The Liberals were too obsessed by the needs of their Nonconformist supporters to make a concerted attack on the weaknesses of the system which the 1902 Act had failed to remedy. Of the leading Liberals, only Haldane appreciated the need, but he was preoccupied with army reform and in 1912 went to the Lords as Lord Chancellor. It is not unfair to conclude that 'indifference to general education advance was the greatest defect of the pre-war Liberal administration'.[83] That indifference would cost Britain dear.

---

80 Read, ed., *Edwardian England*, p. 163.
81 Sidney and Beatrice Webb, *Industrial Democracy* [1897], Longmans, Green & Co., 1902, pp. 770–71.
82 Lowndes, *Silent Social Revolution*, p. 322. The speaker was Isaac Pitman, MP for Bath.
83 Cooper, *The British Welfare Revolution*, p. 207.

A NEW PRIME MINISTER

Salisbury finally retired as Prime Minister in 1902. He would have done so earlier but felt that if he had gone before the end of the Boer War, he would have appeared to be in disagreement with the policy of the majority of the Cabinet. In his last public speech, to the Primrose League, in May 1902, he surveyed the political scene with satisfaction if not complacency. In the year that the Primrose League had been founded in 1883, Salisbury claimed, the country had been faced with the rebellion of the Mahdi in Sudan and Nationalist agitation in Ireland. But by 1902, Britain was supreme in Sudan, while Ireland was peaceful, and there was no longer any reason to fear 'the insane and suicidal projects of Imperial disruption. (Cheers.)' There was, however, he said, one danger which needed to be guarded against. It came from those who sought to hasten through legislation the development of imperial sentiment which depended 'upon the spontaneous growth of affection'. It would be a grave error, Salisbury believed, to

force an anticipation of the results which the natural play of forces and of affections ... will bring before us ... There is no danger that appears to me more serious for the time that lies before us than an attempt to force the various parts of the Empire into a mutual arrangement and subordination for which they are not ready and which may only produce a reaction in favour of the old state of things. (Hear, hear.)[84]

The old statesman was warning of the dangers of attempts to secure imperial union by schemes of federation or tariff reform. His warning was prescient since tariff reform was to break the Unionist coalition. But it was not heeded. Had Salisbury remained, he would almost certainly have avoided the imbroglio over tariff reform. He had succeeded, unlike Gladstone, in controlling and even neutralising Chamberlain, which Balfour was to prove unable to do. And Salisbury would not have allowed Unionists to involve themselves in 1909 in a challenge to the Commons which they could not win. But his skill lay in deferring domestic problems not resolving them; indeed, he tended to assume that a problem delayed was a problem avoided. After his retirement, those problems returned, perhaps with more force because they had been neglected for so long. And because Salisbury's political career was so strikingly devoid of legislative achievement, he has left a slighter mark on Britain than many who were at 10 Downing Street for a much shorter period.

Salisbury was succeeded by Balfour, his nephew. Lord George Hamilton,

84 *The Times*, 8 May 1902.

the India Secretary, told the viceroy, Lord Curzon, of the party meeting that endorsed the succession, 'I have seldom been present at a meeting as unanimous and enthusiastic as that composed of the Peers and House of Commons members of the Unionist Party at which his promotion was announced.'[85] Chamberlain, an obvious alternative, was incapacitated by a cab accident, but he had already accepted that Balfour should succeed. Four months before Salisbury's resignation, in February 1902, Chamberlain had called on Jack Sandars, Balfour's private secretary, to controvert press statements to the effect that he had claims on the premiership. He would have been the choice, no doubt, of the Liberal Unionists, but he had also been approached, apparently, by some Conservatives – 'your people', as he put it to Sandars. According to Sandars:

> Mr Chamberlain then went on further to say in most emphatic tones that I was to understand that he was *'not a candidate'* for that office – 'I have my own work to do and it is not done yet, and I am quite content to stay where I am. It is true that I once said that I meant to be the next Prime Minister in succession to Mr Gladstone, but circumstances have entirely changed and I frankly recognise that such is the case. I say again what I have said before, I shall be quite willing to serve under Balfour – but mark, I would not serve under anyone.' All this was said with great earnestness and almost passionate emphasis, and the impression he made on me was that he was speaking *through me* not only to A. J. B. but to other persons who might be interested in the political drama.
>
> Our conversation ended with Mr Chamberlain begging me to remember that he had always been most deeply touched by A. J. B.'s splendid and unselfish loyalty towards himself, and that every member of his family shared his feeling.
>
> It was an interesting conversation – Mr Chamberlain being to all appearances determined to commit himself.[86]

One implication of Chamberlain's remarks was that he would not have been willing to serve under his own party leader, the Duke of Devonshire, who might well have been acceptable to the Unionist coalition. When he recognised that 'circumstances have entirely changed', what he almost certainly meant was that, not only as a Liberal Unionist but also a Nonconformist, he would be unacceptable to a coalition dominated by Conservatives and Anglicans. The premiership, therefore, would be for ever outside his reach.

85 Adams, *Balfour*, pp. 172–3.
86 Dugdale, *Balfour*, vol. I, p. 254. Italics in original.

Nevertheless, he could have sought a different office, and probably made a mistake in remaining at the Colonial Office. If, as was likely the case, ideas of imperial union and tariff reform were already germinating in his mind, he would have done better to move to the Exchequer, where his position would have been stronger. At the very least, he should have ensured that the Exchequer went to a man in broad sympathy with his ideas of Imperial union. His failure to take either of these courses was to ruin his chances of success and contribute to the collapse of the Unionists.

Balfour handled the transfer of power tactlessly, not in relation to Chamberlain, with whom his relations were at that time cordial, but with another who thought himself well qualified for the premiership: the Duke of Devonshire. The duke had three times turned down the premiership – in 1880, 1886 and 1887 – and believed that he still had claims on the office, even if he did not intend to assert them. But he wanted to be consulted, and perhaps also to refuse the premiership for a fourth time. Balfour, however, did not consult him before accepting the king's commission. Indeed, the duke was not informed until after Balfour had been appointed, and then only as an afterthought. His *amour propre* was offended. At the same time, Lord James of Hereford, a close associate of the duke's, left the government. These may well have been factors – though perhaps not the most important – in the duke's resignation from the government in 1903 over tariff reform. So perhaps the seeds of the Balfour government's disintegration were sown at the very time that the new Prime Minister took office.

Balfour made minimal changes to the Cabinet which he inherited from his uncle, reducing its size by two to twenty. Hicks Beach took the opportunity of his chief's resignation to leave the government. He had long been unsympathetic to the more self-conscious imperialism of the end of the nineteenth century and the extra expenditure it entailed, fighting a losing battle trying to contain it. Hicks Beach's resignation on top of Salisbury's removed another minister who might have been able to curb Chamberlain's headstrong approach. George Wyndham, Chief Secretary for Ireland since 1900, was now brought into the Cabinet, while Lord Dudley, the new viceroy, replacing Lord Cadogan, was outside the Cabinet. The only other new Cabinet member was Austen Chamberlain, Joseph's son, who became Postmaster General. Both Wyndham and Austen were thought of as promising young men, but, whereas Austen would eventually become Chancellor of the Exchequer and Foreign Secretary, Wyndham's career would soon hit the rocks of the Irish problem; and he would die young with his promise unfulfilled.

The most important new appointment was at the Exchequer to fill the place vacated by the long-awaited and long hoped-for retirement of Hicks Beach. The position was first offered to Wyndham, whom, by March 1903, Balfour was to regard 'as the ablest man in the cabinet bar Chamberlain', but Wyndham refused 'and insisted vehemently on staying in Ireland'.[87] The Exchequer then went to Charles Ritchie (1838–1906), the Home Secretary, who had been an MP since 1874. He had been the packhorse of previous Unionist administrations, a safe administrator at the Home Office and before that at the Local Government Board, where he had been responsible for the 1888 Local Government Act providing for elected county councils. But he was an unfortunate choice, a poor speaker, hardly known to the public and of limited vision. He was 'a plain, bluff, honest man', but, according to Sandars, given to 'heavy and affected pleasantry ... His abilities were of the second class, but he was a hard-working minister of pedestrian methods.'[88] Hamilton, the Permanent Secretary at the Treasury, thought he was 'much too second-class', adding in his diary, 'The first qualifications of a Chancellor of the Exchequer are *character* and being a *gentleman*. Then comes influence and financial aptitude.'[89] Ritchie was in fact somewhat better than that, and Sandars and Hamilton were being rather snobbish about a man who had left school at fifteen to work in the family jute business in the East End of London. This had given him an insight into the problems of the poor, lacking in most of the rest of the Cabinet, and was 'hardly to be matched by a major politician until Attlee'.[90] His *Oxford Dictionary of National Biography* entry declares that 'in a party of aristocrats and social climbers, Ritchie's virtues were at a discount. His business skills, his industry and persistence were essential to the legislative output of the Salisbury governments.' In normal times, no doubt, Ritchie's appointment to the Exchequer might have been a good one. But the times would soon be anything but normal with the debate on tariff reform about to burst. For, having flirted earlier in his career with protection, Ritchie was now a determined and implacable free trader and would prove a thorn in the side not only of Chamberlain but also of the Prime Minister who had promoted him. Balfour was to come greatly to regret the appointment.

---

87 Gailey, *Ireland and the Death of Kindness*, pp. 192fn, 197.
88 Gardiner, *Prophets, Priests and Kings*, p. 244; Kenneth Young, *Arthur James Balfour*, G. Bell, 1963, p. 199.
89 Dudley W. R. Bahlman, *The Diary of Sir Edward Walter Hamilton: 1885–1906*, University of Hull Press, 1993, p. 390.
90 Jenkins, *The Chancellors*, p. 103.

CHAPTER 8

THE ALLIANCE WITH JAPAN

NEW ALIGNMENTS

Salisbury's foreign policy had concerned itself with what he believed fundamental to British interests – paramountcy in South Africa, control of the Nile valley, defence of India and avoidance of conflict with the United States. In pursuing his purpose, he had been perfectly prepared to make concessions – to France in West Africa, to Russia in China and to the United States in the Caribbean, areas he thought of as peripheral to Britain's fundamental interests. He charted a middle course, a limited and realist foreign policy in contrast both to those such as Chamberlain who favoured a more 'forward' policy and suspected him of weakness, and to radicals in the Liberal Party who seemed to regard almost any assertion of British power as aggression. Within its frame of reference, Salisbury could be judged successful. But perhaps this frame of reference would not prove as viable in the twentieth century as in the nineteenth. After 1895, great power rivalries were persuading many Unionists of the need to reassess Britain's relations with other nations. Salisbury was slower than others in his Cabinet to appreciate the alteration in Britain's global position flowing from great power rivalry. But Lansdowne, who had replaced Salisbury as Foreign Secretary in 1900, had begun cautiously to chart a new course even before Salisbury departed from Downing Street in 1902.

Salisbury's achievements in foreign policy, though real, proved ephemeral rather than long-lasting. His successors, rather than developing his legacy, repudiated it through limited agreements with other powers, an alliance with Japan in 1902 and ententes – but not alliances – with France in 1904 and Russia in 1907. These arrangements were intended to preserve British security, not to align her with Continental powers. Indeed, they were seen as reinforcing Britain's detachment from the Continent, not ending it. Salisbury, though too old to change, nevertheless had begun to intuit that Britain was entering a new era. On his resignation, he wrote to Curzon:

It may be a misconception – but I cannot resist the impression that we are near some great change in public affairs – in which the forces which contend for the mastery among us will be differently ranged and balanced. If so it is certainly expedient that younger men should be employed to shape the policy which will no longer depend upon the judgments formed by the experience of past times. The times will be very difficult. The large aggregations of human forces which lie around our Empire seem to draw more closely together, and to assume almost unconsciously a more aggressive aspect. Their junction, in menacing and dangerous masses, may be deferred for many years or may be precipitated with little notice at any moment.[1]

The most immediate danger at the beginning of the twentieth century seemed to lie in the Far East, where it appeared that British interests could no longer be protected by the Royal Navy alone. 'If the policy of isolation which has hitherto been the policy of this country', Chamberlain had declared in Birmingham in May 1898, 'is to be maintained in the future then the fate of the Chinese Empire may be, and probably will be, hereafter decided without reference to our wishes and in defiance of our interests.'[2] In addition, the navy would be of little use in deterring Russia on India's north-west frontier. The Crimean War strategy of forcing the straits and landing troops in southern Russia was no longer viable thanks to the Franco-Russian Alliance and growing Turkish hostility towards Britain. Therefore, a new strategy for deterring Russia had to be devised. There were two possibilities. The first would be to join the Triple Alliance of Germany, Austria–Hungary and Italy, and rely on Germany to deter Russia in Europe. The second was to ally with Japan, a counter to Russia in the Far East, which could deter Russia on land. Of the two, Balfour preferred the first. 'The weakest spot in the Empire is probably the Indian frontier,' he wrote to Lansdowne in December 1901.

> In a war with Russia our military resources would be strained to the utmost to protect it ... A quarrel with Russia anywhere, about anything, means the invasion of India and if England were without allies, I doubt whether it would be possible for the French to resist joining in the fray. Our position would then be perilous.

If, however, Britain was connected with the Triple Alliance, that 'very fact' 'would probably prevent France throwing in her lot with Russia'.[3]

---

1 Roberts, *Salisbury*, p. 232.
2 L. K. Young, *British Policy in China 1895–1902*, Oxford University Press, 1970, p. 76.
3 George Monger, *The End of Isolation: British Foreign Policy 1900–1907*, Nelson, 1963, p. 64.

An arrangement with Germany, then, could help Britain resist Russian pressure in the Far East, on the north-west frontier, and in the Mediterranean. After Britain and Germany had cooperated to suppress the Boxer Uprising, they agreed a Yangtze Convention in which they promised to maintain freedom of trade and uphold the territorial integrity of China in those areas where they could exert influence. This was to prove 'the only formal agreement for diplomatic co-operation ever made between Great Britain and Germany'.[4] In the convention, Britain gained recognition of her preponderant position in the Yangtze valley and hoped that it would serve to check Russia in Manchuria. Otherwise, so Chamberlain argued in a memorandum of September 1900, there was a danger that Russia 'will ultimately secure North China and that the Open Door will be a mere name as far as this part of the Chinese Empire is concerned. It is certain that we are not strong enough by ourselves to prevent her from accomplishing such an annexation.'[5] But shortly after the Yangtze Convention, Bülow, the German Chancellor, declared in the Reichstag that it did not cover Manchuria since Germany was unable to exert influence there. Germany was in fact unwilling to help Britain in Manchuria because she did not wish to antagonise Russia, which would bring problems for her on her eastern border.

Thus, any agreement with Germany would be one-sided. Britain would keep an open door for Germany in the Yangtze, a door which in any case she had never had any intention of closing, but Germany would not do anything equivalent for Britain in Manchuria. So, as Sir Edward Grey, the Liberal spokesman on foreign affairs, told the Commons, 'At the first test the agreement has broken down.' Government policy had, he believed, been mistaken. 'They have been relying on the one Power from whom they have got nothing in return.' The convention would, nevertheless, have been worthwhile had it led to better feeling between the two countries, but that had not happened either. Grey's alternative, prefiguring his policy as Foreign Secretary after 1905, was to seek an agreement with Russia.[6]

The unwillingness to risk antagonising Russia rendered Germany of little value as an ally for Britain. But Japan was a different matter. She, like Britain, had an interest in resisting Russian expansion in the Far East. Both Britain and Japan were concerned at the alteration in the balance of power in the region after Russia began to expand in Manchuria. Since Port Arthur was being linked by rail with the Trans-Siberian Railway, troops could be rapidly moved from European Russia to Manchuria, whereas in the past it had

4   Taylor, *Struggle for Mastery*, p. 393.
5   Ian Nish, *The Anglo-Japanese Alliance: The Diplomacy of Two Island Empires, 1894–1907*, 2nd edition, Bloomsbury, 1985, p. 92.
6   House of Commons Debates, 23 July 1903, vol. 126, col. 128

taken nearly four weeks to reach the Far East by sea through the Suez Canal. The Trans-Caspian Railway also was nearing completion from Orenburg to Tashkent, and could prove an even more direct threat, linking as it did European Russia with her central Asian garrisons. Russia now enjoyed a landward approach to China, which would be difficult for Britain, primarily a naval power, to counteract. Russia, Lord Selborne noticed in November 1901, was developing 'her hold over Manchuria, an operation which we can no more prevent than Russia could prevent our conquest of the Transvaal'.[7]

Once it was clear that alliance with Germany was not possible, Japan, which, as early as 1875, Disraeli had predicted would be the strongest force in the Far East, became the only possible counter to Russian expansionism.[8] The strongest advocate of a Japanese alliance in the Cabinet was Lord Selborne, First Lord of the Admiralty and previously a junior minister at the Colonial Office under Chamberlain where, like Chamberlain, he had come to appreciate that Britain could no longer continue with a policy of freedom from entanglements. Selborne feared that the two-power standard would no longer be viable if the United States were to team up with another power, or if Britain were to face a Franco-Russian combination. In Chinese waters, Britain had just four first-class battleships and sixteen cruisers, while France and Russia had between them seven first-class and two second-class battleships and twenty cruisers. Britain must, therefore, Selborne insisted, 'look to diplomacy & alliances to help us out'.[9] Alliance with Japan would allow Britain to redeploy her fleet to the Mediterranean and the English Channel, relying on Japan to protect the Far East. Otherwise, there would have to be either a large increase in naval spending or a weakening of the fleet in European waters. So alliance with Japan would allow Britain to maintain her naval preponderance in Europe and it would also alleviate Britain's military dilemma. With the development of railways allowing more rapid movement of troops, land power was becoming more important than sea power. Britain's small army made it increasingly difficult for her to police her far-flung empire and, in particular, to hold off Russia in Asia. Here too Japan could help.

Lansdowne was to add a diplomatic argument to the naval and the military ones. Without an alliance with Britain, the Foreign Secretary feared, Japan might turn to Russia, an alignment which many of her senior statesmen favoured, so as to divide the spoils in northern China and Korea to Britain's detriment.

---

7 Nish, *Anglo-Japanese Alliance*, p. 181.
8 Marquis of Zetland, ed., *The Letters of Disraeli to Lady Bradford and Lady Chesterfield*, Ernest Benn, 1929, vol. 1, p. 287.
9 Memorandum 4 September 1901, in D. George Boyce, *The Crisis of British Power: The Imperial and Naval Papers of the Second Earl of Selborne, 1895-1910*, Historians' Press, 1990, p. 125; Nish, *Anglo-Japanese Alliance*, p. 184.

But there was also a cultural affinity between many leaders of British opinion and Japan. The idea of national efficiency was, according to the Radical journalist H. W. Massingham, in vogue 'among journalists, platform politicians and unsuccessful merchants at Chambers of Commerce', who would 'speculate or dogmatise according to the mood, upon the question what in particular this National Efficiency might mean, and how to get it, and whether we or Germany, or later on, Japan, had more of it'.[10] Advocates of national efficiency had a favourable image of Japan as a nation which had modernised and militarised herself through her own efforts. A *Punch* cartoon of the period shows John Bull saying to a Japanese woman who is looking at a map of north-east Asia, 'Your army system seems to work splendidly.' The woman replies, 'Every man is ready to sacrifice himself for his country and does it.' John Bull then reflects, 'I must try to introduce that at home.'[11] Rosebery was to write the preface to a book published in 1906 entitled *Great Japan: A Study of National Efficiency*, and an associate of Milner's was to write to him in May 1904:

> I shall turn Japanese, for they at least can think and act and be reticent! … I fail to see any Western people in a position to set the Japs an example in their diplomacy … their organisation, their strategy, their virile qualities, their devotion and self-control, Above all, their national capacity for self-reliant self-sacrifice and their silence.[12]

Fabian collectivists shared this admiration for self-discipline. 'For many a long day,' Beatrice Webb believed, 'the Reformer will be able to quote on his side the innovating collectivism of the Japanese, the Idealist, the self-abnegation of all classes of the community in a common cause.'[13] This, of course, was in reaction to the liberal humanitarianism of the Gladstonian era which, so its critics alleged, had rendered Britain soft and effete.

THE ALLIANCE AND ITS CONSEQUENCES

The Anglo-Japanese Alliance was signed on 30 January 1902 and published shortly afterwards. The alliance referred to the 'Extreme East' rather than the Far East since Japan refused to accept any commitments in relation to British India. The preamble to the accord declared, quite hypocritically, that

---

10   Searle, *Quest for National Efficiency*, p. 170.
11   Quoted in Gordon Daniels, 'The Press', in 'Studies in the Anglo-Japanese Alliance, 1902–23', LSE Discussion Papers, January 2003.
12   Ibid., p. 58.
13   MacKenzie, *Diary of Beatrice Webb*, vol. 2, p. 335.

the signatories were 'specially interested in maintaining the independence and territorial integrity of the Empire of China and the Empire of Korea, and in securing equal opportunities in those countries for the commerce and industry of all nations'. The first article of the alliance then went on to say, somewhat in contradiction, that the two powers recognised 'their special interests of which those of Great Britain relate principally to China, while Japan, in addition to the interests which she possesses in China, is interested in a peculiar degree politically as well as commercially and industrially in Korea'. The two parties agreed that it would be admissible to take measures needed to safeguard those interests if threatened either by other powers or by internal disturbances. The commitment to the 'independence and territorial integrity of the Empire of China' would not prevent Japan from accepting a 'lease' of the Liaodong Peninsula in 1905 from Russia after Japan's victory in the Russo-Japanese War. Article 2 of the alliance declared that if, in defence of their interests, one of the powers became involved in war with another power, the other signatory would remain neutral. But if one of the powers came to be involved in war with *two* other powers, then the other signatory would come to her aid. Britain and Japan also agreed in a secret protocol attached to the treaty to maintain naval forces in the 'Extreme East' superior to those of any third power. The partnership was to last for five years. It was unusual, since it sought not to maintain the status quo but to assist its alteration. It was, therefore, a departure from the ethic that had animated the Concert of Europe.

The alliance appeared to be of greater advantage to Japan than to Britain. There was, after all, a mutual British and Japanese interest in preventing Russian expansion in China, but only Japan had interests in Korea, interests which Britain was now underwriting. Moreover, Japan was being protected in an area which she regarded as fundamental to her existence, whereas for Britain it was Europe not the Far East that was fundamental; and in Europe, Japan could offer no help. Even so, although the collaboration seemed a new departure for Britain, it appeared not to involve her in new commitments. But it would help in sustaining her global position, thereby enabling her to continue free from Continental entanglements. 'The alliance did not mark the end of British isolation; rather it confirmed it. Isolation meant aloofness from the European balance of power; and this was now more possible than before.'[14] A British commitment would only occur were Japan to be attacked by two powers, that is, if in line with the Franco-Russian Alliance, France were to join Russia in a war with Japan. It was this that Lord Salisbury, in one of his last major Cabinet memoranda, found deeply worrying.

---

14   Taylor, *Struggle for Mastery*, p. 400.

It involves a pledge on our part to defend Japanese action in Korea and in all China against France and Russia no matter what the *casus belli* may be. There is no limit; and no escape. We are pledged to war, though the conduct of our ally may have been followed in spite of our strongest recommendations ... I feel sure that such a pledge will not be sanctioned by Parliament, and I think that in the interest of the Empire it ought not to be taken.

There was no case

for surrendering without reserve into the hands of another Power the right of deciding whether we shall or shall not stake the resources of the Empire on the issue of a mighty conflict. We cannot rely on the goodwill, or the prudence, or the wise policy of the present Government of Japan, however conspicuous at present these qualities may be ... I do not think it will be wise to give to Japan the right of committing us to a war, unless the policy which Japan is pursuing has been approved by the British Government.[15]

Balfour, often credited as being the main originator of the idea of a partnership with Japan, was also sceptical, worried that it might entail Britain 'fighting for our existence in every part of the globe against Russia and France, because France has joined forces with her ally over some obscure Russian-Japanese quarrel in Korea'.[16] Some Liberals also had doubts, but the party did not oppose it in the Commons. And perhaps the concerns of Salisbury and Balfour were far-fetched. European powers were generally unwilling to transfer their alliances to the Far East, and France would not wish to sacrifice British support in Europe by getting herself involved in a war in an area in which she had little interest. Instead, the alliance could be presented as one that would preserve the peace. It would deter France from aiding Russia in the Far East, and therefore it would also deter Russian activity on the north-west frontier, helping to protect India.

The British hoped by means of the accord to preserve the status quo. The Japanese, by contrast, hoped to alter it by advancing not only in Korea, whatever the alliance said about her 'independence', but also in Manchuria and northern China. The alliance removed the threat of a Franco-Russian combination against Japan. She could therefore go to war with Russia in 1904–05, in which, to the surprise of most observers, she emerged victorious. And the agreement with Britain meant that she would not have to fear

---

15   J. A. S. Grenville, *Lord Salisbury and Foreign Policy: The Close of the Nineteenth Century*, Athlone Press, 1970, p. 414.
16   Dugdale, *Balfour*, vol. 1, p. 279.

another Treaty of Shimonoseki. As Lansdowne told the king in April 1904, just two months after the outbreak of the Russo-Japanese War:

> The Anglo-Japanese Alliance, although not intended to encourage the Japanese Government to resort to extremity, had, *and was sure to have*, the effect of making Japan feel that she might try conclusions with her great rival in the Far East, free from all risk of a European coalition such as that which had on a previous occasion [i.e. 1895] deprived her of the fruits of victory.[17]

Victory in the war with Russia, Count Hayashi, the Japanese ambassador in London, believed, would not have been possible without the alliance.[18] The accord ensured that the war was localised. Otherwise, with France aiding Russia, a local war might well have become a global one, the Sarajevo of 1904. But in 1904, the Anglo-French entente was to be concluded, a further deterrent preventing France from aiding Russia.

There was a further vital consequence of the new partnership. It meant that, with Japan as a counterbalance to Russia, Britain no longer needed to solicit German aid against Russia. So the prospect of an Anglo-German arrangement, already dim, receded even further into the distance. Further, one barrier preventing cooperation between Britain and Russia and between their ally, France, had been removed. To this extent, the pact with Japan was a precondition for the entente with France.

The alliance was renewed in 1905, two years before the conclusion of the 1902 concord. But perhaps 'renewal' is the wrong word. For 1905 saw what was, in many respects, a new alliance. This second alliance was to bind Britain and Japan more closely together. Article 2 committed each of them to go to the aid of the other, if at war 'in defence of its territorial rights or special interests' which had caused it to be the victim 'of an unprovoked attack or aggressive action', by any *one* power, not two as in 1902. It was now impossible for Russia to launch a war of revenge against Japan, since this would also involve Britain. But the 1907 convention between Britain and Russia would in any case have prevented such a war of revenge.

In the 1905 alliance, the 'special interests' of the two powers were now to include not only 'the regions of Eastern Asia' but also India. Article 4 recognised Britain's 'special interest in … the security of the Indian frontier' and Japan recognised Britain's right to take whatever action might be needed 'for safeguarding her Indian possessions'. This was, of course, a concession

---

17   Lord Newton, *Lord Lansdowne: A Biography*, Macmillan, 1929, p. 309. Emphasis added.
18   Pooley, ed., *Secret Memoirs of Count Tadasu Hayashi*, p. 89.

by Japan, even though she claimed that the pact did not embrace Persia, one of the most sensitive areas on the route to India. And it was a confession of weakness by Britain, since she was for the first time admitting that she could no longer defend her Indian empire entirely unaided. This provoked the ire of the former commander-in-chief of the army, Field Marshal Lord Roberts, who told the Oxford Union in November 1905 that it would be a 'fatal blow to British prestige if India ever regarded her defence as dependent upon the strength of Japan'.

In return for Japanese assistance in the defence of India, Britain recognised Japan's right 'to take such measures of guidance, control and protection in Korea as she may deem proper and necessary' to safeguard her interests. Nothing was said, as in the 1902 alliance, about the 'independence' of Korea, which Britain seemed to have written off. There was just a futile caveat that Japanese action in Korea should not compromise 'the principle of equal opportunities for the commerce and industry of all nations'. This provision would prove no obstacle either to establishing a Japanese protectorate in Korea or to outright annexation in 1910, which one Japanese elder statesman was to compare to the British protectorate in Egypt, although Britain had not in fact annexed Egypt.[19] An influential Japanese newspaper believed that Japan 'could never have annexed Korea' had the alliance 'not been in existence'.[20] Nevertheless, Britain had little alternative but to accept the annexation.

This second alliance was to last for ten years but was to be replaced by yet another one in 1911. The prime reason for this third collaboration was that by 1911, the 1905 concord was incompatible with an arbitration agreement which Britain was negotiating with the United States, an agreement which did not in the event come to fruition. Britain did not wish to get embroiled in conflict with the United States, becoming increasingly concerned at Japanese expansionism in Manchuria and the Yangtze valley, and the threat that this posed to the open door and freedom of trade with China. So the 1911 alliance absolved Britain from aiding Japan were she to be attacked by any nation with whom Britain had an arbitration treaty. But in addition, much of the 1905 agreement was now obsolete. Shortly after it, Japan had signed an agreement with Russia by which the two powers recognised each other's spheres of influence – Russia's in northern Manchuria and Outer Mongolia, Japan's in Korea and southern Manchuria – while the 1907 Anglo-Russian Convention seemed to have removed the Russian threat to the Indian border. Therefore, there was no longer any need for Britain and Japan

19 Nish, *Anglo-Japanese Alliance*, pp. 355fn, 351.
20 Ian Nish, *Alliance in Decline. A Study in Anglo-Japanese Relations, 1908–1923* [1972] Bloomsbury, 2012, p. 82.

to guard against Russia. The third alliance was, therefore, weaker than the other two; in particular, Japan would no longer be obliged to help defend the Indian frontier.

But why was there a need for a third alliance at all? On Britain's side, the main motive was the continued realisation that she could no longer maintain global naval predominance without it. There was, as Grey was to point out in a Commons debate in 1912, an 'intimate' relationship 'between the Japanese alliance and naval strategy'.[21] So the partnership was, from Britain's point of view, a continuing 'instrument of convenience', even though its provisions were 'largely negative'. The 1911 accord enabled Britain to continue to con- centrate her fleet in European waters and ensure the security of her position in the Pacific without any obvious cost and without alienating other powers. But while a prime purpose of the earlier alliances had been to constrain Russia, a main motive for the 1911 pact was to constrain Japan, which was building up her own navy to the concern of Australia and New Zealand. Significantly, the third alliance, unlike the other two, was agreed only after consultation with the dominions, setting a new precedent and giving this third concord greater force and authority. And this third alliance did not stop Japanese expansion in China. If anything, it encouraged it. In the winter of 1913–14, the British ambassador to Japan was to complain, 'While they will never let us into their spheres, they are trying to steal a march into ours, and this is not cricket between Allies.'[22] But the Japanese did not play cricket. Admittedly, the third agreement helped for a time to secure the safety of Australia and New Zealand and preserve peace in the Pacific, insulating it from great power conflict. The *Times of India*, which had believed that the 1905 alliance 'has proved one of the greatest peace movements in history', was to declare in July 1911 that 'its renewal guarantees the peace of Asia for another decade'.[23]

Japan's victory in her war with Russia had seemed advantageous to Britain since it had lessened the Russian threat both in China and on the north- west frontier, and perhaps it encouraged Russia to agree the convention with Britain in 1907. But the humiliation of defeat in 1905 strengthened the revo- lutionary movement in Russia, while her weakened position in the Far East led her to turn her attention back to Europe and, in particular, the Balkans, where she was to come into conflict with Austria and her ally, Germany. But neither Austria nor Germany feared Russia as much as they had done before the Russo-Japanese War, and this perhaps tempted Austria towards more

21 House of Commons Debates, 10 July 1912, vol. 40, col. 1991.
22 Nish, *Alliance in Decline*, pp. 7, 72, 105.
23 Quoted in *The Times*, 26 July 1911.

forward policies in the Balkans. Germany might also have been encouraged to adopt a more forward policy against France, Russia's ally. In consequence, both Austria and Germany were in danger of over-reaching themselves. So, although the 1902 alliance was directed against Russia, it is not perhaps too fanciful to suggest that its long-term victims would be the two Germanic Empires of central Europe. Perhaps the first two consequences were the challenge to France in Morocco in 1905 and the challenge to Russia in the Balkans in 1908. The Russo-Japanese War caused deep-seated alterations in foreign relations both in Asia and in Europe.

The long-term effects of the three Anglo-Japanese Alliances were to prove as significant in Asia as in Europe. In the long run, of course, Japan was to prove a greater menace to British interests than Russia had ever been. The alliance strengthened the military party in Tokyo and set her on the search towards supremacy in Asia, a search which culminated in her attack in 1941 on the American fleet at Pearl Harbor. Perhaps a Japanese partnership with Russia, the prospect of which so frightened British statesmen at the beginning of the twentieth century, might actually have been more beneficial to the Pacific region, since, by preserving a balance of power between the two countries, it would have better served to contain the rise of Japanese power than the alliance with Britain could do. Japan's victory against Russia in 1905, which the first concord had made possible, encouraged nationalists everywhere, and especially in India, since Japan had shown not only that Europeans could be defeated in war but that a country could modernise itself without first being colonised. So, in India and south Asia in general, the rise of Japan encouraged the forces making for the decline of the British Empire.

At the end of the nineteenth century, developments in China had appeared to herald the beginning of an era of diplomatic conflict, similar to that which had occurred in Africa. But the first and second Anglo-Japanese Alliances together with the Russo-Japanese War had the effect of insulating the Far East from European conflicts. For a brief period from 1895, it had seemed that competition between the powers would be global. But now Europe was to become, once again, the centre of the world, even though part of the conflict between European powers was to be fought over Morocco. It was in Europe not the Far East that the tragedy of the early twentieth century was to be played out.

CHAPTER 9

UNIONISM AND REFORM

THE IRISH LAND ACT AND DEVOLUTION

In 1895, Chamberlain had told the electorate, 'We believe that we are in a position which our opponents are not, to give our whole attention to those great social questions which underlie the happiness of the people.'[1] He had hoped to follow in the footsteps of Disraeli by combining an active social policy at home with a strong foreign and imperial policy. But he was to be disappointed in his hopes of converting the Unionists to a policy of social reform. Disraeli too had been disappointed, telling the socialist Hyndman at the end of his life, 'The moment you tried to realise it [social reform in the Conservative Party] ... you would find yourself surrounded by a phalanx of great families who will put you to rout every time – they and their women.'[2] But in any case, as we have seen, it was in large part due to the Boer War and the extra expenditure it entailed that social reform was not on the political agenda. During the three years of conflict, the national debt increased by 25 per cent, the Queen's Speech in 1900 declaring that 'the time is not propitious for any domestic reforms which involve a large expenditure'. Financial constraints made it impossible to spend both on social reform and on the empire. A choice had to be made and the choice was the empire. This meant that Chamberlain found it difficult to preserve his radical constituency. Nevertheless, the Unionists were by no means committed to a defence of the status quo, or to a purely passive role for the state. In addition to the Education Act, they sought to use the state for positive purposes in three areas: Irish land purchase, control of immigration and remedying unemployment.

Of domestic legislation, second in importance only to the Education Act was the Irish Land Purchase Act of 1903, the central legislative achievement of constructive Unionism, the Unionist alternative to Home Rule, and based on the view that Irish problems were essentially social and economic rather than constitutional. Radical Unionists such as Chamberlain believed that the problems of the Irish peasant were no different in kind from those of the

---

1   Quoted by Harcourt, *The Times*, 22 September 1900.
2   H. M. Hyndman, *The Record of an Adventurous Life*, Macmillan, 1911, p. 244.

English agricultural labourer and could be remedied by effective Westminster legislation.

The Land Purchase Act was steered through the Commons by the Irish Secretary, George Wyndham, who sought to continue the policy of killing Home Rule by kindness. Earlier land acts had failed to stem rural agitation, and in April 1902, nine Irish counties had been proclaimed under the Crimes Act. Landlords, tenants and the landless all had grounds for complaint.

Gladstone's Land Act of 1881 had created in effect a system of dual ownership in Ireland by providing for fixity of tenure and judicially determined rents, fixed for fifteen years. A tenant paying his rent could not be evicted but had the right to sell his interest in his holding on the open market. But the Act had given no precise definition of what was to count as a fair rent. Landowners complained that the judges had caused such reductions in rents that property was being rented out below market value, and they were suffering a loss of income. However, a Commons committee in 1894, dominated by Liberals and Irish Nationalists, had complained that rents were in fact too high.[3] Perhaps the truth was that many tenants simply could not afford to pay an economic rent. The Unionist alternative to the Gladstonian policy of dual ownership was land purchase, to create a new landowning class from the tenantry.

In September 1902, Captain John Shawe-Taylor, a Galway landlord, wrote to the *Irish Times* calling for a conference of landlord and tenant representatives to discuss the land question. This took the Chief Secretary, George Wyndham, by surprise, but he welcomed the initiative. 'For the moment home rule and the "land war" have dropped into the background,' Wyndham told Balfour.[4] He hoped that the conference might split the Irish Party. The conference was duly held in December 1902 and was hailed by Redmond as 'the most significant episode in the public life of Ireland for the last century'.[5] Redmond was himself one of the tenants' representatives and Colonel Saunderson, leader of the Irish Unionists, was one of the landlords' representatives. The chairman, on Redmond's nomination, was Lord Dunraven, an Irish peer, a Unionist but a Catholic. The conference reported in January 1903 and declared that current arrangements were adverse to the improvement of the soil and were leading to unending squabbles as well as lawsuits between owners and occupiers. It favoured the Unionist principle of substituting an occupying proprietary in place of dual ownership. In the Commons in March 1902, Wyndham admitted that 'we are getting to the

3   R. B. McDowell, 'Administration and the Public Services, 1870–1921', in W. E. Vaughan, ed., *A New History of Ireland, vol. VI: Ireland Under the Union, II: 1870–1921*, Clarendon Press, 1996, p. 585.
4   Gailey, *Ireland and the Death of Kindness*, p. 190.
5   Joseph O'Brien, *William O'Brien and the Course of Irish Politics, 1881–1918*, University of California Press, 1976, p. 145.

end of the landlords who are prepared to sell for a capital sum which can be advanced under the existing law'. Those who had not yet sold 'are prevented from selling because they cannot afford to do it'.[6] Therefore, he believed, land purchase should be extended so that there were greater incentives for landlords to sell. The conference also called for special provision for the areas covered by the Congested Districts Board in the west and for provision to be made for evicted tenants, who could not pay judicially determined rents.

There were strong pressures from the grassroots in Ireland for an extension of land purchase. In 1898, William O'Brien, a member of the Irish Party, but out of Parliament between 1895 and 1900, had formed a United Irish League, whose electoral base was primarily in the west and whose slogan was 'The Land for the People'. The League's candidates in the first county council elections in 1899 swept the field, eclipsing the Irish Party. To prevent being swamped by the League, the squabbling groups of the Irish Party came together under Redmond's leadership to bring the League under its umbrella. But the League retained a large membership – around 100,000 in 1901. In a separate initiative, T. W. Russell, an independent-minded Unionist MP for South Tyrone, pressed for land purchase in the vastly different conditions of Ulster, where there was very little agitation. Both the League and Russell called for compulsory purchase, but Wyndham was not prepared to accept this. Nevertheless, Redmond could tell the House of Commons that 'never before ... since the Act of Union has an English minister in Ireland the chance that he now has of successfully dealing with this Irish agrarian difficulty. Ireland today is united in her demand in almost all essentials.'[7] The land question seemed to transcend the conflict between Unionists and Nationalists.

The Cabinet agreed to Wyndham's Land Purchase Bill, partly because, as one civil servant put it, 'nobody but George Wyndham understands it'.[8] In introducing the Bill in the Commons on 25 March 1903, Wyndham drew attention to the exceptional condition of the land in Ireland. Governments of both parties had recognised since Gladstone's Act of 1881 that the free market in land did not work there, both for historical reasons, since there was a different system of land tenure in Ireland from that in the rest of the kingdom, and for economic reasons. In England and Scotland, the surplus population on the land could be absorbed into commerce and industry. Outside Ulster, however, Ireland was almost wholly dependent on agriculture, and the only outlet for surplus population was 'exile beyond the sea'.

---

6   House of Commons Debates, 25 March 1902, vol. 105, col. 1035.

7   Ibid., 4 May 1903, vol. 121, col. 1222.

8   Gailey, Ireland and the Death of Kindness, p. 192.

There were, Wyndham went on, over forty Irish Land Acts on the statute book. They followed one of two approaches. Either they provided for an alteration in the relations between landlords and tenants as in the 1881 Act, or they provided for tenant ownership. Acts of the second type, Wyndham argued, had been the more successful. That was because rents were 'unsuited to determination by process of law' and the attempt to fix them had led to 'perpetual and universal litigation'. It was deterring landlords from putting capital into land, while the tenant was tempted to do as little as possible in the last years of the fifteen for which the rent was fixed. For if the tenant improved his land, his rent went up. In consequence, 'the landlords of Ireland are being ruined financially, the tenants are being ruined morally. The land is starved of capital and it is starved of industry.'[9]

At a later stage of the Bill, Balfour waxed eloquent on the faults in the current system. Land in England and Scotland, Balfour declared, was a marketable commodity, but in Ireland it was not. There were no potential purchasers of land other than the tenants, partly because the value of property had fallen as a result of judicially determined rent reductions. 'I can imagine no fault', Balfour went on,

> attaching to any land system which does not attach to the Irish system. It has all the faults of a peasant proprietary; it has all the faults of feudal landlordism; it has all the faults incident to a system under which the landlords spend no money on their property and under which a large part of the land is managed by a Court. It has all the faults incident to the fact that it is the tenant's interest to let his farm run out of cultivation as the term for revising the judicial rent approaches.

In consequence, landlords were

> ranged permanently in opposition to their tenants, who bring them into Court every fifteen years, to diminish their income by a formidable percentage at each operation. In addition, you have a system under which this country is burdened and the landlords and tenants are burdened with a weight of litigation which in itself is intolerable.[10]

The aim of the land purchase legislation was to eliminate what had become, in effect, under Gladstone's 1881 Act, dual ownership. Around 80,000 tenants had already purchased their holdings. But transfer was now grinding to

---

9 House of Commons Debates, 25 March 1903, vol. 120, cols 183–7.
10 Ibid., 4 May 1903, vol. 121, col. 1251.

a halt. In 1898, approximately 8,000 tenants had purchased, in 1900 around 5,000, but in 1901 only around 3,000. Wyndham therefore proposed that the state provide the funds needed to give the policy a fresh impetus.

The Wyndham Act had two basic principles. The first was that credit up to a maximum of £100 million spread out over a period of years would be made available to assist tenants to buy, the money to be repaid at a low rate of interest in annual instalments over sixty-eight and a half years. The maximum to be lent to an individual tenant purchaser was fixed in committee at £7,000. There would be an incentive to buy since those who did not would lose their right to go to a land court to secure a judicially determined rent. The second principle of the Act was that cash aid – a so-called grant in aid, rapidly termed a bonus – would be provided to encourage landlords to sell: up to a maximum of £390,000 in any one year, and a maximum of £12 million in total. A landlord who sold would receive 12 per cent of the purchase price as his bonus, bridging the difference between what the tenant was prepared to pay and what the landlord was willing to accept. In this way, Wyndham hoped, the state would become an honest broker between landlord and tenant. In addition, there would be a special provision for evicted tenants who could receive a loan up to £1,000, which the Land Commission was given discretionary power to increase, while the Congested Districts Board would receive £90,000 per annum and an extra lump sum of £1.25 million to buy untenanted land.

The Bill received widespread support from every part of the Commons – from Liberals, Nationalists and Unionists alike. It was, declared Redmond, 'the greatest effort yet made to settle the Irish land question by purchase. This is a great bill.'[11] It could, the Irish Nationalist leader believed, secure 'all the elements of a settlement of the Irish agrarian difficulty and the ending of the Irish land war, the permanent unity of all classes in Ireland and laying broad and sure foundations of social peace'.[12] T. R. Corbett, the strongly Unionist MP for North Down, declared that 'these are days when old men are seeing visions and young men are dreaming dreams of a new era of peace, plenty and prosperity for Ireland'.[13] The Act received royal assent in August and on 13 September, speaking at a Nationalist meeting at Wicklow, at which resolutions were adopted 'hailing the Land Act as the greatest land measure ever passed', Redmond declared that 'a great parliamentary victory had been won', yielding 'the greatest chance that Ireland had had for a century. They

---

11 Ibid., 25 March 1903, vol. 120, col. 216.
12 Ibid., 4 May 1903, vol. 121, col. 1201.
13 Ibid., 7 May 1903, vol. 121, col. 105.

should extract every possible particle of good in a situation which twelve months ago would have been believed to be impossible.'[14]

The Act was successful in its prime aim of encouraging land purchase. Indeed, it was the most successful of all of the Land Purchase Acts. Up to 1921, when Ireland outside six counties of Ulster became independent, 9,410 estates were sold and 219,000 purchasers received advances totalling over £82 million.[15] But the Act did not finally resolve the land question in Ireland, nor remove it as a political issue. For the Act had a further aim, in Wyndham's words, 'to proceed by special provision to ... improve the worst class of holdings in the west of Ireland, and in a minor degree elsewhere, prior to the sale of the estates in which these holdings were situated'.[16] This further aim was not achieved, largely because the Congested Districts Board lacked sufficient funds. There was insufficient provision for tenants who had previously been evicted in the land wars of the 1880s. By 31 May 1907, of 8,401 applications to purchase by evicted tenants, just 1,033 had been reinstated or provided with new holdings, and by 31 March 1920, just 3,581 had been reinstated out of 13,744 applications.[17] Nor was there effective provision for landless labourers who needed massive financial assistance if they were to take advantage of land purchase; and in the areas covered by the Congested Districts Board, there was simply not enough good quality untenanted land for those who needed it. So even if a tenant were to be advanced sufficient money to purchase, he would be unable to secure a living for himself and his family from his holding. In consequence, land purchase was more rapid in the east where tenants were wealthier and there was less agrarian agitation than in the west where poverty and destitution caused agitation. Lord Ashbourne, a former Unionist Lord Chancellor of Ireland, was to tell the Lords in June 1907, 'The west of Ireland is at the present moment so disturbed as to be in a state almost of civil war.'[18] And in August 1907, the counties of Clare, Galway, Longford, King's County (now County Offaly), Leitrim and Roscommon were proclaimed under the Crimes Act. For all its beneficial effects, therefore, the Wyndham Act did not, as has often been suggested and as the Unionists had hoped, finally resolve the land question in Ireland.

In 1906 and 1911, the Liberals were to introduce legislation to deal with the problem of landless labourers, providing for larger loans to district councils encouraging them to build houses together with provision for compulsory

---

14 *The Times*, 14 September 1903.
15 Patrick John Cosgrove, 'The Wyndham Land Act, 1903: The Final Solution to the Irish Land Question?', PhD thesis, National University of Ireland, 2008, pp. 371, 373. This thesis provides a most valuable analysis of the 1903 Act.
16 House of Commons Debates, 31 March 1909, vol. 3, col. 365.
17 Cosgrove, 'Wyndham Land Act', p. 315.
18 House of Lords Debates, 24 June 1907, vol. 176, col. 828.

acquisition. And in 1909, the Liberals enacted a further Land Act providing for compulsory purchase by the Congested Districts Board. Even so, the problem remained unresolved and it was left to the independent Irish Free State to deal with it.

In September 1903, Wyndham had rather wildly told Balfour that 'the land act will settle the land question and give you 103 votes [i.e. the votes of the Irish Party] for two years'.[19] In 1905, he told the Commons that, under the Unionists, 'the Government of Ireland had ceased to be merely the police force of Ireland'.[20] By tying the Irish peasant to the land, Wyndham hoped to create a conservative class with a stake in the country so that it would sustain law and order. Some Nationalists feared that Wyndham was right and that Home Rule would indeed be killed by kindness. John Dillon, Redmond's chief lieutenant, felt, according to the diarist Wilfrid Scawen Blunt, that 'the land trouble is a weapon in nationalist hands, and that to settle it finally would be to risk Home Rule, which otherwise *must* come. For this reason he was opposed to the Conference with the landlords, and was opposed now in principle to the bill.'[21] For Dillon, the best way to deal with landlords was not to confer with them but to make life so uncomfortable that they were driven out of Ireland. He nevertheless went along with the conference and the Bill since the Irish Party had decided to support it. But both Wyndham's hopes and Dillon's fears were misplaced. While the reforms did create a new class, that class would not feel a real stake in the country until Ireland was able to manage her own affairs. Redmond indeed had supported Wyndham's Act precisely because he believed, unlike its progenitor, that it would assist in the demand for Home Rule, not hinder it.

> He would have never taken off his coat in the land movement if the national movement were not behind it. He valued the Land Act not merely for itself, but because it opened up the way to other great reforms, chief among which was an Irish parliament. The policy underlying this Act was reconciliation of classes which made an absolutely united demand for Home Rule possible. Such a thing was not possible so long as the land war separated Irish classes.[22]

The Irish peasant was indeed to prove conservative, but only when he came to live in his own independent state after 1921.

There was a fundamental contradiction in the Unionist approach, pointed

---

19 Gailey, *Ireland and the Death of Kindness*, p. 197.
20 House of Commons Debates, 20 February 1905, vol. 141, col. 629.
21 Quoted in F. S. L. Lyons, *John Dillon. A Biography*, Routledge & Kegan Paul, 1968, p. 233.
22 *The Times*, 14 September 1903.

out in debates on the Bill by George Lambert, Liberal MP for South Molton. Unionists assumed 'that the Irish tenant in his dealings with the British exchequer will be one of the most punctual and honourable of men' in repaying the loan.

> They almost invest him with a set of wings, but when it comes to a case of Irishmen dealing with Irish affairs in Ireland, then it appears that they are invested with a double dose of original sin, and cannot be trusted to manage their own affairs ... All I hope is that they will carry their principles a little further, and let Irishmen have an opportunity of managing their own affairs in their own country.[23]

Wyndham was shortly to provide this opportunity. But it was to end his ministerial career.

With the Land Act on the statute book, the land conference dissolved itself, but it was reconstituted in August 1904 as the Irish Reform Association, also chaired by Dunraven, whose purpose was to continue with policies of compromise and conciliation such as had produced the Land Act. This would be achieved through reforms in Irish government falling short of Home Rule. The association's first manifesto declared that 'while firmly maintaining ... the parliamentary union between Great Britain and Ireland as essential to the political stability of the empire ... we believe that such union is compatible with the devolution to Ireland of a larger measure of local government than she now possesses'.[24] This declaration perhaps was innocuous. But on 26 September 1904, a second manifesto appeared with concrete proposals involving two forms of delegating power from Westminster. First, there would be a separate Irish Budget and a Financial Council to supervise and control Irish spending. The council would be composed in such a way that it would not have a Nationalist majority. There would be twelve elected and twelve non-elected members, representatives of Irish MPs and local authorities, with the Chief Secretary a member *ex officio* while the Lord Lieutenant would be the chairman with a casting vote. The Commons would only be able to reverse the decisions of the council by a quarter majority. Second, there would be a subordinate legislative body composed of Irish MPs and peers and members of the Financial Council to scrutinise Irish legislation. The precise functions of this body seemed somewhat vague and capable of considerable extension.

---

23 House of Commons Debates, 5 May 1903, vol. 121, col. 1401.
24 Right Hon. the Earl of Dunraven, K. P., *The Outlook in Ireland: The Case for Devolution and Conciliation*, John Murray, 1907, p. 278. The two manifestos can be found on pp. 271–80.

These proposals were based on Indian experience – Sir Antony MacDonnell, Under-Secretary at the Irish Office, had previously been lieutenant governor of the north-western provinces and a member of the viceroy's council – where the Budget was scrutinised by a semi-elective council. But India, by contrast with Ireland, did not at that time contain a large nationalist movement nor any equivalent to the Ulster Unionists. The degree of control exercised by officials in India would not be tolerated in Ireland. The Irish Reform Association's ideas also had some similarity with proposals agreed by Parnell and Joseph Chamberlain in 1885, when Chamberlain had been a Liberal. But that was before Home Rule had appeared on the agenda, which had the consequence that moderate reforms could be seen as a slippery slope towards Home Rule. So what might have been possible in 1885 was not to prove acceptable in 1904.

The association's proposals were put forward tentatively and it suggested that a Royal Commission be established to consider them. And they came not from government but from an independent group with no official status, and only for debate and discussion. But even in this tentative and unofficial form, they caused a political storm since, to Unionists, they seemed to recognise an independent Irish political will, something they were at pains to deny. Wyndham took the unusual step of immediately writing to *The Times* on 27 September to express 'total dissent' from the proposals:

> I have to say without reserve or qualification that the Unionist Government is opposed to the multiplication of legislative bodies within the United Kingdom, whether in pursuance of the policy generally known as 'Home Rule for Ireland' or in pursuance of the policy generally known as 'Home Rule All Round'.

The letter killed the proposals, but it did not kill the furore as to how they had come to be made.

It became apparent that in preparing the proposals, Dunraven had secured the help of the head of the Irish civil service, the Under-Secretary at the Irish Office, Sir Antony MacDonnell, who, when accepting his post, had told Wyndham that he was 'an Irishman, a Roman Catholic and a Liberal in politics'.[25] His brother was a member of the Irish Parliamentary Party. Sir Antony had been appointed because his work in India had impressed the then viceroy, Lord Lansdowne. Upon learning that Sir Antony was about to be appointed governor of Bombay, Lansdowne felt that he could be of more value in Ireland. He had assured Wyndham that it would be a safe

---

25 Adams, *Balfour*, p. 200.

appointment since Sir Antony had refused to join the Irish Party even though it had offered him a seat. Sir Antony was not in fact a Home Ruler and had opposed the policy of obstruction associated with the Irish Party.[26] But he was opposed also to the elements of coercion in Unionist policy. It was later to be revealed that Sir Antony had been appointed to the Irish Office on terms which were, to say the least, unusual. For Lansdowne, in recommending the appointment, had said that Sir Antony could 'scarcely be expected to be bound by the same narrow rules of routine which are applicable to an ordinary member of the civil service'. Therefore, he should be allowed 'greater freedom of action, greater opportunities of initiative than he would have expected if he had been a candidate promoted in the ordinary sense'.[27] He was to be 'lent' to the Irish Office from the Council of India, to which he had been appointed when he had returned to London to advise the India Secretary. Wyndham was to tell the Commons that MacDonnell had been 'invited by me rather as a colleague than as a mere Under-Secretary to register my will'.[28] Sir Antony himself had said that he could 'succeed ... on this condition – that I be given adequate opportunities of influencing the action and policy of Irish Government and (subject of course to your control) am allowed freedom of action within the law'.[29] These terms had not been made public at the time of the appointment or the Irish Unionists would have sought to veto it, and while the Prime Minister, Lansdowne and Wyndham were aware of the terms, the rest of the Cabinet were not.[30] Nor were the terms of appointment ever precisely defined. The appointment was certainly questionable on constitutional grounds as being hardly compatible with the principle of ministerial responsibility, since a minister cannot share power with an official not responsible to Parliament. In Ireland, as elsewhere, there could be only one head of a government department responsible for policy. The appointment was a misjudgement by Lansdowne and also by Balfour who allowed it. He had been sceptical but had let himself be overruled by Lansdowne and Wyndham.

When the Unionist storm broke, Sir Antony insisted that he had informed Wyndham that he was helping the Irish Reform Association, having written to him more than once on the proposals, and had told him on 16 September 1904, just ten days before the manifesto was published, that

26 F. S. L. Lyons, 'The Irish Unionist Party and the Devolution Crisis of 1904–5', *Irish Historical Studies*, March 1948, p. 3. This article provides a clear and concise account of the crisis.
27 Letter by Sir West Ridgeway in *The Times*, 20 February 1905.
28 House of Commons Debates, 20 February 1905, vol. 141, col. 650.
29 Adams, *Balfour*, p. 200.
30 Gailey, *Ireland and the Death of Kindness*, p. 270.

in the Irish Reform Association manifesto I fancy you have recognised the trace of conversations we have had. I have helped – and am helping – Dunraven in this business which has for many a day seemed to me to offer the best hope of an unravelling of the tangled skein of English and Irish relations.[31]

But Wyndham, it appears, failed to appreciate the significance of the letters he had received. He was suffering from nervous exhaustion and had taken a holiday, his first for six years. His health had in fact been poor for some time, and the strains of office were driving him to drink. He was, wrote Sir Edward Hamilton, Permanent Secretary at the Treasury, in his diary in November 1904, 'too fond of the glass'.[32] Wyndham had mislaid the crucial September letter which was not discovered until after his resignation – his private secretary was to find it in a book Wyndham had been reading.[33] Sir Antony assumed that Wyndham's silence indicated consent; and Wyndham was to tell Balfour in November 1904, when MacDonnell was being pressed to leave Ireland, that he could not agree to it, since, 'I could not be silent in a Debate on his removal, and if I spoke I could not say that he had ever disobeyed my instructions, or acted disloyally to me.'[34]

It later came to be revealed that Sir Antony, as well as informing Wyndham, had informed the Lord Lieutenant, Lord Dudley, of his activities; and, although Dudley had not seen the final draft of the manifesto, he had made no objection, since Sir Antony told him that he had written to Wyndham explaining what he was doing. Dudley had, remarkably, told Sir Antony that Wyndham was in sympathy.[35] But Dudley was not in the Cabinet and so in no position to give the consent of the government. Nor could Wyndham alone give consent to the Dunraven proposals which raised sensitive political issues. Only the Cabinet could have done that. And it was odd that Dudley appears not to have discussed the proposals with Wyndham, other than writing to him after they had been finalised; while Wyndham appears not to have known of Dudley's involvement until December 1904. All the same, Sir Antony should have had the political sensitivity to appreciate that the proposed manifesto raised large issues which could offend Unionist sensibilities and would therefore require Cabinet sanction. His experience in India, where the bureaucracy had much freer rein, had misled him as to what was possible in the more politically sensitive conditions of Ireland.

31 J. W. Mackail and Guy Wyndham, eds, *Life and Letters of George Wyndham*, Hutchinson, 1925, vol. 2, p. 765.
32 Quoted in Gailey, *Ireland and the Death of Kindness*, p. 281fn.
33 Lyons, 'Devolution Crisis', p. 9.
34 Dugdale, *Balfour*, vol. 1, p. 315.
35 Gailey, *Ireland and the Death of Kindness*, p. 246.

Dealing with so potentially explosive an issue as devolution, he should have appreciated that he needed at least the specific endorsement of his ministerial chief before engaging in discussions with outsiders about it. Wyndham's private secretary was to tell Balfour's niece when she was preparing her life of the Prime Minister that MacDonnell

> had all the faults of a strong self-made man who had spent all his official life administering a country not under direct parliamentary control ... It was his frequent failure to realise the finesse that is necessary to get any-thing done by parliamentary methods that so constantly irritated him; he never felt the pulse of the political world ... He had no experience of the English code which prevents civil servants from meddling even indirectly with politics.[36]

But Wyndham was also at fault in not making the views of the govern-ment absolutely clear to his Under-Secretary, and in not imposing limits to his activities, especially as Sir Antony often referred to Indian precedents. Wyndham also should have told Sir Antony not to take any new initiatives while he was on holiday.

Wyndham's explanations and disavowals were not sufficient to save him from the wrath of the Irish Unionists. The Attorney General for Ireland denounced the Irish Reform Association's proposals as 'a weak and silly attempt to grant home rule on the sly', and an Irish Unionist conference at Belfast condemned them. The Irish Unionists suspected that Dunraven, with Wyndham's support, was seeking to create a new centre party in Ireland. There was some justification for this suspicion. For Dunraven had in fact discussed this possibility with Wyndham in 1903 after the passage of the Land Act. Sir Antony certainly hoped for such a party, confiding to an Irish historian on 1 September 1904 that he wanted to bring about 'a moderate but progressive party' which could unite Unionists and Nationalists.[37] Irish Unionists were also suspicious that the Dunraven scheme would put them on a slippery slope. There was some justification for this suspicion also. The admittedly not wholly trustworthy diarist Wilfrid Scawen Blunt declared that Wyndham had told him in November 1902 that his schemes 'would probably lead to home rule but – it was not his business to look so far ahead'. The diarist believed that Wyndham was 'theoretically a home ruler' but that 'the less said about it just now the better'.[38] Dining with Wyndham at the

---

36 Quoted in ibid., p. 185fn.
37 Ibid., p. 243.
38 Quoted from the unpublished diaries in ibid., pp. 235, 236.

end of September, after the Chief Secretary's letter to *The Times* denouncing the association's proposals had appeared, Blunt wrote, 'I know this kind of home rule to be in accordance with his views ... He gets out of the difficulty by declaring that it is absolutely contrary to those of the unionist party, a distinction which has so far escaped the criticism of his opponents.'[39] In addition, Lord Dudley, the Lord Lieutenant, had told Redmond through an intermediary, probably in November 1903, that 'once assured of the safety of the "loyal minority" (he did not use the word "loyal") he had hoped to see Ireland commence some sort of autonomous legislation with a council with representatives from each of the four provinces'.[40] It is likely, though it cannot be proved, that Wyndham did know what Dunraven was up to but was nevertheless willing to let Sir Antony explore the issues as he had done with land reform.

The Irish were not slow to show their feelings in Parliament. In February 1905, Redmond moved an amendment to the King's Speech that 'the present system of government in Ireland is in opposition to the will of the Irish people'. When it came to the vote, only six Irish Unionist MPs out of eleven voted with the government; three of the six were office holders, and they threatened to resign. This was the first occasion in twenty years in which Irish Unionists had refused to support a vote of confidence in a Unionist government. And it gave rise to a development of great importance. To resist such threats in the future, northern Unionists formed an Ulster Unionist Council with 200 members – 100 from local Unionist associations, fifty from Orange grand lodges and fifty from MPs, peers and *ex officio* members. This council provided the Unionists 'with an instrument whose political importance in succeeding years it is difficult to exaggerate'. It was indeed to play a significant role in the Ulster crisis after 1912.[41] The establishment of this council began the process of differentiation between northern and southern Unionists which would culminate in partition.

The Dunraven proposals did not even secure the support of Nationalists. Redmond was at first quite sympathetic, regarding them as 'a declaration for Home Rule' – which, of course, was what the Unionists were afraid of – and 'quite a wonderful thing'. But most Nationalists agreed with Redmond's hard-line associate John Dillon, who declared that 'any vote of confidence in Lord Dunraven or any declaration of satisfaction at the foundation of the Irish Reform Association would tear the ranks of the Nationalists of Ireland to pieces' and lead to the indefinite postponement of Home Rule. There is

---

39   Blunt, *My Diaries*, vol. 2, p. 110.
40   Gailey, *Ireland and the Death of Kindness*, p. 239.
41   Lyons, 'Devolution Crisis', pp. 12, 13.

evidence that one of the aims of Dunraven's proposed centre party might be to split the Nationalists.[42]

But it was Irish Unionist anger which most worried ministers. The Cabinet could hardly dismiss Sir Antony since he had told his superiors – Wyndham and Lord Dudley – what he was doing, and it did not wish to throw Wyndham overboard. Wyndham's successor at the Irish Office, Walter Long, was to tell Austen Chamberlain in September 1906 that it would have been unjust to sack MacDonnell since he had acted in accordance with Wyndham's instructions 'in everything he did', a view in which, as we have seen, Wyndham concurred.[43] But clearly the Cabinet could not defend Sir Antony either. So, in December 1904, it compromised by issuing an aide memoire of 'measured censure' of MacDonnell, 'unusual in respect of a civil servant', declaring that the government 'disapprove of your having assisted Lord Dunraven in formulating proposals which include these purposes. The Government believes that you assisted Lord Dunraven in ignorance of the view which we take of such proposals, and are convinced that you acted without disloyalty to your official superiors.'[44] The Cabinet did not offer MacDonnell the courtesy of asking him for an explanation before censuring him. Nor, when it censured him, was it aware of Dudley's involvement. MacDonnell could have defended himself by arguing that he had been supported by the Lord Lieutenant and had informed his political master. He might have claimed that he could take Wyndham's silence as consent. Annoyed no doubt at his censure, Sir Antony then went quite beyond what was acceptable for a civil servant by checking Lord Dunraven's speech of explanation before it was delivered in the Lords and sending the Liberals detailed memoranda to assist them in their case against the government.[45]

The censure of MacDonnell was not sufficient to save Wyndham. Balfour, while possibly not himself unsympathetic to the Dunraven proposals, was not going to risk further division in his party, already reeling from rifts over tariff reform. Wyndham, therefore, had little alternative but to resign, which he did on 6 March 1905. 'Now and again', Sir Horace Plunkett had written, 'an individual tries to broaden the basis of Irish unionism and to bring himself into touch with the life of the people. But the nearer he gets to the people the farther he gets from the Irish unionist leaders.'[46] Wyndham's political career was ruined. He was never to hold office again, took further to drink and died in June 1913. He was, in the Chief Whip's words, 'the most

42 Lyons, *John Dillon*, p. 274.
43 Richard Murphy, 'Walter Long and the Conservative Party 1905–1921', PhD thesis, Bristol University, 1984, p. 29fn.
44 Dugdale, *Balfour*, vol. 1, p. 315.
45 Gailey, *Ireland and the Death of Kindness*, pp. 275–6.
46 Quoted in ibid., p. 210.

accomplished failure of my acquaintance'. He had committed the cardinal sin of allowing Unionists to believe 'that the maintenance of the Union was not a bedrock foundation of his policy'.[47]

Wyndham's place was filled by Walter Long, after Carson had refused it, which gave rise to the jibe that 'the Government having failed in sending Don Quixote to Ireland now propose to send Sancho Panza'.[48] Long was fully committed to the traditional Unionist policy of negation. 'Personally I belong to the stupid party,' he had told Balfour in November 1898.[49] As for Sir Antony, his wings had been clipped but he remained in office until retiring in 1908. Wyndham's resignation did nothing to banish the air of muddle and confusion which surrounded the government's Irish policy, and the crisis further damaged the Balfour government, increasing backbench suspicions of him and so added to the difficulties he was facing after the Education Act and the split over tariff reform.

Constructive Unionism had solid achievements to its credit. It had transformed the administrative and social structure of Ireland, creating a modern system of local government and institutions such as the Congested Districts Board and the Department of Agricultural and Technical Instruction. And it had created a new class of property owners through the Land Acts. Sir Almeric Fitzroy, Clerk of the Privy Council, was to write that 'the modest operations of the Congested Districts Board and the Department of Agriculture ... have so far superseded the efforts of all Mr Gladstone's heroic legislation'.[50] Unionist reforms laid the foundations for much of the success of the Irish Free State following independence in 1922. But the crisis over the Dunraven devolution proposals ended the hopes of those who had believed that Home Rule could be killed with kindness, and so constructive Unionism failed in its main aim. It had strengthened Unionist intransigence without destroying the demand for Home Rule. 'The most striking feature of Irish politics', wrote the Irish novelist George Birmingham in 1919, 'is the stability of parties ... The Nationalist remains steadfastly Nationalist ... The Unionists steadfastly Unionist. No one imagines that the opinions of the voter can be altered by any means.'[51] Gladstone's commitment to Home Rule in 1886 had frozen Irish politics. During the brief period from 1895 to 1905, it appeared that there might be some fluidity and that a centrist combination might be possible. But the crisis over the Dunraven proposals showed that the search for a middle way was a chimera, and there appeared

47 Vincent, ed., *Crawford Papers*, pp. 327, 314.
48 Garvin, *Chamberlain*, vol. 3, p. 671.
49 Vincent, ed., *Crawford Papers*, p. 304.
50 Fitzroy, *Memoirs*, vol. 1, p. 110.
51 George A. Birmingham, *An Irishman Looks at His World*, Hodder & Stoughton, 1919, pp. 9–10.

just two alternatives for Ireland: resolute government by the Unionists or Home Rule. The 'logic of the situation', declared Edward Dowden, professor of English literature at Trinity College Dublin and a staunch Unionist, was that 'two ideas, essentially antagonistic will confront each other – now as in 1886 – until one or other has obtained the mastery'.[52] And so it proved to be. The Dunraven crisis, therefore, marked the end of what had been a brave experiment.

The history of independent Ireland was to show that there was much truth in the Unionist contention that the Irish people were essentially conservative. But their conservatism would be expressed only within the framework of their own state. In relation to the British state, however, Irish opinion was predominantly radical rather than conservative. Therefore, until the Nationalist claim was conceded in some measure, agitation would continue. The Unionists did not fully appreciate the force of Irish Nationalism and proved unable to come to terms with it. They believed, like Karl Marx, that the Irish problem was fundamentally economic and could be resolved by economic rather than political reform. That belief was shown to be unfounded.

THE ALIENS ACT

On the British side of the Irish Sea, there seemed two social problems. The first was that of controlling 'alien', i.e. Jewish, immigration. The second was that of alleviating distress caused by unemployment.

In 1881, there was a small Jewish population of around 60,000 in Britain.[53] Most, while retaining their own religious and cultural customs, had settled comfortably into British life, taking pride in the achievements of their community, and in particular of Benjamin Disraeli, Prime Minister in 1868 and from 1874 to 1880. Disraeli was, admittedly, no longer a Jew by the time he entered No. 10. As a young boy, he had been baptised after a dispute between his father and the local synagogue. Had that not occurred, his political career would hardly have been possible, since Jews were not eligible for membership of the Commons until 1858, by which time Disraeli would have been fifty-three. Even so, most Jews continued to regard Disraeli as a member of their community and he continued to identify with it. For much of the nineteenth century, the majority of British Jews led lives of peaceful and respectable decorum. During the first half of the century, they had been subject, together with other religious minorities, to political discrimination, but they had benefited from emancipation in the Victorian era. As early as

---

52 Gailey, *Ireland and the Death of Kindness*, pp. 256–7.
53 Cecil Bloom, 'The Politics of Immigration, 1881–1905', *Jewish Historical Studies*, 1992–1994, p. 187.

1848, the French statesman François Guizot had told Disraeli, 'Your being leader of the Tory party is the greatest triumph that Liberalism has ever achieved.'[54] In 1855, the first Jewish Lord Mayor, Sir David Salomons, was selected. There was, nevertheless, considerable social discrimination against Jews, and some hostility would flare up from time to time. Such hostility was particularly noticeable during the Boer War, which the left alleged was being fought in the interests of Jewish financiers in Johannesburg, while a few equated the whole imperialist movement with Jewish finance. Morley, for example, argued that 'a ring of financiers ... mostly Jewish, are really responsible for the war'.[55] In September 1900, the Trades Union Congress (TUC) passed a resolution – admittedly by a slim margin – condemning the war as designed 'to secure the gold fields of South Africa for cosmopolitan Jews most of whom had no patriotism and no country'.[56] Anti-Jewish sentiment could be founded on the radicalism of the left and working-class hostility as well as upper-class snobbery. Nevertheless, in a broadly tolerant society, Jews remained largely objects of curiosity rather than targets of persecution.

But from the early 1880s, there was a mass immigration of poorer Jews from Russia and Russian Poland, in response to pogroms following the assassination of Tsar Alexander II in 1881, and also from Romania in response to persecution there. From the early 1880s to 1914, around 2 million Jews emigrated from Eastern Europe. The majority went to the United States, but many came to Britain. By the beginning of the twentieth century, there were around 160,000 Jews in Britain outside Ireland, of whom it appears that nearly 83,000 had been born in Russia or Russian Poland. By 1914, the numbers had increased to around 300,000 Jews in Britain, under 1 per cent of the population of Britain.[57] Precise numbers are, however, difficult to come by, since the system of registration of entrants provided for in the Registration of Aliens Act of 1836 had fallen into desuetude.

Although the total number of Jews in Britain remained small in absolute terms, the new Jewish immigration was highly concentrated – primarily in the East End of London, where around 100,000 of the 160,000 Jews in Britain lived in 1901, but also, though to a lesser extent, in Leeds and in Manchester. In east London, there was pressure to control Jewish immigration, but in areas where Nonconformist influence was prevalent such as Leeds and Manchester, there seemed little such pressure. In January 1902, for

54 Sir Llewellyn Woodward, *The Age of Reform 1815–1870*, 2nd edition, Clarendon Press, 1962, p. 163fn.
55 David Feldman, *Englishmen and Jews: Social Relations and Political Culture 1840–1914*, Yale University Press, 1994, p. 266.
56 Claire Hirshfield, 'The Anglo-Boer War and the Issue of Jewish Culpability', *Journal of Contemporary History*, 1980, p. 627.
57 Bloom, 'Politics of Immigration', p. 193.

example, Gerald Balfour, MP for Leeds Central, replying, as President of the Board of Trade, to a debate on Jewish immigration, declared that in the past fifteen years he had received no more than half a dozen representations on immigration and it 'was not a burning issue in Leeds'.[58] And in Manchester there was to be a large meeting in 1904 in Stevenson Square at which 'the large majority of the audience belonged to the English working classes', to protest against proposals to restrict immigration. Even in London, attitudes were mixed. Rev. Harold Davies, Rector of Spitalfields, a mild restrictionist, was to tell the Royal Commission on Alien Immigration in 1903, that, while,

> there is no question about it that there is a very strong feeling on the part of the English people, not only against the alien Jewish population, but also in their favour ... a very large section of the English people have a great respect for the Jewish people ... I am speaking entirely from my knowledge of Spitalfields.[59]

Jewish immigrants were concentrated not only geographically but also in certain trades – primarily tailoring, peddling and boot and shoe making. They often worked long hours for low wages, sometimes at home, but sometimes in small and insanitary workshops. Few joined trade unions, and some trade unionists accused them of undercutting wages. But perhaps even more important, the Jewish community seemed highly visible – in terms of clothing, accent and religious practice. They were also alleged, on perhaps dubious evidence, to be physically distinguishable in terms of appearance. What was obvious was that 'the Jewish neighbourhoods swiftly evolved a striking new appearance, black hats, long hair, beards, Yiddish signs above the shops, snatches of strange (to the bewildered locals) foreign music from upstairs rooms and kosher butchers'.[60] Because of their high visibility and concentration, the number of Jews in Britain was often exaggerated and there were fears that Britain would face a 'flood' of immigrants in which the indigenous population would be 'swamped'. Similar fears were, of course, to be expressed about later generations of immigrants from the West Indies, East Africa and the Indian subcontinent.

Although net immigration was negative during this period, there being no year between 1890 and 1914 in which immigration exceeded emigration,

---

58 House of Commons Debates, 29 January 1902, vol. 101, col. 1285.
59 John Garrard, *The English and Immigration: A Comparative Study of the Jewish Influx, 1880–1910*, Oxford University Press, 1971, pp. 69–70.
60 Robert Winder, *Bloody Foreigners: The Story of Immigration to Britain* [2004], Abacus, 2005, p. 232.

it was not long before immigration became a political issue.[61] Yet the first opponents of Jewish immigration were Jews themselves, members of a fairly conservative community, who felt their settled position might be threatened by the arrival of impoverished Jews from Eastern Europe. In 1888, the retired Chief Rabbi, 85-year-old Nathan Adler, sent an urgent message to rabbis in Eastern Europe declaring of Jewish immigrants, 'It is difficult for them to support themselves – they sometimes contravene the will of their Maker on account of their poverty and overwork and violate the Sabbath and festivals. Some have been ensnared in the net of the missionaries.' He asked the rabbis to 'warn them not to come' and told the British consul in Odessa that 'England is overcrowded with unemployed workmen and it is most undesirable that people should proceed there'.[62] In addition, Jewish organisations took it upon themselves to repatriate those whom they believed unsuitable for residence in Britain. It was not long, however, before politicians came to take up the issue of Jewish immigration and demand that it be controlled.

But the restrictionists faced a fundamental problem. For, until 1905, any foreigner who could afford the fare could arrive and settle in Britain. Perhaps uniquely in Europe, Britain had no immigration control, while passports were not made compulsory until 1914. The absence of restriction rested on principles of religious tolerance and the right of asylum – principles established in the era of Victorian liberalism. In the House of Lords in 1894, Rosebery as Prime Minister had combated proposals for restriction by quoting Palmerston on

> that law of hospitality by which we have invariably been guided with regard to foreigners seeking asylum in this country. Any foreigner, whatever his nation, whatever his political creed, whatever his political offences against his own Government ... may find in these realms a safe and secure asylum as long as he obeys the law of the land.

And Rosebery went on to claim that Palmerston's principle still held. The 'present more democratic character of the House of Commons', Rosebery insisted, 'has in no degree diminished the jealousy of any restriction of the privilege of asylum which exists in that body. If anything, it has increased that jealousy.'[63] The right of asylum was indeed regarded as a fundamental constitutional principle. In *The Constitutional History of England*, published

61 Harris, *Unemployment and Politics*; B. R. Mitchell and Phyllis Deane, *Abstract of British Historical Statistics*, Cambridge University Press, 1962, Table B, p. 50.

62 Bloom, 'Politics of Immigration', pp. 189–90.

63 House of Lords Debates, 17 July 1894, vol. 145, col. 764.

in 1912, Erskine May, the great codifier of parliamentary procedure, wrote, instancing the Huguenots and refugees from revolutionary France:

> It has been a proud distinction for England to afford an inviolable asylum to men of every rank and condition, seeking refuge on her shores, from persecution and danger in their own lands ... All exiles from their own country – whether they fled from despotism or democracy, whether they were kings discrowned, or humble citizens in danger – have looked to England as their home. Such refugees were safe from the dangers which they had escaped. No solicitation or menace from their own Government could disturb their right of asylum; and they were equally free from molestation by the municipal laws of England.[64]

The *Jewish Chronicle* was to declare in 1904 that the absence of a right of asylum in an abortive Aliens Bill of that year was 'un-English'.[65] Those who favoured restriction, therefore, would have to combat strong traditional beliefs of free movement and the right of asylum, and these were seen as concomitants to the principle of free trade. As J. A. Hobson, the radical economist, wrote, 'If an Alien law is passed, it will bring both logically and historically in its wake such protective measures as will constitute a reversal of our present Free Trade policy.'[66]

The first leading politician to advocate immigration control was Joseph Chamberlain in 1891 as part of his social reform programme. It was, he argued, of little use for the state to sustain wages and improve working conditions if immigrants were undercutting wages and working in conditions lower than those which indigenous workers would tolerate. Chamberlain was in due course to link the immigration issue with tariff reform, declaring that free immigration, like free imports, was inconsistent with policies designed to improve the position of labour. Otherwise, social reform by raising the cost of production would put the British employer at a disadvantage with the foreign employer, thereby forcing him to either lower his prices, which meant lower wages, or employ fewer people. This argument, however, could prove embarrassing for a government which had authorised the importation of cheap Chinese labour into the Transvaal, undercutting the wages of the indigenous population. Chamberlain was later to suggest that legislation to restrict immigration was but 'a step towards much greater things', meaning

---

64 Sir Thomas Erskine May, *The Constitutional History of England since the Accession of George the Third*, Longmans, Green & Co., 1912, vol. 2, p. 156.

65 'The Right of Asylum', *Jewish Chronicle*, 14 July 1905.

66 Quoted in Bernard Gainer, *The Alien Invasion: The Origins of the Aliens Act of 1905*, Heinemann, 1972, p. 129.

tariff reform.[67] But this suggestion was perhaps counterproductive in that it helped to ensure that Liberals and Unionist free traders would oppose immigration restrictions.

The TUC passed a number of resolutions calling for the government to restrict immigration, the last of which in 1895 called for the prohibition of 'pauper aliens' with no visible means of support. But after 1895, the TUC tended to ignore the issue. Chamberlain was, however, supported by other Unionist MPs, primarily but by no means wholly from the East End of London. In 1894, Lord Salisbury had introduced a Private Member's Bill in the Lords, but the Liberals in the Commons who were in the majority refused to support it. In 1895, the Unionists promised immigration control in their election manifesto, but, once returned to office, they did not pursue it and Private Members' Bills introduced in 1897 and 1898 made no progress. Nevertheless, immigration was becoming an issue which Unionist candidates could exploit, particularly in the East End of London where hostility to it cut across class alignments. On a class analysis, the seven constituencies of the borough of Tower Hamlets should have been Liberal or Labour. But in 1895 and 1900, five of the seven – Bow & Bromley, Limehouse, Mile End, St George and Stepney – were Unionist. Of the other two constituencies in the borough, Poplar had a comparatively small Jewish population, but, even so, the MP Sydney Buxton, later a Liberal Cabinet minister, was a discreet supporter of immigration control. He was, admittedly, to vote against the 1904 Aliens Bill, but unlike the vast majority of Liberals, he claimed to have voted against it because it was not strong enough.[68] In the Second Reading debate of the 1905 Aliens Bill on 2 May 1905, Buxton insisted that he was not antisemitic but was to tell the Commons that Jewish immigrants from Russia and Poland 'are in a totally different state of civilisation from what we desire in this country: neither in race, religious feeling, language nor blood are they suitable or advantageous to us'. 'We want', he said, 'to put up the notice that "In future no rubbish will be allowed to be shot here".'[69] He was to vote against his party whip on the Third Reading of the 1905 Bill. Whitechapel, where the Jewish population was nearly 32 per cent, was the only other Liberal constituency in the East End in the 1900 Parliament. Here, too, there was pressure for restriction.[70] Hostility to 'alien' immigration, which included Irish immigration, contributed something to Unionist success in 1895 and 1900. Even so, the 1900 election was dominated by the Boer War which distracted attention from immigration. And it would hardly

67 House of Commons Debates, 2 May 1905, vol. 145, col. 764.
68 See the comments of Chamberlain, reported in 'Mr Chamberlain in the East End', *The Times*, 16 December 1904.
69 House of Commons Debates, 2 May 1905, vol. 145, cols 761, 763.
70 Pelling, *Social Geography*, p. 44.

have been tactful to propose anti-immigration legislation in Britain when one of the complaints against Kruger was that he had refused to give the vote to Uitlanders in the Transvaal. From 1901, however, unemployment rose and this made immigration more salient.

The pressure for immigration control was led from the back benches by Sir William Evans-Gordon, a retired British Indian Army officer who became Unionist MP for Stepney in 1900 and in 1901 founded the British Brothers' League dedicated to the cause. Members were not required to pay dues, which would have been beyond the means of many who favoured control. In consequence, membership rose rapidly to around 45,000. The British Brothers' League claimed, not wholly plausibly, that it was not antisemitic, and its leaders strove, not always successfully, to avoid the word 'Jew' in favour of 'alien'. Evans-Gordon wrote a book entitled *The Alien Immigrant*, published in 1903, in which he proclaimed sympathy for Jews persecuted in Russia and Poland. He had in fact visited the Pale of Settlement and seen at first hand the sufferings of the Jewish population there. But he maintained that Britain could contribute little to help alleviate these sufferings and it would be better for Jews to settle elsewhere. He helped persuade the Unionist government in 1902 to establish a Royal Commission on Alien Immigration, of which he became a member. The Commission was chaired by Lord James of Hereford, the former Liberal Unionist minister, and it contained, in addition to Evans-Gordon, three members favourable to restriction but two others hostile to it – Sir Kenelm Digby, former Permanent Secretary at the Home Office, and Lord Rothschild, a Liberal Unionist peer.

The Commission's 1903 report was to refute most of the allegations made against the immigrants, allegations similar to those made against later immigrants from the Caribbean, Africa and south Asia. Critics had alleged that Jews were liable to introduce infectious diseases into Britain, but Dr Williams, Medical Officer of Health for the Port of London, told the Commission, 'As to their health I should say it was fairly good. The number of cases of infectious diseases introduced that I have detected amongst the people has not been numerous speaking as a whole. I cannot say that much infectious disease has come into the country among these people.'[71] It was alleged that Jewish immigrants were insanitary, but a Custom House official told the Commission that, while the ships carrying the immigrants were often unclean, 'I do not think that they [i.e. the immigrants] are more uncleanly than other similar class of people'.[72] It was alleged that immigrants were impoverished and destitute. The Commission found that while poverty

---

71 Royal Commission on Alien Immigration, Report, vol. 1, Cd 1741, 1903, para. 69.
72 Ibid., para. 72.

was undoubtedly a major cause of immigration, 'destitution is by no means the rule'. Admittedly, in 1901–02, nearly 25 per cent declared on arrival that they had no means of support. But this did not mean they were a charge on the rates since most were provided for by the Jewish Board of Guardians, established in 1859. Out of 54,310 Jewish immigrants in 1901, just 526 were receiving poor relief.[73] Of £13 million spent in 1904 on poor relief, just £29,000 was spent on the Jewish immigrant population.[74] In 1905, there were no immigrants in Whitechapel receiving poor relief. But in neighbouring Poplar, where hardly any Jewish immigrants lived, 6,000 were receiving such relief. In the country as a whole, six out of every 1,000 in the Jewish immigrant population were paupers, but amongst the indigenous population the figure was twenty-four out of 1,000.[75] Sir Kenelm Digby, an opponent of restriction, was to tell *The Times*:

> However poor a Jew from Eastern Europe may be on landing, the evidence seemed to establish that his habits of thrift, industry, orderliness, and, above all, the incalculable advantage of sobriety bring about in the great majority of cases a rapid advance in his position. I confess to having been surprised by the abundance and weight of the evidence to this effect.[76]

Apparently, forty-eight public houses had been closed in the East End since the arrival of the immigrants.[77] Nor was there any evidence that immigrants forced down wages. Indeed, Hubert Llewellyn Smith, a senior civil servant at the Board of Trade, told the Royal Commission that wages were rising in the trades where immigrants were most commonly employed.[78]

It was alleged that there were a large number of criminals amongst the immigrants. In the year ending 31 March 1902, while 0.52 per cent of the native population had been sentenced to imprisonment, the rate amongst immigrants was slightly higher at 1.16 per cent, and there had been 'a substantial increase of Alien crime in London within the last few years'.[79] This may not necessarily have indicated a higher rate of crime amongst the immigrant population, but a higher rate of detection due in part perhaps to antisemitic prejudice. In any case, it was hardly possible for an officer to detect at the ports which immigrants would prove to be criminals. It was alleged that immigrants caused overcrowding, displacing the native population, but the

---

73 Ibid., paras 74, 107.
74 Colonel Seely MP, House of Commons Debates, 19 July 1905, vol. 149, col. 1262.
75 House of Commons Debates, 19 July 1905, vol. 149, col. 1272; 2 May 1905, vol. 145, col. 726.
76 *The Times*, 31 May 1904.
77 House of Commons Debates, 19 July 1905, vol. 149, col. 1274.
78 Royal Commission, Cd 1742, qq. 22494–5.
79 Royal Commission, Cd 1741, pp. 111, 116.

Commission found that this 'has not been proved'.[80] There had been over-crowding before the immigrants arrived and it was indeed 'an evil of long standing'. But there was worse overcrowding in areas such as Holborn where there were few immigrants. And, ironically, 'just as the housing shortage reached its height, it suddenly ended'. In 1903, the Medical Officer of Health for Stepney was able to say that 'for some reason there is at the present time plenty of housing accommodation in the district'. There were in fact many empty houses in Stepney, partly due to numerous new houses having been built there in recent years.[81] In 1905, Stuart Samuel, MP for Whitechapel, told the Commons that there were 1,500 vacant houses in Stepney.[82] More seemed to be moving out of the East End into the outer suburbs than were moving in.

The conclusion of the Royal Commission was that,

> as time proceeds, many of these men [i.e. the immigrants] enter upon a different phase of existence. With the possession of greater skill and knowledge their earnings increase, and they are enabled to improve their modes of life. The balance of evidence before us is favourable to the Aliens after they have reached this stage. They appear to be industrious and thrifty ... They certainly are sober in habit, and are as law-abiding as the natives around them.[83]

But despite this conclusion and the evidence on which it was based, the majority recommended that immigration be restricted, and that certain areas be declared prohibited to immigrants. Sir Kenelm Digby issued a dissenting memorandum, which Lord Rothschild supported, declaring that the majority proposals were impracticable 'and would fail to accomplish the object aimed at'. No case had been made out for exclusion on grounds of health; it would be difficult if not impossible to ascertain by interrogation at the ports which immigrants were criminals or likely to commit criminal offences, while existing legislation was sufficient to deal with overcrowding.[84]

Despite the somewhat flimsy arguments in favour of control, the Unionist government was determined to proceed. In 1904, it introduced a Bill which gave the Home Secretary powers to exclude by regulation without appeal anyone committed of an extraditable crime in a foreign country, anyone associated with prostitution, anyone who could become a charge on public

---

80 Ibid., p. 131.
81 Gainer, *Alien Invasion*, pp. 36, 41.
82 House of Commons Debates, 19 July 1905, vol. 149, col. 1272.
83 Cd 1741, p. 144.
84 Ibid., pp. 48, 46.

purposes, anyone without visible means of support and anyone of 'notoriously bad character'. The Home Secretary could also order the expulsion of any immigrant living in Britain who fell under any of these categories. The onus of proof was to lie with the individual and any expenses were to be borne by the shipping company. But the inspection of immigrants was only to apply to those travelling in steerage – third class. First- and second-class passengers were excluded from the legislation. The Local Government Board was to be given the power, as the majority on the Royal Commission had proposed, to designate as a prohibited area any place where overcrowding was largely due to immigrants, the first time in modern British history that there would be restrictions on where an inhabitant could live. The Liberals divided the House against the Bill, citing the wide powers given to the Home Secretary and the vagueness of the categories which would lead to exclusion. But Liberal opposition was based also on principle, the long-standing principle of the right of asylum. The Bill was withdrawn in committee, largely due to the opposition of Churchill, who, after crossing the floor, was to become the Liberal candidate for North West Manchester, a constituency with a considerable Jewish population. Churchill told *The Times* that the Bill 'proposes to establish in this country a loathsome system of police interference and espionage of passports and arbitrary power exercised by police officers who in all probability will not understand the language of those upon whom they are called to sit in judgement'. The Bill, Churchill went on,

> looks like an attempt on the part of the Government to gratify a small but noisy section of their own supporters and to purchase a little popularity in the constituencies by dealing harshly with a number of unfortunate aliens who have no votes. It will commend itself to those who like patriotism at other peoples' expense ... It is expected to appeal to insular prejudice against foreigners, to racial prejudice against Jews, and to labour prejudice against competition ... the same men who are obstinate opponents of trade unionism will declaim about 'the rights of British labour'. Those who champion the interests of slum landlords will dilate on the evils of overcrowding. Those who have been most forward in bringing Chinese into Africa will pose as the champions of racial purity at home.[85]

On the day the letter appeared, Churchill crossed the floor of the Commons. 'Yes, I wrecked the Bill,' he was to boast to Rothschild.[86]

A second Bill was introduced in 1905 in which the category of 'undesirable

---

85 *The Times*, 31 May 1904.
86 Garrard, *The English and Immigration*, p. 43.

and destitute alien' was more closely defined to include only criminals, the destitute, the ill and infirm. The 'notoriously bad character' category disappeared. The prohibited areas clause was also dropped. In committee, the Bill was modified to exempt from any bar on entry 'an immigrant who proves that he is seeking admission to this country solely to avoid prosecution or punishment on religious or political grounds or for an offence of a political character, or persecution, involving danger of imprisonment or danger to life or limb on account of religious belief'. This clause, remarkably in the light of the motives of those favouring the legislation, actually provided a statutory guarantee of asylum, a right of entry to those fleeing persecution, a right that was to be maintained until the outbreak of war in 1914.[87] But the Act made it harder for those outside the empire to obtain British nationality. Previously, British nationality had been open to almost anyone prepared to pay £3. It would now require five years' residence and applicants would have to show that they could support themselves and their dependents 'decently' and could 'speak, read and write English reasonably well'. Criminals, the insane and those thought likely to apply for poor relief would be excluded. But these provisions did not apply to those born within the empire who remained British subjects with a right of entry and, once resident, the same rights as those born in Britain.[88]

Nevertheless, the burden of proof was to remain with the immigrant. Officials would still be required to make difficult judgements on the character or credentials of would-be immigrants. In committee, the Liberals inserted a clause to the effect that immigrants must be informed of the reason for their rejection and be given a right of appeal to a board which, it was hoped, would usually be chaired by a magistrate; and on the London board, twenty-seven members of the Jewish community were to be appointed.[89] Even so, there was no precedent for an extra-judicial body of this kind, composed of individuals mostly without legal training, rather than a judicial tribunal, to hear appeals. The boards would have no power to administer oaths to witnesses and they could follow whatever procedure they pleased with no clear rules of evidence and no common standards. There was to be no appeal from their decisions. Where immigrants were refused entry, the shipping company would have to bear the cost of repatriation, which, it was hoped, would make them careful in choosing whom they would accept for transit. The Liberals did not oppose the Bill on Second Reading, partly because the most objectionable elements of the 1904 Bill had been removed but also

---

87 Alison Bashford and Jane McAdam, 'The Right to Asylum: Britain's 1905 Aliens Act and the Evolution of Refugee Law', *Law and History Review*, 2014, p. 311.

88 I owe these points to Pat Thane.

89 Gainer, *Alien Invasion*, p. 201.

because the leadership had received a resolution from eight Liberal MPs and candidates in the East End urging them to take account of 'the legitimate demands of East London'.[90] But the Liberals did vote against the Bill on Third Reading.

The Bill received royal assent in August 1905, but three months later, Balfour resigned and was replaced by the Liberals. Seeking to dampen rather than reignite the issue, they decided not to repeal or even amend the Act but rather to make the regulations more generous to immigrants. The Home Secretary in the Liberal government, Herbert Gladstone, raised the number of immigrants on a ship above which inspection was required from twelve to twenty. This had striking consequences. In the first two months of the Act, 86.7 per cent of ships coming from Hamburg, Bremen and Rotterdam were inspected. But in the nine months after Gladstone's ruling, just 25.6 per cent were inspected.[91] Gladstone also told the immigration boards that the legislation was not intended to be enforced if

> refusal of leave to land would involve great personal hardship or suffering in the case of women and children. So too one who is free from any infectious or objectionable disease but may be in a critical state of health, and to refuse him leave to land might expose him to cruel hardship.[92]

More important, Gladstone required boards to give the benefit of the doubt to immigrants alleging that they were fleeing from religious or political persecution. This shifted the onus from the immigrant to the immigration board, which now had to prove that the individual was an undesirable. Evans-Gordon complained that these were 'drastic and fundamental changes', and 'tantamount to the total repeal of the Aliens Act'.[93] In May 1910, there was a further concession. The rules were amended to provide for legal assistance. The immigrants would have to pay for such assistance, but it was in fact paid for by Jewish communal organisations. In 1911, the Home Office reminded board officials that the hearing was not a trial and that officials were not prosecutors but should be impartial. The Liberals, then, 'administered the Act in as generous a spirit as was possible without further legislation'.[94] Even so, there were reports of boards ignoring the strict criteria for exclusion in the Act and applying harsher criteria of their own, and there were all sorts of petty cruelties. For example, the Act declared that lack of means was not

---

90 Ibid., p. 138.
91 Jill Pellew, 'The Home Office and the Aliens Act, 1905', *Historical Journal*, 1989, p. 378.
92 Bashford and McAdam, 'Right to Asylum', p. 319.
93 House of Commons Debates, 14 March 1906, vol. 153, cols 1312, 1317.
94 Garrard, *The English and Immigration*, p. 133.

to be a bar to admission. But one man was sent back to Bialystok because he had only 9s 6d in his pocket. A woman was returned to Russia, where she had no friends, even though her cousin had offered her work in London at a fair wage. There were also numerous inconsistencies in the administration of the Act. In January 1907, one board allowed in a man who had a daughter already resident, but in April rejected a man who had a son already resident. In Hull, a man was admitted after claiming that his stepson would look after him. In London, a man was rejected even though his son said he would look after him. One girl was admitted to join her fiancé in London, another not, even though her sister had been admitted the day before.[95] There were also allegations of procedural irregularities.[96]

The Act did seem to have the effect of reducing the numbers of individuals entering on immigrant ships – from 27,639 in 1906 to 17,982 in 1907 and then an annual average of between 11,000 and 13,500 until 1914. But the reduction might well have been due to the comparative improvement of conditions in Russia following the vicious pogroms after the failure of the 1905 revolution. There is no way of estimating the deterrent effect of the legislation.

Of those rejected, just over half appealed, and nearly 38 per cent of those appealing were successful. Between 1906 and 1913, 19,710 immigrants were convicted of criminal offences, mainly larceny and receiving or soliciting and importuning, 3,107 were recommended for expulsion and there were 2,866 expulsion orders.[97] The fact that 'only a small proportion of convicted alien criminals were recommended for expulsion orders, encourages the view that it was certainly an ineffective, if not extravagant use of government funds'. Nevertheless, it has been held that the Act 'arguably succeeded, for a period, in holding a delicate balance between the opposing and contradictory forces of exclusion and humanity. It achieved this, not despite the lack of coherence in its formulation and of lawfulness in its implementation, but because of it.'[98] The balance was lost when the outbreak of war in 1914 led, understandably, to greater pressure for restriction. Even so, by 1914, London had more Jewish immigrants than any other city in the world except New York and Chicago.[99]

'There is', declared the great constitutional lawyer A. V. Dicey,

something in the tone of the day which assuredly suggests that the Aliens Bill of 1905 may be found to stimulate sentiments of racial and religious

95   These cases were instanced in 'The Aliens Act and its Administration', *Jewish Chronicle*, 11 October 1907.
96   Helena Wray, 'The Aliens Act 1905 and the Immigration Dilemma', *Journal of Law and Society*, June 2006, pp. 315–17.
97   Pellew, 'Home Office and the Aliens Act', pp. 383–4.
98   Wray, 'Aliens Act', p. 320.
99   Bloom, 'Politics of Immigration', p. 187.

hostility. No doubt the Bill does not originate in antisemitic fanaticism, but the constant reference to the evil of admitting to England Polish and German Jews had an ugly sound.[100]

The Bill could certainly be characterised as doubly antisemitic since it was in practice directed against Jews, while its introduction pandered to and perhaps fomented antisemitic attitudes. It would, nevertheless, be an over-simplification to suggest that the Aliens Act was entirely a product of antisemitism. While socially, Jews were tolerated rather than fully accepted and faced considerable discrimination, antisemitism was not widespread at the political level, although there were significant pockets of it. But there was also much sympathy with persecuted Jews. In 1899, there had been a mass protest of 15,000 in Hyde Park after the second Dreyfus trial, and indignation was shared at all levels of society, Queen Victoria regarding the verdict with particular distaste and sending an open telegram to the British embassy in Paris protesting against the verdict, a telegram which, fortunately for Anglo-French relations, was never published.[101] The Dreyfus case, together with the pogroms in Russia, made antisemitism appear disreputable. Indeed, as we have seen, some of those giving evidence to the Royal Commission had been almost embarrassing in extolling the virtues of Jewish immigrants. The restrictionists preferred to speak of 'aliens' rather than Jews, and Evans-Gordon was by no means alone amongst them in expressing genuine sympathy with the condition of Jews in Russia and Poland; and he did not seek to exclude genuine victims of persecution. Chamberlain told an East End audience in December 1904 that Russian Jews were suffering 'the grossest and most brutal persecution', and he mentioned his discussions as Colonial Secretary with the late Theodor Herzl, leader of the Zionist movement. Chamberlain had suggested Uganda as a Jewish national home, a suggestion with which Herzl had sympathised but which had been rejected by the Zionist Congress.[102] It appears that the Unionist government also supported Herzl's idea of a Jewish settlement in El-Arish in the Sinai.[103] Other restrictionists, most conspicuously Balfour, who was to give his name in 1917 to the Declaration expressing British support for a Jewish 'national home' in Palestine, were sympathetic to the Zionist view that Jews should settle in Palestine rather than Britain. Of course, a Jewish national home elsewhere would divert Jews from seeking to come to Britain. The organisation representing British Jews,

100 Gainer, *Alien Invasion*, p. 151.
101 Christopher Andrew, *Théophile Delcassé and the Making of the Entente Cordiale: A Reappraisal of French Foreign Policy 1898–1905*, Macmillan, 1968, p. 102.
102 'Mr Chamberlain in the East End', *The Times*, 16 December 1904.
103 Amos Elon, *Herzl*, Weidenfeld & Nicolson, 1976, pp. 363–72. I owe this reference to Professor T. G. Otte.

the Jewish Board of Deputies, though it disputed the statistics provided by the restrictionists, and argued against what it regarded as fallacies in their arguments, nevertheless supported measures to prevent the immigration of undesirables. It published a pamphlet on the 1905 Bill declaring that there was not

> the slightest desire to champion aliens of immoral or criminal character and we feel that [we] are recording the sentiments of the whole body of Jews in the UK in stating that [we] would readily support any measure, however stringent, so far as it should be effectually directed against these objectionable classes.[104]

On the Second Reading of the 1905 Bill, of the twelve Jewish MPs, four, including one Liberal, voted in favour; four, including one Unionist, voted against; and four Unionists abstained. On Third Reading, the twelve Jewish MPs were again split three ways, four in favour, four against and four abstentions. The Unionists selected Jewish MPs for some East End constituencies, and there were even, apparently, some Jewish members of the British Brothers' League.[105] The anti-immigration movement, therefore, was not in its essence based on hostility to Jews as such. There was no suggestion of restricting the rights of Jews settled in Britain, nor political discrimination against them, nor antisemitic parties or movements as in much of the Continent. 'Nobody', Evans-Gordon told Herzl, 'has hitherto sought or suggested that a single privilege enjoyed by the Jews in this country today should be modified or removed, and I say that that position, which is my position, is perfectly compatible with the desire not to let too many of them come in'.[106] The Aliens Act did not mention Jews, defining the relevant category of immigrant as 'an alien steerage passenger'. Politicians and officials were chary of making legal distinctions on the basis of nationality, race or religion. In the words of the 1901 Inter-Departmental Committee on Naturalisation:

> To the Common Law belongs the fundamental principle that any person who is born within His Majesty's Dominion is from the moment of his birth a British subject, whatever may be the nationality of either or both of his parents, and however temporary or casual the circumstances determining the locality of his birth may have been.[107]

---

104 Bloom, 'Politics of Immigration', p. 190.
105 Ibid., pp. 207, 203.
106 Gainer, *Alien Invasion*, p. 120.
107 Quoted in Feldman, *Englishmen and Jews*, p. 381.

In 1913, the Marconi affair – see pp. 618–20 – was to revive antisemitism on the radical right and in some literary and intellectual circles. But it remained, as one Liberal journal put it, 'tea-table splutter of the golf-house and the club-room', and outside the mainstream of Edwardian politics.[108] No one in Edwardian times suggested sending asylum seekers to Ascension Island, an idea bruited in Britain in 2020. Nor were immigrants put into detention by contrast with Britain in the twenty-first century. In 2019, according to Oxford University's Migration Observatory, 24,019 potential immigrants, including seventy-three children, were in detention centres. In this respect, Edwardian Britain was a far more liberal society than our own; and, despite what Dicey suggested, Britain was to remain, together with the Scandinavian countries, where there were many fewer Jews, the least antisemitic of Europe-an countries. Indeed, one authority has suggested that the period 1870–1914 'may well be described as the golden age of the Jewish people in Britain'.[109]

Chaim Weizmann, leader of the Zionist movement after Herzl, and the first President of Israel, well understood the motives of the restrictionists. He had discussed the issue in a friendly manner with Evans-Gordon and in his autobiography published in 1949, he wrote:

> Looking back, I think our people were rather hard on him [Evans-Gordon]. The Aliens bill in England and the movement which grew up around it were natural phenomena which might have been foreseen ... The reaction ... cannot be looked upon as anti-Semitism in the ordinary or vulgar sense of that word; it is a universal social and economic concomitant of Jewish immigration and we cannot shake it off.

And he insisted:

> Sir William Evans-Gordon had no particular anti-Jewish prejudices. He acted, as he thought according to his best lights and in the most kindly way in the interests of his country ... in his opinion it was physically impossible for England to make good the wrongs which Russia had inflicted on its Jewish population ... I am fairly sure he would equally have opposed the mass influx of any foreign element; but, as it happened, no other foreign element pressed for admission in such numbers.[110]

---

108 Quoted in Kenneth Lunn, 'Political Anti-Semitism Before 1914: Fascism's Heritage?', in Kenneth Lunn and Richard C. Thurlow, *British Fascism: Essays on the Radical Right in Inter-War Britain*, Routledge, 1980, p. 26. But in my view, Lunn over-rates the significance of antisemitism before 1914.

109 Colin Holmes, *Anti-Semitism in British Society, 1876–1939*, Edward Arnold, 1979, p. 109.

110 Chaim Weizmann, *Trial and Error: The Autobiography of Chaim Weizmann*, Hamish Hamilton, 1949, pp. 118–19.

And indeed, prejudice against the Irish was similar to that against Jews in areas where there were strong Irish communities such as Lancashire and parts of east London. It is, one historian has suggested,

> a mistake to regard this hostility to the immigrant as necessarily 'racial' in character, any more than the nineteenth-century anti-Irish feeling was 'religious', as it was thought to be at the time. The fact is that heavy immigration is, in the most literal sense, a disturbing phenomenon: and if those who are disturbed are socially very conservative they are likely to react strongly against it.[111]

But the Aliens Act satisfied hardly anyone. The restrictionists believed that it should have been more strictly applied, the anti-restrictionists wanted it repealed, while Jews felt they had been singled out for unfair treatment. Opponents of the legislation believed that it had been introduced for electoral purposes. But if the motives of Unionists were primarily electoral, it did not do them much good. In the 1906 election, only two Unionists in the East End were returned, one of whom was Evans-Gordon, though with a much-reduced majority. Six seats were lost, four of which had been Unionist since at least 1895. Admittedly, the Unionists polled 45.8 per cent of the East End vote, excluding Bethnal Green, compared with the median for Britain, excluding Ireland, of 43.9 per cent, and so the Act may have played a small part in limiting Unionist losses.[112] But opposition to tariff reform and Chinese labour were far more important than restricting immigration. The legislation may have done some good in assuaging popular fears, particularly in the poorer districts of east London, that they would be 'swamped' or 'flooded' by an endless stream of immigration, which would in future no longer be uncontrolled but managed. But the reaction against immigration proved very limited. Chamberlain had tried to use anti-immigrant feeling as a means of securing support for tariff reform and a wider programme to appeal to the working man, a programme of Tory socialism. But it could be suggested that restriction was contrary to the best instincts of traditional Toryism. 'I wonder what Disraeli would have thought of this bill,' one Liberal MP asked the Commons. 'On April 19th [the date of Disraeli's death] you covered his statue with flowers, but the day before that you introduced a bill which might exclude from this country such families as his.'[113] But it is an exaggeration to call the Act, as one historian did, 'a landmark in the decline

---

111 Pelling, *Popular Politics*, p. 178.
112 Gainer, *Alien Invasion*, p. 284.
113 House of Commons Debates, 2 May 1905, vol. 145, col. 731.

of liberal England'.[114] The forces of liberalism were to prove stronger than those making for radical restrictions on immigration, just as they were to prove stronger than those making for tariff reform. Not even a politician of the strength and intensity of Chamberlain could undermine the foundations of Edwardian liberalism. As that same historian concludes of the Jewish presence in England, 'This is a happy story.'[115]

Of the Aliens Act, Dicey wrote, 'No measure of less immediate importance but of more significance as a sign of the times has ever been passed by the Imperial parliament. It is the outward manifestation of a new spirit' – that spirit was the spirit of collectivism.[116] The Aliens Act as well as the Land Purchase Act and the Unemployed Workmen Act showed that even a Unionist government would use the state to correct social evils. Chamberlain was to take the argument for state intervention to a new and more radical level.

THE UNEMPLOYED WORKMEN ACT

The other social issue requiring state intervention was the need to combat distress caused by unemployment, a matter of public concern since the 1880s – the word 'unemployed' first appearing as a noun in the Oxford Dictionary in 1882 and 'unemployment' in 1888.[117] The work of social investigators such as Booth and Rowntree had cast doubt on the view that unemployment resulted from personal failings. It seemed instead due to economic fluctuations beyond the power of the individual to alter. Before the Unemployed Workmen Act, while there had been some very limited provision of work by local authorities, the unemployed had mainly to rely on help from their trade union, private charity or the Poor Law, which provided for some outdoor relief, though most relief was through the workhouse. By 1908, in England and Wales, 11,413 destitute able-bodied males were obtaining relief inside the workhouse and 2,732 outside.[118] The Poor Law Guardians had no power to find employment and there was a stigma attached to the Poor Law, symbolised by the provision that anyone resorting to relief would be disenfranchised. It seemed crude and unfair to condemn the able-bodied poor to the workhouse as if they were vagrants or work-shy, stigmatising them with the taint of pauperism.

---

114 David Feldman, 'The Importance of Being English', in David Feldman and Gareth Stedman Jones, eds, *Metropolis London: Histories and Representations since 1800*, Routledge, 1989, p. 79.
115 Feldman, *Englishmen and Jews*, p. 3.
116 Quoted in Gainer, *Alien Invasion*, p. 150.
117 Lynd, *England in the Eighteen-Eighties*, p. 55.
118 Harris, *Unemployment and Politics*, p. 373.

The problem of unemployment became more acute after the end of the Boer War in 1902 as discharged soldiers vainly sought work. The public would hardly tolerate ex-soldiers being made subject to the stigma of the workhouse and disenfranchisement. From the 1880s, there had been all sorts of somewhat abortive experiments with relief works, labour colonies and compulsory training. In addition, public spending on poor relief had risen steeply between 1891 and 1906 from £8,643,318 to £14,035,888.[119] There was much duplication of effort in confronting the problem of unemployment.

In 1886, during his brief period as President of the Local Government Board in Gladstone's third government, Chamberlain had issued a Circular calling on Poor Law Guardians to confer with local authorities and arrange work for unskilled labourers during periods of trade depression. Local authority provision of work would then be an alternative to the Poor Law. In 1904, during another period of depression, Walter Long, President of the Local Government Board, inaugurated a London Unemployed Fund, to be financed by voluntary subscription enabling London local authorities to establish distress committees, composed of representatives of London borough councils and members of the boards of Poor Law Guardians together with parochial and charitable organisations. A Central Unemployed Body for London would coordinate the activities of these local committees. The committees would distinguish the 'respectable' temporarily unemployed from the feckless and help the former to find work or, in suitable cases, assist emigration. By February 1905, Long told the Cabinet, voluntary subscriptions had amounted to around £45,000 and the committees had received many applications from those seeking to emigrate. But, Long told the Cabinet, claimants should not have to depend 'on the spasmodic assistance of charity'.[120] So legislation was needed both to put the London arrangements on a more secure base and also to extend them to other urban areas. Long proposed that local authorities be *required* to establish distress committees, to be financed partly from the rates and partly from voluntary subscriptions. To the extent that committees succeeded in finding work for the unemployed, there would be savings for ratepayers. Therefore, it was only reasonable that ratepayers should contribute to it. By contrast with poor relief, those seeking help from distress committees would suffer neither stigma nor disenfranchisement. Lord Salisbury, son of the Prime Minister, objected that such legislation would inaugurate a new principle, that the state had a responsibility 'to secure employment for every deserving man. In practice this

---

119 Ibid., p. 145fn.
120 CAB 37/74/31, 16 February 1905, 'The Unemployed'.

will mean every man who is not demonstratively disreputable.'[121] But Long could retort that this was more likely to happen were the voluntary scheme to break down because of insufficient funds.

The King's Speech of 1905 heralded legislation. 'I have noticed', it declared, 'with profound regret and sympathy, the abnormal distress which has been caused by the want of employment during the present winter. Arrangements of a temporary character have been made to meet the difficulty, but it is expedient now to provide machinery for this purpose of a more permanent character.' By the time the Unemployed Workmen Bill was introduced into the Commons on 18 April 1905, Long had moved on to become Chief Secretary for Ireland and been replaced as President of the Local Government Board by Gerald Balfour. But Balfour paid tribute to Long as the 'real parent' of the legislation.[122] Balfour was at pains to explain that its aims were strictly limited. It was not intended, he insisted, to solve

> the whole of the vast and complicated problem known as the unemployed question; it did not attempt to do more than deal with a part, not altogether an unimportant part, but only a part of that problem and any attempt to extend its principle to the whole field of unemployment would be foredoomed to disastrous failure.

Its aim was 'to assist only a limited class of the unemployed, and, as regards applications of that class, it was not intended that there should be any kind of obligation to find work for them, as was thrown on the [Poor Law] Guardians to provide relief in the case of destitution'. That 'limited class of the unemployed' meant that 'loafers, work-shyers, intermittent workers whose case was not exceptional, and any workman out of work from fault of his own', were excluded from the Act which was instead for 'respectable workmen' – 'the elite of the unemployed'.[123] Balfour was later to say that the main purpose of the Act was 'rather ameliorative than curative'.[124]

The Unemployed Workmen Act in its final form required London boroughs to establish distress committees, with a central body to secure overall coordination. In addition to members from the various organisations which had hitherto comprised the committees, they would now be required to co-opt members 'experienced in the relief of distress'. There could also be members nominated by the Local Government Board. But the co-opted and nominated members were not to comprise more than one-quarter either of

---

121 CAB 37/75/44, 2 March 1905, 'The Unemployed'.
122 House of Commons Debates, 18 April 1905, vol. 145, col. 461.
123 Ibid., 20 June 1905, vol. 147, cols 1116–17.
124 Royal Commission on Poor Laws, Vol. VIII, Minutes of Evidence, Cd 5066, 1910, Qs 7738, 77737.

the committees or of the central body. The Act also extended the scheme to the rest of the country. County boroughs and urban districts with a population of over 50,000 – in Ireland the figure was 10,000 – would be required to form distress committees, while county boroughs with a lower population and county councils could apply to the Local Government Board for permission to establish them. In addition, local authorities without distress committees were required to make committee arrangements for the unemployed and encouraged to establish labour exchanges. All distress committees as well as the central body were required to contain at least one female member.

The distress committees were to sift applications to pick out which amongst them were temporarily unemployed through no fault of their own and were genuinely seeking work. Such applicants should not be on poor relief but were suitable for help, and the committees were empowered to assist them to obtain work. But they had no powers themselves to provide employment and applicants would have no right to employment. The central body was to aid those suitable for emigration and would also have the power to establish farm colonies to train the unemployed in agricultural pursuits, so that they might find jobs in the countryside. But there was no power to spend on any other form of relief works. As statutory bodies, the distress committees could clearly no longer be wholly dependent upon voluntary contributions. Their cost would in future be borne by ratepayers. Councils would contribute in proportion to their rateable value to the value of a halfpenny in the pound rate, which could be raised to 1d with the approval of the Local Government Board. But relief works would continue to be funded from charitable contributions. Queen Alexandra gave a lead with an appeal for funds which raised £154,000. But charitable contributions were never sufficient and in 1906 the Liberal government authorised a grant of £200,000 to distress committees for relief works, to be continued in the four following years. That led to a reduction in charitable contributions since the public saw no reason why it should subscribe to a scheme financed through the rates and central grants.

The Act was to be for an experimental period of three years only. The government had, however, established a Royal Commission on the Poor Laws which was to report in three years – it did not in fact report until 1909 – to consider the whole range of services administered by boards of guardians and local councils. The assumption was that the Commission's recommendations would inform the next stage of provision for the unemployed, and so the Act was intended merely as a stopgap. But both the majority and minority reports of the Commission, although highly influential over the longer term, were to be ignored in favour of the Liberal government's National Insurance Act of 1911, the unemployment provisions of which were far more radical and inclusive than anything that the Unionists would have been willing to consider in 1905. In any case, the Unemployed Workmen Act broke down within two years. For the problem of unemployment was far wider than the authors of the Act could comprehend. Much unemployment was structural or cyclical, persisting for some years, so outlasting the kind of relief provided by the Act. Rate contributions proved insufficient and the Exchequer had to fill the gap, going further towards acceptance of the principle that there was a right to work and that it was the task of government to help secure it, something that Unionists were determined to resist. And it also showed that the problem of unemployment could not be effectively dealt with by local authorities but was a national problem.[125] Giving evidence to the Royal Commission, William Beveridge, who had made a detailed study of unemployment, pointed out that borough committees were registering five or six times as many as could be assisted. The Act, Beveridge declared, was 'best considered as a final effort to meet by the provisions of temporary relief work the difficulty occasioned by exceptional trade depression'.[126] It could not deal with cyclical or structural unemployment.

'I am bound to confess', Long was to write in his memoirs, 'that my policy did not find favour in any quarter. Among my own friends it was regarded as being too much akin to socialism, while the more advanced thinkers looked upon it as incomplete and insufficient.'[127] The Act was far too meagre to satisfy the left, particularly the Labour Party, whose view was that there should be a statutory right to work. But in the long run, so Labour believed, the problem of unemployment was best resolved by transforming society in a socialist direction. But the 1905 Act had its merits and Keir Hardie expressed 'his personal satisfaction that a Government had at length arisen which was prepared to make the unemployed question a matter of serious discussion in the House. It afforded him and his colleagues of the Labour Party considerable satisfaction to find that such was the case.'[128] The Liberals did not oppose the Bill. Campbell-Bannerman told Sydney Buxton, Liberal spokesman on the subject, that the government's proposals were 'satisfactory' and 'we should strike no discordant note'.[129] In the Commons, Buxton declared that he found it 'an important fact that a Government, and a Conservative Government, should introduce a Bill of this sort. To his mind this was a great step in advance and a real departure in social legislation.'[130] But James Bryce

125 Kenneth D. Brown, 'Conflict in Early British Welfare Policy: The Case of the Unemployment Workmen's Bill of 1905', *Journal of Modern History*, 1971, p. 629.
126 Minutes of evidence to Royal Commission on Poor Laws, vol. 8, Cd 5066, 1910, pp. 13, 15.
127 Walter Long, *Memories*, Hutchinson, 1923, p. 139.
128 House of Commons Debates, 20 June 1905, vol. 147, col. 1170.
129 Harris, *Unemployment and Politics*, p. 206fn.
130 House of Commons Debates, 18 April 1905, vol. 145, col. 463.

cautioned, in a letter to Herbert Gladstone in December 1904, that Liberals should be careful 'lest we should seem to admit that it is the duty of the State to provide work – a doctrine which would cause general alarm'.[131] Even so, 'it would be hard to find any government measure that was so contrary to the voiced views of Ministerialists as this measure was'.[132] And, contrary to what its advocates said, the Act did establish new and far reaching principles. It was accepted for the first time that there was to be statutory recognition of employment relief by public authorities without the disqualifications attached to the Poor Law. The implication, however much ministers denied it, was that there was a right to employment; and, although relief was to be administered by local bodies, the Act implied that unemployment was a national problem. Admittedly, as a result of Chamberlain's Circular, many local authorities had been giving relief in times of distress from the rates without disenfranchisement for some years, and this enabled Gerald Balfour to argue that the 'innovations proposed in the Government Bill were more apparent than real'.[133] But local authority relief had been very irregular and spasmodic, lasting sometimes only for a few days, and local authorities had no statutory power to help the unemployed find work. Local authority relief, therefore, had retained the character of a charitable dole. Now there was to be statutory machinery of a permanent character. In London, the uniform rate laid upon the boroughs implied acceptance of the principle of equality of burdens. The poor of London were in future to be a common charge upon the whole city, with wealthier boroughs subsidising the poorer. The Unemployed Workmen Act, in the words of a Unionist critic, 'created a class of persons supported by the rates who were not paupers; a superior class of social dependants'.[134] So, although in a sense the Act looked to the past rather than the future, and although very limited in intention, it would have radical and far-reaching effects.

---

131 Kenneth D. Brown, *Labour and Unemployment, 1900–1914*, David and Charles, 1971, p. 45.
132 R. A. Leach, *The Unemployed Workmen Act, 1905*, Local Government Printing and Publishing Company, 1905, p. 12.
133 House of Commons Debates, 29 June 1905, vol. 147, col. 1121.
134 Sir George Bartley MP, ibid., col. 1140.

CHAPTER 10

TARIFF REFORM

THE GENESIS OF TARIFF REFORM

In 1902, a young Conservative backbencher, Winston Churchill, made a remarkable prophecy in the House of Commons.

> He wondered what would happen if the fair trade [tariff] issue is openly raised by some responsible person of eminence and authority in the country. They would stand once more on old battlefields, and amid broken weapons, grass grown trenches, and the neglected graves of heroes who had fallen in former conflicts. Party bitterness would be aroused such as the present generation could furnish no parallel for except in the brief period of 1885–6 [the Home Rule controversy]. He wondered how the advent of such a tremendous issue would affect the existing disposition of political parties. These were questions for the future … but the time would come when they would have to be answered.[1]

They would be answered very soon, and the answer would almost break the Unionists and keep them in opposition until 1915. From 1903 until 1906 and beyond, political debate was to be dominated by the battle between free traders and tariff reformers. While tariff reform did not lead to a mass breakaway from Unionists as Home Rule had done with the Liberals in 1886, it would split them and lead to Churchill himself crossing the floor in 1904.

Balfour had become Prime Minister in 1902 on a withdrawing tide. The Unionists had been in power for seven years and were badly in need of renewal. The mood of the country seemed to be changing. It was no longer satisfied with the negativism of the Salisbury regime, held in place in large part by fears of Irish Home Rule. But Home Rule did not now appear an immediate danger. Indeed, the Liberals themselves were seeking to disembarrass themselves from it. Imperialism, perhaps a vote-winner in the past, had been discredited by the Boer War – by the time it had taken to win it and by methods that seemed to have tarnished the morality of empire. It was difficult any

---

1   House of Commons Debates, 14 April 1902, vol. 106, cols 240–41.

longer to believe that the empire symbolised some noble ideal with an appeal over and above that of power or material benefit. In addition, by revealing the poor organisation of many British institutions, especially the army, the war had cast doubt on amateurish leadership by the landowning class. In April 1900, Kitchener had written to Lady Salisbury complaining that 'people here do not seem to look upon war sufficiently seriously It is considered too much like a game of polo, with intervals for afternoon tea ... A thorough reorganisation will have to take place before we can call ourselves a fighting nation.'[2] Medical examination of potential army recruits had revealed their dreadful physical condition. In Manchester, for example, no fewer than 60 per cent had been rejected as physically unfit.[3] A stance of non-intervention by government seemed no longer sufficient. The intellectual retreat of non-interventionism opened up an ideological space for new doctrines. But Balfour did not appear able to give the lead that Britain needed to confront these new challenges. He shared Salisbury's scepticism on the value of state intervention, had little sympathy with demands for social reform and was chary of new domestic initiatives. Even if he had not been so out of touch with the new social forces, he would have faced the task of galvanising a coalition formed and held together primarily on a negative basis. With the Irish question seemingly in abeyance for the time being, a question on which all Unionists were agreed, there was a danger of new controversies on which Unionists disagreed. These disagreements were now coming come to a head.

But the restless temperament of Chamberlain was searching for a new initiative which he believed necessary to revitalise Unionism. He had for some time been staking out a position independent of his Cabinet colleagues, a semi-detached position in the government. At the beginning of 1902, Moberly Bell, managing director of *The Times*, wrote that Chamberlain 'is perfectly loyal to the Government and yet somehow manages to keep detached from it. People think and speak of "the Cabinet – and Chamberlain".'[4] He was the strongest figure in the Cabinet and its most popular member in the country, but he was out of sympathy with his government's education policy and with the financial cheeseparing of successive Unionist Chancellors which was stultifying his programme of social and imperial reform. He appreciated that, after the Boer War, the Unionists were on the defensive and was determined that they should not run aground without a fight. In September 1903, he would tell the Duke of Devonshire that, even if the Cabinet and the Unionists had remained united, and tariff reform had not arisen, 'I believe

---

2   Magnus, *Kitchener*, p. 198.
3   Daglish, *Education Policy-Making*, p. 341.
4   E. H. C. Moberly Bell, *The Life and Letters of C. F. Moberly Bell*, Richards Press, 1927, p. 224.

we should have been [defeated] on Education and War Office Reforms', both of which he had warned the Cabinet against. The Education Act, as we have seen, had destroyed Chamberlain's Birmingham base. But his horizons were moving far beyond Birmingham. He had long feared that an industrial society would be insecure if it did not maintain a proper balance between capital and labour. As a Liberal in the early 1880s, he had demanded that the better off finance social reform as a 'ransom' to preserve the social system. As his horizons expanded, he feared that Britain would be unable to maintain her commercial supremacy without radical change. The key in his view lay with the empire, which alone could protect the British economy, enabling it to find the money to pay for social reform. Chamberlain had, for many years, embraced the empire, the reason, after all, why he had sought the Colonial Office in 1895 rather than any other senior posts in government which were his for the asking. Since the late 1880s, he had believed in imperial union. It had become his consuming passion. 'For my own part,' he told the Duke of Devonshire in September 1903, 'I care only for the great question of Imperial Unity. Everything else is secondary or consequential. But for this – to quote a celebrated phrase – I would not have taken my coat off.'[5] Imperial union, he believed, was the only way in which a small island could hope to compete with other great empires – Germany, Russia and the great continental power of the United States. These countries were equipped with protective tariffs, and unless Britain responded in kind, she would find herself 'hemmed in and helpless in an ever closing ring of armed opponents'.[6]

The cry of imperial union had first been raised by Disraeli. In a speech at the Crystal Palace of 1872, he prefigured much of what Chamberlain was to say thirty years later. Disraeli spoke of the relationship between Britain and the self-governing colonies. It had been right, he declared, to grant self-government. But it had been a mistake to regard it as separation. Instead, it 'ought to have been conceded as a part of a great policy of imperial consolidation'. It should have 'been accompanied by an imperial tariff' and also by the establishment of 'some representative council in the metropolis, which would have brought the colonies into constant and continuous relations with the home government'. But free trade had been the policy of every Conservative government since 1852 and neither Disraeli, during his premiership between 1874 and 1880, nor Salisbury had sought to challenge it. Salisbury, however, in his speech to the Colonial Conference of 1887 drew

5 Letter to Duke of Devonshire, 21 September 1903, Holland, *Life of Devonshire*, vol. 2, p. 355.
6 Amery, *Chamberlain*, vol. 5, p. 128. Chamberlain was speaking on his South African tour at the end of 1902 or early in 1903, in Milner's house in Johannesburg to Milner and Sir Percy FitzPatrick, a prominent South African journalist and adviser to the British government on South African affairs. Milner was impressed with Chamberlain's vision but believed that Chamberlain was too old to undertake the task of converting the electorate away from free trade.

attention to the German *Zollverein* or customs union and hinted at the value of a *Kriegsverein* or military union, drawing the self-governing colonies more closely together.

Chamberlain had once hoped that imperial union might be achieved through federation. As early as 1887, he had declared in Toronto that 'the federation of Canada may be the lamp lighting our path to the federation of the British Empire'. In November 1895, Chamberlain said that he had been 'told on every hand that Imperial federation is a vain and empty dream', but he believed that 'dreams of that kind ... have somehow or other an unaccountable way of being realised in their time'.[7] A month later he declared that he liked 'to look forward to the time when there may really be a federation of the Empire', and suggested that it be secured through colonial representation in the Imperial Parliament, something unrealistic in the days before air travel.[8] In the Commons in February 1900, held when Britain had been suffering reverses in South Africa, Chamberlain referred to the contribution of colonial troops to the war, reminding MPs, 'You are the trustees, not merely of a kingdom, but of a federation.'[9] At the 1902 Colonial Conference, he again insisted that a 'political federation of the Empire is within the limits of possibility' and that 'as time goes on, there will be a continually growing sense of the common interests which unite us, and also perhaps, which is equally important, of the common dangers which threaten us'. Chamberlain's approach seemed to have been welcomed by the Prime Minister of Canada, Sir Wilfrid Laurier, who had told Britain, 'If you want our aid call us to your Councils.' Chamberlain interpreted that as a proposal for common institutions. As a first step, he had proposed at the 1897 Colonial Conference a Council of the Empire, advisory at first, but later to acquire 'executive functions, and perhaps also legislative powers'.[10] But the self-governing colonies were not prepared to accept a council or any similar common institution which would threaten their newly won nationhood. A federation would be even more unacceptable since it would formally limit their powers. With imperial federation, the empire would become a kind of super-state, with a government centralised in Britain and an Imperial Parliament strengthened by colonial representatives. What would be the relative weight in a federal institution of Britain and the colonies? Britain would hardly be willing to allow the colonies to override her through majority vote. Chamberlain tended, like many in Britain, to see the self-governing colonies as mere extensions of Britain rather than as countries fast developing their

7   Quoted in Powell, *Joseph Chamberlain*, pp. 101, 106.
8   *The Times*, 9 December 1898.
9   House of Commons Debates, 5 February 1900, vol. 78, col. 623.
10 Quoted from the verbatim report of the conference in Amery, *Chamberlain*, vol. 5, p. 31.

own national consciousness. But Canadians, Australians and New Zealanders were not just men and women of British stock transplanted overseas; they were developing their own nationalisms distinct from that of the mother country and had not surrendered tutelage from Westminster only to have it resurrected in a body in which Britain exerted a predominant influence. But by contrast, Chamberlain's 'zeal for Greater Britain', so it has been said, 'was conditioned inevitably by his devotion to *British* interests. At the root of his imperialism he was a Little Englander.'[11] The colonies, however, had made their position abundantly clear in the 1897 Colonial Conference, when a resolution was passed declaring that 'the present political relations between the United Kingdom and the self-governing Colonies are generally satisfactory under the existing condition of things', with only New Zealand and Tasmania dissenting. 'This resolution', it has been said, 'dispelled forever the dream of imperial federation; though not all the dreamers at once awoke from it.'[12]

A second way of achieving imperial unity would be through a *Kriegsverein*, a union for purposes of defence. But similar and perhaps even stronger objections applied to this as to imperial federation. For a *Kriegsverein* posed the threat of dragging the colonies into a European war at the behest of Britain. Despite his appeal to draw the self-governing colonies more closely together, Laurier in 1902 declaimed against 'a school in England and in Canada ... which wanted to bring Canada into the vortex of militarism, now the blight and curse of Europe. He was not prepared to endorse any such policy.'[13] He even refused to contribute to Britain's defence costs. Indeed, the colonies contributed less than one hundredth of the cost of imperial defence and were certainly not prepared to contribute to an imperial defence policy decided at Westminster, without being given a share in the making of foreign policy. Otherwise, they would become subject to taxation without representation, the very doctrine that had led to the loss of the American colonies. In 1911, at the Imperial Conference, as the Colonial Conference was to be called, Asquith was to insist that Britain could not share responsibility for foreign policy or defence with the colonies. In any case, the colonies were coming to develop their own forces as allies of Britain rather than sharing in a common defence policy. So a *Kriegsverein* was no more possible than federation.

Chamberlain had to accept that any frontal attempt to secure imperial unity would run aground against the rock of colonial autonomy. He therefore switched his hopes in the direction of an imperial *Zollverein*, a customs union involving complete free trade with the colonies and a common

11 Madden, 'Changing Attitudes', p. 401.
12 Ensor, *England*, p. 241.
13 *The Times*, 14 May 1902.

imperial tariff. But a *Zollverein* would, like federation, require a supranational political organ to regulate the uniform tariff. Just over half a century later, the European Community, later the European Union, was to be founded on a similar basis of a uniform common tariff. There was to be a Commission and a Court of Justice to administer that tariff and adjudicate on disputes between the member states. Chamberlain hoped that a supranational organ to regulate trade might be acceptable, where political and defence union was not, since it appealed to mutual economic self-interest. He hoped also that it would lead to political unity with the colonies; just as the German *Zollverein* had led to the unification of Germany. But here too Chamberlain was to be disappointed. For the colonies were no more prepared to abandon their tariff autonomy than their constitutional and political autonomy. So an imperial *Zollverein* was not practical politics either.

But colonies were prepared to offer a tariff preference on British exports and the first suggestion to that effect was made at a Colonial Conference held in Ottawa in 1894.[14] Preference might make possible a step-by-step approach to imperial union, advancing it gradually and empirically by harnessing the forces of economic self-interest; and reciprocal tariff concessions would not raise awkward constitutional questions involving federalism or the sacrifice of colonial autonomy. In 1897, the Canadian government had given British imports a unilateral preference of 25 per cent, raised to 33⅓ per cent in 1900, so that British imports paid only 75 per cent of Canadian duties and then 66⅔ per cent.

At the 1897 Colonial Conference, the other colonies had agreed to follow Canada's example, and Laurier, the Canadian Prime Minister, made it clear that Canada's preference was not part of a bargain.

> We have not done it asking any compensation. We have done it because we owe a debt of gratitude to Great Britain. We have done it because it is not any intention of ours in any way to disturb the system of Free Trade which has done so much for England.[15]

THE CORN DUTY AND ITS REPEAL

The times, however, seemed congenial for Britain to abandon that 'system of Free Trade' and adopt a policy of mutual preference. In the 1902 Budget, his last, Hicks Beach had imposed a corn duty. He was facing a deficit of over £145 million, large by the standards of those days. This substantial deficit was

---

14   Ollivier, ed., *Colonial and Imperial Conferences*, vol. 1, pp. 65–6.
15   Quoted in 'Sigma', 'The Wreck of the Unionist Administration', *Fortnightly Review*, September 1903, pp. 376–7.

due not only to the unexpectedly high cost of the Boer War but also to what Hicks Beach rather archly termed 'the ever-increasing demands made upon the Exchequer flowing from our modern civilisation'.[16] Between 1895 and 1901, even with war spending excluded, government spending had increased by 40 per cent. How was this expenditure to be financed? 'Whenever', Salisbury had warned his Chancellor in September 1901, 'an honest and thorough effort is made to turn it [economy] into a practical policy, the government will go to pieces.'[17] Unionists regarded increases in direct taxation as confiscatory. But increases in indirect taxation would raise the cost of living and prove electorally unpopular. In 1902, however, Hicks Beach proposed both an increase in income tax and also a registration duty on corn of 3d a hundredweight with a 5d duty on imported meat and flour. This was opposed by the Liberals as a threat to free trade and an imposition on the food costs of the people, but it was welcomed by the leader of the protectionists in the Commons, Sir Howard Vincent, who shouted out, 'Well done, Well done,' when the corn duty was announced.

Hicks Beach, however, was a free trader and was careful to dissociate himself from the protectionists, insisting that the corn duty was a temporary imposition for revenue purposes only. He hoped that 'when peace returns', there would be 'no difficulty in settling our financial system on a basis which will be equitable to all the citizens of the country', implying that he would remove the duty as soon as economic conditions allowed. He insisted that 'the great clearance of the tariff with which the names of Sir Robert Peel and Mr Gladstone will always be associated' had yielded considerable advantages 'in increasing trade and commerce and the chances of employment at good wages of our working men'. He denied that the corn tax was inherently protectionist, reminding MPs that it had been retained by Peel in his free trade Budget of 1846 and by Gladstone in 1864, and had not been abolished until 1869. Hicks Beach insisted that he remained a free trader and indeed he was to prove a leading opponent of tariff reform.[18] But when he left the government with Salisbury in August 1902, he told Harcourt that he 'felt bound to go' since his colleagues were 'all protectionists' and 'he feared a breach in the conservative party'.[19]

Less than one month after Hicks Beach's Budget statement, Laurier, speaking in the Canadian House of Commons, declared that the corn duty was 'a step ... which would make it possible to obtain preference for Canadian goods'. He said that at the forthcoming Colonial Conference due to be

16 House of Commons Debates, 14 April 1902, vol. 106, col. 179.
17 Quoted in Gailey, *Ireland and the Death of Kindness*, p. 175fn.
18 House of Commons Debates, 14 April 1902, vol. 106, cols 179–80.
19 Gailey, *Ireland and the Death of Kindness*, p. 175fn.

held in July to coincide with the coronation of Edward VII, he would propose reciprocal preferences – as indeed he did.[20] A resolution in support was passed unanimously by the Canadian House of Commons. The situation was now different from what it had been in 1897. Canada was proposing to give Britain an additional preference; but, by contrast with 1897, this was to be conditional upon Britain agreeing to remit the corn duty on imports from Canada. Balfour, however, winding up for the government in the Budget debate, reiterated the government's position that the corn duty was not protective, and that the forthcoming visit of Laurier to Britain had 'nothing, direct or indirect, to do with this tax. This tax was put on for fiscal reasons.'[21] Then in June, during the committee stage of his Budget, Hicks Beach repeated his denial that the corn duty was 'a prelude to a Customs union of the Empire upon a Protectionist basis', and declared, 'I disclaim altogether the interpretation which Sir Wilfrid Laurier has placed upon the corn duty.'[22]

Nevertheless, at the Colonial Conference, the colonies proposed a specific system of mutual tariff preferences. If Britain did not respond, Laurier declared, Canada would abandon her existing preferences. The conference passed a resolution unanimously calling on Britain to grant a preference to the colonies. Chamberlain responded that he was prepared to open a discussion on altering the fiscal system. Would Britain, then, abandon free trade, a policy to which she had held since the repeal of the Corn Laws in 1846? That would involve an explicit acknowledgment that the corn duty was being retained for protectionist rather than revenue purposes, and that consumers should pay more for their food in the interests of colonial producers. But free trade remained the ark of the covenant for many, and it would not be easy to persuade the public that it should be abandoned. Chamberlain appreciated that the colonial proposal involved an alteration in the fiscal system, and told the delegates to the Colonial Conference in 1902, 'But I do not, myself, regard this as being an insuperable obstacle.'[23] Perhaps he did not yet appreciate how powerful the obstacle would prove to be.

Chamberlain, then, was receptive to the Canadian offer. In April 1902, over two months before the Colonial Conference, he had been entertained at dinner by a group of young Conservative backbenchers, including Winston Churchill. Earlier that day, Churchill had voted against the government. 'I am dining in very bad company,' Chamberlain announced at the dinner. 'What is the use of supporting your own Government only when it is right? It is just when it is in this sort of pickle that you ought to have come to our

20 *The Times*, 14 May 1902.
21 House of Commons Debates, 13 May 1902, vol. 108, col. 154.
22 Ibid., 9 June 1902, vol. 190, col, 167.
23 Amery, *Chamberlain*, vol. 5, p. 49.

aid.' But as Churchill relates in his autobiography *My Early Life*, during the dinner, Chamberlain 'mellowed, he became most gay and captivating' and as he rose to leave, he said, 'You young gentlemen have entertained me royally, and in return I will give you a priceless secret. Tariffs! These are the politics of the future, and of the near future. Study them closely and make yourselves masters of them, and you will not regret your hospitality to me.'[24]

But belief in free trade was held with almost religious fervour in late Victorian and Edwardian Britain. To dispute it, Campbell-Bannerman believed, was, 'after fifty years' experience of it ... like disputing the laws of gravitation'.[25] It was for many the basis of mid-Victorian prosperity and few could believe that one of the preconditions for its success, Britain's industrial supremacy, might now have passed away. As late as 1912, a Yorkshire Conservative bemoaned the fact that 'the poor people hereabouts look upon Free Trade as we do upon Trial by Jury ... an absolute fundamental right to buy eatables as cheaply as circumstance will allow'.[26] But free trade would not have exerted so tenacious a hold had it been merely a matter of economics. It was also a moral ideal, held to be the surest safeguard of international harmony and peace. Other countries, it was believed, would be less apprehensive of Britain's naval supremacy if she remained a free trade country, ensuring that world markets were kept open, than if she became protectionist. 'This', declared Sir Eyre Crowe of the Foreign Office in a memorandum in January 1907, 'is an aspect of the free trade question which is apt to be overlooked.'[27]

Free trade, therefore, was, *The Economist* had declared in 1843:

a good, like virtue, holiness and righteousness, to be loved, admired, honoured and steadfastly adopted, for its own sake, though all the rest of the world should love restrictions and prohibitions, which are of themselves evils, like vice and crime, to be hated and abhorred under all circumstances and at all times.[28]

'Not a bale of merchandise leaves *our* shores,' Cobden declared, 'but it bears the seeds of intelligence and fruitful thought to the members of some less enlightened community; not a merchant visits *our* seats of manufacturing industry, but he returns to his own country the missionary of freedom.' 'The doctrines of free trade', *The Times* had declared in 1879, 'are ... verities as

---

24 Churchill, *My Early Life*, pp. 366–7.
25 McKinstry, *Rosebery*, p. 451. The laws of gravity, of course, were also to be 'disputed' in the twentieth century.
26 Frank Trentmann, *Free Trade Nation: Commerce, Consumption and Civil Society in Modern Britain*, Oxford University Press, 2008, p. 79.
27 Gooch and Temperley, eds, *British Documents*, vol. 3, pp. 402–3.
28 *The Economist*, 2 December 1843, cited in Amery, *Chamberlain*, vol. 5, p. 221.

certain as the axioms of mathematical science, and, like them, are above the accidents of time and place'.[29] Imperialism was seen by many liberals not so much as the rule of one people by another but as a means of spreading the benefits of free trade and free movement of capital and goods – what would now be called globalisation. In spreading free trade, liberal imperialists believed, Britain would also be spreading a common conception of the rule of law, while protection would set nation against nation. So liberal imperialists as well as anti-imperialists could unite against protection. It would not, therefore, be sufficient to refute free trade solely in economic terms. Tariff reformers would also have to undermine its moral foundations – a far more difficult task. But Chamberlain was reacting against liberal imperialism. He believed in neither a natural harmony of classes nor a natural harmony of nations. His was a world of conflict: class conflict, which, if not confronted constructively, would lead to socialism and a destructive class war, and international conflict in a world in which other countries were jealous of Britain's commercial and imperial supremacy.

A further obstacle which Chamberlain had to confront was that tariff reform was seen as a ramp in the interests of wealthy industrialists. The Bishop of Hereford declared that 'this Birmingham Gospel is all in the interest of the rich and without mercy to the poor and needy'.[30] Churchill believed that tariff reform would render Parliament susceptible to endless lobbying from rich businessmen and the Americanisation of politics. It would mean

> a change, not only in historic parties, but in the conditions of public life. The old Conservative Party ... would disappear, and a new party would arise, rich, materialist and secular whose opinions would turn on tariffs and who could cause the lobbies to be crowded with the touts of protected industries.[31]

The Conservatives, Churchill feared, would become like the American Republicans. Indeed, Chamberlain's campaign, had it been successful, would have transformed the Unionists into a radical party of business. It would have become more like parties in the colonies which, unlike Britain, did not have a hereditary aristocracy. No doubt, Chamberlain felt that he had more in common with these colonial parties and with their leaders than with aristocratic leaders of the Unionists such as Lord Salisbury or the Duke of Devonshire, both of whom he had excoriated during his earlier radical Liberal phase.

The great economic historian Sir John Clapham had said of the 'fair

29 Quoted in Read, *Age of Urban Democracy*, p. 231.
30 Quoted in William Scovell Adams, *Edwardian Heritage: A Study in British History, 1901–1906*, Frederick Muller, 1949, p. 196.
31 House of Commons Debates, 28 May 1903, vol. 123, col. 194.

trade' controversy, which had preceded the tariff reform campaign, that 'its strength lay less in its economics, though they were not negligible, than in its sense of a changing world and in its nationalism'.[32] But the appeal was not only to nationalism but also to imperialism. For Chamberlain, like the free traders, was to give his policy a moral tinge – the ideal of empire. His vision bore some resemblance to the vision of European unity held nearly fifty years later by the founders of the European Coal and Steel Community, Jean Monnet and Robert Schuman. They too hoped that cooperation, which began with agreement on limited and beneficial economic objectives, would lead to a wider unity, something which could not be achieved in one fell swoop through a federal system of government but by the day-to-day practice of working together.

Balfour, as we have seen, had agreed with Hicks Beach's interpretation of the corn duty as a measure for revenue, not for protection or for colonial preference. But three days after Balfour's speech in the Commons in May 1902, Chamberlain spoke to his Birmingham Liberal Unionists and offered a quite different interpretation, declaring that the corn duty could form the basis for preferential relations with the colonies. The bulk of his speech was devoted to a review of events in Ireland since the schism of 1886 and the war in South Africa. Both conflicts, he argued, raised the same issue: the urgency of resisting fissiparous tendencies and bringing the colonies together into an imperial union. The need was even greater now than in the past. For Britain was faced not only with 'political jealousy' but also 'commercial rivalry more serious than anything we have yet had, the pressure of hostile tariffs, the pressure of bounties, the pressure of subsidies'. 'The intention', he warned, was 'to shut out this country as far as possible, from all profitable trade with those foreign States and, at the same time, to enable those foreign States to undersell us in British markets'. So 'old ideas of trade and free competition have changed. We are face to face with great combinations, with enormous trusts, having behind them gigantic wealth. Even the industries and commerce which we thought to be peculiarly our own, even those are in danger.' The only answer must be to

> draw closer our internal relations [with the empire], the ties of sentiment, the ties of sympathy, yes, and the ties of interest. If by adherence to economic pedantry, to old shibboleths, we are to lose opportunities of closer union which are offered us by our colonies, if we are to put aside occasions now without our grasp, if we do not take every chance in our power to

---

32 J. H. Clapham, *An Economic History of Modern Britain*, Cambridge University Press, 1938, vol. 2, p. 251.

keep British trade in British hands, I am certain that we shall deserve the disasters which will infallibly come upon us.

The challenges which Britain faced showed, above all, that 'the days are for great Empires and not for little States'. Accordingly, imperial union should be 'the great object of that national party that we call the Unionist Alliance, it is the destiny to which we are summoned, and it is the result for which your sacrifices are asked'.[33] Chamberlain was seeking, it was clear, more than a mere alteration in economic policy. What he wanted was nothing less than a reorientation in Britain's world role.

The immediate problem facing the government was how it should respond to the Canadian request for reciprocity. On 21 October 1902, Balfour put to the Cabinet the Canadian proposal that, 'while retaining the shilling duty on corn as regards *foreign* importation, our *Colonies* should be allowed to import it free'. There was, Balfour told the king in his report on the Cabinet proceedings, 'a very great deal to be said in favour of this proposal', and he said that he as Prime Minister 'leans towards it'. Nevertheless, he conceded, 'it behoves us to walk warily', since 'it raises very big questions indeed – colonial and fiscal – and the government which embarks upon it provokes a big fight'. For this reason it was vital, he believed, that 'no premature decision' be taken. The Cabinet, therefore, postponed a decision. But at a later meeting on 19 November, Chamberlain, before going to South Africa, pressed for a decision, first on remission of the corn duty, and second on the Canadian proposal. Balfour told the king that, after 'long and elaborate discussion ... the Cabinet resolved that, as at present advised, they would maintain the corn tax but that a preferential remission of it should be made in favour of the British Empire'. Ritchie was later to tell Hicks Beach that the Cabinet agreed with Chamberlain, with just two dissentients – himself and one other.[34] Ritchie entered a protest and a caveat. He explained that he could not possibly prejudge his Budget for the ensuing year some months in advance. By the time he came to deliver his Budget, economic circumstances might have so altered that it would be possible to abandon the corn duty. It appears that this caveat was accepted by the rest of the Cabinet, though in the absence of formal minutes it is difficult to be sure. What is clear is that the decision to maintain the corn tax and to offer a preferential remission to Canada was a provisional one, and accepted as such by the whole Cabinet, including Chamberlain. So the free trade ministers believed that the issue

---

33 *The Times*, 17 May 1902.
34 Hicks Beach, *Life of Hicks Beach*, vol. 2, p. 188.

was still open. Nevertheless, the prevailing feeling was that the Canadian proposal should be accepted.

Shortly after this Cabinet meeting, Chamberlain left for a three-month tour of South Africa to obtain greater understanding of the problems involved in post-war reconstruction. His visit confirmed his view of the enormous potentialities of the empire if bound together in a tariff union. On his return, he declared that he had

> felt for some time that this is a critical period in the history of the Empire. What we do now and what our colonies do will probably in the course of the earlier years of this century settle for all time the question whether a new Empire, such as has never entered into the conception of men before – an Empire bound together by invisible ties and yet of extraordinary strength – whether such an Empire shall be consolidated and maintained or whether we are to drop apart into several atoms, each caring only for our local and parochial interests.[35]

But while Chamberlain had been away, his plans had suffered what was to prove a fatal setback.

For in February 1903, Ritchie circulated a memorandum to the Cabinet foreshadowing the proposals of the Budget Speech that he would deliver in April. He wrote that he anticipated a surplus of over £8 million and that this would enable him to reduce income tax by 3d in the pound – he was in fact to reduce it by 4d. But were he to confine tax reductions to income tax, he would lay the government open to the criticism that he was reducing a tax 'which mainly affects the well-to-do' while leaving 'untouched the taxation which falls most heavily on the working classes', that is indirect taxation.[36] He therefore proposed to abolish the corn duty as well and told Balfour that he would resign unless the Cabinet agreed, since he could not in his Budget Speech defend a policy with which he disagreed. Ritchie argued that the only purpose of the corn duty had been as a revenue-raising tax. He could not accept the argument that it should be retained for purposes of preference. Balfour yielded to Ritchie, since he did not believe that he could resist a Chancellor about to present his Budget.[37] But Gerald Balfour had pressed his brother to accept Ritchie's resignation, and perhaps a stronger leader would have done so. The difficulties which this would have caused the government would have been nothing compared to those that were to ensue later in the

---

35   Amery, *Chamberlain*, vol. 5, pp. 117, 119–25, 148.
36   Ritchie's memorandum of 21 February 1903, Amery, *Chamberlain*, vol. 5, p. 153.
37   Dugdale, *Balfour*, vol. 1, p. 258fn.

year when Ritchie and the other free trade ministers were virtually forced out of the Cabinet and Chamberlain also resigned. Ritchie's resignation would not have been anywhere near as dangerous for the government as Chamberlain's was to be. But Balfour drew back from confrontation, as with the appointment of Sir Antony MacDonnell, and this was to have fatal consequences for his government. With Ritchie gone, the government could simply have renewed the corn duty and remitted it for imports from Canada. Later, the duty could have been remitted for imports from the other self-governing colonies. The huge ideological dispute between tariff reformers and free traders which was so to divide the Unionists would have been avoided. Balfour's mistake in submitting to Ritchie was to condemn the Unionists to years of opposition.

Yet Chamberlain too was at fault. The majority of the Cabinet, after all, had supported him on reciprocal preference. Had he himself made it a resigning matter, there can be little doubt that Balfour would have preferred to let Ritchie go rather than lose his most popular lieutenant on whom Unionist electoral hopes largely rested. But Chamberlain acquiesced, not perhaps appreciating that a decisive moment was at hand. On 31 March, the Cabinet duly agreed to the abolition of the corn duty. When announcing the decision to the Commons, Ritchie rubbed salt in the wounds of the tariff reformers by declaring, in the Budget debate on 23 April, that corn

> is in a greater degree a necessity of life than any other article ... it is the food of our people ... I do not think it [the corn duty] can remain permanently an integral portion of our fiscal system unless there is some radical change in our economic circumstances, or unless it is connected with some boon much desired by the working classes.[38]

It is clear, in retrospect, that the abolition of the corn duty destroyed the one means by which Britain might have departed from free trade before 1914. Such a departure could only have been achieved through a step-by-step approach, avoiding a direct confrontation of principle between two opposed economic philosophies. Reciprocity would have been a small step which could have been built upon pragmatically without appearing to raise fundamental issues; and it would have been difficult to oppose it without appearing to be hostile to the self-governing colonies. The appeal to imperial sentiment would probably have made it acceptable to all except diehard anti-imperialists, of whom there were few. This small step could have been the prelude to further small steps, each seemingly insignificant in themselves

---

38 House of Commons Debates, 23 April 1903, vol. 121, col. 256.

but leading eventually to the wider policy on which Chamberlain had set his heart. That wider policy could now only be instigated by a radical policy of new duties rather than the more conservative policy of preserving an existing one. Yet with Ritchie having vetoed reciprocity, Chamberlain was left with no alternative but to mount a frontal attack on free trade, an attack probably foredoomed to failure and one that split the governing coalition. The decision to repeal the corn duty ensured the defeat of imperial preference, a policy which the majority of the Conservative Cabinet and of Conservative MPs came to favour. It ensured that Britain would remain a free trade nation. Ritchie, whom Balfour was later to regard as 'the villain of the piece', is now a forgotten figure.[39] Yet it was he who gave the decisive death blow to the Chamberlain project even before it had been launched. The initiative now lay with the free traders.

THE TARIFF REFORM CAMPAIGN

Chamberlain's response was rapid. Shortly after the Budget, the Liberal Chief Whip taunted him with his lack of influence over the Education Act. Chamberlain smarted, thinking perhaps also of his defeat on reciprocity, and snapped back, 'You can burn your leaflets. We are going to talk about something else.'[40] That something else was the economic future of Britain. On 15 May 1903, Chamberlain spoke again at Birmingham and called for an 'inquiry' into the fiscal system. He made clear what conclusions the inquiry should reach. 'You have an opportunity,' he declared in his peroration. 'You will never have it again. And, for my own part, I believe in a British Empire, in an Empire which ... should yet, even if alone, be self-sustaining and self-sufficient, able to maintain itself against the competition of all its rivals.' The alternative was a 'Little England which shall thus be dependent absolutely on the mercy of those who envy its present prosperity'. He did not explain how self-sufficiency would be possible for an empire which imported most of its raw materials from abroad, while food from the colonies was insufficient to feed the British people, colonial food imports accounting for just one-quarter of total food imports. In addition, duties on raw materials would mean that manufacturers would have to pay more for implements and machinery. To tax food and raw materials, therefore, could seem like cutting off one's nose to spite one's face.

And once again Chamberlain appeared a Little Englander in his imperialism. Imperial preference was proposed as a scheme for uniting 'our own

---

39 Adams, *Balfour*, p. 207.
40 Amery, *Chamberlain*, vol. 5, p. 180.

kinsfolk … that white British population that constitutes the majority in all the great self-governing Colonies of the Empire'. It would not apply to those 'hundreds of millions of our Indian and native fellow subjects'. For India, a free trade country, tariff reform would have had a paradoxical effect. She would be asked to raise her duties on imports which would ruin the Lancashire cotton trade, largely dependent on exports to India. And Lancashire was indeed to remain hostile to the Chamberlain programme. There seemed no place for India in the tariff reform scheme. But even for the self-governing colonies, there would be a problem. For they would be asked not to develop new industries which might compete with those of Britain. As Asquith put it, in a devastating riposte to Chamberlain on 8 October 1903 at Cinderford, the colonies would 'be asked to stereotype their industrial condition, to arrest their industrial development in order that the Mother-country may keep and increase the hold she has on their markets'. Such a proposal 'would certainly tend to engender friction, to foment quarrel, and in the long run to kindle disloyalty'.[41]

Chamberlain had warned the Cabinet that he was intending to make a speech calling for an alteration in fiscal arrangements and there had been no objection.[42] As perhaps with other speeches which detonate political explosions, Chamberlain was to say little that had not been said before, except in his peroration, a warning to the opposition that at the next general election they would 'find that the issues which *they* propose to raise are not the issues on which *we* shall take the opinion of the country'. The implication was clear. The Unionists would fight the election on tariff reform. But the speech caused a political sensation. One young admirer, Leo Amery, later a Conservative MP and minister, was to describe it as

> a challenge to free trade as direct and provocative as the theses which Luther nailed to the Church door at Wittenberg. To many of the younger generation, passionately Imperialist by conviction, beginning to be intellectually sceptical about Free Trade, the speech was a sudden crystallisation of all their ideals in an imperious call to action.[43]

Within an hour, Amery had contacted his friends and they rapidly established a Tariff Reform League. But leading Liberals were also delighted. 'Wonderful news today,' declared Asquith, entering his wife's bedroom with a copy of

41 Garvin, *Chamberlain*, vol. 6, p. 477.
42 Dugdale, *Balfour*, vol. 1, p. 261.
43 *Sunday Times*, 7 February 1932.

The Times the day after Chamberlain's speech, 'and it is only a question of time before we sweep this country.'[44]

'We have reached', Chamberlain's biographer remarks, 'one of those points in history, when material and ideological forces, long damned up, suddenly find their spokesmen and break into the main stream of political life. To harness these revolutionary forces to their interest was the task which challenged Chamberlain and his colleagues.'[45] Chamberlain hoped at first to be able to link social policy with social reform. For him, tariff reform was not only a remedy for economic decline but could also provide money for social reform which, since Unionists were hostile to it being financed from direct taxation, would have to be financed from customs duties.

Balfour accepted that Chamberlain in his Birmingham speech had given 'expression ... to no sentiments which he had not before uttered on public platforms, and that it contained an exposition of no new doctrines'. 'For my part,' Balfour went on, 'I am ready to admit that no one would have had much reason to complain had his utterances stopped there.'[46] But they did not. A week after his Birmingham speech, on 22 May, Chamberlain told the Commons that the matter of old-age pensions was not a 'dead question; and I think it may not be impossible to find the funds, but that, no doubt, will involve a review of that fiscal system which I have indicated as necessary and desirable at an early date'.[47] But of course a main purpose of preference was to keep out goods from foreign countries; if it succeeded, the Exchequer would have less revenue, not more. How could a tariff both protect British industry by keeping out foreign goods and yet also deliver the revenue needed for social reform? To this question posed by the free traders the tariff reformers seemed to have no effective reply. The two aims seemed contradictory. So Chamberlain rapidly dropped the idea of financing pensions and social reform from revenues produced by tariffs; and on 28 May, in the Commons, Chamberlain had to admit that 'if you are to give a preference to the Colonies – I do not say that you are – you must put a tax on food (Opposition cheers)'.[48] For a preference on manufactures would not help the colonies which were primarily agricultural countries. Chamberlain then went even further by suggesting that duties might be levied not only on foreign food imports but also on foreign manufacturers. He was moving towards a full programme of protection. This, so Balfour was to tell the Duke of Devonshire at the end of August, 'was a quite gratuitous challenge both to

---

44 Margot Asquith, *Autobiography*, Thornton Butterworth, 1922, vol. 2, p. 53.
45 Amery, *Chamberlain*, vol. 5, pp. 390–91.
46 Dugdale, *Balfour*, vol. 1, p. 262.
47 House of Commons Debates, 22 May 1903, vol. 122, col. 1553.
48 Ibid., 28 May 1903, vol. 123, col. 185.

his colleagues and the world'. For neither of these two new proposals – food taxes and duties on manufactures – 'was there, in my opinion, justification or excuse'.[49]

Chamberlain's vision was of a self-sufficient empire based on security of supply and guaranteed markets for British manufactures. To the objection that abandoning free trade would impede economic change and therefore hinder progress, Chamberlain replied that such change as described in economic textbooks was destabilising to working people, compelled to shift from one industry to another according to market dictates. Tariff reform could appeal, Chamberlain hoped, not only to imperial and patriotic sentiment, protecting industry against the foreigner, but also to the working class, which sought security of employment. Free trade, he argued, had been a middle-class movement from the 1840s when the working class had been unrepresented. By contrast, tariff reform could unite the classes and yield a rallying cry for the dispirited Unionists. Free traders had argued that labour was easily transferable and that if one industry found that it could not compete with foreign imports, new more competitive ones would spring up in its place. If, for example, as Chamberlain summarised the free trade case at Greenock on 7 October 1903, sugar refining went, jam and pickles would replace it.

> Now, of all these workmen, these intelligent artisans, who were engaged tending and making the machinery for sugar refining in this country, I would like to know how many have found a resting-place, have found equivalent wages and comfort in stirring up jam-pots and bottling pickles … You cannot teach men who have attained to skill and efficiency in one trade, you cannot teach them on a moment's notice, skill and efficiency in another.

For Chamberlain, security of employment was more important than keeping down the price of food. 'What is the whole problem as it affects the working classes of this country?' he was to ask at Liverpool in October 1903.

> It is all contained in one word – employment. Cheap food, a higher standard of living, higher wages – all these things, important as they are, are contained in the word 'employment'. If that policy will give you more employment, all the others will be added unto you. If you lose your employment, all the others put together will not compensate you for that loss.[50]

49 Dugdale, *Balfour*, vol. 1, p. 262.
50 Boyd, ed., *Mr Chamberlain's Speeches*, vol. 2, p. 201.

It was no answer to say that the market would operate so that the unemployed could find other jobs. That was, he declared at Birmingham in November 1903, 'an admirable theory; it satisfies everything but an empty stomach'. It involved

> individual suffering that is caused by every transfer of employment, by taking the working man from some trade in which he has been brought up, and in which he has been engaged all his life, and settling him down to something else to which he is not accustomed, and for which he has no aptitude.

Men would, he had said at Liverpool, be

> dropped into the ranks of casual employment, dropped down into the 13 million [Campbell-Bannerman's estimate] be they more or be they less who are always on the verge of hunger. I say that the personal equation of suffering which all this transference of trade involves is the sort of thing which some political economists never think of at all.[51]

Chamberlain was proposing an alternative to fiscal redistribution, the answer of most free traders, whether Liberal or Labour, to social problems. He was arguing instead for a high-wage economy based on higher output which, he argued, tariff reform would ensure.

In addition, Chamberlain saw the shift from manufacturing to finance and services, a consequence of free trade, as something to be resisted, not welcomed. Manufacturing was for him inherently more rewarding. At Tynemouth in October 1903, he was to declare that without tariff reform

> we shall not only lose our commercial supremacy but the whole character of the country will be changed, and in the course of another generation this will be much less an industrial country inhabited by a race of skilful artisans than a distributive country with a smaller population consisting of rich consumers on the one hand and people engaged in the work of distribution on the other. In itself, the country might still be richer, but it would be a country – I was almost going to say not worth living in, and at any rate not a country to be proud of.[52]

But Chamberlain's approach was open to obvious objections. Tariff reform

---

51 Ibid., pp. 220, 243.
52 Ibid., p. 192.

would not necessarily help all industries. Some, such as coal and cotton, would be harmed not helped by the increase in food and raw material prices resulting from preference. A tariff on iron and steel would mean that farmers would pay more for agricultural implements. Further, to the extent to which tariff reform succeeded in maintaining employment, it would be by diverting labour from new and more profitable industries to the traditional labour-intensive sectors such as agriculture and textiles; and to the extent that tariff reform encouraged agricultural imports from the colonies, it would weaken rather than restore British agriculture.[53] Chamberlain's vision was as likely to inhibit progress as to encourage it.

Tariff reform was fundamentally a pessimistic and defensive policy. Its implication was that Britain could not hope to retain her mid-nineteenth-century dominance in world markets. Therefore, her best strategy was to cultivate the self-governing empire as a regional and self-sufficient economic bloc. The empire could be used as a shield against economic and political decline. In the 1960s, many argued for British entry into the European Community for similar reasons. All the same, Chamberlain was the first politician to show practical awareness of the implications of Britain's economic decline. He appreciated that her advantages were neither permanent nor exclusive, and he was the first leading politician to propose practical measures to do something about it. He was offering an alternative economic strategy based on national efficiency, mercantilist in nature, with an emphasis on wealth creation.[54] Tariff reform was a heroic if doomed attempt to prepare Britain for the new competitive environment in international politics, a world of great empires and militaristic nation states in which blood and iron would prove the arbiter more often than parliamentary majorities. Chamberlain was 'the first British statesman of the front rank to realise that Britain's future no longer lay wholly in her own hands', to appreciate that she could only resolve her economic problems within the framework of a wider trade system, the same impulse that motivated those who believed in the 1960s and 1970s that Britain should join the European Community.[55]

Was Chamberlain speaking for the government? Was tariff reform government policy? Balfour was rapidly made aware of the potential for disaffection amongst Unionists were the government to adopt it. On 24 May, his cousin Lord Hugh Cecil, youngest son of Lord Salisbury and Conservative MP for Greenwich, wrote to him saying, 'If the Government embark on Protection – under whatever specious name – our party must be split & for aught I can

---

53 Nicholas Crafts, *Forging Ahead, Falling Behind and Fighting Back: British Economic Growth from the Industrial Revolution to the Financial Crisis*, Cambridge University Press, 2018, p. 55.
54 Michael Balfour, *Britain and Joseph Chamberlain*, Allen & Unwin, 1985, p. 18.
55 Amery, *Chamberlain*, vol. 6, p. 1,050.

see Protection will do for us what Home Rule has done for the others.'[56] The former Chancellor Hicks Beach complained that Chamberlain's proposal had united the Liberals and divided the Unionists. If persisted in, he believed that it would destroy Unionism, and he began to canvas support for an organisation of Unionist free traders.

Balfour was neither a dogmatic free trader nor a dogmatic tariff reformer. He had informed the king that the Cabinet agreed that he should tell a delegation led by Chaplin, a former Cabinet minister and ardent tariff reformer, that there would be a 'possibility of reviving the tax [i.e. the corn duty] *if it were associated with some great change in our fiscal system*'.[57] Balfour was prepared to depart from free trade, and accepted the argument that imperial union required it. Austen Chamberlain was to tell Blanche Dugdale, Balfour's niece and biographer, in 1929 that Balfour had 'never had any sympathy with the Manchester Free Trade school, either in their economic contentions, or in the political corollaries'. Balfour found no objection in principle to Chamberlain's scheme and 'was as little inclined to treat Tariff reform as a dogma as he was so to regard Free Trade'.[58] He told his niece that 'Joe was becoming an Imperialist, and saw that Imperialism was impossible on the bare naked Free Trade basis – or at any rate that it would lose half its strength'. His niece asked whether he agreed. 'Yes, I did,' Balfour replied, 'I should say I did certainly.' But Balfour did not believe that a tax on food would be acceptable to the electorate; and his main concern was to prevent the Unionists from splitting. In 1899, he had discussed with Austen Chamberlain the premiership of Sir Robert Peel, whom Austen regarded as 'the last great Prime Minister'. Balfour disagreed, 'He smashed his Party, and no man has a right to destroy the property of which he was a trustee.' When, in the 1920s, Balfour's niece read Austen Chamberlain's letter which included this reminiscence, Balfour interrupted, 'I never can hear Peel praised with patience.' Peel had split his party in two over the repeal of the Corn Laws in 1846 and it was to be twenty-seven years before the Conservatives were able to form a majority government again. Balfour was determined not to allow any repetition of that disaster.[59] He was in fact haunted by the ghost of Peel. He sought, therefore, to contain or at least postpone the issue. That meant avoiding a debate on the merits of free trade and protection and discovering a formula on which the Cabinet could agree. His first task was to ensure that Cabinet differences were not publicly exposed. Since the Cabinet was not for the moment presented with any specific proposal to abandon free trade,

---

56   Gollin, *Balfour's Burden*, p. 56.
57   Dugdale, *Balfour*, vol. 1, p. 257. Italics in original.
58   Ibid., p. 258.
59   Ibid., p. 259.

Balfour told the Commons on 28 May, nearly a fortnight after the Birmingham speech, that he saw no reason why Chamberlain's speech should attract complaint or opposition. Chamberlain had called for an inquiry, a perfectly reasonable demand. And he proposed just such an inquiry. It would be in the hands of the President of the Board of Trade, who, by a happy coincidence, was the Prime Minister's brother, Gerald. It was far from being either an independent or a dispassionate inquiry.

The inquiry in fact was to prove perfunctory. It was not, as the Duke of Devonshire was to tell Arthur Balfour on 15 September, a 'real enquiry':

> I cannot admit that the collection of a mass of statistics without any attempt to enlighten ourselves or the country as to what they prove, or an abstract essay such as you intend to publish [a reference to Balfour's pamphlet, 'Economic Notes on Insular Free Trade', discussed below], constitute the kind of enquiry which I, at least, have been promising.[60]

But Balfour used the promise of an inquiry to play for time. He proposed that, during the period of inquiry, there be a truce and that free trade versus protection be treated as an 'open question'. What this meant was that, since the Cabinet had not yet come to a decision, ministers might continue to express differing views in Parliament without committing their colleagues. This device of an 'open question' was by no means novel. Indeed, writing in 1892, one constitutional authority had declared:

> Such great questions as parliamentary reform, the ballot, the abolition of the slave trade, hours of labour in factories, marriage with a deceased wife's sister, women's disabilities, household franchise in counties, and the Public Worship Regulation bill, with other minor matters have severally been considered as 'open questions' by some administrations.[61]

Later, the 1905 Liberal government was to regard women's suffrage as an open question. Balfour was drawing on a precedent, not creating one. Ministers were also asked to refrain from making speeches on the issue until the Cabinet had taken a decision except when required to do so in Parliament. This was accepted, but with a vital caveat. Chamberlain insisted that he be allowed to circulate material presenting the arguments for tariff reform, and indeed, during the period of the inquiry, his Birmingham Liberal Unionist

---

60 Holland, *Life of Devonshire*, vol. 2, p. 345.
61 Alpheus Todd, *Parliamentary Government in England: Its Origin, Development and Political Operation*, 1892 edition, edited by Spencer Walpole, Sampson Low, Marston and Co., vol. 2, p. 79.

Association was assiduous in preparing pamphlets and other propaganda. Free traders claimed that, while they were observing the political truce, their position was being undermined in the constituencies. In the words of one commentator, 'While they are supposed to be inquiring, Mr Chamberlain is agitating.'[62] Ritchie, for his part, insisted that he be allowed to state in the Commons his own position as a free trader. Indeed, on 9 June 1903, the very day that the Cabinet reaffirmed the doctrine of the open question, Ritchie had stated his position in the Commons in trenchant terms, telling the House:

> I avow myself a convinced Free Trader; and I do not share the views of those who think that any practical means can be devised for overcoming the difficulties which present themselves to me in connexion with their proposals; and, as at present advised, I cannot be a party to a policy which in my opinion would be detrimental both to the country and to the Colonies.[63]

Balfour was furious with him, and told a correspondent, 'Had he been more effective he would have almost been dangerous.' Perhaps the doctrine of the open question was suitable only for an era before the development of the modern political machine and extra-parliamentary agitation. It took all Balfour's skill in winding up the debate to resolve tensions. 'Under its magnetism [of his speech] even Mr Chamberlain and the Chancellor of the Exchequer sat side by side in the harmony of a perfectly amicable intercourse.' Balfour's conclusion was that 'the first act of the drama ends therefore fairly satisfactorily, but there are many more to come – and the plot promises to be complicated'.[64] It would clearly not be easy to contain Ritchie in a Cabinet which sought to depart from free trade. Indeed, it might not even be desirable. For the blunt manner in which he had expressed himself showed that he would not be amenable to any middle way formula which Balfour was able to devise. And Balfour had given a hostage to fortune in the debate by declaring that, on the issue of colonial preference, he had 'no settled convictions'. What he meant was that he sympathised with preference if he could be convinced that it would not involve large duties on food and if it were found acceptable to the electorate. For the moment, however, he believed that it did not seem practical.[65] But Balfour's wording was unfortunate and it was easy for the opposition to imply that he had no beliefs at all on tariff

---

62 'Sigma', 'The Wreck of the Unionist Administration', p. 328.
63 House of Commons Debates, 9 June 1903, vol. 123, col. 365.
64 Ridley and Percy, eds, *Letters of Arthur Balfour and Lady Elcho*, p. 200; Fitzroy, *Memoirs*, vol. 1, p. 136.
65 House of Commons Debates, 7 March 1904, vol. 131, col. 412.

reform. His position was caricatured by a radical MP, Sir Wilfrid Lawson, in a devastating doggerel.

> I'm not for Free Trade, and I'm not for Protection;
> I approve of them both, and to both have objections.
> In going through life, I continually find
> It's a terrible business to make up one's mind.
> And it's always the best in political fray
> To take up the line of the Vicar of Bray.
> So, in spite of all comments, reproach and predictions,
> I firmly adhere to Unsettled Convictions.

Sir Edward Grey commented that 'if the length of life of the Government was to be measured by the length of time during which Mr Balfour may continue to have no settled convictions it might have a long life'.[66] Lloyd George taunted that the Cabinet was 'shattered, split – and yet it lives. It is like a worm – cut in twain, but both ends wriggle – blindly, I need hardly tell you.'[67] The truce proposed by Balfour proved ineffective from the start, and the two sides ignored Balfour's pleas by continuing to organise. On 13 July, a Unionist Free Food League was formed. It attracted the support of just fifty-four MPs but would be supported by the two Unionist ex-Chancellors – Goschen and Hicks Beach – and Ritchie. The Tariff Reform League, however, was able to attract many more parliamentary supporters than the free fooders could muster.

Balfour had succeeded in postponing the moment for decision. But he could not delay it for ever. At two meetings in August, the Cabinet began to come to grips with the issue.

At the first meeting, on 13 August, two documents were produced. The first, 'Economic Notes on Insular Free Trade', represented Balfour's personal views and was published. It was written, its author proclaimed, 'from the free trade point of view, though the free trade is perhaps not always that which passes for orthodox in the House of Commons or on the platform'. For orthodox free trade principles assumed that capital and labour flowed without hindrance to wherever profits were greatest and wages highest. But such perfect fluidity did not exist in a world of protectionist empires and nations. Labour, in particular, was not fluid, since men 'are fond of home and country' and 'cannot easily acquire new aptitudes and new languages'. Nor could they 'migrate without cost and risk'. Unless Britain could acquire leverage to

---

66 The Times, 1 July 1903.
67 John Grigg, Lloyd George: The People's Champion, 1902–1911 [1978], Penguin, 2002, p. 64.

persuade other countries to lower their tariffs, she would be 'self-deprived of the only instrument by which [her] policy can conceivably be modified'.[68] That leverage would be tariff retaliation against countries imposing tariffs against Britain. 'The root principle for which Mr Balfour pleads', he was to explain to the king on 15 September,

> is *liberty of fiscal negotiation*. Hitherto it has been impossible for us to nego-tiate effectively with other Governments in respect of commercial treaties because we have neither anything to give which they wish to receive nor anything to take away which they are afraid to lose. Our negotiations are therefore barren; and we have been obliged to look on helplessly while in all the most advanced countries a tariff barrier is being built up against our manufactures which is an ever-growing obstacle to our legitimate trade development.[69]

Balfour was to insist that the government accept the fundamental principle of fiscal freedom. That meant departing from free trade as understood in the textbooks, since it would allow for retaliation. But fiscal freedom could mean much more than this. There were in fact three possibilities: retaliation, impe-rial preference and a general protective tariff. Balfour was strongly in favour of the first. He supported the second but believed that the time was not yet ripe for it. He was opposed to the third. But 'retaliation' was ambiguous. It could mean that tariffs would be imposed specifically against countries with tariffs against British goods, encouraging them to remove their tariffs, in which case it could lead to freer trade. But alternatively, it could mean a gen-eral system of tariffs with exceptions being made only in specific cases when other countries lowered their tariffs, in which case retaliation would lean towards protection. Balfour claimed that he intended the first interpretation. That was how he could declare that his 'Economic Notes' were written 'from a free trade point of view'. But he was sometimes held to mean the second interpretation. And perhaps he might have veered towards the second if the first did not succeed in securing a reduction of foreign tariffs.

There was a further difficulty. It was not clear that retaliation was com-patible with preference. Retaliation to secure a reduction in foreign duties meant bargaining with other countries to reduce their tariffs. Suppose that, for example, the Americans had offered to lower tariffs on British manu-facturing exports if Britain was prepared to put American imports in the same position as those of Canada. Imperial preference would prevent Britain

---

68 A. J. Balfour, 'Economic Notes on Insular Free Trade', Longmans, Green & Co., 1903, pp. 3, 4, 31.
69 Amery, *Chamberlain*, vol. 5, p. 395.

accepting such an offer. Duties on products from outside the empire would always have to be higher than duties on goods from within the empire.

But the idea of retaliation as a means towards freer trade meant that Balfour could sometimes describe himself as a free trader, on others as a protectionist. On some occasions he was praised by free traders and on others by protectionists. Sometimes he was attacked by both. In his 1906 election address, Campbell-Bannerman was to declare that there was no point concerning oneself 'with the question of whether Mr Balfour conceives himself to be a Free Trader, or a Protectionist, or both, or neither'.[70] Balfour's policy was not, as was often said, inherently ambiguous, or a product of unsettled convictions. It was complex and difficult for less subtle minds to comprehend. His policy had the further difficulty of attracting all the odium which free traders felt for someone departing from their creed without winning the support of ardent tariff reformers. And to avoid a party split, Balfour had to struggle to find a form of words which would show that what might appear as fundamental differences between free trade and protection were really matters of degree. This approach upset less subtle minds such as Chamberlain and the Duke of Devonshire. 'You cannot find a safe place on the fence,' Chamberlain told the Prime Minister.[71] 'You can't stop halfway through Niagara,' the duke was accustomed to say during the summer of 1903.[72] Once one accepted retaliation, there was no stopping point, the duke believed, before the full policy of protective tariffs was adopted.

But to add to the complexity, Balfour produced a second document for the Cabinet meeting of 13 August, called the Blue Paper, because of the colour of the paper on which it was printed.[73] Unlike the 'Economic Notes', the Blue Paper was not published. It was, by contrast with the 'Economic Notes', a Cabinet document rather than one representing Balfour's own personal views. The Blue Paper went further than the 'Economic Notes' in the direction of Chamberlain's policy of imperial preference by stressing 'the desirability of knitting our somewhat loosely connected Empire more closely together, not merely in matters political and military, but in matters commercial also'. Otherwise, Canada might 'withdraw her preference' and possibly join in 'intimate fiscal alliance with the United States of America'. If Britain did nothing, 'these contingencies are not only probable; they are almost inevitable'. Therefore, Britain should in principle respond to the Canadian approach and establish a preference, even though it might be currently impracticable.

---

70 Ibid., vol. 6, p. 778.
71 Ibid., pp. 518–19.
72 Ibid., vol. 5, p. 368.
73 CAB 37/65 1903, no. 47.

The Cabinet could not reach agreement at its two meetings in August and the decision was postponed to 14 September 1903, the crucial meeting. In the interim, Balfour received a report from his Chief Whip, whom he had asked to sound out party and popular opinion. This report indicated that while there was considerable support for retaliation, food taxes would be disastrous. Balfour's secretary Jack Sandars wrote that 'it was this report that probably decided the PM's attitude at the Cabinet'.[74] Balfour was to write to the king the day after the meeting that, 'though Colonial preference is eminently desirable in the interests both of British commerce and Imperial unity, *it has not yet come within the sphere of practical politics*'.[75]

RESIGNATIONS FROM THE GOVERNMENT

After the two Cabinet meetings in August, Balfour warned the king that he did 'not feel justified in entertaining any confident hope that he will retain the cooperation of all his colleagues for the scheme which he himself favours'. Nevertheless, he would

> do his best to steer between the opposite dangers of making proposals so far-reaching in their character that the people of this country could not be expected to acquiesce in them – and, on the other hand, of ignoring in a spirit of blind optimism the danger signals which indicate approaching perils to our foreign and to our colonial trade.[76]

Balfour had hoped the policy of supporting retaliation and accepting preference in principle while waiting to apply it until public opinion was favourable could achieve some degree of unity. But it could never secure the allegiance of the dogmatic free traders; and, if he sought to keep them, he would fail to secure the allegiance of the much larger group – those who sympathised with Chamberlain, while Chamberlain himself would come out in opposition to the government. So the free traders had to go. Apart from Ritchie, the free traders in the Cabinet were: Lord Balfour of Burleigh, the Scottish Secretary – no relation to the Prime Minister – and Lord George Hamilton, the India Secretary. All could be expected to resign in the face of a proposed departure from free trade. But they were not of sufficient political weight to threaten the government. There was, however, a fourth member of the Cabinet: the Duke of Devonshire, who sympathised with the free

---

74 Amery, *Chamberlain.*, vol. 5, p. 215.
75 Dugdale, *Balfour*, vol. I, pp. 266–7. Emphasis added.
76 Amery, *Chamberlain*, vol. 5, pp. 369–70.

traders, and whose prestige was such that his resignation might well threaten the government. Balfour, therefore, sought to detach the duke, whose position did indeed appear somewhat distinct, from his free trade colleagues. On 9 June, the duke had written to Sir Edward Hamilton, Joint Permanent Secretary to the Treasury, reiterating his opposition to Chamberlain's programme but distinguishing his own position from that of Ritchie, declaring, 'I am not so confident as Ritchie that the principles of Free Trade, or rather of Free Imports, are unassailable, and I do not object to a fresh inquiry into their effects.'[77] In the Lords on 15 June, he declared that, because of foreign tariffs, the free trade argument no longer held. 'The name of Free Traders cannot with strict accuracy be applied to the supporters of our present fiscal system. We are not Free Traders, because we have not got Free Trade.' That, of course, was also Balfour's view. In addition, the duke spoke with approval of the colonies' desire to enter into 'closer political relations', and reiterated that he welcomed an inquiry, since 'the people of this country are not so deeply impressed with the absolute perfection of our present fiscal and commercial policy'. He made it clear that he could not support food taxes but could 'conceive that an experiment in the way of retaliation might be tried'. This seemed promising from Balfour's point of view. But by 9 September, the duke's position seemed to have hardened, and he wrote to Balfour saying, 'My knowledge of political economy is very small, and I should find it difficult to argue with either an expert Free Trader or Protectionist, and I am too old to begin a new study.' But he was 'more and more convinced that this is and must be a fight between Free Trade and Protection and that no such compromise is possible between them'.[78] So his position remained uncertain.

The crucial Cabinet meeting of 14 September was intended to agree a policy, ending the period when the government's trade policy had been an 'open question'. A political explosion was widely expected. The meeting was indeed to prove fateful. The *Annual Register* for the year declared that 'the British public ... were startled by unquestionably one of the most sensational political events recorded in the long series of volumes of the *Annual Register*', which had been founded in 1758.[79] But what actually occurred is still not entirely clear, and was to be the subject of considerable dispute and recrimination amongst those involved.

Before the meeting, Balfour had received an unexpected benefit – a letter on 9 September from Chamberlain declaring that if food taxes were not to be part of the government's programme, he would resign. Otherwise,

---

77 Holland, *Life of Devonshire*, vol. 2, p. 310.
78 Quoted in A. W. Coats, 'Political Economy and the Tariff Reform Campaign of 1903', *Journal of Law and Economics*, 1968, p. 196.
79 Quoted in Gollin, *Balfour's Burden*, p. 116.

were he to remain in a government which abjured preference, the colonies would think that he had betrayed them. Chamberlain conceded that food taxes were currently 'unacceptable to the majority in the constituencies' and that, 'however much we may regret their decision ... no Government in a democratic country can ignore it'. He proposed to try to win over public opinion. The best way of doing this, he believed, was 'with absolute loyalty to your Government and its general policy' to 'promote the cause I have at heart from outside'. By resigning, Chamberlain would enable preference to be omitted from the government's immediate programme, and so hopefully allow Balfour to retain the duke, together, possibly, with other moderates behind Balfour's policy of fiscal freedom.[80] Chamberlain's letter, however, not merely prefigured his resignation but also laid down a plan of campaign, not only for himself but for the government he was leaving. He would campaign for imperial preference, while Balfour implemented fiscal freedom. The implication no doubt was that, if Chamberlain succeeded in converting the public, Balfour would adopt the full policy including food taxes. As assurance of goodwill, Chamberlain proposed that he would persuade his son Austen, the Postmaster General, to remain in the Cabinet; and he asked that individual ministers be allowed to continue to make the case for preference. Balfour accepted these proposals. But he did not tell the Cabinet on 14 September that he had Chamberlain's resignation in his pocket. Before the Cabinet met, however, Balfour and Chamberlain conferred privately with Gerald Balfour for around an hour, and it was agreed that, if the division of labour between them was to work, Balfour must secure the resignation of the free trade ministers.[81]

At the crucial Cabinet meeting on 14 September, ministers were faced with the two documents from the Prime Minister – the 'Economic Notes' and the Blue Paper. Ritchie and Balfour of Burleigh presented their own memorandum making the case for free trade. But instead of discussing this memorandum as no doubt they expected, Balfour rounded on them and announced that the period of inquiry during which fiscal policy had been an 'open question' was now at an end. Unless they could 'heartily' accept the government's new policy of fiscal freedom, they no longer had a place in it. The free trade ministers were, in the words of Sir Almeric Fitzroy, Clerk of the Privy Council, who relied in his diaries on what the Duke of Devonshire told him, 'practically drummed out' of the Cabinet. The day after the meeting, the duke wrote to Balfour declaring that he had 'never heard anything

---

80 Amery, *Chamberlain*, vol. 5, p. 415.
81 Richard A. Rempel, 'The Abortive Negotiations for a Free-Trade Coalition to Defeat Tariff Reform: October 1903 to February 1904', Proceedings of the South Carolina Historical Association, 1966, p. 8.

more summary and decisive than the dismissal of the two Ministers'. On 17 September, the duke told Lord James, a former minister and free trader, that 'Ritchie and Balfour of Burleigh did not really resign, but were told that they must go'.[82] They were shortly joined by Lord George Hamilton, the India Secretary.

But what was the government's new policy which the free trade ministers could not 'heartily' accept? They took the view, as Balfour had no doubt intended, that the government was to be committed to the policy in the Blue Paper: retaliation *and* preference, which was Chamberlain's policy. They claimed to be unaware that preference had been disavowed as impractical and that Chamberlain proposed to resign. But as only the 'Economic Notes' were published and not the Blue Paper, the public believed that the free trade ministers had resigned because they could not accept that, with preference dropped, the focus was on the more limited policy of retaliation. The free trade ministers were to claim that they had been deceived since they had not been told that preference was being dropped and that Chamberlain intended to resign. To this Balfour replied that Chamberlain had declared at the Cabinet meeting, as he had said in his letter, that he would resign if preference was not adopted. Chamberlain had also reminded the Cabinet that he had previously offered to resign rather than modify his demands, indeed that he rather regretted not having resigned before. But the free trade ministers did not appreciate that, since preference taxes *were* in fact being abandoned, Chamberlain's statement was no longer contingent but a definite commitment to go. He was no longer making a hypothetical threat to resign *if* preference were abandoned but a definite decision because preference *was* in fact being abandoned. As Balfour almost certainly intended, the free trade ministers did not appreciate the significance of Chamberlain's remarks. When they resigned, they believed that Chamberlain was remaining in the government. Balfour's defence was that the free trade ministers had given no indication of being prepared to compromise on strict free trade, even if preference were excluded, and would not support 'fiscal freedom' even in the limited form of retaliation.[83] He was later to write to the Duke of Devonshire, telling him that '*never once*' did any of the free trade ministers 'suggest to me that his objection to tariff reform would be completely met if no attempt were made to put a tax on food'.[84] Balfour argued that the central issue was not whether ministers would accept the whole Chamberlain policy, a policy which indeed he himself did not, for the present at least, accept; but whether they accepted -

---

82 Fitzroy, *Memoirs*, vol. 1, p. 49; Holland, *Life of Devonshire*, vol. 2, pp. 340, 352.
83 Newton, *Lansdowne*, p. 298,
84 Holland, *Life of Devonshire*, vol. 2, p. 353. Emphasis in original.

fiscal freedom in the form of retaliation. The objection of the free trade ministers was not, Balfour alleged, solely to the presence of Chamberlain in the Cabinet or his policy but to *any* departure from free trade. Their dispute was not with Chamberlain but with the Prime Minister. Preference admittedly raised further questions, but it could, Balfour believed, only be profitably discussed by a Cabinet which had already accepted the principle of fiscal freedom; and on this, Balfour regarded the three ministers as irreconcilables. The Cabinet could not, Balfour argued, have plausibly declared its policy to be one of fiscal freedom were the free traders to stay. But Lord George Hamilton later claimed that he *would* in fact have been prepared to consider retaliation.[85] Ritchie also stated, in a memorandum composed in September 1903, that he too would have been prepared to consider retaliation under certain conditions but that he had assumed that preference and food taxes, even perhaps a full-blooded policy of protection, were what was under discussion. However, in a speech to his constituents in Croydon on 8 September, he confessed that he would have resigned once he had seen the correspondence between Balfour and Chamberlain. All the same, it is difficult to acquit Balfour of duplicity in his efforts to hold the party together.[86]

Balfour regarded the Duke of Devonshire as being in a different position to the resigning ministers and now sought to detach him from the irreconcilables. At the end of August, he had told the duke how important it was 'to prevent our divisions reaching a point which may convert them into a national disaster and may deprive the greater interests of the country of the guardianship by which since 1886 they have been protected' – a split in the Unionists which could pave the way for a Home Rule government.[87] Shortly after the Cabinet meeting, Balfour spoke to the duke, and, in the duke's words, 'hinted that Chamberlain might resign'. Nevertheless, the duke met with the three free trade ministers the next day and it was agreed that he too would go. But the duke declared that he would have another conversation with Balfour and that it was 'possible but not probable' that he would reconsider his position. He prepared a letter of resignation but did not send it. Instead, he wrote to Balfour enquiring as to his precise policy with regard to preference. 'The time has come', the duke insisted, 'when the Cabinet must cease to speak with two voices.' That would not be possible with 'any reservations on your part short of rejection' of the Chamberlain programme. He concluded, however, that he had 'reason to believe that a distinct repudiation

---

85 House of Commons Debates, 7 March 1904, vol. 131, col. 422.
86 Gollin, *Balfour's Burden*, pp. 136–8; *The Times*, 9 October 1903.
87 Richard A. Rempel, *Unionists Divided: Arthur Balfour, Joseph Chamberlain and the Unionist Free Traders*, David and Charles, 1972, p. 54.

of it would affect the views of other members of the Government, perhaps more than my own'.

The Duke of Devonshire saw Balfour on 15 September, the day after the Cabinet meeting. Balfour again told the duke that there was a strong probability of Chamberlain resigning but not, as the duke later told the House of Lords, in such a manner as to lead him to believe 'that a definite tender of resignation had been made, still less that it was likely to be accepted'. And Balfour asked the duke not to mention the fact of Chamberlain's probable resignation to anyone, and in particular not to the free trade ministers. For if they had been told that Chamberlain was resigning, they would then realise that food taxes were being dropped and might ask for their resignations to be reconsidered. Balfour's request to the duke was a clear indication that many in the Cabinet had not realised that Chamberlain's talk of resignation was anything other than hypothetical. The Prime Minister told the duke that Ritchie and Balfour of Burleigh were being required to resign not only 'on account of the Memoranda which they had circulated, but on account of the attitude which they had assumed towards the fiscal question throughout all its stages'. The duke maintained his decision to resign, but, with his resignation letter, he attached a covering note offering a loophole, saying that if he was acting under 'a misapprehension of the circumstances', he hoped Balfour could put him right; but he added that if there was in fact a misapprehension, 'it was shared by others, who after consultation with me have taken more prompt action than I did, and that I could not honourably reconsider my position in any way without further communication with them'. His resignation letter declared, however, that since the question was no longer an open one, 'those who, like myself, hold that no sufficient case has been made out for disturbing the foundations on which the fiscal and commercial policy of the country rest, must definitely declare themselves on one side or the other'.

Balfour then called on the Duke of Devonshire and was able to tell him, since the resignation of the free trade ministers had now been accepted by the king, and there was no longer any possibility of their remaining, that Chamberlain had in fact resigned. It was thus clear to the duke that food taxes would not be part of government policy and that Chamberlain would not be campaigning for them as a member of the government. It was indeed a paradox that at the very point that the government was preparing to abandon free trade, the principal advocate of abandoning it was leaving the government because it was not prepared to be even bolder. But the duke now agreed to withdraw his resignation, writing to Ritchie, with copies to the other resigning ministers, seeking to distinguish his approach from theirs and rather awkwardly defending himself from the charge of a breach of faith.

Once the duke had withdrawn his resignation, Balfour wrote to Chamberlain accepting the Colonial Secretary's resignation. Chamberlain's letter of resignation now had to be redrafted to make what had been a contingent resignation an actual one. His letter and Balfour's reply were published in the press before the letters of the free trade ministers, and the public therefore assumed that the free trade ministers had been fully aware of Chamberlain's resignation before themselves resigning. In a speech on 22 October, Lord George Hamilton, one of the resigning free trade ministers, said that 'it was a pity that more care was not taken so to conduct the procedure of resignation as to prevent all cause for subsequent misunderstanding'. The *Annual Register* went further, declaring that there was a 'widespread impression that the Free trade element in the Cabinet had been reduced to conditions hardly compatible with the mutual confidence which was assumed to characterise the relations between ministerial colleagues'.[88] The duke seems to have shared this view. According to Fitzroy, he shared 'the feeling that the Prime Minister's ingenuity is open to criticism'.[89]

But Balfour's legerdemain was in the end to count for nothing. Admittedly, everything seemed, at first, to go well and Balfour proceeded to reconstruct his Cabinet. He asked Milner to replace Chamberlain at the Colonial Office. Chamberlain tried hard to persuade him to accept. But Milner refused, saying that he must continue his work of reconstruction in South Africa. 'All our misfortunes are owing to that,' Chamberlain later declared.[90] The post was then offered to and accepted by Alfred Lyttelton, a disciple of Milner whose name had been suggested by him. Lyttelton had been appointed by Chamberlain to chair a committee on reconstruction in South Africa and, in that capacity, had impressed the High Commissioner. He had other claims to fame, being the nephew of Gladstone and the only Cabinet minister to have represented Britain at both football and cricket. But he could not emulate the lustre of Milner, let alone Chamberlain. Lord Balfour of Burleigh and Lord George Hamilton were also replaced. But the most significant of the new appointments was the replacement for Ritchie at the Exchequer – Austen Chamberlain (1863–1937), son of the resigning Colonial Secretary and a guarantee that Chamberlain retained the Prime Minister's goodwill. Indeed, Balfour had urged this appointment as a clear sign that there was no fundamental 'cleavage on the matter of principle' between them.[91]

Austen was brought in to the government to ensure Joe's legacy, but it proved a poisoned chalice. For, while it gave him, by contrast with his father,

88 Gollin, *Balfour's Burden*, p. 157; Holland, *Life of Devonshire*, vol. 2, pp. 342–7.
89 Fitzroy, *Memoirs*, vol. 1, p. 153.
90 Amery, *Chamberlain*, vol. 5, p. 422.
91 Dugdale, *Balfour*, vol. 1, p. 270.

an early and privileged entry into national politics, it tied him to a policy which divided his party and was to prove unpopular with voters. Austen was a very different character to his father. Joe was a combative and magnetic if divisive personality, the great disrupter of politics. Austen was cast in a different mould. Joe had been an outsider, a self-made industrialist who had not attended university, Oxford and Cambridge being at the time closed to non-Anglicans. Austen, however, was able to take advantage of the removal of Nonconformist disabilities to attend Trinity College, Cambridge. He became an insider – conventional, acquiescent, uninspiring, scrupulously fair to his opponents and determined to adhere to the conventions. Whereas Joe had been radical in temperament, destroying traditional shibboleths, Austen was conservative, seeking to preserve not destroy. 'I do not believe', F. E. Smith was to say of him, 'that, as a young man, Austen Chamberlain saw visions, or that, as an old man, he will dream dreams.' Austen himself explained that he was not as radical in temperament as his father, 'But then you see I am not so young.'[92] One of Joe's mottoes had been 'Never explain, never apologise'. Austen, by contrast, came to believe that he had been wrong on two of the three great issues of his political career – self-government for the Boers and Home Rule. On tariff reform, his father's legacy, he remained steadfast, but his conviction was one of the factors that were to cost him the Unionist leadership in 1911. 'Tariff Reform', he was later to tell the press lord, Lord Beaverbrook, 'has been a millstone round my neck.'[93] He was not as skilful a parliamentarian as Joe, lacking his father's rapier-like swiftness and skill in debate. He was, one official believed, 'slow and sure, not at all clever'.[94] He was to prove a pale imitation of his father. 'His contribution to public life', a commentator was to write in 1926, 'is that of a conscientious and painstaking rectitude, but he belongs to the past, and has no vision of the future. He was born under the shadow of a great name, and from that shadow he will not emerge.'[95] Lord Beaverbrook was to write unkindly of him:

> Nothing in my head I bring.
> Only to my name I cling.[96]

Once in government, he failed to warn his father of Balfour's unwillingness to follow the full tariff reform policy. Seduced by Balfour's charm, he nourished his father's illusion that the Prime Minister was fundamentally in

92 David Dutton, *Austen Chamberlain: Gentleman in Politics*, Ross Anderson, 1985, pp. 13, 31.
93 Gollin, *Balfour's Burden*, p. 127.
94 W. J. Braithwaite, *Lloyd George's Ambulance Wagon: Being the Memoirs of William J. Braithwaite*, Methuen, 1957, p. 188.
95 A. G. Gardiner, *Portraits and Portents*, Harper & Brothers, 1926, p. 113.
96 Quoted in John Charmley, *A History of Conservative Politics, 1900–1996*, Macmillan, 1996, p. 63.

sympathy. By March 1905, it seems that Joe thought his son should resign from the Cabinet.[97] But Austen was not a man for such dramatic gestures. He was to prove an inadequate substitute for his father.

Having reconstructed his government, Balfour's next task was to announce the government's new policy of fiscal freedom at the Conservative Party's annual conference at Sheffield on 1 October. Balfour reiterated that he could not for the moment support colonial preference 'because I believe the country will not tolerate a tax on food', a statement met with silence from the audience. Indeed, his speech received only a tepid response. But every mention of Chamberlain's name met with great applause. When Balfour told the conference that he intended to lead, the protectionist Leo Amery shouted from the back of the hall, 'What about Joe?' to more cheering.[98]

But the Duke of Devonshire was becoming increasingly uneasy, conscious that he had exposed himself to accusations of a breach of faith with the free traders. 'To think', he said to another peer, 'I have gone through all my life, and then at the end of it to have these sorts of accusations levelled at my head.' Balfour's secretary believed that the duke 'literally could not sleep at night for the feeling that in the minds of the three secessionists he had treated them badly'.[99] The duke came gradually to believe that the Prime Minister differed from Chamberlain not on fundamentals but solely on practicability. Balfour had *not*, the duke was coming to believe, abandoned preference in principle. The Prime Minister's Sheffield speech provided the duke with just the excuse he needed to join the free traders by resigning. He complained that Balfour had not mounted any defence of free trade – instead, Balfour had said that Cobden's doctrines had been suitable for his own times but were not relevant to current conditions; nor had Balfour set any definite limits to fiscal freedom. So he had left the way open for the full Chamberlain policy. Had Balfour in fact set out such limits, Chamberlain would no doubt have come out in opposition to him. But in any case, the duke had decided upon resignation before the speech was delivered.[100] In his new resignation letter, written the day after Balfour's Sheffield speech, the duke declared that he could not accept any attempt to 'reverse the fiscal tradition, to alter fundamentally the fiscal tradition, which has prevailed during the last two generations'. He had hoped, the duke went on, 'to have found in your speech a definite statement of adherence to the principles of Free trade as the ordinary basis of our fiscal and commercial system'. Instead, the speech would

97 Amery, *Chamberlain*, vol. 6, p. 681.
98 Ibid., vol. 5, pp. 441, 2.
99 Gollin, *Balfour's Burden*, pp. 172, 181.
100 Ibid., p. 285.

have the effect of materially encouraging the advocates of direct Protection in the controversy which has been raised throughout the country, and of discouraging those who, like me and, I had hoped, yourself, believe that our present system of free imports, and especially of food imports is, on the whole the most advantageous to the country.

Balfour was, understandably, angry, since he had said nothing new in his Sheffield speech. Nor had he departed from 'Economic Notes on Insular Free Trade'. Indeed, that document had been deliberately crafted with the intention of keeping the duke in the government. 'Am I unreasonable', he asked in replying to Devonshire's resignation letter, 'in thinking that your resignation gives me some just occasion of complaint?' The duke was leaving the government, Balfour complained, when 'its fortunes are at their lowest, and its perplexities are at their greatest'.[101] But it was all to no avail. The duke's mind was now made up. His long ministerial career which had begun forty years earlier in 1863 was now at an end. In 1907, he was to join Rosebery on the cross benches, since he believed that the Unionists were now 'up to the neck in tariff reform'.[102] Many years later, in 1926, Balfour told his niece and biographer that he doubted whether the duke had really understood the issues at stake at all.

> Dear Devonshire ... told me once he had been content to leave his financial conscience in the hands of Mr Gladstone. But it was all a muddle. He got himself into such a position that he had to behave badly to somebody – and there it was! But it never made the slightest difference to my love for him.[103]

The duke, however, often pretended, as we have seen, to be more stupid than he was, and may well have had a greater understanding of the issues than Balfour realised. Perhaps he understood perfectly well that retaliation, far from being a means to securing free trade, would open the door to wider protection. But whether that was so or not, all Balfour's subtleties and re-monstrances now turned out to be of little use. All he had achieved was to ensure that the duke's resignation did not occur at the same time as that of the irreconcilable free traders; but that was scant consolation. After five ministerial resignations, he now had the leader of the tariff reform campaign, as well as a potential leader of the Unionist free traders, outside the govern-ment. In just over a year, the government had lost Salisbury, Hicks Beach,

---

101 Holland, *Life of Devonshire*, vol. 2, pp. 365–6.
102 Rhodes James, *Rosebery*, pp. 462, 463.
103 Dugdale, *Balfour*, vol. 1, p. 271.

Lord James, Chamberlain, Ritchie, Lord Balfour of Burleigh, Lord George Hamilton and the Duke of Devonshire.

> All Balfour's skill and subtlety had been in vain. He had sacrificed his most powerful colleague for nothing. He had thrown over the Preference plank of the programme – the only part of it which could inspire passion and idealism, and still failed to keep the only Free Trader who mattered. And now he was accused by his own party of sitting on the fence and letting Chamberlain down.[104]

REALIGNMENT THWARTED

Few believed that the government could survive for much longer. Both sides in the tariff reform controversy now strengthened their organisations. The Unionist Free Food League organised a public rally in London in November at which nine ex-Cabinet ministers spoke in favour of free trade. It seemed that the split might be even more serious than the Liberal divide on the Boer War, for in December 1903 the Duke of Devonshire, President of the Liberal Unionists, supported by two other Liberal Unionists, Lord James and Lord Goschen, urged Unionists not to vote for tariff reform candidates in by-elections. And in 1904 the duke went even further, urging a vote for the Liberals in the Chertsey by-election. Neither the Liberal Imperialists nor the radicals in the Liberal Party had gone so far as to suggest that voters should desert their party. But by contrast with Chamberlain, the Unionist free traders had little understanding of mass politics, and, unlike the Tariff Reform League, were unable to establish constituency branches. They may have had widespread support in the country, but they had little support in the Commons or amongst Unionist activists, the majority of whom were for Chamberlain. The duke was certainly not speaking for the majority of Liberal Unionist members, and was easily outmanoeuvred by Chamberlain.

The duke proposed that Liberal Unionist constituency associations remain neutral in the controversy. They had, he insisted, been formed for one purpose only, preservation of the Union with Ireland, and should not be used for another purpose, tariff reform. If Chamberlain would not agree, the Liberal Unionist organisation should be dissolved. But Chamberlain retorted that the party's policy should be determined by the free choice of local associations, the majority of which supported tariff reform. Therefore, they should be able, if they so wished, to deselect free food candidates, replacing them with tariff reform candidates; and it would be absurd to dissolve the Liberal

---

104 Amery, *Chamberlain*, vol. 5, p. 446.

Unionist organisation when the members wanted it to continue simply be-cause the duke could not accept the majority view. Besides, in advising Un-ionist free traders not to support Unionist candidates in by-elections, the duke, as president of the Liberal Unionist Association, had himself violated its neutrality. Chamberlain, a master of organisational politics, was able to take over the Liberal Unionist organisation for his cause. The Unionist free traders proved to be leaders without followers.

Having lost control of the organisation, the Unionist free traders cast around for support elsewhere. Some contemplated an electoral pact with Liberal Imperialists, many of whom did not want a Campbell-Bannerman premiership, to create a centre party. Indeed, Gerald Balfour told Austen Chamberlain in December 1903 that there was no logic to the duke's advice to voters not to vote for tariff reform candidates,

> unless he means to go further and throw in his lot with the other side. I am inclined to think it is coming to this, and the idea of a coalition party, and (if they succeed in defeating us) a coalition government, formed of Liberals and Free Fooders is once more in the air.[105]

Between December 1903 and February 1904, there were negotiations in which Liberals suggested that if Unionist free traders would vote against the government on a free trade motion or amendment to the address, they would not have to face a Liberal opponent in a general election. This would be a reversal of the pact between Conservative and Liberal Unionists in 1886 which had secured Unionist hegemony for twenty years. On 21 December 1903, there was a discussion between Lord James and Asquith. The next day, James wrote to the duke telling him that Asquith 'does not wish Spencer [Liberal leader in the Lords] to form a Government – and will not do so himself – I said what then – and a shrug of the shoulders was the only reply – I said, "the Duke". "I hope so" was the answer.' According to Asquith, Campbell-Bannerman had told him at around this time that were the Lib-erals to win the election, he would become Prime Minister in the Lords. This would assist with a pact since Campbell-Bannerman was anathema to Unionists as a radical and pro-Boer. 'Our people hate CB,' James declared.[106] But negotiations got nowhere. The duke, though tempted, was too old and too strong a Unionist to want to leave his old party to the tender mercies of Chamberlain. What he hoped for instead was to protect Unionist free trade

---

105 Quoted in Richard A. Rempel, 'Tariff Reform and the Resurgence of the Liberal Party, May 1903 to February 1904', Proceedings of the Canadian Historical Association, 1967, p. 164.
106 Devonshire Papers, quoted in Peter R. Gregory, 'The Eighth Duke of Devonshire and the Tariff Reform Controversy, 1902 to 1908', PhD thesis, Manchester University, 1972, p. 347.

MPs from deselection in their constituencies. So, while prepared to consider electoral cooperation, he was not prepared to reverse the role he had played in 1886 by supporting a Liberal/Unionist free trade coalition; while the Education Act remained a barrier for both Liberals and Unionists. Lord Spencer, Liberal leader in the Lords, told Campbell-Bannerman in December 1903 that the Liberals could not alter their attitude on education or they would lose Nonconformist support.

By January 1905, he was

> sure that in the interests of Free Trade it is essential that we should carry Non Conformists with us on Education, and if we do, then we secure them for a Free Trade vote. If we offend the Non Conformists we strike a serious blow at Free Trade ... Can a union of parties be made between us and the Duke of Devonshire, and his Liberal Unionist Free Traders, also with the Conservative Free Traders ... It involves agreement on (a) Home Rule (b) Education Policy ... (a) and (b) are vital.[107]

Spencer himself was prepared to sacrifice Home Rule for an agreement with Unionist free traders but not education. For their part, few Unionists would support a party intending to legislate to meet Nonconformist grievances in education. Ireland and imperialism were also barriers since Unionist free traders were not convinced that Liberals were really prepared to retreat from Home Rule and from a Little England imperial policy. On 29 June 1904, Lord Hugh Cecil told the Duke of Devonshire that he would have no objection to working with 'moderate' Liberals.

> But ... the main stream of Liberalism does not run in that direction. That stream is Gladstonian in foreign, colonial and Irish questions. It is non-conformist in ecclesiastical and educational questions; it is Radical in questions affecting property; it is Trade Unionist in questions affecting labour and capital. For those of the Free Food League who are Imperialists and Unionists and Churchmen and Conservatives, a permanent co-operation with such a party could not be otherwise than immoral.[108]

Winston Churchill, now a Liberal, pointed out to the duke the difference from 1886 when the Liberal Unionists had '*wanted* to fight with the Conservatives. Nearly all your people – Free Trade apart – would like to see the

---

107 Peter Gordon, ed., *The Red Earl: The Papers of the Fifth Earl Spencer, 1835–1910*, Northamptonshire Record Society, 1986, vol. 2, p. 319.
108 Holland, *Life of Devonshire*, vol. 2, pp. 373–4.

Liberals get a good beating.'[109] Devonshire agreed and, in a letter to Balfour, highlighted the contrast with 1886. Then there had been 'no serious differences between Liberal Unionists and Conservatives which might have prevented a practical alliance. There are no doubt now many more serious differences between Free Trade Unionists and the radicals and it is this fact which has hitherto prevented any similar alliance being formed.'[110] In any case, Unionist free traders seemed to have little to bring to Liberal Imperialists. The Liberal Unionists of 1886 had a firm regional base in the West Midlands. Unionist free traders had no such electoral base. Indeed, neither Liberal Imperialists nor Unionist free traders could guarantee the strong constituency base needed to sustain a new party. So a centre party would be, as Harcourt had said of a similar attempt by Lord Randolph Churchill in the 1880s, 'all centre and no circumference'.[111] But above all, the Liberals saw little reason to cooperate with a party seemingly in irretrievable electoral decline, since they believed that they could defeat tariff reform by themselves, while Campbell-Bannerman was not unaware that an electoral pact would be at the expense of his leadership, and might lead to his replacement by a Liberal Imperialist. Liberal calculations were that by-elections would split the Unionist not the free trade vote, since some Unionists would abstain or vote Liberal rather than support a tariff reformer. Asquith, after a meeting with Hicks Beach in December 1903, told Campbell-Bannerman, of the Unionist free traders, 'they look very well in the shop-window, but I fear that ... their voting strength is insignificant.'[112] The Liberals would only have been prepared to consider electoral cooperation had Unionist free traders been willing to turn the government out as the Liberal Unionists had done in 1886; and of that there was no sign. By January 1905, Hicks Beach was writing to the Duke of Devonshire that 'the only thing to be done' with the Free Food League 'is to let it drop quietly out of existence ... my own impression is that the Free Food League has done so little for so many months that no one will notice its extinction!'[113] The timing was unfortunate for Unionist free traders. The Liberals had been reunited by opposition to the Education Act while the pact between the Liberals and the Labour Representation Committee in September 1903 had increased Liberal confidence. Liberals now believed that they could win a majority without needing Unionist defectors. From January to March 1904, they won four by-elections from the Unionists and

---

109 H. W. McCready, 'The Revolt of the Unionist Free Traders', *Parliamentary Affairs*, 1963, p. 204.
110 Ibid., p. 205.
111 Gardiner, *Harcourt*, vol. 2, p. 586.
112 Gregory, 'Eighth Duke of Devonshire', p. 352.
113 Huw Clayton, 'How Not to Run a Political Campaign: The Failure of the Unionist Free Traders, 1903–6', *Parliamentary History*, 2011, pp. 167, 169.

this increased their confidence even further. Campbell-Bannerman's position was strengthened and the Liberal Imperialists now appeared to be in decline. In addition, hardly any Liberal would be prepared to vote for a Unionist free trader when a Liberal or Labour candidate was in the field. By the time of the 1906 election, twelve Unionist free trade MPs including Churchill had joined the Liberals and a further five were to join afterwards, while twenty-two had retired or gone to the Lords. In the election, fifty-six Unionist free traders were to fight seats; nine faced tariff reform opponents. All but six faced Liberal opponents, and three of the six who did not sat for university seats. After the election, there were just eleven Unionist free trade MPs in the Commons, and after the January 1910 election just one – Lord Hugh Cecil, a member for Oxford University.[114] Ironically, it was only after that election that the Unionists were to retreat from tariff reform, which appeared to be a vote loser.

In the 1906 general election, Unionist free traders were divided as to whether protection or Home Rule was the greater danger and so unable to advise supporters how they should vote. In 1886, by contrast, the defeat of Home Rule had been the *overriding* issue both for Conservatives and Liberal Unionists, and they had been prepared to go to great lengths to defeat it. But in 1903, preserving free trade was *not* seen as similarly overriding. It competed with other issues such as education, the role of the Anglican Church and domestic reform. It competed also with questions of personality and leadership. In 1886, Liberal Unionists had been prepared to accept a government led by Salisbury. But Unionist free traders were not similarly prepared to accept Campbell-Bannerman as their leader, while the Liberals, a party of the left, were not prepared to accept the very conservative Duke of Devonshire as leader of a free trade coalition. So realignment proved a chimera.

DIVIDED COUNSELS AND THE END OF THE UNIONIST GOVERNMENT

Balfour proposed to hold his government together through the policy of fiscal freedom, which meant in practice retaliation. The policy itself was perfectly clear, but if Balfour was to succeed, he had to present it in a manner which was anything but clear. He had to use convoluted language to convince both free traders and protectionists that his instincts were with them. He insisted, therefore, that retaliation was in no way a departure from genuine free trade since its aim was to secure a reduction of foreign tariffs. He declared in

114 Rempel, *Unionists Divided*, pp. 228–30.

addition that he was opposed to protection, in the sense of duties on manufactured goods. His government was not, therefore, protectionist. Nevertheless, it should, he argued, be supported by protectionists since it favoured retaliatory tariffs. Balfour's policy, therefore, could, he hoped, be defended by both free traders and protectionists. There was a certain logic to Balfour's position. But it is not surprising if many found themselves confused.

The greatest danger to the government came not from free traders but from Chamberlain and his tariff reformers, who had much greater appeal to Unionist grassroots. No doubt, both Balfour and Chamberlain had hoped that they could remain in broad accord. The main issue on which they differed, after all, seemed to be not one of principle but rather the electoral acceptability of food taxes, which Balfour claimed not to object to in principle. Chamberlain's task was to speed public acceptance of this policy. Balfour's, it seemed, was to hold the fort until the public had been converted. But Balfour became increasingly convinced that food taxes would be electorally disastrous. 'The prejudice against a small tax on food', he was to insist on 18 February 1905,

> is not the fad of a few imperfectly informed theorists: it is a deep-rooted prejudice affecting the large mass of voters, especially the poorest class …
> The obstacle with which the candidate is confronted is not the opinion of the local leaders, but the absolute impossibility of inducing the mass of the voters to do anything which they can be made to believe would increase the price of bread.[115]

So the gap between Chamberlain and Balfour rapidly widened. Chamberlain, after all, was a man of sixty-seven with few active years of political life left. He was now unmuzzled and impatient, an old man in a hurry, believing the issue was urgent and that if Britain did not respond rapidly to the colonies, the opportunity would not recur.

In his first post-resignation speech at Glasgow, Chamberlain produced a wide-ranging programme of tariff reform. He reiterated that 'if you wish to have preference … you must put a tax on food. The murder is out.'[116] He also widened his policy by introducing a wholly new element, a 10 per cent general tariff on manufactured goods. So he was now committed not only to preference but also to protection. He had come to believe that preference could not succeed without a general tariff. In addition, preference seems not to have found much of an echo in the country, whereas protection

---

115 Quoted in Alan Sykes, *Tariff Reform in British Politics, 1903–1913*, Clarendon Press, 1979, p. 86.
116 Boyd, ed., *Mr Chamberlain's Speeches*, vol. 2, p. 157.

might prove more popular with industrial employers and employees. But the adoption of protection widened even further the distance between himself and the Prime Minister. Chamberlain's policy, however, rapidly won the support of party activists and constituency associations, pressed by the Tariff Reform League to adopt candidates committed to the full programme. In October 1903, Lord George Hamilton lamented to the Duke of Devonshire, 'I am afraid that Chamberlain has captured the machine and inoculated the Unionist constituencies to a greater extent than I had anticipated. My electors are almost to a man against me upon the fiscal question: they are very stupid, but so is a large proportion of the electorate.'[117] The League sought to excommunicate those who disagreed with the Chamberlain programme. Particular pressure was exerted in Greenwich against the candidacy of Lord Hugh Cecil, who complained that 'the older doctrine of the independence of politicians' was being superseded by the 'enforcement of opinions by menaces unmatched even in the history of religion'.[118] Indeed, tariff reform was becoming as much of a religion as free trade had been. 'When a man has become a convinced Tariff Reformer,' Austen Chamberlain was to tell Balfour in 1910, 'nothing will shake him. It is a religion and he becomes its ardent missionary. These are our best workers.'[119] The Chief Whip sought to prevent the Greenwich constituency association from seeking Lord Hugh's resignation but to no avail, since the Chamberlain machine was beyond the control of Conservative Central Office. When Chamberlain called on those who could not accept tariff reform to leave the party, Lord Hugh enraged him saying that he would not leave 'at the bidding of one who ... was after all, in his origin only an alien immigrant', i.e. a Liberal Unionist and a Nonconformist.[120]

Chamberlain appreciated that it would take time to win public support for the new policy. He did not expect to carry the country at the next general election, which, he assumed, would, on the analogy of 1892, lead to a weak Liberal administration unable to govern effectively. If the Unionists were united around his policy, then at the general election after the next, he would be victorious. That timetable envisaged a rapid dissolution once the Unionists in Parliament and the constituencies had been captured for his policy. But Balfour refused to oblige by dissolving, and Chamberlain had no means of exerting leverage upon him until late 1905, when the party conferences of both Conservatives and Liberal Unionists were to come out in his support.

---

117 McCready, 'Revolt of the Unionist Free Traders', p. 191.
118 Richard A. Rempel, 'Lord Hugh Cecil's Parliamentary Career, 1911–1914: Promise Unfulfilled', *Journal of British Studies*, 1972, p. 111.
119 Sir Austen Chamberlain, *Politics from Inside: An Epistolary Chronicle 1906–1914*, Cassell, 1936, p. 197.
120 House of Commons Debates, 7 June 1905, vol. 147, col. 1009.

Chamberlain appears to have believed that, after his resignation, he and Balfour would operate in tandem, with the former Colonial Secretary staking out the land which his leader would then occupy. Balfour did not take the same view. He did not believe that public opinion could be rapidly altered, nor that the floating voter would swiftly come to accept food taxes, and felt a fundamental responsibility to hold the Unionists together. Chamberlain's campaign had the effect of casting Balfour in the role of a timid and fearful party leader. 'It is rather new in politics', a British diplomat had written to a friend after the Sheffield speech, 'that we should have a Prime Minister who openly says he has no convictions until he has found out whether it pays or not. Of the two I prefer Chamberlain.'[121] Balfour became increasingly fearful lest the unpopularity of food taxes drag the Unionists to electoral disaster. In a speech at Edinburgh in 1904, he sought to head off the accusation that a Unionist electoral victory would raise the cost of food by erecting a barrier against colonial preference. If re-elected, he declared that he would summon a Colonial Conference to consider preference. If the conference recommended preference, he would then seek a mandate from the voters in a second election to introduce the policy. At that time, elections were held at seven-year intervals. So, unless Balfour dissolved early, which he was unwilling to do, it would be a considerable time before preference could become a reality. But in the immediate future voters would have nothing to fear. Chamberlain also believed that two elections might be needed for the policy to reach fruition. But for him the first election should be held immediately and should be a campaigning election, while for Balfour the aim would be not to animate the voters but to reassure them. So Balfour's two elections pledge served only to intensify the growing gulf between the two men.

Few in 1903 had expected Balfour's government to last long. The Unionists had an overall majority of around ninety in the Commons. But between forty or fifty of them were free traders, who could, at any moment, bring the government down. Balfour, therefore, had no alternative but to temporise. That meant losing the momentum on which Chamberlain relied for the success of his policy. Chamberlain had hoped that, even though the Unionists would probably be defeated in the ensuing general election, they would then be quit of their 'accumulated unpopularity for the past and free to concentrate on the policy which was now enthusiastically endorsed by the great majority', as he believed.[122] Lloyd George thought that the government clung on for self-interested reasons. They would die, he said, with their drawn

121 Marsh, *Joseph Chamberlain*, p. 583.
122 L. S. Amery, *My Political Life*, Hutchinson, 1953, vol. 1, p. 274.

salaries in their hands.[123] But Balfour had good reasons for remaining in power. He wanted to remodel Britain's foreign relations through the entente with France and remodel her defence machinery through the Committee of Imperial Defence, which was to be established in 1904. He did not trust the Liberals to pursue a responsible foreign or defence policy. Only the Unionists, therefore, were fitted to rule. In August 1903, Churchill had written to Rosebery that the 'Arthurians' are

> so absolutely convinced that England will be ruined if anyone replaces them that their patriotism and self-sacrifice lead them to swallow any quantity of dirt and humiliation to remain in Downing Street for the public interest. It is a strange point of view; and the most curious feature is its absolute sincerity.[124]

But in consequence of the split, legislation almost ground to a halt. The years from 1903 to 1905 were, in Churchill's view, years of legislative sterility. The reason, Churchill, now speaking as a Liberal, told the Commons in July 1905, was that 'they had been working for the past two years in the shadow of a great unsettled controversy'. In his view, 'a great new issue had been raised' in 1903, and the country should have been invited immediately to give its decision on it. But 'the crisis had been delayed, not averted. These two years of delay had not united the Party opposite, or laid to rest the great disintegrative issue' raised by Chamberlain. The 1900 Parliament had 'died a natural death two years ago, but an unnatural and uncanny interval had been interposed between its death and its dissolution. They had been, as it were, in a trance, under the influence of a mesmerist.'[125]

Balfour, though in a humiliating parliamentary position, did all that he could to remain in office, while Chamberlain continued to press for a dissolution. But it was not possible to prevent Unionist divisions from becoming public. In the first debate on fiscal policy after the Sheffield speech, on 15 February 1904, twenty-seven Unionists, including Ritchie, Lord Hugh Cecil, Lord George Hamilton and Churchill, then still a Conservative, voted with the Liberals, seven abstained and five were absent unpaired. Only fourteen Unionist free traders voted with the government. On 9 March, a revolt of over a hundred supporters of Chamberlain compelled Balfour to withdraw an amendment to an opposition motion, tabled in the name of a private member but drafted by the whips.[126] On the main motion, condemning

---

123 Amery, *Chamberlain*, vol. 6, p. 744.
124 Rempel, *Unionists Divided*, p. 51.
125 House of Commons Debates, 31 July 1905, vol. 150, col. 995.
126 Dugdale, *Balfour*, vol. 1, p. 310.

'preferential and protective tariffs', the normal Unionist majority of around ninety was down to forty-six. Later in the year, the Conservative conference passed a tariff reform motion by an overwhelming majority. A Balfourian amendment received just thirteen votes. On 8 March 1905, when Churchill, now a Liberal, moved a motion in the Commons condemning preference, Balfour found it impossible to find an amendment so worded as to unite his MPs. Fearing that Unionist free traders would abstain or even vote with Churchill, the government had to move that 'the Question be not Put'. On 28 March, a resolution condemning preference was passed without opposition when most Unionist MPs walked out of the chamber, though thirty-five Unionist free traders voted for it. By 30 November 1905, Chamberlain told a colleague that the fears of Conservative MPs opposed to dissolution were 'akin to those of the child who postpones as long as possible his visit to the dentist'.[127] On 14 November, he succeeded where Lord Randolph Churchill had failed, by securing the support of the National Union of Conservative Associations at its annual conference, normally a reliable prop for the leadership. The conference not only supported Chamberlain's policy rather than Balfour's but also voted to replace Balfour's men at party headquarters with an elected committee representing the tariff reform majority amongst constituency activists. At the annual conference of the Liberal Unionists at Bristol later in November, Chamberlain's patience finally snapped. He insisted that retaliation was not possible without a general tariff on manufactured goods and declared, 'No army was ever led successfully to battle on the principle that the lamest man should govern the march of the army.' The conference overwhelmingly supported Chamberlain, thereby repudiating both Balfour's policy and his tactics for preserving party unity. Both Conservative and Liberal Unionist conferences had now passed resolutions with near unanimity in favour of tariff reform. Balfour, however, had in any case now come to the view that his government had reached the end, having written to Chamberlain on 3 November:

> Ten years of leading the House of Commons has given me an unutterable desire for a change, and I never go upstairs to bed without thanking heaven that, in a very brief period, I shall have left my official residence and gone back to the comfort and repose of my own house![128]

His release was not to be long delayed. Chamberlain's Bristol speech confirmed his intention that the government should resign. The alternatives of

---

127 Amery, *Chamberlain*, vol 6, p. 761.
128 Adams, *Balfour*, pp. 224–5.

meeting Parliament and continuing until beaten on a division or until his majority was so reduced that resignation became inevitable were not enticing. On 4 December, the government resigned – the last occasion in British history when a government with a secure majority in the Commons resigned instead of seeking a dissolution. The unity of the Unionists had in a sense been preserved but only at the cost of surrendering to Chamberlain, who had successfully steered policy in his direction and had won control over the Conservative and Liberal Unionist organisations.

Balfour decided to resign rather than dissolve for two reasons. The first was that a dissolution would immediately expose Unionist divisions. He was not able to go to the country on an agreed programme which the Unionist free traders could accept. The second was that resignation and the installation of a Liberal government might expose divisions between Liberal Imperialists and Little Englanders. They seemed to disagree not only on imperial issues but also on social reform, on who should lead the party and on Home Rule. Consequently, so Balfour told Chamberlain on 2 November, the Liberals would have difficulties 'in forming either a Government or a policy ... They are increased by personal differences and jealousies which will make the next Cabinet an eminently unfriendly collection of friends. I should infinitely prefer getting them "into the open" before the fight begins.'[129]

---

129 Young, *Arthur James Balfour*, p. 253.

CHAPTER 11

THE LIBERAL REVIVAL

THE ENTENTE BETWEEN THE LIBERALS AND
THE LABOUR REPRESENTATION COMMITTEE

Before the Education Act, Campbell-Bannerman's leadership had appeared uncertain. He had been overshadowed by the Liberal Imperialist leaders, and in particular by Rosebery. But Liberal divisions on the war were always, as Charles Hobhouse, later to be in the Asquith Cabinet, pointed out to the Chief Whip in 1901, 'apparently more pronounced on the front than on the back benches'. Nor were squabbles on the Liberal front bench reflected amongst Liberals in the country. Lord Tweedmouth, another future Liberal Cabinet minister, referred to 'those who are outside the influence of the House of Commons differences and rivalries and who deplore the condition of things which seems to prevail in it'.[1] That was a great contrast with the Unionist split between tariff reformers and free fooders which was strong at all levels of the party; and it made it easier for the various groups in the Liberal Party to come together after the Boer War had ended. The Liberal League was to dwindle into insignificance, giving 'more and more the impression of a disgruntled minority pursuing a vendetta against Campbell-Bannerman'.[2]

The Liberal Imperialists had certainly been dissatisfied with the leadership of Campbell-Bannerman, whose qualities they, together with many others, underestimated. They considered him a last remnant of Gladstonianism: weak, mediocre, insufficiently imperial-minded and uninterested in social reform. 'It would be idle', a well-informed journalist wrote in 1904, 'to affirm that as Leader of the Opposition he commands the respect of his political opponents or the obedience of his party friends.' But the journalist then added, 'This is, however, only the House of Commons' aspect of the case. Throughout the country Sir Henry has a support as wide in range, as hearty in character, as in the House of Commons it is limited and lukewarm.' Even so, the journalist predicted that the next Liberal Prime Minister would not be Campbell-Bannerman, who would go to the Lords as Secretary for War,

---

1   Lloyd, 'The Whip as Paymaster', p. 793.
2   Rhodes James, *Rosebery*, p. 446.

the post he had held in the Gladstone/Rosebery governments, but Lord Spencer, who since 1902 had been leader of the Liberals in the Lords and was like Campbell-Bannerman a veteran of previous Liberal administrations. Indeed, Spencer had been in every Liberal government since Gladstone's first ministry in 1868.[3] There had indeed been some talk by Asquith, Grey and Haldane that Spencer would be a better Prime Minister than Campbell-Bannerman. Spencer had few leadership qualities but might have been a useful stopgap. 'What an amazing example Spencer is', Balfour had said in June 1905 to Edmund Gosse, Librarian of the House of Lords, 'of what can be done in this country by a noble presence and a fine personal record, assisted by no intellectual parts of any kind. It is really very remarkable. Such a sweet and even such a beautiful character and no ability at all.' Gosse argued that Spencer's mind worked somewhat slowly. Balfour put him right. 'It does not work at all. He has no mind. He has character, but no mind. It is only in England that such a man would hold a great position, and' – concluded Balfour wagging his finger at Gosse – 'it is a very good thing that it should be so.'[4] Spencer, however, was to suffer a disabling stroke in October 1905, from which he never recovered, and this put him out of consideration for the premiership just two months before it was to become vacant. He had become, in Churchill's words, 'a ship sinking in sight of land'.[5]

The Education Act had united the Liberals and hostility to tariff reform firmly cemented that unity. On 30 May 1903, just two weeks after Chamberlain's Birmingham speech, Campbell-Bannerman wrote to his constituency chairman, 'This reckless-criminal-escapade of Joe's is the great event of our time. It is playing old Harry with all party relations ... All the old warhorses about me ... are snorting with excitement. We are in for a great time.'[6] That 'great time' was to be considerably assisted by an agreement between the two parties of the left, the Liberals and the Labour Representation Committee (LRC), soon to become the Labour Party.

They faced the problem of how to avoid splitting the progressive vote, which could hamper the Liberals' chances of winning a majority independently of the Irish. The LRC could hardly survive all-out competition with the Liberals, but if it became too close to the Liberals, it would lose its separate identity. The problem was to be resolved by a secret electoral agreement between the two parties. The agreement was made possible largely by Ramsay MacDonald's tactical adroitness in negotiation, although the need for an agreement was 'so compelling that, even before the national

3   Henry Lucy, 'The Next Liberal Ministry', *Nineteenth Century*, October 1904, pp. 675, 680, 684.
4   Grigg, *People's Champion*, p. 81.
5   Randolph S. Churchill, *Winston S. Churchill, Companion*, Heinemann, 1969, vol. 2, part 1, 1901–1907, p. 463.
6   McCready, 'Revolt of the Unionist Free Traders', p. 188.

parties formed an arrangement, constituency organisations were conducting their own negotiations'.[7] After Chamberlain's declaration on tariff reform in May 1903, it was widely believed that an election could not be long delayed, and the Liberals and LRC were united in defending free trade. Jesse Herbert, political secretary to the Liberal Chief Whip Herbert Gladstone, believed that there were no insuperable policy objections to an agreement. In a memorandum in March 1903, he wrote that 'the severe individualists of the party who are wholly out of sympathy with the principles of the LRC are very few'.[8] And almost all LRC MPs would support a Liberal government. Herbert feared that, without an agreement, the Liberals would lose not only 'in those constituencies where LRC candidates fought, but also in almost every borough, and in many of the Divisions of Lancashire and Yorkshire', a pessimism understandable perhaps in the light of the electoral performance of the Liberals in 1895 and 1900.[9] Campbell-Bannerman was sympathetic towards the LRC, which had supported his stance on the Boer War. 'We are keenly in sympathy with the representatives of Labour,' he had declared in a speech in Perthshire in January 1903. 'We have too few of them in the House of Commons.'[10]

Liberals in favour of an accommodation found a natural ally in MacDonald. Socialism as he understood it did not entail a sharp break with liberalism; nor did he believe in the class war. He held to an evolutionary theory of socialism which would, he believed, eventually supersede liberalism, incorporating what was best in it. Socialism would be built on the achievements of the liberal state, not on its ruins as Marx had predicted. MacDonald's view appeared particularly plausible in the light of the development of the New Liberalism of social reform, which seemed to be pushing the Liberal Party in a direction which the LRC could support. In particular, the New Liberal idea of taxing the unearned increment – the increase in the value of land or property without any effort or expenditure by the owner – chimed with Labour's ideas of redistributive taxation. So there need be no basic antagonism between the two parties. And independence for Labour did not mean isolation. In 1897, MacDonald confessed that he had never been 'one of those ... members of the Independent Labour Party who regard "independent" as meaning "isolated" ... I have never given up hopes that a limited and temporary trial might be given to an electoral co-operation

---

7 Tanner, *Political Change and the Labour Party*, pp. 21–2.

8 Peter Clarke, *Lancashire and the New Liberalism*, Cambridge University Press, 1971, p. 223.

9 Jesse Herbert to Herbert Gladstone, 6 March 1903, quoted in Frank Bealey, 'Negotiations between the Liberal Party and the Labour Representation Committee before the general election of 1906', *Bulletin of the Institute of Historical Research*, 1956, p. 266.

10 *The Times*, 3 January 1903.

in certain favoured constituencies'.[11] In April 1901, the Liberal *Manchester Guardian* had commented:

> What must strike a Liberal who reads the report of the Independent Labour Party Conference at Leicester is, one would say, how much of the proceedings is devoted to the advocacy of traditional Liberal principles. Opposition to aggressive war, special abhorrence of the financial factor in aggression, repugnance to conscription, sympathy for foreign reformers, like the Russian students struggling for the first rudiments of liberty – these are the life-blood of Liberalism as understood in the great days of Gladstone and Bright. These are also the main features of a gathering of the most representative group of Socialists.

While the two parties might differ on ideology, they could agree on immediate and practical measures of reform. 'In this spirit,' the *Manchester Guardian* concluded, 'we believe that what is best in Liberalism and Socialism is likely to cooperate better in the future than in the past.'[12] It may seem surprising that Keir Hardie, often depicted as an intransigent socialist, seems not to have been averse to an agreement, telling an audience at York, a two-member constituency, on 26 February 1903, that an agreement whereby an LRC candidate ran in harness with a Liberal would be 'productive of good fellowship and would work to their mutual advantage'.[13] Opposition to the Boer War had brought Liberals and the LRC together, and indeed Hardie, anticipating a Liberal split, had urged an agreement with anti-war Liberals as early as October 1901.[14] In 1900, he had actually asked the Gladstonian Liberal and opponent of state intervention John Morley if he would lead the LRC.

MacDonald held out feelers to the Liberals indicating that he would not be averse to an agreement. He obtained a ready response from Herbert Gladstone, who had told his constituents in 1901:

> If I had the power and the authority I have no doubt that I could come to terms with the leaders of the Labour party in the course of half a morning ... The difficulty lies with the constituencies themselves and in the unfortunate necessity of providing funds ... During the last two or three years I have urged upon the constituencies the claims of labour; but I am sorry to say that, as a rule, a marked want of success has attended my efforts.[15]

---

11   Marquand, *Ramsay MacDonald*, p. 62.
12   *Manchester Guardian*, editorial, 10 April 1901.
13   Poirier, *Advent of the Labour Party*, p. 188.
14   Pelling, *Origins of the Labour Party*, p. 227.
15   *The Times*, 9 October 1901, in ibid., pp. 261–2.

Herbert Gladstone had, in Beatrice Webb's acerbic view, 'a sort of common sense which comes from years of experienced party wire-pulling'. But Gladstone's common sense was to prove of great value.[16] With Campbell-Bannerman's approval, he sent Jesse Herbert to call on MacDonald. At their first meeting in early February 1903, MacDonald played a weak hand with great skill, exaggerating the strength and financial resources of the LRC. MacDonald told Herbert that 'the working men throughout the country and of all shades of opinion (except for the Miners and the SDF) were uniting in support of the LRC' and that 'the LRC represents nearly a million working men' who were contributing to the political fund. So the LRC, MacDonald went on, would have a large fighting fund to contest the next election, and had branches 'all over the United Kingdom'. This was, of course, a gross exaggeration. The Independent Labour Party (ILP) had around 6,000 individual members, for the trade union members had been affiliated by their unions, often without their consent, and the party was nearly bankrupt. In any case, it was by no means clear that the LRC or even the trade union leaders could deliver the union vote en masse to the Liberals. A Conservative trade unionist in Lancashire would not swing to the Liberals merely because the LRC or his trade union told him to. Nevertheless, MacDonald told Jesse Herbert that, if the Liberals were to oppose the LRC, they would 'not only lose the possible accession of the erstwhile Tory working man, but will estrange the hitherto loyal Liberal working man'. It would in any case be pointless, MacDonald argued, for the Liberals to oppose the LRC since LRC candidates would support a Liberal government. The LRC, MacDonald concluded, sought 'no alliance, no treaty but a free hand in certain constituencies, in return for which friendliness in any constituency where they have influence'.[17] The Liberals, MacDonald pointed out, would not be putting up candidates against Liberal Imperialists of the Liberal League, though there was a far greater gap in terms of policy between Liberal Imperialists and Campbell-Bannerman than between Campbell-Bannerman and the LRC. This, of course, ignored the fact that Liberal League MPs would take the Liberal whip while LRC candidates would not. For MacDonald insisted that the LRC be recognised as an absolutely independent national party and that any agreement must be national in scope.

Jesse Herbert was impressed with MacDonald's comments and told Herbert Gladstone that while 'the official recognition of a separate group unpledged to support the Liberal Party ... and whose representatives in parliament will probably decline the Liberal whip, is not lightly to be given'

16 MacKenzie, *Diary of Beatrice Webb*, vol. 2, p. 326.
17 Jesse Herbert to Gladstone, 6 March 1903, in Bealey, 'Negotiations', pp. 264–5.

since 'it would be the recognition of a vital change in the organisation of parties', nevertheless it would be nothing 'other than the official recognition of a fact, indisputable, and clear to every individual politician'.[18] In addition, accepting what MacDonald had said about the LRC's finances, Jesse Herbert believed that LRC candidates could help relieve the Liberals of financial worries, since the Liberals faced the problem that 'people with advanced opinions do not pay'.[19] But for Jesse Herbert, the main advantage of an agreement would be its

> effect upon the public mind of a conviction that the Liberal party will win the election, a conviction which will prevail everywhere when it is seen that the Labour party and the Liberal party are no longer fighting each other. Sentiment has an enormous influence upon the results of a General Election, and if the country sees the opponents of the Government united, not only will the hope and enthusiasm of our own people vote and work, but depression and fear will rob their antagonists of energy and force.[20]

On 13 March, Gladstone wrote a memorandum on 'Labour and Liberalism' in which he concluded, 'There being no material points of difference between Labour and Liberalism in the main lines of Liberal policy, we are ready to ascertain from justified and responsible Labour leaders how far Labour candidates can be given an open field against a common enemy ... We are ready,' he went on,

> to do this as an act of friendship and without any stipulation of any kind because we realise that an accession of strength to Labour representation in the House of Commons is not only required by the country in the interests of Labour but that it would increase progressive forces generally and the Labour Party as the best available instrument of progress.[21]

Campbell-Bannerman agreed and told the annual meeting of the National Liberal Federation in May 1903 that 'honest' Labour candidates and 'honest' Liberals were 'both elements in the progressive force of the country'.[22]

Between the general election of 1900 and July 1903, the LRC had returned three further MPs to the Commons in by-elections, and this seemed to strengthen the case for an agreement. The first was at Clitheroe in August

---

18 Ibid., pp. 265–6.
19 MacKenzie, *Diary of Beatrice Webb*, vol. 2, p. 326.
20 Bealey, 'Negotiations', pp. 266–7.
21 Herbert Gladstone Papers, Add. MSS 46106, f. 7.
22 Poirier, *Advent of the Labour Party*, p. 191.

1902, where the new MP was David Shackleton, a trade unionist and Liberal, neither a socialist nor previously identified with the labour movement. He had been sponsored by the Lancashire weavers and was returned unopposed in what had hitherto been a Liberal seat. Indeed, he did not join the LRC until after the by-election. The LRC had contemplated nominating Philip Snowden, a socialist, but had Snowden been nominated, the Liberals would have put up a competing candidate. One observer of the Clitheroe by-election declared that Shackleton was 'a very mild-spoken gentleman, with ideas very little in advance of the average Liberal ... There was absolutely nothing in his short address to which any reasonable Tory working-man could object.'[23] Shackleton was in fact primarily interested in securing improvements for the cotton operatives, rather than any wider labour representation, let alone socialism.

The second by-election success for the LRC was Will Crooks at Woolwich, who gained the seat from the Unionists in March 1903. Woolwich was a seat which the Liberals had never won – indeed they had not even fought it since 1895 – and in which they now stood aside. In both Clitheroe and Woolwich, a Liberal would have been unable to tap the large working-class support which had gone to LRC candidates.

The third by-election victory for the LRC was that of Arthur Henderson at Barnard Castle in July 1903. This by-election followed the death of Sir Joseph Pease, the long-serving Liberal MP. The LRC had already decided to run Henderson, the candidate of the Ironfounders' Society at the next general election. Henderson, however, had been Pease's electoral agent and was a Liberal. He would have been perfectly acceptable to the Liberals as a candidate, and indeed the Liberals offered to support him as a Lib-Lab, but his trade union which was sponsoring him was financing him as an LRC candidate. The LRC constitution, recently revised at Newcastle, had, as we have seen, forbidden an LRC candidate to stand for any other party. So Henderson had to turn down the Liberal offer. As an LRC candidate, Henderson was opposed by some ILP socialists – he was indeed the only one of the early Labour leaders not to have been nurtured by the ILP – and still more by the Social Democratic Federation, who regarded him as 'a camp follower of the Liberal party' with 'no ideas at all apart from those of capitalist Liberalism'.[24] Indeed, Henderson's programme – trade union legislation to reform *Taff Vale*, old-age pensions, reform of the Education Act, preservation of free trade – was that of the Liberal Party. But he had become a believer in independent labour representation. The local Liberals

23 Bealey and Pelling, *Labour and Politics*, p. 111.
24 Ibid., p. 198.

insisted upon nominating a candidate, against the wishes of some of its members and to the consternation of party headquarters, which had come near to endorsing Henderson. The Liberal candidate was an unusual figure to say the least, since he was sympathetic to tariff reform. In a three-cornered fight, Henderson defeated the Unionist by forty-seven votes while the Liberal came bottom of the poll. Barnard Castle was the first LRC victory against both major parties and 'was the most striking vindication of the policy of independence that the LRC had yet experienced'.[25] Henderson's victory gave particular satisfaction to MacDonald, who believed that it 'would have a salutary effect in discouraging Liberals from opposing Labour in earmarked constituencies'.[26] But the narrow majority showed that a three-party fight could easily yield a seat to the Unionists. The lesson of Barnard Castle, then, was that it would be dangerous for the Liberals to carry constitutional autonomy too far. But the LRC could not afford to be overly ambitious and split the vote in constituencies where the Liberals were strong. The message of all three by-elections, therefore, seemed clear, reinforcing the need for cooperation between the two parties of the left. LRC candidates could gain support in areas where the Liberals could not, such as Lancashire, and also in areas where the Liberals might be seen as too conservative, as in parts of Yorkshire. For the Liberals, the agreement ensured not only that the progressive vote was united but that the LRC would be contained; for the LRC, it ensured that it could establish a firmer foothold in its strongholds.

The agreement between Gladstone and MacDonald was finally concluded in the somewhat lugubrious surroundings of Leicester Isolation Hospital, where MacDonald was recovering from a short illness, on 6 September 1903. Gladstone reminded MacDonald that Liberal headquarters had no power to impose a decision on local associations and that, if an association insisted on putting up a candidate, headquarters would not be able to veto it. But he promised to use his best endeavours to ensure this did not happen. The Liberal Party was not, any more than the other parties, a disciplined army that could command its local associations, much less its voters, to act as party headquarters wished. There had to be some overriding issue – such as Home Rule in 1886 – to persuade voters to follow the advice of their parties in altering their normal allegiances. From 1903, the overriding concern was the removal of the Unionist government. The agreement was in fact more in the nature of an expression of goodwill or an entente than a pact, and it was to be for one election only. It was, moreover, unofficial and, above all, a secret agreement. In the LRC, only MacDonald and Hardie knew of it.

---

25 Ibid., p. 204.
26 Poirier, *Advent of the Labour Party*, p. 205.

Had it been more widely known, it might have been denounced in the ILP as a betrayal not only of socialism but even of independence, and if publicly known it might have deterred working-class Tories from supporting the LRC. Independence was a precondition of the agreement, giving the LRC two elements that the Lib-Labs had lacked: leverage and bargaining power. The agreement was to apply only in England and Wales. In Scotland, the Liberals were stronger and more self-contained, partly because the considerable Irish vote in the west of Scotland remained firmly committed to the Liberals as a Home Rule party. In addition, Liberals in Scotland were more hostile to socialism, stronger there than in England, while the trade unions were weaker. So the Scottish Liberals felt little need to make terms with 'socialists'.

HOME RULE STEP BY STEP

The unifying effects of the Education Act, tariff reform, increasing Unionist disarray and the growing signs of cooperation between the two parties of the left led to a feeling from the beginning of 1904 that the Liberals would be returned to government at the next election. Indeed, much earlier, two weeks before the crucial Cabinet meeting of 14 September 1903, Churchill had written to the Duke of Devonshire, 'We are on the eve of a gigantic political landslide. I don't think Balfour and those about him realise at all how far the degeneration of the forces of Unionism has proceeded, and how tremendous the counter-current is going to be.'[27]

The one potential barrier to a comfortable Liberal majority was Home Rule. Campbell-Bannerman was not prepared to abandon Home Rule, but some Liberals feared that it would continue to damage their electoral prospects. Voters might not be willing to give the Liberals a majority to defend free trade if such a majority would be used to promote Home Rule. It was, therefore, imperative to prevent Home Rule from remaining an irritant. As early as 1899, Herbert Gladstone, on becoming Chief Whip, had initiated a review of the policy. After consulting with Campbell-Bannerman and members of the last Liberal Cabinet still active in politics, he concluded only that 'it was essential to mark time'.[28] A disinclination to retain Home Rule was reinforced by the sympathy which Irish Nationalists showed towards the Boers, further alienating them from English opinion. Moreover, in February 1900, the Irish Party had denounced the Liberal alliance and reverted to a position of independence from the British parties. Significantly, the 1900

27 Holland, *Life of Devonshire*, vol. 2, p. 320.
28 H. W. McCready, 'Home Rule and the Liberal Party, 1899–1906', *Irish Historical Studies*, 1963, p. 319.

Liberal manifesto had made no mention of Home Rule. In 1902, the Irish Party, strongly opposed to the Liberal principle of non-sectarian education, antagonised Liberals by supporting the Education Act which, they believed, would assist the Catholic Church.

The Liberals now proposed to relegate Home Rule from its prominent place in the party's programme, to attract back Liberal Unionists who had left in 1886 and who now resented the Education Act. There was a tendency, Asquith believed, 'on the part of the better sort of liberal unionists (produced by the domestic legislation of the government and its administrative failures) to rejoin their old party', provided that Home Rule no longer stood in the way.[29] In a speech at Ladybank on 29 September 1901, his first for a year in his constituency, Asquith declared that the Liberals should not form a government unless they could do so without relying upon the Irish vote. Haldane was to say the same on 4 October in his East Lothian constituency.

But Liberals were not prepared to go as far as Rosebery and abandon Home Rule entirely. They wanted to relegate it so that it was no longer a priority, but not repudiate it. For, whatever its unpopularity amongst voters, it was still widely supported by most of the Liberal rank and file. So Rosebery's explicit repudiation of it had served not to propel him to the leadership but to separate him even from his Liberal Imperialist supporters, although Haldane was prepared to support him in private but not in public. Others who might privately sympathise were equally unprepared to offer public support but were determined that the next Liberal government should not introduce a Home Rule Bill. In October 1905, Asquith was to tell Herbert Gladstone:

> If we are to get a real majority in the next House of Commons, it can only
> be by making it perfectly clear to the electors that ... it will be no part of
> the policy of the new Liberal Government to introduce a Home Rule Bill
> in the next Parliament ... no one intends to devote either the second or
> third, or any session to framing and carrying a Bill which will be at once
> chucked out by the House of Lords and will wreck the fortunes of the
> party for another twenty years.[30]

But there was an alternative to explicit repudiation. It was, while relegating Home Rule to the future, to enact reforms in the government of Ireland which could lead towards it but would be acceptable to middle-of-the-road voters. This was the so-called step-by-step policy and it seemed capable of uniting the party. Even Morley, a diehard Gladstonian, was prepared to

29 Ibid., p. 321.
30 Quoted in Morgan, *Suffragists and Liberals*, pp. 36–7.

accept it 'with the utmost satisfaction'. It would 'make things easier for sensible Irishmen; it will please or at most it will not displease, sensible liberals in this island; it will keep the centre of gravity in the party where it ought to be; and it is the truth of good statesmanship'.[31] Even more surprisingly, John Redmond, leader of the reunited Irish Parliamentary Party since 1900, was himself to prove one of these 'sensible Irishmen'. Meeting with Herbert Gladstone in February 1905, he accepted that Home Rule would 'come by degrees'.[32] On 14 November 1905, Campbell-Bannerman held a breakfast meeting with Redmond and T. P. O'Connor, a leading colleague, at which the Liberal leader definitely persuaded them to accept the step-by-step policy.

The step-by-step policy had originally been the strategy of the Liberal Imperialists, some of whom no doubt hoped that limited measures would obviate the necessity of Home Rule entirely. It had first been put forward by Grey, supported by Asquith and Haldane, in 1901. But the one person whom the policy did not conciliate was Rosebery, who, in a speech at Stourbridge in 25 October 1905, reiterated his opposition and ridiculed step by step as a policy 'of placing Home Rule in the position of a reliquary, and only exhibiting it at great moments of public stress, as Roman Catholics are accustomed to exhibit relics of a saint'.[33]

Campbell-Bannerman, however, laid out the policy in a speech at Stirling on 23 November 1905, declaring that 'the opportunity of making a great advance on the question of Irish Government will not be long delayed'. Nevertheless, 'in the immediate future the time of Parliament will probably be occupied by ... social questions ... which call for treatment and on which opinion among us is more than ripe ... Undoubtedly they will take time.' He recommended to the Nationalists that 'if an instalment of representative control was offered to you ... I would advise you thankfully to accept it' provided that it was 'consistent with and led up to the larger policy'. He did not state what the first 'instalment' would be, nor when 'the larger policy' would in fact be enacted. It was, however, now clear that Home Rule would no longer be in the forefront of the Liberal programme. The Stirling formula had been agreed with Redmond and with Asquith, Haldane and Grey. But Rosebery was unaware of it. For some reason, the Liberal Imperialists had not told him and he misinterpreted the Stirling formula to mean that a Home Rule Bill would in fact be introduced in the next Parliament. Under the misapprehension that his position was in accord with those of his fellow Liberal Imperialists, Rosebery denounced the Stirling formula which, he

---

31 McCready, 'Home Rule and the Liberal Party', p. 344.
32 Ibid., p. 341.
33 Rhodes James, *Rosebery*, p. 453.

declared, would put the Liberals at the mercy of the Irish Nationalists as they had been in 1886 and 1892, impair the cause of free trade and, as he put it in a speech at Bodmin four days after Campbell-Bannerman's, indefinitely post-pone 'legislation on social and educational reform on which the country has set its heart'. He concluded, therefore, 'emphatically and explicitly and once for all that I cannot serve under that banner'. Just as Rosebery had misin-terpreted Campbell-Bannerman's Stirling speech, so Balfour misinterpreted Rosebery's speech to indicate that the Liberal Imperialists as a whole would not serve in a Campbell-Bannerman government; and this perception played its part in his decision to resign rather than dissolve. But Rosebery was to find himself isolated and his speech ensured that he could not be included in the Liberal government. It may be indeed that Redmond had in fact secured a pledge from Campbell-Bannerman that Rosebery would not be in a Liberal government.[34] And there was a further reason for Rosebery's exclusion. The only post that could reasonably have been offered him would have been the foreign secretaryship. But he was almost the only leading statesman who had opposed the entente with France of 1904. Grey, by contrast, had com-mitted the Liberals to continuity in foreign policy. In a speech in London on 20 October 1905, he was to insist that the Liberals stood by three main achievements of the Unionist government in foreign policy – friendship with the United States, alliance with Japan and the entente with France. In fact, the entente with France, a parliamentary nation, was even more of a Liberal cause than a Unionist one. It is, in any case, doubtful if Rosebery would have wished to serve under Campbell-Bannerman, whose leadership qualities he disparaged. He did not believe that a government containing both Liberal Imperialists and Gladstonians could be effective. Perhaps he thought or even hoped that a government formed out of such seemingly incompatible ele-ments would be bound to fail and that a grateful nation would then call on him as leader of a coalition devoted to national efficiency. But if he did think that, he was to be grievously disappointed. After the Liberal government was formed, he moved ostentatiously to the cross benches in the Lords, where he was to prove a determined opponent of Liberal measures of social reform. 'The light has faded from the morning hills, the vision has faded in grey disenchantment,' declared one commentator. He was to become 'the Flying Dutchman of politics – a phantom vessel floating about on the wide seas, without an anchor and without a port'.[35] He was to be offered the American embassy in 1906 but declined.[36] It was a melancholy end to a political career

---

34 McKinstry, *Rosebery*, p. 469.
35 Gardiner, *Prophets, Priests and Kings*, p. 185.
36 Edward Heath, another awkward colleague, was to be offered the American embassy by Margaret Thatcher in 1979, and, like Rosebery, refused it.

that had begun long ago in the 1870s when Gladstone had hailed him as the man of the future. But he was in fact a man of the past since, unlike Gladstone and unlike Chamberlain, the other great disrupter, he was never at home in the twentieth-century world of mass politics.

THE RELUGAS COMPACT AND THE FORMATION OF THE LIBERAL GOVERNMENT

Balfour, like Rosebery, was unaware that the Stirling formula had been agreed with the Liberal Imperialists. He and other Unionists remained under the misapprehension that the Liberals were irretrievably split and that Rosebery had spoken for all of the Liberal Leaguers. Herbert Gladstone, the Liberal Chief Whip, predicted to Campbell-Bannerman that 'Balfour may be encouraged by Rosebery's astounding speech to precipitate matters', as indeed he was.[37] For a time, it seemed as if Balfour's hopes might be realised. For, despite detaching the Liberal Imperialists from Rosebery, Campbell-Bannerman's personal position remained insecure. Asquith, Grey and Haldane had met in September 1905 at Grey's Scottish hunting lodge at Relugas in Moray, and had agreed, at Haldane's instigation, not to serve under Campbell-Bannerman, an elderly man of seventy-five in uncertain health, unless he would agree as Prime Minister to lead from the Lords. In October 1903, Grey had been firm that 'under no circumstances would I take office with C. B. as Prime Minister in any Govt. in which C-B was leader in the House of Commons'.[38] Haldane wanted Asquith to be Leader of the Commons as well as Chancellor of the Exchequer. Grey would go to the Foreign Office while Haldane himself would go to the Woolsack as Lord Chancellor. Campbell-Bannerman had seemed to indicate that he would not be wholly averse to such a solution. In October 1903, he had told the Chief Whip who repeated to Asquith his view that 'in the event of a change of government he did not think that he would be able to take any part which involve heavy and responsible work. A peerage and some office of dignity ... would be what he would like.'[39]

Haldane communicated the decision of the Relugas conspirators to the king through his private secretary, and the king agreed that it would be best for the Liberal leader to take a peerage. The king's private secretary expressed what was apparently the king's fear that Campbell-Bannerman 'would be inclined to give way to pressures from the extreme left'. Nevertheless, if the

---

37 Quoted in M. Craton and H. W. McCready, 'The Great Liberal Revival, 1903–1906', Hansard Society, 1966, p. 30.
38 Robbins, *Grey*, p. 109.
39 T. Boyle, 'The Formation of Campbell-Bannerman's Government in December 1905: A Memorandum by J. A. Spender', *Bulletin of the Institute of Historical Research*, 1972, p. 295.

Liberal leader refused to be kicked upstairs, the king believed that it would be best, even so, if the Relugas trio took office as 'a restraining influence', to 'moderate the dangerous influence which might be brought to bear' on Campbell-Bannerman.[40]

After Balfour's government resigned, the Liberals were at first uncertain whether they should accept office at all. Some feared it might prove a poisoned chalice. In 1885, Gladstone had resigned instead of dissolving, and the ensuing Conservative caretaker government had lasted just seven months before resigning, having failed to win the 1885 general election. Disraeli had appeared shrewder. When, in 1873, Gladstone resigned, Disraeli had refused to take office, and Gladstone was forced to continue for another year before succumbing to a heavy defeat in the general election of 1874. Herbert Gladstone warned Campbell-Bannerman against taking office, 'Acceptance would bring upon us all the difficulties which we are entitled to avoid. Labour men, Irishmen and cranks of all sorts and last but not least the Nonconformists would hamper you and all our candidates to extort their pounds of flesh.'[41] Asquith and Grey agreed. A survey of some fifteen to twenty Liberal MPs showed them nearly unanimous against taking office, and a majority of the editors of Liberal newspapers and journals were also against. Morley, however, warned that refusal to take office would lead to Campbell-Bannerman's position being called into question. 'People would say, "Why have Campbell-Bannerman and his friends refused? Because *they are not agreed who is to be their leader*."' Further, were Campbell-Bannerman to refuse to take office, it by no means followed that the king would return to Balfour. Instead, he might turn to an alternative Unionist or alternative Liberal leader. With his usual common sense, Campbell-Bannerman wrote to Lord Ripon on 25 November that the voters 'know nothing of tricks and pedantries and judge by facts; and the fact would be that we declined to undertake responsibilities which we had been asking for through these years'.[42]

The Relugas Compact collapsed after Balfour's resignation. Indeed, unbeknown to Grey and Haldane, Campbell-Bannerman, a shrewder man than he was given credit for, had already defused it. He appreciated that Asquith was the key figure, the only ex-Cabinet minister amongst the three conspirators and the only one with a popular reputation as an eloquent spokesman for free trade. Grey was largely unknown to the public, while Haldane, though an effective administrator, was, Campbell-Bannerman believed,

---

40 Dudley Sommer, *Haldane of Cloan: His Life and Times, 1856–1928*, Allen & Unwin, 1960, p. 147. But Otte, *Statesman of Europe*, pp. 220–42 provides the most careful and detailed account available of the compact.
41 Craton and McCready, 'Great Liberal Revival', p. 31.
42 Spender, *Campbell-Bannerman*, vol. 2, p. 191.

'a wonderful intriguer' with 'no more tact than a hippopotamus'.[43] On 13 November, before Balfour resigned, Campbell-Bannerman saw Asquith and offered him the Exchequer, with an implicit reversion to the premiership in due course, adding that Haldane, 'that ingenious person', had suggested that he should go to the Lords but that this would be distasteful to him.[44] Asquith did not mention the Relugas agreement and accepted without conditions, so breaking the compact. In forming his government, Campbell-Bannerman could then resist the entreaties of both the king and the other Relugas conspirators. He flatly refused to go to the Lords. Instead, he confirmed the offer to Asquith of the Exchequer. Grey and Haldane still stood out for the compact, Grey telling Herbert Gladstone:

> C-B for some years had been out of touch with necessary & most important movements of thought & action in the country. He cd not do justice to them. He was all for conciliating everyone, but was not a leader either in council or debate or in character of mind.[45]

Asquith now told Grey and Haldane that conditions were different from those in September, since the government was being formed before the election, and were Campbell-Bannerman to face difficulties, the party's electoral success and therefore free trade would be in jeopardy. This was somewhat disingenuous since Asquith had already broken ranks and agreed terms with Campbell-Bannerman. 'It was evident', Haldane was to declare in a memorandum, written later, 'that Asquith had not been resolute about the solidity of our position.'[46] But Grey and Haldane held out a little longer. On 4 December, Grey told Campbell-Bannerman to his face that he would not take office unless the Liberal leader went to the Lords. On the next day, the king summoned Campbell-Bannerman but contented himself with saying, 'We are none of us as young as we were, Sir Henry.' But Campbell-Bannerman ignored the hint, kissing hands as Prime Minister but determined to remain in the Commons. On 7 December, Asquith wrote to Haldane saying that he had been empowered to offer the Foreign Office to Grey and the War Office to Haldane. Were they to refuse, Asquith argued, the opposition would say that Liberals were divided on Home Rule and the empire and 'the *tertius gaudens* at Dalmeny [Rosebery] would look on with complacency. I cannot imagine more disastrous conditions on which to fight a Free trade election.'

---

43 Campbell-Bannerman to Herbert Gladstone, 20 November, 1905, quoted in José Harris and Cameron Hazlehurst, 'Campbell-Bannerman as Prime Minister', *History*, 1970, p. 368fn.
44 Asquith, *Autobiography*, vol. 2, pp. 66ff.
45 Otte, *Statesman of Europe*, p. 235.
46 Sommer, *Haldane*, p. 149.

Haldane then spoke with Grey and told him that they both 'must come in and we must choose the very hardest jobs which are going. In this Government there are two places of paramount importance, where it is all kicks and no ha'pence. These are the War Office and the Foreign Office.'[47] Grey duly became Foreign Secretary, Lord Cromer having previously refused it when it seemed that Grey was still committed to the Relugas Compact. Campbell-Bannerman was indeed reluctant to appoint Grey, or Cromer for that matter, but realised that if the Liberals were to win the election, there could not afford to be any doubts about their patriotism. Had the government been formed after the election, Grey might well not have been appointed.

Haldane did not secure the Lord Chancellorship as he had hoped. That went to Campbell-Bannerman's friend Sir Robert Reid, ennobled as Lord Loreburn, whose high conception of public service was to rescue the bench from the depredations of Halsbury. Haldane went instead to the War Office, where he was to prove a reforming War Secretary. But the Relugas conspirators had gained two of the three posts that they had sought. Loreburn, the new Lord Chancellor, a pro-Boer who had attacked Unionist policy as one of 'foreign adventure', was later apt to characterise the new government as 'a Cabinet of Liberal Leaguers'.[48] But the foreign policy of the Liberal government was not to be one imposed by Liberal Imperialists upon unwilling radicals. Rather it was to flow almost inexorably from the pressure of events.

Campbell-Bannerman could now afford to ignore Rosebery. A mutual friend of the two men, the journalist J. A. Spender, had hoped that Rosebery would be included. He rushed to Campbell-Bannerman's house when the new government was being formed and, though unauthorised by Rosebery, expressed the hope that the Bodmin speech could be forgotten. But Campbell-Bannerman had been tormented by Rosebery long enough. Spender recorded Campbell-Bannerman's response. The Liberal leader declared:

> He was very glad to have news of the 'Lord' ... Did he come with a sword or an olive branch? ... Then he twinkled all over, as only CB could twinkle, and after some moments of apparent reflection delivered his ultimatum, 'Will you please tell Lord Rosebery that within two hours from now I expect to have accepted the King's commission to form a Government, and that being so I can obviously say no more about the Irish question until I have an opportunity of consulting my colleagues in the Cabinet.'

47 Ibid., pp. 150–51.
48 Otte, *Statesman of Europe*, pp. 242–3; Ensor, *England*, p. 572.

'There could scarcely', Spender commented, 'have been a more skilful answer or the closing of a chapter with a more deadly politeness.'[49]

Campbell-Bannerman was to prove a more successful Prime Minister than had been expected, and both Asquith and Grey were to admit they had underestimated him. In 1907, Grey wrote to Campbell-Bannerman, 'All my forecasts before the Election were wrong, and your presence in the House of Commons has been not only desirable but essential to manage this party, and keep it together, and so it continues to be.'[50] Paradoxically, the Relugas Compact collapsed in part because Balfour resigned instead of seeking a dissolution, and it was therefore a tactical mistake on his part. For, had there been a dissolution, the Liberals might well have found it more difficult to agree on policy in an election campaign, and the pressure on Campbell-Bannerman to go to the Lords would have been more difficult to resist. But as it was, the Liberal government was formed with much less difficulty than many, including Balfour, had fondly supposed.

49 J. A. Spender, *Life, Journalism and Politics*, Cassell, 1927, vol. 1, p. 147.
50 Otte, *Statesman of Europe*, p. 314.

CHAPTER 12

THE LIBERAL GOVERNMENT: UNCERTAIN BEGINNINGS

CAMPBELL-BANNERMAN AND HIS LIEUTENANTS

The new Prime Minister, Sir Henry Campbell-Bannerman, had been born in 1836 as Henry Campbell to a Glasgow draper and warehouseman who had worked his way up to financial and civic respectability, becoming Conservative Lord Provost of Glasgow in 1840. Campbell's older brother was to become a Conservative MP between 1880 and 1906. Campbell attended Glasgow and Cambridge universities but showed no particular academic aptitude, though he did win a prize for Greek at Glasgow, where he began the habit of reading novels in French, a habit which never left him and confirmed him in his Francophilia. Breaking with family tradition, Campbell became a Liberal but maintained good relations with his father and brother who showed no resentment. He played no part in university politics and made little mark at university, though from his early years his congenial and easy-going personality won him many friends and hardly any enemies. After university, Campbell worked as a partner in the family business. In 1871, his wife's uncle died and left him a substantial property in Kent, on condition that he adopted the Bannerman name. He always disliked the double-barrelled name and preferred to be called, if not Henry Campbell, simply CB, the sobriquet by which he was generally known.

In 1868, Campbell became MP for the Stirling Burghs, a constituency he retained without difficulty until his death as Prime Minister in 1908. 'Among the new-comers,' Asquith declared in a eulogy after his death, 'there were probably few ... who seemed less obviously destined than Mr Campbell, as he then was, for ultimate leadership.'[1] He made little mark in Parliament, delaying his maiden speech until 1869, and after that, speaking mainly on Scottish matters. Nevertheless, he soon achieved junior office. In 1871, he was made junior minister at the War Office to Edward Cardwell, whose reforms he enthusiastically supported. He was reappointed to the same position in 1880, and then, in 1882, became a junior minister at the Admiralty. In 1884,

---

1 House of Commons Debates, 27 April 1908, vol. 187, col. 1033.

he became Chief Secretary of Ireland, though still outside the Cabinet. It was in this position that Campbell-Bannerman first showed his qualities of equanimity and imperturbability in the face of abuse and obstruction from the Irish members. He proved a sound if uninspiring and somewhat indolent minister, but he made no mistakes and did not allow himself to be rattled by Irish hostility. All the same, he appeared to at least one observer as 'very undistinguished'.[2] Campbell-Bannerman remained to the end of his life a poor public speaker, indeed 'probably the least fluent speaker who has ever come to lead the House of Commons'.[3] He had little charisma and only moderate administrative ability. His experience at the Irish Office had helped to convert him to Home Rule, and in Gladstone's brief third administration of 1886, he at last at the age of forty-nine entered the Cabinet as War Secretary, a position to which he returned in the Gladstone/Rosebery government of 1892. In none of the offices which he held did he prove an innovator. In 1895, Campbell-Bannerman had hoped to be appointed Speaker, a sign that he believed he would be unlikely to rise further in the ministerial ranks, but his Liberal colleagues decided that they could not do without him. In the ensuing years, he stood aloof from the quarrels which convulsed the party and achieved what seemed the almost impossible task of remaining on good terms with both Liberal Imperialists and Gladstonians.

By the time that Harcourt resigned as Liberal leader in the Commons in late 1898, the party was in despair. It had lost three leaders in the space of four and a half years and seemed without any sense of direction. The leadership was offered to Campbell-Bannerman without any particular enthusiasm, after Asquith had declined to be considered. *The Times* had quite mistakenly prophesied on 17 January 1899 that Sir Henry would '"mark time" respectably and even with dignity ... If "evolution" should bring a leader with more commanding claims to the front ... Sir Henry ... is not the person to stand in the way of a necessary change.' Meanwhile, he would prove 'a temporary leader who will serve adequately enough as a "warming pan" until a more commanding figure emerges'. He seemed to many to lack essential qualities of leadership. He was certainly not a dynamic figure and was accustomed to take long holidays abroad every year. Indeed, the Transvaal crisis of 1899 was to find him on the Continent. After returning to London, he was then to be in Paris on the day of Kruger's ultimatum. Nevertheless, to the surprise of many, Campbell-Bannerman was to prove just the Prime Minister that the party needed. 'There are few contrasts so startling in modern British politics', the biographer of Rosebery has written, 'as the incompetence of

2   Esher, *Journals and Letters*, vol. 1, p. 181.
3   Ensor, *England*, p. 384.

Campbell-Bannerman as Leader of the opposition and his ease, authority and ability as Prime Minister.'[4] It is not perhaps quite fair to suggest that he was an 'incompetent' opposition leader for he had shown great skill in holding his party together. But his abilities did not fully blossom until he became Prime Minister. In opposition, he had remained on good terms with all. 'It is', he was to say later, 'because I have no fault to find with anyone that I am where I am.'[5] Indeed, he was so genial that, as his private secretary was to record, 'he was continually forgetting that he *was* Prime Minister'.[6] He was, however, comparatively uninterested in social reform and in new thinking, remaining comfortable with his Gladstonian heritage. The issues that moved him were the traditional Liberal ones – non-sectarian education, removal of the Lords' veto, temperance reform and Home Rule. 'As to myself,' he wrote to Lord Spencer in February 1900,

> I am half-surprised to find that as I go on I get more and more confirmed in the old advanced Liberal principles, economical, social & political, with which I entered Parliament thirty years ago; and if all these gentlemen can't stand my principles, they must do without me! That would not break my heart.[7]

In February 1895, a Select Committee to consider Unemployment was set up. Campbell-Bannerman was to be chairman. He wrote to his cousin, 'They are going to put me on as Chairman of the Unemployed Committee – a horrible thing. I protested and said I knew nothing about poor law subjects – I had never even picked oakum.'[8] When receiving a deputation of the unemployed in November 1904, he told them that there was nothing he could do for them. But he was sensitive to human suffering, whether in the camps in South Africa or in relation to the poor at home, and courageous, as when he denounced 'methods of barbarism' in South Africa. He could also be radical as was to be shown when he pressed for wide-ranging trade union and House of Lords reform. 'We have not seen in our time', Asquith declared, in his eulogy in the Commons in 1908, 'a man of greater courage – courage not of the defiant or aggressive type, but calm, patient, persistent, indomitable.'[9] Like Gladstone, Campbell-Bannerman became more radical as he grew older. Less glamorous than Rosebery, less combative and powerful

---

4 Rhodes James, *Rosebery*, p. 450.
5 Quoted in Read, ed., *Edwardian England*, p. 105.
6 Francis Hirst, *In the Golden Days*, Frederick Muller, 1947, p. 259.
7 Wilson, *CB*, p. 326.
8 Spender, *Campbell-Bannerman*, vol. 1, p. 166.
9 House of Commons Debates, 27 April 1908, vol. 187, col. 1034.

in debate than Harcourt, he proved to have more staying power than either, as those who had underestimated him were to find out. He resembled in many ways another seemingly stolid and unimaginative leader of the left in the twentieth century, Clement Attlee, also elected as a stopgap but remaining party leader for twenty years, a longer period than any leader of a major party in the twentieth century. Both Campbell-Bannerman and Attlee secured landslide victories for their parties, despite being uncharismatic leaders, and both proved more radical than had been predicted. Indeed, one of Attlee's strongest supporters Ernest Bevin, the trade union leader, was prone to call Attlee 'our Campbell-Bannerman'.[10]

But Campbell-Bannerman did not prove to be a 'strong' Prime Minister in the sense of giving a clear sense of direction to his Cabinet. His government was one of departments

> in which each Minister is very largely a law unto himself and conducts the business of his office without interference from his colleagues and without any desire to interfere with them … The general rule is 'If you don't bother me, I won't bother you.' The result of such a system … is at first to produce an atmosphere of apparent harmony.[11]

And Campbell-Bannerman's government was indeed to prove harmonious, binding up the wounds of the previous years. The new Prime Minister was also skilful in handling the vast Liberal majority gained in the 1906 election which made the new House of Commons

> at the outset a difficult body to lead. It was rich in inexperienced idealists. Radicalism and socialism alike, released from the suppressions of two decades, were radiant with sudden hopes of a new heaven and a new earth. No leader not alive to that morning glory could have carried the house with him; and that was where Campbell-Bannerman in his kindly and generous old age gave the parliament an incomparably better start than the efficient but earth-bound Asquith could have done.[12]

Campbell-Bannerman was a Prime Minister in tune with the times. His weakness was that he had no long-term programme; and once the election pledges of 1906 had been carried out – preserving free trade, reversing *Taff Vale* and ending Chinese labour – he had little idea how to proceed further.

---

10 Quoted in Kenneth O. Morgan, *Labour People*, 2nd edition, Oxford University Press, 1997, p. 146.
11 'The Late Prime Minister', *The Spectator*, 11 April 1908.
12 Ensor, *England*, p. 391.

When, mortally ill, he resigned in 1908, the Liberals were badly in need of a reforming programme.

Campbell-Bannerman's government comprised almost the entire range of Liberal opinion. It was one of the strongest of modern times, in whose ranks would be found three future Prime Ministers – Asquith, Lloyd George and Churchill, the renegade ex-Conservative free trader who now entered the government as Under-Secretary for the Colonies at the age of thirty-one. 'They bought me cheap,' he told Rosebery.[13] But already Churchill had given clear signs of the remarkable energy, bravery and literary and intellectual ability which were to mark his long political career. To some, however, the Cabinet appointments appeared somewhat conservative, over-representing the more traditional Gladstonian wing of the party to which the Prime Minister himself belonged, and including five hereditary peers.

The second man in the government was the Chancellor of the Exchequer, Asquith (1852–1928). His style and background were quite different from those of his leader. His father had been a small businessman, a Congregationalist wool manufacturer in Yorkshire, who had died when Asquith was eight, and his mother suffered chronic ill health. When his father died, Asquith moved to London to stay with an uncle who paid for his education at the City of London School, from where he won a classical scholarship to Balliol College, Oxford. He shone academically, gaining a double first and being elected president of the union. Jowett, the master of the college, predicted that 'Asquith will get on; he is so direct'.[14] He then had a highly successful career as a barrister and, with the help of Haldane, became Liberal MP for East Fife in 1886. An incisive speaker, his maiden speech put him immediately in the front rank of debaters in the Commons. As soon as he entered Parliament, in the words of his biographer, 'he assumed the manner of a front bencher and the House accepted him at his own valuation'.[15] He came to be known as 'the sledgehammer' for the power with which he destroyed his opponents' arguments. He had the barrister's skill of assimilating a mass of information quickly and making rapid judgements upon it which appeared unanswerable. His Treasury officials were to say of him, 'Of course there is nothing like the Prime Minister's machinery once you have put the penny in the slot and got it going.'[16] But one had to put the penny in the slot first. 'He was', declared one commentator, 'incomparably the most powerful intellect in the ... Commons today – not the finest, not the subtlest, nor the most attractive, but the most effective ... The sentences of his orderly speech

13 Rhodes James, *Rosebery*, p. 461.
14 J. A. Spender and Cyril Asquith, *Life of Herbert Henry Asquith, Lord Oxford and Asquith*, Hutchinson, 1932, vol. 1, p. 35.
15 Ibid., p. 56.
16 Braithwaite, *Lloyd George's Ambulance Wagon*, p. 69.

march into action like disciplined units, marshalled and drilled.' But his 'reticence and dislike of display' would prevent him, by contrast with both Gladstone and Lloyd George, from gaining more than 'a small hold upon the affections of the public' – a perceptive verdict.[17] Unlike Gladstone and Lloyd George, he was not a visionary. Nor could he inspire the voters. But he was prepared to carry out great causes originated by others, once convinced of their justice and practicability. Appointed Home Secretary straight from the back benches in Gladstone's last government, he had proved one of the few successes in the unhappy Liberal administration of 1892 to 1895; and when the government fell, Harcourt had told Asquith's wife, 'You need not mind any of the quarrels, your man is the man of the future.'[18] He was, his friend Haldane wrote, 'one of the best Home Secretaries of recent years. He was just, he was thorough, and he was interested in the new bearing which science was beginning to have on industrial life.'[19] He soon came to be regarded as a natural Liberal leader. He had, Rosebery declared in 1895, 'that rare combination of head and heart which ... will conduct him to the highest office of the State'.[20] He could perhaps have become Liberal leader in 1899 after Harcourt's resignation. By 1908, his succession to the premiership was to be a matter of course. By the time he joined Campbell-Bannerman's government, he had lost touch with his Nonconformist roots and, under the influence of Margot Tennant, his second wife whom he married in 1894, had come to adopt an upper-class lifestyle thought by some radicals to be unbecoming in a Liberal leader. His entry into society was symbolised in the marriage register in 1894, signed by four Prime Ministers, past, present and future – Gladstone, Rosebery, Balfour and Asquith himself. In Haldane's words:

> London Society came ... to have a great attraction for him, and he grew by degrees diverted from the sterner outlook on life which he and I for long shared ... From the beginning he meant to be Prime Minister, sooner or later. For this position nature had endowed him to a great extent, but not completely. He had as fine an intellectual apparatus, in the way of grasp and understanding, as I ever saw in any man.

And Haldane then added the double-edged compliment, 'In his earlier political days he was a very serious person.'[21] By the early years of the twentieth

---

17 Cooper, *The British Welfare Revolution*, p. 121; Gardiner, *Prophets, Priests and Kings*, p. x.
18 Stephen Bates, *Asquith*, Haus, 2005, p. 35.
19 R. B. Haldane, *An Autobiography*, Hodder & Stoughton, 1929, p. 104.
20 Stansky, *Ambitions and Strategies*, p. 215.
21 Haldane, *Autobiography*, p. 104.

century, it was clear that Asquith was beginning to take to drink. As early as 1904, a commentator observed that in the Commons he was 'quite drunk on several occasions'.[22] He soon came to acquire the 'popular sobriquet' Perrier Jouet. In April 1911, Churchill wrote to his wife that 'only the persistent freemasonry of the House of Commons prevents a scandal'.[23] By July 1911, at a party he 'is keeping sober and only drank five glasses of champagne last night'. By 1914, he was 'fuddled three or four times in the week'. Even so, as Bonar Law, when Unionist leader, was ruefully to admit in 1911, 'Asquith drunk can make a better speech than any one of us, sober'. He then gave his Chief Whip this tribute to the man he was opposing at the despatch box. 'There is a mellow bonhomie, the nonchalance of Charles James Fox, and withal his many human frailties which all tend to conciliate an Opposition ... he wishes to be calm and imperturbable ... full of good cheer, enjoying his position.'[24]

Unlike Campbell-Bannerman, who strove to preserve a centrist position in the party, or perhaps a position slightly to the left of centre, Asquith was identified with the Liberal Imperialist wing of the party; and indeed, like his friends Grey and Haldane, had come under the influence of Milner, an influence which Campbell-Bannerman mocked as the 'religio Milneriana'. But Asquith was more radical than he seemed or than his lifestyle would indicate. Once in government, he got on well with Campbell-Bannerman and the disagreements apparent before 1906 entirely disappeared. As Prime Minister, he would have the great gift, particularly valuable for a government proposing radical change, of appearing statesmanlike, cautious and conservative. 'He is slow to take up adventurous courses,' one commentator wrote,

> but, once convinced, he has unequalled power to give them shape and, in doing so, to carry the conviction that comes from his own secure and impassioned intellect to that timid public who see the dread form of 'socialism' in every effort after a more just and therefore more firmly rooted State.[25]

His particular skill as Prime Minister was in holding a fissiparous if brilliant Cabinet of the left together. But he was to regard his role as that of chairman rather than leader and could be indecisive on occasion. He tended to act as arbiter of the ideas of others rather than an initiator. According to Churchill, Asquith in Cabinet was

---

22 Vincent, ed., *Crawford Papers*, p. 60.
23 Churchill, *Companion*, vol. 2, part 2, 1907–1911, p. 344.
24 Vincent, ed., *Crawford Papers*, pp. 161, 327, 193, 259.
25 Gardiner, *Prophets, Priests and Kings*, p. 62.

markedly silent. Indeed he never spoke a word in Cabinet if he could get his way without it. He sat, like the great Judge he was, hearing with trained patience the case deployed on every side, now and then interjecting a question or brief comment, searching or pregnant, which gave matters a turn towards the goal he wished to reach; and when at the end, amid all the perplexities and crosscurrents of ably and vehemently expressed opinion, he summed up, it was very rarely that the silence he had observed till then, did not fall on all.[26]

Liberal and tolerant in temperament, he was trusting of others and unwilling to think the worst of them. Believing as he did in the power of rational argument, it was difficult for him to comprehend what he was to regard as irrational behaviour on the part of Conservative peers, Ulster Unionists, suffragettes and radical trade unionists. Asquith was nevertheless to be Prime Minister for a longer continuous period than anyone since Lord Liverpool in the aftermath of the Napoleonic Wars, except for Margaret Thatcher and Tony Blair.

Sir Edward Grey (1862–1933) was the first Foreign Secretary since 1827 to be neither a peer nor the son of a peer. A hereditary baronet, he was the scion of an old Whig family and a collateral descendant of Lord Grey of the Great Reform Act of 1832. His grandfather had been a Cabinet minister in the 1840s and 1850s under Melbourne, Aberdeen and Palmerston, while his father had been an equerry of the Prince of Wales and had prepared his son for a political career. Like Asquith, Grey had been at Jowett's Balliol, but unlike Asquith he did not shine there, idling his time away and being rusticated by his college. He had, however, been allowed to return for his final examination in which he secured a third-class degree in law. He had not been deemed able enough to complete the course in ancient history and philosophy for which he had originally been admitted. In Parliament, however, he was to prove himself very assiduous. Elected Liberal MP for Berwick on Tweed in 1885, he was appointed a junior minister at the Foreign Office under Rosebery in 1892 aged just thirty. In opposition, he became Liberal spokesman on foreign affairs. He was, however, distinctly insular, his visits to the Continent having been confined to just two days in Paris. As Foreign Secretary, he was to go abroad just once, accompanying George V to France in April 1914. He spoke just one foreign language, French, and that not particularly well. Even so, and although labelled a Liberal Imperialist, his orientation, by contrast with Salisbury, was towards Europe rather than the

26 Churchill, *Great Contemporaries*, p. 114.

empire. His latest biographer is right to label him a 'Statesman of Europe'.[27] Regarded as being on the right of his party on foreign affairs, on domestic policy he was radical, more sympathetic towards Home Rule than his fellow Liberal Imperialists and a supporter of labour representation, female suffrage, land reform, the payment of MPs and an elected House of Lords.

Grey carried enormous authority in the Commons. 'If one were asked to say whose word carried the most weight in Parliament today,' declared the Liberal journalist A. G. Gardiner,

> there could, I think, be only one answer. Whether in office or out of office, whether to friend or foe, Sir Edward Grey is intrinsically the weightiest speaker of his time. When he sits down in the House of Commons, it is as though discussion has ceased. Other men speak from the bar; he speaks from the bench. He does not argue; he delivers a judgment. There is no appeal, and no one asks for an appeal.

Gardiner found it difficult to account for

> the source of this authority. There are many brilliant men here. Sir Edward Grey is not one of them. The stuff of his speech is plain to the point of homeliness. His thought is ordinary, almost conventional. He never coins a phrase that sticks nor wears a rhetorical flower in his buttonhole. He has none of the arts of popular appeal. He is remarkable neither for learning nor ambition. His knowledge is limited, and his insularity a tradition ... He seems ... a spectator who is a little bored by its feverish activities and ideal talk.

It was his 'aloofness from life that is the key to his unique position. He comes into affairs, as it were, from the outside, detached, unimpassioned, bringing his own atmosphere with him.' Gardiner compared his influence with that of the late Duke of Devonshire. 'It is the influence of a character of absolute purity of motive and of unyielding independence of thought. It is the influence of one to whom the world can offer no bribe.'[28] This estimate was shared even by Grey's opponents. In 1913, he was to be summed up by Arthur Ponsonby, a Liberal backbench MP on the left of the party who opposed his foreign policy:

> To begin with he is a gentleman in the best sense of the word. Personal

---

27 Otte, *Statesman of Europe*.
28 Gardiner, *Prophets, Priests and Kings*, pp. 72–4.

ambition and a desire to advertise himself I don't suppose he has ever felt for a single instant. This makes him a sharp contrast to many of his colleagues. His House of Commons manner has been a great service to him. It is very simple, very sincere, dignified and direct. He is rather aloof and unapproachable which makes a certain mystery that attracts.[29]

But his aloofness did him harm. He found it difficult to communicate effectively either to Liberal MPs or to the public and this was to lead to much misunderstanding of his foreign policy. He was to be accused of not taking MPs or the public into his confidence. Perhaps, however, no Foreign Secretary can take MPs or the public fully into their confidence. But at least one MP, the Irish Nationalist Swift MacNeill, felt in May 1911 that Grey had communicated well with the Commons.

> The success of the present Foreign Secretary has been very great. The secret of that success has been that he has taken the House of Commons into his confidence in Foreign Affairs to a greater extent than has any other gentleman in his position ... My recollection of the first fifteen years of my parliamentary life [he had entered the Commons in 1887] is that foreign affairs were scrupulously hidden from the House of Commons, that we were kept deliberately in the dark about them ... we have as Foreign Secretary one of ourselves a House of Commons man, ready so far as he can, to answer all questions and to give us so far as he can proper assurances as to how matters stand.[30]

Grey's critics were to allege that he was in the hands of his permanent officials who were anti-German. He certainly took more notice of the professionals than Salisbury had done, but he would weigh their arguments carefully and decide for himself; nor were his permanent officials as uniformly anti-German as his critics alleged, although a number of his senior officials did favour a formal alliance rather than an entente with France, something that the Liberal Party would almost certainly not have accepted. Grey was to remain at the Foreign Office for a longer continuous stretch than any other Foreign Secretary, and both Campbell-Bannerman and Asquith were to give him considerable leeway. Grey inspired confidence in all those he dealt with, whether ambassadors or Cabinet colleagues, largely because of his obvious disinterestedness, integrity and generosity of spirit. Grey's reputation was to be severely damaged by Lloyd George's *War Memoirs*, published in the 1930s,

---

29 Steiner, *Foreign Office and Foreign Policy*, p. 84.
30 Quoted in Gilbert Murray, *The Foreign Policy of Sir Edward Grey, 1906–15*, Clarendon Press, 1915, p. 125.

which attacked him for his pre-1914 foreign policy, but the attack was motivated by Liberal squabbles of the 1920s when they had been on opposite sides rather than anything that happened before the war. Indeed, in 1903, after Grey had spoken for him in Carnarvon, Lloyd George apparently declared that he had more confidence in Grey than in Asquith, and they remained on good terms until 1914.[31] Grey was to prove a great Foreign Secretary.

The third member of the Relugas trio, R. B. Haldane (1856–1928), became Secretary for War. The son of a devout Scottish Calvinist businessman, he entered Edinburgh University at the age of sixteen where he came to be fascinated by philosophy. He continued his studies at the University of Göttingen, and returning to Edinburgh was the only student in his year to graduate with a first in philosophy. Later in life, he was to claim that he had read Hegel's very difficult *Phenomenology of Mind* nineteen times.[32] He won the respect of professionals in the field and was invited to give the Gifford lectures at St Andrews in 1903–04, which were published as *The Pathway to Reality*. He also wrote a number of other philosophical works, as well as a translation of Schopenhauer. H. G. Wells said of *The Pathway to Reality* that it was 'like a very large soap bubble that for some inexplicable reason fails to be iridescent', and was to write of Haldane's later works that they were 'spoken of with profound respect and a careful avoidance of particulars in academic circles, but they mark no turning point in the history of the human mind. They move far away from vulgar reality in a special universe of discourse.' Clarity was indeed not the most obvious virtue of his philosophical work. Lloyd George called him 'the most confusing clever man I have ever met'.[33]

Rejecting the possibility of an academic career, Haldane became a barrister. Despite his somewhat porcine appearance, weak voice and lack of personal magnetism, which were to prove hindrances in his political career, he proved a great success at the Chancery Bar and at thirty-three became the youngest QC for fifty years. He had a gift for rapidly grasping the central points of an argument and an intuitive understanding of which arguments would appeal to a judge. But here too he had the gift of making the straightforward appear complex. In a case before the House of Lords, Lord James told him, 'I never knew how incapable I was of understanding these things until I heard your argument.'[34] And a Liberal commentator wrote that 'no one can invest his subject in a more lucid fog'. He was a poor communicator.[35] One commen-

31 Robbins, *Grey*, p. 112.
32 Sommer, *Haldane*, p. 113.
33 Ibid., p. 7.
34 Ibid., p. 137.
35 Gardiner, *Prophets, Priests and Kings*, p. 283.

tator has suggested that 'the substance of his delivery tended at times to read rather like a parody of a novel by Henry James'.[36] Haldane became Liberal MP for East Lothian in 1885, but unlike his close friends, Asquith and Grey, he had not been offered any post in the 1892 Liberal government.

The central belief which animated Haldane's political creed was that Britain should become more efficient and better organised, whether in industry, education or defence. Less of a party man than his fellow Liberal Imperialists, he was prepared to support Unionist policy provided only that it contributed to these aims. He had worked with Balfour in helping to enact the London University Act of 1898, establishing it as a teaching institution, and had played a major role in helping to create both the London School of Economics and Imperial College, which was to receive its Royal Charter in 1907. In 1903, he secured a University Charter for Liverpool which 'gave State recognition to a new policy ... that the number of the English Universities was to be increased'.[37] He was the only leading Liberal in sympathy with the 1902 Education Act, and infuriated his colleagues by abstaining rather than opposing the ordinance providing for indentured Chinese labour on the ground that only by this means could the Transvaal remain financially solvent. Partly because he would not cleave to the party line, he was disliked by rank-and-file Liberals and distrusted by Campbell-Bannerman, who nicknamed him Schopenhauer and regarded him as an intriguer. But to the extent that Haldane was an intriguer, he was a somewhat flat-footed one and his intrigues were rarely successful. Campbell-Bannerman declared that Haldane always preferred 'the back stairs to the front, but no matter, for the clatter can be heard all over the house'.[38] Haldane's concern for organisation and efficiency could make him appear somewhat remote and impersonal, but he was in fact a kindly man, deeply moved by personal distress. He had been, in his own words, 'haunted' by Oscar Wilde's suffering, visiting him in prison on a number of occasions and making sure that he had a supply of books. He arranged for Wilde to be transferred to prisons where the obligations of hard labour were less onerous and made sure that his wife and children were looked after while he was incarcerated. On Wilde's release, Haldane was sent a copy of *The Ballad of Reading Gaol* by way of thanks. 'His curiously woolly mind', thought Beatrice Webb, 'would make him an unattractive figure if it were not for the beaming kindliness of his nature, warm appreciation of friends and a certain pawky humour with which he surveys the world.'[39]

---

36 Heuston, *Lives of the Lord Chancellors*, p. 196.
37 Sommer, *Haldane*, p. 129.
38 Hirst, *In the Golden Days*, p. 264.
39 MacKenzie, *Diary of Beatrice Webb*, vol. 2, p. 113, entry for 3 May 1897.

Haldane's inability to explain himself clearly meant that he would never become a popular political figure. And he was to give a dangerous hostage to fortune, saying, at a private dinner party, that Germany was his spiritual home. What he meant was that he had found German philosophy congenial. But when the remark was made public during the 1914 war, it did him great damage. That was unfair. He did, it is true, admire German efficiency and the high standard of German education, and was unwise enough to call his favourite dog Kaiser, but he had no sympathy with German militarism. His was the Germany of Goethe and Hegel, not the Prussian parade-ground. He was indeed to be amongst the minority of ministers in 1914 who believed that Britain should fight alongside France even before Belgian neutrality was violated. Although he knew little of army matters, he applied his powerful mind to army reform so that by 1914 it was far more effective than when he had taken office, even if still unprepared for the new kind of war that Britain was to face.

The President of the Board of Trade was David Lloyd George (1863–1945). He had been offered a choice between the Postmaster Generalship or the Board of Trade. He took the latter even at the cost of sacrificing £500 a year in salary. His background was quite different from that of the other Cabinet ministers. He had been born David George in Manchester, the son of a former headmaster of a Welsh non-denominational school who had moved to England. His father died when he was just seventeen months old, and he was brought up in Llanystumdwy, near Criccieth in the Llŷn Peninsula of north-west Wales by his uncle, Richard Lloyd, who doted on him. But Lloyd George was not quite as underprivileged as he was accustomed to claim. Richard Lloyd was a Baptist minister and a master-cobbler who employed five assistants and was known as 'the Hans Sachs of Llanystumdwy'.[40] In tribute to the education which he received from his uncle, David altered his name to David Lloyd George. At home, the family normally spoke Welsh, and indeed Lloyd George was to be the first and so far the only British Prime Minister whose primary language was not English. He lived with his uncle in a modest but comfortable cottage with a garden and an outside closet which he was later accustomed to call 'the House of Lords'. He trained as a solicitor, and became known as a spokesman for Nonconformists and tenant farmers. After the first elections to the new Carnarvonshire County Council in 1889, he was asked to become an alderman – the youngest in Wales – a position he retained for the rest of his life. In 1890, he won Carnarvon Boroughs in a by-election by just eighteen votes. He retained this constituency until 1945, when he accepted a peerage, and first made his mark in the Commons

40 Grigg, *Young Lloyd George*, p. 31.

as a spokesman for Welsh interests and Welsh political culture, a culture distinguished by its popular and egalitarian ethos. Indeed, until 1923, he was to describe himself in *Dod's Parliamentary Companion* as a radical and Welsh nationalist, though he abandoned his nationalism once he became a minister. He consolidated his radical reputation through his pro-Boer stance, which first brought him to wider public attention, and as a spokesman for Nonconformist grievances over the Education Act. 'Lloyd George', Churchill wrote to his cousin Lord Hugh Cecil in January 1904, 'represents three things: Wales, English Radicalism, and Nonconformists, and they are not three things which politicians can overlook.'[41] In 1896, Lloyd George had sought to unify the Cymru Fydd (Young Wales) movement, which sought self-government for Wales, into one national Welsh federation, but he had been defeated by the English-speaking Liberals of south Wales. He had more empathy with the chapel-going small tenant farmers of north Wales than with the industrial working class in the south. In Monmouthshire, so Lloyd George had told his wife in 1895, 'the audiences in these semi-English districts are not comparable to those I get in the Welsh districts. Here the people have sunk into a morbid footballism.' Speaking in Cardiff in 1896, he insisted that the Welsh were 'a nation of Church and Chapel goers and Sunday school lovers' while the English were 'a nation of footballers, stock exchanges, public-house and music-hall frequenters'.[42] His radicalism was directed against the squirearchy and the church, not the employing class, many of whom were Liberals, and before 1902 he was largely ignorant of labour questions. He did not, for example, speak out on the great six-month coal stoppage in south Wales in 1898. Until 1905, he could be regarded as a traditional Liberal. But in office after 1905, his perspective moved well beyond Wales and traditional Liberalism. He ceased to be interested in Home Rule and became concerned with wider issues of poverty and deprivation, so that he came to be, with Churchill, the leading social reformer of the Liberal government.[43]

Like Asquith, whom he was eventually to supplant, Lloyd George was a powerful orator, but while Asquith's speeches represented the triumph of logic and incisive argument, he could not move audiences as Lloyd George did. Lloyd George was the most effective speaker in the Liberal ranks. But his speeches, while they excited his followers, antagonised his opponents, who found it difficult to forgive his biting tongue. From his early days in Parliament, many predicted a significant future for him, noticing a resemblance to Chamberlain. He also had an unerring sense, at least until 1918,

---

41 Churchill, *Companion*, vol. 2, part 1, p. 284.
42 Grigg, *Young Lloyd George*, pp. 201, 202.
43 K. O. Morgan, 'The Welsh Wizard through English Eyes', *Western Mail*, 21 June 1973. This is a review of the first volume of John Grigg's multi-volume biography.

of intuiting what the public would tolerate, an understanding of the art of the possible. He came increasingly to doubt the traditional Liberal nostrums on which he had been brought up, and approached government as a series of problems which needed to be resolved empirically. Every problem had a political solution if one but knew how to find it. His political career was to show him to be a great improviser. At the Board of Trade, he succeeded in enacting legislation in areas such as merchant shipping, company law, copyright, patents and regulation of the Port of London. He showed his talent for conciliation by averting a threatened railway strike. He also established contacts with business leaders whom he came to admire for their capacity to 'get things done'. His effectiveness at the Board of Trade established his claim to the Exchequer in 1908. But he was not merely an empiricist. He had vision and a genuine sympathy for the poor and underprivileged. Yet, from early in his political career, he displayed volatility and disloyalty to friends and colleagues. In consequence, he never inspired trust. He appeared, all too often, to be working for himself, rather than his party or a cause. Sir Robert Chalmers, his Permanent Secretary from 1911 to 1913, was not alone in finding him 'a treacherous man', telling Mrs Asquith in 1913, 'People who think of themselves first are not really worth spending time on.'[44] Asquith regarded him as 'the flame at which all warmed, and many scorched their hands' but added 'he lacks the one thing needful – he does not inspire trust'.[45] This view was shared by Grey, who told the journalist J. A. Spender after the war that Lloyd George has 'some great qualities without being a great man & ... [he] is constitutionally incapable of understanding that straightforwardness is essential and "cleverness" fatal to success in the long run, whether it be in politics, in business or friendship'.[46] All the same, Unionists were to prefer Lloyd George's 'frank and honest hypocrisy' to ostentatious displays of principle by other Liberal leaders.[47] And Liberals and Unionists alike had to admit his remarkable executive abilities. 'He was', Churchill was to say, 'the greatest master of the art of getting things done and of putting things through that I ever knew; in fact no British politician in my day has possessed half his competence as a mover of men and affairs.'[48] He it was who was to wrench the Liberal government from its post-Gladstonian instincts and render it an instrument for social reform.

But the most remarkable new recruit was Winston Churchill (1874–1965), the greatest British statesman of the twentieth century, who joined the

---

44 Cooper, *The British Welfare Revolution*, p. 277.
45 Quoted in Read, ed., *Edwardian England*, pp. 107–8.
46 Spender Papers, 31 July 1920, MSS. 46,389, f. 33.
47 Vincent, ed., *Crawford Papers*, p. 325.
48 Quoted by Tom Jones in the eightieth birthday tribute to Lloyd George in *The Observer*, 17 January 1943.

government as Under-Secretary for the Colonies, a more important position than most junior ministries, since the Colonial Secretary, Lord Elgin, was in the Upper House. Indeed, Churchill had declined the seemingly more important post of Financial Secretary to the Treasury, normally a stepping stone to the Cabinet, for this very reason. For in the Treasury, he would be Junior to Asquith and dominated by him. At the Colonial Office, by contrast, he could easily wrest the initiative from his minister, who was elderly and, even at the best of times, not very assiduous.

Churchill's career had been remarkable even before entering Parliament. Upon leaving school, he had joined the army and was posted to India, where, when nearly twenty-two, 'the desire for learning came upon me. I began to feel myself wanting in even the vaguest knowledge about the many large spheres of thought.' He asked his mother to send him books – beginning with the twelve volumes of Macaulay's history. When the books came, he devoured them, reading for four or five hours a day – Macaulay and Gibbon, then Plato's *Republic*, Aristotle's *Politics*, Schopenhauer on pessimism, Malthus on population and Darwin on the *Origin of Species*; together, as he says, 'with other books of lesser standing' – and then a number of books on religion.[49] His education and historical understanding is the key to his political career. They gave him an inestimable advantage, enabling him to approach problems in a fresh way, untrammelled by class identification or ideological preconceptions. He fought his first parliamentary election in 1899 at a by-election in the double-member constituency of Oldham, both seats being vacant at the same time. His running mate was a Conservative trade unionist, James Mawdsley, who regarded it as 'a compliment to the freedom of British institutions in the standing together on the same platform of a son of the old and well-famed British aristocracy and a spinner from the jinny-gate'.[50] Churchill proclaimed his support for the empire and also social reform. 'To keep our Empire we must have a free people, an educated and well-fed people. That is why we long for Old Age Pensions and the like,' he had declared in a speech at Southsea in 1898 at the age of just twenty-three. 'The improvement of the British breed is my political aim in life,' he had told his cousin Ivor Guest in 1899.[51] Despite being a Conservative, he favoured reversal of the *Taff Vale* judgment. Defeated in 1899, he was returned for Oldham in the 1900 general election. By the time he entered Parliament at the age of twenty-five, he already had more experience of the world than

---

49 Churchill, *My Early Life*, pp. 115–16.
50 Henry Pelling, 'Churchill and the Labour Movement', in Robert Blake and William Roger Louis, eds, *Churchill*, Oxford University Press, 1993, p. 113.
51 Randolph S. Churchill, *Winston S. Churchill, vol. 1, Youth 1874–1900*, Heinemann, 1967, p. 422; Martin Gilbert, *Churchill: A Life*, Heinemann, 1991.

most men twice his age, as a soldier, military correspondent and author. 'He had fought in more continents than Napoleon, and seen as many campaigns as any living general.'[52] He had already published five books – four on the various military campaigns in which he participated, and a novel, *Savrola*. This romantic work is written in the style of *The Prisoner of Zenda* and is not rated very highly. Churchill did not rate it highly himself. In his autobiography, he says, 'I have consistently urged my friends to abstain from reading it.'[53] Through his writings, Churchill had accumulated a fortune of around £10,000, sufficient for his parliamentary expenses and to support his widowed mother. When he entered Parliament, he was hailed as having

> fame already behind him, and absolutely every possibility the Empire can offer in front. This young man has the most dazzling chances in the world, and entering Parliament ... combines more advantages than any politician at his age has done since Pitt. Mr Winston Churchill is not likely to let the grass grow under his feet, and his danger there is likely to be in forgetting that 'a young man in a hurry' is even less impressive than an old one.[54]

As an MP, Churchill rapidly turned himself into an assiduous parliamentary figure, despite a minor speech impediment – a lisp. When he had been on the run having escaped from Boer captivity, the warrant for his arrest declared that he 'talks through the nose and cannot pronounce the letter "s" properly'. The Liberal *Daily Chronicle* wrote after his maiden speech, 'Mr Churchill is a medium-sized, undistinguished young man, with an unfortunate lisp in his voice.'[55] He is often thought to have been a natural speaker. But he found impromptu speaking difficult. He had to apply extraordinary self-discipline to become the fine speaker with whom the world became familiar. At the beginning of his parliamentary career, he learnt his speeches by heart. His great friend, the Tory barrister, MP and future Lord Chancellor, F. E. Smith said, 'Winston has spent the best years of his life composing his impromptu speeches.'[56] On 22 April 1904, however, in the House of Commons, Churchill lost the thread of his argument and had to sit down in the middle of his speech. After that, he always brought with him copious notes in case he should suffer a further breakdown.

During his first term in the Commons, Churchill decided to write a

---

52 Gardiner, *Pillars of Society*, p. 61.
53 Churchill, *My Early Life*, p. 161.
54 Leonard Courtney, 'The Vindication of Democracy', *Fortnightly Review*, 1900, p. 823. Churchill's father, Lord Randolph, had said of Gladstone's Home Rule proposal in 1886 that it was by 'an old man in a hurry'.
55 Churchill, *Young Statesman*, p. 12.
56 Nicholas Soames (Churchill's grandson), 'Sweat and tears made Winston Churchill's name', *Daily Telegraph*, 3 May 2011. This article, condensed from a lecture, gives a fine account of how Churchill prepared his speeches.

biography of his father, Lord Randolph Churchill, who had been Chancellor of the Exchequer and Leader of the Commons in 1886 before an impulsive resignation ended his ministerial career. Churchill had been bullied by his father but nevertheless worshipped him. Indeed, during the first part of his career, he was to model himself on him. One diarist noticed in 1903:

> In mind and manner he is a strange replica of his father with all his father's suddenness and assurance and I should say more than his father's ability. There is just the same *gaminerie* and contempt of the conventional and the same engaging plain spokenness and readiness to understand. As I listened to him recounting conversations he had had with Chamberlain, I seemed once more to be listening to Randolph on the subject of Northcote and Salisbury.[57]

The biography of his father appeared in two volumes, of around 1,000 pages, in 1906. It is a remarkable work for a man of thirty-one – and remains of great scholarly value, being based on extensive quotations from his father's papers and interviews with his political colleagues. But in the course of writing the biography, Churchill's political views began to change, since he came to think that the Conservatives had betrayed his father's legacy. His father had believed that Conservatives could prosper only if they were a party of social reform. Instead, since Lord Randolph's downfall, they had become, in Churchill's view, a reactionary party and were being led by the very same people – Lord Salisbury and his nephew, Arthur Balfour – who, Churchill believed, had betrayed his father. They were leading the Conservative Party in the wrong direction. Churchill was to regard the outcome of the 1906 election as a vindication of his father's warnings. By failing to embrace social reform, the old gang had ensured a Conservative collapse.

Churchill's interest in social reform played a part in his decision in 1904 to cross the floor and join the Liberals, though his main reason was to defend free trade. Perhaps he had made a mistake in joining the Conservatives in the first place. Rosebery had written of Peel that he had been 'sworn to Toryism too young to know the meaning of the oath'.[58] That was true also of Churchill. But many attributed Churchill's change of party to self-interest and desire for office. For, by 1904, the Unionists seemed on their last legs and a Liberal victory was generally expected. Churchill had to face the accusation that he was unreliable, an accusation that would dog him for much of his political career. 'The one real difficulty I have to encounter is the suggestion

57 R. F. Foster, *Lord Randolph Churchill: A Political Life*, Clarendon Press, 1981, p. 383.
58 Lord Rosebery, 'Sir Robert Peel', in *Miscellanies*, 5th edition, Hodder & Stoughton, 1922, vol. 1, p. 189.

that I am moved by mere restless ambition,' he had written in October 1902. Characteristically, this confession was made 'not to a youthful contemporary but to an ex-Prime Minister, Lord Rosebery'.[59] Later, a woman's suffrage journal was to write, 'In all his brief public career all his opinions have been subject to modification, save only his belief in the desirability of office.'[60] It is difficult to overstate the anger kindled by Churchill's change of parties, such that, on one occasion, every single Unionist MP walked out of the chamber when he began to speak.

Churchill appeared to many arrogant, bumptious, self-centred and self-advertising, and he could be noisy and tactless. But unlike Lloyd George, he was not devious and was aware of his weaknesses, weaknesses similar to those which had destroyed his father, and he worked hard to overcome them. In 1908, at the age of thirty-three, he was to enter the Cabinet as President of the Board of Trade, the youngest Cabinet minister for forty years, and then in 1910 he was to become the youngest Home Secretary since Peel in 1822, and almost certainly the only one to have himself been a prisoner, under the Boers in 1899. He was then to hold other Cabinet positions under both Liberal and Conservative governments. But it was not until 1940 that he was finally to come into his own. He was perhaps best summed up in the words of his friend Lady Lytton, who said, 'The first time you meet him you see all his faults, and the rest of your life you spend in discovering his virtues.'[61]

Amongst the other members of the new government in the Commons, Fowler at seventy-five, Lord President of the Council, was now past his best, and in 1908 was translated to the Lords where the Liberals were not very effectively represented. Of Lord Ripon, the new Lord Privy Seal, an elderly dugout who had first served in Palmerston's last government in 1859, one peer wrote to his son in December 1905 that he was 'gaga'; Lord Tweedmouth, First Lord of the Admiralty, 'cannot keep his temper and is hated on our side'; Lord Crewe, the Lord President, 'makes a speech like a mute at a funeral'; while Lord Carrington, President of the Board of Agriculture, had a 'reputation for "gaffe" which was worldwide'.[62]

There was, finally, a symbolism in the appointment to the Cabinet of John Burns, a Lib-Lab who had been involved in the 1889 London dock strike, as President of the Local Government Board, the first working man to enter the Cabinet. But sadly his achievement in that office was to prove minimal.

---

59 Churchill, *Young Statesman*, p. 47; Cameron Hazlehurst, 'Churchill's aim to improve the British breed', *The Times*, 3 September 1969.
60 Quoted in Leslie Parker Hume, *The National Union of Women's Suffrage Societies 1897–1914* [1982], Routledge, 2016, p. 191.
61 Gilbert, *Churchill*, p. 174.
62 Adonis, *Making Aristocracy Work*, p. 22.

THE 1906 GENERAL ELECTION

Campbell-Bannerman confidently dissolved the Commons, opening the Liberal campaign with a speech at the Albert Hall on 21 December, his first public appearance as Prime Minister. Adapting a remark of Chamberlain's on the colonies, he declared that 'we desire to develop our undeveloped estates in this country – to colonise our own country', to make Britain 'less a pleasure-ground for the rich and more of a treasure-house for the nation'.[63] But the Liberal manifesto, in the form of Campbell-Bannerman's election address, gave little hint of the radical social reforms for which the Liberals would be remembered. The address was devoted primarily to an attack on Unionist financial profligacy, which, it alleged, had resulted in higher taxation, indebtedness and unemployment. The section on the new government's programme was remarkable for its emptiness and did little more than repeat old slogans. No doubt Campbell-Bannerman was forced to be non-committal to avoid reopening old wounds and again dividing the party. The address in fact consisted of just two paragraphs, one on domestic and one on foreign affairs, prefaced by the statement that 'our own policy is well known to you, and I need not here repeat the terms of the public declaration which it fell to me to make shortly after assuming office'. It did, however, commit the government 'by a course of strenuous legislation and administration, to secure those social and economic reforms which have been too long delayed'. But it gave no hint of what these reforms might be, and the new Prime Minister was committed, as a good Gladstonian, to retrenchment in public spending. 'The policy upon which the Government has taken office', he was to say in March 1906, 'and upon which they have been supported by their friends is the policy of retrenchment.'[64] On foreign policy, the address called for a 'substantial continuity of policy' with the Unionists, the implication being that the entente with France would be preserved. It was not wholly unfair for Balfour to declare in 1911 that 'the greatest victory at the polls ever won by any Party was won upon no policy at all – CB's victory in 1906'.[65]

The 1906 election was certainly not a victory for social reform. Campbell-Bannerman was more concerned to win over the centrist floating voter than to propose a radical programme. 'The election was fought on the record of the Conservative Government and the fiscal proposals of Chamberlain: and it was the novel rather than the traditional elements of Conservatism that the voters condemned.'[66]

63 Spender, *Campbell-Bannerman*, vol. 2, p. 209.
64 House of Commons Debates, 7 March 1906, vol. 153, col. 554.
65 Dugdale, *Balfour*, vol. 1, p 325.
66 Bealey and Pelling, *Labour and Politics*, p. 265.

The issue of cheap Chinese labour on the Rand played a surprisingly important part in the election campaign, but this did not indicate a sudden upsurge of humanitarianism. Instead, it seems that there was some racial prejudice against the Chinese. In the January 1905 by-election in North Dorset, the Liberals claimed that the Chinese were held as slaves without food, while their money had been taken by Chamberlain, who wanted all whites out of Africa and sought to reduce working men in Britain to a diet of barley bread.[67] The social psychologist Graham Wallas was to write that 'anyone ... who saw much of politics in the winter of 1905–06 must have noticed that the pictures of Chinamen on the hoardings aroused among very many of the voters an immediate hatred of the Mongolian racial type. This hatred was transferred to the Conservative party.'[68] In *The New Machiavelli*, H. G. Wells's *roman-à-clef* published in 1911, the successful Liberal candidate noticed 'delight in the marketplace when he declared that the voters had given the issue of Chinese labour "notice to quit"', but 'whether that delight expressed hostility to Chinamen or to their practical enslavement no student of the General Election of 1906 has ever been able to determine. Certainly one of the most effective posters on our side displayed a hideous yellow face, just that and nothing else.' And while Campbell-Bannerman in his first speech as Prime Minister had promised to 'stop forthwith the recruitment of and embarkation of Chinese coolies', it was found that licences for 14,500 additional workers who had embarked or were embarking from China could not be revoked without new legislation, while the 47,000 already in the Transvaal were to be left under the jurisdiction of the government of that colony.[69]

The voters seemed to want 'a return to nineteenth-century Gladstonianism, to the policies of Little England, to elected School Boards, and to Free Trade'. Bernard Shaw declared that the election was a striking indication of the conservatism of the electorate.[70] But the Liberal Publication Department 'probably reflected the mood of the electorate when it produced for the election 9 million leaflets on the fiscal question, 6½ million on the Tory record, 2 million on Chinese labour, and 2 million on social issues'. Only one Cabinet minister – John Burns – mentioned old-age pensions in his election address.[71] Campbell-Bannerman, speaking in Dunfermline on 29 December, declared that the issue of pensions was 'not so simple as Mr Chamberlain told us it was ... Before you can have any big scheme for old age pensions

67 *The Times*, 28 January 1905, p. 12 and 8 February 1905, p. 8.
68 Graham Wallas, *Human Nature in Politics* [1908], University of Nebraska Press, 1962, pp. 126–7.
69 Spender, *Campbell-Bannerman*, vol. 2, p. 228; Dugdale, *Balfour*, vol. 1, p. 324.
70 Bealey and Pelling, *Labour and Politics*, p. 265.
71 Pelling, *Popular Politics*, p. 130.

the national finances must be put into a better position.'[72] The Liberals managed to conduct a crusading campaign without raising awkward questions which might have split the party. In *The New Machiavelli*, the hero, elected as a Liberal MP in 1906, discovers that 'it was tremendously clear what they were against. The trouble was to find out what on earth they were for!' The election was won on issues of the past, not the future.

The Unionists had greater constructive achievements to their credit than was apparent at the time. Indeed, just as the Liberal programme was far less radical than it seemed, so the Balfour government had greater reforming achievements than were then perceived, particularly in education and relief of unemployment; they had contributed to resolving the Irish land problem and had begun the process of reorientating Britain's foreign relations and reorganising her defence. But all this made little impact on the voters, and the Education Act almost certainly lost votes amongst Nonconformists. The proposed departure from free trade was also a vote loser, owing to fear of a rise in food prices, while Home Rule was no longer the bugbear that it had been, and in any case the Liberals were not intending to introduce it. In consequence, as Austen Chamberlain wrote to his stepmother, 'a speech on Home Rule' had become 'like flogging a dead horse'.[73] The Unionists remained split on tariff reform. The Duke of Devonshire urged Unionist free trade electors to vote for free trade candidates, while tariff reformers ran candidates against eleven Unionist free traders, including Greenwich where Lord Hugh Cecil was to come bottom of the poll behind the Liberal and the tariff reformer.[74] In 1907, Bonar Law was to tell Lord Hugh's brother that 'they would rather lose twenty seats' than 'have him [Lord Hugh] back in the Commons'.[75] But the anti-free-trade Unionists were themselves split on what should replace free trade – whether the Balfour policy or the Chamberlain policy – and on whether Balfour or Chamberlain should lead them. Fewer than half of Unionist candidates declared in their election addresses that they favoured the Chamberlain policy of duties on food imports.[76] As *The Times* commented on 5 February 1906, the Unionists had gone into the election with at least two competing policies and a dual leadership. The key factor in the election was Unionist unpopularity, rather than enthusiasm for the Liberals or social reform. In an unpublished autobiography, Herbert Gladstone attributed Liberal success to '(1) The Liberal-Labour pact. (2) Free Trade. (3) CB's South African policy. (4) Conservative outstay of Welcome, (a)

---

72 Adams, *Edwardian Heritage*, p. 236.
73 Chamberlain, *Politics from Inside*, p. 39.
74 Rempel, 'Lord Hugh Cecil's Parliamentary Career', p. 122.
75 Ibid., p. 124.
76 Ollivier, ed., *Colonial and Imperial Conferences*, vol. 1, p. 297.

inducing a wish for change and (b) arrears of industrial and social legislation. (5) Education.'[77] The Unionists would probably have lost the election of 1906 even without tariff reform. But tariff reform turned a defeat into a rout. 'A candidate had only to be a Free-trader to get in,' the *Manchester Guardian* believed,

> whether he was known or unknown, semi-Unionist or thorough Home Ruler, Protestant or Catholic, entertaining or dull. He had only to be a Protectionist to lose all chance of getting in, though he spoke with the tongues of men and angels, though he was a good employer to many electors, or had led the House of Commons, or fought in the Crimea.[78]

The 1906 election was in a sense a reversal of that of 1886. Both Home Rule and tariff reform had the potential to alter political alignments for a generation. Both stirred up deep-seated fears in the minds of voters – in 1886 the fear of breaking up the kingdom, in 1906 the fear of a rise in food prices and a return to the hungry 1840s. 'The verdict', declared Fowler, 'is a national one against Protection in every shape and disguise.'[79]

The 1906 election resulted in a landslide victory in terms of seats, for the Liberals. There had been a swing of 12 per cent since 1900, a larger swing than was achieved by Attlee in 1945 or Blair in 1997; and the election yielded the only single-party majority government between 1895 and 1914.

Party	Number of seats	Percentage of vote
Liberals	401	49.0
LRC	29	5.9 (39.9 per cent per opposed candidate)
Irish Parliamentary Party	83	0.6 (63.1 per cent per opposed candidate. 74 of its 83 candidates were returned unopposed)
Unionists	157	43.6

All but three of Balfour's Cabinet, including the ex-Prime Minister himself, lost their seats. The election yielded the second largest majority a government of the left was to achieve in the twentieth century; the largest was to be achieved by Tony Blair at the very end of the century, in 1997. But as in that election, the electoral system exaggerated the lead of the winning party. The Unionists, though defeated, won nearly 44 per cent of the vote, slightly more

---

77 Harris and Hazlehurst, 'Campbell-Bannerman as Prime Minister', p. 373fn.
78 *Manchester Guardian*, 15 January 1906.
79 Dutton, 'Unionist Politics and the Aftermath of the General Election of 1906', p. 863.

than the percentage that very much later led in 1983 and 1987 to landslide victories for Margaret Thatcher. Nevertheless, the 1906 election inaugurated a new era. The Liberals with their Labour and Irish allies enjoyed a majority of 356 in a House of 670 members. The Liberal Party alone enjoyed a majority of 132. The election brought new men to the Commons, men of moderate means who had risen by merit rather than inheritance and needed to earn their own living. The 1900 Parliament had been dominated by members of the Anglican Church. The new Parliament, according to the National Free Church Council, contained 176 Nonconformists, mostly Liberals, the largest number in the Commons since the time of Cromwell. In the Cabinet, there were just six Anglicans but ten Nonconformists.[80] The election signalled the end of aristocratic government. In the Balfour Cabinet of 1905, just four of the seventeen members had not belonged to the aristocracy or landed classes. The new Liberal Cabinet contained only six members out of nineteen who did. Its leading members came instead from the professional classes – Asquith, Haldane and Loreburn were barristers, Lloyd George and Fowler solicitors, Morley, who became India Secretary, and Birrell, President of the Board of Education, had been journalists, James Bryce, the new Irish Secretary, was an academic, while John Burns was a working man. Writing in 1948, one commentator believed that, to many Conservatives, the rank and file of the Liberal Party in the Commons were regarded as 'distastefully radical and lower middle class. Looking back indeed, it appears to me that Liberalism was much more socially taboo than Labour has been in recent years.'[81]

The 1906 election showed the long-delayed effects of expansion of the franchise in 1867 and 1884 and the educational changes which underpinned it. That reaction had been delayed by Gladstone's conversion to Home Rule which had split the Liberals, and by the imperialist phase which followed. But now the democratic wave came back in full flood. And the new government, despite the intentions of many of its leaders, would be dominated by social reform. 'If you allow the tramway conductor to vote,' Sidney Webb had warned the Royal Commission on Labour in 1892,

> he will not forever be satisfied with exercising the vote over such matters as the appointment of the Ambassador to Paris, or even the position of the franchise. He will realise that the forces that keep him at work for sixteen hours a day for three shillings a day are not the forces of hostile kings, of nobles, of princes; but whatever forces they are he will, it seems to me,

---

80 *The Times*, 8 February 1906,
81 Victoria de Bunsen, *Charles Roden Buxton*, George Allen & Unwin, 1948, p. 52.

seek so far as possible to control them by his vote. That is to say, he will more and more seek to convert his political democracy into what one may roughly term an industrial democracy, so that he may obtain some kind of control as a voter over the conditions under which he lives.[82]

For the first time since expansion of the franchise, a radical government would be able to carry out policies which the Conservatives and ruling elite did not like. The 1892 government had been hobbled by its dependence on the Irish. After 1906, the left would not be so hobbled. But if the Conservatives were impotent in the elected chamber, the Commons, they still held a vast majority in the unelected chamber, the House of Lords. Of 602 peers, around 475 were Unionists, while ninety at most were Liberals. Whatever the result of the election, so Balfour told an audience in 1906, the Unionists 'should still control, whether in power or opposition, the destinies of this great Empire'; and he told Lansdowne, Unionist leader in the Lords, that 'there has certainly never been a period in our history in which the House of Lords will be called upon to play a part at once so important, so delicate, and so difficult'.[83] The history of the years until 1911 would be in large part a story of how far the Unionists in the Lords would carry their opposition to the elected government – and how the Liberals would react to it.

The Balfour government had ended in electoral disaster. Like Gladstone, he had failed to contain Chamberlain, the wrecker of parties, but he had at least avoided a repetition of the split of 1846. And Balfour's career in government was by no means over. He retained the respect of many Liberals as well as many in his own party. In 1914, Asquith was to declare that he was, in relation to other Conservatives, 'the only quick mind in that ill-bred crowd'.[84] The war was to resurrect his career in government. He was to serve in both the Asquith and Lloyd George coalitions, and then in Stanley Baldwin's Conservative government in the 1920s. He was indeed to serve in Cabinet either as Prime Minister or in a subordinate post for a total of twenty-six years, longer than any other politician in the twentieth century, including Churchill and Lloyd George, and longer than Gladstone, Palmerston and the younger Pitt. He was a remarkable exception to every other Prime Minister in that much of his reputation was gained *after* he left Downing Street, so that his premiership was not in fact the culmination of his career.

82 Quoted in Gilbert, *The Evolution of National Insurance in Great Britain: The Origins of the Welfare State*, pp. 25–6. This book covers a much wider scope than its title suggests and is an indispensable analysis of the social reforms of the Liberal government.
83 Adams, *Balfour*, pp. 233–4.
84 Michael and Eleanor Brock, eds, *H. H. Asquith: Letters to Venetia Stanley*, Oxford University Press, 1982, p. 60.

The election of 1906 had a further significance, one which was to have remarkable consequences for the whole world, though whether for good or ill is still being disputed. During the campaign, Balfour met a young lecturer in organic chemistry at Manchester University, the Zionist leader Chaim Weizmann, who would be the first President of the newly created state of Israel in 1948. Balfour was converted by Weizmann to the Zionist cause. Here lay the seeds of the Balfour Declaration of 1917, committing the British government to supporting a national home for the Jews in Palestine. At the end of his life, Balfour made a remarkable confession to his niece and biographer that, amidst his manifold political achievements, 'on the whole he felt that what he had been able to do for the Jews had been the thing he looked back upon as the most worth his doing'.[85]

THE LABOUR PARTY AND ITS LEADERS

The Labour Representation Committee (LRC) renamed itself the Labour Party after the election, and despite the entente with the Liberals, took its place on the opposition benches. Of its twenty-nine MPs, twenty-three had been sponsored by their trade unions, the other six by the Independent Labour Party (ILP). In the constituencies it fought, the LRC had won nearly 40 per cent of the vote. There were in addition to the Labour MPs, seventeen Lib-Lab trade union MPs, thirteen of whom were miners. But Labour now had more MPs than the Lib-Labs, a crucial step in its progress towards becoming a party to represent the working class. Speaking for J. W. Taylor, MP for Chester-le-Street, a Lib-Lab candidate sponsored by his union who joined the LRC immediately after the election, Ramsay MacDonald declared, 'Cromwell, when he fought on barren Marston Moor, was writing the history of the nation. It was not the history of Chester-le-Street that was being written at the moment, but the history of British Labour.'[86] While there seemed no ideological gap between most Liberals and Labour MPs, and they could without difficulty agree upon a common programme, their priorities were somewhat different. Liberal priorities were education and licensing reform, temperance reform, abolition of plural voting, reform of the Lords, the disestablishment of the Welsh Church and retrenchment. Labour's priorities were the feeding of schoolchildren, old-age pensions, graduated income tax, work for the unemployed and land nationalisation.

But the Liberals were not too worried. 'There is no sign of any violent forward movement – the dangerous element does not amount to a dozen,'

85 Dugdale, *Balfour*, vol. 2, p. 173.
86 Bealey and Pelling, *Labour and Politics*, p. 274.

so Herbert Gladstone told Campbell-Bannerman early in 1906 with undisguised relief. 'If anybody thinks', Morley told Fowler in September 1906, 'we can govern this country against the middle-class, he is wrong.'[87] And the radicals to the left of the new government – whether Liberal or Labour – were so divided in their concerns that they found it difficult to make common cause. The Liberals seemed to be successfully containing Labour. All but five Labour MPs had been elected with Liberal cooperation, and two of the five were in Scotland, where the entente did not operate. Of the other eight LRC candidates in Scotland, all of whom were in three-cornered fights, seven were bottom of the poll. But in the country as a whole, three-cornered fights gave just four seats to the Unionists. The number would have been far greater had it not been for the entente, which had allowed the LRC a free hand in thirty constituencies. The entente had worked most effectively in Lancashire, where there was a Tory working-class tradition and the Liberals were weak. Of sixteen LRC candidates in Lancashire, thirteen won. The Liberals would have been unlikely to win any of these sixteen seats and fighting them would have involved considerable and unnecessary expense. Of the three LRC losses in Lancashire, sectarian issues were prominent in two of them, with Labour proving unable to overcome the stance of the Unionists as defenders of the Protestant working class; the other LRC loss in Lancashire was Eccles, where there was a three-cornered fight. In Yorkshire, by contrast, where the Liberals were far stronger than in Lancashire and less willing to cede seats to the LRC, the entente did not work so well. There were just eight LRC candidates, of whom three won and five lost. The three victories were in Halifax, a two-member seat, Leeds East and Bradford West, which the LRC won in a three-cornered fight. The losses were all in three-cornered fights except York, a two-member seat, won by a Liberal and a Unionist with the LRC candidate at the bottom of the poll. The outcomes in Lancashire and Yorkshire were paradoxical since the roots of the ILP lay in Yorkshire, where 'Liberal opposition had … limited the LRC … to a quarter of the successes that it had in Lancashire – a curious inversion of the real pattern of enthusiasm both for Socialism and for independent politics'.[88] The pact had been greatly assisted by the 1884–85 electoral settlement, which, although establishing the single-member constituency as the norm, had nevertheless retained twenty-seven two-member constituencies where an LRC candidate could fight in tandem with a Liberal. Of the twenty-nine seats won by the LRC in 1906, eleven were in two-member constituencies. In none of the single-member constituencies won by the LRC, except Clitheroe and Barnard

---

87 Harris and Hazlehurst, 'Campbell-Bannerman as Prime Minister', pp. 375, 376.
88 Bealey and Pelling, *Labour and Politics*, p. 268.

Castle won by the LRC in by-elections, would the Liberals have had much chance of success. Of the twenty-five failed Labour candidatures in 1906, nineteen had faced Liberal opponents.

The entente, then, seemed to have restricted the LRC, first to constituencies where it was already strong and would probably have put up a candidate even if the Liberals had also done so but also to constituencies in areas such as Lancashire where the Liberals were less likely to win the votes of the Tory working man than an LRC candidate. There were, Jesse Herbert told Herbert Gladstone triumphantly on 6 February 1906, just two seats which should have been won by a Liberal but were lost because of LRC intervention and only one in which the LRC would have won had a Liberal not also stood. 'Was there ever', Jesse Herbert asked, 'such a justification of a policy by results?'[89] It was, so Gladstone told Campbell-Bannerman on 21 January, 'the successful working out of an understanding with the Labour Party' that was 'the prime cause' of 'the abnormality of the Liberal victory'.[90]

With the great benefit of hindsight, it can be seen that, in the words of Sir Samuel Storey, chairman of the executive of the Northern Liberal Federation, the Liberals were in danger of 'nursing into life a serpent which [would] sting their party to death ... The effect of surrendering to this new party will be the destruction of organised Liberalism in the North.' The Liberal agent at Clitheroe, where the Liberals had avoided putting up a candidate against the LRC's David Shackleton as a result of pressure from Herbert Gladstone, wrote to the Chairman of the Liberal Election Committee, 'If the Liberal Party can only be made strong by giving away its strongest positions, all I can say is that its day of usefulness is gone, and the party which was described by Mr Gladstone as the great instrument of progress is no more.'[91] The entente damaged Labour far less, since where it was weak, the LRC would not in any case have been able to put up a candidate, lacking the funds to do so. Had the Liberals realised in 1903 that they were on track for a landslide and that Labour would in due course supplant them as the main party on the left, they might well have crushed the 'serpent', which they were well able to do, rather than nurturing it. A later Liberal leader, Jeremy Thorpe, has argued that 'the Liberals were to blame for giving room to the Socialist cuckoo in the radical nest. The Herbert Gladstone/Ramsay MacDonald arrangement ... was an act of uncalled for electoral generosity.'[92] Significantly, after 1959, when Labour had lost three elections in a row and a backbench Labour MP, Woodrow Wyatt, urged an electoral pact with the Liberals, Labour's leader,

89 Bealey, 'Negotiations', p. 274.
90 Poirier, *Advent of the Labour Party*, p. 267.
91 Ibid., pp. 202–3.
92 Cited in Roy Douglas, *The History of the Liberal Party 1895–1970*, Sidgwick and Jackson, 1971, p. xii.

Hugh Gaitskell, would have nothing to do with it, and his successors in the Labour leadership have also stood firm against electoral pacts with Liberals.

Three men – Ramsay MacDonald (1866–1937), Philip Snowden (1864–1937) and Arthur Henderson (1863–1935) – were, together with Keir Hardie, to shape the Labour Party until 1931. But the party did not elect a leader until 1922. Until then, it had a chairman, elections for which were held annually, though the first two chairmen – Keir Hardie and Arthur Henderson – were re-elected without opposition for a second year. But Hardie was not a successful chairman. He once confessed, 'Nature never intended me to occupy an official position.' Despite being a main inspiration behind both the ILP and the Labour Party, he was, as one journalist wrote, 'the only man who could have created the Labour Party ... But he is almost the only man in the party who is not fitted to lead it.'[93] In 1911, Ramsay MacDonald was elected chairman and in consequence had to surrender the post, no longer unpaid, of party secretary, which he had held since its formation in 1900. As secretary, he had been the one representative chosen by the whole inaugural conference of the LRC, as opposed to one of its constituent elements – the trade unions or the socialist societies – and this gave him an overall perspective not always apparent amongst other MPs. But in compensation for resigning as secretary, MacDonald became party treasurer as well as chairman, a post elected, as the secretaryship had been, by the whole Labour conference. MacDonald's ascendancy was such that he might well have become Labour's first leader in August 1914 had he not resigned the chairmanship because he could not accept the majority decision to support the war. 'MacDonald,' Beatrice Webb wrote in her diary during the Labour Party conference in February 1914,

> with his romantic figure, charming voice and clever dialectics, is more than a match for all those underbred and undertrained workmen who surround him on the platform and face him in the audience ... Owing to his personal distinction and middle-class equipment he is superior to all his would-be competitors.[94]

He was, another observer thought, 'the Hamlet of the Labour Party – life went out of the play when he left it. He carried the spotlight from the start.'[95]

MacDonald, however, had not begun his life with 'middle-class equipment'. Indeed, at his birth he had appeared to be faced with insuperable challenges. He had been born in 1866 out of wedlock, which then carried a

93 Gardiner, *Prophets, Priests and Kings*, p. 218.
94 MacKenzie, *Diary of Beatrice Webb*, vol. 3, p. 195.
95 Mary Agnes Hamilton, *Remembering My Good Friends*, Jonathan Cape, 1944, p. 120.

serious social stigma, to a poor Scottish servant girl in the remote fishing village of Lossiemouth on the Moray Firth, some forty miles east of Inverness. He saw his father, a ploughman, just once. Leaving school at the age of fifteen, having been a pupil teacher for four years and educating himself in the process, he became a journalist. He lived in penury for many years, surviving on a weekly packet of oatmeal from his mother, but in 1888 became private secretary to a Liberal MP, which gave him a valuable insight into party organisation and management. Unlike Hardie, Henderson or Snowden, Mac-Donald had begun as a Fabian and in 1892 had become a lecturer for the society, though he was to resign from it in 1900 because it would not oppose the Boer War. He had joined the ILP in 1894 only after being rebuffed in his search for a Liberal candidature and stood unsuccessfully in the general election of that year as candidate for Southampton. In 1906, the year he was elected MP for the two-member constituency of Leicester in tandem with a Liberal, he became chairman of the ILP. When he retired from that post in 1909, Keir Hardie described him as 'the biggest intellectual asset which the Socialist movement had in this country today'.[96] But his views had little in common with the somewhat sentimental and utopian outlook of many ILP members, and he came to be supported by trade union MPs as a bulwark against what they regarded as left-wing extremism. Indeed, he, together with Arthur Henderson, was skilled at yoking together seemingly incompatible elements – the ILP left, unhappy at the necessary compromises of pressure group politics in the Commons, and the trade unions, sometimes tempted to place their sectional interests before the wider good of the party.

MacDonald, who was to become Labour's Prime Minister in 1924 but was to be expelled from the party in 1931 for leading a national government, to which Labour was opposed, was, it has been said, both 'the hero and the villain of twentieth-century socialism in Britain'.[97] He was lonely, self-centred and prickly, particularly after the early death of his wife in 1911, combining vanity with self-pity, and was more at ease on the public platform than in personal relations. He was suspicious of rivals, trusted few, saw plots where none existed and remained aloof and distant from most Labour MPs, who nevertheless continued to trust him. His handsome appearance, charisma and star quality elevated him well above his colleagues. He combined Keir Hardie's romantic appeal with a shrewd practical realism, management ability and negotiating skills which Hardie did not possess. Hardie once said to MacDonald, 'If you cannot pull the Party round, no one can.'[98] MacDonald

---

96 McKenzie, *British Political Parties*, p. 345.
97 Emanuel Shinwell, *Conflict Without Malice*, Odhams, 1955, p. 112.
98 Marquand, *Ramsay MacDonald*, p. 130.

was also in the early years of the century a magnificent speaker. Emanuel Shinwell, a Cabinet minister in the Attlee government, who had known him in the 1920s, was to write that 'there has probably never been [another] orator with such natural magnetism combined with impeccable technique'.[99] As late as 1929, the *New York Times* was to declare that 'magnificent speaking like his had seldom been heard in any country from the lips of a citizen of another'.[100] And MacDonald was a fine parliamentarian, which Hardie never was. Even more important, he was, in the early years of the Labour Party, 'the most important single influence on its strategy and tactics'.[101] It was never easy to steer the Labour Party on a tortuous course between a sterile isolation and dependence on the Liberals, and without MacDonald's skills the Labour Party might never have survived its early years. But he was more than a good party manager. He also had a clear view of socialism and how it was to be attained which he put forward in a number of books before 1914. Socialism, he believed, would not be brought about by sudden change, still less through the breakdown of capitalism as Marx had envisaged. Instead, it would be achieved by gradual and evolutionary means when Liberalism had run its course. It would be 'the stage which follows Liberalism', and it 'retains everything of value in Liberalism by virtue of its being the hereditary heir of Liberalism'.[102] So any attempt to speed up the process, to leapfrog the evolutionary process, would be futile. Nor was socialism based on the class war. It took its stand on opinion and belief, not class interest. 'Man is moved by his head as well as by his pocket,' he wrote. 'The richest possession of any man is an approving conscience.' And then came the fundamental statement of his credo: 'Socialism marks the growth of society, not the uprising of a class.'[103]

Philip Snowden, the third leading figure after Hardie and MacDonald, a member of the ILP from 1895, had been born in 1864 in a remote parish in the bleak moors of the West Riding of Yorkshire. He was the son of a Methodist handloom weaver, independent and thrifty, whose main interest lay in poetry – Burns, whose poems he apparently knew by heart, Byron and Milton as well as Shakespeare. Snowden attended what he called 'an apology for a school' and became a pupil teacher, so avoiding employment at the local mill.[104] He then worked in an insurance company and qualified, through night study, for a civil service post, first in the excise department and then in the Inland Revenue. But at the age of twenty-seven, probably as a

99 Shinwell, *Conflict without Malice*, p. 113.
100 Asa Briggs, review of Marquand, *Ramsay MacDonald*, *The Guardian*, 3 March 1977.
101 Marquand, *Ramsay MacDonald*, p. 4.
102 Ibid., p. 92.
103 Ibid., p. 90.
104 Snowden, *Autobiography*, vol. 1, p. 34.

result of spinal tuberculosis, he became paralysed in both legs and compelled to rely on sticks for the rest of his life. Three years later, he enlisted as a travelling socialist preacher for the ILP. His early speeches combined detailed statistics and knowledge of working-class life with a sermon. He preached a 'religion of the future', socialism, combining a powerful ethical appeal with biblical terminology, claiming that a socialist society would be heaven on earth. In 1903, he published a sermon called 'The Christ that is to be'. The title came from Tennyson's poem *In Memoriam*.

> Ring out the darkness of the land,
> Ring in the Christ that is to be!

At the end of his speeches, he would call for a conversion to socialism, parodying the Methodist doctrine of salvation, which came to be known as 'Philip's come to Jesus'. Unfortunately, however, Snowden was never quite able to explain how the socialist millennium was to be brought about. There was a gap between his analysis of current affairs and depiction of the socialist ideal. How did one get from current arrangements to the new society? The first stage, he believed, would entail nationalisation – of the land, the railways and the mines. But beyond that, as he was to write in a pamphlet entitled 'Socialism and Syndicalism', published in 1913, 'the intelligent Socialist' would leave it to 'the wisdom and knowledge of the future to settle. The details and methods will be determined largely by the form which the great industrial operations assume in the process of evolution.'[105]

Snowden was elected as MP for Blackburn in 1906 and came to be regarded as Labour's expert on financial matters, a skill he claimed to have acquired in the excise department, the Inland Revenue and as a member of Keighley Borough Council. But his views on financial matters combined Liberal shibboleths – free trade, sound finance – with redistributive taxation to bring about socialism. His speeches on finance were more rigorous and incisive than those of MacDonald but also more dogmatic. He entirely lacked MacDonald's glamour and his appearance was against him. 'A pallid hatchet-faced young man, small of stature, and leaning heavily on a stick, one foot dragging helplessly along the ground. His face was scarred with the brand of suffering and bitter thought.'[106] He appeared gaunt and ascetic, 'a thin-lipped Yorkshireman, whose crippled body and biting invective gave him the delusive air of an English Robespierre'.[107] He was in fact a

105 Cross, *Snowden*, p. 122.
106 Gardiner, *Prophets, Priests and Kings*, p. 275.
107 Marquand, *Ramsay MacDonald*, p. 60.

moderate, but this was disguised by his Commons speeches which, though severely factual and based on an impressive command of economic statistics, came to be laced with sarcasm and a savage irony which alienated more than they convinced. 'His brain', one early reporter noted, 'seemed packed with ice.'[108] But he could be persuasive. In the 1930s, a writer on the *Manchester Guardian* recalled the impression that he had made at the Oxford Union in 1908 amidst 'the iced champagne, the melodious dip of punt poles in the Cherwell, and the swaying of light muslin'. The journalist continued:

> If John the Baptist had himself appeared in the desert ... the effect could scarcely have been more instantaneous and electric. With a concentrated passion and a pitiless icy irony, Snowden arrayed his facts and figures and drove home his arguments for a social reconstruction ... it is not too much to record that the scales fell away from many eyes, and they were left blinking in a new sun. A new force was revealed in the state ... the overwhelmingly sincere and passionate impression of Snowden's bitter indictment and soul steeped in wrong.[109]

Arthur Henderson, Labour's fourth leading figure, was, unlike Hardie, Mac-Donald and Snowden, not a member of the ILP. He had instead been a trade union delegate to the founding conference of the LRC in 1900, having failed to be selected as Liberal candidate for Newcastle in 1900. He had been born in 1863 in a slum area of Glasgow. His father died when he was nine, and he then moved with his stepfather to the north-east where his schooling ended at the age of twelve. He secured an apprenticeship as an iron moulder and became a paid organiser for his union, educating himself in evening classes and becoming a Methodist Sunday School teacher. A teetotaller and temperance advocate, he became a lay preacher and, from 1896, secretary and agent to the Liberal MP Sir Joseph Pease. In 1892, he was elected to the New-castle City Council, then Darlington Council and in 1897 to the Durham County Council. In 1903, he became a justice of the peace and, despite his membership of the LRC, was elected Liberal Mayor of Darlington, the first working man to hold that position. In the same year, despite having been agent to Pease, a Liberal MP, he was nominated as LRC candidate for the Barnard Castle by-election caused by the death of Pease and won the seat. Although reluctant to sign the LRC constitution, he became totally loyal to it, as to the other organisations to which he belonged – his trade union and the Methodist Church – even though his views remained more akin to those

---

108 Cross, *Snowden*, p. 38.
109 Ibid., p. 89.

of advanced Liberals than to socialists. He was in fact an organisation man. Appointed to the unpaid post of Labour Party treasurer in 1904, he served as Chief Whip in 1906, chairman of the parliamentary party from 1908 to 1910 and then secretary in 1912, when at last he joined a socialist society, the Fabians. He was to hold the post of secretary until 1934. A poor speaker, with little interest in ideas, he nevertheless became indispensable to the Labour Party. His skills were practical rather than imaginative or intellectual. He has been called 'Labour's Bismarck', but he was in fact a packhorse, patient and tenacious, rather than a leader.[110] MacDonald saw him as a rival for the leadership, but it is doubtful if Henderson ever saw himself in that light. He believed that his talents were best exercised, as he put it near the end of his career in 1936, as 'the hewer of wood or the drawer of water to others, content to look after the machine for the benefit of the great movement which I loved so much and felt it an honour to service in the capacity for which I am best suited'.[111] Until 1914, it appeared that his talents were complementary to those of the more glamorous MacDonald, 'a race horse and a cart horse', as the two were described.[112] A man of limited intellect and little imagination, prone to bullying to get his way, 'Uncle Arthur', as he came to be known, nevertheless attracted more affection than any of the early leaders apart from Hardie, thanks to his integrity and because he was seen to be working for the whole labour movement, not for himself. His qualities

> were easy to see. He had psychological and physical resilience, internal poise and self-confidence, and a mind sufficiently narrow not to worry too much about the world, yet expansive enough to show him where it was moving. He had immense capacity for work, and he developed a sureness of touch in dealing with his party that was almost unique.[113]

But above all, he had an instinctive understanding of the feelings and sensitivities of the trade unionists who formed the backbone of the party. He 'cared for the Party as most people can care only for persons … He was there for the Party, not the Party there for him. This was the root of the unequalled authority he built up.'[114] He retained his roots in the working class, something which could not be said of MacDonald nor even of Snowden, while Keir Hardie's bohemianism distanced him from respectable members of the

---

110 Morgan, *Labour People*, p. 82.
111 F. M. Leventhal, *Arthur Henderson*, Manchester University Press, 1989, p. 209.
112 Mary Agnes Hamilton, *Arthur Henderson: A Biography*, Heinemann, 1938, p. 52.
113 McKibbin, 'Arthur Henderson as Labour Leader', pp. 95–6.
114 Hamilton, *Arthur Henderson*, p. 71.

working class. The socialist intellectual G. D. H. Cole, who had little in common with him, gave the best summing up.

> Arthur Henderson was not a particularly clever man, or an inspiring speaker. He had neither the glamour of MacDonald, nor the incisiveness of Snowden, nor the human warmth of George Lansbury. But he had great qualities – honesty, absence of self-seeking, doggedness and patience in action, and an unshakable faith in the ethical ideals of justice and freedom … He never let a colleague down, or attempted to shift on to other men's shoulders the burdens of his own mistakes. Uncle Arthur, much more than any other man, made the Labour Party what it was … Whatever he made it, he made it for the common people, and not for himself.[115]

Balfour believed the real significance of the 1906 election lay in the advance of Labour. 'If I read the signs aright,' he wrote to his cousin Lady Salisbury,

> what has occurred has nothing whatever to do with any of the things we have been squabbling over the last few years. C-B is a mere cork, dancing on a torrent which he cannot control, and what is going on here is the faint echo of the same movement which has produced massacres in St Petersburg, riots in Vienna, and Socialist processions in Berlin. We always catch continental disease, though we usually take them mildly.[116]

This was an absurd judgement. Balfour, of course, did not want to admit that the election was largely a reaction against his own government, and in particular tariff reform, rather than positive enthusiasm for Labour or socialism. The new Labour MPs were far from being revolutionaries. They were, a commentator wrote in 1906, 'English folk, containing moderate and reasonable men, most of them with experience in government acquired either through their trade unions and cooperative societies or as municipal reformers, and are familiar with the expedient … of working with progressive parties in local affairs'.[117] A journalist writing in the 1920s was more pithy, saying that he had been told 'by a witty member of the Labour Party' 'that the British working man is about as revolutionary as a Christmas pudding'.[118] Indeed, 'the most striking link between the great majority of the MPs concerned seemed to be their pride in a nonconformist upbringing: nearly all of them

---

115 G. D. H. Cole, *A History of the Labour Party from 1914*, Routledge, 1948, pp. 305–6.
116 Dugdale, *Balfour*, vol. 1, p. 329.
117 H. W. Massingham, 'Victory and What to do with It', *Contemporary Review*, February 1906, p. 269.
118 Gardiner, *Portraits and Portents*, p. 251.

were Methodists of one sort or another, or Congregationalists'.[119] Ruskin's *Unto this Last* rather than any work by Marx or other socialists was the book that most influenced them. Many also mentioned Dickens and Carlyle. But the Bible was even more fundamental. Even so, Balfour was prescient in remarking in a letter to Austen Chamberlain in January 1906 that the advent of Labour would 'end, I think, in the break-up of the Liberal Party'.[120] The 1906 election was to be the last in which the Nonconformist vote was important; and, even though absurdly exaggerated by Balfour, the first in which the trade union vote and the vote of the labour interest was important. In this sense, the election formed a link between the past and the future.

A NEW LIBERALISM?

The King's Speech of 1906, like Campbell-Bannerman's election address, was a timid affair containing little more than a ragbag of reform proposals. It promised to meet Nonconformist grievances by a new Education Act and trade union grievances by a Trade Disputes Act. It also promised a new Workmen's Compensation Act, improvement of the Unemployed Workmen Act, abolition of plural voting, an inquiry into conditions in rural areas 'as to the means by which a larger number of the population may be attracted to and retained on the soil' and a few other minor matters.[121] There was little to excite the radical spirits of those filling the Liberal benches. The 1907 King's Speech was to herald legislation on Ireland and temperance. 'These were, with education, the very subjects to gladden the hearts of traditional Liberals: they were also the very subjects which had stultified the Liberal party for twenty years, and, not coincidentally, the very subjects on which the House of Lords was least afraid of popular disavowal.'[122]

The small Labour Party sought to act as a pressure group on the Liberals, but its influence should not be exaggerated. Its short manifesto had listed just sixteen measures, only four of which were social reform measures, and these were stated in vague and general terms. They were: 'Adequate Maintenance from National Funds for the Aged Poor', 'Public Provision of Better Houses for the People', 'Useful Work for the Unemployed' and 'Adequate Maintenance for Children'. Apart from trade union reform and, later on, payment of MPs, the party's main influence on the government proved to be in pressing for free school meals and the medical inspection of schoolchildren.

In terms of social reform, the Liberals did not really get into their stride

---

119 Bealey and Pelling, *Labour and Politics*, p. 276.
120 Balfour Papers, Add. MSS. 49735, ff. 216–17.
121 House of Lords Debates, 19 February 1906, vol. 1152, col. 23.
122 Peter Clarke, *Liberals and Social Democrats*, Cambridge University Press, 1978, p. 110.

until 1908, when Asquith became Prime Minister, Lloyd George was promoted to the Exchequer and Churchill to the Board of Trade, so altering the balance of the Cabinet in favour of activism. It was then that the Liberals developed their radical reform programme, a programme to be equalled only by Attlee's 1945 Labour government. With the exception of school meals, medical inspection and trade union reforms, the Liberal programme was to be influenced less by Labour than by middle-class reformers. These reformers were of two types. There were first the so-called New Liberal social philosophers who sought to modernise the party and adapt Liberalism to the era of mass politics; and, second, the social investigators who were to supersede both anecdotal accounts of poverty by prophets such as Carlyle and Ruskin and also amateurish schemes of charitable relief, by underlining the facts of deprivation and showing how much remained to be done to cure what Bernard Shaw had called 'the Crime of Poverty'.

The Liberal Party of 1906 had become a very different animal from that of 1892, when the last Liberal government had been elected. Then, it had been led by Gladstone, a determined opponent of what he called 'construction', the active state. Many in the new Liberal government, by contrast, were social reformers. The very meaning of Liberalism had altered since 1892, with the development of the 'New Liberalism', a term apparently first appearing in print in 1889.[123] The New Liberalism was an eclectic movement, but its essence was, in the words of the social philosopher L. T. Hobhouse, that 'the individual cannot stand alone, but that between him and the State there is a reciprocal obligation'.[124] Whether an individual could fulfil the traditional Liberal aim of developing his talents depended not only on his own abilities and energy but also upon society. Therefore, traditional Liberal aims of individual choice and development would require not just the removal of obstacles such as the limited franchise and dominance of the land and established church but the very policies of 'construction' which Gladstone had deprecated, an extension of state responsibility. The New Liberals sought to adapt liberalism to new conditions. Many Liberals had accepted that the principle of non-intervention in economic and social life needed to be qualified. Mill in *On Liberty* had argued that all economic matters lay within the other-regarding sphere, i.e. that all economic activity was capable of harming others. Therefore, intervention in economic matters could not be excluded on abstract grounds of principle but must be weighed in terms of utilitarian considerations. Intervention could expand individual choice, rather than restricting it as Gladstone had believed.

123 Clarke, 'The Progressive Movement in England', p. 166.
124 L. T. Hobhouse, *Liberalism* [1911], Oxford University Press, 1964, p. 86.

But perhaps the philosophy of the New Liberalism was less important than the work of social investigators such as Charles Booth and Seebohm Rowntree. 'If we can only get down to the facts,' Booth was to write in 1904, 'good must come of it.'[125] Booth, married to a cousin of Beatrice Webb, had carried out studies of London, believing that the socialist Hyndman's figure of 25 per cent living below subsistence levels in the capital was a wild over-estimate. It is commonly believed that Booth found this percentage to be an underestimate rather than an overestimate, and that, in his 1889 study *Life and Labour of the People*, he had discovered that around 35 per cent of those in the East End of London were living below subsistence levels. In fact, how-ever, he discovered the position was not quite as bad as that would indicate. The very poor comprised 8.4 per cent, while 22.3 per cent were poor but not, so he declared, somewhat optimistically, 'in want'. 'They are neither ill-nour-ished nor ill clad, according to any standard that can reasonably be used. Their lives are an unending struggle, and lack comfort.'[126] Booth advocated old-age pensions as a form of what he called 'limited socialism', arguing that, without reform, the poor would turn to real socialism. But his conclusions led him to pour doubt on the idea that there was a unified working class that could threaten the system. The differences between the poor and the casual residuum, on the one hand, and the 'respectable' working class on regular standard earnings on the other, were almost as great as those between the latter and the lower middle class.

Rowntree, who had studied poverty in York and published his conclusions in 1901 in a book, *Poverty: A Study of Town Life*, adopted a more rigorous approach than Booth, his investigators visiting every working-class home in York. Rowntree drew a distinction between primary and secondary poverty. Primary poverty occurred when the income being brought in by a household was insufficient to provide the bare necessities of physical efficiency. Second-ary poverty occurred where poverty resulted from a family not spending its incomes efficiently enough to meet the necessities of life. Rowntree believed that money spent on drink was a main cause of secondary poverty. So also was gambling. His survey of York revealed that over 15 per cent of the work-ing-class population and just under 10 per cent of the total population of York were in primary poverty. But in addition, nearly 18 per cent of the working-class population were in secondary poverty. So over a quarter of the working population of York were living in poverty. Living just above the pov-erty line in secondary poverty involved a stark existence. Such an individual

---

125 Cooper, *The British Welfare Revolution*, p. 11.
126 E. P. Hennock, 'Poverty and Social Theory in England: The Experience of the Eighteen-Eighties', *Social History*, 1976, p. 73.

must never spend a penny on railway fare or omnibus. They must never go into the country unless they walk. They must never purchase a half-penny newspaper or spend a penny to buy a ticket for a popular concert. They must write no letters to absent children, for they cannot afford to pay the postage. They must never contribute anything to their church or chapel, or give any help to a neighbour who owes them money. They cannot save, nor can they join a sick club or Trade Union, because they cannot pay the necessary subscriptions. The children must have no pocket money for dolls, marbles or sweets. The father must smoke no tobacco and must drink no beer. The mother must never buy any pretty clothes for herself or for her children ... Finally, the wage earner must never be absent from his work for a single day.[127]

In addition, Rowntree calculated what was needed for a subsistence diet and claimed that the diet of labourers in York compared unfavourably with that given to prisoners and those in workhouses. The techniques of modern economic historians have shown that Rowntree overemphasised the extent of primary poverty in York by around 50 per cent, that the true figure was around 5 per cent not 10 per cent, and falling, so that Edwardian poverty was not increasing over time. And in any case, there was no reason to regard York as typical.[128] Nevertheless, Rowntree's figures were widely accepted and generalised, exerting great influence on political opinion.

Rowntree put forward the concept of a poverty cycle, to the effect that poverty was likely to strike at certain stages of life – in particular childhood and old age. He drew two conclusions from his work. The first was that poverty and deprivation were far more widespread than had previously been thought; the second was that such poverty and deprivation could not be accounted for by faults of individual behaviour, nor by alcoholism or fecklessness. Instead, poverty resulted, so Rowntree believed, from trade fluctuations, unemployment and poor social conditions. These were social ills which required social remedies. Poverty was not inevitable, but it could not be cured by voluntary or charitable methods. It required the concentrated attention of government, to enquire into its causes and legislate remedies. Rowntree concluded his book with the eloquent cry:

The dark shadow of the Malthusian philosophy has passed away, and no view of the ultimate scheme of things would now be accepted under which

127 Seebohm Rowntree, *Poverty: A Study of Town Life*, Macmillan, 1901, pp. 53–4.
128 Ian Gazeley and Andrew Newell, 'Rowntree Revisited: Poverty in Britain, 1900', *Explorations in Economic History*, 2000, p. 175.

multitudes of men and women are doomed by inevitable law to struggle for existence so severe as necessarily to cripple or destroy the higher parts of their nature.[129]

Rowntree's book *Poverty* was drawn to Churchill's attention. John Morley had told him to read it, and it exerted a profound influence on the young statesman. In an unpublished memorandum in 1901, Churchill had written, with some exaggeration:

> Consider the peculiar case of these poor, and the consequences. Although the British Empire is so large, they cannot find room to live in it; although it is so magnificent, they would have had a better chance of happiness if they had been born cannibal islanders of the Southern seas; although its science is so profound, they would have been more healthy if they had been subjects of Hardicanute.

To an official of the Midland Conservative Association, he had written in December 1901 of how much he had been 'impressed' by Rowntree's book, and declared, 'I see little glory in an Empire which can rule the waves and is unable to flush its sewers.' In a speech at Blackpool in January 1902, he had said, 'I have been reading a book which has fairly made my hair stand on end, written by a Mr Rowntree who deals with poverty in the town of York.'[130] Here lay the germ of Churchill's concern with social reform, a concern which, together with free trade, led him towards the Liberals and was to make him, with Lloyd George, the leading social reformer of the 1905 Liberal government.

In its report in 1909, the Royal Commission on the Poor Law, chaired by Lord George Hamilton, the former Unionist Cabinet minister, was to reveal that there had been around 815,000 paupers in 1908, of which approximately two-thirds were receiving outdoor relief. It had been hoped that education and sanitary reform would, by improving standards in education and health, mitigate the problem of poverty. That had not occurred. On the relief of poverty, education and sanitary reform, Britain was spending around £40 million a year more than forty years before, but there were more paupers in 1908 than there had been then, though, as a result of the increase in population, the percentage was lower, and the numbers receiving outdoor relief had fallen. The increase in pauperism was particularly noticeable in London. 'We, the richest nation in Europe', Hamilton concluded, 'have the heaviest pauperism, yet the more we spend, the worse the position seems to be. It is

---

129 Rowntree, *Poverty*, p. 301.
130 Churchill, *Young Statesman*, pp. 31–2.

in London and the large towns, the supposed centres of progress, that the problems of pauperism are becoming more and more acute and difficult.'[131]

The Liberals, then, were confronted with massive social problems, problems which the traditional philosophy of their party seemed incapable of resolving. The nineteenth-century Liberal Party seemed to have believed that in a free society, individuals were responsible for their own welfare. If forced to seek the help of the state, that should be given only with penalties such as, with the Poor Law, the loss of the right to vote. To be compelled to seek relief was seen as a sign of moral failure. Liberals were to break with this tradition with the introduction of old-age pensions and health and unemployment insurance. But how was social reform to be financed if tariffs were excluded? Redistributive taxation seemed the only answer. In November 1905, Lord Crewe, who was to become Leader of the Lords in 1908, wrote to Campbell-Bannerman, 'The Liberal Party is on its trial as an engine for securing social reforms ... It has to resist the ILP claim to be the only friend of the workers.'[132] Social reform nevertheless seemed the concern only of a limited number of intellectuals, social investigators and political leaders. It appeared to have little resonance at the grassroots of the Liberal Party, where traditional concerns still held sway. In 1902, Herbert Samuel, a young Liberal Imperialist, wrote a book, *Liberalism*, advocating cautious measures of social reform. It sold 2,250 copies. In 1899, by contrast, a book by Arthur Sherwell and Joseph Rowntree, *Temperance and the Social Problem*, had sold 90,000 copies and went through ten editions. 'We do not deceive ourselves', Beatrice Webb had written in her diary on 9 February 1906,

> by the notion that this wave of Liberalism is wholly progressive in character – much of its bulk is made up of sheer conservatism aroused by the revolutionary tariff policy of Chamberlain. But it looks as progressive in its direction and all the active factors are collectivist. Moreover, it is clear that Joe [Chamberlain] is going to try to outbid the Liberals by constructive social reform.[133]

THE UNIONISTS IN DEFEAT

The Unionists seemed in disarray after the election. But despite the electoral unpopularity of tariff reform in the country, it seemed to have captured the

---

131 Lord George Hamilton, 'A Statistical Survey of the Problems of Pauperism', *Journal of the Royal Statistical Society*, 1910, pp. 5, 8, 17, 26, 30.

132 Quoted in N. D. Daglish, 'Robert Morant's Hidden Agenda? The Origins of the Medical Treatment of Schoolchildren', *History of Education*, 1990, p. 141.

133 MacKenzie, *Diary of Beatrice Webb*, vol. 3, p. 25.

two Unionist parties. Of the 157 Unionists returned, it appeared that 109 were Chamberlainites, just thirty-two were Balfourites, while eleven were free fooders with five uncertain.[134] Hitherto, Chamberlain's strength had lain in the constituencies, Balfour's in the Commons. But having already won substantial majorities in both the Conservative and Liberal Unionist Party organisations, the tariff reformers now also enjoyed overwhelming strength in the Commons. Balfour, having lost his seat, was temporarily absent. Despite declaring that he was 'certainly not going to go about the country explaining that I am honest and industrious like a second footman out of a place', he soon found a new constituency in the City of London.[135] During his absence, Chamberlain was urged to seize the leadership. But in a letter to Lord Ridley, published in *The Times* on 8 February 1906 under the heading 'Mr Chamberlain's manifesto', he declared that 'in no circumstances would I be a candidate for the leadership of the Unionist party'. That was partly out of loyalty to Balfour but also 'because I entirely agree with those who say that the leader of the party, seven-tenths of which are Conservative, should be himself Conservative'. He appreciated that he was still regarded by many Conservatives as, in Hugh Cecil's words, an 'alien immigrant', and was indeed opposed to the Conservatives on such matters as the role of the Anglican Church and education. And he was anything but conservative in temperament. But if Chamberlain could not be the Unionist leader, he wanted to determine the policies which the leader would have to follow. He called for a party meeting to decide between three views. The first was that tariff reform was not practical politics and should be dropped, the second was Balfour's Sheffield policy. As Chamberlain never tired of reiterating, that policy would prevent colonial preference since it ruled out 'a moderate duty on corn from foreign countries', i.e. food taxes. It also ruled out a general tariff on manufactured goods without which retaliation, so Chamberlain believed, could not be effective. The third possibility was the full programme.

There was now a tortuous exchange of letters between Chamberlain and Balfour on the metaphysics of tariff reform. Balfour was opposed to a tariff for the purposes of raising revenue as being protectionist and continued to claim that he was not a protectionist. But he remained insistent that his differences with the tariff reformers were simply of methods, not substance, something which the Chamberlainites denied. In response to Balfour's urging that Chamberlain assume temporary leadership of the Unionists in the Commons, Chamberlain replied that he would do so only if confirmed

134 Amery, *Chamberlain*, vol 6, p. 789.
135 Dugdale, *Balfour*, vol. 2, p. 49.

by a party meeting and only if that meeting recognised that 'a clearer acceptance of the policy laid down in my speech at Glasgow in 1903 is the only foundation for future action', i.e. the full policy of tariff reform. While there might perhaps have been something to be said for the policy of balance before 1906, Chamberlain declared, the party must now choose between the various policies on offer. There should, in particular, be 'no more nursing of the Free Fooders'. Balfour replied that there was no precedent for a Unionist Party meeting deciding policy. In the past, such meetings had been called only 'to give emphasis and authority to a decision at which the Party have informally already arrived; still less is there an example to be found of a vote being taken at such a meeting'. Chamberlain responded that it was time Conservative associations democratised themselves, as Lord Randolph Churchill had advocated, so that there was a larger membership of voluntary workers 'chosen from the working classes' as opposed to 'the existing system of privilege for subscribers and so-called men of influence who cannot be relied upon at a time of stress to do any actual work'. In addition, the central organisation should cease to be 'an autocratic and non-representative body' but become 'strictly representative and responsible to the Party as a whole'. Such a 'democratised' party would, of course, be more likely to support the full tariff policy and could be used as a battering ram against the timidities of the leadership.[136] As always with Chamberlain, what appeared to be a dispute about organisation was in reality a dispute about policy.

But the other Unionist leaders were not prepared to adopt the full Chamberlain policy. Lansdowne, party leader in the Lords, believed that the country had pronounced decisively against it, and if the Unionists persisted, the schism in the party 'will become deeper, and the unionist party will degenerate into two feeble and mutually suspicious groups'.[137] The Duke of Devonshire went even further, declaring that he would not attend Lansdowne's eve of session banquet for Unionist leaders in the Lords but would instead invite other free fooders to a separate dinner. When Chamberlain met Balfour after the election, the latter 'seemed perfectly satisfied with the position he took up at Sheffield and absolutely refused to budge an inch from it'. Indeed, it seemed that Balfour was retreating even from that modest position, since he sought to 'drop all discussion on fiscal reform, and to try to build up the party on a purely negative base of criticism of the new Government, leaving all our differences unsolved', a standpoint which, so Austen Chamberlain believed, was 'simple madness'.[138] Balfour claimed that the Liberal majority

136 Amery, *Chamberlain*, vol. 6, pp. 798, 804, 805, 806, 809, 821–3, 825.
137 Newton, *Lansdowne*, p. 348.
138 Austen Chamberlain to Arthur Lee, 7 February 1906, Lee Papers, Courtauld Institute, Box 6.

was fissiparous and that, if the Unionists concentrated their fire on Liberal legislation, rather than exposing their own divisions, the more moderate Liberals would break away to the benefit of Unionists. And while Balfour accepted that the Liberal Unionists were, at least on paper, a representative organisation in which the leader was elected by and responsible to the party as a whole, in the Conservative Party, by contrast, power lay constitutionally with the leader. 'It tended thus', by contrast with the Liberal Unionists, 'to be the instrument of the leader in the constituencies, rather than the voice of the constituencies in London.'[139] Balfour's aim, no doubt, was to wear down the tariff reformers so that a policy which he regarded as electorally disastrous could gradually be consigned to limbo. But Chamberlain argued that a continuation of the Balfourian policy of delay would lead to the party being in the same position in the next election as it had been in 1906 with no advance towards the full programme. If the Conservatives disagreed, Chamberlain declared ominously, he would propose to form 'a Parliamentary Tariff Reform Party', with its own whips and meetings in the Commons, while nevertheless continuing to take the Unionist whip.[140] Chamberlain had become, Gerald Balfour believed, 'a monomaniac and is ready to sacrifice everything to the policy of Tariff Reform, and the machinery by which he could have carried it – namely the Conservative Party – he is actually going to shatter'.[141]

Faced with this pressure, Balfour conceded a party meeting but insisted that if his policy was rejected, he could not remain as leader. He also expressed willingness to establish a committee to consider party organisation – another delaying tactic perhaps – but said nothing about democratising the party. Chamberlain and Balfour then agreed on a form of words which both could accept and which defined the official policy. The form of words was embodied in an exchange of letters labelled the Valentine Compact, so called because it was agreed on 14 February 1906. The compact declared that 'Fiscal Reform is, and must remain, the first constructive work of the Unionist Party', that its aims were 'to secure more equal terms of competition for British trade and closer commercial union with the Colonies'. While it was unnecessary at present to prescribe the means by which these aims were to be achieved, 'a moderate general tariff on manufactured goods, not imposed for the purpose of raising prices or giving artificial protection against legitimate competition, and the imposition of a small duty on foreign corn' were 'not in principle objectionable'. So Balfour had in effect accepted food taxes. The compact was

139 Amery, *Chamberlain*, vol. 6, p. 883.
140 Ibid., p. 814.
141 Denis Judd, *Balfour and the British Empire: A Study in Imperial Evolution, 1874–1932*, Macmillan, 1968, p. 136.

widely interpreted as a surrender by Balfour, who seemed to have been pushed by Chamberlain further than he had wished to go. Chaplin, the elderly protectionist and ex-Cabinet minister, thought it 'the greatest political triumph since the days when Disraeli captured the Conservative Party. He said no one but Joe could have done it.'[142] Lansdowne regretted that the party meeting was held at his London house, which would 'hereafter be associated with the memory of a discreditable and useless episode'.[143] In truth, the compact did not commit Balfour to anything new, although Austen Chamberlain believed that it gave 'his position that clearness and precision which was so terribly lacking in his previous utterances'.[144] What was at least clear was that tariff reform was now the official policy of the Unionists, that the free fooders had lost their legitimacy and that food taxes were not excluded. When Balfour returned to the Commons in February 1906, as MP for the City of London, it became clear that his ascendancy in the House had gone. 'They laugh and jeer at him', Walter Long wrote, 'as if he was something let down from the skylight.'[145] Chamberlain seemed leader in all but name, and Balfour found it difficult to obtain a respectful hearing. 'The majority flushed with victory was intolerant and rude to him,' Austen was later to write. 'It was not so much that they disliked him, as that they despised him, and contempt is less easy to conquer than hatred.'[146] In a debate on an amendment to the address, when Balfour sought to refine the issue through ingenious subtleties, Campbell-Bannerman gave him short shrift:

The Right Hon. Gentleman is like the old Bourbons in the oft-quoted phrase ... he has learnt nothing. He comes back to this new House with the same airy graces, the same subtle dialectics, the same light and frivolous way of dealing with a great question. But he little knows the temper of the new House of Commons if he thinks those methods will prevail here ... I say, enough of this foolery! It might have answered very well in the last Parliament, but it is altogether out of place in this Parliament. The tone and temper of this Parliament will not permit it, dealing with a great question.[147]

A new Liberal MP noted the contrast between Balfour and Chamberlain.

142 Ibid., p. 848.
143 Newton, *Lansdowne*, p. 348.
144 Amery, *Chamberlain*, vol. 6, p. 849.
145 Ibid., p. 861.
146 Austen Chamberlain, *Down the Years*, 2nd edition, Cassell, 1935, p. 216.
147 House of Commons Debates, 12 March 1906, vol. 153, cols 991–2.

Mr Chamberlain is listened to with respect and attention. Mr Balfour, if he continues his present methods, will, I am afraid, be listened to not at all. Mr Chamberlain's political position is entirely repudiated, but members seem to feel that he is fighting about real things, and that he cares. Mr Balfour may care also, and he may be fighting about real things. But he has not succeeded in conveying that impression to the House of Commons. Two remarks one hears repeated everywhere: The first, 'How did this man manage to retain the leadership of the House for ten years?' The second, 'Now, for the first time, the history of the past ten years becomes explicable.' 'But it was not *this* House of Commons,' was the reply of a Tory member to the first of these assertions.[148]

The truth was that while Balfour had more successes as Prime Minister than many were prepared to admit, he was to prove a disastrous Leader of the Opposition. By contrast with Chamberlain, and later with Bonar Law, he offered no inspiration, only negativism. The only alternative policy to the Liberals which he propounded was tariff reform, and his belief in that seemed half-hearted. As his private secretary told him, Conservative MPs 'say that the policy of Fiscal Reform does not fill your heart and mind'.[149] They were right. It did not. For he feared that were the Unionists to become 'a party of one idea, we shall fail to carry even that idea to a successful issue'.[150]

Balfour sought to use the House of Lords against the Liberal government. He hoped that if the Lords accepted Liberal social reforms, while rejecting constitutional reform and reforms such as education and licensing which seemed to come from Liberal faddists, they could avoid alienating working-class support, while blocking those parts of the Liberal programme to which their supporters most objected. In April 1906, Balfour wrote to Lansdowne 'that the Party in the two Houses shall not work as separate armies', and that the Lords would not be 'able to escape the duty of making serious modifications in important Government measures'. He was, incautiously and blatantly, seeking to turn the Lords into an annexe to the Unionist parties. He believed that, just as the rejection of Home Rule in 1893 had strengthened its position, 'I think it quite possible that your House may come out of the ordeal strengthened rather than weakened'.[151] That was a crushing misjudgement. What the Lords could get away with in opposing a weak and divided government in 1893 was no guide to what it could do after a confident Liberal Party had been returned with a large popular mandate. In

148 Masterman, *Masterman*, p. 72.
149 Dugdale, *Balfour*, vol. 2, p. 31.
150 Ibid., p. 33.
151 Ibid., p. 25.

consequence of this crushing misjudgement, Balfour was to be continually worsted by the Liberals.

Chamberlain's ascendancy, however, was to prove short-lived. In July 1906, shortly after the celebrations in Birmingham in honour of his seventieth birthday and thirty years as an MP for the city, he was disabled by a stroke. There were, for a short time, hopes for recovery, and Balfour commissioned a doctor to analyse a photo of him to determine whether he could recover.[152] But it soon became apparent that he would remain permanently disabled, confined to a bath chair. He stayed influential as a background figure advising Austen and other tariff reformers, and a powerful symbol of radical Unionism, but his public life was now at an end. He was to linger on, increasingly helpless, until his death in July 1914, just one month before the world war broke out. 'He never rested,' his son declared. 'To his last day he seemed too young to leave things as they are.'[153] By the time of his death, Home Rule was almost on the statute book, while the tariff reform movement appeared to have been irretrievably weakened. The two great causes of his life seemed ruined.

With Chamberlain effectively removed from the scene, his son was warned to be moderate in his espousal of tariff reform. One Conservative MP wrote in his diary in June 1907 that Austen had been told 'that he must not push matters too far, and he was frankly told that the older section of Conservatives look upon him with suspicion, alleging that in order to achieve his fiscal ideal he would sacrifice the Church, Constitution, the land and the union'. And ominously for Austen, 'another section of the Tariff Reform League were trying to put Bonar Law forward as leader'.[154] But the agenda was now being set by the Liberals, and, at the Colonial Conference of 1907, Winston Churchill, as Under-Secretary for the Colonies, declared that the government had

> banged the door upon Imperial taxation of food. Yes, they banged it, barred it, and bolted it. It was a good stout door of British oak, and the largest Liberal, Radical and Labour majority ever seen in the House of Commons had their backs firmly against it ... They would not concede one inch, they would not give one farthing preference on a single peppercorn.[155]

The election of 1906 seemed indeed to have delivered a final verdict on tariff reform. But Chamberlain had given the Conservatives a faith which

152 David Dutton, *His Majesty's Loyal Opposition: The Unionist Party in Opposition, 1905–1915*, Liverpool University Press, 1992, p. 33.
153 Sommer, *Haldane*, p. 126.
154 Vincent, ed., *Crawford Papers*, p. 102.
155 *The Times*, 20 May 1907.

animated the party even after both he and Balfour had disappeared from the scene. In 1932, to combat the slump, Britain adopted a scheme of imperial preference. By then, in the words of one admirer of Chamberlain, the man in the street 'wonders why he ever adopted Free Trade and is uncertain whether Cobden was a man or a horse'.[156] And the minister who was to pilot imperial preference through the Commons was to be the Chancellor of the Exchequer, Neville Chamberlain, Joseph's son. So Chamberlain continued to exert influence even from beyond the grave. But so in a sense did Balfour, who had known 'by instinct that the fiscal conversion of the majority of people in this country would only be accomplished through economic catastrophe', i.e. after the shock of worldwide depression.[157] Imperial preference, however, did not lead, as Chamberlain had hoped, to the consolidation and unification of the empire. Instead, the empire was to develop in a quite different way in dominion and Commonwealth conferences as a means of consultation between equals, 'an entente rather than an alliance', allowing dominion autonomy to be combined with spontaneous attachment.[158] The failure to introduce colonial preference did not inhibit colonial enthusiasm for the war effort in 1914, just as it had not inhibited colonial support for the Boer War. The self-governing empire was to be held together by sentiment not by formal ties.

Chamberlain had been the dominant figure in politics between Gladstone and Lloyd George, even though he never held high office. But he seemed to have achieved less than either of them. He had failed in the 1880s to convert the Liberals to the new politics of social reform, and that perhaps was part of the reason for the formation of the Labour Party. He had succeeded in preventing Home Rule but only for a period, and Ireland was to become independent a few years after his death. His Unionism failed, and Austen was to be a senior member of the coalition government which in 1921 agreed to Irish independence. Chamberlain failed also in his foreign policy aims of alliance with Germany and a union of the Anglo-Saxon powers. He failed to secure a more tightly organised empire. The dominions rejected closer union while the electorate rejected tariff reform. Above all, he failed to achieve the modernisation of Britain, his deepest aim. He was indeed the first of the twentieth-century modernisers, hoping to jerk the British people out of their complacency. But like other modernisers, he received little reward for his pains. He painted an alternative picture of Britain's future – a creed of national efficiency, with a mercantilist foreign policy, planned industrial

156 Sir Charles Petrie, *The Chamberlain Tradition*, Lovat Dickson, 1938, p. 121.
157 Dugdale, *Balfour*, vol. 1, p. 173.
158 Madden, 'Changing Attitudes', p. 404.

development with an emphasis on wealth creation and an education system in which technical training could play its proper part. The British people listened politely to his sermons but resisted his offers of salvation. They clung to beliefs which had served them well during the period of mid-Victorian supremacy even though the circumstances which supported these beliefs had changed. They preferred to remain as they were – a peaceable and liberal if perhaps somewhat run-down civic kingdom. In challenging the mindset of a generation, Chamberlain doomed himself to frustration. The wider he spread his vision, the smaller his achievement; and even in death he remained an outsider. Memorials for the elite of his day lie in Westminster Abbey. But Chamberlain chose to be buried in Birmingham.

Chamberlain had sought to be a teacher and it is there that his significance lies. He was the first to appreciate that a representative system required new methods of political organisation, and the first to come forward with a concrete programme of social improvement. He was the first to argue against the old liberal ideal of the parsimonious state, and insist that government was an instrument, both at local and at national level, to ameliorate social conditions and, through tariff reform, to regenerate the economy. He was the first also to articulate sentiments of empire into a policy of imperial union. In tariff reform, he founded a faith which was to animate the Conservatives until 1939. He was, above all, the first politician to draw consequences from what he saw as economic decline, perhaps the central theme of British politics in the twentieth century, and sought to persuade others to come to terms with the implications of the fact that Britain was no longer the first industrial nation. His methods were direct and confrontational, methods of a self-made outsider combating a Unionist oligarchy, based largely on inherited wealth, many of whose members sought to do little more than defer the future beyond their lifetime. His loyalty had been to causes – social reform, the Union with Ireland, imperialism, tariff reform – not to parties. He was prepared to break both the Liberals and the Unionists unless they would submit to him. By articulating the themes of the twentieth century, he transformed both parties internally and shattered both. Why did he not achieve more? As a radical outsider, he was unable as, for example, Salisbury and Balfour were, to work with men of his own social background who formed a closed circle. His supporters tended to be younger acolytes rather than men of his own generation. In 1903, the only Cabinet minister loyal to him was his son Austen. He needed a battering ram – a disciplined extra-parliamentary organisation – to supplant the old oligarchs. He was attacking the citadel from outside. Hence his methods – violent agitation in the constituencies designed to pressure an entrenched party elite – together with an extremist unwillingness to compromise, succeeded in converting the Unionists to his policies, at the cost of alienating both colleagues and the floating voter. As early as 1884, Beatrice Webb, who had been in love with him, noted in her diary:

> By nature he is an enthusiast and a despot. A deep sympathy with the misery and incompleteness of most men's lives, and an earnest desire to right this, transforms political action into a religious crusade; but running alongside this genuine enthusiasm is a passionate desire to *crush* opposition to *his will*, a longing to put his foot on the necks of others ... Enthusiasm and self-will are the dominant forces in Chamberlain's mind.[159]

Chamberlain's career from the vantage point of the twenty-first century seems a monument to failure, unequalled in its destructiveness rather than constructive achievement. Yet in one respect, he seemed successful. For Balfour was to be the last aristocratic leader of the Conservatives until Winston Churchill in 1940. Chamberlain, it seemed, had destroyed the notion that aristocrats were born to rule. Yet even here, there was to be a final irony. Churchill was to become Prime Minister because he articulated the very themes of confrontation and defiance which Chamberlain had made his own. It was Churchill, son of an aristocrat, grandson of a duke, who proved the saviour of the nation, while the man he displaced was Chamberlain's younger son, Neville, tainted with appeasement, the one attitude which the father would never have contemplated.

THE TRADE DISPUTES ACT

During the Campbell-Bannerman era, which lasted until 1908, the government proceeded cautiously. The Liberals' first concern was to satisfy the expectations of their Nonconformist supporters through an Education Bill aimed at securing public control over denominational schools together with a Licensing Bill designed to secure greater public control over licensed premises, and providing for the closure of around one-third of public houses, the owners to be compensated through a new tax on surviving public houses. Both measures ran into determined opposition from the strongly Unionist House of Lords and had to be dropped. The Education Bill was greeted with a host of wrecking amendments by the Lords, and was withdrawn by the government, while the Licensing Bill was defeated in the Upper House on Second Reading. Three more attempts to reverse parts of the 1902 Act

159 MacKenzie, *Diary of Beatrice Webb*, vol. I, p. 104.

also failed, owing largely to squabbles between the various denominations. A Plural Voting Bill, seeking to abolish what Liberals regarded as a democratic anomaly, was defeated on Second Reading in the Lords. These measures had all been foreshadowed in the Liberal election manifesto of 1906, and it would be difficult to argue that the government did not have a mandate for them.

Of the Liberal measures emasculated in the Lords, Lord Lansdowne, Unionist leader in the Upper House, insisted that the peers were not claiming 'the right to obstruct'. But they 'did claim' and 'meant to exercise the right of revising measures that came up to them from the other House of parliament'. This process of revision was, Lansdowne believed, 'doubly necessary in these days, when owing to the operation of the closure a great many Bills come up to them which had never been discussed at all'. But the Lords claimed a further right 'to be exercised only in extraordinary cases of asking the country to judge between the two Houses of parliament as it judged between them at the time of the Home Rule bill'.[160] The Unionists were thus claiming both a revising and referendal function for the Upper House, such as they had exercised in 1892–95, functions that had not been exercised during the decade of Unionist dominance. This was a dangerous claim to make against a government which had been so heavily endorsed by the voters. In December 1908, Asquith, who had replaced Campbell-Bannerman as Prime Minister in May, invited an audience at the National Liberal Club 'to treat the veto of the House of Lords as the dominating issue in politics – the dominating issue because in the long run it overshadows and absorbs every other'.[161] But for the moment, the Liberals did nothing further.

The reforms the Liberals were able to implement were due more to pressures from the infant Labour Party than to their own reforming zeal. For, while the Lords were happy to destroy legislation implementing what they regarded as Liberal fads, such as temperance reform or Nonconformist grievances, they did not wish to antagonise the labour interest.

The Liberals faced the problem of what to do about the *Taff Vale* judgment declaring that trade unions could be sued in tort for the actions of their agents. The Balfour government had reacted to it somewhat crassly. In 1903, it had appointed a Royal Commission to consider the state of the law. But it contained no trade union representative. The chairman, Lord Dunedin, had been Lord Advocate for Scotland and had voted against trade union reform in Parliament. Of the other members, one was a former Permanent Under-Secretary, who had called *Taff Vale* 'just and salutary law', another had been president of the Mining Association of Great Britain, the employer's

160 Ridley, 'The Unionist Opposition and the House of Lords', p. 236.
161 Spender and Asquith, *Asquith*, vol. 1, p. 241.

organisation, and was a strong opponent of reform.[162] The only member representing labour was Sidney Webb. But the Webbs, in their monumental *History of Trade Unionism*, had concluded that 'it does not appear that, in the strictly legal sense, the Taff Vale case was unwarranted'.[163] So Webb was hardly a good representative of trade union opinion. The majority of the Commission, whose report – Cd 2825 – was not published until 1906, upheld the Lords ruling but declared that union benefit funds and the right of peaceful picketing should be protected and that further modest reforms were needed. The majority report was to form the basis of the Liberal government's Trade Disputes Bill of 1906, but it was insufficient for most trade unionists who sought complete legal immunity. Nevertheless, had the Balfour government been more conciliatory, it could probably have secured a lesser and more moderate change with union consent. Indeed, Sir Charles Dilke, the veteran radical advising the trade unions, believed that their demands were in fact too modest and that they were 'too easily satisfied'.[164] But the opportunity for a moderate settlement rapidly passed. The Balfour government's reaction to *Taff Vale* alienated it from trade union opinion. The Unionists were now seen as hostile to labour, while tariff reform, despite Chamberlain's attempt to woo the working class, alienated it still further. The unions regarded tariff reform as part of an employer's programme to weaken labour and had also been opposed to the importation of cheap Chinese labour into the Transvaal, which, they believed, meant excluding British workers and forcing down wages. The hostility of organised labour had been a major factor in the heavy defeat of the Unionists in 1906. And Unionist opposition to the claims of labour proved, as we have seen, to be an invaluable recruiting agent for the LRC.

On introducing the Trade Disputes Bill in 1906, Sir John Lawson Walton, Attorney General in the Liberal government, declared that judge-made law had, for the unions, 'seriously disturbed preconceived notions'. For the purpose of the legislation of 1871 and 1875 had been to remove 'the ban of the common law and the stigma of illegality'. But what had hitherto appeared as the agreed and accepted status of the unions had now been seriously compromised. This had 'curtailed' the unions' 'usefulness and efficiency'. It had made them uncertain of their legal position, had 'cut down to the point of extinction ... the undoubted right of peaceful persuasion' and had made union funds contributed to provide against sickness or unemployment liable for confiscation on the basis of 'claims which have rested upon repudiated

162 Clegg, Fox and Thompson, *History of British Trade Unions*, vol. 1, pp. 324–5.
163 Sidney and Beatrice Webb, *The History of Trade Unionism*, revised edition, Longmans, Green & Co., 1920, p. 601, note 1.
164 Gwynn and Tuckwell, *Life of Dilke*, vol. 2, p. 367.

acts of unauthorised officials. The result of this state of things has been to create a feeling of insecurity and sense of injustice.'

Sir John did not, however, propose a return to the status quo ante. Instead, he proposed, first, that criminal liability be limited to actions which would have been criminal if committed by individuals. In addition, trade unions would be free from civil liability in the case of actions which would not have been tortious if committed by individuals, so applying the basic principle of the 1875 Act to the civil law. A trade union would then be able to do anything which it would be lawful for a single person to do. Secondly, Sir John proposed to confirm the right of peaceful picketing. Thirdly, he proposed to reform the law of agency so that unions would be liable under civil law for actions committed by their agents *unless* these actions had been expressly prohibited or immediately repudiated. But he declared that it would be wrong to give the unions complete immunity. While this might seem an injustice, complete liability would be unfair to individuals who did not belong to unions; and he warned against conferring any exceptional privileges upon them. It would be wrong 'to create a privilege for the proletariat, and give a sort of benefit of clergy to trade unions analogous to the benefit of clergy which was formerly enjoyed'.[165]

The trade unions and labour movement as well as the Liberals were divided on the issue of immunity. Some did argue against a return to the status quo ante, which would, thought George Barnes, leader of the engineers and a member of the ILP, be 'anti-socialist and but a glorified individualism, as it seeks to get for groups of men, anti-social rights'.[166] That view was also held by Thomas Burt, the Lib-Lab miners leader, and Richard Bell, leader of the railwaymen, who had been so heavily involved in *Taff Vale*. Sir John was able to quote in support of his position J. H. (Jimmy) Thomas, then an official of the railway union, soon to be its leader, and later a Labour Cabinet minister, who had written in 1903:

> He failed to see how the Labour Members could meet their opponents in the House with an argument for being placed in a position different and apart from all others under the civil law. Having argued that all employers should be responsible for all accidents to workmen, no matter by whom or how they were caused, they were now, on the other hand, asking that, whatever act might be committed intentionally or deliberately, under the rules of an organisation by its executive government or by an official organisation, they should not be responsible for any action thus committed.

165 House of Commons Debates, 28 March 1906, vol. 154, cols 1295, 1305–7.
166 Quoted in Clegg, Fox and Thompson, *History of British Trade Unions*, vol. 1, 1964.

He thought that illogical. In the Taff Vale case the rules were defied; the rules were violated, and if the executive had adhered to the laws, there would have been no Taff Vale judgment.'[167]

But seventy Liberals and five Labour MPs abstained in the vote on the government's Bill.[168] The majority of trade unionists almost certainly held the view that the less the law had to do with the unions the better. One trade union leader told the TUC in 1900 that, 'candidly speaking, he could not trust the judges of this country to give a fair and impartial verdict on any question as to the conditions of labour which might be remitted to them'.[169] This view was to be endorsed by Winston Churchill, as Home Secretary, who was to tell the Commons on 30 May 1911, 'It is not good for the trade unions that they should be brought in contact with the courts, and it is not good for the courts.' 'The courts,' he went on,

hold justly a high, and I think, unequalled prominence in the respect of the world in criminal cases, and in civil cases between man and man, no doubt they deserve and command the respect and admiration of all classes of the community, but where class issues are involved, it is impossible to pretend that the courts command the same degree of general confidence.[170]

There was, therefore, a disagreement on the left between those who favoured complete immunity and those who did not. The government's Bill, which did not propose complete immunity, had been greatly influenced by Asquith and Haldane, both barristers, and Liberal Imperialists. Indeed, the division in the Liberal Party between the Bill introduced by the government and those who believed in complete immunity was largely one between Liberal Imperialists and radicals. The imperialists, supported by the Webbs, believed that the trade unions should be legally regulated in the interests of the community and the common good. The unions should enjoy not privileged immunity but full corporate status. Agreements should be legally enforceable with provision for compulsory arbitration. 'The common sense of the community would not easily be convinced', Asquith had told the Eighty Club, which was aligned to the Liberal Party, in 1903, 'that an association of persons – whether technically unincorporated or not made not the slightest difference ... wielding great powers, controlling considerable funds, should

167 House of Commons Debates, 28 March 1906, vol. 154, cols 1307–8.
168 The Times, 2 April 1906.
169 Clegg, Fox and Thompson, History of British Trade Unions, vol. 1, p. 75.
170 House of Commons Debates, 30 May 1911, vol. 26, col. 1022.

not be answerable for the conduct of agents acting under its authority'.[171] The radicals, by contrast, believed that the bargaining power in the workplace situation was so unequal and skewed towards the employer that the unions needed special privileges to equalise it. Those with so little bargaining power needed to be able to act collectively. 'There is', a radical journalist suggested, 'one kind of administration which cannot survive parliamentary democracy, and that is government by Whig lawyers.'[172] Some argued that, while the radicals wanted to go back to the past, the Liberal Imperialists were more orientated towards the future, a future in which the rights of the community had to be considered as well as the rights of those who were parties to industrial disputes. That debate was to be resurrected in the 1960s and was to be resolved by Margaret Thatcher's trade union reforms in the 1980s, which were to remove the immunities granted to the unions in 1906.

In 1906, Campbell-Bannerman, to the surprise of many, sided with the radicals. Two days after Sir John Lawson Walton introduced the government's Bill, a Labour member, Walter Hudson, of the Amalgamated Society of Railway Servants, introduced a Private Member's Bill providing for complete immunity. The Prime Minister spoke in the Commons in favour of it and implicitly against his own government's Bill. While professing not to understand legal complexities, he argued that the government's Bill was too complex and riddled with too many uncertainties. It left the way open for further judge-made law, and 'the method of restricting agency leaves pitfalls and loopholes from which there is great danger of producing and multiplying litigation'.[173] The trade unions, the Prime Minister declared, were 'beneficent' and had performed 'great services ... in the prevention of conflict and the provision of harmony between labour and capital'. The purpose of legislation should be 'to place the two rival powers of capital and labour on an equality, so that the fight between them, so far as fight was necessary, should be at least a fair one'.[174] Speaking for the opposition, George Wyndham declared that it had been 'incredible that the right hon. Gentleman should on Friday ask the House to vote for this Bill when his Attorney-General had on Wednesday put forward, in solemn argument, reasons for adopting another course'.[175] Nevertheless, in April 1906, Sir William Robson, the Solicitor General, introduced an amended Bill, based on that introduced by Hudson. In his

---

171 *The Times*, 7 February 1903.
172 H. J. Massingham in the *Daily News*, 29 March 1906, quoted in James Thompson, 'The Genesis of the 1906 Trade Disputes Act: Liberalism, Trade Unions and the Law', *Twentieth Century British History*, 1998, p. 196.
173 House of Commons Debates, 28 March 1906, vol. 154, col. 54.
174 Ibid., 30 March 1906, vol. 155, col. 52.
175 Ibid., col. 54.

speech on Second Reading, Sir William gave one of the most ringing defenc es of trade unions to be heard in the twentieth century.

> One of the most essential things to the well-being of the country is the condition of the industrial classes. Trade unions are an essential safeguard against this country's being turned into the paradise of the sweater. It is the greatest mistake in the world to suppose that a matter affecting the vital interests of the industrial classes is not an intensely national question. We cannot injure them without injuring ourselves, for we are all members one of another.[176]

In August, the Bill became even more favourable to the unions when an amendment proposed by Dilke and accepted by the government granted the unions immunity for inducement of a breach of contract of employment in a trade dispute. The argument for this amendment was that legalised picketing would be of very limited value if trade unionists were not allowed to persuade strike-breakers under contract who had not yet begun work, not to do so. The amendment overruled the judgment in *Glamorgan Coal Company v. South Wales Miners' Federation*, which held that the unions could be sued for inducing breach of contract.[177] And a further amendment moved by Sir John Lawson Walton deleted a clause providing that picketing would be immune only if it was conducted 'peaceably and in a reasonable manner'.

Balfour advised the Lords not to oppose the Bill and the Unionist majority there, though deprecating the legislation, which Lord Halsbury declared 'injurious, dangerous and unjust', followed Balfour's advice for fear that Unionists would lose the support of organised labour.[178] Salisbury's referendal theory had suggested that the role of the Upper House was to allow the voice of the people to be heard when there was doubt as to whether the verdict of the Commons represented that of the people. But in this case, the Unionists argued, there was little doubt. Lord Lansdowne, Unionist leader in the Lords, declared:

> He could not help thinking that, whatever their opinion might be of this Bill, they had to admit that the voice of the electors had been heard in regard to it ... He thought if they could claim a mandate for anything they had the right to claim one for dealing with this question.

---

176 Ibid., 25 April 1906, vol. 155, col. 1494.
177 *Glamorgan Coal Company v. South Wales Miners' Federation* [1905] AC 239 (HL).
178 House of Lords Debates, 4 December 1906, vol. 166, col. 704. The very valuable article by Richard Kidner, 'Lessons in trade union law reform; the origins and passage of the Trade Disputes Act', *Legal Studies*, 1982, p. 52fn, wrongly ascribes this speech to vol. 167.

In fact, the measure had not been prefigured in Campbell-Bannerman's election address. But Lansdowne then went on to say:

> If their lordships were to refer this Bill back to the country what would be the result? Could they have any doubt as to the answer which the constituencies would give? They should find the demand for a similar Bill renewed with greater intensity, and in a form embittered by the suggestion that the House of Lords was in conflict with the general desire of the working classes.

Laying down the doctrine which was to guide his leadership of the Lords until it came to the Lloyd George Budget of 1909, Lansdowne insisted that the Lords should conduct themselves with great caution and act only on ground favourable to themselves. This, however, was not favourable ground. Even so, Lansdowne argued that the Act confers 'excessive privileges upon the trade unions ... dangerous privileges on one class and on one class only'. This was 'fraught with danger to the community and likely to embitter the industrial life of the country'. So, even though the Lords would allow the Bill to pass,

> we have at any rate the right to say we declaim all responsibility for its provisions, and to express our hope that the common sense of employers and employed may prevent any untoward consequences from attending the reign of licence which the recklessness of His Majesty's Government is about to inaugurate.[179]

So the Bill was passed by the Lords, even though in terms of Salisbury's referendal theory, the government had no mandate for it, to become the Trade Disputes Act of 1906.

The Act had four clauses.[180] The first amended the law of conspiracy in trade disputes so that an act done in combination would not be actionable unless the same act done by an individual would also be actionable. The second clause strengthened the right of peaceful picketing. The third removed liability for interfering with the business of another, inducing someone to break his contract of employment, interfere with his trade or dispose of his capital or labour as he wished. The fourth and crucial clause, which had differentiated Hudson's Bill from that of the government, conferred a broad immunity on

---

179 House of Lords Debates, 4 December 1906, vol. 166, cols 703–4.
180 See also for an analysis of the historical background to the Act, John Saville, 'The Trade Disputes Act of 1906', *Historical Studies in Industrial Relations*, March 1996, pp. 11–45.

the trade unions so that they could not be sued for actions 'in contemplation or furtherance of a trade dispute'. The great constitutional lawyer A. V. Dicey declared that the Act had made 'a trade union a privileged body exempted from the ordinary law of the land. No such privileged body has ever before been deliberately created by an English Parliament.'[181] Sir Edward Carson, speaking for the Unionist opposition, declared that 'the question of peaceful picketing is a matter of absolute hypocrisy. Peaceful picketing is no use to a trade union.' He went on to declare that 'a wider exemption ... had never been given ... no precedent could be found in the whole course of the laws of this country'. In consequence, in the future, 'the King can do no wrong; neither can a trade union'.[182] On the left also there were qualms, the Webbs believing that the Act conferred 'an extraordinary and unlimited immunity, however great may be the damage caused, and however unwarranted the act, which most lawyers, as well as all employers, regard as nothing less than monstrous'.[183] The immunity, however, would apply only to actions taken in connection with a trade dispute, not to breaches of the criminal law, while the remedy of criminal prosecutions for acts of violence by individual trade unionists was left entirely untouched by the Act.

Until Margaret Thatcher's trade union reforms of the 1980s, Britain was to remain almost unique amongst democracies in the scope and scale of the legal immunities which the trade unions enjoyed. By contrast with much of the Continent, where the rights of unions were to be secured through positive legislation by the state, trade unions in Britain expected government to play a largely negative role, confining itself primarily to securing for them the right of free collective bargaining. They believed that, if granted this right, they could secure for themselves those other rights which on the Continent were secured through the courts or the political wing of the labour movement. They were therefore hostile to a code of regulation laying out rights and duties such as was commonplace in other industrial societies. The relationship which the unions sought has been well summed up by one authority as one of 'collectivist laissez-faire'.[184] In 1965, the general secretary of the TUC, George Woodcock, was to tell the congress:

> In my view and the General Council's view, relations in industry, by their essence, are much more like a marriage between a man and a woman than any other contractual relationship within the law of this country. You

---

181 A. V. Dicey, *Lectures on the Relation Between Law and Public opinion in England During the Nineteenth Century,* second edition, Macmillan, 1914, p. 372.
182 House of Commons Debates, 28 March 1906, vol. 154, col. 1325.
183 Quoted in Gregory Blaxland, *J H Thomas: A Life for Unity,* Muller, 1964, p. 51.
184 O. Kahn-Freund, 'Labour Law', in Ginsberg, ed., *Law and Opinion,* p. 220.

cannot go rushing to the courts and preserve your marriage. You can go to the courts but when you start bringing the white-wigged judge into your marriage it is finished.[185]

The Webbs had seen the trade unions as aids towards the socialist state, instruments of state collectivism. But the unions regarded themselves as voluntary organisations acting as a counter to the power of the state. This raised a fundamental problem for socialists in the Labour Party. For socialism would involve not just mobilising the working class for an attack on capital but state planning, and that would require incursions into free collective bargaining, a contradiction which finally exploded in the winter of discontent of public sector strikes in 1978–79, a response by the unions to the rigours of a statutory incomes policy. The coalition which formed the Labour Party – the ILP and the socialist societies on the one hand, the trade unions on the other – was, from the beginning, a potentially incompatible one. Perhaps the Social Democratic Federation were right after all that there could be no place for trade unions in a planned socialist society.

The settlement of 1906 rested on its acceptance by public opinion. It was assumed that the unions were sensitive to such opinion and that industrial action could succeed only if the public were behind it. Public opinion, it was hoped, could do the job that had previously been assigned to the courts. The settlement of 1906 remained tolerable only so long as the public believed that the trade unions were acting reasonably. In 1906, most Liberals were optimistic on this score. 'The record of England' in respect of industrial order, declared Sir William Robson, the Solicitor General, on 25 April 1906, 'is marvellous.' 'No body of men', declared the *Manchester Guardian* on 30 March 1906, 'has less desire to persecute and nobody is more susceptible to public opinion or has greater respect for fair dealing.' One MP insisted that there would be

no danger in granting a unique position to trade unions, because they could rely on the inherent wisdom and justice of the working classes. If there was one quality which permeated the whole British race more than another it was the quality of political judgment and a great sense of moderation and justice.[186]

The settlement could last only so long as that 'great sense of moderation and justice' remained. It was to collapse amidst the public sector strikes of the winter of discontent in 1978–79.

---

185 Clegg, Fox and Thompson, *History of British Trade Unions*, vol. 1, p. 171.
186 House of Commons Debates, 25 April 1906, vol. 155, col. 1494; 30 March 1906, vol. 155, col. 72.

SCHOOL MEALS AND MEDICAL INSPECTION

The social reforms of the Campbell-Bannerman government were concentrated on those whom Rowntree believed to be prime victims of the poverty cycle: children and the old. Pressure for reform was fuelled by a growing concern with the health and vitality of the population. The Boer War had been the first occasion since the Crimean War at which medical examinations of a large number of men had been required. The results were disturbing. A large number of potential recruits to the army had been rejected on physical grounds – around 29 per cent in 1901 and 32 per cent in 1902. The polemicist Arnold White claimed that three-fifths of those attempting to enlist at Manchester had been rejected as physically unfit.[187] Comparative statistics seemed to show that the British were weaker than they had been fifty years before. In 1845, 105 men per thousand recruited for the army had been under the required height of 5ft 6in. By 1900, 565 per thousand were under this height, and the next year, the army obtained permission to lower the minimum height to 5ft.[188] Detailed evidence had been accumulated by an Inter-Departmental Committee on Physical Deterioration set up by the Duke of Devonshire in 1904. Worries about the physical condition of army recruits were strengthened by the findings of experts. Witnesses told the committee of the poor physical condition of schoolchildren, more obviously noticeable since children from the slums were now attending elementary schools. One witness claimed that around 16 per cent of children were underfed. But the percentage was much larger in certain areas. At one school in Lambeth, it was suggested that 90 per cent of the pupils could not, because of their physical condition, attend to their work. The children were not getting enough to eat – bread and tea for breakfast, bread and margarine for lunch and a penny's worth of food, usually fish fried in cottonseed oil, for supper.[189] There was, a Liberal MP told the Commons in 1905, 'a touch of dumb heroism about these hungry lads', who, in the words of Elizabeth Barrett Browning, 'looked up with their pale and sunken faces and their looks were sad to see'. 'It was', the MP continued, 'heart-breaking to the teacher to attempt to teach such children, and it would be heart-breaking to the British nation when it realised the facts.' A number of charities helped to provide school meals, but they were uncoordinated and spread haphazardly over the country. It was clear that these nutritional deficiencies could not be remedied by charitable agencies, nor through uncoordinated action by local authorities.

187 Cited in Gilbert, *National Insurance*, p. 83.
188 Bentley B. Gilbert, 'Health and Politics: The British Physical Deterioration Report of 1904', *Bulletin of the History of Medicine*, 1965, p. 143.
189 Ibid., pp. 147 8.

One MP cited a Board of Education survey showing that in thirty-three out of fifty-five urban districts and sixteen out of seventy-one county councils, no voluntary provision of any kind was provided.[190] 'You cannot', the social psychologist Karl Pearson insisted, 'get a strong and effective nation if many of its stomachs are half fed and many of its brains untrained', while Sidney Webb in his philippic 'Lord Rosebery's Escape from Houndsditch' in 1901 expressed the fear that 'it is in the classrooms ... that the future battles of the Empire for commercial prosperity are being already lost'.[191] The Physical Deterioration Committee unanimously recommended, amongst other measures, free provision of school meals.

It was illogical and wasteful to require children to receive education when they were not fit enough to receive it, 'wasting the rates and taxes just at the point where they ought to have the most fruitful influence'.[192] If education was compulsory and universal, it seemed that the conditions upon which it depended ought also to be compulsory and universal. So the provision of school meals could be presented not as charity but a simple corollary of the provision for compulsory education. The Labour MP Will Crooks had been the first to propose free school meals, and in May 1905, Arthur Henderson introduced a Bill providing for them for necessitous children, but after its First Reading, the Bill got no further. Many Liberals joined with Labour in supporting free school meals which could be seen, as one Liberal MP put it, as a form of 'real patriotism and general Imperialism'.[193] 'The best and truest Imperialism', Dr Macnamara, the former president of the National Union of Teachers, told the Commons in 1906,

> began at home ... They were thinking imperially now when they thought of the poor little scraps of humanity on whose rickety shoulders the burdens of the Empire would in future rest ... They must not only sing Rule Britannia, but they must weave the chorus into every clause of our social statutes for the betterment of the people.[194]

What philanthropy had been unable to accomplish in the nineteenth century, national interest was making necessary in the twentieth. In 1909, Sir Robert Morant, who had been Permanent Secretary at the Board of Education since 1903, in a speech at the annual dinner of the Society of Medical

190 House of Commons Debates, 2 March 1906, vol. 152, col. 1424.
191 Adrian Wooldridge, 'The English State and Educational Theory', in S. J. D. Green and R. C. Whiting, eds, *The Boundaries of the State in Modern Britain*, Cambridge University Press, 1996, p. 236.
192 House of Commons Debates, 2 March 1906, vol. 152, col. 1423.
193 Ibid., 18 April 1905, vol. 145, cols 532, 534, 536, 539.
194 Ibid., 2 March 1906, vol. 152, col. 1425.

Officers of Health, declared that 'we have now to think of the English people in competition with other races, and if we neglected the health of the race … we should lose in the racial competition of this world'.[195] These two motives – the desire to draw out the logical corollary of free education and the need to strengthen an imperial race – combined to make the case for both school meals and medical inspection.

Faced with the recommendations of the Physical Deterioration report, Balfour had told the Under-Secretary in charge of education, in 1904, that he could 'be as sympathetic as he liked, but there would be no increase in rates'.[196] The Liberals had said nothing about either school meals or medical inspection during the 1906 election, and indeed the Liberal front bench had been absent from the Commons in an earlier vote in April 1905 on a resolution providing for free school meals, a resolution which, on a free vote, was passed by 100 votes to sixty-four. But in 1906, shortly after the Liberal election victory, another Private Member's Bill was introduced by a Labour MP, W. T. Wilson, who had been lucky in the private members' ballot. Of the Liberal front bench, only the Education Secretary was present, but he welcomed it, saying, of the hungry child, 'They must either feed it or turn it away; and, as the Minister for Education, he could not be responsible for the latter alternative. As everybody was agreed that the child could not be taught before it was fed, then fed it had to be.'[197] The government, therefore, took over the Bill, although it did not show any particular enthusiasm for it. Nevertheless, it was enacted later in 1906, over the opposition, largely, of Unionists, which led one Liberal MP, Major Seely, who had left the Unionists on the issue of free trade, to remark that the House had seen 'the opposition of the over-fed Member to the underfed child'.[198] Ireland was, for some reason, excluded from the Bill, provision for her not being made until 1914. The House of Lords struck Scotland out of the Bill on the grounds that it was not needed there, although the vast majority of MPs sitting for Scottish constituencies were in favour of applying it to Scotland. It was not clear why the judgement of the peers as to what was good for Scotland was held to be superior to that of MPs sitting for Scottish constituencies. Campbell-Bannerman, who himself sat for a Scottish constituency, declared that it 'was the strongest case of the inversion of authority on these Constitutional matters that they had ever seen'.[199] Provision for Scotland had to wait until separate legislation was introduced in 1908.

---

195 Quoted in Gilbert, *National Insurance*, pp. 147–8fn.
196 Gilbert, 'Health and Insurance', p. 150.
197 House of Commons Debates, 2 March 1906, vol. 152, cols 1440–41.
198 Ibid., 7 December 1906, vol. 166, col. 1464.
199 Ibid., 21 December 1906, vol. 167, col. 1871.

The Act was less far-reaching than that proposed by the Labour Party. It was permissive only, giving to English and Welsh local authorities the power to provide school meals from the rates, and the power to remit the cost from parents in necessitous cases. Until 1914, local authorities were restricted in the provision of meals to a rate not greater than 1/2d in the pound.[200] Nevertheless, the Act led to an increase in the numbers of those receiving meals from around 3 million in 1906 to approximately 14 million in 1914. Even so, by 1912, only ninety-five of 328 local authorities were using rate money to provide food, and there had been a reduction in voluntary contributions. In 1914, however, by a further Act, the Board of Education could *require* local authorities to feed necessitous children, with a grant in aid from central government to a maximum of 50 per cent of the cost. The 1914 Act also authorised local authorities to feed children during the school holidays, something for which the Labour Party had long pressed. But local authorities were not *required* to provide school meals to all children until the Education Act of 1944.

Despite its limitations, the Act was a landmark, a first step in extending the role of government into an area hitherto regarded as reserved for parents alone. By contrast with other social legislation, there was to be no enquiry into the character of parents failing to provide meals for their children; and even more fundamentally, the parents of children receiving free meals would not be disenfranchised or suffer any form of official stigma, as was the case with those receiving benefits under the Poor Law. 'Never before had the British State offered to support its citizens without reciprocal deprivation of right for those who applied for relief.'[201] Dicey, in his introduction to the second edition of his book in 1914 on changing ideas of the role of law, *Lectures on the Relation between Law and Public Opinion in England during the Nineteenth Century*, saw the Act as the beginnings of socialism. 'Why a man who first neglects his duty as a father and then defrauds the State [by not paying for school meals] should retain his full political rights is a question easier to ask than to answer.' In the past, citizenship had been conditional on the performance of obligations. It was now to be a right against the state. Limited as the legislation was, therefore, its implications could appear revolutionary.[202]

School meals were to be complemented by medical inspection, a reform which, though it required more public expenditure and had more striking consequences, was, nevertheless, less revolutionary in principle, since the

200 Gilbert, *National Insurance*, p. 113.
201 Ibid., p. 112.
202 Quoted in ibid., p. 113.

state already accepted some responsibility for health through sanitary legislation and provision for local authorities to appoint Medical Officers of Health, a provision which was to become compulsory with passage of the 1909 Housing and Town Planning Act. Their main duties were to inspect school premises, but by 1907, forty-eight authorities had begun medical inspection of pupils. The first medical officer in Bradford had discovered in 1894 that around 100 of the children he examined had not taken their clothes off for over six months.[203] An official working for the Board of Education instanced a school in Lambeth in which 92 per cent of the older children and 94 per cent of the infants were below a normal physical condition. At a school in Dundee containing 154 children, forty-seven were suffering from disease of the glands and seventeen from diseases of the lungs. 'At least one-third of all the children examined suffered from such defects of vision as to interfere with their power of receiving instruction under ordinary school methods.' In one Glasgow school, 25 per cent of children were suffering from eye disease, while in a school in Leeds, 50 per cent of the children had rickets.[204] As with school meals, medical inspection had been recommended by the Inter-Departmental Committee on Physical Deterioration.

Jack Tennant, a Liberal MP, proposed an amendment to the abortive 1906 Education Bill in committee, to make medical inspection a duty on the part of local authorities. This was accepted by the government. But the Bill was, as we have seen, withdrawn, following opposition in the Lords. In 1907, however, an Education (Administrative Provisions) Act was passed. This placed local authorities under a *duty* to provide medical inspection for schoolchildren and gave them the *power* to make arrangements 'for attending to the health and physical condition of the children educated in public elementary schools'. It provided, therefore, for treatment as well as inspection, the two being obviously interconnected. Indeed, inspection revealed, as many had suspected, so many children suffering from medical conditions that it would be virtually impossible for a government to refuse the demand for treatment. But if medical inspection uncovered health problems, then parents without resources would have to have their children treated either in voluntary hospitals as a matter of charity or by the Poor Law medical officer which made the parents paupers. School medical inspection was, therefore, in effect, forcing 'parents onto parish relief'.[205] Nevertheless, until 1912, parents were required to pay for treatment, although in practice most education authorities tended to waive charges for minor procedures such as dental care or X-rays. In 1912,

---

203 Ibid., pp. 117, 119.
204 J. E. Gorst (Sir John Gorst), *The Children of the Nation: How their Health and Vigour should be Promoted by the State*, Methuen, 1906, pp. 55–6, 115, 117.
205 Gilbert, *National Insurance*, p. 126.

however, education authorities were given additional powers to provide free medical treatment to schoolchildren, though many authorities did not do so until placed under a duty to do so in 1918.

These two measures – school meals and medical inspections – were the first elements of the welfare state. Both implied that responsibility for the care of the child was no longer exclusively that of parents who, after all, might be negligent or improvident or simply too poor to provide. The child was now being conceived of as a person in his or her own right, and therefore entitled to education and to the means of making that education effective. In 1908, a further measure – the Children Act – strengthened the protection of children against abuse by adults and established a separate judicial and penal system for young offenders.

Neither school meals nor medical inspections raised the sectarian issue, and therefore they did not attract the same degree of opposition in the Lords as the abortive 1906 Education Bill. The measures were carried with the broad agreement of the Unionist front bench and with the support of most, though by no means all, Unionist MPs. There was some opposition in the Lords, and outside Parliament by extreme individualists such as Dicey; but as one authority has argued, passage of these measures 'signalized a permanent change in the politics of welfare legislation. Party contention over the principle of social reform practically vanished.'[206] Nor was party contention to be renewed over the major reforms of the Liberal government – old-age pensions and national insurance. It surfaced only on the question of how the reforms should be paid for – by more steeply graduated progressive direct taxation, as the Liberals believed, or by a protective tariff, the Unionist answer.

OLD-AGE PENSIONS

Neither school meals nor medical inspections had been part of the exiguous Liberal programme of 1906. Nor had old-age pensions, on which, equally, the government was unpledged.[207] But 59 per cent of Liberal candidates had supported it in their election addresses.[208] Even so, a leading Labour Party campaigner for pensions, Frederick Rogers, first chairman of the LRC, wrote of the 1906 election, 'We had no reason to believe that the Liberals would give us pensions for the aged, any more than the Tories had.'[209] Pensions, however, had been a subject of discussion for many years. Saving for old age was particularly difficult for the working class. Some felt that, being unlikely

206 Ibid., p. 157.
207 Pelling, *Popular Politics*, p. 130.
208 A. K. Russell, *Liberal Landslide: The General Election of 1906*, David and Charles, 1973, p. 71.
209 Frederick Rogers, *Labour, Life and Literature: Some Memories of Sixty Years*, Smith Elder and Co., 1913, p. 261.

to reach old age, it was not worth putting money aside; but most could not afford the regular saving needed. Organisations such as trade unions and friendly societies could provide against temporary illness and unemployment, but it was more difficult for them to provide for the problem of poverty in old age. Many poorer people could not afford contributions to friendly societies. Before the Old-Age Pensions Act, trade unions were providing benefits to just 15,604 pensioners, while a few employers also provided benefits. Few women benefited from any of these schemes. So there was a huge need which was not being met.[210]

In his investigations, Charles Booth had found that nearly eight-nineths of the pauperism in the Poor Law unions of Stepney and St Pancras of those aged sixty-five and older was due directly or indirectly to old age, in the sense that, otherwise, these elderly paupers would not be a charge on the rates; while Rowntree discovered that in York, nearly 19 per cent of those in the poorest class were 'ill and old', and poverty amongst the young, which was even greater, showed why they could neither save for old age nor support their elderly parents.[211] It appeared that the Poor Law could be effective only if the elderly were removed from its scope.[212] In 1895, a Royal Commission, on which the future Edward VII and Chamberlain had sat, had concluded that nearly half of those over sixty-five would need relief, much of which would have to come from the Poor Law. Clearly, the existence of such a large number of the elderly and impoverished could not be attributed, as Chamberlain had told the Commons in 1899, to 'drink, idleness or culpable improvidence'. To maintain the contrary would be to 'draw an indictment against the whole of the working class population'. Indeed, five-sixths of those who came on to the Poor Law at the age of sixty-five had never applied for relief before reaching the age of sixty. 'That shows clearly', Chamberlain continued, 'that it is the failure of powers in old age which produces by far the larger amount of pauperism that exists.'[213] A number of schemes had been produced since 1878, when a Canon Blackley proposed that those aged between eighteen and twenty-one should be required to contribute to a state-supervised fund. In 1889, Bismarck had introduced an insurance scheme in Germany and this stimulated a debate in Britain; while New Zealand in 1898 and the Australian states had introduced means-tested non-contributory pensions. From 1891, Chamberlain had advocated voluntary and

210 Paul Johnson, *Saving and Spending: The Working Class Economy in Britain, 1870–1939*, Clarendon Press, 1985, p. 84.
211 Pat Thane, *Old Age in English History: Past Experiences, Present Issues*, Oxford University Press, 2000, p. 213. Chapters 10 and 11 of this book give an excellent account of the background to the Old-Age Pensions Act.
212 E. P. Hennock, *British Social Reform and German Precedents: The Case of Social Insurance, 1880–1914*, Clarendon Press, 1987, p. 122.
213 House of Commons Debates, 22 March 1899, vol. 69, col. 68.

contributory pensions. He chaired a committee on the subject and was credited, more than any other politician, for putting the issue on to the political agenda. But a contributory scheme would not help the poor who would not be able to afford the contributions.

The alternative was a non-contributory system supported by direct taxation, proposed by Booth in a paper delivered to the Royal Statistical Society in November 1891. Booth had become a convert to tariff reform, fearing that it would not be politically practicable to increase direct taxation to the extent necessary to pay for pensions. In 1896, there was a further inquiry by a Treasury Committee chaired by Lord Rothschild, and after that two further Commons Select Committees. In 1898, over a hundred Conservative MPs called on the government to legislate, and Chamberlain promised to do so. In 1899, Rev. F. H. Stead, warden of a settlement in south-east London, and George Barnes, secretary of the Amalgamated Society of Engineers, founded a National Committee of Organised Labour, partly funded by Booth, advocating universal pensions for those over sixty-five. Every year from 1899, the TUC passed a resolution calling for pensions as of right beginning at sixty. But the costs of the Boer War made it impossible to fulfil Chamberlain's promise. 'Joe's war', Balfour declared unkindly, 'stopped Joe's pensions.' Every lyddite shell exploding on the veldt, Lloyd George told an audience at Carmarthen in November 1899, carried away an old-age pension.[214] And as late as 1904, when the Liberal candidate in the Horsham by-election had proposed to mention pensions in his election address, Liberal Party headquarters had made him delete it.[215]

In the words of Lord Wolverhampton, formerly Sir Henry Fowler, Liberal Chancellor of the Duchy of Lancaster, the issue 'had undergone, both in its principle and in the machinery of its administration, greater and more exhaustive inquiry than almost any measure brought before Parliament'.[216] The various inquiries had produced a consensus on the principle if not the details of a scheme. What enabled the Liberals to translate generalised goodwill into legislation was the budgetary situation. After the destruction of the Russian fleet in the Russo-Japanese War in 1904 at the Battle of Tsushima, there was a temporary lull in the naval race. 'Thus in a sense it was Admiral Togo, the victor of Tsushima, who laid the groundwork of Old Age Pensions and deserves to be remembered as the architect of the British Welfare State.'[217] A second factor may well have been Labour Party pressure. There is evidence of

214 Grigg, *Young Lloyd George*, p. 259.
215 Cooper, *The British Welfare Revolution*, pp. 66–8. This book provides the best modern account of the welfare reforms introduced by the Liberal government.
216 House of Lords Debates, 20 July 1908, vol. 192, col. 1335.
217 Pelling, *Popular Politics and Society*, p. 11.

disillusion amongst working-class voters with the Liberal government in two by-elections in July 1907. Jarrow, previously a safe Liberal seat – the Liberals had been returned unopposed in 1895 and 1900 – was won by Labour, and the Liberal, whose support was, admittedly, damaged by the intervention of the Irish Party, came third behind the Unionist. At Colne Valley, another seemingly safe Liberal seat, in which the Liberal had been returned unopposed in 1906, victory was won in a three-cornered fight by Victor Grayson, a maverick 'socialist and Labour' candidate endorsed neither by the Labour Party nor by the trade unions, nor by the ILP. In fact, the Jarrow result was largely the outcome of local factors, while Colne Valley was a quite untypical and isolated constituency which would revert to the Liberals in January 1910. Nevertheless, these by-elections frightened the Liberals. The Chief Whip's secretary wrote in October 1907 to the Prime Minister's private secretary, declaring that 'a few violent anti-Liberal Socialists' had managed to seize control of the Labour Party machine but that the Chief Whip was, nevertheless, cooperating with the Labour Party to 'drive the extremists into a cave of their own'.[218] Earlier, in October 1906, Lloyd George, speaking in Cardiff, had emphasised that, if the Liberals were to contain Labour, they had to 'cope seriously with the social condition of the people, to remove the national degradation of slums, widespread poverty and destitution in a land glittering with wealth', and he mentioned pensions as a first instalment of social reform.[219] Asquith admittedly had announced his intention to introduce pensions in his 1907 Budget Speech before the by-election losses. But the losses may have prodded the government into more rapid action by highlighting the costs of inaction. The day before pensions were proposed in Asquith's 1908 Budget Speech, Lloyd George wrote to his brother, 'It is time we did something that appealed straight to the people – it will, I think, help to stop this electoral rot, and that is most necessary.'[220] And the by-election losses may also have played a part in influencing Lloyd George's People's Budget of 1909 and the National Insurance Act of 1911.

In his 1908 Budget, Asquith laid out decisions of principle guiding the legislation, which would be piloted through the Commons by his successor as Chancellor, Lloyd George. The first was that the scheme would be non-contributory. That had become the consensus view. For, with a contributory scheme, benefits would not be available for some years. Yet action was needed immediately. Further, a contributory scheme would exclude the vast majority of women, under a third of whom were then in paid work. The

218 Bruce K. Murray, *The People's Budget 1909/10: Lloyd George and Liberal Politics*, Clarendon Press, 1980, p. 60.
219 'Mr Lloyd George and Labour', *The Times*, 12 October 1906.
220 William George, *My Brother and I*, Eyre & Spottiswoode, 1958, p. 220.

majority of pensioners were in fact women who had not been in paid work. There was a further objection which Chamberlain had in 1899 regarded as 'fatal' in that, with a contributory scheme, 'the benefit to be received ... is to depend upon the continuance of the payments'. But

> a very large proportion of the persons who subscribe will, by some temporary misfortune, some inability to provide the payments, be thrown out of the benefits; for a failure to pay a single payment may deprive a man not only of the pension but also of the contributions he has already made.[221]

Many working men, perhaps the majority, would be unable to put aside from their earnings sufficient to make adequate provision for their pension. The provident and thrifty would contribute, but a contributory pension would fail to benefit many of those most in need.

The second decision of principle was that the pension would not be universal, since the cost would be excessive. It would therefore have to be means tested. Pensions would be provided only for British subjects over seventy who had lived in the country for at least twenty years – a provision thought by some to be unfair to Jewish immigrants. 'Aliens' – immigrants, primarily Jews – and 'wives of aliens' were excluded. So were criminals under sentence and those committed to a mental institution.

Asquith was opposed to eligibility tests of character or desert, arguing:

> The less you go into that question, short of actual conviction for crime, the better. All those suggested tests which look so well on paper, thrift, prudence, good repute etc. – when you put them into concrete shape, are not only extremely difficult to supply, but in their application produce cases of unwarrantable hardship.[222]

The purpose of the Act indeed was to remove what Asquith called 'discretionary and inquisitorial powers exercised by the outdoor relief committees of the boards of guardians' in administering relief.[223] The Act nevertheless disqualified those who had been on Poor Law relief during the past two years, as well as anyone who had 'habitually failed to work according to his ability, opportunity and need for maintenance or benefit of himself and those dependent upon him'. But this was mitigated by the further provision in a government amendment to the Bill that if a person had 'continuously

---

221 House of Commons Debates, 22 March 1898, vol. 69, col. 76.
222 Ibid., 7 May 1908, vol. 188, col. 470.
223 Ibid., 24 June 1908, vol. 190, col. 1742.

for ten years up to attaining the age of sixty' made payments to a friendly society or trade union, he or she would be entitled to a pension. This provision
was put in less on grounds of deterrence than as a temporary expedient and
seems hardly to have been applied. In 1909, Lloyd George would propose
in his Budget that the 200,000 to 300,000 receiving the pauper allowance
would in future be eligible for pensions, raising them 'from the slough of
pauperism to the dignity and the comparative comfort of State pensioners'.[224] And in 1911, the provision was entirely dropped as a result of a Labour
amendment.[225] With pensions, by contrast with Poor Law relief, beneficiaries
did not lose their right to vote nor any other civil right, except that of voting
for boards of guardians.

Asquith proposed a cut-off point in terms of means for eligibility for a
pension, but in committee, the Bill was to be amended so as to provide for a
sliding scale. The full pension of 5s a week (equivalent perhaps to around £20
a week today) would be paid to those with incomes below £21 a year and was
reduced on a sliding scale for those with incomes between £21 and £31.10s.
Over 6 million pensioners would be eligible for and claim the pension.

The measure was welcomed by most Unionists. Just twenty-five MPs
voted against Second Reading, and just ten against Third Reading. In the
Lords, admittedly, two important amendments were carried against the government. But Asquith had given notice that the Pensions Bill was a Money
Bill and, as such, seemingly beyond the powers of the Lords to amend. The
Commons Speaker declared that the Lords amendments contravened the
privileges of the Commons, and they were rejected. The Unionists in the
Lords resented what their leader, Lord Lansdowne, declared to be a 'most
extreme interpretation of the doctrine of privilege', adding, 'I venture to
maintain that in the strict sense of the word this Bill is not a money Bill ... it
is a Bill which introduces new principles for the relief of necessitous persons'.
Lansdowne pointed out:

> Nowhere is there anything like a clear and authoritative description of
> what is and what is not the privilege of the House of Commons. There is
> no statute dealing with it. There is no written constitution to which we can
> appeal. There is no compact even between the two Houses.

Therefore, what was happening was 'an attempt on the part of one House
to limit the opportunities of the other'.[226] Lansdowne was rehearsing the

---

224 Ibid., 29 April 1909, vol. 4, col. 483.
225 Thane, *Old Age in English History*, p. 228.
226 House of Lords Debates, 31 July 1908, vol. 193, cols 1911, 1915.

great constitutional issue which would resurface with Lloyd George's People's Budget of 1909.

The Bill was enacted on 1 August. Lloyd George gained the credit for it, and many pensioners were to chant, 'God bless that Lord George'. But his role had been primarily confined to steering the Bill through Parliament and, according to one observer, he 'scarcely conceals his unhappiness about the Old Age Pensions Bill. The prospect of putting 3d on the income tax next year must be rather disheartening.' The Chancellor much preferred contributory benefits.[227] Almost all the pre-parliamentary work had been done by Asquith.[228] The Act provided only a very small pension to 'the very poor, the very respectable and the very old'.[229] But the effect was dramatic on those over seventy who had been receiving outdoor relief under the Poor Law. Between 1906 and 1913, the number receiving such relief in England and Wales fell by nearly 95 per cent. There was, however, little impact on those receiving indoor relief, many of whom could not look after themselves in the world outside.[230] Even so, the pension, like the insurance benefits in the National Insurance Act of 1911, was deliberately pitched below subsistence level. The full pension of 5s a week was below the 7s a week which Rowntree had calculated as necessary for subsistence. This was not only for reasons of economy but because the intention and purpose of the pension was to supplement savings, not to supplant them. Liberal social reformers assumed that the pensioner had been able to secure an adequate wage during their working life so that they could put aside something for old age. The reform had much less to offer those in low-wage poverty, or families from which the main breadwinner was absent either through desertion or early death.

The Act had, however, been 'passed without any actuarial consideration of changes of the age distribution in the population', and, from that point of view, was 'a political scandal'.[231] The cost was, so Lloyd George was to declare in his speech introducing his 1909 People's Budget, £8.5 million. But he then added, 'it has cost more than was anticipated, but the greatness of the cost shows the depth of the need'.[232] The cost led Lloyd George to believe that future such measures should be on a contributory basis rather than financed out of taxation. Further, in the view of social reformers, the means test necessary in a non-contributory system would discourage thrift. So the introduction of pensions was 'led by revulsion to social insurance'.[233] Nevertheless,

---

227 Vincent, ed., *Crawford Papers*, pp. 110–11.
228 Pelling, *Popular Politics and Society*, p. 13.
229 Pat Thane, *The Foundations of the Welfare State*, Longman, 1982, p. 83.
230 Gilbert, *National Insurance*, p. 229.
231 Braithwaite, *Lloyd George's Ambulance Wagon*, p. 71.
232 House of Commons Debates, 1 March 1909, vol. 1, col. 1174.
233 Lord Beveridge, *Power and Influence*, Hodder & Stoughton, 1953, p. 53.

the legislation was a landmark, the first cash benefit financed entirely by the state. And while intervention in the interests of children could be justified on the grounds that they were the future of the nation and should not be punished for the failings of their parents, critics argued that the elderly had been insufficiently thrifty and their working life lay behind them. Introduction of the pension was, therefore, a major challenge to the philosophy of the Poor Law.[234] And it was to prove but the prelude to further reforms removing and reclassifying other groups, in addition to the old – in particular the sick and unemployed – from the previously all-embracing Poor Law.

THE REFORM OF TAXATION

The Unionist opposition had not sought to obstruct the Pensions Bill or Bills providing for school meals and medical inspection. Indeed, many Unionists had been sympathetic. Their main disagreement with the Liberals was on how the reforms should be paid for. Unionists argued that they could only be paid for by a tariff. In a telegram to the Unionist candidate in the North Shropshire by-election in May 1908, Balfour had written, 'Those who have hitherto doubted the value of our fiscal policy must now be converted to its wisdom, for though the Radicals have promised old age pensions only the Unionist party can provide for their payment'.[235] The more conservative of the Unionist free traders had indeed opposed social reforms on the very grounds that they could only be financed by a tariff. 'As all true Free-Traders know,' declared *The Spectator*, organ of the Unionist free traders, in April 1908,

> the short cut to Protection is through large national expenditure ... It is idle for Liberals to say that they mean to have large expenditure and still keep our present fiscal system ... If once the country is committed to a system of old-age pensions, the cry of the Tariff Reformers ... will be irresistible.[236]

But the Liberals, of course, wanted to preserve free trade while also promoting social reform. 'I think it is wise for us', Asquith declared when presenting his Budget in 1907, 'who are, as I have said, not only the party of social reform, but the party also of free trade, to make it clear if we can ... that the attainment of the one is not incompatible with the maintenance of the

---

234 Cooper, *The British Welfare Revolution*, p. 106.
235 *The Times*, 14 May 1908.
236 'The Late Prime Minister', *The Spectator*, 11 April 1908.

other.'[237] And in May 1908, he wrote to the editor of *The Spectator* that he had 'realised for the first time that if it could not be proved that social reform (not Socialism) can be financed on a Free Trade line, a return to Protection is a moral certainty'.[238] Earlier reforms – school meals and medical inspection – had been financed from the rates. But some of the wider reforms towards which the Liberals were edging would have to be financed through increases in national taxation.

Liberals were accustomed to draw a distinction between productive and unproductive wealth. Productive wealth was wealth that was earned, unproductive wealth was wealth that was inherited or derived from passive ownership of land. The distinction was explained by Churchill in a speech in 1909. There was, he declared, a 'new attitude of the State towards wealth', so that the Chancellor would be asking not only 'How much have you got?' but also:

> How did you get it? Did you earn it by yourself, or has it just been left you by others? Was it gained by processes which are in themselves beneficial to the community in general, or was it gained by processes which have done no good to anyone, but only harm? Was it gained by the enterprise and capacity necessary to found a business? ... Was it gained by supplying the capital which industry needs, or by denying, except at an extortionate price, the land which industry requires. It is a tremendous question, never previously in this country asked so plainly, a new idea, pregnant, formidable, full of life, that taxation should not only have regard to the volume of wealth, but, so far as possible, to the character of the processes of its origin.[239]

The first steps were taken in Asquith's 1907 Budget, radical in its implications. The Budget, he announced, should in future be regarded not in isolation as a mere accounting process but as an integral part of wider fiscal and social policies. Asquith emphasised that new Liberal policies would cost money, which would be raised by increasing and graduating income tax. But in addition, a new principle would be introduced, differentiating between earned and unearned income. 'The man who earns £500 a year by teaching, or writing, or in business', one radical journal explained, 'is in a totally different position from the man who draws £500 a year from the funds.'[240] For a teacher or businessperson would need to make provision from their income for times

237 House of Commons Debates, 18 April 1907, vol. 172, col. 1192.
238 Matthew, *Liberal Imperialists*, p. 257.
239 Winston Churchill, *Liberalism and the Social Problem: Speeches 1906–1909*, Hodder & Stoughton, 1909, p. 377.
240 Clarke, *Liberals and Social Democrats*, pp. 110–11.

when they could not work, through illness or old age, and for their children, whereas the same sum from investment income or income from land would be received for so long as the investment or ownership of land continued. Before 1907, everyone whose income was more than £700 a year, the level at which abatements ended, was taxed at the same rate whatever the character or source of the income. To treat these different sources of income in the same way was, Asquith believed, 'the annual perpetration of a gross injustice'.[241] When, however, Asquith had first proposed differentiation, 'he was at once met with the objection, which was considered fatal, that Gladstone had always declared that any such scheme was impracticable'.[242] Asquith, however, ignored this objection and his 1907 Budget provided that those whose *earned* income was below £2,000 per annum and whose total income from all sources was below that amount, would in future pay income tax at 9d rather than 1/- in the pound. To pay for differentiation, death duties on estates worth more than £150,000 were raised from 7.5 per cent to 10 per cent and a surtax of a shilling in the pound was imposed on the first £500,000 in excess of £1 million, with an extra 5 per cent on estates of over £3 million. In his final Budget of 1908, Asquith insisted that further reforms in direct taxation were needed. 'In my judgment there cannot be a greater mistake than to suppose that a free trade Finance Minister has come to or is nearly approaching the end of his resources in the matter of new taxation.'[243] This pointed the way to Lloyd George's People's Budget of 1909.

By the time Asquith introduced his 1908 Budget on 7 May, he had already been Prime Minister for a month. Campbell-Bannerman had suffered from bad health for many years, and in 1907 had endured two heart attacks. In 1906, he had been preoccupied with nursing his sick wife, who died in August of that year. 'I have more than once seen him asleep during meetings of the Cabinet,' Augustine Birrell noted in his autobiography. 'His wife's death came too late to restore him to health.'[244] On 5 April, he resigned, mortally ill. He was too weak to leave Downing Street and remained there, a dying man, until finally passing away on 22 April.

---

241 House of Commons Debates, 18 April 1907, vol. 172, col. 1198.
242 Quoted in Murray, *People's Budget*, p. 78.
243 House of Commons Debates, 7 May 1908, vol. 188, col. 480.
244 Augustine Birrell, *Things Past Redress*, Faber, 1937, pp. 245–6.

CHAPTER 13

SOCIAL REFORM AND THE PEOPLE'S BUDGET

THE NEW PRIME MINISTER

Asquith, the first member of the professional middle class to enter Downing Street since Spencer Perceval at the beginning of the nineteenth century, was the undisputed successor to Campbell-Bannerman. He had indeed deputised for him during his various convalescences. Asquith's succession was unquestioned and inevitable – he had been heir apparent since becoming Chancellor in 1905. In opposition, he had consolidated his reputation by his attack on Chamberlain's tariff reform proposals and was widely considered the most powerful advocate for the free trade cause. In 1913, Gardiner was to sum up the difference between Asquith and his predecessor by writing, 'He trusts his intellect where Campbell-Bannerman trusted his faith.'[1] Herbert Samuel in his *Memoirs* described Asquith by quoting from Ben Jonson's remark on Francis Bacon, Lord Chancellor in the seventeenth century. 'He commanded where he spoke.'[2] Asquith was deeply respected and indeed admired by Liberals. But Campbell-Bannerman had been loved.

At the time of Campbell-Bannerman's resignation, Edward VII was staying in Biarritz recuperating from respiratory problems. Unwilling and perhaps unable to return to London, he asked Asquith to travel to France to be appointed. For the only time in British history, a British Prime Minister was to 'kiss hands' in a foreign hotel. This, *The Times* argued in a leader, may 'perhaps be regarded as a picturesque and graceful tribute to the reality of the *entente* with our French friends'. Nevertheless, *The Times* criticised it as a 'very wide departure from hitherto unbroken precedent'. The newspaper did not perhaps realise how very ill the king was. He was occupying a room in the ground floor of his hotel since, due to heart trouble, bronchitis and fits of choking, he was unable to climb the stairs. There was also a tendency to haemorrhage. Indeed, in 1907, he had felt so wretched that he had seriously considered abdicating. In 1908, he was annoyed that his ministers failed to

---

1 Gardiner, *Prophets, Priests and Kings*, 1908, pp. 54–5, 58–60; Gardiner, *Pillars of Society*, p. 118.
2 Samuel, *Memoirs*, p. 87.

defend him from the criticism in *The Times*, and this was to affect his attitude towards Asquith.[3]

Asquith's appointment was confirmed by a party meeting, the first Prime Minister to have his appointment by the sovereign so ratified. *The Times* commented with some justice that he was beginning his premiership 'in conditions much less favourable than those of two years ago. The wave that brought his party into power has spent its force, and the exuberant exaltation of his supporters in Parliament has given place to a more chastened mood'. The Liberal Party was 'now distinctly on the defensive, and its attitude is perforce apologetic rather than confident'. Public opinion, it seemed, was veering towards tariff reform, since rising prices were undermining the argument that free trade could contain the price of food. 'We all feel', Lord Lansdowne had told a Conservative club on 8 March, 'that our cause now is a winning cause.'[4] Asquith's premiership, however, led to a revival of Liberal fortunes and a speeding-up of social reform. Morley had predicted in January 1908 that Campbell-Bannerman's retirement might weaken party unity but would 'tend to the increase of Cabinet efficiency and *drive*'.[5] And so it proved to be. 'I am sure', Churchill told a colleague in December 1907 'no better workman will have been installed since the days of Sir Robert Peel.'[6] Asquith proved a masterly head of Cabinet, with an extraordinary gift for summing up and reconciling divergent views. He was sometimes accused of postponing difficult decisions, but he did so to preserve harmony, and usually succeeded. He encouraged discussion but did not hesitate to give his own view; and, on occasion, was prepared to give a casting voice to decisions opposed by a majority, as with Lloyd George's 1909 Budget. He showed great skill in holding together a Cabinet composed of strong and masterful personalities who in turn respected him because he was loyal to his colleagues, 'a very rare virtue in Prime Ministers', as one commentator noted.[7] In consequence, Grey was able to tell Lloyd George in 1913 that 'the personal relations of all of us have not only stood the long strain but have gained in attachment to an extent that must be very rare if not unprecedented in the history of Cabinets'.[8]

Asquith tended to shyness, taciturnity and understatement. But his calm demeanour and conservative style of life concealed, as with Campbell-Bannerman, a radical temperament. But whereas Campbell-Bannerman's

3   St Aubyn, *Edward VII*, p. 415.
4   *The Times*, 9 April 1908, 9 March 1908.
5   Harris and Hazlehurst, 'Campbell-Bannerman as Prime Minister', p. 382.
6   Churchill to Runciman, 30 December 1907, quoted in Cameron Hazlehurst, 'Asquith as Prime Minister', *English Historical Review*, 1970, p. 502.
7   Spender, *Public Life*, vol. 1, p. 110.
8   Grey to Lloyd George, 20 June 1913, quoted in Hazlehurst, 'Asquith', p. 507.

radicalism had been Gladstonian – a concern to extend civil, religious and political liberty – Asquith was more attuned to social reform. 'He has real sympathy for the ordinary and the poor,' Lloyd George was to say of him in May 1909.[9] Asquith appointed social reformers to two key posts in his government: Lloyd George, as Chancellor, promoted from the Board of Trade, to replace himself, and Churchill, brought into the Cabinet at the age of thirty-three, to replace Lloyd George as President of the Board of Trade. Writing to Asquith in March 1908, Churchill, somewhat unusually for him, declared his lack of qualifications. 'I have never piloted a Bill of any importance through Parliament. (That kind of work exhausts me.) I cannot claim any acquaintance with a proper grounding in the Poor Law or the Law of Rating – two absolutely basic subjects.' He then, more characteristically, set out what needed to be done.

> Five or six first-class questions await immediate attention – Housing, Unemployment, Rating Reform, Electoral Reform, Old Age Pensions administration … On all of these I shall be confronted by hundreds of earnest men who have thought of nothing else all their lives, who know these subjects – as I know military & Colonial things – from experience learned in hard schools, or else men who have served for many years on local bodies.[10]

In addition to Lloyd George and Churchill, Asquith made a few other Cabinet changes, shifting Lord Tweedmouth, who had suffered a mental breakdown, from the Admiralty to the Presidency of the Council, and replacing him with Reginald McKenna, who had been President of the Board of Education. McKenna was himself replaced by Walter Runciman, beginning a long career at the heart of government culminating in his membership of Neville Chamberlain's government after the Munich Agreement and ending only with the outbreak of the Second World War. Asquith dismissed the elderly Lord Elgin, Colonial Secretary in the Campbell-Bannerman administration, replacing him with Lord Crewe, a close confidant. Later in the year, he removed Tweedmouth from the Cabinet entirely, replacing him with Fowler who went to the Lords as Lord Wolverhampton. He retained Augustine Birrell, who had replaced Bryce in the Irish Office in 1907, when the latter had been appointed ambassador to the United States, but that was probably a mistake. Birrell was an amiable littérateur but no administrator. He was a political lightweight and was, significantly, not to be included in

9   Grigg, *People's Champion*, p. 178.
10 Churchill, *Companion*, vol. 2, part 2, p. 755.

the Buckingham Palace Conference on Ulster in 1914. Charles Hobhouse, a junior member of the government, believed that Birrell 'cares nothing about the rights or wrongs of a public matter – his sole concern is whether the Irish party will accept it or not'. He was, according to Hobhouse, 'the most cynical and reckless administrator, all he cares for is a quiet official life, and will throw away money or principles like water to get peace'. He was to prove a disastrous appointment, seldom visiting Ireland, but relying on telegraphic communication or correspondence, and had a fatalistic attitude towards events there, ill-suited to Ireland's problems. His natural inertia was strengthened by worries about the illness of his wife, who was to die in 1913. In May 1914, despite the growth of private armies in both Nationalist and Unionist Ireland and the importation of arms, he 'had not been near Dublin or Ireland for months'.[11] Relations between the absent Birrell and the administration in Dublin Castle were poor. He offered little leadership, and in consequence the Irish administration was to appear paralysed and inert.

CHURCHILL AND SOCIAL REFORM

The Campbell-Bannerman government had seemed to lack a clear sense of direction, partly due to the wrecking tactics of the Lords. Asquith's government, by contrast, was from the first marked by a determination to enact social and welfare reform. This flowed from the predilections of the new Prime Minister and of the promoted ministers, Lloyd George and Churchill. In 1908, Beatrice Webb was to compare the two. After lunching

> with Winston Churchill and his bride ... Winston had made a really eloquent speech on the unemployed the night before and he has mastered the Webb scheme ... He is brilliantly able – more than a phrase-monger, I think – and is definitely casting in his lot with – constructive state action ... After lunch Lloyd George came in and asked us to breakfast to discuss his insurance scheme ... a clever fellow, but has less intellect than Winston, and not such an attractive personality.[12]

In 1909, Churchill was to declare:

> The greatest danger to the British people is not to be found among the enormous fleets and armies of the European continent ... It is here, close

11 Edward David, ed., *Inside Asquith's Cabinet: From the Diaries of Charles Hobhouse*, John Murray, 1977, p. 72, entry for 10 July 1908; p. 74, entry for 17 November 1908; p. 169, entry for 1 May 1914.
12 MacKenzie, *Diary of Beatrice Webb*, vol. 3, p. 100, entry for 16 October 1908.

at home, close at hand in the vast growing cities of England and Scotland, and in the dwindling and cramped villages of our denuded countryside. It is here that you will find the seeds of imperial ruin and national decay – the unnatural gap between rich and poor, the divorce of the people from the land, the want of proper training and discipline in our youth, the awful jumbles of an obsolete Poor Law, the constant insecurity in the means of subsistence and employment ... Here are the enemies of Britain. Beware lest they shatter the foundations of her power.[13]

In 1907, Churchill had told the editor of a Liberal newspaper that 'minimum standards of wages and comfort, insurance in some effective form or other against sickness, unemployment, old age – these are the questions, and the only questions, by which parties are going to live in the future'.[14]

The need for social reform was, Churchill wrote to Asquith in December 1908:

urgent and the moment ripe. Germany with a harder climate and far less accumulated wealth, has managed to establish tolerable basic conditions for her people. She is organised not only for war, but for peace. We are organised for nothing except party politics. The Minister who will apply to this country the successful experiences of Germany in Social organisation may or may not be supported at the polls, but he will at least have left a memorial which time will not deface of his administration.[15]

Churchill had urged Asquith to adopt in Britain 'a sort of Germanised network of State intervention and regulation', instancing six radical measures.

1. Labour exchanges and unemployment insurance.
2. National infirmity insurance.
3. Special expansive state industries, e.g. afforestation and roads.
4. Modernised Poor Law, i.e. classification.
5. Railway amalgamation with state control and guarantee.
6. Education compulsory until seventeen.[16]

The first three formed part of the programme of the Asquith government, and Churchill was himself to be responsible for the first. The fourth had to wait until the 1920s, the fifth to the 1940s, while the sixth was not achieved

---

13   Churchill, *Liberalism and the Social Problem*, p. 363.
14   Paul Addison, 'Churchill and Social Reform', in Blake and Louis, eds, *Churchill*, p. 60.
15   Churchill, *Companion*, vol. 2, part 2, p. 861.
16   Henry Pelling, *Winston Churchill*, Macmillan, 1974, p. 128.

until 2013, over 100 years after Churchill had proclaimed it as an aim of public policy. But Churchill's imaginative sweep went even further, 'Dimly across gulfs of ignorance I see the outline of a policy wh. I call the Minimum Standard. It is national rather than departmental.' That was the policy to be put forward by Beatrice Webb in the minority report to the Poor Law Commission and would be carried into effect by Attlee's Labour government after 1945, which provided a universal right to pensions, healthcare and unemployment benefit. Churchill admitted:

> I am doubtful of my power to give it [his programme] concrete expression. If I did, I expect before long I should find myself in collision with some of my best friends – like for instance John Morley, who at the end of a lifetime of study & thought has come to the conclusion that nothing can be done.[17]

In 1909, Churchill envisaged a 'comprehensive, interdependent scheme of social organisation' to be achieved through 'a massive series of legislative proposals and administrative acts'.[18] He was, so one historian has concluded, 'equalled only by Lloyd George among his contemporaries in his capacity to diagnose and effectively treat the worst social evils of his day'.[19] In some respects, he saw even further. Unlike Lloyd George, he had read widely on social problems; and, unlike Lloyd George, he saw the various social reforms as an interconnected whole leading to a comprehensive welfare state. Even so, and despite his massive achievements, Churchill, like Lloyd George, was never fully trusted by senior Liberals. He seemed volatile and inconsistent, at the mercy of the rhetorical flourish, dominated by ambition and offensive to those who stood in his way. 'He is the unknown factor in politics,' a journalist was presciently to comment in 1913. 'You may cast the horoscope of anyone else; his you cannot cast. You cannot cast it because his orbit is not governed by any known laws, but by attractions that deflect his path hither and thither.'[20]

Lloyd George's proposals for social reform came from experience of poverty and insecurity, Churchill's from wide reading and reflection. Churchill's concern with unemployment led him to offer Beveridge, who in 1907 had published a reassessment of relief works, a permanent appointment at the Board of Trade in 1908. 'If you are going to deal with unemployment,' the

---

17 Churchill, *Companion*, vol. 2, part 2, p. 755.
18 Churchill, *Liberalism and the Social Problem*, pp. 237–8.
19 Pelling, *Churchill*, pp. 128–9.
20 Gardiner, *Pillars of Society*, p. 56.

Webbs apparently said to Churchill, 'you must have the boy Beveridge.'[21] This was to be the beginning of Beveridge's long career of public service, which culminated in his great report on social insurance in 1942. Churchill, Beveridge was to reminisce in 1960, was 'great fun to work with. He told us that he had not himself many years to live; he expected to die young like his father Randolph. But this was before he married.' In 1908, he was to marry Clementine Hozier, and after that he 'gave up any idea of dying young'.[22]

First in Churchill's list of reforms was to be 'a system of labour exchanges', which 'stands at the gateway to industrial security. It opens the way to all immediate practical reforms.' Men seeking work were hindered by friction in the labour market and lack of information on job vacancies. They had to hawk around personal applications for work in a humiliating manner. Part of the reason, so Beveridge wrote in the *Morning Post* in July 1907, why the state was 'forced into the costly and degrading harshness of the Poor Law' was

> because it has no control or supervision of the labour market. It must always rely on the assumption that the applicant for help could find work if he looked for it, because it is never in the position to satisfy itself that there is no work for him. It must apply the test of the workhouse because it is not in a position to apply the test of an offer of real work.[23]

Labour exchanges could reduce friction in the labour market. They could, in Churchill's words, be 'the Intelligence Department of labour. In constant touch with the employers on the one hand, and with the elementary and technical schools on the other, they should be able to "place" numbers of boys in trades which offer a steady livelihood.' Labour exchanges were an essential preliminary to compulsory unemployment insurance, which Churchill had in mind, since they could help distinguish 'between the worker and the loafer', by testing willingness to work.

> The establishment of Labour Exchanges is necessary for efficient working of the insurance scheme; for all foreign experiments have shown that a fund for insurance against unemployment needs to be protected against unnecessary or fraudulent claims by the power of notifying situations to men in receipt of benefit so soon as any situations become vacant. The insurance scheme, on the other hand, will be a lever of the most valuable kind to bring the Exchanges into successful operation ... The administration

21 Beveridge, *Power and Influence*, p. 68.
22 José Harris, *Beveridge: A Biography*, 2nd edition, Clarendon Press, 1997, p. 169.
23 Beveridge, *Power and Influence*, p. 60.

of the twin measures must be increasingly interwoven ... together they organise in due proportions the mobility and stability of labour.

Labour exchanges would facilitate the search for work while national insurance would support the worker and his family while he was searching. Sidney Webb sought voluntary insurance but compulsory labour exchanges with compulsory training for those refusing job offers.[24] Churchill, however, insisted that labour exchanges be voluntary but insurance compulsory. In this way, legislation would respect the rights of working men and of the trade unions. Workmen would be allowed to refuse employment at less than trade union rates so the exchanges would not be providing employers with 'free' or non-union labour. As with other Liberal social reforms, the Unionists offered little opposition, and Second Reading was passed without a division on 16 June 1909. The legislation was a new departure for central government, entering into a new relation with citizens, providing them with a service that was 'personal, discretionary and infinitely various from one locality, or one industry to another'.[25]

In 1909, a second instalment in Churchill's wide-ranging programme, the Trade Boards Bill, provided for minimum wages in the sweated industries. These were industries such as the clothing industry in the East End of London, characterised by long hours, poor sanitary conditions, low wages and many underpaid female and home workers. In such industries, it was difficult for workers to organise in trade unions and bargain collectively for higher wages. In consequence, many working in these trades had to resort to outdoor relief under the Poor Law. In a Cabinet memorandum of 12 March 1909, Churchill wrote that regulating wages by law was 'only defensible as exceptional measures to deal with diseased and parasitic trades. A gulf must be fixed between trades subject to such control and ordinary economic industry. A clear definition of sweated trades must comprise a) wages *exceptionally* low, and b) conditions prejudicial to physical and social welfare.'[26] Moreover, even in the sweated trades, the Act was merely to lay down the principle that wages were to be regulated. The state did not itself fix the wages. They were to be fixed and flexibly adjusted to local and industry-specific conditions by statutory wage boards, composed of an equal number of workers and employers with an impartial chair. The government could refer back any recommendations made by the boards, but it could not amend them. From that point of view, the Trade Boards Act contradicted any idea of a universal minimum wage,

24 Churchill, *Companion*, vol. 2, part 2, pp. 851–3.
25 Beveridge, *Power and Influence*, p. 74.
26 Paul Addison, *Churchill on the Home Front*, Jonathan Cape, 1992, pp. 78–9.

for a statutory minimum wage could hardly exist alongside different minima established in response to local and industry-specific conditions. Churchill steered the Bill through the Commons, where it passed without a division. It was, Churchill wrote in 1907, 'in embryo, the boldest and most far-reaching of all the social reforms which separate modern constructive Liberalism from the older policy that bore that name'.[27] It would be extended by Churchill's successor at the Board of Trade, Sydney Buxton, in 1913 to industries with a high proportion of female workers. And despite Churchill's disclaimer, the Act did create a precedent, establishing a new principle, that wages could be regulated.[28]

The boards were in essence a substitute for collective bargaining in industries where trade unions were weak or non-existent. The first list of such industries included bespoke tailoring, cardboard box making, machine-made lace and chain making, covering around 200,000 workers, of whom around two-thirds were female. As with the Trade Disputes Act, the Trade Boards Bill was 'intended to help the autonomous forces of industry in arriving at a satisfactory agreement'.[29] It was ideologically liberal, rather than socialist or even collectivist.

THE PEOPLE'S BUDGET

These measures were, however, but a prelude to Lloyd George's Budget of 1909 – the People's Budget, as it came to be called – a phrase that had first been used by Cobden in the mid-nineteenth century. The Chancellor faced the problem of having to meet a Budget deficit, the first since 1904, of around £16 million – over 10 per cent of £150 million total government spending. Of this £16 million, around £8.5 million resulted from the commitment to old-age pensions, and there was in addition a shortfall of government revenues owing to a downturn in trade. But £2.8 million of the deficit was due to the cost of four new dreadnought battleships to which the government was committed, in response to an acceleration in the German naval programme. The Unionists had demanded that Britain build eight new dreadnoughts and Wyndham had coined a slogan with considerable popular resonance, 'We want eight and we won't wait'. The First Lord, Reginald McKenna, asked for six. Lloyd George and Churchill, who were at that time economisers, wanted just four. Asquith secured a compromise that four should be laid down immediately and four later in the financial year if the need arose. In

27 Clarke, *Liberals and Social Democrats*, p. 115.
28 Churchill, *Companion*, vol. 2, part 2, p. 879.
29 Kahn-Freund, 'Labour Law', in Ginsberg, ed., *Law and Opinion*, p. 254.

the end, the eight were built. As Churchill was later to put it, 'the Admiralty had demanded six ships; the economists offered four, and we finally compromised on eight'.[30] The cost of naval armaments was to prove a constraint throughout the period of the Liberal government.

Lloyd George reminded MPs that both the pensions and the dreadnoughts were 'incurred with the unanimous assent of all political parties in this House'. Indeed, the Unionists had pressed for more spending, not less, arguing in by-elections for pensions at sixty-five, not seventy, as well as for the additional dreadnoughts. So spending under these heads could not be dismissed as 'wild and extravagant socialistic proposals, but rather an expenditure in which the Government represented the minimum demands and in which its proposals were more moderate from the point of view of expenditure than those which had emanated from any other section of the House'.

The deficit, Lloyd George continued, could not be met by borrowing then regarded with horror. Indeed, the Liberals had criticised Unionists for borrowing to pay for the Boer War. It would be even more unthinkable for a peacetime government, so it was then believed, to borrow. Nor, of course, could a Liberal government increase customs duties. Therefore, the bulk of the revenue must be found through increases in direct taxation. Lloyd George was determined that the extra burden should not fall on what he called the 'industrial classes', who were 'paying more in proportion to their incomes than those who are better off'.[31] He therefore proposed that necessary increases should fall primarily upon the better off, while necessary increases in indirect taxes should fall primarily upon luxuries not necessities – tobacco, spirits and liquor licence duties. Such taxes would have the additional advantage of pleasing Nonconformists in the party. The increases in indirect taxes were in fact to yield a greater total revenue than in any Budget since that of 1900 in the midst of the Boer War.

The Chancellor proposed to raise around £7.5 million of the revenue needed from direct taxation, the remainder from indirect taxes. With regard to income tax, he would extend graduation and differentiation between earned and unearned income, the principle first established by Asquith in his 1907 Budget. Income tax would remain at 9d in the pound for those with incomes under £2,000 a year – around 1.2 million taxpayers – and there would be new child tax allowances for those under £500 a year, an innovation which would become permanent. But those earning more than £2,000 a year would continue to pay 1/ in the pound. A new super-tax would

30 Churchill, *World Crisis*, vol. 1, p. 37.
31 House of Commons *Debates*, 29 April 1909, vol. 4, cols 475, 502.

be introduced for those with incomes over £5,000 a year, at a rate of 6d in the pound on the amount by which such incomes exceeded £3,000. There would also be increased death duties on estates over £5,000 and an increase in legacy and succession duties.

But the most contentious part of the Budget turned out to be the new land taxes, since land had hitherto been virtually immune from taxation. Lloyd George had originally wanted a simple penny in the pound tax on land worth £50 a year or over. But this was rejected by the Cabinet. Instead, there were three new land taxes: a 20 per cent tax on the increment in the value of land 'accruing to land from the enterprise of the community' when it changed hands, a tax that had first been proposed by Mill; a 10 per cent tax on leasehold land imposed when the lease came to an end; and an annual 1/2d in the pound tax on the value of undeveloped land other than agricultural land.[32] There was also to be a tax on mineral royalties. These taxes established a principle dear to the New Liberalism – differentiating between agricultural land, which gave rise to social obligations, and urban land or land containing marketable mineral products which, Liberals believed, did not, and where the increase in value was an 'unearned increment', that is, not due to any effort on the part of the landowner. 'The urban landlord and the mineral royalty owner', the Chancellor declared,

> are invariably rack-renters. They extort the highest and the heaviest ground rent or royalty they can obtain on the sternest commercial principles. They are never restrained by that sense of personal relationship with their tenants which exercise such a beneficent and moderating influence upon the very same landlord in his dealings with his agricultural tenants.

Instead, to quote Mill, such a landlord makes his wealth 'while he is slumbering'. The capitalist, the Chancellor continued, ran a risk, but the royalty owner 'has contributed no capital and runs no risk'. Lloyd George was opposing, then, not the 'productive' capitalist or occupier of property but the 'unproductive' landowner, seen as belonging to a parasitic class.

There were, finally, to be new duties on alcohol licences, which would, it was calculated, bring in around £2.6 million and an increase in stamp duty which would bring in around £650,000. A further £3.5 million would be brought in by increases in duties on tobacco and spirits, though not beer, a luxury, no doubt, but, by contrast with spirits, regarded as a working-class luxury. There would be an increase in the tax on cars and a tax of 3d a gallon on petrol – motoring then being a preserve of the wealthy. These taxes

---

32 Ibid., cols 533, 536, 537.

would, supposedly, be hypothecated by the Treasury and used to pay for an expanded roads programme. The indirect taxes ensured that all classes would contribute to the raising of revenue, but those who did not pay income tax – and that included the vast majority of the working class – would be taxed only on luxuries (tobacco and spirits) not on necessities. The remainder of the deficit would be met by a £3 million raid on the sinking fund.

In pure revenue-raising terms, the Budget proved a great success. When the Liberals came to office in 1905, the net Budget deficit had been £755 million. By 1914, there was a surplus of £650 million.

But, of course, the Budget of 1909 was far more than an exercise in raising revenue. It was radical in extending the principles of differentiation and graduation, and in the land taxes. It was not only Conservatives and traditionalists who felt disquieted but many Liberals as well. Walter Runciman, President of the Board of Education, had written to Asquith, attacking 'the savagery of the scale on men of *moderate means*', while Lewis Harcourt, son of Sir William, the former Chancellor, told Runciman that 'this Budget will ensure the triumph of Tariff Reform', though of course its purpose was precisely the opposite.[33] Because of its radicalism, the Budget was, unusually, discussed in detail in Cabinet before delivery, and in the 1930s, Lloyd George was to tell Randolph Churchill, Winston's son, that when Asquith had gone round the Cabinet table inviting every member to present his view, everyone, including Churchill, was opposed. But Asquith, summing up, had declared, 'We have had a very full and frank expression of opinion from every member of the Cabinet and it seems to me that the weight of argument rests with the Chancellor.'[34] Lloyd George was perhaps exaggerating. The Budget seems to have been supported by Churchill and Haldane as well as the Prime Minister. But there is no doubt that Asquith gave his Chancellor staunch support throughout. There is also no doubt that the Budget proposals were opposed by a majority in the Cabinet, and that the land taxes would have been rejected by 'an overwhelming majority', had they gone to a vote. 'I had to fight and bully and badger my way against everybody,' Lloyd George was to tell a Welsh colleague.[35]

The Budget was, admittedly, more radical in principle than in practice. The super-tax affected at most 12,000 out of around 1 million taxpayers, while the increase in death duties affected only around 80,000. The Budget was also less redistributive than it seemed. The main effect was on the very rich – those earning more than £10,000 a year. The professional and business

---

33 Grigg, *People's Champion*, p. 177. Emphasis in original.
34 Churchill, *Young Statesman*, pp. 323–4.
35 Thomas Jones, *Lloyd George*, Oxford University Press, 1951, p. 36.

classes were little affected. Indeed, lower earners from these classes were the prime beneficiaries. The editor of one radical journal thanked Lloyd George on behalf of 'the man who earns £500 a year by teaching, or writing, or in business'.[36]

Lloyd George presented his Budget to the Commons on 29 April 1909 in a somewhat unimpressive speech lasting four and a half hours, during which his voice failed more than once. Indeed, for some parts of his speech, he was barely audible. He did not content himself with the taxation proposals, radical as they appeared to be, but laid out a further programme of social reform which seemed to have no obvious connection with the Budget. Near the beginning of his speech, he asked, 'What are the dominating causes of poverty amongst the industrial classes?' He answered, 'Old age, premature breakdown in health and strength, the death of the bread-winner and un-employment due either to the decay of industries and seasonable demands, or the fluctuations and depressions in trade.' Bismarck's Germany had tried to meet this problem through a scheme of social insurance. 'And a superb scheme it is.' It had, the Chancellor believed, from his visit to Germany the previous year, not only relieved deprivation but also improved industrial effi-ciency and had, therefore, been welcomed by employers. Britain too needed such a system, he declared, so heralding the National Insurance Act of 1911. In his concluding peroration, Lloyd George said:

> This ... is a war budget. It is for raising money to wage implacable warfare against poverty and squalidness. I cannot help hoping and believing that before this generation has passed away we shall have advanced a great step towards that good time when poverty and wretchedness and human deg-radation which always follow in its camp will be as remote to the people of this country as the wolves which once infested its forests.[37]

It is perhaps hardly surprising that the Commons and, in particular, the opposition spokesman on finance, Austen Chamberlain, was nonplussed by the speech. 'We have never had a Budget statement such as that which the Chancellor of the Exchequer has just made,' Chamberlain remarked. The Chancellor had sketched out not just a Budget but

> a legislative programme trenching ... upon the province of almost every one of his colleagues, a programme of such magnitude and complexity that it is not a question of one or two years before it can be carried out;

---

36 Quoted in Clarke, 'The Progressive Movement in England', p. 175.
37 House of Commons Debates, 29 April 1909, vol. 4, cols 484, 548.

it is much more likely to be two or three Parliaments before that vast programme can be achieved.[38]

Chamberlain was right. The agenda laid out by Lloyd George was indeed to occupy British governments of both left and right for much of the twentieth century. Perhaps it has still not yet been fully implemented.

Opponents of the Budget had three main lines of criticism. The first, stressed by Balfour, was that the Budget was an example of 'tacking', putting measures of social reform such as the land taxes into legislation which ought to do no more than balance the accounts; and Lloyd George had indulged in tacking, Balfour believed, to circumvent scrutiny by the House of Lords. But that argument was double-edged since it tacitly admitted that the Lords had no right to interfere with a Budget which did *not* contain measures of social reform. The second line of criticism, stressed particularly by Unionist free traders and some of the more traditional Liberals, was that it was 'socialistic', a charge given credence when Labour's financial spokesman, Philip Snowden, declared that Lloyd George had been an 'apt pupil'.[39] The third and perhaps strongest line of attack was made by the tariff reformers, who declared that social reform should be financed not by higher direct taxation but a tariff. 'We are told', Austen Chamberlain declared after the Budget, 'that it is the final triumph of free trade and the death blow to the policy of Fiscal Reform. Sir, in the spirit in which it is offered, I accept the challenge and I am ready to go to the country at any moment upon it.'[40] This became the leitmotif of the Unionists – that the Budget was so revolutionary in its implications that it ought to be submitted to the people through a general election.

All the same, the Budget did not at first seem to excite great interest in the country, either amongst opponents or supporters. 'It is difficult to understand', Lord Carrington, President of the Board of Agriculture, wrote in his diary on 1 July, 'why the country is not more with us.'[41] It was opponents of the Budget who first gave it wide publicity in the country. In June, Walter Long formed a Budget Protest League. Balfour, to ensure that it attracted wide support, urged the League to play down tariff reform and concentrate on opposing the land taxes. The League, however, proved somewhat of an embarrassment, its resolutions against the Budget on occasion being defeated at its own meetings.[42] Concentrating on the land taxes, as Balfour wished,

---

38 Ibid., col. 549.
39 Ibid., 5 May 1909, vol. 4, col. 1072.
40 Ibid., 7 June 1901, vol. 6, col. 41.
41 Murray, *People's Budget*, p. 184.
42 Peter Rowland, *The Last Liberal Governments: The Promised Land, 1905–1910*, Barrie & Rockliff, 1968, p. 226.

was playing into Lloyd George's hands, since these were taxes that would affect only the very wealthy. It soon became clear that large landowners had not been paying their fair share. Local taxation was based on rental values, but large mansions were seldom let out for rent, and so there was no real basis for rating them. Many were on the rate books at purely nominal rental values and there had been an unwillingness to challenge landowners by disputing the assessments. Lansdowne House in Berkeley Square, estimated to be worth £8 a square foot, was assessed at a rental value of 7 pence ha'penny, and Devonshire House Piccadilly nearby, at 6d a square foot.[43]

The new land taxes, being comparatively minimal, would certainly not destroy landed property, as critics alleged. But nor would they provide sufficient revenue for the navy or social reform. Indeed, they were to raise a comparatively small sum – around £500,000 – and would cost far more to collect than they were to yield. By 1914, around 5,000 officers were being employed full- or part-time to undertake land valuation at a cost of over £2 million – far more than the amount which the taxes brought in. Indeed, the land taxes would be abandoned in 1920, ironically by Lloyd George's coalition government. Lloyd George would not perhaps have been unduly disturbed by this. For his primary aim had been to secure a valuation of land. But that could not be achieved in a separate Bill which would have been emasculated by the Lords. And if valuation of land had been introduced as part of the Budget without accompanying revenue-raising proposals, the Budget would have been ruled by the Speaker to be hybrid. This would have meant that it could not be protected against the Lords on the grounds of financial privilege. Introduced in the Budget, however, it was hoped that the land taxes would be immune from the Lords. Far from intending to provoke the Lords to reject the Budget, the land taxes were added to the proposal for land valuation precisely to ensure that the Lords would *not* reject it.

THE LORDS REJECT THE BUDGET

If the land taxes did little to raise revenue, they proved a great political success. Opposition to them appeared as selfish class interest and distracted attention from far more important proposals – increases in direct and indirect taxation. A few hitherto unknown peers helped the Liberals by entering the public arena with claims of the depredations which they would be suffering. Lord Onslow declared that he would be dismissing his 'regular and permanent staff of labourers, bricklayers, carpenters, sawyers, painters, drainers and foresters', and would in future be contracting out work in these areas.

43 Edward Porritt, 'The Struggle over the Lloyd-George Budget', *Quarterly Journal of Economics*, 1910, pp. 256–7.

Lord Sherborne declared that, in view of the rise in income tax, he too would be reducing spending on his estate.[44] It was revealed that the Duke of Buccleuch, one of the wealthiest landowners in the country, had discontinued his subscription to his local football club; since, as his chamberlain put it in a letter to the club, 'owing to the large prospective increase in taxation caused by the present Budget it has been found necessary to curtail very largely the amount of his Grace's annual subscriptions', It was also revealed that he had reduced the allowance to elderly retainers on his Drumlanrig estate from fifteen shillings to seven shillings and sixpence following the introduction of old-age pensions. The Duke of Portland declared that he would reduce spending on his estate and was cancelling all of his charitable contributions. The Marquess of Anglesey declared that he would reduce his annual subscription to the London Hospital from £5 to £3. In the newspaper in which this was announced, it was revealed that he had just bought a new yacht costing at least £1,500 a month to sail.[45] The Duke of Westminster had told pensioners on his estate that their *ex gratia* pensions would be discontinued from Christmas 1909 as they were now receiving a national pension.[46] Churchill, who became chair of the Budget League, wrote to his mother on 4 August:

> I never saw people make such fools of themselves as all these Dukes and Duchesses are doing. One after another they come up threatening to cut down charities and pensions, sack old labourers and retainers, and howling and whining because they are asked to pay their share, as if they were being ruined.[47]

As might have been expected, Lloyd George responded fiercely to the wails of the dukes. In a speech at Limehouse on 30 July, he laid into wealthy Unionist landlords who had pressed the government to build dreadnoughts but were unwilling to pay for them.

> We sent the hat round. (Laughter.) We sent it round amongst the workmen (hear, hear), and the miners of Derbyshire (loud cheers) and Yorkshire, the weavers of High Peak (cheers) and the Scotchmen of Dumfries (cheers) ... They all brought in their coppers. We went round Belgravia, but there has been such a howl ever since that it has completely deafened us.

44 *The Times*, 16, 19 June 1909.
45 Letter from J. W. Gulland, First Lord of the Treasury in the government, *The Times*, 16 September 1909; Rowland, *The Last Liberal Governments: The Promised Land*, p. 225.
46 Leslie Field, *Bendor: The Golden Duke of Westminster*, Weidenfeld & Nicolson, 1983, p. 102.
47 Churchill, *Companion*, vol. 2, part 2, p. 902.

Defending the proposed tax on mineral royalties, Lloyd George contrasted the crushing work of the miners, risking their lives, with the landlord living on his royalties.

> When the Prime Minister and I knock at the doors of these great landlords, and say to them: 'Here, you know these poor fellows who have been digging up royalties at the risk of their lives, some of them are old, they have survived the perils of their trade, they are broken, they can earn no more. Won't you give something towards keeping them out of the workhouse,' they scowl at us. We say, 'Only a halfpenny, just a copper.' They retort, 'You thieves!'

Lloyd George told an overflow meeting that the government would not be deterred by the House of Lords, 'the great slaughterhouse of good Bills'.[48]

On 9 October, in a speech at Newcastle, he raised the temperature still further by speaking of the peers as 'ordinary men, chosen from among the ranks of the unemployed', while on 9 January, speaking in Leven, Churchill was to declare that the Lords were 'a played-out, obsolete, anachronistic assembly, the survival of a feudal arrangement ... which only now requires a smashing blow from the electors to finish it for ever'. These speeches were splendid stuff and delighted the faithful. But they probably repelled the floating voter. Indeed, many Liberals believed that Limehouse was in part responsible for the heavy electoral losses the Liberals were to suffer in the south of England in the January 1910 election.

Most Liberals assumed, as Lloyd George did, that the Lords had no power to amend or reject financial legislation, since, from the end of the seventeenth century, it had been a constitutional convention that the Commons had absolute financial privilege. Therefore, only the elected chamber could decide on matters of finance and taxation and only the Commons could determine expenditure since estimates were not submitted to the Lords. Since expenditure and revenue hung together, it would have been odd if the Upper House were to have power over revenue but not spending. Were the Lords as a non-elected chamber able to legislate on revenue, they would be in breach of a fundamental constitutional principle – no taxation without representation; and, by denying the government supply, they would be in danger of bringing administration to a halt. 'Englishmen', *The Spectator*, a Unionist journal, declared on 10 July 1909, 'are not taxed from above, but tax themselves. Therefore only they themselves, through their representatives, can impose a tax.' Each year, the Speech from the Throne requested supply

---

48 *The Times*, 31 July 1909.

for the next session, a request addressed only to the Commons. This principle seemed to have been conceded on a number of occasions by Balfour himself. In 1906, in a speech at Manchester he had declared, 'The House of Lords, as you all know, does not interfere with the general financial policy of the country.'[49] In 1907, Balfour had told the Commons·

> We all know that the power of the House of Lords ... in the sphere of legislation and administration is further limited by the fact that it cannot touch those Money Bills, which if it could deal with, no doubt it could bring the whole executive Government of the country to a standstill.[50]

In 1908, Balfour had said in Dumfries, 'It is the House of Commons, not the House of Lords, which settles uncontrolled our financial policy.'[51]

Most Liberals believed rejection or amendment of the Budget by the Lords highly unlikely. On 10 May, less than two weeks after presenting his Budget, Lloyd George told his brother that F. E. Smith, an influential Conservative, had said to him, 'The Lords are not such fools as to throw it out ... Do you think they are mad?'[52] The Budget was, however, bitterly attacked by Rosebery, who raised the political temperature. On 11 September 1909, he delivered a speech to a Glasgow audience of around 3,000 – *The Times* devoting more than a full page to his remarks – in which he declared that the Budget inaugurated a revolution and one 'without the mandate of the people'. Many, he insisted, would cease to defend free trade if the Budget were held to be the only alternative to a tariff. The great free traders of the past – Cobden, Bright and Gladstone – had also believed in economy in public spending. This Budget contradicted Gladstone's traditional call for retrenchment. It was, he continued, an attack on property, capital and liberty. It made the landowners 'part of the criminal class'. It symbolised 'a new Liberalism and not the one I have known and practised'. The bureaucracy it entailed was 'the antithesis of the old Liberalism'. Indeed, the Budget was not Liberal at all but one 'which in its spirit is Socialistic'. 'Any form of protection', Rosebery concluded in his grand peroration, 'is an evil, but Socialism is the end of all, the negation of faith, of family, of prosperity, of the monarchy, of Empire. (Loud cheers.)'

Rosebery's speech marked, as Asquith told him, 'the parting of the political ways between every one of your old colleagues who have in the past

---

49 *Manchester Guardian*, 23 October 1906.
50 House of Commons Debates, 24 June 1907, vol. 176, col. 930.
51 *The Times*, 7 October 1908.
52 George, *My Brother and I*, p. 226.

fought under you or by your side'.[53] Rosebery had resigned as president of the Liberal League a day before the speech, not wishing to embarrass his former political friends, and the League was wound up shortly afterwards. But Rosebery did not suggest that the Lords reject the Budget, and he told them on 14 November that he would not in fact vote against it, although his speech must have given great encouragement to those favouring rejection. However, he had now annoyed his new Unionist allies as much as his old Liberal ones. And he left a hostage to fortune when he said of dukes, 'I have always found [them] a poor but honest class.'[54] Perhaps he was speaking ironically. Herbert Samuel, who had recently been appointed to the Cabinet as Chancellor of the Duchy of Lancaster, replied to Rosebery at Dundee on 13 September, saying that, although Rosebery belonged to 'neither of the great parties', he belonged 'to another party which existed in every country in the world – a very formidable party which was dominant in some countries, the party ... of the opulent'.[55] It was a telling thrust.

The Liberal government was the first government of the left with a secure majority in Britain since the expansion of the franchise in 1884, the first since Gladstone's second majority administration of 1880 which could enact measures the Conservatives disliked – and it was to prove the last until Attlee's in 1945. It is hardly surprising that the Liberals roused great fears in the propertied classes. Between 1906 and 1909, the Lords had rejected ten Liberal Bills and amended no fewer than 41 per cent of the Bills they had scrutinised. This contrasted with the peers' activities during the Balfour government, when they had amended only around 10 per cent of Bills and rejected none.[56] How would they now respond to the People's Budget?

Neither Balfour nor Lansdowne offered a clear lead in the months immediately following the Budget. The running had been made by the City and by unrepresentative aristocrats, whose arguments appeared a form of special pleading. Balfour and Lansdowne seemed to be awaiting the reaction of public opinion. But Joseph Chamberlain from his sickbed was the first to call for rejection, telling Garvin, editor of *The Observer*, that 'the budget tries to knock the House of Lords out of the constitution' and that he hoped 'the Lords will knock it out'. In September, he sent a message to a meeting at which Balfour was speaking that the Budget was 'the last effort of free trade finance to find a substitute for tariff reform and imperial preference, and it is avowedly intended to destroy the Tariff Reform movement'.[57] Chamber-

53 McKinstry, *Rosebery*, p. 507.
54 Rhodes James, *Rosebery*, p. 465.
55 *Manchester Guardian*, 14 September 1909.
56 G. R. Searle, *A New England? Peace and War 1886–1918*, Clarendon Press, 2004, p. 409.
57 Garvin, *Chamberlain*, vol. 6, pp. 935, 938.

lain was, for the last time, giving a lead to the Unionists, for Balfour was gradually converted to his view and became determined, from at least the time of the Limehouse speech, upon rejection, telling Austen Chamberlain in September that 'if the Lords did not reject the Bill, he could not continue to lead the party'.[58] Lansdowne was more cautious, but even he did not believe the Lords could refrain from interfering with the Budget. Initially, he favoured amendment rather than rejection, but by September, he too had come to accept rejection; and on 1 October, *The Times* declared that 'there can no longer ... be much doubt as to the fate of the Finance Bill when it leaves the House of Commons'. Joseph Chamberlain, though stricken, reinforced the rejectionists by sending a message to a Unionist rally in September expressing the hope that the Lords 'would see their way to force a general election'.[59] Two factors in particular weighed with Balfour in his decision to recommend rejection. The first was the implication of the land valuation proposals. Although, as we have seen, they were very minimal, they could, Unionists feared, open the way to heavier taxation of land in the future. Indeed, Lloyd George had spoken earlier of having to 'rob someone's hen roost next year'.[60] The land taxes introduced, most Unionists believed, a new principle in taxation, that capital in the form of land could be taxed as heavily as income. In the past, governments, whether Conservative or Liberal, had assimilated the tenure of land to that of other forms of property, rather than marking it out for special burdens. In addition, the land valuation clauses were seen as a prime example of 'tacking'. 'I defy', Balfour told the Commons,

> any constitutional lawyer in this house to say it is legitimate for the House
> of Commons to introduce into its Finance Bill great measures of valuation
> and compulsory registration ... How dare you describe it as a Finance
> Bill? By your own admission it is not a Finance Bill. It is a compulsory
> registration Bill.[61]

If the Lords were to accept such a constitutional innovation without protest, Lansdowne in October 1909 told Lord Balfour of Burleigh, who would be the only Unionist peer to vote for the Budget, 'the position of the House of Lords would have been gravely and permanently impaired. We could never

---

58 Austen Chamberlain to Mrs Joseph Chamberlain, 20 September 1909, reprinted in Chamberlain, *Politics from Inside*, pp. 182–3.
59 Rowland, *The Last Liberal Governments: The Promised Land*, p. 239.
60 Le May, *Victorian Constitution*, p. 194.
61 Dugdale, *Balfour*, vol. 2, p. 41.

in future, however outrageous the financial policy of a radical Government might be, claim the right to stand in its way.'[62]

The second reason for rejection, Balfour believed, was that it was the only means of maintaining the credibility of tariff reform. The Budget, after all, presumed that revenues for social reform could be financed without need for a tariff. Were it to prove successful, much of the dynamic behind tariff reform would be lost. Tariff reform seemed the one positive policy that the Unionists had to offer to counter the Liberals. They could deny the charge that they were reactionary by claiming that they too favoured social reform but that they would not finance it by punitive and 'socialistic' levels of direct taxation. The tariff reformers were indeed the only group which offered a positive alternative to the Budget. 'Judicious tariff reform', Balfour told a Birmingham audience on 17 September, was far preferable to the 'bottomless confusion of Socialistic legislation'.[63] 'The House of Lords', Asquith was to declare in his election address for the January 1910 election, 'have violated the Constitution in order to save from a mortal blow the cause of Tariff Reform.' It was no accident that those most vehemently in favour of rejection were also, broadly speaking, ardent tariff reformers.[64] Leading Unionist free traders, Lord Cromer, Lord Balfour of Burleigh and Lord James, as well as Rosebery, now a cross-bencher, all refused to support rejection. Hicks Beach, now Lord St Aldwyn, showed his displeasure with the Unionist leadership by staying away from the Lords entirely. The tariff reformers did not seem to realise that, in the election campaign which was bound to follow, their arguments would be swamped by constitutional arguments over the House of Lords and an attack on aristocratic privilege. In addition, they might lose the support of Unionist free traders who regarded tariff reform as a greater danger than the Budget.

All the same, a decision by Balfour not to reject would have split his party. It was not that he had been pressed by his party into supporting rejection. He made the decision independently. Balfour both anticipated the Unionist consensus and helped to foster it.[65] It was a consensus he could probably not have resisted, even had he wished. Indeed, so strong was Unionist feeling that there was no need even to call a party meeting to support the decision to reject, for it was obvious that the vast majority of Unionist MPs and peers agreed with it. Balfour and Lansdowne were even able to resist the entreaties of Edward VII who, in October, sought to persuade them not to support rejection. The king was a free fooder but, more important, was worried that

62 Newton, *Lansdowne*, pp. 378–9.
63 Blewett, *Peers, Parties and People*, p. 83.
64 Roy Jenkins, *Mr Balfour's Poodle: Peers v. People* [1954], Collins, 1968, p. 98.
65 Murray, *People's Budget*, p. 210.

rejection would lead to a weakening of the hereditary second chamber and, therefore, by implication, weaken the hereditary monarchy also. The Unionist leaders, however, were impervious to the king's plea, and Edward found them 'stiff and uncommunicative'.[66]

In fact, Lansdowne moved not the rejection but rather its referral to the people through a general election, in accordance with Lord Salisbury's referendal doctrine. His motion declared that the Lords would not be 'justified in giving its consent to this Bill, which contains provisions of a dangerous and unprecedented character, until it has been submitted to the judgment of the country'. In the draft of the motion in Balfour's papers, rejection was explicitly altered to referral by substituting the words 'until it has' for the words 'and has not' in an earlier draft.[67] The Unionists, then, claimed to accept the fundamental proposition of a representative system, that the unelected chamber must ultimately give way to the elected chamber. But for them, whether that chamber actually represented the people was a proposition needing to be tested in a general election.

The Unionists argued, and it was not disputed, that they had a *legal* right to reject the Budget. The question was whether it was *constitutional* to do so, as what is lawful may not be constitutional. The sovereign can, after all, lawfully refuse assent to government legislation; but in almost all circumstances, that would be unconstitutional. The Liberals argued that the action of the Lords was similarly unconstitutional. Unionists replied that precedents in relation to the annual Budget did not go back very far. The omnibus Budget, combining all taxation measures for the year in a single measure, had been established by Gladstone as recently as 1861; and he did it to circumvent rejection by the Lords of the Paper Duties Bill the previous year. The measure was then made part of the 1861 Budget. But as Balfour told the Commons in December, 'The English Constitution did not begin in 1860.'[68] The Liberals responded that for the Lords to throw out a Budget was virtually to dismiss a government enjoying a majority in the Commons, since a government lacking the power of the purse could hardly continue. The Unionists could in turn respond that with 'tacking', the constitutional protection given to a Budget did not apply, since more was being asked for than merely granting supply. That argument achieved some retrospective support from the Commons Speaker at the time of the Budget, James Lowther, who, as Lord Ullswater, wrote in his memoirs, published in 1925, that 'the celebrated Finance bill of 1909 which was the immediate cause of the Parliament Act' would not

---

66 Philip Magnus, *King Edward the Seventh*, John Murray, 1964, p. 437.
67 Balfour Papers, Add. MSS. 47930, ff. 28–9.
68 House of Commons Debates, 2 December 1909, vol. 13, col. 562.

have been given the Speaker's certificate as a Money Bill, 'for it contained a number of provisions which were not within the definition of the clause and section'.[69] Indeed, since 1911, only around half of annual Budgets have been classified as Money Bills. Even so, for the Lords to arrogate to itself the right to determine whether a Budget was legitimately a Finance Bill or not meant that it was seeking supremacy over the Commons.

The Unionists appreciated that rejecting the Budget meant an immediate election; and indeed, as we have seen, the terms of the Lansdowne amendment proposed that the Budget be put to the people. While they did not imagine that they might win the election, they did believe that they would radically erode the Liberal majority. They seem to have predicted the outcome, a hung parliament with the Liberals dependent upon the Irish Nationalists and Labour, reasonably accurately. The Liberals would then form a minority government, and such a government would, the Conservatives believed, be weak, as the 1892 minority government had been. Then, in a second election, the Liberals could be removed from office and Unionist supremacy restored. All the same, rejection was foolish, on both constitutional and political grounds. The Lords were arrogating to themselves, as an unelected chamber, not only the power to control taxation but also to compel a dissolution at a time of their choosing and, by that means, to make or unmake a government. Lord Hugh Cecil countered that the Lords were not in fact compelling a dissolution but only forcing a referendum on the Budget.[70] The dissolution, he claimed, occurred only because the government denied the right of the Lords to refer an issue to the people. But a non-elected chamber was hardly in a better position to determine popular opinion than the Commons; and, with its permanent Unionist majority, the Lords were hardly equipped for this quasi-judicial function which they were assuming, nor well-equipped to decide which issues should in fact be referred to the people in a referendum or an election.

In 1884, Gladstone had told the queen:

At no period in our history ... has the House of Commons been dissolved at the call of the House of Lords, given through an adverse vote; that the establishment of such a principle would place the House of Commons in a position of legislative inferiority to the House of Lords; and that the attempt to establish it would end in organic changes detrimental to the dignity and authority of the House of Lords.[71]

---

69 Lord Ullswater, *A Speaker's Commentary*, Edward Arnold, 1925, vol. 2, p. 103.
70 *The Spectator*, 1 January 1910.
71 Buckle, ed., *Letters of Queen Victoria*, 2nd series, vol. 3, p. 518, entry for 14 July 1884.

In his last speech in the Commons, on 1 March 1894, Gladstone had declared that the Lords in rejecting Home Rule had raised 'a most serious question'. They had created 'a state of things which ... cannot continue', so that, rather than 'the closing of a controversy', it was 'handing on that prolonged controversy which in our judgment it will be the duty of parliament to continue until it has arrived at a satisfactory settlement'. The question was 'whether the work of the House of Lords is not merely to modify, but to annihilate the whole work of the House of Commons'. The controversy raised by the actions of the Lords was, Gladstone prophesied, one 'which, when once raised, must go forward to an issue'.[72] In 1909, the Unionists put the 'controversy' at the centre of the political agenda. Salisbury's referendal doctrine meant, according to a Liberal peer, that there was in effect 'single-chamber government when the Conservatives were in power and two-chamber government when the Liberals were in power'.[73] The permanent Unionist majority in the Lords was tolerable only for as long as the Lords were prepared to show self-restraint. But self-restraint had been absent since 1906. The Lords were drawing the attention of voters to the composition and powers of a legislative chamber whose membership seemed hardly compatible with popular government. There is a sense, then, in which the constitutional arguments were beside the point. The key factor was political – that the Liberals had won a large majority in 1906, a majority signifying a transfer of power from the traditional landed interest to new groups in society, including organised labour. The question of constitutionality was to be decided not by a theoretical debate but by the outcome of a political conflict. 'Who talks about altering and meddling with the Constitution?' Lloyd George asked at Newcastle in October 1909.

> The great Constitutional party. As long as the Constitution gave rank and possession and power to the Lords, it was not to be interfered with ... the moment the Constitution begins to discover that there are millions of people outside park gates who need attention, then the Constitution is to be torn to pieces.[74]

Politically, the Unionists were choosing poor ground. An election which left the Liberals dependent on Irish Nationalists and Labour would not, as they seem to have believed, replicate that of 1892. The 1892 Liberal government had been elected on a withdrawing tide, led by the ageing Gladstone, uncertain, and with no strong sense of direction. But the Liberals were by

---

72 House of Commons Debates, 1 March 1894, vol. 21, col. 1150.
73 Lord Lucas, Under-Secretary for War, House of Lords Debates, 25 November 1909, vol. 4, col. 1054.
74 Grigg, *People's Champion*, p. 224.

1910 even more confident, if anything, than they had been in 1906, with sure-footed leaders such as Asquith, Lloyd George and Churchill and a programme of social reform yet to be completed. It was by no means clear that the tariff reform alternative with its concomitant, food taxes, would be a vote winner. Indeed, 1906 had shown that it was not. The Unionists had simply failed to understand the political significance of the great Liberal victory of 1906. Further, they were putting into question the relationship between the two houses of Parliament. Whereas the Liberals might have been prepared to accept Lords' rejection of the Education and Licensing Bills, for which the country had little enthusiasm, on the principle of letting sleeping dogs lie, they would hardly continue to do so were they, as was likely, to be returned to power. 'The Lords may decree a revolution,' Lloyd George declared at Newcastle in 1909, 'but the people will direct it.'[75] Moreover, were the Liberals to succeed in removing the Lords' veto, the road to Home Rule lay open. The Unionists, then, in not accepting the Budget, were risking the Union. For in 1909, they could have thrown out a Home Rule Bill as in 1893. But that would no longer be possible if the Lords' absolute veto were removed. The Unionists' decision, therefore, was, in Asquith's words, 'the most stupendous act of political blindness, and a political blunder of the first magnitude'.[76] By contrast, had the Lords accepted the Budget, the Unionist position would have been far stronger. The Liberals did not have a particularly strong legislative record to put before the voters. In December 1909, McKenna at the Admiralty could write sadly to his wife, 'Starting its work with such promise and an almost unprecedented majority it seems cruel looking back on the four years of arduous toil that so little has been accomplished and that only one of our really important legislative measures should have been placed upon the Statute Book [old-age pensions].'[77] Voters might have felt that the Lords had been sensible in rejecting the Licensing and Education Bills, which could be seen as debts to interest groups associated with the Liberal Party, but that the peers were prepared to be large-minded where their own interests were concerned, by letting the Budget through even though it would hit their pockets. But it was not to be.

On 30 November, the Lords passed the Lansdowne amendment by 350 votes to seventy-five, in effect forcing a dissolution. In doing so, they were ensuring, in Asquith's words, that 'on that fatal day ... the House of Lords as we have known it, as our fathers and our forefathers have known it, committed political suicide'.[78]

---

75 Ibid.
76 House of Commons Debates, 21 February 1911, vol. 21, col. 1746.
77 Martin Farr, *Reginald Mckenna: Financier Among Statesmen 1863–1916*, Routledge, 2008, pp. 185–6.
78 House of Commons Debates, 21 February 1911, vol. 21, col. 1746.

CHAPTER 14

THE STRUGGLE WITH THE HOUSE OF LORDS

THE SUSPENSORY VETO

Asquith responded rapidly. On 1 December, the day after the Lansdowne amendment was passed, he told the Commons that he would propose the following resolution: 'That the action of the House of Lords in refusing to pass into law the financial provisions made by the House for the Service of the year is a breach of the Constitution, and a usurpation of the rights of the Commons'. This resolution was debated the next day and Asquith declared that the House met 'under circumstances which are unexampled in the history of the British parliament'. He dismissed the referendal theory as 'this new-fangled Caesarism which converts the House of Lords into a kind of plebiscitary organ ... one of the quaintest inventions of our times', and a Caesarism which operated only under a Liberal government. 'We are living', Asquith declared,

> under a system of false balances and loaded dice. When the democracy votes Tory we are submitted to the uncontrolled domination of a single Chamber. When the democracy votes Liberal, a dormant Second Chamber wakes up from its slumbers and is able to frustrate and nullify our efforts ... The real question which emerges from the political struggles in this country for the last thirty years is not whether you will have a single or a double chamber system of government, but whether when the Tory Party is in power the House of Commons shall be omnipotent and whether when the Liberal Party is in power the House of Lords shall be omnipotent.[1]

'We have not provoked the challenge,' he concluded, 'but we welcome it.'

The resolution was passed by 349 votes to 134, with the Irish Party abstaining, and Parliament was then dissolved for the longest electoral campaign in British history, lasting ten weeks from 3 December to 10 February. The

---

[1] House of Commons Debates, 1, 2 December 1909, vol. 13, cols 501, 556, 558.

election garnered huge interest amongst the public. Turnout was to be 87 per cent, the highest in the twentieth century. Around 15,000 attended a rally at Trafalgar Square on 4 December to support the Liberals, while on 10 December, Asquith spoke to an audience of 10,000 at the Albert Hall to the background of a banner asking, 'Shall the people be ruled by the Peers?'

The Liberals now had to develop a definite policy on Lords reform. In 1907, following the Lords' wrecking of the Education Bill, a Cabinet committee dominated by Lord Crewe and Asquith had proposed a system of joint sittings of the two houses to resolve deadlocks at which the Lords would be represented by a delegation of peers chosen by them. Just as the judicial functions of the Lords were now exercised by the law lords, the great majority of peers having withdrawn from judicial business, so also the legislative functions of the Lords would similarly be delegated. The Cabinet committee rejected two other proposals for resolving deadlocks, the referendum which would put the two houses on an equal footing and the suspensory veto, that is giving the House of Lords only the power of delay, which was to be the solution eventually adopted in the Parliament Act. But in 1907, the Cabinet committee believed that the suspensory veto amounted in effect to abolition of the Upper House and single-chamber government. It also rejected rationalising the composition of the House of Lords, which would strengthen it and make it more difficult to resolve disagreements between the two houses.

But Campbell-Bannerman opposed his Cabinet committee's recommendation and produced, with the aid of the Clerk of the Commons, a masterly memorandum putting the case against joint sittings, arguing that they would reverse decisions of the seventeenth century by bringing a non-elected, hereditary element into financial legislation. Campbell-Bannerman argued that joint sittings were anti-democratic, since the voting power of the Lords in these sittings would be equal to that of the Commons; while, if the Lords were to be represented by a delegation of, say, 100 peers, elected proportionally, a Liberal government would need a large working majority to overcome peers' opposition. And any figure, whether 100 or more or less, would inevitably be arbitrary. In any case, an assembly of 770 legislators – 670 MPs and, say, 100 peers – would be 'too big for a Conference. It will be a multitude, a mob. Any real deliberation or discussion and any diplomatic give-and-take arrangement will be impossible. The question at issue will be decided by vote, and the voting will be on strict party lines.'[2] The result would almost certainly be that the Lords, instead of being contained by the proposal for joint sittings, would actually be strengthened. More fundamentally, a joint sitting could decide to amend legislation against the government's wishes,

---

2   Campbell-Bannerman's memorandum is reprinted in Spender, *Campbell-Bannerman*, vol. 2, pp. 351–5.

which would be a blow against the whole notion of responsible government, that the Cabinet was responsible only to the Commons.

In place of joint sittings, Campbell-Bannerman favoured the suspensory veto so that legislation passed by the same House of Commons in three successive sessions would automatically become law over the opposition of the Lords. The suspensory veto had first been proposed by the philosopher James Mill, father of John Stuart Mill, in 1836. John Bright had been the first politician to give it public support, in 1883, at a meeting of the Federation of Liberal Associations at Leeds. He had been supported by Chamberlain, then a radical Liberal MP. Campbell-Bannerman in his memorandum did not consider procedure for Money Bills since he could not believe that the Lords would or could tamper with financial legislation. The Cabinet accepted Campbell-Bannerman's advice, overturning the conclusions of the Cabinet committee in favour of the suspensory veto.

On 24 June 1907, Campbell-Bannerman had introduced a resolution in the Commons giving effect to the suspensory veto. Its great advantage, he argued, was that it was a weapon of last resort. The very fact of its existence would persuade the Lords to give way except when dealing with a government with a small majority or towards the close of a parliament. Campbell-Bannerman did not, therefore, expect the suspensory veto to be needed very often, a prediction to be borne out by the history of the Lords following the 1911 Parliament Act. Campbell-Bannerman's resolution was passed after a short and somewhat perfunctory debate, but the Liberals took no further action until the end of 1909.

Opening the election campaign at the Albert Hall in December 1909, Asquith told the Liberals that they faced 'a single task, a task which dominates and transcends, because it embraces and involves, every great and beneficent change upon which our hearts are set. That task is to vindicate and to establish upon an unshakable foundation the principle of representative government.' Asquith committed the government to putting into statutory form the supremacy of the Commons over finance. In addition, since the tampering with the Budget was not an isolated act but the culmination of a series by which the Lords had claimed authority over the Commons, the absolute veto on non-financial legislation 'must go', so that voters could feel 'what they cannot feel now' that 'the will of the people as deliberately expressed by their elected representatives must, within the lifetime of a single Parliament, be made effective'. Asquith implied, then, support for the suspensory veto, although this was not spelt out. Most Liberals favoured this option. A minority, however, sought to reform the composition of the Lords so that possession of a hereditary peerage would not be the only basis for membership. Asquith did not exclude reform of composition, but that, he believed, was an issue for the future.

Suppose, however, as was likely, that the Lords rejected the Liberal reform proposal? In his Albert Hall speech, Asquith insisted that the Liberals would 'not assume office, and we shall not hold office unless we can secure the safeguards which experience shows us to be necessary for the legislative utility and honour of the party or progress'.[3] Asquith's followers naturally interpreted this to mean that he had secured a promise from the king that, were the Lords to reject reform, he would agree to the creation of sufficient peers to enable the Liberals to overcome their opposition. For, since the Upper House could not be dissolved, the only way of diluting the Unionist majority would be by swamping it with newly created Liberals.

But Asquith had obtained no such promise from the king. As we have seen, Edward VII had tried, unsuccessfully, to get Balfour and Lansdowne to persuade the Lords to accept the Budget. But restricting the powers of the Lords, the king believed, meant weakening its authority, while a mass creation would cheapen the peerage, degrading its legislative function. The king's private secretary at first refused even to show his master Asquith's letter which requested a promise to create peers, believing that it would set the king 'still more' against his Prime Minister. Five days after the Albert Hall speech, Edward VII told his secretary that he regarded 'the policy of the Government as tantamount to the destruction of the House of Lords'. He would not, therefore, agree to any creation of peers until after *two* general elections had been held.[4] That was contrary to the precedent of the Reform Bill of 1832, when William IV had agreed to create sufficient peers to pass the Bill without requiring an intervening election at all, although he had done so only after dismissing his Prime Minister and discovering that no alternative government was available. Edward VII's two elections requirement was not known to the Liberal rank and file, nor indeed to anyone other than the Prime Minister himself and the king's immediate associates. To another of Asquith's proposals, that the king might transfer the prerogative of creating peers to the Prime Minister, the king's private secretary said that it 'would be better that the King should abdicate than agree to it'.[5]

Asquith made another important policy statement at the Albert Hall, though much less noticed, saying that the Liberals were now free from their self-denying ordinance not to legislate for Home Rule. Ireland, he said, constituted 'the one undeniable failure of British statesmanship' and 'the

3   *The Times*, 11 December 1909.
4   Ridley, *Bertie*, p. 443.
5   Le May, *Victorian Constitution*, p. 196.

solution of the problem can be found in only one way'. Therefore, 'in the new House of Commons the hands of the Liberal Government and the Liberal majority will in this matter – Home Rule for Ireland – be entirely free'. This commitment, unlike that to remove the absolute veto of the House of Lords, was, according to a report, greeted 'in a meeting which was boiling over with enthusiasm for so many far-reaching changes' with 'a sensation of surprise and coldness. There was comparatively little cheering and even that little was without vigour'. But Home Rule was not regarded as a main priority for the next Liberal government. Nor was Asquith's commitment followed up by other Liberals. In the debate on the address in February 1910, Balfour was to declare that of 149 speeches of Cabinet ministers, just one had voluntarily referred to Home Rule, without being pressed upon it in cross-examination.[6] 'All the Liberals I have met,' one Irish correspondent wrote to Bryce, 'with the exception of Scotchmen, are afraid of Home Rule, and would in fact have much preferred it if Asquith had never made his declaration.'[7] Of sixteen Liberal ministers who issued election addresses in the two elections of 1910, nine did not mention Home Rule, while just 39 per cent of Liberal candidates mentioned it. A quarter of Liberal candidates were either opposed to Home Rule or favoured it within a Home Rule All Round framework; and just 41 per cent of Liberal candidates were to mention it in the December election.[8] But the significance of Asquith's commitment was not missed by Redmond, the Irish leader, who told his supporters in Dublin on 16 December that 'the opportunity for which we have been so long waiting and hoping has at length arrived ... This is the first time since 1892 that full self-government for Ireland has been made a leading issue at a general election'. Further, since the Liberals promised removal of the Lords' veto, 'on this occasion the Liberal ministers are pledged to the means necessary to carry that policy into effect, for they are solemnly pledged never again to accept office until they are furnished with powers to overcome the veto of the House of Lords'. Redmond, therefore, pressed his countrymen on the other side of the Irish Sea to vote for Liberal or Labour candidates in the election.

THE JANUARY 1910 GENERAL ELECTION

The social theorist L. T. Hobhouse wrote that the issues at the January 1910 election were 'larger and cut deeper than any which the country has been

---

6   House of Commons Debates, 21 February 1910, vol. 14, col. 46.

7   Blewett, *Peers, Parties and People*, p. 125.

8   Patricia Jalland, *The Liberals and Ireland: The Ulster Question in British Politics to 1914*, Harvester Press, 1980, p. 29; Blewett, *Peers, Parties and People*, p. 324.

called on to decide since 1832'.[9] The Unionists were placed on the defensive by the Budget and the Liberal attack on the Lords, and their campaign began in a faltering manner. They seemed honour bound to defend the existing constitution and structure of the Lords, for Balfour believed that 'our defence would inevitably be weakened if we coupled it with the admission that the Second Chamber, which has carried out this (in our opinion, necessary) duty, was one which could not claim public confidence unless it were immediately reformed'.[10] But around half of the Unionists in their election addresses declared dissatisfaction with the current composition of the Lords. Indeed, Unionists were even more unclear than Liberals as to whether the Lords should be defended or reformed. But in the new year, the Unionist campaign moved away from defending the Lords' approach to the Budget and began to emphasise tariff reform, which would overcome the 'socialism' of the Budget. Balfour was sceptical, fearing that such a campaign would serve only to unite the opposition and deter moderate voters, especially in free trade Lancashire. But he was hardly in a position to hold out against the tide. Hicks Beach, now Lord St Aldwyn, wrote to Lord Robert Cecil in May 1909:

> This Budget seems to me to have given the final shove of the Unionist Party to Tariff Reform. A man may be a Free Trader by reason and conviction ... but *if he has anything to lose* ... he will certainly prefer an indefinite TR policy ... to the fiscal policy which is initiated by the present Budget.[11]

Tariff reform was a policy designed to meet economic bad times. But by the end of 1909, unemployment was falling and the tariff reformers' cry that the economy was not soundly based appeared to put them in the uncomfortable position of seeking positively to wish for the return of bad times. In addition, they had to meet the charge that tariff reform, by increasing the cost of food, would benefit already wealthy landowners. 'Tariff Reform Means Happier Dukes,' one Liberal poster declared, while Lloyd George attacked those who would 'tax the workmen's children in order to spare the acres of the landlord's child'.[12]

Labour's policy was not to limit the Lords but to abolish it. However, Labour fought the January 1910 election, as it had in 1906, in alliance with the Liberals, even though there was no specific entente. The Liberals put up no official candidates in areas where there were Labour MPs but refused to

---

9   Quoted in Clarke, *Liberals and Social Democrats*, p. 117.
10   Blewett, *Peers, Parties and People*, p. 119.
11   Rempel, 'Lord Hugh Cecil's Parliamentary Career', p. 126fn. Emphasis in original.
12   Blewett, *Peers, Parties and People*, p. 113.

allow Labour to expand beyond its areas of existing strength, threatening that, if it did, they would retaliate by invading Labour strongholds. Of the seventy-eight Labour candidates, just twenty-seven faced three-cornered fights. But Labour had been strengthened by the adherence of the miners' union, the last major union still unaffiliated, which in 1908 had voted to affiliate. The union's MPs, formerly Lib-Labs, were now required to become Labour candidates. In consequence, the Lib-Labs were almost eliminated, though three were to be returned in the January 1910 election. But the miners' leaders were not socialists. So their affiliation, in Bernard Shaw's view, would dilute even further Labour's commitment to socialism. 'What then becomes of Socialism?' the playwright enquired. The miners' leaders 'were out to exploit Capitalism, not to abolish it'.[13]

The Liberals were to lose their overall majority in this election. The results were as follows.

	Votes	Seats	Unopposed returns	Percentage of vote	Percentage of vote per opposed candidate
Liberals	2,880,581	275	1	43.2	49.2
Unionists	3,127,887	273	19	46.9	47.5
Labour	505,657	40	0	7.6	38.4
Irish Party	124,586	82	55	1.9	77.7
Total		670	75		

The Liberal government was the first since 1885 and only the second since 1865 to have been re-elected in peacetime. But it had suffered a net loss of 125 seats, while the Unionists had gained 118. A contemporary commentator believed that, as in 1906, the outcome of the election was caused more by the return of Unionist voters who had deliberately abstained in 1906 than by a switch of floating voters.[14] Instead of floating, voters were falling beneath the surface and then bobbing up again. The Unionists were still sixty-three seats short of an overall majority, but the Liberals were now dependent upon the Irish and Labour for their majority. Labour candidates won only when they were not opposed by Liberals. None were victorious in the twenty-seven three-cornered fights, and in only one – Bow and Bromley – did the Labour candidate secure a higher vote than the Liberal. Labour, so it seemed, 'had launched a cautious exploratory attack on Liberal territory ... which was almost totally repulsed'.[15]

---

13 Quoted in McBriar, *Fabian Socialism and English Politics*, p. 340.
14 Rosenbaum, 'The General Election of January 1910', p. 509.
15 Blewett, *Peers, Parties and People*, p. 265.

The election was, of course, a disappointment for the Liberals. Lloyd George had hoped that the Budget and campaign against wealthy landlords would win working-class votes without upsetting the middle classes. It had not done so, as Herbert Samuel, shortly to enter the Cabinet as Postmaster General, noticed. 'It was', he believed, 'the abiding problem of Liberal states-manship to rouse the enthusiasm of the working classes without frightening the middle classes. It can be done but has not been done this time.'[16]

Limiting the powers of the Lords would now be a priority for the Liber-als. But their first task was to pass the Budget. The election, however, had yielded a majority of MPs opposed to it, for, in addition to the Unionists, the Irish Party had voted against Second Reading, since they regarded it as 'an unjust Budget to Ireland'. After securing concessions in committee, they had abstained on Third Reading but only because, in Redmond's words, 'a great constitutional question had arisen', giving the opportunity of removing the absolute veto of Lords, a necessary pre-condition of Home Rule.[17] The party had opposed the whisky and liquor duties in the Budget, since distilling and brewing were vital manufacturing industries in Ireland – indeed outside Ulster the most important industries in the country. In addition, because the Irish land situation had been transformed by land purchase, Ireland outside Ulster was now dominated by small-scale landed proprietors, frightened by land taxes and increased stamp duties. But it was more important for the Irish Party to get the Lords' veto removed than to amend the Budget, and in a hung parliament they had the power to ensure that the Budget was not passed until abolition of the veto was secure. The Irish Party's policy was now summed up by Redmond as No Veto, No Budget. At the first meeting of the Cabinet in 1910, which did not occur until 10 February, Lord Morley, the India Secretary, read out a letter from T. P. O'Connor, the only Irish Party MP to sit for an English constituency, Liverpool, Scotland. O'Connor declared that the Irish Party would vote against the Budget unless there were guarantees that the Lords' veto would go. Later in the day, Asquith told the king that he could not see how the government could carry on. 'It is possible ... that upon the question of the enactment of last year's Budget, the Government may be defeated by the combined votes of the Unionist and Nationalist parties.'[18] That, of course, would entail a second general election unless the Unionists and Nationalists could themselves form an alliance – an unlikely contingency. For, although there was certainly some talk of this in Unionist circles, Balfour and Lansdowne, a Kerry landlord,

---

16 Quoted in Tanner, *Political Change and the Labour Party*, p. 60fn.
17 House of Commons Debates, 21 February 1910, vol. 14, cols 72–3.
18 A. S. King, 'Some Aspects of the History of the Liberal Party in Britain, 1906–1914', PhD thesis, Oxford University, 1962, p. 123.

were adamant against Home Rule. Balfour accepted that younger Unionists might be sympathetic, telling Austen Chamberlain 'that his whole history forbade his being a party to any form of Home Rule, though younger men less involved in the controversies of '86 and '93 might be free to contemplate what he could not accept'.[19] For Balfour himself, however, dealing with the Nationalists would be, as he put it, 'eating dirt'.[20]

LIBERAL DIFFICULTIES

The government was beset by uncertainty on how to proceed. Churchill told the king that the Cabinet felt it was living 'from day to day under the shadow of the axe'. 'Your Majesty's new Parliament', he continued, 'has been born in a trance. Two prevailing impressions are in everyone's mind – that its hours are numbered, and that in the pass to which we are come, speeches are but words.' Some ministers favoured resignation, believing that the Irish Party was too unreliable to provide a stable majority. Others favoured concessions to the Irish on the Budget. Asquith himself, 'so far as anyone could discover, came back with no ideas and no plan of any kind'.[21]

There were further discussions on Lords reform. Grey, Haldane and Lord Crewe, and on occasion other ministers, favoured reforming the composition of the Lords as well as limiting its powers, Grey at one time threatening resignation on the issue. 'It is the constitution of the House of Lords, and not its powers', he told Asquith in a memorandum sent on 7 February, 'which is an anomaly.' Simply limiting the Lords' powers would lay the Liberals 'open to the charge of being in effect a Single Chamber plan, and from a Single Chamber, I believe the country would recoil'.[22] Reforming composition might even attract Unionist support, since Unionists too were coming to favour this option. If so, a second general election and a long constitutional struggle could be avoided. On 21 February, the King's Speech declared that the Lords should 'be so constituted and empowered as to exercise impartially its functions'.

Upon reflection, however, most ministers came to agree that limitation should not be accompanied by reconstruction. The Liberals had fought hard against the veto. That fight was not too difficult to win against a hereditary Upper House. But a more rationally constituted Upper House would have more legitimacy and therefore be more of a threat to Liberal legislation. Labour MPs and radical Liberal MPs would not support a reform

---

19 Chamberlain, *Politics from Inside*, p. 231.
20 Alfred Gollin, *The Observer and J. L. Garvin 1908–1914: A Study in a Great Editorship*, Oxford University Press, 1960, p. 184; Catherine B. Shannon, *Arthur J. Balfour and Ireland, 1874–1922*, Catholic University of America Press, 1988, p. 149.
21 Masterman, *Masterman*, p. 158.
22 Trevelyan, *Grey*, pp. 194–5; Blewett, *Peers, Parties and People*, p. 149.

strengthening the Upper House, and crucially the Irish Party would accept nothing other than removal of the absolute veto; for a more rationally constituted second chamber might threaten Home Rule as well as Liberal social reforms. So the Liberals had no real alternative but to pursue Campbell-Bannerman's policy of the suspensory veto.

But in the debate on the address on 21 February, Asquith was forced to confess that he had not secured a promise from the king that, were the Lords to reject the Bill limiting their powers, he would create sufficient peers to overcome their resistance. It is not clear whether the Prime Minister had even told his Cabinet colleagues that the king would require two elections, not one, before consenting to a creation. Liberal MPs and the Liberal rank and file were mortified. But Asquith told the Commons that the near universal interpretation of his Albert Hall speech had been mistaken, indeed that

> to ask in advance for a blank authority for an indefinite exercise of the Royal Prerogative in regard to a measure which has never been submitted to or approved by the House of Commons is a request which in my judgment, no constitutional statesman can properly make, and it is a concession which the Sovereign cannot be expected to grant.[23]

This was disingenuous. Asquith had in fact asked 'in advance' for precisely such 'blank authority', but he had been rebuffed. And he was to ask for it again just ten months later. It was generous of him not to make the king's rebuff public, since that would have brought the crown into party controversy, compromising the king's relations with his Liberal government as well as with the Labour Party.

The Unionists argued that the election had given the Liberals a mandate to pass the Budget but not to restrict the powers of the Lords. Therefore, it appeared, the Lords had the right to force a second dissolution before a Bill limiting their powers was enacted. The king believed that the outcome of the January election reinforced his view that a second election was needed before he would agree to create peers. 'The recent elections have caused great relief here,' one courtier wrote to Balfour at the end of January, describing the king's attitude. 'There can be no question with this lowered majority, dependent upon the Irish, of Asquith trying to "bully" the King.'[24] The king himself had told Haldane on 3 February that he 'could not possibly consider the creation of peers without a much more definite expression of opinion from the country'.[25]

---

23 House of Commons Debates, 21 February 1910, vol. 14, col. 55.
24 Brett, *Esher*, vol. 2, p. 440.
25 Sir Frederick Maurice, *Haldane, 1856–1915: The Life of Viscount Haldane of Cloan*, Faber, 1937, p. 260.

It is hardly surprising that there was confusion in the Liberal ranks. On 24 February, C. P. Scott, editor of the *Manchester Guardian*, told Churchill:

> You can have little idea of the confusion & almost despair which has spread through the party ... Men go about declaiming loudly that they have been betrayed and that seats have been won on false pretences. There has been a double disillusion – first the discovery that the Albert Hall declaration was not meant in the sense in which it was universally understood & that there is no question of asking for guarantees from the King at this stage or of refusing office in case they are not forthcoming; then the suggestion of a complete change of policy on the question of the Lords' Veto – the abandonment of the simple policy of the Campbell Bannerman resolution dealing with the power of the House of Lords and the substitution or addition of an elaborate scheme for constituting a new Second Chamber. People simply won't listen to it – for three years they have had the other policy placed authoritatively before them, they have just fought & won an election on it and to be asked when the very moment for action has arrived to sit still & wait till a quite different policy has been contrived & presented is more than they can stand ... The fighting spirit of the party is still strong, but if they are not strongly led & speedily it will evaporate.

On the same day, William Royle, chair of the executive of the Manchester Liberal Federation told Churchill, 'There is a regular "slump" in Lib feeling & there will be a revolt unless the Cabinet gives us relief in a few days ... at present *everyone* is dead against any reform of the House of Lords.'[26]

But the Unionists too had their problems. The *Morning Post*, a Conservative newspaper, declared on 26 January 1910:

> No Unionist can contemplate with equanimity another election fought by the Unionists purely on the issue of upholding the power of the House of Lords as it at present exists. Defeat would be certain ... great sections of the working class of Scotland and Northern England ... simply get out of hand when you try to persuade them that the House of Lords is [a] strong, competent, disinterested and impartial body.[27]

On 2 March 1910, Rosebery, now in effect a Unionist, introduced three resolutions into the Lords, to reconstruct it on a meritocratic basis so that a peerage would no longer of itself give the right to sit and vote in the Lords.

---

26 Churchill, *Companion*, vol. 2, part 2, pp. 977–8.
27 Blewett, *Peers, Parties and People*, p. 155.

But his reception by the peers was not enthusiastic, and Lord Halsbury, the ex-Lord Chancellor, boldly declared, 'I do not believe that it is possible to make an institution more consonant with our habits and more practically useful than the House of Lords at present constituted.'[28] Nevertheless, in March 1910, Lansdowne told the Lords that the Unionists were prepared to disown the hereditary principle provided that they could maintain the veto; and on 22 March, the Lords agreed by 173 votes to seventeen that possession of a peerage should no longer of itself give the right to sit and vote in that house. As for Lansdowne, he was toying with the referendum as a means of breaking deadlocks between the two houses. Of course, both the Rosebery and the Lansdowne proposals involved a far more radical reconstruction of the constitution than anything that was being proposed by the Liberals; and the fact that the Lords passed the Rosebery resolutions was a clear signal that they themselves believed their existing constitutional position was untenable. Even so, the Unionists could not unite on an agreed alternative to the Liberal proposals. But as Asquith was not slow to point out, the very fact that Unionists were contemplating reconstruction of the Lords was an admission of the weakness of their position. Paradoxically, the Unionists were now arguing against the current composition of the Lords while the Liberals were seeking to preserve it. 'The two parties', Churchill told the king, 'seem to be almost exchanging weapons – like in the duel between Hamlet and Laertes.'[29]

Eventually, the government pulled itself together and decided upon a policy. No concessions would be made to the Irish on the Budget. Ministers, as Asquith told the king, were 'strongly and unanimously of the opinion that to purchase the Irish vote by such a concession would be a discreditable transaction, which they could not defend'.[30] Instead, the Cabinet would introduce resolutions proposing limitations on the powers of the Lords before re-introducing the Budget. So the Irish would have the guarantee they sought that the powers of the Lords were to be reduced before having to decide whether to support the Budget. This was sufficient for the Irish Party to vote in favour of the Budget so as to maintain the Liberals in office.

On 29 March, Asquith announced the government's policy in the Commons, explaining why the powers of the Lords needed to be restricted by statute. He mentioned Campbell-Bannerman's resolution of 1907 and added that since then, the Lords had for the first time interfered with a Budget, there had been a general election and the Lords had themselves produced proposals for reform of composition. All this showed 'that the whole-hearted

---

28 House of Lords Debates, 16 March 1910, vol. 5, col. 314.
29 Churchill, *Companion*, vol. 2, part 2, p. 998.
30 Le May, *Victorian Constitution*, pp. 197–8.

complacency with which that body surveys itself is not shared by the nation at large'.[31] He then presented three resolutions. The first would put into statutory form what Liberals had believed was a well-established convention to the effect that the Lords should not be able to amend or reject a Money Bill. Whether a Bill was or was not to be a Money Bill would be decided by the Speaker, whose decision would be final and would not be reviewable in a court of law. The second resolution, by contrast with the first, was 'not a mere reaffirmation with new safeguards of an old constitutional under-standing. On the contrary, it proposed to provide a new remedy for an evil,' namely 'a deadlock between the two branches of the legislature', a problem which arose only when the Liberals enjoyed a majority in the Commons.[32] The solution to that problem was the suspensory veto. If the Commons were to pass the same Bill in three successive sessions, then in the third session, the Lords would lose their power to amend or veto it. The power of veto would be replaced with the power of delay.

The third resolution reduced the maximum duration of a parliament from seven to five years.

The resolutions made no mention of reform of composition, but, when the Parliament Bill came to be published, a preamble, which had no legal effect, was added, noting that it was 'intended to substitute for the House of Lords as it at present exists a Second Chamber constituted on a popular instead of hereditary basis'. But reconstruction would have to be postponed until Home Rule was on the statute book if the allegiance of the Irish was to be retained. Redmond had insisted in the debate on the King's Speech that reform of composition must await Home Rule. 'I want the veto limited,' he had declared. 'When you have limited the veto then you yourself, if you like, can go on reforming the constitution of the Lords, or you can leave it to the ardent supporters of the Conservative party to do so.'[33] In fact, no reconstruction would occur until the 1958 Life Peerages Act and then the removal of all but ninety-two of the hereditary peers by Tony Blair's 'New Labour' government in 1999, although neither of these measures was to put the Upper House on a 'popular' basis.

In 1910, no Liberal had admitted that reconstruction would not occur until after Home Rule had been enacted. So the Unionists could argue that Home Rule was being passed under a constitution that was in suspense. Asquith, however, could reply that, far from putting Britain into some kind of 'anarchical interregnum', in which Parliament must content itself 'with

---

31 House of Commons Debates, 29 March 1910, vol. 15, col. 1162.
32 Ibid., col. 1170.
33 Ibid., 21 February 1910, vol. 14, col. 69.

trivial humdrum' measures, Parliament had become more not less representative, since the removal of the veto would ensure that the will of the people,
as expressed in a general election, would now prevail.[34] And whatever
reform of composition would be enacted, the unlimited veto would not be
restored. The preamble had specifically declared that a measure effecting the
substitution of the second chamber 'on a popular instead of hereditary basis',
would also have to make provision for 'limiting and defining the powers of
the new Second Chamber'.

The Unionists believed that, in Balfour's words, Asquith had 'bought the
Irish vote for his Budget, and he has bought it successfully'. The Irish Party
'are going to get what they do not want in the shape of the Budget', so as to
get what they did want in the shape of Home Rule.[35] The belief that Home
Rule was the product of a discreditable bargain was to fuel Unionist hostility
to it. But there had been no bargain. 'If Mr Redmond's words have carried
weight,' Asquith told the king, 'it is not because he held the power of altering
the balance of voting strength in the House of Commons but because the
counsels which he urged were in full harmony with the views of by far the
greater part of the Ministerial majority.'[36]

The government's resolutions were duly passed in the Commons. Asquith
told Parliament that if the Lords were to reject them, he would seek a promise from the king to create peers so that 'the policy, approved by the House
of Commons by large majorities, shall be given statutory effect *in this Parliament*'.[37] But he already knew that the king would not agree to any creation
until after a second election. The Liberals, however, already dismayed by
the fact that Asquith had not sought guarantees before the January election,
would think it futile to fight a second election before a promise had been secured. Later, in 1911, after the crisis had passed and with a new king, George
V, on the throne, Vaughan Nash, Asquith's private secretary, would write
to Lord Knollys, the king's private secretary, that the Commons had been
'overshadowed and almost paralysed by a sense of helplessness and futility'.

> People in the House and out of it asked themselves what was the use of
> elections if nothing came of them; what would be the force of another
> election (which was seen to be impending), if the same issue was to be put
> to the country with the same results, and what was the good of doing work
> in the House of Commons which the House of Lords occupied itself in
> destroying? The position was perilous in an extreme degree not merely for

34 Ibid., 20 February 1912, vol. 34, col. 517.
35 Ibid., 14 April 1910, vol. 16, cols 1551, 1550.
36 Churchill, *Companion*, vol. 2, part 2, p. 983.
37 St Aubyn, *Edward VII*, p. 430. Emphasis added.

the Government but for the authority and standing of our Parliamentary procedure and institutions.[38]

Nevertheless, one influential courtier told the king that the government was seeking 'to purchase the assent of the Irish representatives to a Budget of which they disapprove, and the price given is to threaten Your Majesty with a view ultimately of inducing Your Majesty to assist in a coup d'état'. Knollys echoed a comment he had made in November 1909, that the king 'would rather abdicate than agree to it [the creation of peers]'.[39] Edward in fact felt betrayed by Asquith's announcement that he would seek guarantees in the current Parliament, writing to Knollys on 22 April that 'they are not only ruining the country but maltreat me personally and I can neither forgive nor forget it'.[40] Knollys was so distressed on the king's behalf that he arranged a meeting under the auspices of the Archbishop of Canterbury on 27 April, sometimes grandiloquently labelled the 'Lambeth Palace Conference', at which Balfour declared that in view of the weakness of the government's mandate, it would be perfectly legitimate for the king to reject advice to create peers. He also assured Knollys that, were the king to reject the government's advice, he, Balfour, would form a government and dissolve Parliament. But on 29 April, Knollys told his royal master that no alternative government was available. For a Unionist government would have been installed in office by what would have amounted in effect to dismissal of the Liberals at the hands of the king, compromising the monarch's political neutrality. It would have been highly dangerous.

A second general election was now widely expected, following a dissolution in the summer, and on 29 April the terms of the Parliament Bill, based on Asquith's three resolutions, were published. The Bill was read for a first time in the Commons on 14 April. On 18 April, the 1909 Budget passed the Commons, most Irish MPs voting for it, and on 28 April the Lords finally accepted it without a division. But there was to be no Second Reading of the Parliament Bill. For, on 6 May, Edward VII suddenly and unexpectedly died. His last words apparently were in response to being told that his horse, Witch of the Air, had won the 4.15 at Kempton Park, 'I am so glad.'[41] The king died with the constitutional crisis unresolved. The Cabinet agreed not to embarrass the new king by persisting with the request for a promise to create peers, and political leaders began to consider alternative means of resolving the crisis.

---

38 Le May, *Victorian Constitution*, pp. 199–200.
39 St Aubyn, *Edward VII*, p. 431.
40 Ibid., p. 432.
41 Ridley, *Bertie*, p. 458.

CHAPTER 15

THE CONSTITUTIONAL CRISIS AND THE END OF BALFOUR'S LEADERSHIP

GEORGE V

Edward VII had been more of a constitutional monarch than his mother. Though holding strong views of his own and fully prepared to argue with ministers, he was generally impartial in his dealings with them, and once it was clear that ministers had made up their minds, and that he could not persuade them otherwise, he gave way with good grace and did his best to support them. In foreign affairs, he had played a greater role than his ministers were prepared to admit, though in his encomium in the Commons, Asquith did accept that 'his powerful influence was steadily and zealously directed to the avoidance not only of war, but of the causes and portents of war, and he well earned the title by which he will always be remembered, "the Peacemaker of the World".' For in 1910, the ententes with France and Russia were seen, not as they were later to be, as dividing Europe into armed camps, but as guarantors of peace by removing causes of dispute between the nations. At home too Edward had sought to be a conciliator, employing what his Prime Minister described as 'the genius of common-sense', though it was perhaps straining the truth somewhat to suggest that the late king had also been 'a keen social reformer'.[1] Unlike Queen Victoria, Edward had been a good parent and had doted on his successor, George V, who noted in his diary, 'We are more like brothers, than like father and son.' On his father's death, the new king wrote, 'I have lost my best friend & the best of fathers.'[2]

George V (1865–1936), who came to the throne in May 1910, had been his father's second son and had been intended for the navy, where he learnt virtues of stability, discipline and duty which were to serve him well during his tumultuous reign. It was indeed during his naval years that his direct and straightforward character had crystallised. In 1892, when George's older brother, Albert Victor, died, he became heir to the throne. He began to study Bagehot, somewhat to the displeasure of his grandmother, Queen Victoria,

1   House of Commons Debates, 11 May 1911, vol. 17, cols 793–5.
2   Harold Nicolson, *King George the Fifth: His Life and Reign* [1952], Pan Books, 1967, p. 153.

who disapproved of 'such a radical writer'. For thirty-three years, he lived, not in a palace, but in what his biographer called 'a glum little villa'. York Cottage on the Sandringham estate was a house in which 'the rooms inside … are indistinguishable from those of any Surbiton or Upper Norwood home … It is almost incredible that the heir to so vast a heritage lived in this horrible little house,' a house which had been furnished from Maples department store.[3]

George V was very unlike his father. He was neither gregarious nor cosmopolitan, preferring the company of his family and disliking foreign travel. 'Abroad', he is supposed to have said, 'is bloody. I know, I've been there.' When asked to pay a state visit to the Netherlands, he spoke of 'Amsterdam, Rotterdam and all the other dams'. On being told that Edward VII had travelled abroad often in the interests of peace, George replied that the result had been the great war.[4] Unlike his father, who was fluent in French and German, he spoke no foreign language. As king, he lived a life of orderly and stately domestic routine, unvarying from year to year, which he stuck to like clockwork. 'First thing in the morning and last thing at night he consulted the barometer; between those two fixed points his daily progress was as predictable as the course of a planet.'[5] Woken at 7 a.m., George began the day by reading *The Times* and then looking at his boxes before breakfast at 9 a.m. In the morning, he saw his secretaries, ministers and ambassadors and attended investitures. He then walked a mile round the garden before lunch. After lunch, he slept for exactly fifteen minutes, waking up after that time as if there were an alarm clock in his head. The afternoon was devoted either to engagements or to his remarkable stamp collection, which, by the time of his death in 1936, comprised 250,000 stamps in 325 volumes. In the early evening, he returned to his boxes. He preferred to dine quietly with his family, dressed in white tie and wearing his Garter star. At 11.10 p.m. precisely, he went to bed. His court, he said, was 'dull perhaps but certainly respectable', a contrast with the court of Edward VII.[6]

Before becoming Prince of Wales on the death of Queen Victoria in 1901, George had taken little interest in politics. 'Apart from occasional public functions and a few official journeys, he lived the life of a private country gentleman, unostentatious, comparatively retired, almost obscure.'[7] But Edward VII had not repeated his mother's mistake of failing to initiate the heir into the mysteries of government. He encouraged his son to read

---

3   Ibid., pp. 86–7.
4   Rose, *King George V*, p. 294.
5   Ibid., p. 95.
6   Ibid., p. 87.
7   Nicolson, *King George the Fifth*, p. 93.

Cabinet papers and Foreign Office telegrams, and to get to know leading politicians. From 1901 as Prince of Wales, the future king was given access to a limited number of state papers, and from 1903 he was shown all Foreign Office cables. 'I am not a clever man,' George V was to say in later life, 'but if I had not picked up something from all the brains I've met, I would be an idiot.'[8] Asquith, who was as condescending to him as Balfour had been to Edward VII, was to write in 1915, 'I don't know a better reflection than his talk of what one imagines to be for the moment the average opinion of the man in the tube.'[9] But in the Ulster crisis, the king was to display more prescience than his Prime Minister.

Regrettably, Edward VII had not discussed the House of Lords crisis with his son; nor, perhaps fortunately, had he informed the heir of the so-called Lambeth Palace Conference at which Balfour had consented to serve as Prime Minister were Asquith to resign. The new king, therefore, was left in the dark. His difficulties were compounded by his mistake of appointing two joint private secretaries of contrasting political views. He inherited his father's private secretary, Lord Knollys, whom Asquith later described as 'a sound and strong Liberal', but he also kept his own private secretary, Sir Arthur Bigge, created Lord Stamfordham in 1913.[10] Bigge had been Queen Victoria's last private secretary and his sympathies, by contrast with those of Knollys, were with the Unionists. The uneasy arrangement of two joint secretaries lasted only until 1913 when Knollys retired, but it led to George V being given conflicting advice on the Parliament Bill crisis of 1911. The crisis was made more difficult for the king since, as Prince of Wales, he had made indiscreet comments at private functions. In 1908, he remarked to Winston Churchill after a dinner party that Asquith was 'not quite a gentleman', and on another occasion, he had said to the Permanent Secretary at the Treasury, 'I can't think, Sir George, how you can go on serving that damned fellow, Lloyd George.'[11] When he came to the throne, one observer noticed that he was

> without the great knowledge and immense patience of his father ... and where Edward could have maintained silence, George is apt to make a pronouncement. I fear that during the last few months he has given opinions which he should have kept for himself, and there may be a feeling already of antagonism between him and his government.[12]

---

8 Rose, *King George V*, p. 109.
9 Brock, ed., *Letters to Venetia Stanley*, p. 487.
10 Ibid., p. 51.
11 Rose, *King George V*, p. 71.
12 Vincent, ed., *Crawford Papers*, pp. 153–4.

Lloyd George was to write when the king died in 1936:

> Before he came to the throne, he had the reputation of being very Tory in
> his views. In those days he was frank to the point of indiscretion in his talk,
> and his sayings were repeated in wide circles. There is no use concealing
> the fact that they gave offence to Liberals and his succession to the throne
> for that reason was viewed with some misgivings.[13]

The new king's entirely correct behaviour as sovereign could not quite efface
his earlier comments; and he admitted in 1914 that Asquith might have been
prejudiced against him because of remarks he had made before coming to
the throne. 'I ought not to have said it, and it was a damned stupid thing to
say.'[14] But it was because of these indiscretions that the Liberals did not trust
him to act on advice by creating peers to overcome Lords' hostility to the
Parliament Bill. They insisted, therefore, on an understanding – sometimes
misleadingly described as a guarantee – that he would in fact create peers if
the government so advised, an understanding to be agreed before the general
election of December 1910.

During his reign, George V was to show that misgivings as to his political
partisanship were groundless. He was to prove in fact an ideal constitutional
monarch. Confronted with constitutional and political crises of a kind not
faced by any other monarch in the twentieth century, he dealt with them with
a sure touch, thereby strengthening the monarchy. His reign saw the extinction
of five emperors, eight kings and eighteen minor dynasties. But in Britain, the
monarchy not only survived but gained considerably in public esteem.

THE CONSTITUTIONAL CONFERENCE

When Asquith learnt of the death of Edward VII, he was on holiday in the
Mediterranean. 'I felt bewildered and indeed stunned,' he recalled.

> At a most anxious moment in the fortunes of the State, we had lost, with-
> out warning or preparation, the Sovereign whose ripe experience, trained
> sagacity, equitable judgment and unvarying consideration, counted for so
> much … Now he had gone. His successor … was without political experi-
> ence. We were nearing the verge of a crisis almost without example in our
> constitutional history.[15]

13 *News Chronicle*, 22 January 1936, cited in Thomas F. Hale, 'The British Labour Party and the Monarchy', PhD thesis,
    University of Kentucky, 1972, p. 89.
14 Rose, *King George V*, p. 71.
15 H. H. Asquith, *Fifty Years of Parliament*, Cassell, 1926, pp. 86–8.

It was felt that everything should be done to avoid embroiling the new king in the crisis. On 8 May, two days after the death of Edward VII, J. L. Garvin, the influential editor of *The Observer*, and a Unionist, wrote what has been regarded as 'the most important and subsequently influential article in its long history', pleading for a change of heart and what he called a 'Truce of God'.

> If King Edward upon his deathbed could have sent a last message to his people, he would have asked us to lay party passion aside, to sing a truce of God over his grave, to seek ... some fair means of making a common effort for our common country ... Let conference take place before conflict is irrevocably joined on terms of war to the knife.[16]

The new king, according to one Cabinet minister, told Asquith 'that his Father would be regarded as the Peacemaker between International Powers & it was his [i.e. Edward VII's] view & his own, an arrangement should be arrived at between contending parties so that there should be domestic peace on the constitutional differences here at home'.[17] On 18 May, at a private audience with George V, Asquith assured him that 'he would endeavour to come to some understanding with the Opposition to prevent a general election & he would not pay attention to what Redmond said'.[18] Redmond and the Irish Party would of course have lost their leverage were the Liberals and Unionists able to achieve an understanding between themselves. It appears, however, to have been Lloyd George who, according to the diary of a wife of one of the junior ministers, suggested in Cabinet a conference between the government and the opposition. 'It cannot be too much emphasised that the Conference was entirely his idea.'[19]

The aim of the Constitutional Conference, as stated in a memorandum from Asquith to the king on 28 May, would be to resolve the House of Lords question, by securing through agreement between the two parties 'a second chamber which shall be so constituted as to exercise the functions appropriate to such a body fairly as between the two great parties in the state', and also 'to provide machinery which will ensure that, in the event of disagreement between the two houses, the opinion and will of the people shall prevail'.[20] But the conference was in fact attempting something even larger than this.

---

16 Gollin, *The Observer and J. L. Garvin*, p. 184.
17 Cameron Hazlehurst and Christine Woodland, *A Liberal Chronicle: Journals and Papers of J. A. Pease, 1st Lord Gainford, 1908–1910*, Historians' Press, 1994, p. 179. This book gives an account of many of the Cabinet meetings of the period.
18 Nicolson, *King George the Fifth*, p. 184.
19 Masterman, *Masterman*, p. 163.
20 J. R. Fanning, 'The Unionist Party and Ireland, 1906–10', *Irish Historical Studies*, 1966, p. 161.

It would be seeking, in the words of Asquith's biographers, 'nothing less than to convert the immemorial unwritten into a written constitution – a task of enormous difficulty in any case, and not to be achieved by men deeply committed to the controversies of the hour'.[21] That it did not succeed is hardly surprising. What was surprising was that it came so near to success.

The conference comprised four Liberals and four Unionists. Labour and the Irish Party were excluded. The Liberals were Asquith, Lloyd George, Lord Crewe (Leader of the Lords) and Augustine Birrell, the Irish Secretary, whom, the Irish Party hoped, would look after their interests. The Unionists were represented by Balfour, Lansdowne, Austen Chamberlain and Lord Cawdor, deputy Unionist leader in the Lords. The conference held twenty-one meetings from 17 June to 10 November, with a break during the summer recess between 28 July and 11 October.

At first, the auguries for success seemed good and Asquith was able to tell the king that it had 'indicated a desire for *rapprochement*'.[22] Balfour declared that the conference was 'exactly like a cabinet, but more united'![23] At the first meeting on 17 June, Balfour accepted that financial legislation should be distinguished from ordinary legislation. It proved surprisingly easy to secure agreement on the procedure to be adopted with regard to such legislation, even though it had been rejection of financial legislation by the Lords which had precipitated the crisis in the first place. But the Unionists now accepted that the Lords should be statutorily prohibited from interfering with Money Bills and agreed also that the decision on whether a purported Money Bill involved tacking could be made by a joint tribunal comprising members of both houses. It is remarkable that, having sought in 1909 to vindicate the right of the Lords to reject Money Bills, so precipitating a constitutional crisis and a general election, the Unionists were now prepared so rapidly to abandon this right. If the Unionists were prepared to agree in 1910 that they ought not in future to reject a 'socialistic' Budget, why had it been right to do precisely that in 1909?

Disagreements over ordinary legislation were to be resolved, the conference appeared to accept, by a joint sitting comprising the whole of the Commons and a delegation from the Lords – twenty from the government, the rest to be selected on a party basis by proportional representation from amongst the peers. This would give the Unionists a majority of around forty-five in the Lords' delegation when the Liberals were in power. There would also be a limit on the number of peers to be created in any one year.[24] The

---

21 Spender and Asquith, *Asquith*, vol. 1, p. 291.
22 Nicolson, *King George the Fifth*, p. 184.
23 Vincent, ed., *Crawford Papers*, p. 144.
24 Chamberlain, *Politics from Inside*, p. 295.

proposal for joint sittings had the great advantage that it could be carried through the Commons by agreement between the two major parties and would be acceptable to the peers themselves. It would, therefore, avoid a clash over the constitution, since it would legitimise, indeed perhaps even strengthen, the second chamber.

There seemed, then, at the conference, agreement on both ordinary and financial legislation. But the Unionists were unwilling to accept the method of joint sittings as a procedure to resolve *all* disagreements between the two houses. They insisted on a third category of legislation, constitutional legislation, which would include Home Rule, and it was on this issue that the conference was to break down. The Unionists believed that the constitution as it stood made fundamental change too easy to achieve, even when such change might not be in accord with the wishes of the people. The Lords, they continued to believe, had a referendal role to play as well as a revising role. On constitutional matters, the Unionists proposed that a referendum should be held to resolve differences between the two houses. But the Liberals would not accept any separate category of 'constitutional' legislation. Lloyd George told the conference that it meant 'bringing in the judicature to settle what was and what was not organic. He regarded the position and power of the Supreme Court in America as wholly alien to the spirit of our constitution.'[25] Further, the referendum would give the Unionist-dominated House of Lords an extra weapon against the Liberals, while the Irish Party would not have accepted what amounted to a new veto – the referendum – to replace the veto of the Lords. 'After all,' Asquith declared at one of the meetings, 'you must think of those with whom you had to work and the Irish would never accept it.'[26] 'Neither side', Austen Chamberlain told his wife on 2 November, 'can get over the "home rule fence", or (to speak more exactly) the Government cannot quarrel outright with the Irish. They are more afraid of them than their own followers.'[27] The Liberals were prepared at best to accept a narrow definition of constitutional legislation, comprising comparatively uncontroversial matters like the monarchy, the House of Lords and relations between the two houses, but excluding Home Rule and the disestablishment of the Welsh Church. They were, however, prepared to make a slight concession on Home Rule to the effect that, *on the first occasion only* on which a Home Rule Bill were passed by the Commons, it should not be implemented until there

---

25 From the Austen Chamberlain Papers, cited in Bogdanor, *The People and the Party System*, p. 23.

26 John D. Fair, *British Interparty Conferences: A Study in the Procedure of Conciliation in British Politics, 1867–1921*, Clarendon Press, 1980, p. 98. Chapter 4 of this book offers a succinct account of the proceedings of the conference. They were held in secret, but there is a full set of notes of the proceedings in the Austen Chamberlain Papers in the University of Birmingham.

27 Ibid.

had been an intervening general election. After that, it would be treated as ordinary legislation. Further than that they would not go. This was insufficient for the Unionists, though they might have accepted the proposal had it been applied to *all* Home Rule Bills rather than only to the *next* Home Rule Bill as the Liberals proposed. For the Liberal proposal meant, in the Unionist view, that 'the Union was a part of the Constitution which only required temporary defence'.[28]

'Behind the Conference', declared Garvin, 'lies the shadow of the Irish question.'[29] It failed not because of disagreement on the role of the Lords but because of Home Rule, resurrected by the election of January 1910 and the resulting hung parliament. 'We are fighting,' Lord Salisbury, son of the former Prime Minister, told Lansdowne in September 1910, 'not for our hereditary privileges, but for the union, and we are prepared to make even the greatest sacrifices.'[30] The Unionists were not willing to concede on Home Rule, without clear evidence that the people supported it either in a referendum or a general election. The Liberals were unwilling to agree that the role of the Commons could be circumscribed by the will of the people. Behind the specific disagreement over Home Rule, there lay a deeper and more fundamental disagreement over the nature of representative democracy. 'We all of us start', Asquith was to claim in the Second Reading debate on the Parliament Bill, 'from one common point – the assumption which lies at the root of representative government that the House of Commons, itself a product of popular election, is, under normal conditions, a trustworthy organ and mouthpiece of the popular will.'[31] But that was just the claim which the Unionists rejected. For them, it could not simply be assumed that the Commons represented the people. That was something which required proof, especially when a Liberal government was proposing fundamental change. In the committee stage of the Parliament Bill in the Lords, the Unionist Lord Selborne declared, 'We are agreed that the sovereign power of government in this country resides in the Crown and in the people.' He was corrected by Lord Morley, who insisted, 'Crown and Parliament'.[32] 'The Government's view of the constitution', Lord Salisbury wrote in September 1910, 'is that the distinct decision of the Commons should prevail ... But our view, over and over again reiterated, is that the distinct decision of the people is the real criterion.'[33] But, as we have seen, the referendal doctrine seemed only to

28 Dugdale, *Balfour*, vol. 2, p. 45.
29 *The Observer*, 31 July 1910.
30 Fanning, 'The Unionist Party and Ireland', p. 164.
31 House of Commons Debates, 21 February 1911, vol. 21, col. 1748.
32 House of Lords Debates, 5 July 1911, vol. 9, col. 276.
33 Ridley, 'The Unionist Opposition and the House of Lords', p. 252.

apply when the Liberals were in power. No measure had been referred to the people under Unionist governments.

The Unionists were perhaps ill-advised to allow the conference to fail. Despite not having won the January 1910 election, they were being given the chance to avoid the suspensory veto and of delaying Home Rule until it had been put to the people in a general election, which might not occur for some time. If the Unionists were right as to the electoral unpopularity of Home Rule, they would have every chance of winning such an election. But with the failure of the conference, there would be an immediate general election which the Unionists were unlikely to win. The Liberals would then claim that they enjoyed a mandate to enact Home Rule without any further appeal to the people. The failure of the conference, therefore, meant that Home Rule might well be enacted. And the ensuing general election also made reform of the Lords on the lines of the suspensory veto a near certainty, rather than joint sittings, which would have been more favourable to the Unionists. In addition, the Liberals had been prepared to accept that reform of the Lords could be put into the category of 'constitutional' legislation, so that it would require a special procedure to enact it, different from that used for ordinary Bills. On 8 November, shortly before the final meeting of the conference, Balfour told Lord Esher that he believed 'a compromise on the lines almost agreed' was 'for the country's sake ... the right thing'.[34] But such a compromise would not, he thought, be acceptable to his party; and as with tariff reform, he was horrified by the thought of being another Peel and splitting the party of which he was the trustee.

The consequences of the breakdown of the Constitutional Conference were to be profound. In a letter to the editor of *The Observer*, Lord Esher concluded, 'No written Constitution is conceivable for our people.'[35] That is a conclusion which the twentieth century did nothing to disprove. But following the Parliament Act, the conflict between the two parties was to take on a more menacing tone which seemed at times near to breaking the bounds of parliamentary convention.

A COALITION GOVERNMENT?

In the middle of the Constitutional Conference, during the parliamentary recess, Lloyd George made a startling proposal for a coalition government, to resolve not only the problem of the House of Lords but the other major issues dividing the parties. In his *War Memoirs*, drawing on the advantages

---

34 Brett, *Esher*, vol. 3, p. 30.
35 Fair, *British Interparty Conferences*, p. 91.

of hindsight, Lloyd George explained the circumstances which persuaded him to write it.

> In the year 1910 we were beset by an accumulation of grave issues – rapidly becoming graver ... It was becoming evident to discerning eyes that the Party and parliamentary system was unequal to coping with them ... The shadow of unemployment was rising ominously above the horizon. Our international rivals were forging ahead at a great rate and jeopardizing our hold on the great markets of the world ... Our working population, crushed into dingy and mean streets, with no assurance that they would not be deprived of their daily bread by ill-health or trade fluctuation, were becoming sullen with discontent ... The life of the countryside was wilting away and we were becoming dangerously over-industrialised ... The Irish controversy was poisoning our relations with the United States of America. A great Constitutional struggle over the House of Lords threatened revolution at home, another threatened civil war at our doors in Ireland.[36]

On 17 August, Lloyd George composed a memorandum, sometimes known as the Criccieth memorandum, although it was not in fact written at Criccieth.[37] It proposed a quite different agenda from that of the Constitutional Conference, which had been concerned with the question – how could the constitution be protected against radical change? Lloyd George, by contrast, was concerned with the actual agenda of change, with answering the question – what are the urgent changes that Britain needs? He was in a sense seeking to resolve the problems raised by the national efficiency school earlier in the century. His memorandum began by declaring that 'some of the urgent problems awaiting settlement, problems which concern intimately the happiness and the efficiency of the inhabitants of these islands, their strength and influence, can only be successfully coped with by the active co-operation of both of the great Parties in the State'. The Irish Party and Labour were to be excluded from the coalition proposal so that, presumably, the pledges made to them – on Home Rule and other matters – would become void. 'The time has arrived', the memorandum continued, 'for a truce, for bringing the resources of the two Parties into joint stock in order to liquidate arrears which, if much longer neglected, may end in national impoverishment, if not insolvency.' Lloyd George then presented a large

---

36 David Lloyd George, *War Memoirs of David Lloyd George*, Ivor Nicholson & Watson, 1933, vol. 1, pp. 34–5.
37 This memorandum can most conveniently be found in the second volume of the multi-volume biography of Lloyd George by Grigg, *People's Champion*, pp. 362–8.

number of 'urgent problems awaiting settlement'. They included 'Social Reform' – housing policy, licensing reform, action against unemployment, a re-casting of the Poor Law and educational reform. There was also national defence, where the solution might include conscription, local government reform, land reform, imperial unity and the Irish question. As to this last issue, 'the advantages of a non-Party treatment of this vexed problem are obvious. Parties might deal with it without being subject to the embarrassing dictation of extreme partisans, whether from Nationalists or Orangemen.' But despite the large number of issues presented, and contrary to the impression given in Lloyd George's *War Memoirs*, to be published in 1933, the memorandum hardly mentioned foreign policy and said nothing about a possible military threat from Germany.

The longest section on the domestic problems which, in Lloyd George's view, needed to be solved was on the national insurance scheme on which he was currently working. He was eager to produce a broad scheme which would include state pensions for widows and orphans – he had himself been orphaned at a very early age. But the insurance companies were resisting this since it would undermine their business, and they had behind them the support of a large army of door-to-door agents and collectors who worked for them and were a powerful electoral force. Consequently, the Act of 1911 did not include provision for widows and orphans. Germany, Lloyd George went on, had been able to establish a system including widows and orphans but in Britain

> one would have to encounter the bitter hostility of powerful organisations like the Prudential, the Liver, the Royal Victoria, the Pearl, and similar institutions with an army numbering scores, if not hundreds of thousands, of agents and collectors who make a living out of collecting a few pence a week from millions of households in this country for the purpose of providing death allowances.

These private insurance schemes were, however, both inefficient and unfair.

> The expense of collection and administration come to something like 50 per cent of the total receipts, and these poor widows and children are by this extravagant system robbed of one half of the benefits which it has cost the workmen so much to provide for them ... The system ought to be terminated at the earliest possible moment. The benefits are small, costly and precarious for if a man is unable, owing to ill-health and lack of employment, to keep up his payments, his policy is forfeited.

By contrast, however, 'state insurance costs 10 per cent to administer'. Yet,

> however desirable it may be to substitute State insurance, which does not involve collection and therefore is more economical, any Party that attempted it would instantly incur the relentless hostility of all these agents and collectors ... a Government which attempted to take over their work without first of all securing the cooperation of the other Party would inevitably fail in its undertaking; so that if a scheme of national insurance is taken in hand by any Party Government it must be confined to invalidity, and the most urgent and pitiable cases of all must be left out ... This is an excellent illustration of the difficulty of dealing with some of these problems except by joint action.[38]

Lloyd George seems to have discussed his memorandum first with Churchill, his ally in social reform, and then with the Master of Elibank, the government Chief Whip. In early October, he apparently showed the memorandum to the rising Conservative backbencher F. E. Smith, who seems to have discussed it with Balfour. According to the wife of a junior minister, Lloyd George, despite their political differences, had been 'absolutely hypnotised' by Balfour, 'by his charm, his quickness, and his undoubtedly very clever intellect'.[39] The bulk of the negotiations on the coalition were in fact to be between Lloyd George and Balfour. But it appears that Lloyd George did not actually give Balfour a copy of the memorandum. Instead, he read out the opening section and then showed him the document without allowing him to take it away. It was agreed that Balfour could consult the other Unionist members of the Constitutional Conference, though none of them, it appears, were shown the document either.[40] Lloyd George, however, agreed that Smith could show the memorandum to Bonar Law. Only after that, in the middle of October, did he discuss the memorandum with Asquith. At that time, he also, it appears, showed it to Lord Crewe and Edward Grey and perhaps other Liberals as well. The king also was informed of the coalition proposal. But as Churchill was to tell Austen Chamberlain in 1913, 'the Cabinet as a whole were never informed'. 'How could we tell them? Some of them would have had to go!'[41] For, with a coalition, it was obvious that some Liberals would have been extruded to make room for Unionists. Government posts would 'be equally divided'. Lloyd George, however, assured Asquith that he would remain as Prime Minister. What he did not tell

38 Grigg, *People's Champion*, pp. 368, 364–5.
39 Masterman, *Masterman*, p. 164.
40 Chamberlain, *Politics from Inside*, p. 192.
41 Ibid., p. 577.

him, however, was that his plan envisaged Asquith being shunted upstairs to
the House of Lords, exactly the fate that the Relugas conspirators had had
in mind for Campbell-Bannerman in 1905. Asquith would be replaced by
Balfour as Leader of the Commons.[42] On 17 October, Lloyd George made
a conciliatory gesture towards the Unionists, declaring in a public speech
that there was much common ground between the parties on social reform,
and paying tribute to Joseph Chamberlain whose 'outstanding service to the
cause of the masses' had been to draw attention to the 'great number of real
crying evils festering among us'.

On 29 October, Lloyd George produced a second memorandum. In addition to the proposals of the first, it proposed a Cabinet inquiry into defence
and advocated a specific settlement of the Irish question 'on some such lines
as were sketched by Mr Chamberlain in his speech on the First Reading
of the Home Rule Bill of 1886'. The 'settlement should be of a kind which
might form a nucleus for the Federation of the Empire at some future date'.
That meant, presumably, legislative devolution in Britain on a federal basis.
There were indications that Redmond would have been prepared to accept
such a settlement, although most of his followers were not. There should,
the memorandum continued, also be an inquiry into the fiscal system, and
'a preference' should be 'given to the Colonies on existing Duties where
found practicable'. Education and Welsh disestablishment would be settled
along Liberal lines but with the possibility of a referendum before a Bill on
the Welsh Church was brought into Parliament. There would be a national
insurance scheme with provision for widows and orphans, state credit for
housing and a reformed Poor Law. The school-leaving age would be raised
with provision made for further training.[43] This second memorandum was,
by contrast with the first, handed to Balfour.[44]

If the Unionists were to accept the Lloyd George proposals, they would
have to make concessions on fundamental issues – Home Rule, Welsh disestablishment and national insurance. The Liberals would in their turn be
required to concede on fundamentals – on tariffs and on conscription.

The most sympathetic of the Unionists to the idea of coalition was F. E.
Smith, a comparatively junior MP, though rapidly gaining in stature. In October, Smith wrote to Austen Chamberlain, declaring with some prescience:

Our position in the country is bad. I myself believe ... that we shall be
a shade weaker in the new parliament assuming a January election. This

---

42   G. R. Searle, 'A. J. Balfour's Secret Coalition Talks Memorandum', *Historical Research*, 1993, pp. 223–5.
43   This second memorandum is printed in Robert J. Scally, *The Origins of the Lloyd George Coalition: The Politics of
     Social-Imperialism, 1900–1918*, Princeton University Press, 1975, pp. 384–6. The passages quoted are from p. 384.
44   Searle, 'A. J. Balfour's Secret Coalition Talks', p. 227.

means a) defeat in the Lords, b) National Defence neglected, c) Tariff Reform beaten three times running and another futile Colonial Conference, d) generally a frittering away of national energy over constitutional crisis injurious to the State and menacing to the Monarchy

That was not a bad prediction of the course of events between 1911 and 1914. But coalition might well, Smith believed, resolve the Irish question – 'a dead quarrel for which neither the country nor the party cares a damn, outside of Ulster and Liverpool'. 'I never in twenty years', Smith concluded,

> remember a time when so many men in England were sick of mere party cries and faction. A great sigh of relief would go up over the whole of business England if a strong and stable Government were formed ... I have a deep and earnest conviction that to refuse this offer at this crisis would almost be a crime against the Empire.

Many younger Unionists shared Smith's enthusiasm.[45] They were, like him, tired of the old issues, eager to move on to new ground, and some were even prepared to accept Home Rule if that was the necessary price. The elderly Tory squire Henry Chaplin, chair of the Conservative 1900 Club, wrote to Balfour ruefully in October 1910 that of eleven young candidates at a meeting, 'the secretary tells me eight ... [are] in favour of home rule'.[46] 'Is home rule exactly where it was?' Balfour's private secretary, Sandars, asked his chief in October 1910. 'I think we shall hug a delusion if we imagine that home rule will alarm the average voter of 1911 as it did in 1886 and 1895.' Some younger Unionists, 'the best of our young men', as Balfour admitted to Garvin, thought that Home Rule could safely be conceded if combined with devolution for the United Kingdom as a whole, so-called Home Rule All Round, which would deprive Irish Home Rule of its separatist connotations.[47] Austen Chamberlain also seemed sympathetic.[48] In return, Unionists would gain a great deal – in particular, colonial preference and perhaps conscription. But the Liberals also had a strong incentive, for coalition would obviate the need to accommodate the Irish Party and Labour. But remarkably perhaps, some leading Liberals had another motive. They believed that their party had reached the end of the road in terms of social reform, indeed of constructive policy as a whole. On 22 October, Lord Crewe wrote to Asquith, 'We have got not far from the end of our tether as regards the

---

45 Frederick Second Earl of Birkenhead, *F. E. Smith first Earl of Birkenhead*, Eyre & Spottiswoode, 1959, pp. 156–7.
46 Fanning, 'The Unionist Party and Ireland', p. 164.
47 Ibid., pp. 167–8.
48 Chamberlain, *Politics from Inside*, p. 281.

carrying of large reforms.' Four days later, Grey wrote to the Prime Minister that he was 'favourable' to 'the big scheme of a coalition for constructive legislation including the settlement of Home Rule', since 'if the Conference breaks up without agreement, I foresee the break-up of the Liberal Party and a time of political instability, perhaps of chaos, to the great detriment of the country'. No doubt the Unionists were not much better placed. Indeed, 'the other party of course is paralysed and useless, but behind us there are explosive and violent forces which will split our party, and I do not believe we can resume the old fight against the Lords by ourselves without division'.[49] Churchill wrote to Lloyd George that 'if we stand together we ought to be strong enough either to impart a progressive character to policy, or by withdrawal to terminate an administration which had failed in its program'.[50]

Lloyd George's methods of securing support for the coalition were, as so often with him, devious if not downright deceitful. It is not wholly clear precisely which of his interlocutors actually saw full copies of either memorandum. It seems that he stressed to the Unionists those measures which they would like to see enacted, such as tariff reform and conscription, while downplaying Home Rule, whereas to Liberals, he underplayed the measures which would have been attractive to Unionists. Lloyd George's aim, no doubt, was to create an atmosphere of conciliation, leaving the detail to be settled later. But it is understandable if what he regarded as skilful diplomacy, his opponents regarded as deceitful. His approach was not conducive to the development of the trust needed for negotiating a coalition. It was, it seems, Balfour in whom Lloyd George had placed so much confidence, who played the leading role in wrecking the coalition scheme. Austen Chamberlain was to tell Churchill in 1913 that Balfour 'had finally rejected the idea because the basis of the proposal was that each side should do what it most disliked to please the other'.[51] Balfour was not only bitterly opposed to Home Rule but sceptical even of the federal principle. Under it, would Ireland 'form one province or two? If two, will any Nationalist of any type accept this administrative solution? And if not, why not?'[52] But according to Balfour, 'we never reached a stage at which precision of detail required to be considered'.[53] Oddly enough, national insurance, which played a large part in the first memorandum, and was perhaps a main motivation for the coalition proposal, played hardly any role in the discussions.

It would been difficult to bring about a coalition even if Balfour had

49   Roy Jenkins, *Asquith*, Collins, 1964, p. 217.
50   Scally, *Origins of the Lloyd George Coalition*, pp. 197–8.
51   Chamberlain, *Politics from Inside*, p. 577.
52   Dugdale, *Balfour*, vol. 2, p. 58.
53   Searle, 'A. J. Balfour's Secret Coalition Talks', p. 225.

been more sympathetic than in fact he was. It would, after all, have had to be accepted not only by leaders but also followers, MPs and constituency supporters. They would be hardly likely to accept the sudden overturning of their sacred shibboleths – Home Rule, tariff reform and a volunteer army. Lloyd George, Churchill and Smith might not have minded, but many MPs and party workers regarded them as matters of high principle. 'Now isn't that like Lloyd George,' Balfour told his biographer in 1928.

> Principles mean nothing to him – never have. His mind doesn't work that way. It's both his strength and his weakness. He says to himself at any given moment: 'Come on now – we've all been squabbling too long, let's find a reasonable way out of the difficulty' – but such solutions are quite impossible for people who don't share his outlook on political principles – the great things.

This was a shrewd appraisal. Balfour was a quite dissimilar character to Lloyd George. He had seen it as his task to hold his party together during the turbulence that followed Joseph Chamberlain's espousal of tariff reform, and he was not prepared to take the risk of splitting it now. 'I cannot become another Robert Peel in my Party,' he told Lloyd George.[54] It is equally doubtful whether Asquith would have taken the risk of splitting his party, let alone being shunted into the Lords. His biographers declare that he would certainly have been unwilling to concede conscription and imperial preference, and was

> wholly sceptical about any Coalition being possible … He thought the ground treacherous and dangerous for both parties, but with his accustomed tolerance, he was willing to let those who thought otherwise try their hand and he watched the progress of the business to its inevitable conclusion with a certain detached amusement.[55]

Lloyd George's coalition could come about only in the quite changed conditions of wartime in 1916 – when its most eager supporters were to be those who had been sympathetic in 1910: Lloyd George himself, Churchill, Smith and Bonar Law. But until war came, coalition was not possible. 'I suppose it is only a dream,' Lloyd George concluded sadly in 1910.[56]

---

54 Dugdale, *Balfour*, vol. 2, pp. 56, 54.
55 Spender and Asquith, *Asquith*, vol. 1, p. 287.
56 Masterman, *Masterman*, p. 164.

THE KING AND THE LIBERALS

The failure of the Constitutional Conference showed that the constitutional issue could not be resolved through inter-party agreement. So the party fight resumed. Indeed, the only consequence of the abortive conference was to delay the date of the second election from the summer of 1910 to December. But before calling this election, Asquith needed an assurance from the king that, in the event of the Lords rejecting the Parliament Bill, he would create sufficient Liberal peers to secure its passage. On 10 November, the day of the breakdown of the conference, the Cabinet decided to seek an immediate dissolution. Asquith had two requests to make of the king – first to dissolve Parliament and secondly to obtain the understanding that he would create peers if the Liberals were returned to office. On 11 November, Asquith travelled to Sandringham to see the king, who was reluctant to agree to the dissolution of a parliament that was just eleven months old. Before giving his consent, he insisted that Asquith send the resolutions to the Upper House for discussion. To this, Asquith reluctantly agreed.

At the meeting on 11 November, Asquith did not ask for a promise. The note of the conversation by Sir Arthur Bigge, later Lord Stamfordham, one of the king's private secretaries, reports Asquith as saying that he 'did not come to ask for anything from the King: no promises, no guarantees during this Parliament'. The king was relieved. But the phrase 'no guarantees during this Parliament' was ambiguous. Did it mean that the king would not be asked to give a promise for the *current* Parliament, which was about to be dissolved? Or did it mean that the king was not being asked to give a promise in relation to the *next* Parliament, the Parliament which would follow the general election? Asquith meant the former; the king and his private secretary assumed the latter.

There were just two precedents for Asquith's proposal. Neither was particularly helpful. The only actual creation had been in 1713, when Queen Anne had created twelve peers to ensure parliamentary ratification of the treaties of Utrecht. But the Liberals would need many more than twelve peers to ensure passage of the Parliament Bill. In 1832, William IV had agreed, with considerable reluctance, to create peers if needed to ensure passage of the Reform Bill, although in the event, no creation proved necessary. But the situation then was quite different from that of 1910. The Second Reading of the Reform Bill had been passed in the Commons by one vote, but the government was defeated in committee, and William IV, after first refusing, agreed to dissolve Parliament. The Bill was the main – almost the only – issue in the general election at which the Whigs were returned with an increased majority. A second Reform Bill, broadly similar to the first, was then introduced, passing the Commons but rejected on Second Reading by the Lords, following which there were widespread riots and disturbances in the country. A third Reform Bill was then introduced, again passing the Commons. The Lords accepted it on Second Reading but passed a wrecking amendment in committee. William was then asked to create fifty peers. He refused to create more than twenty. The government resigned. But the Duke of Wellington, the Tory leader, was unable to form an alternative government and the king was forced to revert to the Whigs. He then agreed to create as many peers as necessary to pass the Bill and the Lords gave way.

In 1910, by contrast, there was no evidence of the sort of popular pressure that had been present in 1832. Indeed, with the government having lost seats in the January election, it was difficult to argue that it had a popular mandate for reform, as distinct from a mandate for the Budget which the Lords had already passed. And, by contrast with the Whigs in the 1830s, the Liberals were seeking a promise in relation to a Bill which had not yet received its Second Reading in the Commons. But in some ways, the position of the Liberals was to be stronger than that of their Whig forebears. For, if they were returned to power in the forthcoming election, the reform proposals would have been before the country at two general elections rather than one, and the principle of the Bill would have been confirmed by MPs in three successive Parliaments. And, by contrast with 1832, an alternative scheme, a proposal by Lord Lansdowne for a reconstructed House of Lords, would also be put to the voters. But there was a further important difference from 1832. For in 1910, by contrast with 1832, a promise was being sought *in advance* of a general election – a hypothetical understanding as it were – in relation to a future which could not at that stage be foreseen. Further, in 1832, advice to create peers was not given until the Reform Bill had actually been rejected in the Lords, while in November 1910, the Parliament Bill had not yet been presented to the Lords, let alone rejected. So there was no strict analogy with the past. The orthodox view would have been that the Liberals, if returned in the December election, should, if necessary, advise the king to use his prerogative to create peers, and the king would be expected to comply. The king argued that it was constitutionally inappropriate to seek to bind him in advance of a general election. His use of the prerogative must depend on the precise circumstances, which could not currently be foreseen. But, as we have seen, George V's Conservative sentiments and unwise utterances as Prince of Wales had made some Liberals believe that he would not accept government advice. And Asquith could not, if he was to retain any credit with his party, enter a second election campaign without a promise. On 14

April, he had told the Commons that 'in no case would we recommend Dissolution except under such conditions as will secure that in the new Parliament the judgment of the people as expressed in the election will be carried into law'.[57]

In November, the Chief Whip, the Master of Elibank, had warned Asquith:

You must get your guarantees, otherwise:

(1) You break faith with your Party; or
(2) You must say that you have asked for guarantees and the King has refused,
(3) You leave the country to conjecture that the King has refused.

The Socialists and Irish will be indignant with the King and drag his name into the controversy.[58]

The king felt that if he gave a hypothetical promise, he would be compromising his neutrality by adding his weight to the Liberal Party's election programme. Were the Liberals not in fact 'asking in advance' for that very 'blank authority for the indefinite exercise of the Royal Prerogative' which Asquith had said in February was constitutionally inadmissible? The Unionists would feel that the sovereign had thrown his weight on the scales against them.

The king's position was made more difficult by the fact that his two private secretaries disagreed on the correct course. Bigge believed that the king should refuse to make any promise as to what he would do in a hypothetical situation. Knollys, on the other hand, believed that the king should agree to Asquith's request. He supported his view, first, by saying that he would have given the same advice to Edward VII, who would have accepted it. In fact, he had given quite opposite advice to Edward. Second, Knollys declared that no alternative government was available. That was not quite correct since, as we have seen, Balfour at the Lambeth Palace Conference in April had agreed that, were the government to resign, he would be prepared himself to form a government. Knollys hid from the king details of this so-called conference. His justification for doing so was that Balfour, whose Unionists were in a minority in the Commons, would have had to seek an immediate dissolution. The king would then have appeared in the invidious

---

57 House of Commons Debates, 14 April 1910, vol. 16, col. 1548.
58 Le May, *Victorian Constitution*, p. 203. Unfortunately, no date is given for Elibank's letter.

position of having in effect compelled the resignation of a Prime Minister, who enjoyed the confidence of the Commons and the voters, only to install a Prime Minister who could not command that confidence. Balfour, therefore, would appear as the king's nominee, and during the election the sovereign's name would have been dragged into the dispute over the powers of the Lords.

On 16 November, the king saw Asquith and Crewe in London. Faced with their determination and Knollys's advice, he very reluctantly gave way, agreeing to the creation of peers if, after a general election in which the Liberals were returned with 'an adequate majority', the Lords refused to pass the Parliament Bill. But he persuaded the government to send the veto resolutions to the Lords and introduce the Parliament Bill before dissolving, together with Lansdowne's Reconstruction Bill, so that voters would know the issues which they would have to decide in the election.[59] The king felt that he had not been treated fairly. A year later, he told Lord Derby, a former Conservative Cabinet minister, that at his meeting with Asquith and Crewe he had 'begged to be allowed to see Arthur Balfour and Lansdowne but this was peremptorily refused'. He had been bullied 'for an hour and a half and he then told them that he would give guarantees if they got a majority and asked to be allowed to make this public'. The king then claimed that he had told Asquith and Crewe, 'I have been forced into this and I should like the country to know it.' But Asquith and Crewe 'declined and said that this was a confidential pledge and must be kept so'. The king told Derby that they had 'behaved disgracefully to me'.[60] But despite Asquith and Crewe's insistence on secrecy, it became clear to informed observers that the government had in fact obtained the understanding. Indeed, the leading article in *The Star* on 19 November was headlined 'We have got the guarantees', while the *Daily News* of 21 November reported Lloyd George as saying, 'Does any man, in his senses, think that we would provoke another election unless we were certain that if we can get a majority it will be a final one?'[61] But at least the promise did not become an election issue, and from that point of view, it was obviously right that it was not made public.

Still, given that the promise was insisted upon not for constitutional reasons but to restore Asquith's position with his MPs, there was no point to the promise unless it became known to them. The promise served no constitutional purpose since the king would have had no alternative once the

---

59 Nicolson, *King George the Fifth*, pp. 208–9.
60 Churchill, *Young Statesman*, p. 343.
61 Le May, *Victorian Constitution*, p. 210.

election was known but to act on advice, whether he had given the promise or not.

In 1930, Lord Stamfordham, who had been the king's joint private secretary in 1911 and felt, unlike Knollys, that the king should not have given the hypothetical understanding, wrote to Asquith's biographer, 'I do not think it should be assumed that King Edward would have agreed to the guarantees that King George did under considerable pressure.'[62] George V was to feel, for the rest of his reign, that he had not been treated fairly either by Knollys, who had not told him of the Lambeth Palace Conference, or by his ministers, who he considered had bullied him, an inexperienced monarch, into acquiescence. He felt, perhaps with justification, that had he been more experienced, he would have asked the government to put the reasons for seeking the hypothetical understanding in writing. Then he could have taken his time to reflect before making his decision. What is clear is that a sovereign is highly unlikely ever to be asked again to give a hypothetical promise, and it is even more unlikely that any future sovereign will be prepared to give it. In any case, the reduction in the delaying power of the Lords to just one session in a second Parliament Act of 1949 means that the sovereign is unlikely ever again to be placed in such a situation. For a sovereign can say to the government: why create peers when, if you have the patience to wait a session, you can secure any legislation you like?

THE DISSOLUTION OF PARLIAMENT AND THE GENERAL ELECTION OF DECEMBER 1910

Armed with the understanding, Parliament could now be dissolved. The Prime Minister, Churchill told the king, had 'effectually extinguished the pallid flickering life of this House of Commons. It has never really lived, & now it is to die. No one cares about it any more.'[63] But before dissolution, the Lords considered the Second Reading of the Parliament Bill. On 21 November, Rosebery's proposal providing for a reconstruction of the Lords was carried without a division. Lansdowne then brought forward proposals of his own in the form of resolutions providing for a 'reduced and reconstituted' Upper House, although giving no details of how it should be 'reconstituted'. Lansdowne also proposed the referendum for situations where conflict over a Bill between Lords and Commons in two successive sessions could not be settled by joint sittings. The Lansdowne resolutions also were carried without a division. His biographer points out that the 'most remarkable feature was

---

62 Letter from Stamfordham to J. A. Spender, 14 April 1930, Spender Papers, Add. MSS. 46,386, f. 23.
63 Churchill, *Companion*, vol. 2, part 2, p. 1,027.

the enthusiasm shown for drastic reform by some of those who had previously deprecated any action of this nature as inopportune and ill-advised.'[64] Indeed, as recently as 29 March 1910 Balfour had asked the Commons, 'Have we proposed changes in the Constitution? Everybody knows that is no part of our party creed, no part of our function; that is not the way social development and evolution are to be effected.'[65]

The Lansdowne scheme went far to concede the Liberal case, since if the Lords had acted wisely and constitutionally in rejecting the Budget, why did it need reform? If, moreover, the composition of the Upper House was so radically defective, did this not justify the Liberal attack on it? In the general election, Asquith was to attack the Unionists with deadly thrusts, 'Ah, gentlemen, what a change eleven short months have wrought. This ancient and picturesque structure has been condemned by its own inmates as unsafe. The parricidal pickaxes are already at work, and constitutional jerry-builders are hurrying from every quarter with new plans.' The Prime Minister quoted Dr Johnson, 'Depend upon it, Sir, when a man is going to be hanged in a fortnight it concentrates his mind wonderfully.' 'The activity recently displayed by the House of Lords', Asquith continued,

> in providing itself with a successor is surely a miracle of this kind of mental concentration. In a single sitting, not unduly prolonged, the venerable institution, which has withstood the storm and stress of ages, was transformed – in principle, of course; some of the details are still withheld – into a brand new modern Senate.[66]

During the election, the old cries of January were repeated. There seemed little new to be said. But there was one unexpected innovation. In a speech at the Albert Hall on 29 November, Balfour, without consulting his shadow Cabinet, seemed to pledge that a referendum would be held before any tariff was introduced. His words, however, were characteristically evasive, declaring that he had 'not the least objection to submitting the principles of tariff Reform to a Referendum'. Was this a definite pledge or conditional perhaps on the Liberals agreeing to submit Home Rule to a referendum – which the Liberals were certainly not prepared to do? But whatever it was, it dismayed the Chamberlainites. The speech, Beatrice Webb believed, 'delivers him from the domination of a political sect that has got hold of the caucus ... It is the last move in his duel with Chamberlain: it is a final checkmate to tariff

---

64 Newton, *Lansdowne*, p. 405.
65 House of Commons Debates, 29 March 1910, vol. 15, col. 1187.
66 Spender and Asquith, *Asquith*, vol. 1, p. 299.

reform.'[67] Balfour's words were intended to dissociate tariff reform from the election, enabling the Unionists, he hoped, to concentrate on the fundamental issues which really mattered to them – defence of the second chamber, opposition to radicalism and socialism and, above all, defence of the Union, the very purpose for which the Unionist coalition had been formed. 'I fully admit', the Duke of Devonshire had told the Liberal Unionist conference as long ago as December 1887,

> that I do not put the two questions of Fair-Trade [i.e. tariff reform] and Home rule on an equal footing … The adoption for some foolish retrograde measure in the direction of Fair-trade … could probably be soon retraced again without much mischief being done … a much less grave misfortune than the separation of the Parliament of Great Britain and Ireland – a step which could never be retraced.[68]

Yet the referendum proposal savoured of panic, 'the counsel of a desperate man', in Grey's words. Asquith contrasted the position of the Unionists in January with their position in December. Then they had defended the Lords as a bulwark of the constitution. Now the hereditary chamber was to be abolished and 'a new cardboard structure run up in its place'.[69] Then tariff reform had been at the centre of the Unionist programme. Now it was to be postponed until approved by referendum. The Unionists, moreover, had claimed to be the constitutional party, a bulwark against dangerous and ill-thought-out innovation. Yet the referendum and proposals to reconstruct the House of Lords were far more radical than anything in the Parliament Bill.

When Balfour made his referendum pledge, an enthusiast in the audience shouted out, 'That's won the election.' But it had not. The referendum pledge probably had some effect in free trade Lancashire where the Unionists made a net gain of six seats, but this was offset by losses elsewhere. The outcome of the December 1910 election was hardly different from that in January. Turnout remained high at 81.1 per cent, the second highest of the twentieth century, after the January election's 87 per cent, despite the December election being fought in wet weather and on a stale register. With an up-to-date register, the drop in turnout would probably have been much less, probably around 2 per cent.[70] The slight drop in turnout was also largely due to the greater number of unopposed returns, from seventy-five to 163.

67 MacKenzie, *Diary of Beatrice Webb*, vol. 3, p. 149, entry for 1 December 1910.
68 Quoted in *The Spectator*, 3 December 1910, p. 966.
69 *The Times*, 2 December 1910.
70 Blewett, *Peers, Parties and People*, p. 380.

	Seats	Percentage of votes	Unopposed Returns	Percentage of vote per opposed candidate
Liberals	272	43.9	35	49.5
Unionists	272	46.3	72	47.9
Labour	42	7.1	3	42.8
Irish Party	84	2.5	53	81.9
Others	0	0.2	0	9.1

The Liberals kept their position as a governing party, the first time a party had won three general elections since before the great Reform Act of 1832. No one suspected that this would be the last election which the Liberals would win, nor that the Conservatives, having been defeated in three successive general elections, would become the dominant party in British politics for the rest of the twentieth century. The election confirmed Labour's dependence on the Liberals. In the twenty-four constituencies where there were three-cornered fights, Labour was bottom of the poll.

The results of the two elections of 1910 show a striking geographical divide in voting patterns. Proceeding southwards from the north coast of Scotland, there is a steady increase in the Unionist vote. In Scotland in the January 1910 election, the Unionist vote was around 40 per cent, in the northern counties 41 per cent, in Yorkshire, Lancashire and Cheshire 44 per cent, in the Midlands 51 per cent, in the metropolitan area of London 53 per cent and in the home counties 58 per cent. The Unionists won every constituency in Hertfordshire, Kent, Surrey and Sussex, while in Middlesex and Warwickshire there was just one Liberal victory. 'Few Liberal members', wrote one commentator, 'can lead a settled life within an hour or two's train journey from London.'[71] In Britain, north of the line linking the Severn and the Wash, the majority was Liberal or Labour; south of that line, the majority was Unionist.[72] Of the 117 seats the Unionists gained in January 1910, just thirteen had been north of the Trent and Mersey; almost all were in non-industrial towns and agricultural or residential county constituencies. Never before had the anti-Unionists done so well in the north, Scotland and Wales, while doing so badly in the south of England. Never before had the Unionists done so well in the south while doing so badly elsewhere. Never before had one half of the nation – the south of England – swung in one direction while in the other, the Liberal gains of 1906 were largely maintained. The Unionists were becoming the party of the centre or core, the Liberals of the

71 E. N. Mozley, 'The Political Heptarchy: An Analysis of Seven General Elections', *Contemporary Review*, 1910, p. 405.
72 Rosenbaum, 'The General Election of January 1910', pp. 487–8.

periphery – and after the war they were to be pushed back even further, to the so-called Celtic fringe: Scotland, Wales, Devon and Cornwall.

This geographical divide corresponded with a socio-economic one, between what Lloyd George called 'the progressive north' and 'the semi-feudal south'.[73] Crudely, it seemed that 'industrial Britain is Liberal, rural and residential Britain Conservative'. Those urban constituencies of the Midlands and north which remained Unionist were 'susceptible of easy explanations based upon the special conditions of employment or unemployment or upon the chance of a three-cornered contest'. There were, the radical economist J. A. Hobson argued,

> two Englands ... a Producer's England and a Consumer's England, one England in which the well-to-do classes, from their numbers, wealth, leisure and influence, mould the external character of the civilisation and determine the habits, feelings and opinions of the people, the other England in which the structure and captivities of large organised industries, carried on by great associated masses of artisans, factory hands and miners, are the dominating fact and forces.

Never before had this social split been so starkly evident. 'This election presents more plainly than ever before the instinctive rally of the classes and interests whose possessions, prestige, privileges and superiority of opportunity, are menaced by the new forces of constructive democracy.'[74] Liberalism had become the party of modern Britain – industrial and commercial Britain. Rural and agrarian Britain remained mainly Unionist. The question for the Liberals was whether they could come fully to terms with modern Britain, or whether it would be the Labour Party that would be seen as the best party to represent Producer's England. But the 1910 elections had shown that, for the present at least, industrial England could no longer give the Liberals and the left an overall majority in the Commons.

THE PARLIAMENT ACT

The December election had been a no-change election. But it was decisive. It made a radical change in the constitution inevitable, since clearly a third general election would not be feasible. In February 1911, the Liberals duly introduced the Parliament Bill into the Commons, a Bill similar to the April 1910 resolutions. On 15 May, the Bill passed its Commons Third Reading

---

73 Clarke, *Lancashire and the New Liberalism*, p. 8.
74 J. A. Hobson, 'The General Election: A Sociological Interpretation', *Sociological Review*, 1910, pp. 108–9, 112–13, 116.

by 362 votes to 243. But a week earlier, on 8 May, Lansdowne had presented his House of Lords Reconstruction Bill, based on both Rosebery's and his own earlier resolutions. The new Upper House was to be composed of a somewhat miscellaneous collection of dignitaries. It would comprise around 350 members, 100 of whom would be so-called Lords of Parliament, elected for a twelve-year term, rather than sitting for life, by the whole body of hereditary peers from amongst those who held or had held various high offices such as former Cabinet ministers, viceroys and ambassadors, together with leading civil servants and figures from the army and navy, and in addition Lords Lieutenant and local authority leaders. A further 120 would be elected on a regional basis by MPs in the regions concerned using the single transferable vote method of proportional representation. Another 100 would be appointed by the government in proportion to the strengths of the parties in the Commons. There would also be the two archbishops, five bishops and sixteen law lords. There was provision for the referendum on matters of great gravity where agreement could not be reached in a joint sitting. The resolutions, in the words of Lansdowne's biographer, which 'really amounted almost to a sentence of death upon the most ancient Legislative Chamber in the world, were received by a crowded and attentive House in a dignified if frigid silence'.[75] Lansdowne could have defended his proposals by arguing that, whereas the Liberals, with their belief in representative government, were giving greater power to the Commons – in reality to the Cabinet – Lansdowne's proposals provided for greater power to be given to the people through the referendum. They indeed represented a radical transformation in the traditional role of the Lords which hitherto had been largely regarded as a barrier against populist democracy. It was now proposed to reconstruct the Upper House so that it could facilitate democracy through the referendum. The Unionists could perhaps regard the resolutions as an example of Tory democracy.

Such limited enthusiasm as there was for the Lansdowne proposals evaporated when Lord Morley, for the Liberals, declared that the provisions of the Parliament Bill would apply just as much to the reconstituted chamber as to the existing House of Lords. After the Second Reading of Lansdowne's Bill, therefore, it lapsed, and attention turned to what the Unionists in the Lords would do with the Parliament Bill. Between 28 June and 6 July, the Unionist majority in the Lords radically amended it in committee. These amendments were to be considered by the Commons on 24 July. But by then, the Unionists knew that the king would create peers if necessary. In consequence, when Asquith rose to move that the Lords' amendments be considered by

---

75 Newton, *Lansdowne*, p. 415.

the Commons, he could not make himself heard amidst opposition cries of 'traitor' and 'who killed the King'. This outcry had been organised by Lord Hugh Cecil and F. E. Smith, the latter seeking to oust Balfour from the Unionist leadership. Indeed, their main target was less Asquith than Balfour whose advice that Unionists should accept the Parliament Bill rather than compel the creation of peers they bitterly resented. After fifty minutes, the Speaker was compelled to adjourn the sitting under Standing Order 21 due to 'grave disorder'.

When MPs did come to consider the Lords amendments, they accepted just one to the effect that any Bill to extend the life of a parliament beyond five years was to be excluded from the operation of the Bill. This provision had a constitutional importance not noticed at the time, indeed not noticed for almost a hundred years. Its effect was to give a handle to the judges. For, if a Bill passed under the Parliament Act procedure purported to extend the life of Parliament, the judges would pronounce it invalid. This meant that the validity of legislation passed under the Parliament Act procedure would not be inherent but would depend upon its compliance with the terms of the Act, and it would be for the judges to ensure that legislation did so comply. In the landmark case of *R (Jackson) v. Attorney General* in 2005, British judges were for the first time to examine the validity of primary legislation passed by Parliament, when it was alleged that the Hunting Act of 2004 did not comply with the terms of the 1911 Parliament Act, a claim that the court rejected.

Other Lords amendments such as one providing that a joint committee, rather than the Speaker, determine Money Bills, and an amendment providing that a referendum be required for any Bill affecting the crown, the Protestant succession, the establishment of new Parliaments within the United Kingdom and other matters raising issues of great gravity, were rejected by the Commons. And MPs rejected an all-important Lords amendment proposing that Home Rule be excluded from the Parliament Bill. This fuelled the opposition allegation that a prime purpose of the Bill was to ensure that voters would have no chance to pronounce again on Home Rule. The government at first decided that the Lords amendments should be rejected *en bloc* without any further reference to the upper chamber, and that it should immediately demand a creation of peers. But on 22 July, the king wisely insisted that, before consenting to a creation, the Lords should be given a final opportunity to consider why the Commons had rejected their amendments and whether they wished to persist in them.[76]

On 29 July, Asquith wrote to Balfour and Lansdowne in identical terms,

76 Nicolson, *King George the Fifth*, p. 212.

declaring that he thought it 'courteous and right, before any public discussions are announced, to let you know how we regard the political situation'. When the Parliament Bill was returned to the Commons, the government would be 'compelled to ask the House to disagree with the Lords' amendments'. He then went on to announce the understanding.

> In the circumstances, should the necessity arise, the Government will advise the King to exercise his Prerogative to secure the passing into law of the Bill in substantially the same form in which it left the House of Commons, and His Majesty has been pleased to signify that he will consider it his duty to accept and act on that advice.

Balfour had in fact learnt of the king's decision in early July, although the Unionist shadow Cabinet did not really believe it for some time afterwards. But Asquith's letter left no doubt. The question now was not whether the Parliament Bill would pass but whether it would pass with or without a creation of peers.

The Unionists were divided on whether to resist to the end. Lord Selborne, a former Unionist Cabinet minister, declared that the question before them was: 'Shall we perish in the dark by our own hand, or in the light, killed by our enemies?'[77] Selborne favoured perishing in the light. So did Austen Chamberlain, F. E. Smith, Carson, Wyndham, Halsbury and the Chief Whip in the Commons. They were 'ditchers', prepared to die in the last ditch, even if that meant a creation of Liberal peers, something which Balfour regarded as 'the Music Hall attitude of mind'.[78] The ditchers were not, however, all short-sighted reactionaries. On the contrary, they comprised some of the most active and radical members of the party, for whom Chamberlain was the symbol and tariff reform the banner. Balfour, Lansdowne, Bonar Law, Curzon, Chaplin and Long, however, were 'hedgers' who favoured acquiescence. At a meeting of the shadow Cabinet on 21 July, when there were rumours that the king would, if necessary, agree to the creation of peers, the majority decided to allow the Bill to pass.[79] The leadership advised abstention. But it appeared that this would not be sufficient.[80] To allow the Bill to pass, some Unionist peers would actually have to vote with the government rather than abstain. Somewhat typically, both Balfour and Lansdowne were away in the country during the final crisis between 3 and 7 August and failed to give any lead as to what peers should do if it appeared that the Bill would

---

77 House of Lords Debates, 10 August 1911, vol. 9, col. 1073.
78 Dugdale, *Balfour*, vol. 2, p. 51.
79 Peter Fraser, 'The Unionist Debacle of 1911 and Balfour's Retirement', *Journal of Modern History*, 1963, p. 357.
80 Vincent, ed., *Crawford Papers*, p. 196.

not pass in the form desired by the government. On 10 August, the date on which the Lords' vote was to be taken, the government announced that it had the king's permission to claim 'a creation of peers sufficient in number to guard against any possible combination of the different parties in opposition'. On a day of sweltering heat in which the temperature reached nearly 100 degrees Fahrenheit, the Lords finally gave way, voting on a motion that the House 'do not insist' on their amendments by 131 votes to 114. Around 300 Unionists abstained to avoid what they regarded as the humiliation of a mass creation of peers, while between twenty-five and thirty voted with the government, together with eleven bishops and the two archbishops. 'We were beaten', declared George Wyndham, 'by the Bishops and the Rats.'[81] Perhaps it was a pity that there was not to be a mass creation. Asquith had prepared a list of 249 prospective peers, which included the philosopher Bertrand Russell, the classical scholar Gilbert Murray, the novelist Thomas Hardy and the playwright James Barrie. Those on Asquith's list were certainly men of higher calibre than most of the members of the House of Lords.[82]

Speaking in Huddersfield in March 1914 at the height of the Ulster crisis, Lloyd George declared that, before the Parliament Act, the Tory leaders had met at Lord Lansdowne's London home 'and decided there whether Liberal Bills were to be allowed to get a free passage on the Statute-book'. The Parliament Act, however, 'has abolished the Lansdowne house Legislature'. It had established 'the right of the people to secure statutory sanction for their legislative projects with or without the consent of the Tory party'.[83] In a sense, the Parliament Act merely drew out the logic of the 1832 Reform Act. Before it, so Disraeli wrote in 1833, the country had the choice of reverting 'to the *aristocratic* principle, or we must advance to the *democratic*'. But 'the moment the Lords passed the Reform Bill ... the aristocratic principle of government in this country ... expired for ever'.[84]

Only three Bills were to be passed under the procedure laid down in the 1911 Parliament Act: the Established Church (Wales) Bill, disestablishing the Anglican Church in Wales, the Government of Ireland Bill, providing for Home Rule – both enacted in 1914 – and a second Parliament Bill in 1949, reducing the delaying power to one session.

The Act had important consequences for the British constitution. Until 1911, a Liberal though not a Conservative government had been subject to the veto of the Lords, a limitation upon its powers. That veto had now been removed. The relationship between the two houses, hitherto based

81 Jenkins, *Mr Balfour's Poodle*, p. 267.
82 Ibid., p. 248.
83 *The Times*, 23 March 1914.
84 William Flavelle Monypenny, *The Life of Benjamin Disraeli, Earl of Beaconsfield*, John Murray, 1910, vol. I, p. 226.

on convention, was now reduced to written statutory form giving a precise definition of the powers of the Lords. The Parliament Act, for the first time in British history, distinguished between different categories of legislation – Money Bills, Non-Money Bills and a Bill to extend the life of Parliament over which the House of Lords retained an absolute veto. Since the Lords also had a veto over the dismissal of judges, it could offer some protection against a government seeking to subvert either the electoral or the judicial process. It could therefore perform, albeit to a very limited degree, the function of constitutional protection.

Since the Parliament Act provided for three different classes of legislation – ordinary legislation, financial legislation and legislation offering an extension to the life of a parliament – it might appear that, in place of a flexible and uncodified system, the Parliament Act would prove a step towards a constitution. For most constitutions distinguish between ordinary legislation and constitutional legislation. Yet the Parliament Act was not in fact to be a step towards a codified constitution, but away from it. The failure of the Constitutional Conference in 1910 ensured, as we have seen, that Britain would not enact a codified constitution in the foreseeable future. And the purpose of a constitution is to make fundamental change more difficult. But the Parliament Act made it easier. For the Liberals believed that the main problem with the machinery of representative democracy in Britain was that it operated too slowly, making radical change too difficult. Most Unionists, however, believed that, except perhaps on the issue of tariff reform, it operated too rapidly and that the powers of a radical government of the left should be curbed by a strong second chamber. But in consequence of the Parliament Act, a government with a majority in the Commons could in practice generally enact any legislation that it wished. From this point of view, the Parliament Act was, in Dicey's words, 'the apotheosis of party', and created 'an absolute legislative dictatorship',[85] words to be echoed by the Conservative Lord Hailsham in the 1970s, when he would characterise British government as an 'elective dictatorship'. Before 1909, the two chambers of Parliament had been, in the case of a Liberal government, but not a Unionist one, in effect a constituent assembly. Now the constituent assembly was just the Commons, in effect the government of the day. Any change, however wide-ranging, with the single exception of a Bill to lengthen the life of a parliament, could be carried through by a simple majority in the Commons.

The preamble to the Parliament Act had, as we have seen, promised reform of the composition of the Lords, replacing a second chamber constituted on a 'hereditary' basis with one constituted on a 'popular' basis – the word

---

85 *The Times*, 3 October 1911, 12 September 1911.

'elected' was not used. In March 1910, Asquith had told the Commons that the veto resolutions were 'not a complete settlement. The problem of reform calls for a complete settlement, and, in our opinion, that settlement does not brook delay.'[86] In May 1911, Asquith had said that reform of composition would take place 'in this Parliament' if time permitted.[87] Lord Crewe was to tell the Lords in 1918 that 'the Parliament Act by the admission of its authors of whom I am one, was never intended to be a permanent measure'.[88] But upon reflection, the Liberals appreciated that rationalising the Upper House would give it more legitimacy, thereby strengthening it. Liberals, so Churchill had told the king on 4 April 1911, were against a 'popular' chamber 'in the proportion of four or five to one'.[89] The preamble had been added largely to appease Grey and one or two others in the Cabinet who favoured an elected chamber. In consequence, in the words of Asquith's biographers, 'the reconstitution of the Upper House was thus bequeathed as a legacy to any Government or party which might be willing to take it up in the future. None so far [up to 1932] has shown any alacrity to do so'.[90] In any case, with legislation pending on national insurance, Home Rule and Welsh disestablishment, time could hardly be found in the pre-1914 legislative programme for another major constitutional measure. Most Liberals took the same view as the 1945 Labour government was to take, and separated the two issues of composition and powers. Until the late 1960s, the left believed, in the words of Richard Crossman, Leader of the Commons from 1966 to 1968, that 'an indefensible anachronism is preferable to a second Chamber with any real authority'.[91] Both the Asquith and Attlee governments sought legislative efficiency, the speedy translation of ministers' wishes into law, not the establishment of new checks and balances in the constitution.

The Parliament Act did not have the radical political consequences that Lloyd George had hoped for. Writing to his brother in 1909, he had detected that there was

undoubtedly a popular rising such as has not been witnessed over a generation. What will happen if they throw it out I can conjecture and I rejoice at the prospect. Many a rotten institution, system and law will be

---

86   House of Commons Debates, 29 March 1910, vol. 15, col. 1166.
87   Ibid., 15 May 1911, vol. 25, col. 1668.
88   House of Lords Debates, 4 July 1918, vol. 30, col. 610.
89   Churchill, Companion, vol. 2, part 2, p. 1,063.
90   Spender and Asquith, Asquith, vol. 1, p. 276.
91   Quoted in Miles Taylor, 'Labour and the Constitution', in Duncan Tanner, Pat Thane and Nick Tiratsoo, eds, Labour's First Century, Cambridge University Press, 2000, p. 169.

submerged by the deluge. I wonder whether they will be such fools. I am almost wishing they should be stricken with blindness.[92]

The peers had indeed been stricken with blindness, but the consequences were not to be as radical as Lloyd George predicted.

A NEW CONSERVATIVE LEADER

Passage of the Parliament Act heralded the end of Balfour's leadership of the Conservatives. Not only had he lost three elections, but he had annoyed both the tariff reformers through his advocacy of the referendum and the diehards by his opposition to the ditchers. Indeed, the diehard revolt could itself be regarded as but a symptom of welling discontent amongst Unionists, who were tired of his endless equivocations and qualifications, and believed, quite falsely, that he and Lansdowne had colluded with the Liberals to secure passage of the Parliament Bill.[93] Unionist MPs sought a more aggressive leader, one who would take the fight to the Liberals and be more in touch with the grassroots of the party. Arthur Steel-Maitland, Chairman of the Conservatives, wrote in a memorandum of 20 September 1911 that Tory MPs 'think that he [Balfour] is not in earnest in wishing to fight and organise the fighting ... they think that a proper lead is not given, especially in those cases where we are on the defensive and where a lead and unity is most essential'.[94] Nor did Balfour seek to resist the forces seeking to remove him. He was a tired and disillusioned man with no clear view as to the direction the party should take, and too old at sixty-two to have much prospect of leading another government for any period of time, given that the next election would probably not be until 1914 or 1915. On holiday in August 1911, he wrote that 'politics have been to me quite unusually odious', and three months later, he announced his retirement as Conservative leader in the Commons after twenty years in the post, three and a half as Prime Minister.[95] 'I think', he wrote to a colleague, 'a slower brain would often be welcome to the party as a whole.' His weakness, he admitted, was that 'I see all the factors of a situation, every potentiality of an argument ... Some people blame the qualifications in my speeches. They are not expressed to save myself, but to protect my party in the future when the statements of leaders are recalled to injure the party.'[96] He resigned as Conservative leader on 8 November 1911.

---

92 George, *My Brother and I*, p. 230.
93 Fraser, 'The Unionist Debacle of 1911 and Balfour's Retirement', p. 354.
94 Balfour Papers, Add. MSS. 49861, ff. 329–33.
95 Dugdale, *Balfour*, vol. 2, p. 61.
96 Vincent, ed., *Crawford Papers*, p. 225.

He had not been an inspirational Leader of the Opposition. His belief in tariff reform had seemed half-hearted. Yet his achievements as Conservative leader were perhaps greater than was then appreciated. Shortly before his resignation, his secretary, Sandars, wrote of a conversation in which Balfour declared:

> He had strained every nerve to prevent Party division. In accents which showed how deeply he felt it, he referred to the abuse which had been poured upon him, and the imputations which had been made upon his sincerity during the years between 1906 and January 1910. But he had seen the success of his Fabian methods, and it would be admitted that he had saved the Party from breaking up and that we went into the General Election of January 1910, a united Party.[97]

Balfour's approach was to have echoes many years later. During the Conservative leadership crisis of 1963, Harold Macmillan, about to resign as Prime Minister, was to tell Selwyn Lloyd:

> Balfour had been bitterly criticised for not having a view on Protection and Free Trade. Balfour had said the important thing was to preserve the unity of the Conservative Party. He had been abused for that. But now whoever argued about Free Trade or Protection? ... Whereas the preservation of great national institutions had been the right priority.[98]

Balfour was by no means the last Conservative leader to be faced with such difficult choices. John Major had to adopt similar tactics to those of Balfour in his 1992–97 government on the issue of Britain's relationship with the European Union and, in particular, the question of whether Britain should rule out joining the eurozone. In his autobiography, John Major was to write ruefully that perhaps 'the day may come when a similar judgment [to that made by Macmillan on Balfour] is made on the single currency'.[99]

There were two obvious candidates to replace Balfour – Austen Chamberlain, son of Joe, preserver of the flame of tariff reform and Chancellor of the Exchequer from 1902 to 1905; and Walter Long, representing the squirearchy, the traditional landed interest of the party, and in contrast to Chamberlain, only a moderate tariff reformer and an opponent of food taxes. Long had

---

97 Quoted in R. Ben Jones, 'The Conservative Party 1906–1911: A Study of the Internal Difficulties of the Party', BLitt thesis, Oxford University, 1960, pp. 5–6.
98 Vernon Bogdanor, 'The Selection of the Party Leader', in Anthony Seldon and Stuart Ball, eds, *Conservative Century: The Conservative Party since 1900*, Oxford University Press, 1994, p. 94.
99 John Major, *The Autobiography* [1999], HarperCollins, 2000, pp. xxi–xxii.

in fact wanted to continue Balfour's work of disengaging the party from tariff reform. He had, by contrast with Chamberlain, supported Balfour's referendum pledge on tariff reform and had been a hedger in 1911. But Long's essential moderation was masked by his choleric manner and eagerness to take offence. The party grandees did not believe that Long had the right temperament to lead the party. Indeed, the prospect frightened them. The Chief Whip believed that his 'nervous and protean excitability must arise from some latent affectation of the nerves', and that as leader he would be 'hopeless, impossible. He is stale and turgid: his temper is peppery and twelve months hence will be uncontrollable.'[100] Long was also thought to be not very bright. One Tory backbencher wrote to a newspaper editor in September 1909 when Long was recovering from an operation. 'The doctors must have taken Walter Long's brains instead of his appendix, they were both small and very swollen, so the mistake is quite permissible.'[101] Chamberlain had much wider governmental experience. He had been a whip, Civil Lord of the Admiralty, Financial Secretary to the Treasury and had held two Cabinet posts – Postmaster General and Chancellor of the Exchequer. He was supported by almost the whole of the Unionist front bench.

But there seemed insuperable objections to both candidates. In the words of Jack Sandars, Balfour's political secretary:

> It may be said against Austen Chamberlain that he comes from Birmingham, that he is a Liberal Unionist, that he is not allied by family tradition or landed estates with the traditional Conservative Party. On the other hand, Walter Long has none of these disqualifications, but he possesses every other conceivable one, and in fact his only claims are squiredom and seniority.[102]

Neither seemed to have overwhelming support, and there was considerable hostility between them. Long greatly resented the hold of Birmingham on the Unionists and had said as early as 1900 of Joe, that the 'Conservative Party ... will not be led by a bloody radical'.[103] It seemed that, were Chamberlain to be chosen, Long would either refuse to serve under him or, if he did serve, that he would make Chamberlain's life a misery. 'Nobody is more apt to take umbrage than Walter.'[104] So, while Chamberlain would have split the party on policy, Long would have split it on personality.

---

100 Vincent, ed., *Crawford Papers*, pp. 186, 237.
101 Dutton, *His Majesty's Loyal Opposition*, p. 142.
102 Memo by Sandars, 'A Note on the Events Leading to Mr Balfour's Resignation', Balfour Papers, Add. MSS. 49767, f. 289.
103 John Ramsden, *An Appetite for Power: A History of the Conservative Party since 1880*, HarperCollins, 1998, p. 188.
104 Vincent, ed., *Crawford Papers*, p. 134.

There was no precedent for the procedure to be adopted in such a situation. It seemed that a ballot would be necessary. Long might well have won a contested election, and the betting at the Carlton Club made him the favourite.[105] Canvassing amongst MPs seems to have shown that he would have won by seventy votes, though given the tendency of MPs to dissimulate, the majority might well have been smaller.[106] Long claimed to be horrified by the idea of a ballot. 'I can think of nothing so undignified', he told his supporters, 'as a ballot for the leadership of the great Unionist Party. I will never be a party to putting the leadership of the Unionist cause up to Dutch auction.'[107] According to a letter by Long's brother-in-law Colonel Chaloner, the MP for Liverpool Abercromby, a leading supporter of Chamberlain's had admitted to him that Long would have won 'by a large majority', and Chaloner thought 'it was very mean and unpatriotic of him [Chamberlain] not to have withdrawn & allowed Walter to go in unopposed'.[108]

A decision needed to be made rapidly since the party conference, meeting shortly, 'would take it out of their hands; there would be resolutions, speeches, every kind of lobbying and intrigue'.[109] Chamberlain and Long were both induced to withdraw in favour of a third candidate, Andrew Bonar Law, a man without the political experience of either of the other two. He had not entered Parliament until 1900 and had held only the minor office of parliamentary secretary at the Board of Trade in the Balfour government. But unlike Long, Bonar Law was seen as a man of competence, and unlike Chamberlain, he was a Conservative rather than a member of the minority Liberal Unionist wing of the Unionist coalition. At the meeting to elect the new leader in the House of Commons on 13 November 1911, at which, for the first time, Chamberlain entered the Carlton Club, Henry Chaplin in the chair said that the prospect had been that

> a variety of candidates might be proposed. This of course was what our radical friends hoped. They would then have rejoiced greatly if three or four candidates had been proposed and we had had to go through what I do not hesitate to describe … as the ignominy of a poll held under secrecy. (Cheers.)[110]

Bonar Law was the first Conservative to have been chosen as party leader in the Commons before being appointed Prime Minister by the sovereign

---

105 Ibid., p. 244.
106 Sir Charles Petrie, *Walter Long and His Times*, Hutchinson, 1936, p. 171.
107 Ibid., pp. 171–2.
108 Walter Long Papers, Wiltshire County Record Office, 947/452, 14 November 1911.
109 Chamberlain, *Politics from Inside*, p. 384.
110 Transcript of shorthand account of proceedings of Unionist MPs held at the Carlton Club, 13 November 1911, to elect leader of the party in the House of Commons. Long Papers, 947/451.

since 1876, when Sir Stafford Northcote replaced Disraeli, who had been elevated to the peerage as Lord Beaconsfield, as leader in the Commons – not a happy precedent since Northcote had proved ineffective. Although Bonar Law was not leader of the whole party but leader in the Commons, it was generally assumed that he rather than the leader in the Lords would be Prime Minister should the Unionists regain power. A Prime Minister in the Lords would be unlikely to be acceptable following the Parliament Act, a judgement confirmed by George V when, in 1923, he appointed Baldwin rather than Lord Curzon as Prime Minister. Bonar Law was to remain Conservative leader, with just one short interval between 1921 and 1922, for over eleven years until struck down by throat cancer as Prime Minister in April 1923. Of twentieth-century leaders, only Baldwin, Churchill and Margaret Thatcher have led the party for a longer period.

Bonar Law might well not have won a contested election, but there are grounds for believing that he was the right leader for the Conservatives at that particular time in their history. 'The fools have stumbled on the right man by accident,' was Lloyd George's verdict.[111] Lloyd George rather liked Bonar Law, writing to him shortly after he had become leader, 'Had the Unionist party always shown the same wisdom in their decisions, I should not have been writing this letter in the Chancellor of the Exchequer's room in the House of Commons.'[112] The biographer of Bonar Law has commented, with some justice, that 'the decision to make Bonar Law leader of the Conservative Party was reached in a strange and tortuous manner, but it probably saved the unity of the party in a way in which no other choice could have done'.[113]

Bonar Law (1858–1923) was an unusual leader, lacking both the landed and Anglican background of most Conservatives. He had been born in Canada, the son of a Presbyterian minister whose family came from Ulster, but he had been brought up in Glasgow from the age of twelve. He did not attend university but joined the iron merchants firm of his mother's family, where he acquired a detailed knowledge of commerce and trade. He had first entered the Commons in 1900 as MP for Glasgow Blackfriars. Like Chamberlain and Lloyd George, he was self-made, but unlike Lloyd George, he had not known poverty and had indeed inherited money from his parents. A widower, he was, like Joseph Chamberlain, his political hero, 'entirely remote from the sentiment and experience of traditional Toryism … He is neither of the land nor of the aristocracy … He is not a Churchman and he is

111 John Ramsden, *The Age of Balfour and Baldwin, 1902–1940*, Longman, 1978, p. 91.
112 Bentley B. Gilbert, *David Lloyd George: A Political Life*, Batsford, 1992, vol. 2, p. 27.
113 Robert Blake, *The Unknown Prime Minister: The Life and Times of Andrew Bonar Law, 1858–1923*, Eyre & Spottiswoode, 1955, p. 85.

a lifelong abstainer. He is more divorced from the old spirit of his party even than Disraeli.'[114] Like Chamberlain and Lloyd George, he was a thoroughly professional politician, a pugnacious fighter, not a man regarding politics as a pleasant pastime between intervals of managing his estates. His modest demeanour led many to underestimate him. He once told the press, 'You make a great mistake about me. You think I am a modest man with no ambition. I am really very ambitious.'[115] Indeed, he had been 'affronted at not being made a cabinet minister in 1903, he who only entered parliament in 1900!'[116]

Unlike Lloyd George, Bonar Law was solitary rather than gregarious, with few worldly interests. Lloyd George once asked him what he enjoyed most in life – music, pictures, women, theatre, politics? Bonar Law gave him a 'sweet sad smile and, after a pause said, I rather like a game of bridge'.[117] He was also proficient at chess. But he had no interest in the aristocratic pursuits of hunting and shooting, country house parties or society. He disliked also what he regarded as the chore of entertaining which fell to Unionist leaders; nor did his guests much enjoy being entertained by a teetotaller, totally uninterested in good food, the arts and music. He was not in the least clubbable. His home at Pembroke Lodge in what Balfour called 'the wilds of Kensington' was thought by more snobbish Conservatives to be on the wrong side of the park, and the atmosphere there was 'wan, cheerless, dejected'.[118] The snobs were also appalled that, since Bonar Law had no catering staff, he had to use outside caterers for shadow Cabinet dinners. At one dinner, so a colleague commented,

> the faces of some of my more aristocratic colleagues, and their faint disgust with the food and the Derry and Tom's furnishings, were a sheer delight to my soul and I was simply fascinated by the only 'object d'art' to be seen in the whole house – a cast-iron bust on the sideboard of Robert Burns, with the ridge from the join of the mould vertically bisecting his forehead and nose.[119]

But Bonar Law had many virtues. He was unfailingly loyal and helpful to his colleagues, easy to deal with, modest and far more approachable than Balfour or Salisbury. Although a keen tariff reformer, he had not, by contrast with Austen Chamberlain and Long, alienated any influential section

114 Gardiner, *Pillars of Society*, pp. 76–7.
115 Chamberlain, *Down the Years*, p. 225.
116 Vincent, ed., *Crawford Papers*, p. 102.
117 Davies, *We, the Nation*, p. 84.
118 Adams, *Balfour*, p. 264; Vincent, ed., *Crawford Papers*, p. 248.
119 Alan Clark, *A Good Innings: The Private Papers of Viscount Lee of Fareham*, John Murray, 1974, p. 120.

of the party. He had indeed won much popularity amongst Unionists by abandoning his safe seat at Dulwich in 1906 for Manchester North West for the December 1910 election so that he could take the Chamberlain doctrine to free trade Lancashire. Narrowly defeated there, he had been elected for Bootle in a by-election in March 1911.

Bonar Law's main weakness was lack of experience in government. But he was a powerful debater, direct and fluent, whose speeches had considerable impact and logical power. Whereas Balfour had used the rapier, Bonar Law preferred to employ the bludgeon, which he could wield somewhat crudely. By November 1912, he was regarded by the Conservative Chief Whip as 'a straight, simple and direct person, transparently honest and sincere; and one behind whom the whole party can rally'.[120] He restored Unionist confidence and also its unity. 'No leader', the Chief Whip wrote to a colleague on 3 January 1913, 'on either side of the House has ever succeeded in killing rivalries or animosity as he has done.'[121] He had the prime quality which the beleaguered and disheartened Unionists so needed in place of their previously flaccid leadership: aggression, 'the chief asset of a leader at this moment – attack in all directions'.[122] This suited a party tired of equivocation and evasion. 'We are', the Chief Whip wrote to a correspondent in December 1911, 'for the first time since 1906 attacking with the conviction of impending success.' By 1912, the Chief Whip could highlight the contrast: 'Whereas Balfour was adored in parliament, he failed to strike the imagination or to fire the zeal of our supporters outside and in the constituencies. With Bonar Law the exact reverse will hold good.'[123] Balfour had seemed not to have any firm views, any 'settled convictions'. One journalist contrasted the Balfour and Bonar Law regimes, perhaps unfairly. Balfour was 'all reflection and no action. The new Toryism is all action and no reflection.'[124] There could certainly be no doubt about Bonar Law's 'settled convictions', convictions which were un-compromising and firmly maintained – the preservation of Ulster within the United Kingdom (his father had been born and died in Ulster) and tariff reform. In 1921, he was to state in a letter to a friend, 'You who knew me so well at one time know that before the war there were only two things which I really cared for as matters of conviction – the rest was mainly a game. One of these was tariff reform; the other was fair play for Ulster.'[125] He was, the Chief Whip thought, 'interested in subjects, not in politics'.[126] But unlike

---

120 Vincent, ed., *Crawford Papers*, p. 284.
121 Ibid., p. 296.
122 Ibid., p. 223.
123 Ibid., pp. 258, 269.
124 Gardiner, *Pillars of Society*, p. 57.
125 Blake, *The Unknown Prime Minister*, p. 433.
126 Vincent, ed., *Crawford Papers*, p. 238.

Joseph Chamberlain, his political hero, Bonar Law had little interest or indeed knowledge of issues other than Ulster or tariff reform – little interest, in particular, in social reform or in economic questions; and he had almost as little understanding of the problems of the mass of the people as Salisbury and Balfour.

Bonar Law was soon to be plunged into the Home Rule maelstrom. But before that, he had to face the fact that many Unionists believed food taxes to be a vote loser, particularly at a time when the cost of living was rising. The danger was that adherence to food taxes could, by depriving the Unionists of support, imperil the Union with Ireland. Privately, Bonar Law believed that food taxes should be dropped, but he feared to say so in public lest he incur the wrath of Chamberlain.[127] Balfour's December 1910 election pledge of a referendum had given Unionists room for manoeuvre. But Austen Chamberlain insisted that the pledge was for one election only and, on 8 November 1911, the day of Balfour's resignation as party leader, he repudiated it. In January 1912, Bonar Law pledged to Austen that he would not abandon food taxes, 'till I have your assent', a pledge he was to break.[128] In spring 1912, the shadow Cabinet agreed privately to repudiate the referendum pledge, despite the protests of Lord Salisbury that if food taxes 'made possible the destruction of the constitution, the prostitution of the Prerogative, the Repeal of the Union, and the Disendowment of the Welsh Church, it will probably rank as the most costly policy in history'.[129] But Bonar Law had reiterated his support for tariff reform even if it meant food taxes and declared that, were the party to decide otherwise, 'I should be quite willing to stand aside', but 'I could not possibly … continue as leader'.[130] And Canada's Prime Minister had insisted that food taxes were essential to imperial preference and that if they were abandoned, he would regard it 'as a serious blow to the whole cause of imperial consolidation'.[131] Indeed, if Britain were to jib at food taxes, Canada might make preferential arrangements with countries outside the empire. The shadow Cabinet's decision was not publicly announced until 14 November 1912, so that it should not be seen as a repudiation of Balfour. But once it was announced, it incited strenuous opposition, especially in the north of England and Scotland, from those who feared that food taxes would be a vote loser. Lancashire, where free trade sentiment was strong, seemed in open revolt – Unionists there were threatening to pass a resolution that food taxes be delayed until a second election. *The Times* and the *Daily Mail*

127 Amery, *Chamberlain*, vol. 6, p. 958.
128 Ibid., p. 978.
129 Dutton, *His Majesty's Loyal Opposition*, p. 184.
130 Blake, *The Unknown Prime Minister*, p. 109.
131 Ibid., p. 111.

began a campaign against 'stomach taxes'. By the end of the year, Bonar Law complained that 'the strongest Tariff reformers are all coming to me saying it is impossible to fight with food taxes ... I am convinced that it must in the end be modified. I doubt whether this modification will be possible under my leadership.'[132] In January 1913, after leading the party for just fourteen months, Bonar Law decided with Lansdowne to call a party meeting and offer their resignations. Carson, however, drew up a memorial which the vast majority of Unionist MPs were to sign begging Bonar Law to remain. That month, all but eight Unionist backbenchers signed a memorandum which came to be known as the 'Bonar Law Memorial', a compromise, insisting that the party would not introduce preferential food taxes until after consultation with the dominions and after it had won a second general election, and Bonar Law remained on these terms. Oddly, the misjudgement served to strengthen Bonar Law's position, not weaken it. For it seemed that he had become indispensable as leader. Austen would have split the party, while Long was temperamentally unsuited to leadership. But for Austen, the Bonar Law Memorial ended hope of tariff reform. 'I have done my best,' Austen wrote to his stepmother, Joe's third wife, 'but the game is up. We are beaten and the cause for which Father sacrificed more than life itself is abandoned! It is a bitter confession to make and it is difficult for me to speak calmly about it.'[133] Austen wrote to Bonar Law pledging loyalty but declaring that his 'dearest political hopes and personal affections have received from fate a cruel blow'.[134] Bonar Law replied, recognising:

> You cannot fail to look upon it as if it were going back upon your father's life-work, and though I believe that the tendency towards closer union on the part of the Colonies is the direct result of what he did, yet that cannot at the moment soften the blow much.[135]

But Bonar Law had both broken the power of the Birmingham machine and preserved party unity.

---

132 Ibid., pp. 114–15.
133 Amery, *Chamberlain*, vol, 5, p. 981
134 Blake, *The Unknown Prime Minister*, pp. 108–9, 111, 115, 117.
135 R. J. Q. Adams, *Bonar Law* [1999], Thistle, 2013, p. 104.

CHAPTER 16

THE NATIONAL INSURANCE ACT

THE NEED FOR NATIONAL INSURANCE

The Liberals hoped that removing the road block of the House of Lords would clear the way for a new era. The Liberals now widened their social reform agenda into new areas – protection against ill health and unemployment, and then land reform.

The Liberals' major legislative achievement was the National Insurance Act, which received royal assent in December 1911. The Act has been characterised by a modern historian as 'perhaps the single most important measure of social reform ever to be carried by Parliament'.[1] It was indeed to be a landmark measure. On 4 April 1911, shortly before it was introduced into the Commons, Churchill, who had been promoted to the Home Office in February 1910, wrote to the king to state his belief that it was 'far more important to the prosperity, contentment & security of Your Majesty's Kingdom than any other measure of our times. Henceforward everyone will have a "stake in the country" in the remarkable rewards wh. Scientific organisation & the strange power of averages can confer on thrift.'[2] And at first, the Bill appeared to enjoy Unionist support. The 'titanic proposals for National Insurance have unquestionably introduced a new & healing force into the political situation,' Churchill reported to the king on 6 May.

> There is no doubt that the general character of the scheme is a true and sincere expression of the principles & feelings which Mr Disraeli & other Tory Democratic leaders inculcated. The two great parties hold each other in such effective equipoise on most occasions, that when they appear ready to join forces, a feeling of enthusiasm & of irresistible strength is created. Such an emotion pervades political circles at the present time and cannot fail to mitigate the fierceness of other disputations.[3]

---

1 Pelling, *Winston Churchill*, p. 126.
2 Churchill, *Companion*, vol. 2, part 2, p. 1,064.
3 Ibid., p. 1,076.

But the seeming consensus was not to last.

National Health Insurance was a response to growing concerns for the health of the nation. Macnamara, the teachers' representative in the Commons, had argued in 1904 that a policy to safeguard the nation's health would not be 'rank socialism, in reality it is first class imperialism',[4] In 1909, Sir Robert Morant, progenitor of the 1902 Education Act, declared that the British were 'in competition with other races and if we neglected the health of the race ... we should lose in the racial competition of the world'. The surgeon Sir William Job Collins, Liberal MP for St Pancras, insisted in 1909 that 'the "*health of nations*" no less than the "*wealth of nations*" now occupies the political stage'.[5] Both the majority and minority reports of the Poor Law Commission, which reported in 1909, drew attention to the inadequacy of medical provision for the poor. Humanitarians as well as many in the professional classes had come to acknowledge that some form of public medical service was needed in place of Poor Law provision. The British Medical Association, although it was to cause Lloyd George considerable difficulties later on, nevertheless proclaimed that 'the National Insurance Bill is in its conception one of the greatest attempts at social legislation which the present generation has known'. 'With the general intentions of the Bill the medical profession will be in full accord ... The Bill is a call to a great social duty.'[6]

The Bill was to deviate from the recommendations of the Royal Commission on the Poor Law. For both the majority and minority reports had recommended the abolition of Poor Law machinery, established as long ago as 1834, and for the ad hoc boards of guardians to be assimilated into local government, just as the school boards had been assimilated into local government in the 1902 Education Act. But the Liberals followed a different path. They retained the system but sought by attacking the causes of pauperism piecemeal, to reduce the numbers of those having to resort to Poor Law provision. National insurance would obviate the need to resort to the workhouse. Lloyd George argued that it was 'the logical and inevitable outcome of the Old Age Pensions Act'. In October 1909, he told an audience at Swansea that, with provision having been made for the aged, 'we are still confronted with the more gigantic task of dealing with the rest – the sick, the infirm, the unemployed, the widows and orphans'.[7] But the cost of non-contributory pensions had proved a drain on the nation's finances. There was a further

---

4   Gilbert, *National Insurance*, pp. 148, 124.

5   Roger Cooter, 'The Rise and Decline of the Medical Member: Doctors and Parliament in Edwardian and Interwar Britain', *Bulletin of the History of Medicine*, 2004, pp. 67–8.

6   Jeanne Brand, *Doctors and the State: The British Medical Profession and Government Action in Public Health, 1870–1912*, Johns Hopkins Press, 1965, p. 463; *British Medical Journal*, 13 May 1911, pp. 1,135, 1,136.

7   Gilbert, *National Insurance*, pp. 291–2, 294.

contrast in that pensions for many younger people would provide a distant and perhaps doubtful benefit, while, with health and unemployment, the need was to protect against more immediate ills, so that the rewards of insurance would be reaped much earlier. So in its national insurance legislation, the government departed from the recommendation of the minority report of the Poor Law Commission that benefits should be non-contributory and financed out of taxation.

The legislation did not come about in the usual way through the laborious procedure of a Royal Commission or departmental inquiry but through initiatives by Churchill and Lloyd George, who had visited Germany in 1908 and been impressed by Bismarck's health insurance scheme. 'I hope our competition with Germany will not be in armaments alone,' Lloyd George had argued in his speech introducing his People's Budget.[8] He sent one of his officials to examine the German scheme and then summoned him to Nice, where he was on holiday. The two of them went together with other officials and junior ministers to the pier. Lloyd George bought drinks all round, and said to the official, 'Now tell us all about it.' But in the event, Lloyd George's proposals turned out to be quite dissimilar to the German system, which had been 'imposed upon an almost clear field', even though in fact health insurance had existed before Bismarck, who extended rather than created it.[9] The British system, by contrast, needed to be 'superimposed upon a great variety of existing organisations', which were already making some sort of provision for sickness and unemployment – friendly societies, insurance companies and trade unions.[10] They had been happy to support non-contributory old-age pensions benefiting those who could not afford to contribute to their funds, but National Health Insurance would interfere with the insurance work of the companies.[11] Enactment of compulsory insurance could only be done by working with and indeed placating the voluntary organisations.

The National Insurance Act was in two parts, the first dealing with sickness, the second with unemployment. The first section was the inspiration of Lloyd George, the second of Churchill. The complexities of developing a scheme for health insurance, however, meant that, by the time the Bill was introduced into Parliament, Churchill was no longer at the Board of Trade, where he had prepared the provisions dealing with unemployment, and unemployment insurance was steered through the Commons by his

8   House of Commons Debates, 29 April 1909, vol. 4, col. 487.
9   George Steinmetz, *Regulating the Social: The Welfare State and Local Politics in Imperial Germany*, Princeton University Press, 1993. I owe this reference to Noel Whiteside.
10 Braithwaite, *Lloyd George's Ambulance Wagon*, p. 82.
11 I owe this point to Pat Thane.

successor, Sydney Buxton. In consequence, Churchill never quite received the credit to which he was entitled. Indeed, Lloyd George sometimes implied that he alone was responsible for both halves of the Bill, rather than just the health insurance component. Unemployment insurance was, however, the more novel of the two parts. For, while there was already a scheme of health insurance in Germany, the unemployment scheme was the first in the world, apart from a brief experiment in the Swiss cantons of Berne and St Gallen, the latter of which had become bankrupt after two years. In Britain, there had been unemployment insurance schemes run by shipbuilding and engineering unions, but there were no other pre-existing models and no precedents. Both the majority and the minority on the Royal Commission on the Poor Laws had believed that compulsory unemployment insurance was neither desirable nor practicable. But purely voluntary insurance seemed equally impractical since it might attract only the bad risks. Compulsory and contributory insurance, therefore, seemed the only practical option.

INSURANCE AGAINST ILL HEALTH AND UNEMPLOYMENT

In presenting the Bill to the Commons on 4 May 1911, Lloyd George emphasised part one, health insurance. He pointed out that both the majority and minority on the Poor Law Commission had regarded sickness as a prime cause of pauperism. Indeed, around 30 per cent of pauperism was held to be due to sickness. Admittedly, many in the working class had made efforts to insure themselves – against death to provide for funeral expenses and benefits for their dependants, and against sickness and unemployment. It appears that around 38 per cent of males over the age of twenty were members of friendly societies, and there were in 1911 around 41 million policies of death insurance – indeed there was 'hardly a household in this country where there is not a policy of insurance against death'.[12] But fewer were insured against sickness – only around 6 million with friendly societies, insurance companies or trade unions.[13] But not all insurance, Lloyd George went on, was 'adequate, and a good deal of it' was 'defective'. Trade unions, for example, provided benefits for their members when sick but not medical aid, as insurance companies and friendly societies did. In addition to the voluntary organisations, there was some minimal public funding of healthcare. And local authorities provided statutory services in areas such as maternity, infant welfare and the treatment of infectious diseases.

---

12 Johnson, *Saving and Spending*, p. 57; House of Commons Debates, 4 May 1911, vol. 25, cols 610, 611.
13 Noel Whiteside, 'Transforming the Unemployed: Trade Union Benefits and the Advent of State Policy', in Keith Layhourn and John Shepherd, eds, *Labour and Working-Class Lives: Essays to Celebrate the Life and Work of Chris Wrigley*, Manchester University Press, 2017, p. 71.

With unemployment, the situation was even worse than with health and fewer than one in ten of the industrial working class were insured against it. Unemployment insurance was provided mainly by trade unions representing skilled workers in precarious trades such as engineering, shipbuilding and metallurgy, where there was much seasonal unemployment. But even in the precarious trades, Lloyd George declared, 'I do not believe more than one-third or one-quarter of the people engaged in them are insured against unemployment.'[14]

Widespread death insurance showed that working people were aware of the need for insurance. But many found that they could not afford regular premiums in addition to death insurance to insure against ill health and unemployment. There were, apparently, around 250,000 lapses in the payment of premiums every year. The order of priorities for the vast majority of the industrial population was death, sickness and then unemployment; and only the better off amongst the working class, perhaps the least susceptible to unemployment, were able to insure against it. Current arrangements, therefore, were perverse since those most in need of insurance were those least likely to be insured. A national insurance scheme, by contrast, would guarantee a wide range of benefits and cost the worker less than membership of a friendly society.

In Germany, contributions and benefits were graduated in proportion to income, but this meant that the poorer contributors who most needed benefits received least and were often forced to turn to parish relief. Lloyd George proposed instead that there be low flat rate contributions which all beyond a certain income level could afford, together with flat rate benefits. But in consequence, the benefits would be comparatively low.

Health insurance was to be compulsory for those employed, aged between sixteen and seventy, and earning less than £160 a year, the level at which income tax began to be paid. At that time, only around 12 per cent of the adult population had incomes above this level, and no manual workers paid income tax.[15] In addition, all those employed in manual labour were to be compulsorily insured whatever their remuneration. The middle classes who could afford to pay medical fees were, Lloyd George believed, not in need of state insurance. Those who could afford to pay should continue to pay. The usual contribution to a friendly society was 6d or 9d a week. Under the Lloyd George scheme, the compulsory contribution for men was to be just 4d a week, the cost, Lloyd George declared, of two pints of cheap beer a week or an ounce of tobacco, and for women 3d. Those earning less than 15s

14 House of Commons Debates, 4 May 1911, vol. 25, col. 611.
15 Richard M. Titmuss, 'Health', in Ginsberg, ed., *Law and Opinion in England in the Twentieth Century*, p. 307.

a week were to pay a lower contribution and those earning 10s a week or less would pay nothing at all, the difference being paid for by the employer benefiting from cheap labour. The employer was to pay 3d and the state would contribute 2d. Lloyd George is said to have declared that the scheme would provide 9d for 4d, and '9d for 4d' was to be the slogan used to promote it.

There was in addition to be a voluntary element for certain categories who did not fall under the compulsory provisions of the legislation – primarily the self-employed (small tradesmen, small shopkeepers and the like) – provided their earnings did not exceed £160 per year. Those under forty-five would pay the employer's contribution in addition to their own, i.e. 7d for men and 6d for women. Voluntary contributions would also be available for married women who had previously contributed but were no longer working.

The legislation was expected to cover, in total, one-third of the population. Excluded from it were those working for the crown, local authorities and other statutory bodies who were able to participate in already existing schemes providing benefits at least as favourable as those provided for by the Bill. And the legislation would not, at the request of the Irish Party, apply in its entirety to Ireland, where there was already an extensive system of Poor Law dispensaries providing medical relief. In Ireland, contributions by employer and employee would, in consequence, be lower than in the rest of the United Kingdom.

Although the national insurance system was to be compulsory, the state would nevertheless be entering a domain which was already partially occupied by voluntary organisations. Liberals were anxious not to undermine them, and indeed Liberal philosophy gave them an important role in maintaining a plural society. But in any case, it would hardly have been possible to ignore them. Under the government's proposals, contributions were to be paid and benefits provided, not by the state, as in Germany, but by so-called approved societies. Contributors would be required either to join such a society or to become so-called deposit contributors, paying their contributions to the Post Office. In the first draft of the Bill, recognition as approved societies was to be granted only to friendly societies, but it was soon apparent that trade unions and insurance companies would also have to be brought in.[16] An approved society was required not to make profits from contributions but to use its funds, after expenses had been deducted, for their benefit. A vital public service should not be commercialised. This meant that insurance companies had to establish a separate section of their business consisting of insured persons in order to qualify as approved societies. The societies were also required to be under the control of their members. The Act, therefore,

16 Social Insurance and Allied Services (Beveridge Report) 1942, Cmd 6404, para. 48.

devolved much of the administration neither to a minister responsible to Parliament nor to local authorities but to voluntary bodies answerable to the insured.

The benefits under the Act were divided into two groups. There were, first, medical benefits to be administered by local insurance committees established for the purpose. These benefits consisted of medical treatment by a general practitioner and any necessary medicines or appliances, as well as a sanatorium benefit primarily for tuberculosis patients. Then there were, secondly, cash benefits for the sick to be administered by the approved societies – ten shillings a week for twenty-six weeks for men, seven shillings and six pence a week for women – but the benefit was in no case to be more than two-thirds of wages to discourage malingering. And sickness benefit would not be paid after the age of seventy, since that was the pensionable age. If sickness persisted after twenty-six weeks, the claimant would move on to a disablement benefit of five shillings a week for men and women alike which would continue for the duration of the illness. There was also a maternity benefit of thirty shillings for the wives of insured contributors, so long as contributions had been paid for forty-two weeks, and also for unmarried insured women. Part of the purpose of this benefit was to reduce the high infant mortality rate by enabling poorer women to obtain skilled care in childbirth. This was a particular concern for the government in the light of the falling birth rate from the 1870s. The maternity benefit was the only benefit to be paid to a non-contributor. If a wife was also insured in her own right, she was entitled to a further thirty shillings. In the no doubt unusual situation of an insured woman whose husband was not insured, she would still be paid the doubled benefit of sixty shillings. But since most married women did not work, they were not an insurable risk and were not covered by the Act. The Act did not provide for any statutory benefits to dependants (other than the maternity allowance), nor funeral benefits, since the insurance companies would not accept benefits interfering with their own commercial business. For the same reason, widows and orphans' pensions did not come about until 1925. Lloyd George had also hoped to include disability benefits for those who became physically unfit for work before the age of seventy, as in the German scheme, but the Treasury indicated that this would require higher contributions than many could afford.[17] In addition to the statutory minimum benefits, approved societies could provide additional benefits such as higher sickness allowances, medical treatment for dependants, dental and ophthalmic treatment and convalescent homes. These additional benefits

---

17   I owe this point to Pat Thane.

provided the societies with an incentive to attract more members and an incentive for those insured to 'shop around'.

Those unable to obtain membership of a society, either because they were poor insurance risks or because they had not bothered to do so, were required to make their contributions to the Post Office. Without this element, the scheme would have been transformed into a voluntary one. Deposit contributors were not, strictly speaking, being insured in the sense that they would become members of a common fund which would make provision for illness. Instead, they would be treated on a strictly cash basis and entitled only to benefits based on what they had contributed. The treatment of deposit contributors was deliberately intended to be worse than that of members of approved societies. All the same, deposit contributors were being generously treated since their contribution was to be enlarged by contributions from the employer and the state. But those who were poor insurance risks – casual labourers, those in precarious employment and the physically unfit – would be more likely to suffer from sickness or disabilities than those who were better risks. In the event, however, only a small minority were to take up the deposit option. By the mid-1920s, there were just 32,000 deposit contributors out of around 15 million who were insured.[18]

Opposition to health insurance came less from MPs – the official opposition welcomed the Bill – than from vested interests affected by it, in particular the great insurance companies and the doctors. This opposition was based less on the principles of the legislation than on the administrative arrangements and the financial provisions. An official preparing the Bill told a friend:

> It was just as if we had poked a stick into a wasp's nest or stirred up a lot of snakes – so many private interests were trying to sting the new proposals to death. The history of the bill is how they were bought off, conciliated and in very few instances over-ruled.[19]

The friendly societies thought, quite mistakenly, that they would be extinguished, while the insurance companies believed that their profits would suffer.

But the main opposition came from the British Medical Association, which now appeared to be rowing back from its previous welcome for a state-guaranteed system, declaring in a summary of the issue for the profession that doctors

---

18 Royal Commission on National Health Insurance, Cmd 2596, 1926, para. 13.
19 Braithwaite, *Lloyd George's Ambulance Wagon*, p. 161.

prefer the independence of private practice with its risks to the security of an official service with its constraints. They believe firmly that the treatment of disease, at all events by the ordinary medical attendant of a patient, will be carried out with most benefit to the patient and most satisfaction to all parties on the lines of private practice. This conviction springs mainly from recognition of the peculiarly personal character of the relation of doctor and patient.[20]

The BMA's qualms may not have reflected the feelings of the medical profession as a whole. 'It is difficult', Lloyd George believed, 'to ascertain the true feelings of doctors as a whole on any proposals affecting them, since a Deputation of Doctors is always a Deputation of swell Doctors; it is impossible to get a Deputation of poor Doctors or of slum Doctors.'[21] And indeed many of the most determined opponents of the Bill were consultants and specialists who would not themselves be involved in the scheme. Aneurin Bevan was to have the same experience in the 1940s. Nevertheless, Lloyd George used great negotiating skills to win the BMA round, even though at one time it seemed as if the doctors would refuse all cooperation and that there would be strike action. Lloyd George promised the BMA that the patient would retain free choice of doctor and that the medical profession would be represented in the administration of medical benefits. Those doctors – in the event, the vast majority – willing to participate in the scheme would be put onto a panel by local insurance committees. Patients would then select the doctor of their choice from this panel. Doctors would have the assurance of a statutorily determined fee far higher than many had been earning in the past. Before the Act, a doctor, when consulted by an obviously sick patient, would treat them, rather than allowing them to suffer, even though the doctor might have a shrewd idea that the patient might not be able to afford to pay more than a few pennies a week, or in some cases, nothing at all. The doctor would be out of pocket as a result. In consequence, the Webbs believed, the medical profession stood 'in a position of grave danger' since 'a very large proportion of its members earn incomes which can only be described as scandalously inadequate'.[22] The system, if such it can be called, degraded the medical profession and was not conducive to the effective practice of medicine. So while some better-off doctors would lose income through a decline in private practice, those practising in poorer areas found themselves both better off and financially more secure.

---

20 *British Medical Journal*, 15 July 1911, p. 378.
21 Gilbert, *National Insurance*, p. 363.
22 Beatrice and Sidney Webb, *The State and the Doctor*, cited in Titmuss, 'Health', pp. 310–11.

The second part of the National Insurance Bill dealt with unemployment insurance. Before 1911, the only provision for the unemployed apart from the Poor Law and the very limited and inadequate provision by local authorities under the 1886 Circular and 1905 Unemployed Workmen Act was in the form of trade union unemployment benefits. By 1908, 66 per cent of all union members, though only 12 per cent of the adult male workforce, were eligible for such benefits. Provision was generally confined to skilled workers – only 5 per cent in labourers' unions were provided for – and even for them the benefits were often insufficient.[23] Contributions were normally of the order of 3d or less. Benefits were rarely more than ten shillings a week and often less, and then only for a limited period not normally exceeding twenty-six weeks in the year. Beveridge believed that the benefit was too small to provide subsistence and had 'to be supplemented ... by the earnings of wife and children, by private saving, by assistance from fellow-workmen and neighbours ... and in other ways'.[24] The benefit was intended to tide trade unionists over short periods of unemployment. After that, the unemployed would have to rely on savings or the Poor Law, but boards of guardians in England and Wales were unwilling to provide outdoor relief for the able-bodied, and there was no provision for such relief at all in Scotland.

The unemployment provisions of the National Insurance Bill were regarded as experimental – 'partial' and 'tentative' in Churchill's words – and 'the counterpart and companion of the national system of Labour Exchanges'.[25] The two were complementary. Labour exchanges tested the willingness of the applicant to work, while insurance would provide an incentive for men to sign on regularly at the labour exchange and find work since otherwise they would exhaust their benefits.

Unemployment insurance would, as with health insurance, have to be compulsory so that bad risks would not predominate, and it would also be contributory, with contributions by employer and employee and a state subvention. If, in addition, unemployment insurance provided for a maximum amount of benefit in relation to contributions, there would be a disincentive to malingering. But by contrast with health, unemployment insurance would not be universal for those earning less than a certain income. It would be confined to particular trades in which there was high, chronic and seasonal but also predictable unemployment. It seemed less practicable to provide insurance for those working in casual trades where unemployment was not

23 George R. Boyer, 'The Evolution of Unemployment Relief in Great Britain', *Journal of Interdisciplinary History*, 2004, p. 414.
24 William Beveridge, *Unemployment: A Problem of Industry* [1909], Longmans, Green & Co., 1930, p. 225.
25 Cabinet Memorandum: Unemployment. Insurance: Labour Exchanges, 11 December 1908, CAB 37/96/159 1908, p. 1; Cabinet Memorandum: CAB 37/99/69, 17 April 1909, p. 1.

so predictable; while in industries such as coal mining and cotton spinning, men tended to be put on short time rather than being laid off during periods of trade depression.

The scale of benefit was deliberately made low so as not to discourage thrift. As with the pension, insurance could, in Churchill's words, 'be only a foundation and an encouragement' but nevertheless sufficient 'in the majority of cases' to 'enable the workman to tide over a temporary depression without selling up his home or losing his status'. And 'it will give him the necessary time to seek new employment if it is evident that the local stringency will be prolonged or perhaps permanent. And thus ... the stabilities of labour will have been conserved and fortified.'[26]

Unemployment insurance would apply to around one-third of males in the industrial population – around 2.25 million employed in the precarious trades of building, construction, shipbuilding and mechanical engineering. Of the remaining two-thirds of industrial workers,

> nearly half are engaged in the railway service or the mercantile marine, or in the textile, mining or other industries, which adopt short time or 'missing shifts' systems in place of discharging workmen. Consequently the scheme may be said, broadly speaking, to cover half the whole field of unemployment and that half the worse half.[27]

But there was also to be a state subsidy for trade unions in trades other than the precarious ones where national insurance did not apply. The legislation made provision for the extension of compulsory insurance to other trades by ministerial order, and in 1914 it was in fact to be so extended. But the scheme did not include dock and wharf labour, where casual unemployment was very prevalent. In 1913, Churchill argued that insurance alone could do 'comparatively little for such occupations. The evils of casual unemployment required other measures of a preventive and curative character.'[28]

Workers and employers in the insured trades would each be required to contribute 2.5d while the state would contribute 1.66d. The employer, however, would be given an abatement were he to pay annually rather than weekly, in which case he would pay just 15s rather than 21s 8d, and this would be an inducement 'to give regular employment; it is a discouragement of casual labour; it is a reward to the employer who keeps his workman for a

---

26 CAB 37/96, pp. 1–3 *passim*.
27 CAB 37/99, p. 2.
28 Cabinet Memorandum: National Insurance Act (Part II) Unemployment, November 1913, CAB 37/117 1913, p. 3.

whole year'. Trade unions would be reimbursed to the extent of three-quarters of the benefits that they were providing.

The rate of benefit would be seven shillings a week after six months' contributions, but there would be no payment of benefit for the first week of unemployment, and no one could draw more than one week's benefit for five weeks of contribution, nor more than fifteen weeks' benefit in any twelve-month period, 'so that the real loafer soon drops out'. These provisions insured against the malingerer or the fraudulent applicant who would simply be using up their contributions. There was then no need to apply a character test, as some wished, as to whether unemployment might be due to personal failings such as laziness, drunkenness or misconduct of some sort; and in any case, Churchill did not 'like mixing up moralities and mathematics'. His concern was 'with the evil, not with the causes, with the fact of unemployment, not with the character of the unemployed'.[29] The fund was so constituted on the basis of what Churchill had, somewhat grandiloquently, called 'the magic of averages to the aid of the millions' so that it would be in balance when unemployment averaged 8.46 per cent.[30] The rate of unemployment had been well below this level in recent years, except possibly in 1908 and 1909.[31]

CONSEQUENCES OF THE ACT

The Bill proposed for the first time a new relationship between the state and the individual. For the first time, the state would enter 'the life of the ordinary adult male able-bodied workman'.[32] It received a warm welcome on its appearance in the Commons. 'Confound Ll George', Austen Chamberlain wrote to his stepmother on 9 May 1911, 'he has strengthened the Government again. His Sickness scheme is a good one and he is on right lines this time. I must say I envy him the opportunity and I must admit that he has made good use of it.'[33] 'You know', Lloyd George told an official drawing up the legislation, 'if this bill goes through we shall do more to relieve human suffering than any measure which has passed in England for hundreds of years.'[34] The Bill received royal assent on 16 December 1911 and came into operation on 18 July 1912. The medical benefits were to become available six months later. Whether they would in fact become available was, however, in

29 Gilbert, *National Insurance*, p. 272.
30 House of Commons Debates, 25 May 1911, vol. 26, col. 509.
31 George R. Boyer and Timothy J. Hatton, 'New Estimates of British Unemployment 1870–1913', *Journal of Economic History*, 2002, especially pp. 662 and 667.
32 Gilbert, *National Insurance*, p. 287.
33 Chamberlain, *Politics from Inside*, p. 338.
34 Braithwaite, *Lloyd George's Ambulance Wagon*, p. 152.

doubt. For the BMA was insisting on an 8/6d capitation fee and threatened not to accept work under the scheme unless they got it, claiming the support of around 27,000 doctors – 80 per cent of their members. A report in July 1912 showed that in six representative towns, 265 GPs were earning just 4/-5d per person per year.[35] The government was offering 6/-. In July 1912, the BMA broke off negotiations and they were not reopened until November. The government then compromised by proposing a fee of 7/-6d. Nevertheless, in December 1912, BMA delegates renewed by four to one their call to doctors to refuse to serve. But it was found, nevertheless, that most doctors, particularly in poorer areas, had already joined the panels being set up under the Act. Indeed, by 15 January 1913 when the medical benefit began, it was apparent that many more than the 15,000 doctors required had in fact applied to join the panels. The threat of a boycott by the medical profession rapidly evaporated, and the medical benefits of the scheme became available on schedule and as planned.[36]

The fundamental principle exemplified by the Act, and one basic to the welfare state, was that the benefit was given as of right in return for weekly premiums, without a means test and, by contrast with the Poor Law, without any penalty or disqualification. In the first year, over 13 million were insured under the health insurance provisions of the Act. This insurance had two aims: to provide a degree of security and to provide effective healthcare. Perhaps the first was more important than the second. In the words of one commentator, 'the evil to be treated was pauperism, not sickness. Sickness was important to the Chancellor only as a cause of pauperism.' The Act was perceived by Lloyd George as 'a social, not a medical measure. The Chancellor's only interest was in supporting the breadwinner during his illness.' The aim 'was, at bottom, to replace lost income, not to cure sickness'.[37] In consequence, families would not suffer when the male breadwinner was unable to work because of illness. But because the benefits were provided at a flat rate, rather than being related to earnings, they were low, otherwise they would be higher than the low-paid employee was earning at work. Therefore, they were hardly enough to guarantee more than a subsistence standard. That was an anomaly from an insurance point of view. 'It would be poor consolation for a man who insures his house against fire, even if his premiums were relatively low, to be told afterwards, that, though his house had been burnt down, he will only get enough out of his insurance to build a hut.'[38] To provide for full

---

35 Report for 1912–13 on the Administration of the National Insurance Act, Part I (Health Insurance), Cd 6907, 1913, para. 508.
36 The story is concisely told in Gilbert, *Lloyd George*, vol. 2, pp. 28–35.
37 Gilbert, *National Insurance*, p. 314.
38 Hermann Levy, *National Health Insurance: A Critical Study*, Cambridge University Press, 1944, p. 70.

compensation would have meant an impossibly large premium. So national insurance would have to be supplemented by voluntary insurance. Those insured could do this by purchasing private policies. Of the 13 million covered by the scheme, nearly three-quarters – 9 million – were already members of mutual aid societies, including 3.4 million who belonged to trade unions.[39] But only those with regular employment and sufficiently high wages could afford the weekly premiums. So 'friendly society membership was the badge of the skilled worker'.[40] Those facing irregular employment, unemployment or low wages benefited less from the legislation. That was unfortunate since, after all, it had been introduced because the old voluntary system had proved inadequate for workers in these categories. By the 1920s, in Scotland, apparently around 75 per cent of those insured who did not have funds of their own needed help from their local parish council.[41]

The Act also did little for the chronic sick or those with disabilities who were unable to work. Medical benefits were restricted almost entirely to treatment by a general practitioner. The benefits did not provide for specialist treatment (with the exception of tuberculosis) or hospital care for the insured, let alone their dependants. Such care was, however, often provided by municipal hospitals, of which there were at that time around 700. These hospitals treated infectious diseases irrespective of means and were usually free. Local authorities also provided maternity and welfare clinics, school medical services, treatment for venereal disease and tuberculosis and institutional care for various infectious diseases and mental health problems. But the extent of these services varied considerably in different parts of the country, being better in the more prosperous areas where local authorities could afford to spend more. The system was, as Aneurin Bevan was to declare in 1946, a patchwork, rather than a truly national service. His National Health Service Act of 1946 would in effect nationalise the hospitals.

Lloyd George was well aware that his scheme was but an interim solution. Speaking in Birmingham on 11 June 1911, he declared, 'I never said this bill was a final solution. I am not putting it forwards as a complete remedy. It is one of a series.' Indeed, he looked forward to a state medical system such as came about under the Attlee government in the 1940s. 'Insurance', he told his private secretary in March 1911,

[is] necessarily [a] temporary expedient. At no distant date hope State will acknowledge a full responsibility in the matter of making provision for

39 David G. Green, 'The Friendly Societies and Adam-Smith Liberalism', in Gladstone, ed., *Before Beveridge*, p. 18.
40 Gilbert, *National Insurance*, p. 167.
41 Royal Commission on National Health Insurance, quoted in Levy, *National Health Insurance*, p. 78.

sickness, breakdown and unemployment. It really does so now, through the Poor Law; but conditions under which this system had hitherto worked have been so harsh and humiliating that working class pride revolts against accepting so degrading and doubtful a boon. Gradually the obligation of the State to find labour or sustenance will be realised and honourably interpreted.[42]

In his 1914 Budget, Lloyd George moved from dealing with the consequences of sickness to preventing it by providing for the first time grants to local authorities for public health equal to 25 per cent of local authority net spending in this area. There were also further grants for the treatment of tuberculosis and for the scientific diagnosis of disease.[43]

The trade unions were sympathetic to the National Insurance Act and hoped by its means to increase their membership. They preferred collective laissez-faire to state socialism. The majority of Labour MPs also supported it, Ramsay MacDonald writing that, 'without some system of premium payment, the whole scheme would degenerate into a national charity of the most vicious kind, which would adversely affect wages and would not help the Socialist spirit'.[44] In addition, MacDonald believed that a non-contributory system would have split the working class. Only the lower paid would have been likely to receive benefits and so their interests would then diverge from the rest of the working class.[45] MacDonald secured a number of amendments to the Bill, including a provision that low-paid workers should be exempt from contributions. But the Independent Labour Party conference joined with the Fabians in opposing what Beatrice Webb called 'Lloyd George's rotten scheme of sickness insurance', and some Labour MPs, led by Keir Hardie, Snowden and Lansbury, took the view of the minority report of the Poor Law Commission, largely the work of Beatrice Webb, that, as part of the guarantee of a national minimum for all, there should be a state non-contributory system, universal and financed wholly out of taxation, rather than a scheme which perpetuated a competitive system.[46] The main opposition in the Commons came not from the Unionists but from some of the Labour members, who would have preferred a non-contributory measure, rather than what they characterised as a regressive flat rate poll tax on industrial workers. During the committee stage of the Bill, Philip Snowden complained:

---

42 Reprinted in the Introduction by Sir Henry Bunbury to Braithwaite, *Lloyd George's Ambulance Wagon*, p. 24.
43 House of Commons Debates, 4 May 1914, vol. 62, cols 77–79.
44 Marquand, *Ramsay MacDonald*, p. 139.
45 Thane, 'The Working Class and "State" Welfare', in Gladstone, ed., *Before Beveridge*, p. 109.
46 Ibid., MacKenzie, *Diary of Beatrice Webb*, vol. 3, p. 160, entry for 26 May 1911.

[In Bradford,] which I understand, judged by the income tax returns, is the richest city in the provinces, there is a very large number of working class families whose income is only sufficient to allow 1 1/2d per day for food per head, and therefore this contribution of 4d [for health insurance] practically means three days' food being taken away from people of that particular class. As a matter of fact there are more than 2 million families in this country whose income is less than £1 per week, and this 4d per week in their case means that the families are to be deprived of one day's food per week.[47]

The Bill was, therefore, Snowden told the Fabians in July 1911, 'a tax on the starvation of the people'.[48] Snowden took what he regarded as the true socialist view that the obligation to insure against ill health and unemployment was for the community as a whole, not for employees and employers alone. Lansbury attacked the incompleteness of the legislation, arguing that it dealt with cure, not with prevention. Insurance, he insisted, could not deal with malnutrition, bad diet and bad housing which were fundamental causes of ill health, and which were, socialists felt, inherent in a commercial society.[49] He, together with the novelist Hilaire Belloc, who had been a Liberal MP from 1906 to 1910, went so far as to advise working men to boycott national insurance and refuse to register at labour exchanges, but hardly anyone followed this advice. In 1913, at the Labour Party conference, Beatrice Webb, speaking for the Fabian Society, was to complain that, under the Act, sick married women and children would still have no recourse but the workhouse. And the conference was to vote for the repeal of the Act and its replacement by a non-contributory system, to be followed by a state medical service, and also for a non-contributory and universal system of unemployment insurance. But a state scheme would have been unacceptable to the more traditional members of the Liberal Party, and Lloyd George's reply to socialist criticism was that a state scheme appeared attractive until one tried to find the money to fund it – around £21 million. How would that be found in addition to the new burdens imposed by old-age pensions and the 1909 Budget, not to mention increased spending on the navy? It would have entailed raising income tax by a further 7d in the pound. Despite the qualms, the Labour Party agreed to support the Bill in exchange for a promise to introduce the payment of MPs, duly achieved in a resolution on 10 August 1911.

The insurance scheme was 'an imperfect compromise between what he

---

47 House of Commons Debates, 6 July 1911, vol. 27, col. 1394.
48 Levy, *National Health Insurance*, p. 6.
49 House of Commons Debates, 31 October 1911, vol. 30, col. 790ff.

[Lloyd George] wanted to do and what the political and social conditions of the time could tolerate'.[50] Providing as it did for consumer choice and competition between voluntary organisations, it created a primitive form of internal market, separating purchase, undertaken by the approved societies, from provision of the service, to be undertaken by other bodies, whether public or private. This solution was adopted, however, not primarily for ideological reasons but because the vested interests – insurance companies, friendly societies and trade unions – had to be brought into the scheme. But the provisions relating to approved societies did not work well. There was little effective competition between them. To transfer from one society to another proved 'time-consuming and expensive', and there was little evidence of shopping around. After 1918, transferees were to lose their right to benefits for five years, and most approved societies gave better benefits and more favourable private policies to long-term members.[51] The insurance companies, required to establish separate non-profit-making sections to administer the Act, nevertheless used it to persuade insured members to purchase extra private policies when they visited their homes to collect premiums. It was as if, one critic suggested, postmen, when delivering the mail, were to canvas for the sale of groceries.[52] But presumably a company seeking to profiteer would lose members. Beveridge in 1942 found that the administrative costs of the societies were high, amounting to 17 per cent of the income of contributors. A National Health Service would, it was hoped, yield economies of scale and enable administrative costs to be reduced. However, from the 1980s onwards, when there was a sharp reaction against what was seen as too centralised and bureaucratic a service, and one in which the entitlement to healthcare had long been disconnected from contributions, new attempts were to be made to replicate an internal market in a publicly run service with the aim of making it both more cost-effective and more accountable.

The National Insurance Act was an experiment in democracy as well as in social reform. But the provision by which the approved societies were to be under the control of their members never became effective. It was not easy to make large organisations such as the Prudential Insurance Company accountable to members. Few were willing to spend time attending meetings or participating in the affairs of their society. When the Liverpool Victoria Society, with 1 million members in London, advertised its first AGM in 1913, just twenty turned up.[53] As with parish councils, general expressions of in-

---

50 Braithwaite, *Lloyd George's Ambulance Wagon*, p. 9.
51 Noel Whiteside, 'Private Provision and Public Welfare: Health Insurance between the Wars', in Gladstone, ed., *Before Beveridge*, p. 36. This chapter provides the best short account of the workings of National Health Insurance.
52 Levy, *National Health Insurance*, p. 337.
53 Whiteside, 'Private Provision and Public Welfare', p. 33.

terest in democratic government were not followed up by wide participation. The vast majority were perfectly content, so long as they received their benefits, to leave the management of the approved societies to those appointed to manage. 'The result was a travesty of Lloyd George's original vision of extending mutuality, independence and self-government' – especially in 'industrial insurance companies, where none of these qualities were found'.[54]

In addition, it soon became apparent that the competitive basis of the system worked against the interests of the poor and the chronically sick. The better-off approved societies attracted the fit and healthy and could offer extra benefits as envisaged in the Act. Those societies subject to numerous claims could offer less. So those who most needed assistance seemed to be getting least. By the mid-1920s, it appeared that the most generous societies were offering five times the amount in terms of benefits of the least generous.[55] It 'soon became intolerable to the public mind that a compulsory contribution should yield a widely different range of benefits according to the Society which the insured person had chanced to join'.[56] This inequality was inconsistent with the policy of a national minimum, the policy of the Webbs, Beveridge and the Labour Party, and proved a powerful argument for the introduction of the National Health Service in 1946. And a supposedly national scheme which did not include the whole population was a misnomer. A national system, therefore, had to be, like the NHS, both free and comprehensive. Nevertheless, in 1945, 199 Labour candidates pledged in their election manifestos to support a continuing role for friendly societies and trade unions in the administration of health services. One Labour MP during the committee stage of the National Insurance Bill in 1946, pleaded

> for human administration, such as was given personally by the industrial agent in the past, a type of service in which, when sickness came, the people found that they had someone in the agent who was friendly and who helped or advised them, or, when death came, the widow found there was someone who took the emotional load off her.[57]

But the basic principle of the NHS was to be that the provision of healthcare should be based not on the, to some extent, fortuitous result of choice of an approved society but upon the needs of the individual for healthcare. That

---

54 E. P. Hennock, *The Origin of the Welfare State in England and Germany, 1850–1914: Social Policies Compared*, Cambridge University Press, 2007, p. 238.
55 Royal Commission on National Health Insurance, Cmd 2596, 1926, para. 245.
56 Bunbury, 'Introduction', *Lloyd George's Ambulance Wagon*, p. 40.
57 Quoted in Whiteside, 'Private Provision and Public Welfare', p. 39.

principle has remained at the basis of the NHS through all the vicissitudes of reform since the 1980s.

The 1911 Act was, despite its deficiencies, a great personal triumph for Lloyd George. 'It is quite certain', wrote one of the leading officials in charge of the legislation, 'that the English Government machine could not, working in the normal way, have produced this bill in three years, and it would probably have choked it to death if it had done so.' During the Bill's passage, Lloyd George's skills at negotiation and conciliation were seen to great advantage. 'I am more and more impressed with the Chancellor's curious genius,' one official noted, 'his capacity to listen, judge if a thing is practicable, deal with the immediate point, deferring all unnecessary decisions and keeping every road open till he sees which is really the best ... it is long since England had so capable a Statesman.'[58] The achievement is the more remarkable since, while the Bill was passing through Parliament, the government was also preoccupied with the Parliament Bill, massive industrial unrest and the Agadir crisis which at one time appeared likely to lead to war. But the Bill was also a triumph for Churchill, whose role has, perhaps, been insufficiently recognised. Admittedly, much of the groundwork on unemployment insurance had been undertaken by statisticians and social scientists in the labour department of the Board of Trade before Churchill arrived. But without Churchill's commitment and drive, the legislation would never have been enacted. Churchill's time at the Board of Trade was, Beveridge believed, 'a striking illustration of how much the personality of the Minister in a few critical months may change the course of social legislation', and he added that Churchill was also 'immense fun to work for'.[59] Even if Churchill's political career had ended in 1914, he would still deserve to be remembered as a prime architect of the welfare state.

The Act seems, however, not to have been electorally popular. Employers as well as employees who, earning less than £160 a year, had hitherto paid no tax, seemed to resent compulsory contributions, labelled by some the 'Lloyd George', and the system of immediate contributions for what seemed an uncertain benefit later. It was even suggested that the contribution would be used to finance MPs' salaries, a measure introduced in October 1911.[60] As the unpopularity of the Act became clearer, the Unionists began to retreat from their support of it. Indeed, on 14 February 1912, Bonar Law, in the debate on the address, even suggested that the Unionists would repeal it, though he was to 'reinterpret' this suggestion in a letter to *The Times* the following day.

---

58 Braithwaite, *Lloyd George's Ambulance Wagon*, pp. 154, 143.
59 Beveridge, *Power and Influence*, p. 87.
60 Gilbert, *Lloyd George*, vol. 2, p. 24.

Nevertheless, between November 1911 and March 1912, the Liberals lost four by-elections, one – in South Somerset – in a constituency which had been Liberal since 1886. It is also possible that the impact of national insurance contributions on wage packets may have encouraged trade union militancy. The *Daily Mail* initiated a campaign on behalf of domestic servants, whose employers were required to lower their dignity by licking stamps under the supervision of inspectors who would apparently invade their drawing rooms to check that they had done so. At a rally at the Albert Hall on 29 November 1911, sponsored by the newspaper, the Dowager Countess Desart and her maid appeared together on the platform to denounce the Bill. When the accompanying orchestra played 'Men of Harlech', the audience hissed, resenting the reference to Wales. The orchestra rapidly switched to 'Rule Britannia', and Lady Desart reminded her audience:

> This England never did, nor never shall,
> Lie at the proud foot of a conqueror.

In a speech at Woodford on 29 June 1912, Lloyd George complained of those 'bad tempered people'.

> They are always dismissing servants. Whenever any Liberal Act of Parliament is passed, they dismiss them. I wonder that they have any servants left. Sir William Harcourt imposed death duties; they dismissed servants. I put on a super-tax; they dismissed more. Now the Insurance Act comes, and the last of them, I suppose, will have to go. You will be having, in the swell West End houses, notices like 'not at home – her ladyship's washing day'.

'There can, I think, be no doubt', Asquith told Lord Crewe on 30 November 1912,

> that the Insurance Bill is (to say the least) not an electioneering asset ... One hears from all constituencies of defections from our party of the small class of employers. Nor is the situation likely to improve, a year hence, when the contributions are in full blast, and the 'benefits' remote and sporadic.[61]

In May 1914, defeated in a by-election at Ipswich, Charles Masterman believed that 'the result was chiefly due to the Insurance Act, which should have been voluntary and free to the poor ... He had noted with surprise that

---

61 Gilbert, *National Insurance*, pp. 396–7.

all the poorest sections of the town were strongly opposed to him ... His supporters were the mechanics, small shopkeepers etc.'[62]

Just as Lloyd George was aware that his health insurance scheme could not be a final solution, so also did Churchill recognise that the unemployment insurance part of the Bill was provisional and that unemployment insurance could be no more than a palliative. He accepted, on 25 May on the Second Reading of the Bill, that 'unemployment and sickness will return to the cottage of the working man'. 'But', he added, 'they will not return alone.'[63] He hoped that the Liberal reforms would

> increase the stability of our institutions by giving the mass of industrial workers a direct interest in maintaining them. With a 'stake in the country' in the form of insurance against evil days, these workers will pay no attention to the vague promises of revolutionary socialism ... It will make him a better citizen, a more efficient worker, and a happier man.[64]

Unemployment insurance was more experimental than National Health Insurance since, as Churchill appreciated, it entered an entirely new field. But it was never to have a really fair trial. While, during the immediate pre-war years, unemployment was low, and the benefit was extended after the war to almost all manual workers and to non-manual workers earning £250 a year or less, between 1921 and 1939, unemployment remained above 10 per cent, and in the staple export trades much higher, far above the 8.46 per cent level at which the fund balanced. The scheme was required, in the words of a Royal Commission appointed in 1931 to evaluate it, 'to carry a load, which it was not designed to bear'.[65] It could deal with temporary fluctuations in employment but not with permanent under-employment due to a deficiency in aggregate demand. In 1921, the maximum limit to benefit was abolished by the introduction of an 'extended' or 'transitional' benefit, and by 1931, if not before, the relationship between contributions and benefits had been severed. The insurance principle had been, for all practical purposes, abandoned. Relief was in effect to be based on need, not contributions. Nevertheless, Churchill had in 1908 identified unemployment as the problem of the age, declaring that it had become 'a paramount necessity for us to make scientific provision against the fluctuations and setbacks which are inevitable in world commerce and in national industry'. There was a need, he argued, in a startling anticipation of modern economics, to have

62 Cooper, *The British Welfare Revolution*, p. 285.
63 House of Commons Debates, 25 May 1911, vol. 26, col. 510.
64 Quoted in Geoffrey Finlayson, *Citizen, State and Social Welfare in Britain 1830–1990*, Clarendon Press, 1994, p. 186.
65 Evidence to Royal Commission on Unemployment Insurance (Holman Gregory Commission), Cmd 3872, 1931, para. 31.

in permanent existence certain recognised industries of a useful but uncompetitive character like afforestation, managed by a public department and capable of being expanded or contracted according to the needs of the labour market, just as easily as you can pull out the stops or work the pedals of an organ.[66]

On 10 October 1908, Herbert Samuel, then a junior minister at the Home office but a future leader of the Liberal Party, had declared that Churchill recognised the crucial elements of the problem:

> First, that it is an essential duty of the State to deal with this evil; secondly, that it is a permanent evil ... and must be dealt with not by machinery improvised for the occasion ... but by a standing organisation; thirdly, that in addition to whatever localities may do, useful works should be organised on a national scale, set into full operation in times of bad trade and reduced to a minimum in times of good trade; fourthly, that a root of the evil is the wrong proportions of unskilled and skilled labour in our society ... and to be cured mainly by technical combination schools.[67]

In recognising the need for better technical education, Churchill showed himself nearly forty years if not nearly a century ahead of his time. For the reforms of further education by the governments of Theresa May and Boris Johnson after 2016 were responding to that very need.

With all its deficiencies, the National Insurance Act marked a fundamental change in the relationship between the citizen and the state. Until 1911, such welfare legislation as was on the statute book concerned those too young to enter the labour market (school meals and medical inspection) or those who had left it (old-age pensions). Everyone else, many Liberals and Unionists believed, was in a free society responsible for making provision for their health and welfare. If they could not do so, that was a sign of moral failure. They would be helped by the state through the Poor Law but would suffer stigma as a result, a loss of freedom entailed by detention in the workhouse and a loss of civil liberty caused by disenfranchisement. The belief that the sick and unemployed, who could not afford welfare, were guilty of moral failings was fatally undermined by the National Insurance Act, which provided for the welfare of working adults. And despite all its manifold deficiencies, the Act did secure improvements. While around 40 per cent of Boer War recruits had been rejected as unfit in 1899, by 1939, just 2.7 per

---

66 Churchill, *Young Statesman*, pp. 303–4.
67 Churchill, *Companion*, vol. 2, part 2, p. 1,841.

cent were rejected for army service; and already, by the 1920s, poverty had been halved. The Act, with all its limitations, protected many wage earners from destitution as a result of ill health, and by providing free treatment it prevented neglect of health through lack of means.

The Liberal reforms were, admittedly, to be superseded by those of the 1940–45 coalition government and the Attlee government which followed it which, by contrast with Liberal enactments, provided for universal public provision rather than selective provision based on the public regulation of a private internal market. They guaranteed a right to work through the commitment to full employment in the 1944 White Paper, and the national minimum living standard as advocated by the Webbs in the National Insurance and National Assistance Acts, to be administered by the state not by voluntary organisations.

The National Insurance Act was of importance for a further reason. The opposition to it, as we have seen, came less from the Unionists than from interest groups – vested interests as the Liberals regarded them. These interests could not be placated through the parliamentary process but only through negotiation. The labour unrest of the years 1911 to 1914 also could only be resolved through negotiation. Lloyd George had to negotiate with three influential interest groups – friendly societies, commercial insurance companies and the British Medical Association. Parliamentary conflicts were coming to appear of less account than extra-parliamentary negotiations. This was to be noticed by the Webbs in their book *Constitution for the Socialist Commonwealth*, published in 1921.

> The real government of Great Britain is nowadays carried on, not in the House of Commons at all, nor even in the Cabinet but in private conferences between Ministers with their principal officials and representatives of the persons specifically affected by any proposed legislation or by any action on the part of the administration.[68]

In May 1911, a Labour MP, George Barnes, told the Commons that the Bill marked

> a great step forward because it brings many millions of workmen into direct contact with the state and is therefore going to be of immense educational value. We believe people have been too much inclined to look upon the state simply as a big policeman and this Bill will enable a great many of them to realise that the state after all is what they like to make it.[69]

---

68 Quoted in Gilbert, *National Insurance*, p. 291fn.
69 House of Commons Debates, 24 May 1911, vol. 26, col. 312.

In his volume in the *Oxford History of England*, A. J. P. Taylor declared, 'Until August 1914 a sensible law-abiding Englishman could pass through life and hardly notice the existence of the state, beyond the post office and the policeman.' But in 1914, 'the history of the English state and the English people merged for the first time'.[70] Yet the crucial date was, surely, 15 July 1912, when the National Insurance Act came into operation, not 4 August 1914, when Britain declared war. The Act brought the people into a compulsory relationship with the state and was far-reaching in that it affected a large swathe of the population. Liberal reforms had been based on the radical principle of transferring income from the taxpayer via the state for the benefit of specifically targeted individuals on the basis of need and as of right.

Perhaps the significance of the National Insurance Act was best expressed in Churchill's eloquent speech on Second Reading.

> The penalties for misfortune are terrible today ... A man may have neglected to make provision for unemployment; he may have neglected to make provision for sickness; he may be below the average standard as a workman; he may have contracted illness through his own folly or his own misconduct ... But what relation is there between these weaknesses and failings and the appalling catastrophes which exceptionally follow in the wake of these failures; so narrow is the margin upon which even the industrious respectable working class family rely that when sickness or unemployment come knocking at the door the whole economy and even the status of the family are imperilled ... No one can measure the suffering to individuals which this process causes; no one can measure the futile unnecessary loss which the State incurs. We do not pretend that our Bill is going to prevent these evils. Unemployment and sickness will return to the cottage of the working man, but they will not return alone. We are going to send him by this Bill other visitors to his home, visitors who will guard his fortunes and strengthen the force of his right arm against every foe.[71]

The Liberal reforms were creative and path-breaking, and there had been few precedents, principles or past experience to guide them. They were a clear departure from much of what had gone before, in what Churchill in 1908 rightly characterised as 'the Untrodden Field in Politics'.[72]

---

70 A. J. P. Taylor, *English History 1914–1945* [1965], Oxford University Press, 1992, pp. 1–2.
71 House of Commons Debates, 25 May 1911, vol. 26, col. 510.
72 Churchill, *Young Statesman*, p. 276.

CHAPTER 17

LAND REFORM

THE PROBLEM OF THE LAND

The National Insurance Act was the second of two great Liberal reforms spearheaded by Lloyd George, the first having been the Budget. Both were, inevitably and indeed intentionally, incomplete. The Budget had pointed the way to insurance, to a renewed attack on poverty and to land reform. National insurance steered the way to an inquiry into the causes of ill health, which were social as much as medical.

Many Liberals believed that social evils resulted primarily from an unjust system of landholding. Conditions in the countryside were forcing too many into the towns where they were living in overcrowded dwellings with inadequate public facilities, while the wages of agricultural labourers were amongst the lowest of all employees. The National Insurance Act, so Masterman, a junior minister close to Lloyd George and Churchill, argued, should be seen not as the end of social reform but as coming between two great measures of emancipation: the destruction of the power of the Lords and 'the coming changes in the land system'.[1] Lloyd George himself believed that Liberalism could survive only if it maintained its momentum. 'For Liberalism stagnation was death. The worst kind of Tory was the nominal Liberal.'[2]

Radical Liberals believed that land reform should be the next instalment of social reform. 'I am convinced', Lloyd George told a friend in May 1912, 'that the land question is the real issue. You must break down the remnants of the feudal system ... I feel that the land and the agricultural labourer are at the root of the whole social evil.'[3] It was on the land that inequality seemed most blatant. In 1873, an official survey had seemed to show that fewer than 6,000 men owned two-thirds of the land in England and Wales. By the time of the Edwardian period, 1 per cent of proprietors still owned 30 per cent of British land by value and perhaps up to 60 per cent in acreage.[4] The land,

1   Gilbert, *National Insurance*, p. 445fn.
2   Trevor Wilson, ed., *The Political Diaries of C. P. Scott, 1911–1928*, Collins, 1970, p. 70.
3   Gilbert, *Lloyd George*, vol. 2, p. 58.
4   Avner Offer, *Property and Politics 1870–1914: Landownership, Law, Ideology and Urban Development in England*, Cambridge University Press, 1981, pp. 5–6.

Churchill had declared at Edinburgh on 17 July 1909, was 'by far the greatest of monopolies – it is a perpetual monopoly, and it is the mother of all other forms of monopoly', since it offered enrichment without service. It was to such enrichment that Liberals took objection. They were not opposed to wealth or to large incomes on principle. Indeed, one of their objections to the land monopoly was that it made it difficult for a manufacturer hoping to begin a new industry, or a railway company wishing to build a new line. 'It does not matter where you look or what examples you select,' Churchill argued, 'you see that every form of enterprise, every step in material progress is only undertaken after the land monopolist has skimmed the cream off for himself.' What the Liberals objected to was to unearned wealth, wealth accruing to a class that was not contributing to the community. They sought what would now be called a socially responsible capitalism. Coming as he did from rural north Wales, Lloyd George had been able to see the iniquitous system of land ownership at first hand. Land reform was, as it were, in his blood. It had been his first political cause. He had resented the power and assumptions of social superiority of the large landowner, and his clients, the squires, the Church of England and the church schools. He used to reminisce on the theme of tenants being turned out of their homes for voting Liberal, tales which lost nothing in the telling. His first act, after becoming an alderman in the Carnarvonshire County Council in 1889 was to call for leasehold enfranchisement. His first major speech in Parliament had been to attack Unionist legislation of 1896 which derated a quarter of agricultural land, something he regarded as a free gift to an unproductive section of the community. It is not too much to say that it was the problem of the land which had driven him into politics. And it continued to animate him. In a speech at the National Liberal Club on 31 July 1913, he declared that 'foremost among the tasks of Liberalism in the near future is the regeneration of rural life and the emancipation of the land in this country from the paralysing grip of a rusty, effete and unprofitable system'.[5]

Lloyd George sought to democratise the system of land ownership so that the landowner became responsible to the community. In 1912, he established an unofficial Liberal land inquiry, which was to publish two reports, one on rural land in England in October 1913, the other on urban land in England in April 1914. There was also a separate Scottish inquiry. The inquiries, unlike Royal Commissions, were partisan. They were designed, like the Tariff Commission, to prove a case, but unlike the Tariff Commission, they did not cross-examine witnesses, claiming that agricultural labourers and tenant farmers would have been fearful at giving evidence in public. The approach

5   John Grigg, *Lloyd George: From Peace to War, 1912–1916* [1985], Penguin, 1997.

was selective and much of the material collected was impressionistic, not based on scientifically collected statistics, while most respondents to the inquiries' questionnaires appeared to be Liberal sympathisers. Five Liberal MPs were members of the inquiries and much of the work was done under the aegis of Seebohm Rowntree, also a member of the inquiries. But however partisan the inquiries, it was difficult to argue with the broad picture painted in the two reports.

In his study of York, Rowntree had argued that a wage of 21s 8d a week was needed to avoid primary poverty. He had already expressed his conviction in his book *Labour and the Land*, published in 1910, that most village labourers were living below the primary poverty line.[6] The rural report confirmed that agricultural labourers were the worst paid of any workers in England, with over 60 per cent of agricultural labourers earning less than eighteen shillings a week.[7] Their position was similar to that of workers in sweated industries before the Trade Boards Act. Part of the reason was that they could not easily organise for collective bargaining in trade unions. With wages low, it was difficult for them to maintain weekly union contributions, while the tied cottage system made the labourer dependent on his employer. There was a strong case, the inquiry believed, for a statutory minimum wage administered by wage boards as with the sweated industries. If tenant farmers found the increase in wages too heavy a burden, they should have the right to apply to a judicial body such as a land court for a readjustment of rent. Such land courts were already in existence in Ireland and in Scotland. Tenant farmers should in any case be given security of tenure, as in Ireland in Gladstone's 1881 Land Act, so that their farms could not be sold over their heads, a factor which inhibited tenant farmers from making improvements.

There was also, the land inquiry believed, a serious rural housing problem such that 120,000 new cottages were needed. Private builders had in the past ten years built a 'practically negligible' number – and rural district councils had been unable to fill the gap since housing was 'practically never an issue at the local elections, which are very frequently uncontested'. Labourers lacked the confidence and organising power to bring housing matters before the council, while local ratepayers feared the effects of house building on the rates, and councils had found it difficult to acquire land for housing.[8] Local authorities needed housing grants from central government, which should ensure that local authorities used them effectively. But the Local Government Board was, 'both by its composition and the nature of its duties', 'a

6 Briggs, *Social Thought and Social Action*, p. 47.
7 *The Land: The Report of the Land Enquiry Commission, Vol. 1 Rural*, Hodder & Stoughton, 3rd edition, 1913, p. 7.
8 Ibid., pp. 115, 122–3.

supervising and controlling rather than an initiating or creating body', and had no powers to force local authorities into activity.[9] So there should be a new ministry with powers to acquire land. The Cabinet accordingly decided in October 1913 to establish a new Ministry of Land and Natural Resources, taking over most of the functions of the Board of Agriculture. Had it not been for the war, the Liberals might have established such a ministry in 1914 or 1915. It would have been the first government department to bear the title of 'Ministry'. In the event, it was not established for fifty years, in October 1964 by Harold Wilson's first Labour government. But it lasted less than two and a half years, being merged into the Ministry of Housing and Local Government in February 1967.[10]

The rural report concluded that the system of land ownership 'is of the nature of a monopoly, and the legal power which a landowner has over his tenant ... is detrimental to the best national interests'. There was too great a concentration of land ownership, too many large estates and too many absentee landlords, problems highlighted by the purchase of large estates by newly rich merchants and industrialists. The report quoted the novelist Rider Haggard that 'it is foolish to hope that the regeneration of rural England as a whole will be brought about through the purchase of properties by *nouveaux riches*. This class wants good value for its money in pleasure or social consideration, and will go only where this is to be had.' An informant had told Haggard that the typical new owner made 'no legitimate use of the land. His interest was primarily sporting, the rest being a matter of indifference to him, he seeks to grow not produce but partridges.'[11]

The rural report was launched with great fanfare and considerable publicity. The urban report received much less attention but was equally radical. It claimed that, of the urban working class, 'a considerable proportion still have to live in houses which are so injurious to health as to be unfit for human habitation, and that one-tenth of the population have to live under conditions of gross overcrowding'. The Housing of the Working Classes Act of 1890 had empowered local authorities to clear unhealthy areas and to carry out improvements, while the Housing and Town Planning Act of 1909 had placed them under an obligation to deal with dwellings unfit for habitation and to use compulsory powers for this purpose. Local authorities also had powers to borrow money to buy land and build houses for rent to the working classes. But these powers had hardly been used and were in any case insufficient. Local authorities should, the inquiry argued, be *required* to

9   Ibid., p. 125.
10 J. A. Cross, 'The Ministry of Land – 1914 Version', *Public Administration*, 1965, pp. 215–20.
11 *The Land*, pp. 383, xlviii–xlix.

survey housing conditions, and central government should provide grants so as to avoid large rate increases, since 'the fear of adding to the rates ... is almost an obsession with large sections of the population'.[12] The urban report also advocated a minimum wage for low-paid workers and security of tenure for leaseholders with full compensation for improvements.

Lloyd George was in broad sympathy with these proposals and, with the support of the Cabinet, he launched his land campaign on 11 October 1913 in a speech at Bedford. He contrasted the economic helplessness of the agricultural labourer with the social power of the landlord enjoying a monopoly position. He seemed to be advocating that the wages of agricultural labourers be fixed by statute, that they should enjoy security of tenure so that they could benefit from improvements and that land tribunals should be empowered to fix rents. In addition, the state should be given powers to acquire land. He rejected the Irish precedent of land purchase. It is sometimes suggested that Lloyd George was concerned only with rural areas, believing that urban problems were largely the result of overcrowding and could be resolved by a return to the land. But he intended also to propose reforms to improve urban life, strengthening urban local authorities and encouraging house building in the towns as well as the countryside. Such reforms might unite the middle and working classes, so cementing the Liberals' electoral base. But the campaign attracted more support in the countryside than in the towns, where reform proposals were often misrepresented. At the Reading by-election in November 1913, for example, it was suggested that money from the national insurance fund would be used to finance working-class housing. A pamphlet was circulated asking electors, 'Do you want your Insurance taxes fooled away on wild-cat country cottage schemes?'[13]

THE BUDGET OF 1914

Lloyd George had intended to give effect to his land proposals in his 1915 Budget, which, he believed, would provide a platform for the election due that year, ensuring that it would be fought on land reform not Ulster. But at the end of 1913, he found himself in conflict with Churchill, First Lord of the Admiralty, on the naval estimates, a conflict occasioned by Churchill's demand that four dreadnoughts be constructed rather than the two already planned. This was conceded by the Cabinet in return for a somewhat vague promise that the naval estimates would not be greatly increased for the

---

12 *The Land: Vol. 2 Urban*, Hodder & Stoughton, 1914, pp. 44, 205, 50.
13 Bentley B. Gilbert, 'David Lloyd George: The Reform of British Land-Holding and the Budget of 1914', *Historical Journal*, 1978, p. 127fn.

financial year 1915/16. But the extra dreadnoughts meant that Lloyd George would have to raise taxes in 1914 for them as well as for land reform. It seemed politically unwise to have two successive Budgets, each of which raised taxation. So Lloyd George decided to repeat what he had done in 1909 – bring the two together into one Budget, hoping that Liberal distaste for the naval expenditure would be assuaged by their delight at land reform. But he had insufficient time to prepare his proposals thoroughly; they proved so rushed and ill-thought-out that they could not be put into effect.

Lloyd George began his Budget Speech on 4 May 1914 by highlighting the new duties that had been placed on local authorities in recent years – education thanks to the 1902 Act, measures providing for the feeding and medical inspection of schoolchildren, greater welfare responsibilities, new responsibilities in housing and, with the development of motor cars, roads also. These local government functions, however, were really, so Lloyd George argued, national in character. Local government was no longer dealing, if it ever had been, only with purely local services but with local aspects of what were national services. Moreover, insufficient finance was being given to local authorities for their new functions. 'The credit is ours and the burden is theirs,' Lloyd George continued 'and we are surprised when we discover that many of our previous Statutes are really dead letters.'[14] The local rating system and meagre levels of government assistance to local authorities were incapable of sustaining the burden of providing for national services. Since 1889, there had been a grant to local authorities whereby the revenues of certain duties, primarily licence duties, were assigned to local government. But this system of assigned revenues bore no relationship to expenditure needs and was insufficiently buoyant for the new responsibilities of local authorities. Moreover, the centre had no means of supervising how the money would be spent. The rating system discouraged improvements, which would raise the amount payable on a property. In effect, it rewarded the landowner who failed to put his land to good use. 'The less a man improves his property,' Lloyd George declared in his Budget Speech, 'the less he contributes; and the more a man improves his property the more he is subjected to a levy for the local rates.' Unused land, even if with development potential, paid no rates at all. Agricultural land paid a much-reduced rate.

Moreover, rates were the only direct tax paid by those earning below the level of eligibility for income tax, and they affected poorer householders disproportionately. The system was, therefore, highly inequitable. A supertax payer contributed just 1 or 2 per cent of his income in rates, a workman 5 per cent, a provincial tradesman 9 per cent and a London tradesman 13 per

---

14 House of Commons Debates, 4 May 1914, vol. 62, col. 62.

cent.[15] The system was also inequitable between local authorities. Needs were greatest in poorest areas, but rateable values there were lower, particularly as better transport facilities and the invention of the motor car enabled the wealthy to live well away from their industries or workplaces. In a speech at Sheffield on 14 May, Herbert Samuel, President of the Local Government Board, was to declare that the system of local taxation had been appropriate 'for a simple agricultural community of three hundred years ago'. 'If', he went on to say,

> we had deliberately set out to devise a system of rating for local purposes which should discourage building, lower the standard of houses for the working classes, tax the poor heavily and the rich lightly, and should place heavier burdens on the man with a large family than on the man with a small family; if we had devoted our utmost ingenuity over a long period to secure these injustices and follies, he believed they would arrive at last at such a system as we had at present.[16]

Lloyd George proposed to replace a rating system based on the value of premises with one based on site values, encouraging landowners to bring property onto the market since it would become more expensive to keep it unused. Lloyd George also proposed partially to derate new construction and improvements to property and repeal the 1896 Act by which agricultural land was partially derated. Even so, the new rating system would still be insufficiently buoyant to meet the new responsibilities of local government and would need to be supplemented by larger government grants given according to the resources of the area to achieve greater equalisation. In addition, the grants would give central government a handle to ensure that local authorities were administering public services effectively. The policy of large grants was a considerable departure from classical Liberalism. It had originated indeed with Disraeli, and, according to Sidney Webb writing in the *Municipal Journal* in December 1899, 'No subject except perhaps war so annoyed Mr Gladstone as that of grants-in-aid and he continually fulminated against them as iniquitous and "a positive excitement to extravagance". What he did not realise is that sometimes it is desirable to encourage expenditure.'[17]

To pay for reform, Lloyd George proposed: to raise direct taxes and extend the graduated income tax on earned income, with a top rate 7d higher than

---

15 Ibid., col. 66.
16 *Manchester Guardian*, 15 May 1914.
17 Quoted in Offer, *Property and Politics*, pp. 405, 216–17.

the lowest rate at 1/-4d, higher than ever before, even than during the Boer War when there had been no supertax either; higher taxes on unearned income; lowering the rate at which supertax was to be paid from £5,000 to £3,000 and imposing a graduated supertax; and higher death duties on estates over £60,000. In nine years, the maximum rates of direct taxation would have risen from 9d to 2s 8d in respect of earned incomes and supertax and from 8 per cent to 20 per cent in respect of death duties. Government spending had risen by around a third. Between 1888 and 1913, expenditure on social services, excluding the Poor Law – health, education, pensions and insurance – had risen from £5 million to £33 million. The 1914 Budget was the first to project a total national outlay of over £200 million.[18] Such was the scale of the Liberal government's social revolution.

But overhaul of the rating system presupposed assessing site values separately from premises, from improvement values. That meant adapting the valuation put in train following the 1909 Budget, which could not be completed until September 1915 at the earliest. So Lloyd George proposed provisional grants for four months, beginning on 1 December 1914. His original intention was to include the grants together with the derating powers in a separate Revenue Bill. But that Bill had not yet been prepared, let alone considered by Parliament – and there could be no guarantee that it would not itself be held up by the Lords. So while the Budget's increases in income tax to pay for the grants would take effect, there could be no guarantee that the Revenue Bill would become law; and until it did, the Exchequer would have unspent revenues. It was unconstitutional for Parliament to be asked to vote for an increase in taxation without knowing whether the purpose for which it was being voted would actually be achieved. And the Budget was on an annual basis; taxes for the year could only be spent on services for that same year.

On the second day of the Budget debate, Lloyd George was pressed by the opposition to admit that if the Revenue Bill was not passed, money voted would not in fact be spent on the provisional grants. For MPs could not be asked to vote money for grants which might not be enacted. In consequence, in early June, the government had to change tack, grafting the grants on to the Budget, the Finance Bill. But this gave rise to three massive problems.

The first issue was that Parliament was still being asked to vote for a rise in taxation, part of which it might not legally be able to spend, since the valuation on which the grants would be based might not have been completed in time. The second problem was that the Budget might not be given the Speaker's certificate as a Money Bill. In that case, the Finance Bill would

---

18 H. V. Emy, 'The Impact of Financial Policy on English Party Politics Before 1914', *Historical Journal*, p. 129.

be at the mercy of the Lords, which could hold it up until 1916, beyond the date of the next general election due at the latest by December 1915. The third problem was that the Finance Bill now contained a provision, the local authority grants, which made it different from the Budget resolutions introduced five weeks previously. So either the resolutions or the Bill would have to be amended. In the end, as we shall see, the Finance Bill had to be amended to exclude the grants. There were also political difficulties since the more conservative Liberal MPs objected to increased taxation and expenditure. They drew attention to the constitutional problem in a letter to *The Times* on 18 June 1914. They pointed out that, if the grants were passed and the derating was not achieved before the general election because the valuation on which they were based was not complete, then if the Unionists won the election, the grants without the derating would give rate relief under the unreformed rating system and benefit primarily better-off landowners. The expenditure provided for in the Finance Bill was therefore dependent upon the passage, Lloyd George's Liberal critics argued, in their letter to *The Times*, 'of a highly contentious measure, which has not yet even been introduced, and which, in all probability, will be rejected by the House of Lords'. The expenditure might never materialise. So there were, the critics continued, 'dangerous innovations in constitutional practice' in the Finance Bill. It was a fundamental constitutional principle that Parliament not be asked to vote for higher taxation until, in the words of the Liberal MPs, it had 'first approved the scheme which it is intended to finance, until the machinery for expending it in a manner acceptable to parliament has been provided, and until its expenditure is no longer dependent upon contingencies'.[19] When the Revenue Bill was finally published on 19 June, it did not authorise either site value rating or the derating of improvements but merely asked the Inland Revenue to make inquiries. This was hardly satisfactory.

Faced with these insuperable constitutional and political problems, the Cabinet decided on 22 June to drop the provisional grants from the Finance Bill. This, in consequence, meant that the top rate of income tax could be lowered from 1/-4d to 1/-3d to avoid unspent revenues. 'It is a long time', *The Economist* commented on 27 June, 'since a Budget has been so much battered and shattered.' The Budget was passed in its truncated form by the Commons on 23 July by a majority of just thirty-eight, following a guillotine, the first occasion on which a guillotine motion had ever been applied to a Finance Bill. The normal government majority was ninety-five. The Budget received royal assent on 31 July. Land reform would have to await the Budget of 1915, which would appear in the shadow of a general election and with the

19 *The Times*, 18 June 1914.

strong possibility that the Lords would not pass the revenue proposals. In the event, of course, the Budget of 1915 was to be a war Budget and land reform was postponed. The whole episode was a shambles. 'It all springs', declared Sir Robert Chalmers, the somewhat conservative Permanent Secretary of the Treasury from 1911 to 1913, to Walter Runciman, a minister out of sympathy with Lloyd George's aims and himself a large landowner, 'from the besetting sin of the creature [i.e. Lloyd George] that he will not work at his business beforehand & betimes.'[20] That was not wholly fair. The shambles resulted in part from the dispute over the naval estimates, and Lloyd George had always believed that a reforming Budget in 1914 rather than 1915 would be 'premature', telling a friend in June 1914, 'I did not want a taxing Budget this year. It was not the time for it.'[21] The debacle brought Lloyd George's reputation down from the pinnacle it had reached after the 1909 Budget and the National Insurance Act.

The Chancellor's reputation had already been damaged by the Marconi affair. In 1912, he had injudiciously and improperly – though not, in terms of the mores of the times, corruptly – speculated, together with the Attorney General, Rufus Isaacs, and the Chief Whip, the Master of Elibank, in shares of the American Marconi Company. At that time, the English Marconi Company was negotiating a contract with the government for the supply of telegraph stations linking together various parts of the empire. The shares had been offered to the ministers by Godfrey Isaacs, brother of the Attorney General, joint managing director of the English business and a director of the American one, at a price lower than that at which they were to be made available to the public. The English and American firms were legally separate entities, but there were strong connections between them. Until April 1912, the English enterprise, which had founded the American one, held the majority of shares in it and nominated three of its directors. Patents belonging to the American company were the same as those of the English business. It could be assumed, therefore, that, if the value of the English company's shares rose, as they would if its negotiations with the government were successful, the value of the American company's shares would also rise, as indeed they did. The Master of Elibank had, unbeknown to Lloyd George, used Liberal Party funds for his purchase, setting the dangerous precedent of allowing a government contractor in effect to contribute, however indirectly, to party funds. Lloyd George no doubt assumed that if it was in order for the Attorney General, chief legal adviser to the government, to purchase

---

20 Bruce K. Murray, '"Battered and Shattered": Lloyd George and the 1914 Budget Fiasco', *Albion*, 1991, p. 485.
21 Bruce K. Murray, 'Lloyd George, the Navy Estimates and the Inclusion of Rating Relief in the 1914 Budget', *Welsh History Review*, 1990, p. 58; Lord Riddell, *More Pages From My Diary, 1908–1914*, Country Life, 1934, pp. 214–15.

shares, it was also in order for him. And the Attorney General had told him that there was no connection between the English and the American companies. Lloyd George and the other ministers compounded their offence by being evasive in the House of Commons when knowledge of the transactions came to light. The offence was not mitigated by the revelation that, far from profiting from his purchase, the Chancellor actually lost money on it. Lloyd George together with the Master of Elibank had done 'what every tyro indulging in a half-guilty flutter does. They had bought half-way up a boom and sold excitedly at a profit. Then at the first serious drop they had bought again in larger quantities, on this occasion half-way down a slump.'[22] It appeared during the inquiry into the affair that 'the highest financial officer in the British government showed a lamentable ignorance' in the operation of the stock market.[23] But, of course, ministers had not purchased the shares intending to make a loss.

The ministers had speculated in the shares of a company associated with another company seeking to enter into contractual relations with the government, on the basis of information received from the managing director of the contracting company. There was, in addition, some danger of a conflict of interest. For Lloyd George might have had to adjudicate on aspects of the Marconi contract were the Treasury to raise objections to it. But, in any case, the Chancellor had no business to be dabbling in shares. In the words of a contemporary journal:

> The Chancellor of the Exchequer is, in a sense, the ex-officio head of the City of London; for he is the highest financial officer of the British Empire. City opinion is therefore affronted by the disclosure of this sublime functionary behaving for all the world like the poor, greedy, excited Mr Juggins of ordinary life.[24]

The Marconi affair highlighted the division between financially secure ministers, such as Asquith, Grey and Haldane, and the new less secure, more pushy men, a division that coincided in large part with the division in 1916 between supporters of Asquith and supporters of Lloyd George.[25] On 19 June 1913, *The Times* declared that if a man steps into a puddle and

---

22 Frances Donaldson, *The Marconi Affair*, Rupert Hart-Davis, 1962, p. 135. This book still gives the best account of the affair.
23 Don M. Cregier, *Bounder from Wales: Lloyd George's Career Before the First World War*, University of Missouri Press, 1976, p. 206.
24 Quoted in Donaldson, *The Marconi Affair*, p. 135.
25 Otte, *Statesman of Europe*, pp. 485, 762.

says that it was after all quite a clean puddle, then we judge him deficient in the sense of cleanliness. And the British public like their public men to have a very nice sense of cleanliness ... If Ministers are so innocent and careless as not to know a puddle when they see one, then they ought not to occupy their extremely responsible position

An opposition vote of censure was deflected only by a government amendment, shaped by Asquith, to the effect that the Commons accepted expressions of regret by Lloyd George and Isaacs, although it was not clear that either had in fact expressed regret. Had the censure motion been passed, they would have had to resign; and a number of Liberals did in fact believe that they should go.

Marconi and the shambles over the 1914 Budget meant that Lloyd George's 'reputation for magic was destroyed'.[26] His political position indeed was always 'fundamentally insecure – depending not on patronage, family connection, or wealth, but on unique personal qualities'.[27] By the time of the outbreak of war in August 1914, he seemed in decline. But whether the debacle of the 1914 Budget would, without war, have also heralded the decline of the new liberalism of which he was the champion will, of course, never be known.

---

26 Gilbert, Lloyd George, vol. 2, p. 92.
27 Cameron Hazlehurst, Politicians at War, July 1914 to May 1915, Jonathan Cape, 1971, p. 107.

CHAPTER 18

THE CHALLENGE OF LABOUR

THE *OSBORNE* JUDGMENT

Passage of the Parliament Act did not, as many Liberals hoped, lead the government into calmer waters. On the contrary, during the years 1911 to 1914, it faced a series of profound conflicts seemingly challenging the very foundations of parliamentary government – conflicts with organised labour, with women seeking the vote and with Nationalists and Unionists in Ireland. A new spirit seemed abroad in the land. Social unrest was coinciding with intellectual unrest. 'On or about December 1910,' Virginia Woolf declared, 'human character changed ... All human relations have shifted – those between masters and servants, husbands and wives, parents and children. And when human relations change there is at the same time a change in religion, conduct, politics and literature.'[1] Looking back in 1916, H. G. Wells believed that militancy was a consequence of a long period of peace, peace which had led to stuffiness and an overwhelming urge to fling open the windows.

> We live at the end of a series of secure generations in which none of the great things of life have changed materially. We've grown up with no sense of danger – that is to say, with no sense of responsibility. None of us ... really believe that life can change very fundamentally any more forever ... It seems incredible that anything we can do will ever smash the system. Old Asquith thinks that we always have got along, and that we shall always get along by being quietly artful and saying, 'Wait and See.' And it is just because we are convinced that we are so safe against a general breakdown that we are able to be so recklessly violent in our special cases.[2]

Trade unionists, suffragettes and Ulster Unionists were coming to feel that Parliament was failing to deal with their demands. Women were no longer content to remain the chattels of men, accepting rules drawn up by them. Labour wanted what one Liberal MP called 'a place in the sun'.

---

1 Virginia Woolf, 'Mr Bennett and Mrs Brown', in *Collected Essays*, vol. 1, Hogarth Press, 1966, p. 320.
2 Wells, *Mr Britling Sees It Through*, pp. 46–7.

It is part of a long developing movement, which began with the first Factory Act, and which has gained force and effect ever since. From being a blind and groping movement it has become a conscious and connected effort. Not only has labour learnt its power, but labour has obtained an ethical conviction of the rights of its cause.[3]

Trade union membership had been steadily growing since the beginning of the century, more than doubling from just under 2 million in 1900 to over 4 million in 1914. With unions becoming stronger, activists began to use the strike weapon to force the government to intervene and secure fair conditions at work. Militant suffragettes sought to force the government to give women the vote. And Ulster hostility to Home Rule challenged the Liberal notion that all political disputes could be resolved by parliamentary methods.

The Labour Party had two main immediate and inter-related aims: the first was to secure the payment of MPs, the second was to secure a reversal of the *Osborne* judgment. Delivered by the law lords in December 1909, shortly before the January 1910 election, the *Amalgamated Society of Railway Servants v. Osborne* ruling had declared that a trade union was prohibited from making financial contributions for political purposes.[4]

Faced with these two demands from Labour, the government moved rapidly on the first. In 1911, Lloyd George, as Chancellor of the Exchequer, introduced a resolution providing for the payment of £400 a year to MPs, declaring that Britain was the last major representative system not to pay MPs, except for Italy, though Italy paid travel expenses. Another Liberal minister, Herbert Samuel, pointed out that 'an unpaid legislature is an institution essentially aristocratic, a contrivance for keeping the legislature exclusively in the hands of those who can afford to serve without payment'. Ramsay MacDonald, the future Labour leader, complained that an MP had to live on his wits 'by being a company promoter, a lawyer, a half-pay officer, the son of a rich father, or that father himself'.[5] By paying MPs, Lloyd George claimed, constituencies would enjoy a wider choice of candidate. Trade union sponsorship was an inadequate substitute since, although it enabled those of limited means to enter the Commons, sponsored MPs were bound to their union. But such was the prejudice against state payment that Lloyd George insisted the £400 was not remuneration, recompense or 'even a salary. It is just an allowance.'[6] Payment of members was relatively uncontroversial in

---

3 House of Commons Debates, 8 May 1912, vol. 38, col. 489.
4 *Amalgamated Society of Railway Servants v. Osborne* [1910] A.C. 87.
5 House of Commons Debates, 10 August 1911, vol. 29, cols 1475, 1408.
6 Ibid., cols 1375, 1383.

Parliament; the Unionists supported it, hoping perhaps that it might weaken pressure for reversing *Osborne*, since it would relieve some of the financial pressures on the Labour Party.

The *Osborne* judgment seemed to threaten the financial viability and therefore the very existence of Labour, since without such contributions it would be nearly impossible for a party dependent on working-class votes to survive. Not only did candidates have to pay campaign expenses and the expenses of returning officers but MPs had to pay for their food and accommodation in London, travelling expenses, stationery and postage. So, without funding from the trade unions, Parliament would remain a reserve of the well-to-do. Admittedly, in 1903 Labour had established a parliamentary fund. But this was insufficient for many Labour MPs who could not afford meals in the Commons restaurant but had to eat in a nearby cheaper cafeteria. Ideally, no doubt, working men who wished to finance political activity could do so by voluntary subscription. But that seemed unlikely. A ballot held by the engineers, whose membership was around 107,000, attracted a turnout of just 7,166, of which 5,110 declared that they were prepared voluntarily to contribute a levy of one shilling to a parliamentary fund. Amongst the boilermakers, whose membership was around 50,000, only around 4,000 voted, with 3,371 in favour of a voluntary levy.[7] Nevertheless, many unions, including the Amalgamated Society of Railway Servants (ASRS), imposed a compulsory political levy.[8] Members were required to contribute whether or not they supported the Labour Party. Critics argued that the party could only survive by compelling trade unionists to contribute.

Walter Osborne was head porter at Clapton Station in north London and secretary of the Walthamstow branch of the ASRS. He had at one time been a supporter of the Social Democratic Federation but was now a staunch Liberal and determined opponent of socialism. When he had joined the union in 1892, it had seemed apolitical. In 1903, however, the ASRS added to its list of purposes, 'to provide parliamentary representation'. In 1906, it had established a fund to sponsor parliamentary candidates and contribute to the Labour Party, to which it had been affiliated since the founding conference of 1900. The union also added a proviso that sponsored candidates 'must sign and accept the constitution of the Labour Party and be subject to their Whip'. This was designed to constrain the activities of Richard Bell, the general secretary, and one of the two Labour Representation Committee MPs elected in 1900, who seemed insufficiently independent of the Liberals and indeed would send messages congratulating Liberal victors in by-elections.

7   Ibid., 30 May 1911, vol. 26, col. 933.
8   Ensor, *England*, p. 438fn.

In a ballot on the compulsory levy, it was supported by 80 per cent on a turnout of around 46 per cent. Osborne objected to being required to contribute towards a cause which he did not support. Individual resistance to the collective, Osborne believed, 'has always been of the vital stuff of which Liberalism is made, and a refusal to sympathise with it would be a sign of approaching dissolution of their creed'.[9] He sought an injunction against his union, losing in the High Court but winning in the Court of Appeal and the House of Lords. 'Not content with the judgment of the highest court of commoners,' Osborne remarked with heavy irony, 'they appealed to the Lords, the last refuge of the Socialist.'[10] In December 1909, the law lords, three of whom had been Liberal MPs, ruled that the union's policy was unlawful on two main grounds. The first was that the legislation of 1871 and 1876 regulating trade union activity had specified and therefore limited the legitimate activities of trade unions. Since these did not include collecting and administering funds for political purposes, they were *ultra vires*. Three of the five law lords took this view. The argument against it was that such *ultra vires* restrictions applied only to statutory bodies, and the unions, though regulated by statute, had not been created by statute. The unions were, critics of the *Osborne* judgment argued, unincorporated and voluntary associations, and as such allowed to make financial contributions to a political party. Lord James of Hereford, who as Sir Henry James, a former Liberal MP though Liberal Unionist from 1886, had helped to frame the 1876 Act, believed that the purposes clause was 'not a clause of limitation or exhaustive definition'.[11]

The second ground for declaring the union's political activities unlawful, on which the law lords were unanimous, was that sponsored MPs had to pledge to accept the Labour Party's constitution and agree to be subject to its whip. That, the law lords believed, would make ASRS MPs delegates rather than representatives free to use their own judgement. In the Court of Appeal, Lord Justice Farwell had quoted Burke's famous oration to the electors of Bristol. 'Parliament is not a congress of Ambassadors from different and hostile interests but a deliberative Assembly of one nation.'[12] The pledge, therefore, in the view of Lord Shaw, was not 'compatible either with the spirit of our parliamentary constitution or with that independence and freedom which have hitherto been held to lie at the basis of representative government in the United Kingdom'.[13] An MP's duties, the two judges

---

9   W. V. Osborne, *My Case*, pp. 65–6, quoted in Michael J. Klarman, 'Parliamentary Reversal of the Osborne Judgment', *Historical Journal*, 1989, p. 899.

10 Quoted in Henry Pelling, 'The Politics of the Osborne Judgment', *Historical Journal*, 1982, p. 893.

11 Philip S. Bagwell, *The Railwaymen: The History of the National Union of Railwaymen*, George Allen & Unwin, p. 252.

12 Pelling, 'Politics of the Osborne Judgment', p. 893.

13 *Amalgamated Society of Railway Servants v. Osborne* [1911] A.C. 111.

alleged, were primarily to his judgement and to his constituency. Some constituencies, therefore, were being in effect disenfranchised, since instead of a representative, their MP would be a paid delegate putting the interests of those who paid him before other considerations, which was contrary to public policy. Curiously, the courts did not give particular attention to the problem of the Liberal or Conservative minority in the union, which had been an important part of Osborne's complaint, even though a number of unions sought to impose a closed shop so that a man who conscientiously refused to contribute to a fund aiding a party he did not support might not only be expelled from his union but would also lose his job. Indeed, the ASRS was spitefully to expel Osborne in June 1910, seven months after the law lords' judgment. The union also disbanded its Walthamstow branch, 'confiscating their eighteen years' contributions and terminating their benefits'.[14] Osborne had to fight the union again to secure reinstatement. But the judges gave him more than he had sought. He had objected to trade union contributions to the Labour Party. The Court of Appeal had gone further, declaring that *any* union spending for the purposes of parliamentary representation was illegal.

The *Osborne* judgment was a great blow to Labour. Trade unions had since the 1870s been spending money in election campaigns, and in the 1874–80 Parliament, two trade union officials had sat as MPs supported by union funds. George Barnes, chairman of the Labour Party, told the Commons in November 1910 that while Labour agreed with the Liberals that the Commons should be supreme against the Lords, the effect of the *Osborne* judgment was that,

> speaking as a representative workman, it makes precious little difference to us at the moment whether the House of Commons is supreme or not if the working people of the country have no means of access to it. Up to a very few years ago, access to this House was denied to the workman because there was a golden key which had to be turned and we had not the means of turning it. It is only within recent years that a working class party has been possible in this House. It was recognised a few years ago that, individually, workmen had not the money to enable them to reach this House, and consequently the money was provided collectively … That door has now been closed.[15]

Payment of members, which Labour also favoured, was of use only once a

---

14 Ensor, *England*, p. 438fn.
15 House of Commons Debates, 18 November 1910, vol. 6, col. 118.

working-class candidate had been elected. But how was he to get elected without money? He could not afford the entrance fee.

The TUC immediately called nearly unanimously for reversal of the judgment at its 1910 conference by a card vote of 1,717,000 to just 13,000 – seemingly a great contrast to its divided counsels after the *Taff Vale* judgment. But the vote underestimated the size of the minority opposed to reversal, since each delegate voted in accordance with the majority view in their union. So the figures were illusory and misleading. J. A. Pease, Chancellor of the Duchy of Lancaster, circulated a memorandum to the Cabinet arguing that 'it is fair to assume that the aggregate number of Trade Union members who desire their liberty to contribute or not to the maintenance of a Member of Parliament to whom they are politically opposed may be counted by many tens of thousands, if not hundreds of thousands' – a view later to be confirmed by the size of the minority vote in union ballots.[16]

In 1911, Labour sought to improve the chances of reversing the *Osborne* judgment by abandoning, at Henderson's urging, the pledge which had so annoyed the law lords. The pledge had in fact originated with the trade unions, not the Labour Party or the ILP. Indeed, both MacDonald and the ILP had been sceptical of it. Philip Snowden was later to say, 'I had never found the pledge to be an embarrassment to my individual judgment. Indeed I doubt if I ever signed it.'[17] The pledge seemed symbolic, probably not enforceable in law, and hardly necessary since Labour could use the same means of enforcing discipline, the whipping system, as the other parties.

The government was less eager to reverse *Osborne* than it was to pay MPs. Some Liberals believed that it would be unwise to help a party which might in due course compete with them at the polls, but more believed that a return to the situation before *Osborne* would offend against the liberal principle of the rights of the dissenter. A member of a trade union, after all, was not in the same position as the member of a club. Were they to resign, they would lose their right to unemployment and sickness benefit and their right to be represented in case of a dispute with their employer. They might regard their trade union as an industrial organisation and not want it converted into a political one. Political views, Liberals believed, were like religious views in that they should not be at the mercy of the majority. The parliamentary timetable was in any case so congested with the National Insurance Bill, Home Rule, Welsh disestablishment and franchise reform that it was difficult to find a place for trade union legislation. Nevertheless, in 1913 a Trade Union Act was passed. But it did not restore the status quo ante

16 CAB 37/103/42, 6 October 1910, reprinted in Hazlehurst and Woodland, *A Liberal Chronicle*, pp. 200–201.
17 Snowden, *Autobiography*, p. 224.

before *Osborne*, as the Labour Party had desired. An amendment proposing precisely this was only narrowly defeated in committee, with the aid of the Unionists, most Liberals voting with Labour for complete reversal. Had the amendment succeeded, the Attorney General indicated that the government would withdraw the Bill.[18]

Instead of reversing *Osborne*, the Act provided that trade unions could make payments for political purposes provided that three conditions were met. The first was that such payments should be made through a special political fund separate from the other funds of the union. The second was that such a fund could be established only after a majority in favour had been secured in a ballot. The third was that any member who objected to contributing should be able to contract out without suffering any disadvantage from doing so. The Unionists had favoured contracting in, which the Conservative government introduced in 1927 after the General Strike – Labour, in turn, was to restore contracting out in 1946. The Unionists did not oppose the 1913 Bill and Third Reading passed without a division.

Sixty-three trade unions held ballots in the fifteen months after the passage of the Act, and in sixty there was a majority in favour of setting up a fund. Unions where there had been no majority for a fund held repeated ballots until such a majority had been secured. By mid-April 1916, just six trade unions out of 101 had voted against establishing such a fund.[19] There were, however, often sizeable minorities voting against the fund, and turnout was often low, as shown below.[20]

	Number supporting establishment of a political fund	Number opposing establishment of a political fund	Total union membership	Percentage of total membership supporting the fund
Railwaymen	102,270	34,953	267,611	38.2
Engineers	20,586	12,740	143,783	14.3
Gas workers	27,802	4,339	134,538	20.7
Carpenters	13,336	11,738	66,380	20.1
Card and blowing-room operatives	2,993	1,437	58,062	3.9
Dock labourers	4,078	501	51,755	7.9
Other ballots in 1913	128,337	59,602	485,712	26.4

18 House of Commons Debates, 31 January 1913, vol. 47, col. 1705.
19 Pelling, 'Politics of the Osborne Judgment', pp. 906–7.
20 Taken from Michael Pinto-Duschinsky, *British Political Finance, 1830–1930*, American Enterprise Institute for Public Policy Research, 1981, p. 69. This book provides an exhaustive description of political finance in the years before 1914.

In the Miners' Federation of Great Britain, 44 per cent of whose members had voted against affiliation with the Labour Party in 1908, 42 per cent were to vote against establishing a political fund. Overall, around 37 per cent of union members voted against.

The legislation did not provide for any periodic testing of trade union opinion on political contributions once a majority for establishing a political fund had been secured. No further ballots were to be held until 1984, when Margaret Thatcher's government legislated for regular ballots at ten-year intervals. And, despite the provision for contracting out in the 1913 Act, inertia meant that few took this option, and it is probable that many were contributing who did not support the Labour Party. In 1924, it was established that only around 2 per cent in the major unions contracted out, yet, during this era of Conservative hegemony, around one-third of trade union members probably voted Conservative.[21] With the substitution of contracting in for contracting out in 1927, inertia was on the side of those who opposed the Labour Party and trade union contributions fell drastically, as the Conservatives had hoped.

The figures for trade union ballots point to two conflicting conclusions concerning the state of the Labour Party in the immediate pre-war years. Support for the fund shows that Labour rather than the Liberals was becoming the party of choice for trade unionists. But the large minority vote shows that Liberalism and indeed working-class Conservatism were also strong, and that it would not be easy for Labour to win a majority of the working-class vote.

STRIKES

For the moment, however, the Labour Party, tied to the Liberals, seemed almost powerless in the Commons. The Irish Party had leverage, since, if it voted against the Liberals, the government would fall. Labour had no such leverage because the Liberals, together with the Irish, had a majority independent of the Labour Party.

Liberal priorities in the hung parliament after the December 1910 election were Home Rule and Welsh disestablishment, not labour issues. The impotence of Labour in Parliament was a prime cause of the militancy of labour outside Parliament. The years from 1910 to 1914 were to see a series of strikes, seeming, to some contemporary observers and a few later historians, to herald a revolutionary outbreak. The strikes included Britain's first national rail strike and first national miners' strike. Some strikes were accompanied by serious rioting and violence. In 1911, during a seamen's strike, for example, a town councillor in Hull told the government's chief arbitrator 'that he had

---

21 Ibid.

been in Paris during the Commune and had never seen anything like this ... he had not known there were such people in Hull – women with hair streaming and half nude, reeling through the streets, smashing and destroying'.[22] Austen Chamberlain told the Commons in August 1911 that Britain had seen 'violent actions which are only comparable to civil war', while, from the left, Ramsay MacDonald spoke of 'a sort of revolutionary spirit'.[23] In 1911, it has been argued, disruption was even more widespread than in 1926, the year of the General Strike.[24] Some believed that the trade unions had become, under the influence of a militant younger generation, syndicalists and converts to direct action. The strikes of 1913–14 seemed 'designed', the Webbs thought, 'to supersede Collective Bargaining – to repudiate any making of long-term agreements, to spring demand after demand upon employers, to compel every workman to join the Union, avowedly with the view of building up the Trade Union as a dominant force'.[25] 'There exists today', Ben Tillett of the National Transport Workers' Federation declared in 1912, 'a tendency to "down tools" at what they [the men] deem justifiable provocation.' He then went on to say, 'While we admire the spirit of revolt, it is not always activated by wisdom.'[26] 'A new philosophy of industrial action for political ends came into prominence', one historian has suggested, 'seeking to use collective bargaining for political ends.'[27]

The table below shows the number of workers on strike and the number of working days lost from 1910 to 1913.

	Number on strike	Number of working days lost
1910	515,165	9,894,831
1911	961,980	10,319,591
1912	1,464,000	40,915,000
1913	688,925	11,630,732

Working days lost had not risen above 4 million since 1901, except in 1908, but were above 9 million in every year from 1910 to 1914, reaching a peak of nearly 41 million days lost in 1912.[28]

22 George Askwith, *Industrial Problems and Disputes*, John Murray, 1920, p. 150.
23 House of Commons Debates, 16 August 1911, vol. 29, col. 1948; 22 November 1911, vol. 31, col. 1211.
24 Jane Morgan, *Conflict and Order: The Police and Labour Disputes in England and Wales, 1900–1939*, Clarendon Press, 1987, p. 164.
25 Sidney and Beatrice Webb, *The History of Trade Unionism, 1666–1920*, Longmans, Green & Co., 1920, p. 665.
26 Hugh Clegg, *A History of British Trade Unions since 1889*, vol. 2, Clarendon Press, 1985, p. 54.
27 Pelling, *Popular Politics and Society*, p. 147. Pelling's chapter, 'The Labour Unrest, 1911–14', pp. 147–164, offers a fine analysis of the strikes and their causes but ignores causes not susceptible of statistical proof.
28 Board of Trade (Labour Department): Report of Strikes and Lock-Outs, 1910, 1911, 1912, 1913, Cd 5850, p. 2; Cd 6472, p. 2; Cd 7089, p. ii; Cd 7658, p. x; Clegg, *History of British Trade Unions*, p. 24; Pelling, *Popular Politics and Society*, p. 145.

The first phase of industrial action was centred on the mines and caused by employers seeking to impose an extra shift in consequence of the Coal Mines Regulation Act of 1908, generally known as the Eight Hours Act, which had restricted miners' hours to eight hours a day. Industrial action began in January 1910 with an unofficial strike by 85,000 miners in Durham and 30,000 in Northumberland, lasting until April. The Miners' Federation called on strikers to go back to work, but they refused. There were strikes in south Wales where hitherto conciliation had been 'more than industrial policy; it was a manner of life'.[29] In the Rhondda valley, the owners had sought to make the miners bear the loss from rising costs, in part due to the Eight Hours Act, since, if rising costs were shifted to the consumer, sales would suffer. The immediate cause of the disputes seems to have been a grievance over piece rates and the wage to be paid to miners for digging difficult seams of coal. The owners imposed a lockout at one pit. The miners then balloted and called an official strike for the end of October 1910. In the Aberdare valley, what began as an unofficial strike was made official by the South Wales Miners' Federation (SWMF), acting perhaps weakly since the vast majority of miners had no dispute with management. The strike was in consequence of a seemingly trivial dispute over a forty-year perk allowing miners to take home waste wood, which the owners insisted must now be paid for. The strike in the Rhondda lasted from November 1910 to August 1911. In some districts, there was bullying and looting and militants at one point threatened to prevent pumping and ventilating, putting at risk the safety of men still at work. At Maesteg, the mines were flooded, making it impossible to resume work when the strike ended. They took nearly a year to repair. A Great Western Railways train was stormed and its passengers attacked. A ballot in March 1911, in which the miners voted to reject a return to work was held in an 'atmosphere of terror and intimidation'. 'In their violence and in the numbers of the workmen directly affected by them, the sectional strikes ... were unprecedented.'[30] The strikes ended with hardly any gains for the strikers but with the long-accumulated funds of the SWMF exhausted and 'acute and widespread' distress amongst the miners' families.[31]

In September 1910, there was a lockout of around 35,000 boilermakers in the north-east, followed by a national strike. There had been a series of sectional and unofficial strikes in Scotland and in the north-east in breach of the 1909 Shipyard National Agreement providing for all disputes to be discussed

---

29 Hywel Francis and David Smith, *The Fed: A History of the South Wales Miners in the Twentieth Century*, Lawrence and Wishart, 1980, p. 7.
30 David Evans, *Labour Strife in the South Wales Coalfield, 1910–11*, Educational Publishing, 1911, Preface, pp. 35, 36, 155, 38. This paragraph is based on this book.
31 Ibid., p. 133.

in conference before strike action was called. That agreement, according to *The Spectator*, had 'seemed to point clearly to the passing of Trade Unionism to a higher plane. The old crude methods of the strike and the lock-out were abandoned by men and masters respectively, and both sides agreed that they would defer any differences which arose to peaceable discussion.' The general secretary of the Boilermakers' Union wrote to the branches that 'this lock-out is directly attributable to small bodies of our own members taking the law into their own hands and acting contrary to the advice of all the officials in the Society, both local and national'. The strikes were, declared Thomas Burt, the veteran Lib-Lab miners' leader and a minister in Gladstone's last government, 'typical of ebullitions which have broken out in many trades throughout the country. Not only have there been sudden stoppages of work, but accompanying this there have also been breaches of contract and more or less disloyalty to the society of which the strikers are members.'[32] The real conflict, as in the miners' strike at Aberdare, seemed less between the union and the employers than between the union and the rank and file. The members twice rejected settlement terms offered by the employers, but the lockout ended after nearly fifteen weeks, in December 1910, with a return to work on terms little different from those that had been twice rejected. However, by contrast with the south Wales miners' strike, the boilermakers' strike was carried out peacefully. 'We feel bound', *The Spectator*, a Unionist journal declared, a trifle sententiously, 'to express our admiration for the manner in which they have conducted the dispute', which was

> a model for the manner in which 'direct action' should be employed, if it is employed at all. And we cannot help thinking that an occasional conflict of this kind is perhaps inevitable, if only for the purpose of bringing home to employers the fact that their men must always be handled with care and consideration.[33]

Finally, in this phase of strike action, there was in October 1910 a ten-day employers' lockout of cotton operatives in Lancashire and Cheshire following a series of unofficial strikes in protest at what was alleged to be an unjustified dismissal. Remarkably, of the strikes during this phase, only around 20 per cent involved wage claims, 24 per cent were concerned with hours and 30 per cent were on the issue of the employment of particular individuals or classes of individuals.

During the next phase of strike action in 1911, the focus shifted to

---

32 *The Spectator*, 10 September 1910, pp. 376, 377.
33 Ibid., 17 December 1910, p. 1,067.

transport. In June, there was a national strike of dock labourers ending in August, by which time riverside trade was almost at a standstill. The National Sailors' and Firemen's Union had demanded a National Conciliation Board to consider a minimum wage and a scale of wages for those working in the ports. The employers in the Shipping Federation had refused to consider these proposals. The dock strikes led to serious riots in Hull and disorder in Manchester. The London docks came to a standstill and there was real danger of a shortage of food supplies. London, one newspaper declared, was 'within measurable distance of a meat and butter famine'.[34]

The dock strike had consequences for the railways. When the port of Liverpool ceased to function, railwaymen in sympathy refused to handle goods from the ships. In August, around 1,000 railwaymen in Liverpool went on an unofficial strike for an increase in wages and reduced hours. Leo Chiozza Money, Liberal MP for East Northamptonshire and a trained economist, told the Commons that railway profits in 1910 had been larger than ever before and were quite sufficient to pay increased wages.[35] But the average weekly earnings of railway workers were lower in 1910 than in 1907.[36] There was then a spate of unofficial strikes in the railways which led to the first national rail strike. The rail unions had been carried along by events when the dockers came out on strike and, so the general manager of the Grand Central Railway believed, they now 'had to race to get up level with the men'.[37] Railway union leaders were dissatisfied with the workings of conciliation boards, established to prevent strikes in 1907, believing that the employers had not acted in a spirit of conciliation. Indeed, the leader of one of the railway unions branded them 'Confiscation Boards'.[38] The railway companies were almost unique amongst employers in refusing, with the exception of the North Eastern Railway, to recognise the unions, arguing that only a minority of railwaymen belonged to unions and that recognition was incompatible with the discipline needed to run the railways effectively. A manager on the London and North Western Railway declared, 'You might as well have a trade union or an "Amalgamated Society" in the Army as have it on the railways.'[39] The owners prided themselves on the welfare services they provided for the men, such as free clothing and free rail travel, which, in their view, showed that unions were unnecessary. But the value of the clothing was small, while the long hours worked by the men gave them little

34 Askwith, *Industrial Problems and Disputes*, p. 156.
35 House of Commons Debates, 22 August 1911, vol. 29, col. 2306.
36 G. D. H. Cole, *Trade Unionism on the Railways: Its History and Problems*, Allen & Unwin, 1917, pp. 21–3.
37 Bagwell, *The Railwaymen*, p. 291.
38 J. R. Raynes, *Engines and Men: The History of the Associated Society of Locomotive Engineers and Firemen*, Goodall and Suddick, 1921, pp. 147–8.
39 Blaxland, *J. H. Thomas*, p. 30.

spare time for free travel. A Board of Trade study in 1905 had revealed that over 70,000 railwaymen were working thirteen hours a day or more.[40] One author, who had himself worked on the railway, declared that free travel was of little use unless the railwaymen were to travel in their sleep. He concluded that 'the companies have treated their servants as if they were cattle. Indeed, they have done worse; for many companies are noted for their fine, sleek, well-kept horses, whereas few of them have any reason whatever to be proud of the condition of their men.'[41] Sir George Askwith, the government's chief arbitrator, believed that the directors 'despised' the men, thinking them too weak to sustain a strike.[42] They were to be proved wrong. The rail unions demanded immediate recognition so that wages and conditions could be improved and gave 24-hours' notice of a national strike at a time when the government was grappling with the final stages of the conflict with the Lords and a crisis in Morocco threatening war. The government was maladroit, apparently promising to put troops at the services of the railway companies to protect the railways. Large areas of the country were placed under martial law on the orders of Churchill, the Home Secretary. This created a new and perhaps dangerous precedent since in the past troops could only be employed at the request of local magistrates. The government offered a Royal Commission in a take-it-or-leave-it fashion, an offer the unions rejected, regarding it as a delaying device. Asquith responded, 'Then the blood be on your own head.'[43]

But public opinion was sympathetic to the unions, believing that the managers were in the wrong in not conceding recognition. One newspaper asked, 'What possible harm can come of two parties meeting in a room? The labour leaders are not lepers; there is surely no physical pollution in their presence even for a railway director.'[44] The government, unnerved by the serious repercussions of the rail strike on industry, rapidly backed down, offering an inquiry with labour representation and an impartial chairman, to report rapidly. In October 1911, the inquiry recommended a new conciliation procedure, which was accepted, with modifications, by the unions. The inquiry did not, admittedly, concede the principle of recognition, but the men could now elect as secretary to their side on conciliation boards a trade union official. J. H. 'Jimmy' Thomas, a Labour MP and assistant general secretary of the ASRS, was to act in this role on the boards of four railways. Election to the boards, however, was by all railway employees, amongst whom trade

40 Ibid., p. 47.
41 Rowland Kenney, *Men and Rails*, T. Fisher Unwin, 1913, p. 29.
42 Askwith, *Industrial Problems and Disputes*, pp. 157, 120.
43 Ibid., p. 164.
44 Bagwell, *The Railwaymen*, p. 298.

unionists were still in a minority. But in January 1914, the employers did finally agree to negotiate with the main railway unions.[45]

In 1912, there was a further outbreak of strikes, 'the outstanding feature' being 'the dispute in the coal-mining industry, in which about 1,000,000 workpeople were involved, or more than twice as many of the total for all other disputes'. A national coal strike, which followed a series of unofficial strikes, lasted for four weeks. It was the largest strike that Britain had yet seen. The strikers sought a minimum wage and national settlement to apply to all districts and all miners, regardless of economic conditions or profitability of particular mines. This was conceded, if hastily and unwillingly, through a Coal Mines (Minimum Wage) Bill, rushed through Parliament in two weeks in March. Keir Hardie, it was said, 'jumped with joy at the result ... because legislative enactment had recognised the minimum wage'.[46] Even so, a ballot of miners showed a small majority for continuing the strike, but the Miners' Federation of Great Britain decided that, as a two-thirds vote was needed to inaugurate a strike, so also a two-thirds vote should be needed to continue it; and it ended the strike. The Bill, like so much else enacted by the Liberal government, though limited, had vast implications. Returning from a world tour in 1912, Sidney Webb commented:

> The historian of the future will notice that in March 1912, it appeared to everybody quite a simple matter for the Government to impose on every coal-owner in the Kingdom, without compensation, and as a condition of being allowed to use his own property at all, the obligation of paying a Legal Minimum Wage, over the fixing of which, even though it might stop his income and destroy the value of his mine, he had individually and personally no control. And in marked contrast with every piece of Factory Legislation for a hundred years, there was practically no opposition.[47]

There was another transport workers' strike in the Port of London from May 1912 on the employment of non-union labour. The dockers' union, part of the National Transport Workers' Federation, a loosely organised grouping of twenty-six separate unions, had demanded a closed shop and sought to regulate the terms of employment of casual labourers who could be discharged at a moment's notice. Employers refused to recognise the federation. Nevertheless, the strike was initiated not by the unions but unofficially by men exasperated at the working conditions for casual labour. But some of

---

45 Geoffrey Alderman, *The Railway Interest*, Leicester University Press, 1973, p. 218.
46 Askwith, *Industrial Problems and Disputes*, p. 215.
47 Quoted in Read, ed., *Edwardian England*, p. 207.

the affiliated unions of the federation held ballots in which strike action was rejected, the men refusing to support a sympathetic strike in aid of the dockers. So the strike failed, ending in August without any of the strikers' aims having been achieved.

The year of 1913 saw strikes by London motor cab drivers, Midlands metalworkers and workers in hitherto unaffected sectors such as engineering, the building trade, agriculture and municipal work. From August 1913 to February 1914, there was a lockout of transport workers in Dublin, the culmination of a long period of industrial unrest, during which James Larkin, general secretary of the Irish Transport and General Workers' Union (ITGWU), representing primarily the unskilled, had, in the words of the TUC, 'adopted a very aggressive policy. This policy is being met by the employers with an equally aggressive policy of a sympathetic lock-out.' The tramway employers demanded that their employees should not join the ITGWU, whose members struck in sympathy, demanding union recognition and reforms including better working conditions, higher wages, an eight-hour day, pensions for employees and compulsory arbitration. In October 1913, Larkin was arrested for sedition and sentenced to seven months' imprisonment for inciting a riot and the pillaging of shops. Trade unionists contrasted the prosecution of Larkin with the laxity shown to Carson and Ulster Unionists, who were far more blatantly encouraging sedition. Larkin was released from prison after seven days following a public outcry. But the strike failed as had other sympathetic strikes. Much hardship resulted and many workers lost their jobs. The Board of Trade report for 1913 concluded of sympathetic strikes:

> The ramifications of this method of industrial warfare have been shown to involve loss and suffering to large numbers of both employers and workpeople who not only have no voice in the original dispute but have no means of influencing those concerned in the original cause of the difference ... No community could exist if resort to the sympathetic strike became the general policy of trade unionism.[48]

Some trade unionists believed that they could increase their bargaining power through coordinated action. In 1911, the dock strike had affected the railways and the mines which produced coal for transport by water. Then strikes on the railways had thrown dockers and miners out of work, since coal was no longer being transported on the railways, and the amount that could be stored at the pithead was very limited. The four-week miners' strike in

---

48 Cd 5850, p. 2 and *passim*; Cd 6472, *passim*; Cd 7089, p. ii and *passim*; Cd 7658, pp. x, xvii, iv, xxiii, xxvii, xxviii and *passim*; Pelling, *Popular Politics*, p. 149.

1912 had harmed the railway unions, reducing the demand for rail transport and, although the railwaymen had no dispute with their employers, many working on local railways had been dismissed, costing the ASRS £94,000 in unemployment pay. These strikes had shown the interdependence of railwaymen, miners and transport workers employed in the docks. On 23 April 1914, the executives of three unions – the miners (Miners' Federation of Great Britain), the railwaymen (National Union of Railwaymen, formed in 1913 from a merger of three railway unions including the ASRS) and the transport workers (National Transport Workers' Federation) – agreed on a Triple Alliance to coordinate common action in bargaining and industrial disputes. The precise terms of the alliance had not, however, been settled by the time of the outbreak of war. The alliance aroused fears of further large-scale strikes, and on the eve of war, Lloyd George predicted that 'the autumn would witness a series of industrial disturbances without precedent'.[49] Even so, the leadership of the National Union of Railwaymen had, in the words of its historian, no intention of 'using every strike in the coalmining, dock and railway industries as an occasion to draft reinforcements to the strikers from the million-and-a-half trade unionists covered by the agreement'.[50] The same was almost certainly true of the leaders of the other two unions. The alliance was regarded as a bargaining weapon, not a commitment to a general strike. The unions wanted to increase their power to negotiate, not their power to strike, still less to undermine the government. Indeed, as we shall see, during the years after 1910, tentative and uncertain steps were being taken towards a limited form of what was later to be labelled corporatism, involving a coop-erative rather than a confrontational relationship between government and unions. In any case, the extent of trade union militancy, the product of a minority of the politically active, should not be exaggerated. Men who, as the post-*Osborne* trade union ballots had shown, were unwilling to establish a political fund or voluntarily subscribe a shilling a year for parliamentary representation were hardly likely to support a general strike.

CAUSES OF LABOUR UNREST

What caused the unprecedented outbreak of strikes? Each strike had its own particular causes, in some cases seemingly quite local and almost trivial. But there were also general causes, some economic, others intangible and non-economic. The most obvious economic cause was the rise in the cost of living at a time when wages were stagnant. From 1907 to 1913, there had been

49   Walter Kendall, *The Revolutionary Movement in Britain 1900–1921*, Weidenfeld & Nicolson, 1969, p. 28.
50   Bagwell, *The Railwaymen*, p. 307.

a rise in average retail prices while average money wages had fallen. Between 1905 and 1910, wages rose on average by around 3 per cent, food prices by more than double this. These averages concealed considerable differences amongst different groups of workers; and, in July 1911, Sir George Askwith observed that 'the present disturbances are, to a large extent, among sections in which wages have lagged behind the general advance'.[51] Low unemployment, which had fallen from a peak of 7.8 per cent in 1908 to 2.1 per cent in 1913, made it difficult for employers to recruit non-union labour. Nevertheless, despite Askwith's observation, economic causes alone are insufficient to explain trade union militancy. Indeed, he was himself later to write of the disputes of 1910 that 'curiously, questions of wages involved only 20 per cent of the workpeople directly affected by these disputes'.[52]

The expansion of union membership increased the confidence of trade unionists. So did amalgamation, as the unions adapted to what they saw as an era of oligarchy and industrial concentration. Trade unionists were becoming more conscious of their numbers and strength and better prepared to resist employers. Some strikes resulted from employer resistance not to wage increases but to union recognition. And perhaps trade unionists in general were coming to consider themselves as having something in common with workers in other unions, as part of a united class, and perhaps even, as part of a wider labour movement, which included the Labour Party. But the degree of working-class solidarity should not be exaggerated.

A number of strikes had, as we have seen, been called against the advice of union leaders, many of whom retained cautious attitudes inherited from the Victorian era. Writing of a coal strike in Northumberland in 1910, Sir George Askwith noted that, 'as in so many cases of these years, the official leaders could not maintain authority, indicating the fact that there is often more difference between the men and their leaders than between the latter and the employers.' In south Wales, the miners had refused to follow the advice of a conciliation board which included members of the union executive.

Some strikes had been accompanied by violence against employers, though more frequently against strike-breakers and so-called free labour imported from outside. 'Peaceful picketing' had become almost a contradiction in terms. Snowden referred to 'the new Industrial Unionism – which is the gospel of fighting armed men with fists fed from empty stomachs'.[53] The police found it difficult to preserve order, and, on occasion, troops had to be used to quell rioting, intimidation and looting. In one notorious episode

51 Pelling, *Popular Politics and Society*, p. 149; G. R. Askwith, 'The Present Unrest in the Labour World', 25 July 1911, NA CAB 37/107/70, para. 2.
52 Askwith, *Industrial Problems and Disputes*, p. 134.
53 Ibid., pp. 135, 147.

in the south Wales coal strike in November 1910, which attracted many myths, Churchill, the Home Secretary, was to be unfairly accused of sending troops to shoot down striking miners at Tonypandy. In fact, though he did in the event send troops, he did so reluctantly and as a last resort when it had become clear that the police were unable to maintain order. Troops had been requested by local magistrates, who believed that the police had lost control, but the magistrates 'seemed to have lost all sense of proportion, and to be obsessed with but one idea: to flood the valleys with troops'.[54] The major general commanding Southern Command ordered troops to the area without authorisation from the Home Office, but Churchill countermanded this order, declaring, 'If I succeed in using the police, and the police alone, though blood may be shed, most of it will be from the nose, which can subsequently be replaced.'[55] However, the following day, with continued rioting, after the police seemed to have lost control, he agreed reluctantly to send the cavalry to Tonypandy as a precautionary move, but the cavalry was told not to act except in case of dire necessity. The troops remained in the area until October 1911, but Churchill did his best to ensure that they acted with restraint. They were there only to keep order, not to take sides in an industrial dispute. Indeed, there was hardly any contact between troops and strikers except for a football match held between them which the troops won. No miner was shot, though one died from a fractured skull after a battle with the police before the troops had arrived.

The Unionists criticised Churchill for not sending troops earlier to quell the rioting. In previous strikes, in 1893 and 1898, troops had had a pacifying effect. Churchill responded, 'For soldiers to fire on the people would be a catastrophe in our national life. Alone among the nations, or almost alone, we have avoided for a great many years that melancholy and unnatural experience.'[56] *The Times*, on 10 November 1910, called the deployment 'the rosewater of conciliation'. But the canard that Churchill had sent troops to shoot striking miners was to prove long-lasting and was often to be used against him even in the post-war years. Later, however, in 1911, both in south Wales, at Llanelli, and also on Merseyside, troops were to be used. In Llanelli, two men were shot and killed; and Churchill was to authorise the use of troops in towns where local authorities had not requested them, in response to strikes by dockers and other transport workers which, he believed, threatened essential supplies of food and fuel. The troops did not involve themselves in the dispute but helped to move supplies in Liverpool. And Churchill wanted to move 25,000 men into the Port of

54 Sir Nevil Macready, *Annals of an Active Life*, Hutchinson, 1924, vol. 1, p. 138.
55 House of Commons Debates, 24 November 1910, vol. 20, col. 421.
56 Ibid., 8 November 1910, vol. 20, col. 239.

London in the summer of 1910, but Asquith and Lloyd George dissuaded him. However, antisemitic riots at Rhymney in south Wales were put down almost exclusively by the military, not the police. During the railway strike of 1911, 58,000 troops were deployed to guard the railways, protect railwaymen who wanted to continue to work and maintain essential supplies of food and fuel.[57] But only in a very small number of cases were troops used to break strikes.

The rioting and violence in south Wales and Liverpool, though not unique in the strike wave from 1910 to 1914, were, however, not typical. They were the exception not the rule. Most strikes, especially those officially endorsed by trade unions, were conducted in an orderly manner.

Older trade union leaders had sought 'to create an aura of respectability by their dress. High silk hats, large watch chains, high starched collars – there was no telling a trade union leader from a magistrate.' In 1898, the annual congress of the Amalgamated Society of Railway Servants had been opened with an address from the Lord Mayor.[58] But a new generation of trade union-ists, the product of the 1870 Education Act, was no longer prepared to put up with the conditions which their fathers had accepted. Nor did they share the deferential attitudes of an older generation. Trade unionists were refusing to regard labour as a mere resource, a means of production. And the older gen-eration seemed unable to secure solid gains. In Parliament, the Labour Party, on which high and no doubt unrealistic expectations had been based, was tethered to the Liberals. 'A large section of the working class', one Liberal MP told the Commons, 'have a feeling of dissatisfaction at the results of political action. They began with false dreams. When they saw the advent of the Labour Party in this House they expected miracles.'[59] The judges in the *Taff Vale* and *Osborne* cases had seemed to show that working people could not look to them for fairness. The *Osborne* judgment had prohibited trade unions from establishing a fund to finance labour representatives. But railway companies regularly paid their chairmen and directors who had become MPs. In the 1900–06 Parliament, there were fifty-three railway directors in the Commons, in the 1906–10 Parliament twenty-one, and around forty in the Lords. A White Paper published in December 1908 showed that in that year railway companies had contributed £277 11s 1d to ratepayers' associations to influence local poli-tics.[60] Parliament, the dockers' leader Ben Tillett declared, was 'the rich man's Duma, the employers' Tammany, the Thieves' kitchen and the working man's

57 See Churchill, *Young Statesman*, pp. 373–8 and 383–6 for an account sympathetic to Churchill. Chapter 2 of Evans, *Labour Strife in the South Wales Coalfield* gives a contemporary and fairly objective account. The best modern account is in Morgan, *Conflict and Order*, especially pp. 44–9, 154–6 and 172–5.
58 Blaxland, *J. H. Thomas*, p. 33.
59 House of Commons Debates, 8 May 1912, vol. 38, col. 495.
60 Bagwell, *The Railwaymen*, p. 251.

despot'.[61] Further, in resisting the Budget, the Parliament Bill and Home Rule, the Unionists seemed to be claiming to choose which laws and conventions they were prepared to obey. 'Should there be one law for Unionist gentlemen in the House of Commons and another for poor strikers on Tower Hill?' asked Lloyd George in the midst of the strike wave of August 1911.[62] Speaking to the Yorkshire Liberal Federation in the middle of the Curragh crisis in March 1914, Lloyd George spoke of the doctrine of optional obedience. 'All subjects must obey the law whether they like it or not, unless they be members of the British aristocracy, their associates or retainers.' But fashions, he insisted, 'have a habit of percolating down from the top through the various strata to the bottom ... Why should there be one law for the poor and another law for other people?'[63] 'I do think', one Liberal MP told the House of Commons,

> that the attitude of one section of the rich on matters of taxation has had no little effect on the poorer classes of this country. I think that if we had not heard so much outcry over the Budget, we should not have had quite so much industrial unrest as that with which we are faced today. The result of all this has been the awakening of the people to what I might call a sense of their birthright. It is an idealism ... in the main and on the whole, it is a right idealism, for it is founded on facts and on right assumptions.[64]

It is perhaps hardly surprising if militants on the right were to be copied by militants on the left.

The new spirit in the land was manifested in a new approach to strike action. The older generation had regarded strikes as very much an instrument of last resort, to be used infrequently, and only after negotiations had failed. Younger men saw it as a threat to compel employers to give way. In November 1913, in a speech at Bristol, Sir George Askwith noted 'a spirit abroad of unrest, of movement, a spirit and a desire of improvement, of alteration. We are in perhaps as quick an age of transition as there has been for many generations past.' He then went on to consider the causes which, he said, 'are manifold'. The first was the spread of education. 'The schoolmaster has been abroad in the land, and ... as education improves, the more a man wishes to get a better and higher position ... By newspapers, by magazines, by books, the workpeople are self-educating themselves far more than they did a score of years ago.'[65] 'After all,' a Labour MP told the Commons in March 1912,

---

61 Quoted in Alan Bullock, *The Life and Times of Ernest Bevin: Trade Union leader, 1881–1940*, Heinemann 1960, vol. 1, p. 35.
62 House of Commons Debates, 16 August 1911, vol. 29, col. 1961.
63 *The Times*, 25 March 1914.
64 House of Commons Debates, 8 May 1912, vol. 38, col. 495.
65 Alison Heath, *The Life of George Ranken Askwith, 1861–1942*, Pickering and Chatto, 2013, p. 162.

nearly every workman today has almost as much facility for education and reflection as was enjoyed by the well-to-do classes half a century ago. It is quite right that the working classes, when they possess that intellectual equipment, should ask themselves why it is that, after days of hard toil, they are only able to win such a miserable pittance for themselves and those who are dependent on them.[66]

Social and economic differences no longer seemed divinely ordained but could be ameliorated through political action. 'You cannot', Ernest Bevin was to declare in 1918, 'have the schoolmaster ahead for fifty years and still keep the working classes at only a living wage.'[67] Trade unionists were coming to think more deeply about social questions, encouraged to do so by the conspicuous consumption of the rich, a notable feature of the Edwardian age. The new plutocrats seemed devoid of that sense of self-restraint which had characterised their fathers, displaying their luxury, in the words of one correspondent to *The Spectator*, 'at times ... in excesses almost rivalling those of the emperor Elagabalus'.[68] There were, Churchill told the king, to the latter's annoyance, in February 1911, 'idlers and wastrels at both ends of the social scale'.[69] Ramsay MacDonald warned that trade unionists 'read in the sensational Press, day after day, accounts of the enormous wealth of this country, and of the brutal Byzantine display of vulgar wealth which is going on in the West End', but 'when they go to the very men who are displaying this extravagance and ask for an extra shilling a week on their wages they cannot get it'.[70] Shortly after the war, when militancy was, if anything, even greater than before 1914, Bonar Law was dining at a smart country house. His hostess, referring to the strikers, asked, 'Now do tell me, Mr Bonar Law, what do these people really want?' Bonar Law 'looked at the table with its glittering load of glass and silver, at the portraits on the walls, at the silently efficient servants'. 'Perhaps,' he said in his soft voice, 'they want just a little of all this.'[71] It would be difficult to find a better explanation. Even so, the unrest hardly indicated a revolutionary spirit. 'There is little evidence', an economic historian investigating coalfield militancy has concluded,

> of a major challenge to the status quo except in respect of bargaining power ... by the unions who challenged employers' associations, and by rank and

---

66 House of Commons Debates, 27 March 1912, vol. 36, col. 556.
67 Bullock, *Bevin*, vol. 1, p. 91.
68 Letter 'Industrial Unrest and National responsibility', *The Spectator*, 26 August 1911, p. 307.
69 Churchill to George V, 10 February 1911, quoted in Churchill, *Companion*, vol. 2, part 2, p. 1,037.
70 House of Commons Debates, 16 August 1911, vol. 29, col. 1956.
71 Blake, *The Unknown Prime Minister*, p. 412.

file; those who envisaged as the outcome a transformation of society and the advancement of class as distinct from industrial trade union aims, were a small minority.[72]

Trade unionists wanted a larger share of the fruits of a private enterprise society rather than a transformation of it.

The unrest brought government into industrial relations. In 1906, the attitude of the Liberal government had seemed no different from that of Liberal governments in the 1880s. Industrial relations were a matter for employers and workers and had little to do with government, which was loath to intervene in disputes. The pressures of industrial action and threat to the national economy broke down that attitude. For a strike, fought to the finish, would either ruin an industry or force strikers back to work through the threat of starvation. The outcome depended on the strength of trade union funds and the viability of the industry concerned. It did not necessarily reflect the merits of the trade unionists' case. Strikes, Lloyd George insisted, were 'a thoroughly barbarous method' of settling disputes.[73] In addition to the interests of labour and capital, there was a public interest involved in industrial relations. The duty of government, Lloyd George had insisted at the time of the national rail strike in August 1911, did not end with the protection of property but embraced also the need to ensure that fair play was given to both parties. This was a new philosophy of government. Successful intervention and conciliation were particularly associated with Lloyd George, not slow to take the credit for successful settlements. But success was due as much to officials as to ministers, and in particular to the indefatigable Askwith, who seemed to have a magic touch in softening industrial conflict, being trusted by both sides of industry. Indeed, Askwith deplored the intervention of ministers as opposed to officials in strikes, believing that they introduced a political element which made settlement more difficult to achieve. The government in the Coal Mines (Minimum Wage) Act of 1912 was conceding a new principle – government resolution of wages in response to pressure from a powerful trade union.

In industrial relations, the government had no powers of compulsion. And the unions were as resistant as the employers to compulsory arbitration, fearing that the cards would be stacked against them by the political and administrative establishment. Even so, the government in May 1912 for the first time established, under the provisions of the 1906 Conciliation and Arbitration Act, a court to inquire into the trade dispute in the Port of London, though not requested

---

72 Roy Church, 'Edwardian Labour Unrest and Coalfield Militancy, 1890–1914', *Historical Journal*, 1987, p. 855.
73 House of Commons Debates, 6 June 1912, vol. 39, col. 1114.

to do so by either side.[74] There was a tension between the needs of the public interest and the comparatively weak institutions available to sustain it.

Sir Edward Grey believed that the 1912 coal strike was 'the beginning of a revolution'.

> Power ... is passing from the House of Commons to the Trade Unions. It will have to be recognised that the millions of men employed in great industries have a stake in those industries and must share in control of them ... The Unions may of course like blind Samson with his arms round the pillars, pull down the house on themselves and everyone else, if they push things too far; or if the owners are too unyielding, there will be civil war ... There are unpleasant years before us; we shall work through to something better, though we who have been used to more than £500 a year may not think it better.[75]

It was coming to be accepted that trade unions had a right to be consulted by government on legislation affecting organised labour. The trade unions were, in effect, coming to be part of the constitution. The line between state and society was starting to be blurred. A new philosophy of group consultation was burgeoning, a philosophy which was to grow during the interwar period and reach its apogee in the 1960s and 1970s when it came to be labelled corporatism, before being dismantled in the 1980s by Margaret Thatcher. So the adversarial relationship in industry was to be diluted by the political system. The philosophy of group consultation enabled Britain to avoid the class warfare which afflicted many Continental countries, at the cost, perhaps, of undermining Britain's industrial dynamism by making decisions on the economy subject to the veto of powerful industrial interests. The policy of conciliation and the incorporation of the labour movement into the state was particularly associated with Lloyd George. When in the twilight of his career during the 1930s, Lloyd George met the novelist C. P. Snow, he was asked what history would say of him. Lloyd George replied:

> I think our wars will seem rather local affairs to posterity, because the centre of gravity of the world is going to change, if it hasn't changed already, I am inclined to think that, if they are interested in me at all, they will be interested because, in the first country to be highly industrialised, I did something to mollify class conflict – and whether they approve or not, will depend on whether they believe that was a good thing to do.[76]

---

74 Ibid., 21 May 1912, vol. 38, col. 1871.
75 Otte, *Statesman of Europe*, p. 477.
76 Bernard Semmel, *Imperialism and Social Reform: English Social-Imperial Thought, 1895–1914*, Allen & Unwin, 1960, pp. 239–40.

CHAPTER 19

THE CHALLENGE OF FEMALE SUFFRAGE

SUFFRAGISTS AND SUFFRAGETTES

The industrial revolt was largely motivated by a feeling that working-class voices were not being effectively heard in Parliament or government. Women's voices were hardly being heard at all. Britain claimed to have fought the Boer War for the Uitlanders, who had sought the vote so that their grievances could be heard and remedied. The franchise was, it was argued, the one essential if other rights were to be secured. The Uitlanders believed that lack of the vote marked them with a badge of inferiority. British women were Uitlanders in the land of their birth. They too believed that lack of the vote symbolised their inferior position in society and politics. They too sought the vote so that their grievances could be heard and remedied. 'We have', Millicent Fawcett was to tell Asquith in 1913, 'ceased to have the serf's mind and the serf's economic helplessness, and it follows of necessity that the political status offered no longer contents us.'[1]

Women, however, were by no means entirely without political influence, since they enjoyed the vote in local government. But the franchise arrangements and rules for female voters and candidatures were somewhat incoherent and indeed anomalous.

For borough and county council elections outside London, and in elections for the school boards established under the Education Act of 1870 (but abolished in 1902), unmarried women and widows who qualified on the same basis as men as owners or occupiers of rateable property had the vote. By a strange anomaly, although only female ratepayers had the vote for the school boards, married and unmarried women, whether they were ratepayers or not, could be candidates.[2] For the Poor Law boards, all female ratepayers, whether married or not, had the vote, and qualified women could stand for election to the boards. For the London County Council and London borough councils, married women otherwise qualified had the vote, as well

---

1 *Manchester Guardian*, 9 August 1913.
2 Martin Pugh, *The March of the Women: A Revisionist Analysis of the Campaign for Women's Suffrage, 1866–1914*, Oxford University Press, 2000, pp. 74–5.

as unmarried women and widows. For urban and rural district and parish councils, married women otherwise qualified had the vote and were also eligible to serve as councillors, as were unmarried women and widows. But no married woman could qualify to vote or be elected on the basis of the same property as her husband.

So women, whether married or not, could vote on very local matters – urban and rural district councils and parish councils. For less local matters – county and borough councils – only unmarried women and widows could vote. However, for national matters in Parliament, women could not vote.

By the mid-1880s, female voters constituted around 17 per cent of the local electorate.[3] By the late 1890s, around 1,500 women were being elected to local bodies and there were, apparently, a larger number of women elected in 1900 than there were to be in 1975![4] When the Education Act of 1902 abolished school boards, county councils became statutorily required to include at least one woman on their education committees; and the Unemployed Workmen Act of 1905 required that women be included in all distress committees. In 1907, by virtue of the Women (County and Borough Councils) Act, women became eligible for election to these bodies. This seemed to both opponents and supporters to concede the case for female suffrage. Lord Halsbury, an opponent, declared that if the 1907 Bill passed, 'there is no answer to the demand for Parliamentary franchise', while Lord James of Hereford regarded it not as the thin end but 'the thick end of the wedge' and predicted that 'the inevitable consequence ... will be that ... the day upon which this Bill becomes law all arguments against the granting of the parliamentary franchise to women will be sorely weakened'.[5] Supporters of female suffrage, on the other hand, hoped that the local government franchise would be a stepping stone to the parliamentary franchise. 'Political freedom begins for women', Lydia Becker, a leader of the women's movement, had declared in 1879, 'as it began for men, with freedom in local government.'[6] And the Liberal government of 1905 was extending the activities of the state into the very areas of education and public health, which were in part the concern of local government, so appearing to make the case for female suffrage unanswerable.

As well as local government, women were playing an important part in canvassing and other voluntary party work and in organisations such as the Primrose League for the Conservatives and the Women's Liberal Federation. They had been in demand as unpaid volunteers since the 1883 Corrupt

---

3 Hollis, *Ladies Elect*, p. 11.
4 Ibid., p. 30.
5 House of Lords Debates, 12 June 1907, vol. 175, cols 1355, 1362.
6 Quoted in Hollis, *Ladies Elect*, p. 30.

Practices Act, which had prohibited paid canvassing. Women were also sitting on Royal Commissions and various administrative bodies and coming to be admitted, after many difficulties, into the professions. In elections to the House of Keys in the Isle of Man, women had enjoyed the vote since 1881.

The movement for women to be given the vote in parliamentary elections had begun well before the twentieth century, in the 1860s. Between 1870 and 1897, fifteen Female Suffrage Bills and resolutions were introduced in the Commons. In 1897, a Private Member's Bill providing for the principle of female suffrage secured a majority of seventy-one, comprising majorities amongst the Liberals, the Conservatives and the Irish Party. Only the Liberal Unionists recorded a majority against the Bill, Chamberlain himself being a determined opponent.[7] But this majority did not translate into legislation since the government, which controlled the timetable, refused to give it parliamentary time. Later Private Members' Bills in 1904, 1909, 1910 and 1911 were also to record pro-suffrage majorities, but again without effect.

There were, admittedly, a number of prominent women from the time of Florence Nightingale who opposed female suffrage. They included Mrs Asquith, Lady Randolph Churchill, the archaeologist Gertrude Bell, the novelist Mrs Humphry Ward and, until November 1906, Beatrice Webb. Some female opponents went so far as to work for anti-suffrage organisations, thereby exposing themselves to the paradox that, by their very activity, they were proving that women had as much aptitude for national politics as men. 'There is something a little comic', Lord Robert Cecil, a younger son of Lord Salisbury and Conservative MP in favour of female suffrage, declared, 'in the energy and the ability and the eloquence with which a writer like Mrs Humphry Ward proclaims to the world that she ought not to be trusted to exercise the franchise.'[8] Opponents of women's suffrage put forward the doctrine of 'separate spheres', according to which women were equipped to make decisions on such matters as education and public health, which was why they had the vote in local government but not the high political issues of state and empire.[9] 'With a high disdain of logic,' declared Ethel Snowden, wife of the Labour politician, anti-suffrage women 'have proclaimed that the sphere of woman is the home. And have come out of the house to prove it.'[10]

In 1897, various women's organisations, known at that time as suffragists, joined together to form the National Union of Women's Suffrage Societies

---

7   Pugh, *March of the Women*, p. 80.
8   Ibid., p. 149.
9   Brian Harrison, *Separate Spheres: The Opposition to Women's Suffrage in Britain*, Croom Helm, 1978.
10   Read, ed., *Edwardian England*, p. 222.

(NUWSS), a loose non-party federation of local, autonomous and independent branches, democratically organised. It sought by constitutional and legal methods to secure the enfranchisement of women. Its leader, Millicent Garrett Fawcett, was the widow of Henry Fawcett, the blind Postmaster General in Gladstone's second government, who had become a Liberal Unionist in 1886. The NUWSS attracted a large and growing membership but appeared to many to be dominated by middle-class women. Its social composition attracted criticism from opponents of women's suffrage, but few working-class women, living in households without servants, could spare the time needed for political campaigning. The NUWSS sought, through patient propaganda and education, to win over sufficient MPs to secure enactment of women's suffrage. It was, until 1912, a non-party organisation seeking to identify in every constituency the candidate most sympathetic to the cause, generally the Liberal. The NUWSS saw itself as being in a long tradition of radical protest, much influenced by such nineteenth-century movements as the Anti-Corn Law League. It therefore sought to pressure individual MPs so as to secure a majority in the Commons. But this was less likely to succeed in an era of disciplined parties in which the government controlled the parliamentary timetable than in mid-Victorian times when parties were more loosely organised. The NUWSS needed to convince the government, not backbench MPs.

In 1903, a new organisation had been established to press the cause more forcefully: the Women's Social and Political Union (WSPU), led by Emmeline Pankhurst, the widow of a Manchester suffrage campaigner whose grandmother had supported the Anti-Corn Law League and whose grandfather had narrowly escaped death at Peterloo, and her three daughters, Adela, Christabel and Sylvia. Emmeline Pankhurst had done voluntary work as a Poor Law Guardian, but on the death of her husband, she had taken paid employment as a registrar of births and deaths in a poorer district of Manchester. Her conscience was stirred by the plight of many young mothers who came to register births, some as young as thirteen, and by unjust marriage and divorce laws. She often spoke of her experiences and was a spellbinding orator. She became convinced that the only way to improve the position of women was through female suffrage. She had been elected to the National Executive of the Independent Labour Party and was won for the cause when she discovered that a hall built in memory of her late husband, a founder member of the party, was used by a branch of the ILP whose membership was confined to men.

It seemed, by the beginning of the twentieth century, that with widespread acceptance of the right of women to participate in public affairs, the

Liberals should easily have been able to resolve the issue. The claim, after all, seemed very much in accordance with liberal philosophy. 'The function of the nineteenth century', one historian has written, 'was to disengage the disinterested intelligence, to release it from the entanglements of party and sect – one might almost add, of sex – and to set it operating over the whole range of human life and circumstance.'[11] In fact, however, female suffrage posed difficult problems for both the major parties, particularly for the Liberals, who could not resolve them, a failure which played an important part in the party's downfall, depriving it of many active local organisers and canvassers and – perhaps even more important – the support of an important swathe of progressive opinion.

There were two main difficulties. The first was that both major parties were divided on the issue and, as Herbert Gladstone was to declare in 1909, 'our machinery is not adapted for the immediate and successful treatment of questions on which parties are divided'.[12] That was particularly true of an era when party leaders remembered recent splits which had led to heavy election defeats – Home Rule in 1886 and tariff reform in 1906. Amongst Liberals, a majority of MPs favoured female suffrage, as did the general committee of the National Liberal Federation, representing Liberals outside Parliament. But since Gladstone, Liberal leaders had been hostile – the Grand Old Man himself, Rosebery, Harcourt and Asquith. Campbell-Bannerman was the only exception, telling a deputation in May 1906 that the suffragists had established their case.[13] But since other leading figures in the party were opposed, the only advice he could offer was to 'go on pestering'. 'He had only one thing to preach to them', he declared to a later deputation in 1907, 'and that was the virtue of patience.'[14] His government already had a crowded legislative timetable. Education reform and reform of trade union law occupied a more prominent place on the Liberal agenda. 'Well, to tell you the truth, your cause is not in the swim,' Balfour had told Emmeline Pankhurst in 1905.[15] It was unfortunate for the cause that Campbell-Bannerman's successor, Asquith, was a determined opponent of women's suffrage, which he was to call in 1910 a 'most repulsive subject'.[16] 'Our greatest enemy in the Liberal Party', reminisced Millicent Fawcett in her autobiography, 'was Mr Asquith.'[17] A colleague of Asquith's told Lady Frances Balfour, Gerald Balfour's wife, that Asquith 'had only one sincere conviction and that was his

11 Young, *Victorian England*, p. 186.
12 Morgan, *Suffragettes and Liberals*, p. 59.
13 Pugh, *March of the Women*, pp. 149, 139, 135, 83.
14 Elizabeth Crawford, *The Women's Suffrage Movement: A Reference Guide*, UCL Press, 1999, p. 734.
15 Morgan, *Suffragists and Liberals*, p. 40.
16 Hazlehurst and Woodland, *A Liberal Chronicle*, p. 185.
17 Fawcett, *What I Remember*, p. 201.

antagonism to the vote being given to women'.[18] But Asquith was not a total misogynist. As Home Secretary in 1893, he had appointed the first female factory inspectors and was later to support equality of status for women with men at Cambridge University and the admission of peeresses to the House of Lords. But he seems to have held to the doctrine of separate spheres for men and women. In 1892, he had told the Commons that women 'operate by personal influence, and not by associated or representative action, and their natural sphere is not the turmoil and dust of politics, but the circle of social and domestic life'. To give them the vote, would, he insisted in 1910, give rise to 'the danger of having fitfulness and capricious movement followed by intervals of indifference'.[19] Asquith was to prove a fatal stumbling block to female suffrage, and it was a paradox that a pre-eminently liberal reform was to be persistently thwarted by a leading Liberal.

By contrast with the Liberals, the past four Conservative leaders – Disraeli, Lord Salisbury, Balfour and Bonar Law – had all been favourable to female suffrage. So was the National Union, representing the Conservative Party in the country. But the Liberal Unionist leaders, Joseph and Austen Chamberlain, were opposed, and seemingly to women playing any part in public affairs at all. When, in January 1884, Beatrice Webb, then Beatrice Potter, paid a visit to Joe's home at Highbury and an engagement seemed in prospect, with Beatrice to become his third wife, Joe burst out with some irritation, 'I have only one domestic trouble: my sister and daughter are bitten with the women's rights mania. I don't allow any action on the subject.'

'You don't allow division of opinion in your household, Mr Chamberlain?' Beatrice asked.

'I can't help people *thinking* differently from me,' Chamberlain replied.

'But you don't allow the expression of the difference?' Beatrice enquired.

'No,' was Chamberlain's response.

'And that little word', Beatrice declared, 'ended our intercourse.'[20]

There was to be no engagement.

Millicent Fawcett assumed that most Conservative MPs were opposed to female suffrage, thinking of the Liberals as an army without generals and the Unionists as generals without an army on the issue.[21] But, in fact, a majority of Conservative MPs had supported the enfranchisement of women in 1897 and 1904. 'The gradual conversion of the Conservative members', it has been said, 'must be counted the greatest achievement of the constitutional

18 Balfour, *Ne Obliviscaris*, p. 158.
19 House of Commons Debates, 27 April 1892, vol. 3, col. 1513; 12 July 1910, vol. 19, col. 251; Harrison, *Separate Spheres*, pp. 16, 17.
20 MacKenzie, *Diary of Beatrice Webb*, vol. 1, p. 103.
21 Millicent Garrett Fawcett, *The Women's Victory – and After*, Sidgwick and Jackson, 1920, p. 125.

suffragists before 1900.'[22] But because both major parties were divided, no party leader was prepared to make women's suffrage a priority. The Liberals were neither prepared to sponsor a government measure, nor to offer parliamentary time to ensure passage of a Private Member's Bill.

And there was a second problem, a division within the two major parties not only on whether women's suffrage should be granted but also on the *terms* on which it should be granted. The various Private Members' Bills had not confronted this question but had merely proposed the general principle of enfranchising women. The position of both the NUWSS and the more militant WSPU, founded in 1903, was that women should be granted the suffrage on the same terms as men. They did not support full adult suffrage for men and women, which would have involved a far larger addition to the electorate than in any of the previous Reform Bills, and which would, they believed, have been too controversial to pass the Commons, let alone the Lords. Moreover, Millicent Fawcett believed that adult suffrage was both undesirable and unnecessary, and in 1909 wrote that she did not believe that 'there is much genuine demand for universal suffrage ... In any case our position is clear ... Any change in the direction of adult manhood suffrage would make our task infinitely more difficult of attainment.' Many suffragists, admittedly, favoured adult suffrage but thought it best to achieve it in stages, the first stage being the abolition of the bar on women voting in parliamentary elections.[23] But the property-based franchise envisaged by the female suffrage movement meant enfranchising only a small number of women – around 1 million out of 13 million – and only a minuscule proportion of married women, few of whom were property owners, occupiers or householders in their own right. Most of the women enfranchised would be unmarried or widowed. This seemed to the female suffrage organisations an unthreatening approach, since women would only be a small minority of the electorate. But it meant that a woman would lose her rights of citizenship when she married and only regain them when she was widowed. As one MP unkindly put it, as early as 1875, in relation to a Bill proposing female enfranchisement on this basis, 'elderly virgins, widows, a large class of the *demi-monde* and kept women ... would be admitted to the franchise, while the married women of England – mothers who formed the mainstay of the nation – were rigidly excluded'.[24] And enfranchisement on this limited basis could hardly be attractive to the Liberals since the vast majority of the propertied women enfranchised would support the Unionists. Indeed,

---

22 Pugh, *March of the Women*, p. 115.
23 Sandra Holton, *Feminism and Democracy: Women's Suffrage and Reform Politics in Britain, 1900–1918*, Cambridge University Press, 1986, p. 64.
24 House of Commons Debates, 7 April 1875, vol. 223, col. 449.

some Unionists supported this option precisely on those grounds. The only countries which before 1906 had enacted female suffrage, New Zealand and Australia in 1893 and 1902, respectively, had not faced this problem since they had started from a position of full adult suffrage for men.

The suffragists saw the problem in terms of gender, the Liberals in terms of democracy whose claims some suffragists seemed to be denying.

An obvious alternative to giving the vote only to a small minority of propertied women would, of course, have been full adult suffrage for all men and women over twenty-one, the solution eventually achieved in the 1928 Representation of the People Act. Adult suffrage was the policy of the infant Labour Party endorsed at party conferences in 1904 and 1907, the conference in 1907 declaring that 'to extend the franchise on a property qualification to a section only is a retrograde step and should be opposed'.[25] This policy led Emmeline Pankhurst, leader of the WSPU, and her daughter Christabel to resign from the ILP and break with Labour. The difficulty with adult suffrage was that, before 1914, it would have alienated the more conservative supporters of female suffrage and would almost certainly have been rejected in the Lords. Those who believed – however mistakenly – that women would vote as a bloc rather than on party lines were particularly opposed to adult suffrage, since it would mean more women than men on the electoral register, something shocking to the sensibilities of conservative men. With full adult suffrage, declared the otherwise radical MP Henry Labouchère in 1904, 'the country would be absolutely in the hands of women'.[26]

Adult suffrage would have required the Liberals to have introduced a fourth Reform Bill. But that too did not seem a priority. Since the existing franchise did not exclude any specific social class or community, there was little pressure for it. A new Reform Bill would also have had to deal with what Liberals regarded as anomalies in the franchise, such as plural voting and the university constituencies. The Unionist-dominated House of Lords would not have passed such a Bill, unless there was an accompanying measure of redistribution which would drastically reduce the number of Irish constituencies, something which the Irish Party would not contemplate until Home Rule was safely on the statute book. Ireland, therefore, blocked franchise reform and for this reason it was not part of the Liberal agenda in the 1906 Parliament.

The problems faced by the female suffrage movement were not, then, due solely to misogyny, though misogyny was certainly present, but represented

25 Andrew Rosen, *Rise Up, Women! The Militant Campaign of the Women's Social and Political Union, 1903–1914* [1974], Routledge & Kegan Paul, 2012, p. 85.
26 House of Commons Debates, 16 March 1904, vol. 131, col. 1339.

real difficulties, which campaigners, for understandable reasons, did not always appreciate. For the argument from principle seemed to have been won, but the political system seemed not to be working by preventing implementation. 'I know of no question', Lord Robert Cecil was to tell the Commons in January 1913, 'which has given greater cause for distrust in our Parliamentary institutions to a large section of the population.'[27] A Liberal MP in May 1911 asked the Commons to imagine

> a foreigner comes to this country, and asking what the opinion of the House of Commons is in regard to Woman Suffrage. He would be told the question was debated in this House for forty years. He would be told for the last quarter of a century it had a permanent majority in this House. He would then say, very likely, 'I suppose this is a democratic and representative assembly. Can you explain to me why this does not become law?'[28]

Some women, not surprisingly, were losing patience, and a few their tempers. Having acted respectably and got nowhere, they decided to take an alternative path, that of militancy, feeling that they had exhausted constitutional methods.

THE GROWTH OF MILITANCY

The WSPU had been formed by a group of ILP female supporters and, by contrast with the NUWSS, its membership was restricted to women. It decried the staid, ladylike and traditional tactics of the NUWSS. Women should be less submissive and more forthright, it believed. Deeds not words was its motto. Its formation has been regarded as a *symptom* of the revival of suffragism around the turn of the century rather than simply or primarily a *cause* of that revival.[29] Supporters of the WSPU came to be known as suffragettes, a title coined by the *Daily Mail* in January 1906, to distinguish them from the NUWSS, and with the intention of belittling them. In modern times, of course, 'suffragette' has been used to cover all campaigners for women's franchise, while the term 'suffragist' has fallen into disuse.

At first, there was no sharp division between the NUWSS and the WSPU, which appeared complementary rather than competitive organisations. Indeed, for its first two years, the WSPU was hardly more militant than the NUWSS, and was committed to constitutional methods. Unlike the

---

27 Ibid., 27 January 1913, vol. 47, col. 1034.
28 Ibid., 5 May 1911, vol. 25, col. 744.
29 Pugh, *March of the Women*, p. 82.

NUWSS, it did not publish membership figures and sometimes not even accounts, so it is difficult to calculate how much support it had. Its subscribers' lists indicate that in 1906–07 there were just 405 members, rising to a peak of 4,831 in 1912–13 and 4,134 in 1913–14.[30] So it never became a mass movement, and it remained an organisation of outsiders not, as with the NUWSS, one primarily of the well-connected.[31] But many women were members of both organisations. The division between militants and constitutionalists was always more clear-cut amongst the leaders than the grassroots, and until 1909, the two organisations appeared not as hostile but as overlapping ones, 'in which women continually crossed back and forth according to their changing views or local circumstances'.[32] But they were to employ different strategies in their quest for the vote.

The WSPU took the view, understandably, that the NUWSS policy of pressure on backbenchers was of little use for as long as the government refused to offer facilities for legislation. Instead, the suffragettes needed leverage over the government. That, the WSPU believed, was best done by *opposing* Liberal candidates in by-elections, and in January 1910, it was to campaign against the Liberals in the general election. On occasion, Christabel supported a Unionist even when a Liberal sympathetic to female suffrage was standing. The WSPU was following the tactics of Parnell who, in 1885, had told the Irish in Britain to vote against the Liberals to secure a hung parliament in which the Irish Parliamentary Party would hold the balance of power. And, indeed, the Liberals had introduced Home Rule Bills only in 1886, 1893 and 1912 when dependent on Irish support. In 1906, when the Liberals enjoyed an overall majority, they had not introduced a Home Rule Bill. But women's position was quite different from that of the Irish. For women had no party of their own. Nor, unlike the Irish Party, did they have the united support of a major party.

If the WSPU believed that its tactics would lead to the Liberals appreciating the folly of opposing female suffrage, it showed a misunderstanding of both psychology and politics. Such tactics were unlikely to convince Liberal waverers. Instead, they stiffened their hostility, leading some Liberals to believe that the WSPU was a Tory front. Admittedly, many in the WSPU supported the infant Labour Party, the only party united in supporting female suffrage. But the strategy of the WSPU would assist Unionists. For in three-cornered fights, Labour was in no position to challenge effectively in more than a very small number of constituencies. At a by-election in East

30 Ibid., p. 211.
31 Hume, *National Union*, p. 55.
32 Pugh, *March of the Women*, p. 184.

Wolverhampton in 1908, WSPU campaigners were asked, 'If the Conservatives get in power will they give women the vote?' Only to respond with the lame answer, 'Yes, if we make them.'[33] In fact, many successful Unionist candidates were hostile to women's suffrage.

But, as we have seen, the WSPU also distanced itself from Labour after the Labour conference voted in 1907 to support adult rather than female suffrage. WSPU members were then required to sign a pledge that they would not support the parliamentary candidates of any party. This was very much a personal decision by Emmeline and Christabel Pankhurst, who were running the WSPU in an increasingly autocratic fashion, rather than of the members who might well have disagreed. At the 1907 WSPU conference, its draft constitution 'was torn up and thrown to the ground'. The members were told by Christabel 'that they were in the ranks in an army of which she was the permanent C-in-C'.[34] There were to be no more annual conferences, and in future Emmeline Pankhurst would herself choose the committee, and even that hand-picked committee was to meet just once in 1912, to expel two members of the leadership cadre who had disagreed with the Pankhursts.[35] The Pankhursts transformed a movement whose origins had been democratic and in sympathy with the labour movement into an authoritarian one. One suffragist was in 1935 to characterise the WSPU leadership as

> the first indication of the dictatorship movements which are by way of thrusting Democracy out of the European continent. Not the Fascists but the militants of the WSPU first used the word 'leader' as a reverential title ... Emmeline Pankhurst was a forerunner of Lenin, Hitler and Mussolini – the leader whose fiat must go unquestioned, the leader who could do no wrong.[36]

This was a trifle unfair since the WSPU often followed rather than initiated militant measures, many of which were begun by rank-and-file members without authorisation but then endorsed by the leadership. Nevertheless, the Pankhursts' authoritarian approach led to a defection in 1907 from those who wished to remain loyal to Labour – Christabel saw them as 'renegades who plotted to sell the movement to the Labour Party'.[37] The seceders formed a Women's Freedom League which, after 1909, adopted a policy of non-violent

---

33 Ibid., p. 239.
34 Teresa Billington-Greig, quoted in Joyce Marlow, ed., *Suffragettes: The Fight for Votes for Women*, Virago Press, 2000, p. 54.
35 Holton, *Feminism and Democracy*, p. 95.
36 Pugh, *March of the Women*, p. 178.
37 Teresa Billington-Greig, *The Militant Suffrage Movement*, Frank Knight, 1912, p. 84.

militancy, such as non-payment of taxes, refusing to complete census forms, organising demonstrations and chaining themselves to the railings outside Parliament. Unlike the WSPU, they were opposed to attacks on persons or property. After a members' referendum in 1912, the WFL were to come out in support of Labour. Later, in 1914, there was to be a further defection by Sylvia Pankhurst, who formed an East London Federation, designed to restore links with the ILP and win the working classes on the basis of support for adult suffrage. She was duly expelled from the WSPU. But her federation completely failed in its attempt to become a mass movement, its membership in 1914 being apparently around sixty.[38]

The WSPU began to adopt different tactics from the NUWSS and first made an impact upon the wider public at a meeting in October 1905 at Manchester Free Trade Hall addressed by Sir Edward Grey. Christabel Pankhurst and her close associate Annie Kenney wanted to ask whether a Liberal government would give votes to women. They unfurled a banner but were shouted down by the audience. A police officer intervened, offering, if the two women would write their question on a piece of paper, to pass it to Grey for an answer at the end of the meeting. This they did, but Grey mishandled the situation and did not answer the question, largely, it appears, on the grounds that female suffrage was not a party issue. It would have been more prudent to have replied that while he himself was in favour, he could not commit a Liberal government. The two women heckled Grey and were taken from the meeting, kicking and struggling, even though heckling was of course perfectly lawful and male heckling was quite normal at political meetings. Removed to an anteroom, the women were told they were free to leave, but Christabel spat in the face of two policemen and struck one on the mouth. At her trial, Christabel declared, 'At the time I committed the assault ... I was not aware that the individuals assaulted were police officers. I thought they were Liberals.'[39] She said that she was only sorry that she had not assaulted Grey himself. The two women were charged with disorderly behaviour and obstruction, the prosecuting counsel alleging that their conduct 'instead of what one expected from educated ladies, was like that of women from the slums'. But the defendants declared 'that, as they were denied votes, making a disturbance was the only way in which they could put forward their claim to political justice'.[40] They were fined with the alternative of a short prison sentence. They chose prison. When Emmeline Pankhurst said that she would have paid the fines, Christabel replied that,

38 Pugh, *March of the Women*, p. 115.
39 *Manchester Guardian*, 16 October 1905.
40 *The Times*, 16 October 1905.

if so, she would never have returned to the family home. This episode made the female suffrage cause newsworthy, which it had not been before; and, in the short run at least, it led to an increase in support and membership. Then, at the Albert Hall in December 1905, when Campbell-Bannerman was laying out the Liberal programme, Annie Kenney and Teresa Billington, later Teresa Billington-Greig, making a similar protest, were thrown out of the meeting. In February 1906, at the time of the King's Speech, WSPU members marched to the Commons and sought to enter the Members' Lobby, but they were prevented from doing so by the police.

Until 1908, however, the WSPU did not adopt violent or law-breaking tactics. Indeed, as the constitutional suffragist Millicent Fawcett was later to write, during the first five years of the WSPU's existence, although its members 'suffered extraordinary acts of physical violence, they used none'.[41] The rough ejection of hecklers from a meeting addressed by Asquith at Aberdeen in 1908 evoked the comment from many women that the Liberals were using 'methods of barbarism', the description by Campbell-Bannerman in 1901 of the camps in South Africa.[42] The violence and disorder, Millicent Fawcett believed, had been created by the refusal of Liberal ministers to answer straightforward questions. 'If you treat women as outlaws,' she declared in 1906, 'you must not be surprised to find them behaving as outlaws ... The real responsibility for these sensational methods lies with the politicians, misnamed statesmen, who will not attend to a demand for justice until it is accompanied by some form of violence.'[43] There was a burgeoning division of labour between the two organisations, the WSPU providing the spectacle, the NUWSS pressuring MPs and continuing to educate the public. Certainly, in the early stages, the activities of the WSPU were helpful to the NUWSS, for whom 'every post brought applications for information and membership ... Money rolled in in an unexpected way; where we were formerly receiving half-crowns and shillings, we were now getting £5 and £10 notes.'[44]

Police hostility and on occasion brutality persuaded the WSPU to alter its tactics in 1908. 'Let it be the windows of the Government', Sylvia Pankhurst was to write, 'not the bodies of women which shall be broken.'[45] In January, four women padlocked themselves to the railings at No. 10 Downing Street while the Cabinet was in session and were sentenced to three weeks' imprisonment. In June, Edith New and Mary Leigh threw stones at the windows

41 Fawcett, *What I Remember*, pp. 181, 79.
42 Pugh, *March of the Women*, p. 189.
43 *The Times*, 27 October 1906.
44 Marlow, ed., *Suffragettes*, p. 49.
45 E. Sylvia Pankhurst, *The Suffragette Movement: An Intimate Account of Persons and Ideals* [1931], Read Books, 2019, p. 417.

of No. 10 and were sentenced to two months' imprisonment. This was the first episode of wilful damage to property. The women had acted on their own initiative, but Emmeline Pankhurst and Christabel endorsed them, and such activities rapidly became WSPU policy. 'One had sometimes', Emmeline Pankhurst declared, 'to be a law-breaker before one could be a law-maker.'[46] This began a new phase of militancy, which included wilful damage of property and preventing ministers from speaking. The next phase involved physical attacks on ministers, with Asquith being a particular target. On 5 September 1909, he was struck by three women on leaving church; Jessie Kenney, Elsie Howey and Vera Wentworth then pursued him and Herbert Gladstone onto a golf course, hitting them with umbrellas. The two ministers parried the women with their golf clubs. Later on that day, the women threw stones through the window of the house where Asquith was dining. On 17 September, while he was speaking at the Bingley Hall in Birmingham, Mary Leigh and Charlotte Marsh threw slates from the roof at police and at Asquith's car, while Mary Edwards assaulted policemen in the crowd below. In court, Edwards said, 'I had the opportunity, had I chosen to take it, of seriously injuring Mr Asquith. I am now sorry that I did not do it. As he will not listen to words I think it is time that blows should be struck.'[47] Then a metal object was thrown at a train in which Asquith was travelling. These episodes led to the parting of the ways between the NUWSS and the WSPU. The NUWSS decided to exclude militants from membership.

In July 1909, Marion Wallace Dunlop, who had been imprisoned for wilful damage, demanded to be classed as a political prisoner. When this demand was rejected, she went on hunger strike. This too had been unauthorised by the WSPU leadership, but, as with damage to property, it was rapidly endorsed by the leadership and adopted as official policy. In September, a policy of forcible feeding was adopted to ensure that women did not die in prison. This created an outcry – 116 doctors signed a memorial against it and many others in the medical profession protested. In 1912, the medical journal *The Lancet* was to argue that it was dangerous since forcible feeding could lacerate the nasal mucous membrane, causing abscesses and leaving women in great pain.[48] 'We cannot', one radical journalist insisted, 'denounce torture in Russia and support it in England.'[49] The protests reached the king, whose private secretary wrote in March 1913 to Reginald McKenna, the Home Secretary, that 'His Majesty cannot help feeling that

46 Crawford, *The Women's Suffrage Movement*, p. 492.
47 Rosen, *Rise Up, Women!*, p. 123.
48 As cited by the pro-suffrage Liberal MP Charles McCurdy, House of Commons Debates, 2 April 1913, vol. 51, col. 418.
49 Rosen, *Rise Up, Women!*, pp. 124, 125.

there is something shocking, if not almost cruel, in the operation to which these insensate women are subjected through their refusal to take necessary nourishment'. Forcible feeding would 'horrify people otherwise not in sympathy with the Militant Suffragettes. The king asks whether ... it would not be possible to abolish forcible feeding?'[50] McKenna himself had been in favour of female suffrage but had been repelled by violence and had refused to support the cause until militancy was abandoned. By November 1912, militancy had turned him into an opponent. He had, however, sought to mitigate prison conditions by freeing suffragette prisoners from uniform and leaving cell doors unlocked except for prisoners undergoing hard labour and those convicted of serious violence. In addition, any prisoner signing an undertaking not to commit further militant action would be released.[51] In April 1913, McKenna introduced a Prisoners (Temporary Discharge for Ill Health) Bill, commonly known as the Cat and Mouse Bill, intended, as he put it, 'to deal with an unprecedented set of circumstances' – the refusal of women to take food. The government, he declared, was not prepared to risk the lives of women on hunger strike, 'many of whom have been convicted of no greater offence than breaking windows'.[52] In the case of Emmeline Pankhurst, who had been sentenced to three years in prison following an arson attack on Lloyd George's house, and had begun a hunger strike, her weak heart meant that she could not be forcibly fed, and there was fear that she might die in prison.

McKenna was not prepared to release prisoners by remitting the whole of their sentence, so enabling them to escape due punishment. Under the Cat and Mouse Bill, a woman licensed for release remained liable to serve the rest of her sentence once her health had recovered. The Bill received royal assent rapidly – a great contrast to the endlessly delayed progress of female suffrage. But it exposed the hapless Home Secretary to abuse both from those who thought it unkind to the women and from those who thought it was not unkind enough and that women should not be released since that would seem to show that the law could be successfully defied. In fact, the legislation was used only for a very small number of women. Of 186 women imprisoned between January 1913 and March 1914, just forty-two were temporarily released. Some agreed to abandon militancy in return for remission of their sentences, others were released as being unlikely to commit further offences. 'In effect the Cat and Mouse Act was steadily whittling away the number of active militants by securing promises of good behaviour.'[53]

50 Nicolson, *King George the Fifth*, pp. 286–7.
51 Farr, *Reginald McKenna*, pp. 231, 241.
52 House of Commons Debates, 2 April 1913, vol. 51, col. 405.
53 Pugh, *March of the Women*, p. 208.

LEGISLATING FOR FEMALE SUFFRAGE

Meanwhile, the NUWSS appeared to be making progress. At his Albert Hall meeting in December 1909, Asquith indicated that if and when the next Liberal government introduced a Reform Bill, it would allow female suffrage amendments to be decided on a free vote. The NUWSS could claim that the next Liberal government would have a mandate for reform. In the short Parliament of 1910, dominated by the constitutional issue, little progress appeared possible, but nevertheless a radical journalist, H. N. Brailsford, pushed the cause forward. He brought together MPs from all parties into a Conciliation Committee to sponsor a Bill, and from January 1910 the WSPU declared a truce in militancy, lasting until November 1911, apart from a week in November 1910, indicating that it would support the Conciliation Bill. This Bill proposed to enfranchise female householders and occupiers of property worth at least £10, around 1 million women. But married women would continue to be represented by their husbands. The Bill was supported by Lady Selborne, president of the Conservative and Unionist Women's Suffrage Society, which supported enfranchisement only on the basis of a property qualification. She wrote to the anti-suffragist Austen Chamberlain urging him to 'enlist the naturally Conservative force of property owning women on the Unionist side ... we might stave off adult suffrage for another generation'. Not surprisingly, many Liberals agreed with Lloyd George that a Bill framed on this basis 'spells disaster to Liberalism'.[54] Churchill, the Home Secretary, regarded the Conciliation Bill as

> an anti-democratic Bill. It gives an entirely unfair representation to property, as against persons ... We are asked by the Bill to defend the proposition that a spinster of means living on the interest of man-made capital is to have a vote, and the working man's wife is to be denied a vote.

An unmarried woman 'living in a state of prostitution', he went on, would have a vote but lose it if she married, getting it back again if she was divorced. In addition, the property qualification would extend plural voting. Currently, no one could vote more than once in the same constituency. But a man with an office and two residences in the same constituency would in future be able to register himself in the office and his wife and daughter in the two residencies. Such expedients would not be available to working-class or poorer voters so that, consequently, their wives and daughters would not

---

54   Morgan, *Suffragists and Liberals*, pp. 69, 82.

be enfranchised.[55] The Conciliation Bill nevertheless passed its Second Reading with a majority of 110. But on 18 November 1910 – Black Friday in the annals of the female suffrage movement – Asquith declared that Parliament would be dissolved, with the remaining time devoted to government business. The Conciliation Bill accordingly lapsed. Emmeline Pankhurst then led a demonstration of around 300 women to Parliament to petition Asquith. But the Prime Minister refused to meet them since they were lawbreakers. He would meet only deputations from the NUWSS. While there are conflicting accounts of what happened after Asquith refused to meet the WSPU demonstration, there can be little doubt that bystanders and some policemen dispersed it with some brutality and there were instances of indecent assault and sexual intimidation. One disabled woman was pushed into a side street where she was assaulted and the valves from the wheels of her wheelchair were taken, leaving her stranded. This, however, was not typical of police behaviour, and a leading suffragette was later to write that, 'the police were our protectors far more than they were ever our adversaries ... altogether kinder and more lenient than the general public'.[56] Over 100 women and four men were arrested. Churchill as Home Secretary used his power, however, to prevent prosecutions for assaulting and obstructing the police, declaring that this would yield no public advantage. But he refused to institute an inquiry into alleged police brutality. From this point, the WSPU abandoned marches for stone throwing and other militant activities less likely to lead to violence against women.

A further Conciliation Bill was introduced in 1911, enfranchising only householders but not £10 occupiers. This too passed its Second Reading, by a majority of 167, but in the absence of government support, it too proceeded no further. Yet another Conciliation Bill was due in 1912. These Bills, as we have seen, placed the Liberal government in a dilemma, since the limited franchise it proposed would help Unionists and damage the Liberals. Even those in the government who supported female suffrage had little enthusiasm for Conciliation Bills, while in the constituencies, Liberal agents were almost unanimously hostile.[57] In September 1911, Lloyd George told the Chief Whip:

We seem to be playing into the hands of the enemy. The Conciliation Bill would, on balance, add hundreds of thousands of votes throughout the country to the strength of the Tory Party ... I think the Liberal Party

55 House of Commons Debates, 12 July 1910, vol. 19, cols 224–5, 227.
56 Pugh, *March of the Women*, p. 194.
57 Hume, *National Union*, p. 113.

ought to make up its mind as a whole that it will either have an extended franchise which would put working men's wives on to the Register as well as spinsters and widows, or that it will have no female franchise at all.[58]

It was, moreover, becoming increasingly clear that a Private Member's Bill offered little chance of success. But a government Bill was hardly possible, even though the majority in the Cabinet and amongst Liberals favoured supporting female suffrage, since Asquith was so hostile. One precedent, to be suggested by the NUWSS, was that Asquith should follow the example of Peel and the Duke of Wellington who, in 1829, had introduced a Bill providing for Catholic emancipation, even though they were themselves opposed to it. But Asquith understandably regarded such a course as humiliating, particularly as he might have to use the Parliament Act to get such a Bill through the Lords. Instead, Asquith came up with a solution which he hoped would meet with general assent. He declared that the government would introduce a Bill to reform the franchise and registration systems, drafted to permit women's suffrage amendments. The government would not oppose such amendments, and if, on a free vote, they were passed, it would regard them as an integral part of the Bill and defend them at all stages in Parliament. The assumption was that the 1912 Conciliation Bill would be considered after the Franchise and Registration Bill, so that if the amendments to the latter Bill failed, female suffrage would have a second chance with the Conciliation Bill. So the Conciliation Bill would become a kind of safety net for the supporters of female suffrage. But in November 1911, Asquith announced that the Conciliation Bill would in fact come first; and some time after this announcement, the Prime Minister, according to a suffragist delegation in August 1913, was to declare that female suffrage would be a 'political mistake of a disastrous kind'. This encouraged Liberals to vote against the Conciliation Bill and await the forthcoming larger measure. Asquith's announcement seemed to have exploded a mine beneath the Conciliation Bill, and Lloyd George was unwise enough to boast in Bath on 24 November that the plan of the militants, who were 'less pro-suffrage than anti-Liberal', for a 'limited suffrage' in the Conciliation Bill had been 'torpedoed'.

Meanwhile, leading anti-suffragists in the government were lobbying Irish MPs to oppose the Conciliation Bill. The Chancellor of the Duchy of Lancaster, Charles Hobhouse, was, it was said, 'hard at work intriguing with them. No doubt what he says to them is that if the Bill gets past a Second Reading, and the Government in accordance with their pledge have to find

---

58 Rosen, *Rise Up, Women!*, p. 150.

time for it, it will seriously jeopardise the prospects of Home Rule.'[59] Two leading Irish Nationalists told the editor of the *Manchester Guardian* that 'two motives weighed' with them in their decision to oppose the Bill. The first was 'gratitude and loyalty to Mr Asquith ... They would not willingly do anything to hurt or wound him.' The second was that

> they felt that his personal position and authority was involved – that he had placed himself in an almost impossible position and that, as the maintenance of his personal credit and authority were vital to the prospects of Home Rule, it was clearly to their interest to rescue him from his difficulties.[60]

John Redmond indicated that he would vote against the Bill and a majority of the Irish Nationalist MPs followed his lead – forty-one voted against the Bill while ten abstained. In 1911, by contrast, thirty-one had voted for the Conciliation Bill and nineteen had abstained. The votes of the Nationalists were to be decisive in the defeat of the 1912 Conciliation Bill. Further, some Labour MPs from mining districts were absent, supporting a strike in the north of England. Only twenty-five of the forty-one Labour MPs were present to vote. Labour, in any case, could not be enthusiastic about a Bill which enfranchised only a small propertied minority of women. But perhaps more important, by contrast with 1897 and 1904, a majority of Unionist MPs voted against the Bill. That was undoubtedly a reaction to the militancy of the WSPU. The Unionist MP for Kensington North had written to the NUWSS a week before the Bill came before the Commons to say:

> I know well that none of your body is in sympathy with those unsexed harridans but the odium of association attaches to the whole of those who hold the principle of their views ... In the House of Commons the matter was for days the subject of comment and a resolve entered the minds of a growing number of those who formerly supported the Conciliation Bill to withdraw their support during the present Parliament. I can only tell you that my attitude is shared by over four score of the former supporters of this measure and the damage done to the movement will be seen in the Division.[61]

'If a few more windows were smashed,' Austen Chamberlain wrote to his stepmother, 'the bill would be smashed at the same time.'[62] Such attitudes were not confined to Unionists. 'The Suffragettes', Haldane told his sister in

59 Morgan, *Suffragists and Liberals*, p. 97.
60 Pugh, *Electoral Reform*, p. 39.
61 Hume, *National Union*, p. 131.
62 Chamberlain, *Politics from Inside*, p. 447.

March 1912, 'are behaving like mad women. They are spoiling the chances of the Conciliation Bill.' Both Churchill and Sydney Buxton declared that they would vote against the Bill, since a positive vote would be claimed by the militants as a justification for their actions.[63] The Conciliation Bill was defeated in March 1912 on Second Reading by fourteen votes. The militants, Millicent Fawcett believed, had a 'large share' in the defeat of the Bill and were now 'the chief obstacles in the way of the success of the Suffrage movement in the House of Commons, and far more formidable opponents of it than Mr Asquith or Mr Harcourt'.[64] But understandably, the suffrage organisations felt that Asquith's pledge on female suffrage amendments to the Franchise and Registration Bill had been a mere ploy to kill the Conciliation Bill. For Asquith used the defeat of the Conciliation Bill as an argument against supporting female suffrage in the Franchise and Registration Bill, declaring during its Second Reading debate, 'I dismiss … as altogether improbable the hypothesis that the House of Commons is likely to stultify itself by reversing in the same Session the considered judgment at which it has already arrived.'[65] He did not, however, explain why a defeat by fourteen votes represented a 'considered judgment' while Second Reading majorities of 110 and 167 in 1910 and 1911 did not.

In consequence of the defeat of the Conciliation Bill, militancy intensified, beginning with an attempt to burn down the home of Lewis Harcourt, the anti-suffragist Colonial Secretary. Then a hatchet was thrown into an open carriage in Dublin in which Asquith was seated, narrowly missing him but hitting Redmond, the Irish Nationalist leader. That evening, there was an attempt to burn down the empty Theatre Royal. In October 1912, Emmeline Pankhurst told suffragettes at the Albert Hall, 'I incite this meeting to a rebellion. I say to the government: You have not dared to take the leaders of Ulster for their incitement to rebellion. Take me if you dare.'[66] In the same month, George Lansbury, Labour MP for Bow and Bromley, pressed the party to vote against every single government measure until female suffrage was granted. The party refused – even Keir Hardie was unsympathetic – and told him to support official policy. Instead, Lansbury resigned his seat to seek re-election as an independent Labour candidate. But he lost to a Unionist, who had railed against 'petticoat government', and gained a swing of 10.5 per cent.

The committee stage of the very wide-ranging Franchise and Registration Bill, in which amendments providing for female suffrage could be discussed, was not to be reached until January 1913. But the Bill had been introduced

63 Rosen, *Rise Up, Women!*, pp. 159, 160.
64 Ibid., p. 171.
65 House of Commons Debates, 12 July 1912, vol. 40, col. 2268.
66 Rosen, *Rise Up, Women!*, p. 176.

into the Commons on 17 June 1912 by J. A. Pease, President of the Board of Education and an opponent of female suffrage. He declared somewhat optimistically that he hoped the principles of the Bill would be regarded as uncontroversial. The Bill provided that no one could in future be registered to vote in more than one constituency, so plural voting and the university constituencies would come to an end; that the only qualification for the vote would be residence or the occupation of property; and that the qualifying period of residence or occupation would be a continuous six-month period.[67] The electoral register would then be increased from just under 8 million to between 10 and 10.5 million. Were the franchise to be extended to women on the same basis as men, around 10 million women would also be added to the register.

Four amendments providing for female suffrage had been prepared for the committee stage of the Bill in January 1913.

The first, to be proposed by Grey, would simply remove the statutory restriction of the parliamentary vote to men. Passage of this amendment was essential if any of the other amendments were to be considered. If the Grey amendment failed, the other three would automatically fail as well.

The second amendment, to be proposed by the former Colonial Secretary, Alfred Lyttelton, would have provided for the enfranchisement of female householders.

The third amendment, to be proposed by a backbench Liberal enthusiast for female suffrage, Willoughby Dickinson, would have provided for wives to vote on the basis of the property owned by their husbands, an extension of the principle of household suffrage, since in practice most wives were joint occupiers with their husbands, but the franchise would be restricted to women over twenty-five by contrast with the qualifying age of twenty-one for men. The Dickinson amendment would have enfranchised around 6 million women. But it would have given rise to the anomaly that women qualified to vote for the House of Commons would not be qualified to vote for local elections in the boroughs and counties, where the wives of householders had no vote.

The fourth amendment, to be proposed by Labour's Arthur Henderson, would have provided for complete adult franchise, and would have enfranchised around 10 million women.

But MPs were never to have the chance to vote on any of the amendments. For the Speaker, to the surprise of most Liberal MPs, ruled that the amendments would be out of order as illegitimately widening the scope of the Bill. Asquith was delighted. 'The Speaker's coup d'état has bowled over the Women for this Session: a great relief.'[68] He was later to tell a deputation from the

---

67 House of Commons Debates, 17 June 1912, vol. 39, col. 1332.
68 Brock, ed., *Letters to Venetia Stanley*, p. 17.

NUWSS in August 1913 that he did not believe any of the amendments would in fact have been carried. One can of course never know whether he was right or wrong in that judgement.[69] The suffragists still faced the difficulty that a narrow franchise would alienate Liberal and Labour MPs, while a wider one would alienate the Unionists, and Unionist supporters of female suffrage would in any case have been unwilling to support a government Bill on Third Reading. In addition, the Irish Nationalists might well have repeated their hostile vote on the Conciliation Bill for fear of endangering Home Rule. Before the Speaker's ruling, according to one contemporary suffragist observer, 'it was freely alleged, and Mr Churchill and Mr Harcourt had used the suggestion to the utmost, that the Premier would resign if the amendments were carried', a threat which carried particular weight amongst Irish MPs.[70] Perhaps the Dickinson amendment had the best chance of success as a compromise acceptable to Unionists fearful of full adult suffrage but acceptable to the Liberals and Labour fearful of the enfranchisement only of female householders as proposed by Lyttelton. Had any of the amendments been passed, Asquith might have had to use the Parliament Act to force the Bill through the Lords.

Following the Speaker's ruling, the Franchise and Registration Bill was withdrawn. It could not be re-introduced since Cabinet supporters of female suffrage declared they would not vote for any Bill which excluded it. Asquith escaped from this stalemate by declaring that the government would now bring in a Bill dealing only with plural voting. By the outbreak of war, this Bill had passed nearly all its stages in the Commons but had not reached the statute book. There was, however, to be a further Private Member's Bill in 1913 to enfranchise women. This, in contrast to the Conciliation Bill, provided for the enfranchisement of wives, as with the Dickinson amendment, on the basis of the same property as their husbands. But this Bill, like the 1912 Conciliation Bill, was defeated, and again the opposition of the majority of Irish Nationalists was to prove decisive. In any case, a Private Member's Bill could not reach the statute book unless the government supported it; and it was perhaps hardly desirable for so radical a change to be undertaken through a Private Member's Bill. There were no further parliamentary attempts to enfranchise women before the war. The NUWSS accepted that Asquith had kept his pledge to provide governmental facilities for female suffrage but had failed, perhaps through no fault of his own, to take matters further. But the Speaker's ruling did not, they believed, relieve him of his obligation. Whether or not Asquith was under such an obligation, he made no further attempt to meet it.

---

69 *Manchester Guardian*, 9 August 1913.
70 W. Lyon Blease, *The Emancipation of English Women*, revised edition, David Nutt, 1913, p. 291.

The NUWSS believed, however, that there had been a striking advance in public opinion since the beginning of the century. Their membership, which had been around 6,000 in 1907, reached 50,000 in 1913. In place of ridicule and abuse, they now attracted much sympathy. At suffragist meetings, men were accustomed to ask, 'whether my wife will get a vote'. To withhold votes seemed to many working men to be withholding democracy. Labour insisted that those Liberals and Conservatives who refused to enfranchise women were simply resisting democratic advance.[71] In 1912, Labour's conference passed a resolution declaring 'that a bill which did not include women would be unacceptable to the great Labour and Socialist movement'. Labour MPs would not therefore vote for any suffrage measure if women were excluded. But the resolution was conditional on an end to militancy.[72] It was to begin a process of rapprochement between the NUWSS and the Labour Party, the only party united in favouring reform. Defeat of the Conciliation Bills in 1911 and 1912 had destroyed, for the time being at least, the chance of a non-partisan solution. The NUWSS's non-party stance had meant, as we have seen, that it supported in by-elections whichever candidate seemed the best friend of female suffrage. But forty-two 'best friends' had voted against the Conciliation Bill on Second Reading, while ninety-one had abstained.[73] In 1912, therefore, the NUWSS abandoned its non-party stance in favour of Labour and now accepted adult suffrage. It declared that in future it would support Labour candidates in by-elections, with only a very few exceptions for tried and trusted allies, and it formed an Election Fighting Fund for this purpose. The aim was not so much to win the support of individual members of the Labour Party, which the NUWSS would probably have gained in any case, but by cooperating with Labour to enable it to run candidatures in a large number of constituencies and so threaten the Liberal majority. The effect might of course be the election of anti-suffrage Unionists where Labour was too weak to challenge the Liberals, as was the case in many constituencies.

THE RESUMPTION OF MILITANCY

The WSPU, understandably aggrieved at what it saw as evasions and obfuscations by Asquith, from 1911 took the alternative path of greater militancy, furious at what it regarded as the failure of parliamentary methods. Female suffrage had brought out the worst in Asquith – his tendency not to confront difficult issues but instead take refuge in delay and postponement. 'It

---

71 *Manchester Guardian*, 9 August 1913.
72 Morgan, *Suffragists and Liberals*, p. 92.
73 Hume, *National Union*, p. 145.

is cruel', Beatrice Webb had declared in November 1906, when she recanted her opposition to female suffrage,

> to put a fellow-citizen of strong convictions in the dilemma of political in-effectiveness or unmannerly breaches of the peace. If the consciousness of non-consent is sufficiently strong, we can hardly blame the public-spirited women who by their exclusion from constitutional methods of asserting their views are driven to the latter alternative, at the cost of personal suf-fering and masculine ridicule.[74]

The suffragettes could argue that they had, for over forty years, used such consti-tutional means as were available to them – petitions, education, propaganda and public meetings – all to no avail. And the militants could claim to be following in the footsteps of men who, in seeking the franchise in 1831, had burnt down the Bishop's Palace in Bristol and rioted elsewhere; while in 1867 they had broken the railings at Hyde Park, and the Reform League had stormed the platforms of politicians opposing reform to prevent them from speaking. 'By what means', the *Daily Mirror* asked in 1906, 'but by screaming, knocking and rioting, did men themselves ever gain what they were pleased to call their rights?'[75] Lord Robert Cecil, an opponent of militancy, was to tell the Commons that while,

> it is all very well to denounce the militancy of militant women; conceive what any body of men would have done if they had been treated in the way women have been ... you have no right to treat women in the provocative and treacherous way in which they have been treated.[76]

There was also for militants the example of Ireland, which, so leaders of the WSPU argued, had won support for Home Rule by agitation, while the Ulster Unionists, by drilling, gun-running and threats of violence, seemed to have pressured the government into conceding the exclusion of Ulster from Home Rule. 'The Liberals', Christabel Pankhurst declared in March 1914, 'can no longer say that the Government will not yield to violence because [they] are doing so. Unionists ... can no longer say that violence is not legitimate when used by women because they have threatened it themselves.'[77] But Ulster Unionists had the power to prevent Home Rule in their province and enjoyed the support of His Majesty's opposition. The WSPU had no such leverage. 'Women never show up their real weakness so much', one American

---

74 *The Times*, 5 November 1906.
75 Rosen, *Rise Up, Women!*, p. 74.
76 House of Commons Debates, 27 January 1913, vol. 47, cols 1037–8.
77 Pugh, *March of the Women*, p. 174.

observer commented, 'as when they attempt force.' 'Two hundred women of whom a few were armed with clubs and paint had little but revolt itself in common with the armed bands of hard-faced men drilling in Ulster.'[78]

Some rather incautious anti-suffrage ministers had declared that they were not satisfied of a real demand by women for the vote since they had not adopted similar tactics to men before 1831 and 1867. That proved but an encouragement to militancy to prove that there was indeed such a demand. But it went much further than in 1831 or 1867, becoming even more violent and illegal. 'Terrorism', declared Christabel, 'is, in fact, the only argument that Parliament understands.'[79] The WSPU's campaign now involved smashing windows not only in government buildings but also in hotels and shops in the West End, premises quite unconnected with the government or the Liberal Party. What the *Manchester Guardian* called 'the madness of the militants' alienated the uncommitted. The newspaper referred to 'the small body of misguided women who profess to represent the noble and serious cause of political enfranchisement of women, but who in fact, do their utmost to degrade and hinder it'. One newspaper suggested that the militancy was encouraged by antis in disguise to discredit the movement. Window smashing became indiscriminate. 'The argument of the broken pane', Emmeline Pankhurst wrote in February 1912, 'is the most valuable argument in modern politics.'[80] The militants also destroyed postboxes and cut telephone wires. In June 1913, Emily Davison was killed when, running onto the racecourse at Epsom on Derby Day with suffragette symbols, she was knocked down by the king's horse, dying a few days later from a fractured skull. She became a martyr to the cause, her funeral attracting huge crowds to Hyde Park, many taking off their hats as a sign of respect.[81] Attacks on paintings began in March 1914 with the slashing of Velázquez's *Rokeby Venus* at the National Gallery by Mary Richardson, later to become in the 1930s a supporter of Sir Oswald Mosley's British Union of Fascists. Fourteen more paintings were slashed. The National Gallery was then closed for two weeks, other institutions such as the Tate Gallery following suit. There were arson attacks on churches, libraries, large empty country houses, railway stations, seaside piers, race courses, cricket pavilions and boat houses. Bombs were placed at reservoirs, waterworks, trains and churches, including St Paul's and Westminster Abbey.[82] The WSPU claimed that it had a policy of not endangering human life and that Emmeline

---

78 Rosen, *Rise Up, Women!*, p. 233.
79 June Purvis, 'Did Militancy Help or Hinder the Granting of Women's Suffrage in Britain?', *Women's History Review*, 2019, p. 1,205.
80 Pugh, *March of the Women*, p. 203.
81 House of Commons Debates, 2 April 1913, vol. 51, cols 405–6.
82 Purvis, 'Did Militancy Help or Hinder?', p. 1,219.

Pankhurst had given strict orders to that effect. They were to attack empty property, not people.[83] 'Martyrdom, not murder,' it has been said, 'was their style.'[84] But some of the arson attacks could have threatened human life. In February 1913, for example, there was a bomb attack on Lloyd George's house, in the process of construction at Churt in Surrey, wrecking part of it, an action unauthorised by the leadership of the WSPU but which Emmeline Pankhurst accepted responsibility for. Lloyd George told a friendly newspaper proprietor that it could have led to death by miscalculation. 'The bombs had been concealed in cupboards, which must have resulted in the death of twelve men [i.e. workmen] had not the bomb which first exploded blown out the candle attached to the second bomb, which had been discovered, hidden away as it was.'[85] Threats of kidnapping were made against Lloyd George's daughter and Asquith's daughter.[86] Parcels of volatile chemicals which would burst into flames were sent to Asquith and Lloyd George, and signals at railway stations were tampered with.[87] The intention, the militants declared, was not to maim or kill, but their actions could have had that effect.

Until 1912, one leading moderate suggested, the NUWSS had been 'parasitic' upon the WSPU, 'the fire kindled by Mrs Pankhurst's organisation helped to heat the furnaces of Mrs Fawcett's', while Millicent Fawcett herself had declared in 1909 that the courage of the prisoners had 'touched the imagination of the country in a manner which quieter methods did not succeed in doing'.[88] But Millicent Fawcett was quite alienated by the new militancy, declaring that it enabled Asquith to treat the militants as if they were representative of the whole movement, so converting the issue to one of law and order. Indeed, Asquith and other opponents saw in militancy a means of defeating the whole movement. Millicent Fawcett objected that 'it is the opponents of women's suffrage who argue that the ultimate basis of government is physical force. We, on the contrary, believe that physical force can produce no permanent settlement of any great political issue, and that the ultimate appeal is to the principles of right and reason.'[89] She told a meeting of the London Society for Women's Suffrage that a victory gained by militancy would be worse than defeat since it would countenance the assumption that government was based on force.[90]

---

83 Ibid., p. 1,206.
84 'The Act of Militancy: Violence and the Suffragettes 1904–1914', in Brian Harrison, *Peaceable Kingdom: Stability and Change in Modern Britain*, Clarendon Press, 1982, p. 26.
85 John M. McEwen, ed., *The Riddell Diaries, 1908–1923*, Athlone Press, 1986, p. 57.
86 Holton, *Feminism and Democracy*, p. 275.
87 Pugh, *March of the Women*, p. 201.
88 Ibid., p. 182.
89 Elizabeth Crawford, 'Did Militancy Help or Hinder the Granting of Women's Suffrage in Britain?', *Women's History Review*, 2019, p. 1,223.
90 *The Times*, 13 June 1914.

The militants, although not powerful enough to coerce the government, were powerful enough to antagonise it and damage their cause. Britain in the early twentieth century was a profoundly liberal society, deeply suspicious of a cause whose adherents felt compelled to break the law. Militancy led to a hardening of attitudes and was, as we have seen, in part responsible for the defeats of women's suffrage in the Conciliation Bill of 1912 and the Private Member's Bill of 1913. In 1912, the annual report of the West Lancashire, West Cheshire and North Wales Federation for Women's Suffrage declared: 'It is impossible for anyone who has not worked in North Wales to realise the strength of the antagonism which is aroused by militant outbreaks and the revulsion of feeling which they cause.' 'You can hardly realise', Lloyd George told Millicent Fawcett, after Asquith had been shouted down at a meeting at City Temple in November 1911, 'what the feeling is, even amongst Members of Parliament who have hitherto been steadiest in their support of Women's Suffrage.'[91] By 1913, Lloyd George was declaring that 'the militants have created a situation which is the worst I have ever seen for woman suffrage in Parliament'.[92] Illiberal activity by the militants led to the government adopting illiberal methods to combat militancy, seeking to suppress publication of the WSPU journal *The Suffragette*, diverting its mail and cutting its telephone lines. The police raided the houses of leading militants in an attempt to discover compromising material. Although this led to Commons protests, public opinion, it seemed, was behind the government, and by 1914, the suffragists appeared but 'a harried rump of the large and superbly organised movement it had once been'.[93] The Pankhursts might have helped the cause in the early days of the WSPU by increasing its salience, but they were not primarily responsible for the success which it finally achieved in 1918.

With the benefit of hindsight, the Liberals would have been well advised to follow Sylvia Pankhurst's advice and produced early in the 1906 Parliament a Bill providing for universal male and female suffrage. It is, of course, understandable why they did not do so amidst the numerous other issues clamouring for attention. By 1914, however, it appeared that even Asquith was becoming a convert. In June, he met a delegation from Sylvia Pankhurst's East London Federation which told him that working conditions in the East End could not be improved unless women had the vote. Asquith replied that, while not resiling from his opposition, 'if the change has got to come we must face it boldly and make it thoroughly democratic'. If a measure were to be introduced, he went on:

91 Pugh, *March of the Women*, p. 187.
92 Rosen, *Rise Up, Women!*, p. 216.
93 Ibid., p. 242.

Make it a democratic measure. It is no good paltering with it. If the discrimination of sex is not sufficient to justify the giving of the vote to one sex and the withholding it from another, it follows *a fortiori* that the discrimination of sex does not justify and cannot warrant giving to women a restricted form of franchise while you give to men an unrestricted form of franchise.

Asquith had in effect given his grudging imprimatur to female suffrage. But it was too late. Britain was to be at war just six weeks after Asquith made these remarks.[94]

Asquith's failure 'to see either the necessity or the urgency' of women's suffrage was, it has been said, 'the most serious criticism that can be made of his leadership'.[95] 'The failure of the Liberal Government', a leading suffragist wrote to a Liberal supporter in August 1913,

> to recognise the biggest movement for political liberty of its day is very bitter to those of us who are Liberals. I was burning with zeal for the great principles of Liberalism and as soon as I left school I started working for the Liberal Party almost as hard as I am working for women's suffrage now. It has been the greatest disillusionment of my life to find how little those principles count with the majority of the Liberal men.

It is a paradox that female suffrage was 'a pre-eminently liberal cause which was persistently thwarted by influential Liberals'.[96] And in April 1914, a Liberal commentator could write:

> In the constituencies which determine all things, Liberals and Conservatives are today threatened by Labour, and the central fact of the times which are ahead of us is the rapidly extending association of the workers with the political aims of women … The restlessness of women, if it stood alone, might have been negligible but when as now, it is associated with seething undercurrents of industrial discontent, when its satisfaction is the condition precedent to fundamental Liberal reforms, it can only be answered with evasion at the risk of a Liberal debacle … The suffragists … are in every direction reinforcing and influencing the balancing vote on which depends the fate of Governments.

---

94 *Manchester Guardian*, 22 June 1914.
95 Clarke, *Lancashire and the New Liberalism*, p. 399.
96 Pugh, *March of the Women*, p. 120.

There can be little doubt that 'unwittingly the suffragists had driven a nail in the coffin of the Liberal party'.[97] Labour was to be the beneficiary.

When women were finally to be given the vote in the Representation of the People Act of 1918 – the fourth Reform Act – it was on a different basis from that of men. There would be universal suffrage for men over twenty-one based on residence but for women only when they reached the age of thirty and then only if they were local government electors or the wives of local government electors, a franchise based on the ownership or tenancy of property rather than residence. Equal franchise had to wait until 1928.

Success for the women's cause was due less to the militants than to the decades of quiet, patient and educative work by the NUWSS, which had produced a consensus for reform. This enabled the political deadlock to be broken when coalition governments were formed in 1915 and 1916. And although there were elements of the WSPU which were hostile to men, the movement was not as a whole hostile. It would not have succeeded in securing the vote from men if it had been.

Millicent Fawcett had accurately predicted that female suffrage would not come about

as an isolated phenomenon, it will come as a necessary corollary of the other changes which have been gradually and steadily modifying, this century, the social history of our country. It will be a political change, not of a very great or extensive character in itself, based on social, educational and economic changes which have already taken place.[98]

And so it was to be. But success did not have the consequences anticipated either by the suffragists or by their opponents. Both believed that women's suffrage would have radical consequences, leading to extensive changes in the role of women in society. But these changes did not occur for many years, not perhaps until the 1960s. Until then, the main political effect of female suffrage was almost certainly to strengthen the Conservatives. Survey evidence from 1945 onwards shows that at every general election for at least twenty-five years, women were more likely than men to vote Conservative. In 1969, a secret internal Conservative Party report was to conclude that if women had not enjoyed the vote, Labour would have been in power nearly continuously since 1945.[99]

---

97 Hume, *National Union*, pp. 215, 207, 187.
98 Pugh, *March of the Women*, p. 63.
99 G. E. Maguire, *Conservative Women: A History of Women and the Conservative Party 1874–1997*, Macmillan, 1998, p. 2.

CHAPTER 20

THE CHALLENGE OF HOME RULE

THE IRISH QUESTION

The most obvious consequence of the two general elections of 1910 and the Parliament Act was to make it inevitable that Welsh disestablishment and Irish Home Rule would return to the forefront of the political agenda.[1] Welsh disestablishment had been Liberal policy since the Newcastle programme of 1891, and a Bill providing for the disestablishment and disendowment of the Anglican Church in Wales was introduced in April 1912 at the same time as the Government of Ireland Bill providing for Home Rule. Disestablishment sparked hostility amongst Unionists but little interest in the country even in Wales, where religious fervour was in decline. *The Times* declared that 'it would be an exaggeration to describe the attitude of the country towards the Welsh Church Bill as one of interest, or even of concern'.[2] The House was almost empty for many of the debates, but they were enlivened by the Unionist barrister F. E. Smith, who declared that the Bill 'has shocked the conscience of every Christian community in Europe', a claim which caused G. K. Chesterton to write a memorable poem, 'The Antichrist'.[3]

> Are they clinging to their crosses, F. E. Smith,
> Where the Breton boat-fleet tosses,
> Are they, Smith?
> Do they, fasting, trembling, bleeding,
> Wait the news from this our city?
> Groaning, 'That's the Second Reading!'
> Hissing, 'There is still Committee!'
>
> ...
>
> It would greatly, I must own,
> Soothe me, Smith,
> If you left this theme alone,

---

1   See p. xvii for a map of Ireland.
2   *The Times*, 30 April 1912.
3   House of Commons Debates, 13 May 1912, vol. 38, col. 819.

Holy Smith!
For your legal cause or civil
You fight well and get your fee
For your God or dream or devil
You will answer, not to me
Talk about the pews and steeples
And the Cash that goes therewith!
But the souls of Christian peoples...
Chuck it, Smith!

Wales did in fact have a genuine grievance. The report of the Royal Commission on the Churches in 1910 showed that there were 550,280 Nonconformist communicants in Wales but just 198,081 Anglicans, 4,526 chapels but just 1,546 churches, a Nonconformist preponderance of almost three to one. In Wales, the Anglican Church was clearly not the national church but was seen as an alien encumbrance imposed upon her by England, following conquest. In the past, many Anglican bishops had been unable to speak Welsh, and so could not deliver sermons in Welsh. They seemed to have little identification with Wales, seeing a Welsh bishopric as a mere prelude to advancement in England. It was, Nonconformists argued, unjust that a church in a minority amongst the people received an endowment from public funds.[4] The Bill went through Parliament three times, being rejected twice in the Lords. On the third occasion on which the Bill reached the Lords, Second Reading was adjourned *sine die* due to the outbreak of war. But on 18 September, the Bill was passed under the provisions of the Parliament Act together with a Bill suspending its operation until the end of the war.

Irish Home Rule was far more contentious and divisive. Leading ministers – Asquith, Lloyd George, Churchill, Grey and Haldane – had been far from enthusiastic Home Rulers, and the 1906 government had made no attempt to introduce such a Bill despite its huge overall majority. It had contented itself with an Irish Council Bill in 1907, providing for a largely elected administrative body with powers over the major Irish departments but limited financial powers. This Bill had been a further attempt by Sir Antony Mac-Donnell to pursue his 'devolution' scheme of 1905. Campbell-Bannerman called it a 'little modest, shy, humble effort to give administrative powers to the Irish people'.[5] But it had no more success under the Liberals than under the Unionists. In 1905, Irish Unionists had rejected devolution. In 1907, it was unanimously rejected by Nationalists at the Irish National Convention

---

4   Cd 5432, 1910, vol. 1, p. 7.
5   Wilson, *CB*, p. 115.

and withdrawn by the government. Asquith had told the Commons in 1908, to the annoyance of the Irish, that, while he favoured Home Rule in principle, it should be part of a more general policy of devolution and in any case, until the British people 'are convinced you cannot travel an inch of the road'.[6] There was no evidence that the British people were any more convinced in 1912 than in 1908. But the Parliament Act had removed the barrier blocking Home Rule. Had the Lords not rejected the Budget, and had the electors not destroyed the Liberal majority, Home Rule might have remained dormant, and perhaps even in the long run disappeared as an issue. One critic noticed 'the absence of public excitement or enthusiasm' and felt that on the part of its 'English advocates at least', it was 'treated rather as a wearisome necessity than as the glorious building of the Irish nation'.[7] Despite the passions which it aroused, few in England outside the political class appeared interested. On 26 October 1912, an Irishman wrote to the *Manchester Guardian*, claiming that 'ninety-nine Englishmen out of 100' knew nothing about Ireland and that 'to the average Englishman Ireland means a troublesome island somewhere in the Atlantic, where the natives run half naked over bogs flourishing shillelaghs whilst behind them all lurks a mysterious conspirator known as "the Priest".' But there was enthusiasm amongst some Liberal MPs and the rank and file, who saw Home Rule, based as it was on the principle of self-government, as an important instalment of democratic reform and, so, central to the Liberal philosophy. But the consequences of seeking to fulfil the Liberal commitment would be momentous. There was to be rebellion in Ulster, supported by the Unionists, gun-running, private armies and a threat of civil war; then after 1918, a violent rebellion against British rule and guerrilla warfare; and, following Irish independence in 1922, a vicious Civil War between factions of the Irish Nationalist movement.

In 1912, then, a Home Rule Bill was introduced, to answer the Irish question. But what was that question? It has become a tired quip that, as soon as the English thought that they had answered it, the Irish changed the question. But in reality, the question had hardly changed since Gladstone had announced his conversion to Home Rule in 1885, although it soon became clear that there were two parts to it.

The first part of the question asked whether a liberal society had the right to rule an unwilling, geographically concentrated minority, through a form of government that it rejected. Since the Act of Union of 1800, Ireland had been governed without the consent of the bulk of Irish Catholics, comprising

6 House of Commons Debates, 30 March 1908, vol. 187, col. 228.
7 A. V. Dicey, *A Fool's Paradise: Being a Constitutionalist's Criticism on the Home Rule Bill of 1912*, John Murray, 1913, Preface, p. xx.

around three-quarters of the population. British governments had sought to meet popular grievances, first, by disestablishing the Anglican Church, in Gladstone's first government in 1869, and then by land reform. Unionist governments, as we have seen, had enacted a series of social and economic measures, in particular land purchase, buying out many English landlords and creating a class of native peasant proprietors. But the improvement in living conditions which followed seemed not to have undermined Nationalism and, although Ireland had been transformed economically since 1886, the majority of her Catholic population remained alienated. It was difficult, in consequence, to secure indigenous support for the forces of law and order, and more difficult to detect wrongdoing than elsewhere, since juries were often unwilling to convict. Those elements in society who would normally support law and order were, in Ireland, out of sympathy with the governmental machinery administering justice and policing. Home Rule – limited self-government within the empire – so Liberals believed, not only was right in principle but would also render Ireland more peaceable and law-abiding. Above all, Home Rule would transform Irish attitudes towards the Union, which would then become, as Gladstone had hoped, one based not on domination but a real Union of Hearts.

The Nationalist cause was championed in the Commons by John Redmond (1856–1918), the MP for Waterford, leader of the Irish Party, characterised by a colleague as 'slow, cautious, cynical, with a prejudice in favour of truth that was almost English'.[8] Born in 1856 to Catholic gentry and the son of a Home Rule MP, he had attended Trinity College Dublin at the same time as his great opponent, Carson, although, unlike Carson, he did not complete his degree, dropping out after two years. And, unlike Carson, instead of pursuing a career at the Bar, he devoted himself full-time to politics, entering the Commons in 1891. By temperament a conciliator, he was, for this reason, despite belonging to the Parnellite minority, a natural choice as leader of the Irish Party when it was reunited in 1900. Some believed that he had become too enmeshed in parliamentary life, a consequence perhaps of his first post which had been that of a clerk in the Commons. He took little part in social life and came to be somewhat detached from new currents of political thought in Ireland. Imprisoned for five weeks in 1888 for intimidation in an agrarian case, he became, nevertheless, an adherent of parliamentary and constitutional methods. But he did not totally renounce violence. He retained links with the Fenians in the 1890s, while in 1905, he told the Commons that 'if I believed there was the smallest reasonable chance of success, I would have no hesitation in advising my fellow-countrymen to

8 Paul Bew, *Ideology and the Irish Question: Ulster Unionism and Irish Nationalism, 1912–1916*, Clarendon Press, 1994, p. 63.

end the present system by armed revolt', and was again briefly imprisoned in 1909 for his part in the land agitation.[9] The Irish Nationalists perhaps were to remain, in words used by Seán Lemass of Fianna Fáil in 1926, when it entered the Dáil after the Civil War, 'a slightly constitutional party'. Redmond's mother was a Protestant who had converted to Catholicism, and a Unionist. His second wife also was a Protestant, and he probably had greater understanding of and indeed sympathy with the Protestants of Ulster than most Nationalists. He was on the moderate wing of his party and had supported Plunkett's Recess Committee and been sympathetic to Wyndham's Land Purchase Act, which he regarded, by contrast with the majority of his followers, as the 'greatest measure since the Union'.[10] Less hostile to Britain than many Nationalists, he also had a more positive attitude to the empire than was common in Nationalist circles. Although a supporter of Parnell, he lacked the glamour, emotional force and charisma of that by now legendary figure. His strength lay less in Ireland and more in the Commons. The journalist W. T. Stead had believed in 1906 that, were Redmond an MP for a major party, he 'would have had a better chance than most men to be prime minister. He has the qualities for the post ... He is the greatest of our parliamentarians.'[11] But in the Commons he appeared, quite unlike Parnell, as a supplicant, confessing to his lieutenant John Dillon that he felt 'really humiliated in having to run after them in the way I have done it'. Redmond, it has been said, was 'in some ways ... loyal to the letter but not necessarily to the spirit of Parnellism'.[12] And the party had changed since Parnell, when it had appeared composed of young and lively enthusiasts. Now it seemed middle-aged, too ensconced at Westminster and out of touch with new elements in Irish society.

Opponents of Home Rule believed that, far from proving a barrier to separation, it would encourage it and intensify the conflict between Ireland and the rest of Britain. For a Dublin Parliament would provide a new forum for Irish Nationalists. Inadequacies in the government or administration of Ireland would always be attributed to the British government's failure to concede sufficient funds or to concede sufficient powers to the Irish Parliament; and the Dublin Parliament would give Nationalists greater leverage to protest and agitate. Moreover, Home Rule would not be accepted as a final settlement, despite what Nationalists said. Their ultimate, albeit unspoken,

---

9   House of Commons Debates, 12 April 1905, vol. 144, cols 1508–9.

10 Paul Bew, *John Redmond*, Dundalgan Press, 1996, Preface, pp. 27, 6.

11 J. O. Baylen, '"What Mr Redmond Thought": An Unpublished Interview with John Redmond, December 1906', *Irish Historical Studies*, 1974, p. 173.

12 Alvin Jackson, 'Redmond and Carson: Bloodshed, Borders and the Union State', *Revue Française de Civilisation Britannique*, 2019, pp. 8, 4. This article provides a penetrating comparison of the two leaders.

objective, critics suggested, was not a mere revision of the legislative relationship but, perhaps through peaceful evolution, dominion status or even
outright independence. After all, Parnell, speaking in Cork In 1885, had insisted that 'no man has the right to fix the boundary to the march of a nation
... No man has the right to say to his country, "Thus far shalt thou go and
no further."' Independence was as unacceptable to Liberals, who wanted to
retain the legislative union but revise its terms, as it was to Unionists. An
independent Ireland, even if remaining in the empire, would, many believed,
constitute a danger to Britain as a hostile base for enemy troops as it had
been during the rebellion of 1798, when part of the country had been occupied by French troops. Unionists argued that Home Rule would merely
create an appetite for more, an appetite which could be satiated only by
separation. There was, Unionists believed, no halfway house between the
unitary state and separation, apart from federalism, which, they believed,
was quite unsuited to Britain. So Home Rule, far from proving a barrier to
separation, would encourage it and lead to greater conflict between Ireland
and the rest of the United Kingdom.

The Unionist alternative to Home Rule was to continue the twofold
policy of resolute government combined with social and economic reforms,
reforms which, they argued, needed more time for their full beneficial effects
to be felt. In due course, they hoped, Ireland would be reconciled to the
Union. And indeed by 1910, Ireland was more peaceful than it had been
during the last two decades of the nineteenth century, although, admittedly,
the demand for Home Rule seemed not to have abated, while parliamentary
elections showed that the Irish Party still retained an electoral stranglehold
over Ireland outside Ulster.

In theory, the argument that Home Rule would lead to separatism could
have been met by a policy of 'Home Rule All Round', sometimes called
federalism, not in the sense of a juridical division of powers on the American
or Canadian model, but Home Rule Parliaments throughout the United
Kingdom with powers roughly similar to those of the proposed Irish Parliament. This policy was, its advocates believed, consistent with retaining
legal sovereignty at Westminster. The term 'federalism', used rather loosely,
had the advantage over 'Home Rule All Round', according to an advocate,
as being 'a good fighting word ... Devolution has noisome associations.
Home Rule all round, worse. Federalism has been a success everywhere, and
people therefore will not be inclined to fight shy of the word.'[13] Under this
policy, Scotland, Wales and also either England or the English regions would
be given subordinate Parliaments, and there would, therefore, be equal

13 Quoted in J. E. Kendle, 'The Round Table Movement and "Home Rule All Round"', *Historical Journal*, 1968, p. 338.

treatment for every part of the United Kingdom, checking separatism since Ireland would no longer be singled out as a special case and would be given nothing which was not also given to the rest of the kingdom. So the effect would be centripetal, not, as with Home Rule for Ireland alone, centrifugal. In addition, its advocates believed, the federal solution could resolve the Ulster problem since Ulster could be given its own Parliament with powers similar to the Dublin Parliament and those of Scotland, Wales and England. The success of federalism in Canada, where it seemed to have conciliated the French minority, and also in Australia was cited as something for Britain to follow. So also was the new constitution of South Africa, even though not precisely federal, enacted in 1910, which seemed to have conciliated the Boers, who, like the Irish, had been hostile. Indeed, Asquith believed that the Transvaal was 'strictly analogous to the case of Ireland', while Botha, first Prime Minister of South Africa, was himself sympathetic to Home Rule as were the leaders of the other dominions. Liberals hoped that Redmond could become the Irish Botha.[14] As we have seen, Home Rule All Round in 1910 was supported by some younger Unionists who could call in aid Disraeli, who had, apparently, been prepared to consider it in 1880.[15] It also attracted some leading Liberals, including Lloyd George and Churchill. Accordingly, the second draft of the 1912 Government of Ireland Bill, influenced by Lloyd George, proposed Commons Grand Committees in England, Scotland and Wales with powers not dissimilar to those offered to Ireland, a prelude perhaps to legislative devolution. Indeed, the original title of the Home Rule Bill was the Government of Ireland and House of Commons (Devolution of Business) Bill. The scheme was to be dropped from the final draft of the Bill, but in introducing it, Asquith declared that it was 'the first and only the first step in a larger and more comprehensive policy' of devolution, and during the debates on the Bill, he looked forward to dealing 'with this problem in relation to Scotland'.[16] But the government produced no concrete plans for further devolution, and Unionists regarded Asquith's statement as a deceitful attempt to head off opposition to Irish Home Rule.

In any case, Home Rule All Round was unrealistic. It would involve an upheaval, which few sought, in the government of Britain for the sake of Ireland, yielding a constitution for Britain, which it did not want, to placate hostility to Irish Home Rule. *The Spectator* on 21 September 1912 declared that to reconstruct the whole kingdom to accommodate Irish needs was akin to arguing that the best way to roast a pig was to burn down the

---

14 House of Commons Debates, 11 April 1912, vol. 35, col. 1406.
15 Monypenny and Buckle, *Life of Disraeli*, vol. 6, p. 510.
16 Patricia Jalland, 'United Kingdom Devolution 1910–14: Political Panacea or Tactical Diversion?', *English Historical Review*, 1979, pp. 765–7; House of Commons Debates, 11 April 1912, vol. 35, col. 1043; 18 June 1912, col. 1568.

whole house. Irish Nationalists were equally unsympathetic to Home Rule All Round. They wanted to redress Irish grievances, not to reconstruct the whole constitution. Some Nationalists believed that Home Rule All Round was a tactical diversion intended to delay satisfaction of the Irish demand which was far more urgent than devolution elsewhere. Significantly, the two leading ministers most associated with Home Rule All Round, Churchill and Lloyd George, were far from orthodox Liberals, one a former Conservative who retained imperialist instincts, the other a former Welsh nationalist who had been unsympathetic to Home Rule in 1886 and had been attracted to Chamberlain's ideas. More orthodox Liberals such as John Morley were suspicious of Home Rule All Round, agreeing with the Nationalists that the condition of Ireland was special and urgent, and that the form of Home Rule suitable for Ireland would not also be suitable for other parts of the kingdom which did not have Ireland's problems. The 'federal' solution always had about it an air of unreality, an unreality brutally pointed out by Lord Salisbury in 1880, in reply to a correspondent who was urging it. 'As to Home Rule in your sense – which is Federation – I do not see in it any elements of practicability. Nations do not change their political nature like that except through blood.'[17]

THE ULSTER QUESTION

The first part of the Irish question asked how Ireland could be governed in a liberal polity. But there was a second part of the question, occasioned by the presence of a large Protestant minority, amounting to just over a quarter of its population. In most of Ireland, the Protestants were a scattered minority, but in the province of Ulster they were in a majority of around 56 per cent. In three counties of Ulster – Cavan, Donegal and Monaghan, later to become part of the Irish Republic – they were a distinct minority comprising between a fifth and a quarter of the population. In Fermanagh and Tyrone, they were a more substantial minority comprising around 45 per cent of the population. But in the remaining four counties – Antrim, Armagh, Down and Londonderry – they were in a concentrated majority, and in Antrim and Down an overwhelming majority.[18] Nationalists tended to believe that the Protestant minority had been 'planted' there by James I in the early seventeenth century to subjugate the Catholics, and that they were, therefore, an alien element in Ireland. But Unionists argued that there had been an English

17 Salisbury to Rev. M. MacColl, 12 April 1889, in G. W. E. Russell, ed., *Malcolm MacColl: Memoirs and Correspondence*, Smith Elder, 1914, p. 137.
18 L. P. Curtis Jr, 'Ireland in 1914', in Vaughan, ed., *A New History of Ireland, vol. VI*, pp. 146, 178.

and Scottish presence in Ulster before the seventeenth century and before the Reformation. There had, they insisted, been a Scottish presence in Ulster from earliest times, with immigration from Scotland being 'fairly continuous for centuries before 1609'.[19] Nor had the plantation in the seventeenth century covered the whole of Ulster, since three of its counties – Antrim, Down and Monaghan – had not been plantation counties at all. But the Protestant population had come to occupy the more fertile areas, the Catholics the less fertile, and had come to assume the character of a dominant minority which was enjoying a monopoly on political power. The Ulster Protestants felt their main links to be with Scotland and the rest of the United Kingdom rather than the Catholic population of Ireland, from whom they felt separate, not only in religion but also in nationality and ethnicity. Unlike the vast majority in the rest of Ireland, they accepted the premise on which the Act of Union had been based as an expression of a single British nationhood. And while, in the rest of Ireland, the Protestant population was largely concentrated amongst the better off, in Ulster it embraced every social class. Everywhere the Protestants seemed 'isolated from the mainstream of Catholic and Gaelic culture', which had remained immune to the Reformation.[20] In the nineteenth century, differences were accentuated as Belfast became an industrial city, while in agriculture there was a different system of land tenure in Ulster from that prevailing in the other provinces. The rise of Irish Nationalism and the growth of a modern sense of Irish identity from the end of the eighteenth century exacerbated the conflict. For, although some Irish Nationalist leaders – for example, Wolfe Tone and Parnell – were Protestants, Irish Nationalism came to be identified with the Catholic majority and by 1886, the terms Protestant and Unionist had become largely interchangeable. It is the superimposition of a Nationalist conflict upon a religious one which explains the persistence and depth of the Irish problem.

The conflict between the two communities, therefore, had deep historical roots. In 1919, Lloyd George was to declare that what had begun as 'a family quarrel' had 'degenerated into a blood feud'.[21] The Protestants were determined to resist submission to a Dublin Parliament, entailing rule by men they regarded as disloyal, a view intensified when Nationalist MPs cheered Boer victories in the war. They also believed that a Nationalist government would be corrupt and priest-ridden. Home Rule would mean Rome rule. And Ulster Unionists regarded Home Rule as being tantamount to expulsion from the kingdom. They were not mollified by being told that Home Rule

---

19 A. T. Q. Stewart, *The Narrow Ground: Aspects of Ulster 1609–1909*, Faber, 1977, p. 39.
20 Ibid., p. 39.
21 House of Commons Debates, 22 December 1919, vol. 123, col. 1168.

was distinct from separation. The 21st-century experience with Scotland may show that they were right. It is too early to tell.

The scattered Protestant minority outside Ulster, comprising largely the middle and upper classes, would find it difficult to resist Home Rule, but in Ulster where opposition to Home Rule came from every section of society, Unionists could certainly resist.

Sir Edward Carson (1854–1935), who championed the Ulster cause in Parliament, was not himself an Ulsterman, and indeed had little previous contact with the province. He had been born in Dublin where he had qualified as a barrister, becoming a leading advocate at the English Bar. He had first won fame in 1895 through his successful defence of Lord Queensberry against Oscar Wilde's accusation of criminal libel. Carson had been a fellow student of Wilde's at Trinity College Dublin, and Wilde had allegedly declared that Carson would 'pursue his case with all the added bitterness of an old friend'. Carson was not in fact a friend, had enjoyed no social contact with Wilde and would certainly not have prosecuted him had he been a friend. He interceded, unsuccessfully, after the libel case, by asking the Solicitor General not to prosecute Wilde for indecency, pleading, 'Can you not let up on the fellow now, he has suffered a great deal?'[22] He had also successfully defended in 1910 George Archer-Shee, a naval cadet accused of theft, a case later to be immortalised in Terence Rattigan's play *The Winslow Boy*. Carson had won the admiration of Irish Unionists by successfully prosecuting at the Irish Bar Nationalists accused of agrarian crime. Elected as Liberal Unionist MP for Dublin University in 1892, he became Solicitor General for Ireland in the same year and then, from 1900 to 1905, Solicitor General for England. In 1910, he became leader of the Ulster Unionists following the resignation of Walter Long, infusing the cause with a passion and fire of which Long had been incapable. Although often identified with Orangeism, Carson was in fact unsympathetic to it, and had belonged to an Orange Lodge for only a short time in his late teens. A liberal on many issues, he supported the demand for a Catholic University in Ireland. An 'independent nationalist' declared in the *Irish Times* on 9 October 1913 that there 'was no member of the House of Commons who was more respected by the Nationalists' and remarked 'how careful he [Carson] was to avoid saying a single word that could even seem to be offensive to the Roman Catholic religion'. But Carson was implacably opposed to Home Rule and deeply committed to the Union. To the cause of Ulster Unionism, he provided both courage and forensic ability. But his activities were primarily in London not Belfast, and the organisation of opposition in Ulster was in the hands of his associate, James

22 Gerry Moriarty, Interview with Merlin Holland, Oscar Wilde's grandson, *Irish Times*, 23 January 2021.

Craig, who was to become the first Prime Minister of Northern Ireland in 1921. Craig, unlike Carson, was an Ulsterman, born in Belfast, a member of the Orange Order and close to the grassroots. He had fought and been taken prisoner by the Boers, and on his return to civilian life, was elected Unionist MP for East Down in 1906. After the Ulster Covenant was signed in 1912, Craig was charged with preparing a constitution for a provisional government of Ulster.

To liberals in London, Carson appeared as a dangerous extremist. But this was somewhat deceptive. His aim was, by ratcheting up the threat of militancy and violence, to secure a compromise solution – a tactic often used by the Nationalists, in accordance with Tim Healy's dictum that in Ireland violence was the only way to secure a hearing for moderation. Carson was in fact to ensure that the Ulster movement was contained and disciplined. It was, nevertheless, a paradox that, while the Nationalists, who in the nineteenth century had combined parliamentary politics with extra-parliamentary agitation, were now ensconced in Parliament, the Unionists seemed to depend upon popular mobilisation outside Parliament. But Carson's defence of Ulster was intended not to secure partition but to defeat Home Rule. 'If Ulster succeeds,' he declared in 1911, 'Home Rule is dead.'[23] For many Unionists believed that, without industrial Ireland centred on Belfast, an Irish Parliament would not be viable and so Home Rule also would not be viable. But once it was clear that the southern Unionists could not prevent Home Rule, Carson was determined to save Ulster from the wreckage. Partition, originally a tactic to defeat Home Rule, was to become a compromise solution. Carson's statue lies outside Stormont, and he is often seen as the founder of the Northern Ireland state, which Unionists are committed to defend. Yet he was ambivalent about partition and told a correspondent after the war that he had agreed 'to the exclusion of six counties although I think that arrangement unstatesmanlike and a poor solution'.[24] He had hoped that exclusion would be but a temporary solution and declared that, if only Nationalists would woo Unionists and empathise with their concerns, Ulster would come to accept a Dublin Parliament. But Nationalists did not empathise with the Unionist tradition. That was perhaps hardly surprising since both Joseph Chamberlain and Lord Randolph Churchill had used Ulster to prevent Home Rule in the rest of Ireland, rather than arguing for exclusion. Carson at first did the same, though Bonar Law, paradoxically in the light of his even more extreme

---

23 Cited in Nicholas Mansergh, *The Government of Northern Ireland: A Study in Devolution*, George Allen & Unwin, 1936, p. 93.
24 Alvin Jackson, 'Redmond and Carson', p. 9.

utterances, concentrated more on exclusion, using extreme language to secure a moderate outcome.

To many in Britain, Ulster seemed to have right on its side. The case for Home Rule, after all, was based upon self-determination. But did not Ulster also have a right to self-determination? Ireland, after all, contained one-fifteenth of the British population, Ulster one-quarter of the Irish population. The Irish Nationalists declared that they did not wish to be ruled by Westminster. The Ulster Protestants declared that they did not wish to be ruled by Dublin. Bonar Law went even further, declaring that 'these people in the North-east of Ireland ... would prefer, I believe, to accept the government of a foreign country rather than submit to be governed by honourable gentlemen below the gangway [the Irish Nationalist party]', a sentiment echoed by some of the Ulster Unionists themselves, who declared that they would prefer the rule of the kaiser to that of Redmond.[25] 'We are sure', Carson and his followers declared, in a letter to *The Times* on 30 December 1912, that Ulster 'will, regardless of all consequences, refuse to submit to the government it is proposed to force upon them'. 'Their resistance', they went on to say,

> seems to us righteous. To drive out a loyal, industrious, thriving, and contented population from under the authority of the Imperial Parliament and Executive to which they cleave and to place them under a Government which they abhor, is an act of gross tyranny unparalleled in the history of our country. Such tyranny it is right to resist.

The signatories to the letter urged the British people not 'to be deaf to the claims of a free population to remain under a Government they love; to be saved from a Government they hate'. This appeal was a powerful one at a time when British identity was still, to a large extent, defined by religion. Britain before 1914 was a determinedly Protestant country, while Catholics were a tolerated minority, still facing some degree of social discrimination.

The Irish Nationalists had indicated that they did not regard themselves as British but as Irish, and their Irish identity was, they believed, incompatible with rule from Westminster. The Ulster Protestants responded that they were British. The Nationalists insisted that Ireland was a unity, comprising a single nation. Ireland, being an island, must, they argued, remain under a single unit of government. But that view, Unionists argued, ignored the realities of ethnicity, religion and nationality. A united Ireland, Unionists insisted, could only be maintained by the continuation of British rule and the defeat

---

25 House of Commons Debates, 1 January 1913, vol. 46, col. 464.

of Home Rule. The Ulster argument was, in a sense, stronger than that of the Nationalists. For Ulster Unionists, unlike the Nationalists, were not asking for a privilege – the privilege of a separate legislature within the United Kingdom – but only to maintain their existing constitutional position.

In 1886, Joseph Chamberlain had insisted that Ireland 'consists of two nations'.[26] But for an Ulster Unionist, Ulster could not, by definition, be a separate nation. The essence of Unionism was that Ulster was part of the British nation. Ulster did not, therefore, seek a Home Rule Parliament of its own. What it wanted was continued rule from Westminster as part of the United Kingdom. In the words of the Ulster Solemn League and Covenant signed in 1912, Unionists sought 'to preserve for ourselves and our children our cherished position of equal citizenship in the United Kingdom'. They sought, by contrast with the Nationalists, not special treatment but the same right to be governed and taxed from Westminster as was enjoyed by every other British citizen. The Nationalist claim was based on nationhood, the Unionist claim on citizenship. While the Unionists neither understood nor sympathised with the Nationalist claim, few Liberals understood or sympathised with the Unionist claim. Nor did they understand the strength of Ulster's case. Many Liberals regarded Ulster Unionists as a disaffected minority within Ireland and were prepared to offer extensive guarantees for minority rights in the Home Rule constitution. But the Ulster Unionists did not regard themselves as a minority in Ireland but as part of a majority within the United Kingdom. They were not, therefore, to be conciliated by minority guarantees, however generous. They would not under any circumstances accept rule from Dublin.

Liberal dependence upon the Irish Party's vote strengthened Unionist hostility. They believed that Home Rule was being introduced as part of a corrupt bargain with the Irish Party by which the Irish had been induced to pass the Budget in exchange for a promise to abolish the Lords' veto. They ignored the fact that the Liberals had been committed in principle to Home Rule since 1885, and, given that Unionists believed that the Irish should remain in the Imperial Parliament, it was somewhat illogical to contend that the Irish Party should not be entitled to exert such influence in the Commons as it was able to achieve. There is no evidence of any explicit bargain between the Liberals and the Nationalists, but, even if there had been, there was no reason why the two parties should not bargain together in a hung parliament situation.

But Unionists also believed that the Liberals were acting unconstitutionally for two further reasons. The first was that the Liberals were using the

---

26   Ibid., 8 April 1886, vol. 34, col. 1200.

mandate for Lords reform in the general election of December 1910 as if it also conferred a mandate to implement Home Rule. The second was that, in their view, the Parliament Act had left a gap in the constitution. For the preamble to that Act had declared, as we have seen, that the Lords should be replaced by 'a Second Chamber constituted on a popular instead of hereditary basis'. The Unionists argued that, until such a chamber actually came into existence, the constitution was in suspense, lacking its normal checks and balances. Britain was, therefore, as Balfour was to argue in 1913, living under an 'interim constitution'.[27] George V tended to share this view, writing to Asquith in September 1913:

> Does not such an organic change in the Constitutional position of one of the Estates of the Realm also affect the relations of all three to one another; and the failure to replace it on an effective footing deprive the Sovereign of the assistance of the Second Chamber? ...
>
> Is there any other Country in the world which would carry out such a fundamental change in its Constitution upon the authority of a single chamber?
>
> Is there any precedent in our own Country for such a change to be made without submitting it to the Electorate?[28]

The Parliament Act, the king believed, placed him 'in a false position and in one never contemplated by the framers of our Constitution. As I regard it, the King alone can now compel a Government to refer to the Country any measure which hitherto would have been so referred by the action of the Lords.'[29]

Whereas, before 1911, the House of Lords had been able to compel a dissolution, now only the king could do so. But that would involve the king taking the dangerous course of dismissing his government and replacing it with a Unionist government. The Unionist government would immediately seek a dissolution which, presumably, the king would grant. His political neutrality, therefore, would have been compromised, since he would be granting to a Unionist government which lacked the confidence of the Commons what he had refused to the Liberals.

The Parliament Act, as we have seen, made it possible for Home Rule to be put on the statute book in a single Parliament whether the Lords agreed to it or not, and without any need for a further appeal to the people. If, as was highly probable, the Lords rejected Home Rule, the Bill would nevertheless

---

27 Undated memo on 'The Constitutional Question, 1913', Balfour Papers, BL Add MS 49869, f. 127.
28 Nicolson, *King George the Fifth*, p. 227.
29 Undated memo in the Royal Archives, but probably late 1913. Quoted in Vernon Bogdanor, *The Monarchy and the Constitution*, Clarendon Press, 1995, p. 124.

become law after the third occasion at which it was presented for approval to them. So Home Rule was for the first time a very real, indeed a likely, possibility. Bonar Law had called the Parliament Act a Home Rule Act in disguise. On 9 April 1912, he addressed a Unionist demonstration in Belfast, which *The Times* the next day called 'more than a political meeting, more even than a demonstration on an unprecedented scale; it was the assemblage of a nation to defend its existence, to plead against an attempt to suppress its identity, to lead and also to warn'. The opposition leader declared that the Parliament Act had rendered Belfast a besieged city as it had been during the Siege of Derry in 1689. But Ulster could break the siege as it had done then. 'The Government have erected by their Parliament Act a boom against you to shut you off from the help of the British people. You will burst that boom.' Ulster could burst the boom by forcing an appeal to the people. The demand for such an appeal before Home Rule was passed was to become a unifying cause for the Unionist Party following the traumas of tariff reform.

Ulster was to generate an even graver constitutional crisis than Lords reform, a crisis which raised, some believed, the spectre of civil war in Britain for the first time in over 300 years. For, since the Unionists believed that the Liberals were acting unconstitutionally, they felt no reason why they should be bound by the normal constitutional conventions. The government, Bonar Law wrote to a Conservative MP in March 1914, 'are trying to carry through the measure [Home Rule] in an entirely unconstitutional way and they cannot be prevented from succeeding unless action is taken by us which goes much beyond ordinary Parliamentary opposition'.[30] The Unionists sought to force the Liberals to secure a popular mandate through a general election, as the Lords had been able to do before the Parliament Act. Were an election to return a Liberal government, the Unionists would reluctantly accept that as a mandate for Home Rule. But they would never accept that there could be any mandate to put Ulster under a Home Rule Parliament. That, in their view, raised quite different considerations which could not be resolved by an appeal to the people. For Ulster raised fundamental questions of identity and allegiance lying beyond the to and fro of electoral politics. The majority in the United Kingdom had no right, Unionists believed, to extrude a part of the country against its wishes. Ulster had an absolute right to remain in the United Kingdom for so long as its people wished. Were that right to be threatened, Ulster had, Unionists believed, every right to disobey the law, since the contract binding them to government had been broken. The Unionists would, therefore, 'vote against Home Rule for Ireland to the end

---

30 Jeremy Smith, 'Bluff, Bluster and Brinkmanship: Andrew Bonar Law and the Third Home Rule Bill', *Historical Journal*, 1963, p. 162.

of time, but they would only *fight* for the exclusion of Ulster'.[31] And Ulster would fight against the government in the name of the king, in the name of a higher law. They would become king's rebels, as their ancestors had been when, in 1689, they had disobeyed the orders of James II. Their loyalty was contractual rather than unconditional. It depended upon the British government respecting their constitutional position.[32] Ulster's stance was strongly supported by many army officers, a number of whom came from Anglo-Irish families and were steeped in the history of the American Civil War, which was part of the syllabus at Sandhurst. And indeed Ulster Union-ists were accustomed to assume the mantle of Abraham Lincoln, especially since 1 July 1913 marked the fiftieth anniversary of the Battle of Gettysburg. Home Rulers, on the other hand, were seen as rather like the secessionists in the Civil War. In their rebellion, Unionists believed, Ulster would be sup-ported by the rest of the country. In July 1912, Bonar Law declared at a rally at Blenheim Palace in Oxfordshire, 'They [the Liberals] may perhaps carry their Home Rule Bill through the House of Commons but what then? I said the other day that there are stronger things than Parliamentary majorities.' He ended his speech with these fighting words: 'I can imagine no length of resistance to which Ulster can go in which I should not be prepared to support them and in which, in my belief, they would not be supported by the overwhelming majority of the British people.'[33] This and other speeches were thought by supporters of Home Rule to be outrageous, and indeed Bonar Law as Leader of the Opposition was suggesting that it was permissi-ble to resist an Act of Parliament by any means. He insisted that what he was saying was little different from what had been said in 1886 and 1893 by Lord Randolph Churchill, Lord Salisbury, Balfour and others. In 1893, the late Duke of Devonshire had invoked the Whig doctrine of resistance to oppres-sion and, like Bonar Law, had used the analogy of 1689, asking, 'How ... can the descendants of those who resisted King James II say ... that they have not a right, if they think fit, to resist ... the imposition of a Government put upon them by force.'[34] Even further, Bonar Law was to declare that not only would the army refuse to obey orders to march against Ulster but he would encourage them in this course. In November 1913, speaking in Dublin, he repeated the analogy with 1689, declaring that James II

had behind him the letter of the law just as completely as Mr Asquith has now ... In order to carry out his despotic intention the King had the

31 Michael Laffan, *The Partition of Ireland, 1911–1925*, Dublin Historical Association, 1983, p. 33
32 David W. Miller, *Queen's Rebels: Ulster Loyalism in Historical Perspective*, University College Dublin Press, 1978.
33 Blake, *The Unknown Prime Minister*, p. 130.
34 Ibid., p. 162; Holland, *Life of Duke of Devonshire*, p. 250.

largest army which had ever been seen in England. What happened? There was no civil war. Why? Because his own army refused to fight for him.[35]

In 1914, the shadow Cabinet seriously considered amending the annual Army Act, on which military discipline depended, to ensure that the army could not be used against Ulster.[36] Nor did Unionist threats after 1912 appear to be idle. Even before the Home Rule Bill had been introduced into the Commons, Carson had told Ulster Protestants to be prepared 'the morning Home Rule passes ... to become responsible for the government of the Protestant province of Ulster'.[37] 'The people of Ulster', Bonar Law told Asquith in July 1914,

> knew that they had a force which would enable them to hold the province, and with opinion divided in this country [i.e. the rest of Britain] it was quite impossible that any force could be sent against them that would dislodge them ... Therefore they knew that they could get their own terms, and it was certain that they would rather fight than give way.[38]

Carson and other Unionists who had uttered such threats, including Bonar Law himself, were making themselves liable to be charged with sedition. Arresting the opposition leaders, however, would have been, as Asquith's biographer pointed out, 'fatal'. It would have provoked a mass withdrawal of Unionists from the Commons, disaffection if not mutiny in the army and the hostility of the king.[39] But the government's inactivity in the face of the rebellion in Ulster left it looking weak.

It appeared, then, that if Ulster was determined to resist Home Rule by force, the British government could only include it in a Home Rule Bill by an even greater display of force which would require use of the army. This raised three questions. The first was whether the army, some of whose senior officers were themselves Irish Protestants, would obey orders to coerce Ulster into a Dublin Parliament. The second was whether the British people would be prepared to support coercing Ulster. The third and perhaps most important question was how Ulster could be permanently held under a Dublin Parliament against its wishes. The answer could only be by British armed forces subduing it and turning it into a conquered province while a Home Rule Parliament was being established in Dublin; and then, once that

---

35   *The Times*, 29 November 1913.
36   Robert Blake, 'The Curragh Incident and UDI', *The Listener*, 21 March 1974, p. 366.
37   Ian Colvin, *Life of Lord Carson*, Gollancz, 1934, vol. 2, p. 79.
38   Blake, *The Unknown Prime Minister*, p. 214.
39   Jenkins, *Asquith*, pp. 281–2.

Parliament had been established, the Protestants of Ulster would somehow accept Home Rule so that the troops could be withdrawn. One only has to state such an assumption to appreciate its absurdity.

THE PARTITION OF IRELAND

Despite what Unionists believed, the Liberals had no intention of forcing Ulster to live under a Dublin Parliament. Even before the Home Rule Bill was presented to Parliament, they had been discussing the exclusion of Ulster – what form it should take and when it should be publicly announced. Exclusion was, apparently, first suggested, somewhat tentatively, by Birrell, the Irish Secretary, in a letter to Churchill in August 1911. The letter proposed that Antrim and Down be allowed to opt out for five years following which there should be a referendum. 'If this was done,' Birrell thought, 'there could be no Civil War.' But Birrell did not pursue his tentative suggestion. In January 1912, a Liberal backbencher, lunching with Lloyd George and the Scottish Secretary McKinnon Wood, found them 'all agreeing that Home Rule ... could not be imposed upon Ulster by force and that if possible the Protestant counties in Ulster should be exempted'.[40] In February 1912, the Cabinet came, perhaps rather late in the day, to consider Ulster. Lloyd George 'proposed that every county should be given the option of 'contracting out' – really to apply to Ulster, but nominally for every part. He was supported by Asquith, Churchill, Haldane and Hobhouse but opposed by Lord Chancellor Loreburn, Lord Crewe, the Liberal leader in the Lords, who normally sided with Asquith, and the old Gladstonian Morley at the India Office. Faced with this opposition, Asquith decided not to decide.[41] The Cabinet, therefore, made no commitment but left open the possibility of exclusion. The Bill, as introduced, Asquith told the king, would apply to the whole of Ireland, but the Irish leaders 'should from the first be given clearly to understand that the Government held themselves free to make such changes in the Bill as fresh evidence of the facts, or the pressure of British opinion, may render expedient'. And that 'if in the light of such evidence or indication of public opinion, it becomes clear as the Bill proceeds that some special treatment must be provided for the Ulster counties, the Government will be ready to recognise the necessity'.[42] Asquith himself, as he was to tell Churchill in September 1913, 'always thought (and said) that, in the end, we should probably have to make some sort of bargain about Ulster

40 Jalland, The Liberals and Ireland, pp. 59, 61.
41 David, ed., Inside Asquith's Cabinet, account of the Cabinet meeting of 11 February 1912, p. 111.
42 Jenkins, Asquith, p. 277.

as the price of Home Rule'. 'But', he continued, 'I have never doubted that, as a matter of tactics and policy', the Bill should, in the first instance, apply to the whole of Ireland.[43] He wanted to postpone exclusion to a time when it might help secure a settlement. And exclusion by no means implied permanent partition. The dominions apart from New Zealand – Canada, Australia and South Africa – had all begun with partition but were now unified. In particular, Natal had, until 1910, taken up Ulster's attitude, refusing to be part of a unified South Africa, and had decided only at the last moment to join the Union. So the issue of exclusion, despite appearances, was not one of principle.

Partition was first proposed in Parliament by Thomas Agar-Robartes, Liberal MP for St Austell and a Roseberyite, at the committee stage of the Bill, in June 1912. 'I have never heard', he declared, 'that orange bitters will mix with Irish whisky.'[44] He proposed exclusion of the four counties with Protestant majorities. His amendment led to anguished debate amongst Unionists who decided they could hardly fight for something they had been offered by legislation. So they supported the amendment. But the Liberal majority ensured that the amendment was defeated by sixty-one votes, although both Lloyd George and Churchill abstained.

The Unionists were themselves formally to propose exclusion for the first time in December 1912, at the report stage of the Bill, when Carson proposed an amendment to exclude the whole of Ulster. Carson's amendment symbolised the gradual and generally unnoticed evolution of Unionist policy, implicitly recognising that the Unionists could not prevent Home Rule for the rest of Ireland and should therefore concentrate on exclusion. So it was that 'the Irish question of 1912 became the Ulster question of 1913–14; and by 1914 the Ulster question for Conservatives like Balcarres [the Chief Whip] was one of how much to settle for'.[45] The Cabinet was, once again, uncertain in its response. Asquith 'was convinced that the amendment was merely a wrecking or embarrassing amendment'. There appeared to be agreement in the Cabinet that the amendment would be resisted, when, according to his diary, a junior member of the Cabinet, Charles Hobhouse, Chancellor of the Duchy of Lancaster, said, 'I thought it was a very important and significant step for Carson to take.' The Unionists were, in his opinion:

right in saying the responsibility would be ours if serious disturbances broke out later in Ulster which could be attributed to our refusal to

43 Jalland, *The Liberals and Ireland*, p. 67.
44 House of Commons Debates, 11 June 1912, vol. 39, col. 773.
45 John Vincent in Vincent, ed., *Crawford Papers*, p. 309.

exclude Ulster; moreover I was certain that we had no means of coercing Ulster, for the troops were not to be relied on, even if we wished to coerce.

Birrell, the Irish Secretary, declared that 'it was impossible to overestimate their real racial, religious and local abhorrence of a Dublin Parliament' Lloyd George and Churchill then 'took up the running and advised no banging of the door against Ulster, Ll.G. particularly strongly, and ultimately it was agreed that the PM should speak rejecting the actual amendment but hinting that if settlement was in the air, our attitude would be one of meeting them half-way'.[46] So once again the Cabinet decided not to decide and the Liberals voted against the Carson amendment, which was defeated by ninety-seven votes.

Asquith had made a crucial mistake in not at this time publicly proclaiming his willingness to consider exclusion. His reasons seemed at first sight plausible. Exclusion would not at that stage have reconciled the Unionists to Home Rule. Carson and the co-signatories to his amendment had reiterated in a letter to *The Times* on 30 December that, despite their amendment, their opposition to Home Rule was 'fundamental and unalterable'. So the Unionists would simply have pocketed the concession and continued their agitation. Moreover, exclusion would have been opposed by the Irish Nationalists and the bulk of the Liberal Party. So the government would be weakening the authority of Liberals in the Commons, which was where their strength lay. In any case, the provisions of the Parliament Act meant that the first two circuits of the Home Rule Bill, until 1914, would be in the nature of dummy runs. Asquith believed, therefore, that it would be more sensible to wait until the Home Rule Bill was approaching the statute book and only then consider a concession which, if made when the Bill was nearing the statute book, might persuade the Unionists to accept it as a compromise. In the words of one of Asquith's biographers, 'The Parliament Act procedure put a premium on delay ... Why should anyone settle until they saw what the disposition of the forces was likely to be when it came to the final confrontation?'[47] The Nationalists would not accept partition, so Asquith believed, unless convinced that it was the only way of avoiding civil war.

But there was a fatal flaw in Asquith's reasoning. A concession along the lines of the Carson amendment in 1912 would ensure that the Bill, as amended, could become law in 1914, even against the wishes of the Lords. The next two sessions would then be the dummy runs. But a concession made at a later stage would mean that the Bill in its newly amended form could not become

46 David, *Inside Asquith's Cabinet*, account of meeting of members of the Cabinet on 31 December 1912, pp. 126–7.
47 Jenkins, *Asquith*, p. 279.

law against the wishes of the Lords until after the next general election, due by January 1916. For the Home Rule Bill, as amended, would not be the same Bill as that which the Lords would have twice rejected. An amended Home Rule Bill, introduced after January 1913, could not complete its three circuits until after January 1916. The only way of avoiding a general election before Home Rule had been enacted would lie in agreement between Liberals and Unionists, so that the Lords would abandon their opposition to Home Rule. So the Unionists would enjoy in effect a veto on the Bill. Acceptance of the Carson amendment in 1912, by contrast, would have rendered innocuous the threat of armed resistance, since the Ulster Unionists would have been left with nothing to resist. 'It is hard to see', Carson declared, 'if separate treatment was given to Ulster, how could I be justified in asking men to go on preparing for resistance when their only object could be to obtain what had been offered to them.'[48] It would have undermined the Unionist claim that the government intended to coerce Ulster and so deprived the Unionists of their best cry. Indeed, it might have split the Unionists between those who wanted to continue to resist Home Rule, and those prepared to accept Home Rule provided that Ulster was excluded. There were already in 1912, according to the opposition Chief Whip, signs of 'a serious split in the Unionist party' along these lines, a split which the Liberals could have exploited.[49] Since the Liberals had no intention of coercing Ulster, therefore, it would have been better to have said so directly in 1912, after which the Ulster resistance and Ulster Volunteers, a private army, would have been unnecessary. But by inaction, the government lost the initiative. It had raised expectations amongst Nationalists of a united Ireland which it knew that it would probably be unable to fulfil. Later, the piecemeal extraction of concessions from the Irish Party weakened the credibility of the party in Ireland.[50] But since the Liberals did not intend to coerce Ulster, despite all the sound and fury which led some to think that Britain was on the brink of civil war, the conflict between Liberals and Unionists was to a large extent shadow boxing, albeit highly dangerous shadow boxing.

THE HOME RULE BILL AND THE ULSTER COVENANT

The Home Rule Bill introduced into the Commons on 11 April 1912 was on broadly similar lines to the Bill of 1893. The Irish Parliament would be given delegated powers to legislate on all domestic matters except land purchase,

48 Alvin Jackson, *Home Rule: An Irish History, 1800–2000*, Oxford University Press, 2003, p. 125.
49 Vincent, ed., *Crawford Papers*, p. 261.
50 This is essentially the argument of Jalland in *The Liberals and Ireland*. It seems to me irrefutable.

pensions and national insurance. These could be transferred to the Irish Parliament at a later stage if it so wished, though this was somewhat unlikely given the heavy expenditure these services incurred. There were a number of safeguards for minorities. The Irish Parliament was to be prohibited from passing any legislation which either directly or indirectly established or endowed any religion, affected the free exercise of any religion or gave preferences or privileges to any religion. The Lord Lieutenant, appointed by the British government, would have a veto on Irish legislation, while the Secretary of State could refer any suspected breach of the terms of the Home Rule legislation to the Judicial Committee of the Privy Council for adjudication. Ireland would have a two-chamber system, a Lower House of 164 directly elected members, of which fifty-nine would be elected from Ulster, but also an Upper House of forty members with equal powers to those of the Lower House, nominated by the government for a period of eight years, with retirement by rotation. In cases of disagreement, the Upper House could be overruled by the lower in joint session. Westminster would remain supreme so that it could, in theory at least, overrule the Irish Parliament even on matters for which that Parliament was responsible. Ireland would continue to be represented at Westminster, but her representation would be reduced from 103 to forty-two, of which sixteen would be from Ulster. It was, therefore, far less likely that Irish MPs would hold the balance at Westminster. The Irish university seats would be abolished.

The financial arrangements, however, had to be different from 1893 since there had been a transformation in Ireland's financial position. The surplus on the Irish Budget of around £2 million in 1893 had now become a deficit of around £1.5 million. Expenditure in Ireland had increased by around 90 per cent, while revenue raised there only by around 30 per cent, largely due to heavy expenditure on financial commitments resulting from land purchase, pensions and national insurance. Ireland indeed had benefited disproportionately from pensions since it had a larger than average proportion of the elderly and also because registration of births had not begun there until 1864 and so there was nothing to prevent applicants from overstating their age.[51] One diarist recorded that 'an old lady in the West of Ireland who is duly in receipt of an old age pension has just been safely delivered of a strapping son'.[52] 'I always thought I was sixty,' one man told Birrell, 'but my friends came to me and told me they were certain sure I was seventy and as there were three or four of them against me, the evidence was too strong for me,

---

51 John W. Budd and Timothy W. Guinnane, 'Intentional Age-Misreporting, Age-Heaping and the 1908 Old Age Pensions Act in Ireland', *Population Studies*, 1991, pp. 497–518.

52 Vincent, ed., *Crawford Papers*, p. 121.

I put in for the pension and got it.'[53] In 1913, Birrell indicated that while
89.3 per cent of those of the appropriate age were in receipt of pensions
in England and Wales, in Ireland the percentage was 101.6 per cent![54] The
government proposed to transfer to Ireland a sum of £500,000 a year for the
payment of devolved services, which would be reduced by stages to a sum
of £200,000. The Irish Parliament would be given the power to vary income
tax and various other taxes, though not customs duties, by 10 per cent. If,
however, it decided to reduce taxes, there would be an equivalent reduction in the transferred sum. The hope was that these proposals would give
the Irish government an incentive to economise in spending, since Ireland
would herself benefit from such economies, while, if she decided to spend
more, she would have to find the extra money for herself. But these financial
arrangements increased Unionist anger. Not only would Ireland be given her
own legislature, but the rest of the country would continue to finance her
old-age pensions and national insurance, and in addition she would be given
a subsidy of £500,000 a year from taxpayers in the rest of the United Kingdom. Divorce, so F. E. Smith complained, was not normally accompanied
by wedding presents.[55] The financial arrangements could only be revised by a
parliament in which Irish representation in the House of Commons would
be increased from forty-two members to at least sixty-five.

Asquith concluded the First Reading of the Bill with a peroration. There
were, he declared, between twenty and thirty self-governing legislatures in
the empire. 'Are we going to break up the Empire by adding one more?'
he asked rhetorically. Surely not. For the Parliament elected in 1910, he
concluded, there had been reserved a 'double honour', that of 'reconciling
Ireland and emancipating herself'.[56] After a speech by Carson for the opposition, Redmond spoke and accepted the Bill as 'a final settlement of Ireland's
claims'. While there remained, he admitted, a small number of separatists in
Ireland, they were separatists only because they saw no alternative to current
misgovernment in Ireland and were massively outnumbered by supporters
of Home Rule. Once the Irish Parliament came into existence, the demand
for separation would, he predicted, disappear. The principle of Home Rule,
he insisted, was 'the foundation of the Empire today, and it is the bond, and
the only bond, of union'.[57]

The arguments against Home Rule had been well rehearsed since 1886,

53 Birrell, *Things Past Redress*, p. 221.
54 Hoppen, *Governing Hibernia*, p. 217.
55 James Doherty, *Irish Liberty and British Democracy: The Third Home Rule Crisis, 1909–14*, Cork University Press, 2018,
    p. 43.
56 House of Commons Debates, 11 April 1912, vol. 36, col. 1426.
57 Ibid., cols 1445, 1443.

and the long and wearisome progress of the Bill in three successive sessions revealed little new. The government faced little difficulty in securing passage of its legislation through the Commons, but it was, predictably, rejected by the Lords. Under the Parliament Act provisions, it could be expected to become law over the Lords' veto in 1914. But the real opposition and the real action against Home Rule was taking place outside Parliament, in Ulster.

On 23 September 1911, a large Unionist rally was held outside the house of Sir James Craig, overlooking Belfast Lough. Carson declared:

> We must be prepared, in the event of a Home Rule Bill passing, with such measures as will carry on for ourselves the government of those districts of which we have control. We must be prepared ... the morning Home Rule passes, ourselves to become responsible for the government of the Protestant Province of Ulster.

That government would rule Ulster until the day when it could resume its rightful place in the United Kingdom. A second rally in Belfast in April 1912, attended by around seventy Unionist MPs, including Bonar Law, attracted an audience of around 100,000. In a letter to Lady Londonderry, Bonar Law professed himself 'astounded at the magnitude of the Demonstration and it surpassed all he had imagined or expected'.[58] At this meeting, the Unionist leadership committed itself to the support of Ulster's claims. The Ulster Unionists proclaimed 28 September 1912 as Ulster Day. It began with a religious service at Belfast Cathedral and in the Ulster Hall, at which the congregation, led by Carson, sang, 'O God, Our Help in Ages Past'. The sermon took as its text Timothy 6:20, 'Keep that which is committed to thy trust.' The former moderator of the Irish Presbyterian Church preached a sermon in which he declared that 'the Irish question' was 'at bottom a war against Protestantism; it is an attempt to establish a Roman Catholic ascendancy in Ireland to begin the disintegration of the empire by securing a second parliament in Dublin'. Behind the pulpit stood the standard, said to be that of the Battle of the Boyne of 1690, at which the troops of William III had defeated those of the former James II, who was attempting a Catholic restoration. Similar services were held in other parts of Ulster.

After the service, Carson walked to Belfast City Hall, where a guard of honour and city dignitaries were waiting, to sign the Solemn League and Covenant. This document, based on the 1643 Scottish Covenant, pledged its signatories to use 'all means which may be found necessary to defeat the present conspiracy to set up a Home Rule Parliament in Ireland'. 'And', it

---

58 H. Montgomery Hyde, *Carson: The Life of Sir Edward Carson, Lord Carson of Duncairn*, Heinemann, 1953, p. 312.

went on, 'in the event of such a Parliament being forced upon us, we further solemnly and mutually pledge ourselves to refuse to recognise its authority.' In practice, of course, the 'authority' of the legislation could only be resisted in Ulster, not in the rest of Ireland. The covenant, signed by prominent lawyers, amongst them Carson and Lord Macnaghten, a law lord, implied that it was permissible to resist an Act of Parliament, and this was to be supported by Bonar Law. The covenant did not call for exclusion but for the defeat of Home Rule in the whole of Ireland. Around 450,000 signatures were affixed to it, representing around half of the total Protestant population – although some of the signatories were southern Unionists. But it was not, contrary to what is often said, signed in blood. The wooden ink stand used for the signing was to come eventually to be in the possession of Rev. Ian Paisley, founder and leader of the Democratic Unionist Party in Northern Ireland, who regarded himself as Carson's heir. The signing continued until nearly midnight to the accompaniment of crowds outside singing 'Rule, Britannia!' and 'God Save the King'. The square below City Hall and the nearby streets were crowded until late in the evening. In 1914, a similar British Covenant was to receive 2 million signatures from those living in the rest of the United Kingdom.

To commemorate the Ulster Covenant, Rudyard Kipling, a neighbour of Carson's at Rottingdean in Sussex, wrote a poem entitled 'Ulster', which well sums up the mood of some of Ulster's more extreme supporters.

> The dark eleventh hour
> Draws on and sees us sold
> To every evil power
> We fought against of old.
> Rebellion, rapine, hate,
> Oppression, wrong and greed
> Are loosed to rule our fate,
> By England's act and deed.
>
> The Faith in which we stand,
> The laws we made and guard,
> Our honour, lives and land
> Are given for reward
> To Murder done by night,
> To Treason taught by day,
> To follow, sloth and spite,
> And we are thrust away.

A Liberal backbencher asked the Attorney General to prosecute Kipling for sedition. The Attorney General refused. But Redmond's brother then asked, 'Will the right hon. gentleman bear in mind that in general opinion this doggerel ought not to be called verses at all?'[59]

In early 1912, Unionists had established small local militias which had begun drilling, claiming that they were within the law since they had obtained the sanction of local magistrates.[60] On 13 January 1913, the Ulster Unionist Council amalgamated these various militias into an Ulster Volunteer Force (UVF), recruitment to which would be open to all men aged between seventeen and sixty-five who had signed the covenant but would be limited in total to 100,000. The commander was to be Lieutenant General Sir George Richardson, who had been recommended by Lord Roberts, former commander-in-chief of the British Army. The UVF was a private army, its purpose being military training and the importation of arms. Remarkably, the firearms legislation of the period allowed anyone to own a firearm on payment of 10s for a gun licence. For many in Ulster, the UVF had echoes of Cromwell's Roundheads and the Apprentice Boys of Derry, founded in 1814 to commemorate the siege in 1690. It became a highly organised force under Carson and Craig who, far from inciting militancy as Liberals believed, ensured that it remained properly disciplined. Nevertheless, the activities of the UVF were, without a doubt, illegal. A Cabinet paper prepared by Sir John Simon, the Attorney General, made it clear that those in the UVF were liable to prosecution for 'treason-felony', since their aim was to compel the government by force to alter its policy. Illegal drilling was unlawful under an Act of 1819 and could not be made lawful by the permission of magistrates. Indeed, the magistrates would themselves be legally liable as accessories to a 'seditious conspiracy'. In addition, members of the UVF would be guilty of unlawful assembly and, under the Explosives Act of 1875, illegally storing ammunition.[61] Some Liberals argued that the UVF should be proclaimed and declared illegal. That would have required force by the army to put it into effect and could only have increased Unionist hostility. The government decided to take no action unless and until there was actual violence. They could hardly have arrested members of the UVF without also arresting Carson and Craig, and perhaps even the Leader of the Opposition himself; and from that they understandably shrank.

It was nevertheless becoming even clearer to ministers that it would not be possible to coerce Ulster. How could one coerce those who wished for

---

59   House of Commons Debates, 15 April 1912, vol. 37, col. 17.
60   Patrick Buckland, *Irish Unionism: Ulster Unionism and the Origins of Northern Ireland, 1886 to 1922*, Gill and Macmillan, 1973, p. 58.
61   CAB 37/117/82, 29 November 1913.

nothing more than to remain equal citizens in the United Kingdom? No British administration could have imposed on Ulster a government to which it refused consent. The strength of Ulster's case lay not in its private armies but in the adamant refusal of its population to accept Home Rule and insistence on remaining full citizens of the United Kingdom.

A COMPROMISE SOLUTION?

From the autumn of 1913, therefore, the Liberals sought compromise. By then, the Home Rule Bill had twice been passed by the Commons and twice rejected by the Lords. But the first impulse for compromise came from the king. He knew that the army could not be used to coerce Ulster, and was being pressed by the Unionists to prevent Home Rule passing in its unamended form either by using the royal veto, which had not been exercised since the time of Queen Anne in 1707, or, alternatively, by dismissing Asquith and appointing Bonar Law as Prime Minister, who would then seek an immediate dissolution. That would be an exercise of royal power not attempted since William IV had dismissed Lord Melbourne in 1834, not an encouraging precedent, since the king had been forced to reappoint Melbourne after a few months. Even so, the king was disturbed. 'Whatever I do,' he complained to Asquith in August 1913, 'I shall offend half the population. One alternative would certainly result in alienating the Ulster Protestants from me, and whatever happens the result must be detrimental to me personally and to the Crown in general.'[62] A memorandum by the king's private secretary, Lord Stamfordham, written after the Home Rule Bill had been enacted in September 1914, expressed the king's view 'that it was for the *politicians* to decide whether Ireland should have Home Rule or not. But that he intended to do everything in his power to prevent Civil War.' Accordingly, from August 1913, he 'insisted upon discussing the question with the Prime Minister who up to that time had never alluded to it in his frequent interviews with His Majesty'.[63] The king told Asquith that 'Ulster will never agree to send representatives to an Irish Parliament, no matter what safeguards or guarantees you may provide'.[64] He also believed that any attempt to coerce Ulster could cause disaffection in the army. Asquith believed the king to be alarmist. But the king's judgement was in fact superior to that of his Prime Minister. The king insisted that the issue be resolved through a settlement by consent. His influence was in part responsible for the Prime Minister

---

62 Memorandum to Asquith, 11 August 1913, quoted in Nicolson, *King George the Fifth*, p. 223.
63 Memorandum by Lord Stamfordham, 17 September 1914, quoted in Bogdanor, *The Monarchy and the Constitution*, p. 127.
64 George V to Asquith, 26 January 1914, quoted in ibid., p. 128.

agreeing to three meetings with Bonar Law between October and December 1913.

At the first of these meetings, on 14 October, Bonar Law pointed out how difficult it would be for him to accept exclusion, which would appear to be betraying the southern Unionists. He added, rather remarkably, that, if a compromise was agreed on Ulster, the disestablishment of the Welsh Church would go through under the Parliament Act and that Unionist MPs 'would, if they had to choose, prefer Home Rule rather than the disestablishment of the [Welsh] Church'. He then declared, no less candidly, 'that if the question of Ulster were removed one of the strongest points in our favour in an Election would be gone and our chance of winning it would, in my opinion, be diminished'. In addition, there was a danger of a party split in Unionist ranks. He told Asquith that his pledge

> to support Ulster to the utmost if there were no Election ... was contingent and if an Election took place and the Government won, our support would be withdrawn; and I added that Mr Asquith must understand as well as I did that this made all the difference, and that it was really the certainty of British support which made the strength of the Ulster resistance.[65]

Asquith, however, was adamant. There would be no election before Home Rule was enacted. Nevertheless, this first meeting left open the possibility that were Ulster to be excluded, the Unionists would not seek to prevent Home Rule in the rest of Ireland. On 6 November, the two leaders met again. Asquith then declared that he was prepared to accept the exclusion of either four or six counties of Ulster, with an option to come under a Dublin Parliament after a period of years. Bonar Law accepted that the three counties with large Catholic majorities – Cavan, Donegal and Monaghan – could not be regarded as part of Ulster for this purpose.[66] There was a third and final meeting between the two men on 10 December, but this did not advance matters further, and on 15 January 1914 in a speech at Cardiff, Bonar Law announced that negotiations for compromise had come to an end. The three meetings were not, however, completely fruitless. They showed Asquith that Bonar Law was by no means the extremist that he appeared in public utterances – indeed that he was more moderate than many of his followers in that he was no longer wedded to opposing Home Rule outside Ulster; and the talks showed to Bonar Law that the Liberals were by no means opposed in principle to exclusion. They paved the way, therefore, to a possible

65 Blake, *The Unknown Prime Minister*, pp. 161–2.
66 Jenkins, *Asquith*, p. 292.

settlement by agreement. But it was, no doubt, too early for the leaders to impose a settlement on their followers. For that to happen, both Asquith and Bonar Law appeared to believe, the followers had to be made to peer into the abyss and realise that no alternative to compromise was possible if civil war was to be avoided. This was, however, a dangerous strategy requiring a sure-footed approach from the leaders, who would have to keep their extremists under control, and an understanding by the followers that a compromise settlement was better than no settlement at all.

When the Cabinet came to consider Asquith's conversations with Bonar Law on 12 and 13 November, it accepted a proposal by Lloyd George for exclusion 'for a definite term of five or six years', with automatic inclusion after that. This course, Lloyd George pointed out:

> would have two distinct advantages: (1) no one could support or sympathise with the violent resistance of Ulster to a change which would in no way affect her for years to come; (2) before the automatic inclusion of Ulster took place, there would be two General Elections which would give the British electorate – with experience of the actual working of Home Rule in the rest of Ireland – the opportunity – if so minded – of continuing the exclusion of Ulster.[67]

In a memorandum to the Cabinet, Lloyd George admitted the tactical nature of his proposal.

> It must be an offer the rejection of which would put the other side entirely in the wrong, as far as the British public is concerned ... It would be almost impossible for them [the Unionists] to justify armed resistance in these counties at the present moment if such an option were given to them, and the same observation applies even if they rejected it. It would hardly be possible to rebel in anticipation of something which could not occur for six years.[68]

Asquith took this proposal to Redmond, telling the Nationalist leader that he feared a 'baptism of blood' in Ulster, which could only be avoided by 'the prevention, or at any rate the indefinite postponement, of the bloody prologue'. Redmond rejected this assessment, telling the Prime Minister that his 'friends in Ulster' had told him that 'apprehensions' of rebellion in Ulster are 'without any real foundation'. Nevertheless, very unwillingly, he accepted

---

67 From Asquith's letter to the king after the Cabinet meetings, quoted in Jenkins, *Asquith*, p. 293.
68 Denis Gwynn, *The Life of John Redmond*, Harrap, 1932, p. 257.

the proposal on exclusion on condition that he was not asked to make any further concessions.[69]

By the time the Home Rule Bill had reached its third parliamentary circuit in the Commons on 11 February 1914, Bonar Law was prepared to accept that the opposition could not prevent Home Rule reaching the statute book. But Ulster, he said, straining at the truth, 'had never' made the claim to veto Home Rule, 'and, if she had, we should never have supported her in it'. 'The position of Ulster' was

> that they are opposed to Home Rule, and that they will do their best, by every constitutional means, to defeat it. But they have never said that they will resist by force the right of Nationalist Ireland to govern itself. What they have said and what they mean is that they will resist by all means, if necessary by the sacrifice of life itself, the attempt to make Nationalist Ireland govern them.

Bonar Law pointed out that exclusion was the only solution, since if Ulster was coerced, 'You will simply have added another and a terrible page to the long list of bitter memories which are the curse of Ireland ... You will by that means have made even the possibility of a united and contented Ireland utterly inconceivable.'[70]

In moving the Second Reading of the Home Rule Bill in its third parliamentary circuit, on 9 March 1914, Asquith declared himself prepared to consider any proposal not imposing a 'permanent or an insuperable bar in the way of Irish unity'. This meant that 'exclusion in any form must be put forward, and can only be put forward, not as a solution, but as an expedient which may pave the way in time for a final settlement'. He proposed that, on the petition of one-tenths of the electorate, any county in Ulster – and the county boroughs of Belfast and Derry – could choose to vote itself out of a Home Rule Parliament for a period of six years from the first meeting of the Irish Parliament. After that period had ended, it would be automatically included unless Westminster decided otherwise. Since there would be two general elections during that six-year period, it was open to British electors to decide, if they wished, to alter these arrangements. The practical consequence would be that just four counties – Antrim, Armagh, Down and Londonderry – would vote for exclusion. Redmond accepted this proposal very unwillingly, but Carson declared that Ulster's position must be settled immediately and permanently, and made a remark which has resonated in

---

69 Jenkins, *Asquith*, pp. 293–4.
70 House of Commons Debates, 11 February 1914, vol. 58, cols 274–5.

history, 'We do not want sentence of death with a stay of execution for six years.'[71] Unionists objected to the fact that, after the six-year period, Ulster could be *compelled* to enter a Home Rule parliament. They insisted that Ulster could enter such a parliament only on the basis of *consent*. Under Asquith's proposal, the British voter, but not Ulster, would be required to consent in the two general elections during the six-year period.

In the Commons on 19 March, Bonar Law proposed that the Home Rule Bill be put to referendum in the whole of the United Kingdom. Were it passed, Unionists would accept it and would even accept the coercion of Ulster.[72] Asquith rejected this, arguing that his six-year exclusion proposal was in effect an equivalent. In the middle of the debate, Carson further raised the temperature by staging a dramatic departure from the Commons to catch the overnight boat train to Belfast, saying that he should be with his own people. This led Liberals to believe that Carson was about to proclaim a provisional government. But that was far from his intention; nor was it the intention of other Ulster leaders until the Bill had actually reached the statute book. It was vital, they believed, for the Ulster movement to retain its discipline and not to make any move giving the Liberals an excuse to act against it. No doubt some of the hotheads were not particularly disciplined, but Carson and Craig saw their role as one of countering indiscipline, not encouraging it.

THE CURRAGH 'MUTINY'

The rejection of Asquith's proposal led to serious and bitter misunderstandings on both sides, leading to the Curragh incident or 'mutiny' and encouraging both Unionists and Nationalists to believe that concessions could be won from the government by a threat of force. And relations between government and the military were to be poisoned with unfortunate consequences in the world war which broke out less than five months later.

The Liberals misinterpreted Carson's approach, noticing the rejection of Asquith's proposal but not his accompanying statement that 'we have made some advance ... by the acknowledgment of the principle of exclusion. That, in my opinion, is an important matter, because the moment you admit the principle of exclusion the details of the principle may be a matter that may be worked out by negotiation. (Cheers.)' Liberals ignored that part of Carson's speech pointing the way to negotiation. Instead, they interpreted it as a rejection of all compromise and were furious. No one was more furious than

---

71 Ibid., 9 March 1914, vol. 59, cols 908, 912, 933, 934.
72 Ibid., 19 March 1914, vol. 59, col. 2263.

Churchill, and, in a speech delivered at Bradford on 14 March, approved by the government and encouraged by Lloyd George, he gave full vent to his fury. This speech was in turn to be misinterpreted by the Unionists.

Churchill began by saying that he had been the first minister publicly to advocate exclusion in a speech in his Dundee constituency in autumn 1913. 'That', he told his Liberal audience to a chorus of 'Hear, hears', 'was perhaps going further than many there considered wise.' 'If Ulster seeks peace and fair play,' he went on, 'she can find it. She knows where to find it.' That was the conciliatory part of his speech. But it was drowned out by the confrontational part which, as so often with Churchill, was the more memorable. Asquith's offer was, he said, the government's last, 'I do not say in detail, but in principle.' The government would make no further substantive amendments to the Bill. Rebellion or disaffection in Ulster would be firmly put down. Were the Unionists to persist in rejecting the government's offer, Churchill went on, this would show that they 'prefer shooting to voting ... they would rather use the bullet than the ballot'. Indeed, they were seeking to substitute for 'the veto of privilege', destroyed by the Parliament Act, 'the veto of violence'. The Unionists had demanded that trade unionists and Irish Nationalists obey the law – but when it came to their own claims,

> there is no measure of military force which the Tory party will not readily employ. They denounce all violence except their own. They uphold all law except the law they choose to break. They always welcome the application of force to others. But they themselves are to remain immune. They are to select from the Statute book the laws they will obey and the laws they will resist.

He ended with a magnificent peroration.

> If there is no wish for peace, if every concession that is made is spurned and exploited, if every effort to meet their views is only to be used as a means of breaking down Home Rule and of barring the way to the rest of Ireland, if Ulster is to become a tool in party calculations, if the civil and Parliamentary systems under which we have dwelt and our fathers before us for so many years are to be brought to the crude challenge of force; if the Government and the Parliament of this great country and greater Empire, is to be exposed to menace and brutality, if all the loose, wanton and reckless chatter we have been forced to listen to all these many months is in the end to disclose a sinister and revolutionary purpose – then, gentlemen, I can say to you let us go forward together and put these grave matters to the proof.

Never one to waste a good line, he was to repeat this last phrase in his challenge to Hitler in January 1940.

Churchill's speech won him great popularity amongst Liberals. But it inflamed the Unionists who were led to believe that the government was about to embark on drastic measures by arresting Carson and other Ulster leaders and overawing Ulster through a display of military force. *The Times* on 23 March declared that the speech gave 'the impression of wanton recklessness' and that it had been read in Ulster as 'a declaration of war'. In the Commons on 23 March, Balfour was to complain that the government had two policies: the conciliatory policy of the Prime Minister and the incendiary policy of Churchill.[73]

There was now a double irony in that Churchill, one of the earliest and strongest advocates of the exclusion of Ulster, appeared to be the most strenuous advocate of coercing Ulster, while Carson, whose intention had been to save the whole of Ireland for the Union, now appeared as the most determined advocate of a separate government for Ulster. It was not, however, misunderstanding alone which produced the Curragh incident but also the personalities of the ministers involved and of the army officer charged with carrying out the government's instructions. Churchill, as First Lord of the Admiralty, bears much of the blame. He was impulsive and inclined to charge frontally at obstacles. In 1921, Lloyd George, his closest colleague amongst senior ministers before the war, was to characterise him as like 'a chauffeur who apparently is perfectly sane and drives with great skill for months, then suddenly he takes you over a precipice'.[74] Churchill had not yet arrived at that mature judgement, tempered by listening to advice from the more level-headed, which was to characterise his later years.

The War Secretary was Jack Seely, who had succeeded Haldane when the latter was elevated to the Lord Chancellorship in June 1912. Like Churchill, his close friend, Seely had served in the Boer War, and, like Churchill, having been elected to the Commons in 1900 as a Unionist, had crossed the floor to join the Liberals in protest against tariff reform. Again, like Churchill, he was somewhat impulsive; but, unlike Churchill, he was a political lightweight. It was apparently said of him that 'if he had rather more brains, he would be half-witted'.[75] Many believed that, if Haldane had been at the War Office, the Curragh incident would never have occurred. The third leading actor in the drama was the General Officer Commanding in Ireland, Sir

---

73 Ibid., 23 March 1914, vol. 60, col. 88.
74 Richard Toye, *Lloyd George and Churchill: Rivals for Greatness*, Pan, 2012, p. 232.
75 Blake, 'The Curragh Incident and UDI', p. 366.

Arthur Paget, who was quite unsuited for so delicate a post. A gallant officer, entirely loyal to his subordinates, he was bull-headed and insensitive.

The Curragh, around thirty miles south-west of Dublin in County Kildare, was headquarters of the 5th Division of the army, one of two British Army divisions stationed in Ireland. On 14 March, the day of Churchill's Bradford speech, the Army Council warned Paget that attempts might be made 'by evil-disposed persons to obtain possession of arms, ammunition and other Government stores'. He was advised, as a precautionary measure, to move troops to Ulster to guard these stores. Paget declined, declaring that 'in the present state of the country, I am of the opinion that any such move of troops would create intense excitement in Ulster and possibly precipitate a crisis. For these reasons I do not consider myself justified in moving troops at the present time.' The next day, the Cabinet met and was told that there were only 9,000 troops in Ulster and that additional troops from the other side of the Irish Sea might be needed to safeguard the stores. On 18 March, Paget was summoned to the War Office where, over the next two days, he had a series of meetings with ministers, including what appears to have been a crucial conference with Seely, Churchill, Sir John French (Chief of the Imperial General Staff) and the adjutant general (the head of army administration).[76] Remarkably, indeed unbelievably, no written record was taken of these meetings, nor of the instructions which Paget was to take with him back to Ireland. He may possibly have been offered written instructions but declined them; it seems more likely, however, that he was not offered written instructions. What is clear is that he was told to move troops north to protect the depots, and also told that he could have both military and naval reinforcements if this led to disturbances. At a meeting the next day with Asquith, Birrell, Seely, Churchill and French, it was said 'that the Govt believed that Sir E. Carson had gone over to Ireland to proclaim the Provisional Govt, that this might mean civil war & that it therefore behoved the government to take every precaution'. A week earlier, the Cabinet had decided, without fixing a date, that the 3rd Battle Fleet should steam from Spanish waters to Lamlash on the Isle of Arran, around sixty miles from Belfast. On 19 March, Churchill ordered it to steam there immediately. 'It was thought that the popularity and influence of the Royal Navy might produce a peaceable solution even if the Army had failed.'[77] On the next day, French was told by Churchill that if Belfast were to fight, 'his fleet would have the town in ruins in twenty-four hours'.[78] But no evidence has ever been produced

---

76 Ian F. W. Beckett, *The Army and the Curragh Incident 1914*, Bodley Head, 1986, pp. 57, 58, 73. This book gives a full documentary account of the incident.

77 Churchill, *World Crisis*, p. 154.

78 Beckett, *The Army and the Curragh Incident*, p. 74.

that arms depots were in danger from the UVF, much less that a provisional government was about to be declared, and it was never clear precisely what the army was to be asked to do – largely because the government itself did not know what it should do. But, no doubt, Churchill was trying to show that if there were a revolt, the navy would, with the army, be able to frustrate it. Seely, responsible for the army, had warned French a fortnight before that there were in Ulster 'a great number of hotheads who were not content to sit still'. That was no doubt true. But he then went on, absurdly, to suggest that 'these had planned a great coup, nothing short of marching down to the Boyne, concentrating there and then move in on to Dublin which they intended to take'.[79]

In discussing the forthcoming operation, according to a note made by Seely shortly afterwards, Paget was well aware that his officers were disproportionately drawn from the Protestant population and hostile to Home Rule, which they regarded as a reward for those who had denigrated the army in the Boer War. Paget had therefore urged

> that in the few exceptional cases where officers have direct family connection with the disturbed area in Ulster, so that in the event of serious trouble arising their future private relations might be irretrievably compromised if they were engaged with our troops, they be permitted to remain behind either on leave or with details.

This was agreed. That was not of itself a novel precedent. In other circumstances where the army was to be called upon to aid the civil power, for example in a strike, it might well be appropriate to exclude soldiers – not just officers – who had family members in close communities. But there was an implication that more than merely guarding depots and stores would be involved. For why was it necessary to allow troops to 'remain behind' or to warn officers that they must comply with orders? And if just policing duties were involved, British soldiers would have been welcomed in Ulster, perhaps the only part of Ireland where British soldiers would, in fact, have been welcomed.

For troops not resident in Ulster and without family connections there, then, according to Seely's note, 'Sir A. Paget wished to be able to say that any officer hesitating to comply with orders or threatening to resign should be removed'. That was authorised in writing by the War Office.[80] Sir John

---

79 Ibid., p. 278.
80 Ibid., pp. 61–2.

French believed that officers who took this option should be dismissed from the army and court-martialled. But that was not accepted.

These arrangements established a new and unfortunate precedent, made available only to officers. Military law did not then and does not now allow soldiers to decide for themselves whether or not to obey a lawful order. No doubt in the world war which was to follow just over four months later, many in the trenches would have been glad to have the choice of whether to follow orders to go 'over the top' or instead face a penalty no more severe than dismissal from the army with loss of pension rights.

The Unionists believed that something more drastic was being contemplated than mere policing duties in Ulster. It may be that Churchill, after his Bradford speech, had persuaded Seely that a rapid settlement of the Irish question could be achieved if the authority of government was firmly asserted by disbanding the UVF and overawing Ulster with a huge display of force. If the Ulstermen were to respond by firing on the troops, they would put themselves in the wrong with public opinion, undermining their case. Whether or not this was Churchill's policy will probably never be known. But the circumstances were highly suspicious. 'The point which hasn't been cleared up yet', the future Field Marshal Wavell, then a captain in the War Office, wrote to his father on 23 March after the 'mutiny' was over, 'is exactly what the Government meant to do and exactly what instructions were given to Paget, but there seems little doubt that they had decided on a policy of immediate coercion or it is inconceivable that even an ass like Paget could have said what he did.'[81]

Because there was no written record of the instructions given to Paget, it will probably never be wholly clear precisely how the agreement reached between him and Seely was to be put to the officers. The government hoped and indeed assumed that there would be few refusals to serve in Ulster on the basis of conscience. But when Paget returned to Ireland, he put the options to his senior officers in so tactless and threatening a manner that disaffection became almost inevitable. According to one of those present, Paget implied that civil war was a distinct possibility, declaring that 'the whole place would be in a blaze, he thought, tomorrow'. And 'in the event of such disturbance such an enormous force would be displayed that Ulster would be convinced of the impossibility of resistance'. But 'if anyone started the fighting, it should be the Ulstermen. Should they anticipate the Government by occupying these buildings the Government would be forced to turn them out, and bloodshed would result. By occupying these buildings now, the onus of any aggressive act would fall on the Ulstermen.' Paget then said that he had

---

81 Ibid., p. 278.

obtained concessions from Seely. Officers domiciled in Ulster could 'disappear'. Others unwilling to take part would have to resign, though he hoped that there 'will be very few' taking that option. Paget added insult to injury by saying that officers who chose to resign would lose their pensions, while those who chose to 'disappear' would have to give their word of honour that they would not fight on Ulster's side, under pain of court martial, as if they could not otherwise be trusted.[82] Paget also said that his senior officers had to come to a decision within two hours so that he knew on whom he would be able to rely. Even worse, when questioned by one of his officers, Paget apparently expostulated, 'Don't think, officers, that I take orders from those swines of politicians! No – I only take orders from the Sovereign.'[83] Indeed, he seems to have used the king's name frequently in his various perorations. The king's name was also used by Sir Charles Fergusson, Major General of the 5th Division, who insisted that 'the Army must hold together', and that if officers were allowed to decide for themselves on the basis of their political predilections what orders they would or would not follow, the empire would be in danger. Like Paget, he used the king's name but to persuade his fellow officers not to resign. Fergusson had apparently formed the impression from Paget that the orders to occupy Ulster had in fact come directly from the king. That, he declared, left officers with no choice. Loyalty to the king may indeed have been a determining factor in the decision of the majority of officers not to resign.[84] But while, of course, all orders in the army are technically orders from the king, George V knew nothing whatever of Paget's instructions and was furious when he learnt that his name had been brought into so sensitive a matter.[85] On 21 March, the king wrote in his diary that he had seen Seely, and 'I spoke very strongly to him'.[86]

Wavell was shocked at what had happened. Writing to his father, he declared:

> If we are going to have wholesale resignations over what I maintain is still a political matter, it shakes all discipline and drags the Army into politics ... The idea of the officers of the Army going on strike, which is I think what it really amounts to, is to my mind absolutely disastrous. What about the men? They can't resign, whatever their opinions are. Of course the Government's ultimatum to the officers, if they put one, was absolutely

82 Sir James Fergusson, *The Curragh Incident*, Faber, 1964, pp. 66–7, 69.
83 Ibid., p. 114.
84 Ibid., p. 70.
85 Blake, *The Unknown Prime Minister*, p. 193.
86 Fergusson, *Curragh Incident*, p. 128.

unfair ... I am afraid that the Government have trapped the simple, honest officer over this.[87]

Paget's blustering and insensitive approach had the opposite effect to that intended. He certainly did not intend to incite his offers to resign but hoped instead to ensure that all obeyed. Had he said no more than that officers domiciled in Ulster could 'disappear', it is probable that, as one of the leaders of the 'mutiny' was later to indicate, the others would have obeyed orders. But as it was, five officers, resident in Ulster, claimed the right to 'disappear', while sixty officers, led by Sir Hubert Gough, Brigadier General of the 3rd Cavalry Brigade, attached to the 5th Division, and a Protestant from southern Ireland, declared that they would resign rather than take part in active operations against Ulster. They were immediately suspended from duty. Paget reported the attitude of his officers to the War Office. Gough and his three colonels were then summoned to London. The government was, by now, frightened that Gough's example might be followed by other officers, with the danger of widespread disaffection amongst the military. In Ireland, Paget insisted that there had been a misunderstanding, and in London, French and the adjutant general said the same. But Gough was now in a strong position. He refused to withdraw his resignation without a written guarantee that the army would not be used to enforce Home Rule upon Ulster. A Cabinet meeting on 23 March agreed a memorandum insisting that 'the incident which has arisen in regard to their resignations has been due to a misunderstanding', and reiterated that all soldiers must obey lawful orders. Gough declared that this was insufficient. While he claimed not to doubt the word of ministers, he would, he said, be unable to convince officers in Ireland without written confirmation that the army would not be used to enforce Home Rule upon Ulster. And if he went back without such confirmation, he claimed, officers might be placed in a similar quandary later on. By a stroke of ill fortune, Seely had not been at the Cabinet meeting at which the memorandum had been drawn up, having been required to go to Buckingham Palace to mollify the king. Remarkably, indeed almost unbelievably, Seely, together with Morley, the India Secretary, who had been present at the Cabinet meeting, then altered a Cabinet document on the grounds that they were merely 'clarifying' what the Cabinet had intended. Seely added two paragraphs to the memorandum, which came to be called the 'peccant paragraphs'. They were then initialled by Seely, French and the adjutant general. The first of the paragraphs was innocuous, reiterating the government's right to use troops in Ireland to maintain law and order in

---

87 Ibid., p. 125.

support, where necessary, of the civil power. The second paragraph, however, was not innocuous, declaring, 'But they have no intention whatever of taking advantage of this right to crush political opposition to the policy or principles of the Home Rule Bill.' Gough was still not satisfied and asked whether this 'relieved him from a liability to order his brigade to assist in enforcing submission to a Home Rule Bill'. French, without consulting the War Secretary, wrote below the second paragraph, 'I should so read it.'[88] Gough and his colonels then returned to Dublin in triumph. That was the end of the Curragh incident, since Gough now had the assurances he wanted. Strictly speaking, it was not a 'mutiny', since no actual orders were disobeyed – officers were offered an option and accepted it. Nor did officers incite others to disobey nor conspire to suborn the army from its duties. Gough was indeed scrupulous in not trying to persuade his fellow officers to follow his lead. There might have been a preventive mutiny had the Liberal government seriously intended to coerce Ulster, but, as we have seen, that was not its policy. Even so, the incident was the gravest issue of civil–military conflict to arise in Britain in modern times.

When the existence of the 'peccant paragraphs' became known in London, the government was, naturally, deeply embarrassed. The day after they were signed, the Cabinet learnt of their existence and repudiated Seely. Asquith tried to pass the issue off as a 'misunderstanding', and in the Commons, where Liberal MPs spoke of a revolt by aristocratic army officers and asked why the government had surrendered to them, he disowned the 'peccant paragraphs'. In the Lords, Haldane misleadingly declared that the officers had gone back 'without conditions'.[89] Gough was asked to return the document with the addition of the paragraphs and the further clarification by French. But he had wisely deposited it for safe keeping with his bank. French and the adjutant general insisted on resigning, and the government then had no alternative but to require also the resignation of Seely, as the responsible minister. Surprisingly perhaps, Paget was not required to resign. It may be that, freed of the constraints of army discipline, he would have revealed matters embarrassing to the government. Asquith himself replaced Seely at the War Office. Seely would hold no further political office. Remarkably, Morley, who had been present when Seely had added the 'peccant paragraphs', did not follow Seely in resigning. Even more remarkably, he seems to have made no protest to Seely at the time, nor to inform his Prime Minister of what was afoot, an indication perhaps that the Cabinet may have tacitly approved of Seely's actions which, after all, did have the effect of preventing mass

---

88 Spender and Asquith, *Asquith*, vol. 2, p. 46.
89 House of Lords Debates, 23 March 1914, vol. 15, cols 642–3.

resignations from the army. No doubt for this reason, the 'peccant paragraphs' were never formally repudiated except by ministers in Parliament. If they had done so in public, they might have instigated a further army revolt; and ministers were to prove remarkably evasive when offering explanations of the incident.

The Curragh Incident is widely held to have proved that the government could not use the army to coerce Ulster. But, as we have seen, it had never intended doing so. Indeed, it had very recently publicly accepted the principle of exclusion. If, as was possible, Churchill intended to overawe Ulster, it was to disarm a private army which, he believed, was intending to prevent the government from carrying out its policy. That army, however, was largely under the control of Carson and Craig and would not have undertaken military action unless Ulster had actually been coerced. To that extent, the incident was indeed based on a misunderstanding.

The incident, nevertheless, had considerable repercussions. 'We soldiers', declared Major General Henry Wilson, Director of Military Operations at the War Office, wrote in his diary on 23 March, 'beat Asquith & his vile tricks.'[90] Senior officers had been in communication with the Unionist opposition and many in the army believed that they had triumphed over the government. A Liberal trade union MP, John Ward, asked ironically, 'Is it proposed to ask General Gough to form a Government?'[91] It appeared, however inaccurately, that the threat of military disaffection had turned the government from its course. That lesson was not lost on Irish Nationalists, who concluded that force could succeed where persuasion failed. Patrick Pearse, later to be the leader of the 1916 Easter Rising, declared, 'I think the Orangeman with a rifle a much less ridiculous figure than the Nationalist without a rifle.'[92] In November 1913, a private army was formed by Nationalists, the Irish Volunteers, which included members of Sinn Féin and members of a secret society, the Irish Republican Brotherhood, the Fenians. It reached a peak of strength in mid-1914 of 200,000 but was to split in August on the issue of whether Ireland should support the war. The Irish Volunteers were less disciplined than their Ulster counterparts and for some time had no single leader. Redmond did not welcome their formation, believing that it might imperil the chances of Home Rule. It was indeed a protest against parliamentarism. In June 1914, Redmond was to insist that the volunteers co-opt sufficient nominees from the Irish Party to ensure that he could control it. An anonymous letter signed 'Irish Volunteer' published in the *Irish Times*

90 Keith Jeffery, *Field Marshal Sir Henry Wilson: A Political Soldier*, Oxford University Press, 2006, p. 123.
91 House of Commons Debates, 24 March 1914, vol. 60, col. 205.
92 Stewart, *The Ulster Crisis: Resistance to Home Rule*, Faber, 1967, p. 207.

on 5 June commented, 'The attempt of the Redmondite leaders to capture the movement, now that it is too strong for them, which they opposed and sneered at when it was weak, is a most serious and sinister affair.' Redmond himself argued that while he had originally believed the volunteer movement to be premature, the Carsonite campaign had changed his mind.[93] The government responded to the creation of the Irish Volunteers by two Arms Proclamations on 5 December 1913, prohibiting the importation of arms into Ireland by sea, although rifles could continue to be imported for 'sporting purposes'. There were now two private armies in Ireland, leading the *Morning Post*, a Unionist newspaper, to comment on 2 June, 'Ministers have placed themselves in that most odious of situations, when they can neither advance with safety or retreat with credit, while to remain inactive is to put the peace of the realm at the mercy of any untoward event'.[94]

The Curragh incident made an agreed settlement more difficult to achieve, even though the actual gap between government and opposition was not as great as it appeared. The opposition demanded exclusion of the whole of Ulster, with inclusion to depend on a vote by the whole province. The government proposed exclusion by county option, with automatic inclusion after six years. But the term 'automatic inclusion' is misleading since, as Lloyd George had pointed out, there would be two general elections before the six-year period came to an end; and were the Unionists to win, they could alter the arrangement as they wished. Disagreement was no longer about the principle of exclusion but about the area to be excluded and the time limit. Even this latter issue, however, had an air of charade about it. Were Ulster to be excluded following enactment of the Home Rule Bill, it was hardly credible that she could be coerced after six years whatever the Bill said. But the Curragh incident made this comparatively narrow area of disagreement more difficult to bridge. The Unionists remained suspicious that the government was insincere and intended to coerce Ulster. Indeed, they believed that by their action, Gough and his colleagues had saved the country from civil war. 'We are convinced', Walter Long wrote to Carson that '(a) warrants were signed for the arrest of political people, such as you and me, and (b) that a deliberate play was arrived at to attack Ulster on Saturday last with a considerable force.'[95] They were particularly suspicious of Churchill, who, they believed, was the mastermind behind a 'plot' to coerce Ulster, and this suspicion conditioned Unionist attitudes towards him for many years to come. Churchill was, after all, the wayward son of Lord Randolph, who had

---

93 Geraldine Dillon, 'Legal and Political Position in Pre-1916 Ireland', *University Review*, Spring 1963, pp. 59, 60.
94 Ibid., pp. 57–8.
95 Stewart, *Ulster Crisis*, p. 173.

stood by Ulster and indeed coined the phrase, 'Ulster will fight and Ulster will be right'. In Unionist eyes, Churchill was a maverick and bumptious renegade, who had crossed the floor for reasons of personal advancement, and whose impulsiveness was a danger to the state.

The Liberals were just as suspicious as the Unionists. They believed that Ulster intended to use illegal means to frustrate Home Rule. They also become aware that senior army officers were in regular communication with opposition leaders. Indeed, Henry Wilson, whose family had roots in Ulster, was providing Bonar Law with advance warning of government moves, French was consulting with the editor of the Unionist *Morning Post*, while the adjutant general leaked to the press the 'peccant paragraphs', which Gough had promised to keep confidential. Disloyalty to the government came from the very top of the army. Wilson and other officers could have been prosecuted under Section 2 of the Official Secrets Act of 1911, which had prohibited the unauthorised disclosure of official information. Officers such as Fergusson who had refused to resign and had encouraged others not to do so were regarded as disloyal. Wavell expostulated to his father:

> The attitude of the majority of officers is that the Army by the action of these officers has saved the situation, won a great victory, etc. I cannot agree. I think they have won a political battle to the ruin or great danger of ruin of the Army and the country. For it is a political victory. How can you call it other when the Army refuses to enforce the present Home Rule Bill? It seems to me deplorable that those words should be issued. And Wilson made no secret of his opinion. He actually said, 'the Army have done what the opposition have failed to do' and 'will probably cause the fall of the present Government'. What right have the Army to be on the side of the Opposition, what have they to do with causing the fall of Governments?

He summed up an important cause of the trouble by telling his father, 'It is a thousand pities that the protagonists were a fool like Paget and a hothead like Gough.' For the government, he had nothing but contempt.

> Their attitude in the House this afternoon was that there was no intention to coerce Ulster, that Paget made unauthorised statements and that the officers resigned under a misunderstanding. Lawyers and liars all ... We have to realise that we have a Government which has not even the courage of its convictions, an army which takes sides in politics, and leaders of that army who do not lead but yield to pressure from their subordinates.[96]

96 Fergusson, *Curragh Incident*, pp. 154–5.

The personal animosities stirred up were to intensify suspicion between civilians (the 'frocks') and the military (the 'brasshats') in the great conflagration which was to break out in August 1914.

Liberal suspicious were heightened when, on 29 April, just over a month after the Curragh incident, a supply of ammunition purchased from Germany was landed, in dead of night at Larne, the crew singing 'Three cheers for the King'. The password for the operation was 'Gough'.[97] The police and the army did nothing to interfere with this operation. The gun-running seemed to confirm government fears of a coup in Ulster and had the effect of enabling 'the Government to regain the moral advantage lost in March'.[98] There had in fact been arms deliveries to Belfast from at least August 1913, which, remarkably, the Irish Secretary Birrell had neither informed the Cabinet of nor had he taken any 'steps to delay them at the Customs', even though the law empowered the government to prohibit the import or export of arms, though not to seize or destroy them. Birrell seems indeed to have endorsed a private understanding by the Royal Irish Constabulary that the Ulster Volunteers should be allowed to 'take charge of the great part of Belfast ... Neither he nor the police seemed to think that there was anything unusual in such a division of authority.'[99] There is some evidence, although it is not conclusive, that Bonar Law both 'knew about and blessed' the landing of weapons.[100]

FURTHER ATTEMPTS AT COMPROMISE

In the aftermath of the Curragh incident, negotiations between Asquith and opposition leaders continued, but no agreement was achieved. On 12 May, Asquith declared that he would make a concrete proposal for exclusion by introducing an Amending Bill, but he refused to indicate its contents to MPs until the Home Rule Bill itself had been passed. On 25 May, this Bill was duly passed for the third time by the Commons and it could now be presented for royal assent whether the Lords accepted it or not. On 23 June, Lord Crewe introduced the Amending Bill in the Lords, even though the Home Rule Bill had not yet been considered for the third time by the Lords and had therefore not yet been enacted. It was an odd procedure to ask Parliament to amend legislation which had not yet reached the statute book, and even odder, perhaps, for important government legislation to be

---

97 Dillon, 'Legal and Political Position in Pre-1916 Ireland', p. 57.
98 Stewart, *Ulster Crisis*, p. 214.
99 David, *Inside Asquith's Cabinet*, p. 168, entry for 1 April 1914; p. 152, entry for 25 November 1913; p. 169, entry for 1 May 1914.
100 Jackson, *Home Rule*, p. 327.

introduced in the Lords. The day before the Bill was introduced, the stricken Joseph Chamberlain told a supporter, 'Amery... if I... were the... House of Lords... I would... *fight*,' a strange conclusion to the career of the former radical, who at Denbigh on 20 October 1884 had asked, 'Are you going to be governed by yourself, or will you submit to an oligarchy which is the mere accident of birth?'[101] But it proved to be his last political utterance. Joseph Chamberlain died on 2 July with Home Rule still unresolved.

The Amending Bill was no different from Asquith's March proposal, providing for exclusion on the basis of county option, after a referendum which could be triggered by one-tenth of voters in any county, and automatic inclusion after six years. Crewe, however, declared that the government welcomed amendments and would consider them seriously. Perhaps that was why the Bill had been introduced in the Lords. Lord Lansdowne, whose connections, unlike those of Bonar Law, were in the south of Ireland where he had large estates rather than in Ulster, remained adamant against Home Rule even with exclusion. 'Any attempt', he declared,

> to arrive at a final settlement of the Irish Question by means of separate treatment for a part of that country is pre-determined to failure. My own impulses led me to desire to see the Irish nation one and undivided and to see that one and undivided nation remain under the British flag.[102]

Nevertheless, in committee Lansdowne introduced an amendment removing the time limit and providing for exclusion of the whole province of Ulster, an amendment passed by the Unionist majority in the Lords. In this form, the Bill was to be presented to the Commons on 20 July. But meanwhile, tension was growing in Ireland. On 6 July, the UVF marched with rifles and bayonets in Belfast. On 9 July, the constitution of a provisional government was announced.

The government could not, having accepted the principle of exclusion, simply drop the Amending Bill. But if the Bill was presented in the form in which it had been agreed in the Lords, it would have been opposed by the Liberal majority in the Commons. Nevertheless, the argument had narrowed to the precise terms of the exclusion of Ulster rather than the desirability or otherwise of Home Rule, or whether Ulster should in fact be excluded. Lord Murray of Elibank, the former Liberal Chief Whip, told Redmond on 30 June 'that Sir Edward Carson had stated to him in the presence of Mr Bonar Law, and with his approval, that it was the opinion of them all that

---

101 Amery, *My Political Life*, vol. 1, p. 465.
102 House of Lords Debates, 23 June 1914, vol. 16, col. 391.

Home Rule was inevitable, and that the inclusion of Ulster in a comparatively short time was, in their judgment, inevitable also'.[103]

The king had long been anxious for a settlement by agreement. So when Asquith asked him to summon a conference at Buckingham Palace, he readily agreed. The king's initiative, though made on the advice of his Prime Minister, was crucial. For Bonar Law was only prepared to agree to such a conference if invited by the king. Indeed, both he and Redmond insisted in the Commons that they were only attending it because of a royal 'command'.[104] The conference met from 21 to 24 July. Its members were Asquith and Lloyd George, Bonar Law and Lansdowne; for the Nationalists Redmond and Dillon, and for the Unionists Carson and Craig. The Speaker presided. The king opened the conference by saying, 'The trend has been surely and steadily towards an appeal to force, and today the cry of Civil War is on the lips of the most responsible and sober-minded of my people.'[105] He then withdrew and the conference began.

While no minutes were kept, Redmond preserved very full notes, and it is not difficult to reconstruct what happened. There were two issues to be discussed in connection with exclusion – the time limit and the area to be excluded. Remarkably, even though exclusion had been conceded, only two of the eight participants – Bonar Law and perhaps Craig – favoured it for its own sake, having 'no natural sympathy for the traditions of a united Ireland'.[106] The others saw exclusion as a second best and hoped it would prove temporary and that Ireland would soon come to be reunited. After some dispute, it was agreed, as the Nationalists wanted, to consider first the area to be excluded, and only then to consider the time limit. But the conference rapidly became deadlocked, Nationalists continuing to insist on county option, Unionists on a clean cut of the whole province. Carson argued, not implausibly, that exclusion of the whole province was 'in the interest of the earliest possible unity of Ireland. He argued that, if a smaller area were excluded, the reunion of the whole of Ireland would be delayed.'[107] Redmond and Dillon admitted, according to a memorandum by Bonar Law, that had they been 'free agents', they would have accepted the clean cut.[108] But they were not free agents and believed that Irish public opinion would not accept it. The discussion then considered dividing Ulster. But the conference came to be deadlocked on Tyrone – Redmond insisting that he could never agree

103 Denis Gwynn, *The History of Partition, 1912–1925*, Browne and Nolan, 1950, p. 106.
104 House of Commons Debates, 20 July 1914, vol. 65, cols 69–70.
105 Gwynn, *History of Partition*, p. 117.
106 Ibid., p. 27.
107 Ibid., p. 119.
108 Fair, *British Interparty Conferences*, p. 115.

to it being *excluded* from Home Rule, Carson that he could never agree to it being *included*. The Nationalist Convention would not have countenanced exclusion, the Unionist Council would not have countenanced inclusion. There was a similar deadlock over Fermanagh. Carson then proposed a six-county exclusion so that both Tyrone and Fermanagh would be excluded, but that too was unacceptable to the Nationalists. This was the first time that a six-county Ulster, the current Northern Ireland, was suggested as the proper unit for exclusion. In an attempt to break the deadlock, Asquith proposed 'with great diffidence' that, if the conference could agree on everything except Tyrone, 'some impartial authority might be selected who would undertake the task of fairly dividing Tyrone'.[109] That too was rejected both by Redmond and by Carson. The conference broke down on 24 July. It had not even discussed the time limit. On the day before the conference ended, Asquith wrote to Venetia Stanley of

> that most damnable creation of the perverted ingenuity of man – the County of Tyrone. The extraordinary feature of the discussion was the complete agreement (in principle) of Redmond & Carson. Each said, 'I must have the whole of Tyrone, or die; but I quite understand why you say the same.' The Speaker, who incarnates bluff unimaginative English sense, of course cut in, 'When each of two people say they must have the whole, why not cut it in half?' They wd. neither of them look at such a suggestion ... I have rarely felt more hopeless in any practical affair: an impasse, with unspeakable consequences, upon a matter which to English eyes seems inconceivably small, & to Irish eyes immeasurably big. Isn't it a real tragedy?[110]

Asquith perhaps exaggerated how near the parties were to agreement, since the time limit had not been discussed. All the same, the conference undoubtedly led to some fellow feeling between Nationalists and Unionists. According to Asquith, Redmond told him that, when he and Carson parted company, Carson was in tears, while Craig, who had not previously spoken to Dillon, approached him saying, 'Mr Dillon, will you shake my hand, I should be glad to think that I had been able to give as many years in Ulster as you have to the service of Ireland.' 'Aren't they a remarkable people,' Asquith told Venetia, 'and the folly of thinking that we can ever understand, let alone govern them.'[111]

After the breakdown of the conference, the king met each of the

109 Ibid., p. 117.
110 Brock, ed., *Letters to Venetia Stanley*, p. 107.
111 Ibid., p. 122.

participants. It was Redmond's first audience with the king, who impressed the Irish leader by telling him that 'everyone in the world, himself included, regarded Home Rule as inevitable, and that any idea that he was opposed to it was quite wrong'.[112] After the conference, Asquith told the king that, if county option was accepted, he was prepared to allow continued exclusion after six years. This was a most important and significant concession. Redmond too was prepared to abandon the time limit.

The Amending Bill was due to be debated in the Commons on 27 July. But it had to be postponed for three days. For, on the day before, a Sunday, Dubliners had been shot by the army. In response to the growth of private armies in both parts of Ireland, the government had issued proclamations banning the import of arms. But on 26 July, Sir Roger Casement landed rifles and ammunition at Howth, just north of Dublin, from a yacht owned by Erskine Childers, who, born in Britain and a former House of Commons clerk, had become a convert to Irish Nationalism. He had declared that the arms were destined for Mexico. The rifles and ammunition were unloaded by Irish Volunteers. They were later to be used in the attack on the General Post Office in the Easter Rising of 1916. Returning to Dublin, the volunteers were met by police and troops called out by the assistant commissioner of the Dublin Metropolitan Police, William Harrell, who demanded that the arms be surrendered, a demand which was refused, with Nationalists 'resenting the unfair discrimination between the two kinds of Volunteers'.[113] The army then charged the volunteers but were resisted, with slight injuries on both sides. Returning to Dublin, the troops were pelted with stones and other missiles. Around one-quarter of the troops were injured. Without waiting for orders, the troops fired on the crowd, most of whom were unarmed, killing three and wounding thirty-eight. The use of force against Nationalists was contrasted with the failure to confront the much more serious gun-running at Larne in April, and the tolerance towards marches of armed UVF men in Belfast, one of which had occurred the day before. A furious Redmond demanded the adjournment of the Commons and an inquiry, which the government conceded. The Lord Mayor of Dublin had telephoned Redmond to tell him that those responsible for the killings should be tried for murder. The Archbishop of Dublin opened a fund for the victims. Birrell accepted that it had been a mistake to call on the military, Harrell resigned and his assistant was suspended. The Dublin shootings were the fourth in a series of disasters, following the Curragh incident and the gun-running at Larne and at Howth, disasters which underlined the weakness and incapacity of

---

112 Gwynn, *History of Partition*, p. 130.
113 Geraldine Dillon, 'The Howth Gun Running', *University Review*, Spring 1964, p. 49.

British government in Ireland. 'It is unnecessary', wrote Tomás MacDonagh, a company commander of the Irish Volunteers, later to be executed for his role in the Easter Rising in 1916,

> to comment on the incompetence and dishonesty of the British authori-
> ties. The moral of this step, as of the whole rise and progress of the Irish
> people is that if people act strongly and decisively, they can succeed in their
> action ... Ireland has now the strength to enforce her choice of destiny.
> The men who ruled Ireland in the past under Tory regime and under Lib-
> eral regime lost their power on the 26th July [a verdict widely supported in
> Ireland]. At Clontarf in 1914 [the suburb of Dublin where police, military
> and Irish Volunteers had engaged, and the site of a victory in battle in 1014
> by Brian Boru, king of Ireland], as at Clontarf in 1014, has been won a
> National victory.[114]

The report of the inquiry, published in October, confirmed that use of the police and military was not in accordance with the law, and that military intervention had been unjustified, since neither the gathering of the Irish Volunteers nor the march to Dublin had been unlawful assemblies requiring dispersal. Further, the danger to the military from insults and missiles had not been sufficient to justify the use of firearms.

Because of the shootings in Dublin, discussion of the Amending Bill had been postponed to 30 July. But on that day, Bonar Law took the initiative to secure a truce. He telephoned Asquith and asked him to visit his house in Kensington, where the Prime Minister found Carson present also. They sug-gested that discussion of the Amending Bill be postponed in view of the grave international situation. Two days earlier, Austria had declared war on Serbia and was bombing Belgrade. A general conflagration appeared unavoidable, and on 29 July, the Cabinet for the first time discussed Belgian neutrality, and how it should react if that neutrality was violated. A parliamentary truce was agreed, and it was also agreed that all controversial legislation be abandoned. Yet, even now, there was to be a misunderstanding. Bonar Law and Carson assumed that the truce extended not only to postponement of the Amending Bill but also the Home Rule Bill. Yet Asquith had no intention of postponing Home Rule, and was begged by Redmond, who had incurred unpopularity in Ireland by announcing Nationalist support for the war, not to miss so great an opportunity to win over the Irish people. On 15 September, over six weeks after the war began, Asquith announced that the Home Rule Bill and the Bill for the disestablishment of the Welsh Church, which, like Home Rule, had

114 Ibid., p. 53.

taken three years to reach the statute book, would be enacted. The two Bills would, however, be suspended for at least twelve months but no later than the end of the war, which, it was assumed by many, would be short. Asquith also promised that he would introduce an Amending Bill in the next parliamentary session before Home Rule came into effect, so that it could be modified with 'general consent'. He insisted that it would be 'absolutely unthinkable' amidst 'this great patriotic spirit of union' to use 'force, any kind of force, for what you call the coercion of Ulster'.[115] Bonar Law responded that the government had used 'our patriotism to betray us'. And that it had broken its pledge. When Redmond rose to reply, the opposition leader led his followers out of the House, in Asquith's words, 'by way of washing their hands of responsibility for our wicked ways. It was not really a very impressive spectacle – a lot of pro-saic & for the most part middle-aged gentlemen trying to look like the early French revolutionaries in the Tennis Court.'[116] On 18 September, Parliament was prorogued. But Redmond told the Commons that Home Rule had 'transformed Ireland from what George Meredith described a short time ago as "the broken arm of England" into one of the strongest bulwarks of the Empire'.[117]

On the day of Asquith's announcement, the king signed the Home Rule Bill. The Liberals had been concerned as to whether the king would in fact give his assent. On 5 February 1914, he had summoned Asquith to Windsor 'and told him bluntly that when the bill was presented for assent he should feel it his duty to do what in his own judgment was best for his people generally, and this broad hint took the Prime Minister considerably aback'.[118] Asquith strongly advised the king not to withhold his assent, something that had not been done since 1707. It would have been an extraordinary step to take and would have amounted in effect to dismissal of the government. The king had been unwilling to signify his assent in the absence of an accompanying Amending Bill, and was to write on 5 September to Sir Francis Hopwood, the Additional Civil Lord of the Admiralty, and a friend of his private secretary, 'I do not conceal from you my regret at having to give my Assent to the Home Rule Bill.' The king wrote to his Prime Minister on 31 July, insisting that he retained the right to veto legislation but felt that such an 'extreme course should not be adopted unless there is convincing evidence that it would avert a national disaster, or at least have a tranquillizing effect on the distracting conditions of the time. There is no such evidence.' But this letter was not in fact sent owing to the imminence of war. Instead, the

---

115 House of Commons Debates, 15 September 1914, vol. 66, col. 892.
116 Brock, ed., *Letters to Venetia Stanley*, p. 239.
117 House of Commons Debates, 15 September 1914, vol. 66, col. 912.
118 National Archives, T 273/237.

king declared on the same day that he would consent to the Bill but only on condition that the Cabinet provide a written 'statement of [their] full and considered reasons for it ... in a form which can be put on record for the use of his successors, and referred to If any necessity should hereafter arise'.[119] That was a highly unusual course to take.

But Home Rule was not to prove a final answer to the Irish question or questions – if indeed they can ever be finally answered. Home Rule was to be implemented after the war, ironically, only in the six counties of Northern Ireland. For, by 1918, the Irish Party had been electorally obliterated by Sinn Féin, whose aims and methods were far more radical than could be satisfied by Home Rule. Nevertheless, the promise of Home Rule did much, for a short time at least, to mollify historically embittered Anglo-Irish relations. It was because of Home Rule indeed that Redmond was able to express the support of his party for the British war effort. Whether Home Rule, in the absence of war, would have a proved a final settlement is of course impossible to know. It might well have stimulated an Irish demand for dominion status, independence within the Commonwealth, as was eventually to be achieved in the Anglo-Irish Treaty in 1921. But without the war, there might have been a peaceful evolution to this status rather than the bloody conflicts that were to ensue – the Easter Rising of 1916, the Anglo-Irish guerrilla war, the Black and Tans and the Irish Civil War. The Home Rule Act gave Ireland what Michael Collins, one of the signatories to the Anglo-Irish Treaty, was to declare that the treaty gave: the freedom to achieve freedom. In future, Britain seems to have accepted, Ireland would be governed by consent, not by force. That is the measure of the Liberal achievement. But partition had also been accepted as a regrettable necessity by the Liberals, to be recognised in the 1920 Government of Ireland Act, the fourth Home Rule Act, providing for separate Parliaments in six of the Ulster counties and, abortively, in the rest of Ireland. Partition was not, however, to be accepted by the Nationalists until the Belfast or Good Friday Agreement of 1998, in which the Irish Republic accepted that Irish unity could not be achieved until a majority in Northern Ireland consented to it. This agreement yielded a retrospective mandate for partition and retrospective legitimation of the solution so tortuously reached by 1914, a solution which recognised, as far as was possible, the right of self-determination of both Nationalists and Unionists. Partition indeed appeared inherent in the very nature of the Irish problem.

---

119 Bogdanor, *The Monarchy and the Constitution*, p. 131; Nicolson, *King George the Fifth*, p. 234fn, Brock, ed., *Letters to Venetia Stanley*, p. 126.

WAS BRITAIN NEAR TO CIVIL WAR IN 1914?

By 1914, the social reform agenda of the Liberals appeared to be exhausted. Ireland blocked the way. Speaking in Huddersfield on 23 March 1914, Lloyd George said:

> A generation has passed away since 1885, a generation that expected deliverance from penury, misery, wretchedness, privation. They wait in vain. Why? The great leaders of the people on both sides – Gladstone with his magic power, Chamberlain in his great power and skill such as few men have acquired in this generation ... Balfour, Morley – great names – why was it that they did not open the door to this wretched throng – the door of hope? I will tell you why. Heart and brain were concentrated on this wretched controversy [i.e. Ireland]. Let us settle it in order to get rid of it. Has another generation to pass away in wretchedness? Not if we can help it.[120]

It was the insistence by the Nationalists, on whom the Liberals depended, on the priority of Home Rule which made it so difficult to secure franchise reform or female suffrage. But with that block removed by Home Rule, the Liberals would have been free to continue their programme of constitutional reform and social legislation. Perhaps there would have been a new era of social reform. We shall never know.

It is a paradox that, as the franchise was widened, the legitimacy of the constitution came to be threatened.[121] Some indeed have argued that the constitution was under such threat in 1914 that Britain's liberal society was near to collapse. But this view is hardly possible to sustain. There were, as we have seen, revolts against the liberal order, two from the right – peers breaching the convention that they should not reject a financial measure, and Ulster Unionists threatening not to accept an Act passed by Parliament – and two from the left: militant trade unionists and militant suffragettes. The concatenation of these challenges, one historian believed, 'slowly undermined England's parliamentary structure until, but for the providential intervention of a world war, it would certainly have collapsed'.[122] But they did not in fact shake the foundations of the liberal polity. The Liberal government and indeed the political system as a whole were far more resilient than is often suggested. The Lords had backed down, after much grumbling, in response to the voice of the people. The militant suffragettes, it has been

---

120 *The Times*, 23 March 1914.
121 Robert Saunders, 'The British Constitution in the Long Nineteenth Century', *Journal of Modern European History*, 2008, p. 73.
122 George Dangerfield, *The Strange Death of Liberal England, 1910–1914* [1935], Paladin, 1970, p. 75.

suggested, 'broke more than windows with their stones, they broke the crust and conventions of a whole era'.[123] But they were but a small part of the female suffrage movement, they were losing support by 1914 and, in any case, their cause was in no way revolutionary. Their methods may have been radical, but their aims were not. They sought not to undermine or overthrow the liberal polity but the right to participate in it. Female suffrage was in fact a long overdue and sensible reform, in no way equivalent to the storming of the Bastille, and its main advocates, the suffragists of the NUWSS and the Labour Party, were strictly constitutional and law-abiding. With a general election due by January 1916, it is probable that the Liberal programme would have included a commitment to women's suffrage, and that it would have been enacted during that Parliament. Indeed, Lloyd George seemed to have promised Sylvia Pankhurst that he would not join a new Liberal Cabinet unless female suffrage were to be introduced – though characteristically he had left himself a loophole – provided that militancy were ended. And it would no doubt have been up to him to define 'militancy'.[124] The main consequence of female suffrage, as we have seen, far from being revolutionary, would almost certainly have been to weaken the forces of the left and strengthen the Conservatives.

Militant trade unionism also was on the wane in 1914. The strikes of 1911 and 1912 had been far more serious than those of 1914, though even then the leaders of the trade unions had sought to contain the revolt rather than encourage militancy. Admittedly, the Triple Alliance of January 1914 between the railwaymen, the transport workers and the miners seemed to threaten a general strike such as actually occurred in 1926. But workers were far less heavily unionised in 1914 than in 1926. In 1910, total union membership was around 2.5 million out of around 8 million adult male workers, divided between over 1,200 unions. Faced with a general strike, Conservatives and Liberals would have closed ranks to defeat it as they were to do in 1926. The result would have been an even greater setback for the working-class movement than it was to be in 1926. But it is unlikely that there would have been a general strike. In 1910, Harry Quelch, a militant member of Hyndman's Social Democratic Federation, later praised by Lenin as having been 'for decades' 'carrying on systematic propaganda and agitation in the Marxist spirit', lamented that not even the 1.5 million trade union members affiliated to the Labour Party could 'be relied upon to pay twopence a year each for Parliamentary Representation! ... How absurd, then, to suppose that they are in a state of incipient revolt, or would fight, or even strike, for principles for which they – while believing

---

123 Lady Rhondda, quoted in Harrison, *Peaceable Kingdom*, p. 48.
124 Purvis, 'Did Militancy Help or Hinder?', p. 1,210.

in them – will not even vote!'[125] In any case, the Triple Alliance was primarily seeking greater power to negotiate, not greater power to strike.

The most dangerous threat came from Ulster. The Unionist 'Campaign Guide' of 1914, written in preparation for the general election, declared that the government had 'smashed the constitution' and that 'no method remains, except armed revolt, by which the country can make its will prevail'. It predicted 'the blood of civil war'.[126] But Ulster was only a threat if it could command support from the other side of the Irish Sea, and by 1914 that was becoming doubtful. The Unionists indeed were increasingly worried as to the international implications of the Ulster conflict, and fearful that enemy powers might take advantage of it. On 15 March 1914, the day after Churchill's Bradford speech, Austen Chamberlain noted in his diary that 'the extraordinary Austro-German outburst of feeling against Russia at this moment is not wholly divorced from the spectacle of our domestic difficulties, and that, if for any reason our participation were impossible, Germany might provoke a quarrel with Russia or France'.[127] On 21 March, in the middle of the Curragh crisis, Austen told a meeting of Unionist leaders that he would like 'to offer the Government the alternative of Provincial Councils or Federal Home Rule on the South African model' as a 'safe settlement'.[128] On 25 March, at the time of the Curragh 'mutiny', Asquith reported to Venetia Stanley that 'the Tories are thoroughly cowed over this army business: they think it is going to do them harm in the country'.[129] The Unionists would not have pressed their Ulster policy were it to damage the unity of the country in face of a hostile Germany. Bonar Law, Carson and Craig believed that precipitate action would lose the support of public opinion on the other side of the Irish Sea. In any case, what would Ulster be rebelling against? By August 1914, its right to exclusion had been accepted by Liberals and, admittedly very unwillingly, by Nationalists. Asquith's important concession, after the Buckingham Palace Conference, that there would be exclusion on the basis of county option without the time limit gave the Unionists most of what they were fighting for. There was, admittedly, no agreement on the area to be excluded, but as Lloyd George was later to put it, 'Men would die for the Empire but not for Tyrone and Fermanagh.'[130] There would, no doubt, have been riots and fighting in Ulster and perhaps elsewhere in Ireland between the UVF and the Irish Volunteers, and

125 Lenin, *Collected Works*, vol. 19, p. 371; John Callaghan, 'The Edwardian Crisis: The Survival of Liberal England and the Rise of a Labour Identity', *Historical Studies in Industrial Relations*, 2012, p. 13.
126 Saunders, 'The British Constitution', p. 73.
127 Chamberlain, *Politics from Inside*, p. 620.
128 Ibid., pp. 626–7.
129 Brock, ed., *Letters to Venetia Stanley*, pp. 60–61.
130 Kenneth O. Morgan, 'Lloyd George and the Irish', in *Ireland After the Union: Proceedings of the Second Joint Meeting of the Royal Irish Academy and the British Academy, London, 1986*, Oxford University Press, 1989, p. 97.

the borders of the excluded area might well have been eventually determined by force. But the fighting would probably not have spread to the other side of the Irish Sea. The Ulster Unionists, to be successful, would have needed wide public support outside Ireland. The public on this side of the Irish Sea would have asked itself why it was proposing to fight for something that had already been conceded. Unionists outside Ireland would not have supported armed rebellion against an Act of Parliament which was giving Ulster most of what it sought, and the public would not have supported it either. It was, therefore, not clear who would fight who in a civil war, nor what they would be fighting about. Lord Stamfordham, the king's private secretary, noted that 'it is obvious that civil war cannot be permitted on the subject of the delimitation of a county'.[131] The private papers of Unionist politicians show them to be well aware of the weakness of their position. In April 1914, Carson told the Commons that he would be prepared to settle for exclusion with inclusion after six years at the will of Westminster. He expressed the hope that Home Rule, if it came about in the south and west 'might prove such a success in the future ... that it might be even for the interests of Ulster itself to move toward that Government to come in under it and form one unit in relation to Ireland'. He claimed to be 'as anxious as any man living to find a way out of this Ulster difficulty which will avoid bloodshed'. 'Nobody supposes', Carson declared, 'that at my age I prefer strife to peace.'[132]

One reason the parties were unable to agree at the Buckingham Palace Conference was that, for both, Ulster seemed to offer a powerful electoral cry. With Ulster unresolved, the Liberals could appeal to the country on the basis that they were defending the rule of law. As for the Unionists, they had few other positive policies and, once Ulster disappeared from the agenda, divisions over tariff reform would once again be exposed, and they would have been hoisted again with the damaging policy of higher food prices. So the next election would have been as much a challenge to the Unionists as to the Liberals.

In fact, however:

The British parties were far closer in Irish matters than either had cared to admit for a generation past ... At the outbreak of war, home rule on the basis of partition was a fait accompli so far as Britain was concerned, and the three years of party struggle had produced the essential materials for a settlement by consent.[133]

---

131 Rose, *King George V*, p. 157
132 House of Commons Debates, 29 April 1914, vol. 61, cols 1752, 1750.
133 Vincent, ed., *Crawford Papers*, p. 322.

Paradoxically, Bonar Law's extremism had forced a compromise settlement based on the exclusion of Ulster. And perhaps a Dublin Parliament which would follow, as Redmond hoped, conciliatory and consensual policies would not, in the end, have appeared as dangerous to the Protestant population of Ulster as had been believed, in which case Ireland could have been reunited just as Canada, Australia and South Africa had been reunited after initially being partitioned. But it was not to be.

CHAPTER 21

THE LIBERAL AND LABOUR PARTIES ON THE EVE OF WAR

Although constitutional reform had been in a sense the *raison d'être* of the mid-Victorian Liberal Party, the Liberals had proved more sure-footed in social than in constitutional reform. Even so, the New Liberalism had set an agenda of constitutional change – House of Lords reform, devolution and electoral reform – which was to bear fruit at the end of the twentieth century in the New Labour government of Tony Blair, which completed what many would regard as a Liberal, in part even a Gladstonian, agenda.

But before Home Rule was on the statute book, Britain was at war. And war, Churchill believed, 'is fatal to Liberalism'.[1] It may have indeed proved fatal to the Liberal Party. Was it the war or wider social factors which led to the rapid decline of the party in the post-war years? Perhaps the Liberal decline was inevitable as a result of the growth, cohesion and self-confidence of a working class which would come automatically to attach itself to the Labour Party. But was Labour by 1914 really in any position to overtake the Liberals?

Before 1914, Labour's vote was rising in by-elections, and it was achieving some limited success in local elections with 184 elected councillors in 1913, up from just seventy-three in 1907. But its local successes were generally achieved in cooperation with, rather than competition with, Liberals.[2] Labour's organisation was developing but painfully slowly. By 1914, it had only sixty-five local organisations designed for political work.[3] Admittedly, trade union membership was expanding before the war from 2.5 million in 1910 to just over 4 million in 1914, but the proportion of trade unionists affiliated to Labour had fallen from around 50 per cent between 1910 and 1912 to 38 per cent in 1914, a lower percentage than in 1903.[4] At no time before 1914 did the Labour Party secure the allegiance of anywhere near a majority of the working class. Nor is there evidence that universal male suffrage would nec- essarily benefit Labour. Remarkably, those areas of London with the lowest pre-war levels of enfranchisement were also those which gave the Liberals

1   Quoted in Beveridge, *Power and Influence*, p. 113.
2   Henry Pelling, 'Labour and the Downfall of Liberalism', in *Popular Politics and Society*, p. 117.
3   Cole, *History of the Labour Party from 1914*, p. 10.
4   K. D. Brown, ed., *The First Labour Party 1906–1914*, Croom Helm, 1985, p. 4.

their only London footholds after 1918 – Tower Hamlets, Bethnal Green and Southwark. There seems no clear link between low enfranchisement and Labour strength after 1918. The heavily unionised voters most likely to support Labour were also those in the working class most likely to already have had the vote before 1918.

Class cohesion was, admittedly, strengthening before 1914 and religious allegiances were weakening. But until 1910 at least, class seems to have remained secondary to religion. The Nonconformist share of the population was a better predictor of variances in the vote than social class and 'religion was the major electoral factor in elections from 1885–1910', with class secondary 'in its capacity to structure the vote'.[5] Perhaps the denominational rift was in fact 'a surrogate for centre-periphery attitudes', a split displayed particularly sharply in the two general elections of 1910.[6] In any case, before 1914, 'the class cleavage seems to have been politically relevant for only a small core of the electorate'. Admittedly, after 1910, it appeared that in some areas of the country such as Lancashire, class was replacing religion as a predictor of the vote, but in such areas the Liberals seem to be adapting effectively to that change. In Lancashire, indeed, Labour and the Liberals seemed but two wings of a single progressive cause.[7] In addition, working-class Unionist voters, who were certainly not Nonconformists, were swinging to the Liberals. There was, admittedly, a slow countermovement of wealthier Nonconformists away from the Liberals to Unionism, but this was not always due to economic causes. For example, the comparatively high level of Wesleyans voting Unionist in the two general elections of 1910 – 15 to 20 per cent in January and probably higher in December – owed less to class than to hostility to Home Rule and the threat to Protestantism which Wesleyans believed would follow in its train.[8] But most Nonconformists continued to support the Liberal Party well into the twentieth century. Irish Catholic voters, however, would feel free to desert the Liberals for the Labour Party once Home Rule had been enacted. That shift indeed was to be one of the reasons why Clydeside became a Labour stronghold during the 1920s.

Labour's whole future as a parliamentary party before 1914 depended upon the need to maintain an electoral arrangement with the Liberals. Admittedly, there had been no explicit pact between the two parties in the two elections of 1910, but there had been an implicit understanding in much of England

---

5 Kenneth Wald, *Crosses on the Ballot: Patterns of British Voter Alignment since 1885*, Princeton University Press, 1983, pp. 17, 161.

6 As suggested by Iain McLean in, 'The Great Victorian Realignment', a chapter of his book, *Rational Choice and British Politics: An Analysis of Rhetoric and Manipulation from Peel to Blair*, Oxford University Press, 2001, p. 100.

7 This is the central theme of Clarke, *Lancashire and the New Liberalism*. Historians dispute the extent to which Lancashire was typical or unusual.

8 D. W. Bebbington, 'Nonconformity and Electoral Sociology, 1867–1918', *Historical Journal*, 1984, p. 652.

and Wales. In the words of the Liberal Chief Whip, 'We never negotiate. Things simply "happen".'[9] It was, of course, in the interest of Liberals to negotiate such an understanding to avoid the Conservatives taking advantage of a split vote on the left. But it was also in the interests of Labour. Had Labour sought to challenge the Liberals nationally, it would have met with retaliation and would have lost many of the seats which it held. Snowden, together with many in the ILP, would have preferred Labour to disentangle from the Liberals, even if the party was reduced as a result to just a handful of seats. But MacDonald was realistic to reject this option, for, as Beatrice Webb noticed at the Labour Party conference of 1914, 'the solid phalanx of miners and textiles don't want the Labour members to cut loose from the Liberal party, and MacDonald knows it'.[10] Competing with the Liberals would have seen Labour eliminated as a serious factor in politics.[11] Between 1912 and 1914, Labour had been third in all three-cornered by-elections that it fought, even in the three seats which it was defending. By 1913, there was not a single Labour MP who had won his seat in a three-cornered fight against both of the major parties.[12] But the price of a renewal of the electoral arrangement with the Liberals was to confine Labour within its areas of existing strength.

There was a deep-seated tension within the Labour Party between, on the one hand, the desire for independence and the urge to make converts so as to become a truly national party, and on the other, maintaining cooperation with the Liberals. The problem which Labour faced was that its leaders had to maintain the party in what has been called a state of 'suspension' and 'unnatural restraint', which irked many party members.[13] Could Labour remain in such a situation indefinitely? It claimed, after all, to represent the working class, which comprised a majority of the voters. But it was precluded by its agreement with the Liberals from seeking to represent more than a small fraction of that class. Labour's electoral problems in 1914 seemed at least as great as anything faced by the Liberals.

In April 1914, it did indeed seem as if Labour might at the next election seek to break away from dependence on the Liberals. Labour's National Executive rejected the renewal of an electoral arrangement and proposed to run 120 to 130 candidates at the next election. That might have been a bargaining ploy designed to persuade the Liberals to allow an increase in Labour

---

9   Tanner, *Political Change and the Labour Party*, p. 67.
10 MacKenzie, *Diary of Beatrice Webb*, vol. 3, p. 321, entry for 6 February 1914.
11 R. I. McKibbin, 'James Ramsay MacDonald and the Problem of the Independence of the Labour Party', *Journal of Modern History*, 1970, p. 235.
12 Pugh, *Electoral Reform*, p. 9.
13 McKibbin, 'James Ramsay MacDonald and the Problem of the Independence of the Labour Party', p. 235.

candidatures. Whether Labour would actually have run 120 to 130 candidates must remain open to doubt. The trade unions would have been unlikely to finance so large a number, which would have led to heavy retaliation by the Liberals and a radical reduction in the number of Labour MPs.[14] Fighting as a party in opposition to the Liberals would have been ruinous for Labour.

Labour, then, was in a weak position in 1914. It was a sectional party, supported only by a minority of the working class, not a serious aspirant for government. It had made little impact in areas of heavy industry such as iron and steel, engineering and textiles and was not even dominant in all of the coalfields. It did not have the support of the working class as a whole, or even of all trade unionists, as was shown by the large minorities voting against affiliation to the party.[15] One historian has concluded:

> Before the First World War, the question of whether the Labour Party could or would displace the Liberal Party as one of the two main parties of the State hardly seemed to arise. The Labour Party was as yet no more than a pressure group which, as if in a fit of exasperation, had pushed its way from the lobbies onto the benches in Parliament, but once there had been seriously perplexed by the great questions of state such as foreign policy, Home Rule and even social welfare, and had as a consequence huddled in support of the Liberals whom by and large they trusted to deal with such complicated matters.[16]

And the biographer of Ramsay MacDonald has argued that 'the notion that the Liberal Party was doomed and that the Labour Party was bound by some inexorable sociological law to replace it as the main anti-Conservative party in Britain would have seemed absurd, not only to most Liberals, but to most Labour men as well'.[17] It was the Liberals, not Labour, who seemed in the van of the social reform movement. Labour appeared to have few ideas of its own. In June 1911, McKenna, the First Lord of the Admiralty, told the official piloting the National Insurance Bill through Parliament 'that the Liberals would never have to fear the Labour party, for the Labour party had no brains'.[18] Just over a year later, in July 1912, the Liberal Chief Whip declared his belief that 'the bulk of the Labour members of parliament are in reality no more than advanced Liberals; and there are many orthodox radicals who go a great deal further than the so-called socialists'. In January 1914, a Liberal

---

14 Tanner, *Political Change and the Labour Party*, p. 321.
15 Ibid., pp. 317, 318.
16 Pelling, *Social Geography*, p. 435.
17 Marquand, *Ramsay MacDonald*, p. 151.
18 Braithwaite, *Lloyd George's Ambulance Wagon*, p. 180.

journal declared, 'The reason why the Labour Party has been able to make so little of a fight against Liberalism has been that Liberalism has gone so far in the direction of a Labour policy,' while in June, Snowden wrote that 'Labour has been checkmated by Lloyd George'.[19]

The Liberals admittedly faced considerable problems, but they were to some extent the problems of success. As they sought to move forward, they faced the problem of retaining the allegiance of those who believed that they were moving too fast and who might in consequence shift to the Unionists. There were also those who believed that the Liberals were not moving fast enough and might well shift to Labour. Still, that kind of dilemma was not peculiar to the Liberals but is faced by any successful party of the left. There is no reason to believe that the Liberals could not have resolved it. Admittedly, in many of the areas where the Liberals remained strong, the New Liberalism had not taken root, and in those areas, the Liberals did not seem part of a wider progressive movement.[20] New Liberalism tended to be an urban phenomenon, much less noticeable in rural England, Scotland or Wales than in the towns. Even so, Liberalism had proved itself to be highly adaptable in the years before 1914. Indeed, there is some evidence, albeit limited, that the New Liberalism had first developed at a local level, some years before it became of importance nationally.[21] Perhaps Lloyd George might have been a bridge between the older world of Nonconformist liberalism and the new world of social reform, which was turning the Liberal Party into a kind of social democratic party. Perhaps such a party could have remained allied with, or at the very least, continued to constrain, the Labour Party. The two parties were grounded, socially, in the culture of Nonconformity and ideologically in their commitment to free trade and social and constitutional reform. But the war was to undermine that culture, divide Nonconformists and weaken them as a political force.

The Liberals, then, seemed in little danger from Labour. Indeed, many believed that the parliamentary Labour Party had failed. 'Whenever they [Labour MPs] have had to do more than act as critics,' a Unionist observer believed, 'their failure has been manifest. Nobody knows this better than their chairman, Ramsay MacDonald, who is the biggest failure of the parliament.'[22] That view was shared by Beatrice Webb, although unlike the Unionist critic, she tried to explain MacDonald's dominance. Labour MPs,

19 Quoted in Martin Petter, 'The Progressive Alliance', *History*, 1973, p. 49.
20 See, for example, Kenneth O. Morgan, 'The New Liberalism and the Challenge of Labour: The Welsh Experience, 1885–1929', *Welsh History Review*, 1972–3.
21 James R. Moore, *The Transformation of Urban Liberalism: Party Politics and Urban Governance in Late Nineteenth-Century England*, Ashgate, 2006.
22 Vincent, ed., *Crawford Papers*, pp. 276–7.

she wrote in her diary, were primarily 'ordinary workmen who neither know nor care about anything but the interests of their respective trade unions and a comfortable life for themselves'. In consequence, MacDonald 'rules absolutely and the other Labour members stick to him as their only salvation from confusion'.[23] But the trouble was that MacDonald 'does not want anything done in particular. He honestly disapproves of nearly all the planks in the ostensible party programme ... He is bored by his Labour colleagues and attracted to Front Bench Liberals.' MacDonald was, she thought, 'the Parnell of the Labour Party – but a Parnell who does not believe in his cause'.[24] That was unfair. MacDonald did have a clear view, albeit one that Beatrice Webb did not share. He believed that the Labour Party and the left wing of the Liberals, led by Lloyd George, were converging and that, just as there had been a merger between the Conservatives and the Liberal Unionists in 1912, so also there should and would eventually be a merger between Labour and the Liberal left. Labour would in the course of evolution succeed the Liberals as a majority party when the work of Liberalism had been completed, and at that stage no doubt many Liberals would join the party. But meanwhile, Labour should not seek to short-circuit the evolutionary trend by competing with Liberals, since the aims of the two parties were perfectly compatible.

Before the outbreak of war, there were a number of informal discussions on the possibility of coalition between Liberals and Labour. In October 1911, after a breakfast with Lloyd George, MacDonald wrote in his diary, 'He sounded me on coalition Government,' and commented revealingly, 'not just yet'. In November 1911, the Liberal Chief Whip made another approach, 'Wanted to know privately if coalition were possible at next Election.'[25] In March 1914, at a time when it seemed as if the government might be forced to go to the country on what MacDonald called 'the Tory Army plot', the Curragh 'mutiny', Lloyd George made a definite offer. Claiming the authority of Asquith, he proposed a new electoral pact with an increased number of Labour candidatures, and an agreed programme, while if Labour wanted representation in the Cabinet, according to MacDonald, 'it was to be given to us'.[26] But this offer was rejected by Labour's National Executive in April. When war broke out, MacDonald was again offered a place in the government, but, as an opponent of the war, he had to decline.[27]

There is little doubt that MacDonald could have become a member of the Liberal government had he wanted to, although he might have been unable

---

23 MacKenzie, *Diary of Beatrice Webb*, vol. 3, p. 196, entry for 18 February 1914.
24 Ibid., entry for 18 February 1914.
25 Marquand, *Ramsay MacDonald*, p. 142.
26 Ibid., pp. 161, 160.
27 Maurice Hankey, *The Supreme Command*, George Allen & Unwin, 1961, vol. 1, p. 162.

to persuade his party to agree upon a coalition. Nevertheless, many Labour MPs did not see the two parties as mutually exclusive. Their concern, as we have seen, was with representation, not doctrine. The socialists in the Labour Party certainly saw an incompatibility and the ILP would almost certainly have rejected coalition and formed an independent socialist party of its own, but the socialists were a distinct minority in the Labour Party. A coalition, however, held out the possibility of a new progressive social democratic party. Had it come into existence, the history of the British left might have been quite different from what it came to be. But even without coalition, the parties might have grown closer together. And an intelligent observer of the political scene before the war could plausibly conclude that Asquith would be succeeded by Lloyd George, who would himself be succeeded by MacDonald as Prime Minister of a progressive government combining the Liberal and Labour parties. The interests of Labour could have been accommodated within the Liberal Party as they had been in Canada and with the Democrats in the United States. The assumption that this could not occur is based on the view that the political culture of Britain is more like that of the Continent than of Canada or the United States. But, as we have seen, Labour was very different from the doctrinal socialist parties of the Continent, where Marxism and class war theories enjoyed greater influence.

There is, however, one indication, albeit very slender, that MacDonald foresaw Labour replacing the Liberals. Every other Labour or socialist party in Europe favoured proportional representation. Labour did not and that was largely MacDonald's doing. The TUC supported proportional representation at its 1911 conference by a majority of three to one. The ILP also supported it at its 1913 conference. Proportional representation would have allowed Labour to campaign nationally against the Liberals without fearing that a split vote would lead to Conservative victories. But Labour, at its 1914 conference, rejected proportional representation, though Henderson and Snowden were in favour. Towards the end of his life, the historian Michael Brock, editor of the letters of Asquith and Venetia Stanley and the diaries of Margot Asquith, told me of a conversation many years earlier with Sir Robert Ensor, author of the volume on 1870 to 1914 of the *Oxford History of England*, which had been published as long ago as 1936. Ensor had, before 1914, been a supporter of the ILP, and had known MacDonald well. MacDonald had told him that he had been against proportional representation because he foresaw that Labour would eventually become a majority party in the state and would then benefit from first past the post. This, of course, hardly counts as historical evidence, but nevertheless, Labour's rejection of proportional representation ensured that it would eventually be able to form a majority government, although it took until 1945 for it to do so. Proportional representation, by contrast, while it might have eased Liberal–Labour relations, would have prevented a single-party majority government since Labour has never secured a majority of the popular vote. MacDonald even rejected the second ballot which, like the alternative vote, would have avoided electoral clashes between Labour and the Liberals, arguing:

> A Third Party which has won its way into Parliament in spite of our single ballot system, has undoubtedly come to make a permanent contribution to legislation, and its strength is all the greater because it can use the terms of the single ballot in its own self-defence at future elections.

Here, too, the implication was that Labour would eventually win a general election on its own without needing assistance from other parties.[28] The 1914 Labour conference also voted against the alternative vote, but the parliamentary party supported a Bill providing for it in 1914.

Had cooperation between the Liberals and Labour continued after 1914, the Unionists would have been under severe electoral pressure. At the end of the January 1910 election campaign, Austen Chamberlain had written to Balfour:

> There is one feature of the situation which causes ... some anxiety. The combination of the Liberal and Labour parties is much stronger than the Liberal Party would be if there were no third Party in existence. Many men who would in that case have voted with us voted on this occasion as the Labour Party told them i.e. for the Liberals ... The existence of the third Party deprives us of the full benefits of the 'swing of the pendulum', introduces a new element into politics and confronts us with a new difficulty.[29]

In addition, tariff reform with its seemingly inevitable concomitant, higher food prices, remained an electoral obstacle for the Unionists. The two general elections of 1910 with their high levels of turnout had shown how difficult it would be for them to increase their vote and mount an effective challenge to the Liberals, even though they had polled a higher share of the *electorate* than they had done at any general election since the 1884 Reform Act. A further difficulty for the Unionists would have been the abolition of plural voting, which the Liberals were determined to enact. And the Unionists needed to win more seats than not only the Liberals but the Liberals, Labour and the

---

28 Chadwick, *Augmenting Democracy*, pp. 161–2.
29 Green, 'Radical Conservatism', p. 685.

thirty or so Irish Nationalists remaining in the Commons after Home Rule had come into effect combined. Arguably, not only Labour but also the Unionists faced more difficult electoral problems than the Liberals.

But whatever the fortunes of the Liberal Party might have been, the Liberal government was able to show, even after nearly nine years in office, that it remained full of energy and had not lost the power of decision. When Germany demanded passage of her troops through neutral Belgium, the Asquith government acted rapidly and decisively, with the support of the opposition. It sent an ultimatum to Berlin and secured parliamentary authority to increase the size of the army by half a million men. These were not the actions of a party or a polity in decay but rather of a government, Parliament and people united and ready to meet what they rightly perceived as a challenge to the public law of Europe.

CHAPTER 22

FROM THE ENTENTE TO WORLD WAR

THE ENTENTE WITH FRANCE

The Unionist government had been badly shaken by the hostility of the Continental powers during the Boer War. Britain's friendlessness had been cruelly exposed. 'I am gradually coming to the conclusion', Lord George Hamilton, the India Secretary, wrote to Curzon in April 1901, 'that we must alter our foreign policy and throw our lot in, for good or bad, with some other Power.'[1] The obvious ally seemed to be Germany. For, by contrast with France and Russia, Britain had hardly any colonial conflicts with Germany. In no part of the world did the interests of the two powers seriously conflict.

From March 1898 until the end of 1901, there were four attempts at reaching an agreement with Germany. The first was initiated informally by Chamberlain in a conversation in November 1898 with the German ambassador, the second in December 1899 when the kaiser was on a visit to Britain, the third in March 1901 two months after the accession of King Edward and the fourth in May 1901 when a draft convention for an agreement was prepared by Lansdowne. Until the summer of 1901, the Cabinet was debating 'not whether they should co-operate with Germany but upon what terms they should do so'.[2] King Edward was sympathetic to these approaches, telling the first secretary at the German embassy in March 1901 that he had 'for years had the greatest sympathy for Germany, and I am still today of [the] opinion that Great Britain and Germany are natural allies. Together they could police the world and secure a lasting peace.'[3] Balfour favoured an alliance if it would help Britain in the Far East but had doubts whether it would be ratified by Parliament. Salisbury, however, was sceptical from the start, and his scepticism was strengthened by the failure of the Anglo-German Agreement of 1900 on China, which had been unsuccessful in limiting Russian expansion in the Far East.

In November 1898, in a conversation with the German ambassador,

---

1   Quoted in Keith Wilson, ed., *International Impact of the Boer War*, Acumen, 2001, p. 160.
2   Grenville, *Lord Salisbury and Foreign Policy*, p. 345.
3   Lee, *King Edward VII*, vol. 2, p. 120.

Chamberlain proposed, unofficially and almost certainly without Cabinet authority, an alliance 'of a defensive character based upon mutual understanding as to policy in China and elsewhere',[4] But Chamberlain did not impress the ambassador, who told the German Chancellor:

> In natural intelligence as in energy and great parliamentary skill he assuredly does not fail, but in respect to foreign policy he makes on me the impression of a raw beginner who follows the dictates of his personal vanity, taking no sufficient account of consequences in what he says and does. Obviously he would have regarded it as a personal triumph, bringing him a good step nearer the Premiership, could he have succeeded in establishing as the author of the English alliance with the Dreibund [Triple Alliance].[5]

But a little later another German Chancellor thought Chamberlain was 'like all big men ahead of his time; and that which is not yet may come to be'.[6]

Chamberlain carried his proposal further in a major speech at Leicester in November 1899, shortly after the outbreak of the Boer War. He declared that 'no far-seeing statesman could be content with England's permanent isolation on the continent of Europe' and argued for a 'new Triple Alliance between the Teutonic race and the great branches of the Anglo-Saxon race'. The Americans, however, who had not been consulted, were not interested. Much American opinion was isolationist and she was certainly not prepared to undertake European commitments. But in his Leicester speech, Chamberlain went on to say that 'the natural alliance is between ourselves and the German Empire ... Both interest and racial sentiment united the two peoples.' What, however, were the terms on which an agreement could be made? On that, Chamberlain was uncharacteristically vague. 'To me it seems to matter little whether you have an alliance which is committed to paper or whether you have an understanding which exists in the minds of the statesmen of the respective countries.'[7] Germany, however, saw no value in a mere 'understanding'. What she wanted was a commitment from Britain to help defend her against Russia and France. That could best be achieved, Germany believed, by Britain joining the Triple Alliance. But Britain would then be committed to defending Austria, Germany or Italy were they to be attacked. To fulfil such a commitment, substantial defence spending would be required and perhaps a large army to be sent to the Continent. It would

4 H. W. Koch, 'The Anglo-German Alliance Negotiations: Missed Opportunity or Myth?', *History*, 1969, p. 381.
5 Garvin, *Chamberlain*, vol. 3, pp. 268-9.
6 Ibid., p. 515.
7 Ibid., pp. 507-8.

mean a massive change in Britain's defence and foreign policy orientation. There was not the slightest possibility of either the Cabinet or the public accepting so wide-ranging a commitment.

By emphasising Britain's isolation, Chamberlain had given Germany the impression that Britain was weak and desperate for an agreement. German diplomats, in consequence, believed that Britain would have to sue for terms. Friedrich von Holstein, the head of the political department in the German Foreign Office and a key figure in German foreign policy, had written in a memorandum in December 1895:

> So long as England retains India, it is necessary for her, unless she is to retreat without fighting, to effect a *rapprochement* with the Triple Alliance. She will only appreciate this necessity if she has learned ... that the Triple Alliance *will not under all circumstances render support to her*.[8]

What he meant was that Britain needed the Triple Alliance countries of Germany, Austria and Italy to counterbalance Russia in Europe so that Russia would no longer be able to concentrate her forces against Britain in India. Holstein's pronouncement remained the key to German policy. It meant that Germany was prepared to exact a high price for her friendship since, it seemed, Britain had no alternative to it. Few in German ruling circles believed that there could be a rapprochement between Britain and France or Britain and Russia. The Kruger telegram, sent by the kaiser after the Jameson Raid, was a maladroit attempt to emphasise that Britain needed German friendship. But its clumsiness had the opposite effect, and it appeared as an insulting interference in Britain's affairs.

Even so, until the end of 1901, it still seemed that Britain's natural partner would be Germany to secure British interests in China. 'Within China,' Balfour had told the Commons in 1898, 'British interests and German interests are absolutely identical.'[9] In a memorandum in September 1900, Chamberlain had declared that 'both in China and elsewhere it is in our interest that Germany should throw herself across the path of Russia'.[10] Chamberlain continued his efforts, urging local understandings which might eventually lead to an alliance. The German ambassador was told that Chamberlain and his colleagues were perfectly aware that the era of isolation was over and that Britain needed allies. In November, Selborne at the Admiralty felt that an alliance with Germany was 'the only alternative to an ever increasing Navy

---

8   Quoted in Raymond J. Sontag, 'The Cowes Interview and the Kruger Telegram', *Political Science Quarterly*, 1925, p. 241. Emphasis in original.
9   House of Commons Debates, 3 April 1898, vol. 56, col. 232.
10 George Monger, *End of Isolation*, p. 15.

and ever increasing Navy estimates'.[11] But Salisbury remained sceptical and told Curzon in October 1900 that he did

> not feel the same danger in the case of Russia ... As to Germany I have less confidence than you. She is in mortal danger on account of that long undefended frontier of tier's [sic] on the Russian side. She will therefore never stand by us against Russia; but is always rather inclined to curry favour with Russia by throwing us over. I have no wish to quarrel with her: but my faith in her is infinitesimal.[12]

And indeed for Germany, her interests in China were of far less importance than they were for Britain. Germany was concerned primarily to protect her frontiers in Europe, and less worried by quarrels in the Far East. 'The further the Russians engage themselves in Asia,' the kaiser declared, 'the quieter they sit in Europe.'[13] Germany was certainly not prepared to endanger her relations with Russia in the Far East for Britain's sake, while Britain had no intention of assuming wide Continental commitments. Salisbury, for his part, wanted to antagonise Russia as little as possible, since a hostile Russia, in alliance with France, would threaten his chances of ejecting France from the Nile valley.

Nevertheless, Lansdowne as Foreign Secretary continued patiently to secure an understanding with Germany, even going so far as to produce a draft convention. But it never came to fruition. Sanderson, the Permanent Under-Secretary at the Foreign Office who had prepared the draft, believed that, however it was worded, 'it will practically amount to a guarantee to Germany of the provinces conquered from France [i.e. Alsace-Lorraine] and that is the way in which the French will look at it. I do not see exactly what Germany would guarantee us.'[14] Lansdowne's aims were far less wide-ranging than Chamberlain's had been. He wanted a limited agreement of the type that he was later to achieve with France. He sought not a wholesale reorientation of Britain's diplomatic position but the resolution of specific problems. The difficulty was that, while Lansdowne wanted to limit Britain's commitments, any agreement with Germany would increase them. Salisbury penned a magisterial memorandum arguing against 'novel and most onerous obligations' and insisting that Britain could not commit herself to war

---

11 Quoted in Nicholas A. M. Rodger, 'Anglo-German Naval Rivalry 1860–1914', in Michael Epkenhans, Jörg Hillmann and Frank Nägler, eds, *Jutland: World War 1's Greatest Naval Battle*, University Press of Kentucky, 2015, p. 11.
12 Neilson, *Britain and the Last Tsar*, p. 216.
13 Garvin, *Chamberlain*, vol. 3, p. 275.
14 Steiner, *Foreign Office and Foreign Policy*, pp. 60–61.

'unless it is a purpose of which the electors of this country would approve'.[15] Britain's attitude in the event of war must depend on circumstances. This was to remain Britain's policy until the violation of Belgium's neutrality in 1914 left her with little choice.

By September 1901, Baron von Eckardstein, secretary to the German embassy, reported to the German Chancellor that Chamberlain's attitude, previously sympathetic, had given place to 'resentment against Germany'. That was in large part the result of German criticism of Britain during the Boer War. 'I had', wrote Eckardstein,

> for some time seen and spoken to Mr Chamberlain only in a casual way, and had noticed that he had abandoned his earlier friendly tendencies towards Germany ... The utterances as well as the vehemence with which the Minister expressed himself to me about it, leaves one convinced that his opposition to Germany has taken a much deeper root and bears a far more dangerous character than could be supposed.

Further, 'the attitude against Germany in all circles of the nation had taken too deep roots'.[16] On 25 October, speaking in Edinburgh, Chamberlain widened the gap, referring to German criticism of British tactics in South Africa and responding that Britain had nothing to learn from Germany in terms of 'barbarity' and 'cruelty'. In the Reichstag on 8 January 1902, Chancellor von Bülow contemptuously dismissed Germany's critics, using the words of Frederick the Great, as 'biting on granite'. With that, all hope of an agreement between Britain and Germany evaporated. But it had never really been feasible. Germany had never been willing to consider an entente or an understanding as opposed to an alliance. That was probably a misjudgement on her part. She did not believe that Britain could achieve such understandings with France or Russia. But nor did anyone in the British Cabinet at the time. Even so, Britain believed that a powerful Germany balancing France and Russia was in her interests, so long as France was not excessively weakened. British policy remained one of balance, not, as many Germans were to believe, encirclement.

In January 1902, Chamberlain spoke in Birmingham Town Hall:

> We have the feeling, unfortunately, that we have to count upon ourselves alone, and I say, therefore, that it is the duty of British statesmen and it is the duty of the British people to count upon themselves alone, as their

---

15 Gooch and Temperley, eds, *British Documents*, vol. 2, pp. 68–9.
16 Ibid., p. 132.

ancestors did. I say alone, yes in a splendid isolation, surrounded by our kinsfolk.[17]

Chamberlain had come to adopt the same attitude as Salisbury, whom he had earlier opposed. But when alliance with Germany proved impossible, Lansdowne, who had hoped for a Triple Alliance of Britain, Germany and Japan, had pressed instead for an alliance with Japan to contain Russia.

Remarkably, the European power most eager for an arrangement with Britain proved to be not Germany but France which, following Fashoda and the Boer War, had seen Britain as 'the eternal enemy', a feeling intensified by the vagaries of British cooking. The cuisine was 'detestable', declared Paul Cambon, the French ambassador to London and one of the architects of the entente, of a meal at Windsor Castle in 1898. 'In my household such a dinner would not have been tolerated.'[18] French enmity had been reciprocated. 'Don't like the French,' sings Captain Vere in Benjamin Britten's opera *Billy Budd*, set in the Napoleonic Wars. Until well into the nineteenth century, the French had been hereditary enemies at Agincourt, Blenheim and Waterloo. Relations had improved briefly when Louis Philippe became king in 1830, but by the end of the century, enmity had returned and French public opinion was solidly in sympathy with the Boers. But the Anglo-Japanese Alliance posed a problem for France. For, were there to be conflict between Japan and Russia, France would, because of her alliance with Russia, have to support her and that would bring her into conflict with Britain. The British too feared that France might be drawn into war against Japan, and in consequence, under the terms of the Anglo-Japanese Alliance, Britain would then have to become involved. At a Cabinet meeting on 11 December 1903, Lansdowne was authorised to tell the French ambassador of this; and as Balfour reported to the king, 'It was impossible to contemplate anything at once so horrible and so absurd as general war brought on by Russia's impracticable attitude in Manchuria.'[19] An entente would ensure that so pointless a conflict could be avoided.

The conflict between Britain and France had been over colonies. But both countries now seemed satiated powers. In any case, the outcome of the Fashoda crisis had shown France that she could not hope to challenge British predominance in Egypt. The French, Cambon told Lansdowne in August 1902:

17 Grenville, *Lord Salisbury and Foreign Policy*, p. 366.
18 Robert and Isabelle Tombs, *That Sweet Enemy: The French and the British from the Sun King to the Present*, Vintage Digital, 2010, p. 442.
19 Nish, *Anglo-Japanese Alliance*, pp. 286–7.

had a colonial dominion amply sufficient not only for their present wants, but for their wants for generations to come. They had passed out of the period of expansion and had no wish to add to their responsibilities by further acquisitions. The colonial policy of France was therefore essentially conservative, and in the pursuit of such a policy, M. Delcassé [the French foreign minister] believed that it would be possible for them to move in accordance with us. This seemed to him all the easier because we were not really competitors.

All that France wanted was 'to ensure the security of what she already possessed'.[20] That, presumably, was also Britain's aim. For France, preservation of a balance of power in Europe was more important than colonial expansion; while for Britain, breaking the hostility of the Continent towards her had become more important than extending her empire. There seemed, therefore, no longer any obstacles to an understanding, and in exchange for British support for the French position on Morocco, France was prepared to confirm her acceptance of British hegemony in Egypt.

But the entente rested on something more than a mere pragmatic settling of differences. Britain and France were, amongst the major powers of Europe, the only parliamentary nations – Austria–Hungary, Germany and Russia were military autocracies. And Britain and France were also the only major European powers with a deep commitment to the rule of law and civil and religious liberty. In 1898, at the time of Fashoda, Lloyd George had declared:

> If we defeat France, we shall be defeating the only power on the Continent with a democratic Constitution. Emperors, Kings and aristocratic rulers will mock at the whole thing – two great democratic Powers at each other's throats, the only countries where you have perfect civil and religious liberty in Europe quarrelling with each other to make sport for the titled and throated Philistines of Europe.[21]

The feeling that Britain and France had something deep in common was given expression by the visit of Edward VII to Paris in May 1903, a visit welcomed by President Loubet, who believed that it 'would, in the present temper of France, do an amount of good which is probably not realised in England'.[22] Edward had been brought up a Francophile. As a boy, Queen

---

20 Gooch and Temperley, eds, *British Documents*, vol. 2, no. 322. In fact, France was to acquire much of her empire in north-west Africa *after* the entente was agreed.
21 Grigg, *Young Lloyd George*, p. 223.
22 Newton, *Lansdowne*, p. 275.

Victoria had made him kneel before the tomb of Napoleon in Les Invalides. In 1878, he had been president of the British section of the Paris International Exhibition, and in his speech at the banquet held to celebrate the occasion, he declared his faith in an 'entente cordiale'. The king's visit, undertaken on his own initiative, perhaps strained the conventions of constitutional monarchy; and yet helped create the atmosphere which made the entente possible. The change in attitude of the Parisian crowd was startling in its rapidity. Greeted at first by cries of 'Vivent les Boers', 'Vive Marchand' and 'Vive Fashoda', by the end of his visit, the crowd was shouting 'Vive notre roi'.[23] 'Seldom', according to a report from a Belgian representative in Paris to his Foreign Ministry, 'has such a complete change of attitude been seen as that which has taken place in this country during the last fortnight towards England and her Sovereign.'[24] The French ambassador to London was later to say 'any clerk at the Foreign Office could draw up a treaty' but only the king 'could have succeeded in producing the right atmosphere for a rapprochement'.[25] A future Permanent Secretary at the Foreign Office declared that the entente was due 'entirely to the initiative and political flair of King Edward who, had he listened to the objections of his Cabinet, would never have gone to Paris'.[26] The success of the entente would depend upon a sense of good feeling which was to transmute and transcend diplomacy; and this sense of good feeling the king had helped to create.

France had initiated the discussions which led to the entente and found Lansdowne receptive. For, by contrast with Germany, France did not require anything more than a limited commitment, a settlement of colonial conflicts. On 8 April 1904, three conventions comprising the entente were signed. The first, the most important and most complex, declared that the French government would do nothing to obstruct Britain in Egypt, something Britain had sought to achieve since her occupation in 1882. In particular, France would place no obstacles to the reform of Egypt's financial system which Cromer sought but which depended upon the acquiescence of the powers. Britain, for her part, recognised that in Morocco it was for France 'to preserve order in that country and to provide assistance for the purpose of administrative, economic, financial, and military reforms which it may require'. Britain promised not to 'obstruct the action taken by France for this purpose', so long as her commercial rights were protected. Both countries promised complete commercial freedom in their spheres of influence as well

23 Lee, *King Edward VII*, vol. 2, pp. 237, 240.
24 Ibid., p. 241.
25 St Aubyn, *Edward VII*, p. 329.
26 Lord Hardinge of Penshurst, *Old Diplomacy: The Reminiscences of Lord Hardinge of Penshurst*, John Murray, 1947, p. 96.

as free navigation in Suez and the Straits of Gibraltar. France, in addition, promised not to fortify a large part of the coast of Morocco.

The second convention concerned Newfoundland, where France surrendered privileges she had been given under the treaties of Utrecht in 1713 in return for an indemnity and territorial compensation in West Africa.

The third convention provided for a partition between spheres of interest in Siam and an adjustment of territorial claims in East Africa, Madagascar and Zanzibar, together with the establishment of an Anglo-French condominium in the New Hebrides.

These conventions were, as regularly occurred during the era of imperialism, signed without bothering to seek the consent of the peoples affected, and with little concern for their interests.

There was an asymmetry to the entente. French acceptance of the British position in Egypt was little more than a recognition of the status quo, confirming what Fashoda had established. But recognition of a French sphere of influence in Morocco represented an alteration in the status quo. For the Treaty of Madrid in 1880, which the entente undermined, had left Morocco open to all the powers. French interests in Morocco arose because it was, as the convention stated, 'coterminous for a great distance' with Algeria, an overseas *departement* of the French Republic, which sent representatives, elected almost wholly by the European population, to the National Assembly. France, therefore, felt that she could not allow Morocco to fall under foreign influence which would threaten her North African empire, just as Britain believed that an Afghanistan controlled by a hostile power would threaten her Indian empire.

In Morocco, Cambon had told Lansdowne in July 1902, 'the attitude of the tribes had become extremely threatening of late', and it was primarily for this reason that he had proposed 'a frank discussion' between Britain and France.[27] In 1902, tribal warfare had broken out, encouraged, so it was suggested, by French agents and exaggerated in the French press.[28] But the sultan's forces were rapidly defeated and his rule became almost wholly nominal. Morocco was, like Turkey and China, another decaying state, a dying empire with a government unable to maintain order amongst warring groups and chaotic finances. By 1902, it appeared to be in dissolution. Whether there was actually a status quo there to be preserved was very questionable. But the entente meant, insofar as Morocco was concerned, the dominance of France and the exclusion of Germany.[29] So it led to conflict between France and Germany.

---

27 Gooch and Temperley, eds, *British Documents*, vol. 2, 23 July 1902, no. 321.
28 James J. Cooke, *New French Imperialism 1880–1910: The Third Republic and Colonial Expansion*, David and Charles, 1973, pp. 109, 123.
29 Samuel R. Williamson Jr, *The Politics of Grand Strategy: Britain and France Prepare for War, 1904–1914*, Harvard University Press, 1969, pp. 8–9.

There was a large element of hypocrisy in the entente. Britain declared that she had 'no intention of altering the political status of Egypt'. But she wanted to tighten her grip on it through reform of her financial system and had no intention of ending the occupation. France, in turn, declared that she had 'no intention of altering the political status of Morocco'. But, as we have seen, Morocco was highly unstable, and France was intending to increase her control there. Britain too had an interest in Morocco – to ensure that no hostile power could threaten Gibraltar. That meant not losing control of Tangier, since a foreign power could use it to threaten Gibraltar and seal off the western entrance to the Mediterranean. The convention, therefore, stipulated that the Mediterranean seaboard would lie outside the French sphere of influence and would be neutralised. France was also required to come to an arrangement with Spain concerning her sphere of influence on the Mediterranean coast. In October 1904, she did so, acknowledging the Spanish sphere of interest, while Spain agreed not to extend her fortifications on the Atlantic or cede authority in her area to any other power than France. The secret clauses of the convention, not disclosed to the Cabinet and not made public until November 1911, in the French newspaper *Le Temps*, made provision that, were the sultan prove unable to exercise his authority in the Spanish sphere of influence, Spain, which already owned a few scraps of Moroccan territory, would receive in addition a strip of northern Morocco which she would administer as a neutral and unfortified zone lying between France and Gibraltar. The entente, therefore, did not ensure the preservation of the political status of Morocco. What it did ensure was that any disturbance to it would not embitter Anglo-French relations.

The distinctive feature of the entente was not merely that the two countries pledged themselves to abstain from interfering in the spheres of influence of the other but that they would do all they could to *further* each other's interests through 'diplomatic support'. It was, the Under-Secretary for Foreign Affairs declared, recommending the agreement to the Commons, in terms of 'pledges of friendship rather than as the terms of a compromise between jealous and exacting litigants'.[30] Nor was it 'a mere commercial bargain'. It was intended to lead to a broader habit of cooperation between the two countries, as it did. The *Manchester Guardian* declared that 'the value of the new friendship lies not in the mere avoidance of disputes, but in the chances that it affords a genuine alliance between the democracies in both countries for furtherance of the democratic cause'.[31]

The entente is too often judged with hindsight in terms of the 1914 war.

---

30 House of Commons Debates, 1 June 1904, vol. 135, col. 515.
31 *Manchester Guardian*, 10 April 1904.

But it is quite wrong to regard it as being, from Britain's point of view, a step towards a defensive alliance. It was regarded instead in Britain as a contribution to the peace of Europe, a peace endangered by conflicting colonial aspirations. It would also help achieve peace in the Far East since it ensured that France would not join Russia in war against Japan, so freeing Britain from her obligation to assist Japan were she to be attacked by two powers. Britain hoped that the entente would yield a precedent for settling other colonial issues peacefully. It was seen indeed as a working model for further agreements, such as that with Russia in 1907. So the entente could help to reduce, the *Manchester Guardian* hoped, the 'increasing and well-nigh intolerable burden of military expenditure which is thrown on the shoulders of the peoples of Europe'.[32] Largely for this reason, it was welcomed both in Parliament and in the country. The pacifically minded Campbell-Bannerman told the Commons in June 1904:

> The most remarkable feature of this debate is that there has not been a single discordant note as to the main purport and object of the convention … The House will echo the general feeling of the country, which is one of intense satisfaction at the conclusion of this convention.[33]

The only discordant voice was that of Lord Rosebery, who predicted that it would lead to war, but by this time, he counted for little in Liberal counsels.

In form, then, the entente was simply a settlement of colonial disputes. Unlike the agreement with Japan, it was not a definite treaty 'embodying the terms under which each country undertook to defend the other if attacked under certain circumstances'.[34] But it would make detente with Germany more difficult to achieve. Article 9 of the convention concerning Egypt and Morocco committed the two countries to 'diplomatic support' of each other. But 'diplomatic support' is an elastic phrase, capable of alternative interpretations. What did it entail? Was it worth anything if it was not backed up by a threat, in the last resort, of naval or military force? Churchill was to tell Grey in August 1912 that 'everyone must feel who knows the facts that we have the obligations of an alliance without its advantages, and above all without its precise definitions'. 'No Glasgow merchant', Rosebery had declared in January 1912, 'would do what we do in foreign affairs – that is, to engage in vast and unknown liabilities and affix his signature to them without knowing their nature and extent.'[35] But Grey was to take the view

32 House of Commons Debates, 1 June 1904, vol. 135, col. 516.
33 Ibid., cols 566–7.
34 Newton, *Lansdowne*, p. 291.
35 Williamson, *Politics of Grand Strategy*, pp. 291, 250.

that the very ambiguity of the entente and later the convention with Russia were positive advantages. Uncertainty as to the precise British commitment would, Grey believed, prevent aggression by France and Russia, since they could not be sure whether Britain would support them. In 1912, for example, Grey was to warn the Russian ambassador that if she were to occupy northern Persia, which was within her sphere of influence, he would resign as it would be a breach of the 1907 convention.[36] Grey believed, therefore, that the entente was not only compatible with the Concert of Europe but would actually strengthen it; and until 1914, he sought to balance the entente with France and the convention with Russia with the needs of the Concert. It was perhaps always an uneasy balance and it proved impossible to maintain after the murder of the Austrian archduke at Sarajevo in 1914.

The French view of the entente was very different. The French foreign minister Théophile Delcassé and others hoped it would prove the first step to an alliance, strengthening the Franco-Russian Alliance against the central powers. But this was something which no British government could support for the same reason that it had been unwilling to join the Triple Alliance. The British government did not regard the entente as a departure from its policy of no Continental entanglements. If anything, it was intended to strengthen that policy. Britain believed that the entente left her hands free, except on the Moroccan question, specifically mentioned in the convention, and committed her to nothing else; while the commitment on Morocco seemed diplomatic, not military. In any other international crisis, Britain would decide, in the light of circumstances, whether or not to support France. All would depend on circumstances, on the view of the Cabinet and Parliament; and, in the last resort, on public feeling. The probability is that Britain would support France only if Parliament and the people felt that she had been the victim of aggression. Perhaps the significance of the entente was best summed up by Sir Eyre Crowe, a senior and influential Foreign Office official in a letter to Grey in February 1911:

> For purposes of ultimate emergencies, it may be found to have no substance at all, for an entente is nothing more than a frame of mind, a view of general policy which is shared by the government of two countries, but which may be or become so vague as to lose all content.[37]

So the entente, from the beginning, was interpreted differently in the two countries.

36 Steiner, *Foreign Office and Foreign Policy*, p. 132.
37 Williamson, *Politics of Grand Strategy*, p. 127.

THE FIRST MOROCCAN CRISIS

The entente was soon to be tested by Germany, which did not at first regard it as directed against her. In June 1903, one month after King Edward's visit to Paris, Count Metternich, the German ambassador in London, wrote to his Chancellor:

> I am convinced ... that the English government in the approaching recon-
> ciliation with France desires to create no opposition to Germany ... Rec-
> onciliation with an enemy does not imply quarrelling with a third party.
> I know, moreover, that the English government does not wish to break its
> connection with Berlin, but rather to hold that connection tight.[38]

But German diplomacy after 1904 was to give the entente an anti-German orientation which, in Britain at least, had not been intended.

Germany had some reason to feel aggrieved at the arrangements made for Morocco without her consent. By the terms of the Treaty of Madrid of 1880, the powers had been given 'protection', i.e. freedom from taxation, for their diplomats and their Moroccan employees, and Germany, together with other powers, had been given a guarantee of her commercial rights. Yet neither Germany, which had trading interests in Morocco, admittedly less extensive than those of France or Britain, nor any of the other powers had been consulted before Morocco was put, in effect, within the French sphere of influence. Delcassé could claim, however, that he had enquired informally of Germany before the entente as to her interests in Morocco, and had re-ceived the reply in January 1903 that 'Germany has so to speak no interests in Morocco, they are so trifling and insignificant'.[39] And much earlier, in 1880, at the time of the Madrid conference, Bismarck had assured France that Germany had no interests there. For Germany, unlike France and Spain, was not primarily a Mediterranean power. And Bülow, the German Chancellor, made no objection to the entente in his address to the Reichstag on 12 April 1904.

> We know of nothing that should lead us to think that this agreement
> is directed against any Power whatever. What it seems to indicate is an
> attempt to settle a series of disputes between France and England by means
> of an amicable understanding. From the point of view of German interest,
> we have no objection to make against it. As a matter of fact, we cannot

---

38 Lee, *King Edward VII*, p. 242.
39 Taylor, *Struggle for Mastery*, p. 405.

be desirous of a tension between France and England, which would be a danger for the peace of the world, whereas we are sincerely anxious that peace should be maintained.[40]

Nevertheless, German *amour propre* was undoubtedly affected by the entente.

Under Bismarck, Germany's aims had been limited. He had told promoters of colonies, 'Your map of Africa is very nice but there is Russia and there is France, and we are in the middle, and that is my map of Africa.'[41] There was no point in alienating Britain through colonial competition so that she aligned herself with Germany's enemies. But Bismarck's successors lacked his wisdom. They wanted Germany to become a global power. In 1897, the German foreign minister, Bülow, had declared:

> The times when the German left the earth to one of his neighbours, the sea to the other, and reserved for himself the heavens where pure philosophy reigns – these times are over ... We don't want to put anyone in the shade, but we too demand our place in the sun.[42]

To achieve that, Germany had to be secure in Europe. Some believed that could only be achieved through dominance. But a Germany dominant in Europe would mean that the continued existence of the British Empire would become dependent upon Germany. The effect of the entente with France and the convention with Russia was to ensure that such German dominance could not be achieved.

Many in Germany believed that the Franco-Russian Alliance rendered her insecure by encircling her. Between 1900 and 1906, Germany had attempted to negotiate an alliance with Russia, based on common aims in the Far East. But Russia had been no more willing than France or Britain to accept German hegemony in Europe. So there had been no alliance. In 1905, with Russia gravely weakened by the war with Japan and revolutionary ferment at home, Germany decided to test the entente by intervening in Morocco. Holstein hoped this would make it 'impossible for the French to cash their agreement with Britain, and France could be taught that an agreement with Britain without the sanction of Germany was worthless'.[43] Germany used as a pretext an ill-considered decision by France to despatch a military policy force to Morocco, supposedly to sustain the sultan but in reality to help transform the country into a French protectorate. This, like the entente

---

40 Lee, *King Edward VII*, vol. 2, p. 256.
41 Quoted in Nicholas A. M. Rodger, 'Anglo-German Naval Rivalry', p. 8.
42 Clark, *The Sleepwalkers*, pp. 150–51.
43 Williamson, *Politics of Grand Strategy*, pp. 31–2.

itself, was a breach of the Treaty of Madrid since neither Germany nor the other signatories had been consulted on the sending of the force. Delcassé had deliberately not consulted Germany because he believed that Britain would support him if it came to conflict. On 12 March in the Reichstag, the German Chancellor, Bülow, announced that German influence must be asserted in Morocco. A week later, he declared that the kaiser would champion Moroccan independence and would discuss with the sultan how it could best be preserved. Acting on the advice of his Chancellor – 'At your request, I risked my life,' he was later to tell Bülow somewhat melodramatically – the kaiser landed in Tangier on 31 March 1905.[44] He was, according to *The Times* on 1 April, welcomed by the local population, 'garlanded with flowers and beflagged' and greeted with volleys of guns. He told the German colony there that he would uphold

> the interests of the Fatherland in a free country. The Empire has great and growing interests in Morocco. Commerce can only progress if all the Powers are considered to have equal rights under the sovereignty of the Sultan and respect the independence of the country. My visit is the recognition of this independence.[45]

In fact, the German share of Moroccan trade was far below that of France and Britain and she hardly competed in the main areas of Moroccan demand – tea, textiles and sugar. And until 1905, she had taken little interest in Morocco.

The implication of the kaiser's statement was that the sultan should ignore the Anglo-French entente, and on 1 April the kaiser told Prince Louis of Battenberg, who reported it to Edward VII, 'I know nothing of any agreement between France and Morocco. For me, the Sultan is an independent sovereign.'[46] Richard von Kühlmann, the German minister in Tangier, told the kaiser that his landing 'has been a deadly blow to Delcasse ... according to my information from Paris, he has guaranteed that Germany would do nothing. No Minister can long survive a prophecy so false ... He is mortally wounded.'[47] On 6 June, Delcassé who, unlike Grey, did not have the support of his Prime Minister, resigned. He was seen in France as a victim of German bullying. Delcassé's resignation was regarded as a triumph for Germany and a setback for the entente. Lansdowne told the British ambassador in Paris:

---

44 Lee, *King Edward the Seventh*, vol. 2, p. 339fn.
45 Ibid., pp. 339–40.
46 Newton, *Lansdowne*, p. 333.
47 Quoted in *Times Literary, Supplement*, 30 September 1949.

Delcasse's resignation has, as you may well suppose, produced a very painful impression here. What people say is that if one of our Ministers had had a dead set made at him by a foreign Power, the country and the Government would not only have stood by him, but probably have supported him more vigorously than ever, whereas France has apparently thrown Delcasse overboard in a panic. Of course, the result is that the *entente* is quoted at a much lower price than it was a fortnight ago.

In a remarkable departure from convention, King Edward had telegraphed to the governor general of Algiers a message to Delcassé pressing him not to resign.[48] Delcassé's resignation was, in the view of one authority, 'the greatest German victory since Sedan [the decisive battle in the 1870 war between France and Prussia]'.[49]

In France, the entente had not achieved unanimous support, but the alternative to Delcassé's policy could only have been subordination to Germany. That seemed for a time the stance of the French Prime Minister, Maurice Rouvier, fearful of war with Germany, and then of later French leaders such as Caillaux during the First World War. Collaboration with Germany was to reach its apotheosis with the men of Vichy in the 1940s – Flandin and Laval. Had Germany proved more successful at the Algeciras conference, which was, temporarily at least, to resolve the Moroccan problem, and had France been rendered subordinate to her, or had Britain not supported France, Germany might well have been able to construct, under her leadership, the Continental league which had eluded the nations of the Continent during the Boer War. Such a league would have excluded Britain from Europe. But the entente was to hold firm since most in France refused to accept German hegemony, which would mean subordination to a military autocracy and permanent renunciation of Alsace-Lorraine. So, in the long run, the entente proved of enormous significance. It ensured that Germany would be unable to achieve the dominance of Europe by peaceful means and that her two attempts to dominate Europe by war would also fail.

Following the kaiser's visit to Tangier, Germany demanded an international conference to consider the status of Morocco. France sought to buy her off by transferring to her the right of first refusal to the Congo in exchange for a free hand in Morocco. But Germany, having committed herself to Moroccan independence, rejected this proposal. France then had to concede a conference of the European powers, together with Morocco and the United States, convened at Algeciras in January 1906, the first conference of the

---

48 Newton, *Lansdowne*, pp. 341, 342.
49 Taylor, *Struggle for Mastery*, p. 431.

powers since that at Berlin in 1884 to consider spheres of influence in Africa, and the first conference dealing with European affairs since 1884 in which the United States participated – a portent for the future. The convening of the conference was a second triumph for Germany, following the resignation of Delcassé, and a second defeat for France, which had sought to remove Morocco from the purview of the powers. Germany had succeeded, therefore, in reopening the Moroccan question.

By the time the Algeciras conference was convened, the Unionists were no longer in office and Lansdowne had been replaced at the Foreign Office by Grey. The new Foreign Secretary had made clear in a speech in October 1905 that there would be continuity in foreign policy. Indeed, the Liberals had welcomed the entente with hardly a dissenting voice, in part because France, like Britain, had a parliamentary regime and, despite the Dreyfus affair, a liberal state. Speaking in Portsmouth in November 1902, Campbell-Bannerman had declared that 'friendship with France is, to the Liberal party, something more than a cherished ideal or an historical tradition ... To Liberals it has been given to a special degree to appreciate the incalculable benefits which the great nation of France has bestowed upon mankind.'[50] He believed that the entente was 'a great instrument for bringing together ... the two nations of Europe most identified with progress and freedom'.[51] The Radical weekly *The Speaker* had written in 1904 of the entente, 'Every Englishman rejoices and particularly every Gladstonian Englishman. It is an alliance which Liberals may foster and develop into a partnership in great causes and splendid memories. Liberalism has found an inspiration in France as imperialism has found an example in Germany.'[52] The Liberals were in fact even more enthusiastic for the entente than the Unionists.

Grey, like Lansdowne, sought to reassure Germany that the entente was not directed against her, telling the German ambassador:

> On behalf of the Government, I have said that we shall not use the Anglo-French Entente against German policy or interests; that though at the Conference we must keep our public engagement to France, we shall not egg on France against Germany ... Also that we wish to improve relations between France and Germany.[53]

And the German ambassador wrote to his Chancellor that 'we are at the turning point in our relations with England', warning 'if we ... now coolly

---

50 *The Times*, 12 November 1902.
51 House of Commons Debates, 1 June 1904, vol. 135, col. 567.
52 Taylor, *Trouble Makers*, pp. 110–11.
53 Grey, *Twenty-Five Years*, vol. 1, p. 117.

reject significant and spontaneous demonstrations of conciliatory attitudes, then we must give up forever any hope of improving our relationship with England'. He asked the Chancellor to tell the kaiser that Germany should 'grasp the proffered hand'. But the opportunity was not taken.[54]

At Algeciras, Germany hoped to secure support for her demand for a German stake in Morocco, isolating France and rendering her dependent. But largely due to blundering diplomacy, it was Germany which found herself isolated. She was supported only by Austria–Hungary, and that half-heartedly, and by Morocco, but the Moroccans were to be grievously disappointed. They had hoped that the Germans would, in the light of the kaiser's speech at Tangier, be their advocates, but instead they found that the Germans were engaged in bartering Moroccan rights with other powers. 'We are not benighted savages,' the Moroccan delegation complained to *The Times* on 30 January. 'We have much to do before we can compare ourselves with you but we possess a civilization, a legal system and a religion deserving all respect. Why would they not let us speak?' But in the age of imperialism, such views could be ignored. Admittedly, the conference was to reiterate principles laid down by Germany confirming the territorial integrity of Morocco, principles to be reaffirmed in a Franco-German agreement in 1909, with equal trading rights for all. But these fine principles were to mean little in practice. In practical terms, the conference decided that there would be a new Moroccan state bank, under the control of Europeans, and policing rights in eight Moroccan ports. These would be under the control of France and Spain, but in Casablanca and Tangier, there would be a European police force commanded by a Swiss officer. This gave Germany a small stake in Morocco as part of the European force. The decisions were formalised in the Algeciras Act, signed in April 1906, which removed key elements of national sovereignty from the sultan, whom it was held, not without reason, was incapable of exercising them.

The crisis ending with the signature of the Algeciras Act has been labelled 'a decisive moment in European diplomacy', 'a turning-point in European history' and even as a first step on the road towards 1914.[55] This is at first sight a surprising verdict. The crisis was, after all, settled peacefully by the conference method, and war in 1914 arose out of European not imperial conflicts. Further, the conference did not appear to be a total defeat for Germany. She had, after all, been given a role, admittedly minor, in Casablanca and Tangier, and, more important perhaps, the conference was evidence that the powers saw the future of Morocco as a European issue, not one for France

---

54 John C. G. Röhl, *Wilhelm II: Into the Abyss of War and Exile, 1900–1941*, Cambridge University Press, 2014, pp. 408–9.
55 A. J. P. Taylor, *Englishmen and Others*, Hamish Hamilton, 1956, p. 88; Taylor, *Struggle for Mastery*, p. 441.

alone. But Germany saw the outcome differently, feeling that other powers had ganged up on her. That may be one of the reasons why, when Grey was to propose an international conference to resolve the conflict between Austria and Serbia after the murder of the archduke in 1914, Germany was unsympathetic.

Little noticed at the time, the Algeciras conference marked the appearance of the United States on the world stage. It followed President Theodore Roosevelt's mediation ending the Russo-Japanese War by the Treaty of Portsmouth, New Hampshire, in 1905. At Algeciras, Roosevelt helped to break deadlocks and, although out of sympathy with French colonialism, found himself even more out of sympathy with the bullying style of German diplomacy. 'The Washington government', according to the secretary of the French delegation, 'dislikes the brutal and realistic policy of the Berlin government and answers it by a policy equally realistic, but pacific, because peace and time are working for the United States and against Germany.'⁵⁶ Roosevelt was leaning towards the entente and preparing for the United States to alter her attitude of abstention from European affairs were the balance of power in Europe to be threatened.

But the main effect of the Moroccan crisis was on the entente. Germany had hoped to weaken it. Instead, it was strengthened and transformed from a mere friendly understanding into something stronger. For the first time, moreover, it appeared as if Britain and Germany might come into conflict. When the entente had been signed, there appeared to be no diplomatic clouds on the horizon, but the entente seemed now to have a greater significance, and some in Britain were coming to believe that it should be backed up by defence coordination between Britain and France. Already, under the Unionist government, British and French military and naval experts had joined together and discussed possible cooperation. In the French view, 'diplomatic support' had little meaning unless it could be backed up, in the last resort, by a threat of force. Britain, therefore, should be prepared to back up her support of France with more than words. At one time, it had indeed appeared that the Moroccan crisis would lead to war, the first in Europe outside the Balkans since 1871. Suppose that in such a war, it appeared that France was about to become the victim of German aggression, what would Britain do? Was she not committed to support France? The French were prepared to discuss their military dispositions with the British, but, if she was to do so, she must be given, in return, some knowledge of British dispositions. The military and naval discussions had not been authorised by Lansdowne, and

---

56 Ibid., p. 106.

he seems to have been unaware of them.[57] But on 9 January 1906, Grey was informed of them by the Secretary of the Committee of Imperial Defence. The next day, the French ambassador bluntly asked Grey whether France could rely on British armed support to resist German aggression. Grey answered that his government could not commit itself beyond diplomatic support as promised in the entente. Armed support would depend upon circumstances and public opinion. Grey told the ambassador:

> I did not think that people in England would be prepared to fight in order to put France in possession of Morocco. They would say that France should wait for opportunities and be content to take time, and that it was unreasonable to hurry matters to the point of war. But if, on the other hand, it appeared that the war was forced upon France by Germany to break up the Anglo-French 'entente', public opinion would understandably be very strong on the side of France.

Even so, it was not clear whether 'the strong feeling of the Press and of public opinion would be strong enough to overcome the great reluctance which existed among us now to find ourselves involved in war'.[58] In January 1906, Grey told the British ambassador in Paris that a 'promise in advance committing this country to take part in a Continental war is ... a very serious [matter] ... it changes the Entente into an Alliance – and Alliances, especially continental Alliances are not in accordance with our traditions'.[59] This remained the basis of British policy until 1914.

But Grey authorised continuing staff talks on the strict understanding that they implied no military or naval commitment of any kind. On that understanding, the talks were put on an official basis.[60] But during them, Sir George Clarke, Secretary of the Committee of Imperial Defence, told French officials that a German incursion into Belgium would bring automatic British assistance. There was some talk of a contingency plan involving the despatch of a British expeditionary force of 100,000 men to the Continent in case of war.[61] That was by no means the position of the Foreign Office or the Prime Minister, who had not been consulted. The French were, understandably, confused. But it was only after Algeciras that Britain, for the first time, came to believe that she might be involved in conflict with Germany;

---

57 Simon Kerry, *Lansdowne: The Last Great Whig*, Unicorn, 2017, p. 180.
58 Gooch and Temperley, eds, *British Documents*, vol. 3, p. 181, 31 January 1906.
59 Quoted in T. G. Otte, 'Problems of Continuity: The 1906 General Election and Foreign Policy', *Journal of Liberal History*, no. 84, Spring 2007, p. 12.
60 John W. Coogan and Peter F. Coogan, 'The British Cabinet and the Anglo-French Staff Talks, 1905–1914: Who Knew What and When Did He Know It?', *Journal of British Studies*, 1985, p. 111.
61 Otte, *Statesman of Europe*, p. 271.

and the Committee of Imperial Defence, without consulting the government, established a sub-committee to coordinate plans for a possible war against Germany.[62] This was 'a momentous transformation of the Entente', transforming it from a purely colonial settlement and assurance of goodwill into something a little closer to an alliance.[63]

Grey had been informed of the staff talks at the end of the 1906 election campaign. He told the two new service ministers, the War Secretary, his friend, Haldane, and the new First Lord of the Admiralty, Lord Tweedmouth, but did not inform the Cabinet, and, when he told Campbell-Bannerman, he was presenting him with a fait accompli. The Prime Minister acquiesced somewhat reluctantly, telling Lord Ripon, 'He did not like the stress laid upon joint preparations; it comes very close to an honourable undertaking and it will be known on both sides of the Rhine.'[64] The king and Asquith also seem to have been informed. One or two other ministers may have come to learn of the staff talks, which continued until May 1906. But details of the talks were not to be revealed to the Cabinet until November 1911. It appears, however, that not even Campbell-Bannerman was aware that the staff talks envisaged sending a British expeditionary force to the Continent in the event of war, something that he was eventually to learn from the French Prime Minister, Clemenceau, in April 1907.[65] But approval of the talks by Campbell-Bannerman, a Gladstonian in foreign policy, was, according to Churchill, to prove crucial in persuading the Cabinet, on being officially informed in 1911, to agree to their continuance. 'If the military conversations with France had not been authorised by Sir Henry Campbell-Bannerman, and if his political virtue could not be cited, in their justification, I doubt whether they could have been begun or continued by Mr Asquith.'[66]

In his memoirs, Grey declares that he had not informed the Cabinet since it was difficult to bring ministers together during an election campaign – a feeble excuse, and neither Grey nor Campbell-Bannerman saw fit to inform the Cabinet even after the election was over. Grey himself professed to believe that the conversations would in fact increase Britain's freedom of action.

We must be free to go to the help of France as well as free to stand aside ... If there were no military plans made beforehand we should be unable to come to the assistance of France in time ... We should in effect not have

62 McDermott, 'Revolution in British Military Thinking', p. 175.
63 Ensor, *England*, p. 400.
64 Spender, *Campbell-Bannerman*, vol. 1, p. 257.
65 Coogan and Coogan, 'The Anglo-French Staff Talks', p. 128.
66 Churchill, *World Crisis*, vol. 1, p. 21.

preserved our freedom to help France, but have cut ourselves off from the possibility of doing so.[67]

The argument for not informing the Cabinet was that the staff talks did not indicate a new departure in policy but were purely exploratory. But the Cabinet might well have repudiated the talks had it been told about them and the king was worried about their 'constitutional gravity'. Nevertheless, the French ambassador, Paul Cambon, was told that at the end of January the king, Campbell-Bannerman and Grey had agreed to conceal the talks from the Cabinet since otherwise there would be 'a Cabinet discussion and that at present this consultation would have some inconvenience for certain Ministers would be astonished at the opening of official talks between the military administrations of the two countries and of the studies which they have worked out in common'.[68]

Much was later to be made by Grey's critics of his failure to consult the Cabinet. But some of its members, whatever they said later, probably knew of the staff talks and some journalists certainly did. In any case, as Grey's biographer has pointed out, the responsibility for not informing the Cabinet lay less with Grey, the Liberal Imperialist Foreign Secretary, than with the Prime Minister. Campbell-Bannerman, after all, had been in previous Cabinets. Grey and Haldane had not.[69] But Campbell-Bannerman no doubt did not want to reignite the old disputes between Liberal Imperialists and pro-Boers. And Grey did not believe that the staff talks would prevent the entente remaining an instrument of peace. In December 1906, he told President Theodore Roosevelt, with whom he had established cordial relations, that Britain would work for peace. As a result of the Boer War, 'this generation has had enough excitement, and has lost a little blood, and is sane and normal'. But it would be dangerous if the entente were to break up and France came to terms with Germany – if so, 'Germany will again be in a position of keeping us on bad terms with France and Russia & sooner or later there will be war with us'.[70]

The staff talks, however, had a greater import than Grey or Campbell-Bannerman were prepared to admit. The premise behind them was that, in some circumstances, Britain might fight with France against Germany. Indeed, that was what Grey himself believed. For him, the entente meant that Britain could not allow France to be overcome by Germany. 'The British people', Grey told the German ambassador on 3 January 1906, less than a month

---

67 Grey, *Twenty-Five Years*, vol. 1, p. 75.
68 Williamson, *Politics of Grand Strategy*, p. 83.
69 Otte, *Statesman of Europe*, p. 277.
70 Ibid., pp. 281–2.

after the Liberals had come to office, 'would not tolerate France's being involved in a war with Germany because of the Anglo-French agreement, and in that case any English government, whether Conservative or Liberal would be forced to help France.'[71] Otherwise, as Grey wrote in a memorandum shortly after Algeciras, 'the French will never forgive us'.

> There would also ... be a general feeling in every country that we had behaved very meanly and left France in the lurch. The United States would despise us, Russia would not think it worth while to make a friendly arrangement with us about Asia. Japan would prepare to re-insure herself elsewhere, we should be left without a friend and without the power of making a friend and Germany would take some pleasure in ... exploiting the whole situation to our disadvantage.[72]

But that was very far from meaning an unconditional commitment to France. Britain would not, for example, have joined France in a war to recover the lost provinces of Alsace-Lorraine. Nor would she necessarily have become involved in a war in the Balkans in which France was involved through her alliance with Russia. In 1913, Grey was to tell the British ambassador in Paris, 'If France is aggressive to Germany there will be no support from Great Britain.'[73]

Further, the staff talks were radically altering British strategy in a manner that was to remain unknown to the politicians for some time. The navy, hitherto the key element in British strategy, would be of little use were France to be invaded – Rouvier had remarked that the navy 'could not run on wheels'.[74] France could only be assisted by the army; and the talks seemed to be proceeding on the basis that, in the event of war, Britain would send an expeditionary force to the Continent to cooperate with the French Army. Hitherto, however, the army, as we have seen, had been intended not for use on the Continent but for imperial purposes – in particular, to protect India.

So the talks were leading to a striking reorientation in foreign policy. Thus far, Britain's imperial position seemed to have taken precedence over Continental commitments. Such agreements as had been made with Continental powers had been determined primarily by imperial interests, in particular India. Now, bargains were made in relation to Britain's extra-imperial interests so as to maintain a balance of power in Europe.

---

71 Taylor, *Struggle for Mastery*, p. 437.
72 Otte, *Statesman of Europe*, pp. 273–4.
73 Ibid., p. 462.
74 Taylor, *Struggle for Mastery*, p. 437.

In Salisbury's time, Great Britain made arrangements with European Powers in order to defend her empire; now [1906] she made concessions outside of Europe in order to strengthen the balance of Power ... Though imperial interests still counted ... they had henceforth to be fitted into the framework of relations with the European powers, instead of determining them, as they had done previously.[75]

Although there seemed continuity in foreign policy, this transformation was largely symbolised by the transition from the Unionist to the Liberal government. Britain was becoming a European and Continental power almost without realising it.

In opposition, Grey had welcomed the entente on the grounds that it would tend to obliterate hard and fast lines between the power groupings in Europe. But it did not seem to be having that effect. During the Moroccan crisis, Austria–Hungary had stood by Germany, while Russia had stood by France. The freezing of alliances was to prove a contributory factor to war in 1914 by making it more difficult to contain local conflicts between the powers.

THE GERMAN QUESTION

The Moroccan crisis brought Britain face to face with the German question – the question that was to dominate Europe for much of the twentieth century. At first, the crisis had seemed to have little effect on Britain's relationship with Germany. Grey had told the British ambassador in Berlin in January 1906 to convey to the German government that, if the Algeciras conference went well, 'you may be sure of this, that the Anglo-French entente will not be used afterwards to prejudice the general interests or policy of Germany'.[76] And in the aftermath of Algeciras, and then again after the Agadir crisis in 1911, relations between the two countries seem to have improved. Nevertheless, the challenge to the entente made Europe once again the centre of world conflict. And while in February 1903, the War Office had considered conflict with Germany to be unlikely, after the 1905 crisis, Germany was being thought of as a potential enemy, very tentatively by Grey, but more definitely by army leaders. Already in 1904 in army circles, even before the Moroccan crisis, 'talk of the inevitability of an Anglo-German war was in the air'. The crisis reinforced that feeling and led to the staff talks; while in September 1905, after prodding by the Secretary of the Committee of

75 Ibid., p. 438.
76 Gooch and Temperley, eds, *British Documents*, vol. 3, no. 229.

Imperial Defence, Balfour asked the army General Staff to undertake a study of Belgian neutrality in the Franco-Prussian War of 1870. By January 1906, Sir James Grierson, Director of Military Operations at the War Office, who had been military attaché in Berlin from 1896 to 1900, had come to the view that war between France and Germany was very possible and that, in such an eventuality, he hoped and believed that Britain would immediately come to the aid of France.

The Moroccan crisis focused attention on the conflict between France and the German Empire. That empire had been proclaimed following victory in war against France in 1870, by the new German Emperor William I, the victorious king of Prussia, at Versailles. France had been compelled to surrender to this new empire the provinces of Alsace-Lorraine, a surrender to which she was never fully reconciled. Many in Britain, focusing primarily on the empire and not perceiving Britain as primarily a European power, had not fully appreciated that Germany was now dominant on the Continent, and that a threat to the balance of power on the Continent was more likely to come from her than from France or Russia.

In 1748, the Scottish philosopher David Hume had said, 'Germany is undoubtedly a fine country, full of industrious honest people; and were it united, it would be the greatest power that ever was in the world.'[77] The first British statesman to appreciate the significance for Britain of German unification and her victory against France in 1870 had been Benjamin Disraeli, perhaps the most far-sighted politician of the age. In February 1871, in the debate on the address, he declared:

> This war represents the German revolution, a greater political event than the French revolution of last century ... Not a single principle in the management of our foreign affairs, accepted by all statesmen for guidance up to six months ago, any longer exists ... We used to have discussions in this House about the balance of power. Lord Palmerston, eminently a practical man, trimmed the ship of State and shaped its policy with a view to preserve an equilibrium in Europe ... But what has really come to pass? The balance of power has been entirely destroyed, and the country which suffers most, and feels the effects of this great change most, is England.[78]

Germany was primarily a European power. Unified later than France or Russia, she had few colonies, and therefore had not been in competition with the British Empire as were France and Russia. Germany was to prove

---

77 J. Y. T. Greig, *The Letters of David Hume*, Oxford University Press, 1932, vol. I, p. 125.
78 House of Commons Debates, 9 February 1871, vol. 204, cols 81–2.

a threat to Britain not in Africa or the Far East but in Europe. The French response to the rise of Germany was alliance with Russia in 1894, ensuring that, by contrast with 1870, Germany in any future war would be forced to fight on two fronts as indeed she had to do in 1914. The 1894 alliance seemed to Germany's leaders to create a problem on both her western and her eastern frontier. To her west, was France seeking to recover Alsace-Lorraine. To her east, lay the long frontier with Russia. She came to think that her only chance of victory in a war on two fronts was to knock out France rapidly before the massive resources of Russia could be brought to bear – hence her plan of a rapid strike through Belgium, encircling Paris, a military plan which, it was hoped, could defeat France within six weeks.

The unification of Germany had probably been inevitable. But the form which that unification took was not. Germany had been unified by her great conservative statesman Bismarck. But Bismarck had been a master of restraint, acting in the spirit of Goethe's aphorism that genius lies in limitation. He had helped to give Europe a generation of peace, a peace which was coming to be taken for granted. It is often said that if Bismarck had been Chancellor in 1914, there would not have been a world war. For he had preserved peace and security through a system of alliances to contain France so as to prevent a war of revenge. But his successors were unable to preserve the structure of security he had created. And perhaps an international system depending for its success upon a man of genius is not, in the last resort, very stable. Bismarck's methods were later to be adopted by those lacking his genius or indeed his sense of restraint and led to destruction of the empire which he had so laboriously created.

By the beginning of the twentieth century, it appeared that Germany was no longer content to remain, in Admiral Tirpitz's words, 'a European continental power of second rank'.[79] The search for global power meant colonies and a large navy. Germany complained that, as a late arrival, she had been deprived of her rightful share of colonies and indeed possessed only a small number – in West, South West and East Africa and New Guinea and various Pacific islands as well as a 'lease' in China. Few Germans had been persuaded to settle in these colonies. Nevertheless, it seemed that the rest of the world had been barred and bolted against her.

Germany's attempt to become a global power also involved naval construction through a series of naval laws beginning in 1898, which put her in competition with Britain. Germany already had the largest army in the world. She was now, it seemed, seeking a large navy as well. The German

---

79 John C. G. Röhl, 'Goodbye to all that (again)? The Fischer thesis, the new revisionism and the meaning of the First World War', *International Affairs*, 2013, p. 165.

attempt to become an imperial and global power seemed to pose a problem which had not arisen with other powers such as Britain, France or Russia. For it appeared that Germany could not become a global power without also becoming hegemonic in Europe, dominant even beyond the gains which the 1870 war with France had given her. This was bound to bring her into conflict with other European powers, and eventually with the United States.

It was understandable if Germany's naval programme stirred up British fears. In September 1902, Arnold-Forster, a junior Admiralty minister, had visited Kiel and Wilhelmshaven and declared in a Cabinet memo that 'Germany must be regarded as a possible enemy'. A Cabinet memo by the First Lord, Selborne, one month later, found him 'convinced that the great new German navy is being carefully built up from the point of view of a war with us'.[80] He was right. Of the 1900 Naval Law, the German socialist leader August Bebel wrote to the British consul general in Switzerland that, 'as a regular member of the Budget Commission [of the Reichstag,] I can assert that' it 'was directed against England alone'.[81] During the final months of the Unionist government in 1905, Lord Cawdor, the First Lord, had sanctioned the construction of dreadnoughts, a new type of battleship which made all others obsolescent. In October 1906, Grey confessed to a Unionist MP that this might have been a mistake. Britain had, he thought, forced the pace 'unnecessarily in my opinion, by building the Dreadnought and introducing a new type, which increased the size'. But he believed, nevertheless, that it was 'Germany who is forcing the pace ... We do not want to force the pace now and if Germany will meet us in any way we will respond generously.'[82] The British Navy could not be used to invade Germany or any major Continental power. But the German Navy could be used in an invasion of Britain or to block British trading routes. So there was 'no comparison', as Grey told the Commons on 29 March 1909, 'between the importance of the German navy to Germany, and the importance of our Navy to us. Our Navy is to us what their Army is to them.'[83] It seemed, however, that Britain's need for naval preponderance was in irredeemable conflict with the German wish that no limits be placed on her naval building programme. Germany sought to use her growing naval power as a bargaining counter with Britain. She would reduce her programme only if Britain agreed to remain neutral in any war in which Germany was not the aggressor. No British government could give such a commitment, not least because, in most armed conflicts, each side would accuse the other of being the aggressor. Britain responded to

---

80 Williamson, *Politics of Grand Strategy*, p. 17.
81 R. J. Crampton, 'August Bebel and the British Foreign Office', *History*, 1973, p. 219.
82 Grey to Arthur Lee, 24 October 1906, Lee Papers, Courtauld Institute.
83 House of Commons Debates, 29 March 1909, vol. 3, col. 60.

the German proposal by pointing out that she could go to war only with the support of the Cabinet, Parliament and the people, and there would never be support for a war of aggression against Germany. Understandably perhaps, the German government was not content with this assurance, even if it fully understood the niceties of Britain's constitutional and parliamentary system and the role of public opinion, all of which were somewhat different from that prevalent in Germany.

By 1914, the naval race, however, had ended in Britain's favour. On the eve of war, Britain had twenty-four dreadnoughts, nine battlecruisers and forty pre-dreadnought battleships. Germany, the next strongest naval power, had sixteen modern battleships, six battlecruisers and thirty pre-dreadnoughts.[84] Germany had decided that it was too expensive for her to both compete with Britain's navy and retain a large army. In September 1911, Admiral von Müller, Chief of the kaiser's Naval Cabinet, told Chancellor Bethmann Hollweg that 'it lay in the Navy's interest' to postpone war, since this would mean war with Britain, 'which was probably unavoidable in the long run, until the [Kiel] Canal is finished'.[85] The widening of the Kiel Canal to which Admiral von Müller was referring was to be completed in the summer of 1914, six weeks before the outbreak of war.

THE CONVENTION WITH RUSSIA

In December 1906, Grey had told President Theodore Roosevelt that, to complete the foundation for peace in Europe which he believed had been laid by the entente:

> we want to get an arrangement with Russia, which will remove old traditions of enmity & ensure that if we are not friends at any rate we do not quarrel. If all this can be done we shall take care that it is not used to provoke Germany or score off her, if she will only accept it & not try to make mischief.[86]

Grey had in fact argued for an agreement with Russia since January 1902 if not before.[87] Shortly after taking office in December 1905, he told a senior diplomat that he continued to hope that Russia would be 're-established in the councils of Europe, and I hope on better terms with us than she has been

84 Keith Neilson, '"Greatly Exaggerated": The Myth of the Decline of Britain Before 1914', *International History Review*, 1991, p. 705.
85 Röhl, 'Admiral von Müller', p. 655.
86 Otte, *Statesman of Europe*, p. 281.
87 House of Commons Debates, 22 January 1902, vol. 101, cols 608ff.

yet'.[88] Grey had been the one Liberal Imperialist who had doubts about the Anglo-Japanese Alliance and had told the Commons in July 1903:

> Our interests in Asia ... touch more closely and more often with Russia than with any other country ... It should be our object ... to lose no opportunity of using every possible effort to come to a clear understanding with Russians to what the boundaries of our interests are.[89]

One motive behind the entente had been to give Britain leverage over Russia, so as to constrain her in central Asia. Delcassé, the French foreign minister, had told Lansdowne in July 1903 that, were an entente to be agreed, 'he will exercise a restraining influence upon Russia, if not in fact intimate to Russia that, under certain conditions, she could not rely upon French support if she picked a quarrel with us'.[90] Both Salisbury and Lansdowne had sought an arrangement with Russia but had not been able to achieve it. What altered was Russian not British attitudes following the Russo-Japanese War. After her defeat by an Asian power, Russia was ceasing to be a threat to Britain in China. She also became less of a threat to India and turned back to Europe. In her weakened position, she was more willing to seek accommodation with Britain. But the difficulty now came primarily from the British side. For Russia, unlike France, was an autocracy. In the words of the British ambassador to St Petersburg, its government was 'an anachronism existing now only in semi-barbarous states'. In 1906, the year before the convention, the tsar had dissolved the fledgling Parliament, the Duma, on which British liberals had pinned their hopes; and Russian antisemitism, officially encouraged and even inspired, alienated many in Britain. 'It was easy', one diplomat believed, 'for two civilized and liberal nations like France and England to come to terms and act together: but common action between an English Liberal and a Russian bureaucracy is a pretty difficult thing to manage. A wild ass and a commissary mule make a rum team to drive.'[91]

All the same, from a diplomatic perspective, the convention with Russia, to be concluded in August 1907, was a natural development from the entente. The convention, like the entente, took the form of a settlement of territorial conflicts – in Afghanistan, Tibet and, above all, Persia. In the buffer state of Afghanistan, the emir had long accepted that his foreign relations would be conducted through Britain in return for a subsidy and a British guarantee

---

88 T. G. Otte, '"Postponing the Evil Day": Sir Edward Grey and British Foreign Policy', *International History Review*, 2016, p. 254.
89 House of Commons Debates, 23 July 1903, vol. 126, col. 129.
90 Monger, *End of Isolation*, p. 129.
91 Neilson, *Britain and the Last Tsar*, pp. 81, 108–9.

to defend her against external threat. Russia, which from 1903 bordered Afghanistan, now agreed to respect British political predominance there, and guaranteed, as Britain had done, not to seek to annex or occupy her nor to seek to alter her political status. Russia also agreed to conduct all political relations with Afghanistan through the British government. The emir had not been consulted on the convention. His consent was assumed. In Tibet, under Chinese rule, Britain sought to minimise her commitments while ensuring that Russia did the same, and agreed that she would not seek to annex, establish a protectorate or control Tibet's internal administration or send a permanent mission there, so long as Russia agreed to exercise similar restraint. But Russia agreed that Britain could retain her predominant commercial interests there. Persia, the most contentious problem, was divided into three spheres of commercial influence on a negative basis – Britain was to keep out of the north, which included the capital, Tehran, while Russia was to keep out of the south, which included the mouth of the strategically important Persian Gulf, vital to the defence of India. The central area would remain neutral. The political integrity and independence of Persia would, it was agreed, be maintained. The convention, like the entente, was not intended as a challenge to Germany but a settlement of past disputes. Britain, Grey told the ambassador in St Petersburg in May 1906, would not 'use our friendship with Russia as a lever to create difficulties with Germany, either for Russia or for ourselves'.[92] For his part, the Russian foreign minister 'had taken care to seek German approval before he made the agreement'.[93] But, though modest in form, the convention, like the entente, marked a revolution in British foreign policy, a shift from a relationship of suspicion to one based on detente, though not perhaps entente. The convention meant that Britain no longer had to fear Russia in central Asia or China, nor, hopefully, on the north-west frontier of India. And the convention also made it more likely that the two countries would cooperate diplomatically. Whatever the intentions of those concluding the convention, that cooperation would be most likely to operate against Germany, the strongest military power in Europe and coming to be seen as a threat to the balance of power on the Continent. Russia hoped, like France, to convert the understanding into an alliance. The Russian foreign minister wrote to his ambassador in London in February 1914 that 'the peace of the world will be secure only when the Triple Entente ... is transformed into a defensive alliance without secret clauses. Then the danger of a German hegemony will be finally ended.'[94] But Grey

92 Nellson, *Britain and the Last Tsar*, p. 277.
93 Taylor, *Struggle for Mastery*, p. 445.
94 Ibid., p. 511.

was even less likely to countenance an alliance with Russia than with France. All the same, Germany would now potentially be challenged both by France and Russia; and Britain would be more likely to align herself with them than with Germany.

The hope behind the convention was, as with the entente, to build friendlier relations by settling extra-European disputes, but in Russia's case, that hope hardly materialised. For Russia did not keep strictly to the terms of the convention but continued with her policy of infiltration into Persia and the buffer states. In addition, the convention, like her defeat by Japan, turned Russia further towards Europe and the championing of fellow Slavs there. This, in turn, caused conflict with Austria–Hungary, a conflict which was to lead to war in 1914.

The convention with Russia never fostered the same warm feelings amongst Parliament and the British people as the entente. The Liberal government defended it on the ground that it would relieve pressure on India and would therefore obviate the need for large military expenditures to combat the threat posed by the extension of the Russian railway system into central Asia. But radicals resented what they regarded as the sacrifice of Persian independence, to say nothing of association with what they regarded as an odious regime. The convention increased left-wing disenchantment with Grey and seems not to have been particularly popular with the public. The entente became a matter of the heart, the convention a matter of the head. It was more tenuous, it never became cordiale and, indeed, in the summer of 1914 it came near to breakdown. In Britain indeed, feelings towards Germany were almost certainly warmer than feelings towards Russia.

The Russian foreign minister had used the term 'triple entente'. Grey disliked the term, and early in 1910 discouraged his officials from using it, since 'if it appeared in a Parliamentary Bluebook it would be assumed to have some official meaning and might provoke inconvenient comment or inquiry'.[95] In January 1914, Lewis Harcourt, the Colonial Secretary, wrote to Grey:

> I object to 'Triple Entente' because no such thing has ever been considered or approved by the Cabinet. In fact the thing does not exist. We had an 'Entente' with France over Morocco, with some obligations which are now happily resolved. This 'Entente' left behind it greatly improved relations between the two countries, but no mutual obligations of any kind whatever. At a later date we came to an 'understanding' with Russia over Persia – and *over* nothing else. It is true that there is an alliance between France

---

95 Harold Nicolson, *Sir Arthur Nicolson Bart, First Lord Carnock: A Study in the Old Diplomacy*, Constable, 1930, p. 308.

and Russia (in which we are not concerned) and that when we are acting with one of these Powers we are likely to find ourselves in agreement with the other. But none of these facts entail any community of action between the three in European diplomacy.

Grey replied:

The best course … is to let things go on without any new declaration of policy. The alternatives are either a policy of complete isolation in Europe, or a policy of definite alliance with one or the other group of European powers. My own desire has been to avoid bringing the choice between these two alternatives to an issue; and I think we have been fortunate in being able to go on as long as we are.[96]

The entente and the convention had, therefore, enabled Britain to escape from isolation without committing herself to alliances. That was a remarkable achievement, executed with some agility by both Unionists and Liberals.

THE ANNEXATION OF BOSNIA-HERZEGOVINA

The entente and the convention were to be tested in the Balkans.[97] There, the cause of conflict lay not in rival imperialisms but in rival nationalisms, and, in particular, the growth of Slav nationalism. The Slavs were seeking what Germany, Italy and Hungary had recently achieved: the realisation of their national aspirations. In their way stood Turkey – the Ottoman Empire – but also the supranational Austro-Hungarian Empire. It has become perhaps fashionable to feel some nostalgia for that empire. Its defenders claim that it secured a roof over the nationalities and so helped to contain national conflicts, as the European Union seeks to do. The late Marxist historian Eric Hobsbawm once asked me whether any of the nationalities in central or Eastern Europe had actually benefited from the collapse of that empire. But perhaps this nostalgia is a little misplaced. The empire, being supranational and dynastic, would have found it difficult to survive the transition to popular government without disintegration. It was dominated by two 'master races' – the Germans and Hungarians. Since 1867, it had been a dual empire with two separate governments united in the person of the Habsburg ruler Franz Joseph, emperor of Austria and king of Hungary, and by common foreign, defence and financial policies. Many Slavs lived within the empire

---

96 Hazlehurst, *Politicians at War*, pp. 112–13; Hazlehurst and Woodland, *A Liberal Chronicle*, p. 197.
97 See p. xviii for a map of the Balkans in 1912–13.

– in what is now the Czech Republic, Slovakia, part of what is now Poland, part of what is now Ukraine and part of what was to become Yugoslavia. But there were also many Slavs living in territories bordering on the empire to the south-east – in particular, in the independent Slav state of Serbia and her small ally Montenegro, both of which had gained international recognition in the 1878 Treaty of Berlin. In Austria, Czechs and Serbs felt themselves to be subordinate. In Hungary, the Slavs were certainly subordinate, subject to a policy of Magyarisation which emphasised their inferior status. Some in Austria sought to convert the empire into a trialist one, to include the Slavs; and a number of such schemes were drawn up before 1914. It has been argued – wrongly in my view – that the heir to the throne, the Archduke Franz Ferdinand, killed at Sarajevo, was of their number. But what Franz Ferdinand sought was in fact a more centralised state with stronger executive authority, privileging German-speakers, so as to insulate the empire from challenge. It is hardly likely that a dynastic state in which loyalty was to the emperor personally could have been transformed into a federal or qua-si-federal state in which the various nationalities all had equal rights. In any case, the Hungarians would not have accepted equality with the Slavs. The empire, therefore, remained dualist and, as such, stood in the way of Slav and Serb aspirations. Many Serbs sought a union of South Slavs, an aspiration which came to fruition in 1918 with the creation of Yugoslavia – which means land of the South Slavs. But in the early twentieth century, nearly four-fifths of South Slavs lived in the Austro-Hungarian Empire under foreign rule – in Bosnia–Herzegovina, Croatia and Slovenia. Bosnia itself contained a mixed population – between 43 per cent and 49 per cent were Orthodox Serbs, 33 per cent were Muslims, while 23 per cent were Catholics, mainly Croats. Bosnian Muslim leaders called their people 'Serbs of Muslim faith', while Serbs regarded Bosnians as fellow Slavs, living under foreign rule.[98] They had indeed fought the Ottoman Empire in 1876 in an unsuccessful attempt to liberate Bosnia. Any union of the South Slavs was of course incompatible with the continuation of Austrian or Hungarian rule.

Under Article 25 of the Treaty of Berlin in 1878, the Slav provinces of Bosnia–Herzegovina, which were part of the Ottoman Empire, were to be occupied and administered by Austria–Hungary but with the ultimate sov-ereignty of the sultan remaining unimpaired. It was widely expected at the time that the occupation would be permanent, and indeed Lord Salisbury as Foreign Secretary in 1878 had urged Austria to annex it, but Turkey had re-fused to sign the treaty until Austria–Hungary accepted that the annexation

---

98 John Zametica, *Folly and Malice: The Habsburg Empire, the Balkans and the Start of World War One*, Shepheard-Walwyn, 2017, pp. 235–6.

'shall be considered provisional'.[99] In 1881, as part of the condition for joining the League of the Three Emperors with Germany and Russia, Austria reserved 'the right to annex the provinces at whatever moment she shall deem appropriate'; and Russia had raised no objection, though from the late 1890s, she did begin to object. Nevertheless, for practical purposes, the two provinces had become part of the Habsburg Empire, although both Serbs and Bosnians hoped the occupation would prove temporary. It was, of course, a weakness in the 1878 settlement that it had disregarded the wishes of the people of Bosnia–Herzegovina, transferring them in effect from one polity to another without bothering to consult them.

Some historians have praised Austro-Hungarian rule in Bosnia, speaking of the great benefits that it brought Slavs – rather in the spirit of those who praised British rule in Ireland. As in Ireland, there was a model form of government if one excluded the fact that the majority did not consent to it; and there is some danger of nostalgia blinding one to the facts. In 1908, there were just twelve high schools in the whole of Bosnia, compared to six in the capital of Serbia, Belgrade, alone. Moreover, 90 per cent of Bosnians were illiterate and just 30 per cent proceeded to higher education. Part of the reason for this was that Bosnians were not allowed to attend universities in Austria–Hungary where instruction was given in the Slavic languages.[100] Shortly before the annexation in 1908, emigrants from Bosnia–Herzegovina, claiming to represent its people, addressed a petition to The Hague, declaring, with some exaggeration, that 'the Austrian domination is a thousand times more insupportable than that of the Turks'. They claimed that Austrian authorities discriminated in favour of Catholics and against Muslims and the Orthodox, who were the great majority.[101] When war came in 1914, 'whole towns' in Bosnia were displaying 'their sympathy for the enemy', i.e. Serbia, and there was to be a rebellion in those areas of Bosnia adjoining Serbia.[102]

In October 1908, there was a dress rehearsal for the Sarajevo crisis when Austria–Hungary converted her occupation of Bosnia–Herzegovina into annexation. In September 1908, this had been discussed between the Habsburg and Russian foreign ministers, Counts Aehrenthal and Izvolsky, at a meeting at the castle of Buchlau (now Buchlovice) in Moravia. Since no records were kept, it is unclear precisely what was agreed. But it appears that Izvolsky agreed to support conversion of occupation into annexation, in return for

99 Bernadotte E. Schmitt, *The Annexation of Bosnia, 1909–1909*, Cambridge University Press, 1937. This book provides what still remains an authoritative account of the Bosnian crisis.
100 Z. A. B. Zeman, 'The Balkans and the Coming of War', in R. J. W. Evans and H. Pogge von Strandmann, eds, *The Coming of the First World War*, Clarendon Press, 1988, p. 24fn.
101 'The Question of Bosnia and Herzegovina', *The Times*, 7 October 1908.
102 Solomon Wank, 'The Nationalities Question in the Habsburg Monarchy: Reflections on the Historical Record', Working Paper 93–3, Center for Austrian Studies, University of Minnesota, 1997, p. 5.

Austria accepting an end to the prohibition on Russian ships entering the Dardanelles. What is unclear is how and when this agreement was to be put into effect. The Russians claimed that the Buchlau meeting was just a preliminary exchange of views and that alterations to the Treaty of Berlin had to be acceptable to the powers that had negotiated it, since annexation was a European issue. Were the problem to be put to the powers, annexation could not of course be carried out immediately. The Austrians, however, claimed that the annexation was a purely local issue, that Russia had conceded this in the past and had renewed her consent at Buchlau. The Austrians, therefore, unilaterally annexed the provinces in October, a month after the meeting. In an attempt to show that she did not seek territorial expansion, Austria evacuated her troops from the Ottoman Sanjak of Novi Pazar, which in 1913 was to come under Serbian rule. The Austrians promised constitutional government in Bosnia, but the Bosnian legislature was to be elected, not directly, but by various curiae – that is, interest groups – a system which Austria had recently rejected for herself as antiquated and unworkable. The annexation was justified by a clumsy forgery designed to show that the leaders of Slav parties in Austria–Hungary were in the pay of Serbia and conspiring to annex parts of the empire to Serbia. Thirty-one Slavs were arrested, convicted of treason and sentenced to terms of imprisonment totalling 184 years. They were released on appeal after the forgery was discovered. The forgery had been manufactured in the Austro-Hungarian Foreign Office, and the official responsible was in 1913 to become an adviser to the Austrian foreign minister, Count Berchtold, and a vocal advocate of preventive war against Serbia. Russia was unable to benefit from her side of the bargain at Buchlau since, by contrast with the annexation, she could not unilaterally occupy the Dardanelles without the agreement of the powers, and they refused to give their consent.

Although the annexation of Bosnia involved no territorial change, it gave rise to an international crisis lasting six months which nearly led to war. The annexation has been described as a 'nominal change from occupation to outright annexation',[103] since the powers had long recognised that Bosnia–Herzegovina was no longer in effect part of Turkey, and had accepted that Austrian law and coinage rather than Turkish applied there. So the annexation seemed to do no more than transform a de facto situation into a de jure one. But it was nevertheless a clear breach of a treaty, done by force rather than agreement. *The Times* on 7 October 1908 called it a 'naked violation of law and right'. Georges Clemenceau, shortly to become Prime Minister of France, declared it 'a gross breach of a treaty engagement and an offence to

103 Clark, *The Sleepwalkers*, p. 36.

public morality which if allowed to pass would form a very bad precedent'.[104]
There was perhaps an element of hypocrisy in this criticism. For the French
themselves had, as we have seen, breached a treaty in Morocco in 1905 and
were to do so again in 1911. But those treaty breaches did not entrench upon
the national rights of a European power. Annexation of Bosnia–Herzegovina,
by contrast, was a blow to the Slavs and to Serbia, since it made non-Slav
rule in Bosnia seem permanent. For the Habsburg Empire appeared to have
much more staying power than the Ottoman. Indeed, part of the purpose
of annexation was to end pressure for irredentism from Serbia and ensure
Teutonic supremacy over the Slavs. A permanent obstacle now seemed to
have been erected against Slav unity. It would, in Aehrenthal's view, 'strike at
the root of the evil and put an end to the Great Serbian dreams of the future'.
In fact, Aehrenthal had gone even further. In December 1907, he had told
his Chief of General Staff that he was considering not only the annexation of
Bosnia but also the 'incorporation of the non-Bulgarian parts of Serbia' with
the rest going to Bulgaria. For him and for others in Habsburg ruling circles,
annexation was to be a first step towards, in his words to the Secretary of the
German Foreign Ministry, 'the complete elimination of the Serbian revolutionary nest'. Having secured self-determination for themselves, Germans
and Hungarians were unwilling to extend it to Slavs.[105]

The annexation converted the South Slav issue into an international
problem. Serbia's foreign minister declared that it had made 'slaves out of
the people of the two Serbian lands'.[106] It was a blow also to Russia. Many
Russians saw themselves as protectors of the Slavs. Indeed, it was because he
saw Russia in this light that the Russian Prime Minister, Peter Stolypin, had
disagreed with Izvolsky's policy at Buchlau, even though Izvolsky had the
support of the tsar. Stolypin argued that Russia should never give her consent
to the annexation of Slav lands by a Germanic power. But the Russian government could hardly protest since her foreign minister was deemed to have
agreed to the annexation at Buchlau. Whenever Russia appeared to be about
to protest, Aehrenthal threatened to publish details of the Buchlau meeting
and memoranda exchanged after it. Russia was in any case, owing to her military weakness after the war with Japan, unable to offer any practical military
help to her fellow Slavs, though if Austria had in fact attacked Serbia, public
outrage might well have forced a Russian military response.

Britain resented the breach of the treaty, and the way it had been done.
Edward VII was particularly incensed since he had recently visited the

104 Schmitt, *Annexation of Bosnia*, p. 36.
105 Ibid., p. 5.
106 Ibid., p. 145.

Habsburg emperor, Franz Joseph, at his summer residence in Bad Ischl, and had not been told of the imminent annexation. But on the Continent, Britain's attitude appeared hypocritical since, as we have seen, Salisbury had advocated it in 1878. In any case, Britain was both unable and unwilling to enforce the Treaty of Berlin with military action.[107] Britain and France accepted, as Russia had to do, that the annexation could not be reversed. Grey stressed to the British ambassador at St Petersburg that Britain would not support Russia militarily. 'If war were to take place, it would probably in the end embroil the greater part of the Continent, and even Russia must see that such a risk for the sake of Serbia's demands for territorial compensation is utterly disproportionate to the end in view.'[108] Grey sought to work with the powers – France, Germany and Russia – to ensure a peaceful settlement by conference, to regularise the annexation and perhaps provide some form of compensation to Serbia, though, since Serbia had not been a signatory of the Treaty of Berlin, she had no right in law to compensation. But the entente allies failed to secure a conference. Austria–Hungary refused, unless it were agreed beforehand that the annexation was a fait accompli and not open for discussion. Germany, though she had not been consulted before the annexation, agreed, and declared that if the crisis led to war, she would unhesitatingly support Austria–Hungary with, in the words of Chancellor Bülow in the Reichstag, '*Nibelungen* loyalty'. Britain, the kaiser believed, was trying to secure 'a second Algeciras', a conference designed to isolate and humiliate the central powers.

Three days after annexation, the Serbian Parliament voted by ninety-three votes to sixty-six against taking military action. Instead, Serbia sought territorial compensation and autonomy for Bosnia. But it rapidly became clear that Serbia could not achieve anything more than an economic agreement with Austria. Indeed, Aehrenthal was determined to press home his advantage, insisting that both Russia and Serbia accept annexation and that Serbia disarm, control and disband her irregular military units and accept normal relations with Austria. He told the Serbs that if they did not accept these conditions, there would be an ultimatum. He seemed indeed at one point to be hoping that Serbia would not in fact accept his stringent conditions. On 2 April, the German ambassador in Vienna told Chancellor Bülow that it was 'no secret' that 'originally and also recently' Aehrenthal had regarded war as 'unavoidable and, for internal as well as external reasons, desirable', though Franz Joseph preferred a peaceful solution.[109] Britain helped to per-

107 R. W. Seton-Watson, *The Southern Slav Question and the Habsburg Monarchy*, Constable, 1921, pp. 176–7.
108 Grey, *Twenty-Five Years*, vol. 1, p. 181.
109 Cited in Schmitt, *Annexation of Bosnia*, p. 255.

ouade Russia and Serbia to accept Austria's conditions so that the Bosnian crisis could be resolved peacefully. Accordingly, Serbia promised to disarm and dismiss irregular bands agitating from her territory against Austria, to prevent their formation on her territory and to resume friendly relations with Austria. These promises were made to the powers as a whole, not to Austria. The crisis, therefore, was resolved on the terms laid down by the central powers and seemed a defeat for the entente powers. The tsar, according to the correspondent of *The Times* in Vienna, 'had said that he would never forget or forgive that humiliation in 1908'.[110]

The Bosnian crisis was the first in which the two alliance groups were arrayed against each other. It seemed to end in triumph not only for Austria–Hungary but for Germany. But the Chief of the German General Staff, Helmuth von Moltke, regarded the peaceful settlement as a lost opportunity. He complained to his Austrian counterpart that 'an opportunity has passed unused [to make Serbia a subordinate power] that should not present itself again soon under such favourable conditions'.[111] A more sober view would have asked whether it was prudent to humiliate Russia, pushing her further into alliance with France. Had she instead been relieved of anxiety in the Balkans, she might then have reverted to a Far Eastern policy which would have involved her in conflict with Britain and relieved Germany of worries on her eastern frontier.

The crisis had deeply worried Asquith, as he told Balfour in November 1908, who reported the Prime Minister's comments in a letter to Lansdowne:

> He was ... extremely perturbed about the European situation, which, in his view, was the gravest of which we have had any experience since 1870. He said that, incredible as it might seem, the Government could form no theory of the German policy which fitted all the known facts, except that they wanted war, and war at the present time clearly means much more than it did in 1870, as it would certainly involve Russia, Austria and the Near East – to say nothing of ourselves ... The almost incredible frivolity of the excuse for hostilities which the Germans had devised would shock the civilised world beyond expression ... I [Balfour] said that, quite apart from the entente, we should, as I understood it, be involved under treaty obligations if Germany violated Belgian territory. Asquith assented, and said that (as we all know) the Franco-German frontier is now so strong that the temptation to invade Belgium might prove irresistible.

110 Steed, *Through Thirty Years*, p. 362.
111 Annika Mombauer, 'A Reluctant Military Leader? Helmuth von Moltke and the Crisis of July 1914', *War in History*, 1999, p. 419.

Asquith had given Balfour 'no information and I believe had no information which is not in the newspapers', but Balfour 'was very much struck by
the pessimistic tone in which he spoke of the position'. Balfour assured the
Prime Minister that 'he might count upon the Opposition in case of national
difficulty'.[112] All this was a clear pointer to British policy in 1914.

Austria had seemingly gained what she wanted. But the annexation of
Bosnia had the paradoxical effect of increasing her sense of insecurity. For it
was not accepted by the local population, many of whom looked to neighbouring Serbia as their home. So the annexation made Serbia appear even
more of a threat to Austria and a rival for the affections of her Slav population, though discontent in Bosnia was as much a result of Austrian policy as
it was of anything that Serbia did.

Russia, having been humiliated, reorganised her army, sped up her re-
armament and encouraged the Slav states of the Balkans to join together
in a Balkan league. In July 1909, a Pan-Slav Congress, whose conclusions
embodied 'at least to some extent the official policy of the Russian government', pressed Russia to 'take up energetically her mission as protectress of
the Slav world', called for the Slav states to expand their territory, supported
the exclusion of German industry and commerce and predicted that 'in two
or three years at the most the time will come when the Slav world under the
leadership of Russia, must strike the great blow'. So, far from resolving the
problem of the southern Slavs, the Bosnian crisis had exacerbated it.

The Bosnian crisis prefigured that of 1914. In 1914, as in 1908, it seemed
that Europe east of the Rhine was divided into two camps – Teutons and
Slavs. The annexation of Bosnia had pitted Slav nationalism, seeking to unite
the South Slavs either in a Greater Serbia or a Yugoslavia, against the Austro-Hungarian Empire. That clash was to lead in 1914 to world war. There
were great similarities between the crises. Bülow was to boast in 1913 that,
in the Balkans, 'the German sword had been thrown into the scale of European decision'. But, in consequence of the German triumph, 'other swords
were sharpened'.[113] In the Bosnian crisis, Germany showed that she was no
longer disinterested in the Balkans, which, Bismarck had told the Reichstag
in 1876, were 'not worth the healthy bones of a single Pomeranian grena-
dier'. Germany was dragged into Balkan affairs by the need to shore up her
Austrian ally, to prevent Austria from becoming a power of no consequence
on the European stage. From the beginning of the crisis, Germany allowed
Austria–Hungary to dictate its progress. The decision as to peace or war was

---

112 Newton, *Lansdowne*, pp. 371–2.
113 Schmitt, *Annexation of Bosnia*, pp. 216fn, 36, 11, 5, 15, 145, 223, 57, 210fn, 222, 245, 196, 248–9, 252; Seton-Watson,
   Southern Slav Question, pp. 194–5.

to be left to the Habsburgs – just as in 1914, Germany was to give her ally a 'blank cheque'. And Germany's campaign plan was not dissimilar to that adopted in 1914. Were Austria to be involved in war with Serbia, and were Russia to support a fellow Slav state, this would be a *casus belli* for Germany. In case of war, Germany would launch her principal attack not on Russia but on France, even though she had no cause for quarrel with her. It is often said that the war of 1914 broke out by accident, but the crisis of 1908–09 showed that the Balkans were a powder keg and that little would be needed to set it alight. To avoid war, considerable diplomatic skills would be required, skills displayed by Grey but by hardly any other foreign minister. Indeed, 'that the continent did not descend into war' before July 1914 'was largely due to Grey's shrewd and subtle crisis diplomacy'.[114]

After the Sarajevo assassination in June 1914, the same scenario was to be played out as had seemed possible in 1908–09. There was to be just one great difference. In 1908, Russia had backed down, in part because of British pressure. In 1914, she did not back down. This meant not only that there would be war but that the war would not be localised. It became a European and then a world war. Aehrenthal, Grey believed, had been far too insouciant concerning the effects of the annexation. 'A breach of the peace', the Foreign Secretary told his ambassador in Vienna in December 1908, 'will provoke a conflagration greater than anyone can foresee: he [Aehrenthal] is living in a fool's paradise. It is dangerous to light a fire out of doors when there is a lot of combustible material about.'[115] The fire was to be lit again in 1914.

THE SECOND MOROCCAN CRISIS

In July 1911, there was a further conflict between France and Germany over Morocco following another tribal revolt there. The sultan appealed for assistance, though his appeal had been drafted by the French consul and then given to him for signature. France then occupied Fez on the pretext of rescuing French citizens threatened by dissident locals. She had failed to warn Germany of this occupation, infringing on an agreement in 1909 by which France promised to respect Germany's economic interests, and her occupation was clearly a prelude to the establishment of a French protectorate. In addition, France insisted that the sultan not sign treaties with other countries without French approval, an infringement of the Act of Algeciras.

German protests were met by a French promise to start negotiations. But after waiting for ten days with no further French response, Germany sent a

114 Otte, *Statesman of Europe*, p. 451.
115 Ibid., p. 343.

gunboat, the *Panther*, to the port of Agadir, south-west of Marrakesh, normally closed to European shipping, on the pretext of protecting German traders threatened by disorder but in reality to reopen the Moroccan question and stake a German claim to Morocco. 'The sudden discovery of German "subjects" and "threatened interests" in the immediate neighbourhood of the only place on the west coast of Morocco which can be developed into a naval and commercial base' was, so Asquith told the king on 4 July 1911, 'an interesting illustration of "realpolitik"'.[116] In fact, German economic interests in Morocco were somewhat greater than they had been in 1905, and greater than Asquith appreciated. But it appears that the appeal for help from the German colony in Morocco that led to the despatch of the *Panther* had been organised in advance by Germany's Foreign Office, and a German civilian based seventy miles to the north travelled south to be 'rescued' three days after the *Panther* arrived.[117]

Germany, however, claimed that she sought no special rights, only an assurance that economic rights there would not be monopolised by France. More important, she sought territorial compensation elsewhere in Africa. She assumed that the *Panther* would not be seen as a threat to Britain since Agadir was far south of Gibraltar. Germany's methods were heavy-handed but were intended to open negotiations with France, which was, after all, in breach of a treaty. She demanded almost the whole of the French Congo, leaving for France just an isolated scrap. That would lay the foundation for a German Empire stretching from east to west in central Africa, countering British attempts to create an empire from the Cape to Cairo. The French Prime Minister Joseph Caillaux was more conciliatory in style to Germany than Delcassé had been but would not negotiate under threat. Britain, while prepared to recognise a German interest in Morocco, was not prepared to concede her a port on the coast, which could be fortified. Nor was she prepared to be excluded from discussions on Morocco in which she had an interest as a signatory of both the Algeciras Act and the entente, and because of Gibraltar. Grey had hoped that the problem could be solved if France rapidly withdrew from Fez. But she did not. She was not prepared to return to the position agreed at Algeciras but was clearly seeking complete control in Morocco. Yet in 1911, as in 1905–06, bullying tactics by Germany destroyed her promising diplomatic position. On 4 July, Grey told the German ambassador that Britain would not recognise any new arrangements on which she had not been consulted. Ominously, there was no reply from Germany.

116 Keith M. Wilson, *The Policy of the Ententes: Essays on the Determinants of British Foreign Policy, 1904–1914*, Cambridge University Press, 1985, p. 34.
117 See the letter by James Joll, *Times Literary Supplement*, 25 September 1953.

Both Germany and France kept Britain in the dark. There were rumours that the German fleet had been mobilised, and Grey decided to send a ship to Agadir. On 21 July, Lloyd George, speaking at the Lord Mayor's dinner, reinforced Grey's warning, delivering a speech that had been carefully drafted in agreement with Asquith and Grey. Lloyd George insisted:

> If a situation were to be forced upon us in which peace could only be
> preserved by the surrender of the great and beneficent position Britain has
> won by centuries of heroism and achievement, by allowing Britain to be
> treated as if she were of no account in the Cabinet of nations, then I say
> emphatically that peace at that price would be a humiliation intolerable
> for a great country like ours to endure.

He was interrupted three times during his speech by cheers. It was a courageous speech, given that his political support came so largely from the Nonconformist element which was pacifistic and sympathetic to Germany. 'His courage is great', Grey's private secretary told the British minister to Sweden, 'he risked his position with the people who have mainly made him'.[118] For a time, armed conflict seemed a distinct possibility and on 27 August, the kaiser announced an expansion of German naval construction 'so that we can be sure that nobody will dispute our rightful place in the sun'.[119] In fact, the kaiser was opposed to war and a compromise settlement was to be reached in November 1911. Germany recognised French rights in Morocco, which became a French protectorate in 1912, in exchange for two strips of the French Congo, far less than she had wanted.

The settlement was denounced both in France and Germany as appeasement, and Caillaux was to be overthrown shortly afterwards. Germany amended her naval law so as to provide for a rapid increase in dreadnoughts, which Britain saw as a challenge. The settlement did nothing to mollify Franco-German tensions, and it increased tensions between Germany and Britain.

The Agadir crisis had fateful consequences. In Britain, the German action was seen as an attempt to drive a wedge between the entente partners. Then France would have to make the best deal that she could with Germany and be drawn into the German orbit, which would leave Britain facing a Continent dominated by Germany. At a breakfast meeting with C. P. Scott, editor of the *Manchester Guardian*, Grey explained the principles of his policy.

118 Stephen Gwynn, *The Letters and Friendships of Sir Cecil Spring-Rice*, Constable, 1929, vol. 2, p. 163.
119 Bentley B. Gilbert, 'Pacifist to Interventionist: David Lloyd George in 1911 and 1914. Was Belgium an Issue?', *Historical Journal*, 1985, p. 871.

He at once admitted that this was to give to France such support as would prevent her from falling under the virtual control of Germany and estrangement from us. This would mean the break-up of the triple entente as if France retired Russia would at once do the same and we should again be faced with the old troubles about the frontier of India. It would also mean the complete ascendancy of Germany in Europe ... The history of the Napoleonic wars showed that any power which achieved European dominance in the last resort came against England, which so long as she retained her sea-power could not be coerced, and that was the inevitable sequel to German as to a French supremacy.[120]

In Parliament, Grey told MPs that isolation was 'not a policy. It is the negation of policy.' It would mean 'that in the course of a few years we should be building warships not against a two Power standard, but probably against the united navies of Europe'.[121]

The Agadir crisis seemed to show, as the first Moroccan crisis had done in 1905, that there was a real possibility of war between Britain and Germany. It led to a special meeting of the Committee of Imperial Defence on 23 August 1911 to consider how France should be aided, the only occasion on which grand strategy was discussed before 1914. Non-interventionists such as Harcourt, Crewe and Loreburn were not invited; Morley was on holiday, but Lloyd George and Churchill attended for the first time. Asquith, Grey, Haldane, McKenna were also present, together with leading army and naval officers. The meeting was dominated by Brigadier Henry Wilson, Director of Military Operations at the War Office. He had in 1910 resumed military conversations with the French, without informing the Foreign Secretary. He now insisted that any German attack on France would sweep through Belgium. While he hoped that Belgium would resist, Wilson believed that only a rapid British military contribution of six divisions would enable the French to contain the German attack. British intervention, therefore, would be decisive. Asquith and Grey were unhappy, preferring that only four divisions be sent, but acquiesced. This confirmed the shift in strategy, begun during the first Moroccan crisis. Indeed, the first strategic war game in Britain on the problems of continental warfare had been held in April and May 1905, shortly after the kaiser had landed in Tangier. It now appeared that the army would play an active role on the Continent in alliance with France – the so-called Continental strategy. But the First Lord of the Admiralty, Reginald McKenna, 'abhorred the use of British troops in France' and opposed any

120 Wilson, ed., *C. P. Scott*, pp. 50–51.
121 House of Commons Debates, 27 November 1911, vol. 32, col. 60.

continuation of staff talks with the French. He was, therefore, moved to the Home Office, swapping places with Churchill, who became the new First Lord.[122] The government, despite seeming to agree with the conclusions of the Committee of Imperial Defence, took no further action to implement the strategy proposed. Indeed, the Cabinet could not agree on a strategy before war broke out in 1914. For a Continental strategy seemed to require the creation of a mass army, probably involving conscription. Yet military leaders made no proposals for creating such a mass army. Nor did the politicians. If, however, as Asquith, Grey, Haldane and Lloyd George believed, there was a real danger of war with Germany, should they not have accepted the corollary, a mass army, which might indeed have had a deterrent effect, preventing war altogether? Lloyd George had hinted at conscription in his 1910 coalition proposals, but no further attempts were made to secure it – no doubt because it was hardly politically feasible. In consequence, the government did not adopt the means to make the military strategy put forward by the Committee of Imperial Defence effective.

The Agadir crisis had a strong effect both on Churchill and on Lloyd George, previously amongst the more pacifistic members of the Cabinet. In May 1908, Churchill had called the idea of a British expeditionary force on the Continent 'a dangerous and provocative force'.[123] But now, 'he moved quickly and permanently from the pacifist to the interventionist camp within the cabinet, a change that would only be confirmed and was not caused by his appointment to the Admiralty in October'.[124] Churchill's conversion seems to have influenced Lloyd George. Two days after the Committee of Imperial Defence meeting on 23 August, he wrote to Churchill declaring, 'I am inclined to think the chances of war are multiplying ... "Be ye therefore ready".'[125] The effect of the meeting of 23 August on Lloyd George was considerable. Lloyd George told C. P. Scott, whose *Manchester Guardian* had taken a less interventionist line in the crisis, that while 'Asquith was quite conscious of the anti-Germanism of the Foreign Office staff and was prepared to resist it', neither Asquith nor Grey nor Lloyd George himself was prepared for Britain to be ignored.[126]

It seemed that Britain was moving closer to becoming a military ally of France. But in November 1911, when the staff talks were at last revealed to the Cabinet, just five supported them and fifteen were against. The pacifistic members of the Cabinet secured a commitment that Britain not be

122 Gilbert, 'Lloyd George in 1911 and 1914', p. 876.
123 Williamson, *Politics of Grand Strategy*, p. 99.
124 Gilbert, 'Lloyd George in 1911 and 1914', p. 868.
125 Ibid., p. 874.
126 Wilson, ed., *C. P. Scott*, pp. 46–8.

committed 'directly or indirectly' 'to military or naval intervention' and that any further communications with the French General Staff be submitted to the Cabinet for approval. 'It is depressing', a diplomat wrote to a Foreign Office colleague in July, 'that after six years' experience of Germany the inclination [in the Cabinet] is still to believe that she could be placated ... What she wants is the hegemony of Europe.'[127]

In November 1912, there was to be an exchange of letters between Grey and the French ambassador, approved by the Cabinet but not made known to Parliament until 3 August 1914. In this exchange, it was emphasised that consultation between naval and military experts

> does not restrict the freedom of either Government to decide at any future time whether or not to assist the other by armed force ... The disposition, for instance, of the French and British Fleets respectively at the present moment is not based upon an engagement to co-operate in war.

Cambon had asked what Britain would do if France 'had grave reason to expect an unprovoked attack by a third Power'. Could she 'depend upon the armed assistance of the other'? Grey answered that there should then be discussions on 'whether both Governments should act together to prevent aggression and to preserve peace, and, if so, what measures they would be prepared to take in common'. In reporting to the Commons in 1914, Grey inadvertently omitted the final sentence of the exchange: 'If these measures involved action, the plans of the General Staffs would at once be taken into consideration, and the governments would then decide what effect should be given to them.'[128] This exchange put future conversations between the General Staffs of both countries on a stronger basis, since they now had the approval of the British government. Ministers believed that Britain now had the best of both worlds. The entente preserved security, but Britain still retained full freedom of action in a crisis. The French, by contrast, believed that the British commitment had been strengthened in conjunction with a further agreement in 1912 that the French fleet would be concentrated in the Mediterranean while the British fleet would patrol the English Channel and the North Sea. However, in 1914, the French ambassador never suggested that Britain was *legally* committed to aid France. What both the French and Grey thought was that Britain was under an obligation of honour to France. Even so, the French did not in their war plans assume that Britain would

---

127 Edward Corp, 'Sir William Tyrrell: The Éminence Grise of the British Foreign Office, 1912–1915', *Historical Journal*, 1982, p. 700.
128 House of Commons Debates, 3 August 1914, vol. 65, col. 1813.

send an expeditionary force to the Continent. The position remained ambiguous, but Balfour, whose government had signed the entente, wrote to a friend in 1912 that 'it came upon me as a shock of surprise – I am far from saying of disapproval – when I found how rapidly after I left office the Entente had, under the German menace, developed into something resembling a defensive Alliance'.[129]

In Germany, the Agadir crisis showed, as the earlier Moroccan crisis had done, that little was to be gained by making threats and then backing down. Moltke, the Chief of the German General Staff, was furious, telling his wife, 'If we creep out of this affair with our tails between our legs, if we cannot be aroused to an energetic set of demands which we are prepared to enforce by the sword, then I am doubtful about the future of the German Empire. And I will resign.'[130] The Agadir crisis induced in Germany a shift from naval competition to an emphasis on the army, a decision made at a meeting of the so-called War Council in December 1912. Germany's resolve was, as we shall see, to be bolstered by the outcome of the First Balkan War, which seemed to strengthen Russia and Serbia and weaken her alliance partner, Austria, so also weakening the Triple Alliance. The preamble to Germany's 1913 Army Bill declared that 'the events taking place in the Balkans have changed the balance of power in Europe. In a war which may be forced upon her Germany will have to defend her extensive frontiers, in great part devoid of natural defences, possibly against several adversaries.' Germany, therefore, provided for a huge increase in her army. The 1912 Army Bill added 29,000 to the army. Then, in 1913, Moltke asked for an extra 117,000 men and 19,000 officers. These increases equalled the whole of that made by a succession of German army laws between 1873 and 1912. The increases were accepted even by the Social Democrats, the largest party in the Reichstag. They required a capital levy to pay for it, which raised over three times that exacted by Lloyd George from tax increases in his 1909 Budget.[131] 'No statesman in Europe had ever before dreamed of raising by extra taxation, in one year and during peace, so enormous an extra cost as this then seemed.'[132] 'The sacrifices to which the German people have this year willingly consented to make', declared *The Times* military correspondent on 20 August 1913, 'are unexampled in modern history.' The 'result will be to endow Germany with a weapon of offence' to which modern Europe had not seen the like since the days of Napoleon. But the correspondent added that 'it is only just to remark that no aggressive intentions have been displayed of late'. Moltke, however,

129 Dugdale, *Balfour*, vol. 2, p. 281.
130 Craig, *Germany*, p. 329.
131 Ibid., pp. 295–6.
132 Ensor, *England*, p. 470.

believed that, because of the growth of Russian strength, Germany needed preventive war and 'the sooner the better'.[133] A prominent German journalist, Maximilian Harden, proclaimed, 'Now our future lies on the continent. This awareness has returned to the German people.'[134] In response to the increase in Germany's army, France increased her period of national service from two to three years, and the Russians also expanded their army. Agadir and then the Balkan wars were to give a great impetus to the Continental arms race.

Once again, as in 1905–06, what had seemed a purely European crisis impinged upon the United States. After the Agadir crisis had been resolved, Theodore Roosevelt, now ex-President, told the German ambassador that if Germany had overrun France, the United States would not have remained neutral. The ambassador answered that this seemed contrary to the Monroe Doctrine. Roosevelt replied:

> As long as England succeeds in keeping up the 'balance of power' in Europe, not only in principle, but in reality, well and good; should she however for some reason or other fail in doing so, the United States would be obliged to step in at least temporarily, in order to re-establish the balance of power in Europe, never mind against which country ... In fact we ourselves are becoming, owing to our strength and geographical position, more and more the balance of power on the whole globe.[135]

That was an astonishing prediction of the course of twentieth-century history. Twice indeed during the twentieth century, Americans felt compelled, as Theodore Roosevelt had intuited, to 'step in' to protect the balance of power in Europe and resist German attempts to become the dominant power on the Continent. Twice, if the world wars had been confined to European powers, Germany might well have won.

Some historians have seen the Agadir crisis as a prelude to the world war which broke out three years later.[136] And indeed many at the time believed that, since European borders outside the Balkans seemed settled, Europe would no longer be an arena for future conflicts. The Concert of Europe would guarantee that conflicts in Europe would be settled peacefully. The danger was rather that war would be caused by imperial conflicts. But instead, the Agadir crisis was to prove 'the last of the colonial disputes which had disturbed international relations for the preceding twenty-five years, and all of which had been settled peacefully. But it established a myth that the

---

133 Craig, *Germany*, p. 332.
134 Evans and von Strandmann, eds, *Coming of the First World War*, p. 111.
135 Quoted in John Lukacs, *The Last European War: September 1939/December 1941*, Routledge & Kegan Paul, 1976, p. 507fn.
136 The main theme of Geoffrey Barraclough, *From Agadir to Armageddon: Anatomy of a Crisis*, Weidenfeld & Nicolson, 1982.

basic causes of European tension were imperialist and extra-European.'[137] Imperial conflicts could be, and were, contained through bargaining between the powers. Nationalist conflicts in Europe could not be so contained. The world war was to be caused by conflicts not in Africa or Asia but in Europe, and specifically the Balkans. The cause lay not in rival imperialisms but in rival nationalisms.

Even so, following the Agadir crisis, relations between Britain and Germany appeared to be improving. There seemed to be what one historian has called a 'hollow detente',[138] indeed something of a kind of fellow-feeling between the two nations. Germany, together with the British Empire and the United States, had been included in Cecil Rhodes's scholarship scheme initiated in 1903. In 1907, the kaiser had been given an honorary doctorate by Oxford University, while in May 1914 the Oxford Union was to vote by ninety-six votes to sixty to 'condemn the Triple Entente as both an unnecessary and an unnatural policy'. The president, a Unionist, spoke for the majority. The next month, five of the seven who received honorary degrees at Oxford were German. Admiral von Tirpitz, the head of the German Navy and the man probably the least sympathetic to Britain amongst the German elite, had nevertheless acquired a British governess for his daughters, who were educated at Cheltenham Ladies' College.[139]

But the German question was to interact with another question which was to be the immediate cause of the war – the conflict in the Balkans between Austria and Serbia.

THE BALKAN WARS

The annexation of Bosnia weakened the Ottoman Empire. Bulgaria took the opportunity to declare her independence, while Crete broke her last ties with that empire so as to proclaim her union with Greece.[140] In 1911, during the Agadir crisis, while the powers were distracted, Italy also took advantage of Ottoman weakness by declaring war on her to secure her own colonial empire in what was to become Libya. She was soon victorious. The effects of this war were far-reaching in helping to undermine the European balance of power, and once more to set the Balkans alight.

Seeing the weakness of the Ottoman Empire, the Slav powers in the Balkans – Serbia, Montenegro and Bulgaria – joined with Greece to form in March 1912 the Balkan League, which, in October, declared war against

---

137 A. J. P. Taylor, 'The Panther's Spring', *The Guardian*, 1 July 1961.
138 R. J. Crampton, *The Hollow Detente: Anglo-German Relations in the Balkans, 1911–14*, Prior, 1979.
139 Hew Strachan, *The First World War: Volume 1, To Arms*, Oxford University Press, 2001, p. 78.
140 Hazlehurst and Woodland, *A Liberal Chronicle*, p. 187.

Turkey. The League, to the surprise of many, gained a rapid and complete victory and Turkey lost around four-fifths of her European territories. The Balkan members of the League had at last secured their national liberation from Ottoman rule. But, as Grey notes in his memoirs, 'in acting thus, the members of the Balkan League liberated forces the full effect of which they did not foresee, and set in motion rivalries among themselves which they could not control'.[141] The victory of the Balkan powers strengthened Slav and Russian influence and weakened Austria. The immediate fear was that war in the Balkans would engulf the powers. 'It had', so Grey told the Commons in August 1913, 'been an axiom of diplomacy for many a year past that if ever war broke out in the Balkans, it would be impossible, or almost impossible, to prevent one or more of the Great Powers being dragged into the conflict.'[142] To ensure that conflict was localised, Grey proposed that ambassadors of the five major powers – Austria–Hungary, France, Germany, Italy and Russia – meet with Britain in London as 'the symbol of the existence of the Concert of Europe'.[143] The ambassadors' meetings – sometimes misdescribed as a conference – opened in December 1912 and succeeded in maintaining peace between the major powers. The key to success was cooperation between Britain and Germany, neither of which had direct interests in the Balkans. The Triple Alliance enabled Germany to constrain her ally Austria; the entente enabled Britain to constrain Russia; while Russia in turn constrained Serbia. For the last time, the alliance system worked to preserve peace.

The ambassadors' meetings made three fundamental decisions. The first was the establishment of an independent Muslim state of Albania in the western Balkans, separate in language and religion from Serbia, so as to counterbalance Serbia's newly enhanced power. France was opposed to the creation of Albania, but Grey used his influence on the side of Germany and Austria rather than his entente partner, a clear indication that he sought balance rather than alignment. The second decision was to draw a line in the Ottoman Empire beyond which the Balkan League could not go so as to ensure that Turkey remained in control of Constantinople and eastern Thrace, Turkey's only remaining footholds in Europe. These two decisions were exceptions to the ambassadors' acceptance that the new contours in the Balkans would be determined by the vicissitudes of war. The third decision was that, at the insistence of Austria–Hungary, Albania's protector, Serbia would not be allotted a port on the Adriatic. Instead, she would have trade access by means of an international railway through a free and neutral port,

---

141 Grey, *Twenty-Five Years*, vol. I, p. 260.
142 House of Commons Debates, 12 August 1913, vol. 56, col. 2283.
143 Ibid., cols 2282, 2283.

though the railway was never in fact built. These decisions were embodied in the Treaty of London signed at the end of May 1913. But just one month after, the Second Balkan War broke out between Bulgaria and her former allies, Serbia, Montenegro and Greece, over the division of the spoils in the first war. In this second war, Bulgaria was defeated and, by the Treaty of Bucharest in August 1913, Serbia gained further territory in Macedonia, controlling many areas with a Bulgarian majority. This was a repudiation of the Treaty of London, and Turkey, also disregarding that treaty, recovered western Thrace and Adrianople (now Edirne), which she had lost in the First Balkan War. Both Balkan wars had been characterised by savagery on all sides, against those who differed in religion or race. What had begun, in Grey's words, 'as a war of liberation' had become rapidly 'a war of conquest' and had ended in being 'a war of extermination'.[144] The Serbs in particular had committed terrible atrocities in Kosovo, where Serb soldiers boasted, 'We have not left a nose on an Albanian there,' and in Scutari, where Serb soldiers threw food on a bridge to attract hungry children and then bombed them.[145] The Concert of Europe, despite the Treaty of London, now seemed impotent to prevent atrocities or to prevent Turkey and Serbia from breaking the treaty.

The Balkan wars had increased the size and prestige of Serbia, which gained 1.5 million new subjects, and was, even more than before, the Piedmont of the Slavs, a rallying point for Slav aspirations. Corresponding fears were awakened in Austria that Serbia was a threat to the empire, and, with the defeat of the Ottoman Empire and Bulgaria, which could have been counterweights, Austria felt weakened. Commentators on the outbreak of the world war in 1914 have often written about how peaceful Europe had seemed before it, stressing the contingent, even accidental nature of the outbreak. They cannot have been paying close attention to the Balkans, which was a combustible powder keg containing all the ingredients for a conflict which it would not be easy to localise. Austria remained convinced that her empire would not be safe until Serbia had been contained if not eliminated. Germany, for her part, feared that Russia's growing economic and military strength, together with her alliance with France, constituted a threat, encircling her. In the radical journal *The Nation*, the editor H. W. Massingham declared on 1 March 1914, in relation to the Russian Army, that 'the Prussian military would be less than human if it did not dream of anticipating the crushing accumulation of force'. In 1912, the size of peacetime forces in France and Russia exceeded those in Germany and Austria–Hungary by

144 Ibid., col. 2284.
145 R. W. Seton-Watson, *Sarajevo: A Study in the Origins of the Great War*, Hutchinson, 1926, p. 55.

around 700,000. France had 1.4 per cent of her population under arms, Germany just under 1 per cent. But German defence estimates were increasing. In 1914, they were £110.8 million, up from £64 million in 1910. Many in Britain were unaware of the vast increases in German military spending and the hostility to Britain in some military and intellectual circles.

Grey sought by diplomacy to reduce tensions. During the London meetings in 1913, he had tried to balance his commitment to the entente with mediation, to maintain the Concert of Europe, an easy position perhaps for Britain to adopt since, in the Balkans, she was a disinterested power, her only concern being to localise conflict. On many contentious issues, Grey did not take the side of his supposed partners in the entente, France and Russia. He was, so Count Mensdorff, the Austrian ambassador, told his Foreign Office, 'utterly impartial'.[146] He helped to ensure that the borders of Albania were drawn so that she could be a buffer between Austria and the Slavs. When Serbia's ally Montenegro captured the strategic city of Scutari (now Shkodër), allocated to Albania by the powers, Grey, ignoring the advice of his officials, joined the powers (with the exception of Russia, which, however, acquiesced) in a naval demonstration to compel Montenegro to withdraw. This demonstration, admittedly, did not succeed and Austria had to act unilaterally to compel Montenegrin withdrawal. Even so, during the crisis, 'the powers had shown themselves capable of action to enforce their will. It was the high-water mark of the Concert's effectiveness; in the months after the Scutari crisis the unity of the powers was gradually but inexorably destroyed'.[147] The Concert had rested upon Germany's willingness and ability to restrain Austria–Hungary and Britain's willingness and ability to restrain Russia. These were wasting assets, and the crisis was to have its effect on Austria's attitudes during the Sarajevo crisis. She drew the conclusion from the Scutari episode that force rather than international consultation was needed to secure results.

In the Commons, Grey defended his stance on Scutari by saying that the Albanian population there was mainly Catholic and Muslim, not Slav, and that Muslims in Albania had the same right of self-determination as Slavs in Montenegro. The Montenegrin conquest of Scutari was not, therefore, part of a war of liberation but a war of conquest. But Grey also declared that the agreement on Albania had been 'essential for the peace of Europe, and, in my opinion, it was accomplished only just in time to preserve that peace between Great Powers'.[148] But perhaps there was a further motive. Grey wanted to prove

---

146 E. C. Helmreich, *The Diplomacy of the Balkan Wars, 1912–13*, Harvard University Press, 1938, p. 251.

147 R. J. Crampton, 'The Decline of the Concert of Europe in the Balkans, 1913–1914', *Slavonic and East European Review*, 1974, p. 396.

148 House of Commons Debates, 7 April 1913, vol. 51, col. 816.

to Germany and Austria–Hungary that their fears of encirclement by hostile powers were baseless. While the ententes committed Britain to supporting France in Morocco, and perhaps Russia in the unlikely event of an attack on her interests in northern Persia, they did not commit Britain to supporting Russia or Russia's allies in the Balkans. Grey sought to avoid coming down firmly on the side of the entente while at the same time ensuring that Britain did not lose her allies. Britain, he believed, must continue to judge issues on their merits. Grey was, therefore, perfectly prepared to take the side of Austria–Hungary and Germany in the Balkans. That was what the Gladstonian concept of the Concert of Europe meant. Admittedly, the Concert had not been able to impose peace in the Balkans or avoid the acquisition of territory by conquest, but it had at least succeeded in localising the conflict.

Grey hoped that the settlement in London after the First Balkan War might be the prelude to a much wider detente and the establishment of the Concert of Europe on a firmer basis. He was later to regret not having pressed more strongly for the ambassadors to remain in London to continue negotiations as a kind of clearing house to resolve disputes, believing that this might just have succeeded in avoiding war in 1914. 'The mere fact that we were in existence,' Grey was to write in his memoirs about 1912–13, 'and that we should have to be broken up before peace was broken, was in itself an appreciable barrier against war.'[149] In July 1912, he had expressed the hope that 'though there may be separate groups, they need not necessarily be in opposing diplomatic camps'. And indeed, such differences as had arisen at the meetings had not, in his view, shown 'a tendency to divide the different groups of the Great Powers into opposing camps'.[150] In particular, in December 1912, Grey welcomed the fact that 'relations with Germany are excellent just now because we have both been working for peace in Europe. We shall continue to do that and all that is necessary is that Germany should continue also.'[151] The London meetings showed that Europe need not necessarily be divided by alliances. The powers made concessions, sometimes at the cost of their alliance partners. The diplomatic situation, then, appeared to be in the process of becoming more fluid.

Britain, it seemed, was not required to align herself with France and Russia on all matters. The French ambassador indeed expressed annoyance that Britain had not proved more favourable. Russia, in her turn, complained that when, in July 1913, Turkey had recaptured Adrianople in breach of the Treaty of London, Britain had refused to act with her against Turkey. Sazonov, the

149 Grey, *Twenty-Five Years*, vol. 1, p. 262.
150 House of Commons Debates, 10 July 1912, vol. 140, col. 1995; 12 August 1913, vol. 56, col. 2282.
151 Otte, *Statesman of Europe*, p. 467.

Russian foreign minister, complained to the British ambassador in February 1914 that 'Britain would never ... allow the Triple Entente to take any action in which the Triple Alliance would not join, for fear of causing a division among the Powers' – an accurate and fair summary of Grey's approach. The Triple Alliance, the Russian ambassador continued:

> either by its action or its inaction always succeeded in getting the better of us and the reason for this was to be found in the fact that England was only the friend and not the Ally of France and Russia. If we were ever to hold our own in the world, we should have one day to convert the Triple Entente into a regular Alliance. Were it once proclaimed to the world that there was such an Alliance between us, we should be able to sleep comfortably in our beds without fear of some new 'coup' on Germany's part. The Alliance should be of a purely defensive character.[152]

But Grey was not prepared to convert the entente into an alliance. Nor would Liberals have allowed him to do so. Were Britain to be formally allied to France and Russia, she would no longer be able to act as mediator. Grey was in fact slightly distancing himself from the entente with France after 1911 and becoming rather less pro-French than in the past. The Grey of 1912–14 was a very different animal from the Grey of 1905–06. Part of the reason for this was that both France and Russia were stronger militarily than at the time of the ententes. But perhaps the main reason is that he was not, as some have suggested, a believer in a Europe divided by alliances. As a Liberal, he believed in the essentially Gladstonian idea of the Concert of Europe. It is no accident that he was later to prove one of the most ardent advocates of a League of Nations. The Unionists, by contrast, had come to believe that the entente with France should be converted to a full-scale alliance.

Grey's radical critics appreciated the shift in his approach, even if some later historians have not. The radical journal *The Nation* – a predecessor of the *New Statesman*, which used to be called the *New Statesman and Nation* – declared on 10 May 1913, following the London meetings, 'The credit belongs in equal parts to the statesmen of Germany and Sir Edward Grey. They have found at last a consciousness of their common duties ... There might evolve from this temporary association some permanent machinery of legislation' – a kind of proto-League of Nations perhaps. On 15 December 1913, *The Nation* declared that 'nothing more than a memory is left of the old Anglo-German antagonism'.[153] As late as 27 June 1914, just one day before the

---

152 Crampton, 'Decline of the Concert of Europe', p. 417.
153 Taylor, *Trouble Makers*, p. 126.

assassination at Sarajevo, Grey was reported as believing that 'the German government [was] in a peaceful mood and ... very anxious to be on good terms with England'.[154] Lloyd George, on 23 July 1914, the very day in which the Austrian ultimatum was presented to Serbia, and just twelve days before Britain was to declare war on Germany, told Parliament, 'Our relations are very much better than they were a few years ago.' The two empires were beginning 'to realise that they can co-operate for common ends, and that the points of co-operation are greater and more numerous and more important than the points of possible controversy'.[155] While Britain hardly needed an entente with Germany, since the two powers were not, by contrast with France or Russia, colonial rivals, Grey hoped to improve relations through a series of local agreements. The outcome of the London meetings seemed to point in that direction; and there were in fact two such agreements with Germany, completed shortly before the world war – one on the Berlin–Baghdad railway, signed on 29 May 1914, though never ratified, and one on the eventual partition of Portuguese colonies. Grey, however, declared that this latter agreement must be submitted to Parliament since it conflicted with the Anglo-Portuguese declaration of 1899, according to which Britain would defend Portuguese colonies. Germany objected that a parliamentary debate would expose her policy to ridicule and on 3 March 1914, the German ambassador in London asked for it to be dropped. It was ironic that Grey, so often accused by his critics of withholding secret agreements from Parliament, was so scrupulous on this occasion that the agreement collapsed. The agreement on the railway and on the colonies could easily have been the basis of a rapprochement between the two countries.

Grey was, however, careful in his approach to cooperation with Germany. He went no further than promising that Britain would make no unprovoked attack on her. He could not give any assurance of neutrality in any war in which Germany was involved, the German condition for a general agreement. It would mean that while Germany could retain Austria and Italy as her allies, Britain herself would be prevented from finding allies. Grey said instead that Britain would make no unprovoked attack on Germany and would not pursue an aggressive policy towards her. But Germany found that insufficient. Haldane had told the German ambassador in December 1912 that 'speaking for Grey', Britain could not tolerate France being crushed by Germany. Nor would she tolerate the hegemony of a single power on the Continent. On the next day, Grey summoned the ambassador to the Foreign

---

154 Robbins, *Grey*, p. 287.
155 House of Commons Debates, 23 July 1914, vol. 65, cols 727–8.

Office and repeated this message, though not quite so explicitly. He also told the ambassador with some emphasis:

> Russia would not a second time beat a retreat [as she had done in 1909] but would rather take up arms ... if ... a European war were to arise through Austria's attacking Serbia, and Russia, compelled by public opinion, were to march into Galicia rather than again put up with a humiliation like that of 1909, thus forcing Germany to come to the aid of Austria, France would inevitably be drawn in *and no one could foretell what further developments might follow.*

This was taken by the kaiser as a hostile declaration.[156]

THE ASSASSINATION AT SARAJEVO

TIMELINE OF THE SARAJEVO CRISIS, 1914

28 JUNE
: Archduke Franz Ferdinand, heir to Austro-Hungarian throne, assassinated at Sarajevo.

5 JULY
: Germany gives Austria blank cheque to attack Serbia.

23 JULY
: Austrian ultimatum to Serbia.

1 AUGUST
: Germany declares war on Russia.

2 AUGUST
: Germany invades neutral Luxembourg and sends ultimatum to neutral Belgium.

3 AUGUST
: Germany declares war on France. Germany invades neutral Belgium.

4 AUGUST
: Britain declares war on Germany.

Around two weeks before the outbreak of the world war, a German shipping magnate told Churchill that, towards the end of Bismarck's life, he had heard the statesman predict, 'If there is ever another war in Europe, it will come out of some damned silly thing in the Balkans.'[157] War did not break out primarily because of a quarrel between Britain and Germany but through conflict between Austria–Hungary and Russia in the Balkans. The origins of the war lay in south-eastern Europe, not central or western Europe. And in July and August 1914, the alliance system, far from restraining the powers, pushed them into a war which might otherwise have been avoided. So the London meetings, far from heralding a revival of the Concert of Europe,

---

156 Keith M. Wilson, 'The British Démarche of 3 and 4 December 1912: H. A. Gwynne's Note on Britain, Russia and the First Balkan War', *Slavonic and East European Review*, 1984, pp. 553, 555. Emphasis added.

157 House of Commons Debates, 16 August 1945, vol. 413, col. 84. Churchill had been told this by a friend of the kaiser's just two weeks before the First World War.

were its last act. For the Concert depended upon Europe being dominated by states of roughly equal power committed to the status quo. It was fatally injured – first by the weakening of Turkey and Austria relative to Russia; second by the weakening of Austria, France and Russia relative to Germany; and third by the desire of Austria to alter the status quo in the Balkans. The Concert of Europe had become unstable and perhaps unsustainable.[158]

Grey, sadly, was not the only voice in Europe during the Balkan wars, nor even an entirely representative one. In Austria, very different opinions were being heard. The outcome of the Balkan wars led many in Vienna to conclude that Serbia, because of alleged subversive activities, designed to secure the secession of Austria's southern Slav territories and create a Greater Serbia, was a dagger aimed at her heart; and behind Serbia, it was believed, was Russia. Austria did not believe that the settlement after the Balkan wars could prove permanent. 'From the day of the conclusion of the peace in Bucharest,' Austrian foreign minister Berchtold's *chef de cabinet* was to write in 1928, 'it was clear to all well-informed Austrian and Hungarian statesmen that it must come to a world war unless something happened to offset the sinister impact of that peace.'[159] The assassination at Sarajevo was only to confirm a conclusion that many in the ruling group in Vienna had already reached. The assassination, therefore, was not the only or even perhaps the prime cause of the Austrian decision to declare war on Serbia. There had been pressure for some years from the chief of staff, Conrad von Hötzendorf, for a preventive war against Serbia, and at times the civilian leadership had been inclined to agree with him. Whereas the London meetings had increased Grey's faith in the value of the conference method, it had the opposite effect in Austria, who believed that she would do better by herself threatening force as Serbia had done. In January 1913, the new war minister General Krobatin declared that a war against Serbia was needed to protect Austria's southern borders, and there was widespread support amongst the Austrian military, diplomatic and even intellectual elite for 'smashing' and 'annexing' Serbia. In February 1913, Conrad's German counterpart, Helmuth von Moltke, had told him that 'a European war must come sooner or later in which ultimately the struggle will be one between Germanism and Slavism'.[160] In August 1913, as the Italian Prime Minister Giolitti was later to disclose, Count Berchtold invited his allies in the Triple Alliance – Germany and Italy – to join Austria in an attack on Serbia.[161] They refused. But that was to prove merely a postponement. In October 1913, Count Stürgkh, the Austrian Prime Minister,

158 I owe this thought to Gareth Cadwallader.
159 Zametica, *Folly and Malice*, p. 264.
160 Taylor, *Struggle for Mastery*, p. 496.
161 Ensor, *England*, p. 469. See also Helmreich, *Diplomacy of the Balkan Wars*, p. 453.

declared that Serbia must be reduced in size and its dynasty replaced. In November, Emperor Franz Joseph himself told his minister in Budapest, 'The Peace of Bucharest is untenable, and we are heading for a new war. God grant that it remains confined to the Balkans.'[162] In that same month, Berchtold told a diplomatic colleague, departing on a mission to Bucharest:

> The solution of the South Slav issue, subject to the limitations of human wisdom and in face of the tenacity and confidence with which Serbia is pursuing the idea of a Greater Serbia, can only be by force. It will either almost completely destroy the present state of Serbia or shake Austria–Hungary to its foundations.[163]

The Austrian 'solution' to the South Slav question was to do both.

Sunday 28 June 1914 was a beautifully sunny day in the Balkans, following days of rain. Franz Ferdinand, heir to the Austrian throne, and his morganatic wife Sophie were visiting Sarajevo as part of a tour of military inspection in Bosnia. He had paid an informal visit with his wife the day before on a shopping expedition and been greeted with enthusiasm by the local population. He had, however, been advised not to return on 28 June, which was the Serb national day commemorating the Battle of Kosovo in 1389, a battle with the same significance in Serb mythology as the Battle of the Boyne in Northern Ireland. The archduke's advisers suggested that his visit might be seen as a provocation to the Slavs. The archduke, however, ignored the advice. Security in Sarajevo was lamentable. Seven youthful Bosnian Serb terrorists – two were aged seventeen and still at school, two had been expelled from school and were now students, while the oldest was twenty-seven – were waiting for the archduke. They had been trained in neighbouring Serbia, not by the government, but by dissident elements in the Serbian army. They had been given revolvers and bombs in Serbia and also cyanide pills, to kill themselves after murdering the archduke. They were assisted in crossing the border from Serbia into Bosnia by minor Serb customs officials. Six of the seven wanted an independent South Slav state: Yugoslavia, which would comprise – in addition to Serbia and Montenegro – Bosnia–Herzegovina, Croatia and Slovenia, all part of the Austro-Hungarian Empire. They were not, as is often suggested, Serb nationalists. Indeed, the Yugoslav idea owed more to movements in Croatia than to Serbia.[164] Just one of the conspirators – Muhamed Mehmedbašić, the only Muslim in the group – favoured a Greater Serbia.

162 Zameica, *Folly and Malice*, p. 264.
163 Quoted in Keith Wilson, 'Hamlet – With and Without the Prince: Terrorism at the Outbreak of the First World War', *Journal of Conflict Studies*, Winter 2007, p. 32.
164 Zametica, *Folly and Malice*, p. 330.

As the archduke's car drove to the town hall, one of the terrorists, Nedeljko Čabrinović, threw a bomb at it. The driver accelerated. The bomb exploded under the second car, causing injuries to spectators and those inside. Čabrinović threw himself into the river but did not drown, and his cyanide pill did not work. He was immediately arrested, the police saving him from a lynching by the crowd. The archduke reached the town hall and was greeted with a pompous speech of welcome from the mayor. The archduke interrupted – You invite me here and greet me with bombs? He decided to cut short his visit and take a different route out of the town. His driver was either not told of this or forgot. He took the wrong route and had to back up the car to return to the right road. By chance, one of the conspirators, nineteen-year-old Gavrilo Princip, was standing on the pavement beside the car. Shooting at point-blank range but with his eyes closed, he killed both the archduke and his wife. At his trial, Princip was to say that under Austrian rule the people 'have been completely impoverished' and were treated 'like cattle'. 'The peasant is impoverished, they have ruined him completely. I am a villager's son and I know what it is like in the villages. That is why I wanted to take revenge, and I am not sorry.'[165] Princip too was saved by arrest from being lynched by the crowd following the assassination, and his cyanide pill also failed to work. Had it done so, war might possibly have been avoided, since the connection with Serbia might not have been discovered. Princip and Čabrinović, however, were Bosnian Serbs, subjects of the Austro-Hungarian Empire, not of Serbia or any other Slav country. Both were tubercular and knew that they had not long to live.

Five weeks after the assassination, on 2 August, four of the six great powers – Germany, Russia, France and Austria–Hungary together with Serbia – were at war. Two days later, on 4 August, the day after a sunny August Bank Holiday Monday, Britain declared war on Germany, and later in the month on Austria–Hungary. Italy was to keep out for the time being.

There seemed no obvious reason why the assassination should lead to a world war. Assassinations of heads of state and government were by no means uncommon in this period and were generally without major consequences. Indeed, for a month after the assassination, nothing seemed to happen. In Britain, the king, Prime Minister and Foreign Secretary paid their condolences and there was a week of court mourning. But the assassination soon disappeared from the front pages of the newspapers. British ministers remained engrossed in the Ulster problem and the 1914 Budget. The Austrian government, however, decided immediately after the assassination, with just one dissentient, that a diplomatic protest would be insufficient and that military

165 Ibid., pp. 364, 366.

action would be necessary to subdue Serbia. Berchtold was to confess in 1928 that he had wanted to take immediately military action but was dissuaded both by the army chief of staff on military grounds and by the Hungarian Prime Minister, Count Tisza – the Hungarians being unwilling to add more disaffected Slavs to their kingdom.[166] Ironically, however, it is just possible that an immediate Austrian attack on Serbia might not have generated a world war, sympathy for Austria being so great after the assassination. But in response to doubts amongst the military in Vienna and the Hungarians, Berchtold sent his *chef de cabinet*, Count Hoyos, to Berlin with two letters seeking German support, which would, hopefully, convert Tisza to supporting military action. Austria would not, of course, need German support to crush a small country like Serbia. But German support was needed to ensure that Russia was deterred from intervening. It was, then, already clear that there were doubts as to whether a war against Serbia could be localised.

Hoyos arrived in Berlin on 5 July. The letter which he carried from Franz Joseph made it clear that war was contemplated, stating that Serbia was to be 'eliminated as a political factor in the Balkans'.[167] Hoyos told the Under-Secretary at the Foreign Ministry that 'a surprise attack against Serbia without prior diplomatic action' was the 'right modus procedendi'. Austria 'had to strike and present Europe with a fait accompli. In Austria a complete partition of Serbia was contemplated.' In 1917, Hoyos recollected that he had emphasised Austria's determination 'even at the risk of a war with Russia' and that Vienna appreciated 'that such a policy might bring about a world war'.[168] The Under-Secretary told Hoyos that European war was a 90 per cent certainty if Austria 'did something' against Serbia.[169] Meanwhile, the Austrian ambassador was lunching with the kaiser. After lunch, the kaiser instantly gave the ambassador what was sought – a so-called blank cheque that Austria–Hungary could do with Serbia as she wished and that Germany would support her. He said that Russia was 'not remotely' ready for war and that he personally would 'regret it' if Austria did not use this favourable moment. 'Now or never,' he had commented on a memorandum on 30 June. 'The Serbs must be put away *and* right *now*.'[170] The kaiser's adjutant wrote in his diary, 'Here the view prevails that the sooner the Austrians strike against Serbia, the better, and that the Russians – although friends of Serbia – would not join in after all.'[171] But the kaiser's action was not perhaps as significant

166 Bernadotte E. Schmitt, *Interviewing the Authors of the War*, Chicago Literary Club, 1930, p. 28.
167 As he recalled in 1928, ibid., p. 25; Seton-Watson, *Sarajevo*, p. 174.
168 T. G. Otte, *July Crisis: The World's Descent into War, Summer 1914*, Cambridge University Press, 2014, pp. 78, 79.
169 Röhl, 'Goodbye to all that (again)?', p. 158.
170 Zametica, *Folly and Malice*, pp. 545, 546.
171 Otte, *July Crisis*, p. 83.

as is often suggested. It was his habit when a foreign policy crisis arose to call for immediate warlike action but then to retreat when the actual prospect of war arose; and indeed, at a later stage of the crisis, the kaiser strove hard to avoid war. His volatile nature meant that he was not taken wholly seriously either by his ministers or by the military, both of whom spent much time humouring his obsessions and trying to talk him out of them. More important was the attitude of the German Chancellor, Bethmann Hollweg. Bethmann was, somewhat casually, given the issues at stake, to endorse the blank cheque on the evening of 5 July, writing later that 'the views of the Kaiser were in accordance with my own thinking'.[172] He felt indeed that an 'immediate intervention' was the 'most radical and best solution'.[173] Bethmann's decision was crucial, amounting to incitement as well as a blank cheque, and it was given even though German interests were in no way involved in Austria's dispute with Serbia. Had Germany not been willing to give that cheque, Austria could not have taken the risk of armed conflict with Serbia, as Hoyos was later to admit, for fear of Russian intervention.

When Hoyos saw Zimmermann, deputy to Jagow, the foreign minister, who was away on his honeymoon, no objection was made to the Austrian plans. Zimmermann then told the German ambassador to London who happened to be in Berlin at the time that 'if war was now after all inevitable ... in consequence of the unfriendly attitude of Russia, it would be better to have it now rather than later'. In July 1917, Hoyos indicated that on the next day, Bethmann expressed similar sentiments.[174] The responsible ministers and officials in Germany gave the so-called blank cheque without any critical examination of the Austrian contention that the Serbian government had been involved in the assassination and that the continued existence of Serbia in her present borders was a menace to Austria. The purpose – or perhaps it would be better to say, the hope – of the blank cheque was to localise the war by deterring Russia.

Hoyos, then, was left in little doubt that Germany would support Austria. The blank cheque helped him, as he had hoped, persuade the Hungarian Prime Minister, Count Tisza, to withdraw his objections to military action. And perhaps there would be no wider conflict, since, if Germany stood behind Austria, Russia might back down. But it was a terrible gamble. The Russian foreign minister was to tell the British ambassador at St Petersburg on 18 July that 'anything resembling an Austrian ultimatum in Belgrade

---

172 Ibid., p. 91.
173 Zametica, *Folly and Malice*, p. 547.
174 Bernadotte Schmitt, 'July 1914: Thirty Years After', *Journal of Modern History*, 1944, p. 175; Jan Opocénský, 'A War-Time Discussion of Responsibility for the War', *Journal of Modern History*, 1932, pp. 426–8.

could not leave Russia indifferent'.[175] And it appears that Germany was in fact perfectly prepared to contemplate war with Russia. The Bavarian chargé d'affaires in Berlin reported to Munich on 18 July after talking to Zimmermann, 'That Serbia cannot accept demands so incompatible with her dignity as an independent state, is obvious. The consequences would therefore be war ... Berlin declared itself satisfied with whatever action Vienna might decide upon, even at the risk of war with Russia.'[176] And Bethmann's endorsement of the blank cheque meant that the decision for peace or war would in effect lie not in Berlin but in Vienna, over which Germany would have no control.

Hoyos apparently reported back to Vienna that Germany favoured 'immediate action' against Serbia, 'although it is clearly recognised that a world war might arise from this'.[177] On 15 July, in Vienna, Hoyos said, 'If this leads to a world war, we don't care.'[178] In 1918, Baron Leopold von Andrian-Werburg, the Austro-Hungarian Consul General in Warsaw, who had been privy to discussions in the Austrian Foreign Office following the murder of the archduke, wrote, 'We began the war, not the Germans and even less the Entente – that I know.'[179] While Austria bore the prime responsibility, Bethmann too seems to have become aware of the monumental gamble that he was taking. For, on 7 July, he had told his secretary, 'An action against Serbia can lead to a world war' – '*Ein Aktion gegen Serbien kann zum Weltkrieg führen*'.[180] Zimmermann had told Hoyos on 5 July that there was a 90 per cent chance of 'a European war' if Austria moved against Serbia.[181] On 18 July, the German foreign minister wrote to his ambassador in London, 'I do not want a preventive war, but if the opportunity offers itself, we must not shirk it.'[182] This makes Bethmann's endorsement of the blank cheque even more culpable. Indeed, in the search for 'war criminals', Bethmann was far more culpable than the kaiser.

Back in Vienna, Tisza was somewhat reluctantly won round to support war on condition that Austria did not annex Serbian territory after victory. Berchtold accepted this condition, perhaps not intending to honour it. But if Austria did not annex Serbian territory herself, the country would instead

175 Clark, *The Sleepwalkers*, p. 481.
176 Seton-Watson, *Sarajevo*, p. 179.
177 Ibid., p. 179.
178 Quoted in Avner Offer, 'Going to War in 1914: A Matter of Honour?', *Politics & Society*, 1995, pp. 226–7. This article offers a profound analysis of the unspoken assumptions behind the decisions taken in 1914.
179 Quoted in Solomon Wank, 'Desperate Counsel in Vienna in July 1914: Berthold Molden's Unpublished Memorandum', *Central European History*, 1993, p. 281.
180 Diary entry of Bethmann's secretary, Kurt Riezler, for 7 July 1914, quoted in Hew Strachan, '*Die europäischen Mächte und der Habsburgerstaat in der Juli-Krise 1914*', in Helmut Rumpler and Anatol Schmied-Kowarzik, eds, *Die Habsburgermonarchie und der Erste Weltkrieg*, Verlag der Österreichischen Akademie der Wissenschaften, 2016, p. 158. I am grateful to Sir Hew Strachan for drawing my attention to this comment.
181 Zametica, *Folly and Malice*, p. 55.
182 Otte, *July Crisis*, p. 172.

be partitioned amongst the neighbouring powers or reduced to the status of a vassal state. Austria aimed, in the words of the Austrian ambassador to London, on 28 July, at 'crushing Serbia'. Serbia was to be 'ironed flat' with portions of her territory being ceded to Bulgaria and perhaps also to Albania.[183]

Berchtold now had to make a convincing case for war to the other powers. He accordingly sent his Secretary of State in the Foreign Office, Friedrich von Wiesner, to Serbia to discover evidence of Serbian complicity. Wiesner reported in a long telegram on 13 July to Vienna what must have been already known, that the assassination had been decided upon and prepared with the help of Serbian state officials, and that the terrorists had smuggled bombs and weapons across the border with the help of Serb border guards. There had also been much propaganda against Austria–Hungary by various Serb organisations as well as the Serb press with the support, knowledge and approval of the Serb government. But he concluded:

> There is nothing to show the complicity of the Serbian Government in the directing of the assassination or in its preparation or in the supplying of weapons. Nor is there anything to lead one even to conjecture such a thing. On the contrary, there is evidence that would appear to show that such complicity is out of the question.

This is misinterpreted by Christopher Clark who, in his book *The Sleepwalkers*, declares that Wiesner in his report found '*as yet* no evidence to prove the responsibility or complicity of the Belgrade government' (my emphasis). The words 'as yet' did not appear in Wiesner's report. And Hoyos was later to admit, 'I never believed that the murder of the Archduke Franz Ferdinand had been prepared or intended by authorities in Belgrade or Petersburg.'[184] But Wiesner's report was suppressed by Berchtold.

It would indeed have been surprising had the Serbian government been involved in the assassination. Having just fought two wars in the Balkans, she was in no condition to embark on a third. Preoccupied with incorporating the new territories to her south, in particular parts of Macedonia with its large Bulgarian population, she could hardly afford to challenge the great power lying to her north and west. Further, had the Serbian government masterminded the assassination, she would hardly have chosen such amateurish and immature conspirators, and in any case, as we have seen, only one of the conspirators actually favoured a Greater Serbia, the others being

---

183 Ibid., p. 349.
184 Clark, *The Sleepwalkers*, p. 454; Zametica, *Folly and Malice*, pp. 556–8.

supporters of a Yugoslavia in which Serbia would be just one component. In addition, at the end of June, the government was just four days into an election campaign, not an ideal time to take on the risk of war with her larger neighbour.

It appears that Serbia had given informal warnings to Vienna of the likely dangers to the archduke if he visited Sarajevo, but these were of a desultory and general kind, since the Serbian government had no detailed knowledge of what was afoot. But in any case, it was difficult for a foreign government, not on the best terms with Austria, to warn against a visit by a member of her royal family in her own territory. According to Grey, one of the assassins who had been arrested 'had already been regarded as an undesirable by Serbia: but the Serbian Government had then been informed by Austria that he was harmless and had been warned that he was under Austrian protection'.[185] It was not, however, suggested, even by Austria, that the Serbian government approved of the plot or assisted in its preparation. The most that the Serbian government could be accused of was negligence in not controlling its extremists. It was also at fault in not instituting an immediate investigation into the assassination. Still, it did not require great foresight to appreciate that the archduke would be in some danger on Serb national day, 28 June. If the Prince of Wales had decided to visit Dublin in 1920 at the time of the Black and Tans, he too would have been taking a risk. But neither in Vienna nor in Sarajevo had the authorities taken the security precautions that would seem so obviously indicated.

Wiesner's report reached Vienna on 13 July. There was then a gap of ten days until Austria sent her demands, in effect an ultimatum, to Serbia, on 23 July with a forty-eight hour time limit demanding unconditional acceptance. When he had read the ultimatum on 20 July, Emperor Franz Joseph declared that a European war was 'certain' since it would be 'impossible' for Russia to put up with such an affront. The war minister, General Krobatin, was to declare in 1916 that Russian intervention was 'inevitable'. And Hoyos had on 15 July told the Anglophile academic Josef Redlich, 'If a world war breaks out, it is all the same to us.'[186]

The Wiesner telegram did not affect the situation, since the crucial decisions had already been taken in Vienna. Austria lacked the definite evidence she had hoped for to prove official Serb complicity in the assassination and the ultimatum was not supported by any evidence of complicity since there was none. But Austria still went ahead. For she had needed evidence not to decide whether to go to war with Serbia – that had already been decided

185 Grey, *Twenty-Five Years*, pp. 310, 312.
186 Zametica, *Folly and Malice*, p. 566.

– but to provide a justification for it. And the prime justification for the ultimatum was not the assassination itself but the danger which, in the Austrian view, Serbia posed to her empire. The ultimatum claimed that there had been 'a subversive movement in Serbia', meaning the so-called Black Hand, which had sought to detach Bosnia and Herzegovina from the empire. But the Black Hand was also hostile to the civilian government in Belgrade, which it wanted to bring down, as well as Austria. And, in any case, the committee of the Black Hand had turned down an attempt on the life of Franz Ferdinand on 14 June.[187] Princip was apparently aware of this but took no notice. Nor is there any evidence that Princip and his fellow conspirators were members of the Black Hand, which barred minors and was no longer recruiting members; and while the Black Hand favoured a Greater Serbia, six of the seven conspirators, as we have seen, wanted to create a union of the South Slavs, a Yugoslavia.[188]

The ultimatum required the Serbian government to publish an official declaration condemning propaganda against Austria–Hungary, and suppress all organisations disseminating such propaganda, in particular the Narodna Odbrana (People's Defence), an organisation founded after the annexation in 1908 which sponsored paramilitary activities and was also alleged to have been involved in the assassination. Serbia was in addition required: to 'suppress any publication which fosters hatred of, and contempt for the Austro-Hungarian monarchy, and whose general tendency is directed against the latter's territorial integrity', a demand which Serbia regarded as an interference with constitutionally guaranteed freedom of the press; to remove from military service the names of those supplied by Austria whom Austria regarded as having been 'guilty of propaganda' against her; to accept the collaboration of Austrian officials 'for the suppression of the subversive movement directed against the territorial integrity of the Monarchy'; and to undertake, together with Austrian delegates, judicial proceedings against accessories to the assassination plot. These last two demands were hardly consistent with the maintenance of Serbian sovereignty. Even if the ultimatum had been accepted, the Austrian minister in Belgrade was instructed to break off relations. But it was not intended to be accepted. As Berchtold's wife related in October 1914, 'poor Leopold could not sleep on the day he wrote his ultimatum to the Serbs, as he was so worried that they would accept it. Several times in the night he had got up and altered or added some clause, to reduce this risk.' In the unlikely event of acceptance of the ultimatum,

---

187 M. S. Anderson, *The Eastern Question 1774–1923: A Study in International Relations*, Macmillan, 1966, p. 306.
188 Zametica, *Folly and Malice*, p. 354.

Berchtold would so 'harry and injure Serbia that, in the end, she gave Austria pretext for invading her'.[189]

Serbia agreed to publish the required official declaration as dictated from Vienna, a humiliation. She also offered to alter her constitution so as to punish those responsible for publications 'whose general tendency is directed against the territorial integrity of Austria–Hungary'. She agreed to supress the Narodna Odbrana, even though this violated her constitution which guaranteed freedom of association and even though she claimed there had been no evidence of criminal acts on its part. She agreed to remove from military service officers found guilty of actions directed against Austria's territorial integrity. She even agreed to the collaboration of Austrian officials on her territory, provided that it was in conformity 'with the principle of international law, with criminal procedure and with good neighbourly relations'. But she could not accept participation by Austrian officials and police in the inquiry of those implicated in the assassination plot, 'as it would be a violation of the Constitution and of the law of criminal procedure'. Perhaps Serbia was as fearful of what might be found concerning the complicity of officials in the assassination, as of a breach of her sovereignty. Nevertheless, even on this, Serbia made a qualified acceptance, declaring that she was willing to accept 'every cooperation which does not run counter to international law and criminal law, as well as to the friendly and neighbourly relations', a response which the Austrians declared was too vague. Finally, Serbia offered to refer the whole question to the International Tribunal at The Hague or the great powers. She had done the same at the time of the annexation in 1908 and at the time of the forged documents. This 'does not suggest a guilty conscience on its own part or even a desire to shield any of its own guilty subjects'.[190] On both occasions, Vienna had refused to accept the jurisdiction of The Hague.

On 24 July, Grey had told the British chargé d'affaires in Belgrade to urge Serbia to yield as much as possible to the ultimatum. He now believed that the Serbs had complied with this advice. The Serbian response, Grey believed, 'went further than we had ventured to hope in the way of submission'. He told the Austrian ambassador on 27 July that 'the Serbian reply already involved the greatest humiliation to Serbia that I had ever seen a country undergo, and it was very disappointing to me that the reply was treated by the Austrian Government as if it were as unsatisfactory as a blank negative'.[191] Writing to the British ambassador in Berlin on the same day, he declared:

---

189 Ibid., pp. 567, 592.
190 Schmitt, 'July 1914', p. 185; Seton-Watson, *Sarajevo*, p. 133.
191 Gooch and Temperley, eds, *British Documents*, vol. 11, p. 188.

If Austria put the Serbian reply aside as being worth nothing and marched into Serbia, it meant that she was determined to crush Serbia at all costs, being reckless of the consequences that might be involved. Serbian reply should at least be treated as a basis for discussion and pause.

Germany should, Grey believed, urge this in Vienna. The kaiser took a similar view, declaring, 'This is more than one could have expected!' 'With it every reason for war disappears ... I am convinced that on the whole the wishes of the Dual Monarchy have been acceded to. The few reservations which Serbia makes in regard to individual points can, in my opinion, be cleared up by negotiation.' The kaiser nevertheless proposed that Austria occupy Belgrade to ensure that Serbia kept her commitments. Bethmann, like the kaiser, believed that 'the Serbian reply had in fact agreed to the Austrian wishes except on unimportant points'.[192] Nevertheless, the Austrian ambassador was instructed to leave Belgrade, and on 28 July, Austria declared war on Serbia, the first time a great power in Europe had been involved in war on the Continent since 1871. On the same day, Bethmann had told his ambassador in Vienna that he must

> carefully avoid giving the impression that we wish to hold Austria back. It is solely a question of finding a method which will make possible the accomplishment of Austria's purpose of cutting the vital nerve of Great Serbian propaganda without at the same time unchaining a world war, and in the end, *if this is unavoidable*, of improving as far as possible the conditions under which it is to be waged.[193]

On 29 July, Austria bombed Belgrade from the Danube, at a time when mediation proposals were still in play, making a peaceful solution to the crisis almost impossible. The short time limit fixed by the ultimatum meant that it was extremely difficult to place the dispute between Austria and Serbia on an international footing so as to devise a peaceful solution.

In 1928, an American historian, Bernadotte Schmitt, interviewed some of those involved in the Sarajevo crisis. One of those he interviewed was Wiesner. Schmitt suggested that Austria, instead of breaking off relations, could have put Serbia to the test of living up to her commitments with the support of the powers. Wiesner admitted, with the benefit of hindsight, that this might have proved a better course.[194]

---

192 Schmitt, 'July 1914', pp. 185, 191.
193 Sidney B. Fay, 'New Light on the Origins of the World War, II. Berlin and Vienna, July 29 to 31', *American Historical Review*, 1920, p. 42. Emphasis added.
194 Schmitt, *Interviewing the Authors of the War*, p. 25.

BRITAIN AND THE CONTINENT

'It is not to be supposed', a correspondent in the *Manchester Guardian* wrote on 29 June, the day after the assassination, 'that the death of the Archduke Francis Ferdinand will have any immediate or salient effect on the politics of Europe.' That was probably the general opinion in Britain, which thirty-seven days later was to declare war on Germany. But Grey had been one of very few to appreciate that the assassination could lead to a dangerous escalation. On 8 July, well before the presentation of the Austrian ultimatum, he told the Russian ambassador of his thoughts. The ambassador reported, 'The idea that this terrible crime might unexpectedly produce a general war with all its attendant catastrophes after all the great efforts in recent years to avoid it and after things on the whole got back onto an even keel again – "made his [Grey's] hair stand on end".'[195] But until the actual presentation of the ultimatum on 23 July, nearly a month after the assassination, it was difficult to see what diplomacy could achieve. Grey appreciated that Austria might well take military action against Serbia but assumed that she would state her case publicly beforehand, based on what she had discovered at the trial of the assassins. He told the German ambassador on 20 July that it would be easier to ensure moderation if Austria could produce a strong justification for military action and keep her demands upon Serbia within reasonable limits.

The ultimatum, however, was the first sign to those outside the inner circles in Austria and Germany that the crisis could threaten the wider peace of Europe. Sazonov, the Russian foreign minister, declared when he heard of the ultimatum, '*C'est la guerre Européenne*.'[196] When Grey saw it, he told the Austrian ambassador that it was 'the most formidable document that was ever addressed from one state to another'.[197] It was at this point that the European crisis came before the Cabinet, at an afternoon meeting on 24 July. In the morning, the Buckingham Palace Conference had broken down, and it seemed as if there was danger of civil war in Ulster. Indeed, the day before the Cabinet meeting, on 23 July, *The Times* had written of 'the great crises in the history of the British race'. It was referring to Ireland, not the possibility of Britain being involved in war; and indeed, much of the discussion at the Cabinet meeting was about Ulster. The atmosphere has been graphically described by Winston Churchill, First Lord of the Admiralty.

---

195 Otte, *July Crisis*, p. 146.
196 James Joll, '1914: The Unspoken Assumptions: An Inaugural Lecture delivered 25 April 1968', Weidenfeld & Nicolson, 1968, pp. 6–7; Luigi Albertini, *The Origins of the War of 1914*, Oxford University Press, 1965, vol. 2, p. 290.
197 National Archives, FO 371/2158, f. 97.

The discussion had reached its inconclusive end, and the Cabinet was about to separate, when the quiet grave tones of Sir Edward Grey's voice were heard reading a document which had just been brought to him from the Foreign Office. It was the Austrian note to Serbia. He had been reading or speaking for several minutes before I could disengage my mind from the tedious and bewildering debate which had just closed. We were all very tired, but gradually as the phrases and sentences followed one another, impressions of a wholly different character began to form in my mind. This note was clearly an ultimatum, but it was an ultimatum such as had never been penned in modern times. As the reading proceeded it seemed absolutely impossible that any State in the world could accept it, or that any acceptance, however abject, would satisfy the aggressor. The parishes of Fermanagh and Tyrone faded back into the mists and squalls of Ireland, and a strange light began immediately but by perceptible gradations, to fall and grow upon the map of Europe.[198]

Nevertheless, it did not at first seem that Britain need be involved in an obscure squabble in the Balkans; and that evening, Asquith wrote a letter to his confidante Venetia Stanley, mainly about Ulster – a 'cause of blackness', as he put it. Only towards the end of the letter did he mention 'the European situation, which is about as bad as it can possibly be. Austria has sent a bullying and humiliating Ultimatum to Servia [sic], who cannot possibly comply with it, and demanded an answer within forty-eight hours – failing which she will march'. He then foresaw the likely consequences.

This means, almost inevitably, that Russia will come on the scene in defence of Servia, & in defiance of Austria; and, if so, it is difficult both for Germany & France to refrain from lending a hand to one side or the other. So that we are within measurable or imaginable distance of a real Armageddon, which would dwarf the Ulster & Nationalist Volunteers to their true proportion.

But he concluded, 'Happily there seems to be no reason why we should be anything more than spectators, but it is a blood-curdling prospect – is it not?'[199] As for Grey, he did not allow the Serbian ultimatum to interrupt his planned weekend fishing break in Hampshire. When told by the Foreign Office that Serbia had accepted most of the demands in the ultimatum, he felt relieved.

---

198 Churchill, *World Crisis*, vol. 1, p. 193.
199 Brock, ed., *Letters to Venetia Stanley*, pp. 122–3.

Britain seemed in no way involved in the quarrel between Austria and Serbia. Opposition newspapers, sympathetic to the Unionists, tended to regard the ultimatum as excessive, but the Liberal press tended to be more pro-Austrian, no doubt because that would excuse Britain from being involved. The *Manchester Guardian* summed up Liberal opinion on 30 July 1914, just five days before Britain declared war:

> We wish Servia no ill; we are anxious for the peace of Europe. But Englishmen are not the guardians of Servian well-being, or even of the peace of Europe. Their first duty is to England and to the peace of England. Let us for a moment drop solicitude for Europe and think of ourselves. We ought to feel ourselves out of danger, for, whichever way the quarrel between Austria and Servia were settled, it would not make a scrap of difference to England.

And it concluded, 'We care as little for Belgrade as Belgrade does for Manchester.' In any case, 'if we had to choose foreign clients we should prefer others than the Servians and another cause than that of regicide with impunity'. On 1 August, it expressed the wish that Serbia could be towed into the middle of the ocean and sunk. Hardly anyone believed that Britain should fight over a quarrel in the Balkans. Had Austria's war with Serbia been localised, Britain would certainly not have intervened. The government hoped, therefore, that the Concert of Europe would contain the Balkans crisis as it seemed to have done in 1908–09 and 1912–13.

But events were moving rapidly. On 26 July, a Sunday, Churchill prevented the fleet from dispersing. From the 27th, the Cabinet met daily to discuss the European situation, and, on occasion, twice daily. Grey appreciated that this crisis would be more difficult to resolve than that following the Balkan wars, since at least one great power, Austria–Hungary, was involved, and very possibly a second, Russia. He did not believe that Russia would stand aside as she had done in 1908–09. But even if Russia intervened, as Grey was to tell the British ambassador in Paris, that would not necessarily involve Britain. 'It would then be a question of the supremacy of Teuton or Slav – a struggle for supremacy in the Balkans; and our idea had always been to avoid being drawn into a war over a Balkan question.'[200] Difficulties would only arise if Germany and France became involved. Even so, the position would be different from the Moroccan crises since Morocco was a French interest that had been the subject of a specific agreement between France and Britain. That was not the case with the Balkans. Nevertheless, Britain

---

200 Gooch and Temperley, eds, *British Documents*, vol. 11, p. 283.

could not allow France to be crushed or Germany to become the hegemonic power in Europe.

By contrast with the crisis after the Balkan wars, therefore, the Sarajevo assassination called into question the balance of power between the major powers. So it was far more dangerous. Nevertheless, Grey pursued the same course as he had done after the First Balkan War. On 26 July, he proposed a conference between the French, German and Italian ambassadors and himself. Significantly, he did not include Britain's entente partner, Russia. His aim was to secure German cooperation, not, as some in Germany were to believe, to encircle her. The members of the ambassadors' meetings of 1912–13 were still available, and Grey proposed that there be an ambassadors' conference, not necessarily in London, and not necessarily under his chairmanship. They should propose to Austria, Serbia and Russia that all military activities, including mobilisation, be suspended pending the outcome of the conference. Russia responded that she would prefer direct talks with Austria; but, if that were rejected, she would accept the conference proposal. France also accepted it. But in Vienna, Hoyos said, 'Nonsense – no negotiations, but rather war!' Berchtold expressed his fear to Franz Joseph that 'the Powers of the Triple Entente might yet make another attempt to achieve a peaceful settlement of the conflict unless a clear situation is created by a declaration of war'.[201] On 28 July, Berchtold told the British ambassador that the proposal had come too late as Austria had already declared war on Serbia. But it seemed for a time as if Germany might accept, Grey having told the German ambassador that it represented the only chance for peace. On the evening of the 27 July, however, the German foreign minister rejected it, saying that it 'would practically amount to a court of arbitration', although what in fact Grey was proposing was, as he was to tell the British ambassador in Berlin on 28 July, 'a private and informal discussion to ascertain what suggestions could be made for a settlement. No suggestion would be put forward that had not previously been ascertained to be acceptable to Austria and Russia.' The French ambassador in Berlin berated the German foreign minister, who, incredibly, had not yet read the Serbian response to the Austrian ultimatum, 'I beg of you in the name of humanity, do not assume for your person part of the responsibility for the catastrophe which you are letting happen.'[202]

Grey's policy, the policy he had followed after the First Balkan War, could only have worked if, as then, Germany had worked in cooperation with him. But she did not. Her aim instead was to ensure that Austria could settle her quarrel with Serbia without the other powers intervening. The dispute,

201 Zametica, Folly and Malice, p. 628.
202 Otte, July Crisis, p. 325.

Germany believed, was one between Austria and Serbia alone. In order to avoid a wider war, Russia should show restraint and Britain should press Russia to do so. The onus, therefore, would be on Russia to allow Serbia, a victim of aggression, to be dealt with as Austria pleased – in other words, to allow Austria a free hand. But Russia took the view that her essential interests were involved in the Balkans and was not prepared to countenance Austrian domination of Serbia. Grey could only press Russia to show restraint were Germany to press her ally Austria to show similar restraint. But the blank cheque prevented Germany from doing so.

Nevertheless, Grey, unaware of course of the blank cheque, continued desperately to seek to localise the war. 'European peace', he was to write in his memoirs twenty-five years later,

> had weathered worse storms than any that now were visible above the horizon. I had been more than eight years at the Foreign Office, in the centre of all the troubles; it was natural to hope, even to expect, that the same methods which had preserved peace hitherto, when it had been threatened, would preserve it still.[203]

Grey six times proposed either a conference or mediation, and also asked Germany, if she rejected these proposals, herself to suggest some alternative. On each occasion, he was rebuffed or his proposal was accepted with conditions entailing Russia's non-participation. Grey comments in his memoirs that 'although the suggestion of settling [the crisis] by the same machinery as in 1912 was made, it was dismissed peremptorily by Germany and Austria'.[204] Germany feared that in a conference, as at Algeciras in 1906, she would be Austria's only defender, and the powers would gang up against her. But Grey, as we have seen, had not taken the entente side on every issue at the London meetings of 1913. He had been perfectly prepared to sacrifice entente needs to the overall requirement of peace, as when he opposed Montenegro in Scutari and opposed Serb demands on Albania. Had there been a conference, Grey would have strained every nerve to preserve peace and done all that he could to give Austria satisfaction, short of dismembering Serbia. Though he felt 'that Serbia was being dealt with more harshly than was just', nevertheless 'it was better that Serbia should give way than that European peace should be broken'.[205] He produced a formula that the powers would 'examine how Serbia can fully satisfy Austria without impairing Serbia's sovereign rights or independence'.

---

203 Grey, *Twenty-Five Years*, vol. 1, p. 302.
204 Ibid., vol. 1, p. 267.
205 Ibid., vol. 1, p. 310.

He would have insisted that Serbia make those concessions, so long as her territorial integrity or independence were not affected. He was prepared to go very far in achieving a settlement on Austrian and German terms, provided only that it was negotiated as with the 1913 Treaty of London. He was in fact offering Germany 'a diplomatic triumph on a silver salver'.[206] The Russians might also have been restrained in supporting Serbia, since they could hardly have condoned regicide – the tsar's grandfather had himself been assassinated in 1881 by terrorists. But Germany's rejection of the conference proposal took from Grey's hands the lever with which he could have persuaded Russia not to mobilise. 'Had such a conference taken place,' Churchill was later to write, 'there would have been no war. Mere acceptance of the principle of a conference of the Central Powers would have instantly relieved the tension.'[207] Grey shared that view. After the war, he told the Liberal journalist J. A. Spender:

> As to the War Guilt – I think the crucial point was when Germany allowed Austria to refuse a Conference after the Serbian reply – a document which the Kaiser had annotated to the effect that there was now no cause for war. Russia had agreed to a Conference & if Austria had also agreed there would have been no general Russian mobilisation; France and we should have had a strong card in our hands with which to control Russia if she needed to be controlled.[208]

It is difficult to argue with this verdict. With the conference proposal rejected, Grey declared that he would accept any proposal for peaceful mediation offered by Austria or Germany. He more than once invited Germany to make proposals of her own. But there was no response. Russia offered to put the dispute to the International Court of Arbitration at The Hague, but Austria refused.[209] According to Arthur Murray, Grey's parliamentary private secretary, the German ambassador had admitted to Grey on 24 June that Russia was not contemplating war against Germany.[210] It is difficult to see what Austria and Germany could have lost by agreeing to a conference or submitting claims to arbitration. Had the conference failed, they would then have been in a good position to use force against Serbia, with the support of the powers. But the consequence of rejecting the conference proposal was to condemn millions to death and destroy the Concert of Europe. In 1915, Grey asked, 'Is there one candid soul in Germany and Austria–Hungary who,

---

206 Otte, *Statesman of Europe*, p. 521.
207 Churchill, *World Crisis*, vol. 1, p. 201.
208 Spender Papers, Add. MSS. 46, 389, f. 93–4, 5 September 1928.
209 Seton-Watson, *Sarajevo*, p. 133.
210 Letter from Arthur Murray to *The Times*, 1 April 1936.

looking back on the past year, does not regret that neither the British nor the Russian proposal [for arbitration at The Hague] was accepted?'[211]

Grey's error – a natural one perhaps – was to assume that, as in 1912–13, Germany would work for peace by exercising restraint upon Austria–Hungary. In his interview with the American historian Bernadotte Schmitt in 1928, Grey was full of self-reproach and believed that it would have been better to have approached Austria directly rather than through Germany. But that would probably have made little difference, since Austria had been committed with German support to a military solution ever since the murder of the archduke. She could only have been restrained if Germany had definitely and authoritatively withdrawn her support; and of that there was no sign. Grey's view was that if Germany, an ally, was unable to restrain Austria, he would be unlikely himself to succeed.

Russia was not prepared to back down as she had in 1908–09. She could not allow Serbia to be crushed. On 30 July, she mobilised to prevent further military action by Austria against Serbia. Her General Staff had planned, in case of war, to abandon her Polish salient including Warsaw as indefensible. She was only to make her disastrous incursion into East Prussia later in 1914 to aid her allies on the western front, deciding at the last minute to try to hold Warsaw after all. This was proof that she had no intentions, contrary to what some in Berlin believed, of attacking Germany in 1914. Her military preparations were in fact far behind those of Germany.[212] But Russian mobilisation transferred the quarrel from one between Austria and Serbia to one between Russia and Germany and heralded a wider war. Although Russia had not attacked Austria and although the tsar promised that he would not march against Germany if negotiations were begun, and for as long as they continued, Germany in response sent an ultimatum demanding that the decision to mobilise be reversed. This destroyed hopes of avoiding a Continental war. When the German ultimatum was refused, she declared war on Russia on 1 August. Admiral von Müller congratulated the kaiser and Bethmann, 'The government has succeeded very well in making us appear as the attacked.'[213] Germany then asked France to give a promise of neutrality, which meant abandoning her alliance with Russia. Had France agreed, she would have been asked to surrender her two border forts at Toul and Verdun as security for her neutrality. But France did not agree and on 3 August, Germany declared war on her also. As the German ambassador to Paris took his leave of the French Prime Minister, after handing him the declaration

---

211 Edward Grey, *Sir Edward Grey's Reply to Dr von Bethmann Hollweg*, T. Fisher Unwin, 1915, p. 12.
212 Seton-Watson, *Sarajevo*, p. 218.
213 Röhl, 'Goodbye to all that (again)?', p. 160.

of war, he presented him with his visiting card on the back of which he had written, '*C'est la suicide de l'Europe*.'[214]

THE NEUTRALITY OF BELGIUM

The issue facing the British government was now no longer whether the war could be localised but whether the country should take part in it. Britain seemed to have a real choice. She was in no fear of invasion. In Britain, alone of the states involved, the decision lay with the Cabinet and Parliament. France, the only other parliamentary state amongst the combatants, had been faced with an ultimatum which no French government could possibly have accepted. The Cabinet was deeply divided on intervention. The majority were opposed. On 29 July, when it was becoming clear that Grey's efforts at mediation would not succeed, the Cabinet had to decide what do about the crisis. Just five ministers favoured intervention – Asquith, Grey, the Lord Chancellor Haldane, the India Secretary Crewe and the First Lord of the Admiralty Churchill. They argued that Britain was under an obligation to support France. The majority did not agree. At this Cabinet, for the first time, Belgium was discussed and it was agreed that, as Asquith was to tell the king, the preservation of Belgian neutrality was 'one of policy rather than of legal obligation'.[215] Otherwise, the Cabinet, in the words of Burns, who was to resign when Britain declared war, 'decided not to decide'.[216] It was to take the German invasion of Belgium to transform Liberal opinion.

Germany's military plan required her to invade the neutral countries of Luxembourg and Belgium. In December 1912, Moltke, the German chief of staff, had told Bethmann that a speedy decision could be hoped for by an offensive against France. But to achieve that quick victory, 'it will be necessary to violate Belgian territory'. Moltke accepted that this could mean British intervention, 'This way we will face the English Expeditionary Corps.'[217] In Bethmann's presence, Moltke told the kaiser that 'our plan of deployment against France is based, as is well known, on our advance through Belgium'.[218] In 1913, Moltke had written in a memorandum:

Should we renounce the march through Belgium, in case England promises neutrality? That would be very dangerous, for it is quite uncertain

214 Otte, *July Crisis*, p. 489.
215 Otte, *Statesman of Europe*, p. 513.
216 Quoted in Annika Mombauer, 'Sir Edward Grey, Germany and the Outbreak of the First World War', *International History Review*, 2016, p. 309.
217 Quoted in Annika Mombauer, 'Of War Plans and War Guilt: The Debate Surrounding the Schlieffen Plan', *Journal of Strategic Studies*, 2005, p. 870.
218 Röhl, 'Admiral von Müller', p. 665.

whether England would keep her promise; but we should give up the only chance of a quick and decisive victory, which we need. Only if England went with us, would a renunciation of the march through Belgium be possible. That however is inconceivable.[219]

British intervention did not worry Germany since Britain's army was so small. Indeed, the German admiralty was told in August not to risk its vessels by trying to stop the transfer of the four divisions of the British Expeditionary Force to the Continent.[220]

Bethmann, then, knew that the German war plan involved the violation of Belgian neutrality and that it could well bring Britain into the conflict. He sought British neutrality primarily because that might deter Russia or France from war, not because he was fearful of the British Army.[221] On 29 July, he made a specific bid for British neutrality, offering to guarantee the territorial integrity of both France and Belgium. He did not offer to guarantee the French colonies, nor, more importantly, the neutrality of Belgium. Germany would, Bethmann declared, respect the 'integrity and neutrality' of the Netherlands, as indeed she did, but only the 'integrity' of Belgium – a clear pointer to her policy five days later. Indeed, Bethmann's bid for British neutrality made sense only if he was already convinced that a European war was likely. On 6 August, two days after Britain had declared war on Germany, Asquith told the Commons that for Britain to have accepted neutrality on the basis proposed by Bethmann would have been contemptible. It would have meant that

> behind the back of France – they were not made a party to these communications – we should have given, if we had assented to that, a free licence to Germany to annex, in the event of a successful war, the whole of the extra European dominions and possessions of France. What did it mean as regards Belgium … We should have been obliged to say that, without her knowledge, we had bartered away to the Power threatening her our obligation to keep our plighted word … Yes, and what are we to get in return for the betrayal of our friends and the dishonour of our obligations? … A promise – nothing more; a promise as to what Germany would do in certain eventualities … given by a Power which was at that very moment announcing its intention to violate its own treaty and inviting us to do the same.[222]

---

219 Gerhard Ritter, *The Schlieffen Plan: Critique of a Myth*, Oswald Wolff, 1958, p. 69.
220 Ensor, *England*, p. 483.
221 Taylor, *Struggle for Mastery*, p. 525.
222 House of Commons Debates, 6 August 1914, vol. 65, col. 2076.

The German promise to respect British neutrality and independence, made at the very same time as she was violating the neutrality and independence of another power whose neutrality she had promised to respect, and whose violation she was inviting Britain to accept, was worth similarly little. 'There is something very crude & almost childlike about German diplomacy,' Asquith had written to Venetia Stanley on 30 July.[223] Grey was disgusted by the German proposal. His secretary reported that 'never before had he been seen in a white heat of passion'.[224]

In his speech to the Commons on 3 August, before the declaration of war, Grey did not mention the German proposal, claiming in his memoirs that he did not wish to incite prejudice against Germany when it seemed as if the issue of peace or war might still just be in the balance. But in replying to the British ambassador in Berlin to Bethmann's proposal on 30 July, he declared that, were France to lose her colonies, she 'could be so crushed as to lose her position as a Great Power, and become subordinate to German policy'.

> Altogether apart from that, it would be a disgrace for us to make this bargain with Germany at the expense of France, a disgrace from which the good name of this country would never recover. The Chancellor also in effect asks us to bargain away whatever obligation or interest we have as regards the neutrality of Belgium. We could not entertain that bargain either.

Grey then added what appears in retrospect as a deeply tragic coda in which he laid bare his hope for a new Concert of Europe if only the current crisis could be overcome. He told the ambassador that, after rejecting the German proposal for neutrality:

> You should add most earnestly that the one way of maintaining the good relations between England and Germany is that they should continue to work together to preserve the peace of Europe ... If the peace of Europe can be preserved and the present crisis safely passed, my own endeavour will be to promote some arrangement to which Germany could be a party, by which she could be assured that no aggressive or hostile policy would be pursued against her or her allies by France, Russia and ourselves, jointly or separately. I have desired this and worked for it as far as I could, through the last Balkan crisis, and, Germany having a corresponding object, our relations sensibly improved. The idea has hitherto been too Utopian to form

---

223 Brock, ed., *Letters to Venetia Stanley*, p. 136.
224 Robbins, *Grey*, p. 294.

the subject of definite proposals, but if this present crisis, so much more acute than any that Europe has gone through for generations, be safely passed, I am hopeful that the relief and reaction which will follow may make possible some more definite rapprochement between the Powers than has been possible hitherto.[225]

On 30 July, he wrote again to the ambassador saying that, at a conference, the four powers would tell Austria–Hungary 'that they would undertake to see that she obtained full satisfaction of her demands on Servia, provided that they did not impair Servian sovereignty and the integrity of Servian territory'. But if Germany rejected the conference, Grey was to tell the historian Harold Temperley in 1929, his policy to her was 'put up a conciliatory proposal in any form you like and we will support you'.[226] On 31 July 1914, he told the German ambassador:

If Germany could get any reasonable proposal put forward which made it clear that Germany and Austria were striving to preserve European peace, and that Russia and France would be unreasonable if they rejected it, I would support it at St Petersburg and Paris, and go the length of saying that if Russia and France would not accept it His Majesty's Government would have nothing more to do with the consequences; but otherwise I told the German Ambassador that if France became involved we should be drawn in.[227]

He also made it clear to Austria and Germany that if they rejected mediation, they would face a coalition of powers in Europe against them, though in fact he had no authority from the Cabinet for this statement. Indeed, on the same day that he wrote this letter, 31 July, Grey had a painful interview with the French ambassador in which he said that the Cabinet could not commit itself to support France and was indeed under no obligations towards France.

On 31 July, Grey enquired of France and Germany whether they would respect Belgian neutrality. France replied that she would. Germany gave no response, since her war plan relied on an invasion of Belgium to secure a rapid victory over France. Before that strategy had been adopted, she had aimed at a defensive war in the west and an attack on Russia. The kaiser still hankered after such an approach. Had such a plan been retained, there

---

225 Otte, *Statesman of Europe*, pp. 519–20.
226 Spender Papers, Add. MSS. 46,386, f. 79.
227 Gooch and Temperley, eds, *British Documents*, vol. 11, nos 303, 304.

would have been no invasion of Belgium and Britain might well not have been involved in the war.

On 1 August, a further Cabinet meeting was held. But it was as inconclusive as that of 29 July, although it was agreed that a wholesale invasion of Belgium – that is, of the entire country – would be a *casus belli*. Grey was authorised to warn the German ambassador that it would be difficult to restrain public feeling were any power to violate Belgian neutrality. But the non-interventionists now had an escape route. The Cabinet had little doubt that the German Army would in fact invade France through Belgium. But some believed that Germany would only invade a narrow corner of Belgium, south and east of the Sambre-Meuse line. That had been the view of Brigadier Henry Wilson, Director of Military Operations at the War Office, in August 1911. He had told Asquith and other members of the Committee of Imperial Defence that German intervention would in fact be confined to the south-east corner. In that case, it was possible that Belgium would offer only token resistance to the invasion and would not actually seek Britain's aid as a guarantor power. Britain could hardly be expected to defend Belgian neutrality if the Belgians themselves were not prepared to defend it.

On 2 August, Germany invaded Luxembourg, whose neutrality she was committed to respect by the Treaty of London of 1867, signed by Prussia whose obligations Germany had inherited. This made invasion of Belgium more likely, since the German Army could not leave Luxembourg without entering Belgian territory except via a narrow bottleneck into France. On that day, 2 August, a Sunday, the Cabinet held two meetings. At the first meeting, Asquith laid out the principles which should guide British policy. Britain, he believed, had no obligations of any kind to France or Russia but had a 'long-standing & intimate friendship with France'. In addition, it was 'against British interests that France shd. be wiped out as a Great Power'; nor should Germany be allowed 'to use the Channel as a hostile base'. That was to cause no problems to Germany since the Channel formed no part of her war plans. But in addition, Britain had 'obligations to Belgium to prevent her being utilised & absorbed by Germany'.[228] For his part, Grey argued that Britain had towards France 'both moral obligations of honour and substantial obligations of policy'. 'We have', he told the Cabinet with some emotion, 'led France to rely upon us, and unless we support her in her agony, I cannot continue at the Foreign Office.'[229] Herbert Samuel, the Postmaster General, wrote to his wife that Grey 'was outraged by the way in which Germany and Austria have played with the most vital interests of civilisation, have put

---

228 Brock, ed., *Letters to Venetia Stanley*, p. 146.
229 George Riddell, *Lord Riddell's War Diary*, Ivor Nicholson & Watson, 1933, p. 6.

aside all attempts at accommodation made by himself and others and, while continuing to negotiate, have marched steadily to war'.[230] It appears that Harcourt, the Colonial Secretary and a non-interventionist, then passed a note to Lloyd George, 'Speak for us. Grey wishes to go to war without the violation of Belgium.'[231] But there was no majority for intervention either in the Cabinet or amongst MPs. Had Asquith and Grey pressed for war at this stage, they would have faced opposition from a majority of the Cabinet. Without the invasion of Belgium, the Liberal Cabinet would have split. For Grey, so Asquith wrote to Venetia Stanley, 'would never consent to non-intervention & I shall not separate myself from him'.[232] Both Asquith and Grey would, therefore, have resigned. So would Churchill, and probably Haldane, possibly others also. Lloyd George's position, however, was mysterious. Although he seemed to be siding with the non-interventionists, it is very possible that he was confident that opinion would eventually change, and was therefore biding his time until his pacifistic support base in the Liberal Party came round to support for intervention.[233] On 1 August, he had passed a note to Churchill, the most belligerent of the interventionists, 'If patience prevails and you do not press us too hard we might come together.'[234] As it was, the Cabinet at its two meetings on 2 August compromised by deciding to intervene if Germany bombarded the French Channel coast. That represented an attempt by the anti-war ministers, except for Burns, who dissented even from this, to escape from war rather than to commit themselves to it. The German embassy responded with an assurance 'that she will not attack France by sea in the north, or make any warlike use of the sea coast of Belgium or Holland' if Britain remained neutral 'for the time being'.[235] She was, in any case, unlikely to attack a coast so far from her bases. But the Cabinet also agreed that, in the words of Herbert Samuel to his wife:

> We should be justified in joining the war … for the maintenance of the independence of Belgium, which we were bound by treaty to protect and which again we could not afford to see subordinated by Germany. But I held we were not [obliged] to carry England into war for the sake of our good will from France or for the sake of maintaining the strength of France and Russia against that of Germany and Austria. This opinion is shared by a majority of the Cabinet.[236]

---

230 Otte, *Statesman of Europe*, p. 530.
231 Gilbert, 'Lloyd George in 1911 and 1914', p. 880.
232 Brock, ed., *Letters to Venetia Stanley*, p. 146.
233 Gilbert, 'Lloyd George in 1911 and 1914', p. 881.
234 Otte, *Statesman of Europe*, p. 525.
235 Brock, ed., *Letters to Venetia Stanley*, p. 147.
236 Gilbert, 'Lloyd George in 1911 and 1914', p. 881.

The Cabinet further decided that on the next day, Monday 3 August, Grey should tell Parliament, without using the term 'casus belli', 'that a substantial violation of the neutrality of that country [Belgium] would place us in the situation contemplated as possible by Mr Gladstone in 1870 when interference with Belgian independence was held to compel us to take action'.

At the 3 August meeting, Asquith announced the resignation of four Cabinet ministers – Burns, Lord Morley, the First Commissioner of Works Lord Beauchamp and the Attorney General Sir John Simon. Beauchamp and Simon were later to withdraw their resignations. Burns wrote presciently in his diary that day that the war 'will end the Hohenzollerns [the German ruling house], terminate Junkerdom, finish the Monarchy and inaugurate a Federal German Republic – and may lead to a United States of Europe with Britain the last in the hegemony of emancipated European states' – though it was to take a Second World War to fulfil all of his predictions.[237]

Lloyd George now declared that 'events' were now 'too strong for him', although he perhaps knew that Britain would in due cause have no alternative but to intervene.[238] His mistress Frances Stevenson was later to write in her autobiography that she had prayed on Sunday 2 August that the invasion of Belgium would give Lloyd George 'a heaven-sent excuse for supporting a declaration of war'.[239] Grey's parliamentary private secretary was later to write, 'The invasion of Belgium – and that event alone – brought Lloyd George into the First World War against Germany.'[240] On 3 August, Churchill on his own initiative ordered the fleet to be mobilised, receiving retrospective endorsement from the Prime Minister. On the evening of 2 August, the Foreign Office had received news of the German ultimatum to Belgium with its demand that her troops be allowed through the country to attack France. At the Cabinet meeting on 3 August, ministers had in front of them a request from the king of the Belgians for assistance in defending his country. It was clear, then, that Belgium would resist the passage of German troops on her territory. That evening, there were large cheering crowds outside Buckingham Palace calling for war. Asquith was reminded of Walpole's remark: 'Now they are ringing their bells; in a few weeks they'll be wringing their hands.'[241]

On the morning of 4 August, German forces invaded Belgium, the Belgian government having rejected the German ultimatum. Asquith told Venetia that the invasion of Belgium 'simplifies matters so we sent the Germans an

237 Otte, *July Crisis*, p. 457.
238 Williamson, *Politics of Grand Strategy*, p. 357.
239 Frances Stevenson, *The Years that are Past*, Hutchinson, 1967, pp. 73–4.
240 *Manchester Guardian*, 30 November 1958.
241 Brock, ed., *Letters to Venetia Stanley*, p. 148.

ultimatum to expire at midnight'.[242] When the German government refused to give the required undertaking, Britain declared war. This would have been no surprise to Moltke, Chief of the German General Staff, who predicted to his adjutant in the early hours of 31 July, shortly before Germany mobilised, that 'this war will turn into a world war in which England will also intervene. Only few can have an idea of the extent, the duration and the outcome of this war. Nobody today can have a notion of how it is all going to end.'[243] On 4 August, Bethmann made his celebrated remark to the British ambassador in Berlin that Britain was going to war 'just for a word "neutrality" – a word which in wartime had so often been disregarded – just for a scrap of paper' – whether Bethmann actually used that phrase has been disputed, but the probability is that he did.[244] The British ambassador replied to Bethmann that 'it was part of the tragedy which saw the two nations fall apart just at the moment when the relations between them had been more friendly and cordial than they had been for years'.[245] It 'all happened in such a short time', Margot Asquith, the Prime Minister's wife, wrote in her diary on 4 August. 'On 30 July everyone was talking of Ireland. The cry of "Civil war! Civil war!" to which *The Times* and the Tories treated us every day has been stilled in five days.'[246]

By a convention of 1831, confirmed by Article 7 of the 1839 Treaty of London, Belgium was recognised as 'an independent and perpetually neutral State' by all the major European powers – Britain, Austria, France, Russia and Prussia (Germany was not then united but would inherit Prussia's obligations). The signatories were committed collectively to defend that neutrality. In 1870, at the time of the Franco-Prussian War, Gladstone had asked both France and Prussia whether they would respect Belgian neutrality. Both had said that they would. In 1887, Bismarck had guaranteed Belgian neutrality during an international crisis, while France ironically had not done so, and Britain had wavered. As late as 28 April 1914, the German foreign minister, Jagow, had told the Reichstag that 'Belgian neutrality is provided for by international conventions, and Germany is determined to respect those conventions'.[247] Speaking in the Reichstag on 11 August, Bethmann was to admit that Germany was in breach of international law but declared that 'we are now in a state of necessity, and necessity knows no law'.

In 1870, Gladstone had defended Britain's interest in the neutrality of

242 Ibid., p. 150.
243 Mombauer, 'A Reluctant Military Leader?', p. 437.
244 See the meticulous examination in T. G. Otte, 'A "German Paperchase": The "Scrap of Paper" Controversy and the Problem of Myth and Memory in International History', *Diplomacy and Statecraft*, 2007, pp. 53–87.
245 Gooch and Temperley, eds, *British Documents*, vol. 11, p. 350.
246 Michael and Eleanor Brock, eds, *Margot Asquith's Great War Diary*, Oxford University Press, 2014, pp. 13–14.
247 Foreign Office, *Neutrality of Belgium*, HMSO, 1920, p. 18.

Belgium in the House of Commons, in words much quoted in 1914. There were, he said, 'common interests against the unmeasured aggrandisement of any Power whatever', But there was more than that.

> We have an interest in the independence of Belgium which is wider than that which we may have in the literal operation of the guarantee. It is found in the answer to the question whether, under the circumstances of the case, this country, endowed as it is with influence and power, would quietly stand by and witness the perpetration of the direst crime that ever stained the pages of history, and thus become participators in the sin.[248]

The guarantee of Belgium was, however, a collective one and, although every signatory had the legal right to enforce it, there was no legal obligation for any single power to do so. The matter was, as the Cabinet had recognised, one of policy not obligation. But in practice, no British government could conceivably have accepted the breach of Belgian neutrality.

The twentieth and twenty-first centuries have seen numerous atrocities, and they have perhaps so dulled sensibilities that it is difficult to understand fully the sense of moral outrage caused by the invasion of Belgium. Apart from the breach of a treaty, the invasion was an act of unprovoked aggression against a small power, and a small power which, by contrast with Serbia, was in no way subversive. The invasion of Belgium, in Lloyd George's words, 'set the nation on fire from sea to sea'.[249] There was a general feeling that if a great power could simply ignore the neutral status of a small country to which it had pledged its word, Europe would not be safe; and in 1914, no government that failed to help Belgium could have survived in the Commons. For Liberals, the declaration of war was seen as an affirmation, not a denial of Liberalism, and Asquith declared that his policy was similar to that of Gladstone's in 1870. The Commons was almost unanimous. Shortly before the invasion of Belgium, Grey reports in his memoirs:

> A very active Liberal member came up to me in the lobby and told me that he wished me to understand that under no circumstances whatever ought this country to take part in the war, if it came. He spoke in a dictatorial tone, in the manner of a superior addressing a subordinate whom he thought needed a good talking to ... I answered pretty roughly to the effect that I hoped we should not be involved in war, but that it was nonsense to say that there were no circumstances conceivable in which

---

248 House of Commons Debates, 10 August 1870, vol. 203, cols 1787–8.
249 Lloyd George, *War Memoirs*, vol. 1, p. 66.

we ought to go to war. 'Under no circumstances whatever' was the retort. 'Suppose Germany violates the neutrality of Belgium?' For a moment he paused, like one who, running at speed, finds himself suddenly confronted with an obstacle, unexpected and unforeseen. Then he said with emphasis, 'She won't do it.' 'I don't say she will, but supposing she does?' 'She won't do it,' he repeated, confidently, and with that assurance he left me.[250]

The backbencher illustrated what is perhaps a peculiarly British unwillingness to face unpleasant realities, a consequence perhaps of her island situation. 'The English', Oscar Wilde once said, and he meant the British, 'are always degrading truths into facts. When a truth becomes a fact it loses all its intellectual value.' The 'fact' was that Germany was a peace-loving power, prepared to observe the rules of international morality. That same 'fact' was to be held by many in the 1930s.

The invasion of Belgium caused a rapid reversal of view on the left. In 1913, the Radical weekly *Nation* declared confidently, 'Germany would not violate the neutrality of Belgium for the sake of some small military advantage if she might otherwise reckon on our neutrality.'[251] The left had argued that Germany was not as bad as she was painted by Unionists, and that Britain should make more effort to secure detente. Grey had come to agree with much of their case. On 27 June 1914, the day before the assassination, the British ambassador to Paris reports Grey as thinking 'that the German Government are in a peaceful mood and that they are very anxious to be on good terms with England, a mood he wishes to encourage'.[252] But the invasion of Belgium showed that Germany was in fact far worse than she had been painted. The shock amongst those previously sympathetic to her was profound. On 3 August, Simon, who had withdrawn his resignation, told C. P. Scott, editor of the *Manchester Guardian*, that 'he had been entirely deceived about Germany and that I ought to know that the evidence was overwhelming that the party which had gained control of the direction of affairs throughout the crisis had deliberately played for and provoked war'.[253] Gilbert Murray, an academic on the Liberal left, who had been opposed before 1914 to Grey's policy, wrote a book in 1915 confessing his mistake. 'I have never', he was to write,

till this year seriously believed in the unalterably aggressive designs of

250 Grey, *Twenty-Five Years*, vol. 1, p. 338.
251 Michael Brock, 'Britain Enters the War', in Evans and von Strandmann, eds, *Coming of the First World War*, p. 168. Brock's chapter still remains the best account of how Britain came to be at war.
252 F. H. Hinsley, ed., *British Foreign Policy Under Sir Edward Grey*, Cambridge University Press, 1977, p. 21.
253 Ibid., p. 403.

Germany ... And I also felt with some impatience, that though, as an outsider, I could not tell exactly what the Government ought to do, they surely could produce good relations between Great Britain and Germany if only they had the determination and the will. And now I see that on a large part of this question ... I was wrong and a large number of the people whom I honour most were wrong. One is vividly reminded of Lord Melbourne's famous dictum, 'All the sensible men were on one side, and all the d-d fools on the other. And egad, Sir, the d-d fools were right'.[254]

The invasion of Belgium was the one issue which could unite the Cabinet, Parliament and the people so that interest, honour and obligation coincided. It was now impossible for Britain to keep out of the war. 'If Germany had not violated Belgian neutrality,' Grey told the American ambassador in early August 1914, 'the British Government would not have been able to come to the support of the Allies.'[255]

In the Commons in August 1914, the Liberals held 257 seats out of 670, some way short of an overall majority. They were supported by the Irish Party, which held eighty-four seats, and Labour, which held thirty-seven. The Unionist opposition held 287 seats, and there were five vacancies. The Liberals, without an overall majority, relied on the Irish and Labour. Neither would have supported a war before the invasion of Belgium. Nor would most Liberal MPs. After a Cabinet meeting on 27 June, before Austria had declared war on Serbia and when there still seemed a possibility of the international conference which Grey was seeking, Lloyd George told C. P. Scott, editor of the *Manchester Guardian*, that 'there could be no question of our taking part in any war in the first instance. He knew of no Minister who would be in favour of it,' this last sentence being somewhat of an exaggeration.[256] Writing to Venetia Stanley on 2 August, Asquith believed, 'a good three-quarters of our own party in the House of Commons [are] for absolute non-interference at any price'.[257] On 3 August, a Conservative observer believed:

The whole attitude of the radical rank and file is intensely hostile to the government ... Had there been a vote by a ballot tonight I do not believe the government would have been supported by fifty of its adherents. The Radical press also bitterly criticise the government and anxiously argues that we are entering upon a 'Tory war'.[258]

254 Murray, *The Foreign Policy of Sir Edward Grey*, p. 9.
255 Otte, *Statesman of Europe*, p. 534.
256 Wilson, ed., *C. P. Scott*, p. 91.
257 Brock, ed., *Letters to Venetia Stanley*, p. 146.
258 Vincent, ed., *Crawford Papers*, p. 340.

It is sometimes suggested that the outcome, had there been no invasion of Belgium, would have been a Conservative-dominated coalition that would have led Britain into war. But until news of the ultimatum to Belgium arrived, it is not clear if even the Unionists would have been united for war. At around 29 July, Bonar Law told Grey that he doubted whether his party 'would be unanimous or overwhelmingly in favour of war, unless Belgian neutrality were invaded; in that event, he said it would be unanimous'.[259] A pro-war coalition would have needed the unanimous support of the Unionists and of forty-nine Liberals to secure a bare majority in the Commons. Without the invasion of Belgium, it is not clear whether or not that would have been possible. There might instead have been a Liberal anti-war government, supported by the Irish and Labour and perhaps led by Lloyd George, who was waiting to see which way the wind was blowing before committing himself.

On 3 August, after Grey's statement in the Commons, Bonar Law spoke to support the war on behalf of the opposition. That was no surprise. What surprised many was the speech which followed from Redmond, in support of the war. The government, he declared, could take all British troops out of Ireland. Nationalists would defend it, joining with Ulstermen to do so. Unionists cheered and waved their order papers. Grey could declare that 'the one bright spot in the very dreadful situation is Ireland'.[260] On 18 September, the day on which Parliament was to be prorogued, the Labour MP Will Crooks would ask MPs to sing 'God Save the King'. The Irish Nationalists joined in and Crooks cried out, 'God Save Ireland!' to which Redmond replied, 'And God Save England Too!' At Woodenbridge, Co. Wicklow, on 21 September, Redmond was to urge members of the Irish Volunteers to join the army, arguing that 'this war is undertaken in defence of the highest principles of religion, morality and right'. And on 15 September, when the Commons was debating the Home Rule and Suspensory Bills, he declared:

In this war, I say, for the first time, certainly for over a hundred years, I feel that her [Ireland's] interests are precisely the same as yours. She feels and will feel that the British democracy has kept faith with her. She knows that this is a just war. She is moved in a very special way by the fact this war is undertaken in the defence of small nations and oppressed peoples.[261]

Redmond had always hoped that Home Rule would transform feelings between Britain and Ireland, that enmity would be replaced by friendship.

---

259 Blake, *The Unknown Prime Minister*, p. 220.
260 House of Commons Debates, 3 August 1914, vol. 65, col. 1824.
261 Ibid., 15 September 1914, vol. 66, col. 911.

Home Rule had won goodwill for Britain. But it was too late. After the war, the more radical voices of Sinn Féin were heard and Ireland broke off from the rest of Britain. Redmond supported Britain's war effort in 1914, Éamon de Valera in 1939 did not.

After Redmond's speech in the Commons on 3 August, Ramsay Mac-Donald, the Labour leader, and Keir Hardie, spoke against the war. But they were to be repudiated by their parliamentary colleagues. The Labour Party, faithfully representing its working-class constituency, supported the war. Only the City appeared dubious and aloof from the popular clamour, in accordance with the view put forward by the publicist Norman Angell in his book *The Great Illusion*, published in 1910, that the interlocking forces of international business and finance made war not necessarily unlikely but certainly unprofitable. In 1914, Labour turned out to be patriotic, while capital remained international.

Although the majority of Labour MPs supported the war, the ILP maintained its opposition. MacDonald declared that he was not a pacifist and would have supported war had he really believed that Britain was in danger, but he did not believe that she was. He did not explain how British safety was compatible with the occupation by a hostile power of Belgium and the Channel ports. For the decision to go to war for Belgium was based not only on morality but also the national interest. Almost every British politician, and most British people, felt that to allow Germany to conquer France and Belgium would compromise British independence, so that she would become dependent upon Germany. In 1870, Disraeli had told the House of Commons:

> It had always been held by the Government of this country that it was for the interest of England that the countries on the European coast extending from Dunkirk and Ostend to the islands of the North Sea should be possessed by free and flourishing communities, practising the arts of peace, enjoying the rights of liberty, and following those pursuits of commerce, which tend to the civilisation of man, and should not be in the possession of a great military Power, one of the principles of whose existence necessarily must be to aim at a preponderating influence in Europe.[262]

That principle had, of course, increased in importance in 1914 with the advent of long-range artillery, large warships and submarines. So the decision to go to war for Belgium seemed to be one where honour, moral obligation and the national interest coincided.

---

262 Ibid., 1 August 1870, vol. 203, col. 1289.

After the invasion of Belgium, any British government which had tried to keep the country out of the war would have been overthrown by an outraged House of Commons and public. 'It is a mistake', one writer was to declare in 1920, 'to say that Mr Asquith carried England into the war. England carried Mr Asquith into the war ... A House of Commons that had hesitated an hour after the invasion of Belgium would have been swept out of existence by the wrath and indignation of the people.'[263] And the invasion of Belgium would have brought Britain into the war even if there had been no ententes and no military or naval conversations with France, and whoever had been Foreign Secretary. What Grey and the Liberal government did achieve, however, was to bring a united country into the war, while Lloyd George by his tactics persuaded most of the pacifistically inclined Liberals to support it. The Unionists would have found it more difficult to secure such national unity since they would have been opposed by a number of Liberal MPs, suspicious of their balance of power approach.

British opinion at the outbreak of war was well summed up by the great American novelist Henry James, who wrote to his nephew on 6 August.

The entrance of this country into the fray has been supremely inevitable – never doubt for an instant of that; up to a few short days ago she [Britain] was still multiplying herself over Europe, in the magnificent energy and pertinacity of Edward Grey, for peace, and nothing but peace, in any way in which he could by any effort or any service help to preserve it, and has now only been beaten by what one can only call the huge immorality, the deep conspiracy for violence, for violence and wrong, of the Austrian and German Emperors. Till the solemnly guaranteed neutrality of Belgium was three or four days ago deliberately violated by Germany, in defiance of every right, in her ferocious push to get at France by the least fortified way, war still hung in the balance here; but with that no 'balance' was any longer possible, and the impulse to participate to the utmost in resistance and redress became as unanimous and as sweeping a thing in the House of Commons and throughout the land as it is possible to conceive. That is the one light, as one may call it, in so much sickening blackness – that in an hour, here, all breaches instantly healed, all divisions dropped ... so that there is at once the most striking and interesting spectacle of united purpose.[264]

And in July 1915, as a sign of solidarity, the novelist made a gesture which, although he had lived in England for forty years, he had not before

---

263 'A Gentleman with a Duster' (Harold Begbie), *The Mirrors of Downing Street*, Mills and Boon, 1920, pp. 42–3.
264 Percy Lubbock, *The Letters of Henry James*, Charles Scribner, 1920, vol. 2, pp. 773–4.

contemplated he became naturalised as a British subject. Asquith was one of his sponsors.

The king was to sum up the general opinion, as he so often did, when he asked the American ambassador, 'My God, Mr Page, what else could we do?'[265]

Neither the government nor the British people appreciated what war would involve. Grey indeed told the Commons on 3 August that, 'for us, with a powerful Fleet, which we believe able to protect our commerce, to protect our shores, and to protect our interests, if we are engaged in war, we shall suffer but little more than we shall suffer if we stand aside'.[266] But the war was to prove quite different from any previous conflict in which Britain had been involved. It was the first war requiring the creation of a mass army and involving the participation of almost the whole of the civilian population. For that war, Britain was unprepared.

THE CRITIQUE OF GREY

Asquith pointed out as early as 29 July 1914 how unfair it was 'that we being the only Power who has made so much as a constructive suggestion in the direction of peace, are blamed by both Germany & Russia for causing the outbreak of war'.[267] Of all foreign ministers in the countries going to war, Grey was the most regretful. War for him represented a terrible failure. For too many on the Continent, it represented a solution. Many observers at the time regarded Grey with admiration as the one man in Europe who had worked hard and disinterestedly for peace. The American ambassador wrote privately to his President, 'Here is a great and sincere man working with a great government as his tool, working to save Europe from itself and (most likely) failing.'[268] Later, however, Grey was to be reproached by critics for not coming out earlier with a clearer declaration of British policy. He was attacked from two contradictory angles. One set of critics blame him for not declaring that Britain would under no circumstances support France or Russia. In that case, it was suggested, Russia would not have mobilised. The opposite line of criticism condemns Grey for not telling Germany that Britain, far from remaining neutral, would definitely support France and Russia, and, more particularly, for not telling Germany that attacking France or invading Belgium would bring Britain into the war. Both criticisms are misguided.

---

265 Hendrick, *Life and Letters of Walter H. Page*, vol. 2, p. 309.
266 House of Commons Debates, 3 August 1914, vol. 65, col. 1823.
267 Brock, ed., *Letters to Venetia Stanley*, p. 132.
268 Otte, *Statesman of Europe*, p. 515.

The other powers determined their policies during the July crisis, based on what they regarded as their national interests. Russia and France could not know whether or not Britain would remain neutral. Russia mobilised well before Britain had decided on her policy, since she could not afford to allow Serbia, her Slav ally, to be wiped off the map. France would never have agreed to neutrality while her ally Russia was at war with Germany. Nor would she have accepted the surrender of her border forts. The main contribution that Britain could be expected to bring to the war effort was sea power, and while that could interfere with German commerce, it could, France assumed, do little to hinder the German sweep to Paris. As for Germany, she decided on her policy despite knowing that Britain would almost certainly respond to the invasion of Belgium. Grey is sometimes criticised for not having warned Germany that a serious breach of Belgian neutrality or even a threat to France would lead to a British declaration of war. But no one with the slightest familiarity with Britain could have had any doubt. In 1911, at the time of the Agadir crisis, 'one of the best-known German correspondents in London' asked the British journalist J. A. Spender whether Britain would join in a war if France were threatened. Spender replied, 'You have lived in England for ten years and you know the English people. Can you really see them sitting still while the ... German army wiped out the French and planted itself on the French coast?' 'You have answered my opinion,' the German replied, 'and we won't argue it further.'[269] Haldane had told the Anglophile German ambassador shortly after the First Balkan War had broken out 'that as the maintenance of France was of vital importance to England, England could not stand aside should the Balkan war lead to a European war'.[270] The British public was even less likely to 'stand aside' in the case of a German invasion of Belgium which would enable her to 'occupy Antwerp and thus permanently threaten the mouth of the Thames with its navy.'[271] British policy was perfectly clear. But as Bethmann admitted, in his book on the war published in Germany in 1919 and in Britain in 1920, 'Our military men had, as I had long been aware, only one plan of campaign.'[272]

So Britain was in no way crucial in the decisions of the powers which turned a local war into a Continental war. Grey believed that any early declaration of a definite British policy would prevent him from exerting any influence upon the crisis. Were he to offer unconditional support to France or Russia, they might be encouraged to precipitate conflict. He would have been unable to urge them to show caution, or urge Germany to show moderation.

---

269 Spender, *Life, Journalism and Politics*, vol. 2, p. 12.
270 Prince Lichnowsky, *Heading for the Abyss: Reminiscences*, Constable, 1928, p. 5.
271 Halévy, *History of the English People in the Nineteenth Century*, vol. 6, p. 675.
272 Theobald von Bethmann Hollweg, *Reflections on the World War, Part 1*, Thornton Butterworth, 1920, p. 146.

Grey's policy, as we have seen, was to restrain Russia while Germany restrained Austria. Any declaration of neutrality or blanket commitment to France or Russia would have removed that potentially restraining hand both in relation to France and Russia and also in relation to Germany. In addition, as we have seen, Grey believed, until a late stage of the crisis, that Germany was willing to work for peace by cooperating with Britain to restrain Austria. Committing Britain to Russia or France would have destroyed all chances of securing cooperation from Germany.

But even had he wished, Grey could not have made the clear commitment called for by his critics, since the Cabinet, the party and the country were divided. He was not in the position of foreign ministers in the military autocracies of Austria–Hungary, Germany or Russia who could make decisions on vital matters of peace and war without fearing parliamentary scrutiny. 'The idea', Grey declared some months later, 'that one individual ... in the Foreign Office could pledge a great democracy ... in advance either to take part in a great war or to abstain' was absurd. In 1915, he was to declare that 'one of his strongest feelings' was 'that he himself had no power to decide policy and was only the mouthpiece of England'.[273] Many years later, Grey's parliamentary private secretary was to write, 'It is not open to doubt ... that if Grey had insisted on sending an ultimatum to Germany' to the effect that if she attacked France, Britain would fight on the side of France, then 'Lloyd George would have a led a revolt in the Cabinet; the Cabinet would have disintegrated; and the country would have been split from top to bottom. This was the very thing that Grey was determined at all possible costs to avoid. And how right he was!'[274]

From the interwar years until today, Grey has been unfairly traduced. He alone amongst the diplomats of 1914 had actively worked for peace and had made concrete proposals which could have achieved peace, or at least localised the war. His straightforwardness and the fact that he was trusted by the diplomats of the other powers were compelling factors in his favour. Interviewing him in 1928, the American historian Bernadotte Schmitt concluded, 'One did not have to speak long with him to be aware that here was a deeply sensitive person ... who hated war and the thought of it and was as likely to have worked for it as to have murdered his wife or sovereign.'[275] The fact that Grey had striven so hard for peace meant that Britain could enter the war united. So the conventional criticisms of Grey and the Liberals – either that they embedded Britain too closely into an alliance system with France

---

273 Hazlehurst, *Politicians at War*, pp. 51–2.
274 *Manchester Guardian*, 30 November 1958.
275 Schmitt, *Interviewing the Authors of the War*, p. 18.

and Russia, or that they failed to warn Germany in time – lack substance. Much of the criticism assumes that Britain was the crucial factor in decisions made by the Continental powers. She was not. The key decisions were taken elsewhere and the British stance of non-commitment until the invasion of Belgium did not affect the outcome.

The critique of Grey had few supporters in 1914. But some Labour and Liberal opponents of the war, led by MacDonald and the philosopher Bertrand Russell, formed in August 1914 a movement called the Union of Democratic Control (UDC), which developed a radical critique of Grey's policy. In the years of disillusionment after the war, the UDC view became the new orthodoxy. Its members questioned the view that Germany or Austria had triggered the war and argued that Britain's intervention had been a mistake. War could have been avoided, they said, if Grey's diplomacy had been more conciliatory towards Germany, and if he had understood that Germany and Austria had genuine grievances against Serbia. In any case, what happened east of the Rhine was not really Britain's affair.

In the first volume of his *War Memoirs*, published in 1933, which contains a vehement attack on Grey, Lloyd George seemed to agree with much of this critique, arguing that the powers had somehow 'slithered over the brink into the boiling cauldron of war. Not one of them wanted war; certainly not on this scale.'[276] But if that were so, why had Lloyd George been sympathetic to conscription in his 1910 coalition proposals and declared many times before 1914 that Germany sought war? On 13 September 1911, after the Agadir crisis, Lloyd George had a conversation with Brigadier Henry Wilson, Director of Military Operations at the War Office, in which, according to Wilson, he 'was quite in favour of war now. I asked him if he would give us conscription, and he said that, although he was entirely in favour of a ballot, yet he dare not say so until war broke out, which I told him was too late.'[277] In October 1911, Lloyd George told Balfour, according to Balfour's report to Austen Chamberlain, 'Germany meant war; wouldn't it be better to have it at once? And so on.' Balfour was, understandably, 'rather shocked' by the Chancellor's language.[278]

> Repeatedly in the course of the conversation Lloyd George spoke of France's weakness and terror in the face of Germany. She had her eyes fixed on 'those terrible legions across the frontier'. 'They could be in Paris in a month and she knew it.' Then Germany would ... see to it that France

---

276 Lloyd George, *War Memoirs*, vol. i, p. 32.
277 Gilbert, 'Lloyd George in 1911 and 1914', p. 874.
278 Chamberlain, *Politics from Inside*, p. 363.

as a Great Power ceased to exist. This was a real danger that Prussia (and it was Prussia really, not Germany, which was in question) should seek a European predominance not far removed from the Napoleonic.[279]

Lloyd George feared, and many military authorities agreed, that without British aid, France would be rapidly defeated in war. His approach in his *War Memoirs* was quite different from that which he had adopted at the time, and owed more to post-war squabbles in the Liberal Party than to any objective assessment.

The 'slithered into war' thesis has, however, been endorsed in our own times in somewhat more sophisticated terms by Niall Ferguson in his book *The Pity of War* and by the Cambridge historian Christopher Clark in *The Sleepwalkers*. The implication of calling the main actors sleepwalkers is that, as Lloyd George suggested, the powers 'slithered' into war, unaware of what they were doing. It seems clear, however, that the German and Austrian decision makers were very aware of what they were doing, that they might be triggering a war which could not be contained. Clark, indeed, comes to be involved in the same kind of contradiction as Lloyd George. Both argue that the sleepwalkers were unaware of what they were doing. But both seek also to blame the decisions of the leading actors – in Clark's case, the leaders of the entente powers who he believes converted a local crisis in the Balkans into a world war.

More recently, in his book *Time and Power*, Clark denies this interpretation, and claims that he did not intend to acquit Germany of at least some responsibility for launching a preventive war.[280] The war, he now believes, was not accidental but a consequence of a hugely complex chain of decisions made in full consciousness of the risks. But in that case, calling the leaders sleepwalkers seems singularly inappropriate. Sleepwalkers, after all, cannot be held responsible for their actions, nor are their actions taken in full consciousness of the risks involved.

While in the past, criticism of Grey came mainly from the left, in modern times, it has come mainly – though not exclusively – from the Eurosceptic right, who argue that Britain was primarily an imperial not a Continental power and that, if only Britain had not fought, she could today have been an honoured member of the kaiser's European Union. Niall Ferguson has criticised Grey for turning a Continental war into a world war, the implication being that Britain was not part of the Continent. But if Britain could

---

279 Wilson, ed., *C. P. Scott*, pp. 46–8.
280 Christopher Clark, *Time and Power: Visions of History in German Politics, from the Thirty Years' War to the Third Reich*, Princeton University Press, 2019.

not afford to allow France or Belgium to be overrun or the Channel ports to be in the hands of a hostile power, then she was inescapably a Continental power.[281]

'It is not at all surprising', one historian has argued, 'that those who felt most betrayed by Grey in 1914 became the leading appeasers of the next decades.'[282] A permanent peace seemed to be the only justification for the mass slaughter of 1914–18 in what H. G. Wells was to christen the war to end war. Between the wars, the critique of Grey became the leitmotif of appeasement, led by liberal-minded Conservatives, and by the former Liberal Sir John Simon, who had nearly resigned on the declaration of war in 1914, and was to resign over the introduction of conscription in 1916. In 1914, Grey had proposed a conference to settle the problems of Europe, a proposal rejected by Germany and Austria. In 1938, Neville Chamberlain also proposed a conference to settle the problems of Europe, a proposal accepted by Hitler and resulting in the Munich settlement, which postponed although it did not avoid war. The appeasers believed, together with left-wing opponents of the war in 1914, that Britain was not fundamentally part of Europe but an imperial and maritime power. Czechoslovakia, Chamberlain was famously to declare in 1938, was a far away country of which we knew nothing. But in 1914, what happened in a far away country had led to war, as it was to do in 1939 when another far away country, Poland, was invaded. On both occasions, it was clear that German hegemony in Europe was not compatible with British independence. But the arguments about the First World War and the left's critique of Grey provided ideological support for appeasement and so, in this sense, they contributed to the Second World War. In the 1930s, Chamberlain and the appeasers were to be opposed by Churchill – a hawk in the Cabinet of 1914 – who believed, both in 1914 and 1939, that Germany sought Continental hegemony and that Britain must resist her.

THE FAILURE OF UNDERSTANDING

But if the standard critique of British policy lacks substance, Grey and indeed the Liberal government are open to criticism from a quite different perspective. For there was a disconnection between the foreign policy of the Liberals and their defence policy. The events of 1914 made it clear that Britain was a European as well as an imperial power. British security depended not only upon mastery of the seas but upon developments on the Continent. If, then, British security was bound up with the security of France, should not the entente have

---

281 Ferguson, *Pity of War*, passim.
282 Steiner, *Foreign Office and Foreign Policy*, p. 211.

been transformed into an alliance? French security, moreover, depended upon her eastern alliance – the alliance with Russia. It followed then that, if British security depended upon the security of France whose security in turn depended upon that of Russia, it was also in Britain's interest to transform the convention with Russia into an alliance, however distasteful her political system.

Britain before 1914 continued to think of herself as an island nation. Her powerful navy, it was generally believed, exempted her from the need to either secure alliances or create a mass conscript army on the Continental model. But if British security was so closely bound up with the balance of power on the Continent, she needed not just a strong navy but also a strong army. British security could not, in fact, be secured without a greater military effort than she was prepared to make. In liberal Britain, 'there was a consistent failure to comprehend that a nation must balance its foreign policy objectives with the military and other means available to achieve those objectives'.[283] If the policies embodied in the ententes were seriously meant to show that Britain could not disinterest herself in what happened on the Continent, that she could not afford to allow Germany to control the French coast or the Low Countries, then Britain would have to become a military as well as a naval power, since France could only be defended on land. While Grey was right to believe that 'any power which achieved European dominance in the last resort came against England', he was wrong to believe that 'so long as she retained her sea-power' she 'could not be coerced'.[284] The navy alone would not be sufficient to ensure British security, and the army was far too small to deter Germany. 'We are', General Sir Henry Brackenbury had told the Royal Commission on the South African War, 'attempting to maintain the largest Empire the world has ever seen with armaments and reserves that would be insufficient for a third class military power.'[285] For there was a strong belief, as Churchill put it in his autobiography, that 'the British Army would never again take part in a European conflict ... Certainly no Jingo Lieutenant or Fire-eating Staff Officer in the Aldershot Command in 1895, even in his most sanguine moments, would have believed that our little Army would again be sent to Europe.'[286] Despite Haldane's reforms, that assumption had hardly changed by 1914. The army remained fundamentally one intended to reinforce troops in India and Egypt and was not equipped for Continental warfare against a nation in arms. In September 1908, the French Prime Minister Clemenceau, whom Edward VII regarded as 'a true friend of his own country and of ours', had begged Britain to strengthen

283 Coogan and Coogan, 'The British Cabinet and the Anglo-French Staff Talks', p. 129.
284 Wilson, ed., C. P. Scott, p. 51.
285 McDermott, 'Revolution in British Military Thinking', p. 162.
286 Churchill, My Early Life, p. 75.

her army and produce the requisite weapons and ammunition needed. 'The fact is', Clemenceau insisted, 'that England cannot maintain her position in Europe and in the world, nor can her friendship with France be secure against surprises unless she has an adequate army.' He reminded Britain that Napoleon had been finally defeated not at Trafalgar but at Waterloo.[287] Grey, however, told Asquith in September that Clemenceau did not understand Britain 'if he imagines that we are going to keep a standing army of half or three quarters of a million of men, ready to meet the Germans in Belgium, if and when they are minded to adopt that route for invasion of France'.[288] That was probably a just estimate of British attitudes. But the consequence was that the army was too small for what was needed in 1914. Its target had been 35,000 recruits a year, but only once between 1908 and 1913 had there been more than 30,000 recruits in a year. In any case, Haldane, despite what he said in his book *Before the War*, published in 1920, continued to regard the army as needed primarily for the defence of the empire, not for the Continent. The Territorial Army, which Haldane had grandly portrayed as 'the nation in arms' was also inadequate. It was 67,000 short of the hoped-for 300,000; some of its members had not, by 1914, completed their training or attended an annual camp; and there was an annual wastage rate of around 12.5 per cent.[289] In any case, the Territorial Army was intended primarily to help defend Britain and its members were under no obligation to serve overseas. Britain had no mass army.

Such a mass army could probably only have been achieved through conscription and that was hardly practical politics. It was, as Grey said in 1914, 'unnatural'. It would have split the Liberal Party.[290] And most Unionists were as hostile to it as the Liberals. In his book on the genesis of the war, published in 1923, Asquith wrote that it 'would have split the Cabinet, split the House of Commons, split both political parties and split the whole nation'.[291] But in any case, the conscriptionists were more concerned with home defence, with the protection of Britain, than with sending a large force to the Continent. More fundamentally, conscription went against Britain's liberal culture. In 1891, the French historian Hippolyte Taine, in a startling prediction of twentieth-century history, had written that 'universal conscript military service, with its twin brother universal suffrage, has mastered all Continental Europe – with what promises of massacre and bankruptcy for the twentieth

287 Lee, *King Edward VII*, vol. 2, pp. 630, 629.
288 Otte, *Statesman of Europe*, p. 326.
289 Strachan, *First World War*, p. 159.
290 Grey, *Twenty-Five Years*, vol. 1, p. 281.
291 H. H. Asquith, *The Genesis of the War*, Cassell, 1923, p. 139.

century'.[292] Nevertheless, a strong army and a British commitment to the defence of France might just have had a deterrent effect in 1914 and therefore have served to prevent war. For it would have cast doubt on the feasibility of the German war plan to overcome France rapidly before turning on Russia.

The Liberals before 1914 had followed a policy of limited liability, since many of them, including a majority of the Cabinet, did not fundamentally believe that Germany was an aggressive power. Further, it was not in the tradition of British foreign policy to commit herself to the Continent, a tradition that was to last until the agreement with Poland in April 1939. It was even alleged that the British constitution forbade an alliance since, when it came to the decision of peace or war, it must be for Parliament to decide. 'The fact that we cannot strengthen our agreement by an alliance', the Permanent Under-Secretary at the Foreign Office told the ambassador to Russia, 'is due to our Constitution, and we cannot help it.'[293] So Britain's foreign and defence policy remained before 1914 the policy of a maritime and imperial power, not a Continental power, and rendered her unprepared for the catastrophe that was to follow. It was the policy almost of an isolationist power. A Continental commitment could only be made coherent through conscription. Britain's foreign and defence policies were inadequate if, as Asquith and Grey believed, from at least the time of Agadir, if not before, Germany was an expansionist and aggressive power. But forebodings about German power could not overcome the hopefulness and optimism that were so integral to Liberal politics. The war was to come as a terrible shock to the liberal sensibility. The son of the New Liberal philosopher L. T. Hobhouse declared that the war had come to his father as 'a shattering blow ... It struck directly at the whole foundation of his thought.' Mary Agnes Hamilton, a young intellectual member of the ILP, declared of her generation:

> Its impact destroyed our foundations; left us staring at a world, alien, hostile, terrifying, in which we did not know our way about ... Everything that had been, everything in which we trusted, now seemed suspect ... War, in 1914, was a revelation of evil outside our categories ... It was a charge of dynamite applied not only to the forms of our lives but to the ideas by which we had lived.[294]

The catastrophe might just have been avoided but only by policies which lay beyond the perspective of liberalism. Only a very small number advocated a

292 Quoted in Semmel, *Imperialism and Social Reform*, p. 216.
293 Wilson, *The Policy of the Ententes*, pp. 42–3.
294 Quoted in Peter Weiler, 'The New Liberalism of L. T. Hobhouse', *Victorian Studies,* 1972, p. 159.

firm military alliance with France accompanied by conscription and the creation of a large army, and most of them were to be found amongst the military and Unionists of the radical right. They were seen as unrepresentative warmongers. Yet, paradoxically, these 'warmongering' policies were the only ones that might have succeeded in preserving the long peace, so rendering the twentieth-century world a safe one for Britain's liberal ideals. Britain's liberal political culture, which had done so much to assist her industrial and social progress and had made her so peaceable and tolerant a country, proved inadequate to defend it against those powers which were challenging it.

It was Disraeli who had first noticed in 1870 that the balance of power in Europe had been irretrievably altered to the advantage of Germany. Britain was not prepared either in 1914 or 1939 to accept German hegemony in Europe, whatever the consequences for herself. She fought to secure a liberal polity in Europe. But the war was to end hopes of liberal progress on the Continent. A liberal Europe was not to be restored in western Europe until 1945, after a second and even more terrible war; and in central and Eastern Europe not until the fall of communism in 1989. But in ensuring that Germany would not succeed in dominating the Continent, Britain was able to perform a last service for Europe, after which she ceased to be a world power. For the two world wars showed that Britain could not defeat Germany without the aid of Russia, a part-European power, and the United States, a non-European power. When the Americans and Russians met in the middle of Germany in April 1945 in the ruins of Hitler's Reich, they signalled the end of the era of European supremacy in world affairs. They signalled the end also of Britain's role as a global power. We are still living with the consequences.

PRESERVING LIBERAL BRITAIN

B ritish liberal culture, then, was not a tough enough creed to confront the problems which she faced on the Continent. The war was to undermine liberalism in Europe. Would it also undermine liberalism at home? Was liberalism indeed already decaying even before the war? In 1935, George Dangerfield in his book *The Strange Death of Liberal England* argued that liberalism had reached the end of its natural span by 1914, that the war finally destroyed liberal Britain, already under mortal threat from suffragettes, strikers and Ulstermen, and that the interwar years were to see a struggle between two illiberal forces – reactionary Conservatism and illiberal socialism. Similar views had been held by a number of those reaching maturity in Edwardian times, intellectuals who saw their age as one of decadence. The Conservative tariff reformer Leo Amery, one of Chamberlain's chief lieutenants, believed that the political principles and traditions of Liberalism had become irrelevant in the twentieth century and had been kept alive solely by the conserving effect of the party system. From this point of view, the great Liberal victory of 1906 had been 'not the herald of some great advance, but the last backwash of a tide that has run out', a conservative reaction against the Boer War and against attempts of the Unionists to modernise Britain through education reform and tariff reform.[1]

George Wyndham believed after the 1906 election:

Two ideals, and only two, emerge from the vortex:

1. Imperialism, which demands unity at home between classes, and unity throughout the Empire; and which prescribes fiscal reform to secure both.
2. Insular socialism and class antagonism ...

As for the 'Liberals' and 'Unionist Free Traders' – the 'Whigs' of our day – Well! Their day is over. It is they who are drowned.

The Imperialists and Socialists emerge. That is the dividing line of future parties.[2]

---

1   A. L. Rowse, *All Souls in My Time*, Duckworth, 1993, p. 61.
2   Mackail and Wyndham, eds, *Life and Letters of George Wyndham*, vol. 2, p. 540.

But in the Edwardian years, it was the attack on liberalism that failed, not liberalism itself. The policies of Amery and Wyndham, the policies of the radical right – imperial unity, conscription, national efficiency – were conclusively rejected. Julian Amery, the biographer of Joseph Chamberlain and son of Leo, came ruefully to accept this in the last three volumes of his monumental biography of Chamberlain. Britain remained wedded to free trade while the dominions, continuing their progress towards full independence, had no wish to become part of a centralised Chamberlainite empire. It was in consequence the social imperialists, not the liberals, who found their political careers stunted, while the Fabians, who had many affinities with the social imperialists, could exert influence only by working through the Liberals and later the Labour Party, itself deeply influenced, as we have seen, by liberalism. The social reforms of the 1905 Liberal government were to derive from the British radical tradition, not from social imperialism.

In 1910, Lloyd George had offered Britain in his coalition proposals the chance of transforming her institutions and way of life through a policy of national efficiency. Imperial links would have been tightened, the technical education and training system would have been radically improved and conscription would have been introduced. But such proposals had little chance of success in a culture in which fear of the abuse of state power was so strong. The critics of liberalism tended to look to the autocratic states, Germany and Japan, as models. But significantly, those two countries, which proved so efficient at organising themselves domestically, were also to prove efficient at organising themselves for war. Britain, by contrast, remained content with the old ways. Voters listened to the sermons urging them to modernise, to, as it were, brush their shoes, straighten their shoulders and discipline themselves, but politely ignored them. They retained a healthy suspicion of those who promised them salvation. The forces that made Britain a liberal country were also perhaps the forces that prevented her from embracing the philosophy of national efficiency. And the scepticism towards national efficiency cut across party. Most Unionists were as committed to the old ways as the Liberals.

'Insular socialism and class antagonism' made equally little headway, as anyone who had considered Labour's origins amidst the liberal culture of late Victorian Britain could have predicted. In any case, socialism seemed in decline. By 1914, the left of the Labour Party – Hardie and Lansbury – were isolated. Hardie, who had hoped that the Labour Party would become socialist, had become, in Beatrice Webb's view, 'little more than a figurehead'.[3] The ILP had not succeeded in building a mass following for socialism, but

---

3   MacKenzie, *Diary of Beatrice Webb*, vol. 3, p. 196, entry for 18 February 1914.

it was in any case unsympathetic to 'class antagonism'. Labour, Keir Hardie was accustomed to say, opposed not a class but a system. The Labour Party indeed did not even formally commit itself to socialism until its 1918 constitution, and then only in a mild evolutionary form. So even if Labour had been replaced by the Liberals, that would have been far from heralding a 'strange death' of liberal Britain.

Admittedly, the Liberal Party itself was to fail after 1918. It had been able to accommodate itself to the welfare state but not to the exigencies of war. And parts of the liberal economy came to be superseded. In 1932, Britain would adopt tariff reform in the form of imperial preference. But this was a defensive measure during the slump, not part of a grand project of imperial unity. And, as the Liberal Party failed, liberal ideas spread to the Conservative and Labour parties. Labour in power during the interwar years was to adhere to modest and primarily defensive policies, concerned with protecting the position of the working class during a period of depression and unemployment. There was little hint of Wyndham's 'class antagonism', and, far from espousing 'insular socialism', Labour remained an internationalist party dedicated to conciliation in foreign policy and maintenance of the international gold standard. So the Liberal Party was to begin its long decline in a democracy more committed than ever to realising liberal ideals. What need was there for a Liberal Party when liberalism had become so pervasive? From this point of view, the Liberal Party could be said to have 'buried itself with a kind of triumph: because Britain as a whole is liberal, the Liberal Party dies', so a French commentator was to write in 1953.[4] During the interwar years, Britain was to remain a haven of liberal tolerance compared to the countries of the Continent, ravaged by fascism and national socialism. The pre-1914 attack on liberalism was to prove superficial and lacking in firm roots; and while the war destroyed liberalism in so many countries of the Continent, it did not destroy it in Britain.

Domestically, the central problem that had faced Britain during the years from 1895 to 1914 had been one of how to bring new groups within the pale of the constitution – to achieve universal suffrage so that women and unenfranchised men had the vote, to ensure that the representative chamber prevailed over the unrepresentative one, to construct institutions which would conciliate Ireland and, above all, to bring the working class into the political system – and to achieve all this without sacrificing the liberal values that had characterised Victorian Britain. With the exception of Ireland, all these ambitions were to be peacefully resolved after 1918 amidst general

---

4   Jean-Jacques Chevallier, Preface to Albert Mabileau, *Le Parti libéral dans le système constitutionnel britannique*, Colin, 1953, p. x. My translation.

acceptance. And even in the case of Ireland, there was, as we have seen, a good chance that Home Rule combined with exclusion would have removed the long-standing grievances of those living in the emerald isle. On the eve of war, the Irish Parliamentary Party was certainly optimistic on this score.

In 1920, the departing French ambassador Paul Cambon, who many years earlier had helped to negotiate the entente, was to tell Winston Churchill:

> In the twenty years I have been here, I have witnessed an English Revolution more profound and searching than the French Revolution itself. The governing class have been almost entirely deprived of political power and to a very large extent of their property and estates; and this has been accomplished almost imperceptibly and without the loss of a single life.

'I suppose', Churchill reflected, 'this is true.'[5] By 1947, George Orwell could write about 'the special thing' that the English – he meant the British, although he would perhaps not have included the Northern Irish – 'could contribute'.

> The outstanding and – by contemporary standards – highly original quality of the English is their habit of *not killing one another*. Putting aside the 'model' small states, which are in an exceptional position, England is the only European country where internal politics are conducted in a more or less humane and decent manner.[6]

The Edwardians had succeeded, in circumstances at least as complex as those which had faced their Victorian predecessors, in preserving if not strengthening that deep-seated liberal political culture which was to characterise Britain in the twentieth century. Liberal Britain had indeed survived as her people prepared to face, with courage and determination, the terrible challenge of war.

---

5 Churchill, *My Early Life*, pp. 97–8.
6 Orwell and Angus, eds, *Essays, Journalism and Letters of George Orwell*, vol. 3, p. 30.

SUGGESTIONS FOR FURTHER READING

I t would take a lifetime to master even the voluminous secondary literature for this period. Those without a lifetime to spend may appreciate suggestions for further reading of those books which have proved most useful in preparing this volume. Inevitably, this selection is personal, and no doubt idiosyncratic.

Most of the older books recommended and some of the newer ones are obtainable online at the Internet Archive.

There is a massive and fully comprehensive bibliography covering this period, of works published until the early 1970s – H. J. Hanham, *Bibliography of British History, 1851–1914*, Oxford University Press, 1976. This is, of course, now seriously out of date and a revised edition would be of great value.

Butler's British Political Facts, edited by Roger Mortimore and Andrew Blick, Palgrave Macmillan, 2018, is a quite indispensable work of reference. For electoral facts, there is F. W. S. Craig, *British Electoral Facts, 1885–1975*, 3rd edition, Macmillan, 1976, while Dermot Englefield, Janet Seaton and Isobel White, *Facts about the British Prime Ministers: A Compilation of Biographical and Historical Information*, Mansell, 1995, and *The Royal Encyclopedia*, edited by Ronald Allison and Sarah Riddell, Macmillan, 1991, contain much useful information on Prime Ministers and the monarchy, respectively.

The *Oxford Dictionary of National Biography* has biographies of all the politicians discussed in this book but should be used with caution. There are occasional factual mistakes, and some of the interpretations are questionable. But it is regularly updated online.

There is one primary source containing a rich seam of material which is astonishingly underused – Hansard. The parliamentary debates of the period were of an infinitely higher quality than those of the twenty-first century. Indeed, the depth of argument in late Victorian and Edwardian debates is truly humbling. Whatever else may be said of this period, its Parliament was far from decadent. Indeed, to compare Parliament then with Parliament today is to refute Darwin's theory of evolution.

GENERAL BOOKS

Two classic works illuminate the period. The first, R. C. K. Ensor's *England 1870–1914*, Clarendon Press, 1936, although published nearly ninety years ago, is an undervalued masterpiece. Ensor was a member of the ILP before 1914 and knew many of the leading Liberal and Labour politicians of the day. He had an uncanny understanding of how the political system worked. Many of the conclusions he reached still stand today.

The second classic is by a great French historian, Élie Halévy, whose epilogue to his *History of the English People in the Nineteenth Century, vol. 5: Imperialism and the Rise of Labour, 1895–1905* and *vol. 6: The Rule of Democracy, 1905–1914* [1952], 2nd edition, Ernest Benn, 1961, was first published in English translation in 1932. The second edition was published in English translation in 1952.

The volume in the *New Oxford History* series by G. R. Searle, *A New England? Peace and War, 1886–1918*, Clarendon Press, 2004, attempts a more unified history aiming to grasp the *mentalité* of the period, discarding narrative and instead analysing various themes such as nationalism, generation, gender, leisure, art and culture, and science and learning. It even includes a chapter on the seaside! In my view, this is not a sensible approach, and, while valuable in its way, *A New England?* it is not as perceptive on politics as Ensor.

More recently, Simon Heffer's *The Age of Decadence: Britain 1880–1914*, Cornerstone Digital, 2017, argues a point of view directly contrary to that put forward in this book.

Richard Shannon, *The Crisis of Imperialism, 1865–1915*, Hart-Davis, MacGibbon, 1974, is full of insight. Brian Harrison, *The Transformation of British Politics, 1880–1995*, Oxford University Press, 1996, provides a good overview, particularly strong on constitutional issues.

There are two other general books covering the period, Edgar Feuchtwanger, *Democracy and Empire: Britain, 1865–1914*, Edward Arnold, 1985, and Donald Read, *The Age of Urban Democracy: England 1868–1914*, revised edition, Longman, 1994.

There are also three books of edited essays on this period: Simon Nowell-Smith, *Edwardian England: 1901–1914*, Oxford University Press, 1964; Alan O'Day, *The Edwardian Age: Conflict and Stability, 1900–1914*, Macmillan, 1979; and Donald Read, *Edwardian England, 1901–1914*, Croom Helm, 1982.

Paul Thompson's *The Edwardians: The Remaking of British Society*, Weidenfeld & Nicolson, 1975, illuminates social divisions through oral interviews.

Two books covering central themes of the period are Aaron Friedberg, *The Weary Titan: Britain and the Experience of Relative Decline, 1895–1905*, Princeton University Press, 1988, and Kori Schake, *Safe Passage: The Transition from British to American Hegemony*, Harvard University Press, 2017, which seeks to compare the challenges to British hegemony from the 1890s onwards to the challenge to American hegemony from China today. But an important corrective to what has become a conventional view is the article by Keith Neilson, '"Greatly Exaggerated": The Myth of the Decline of Britain Before 1914', *International History Review*, 1991.

The economy is little discussed in this book. But Roderick Floud, Jane Humphries and Paul Johnson, eds, *The Cambridge Economic History of Modern Britain, vol. 2: 1870 to the Present*, Cambridge University Press, 2014, give a good general survey.

There is a most valuable book of general essays with very full bibliographies edited by Chris Wrigley, *A Companion to Early Twentieth Century Britain*, Blackwell, 2003.

Finally, *The Diary of Beatrice Webb*, edited by Norman and Jeanne MacKenzie, particularly *vol. 2, All the Good Things of Life, 1892–1905*, Harvard University Press, 1983, and *vol. 3, The Power to Alter Things, 1905–1924*, Harvard University Press, 1984, offers acute observations spiced with malice.

THE CONSTITUTION, GOVERNMENT AND ELECTORAL SYSTEM

On the constitution, G. H. L. Le May, *The Victorian Constitution: Conventions and Contingencies*, Duckworth, 1979, is the best guide. The last chapter has a penetrating analysis of the constitutional crises between 1909 and 1914.

The complex electoral system of the period is best approached through a seminal article by Neal Blewett, 'The Franchise in the United Kingdom, 1885–1918', *Past and Present*, 1965. Chapter 5 of Duncan Tanner, *Political Change and the Labour Party 1900–1918*, Cambridge University Press, 1990, also gives an excellent account of the complexities of the electoral framework. In addition, this book is of great value for the history of the Labour Party during this period and for relations between the Labour and Liberal parties.

Henry Pelling, *Social Geography of British Elections, 1885–1910*, Macmillan, 1967, is a classic, describing in some detail every constituency in the country, except for Irish constituencies. It is a fascinating book for anyone interested in the quirks and quiddities of electoral behaviour.

A good guide to electoral behaviour during this period is Kenneth Wald, *Crosses on the Ballot: Patterns of British Voter Alignment since 1885*, Princeton

University Press, 1983, whose conclusion is that, until 1910 at least, religion was more important than social class in structuring the vote.

A specialised work, Peter Clarke, *Lancashire and the New Liberalism*, Cambridge University Press, 1971, is of great importance for the argument that in Lancashire, the Liberals had adapted to social democracy and class politics before 1914 and were thriving. Historians have long debated whether Lancashire was typical of the country but have reached no definitive conclusion.

The Report of the Royal Commission Appointed to Enquire into the Electoral System, Cd 5163, 1910, is a guide to how the system was seen by an official body which recommended the alternative vote. Martin Pugh, *Electoral Reform in War and Peace, 1906–18*, Routledge & Kegan Paul, 1978, provides an excellent guide to Edwardian debates on proportional representation and female suffrage, on which it is particularly valuable. Vernon Bogdanor, *The People and the Party System: The Referendum and Electoral Reform in British Politics*, Cambridge University Press, 1981, analyses the historical debate.

On the working of government, two books written in the first decade of the twentieth century retain their value. The first, by a Harvard professor, A. L. Lowell, *The Government of England*, published in two volumes by Macmillan in 1908, provides a complete description of British institutions at the time. *The Governance of England* by Sidney Low, a true successor to Bagehot, published by T. Fisher Unwin in 1904, is concerned more with interpretation than description. It is strikingly perceptive as well as being a pleasure to read.

The essays in Vernon Bogdanor, ed., *The British Constitution in the Twentieth Century*, published for the centenary of the British Academy by Oxford University Press in 2003, may also be found of value.

An Austrian scholar, Josef Redlich, gives a contemporary description of the Commons in *The Procedure of the House of Commons: A Study of its History and Present Form*, Constable, 1908, while the essays in S. A. Walkland, ed., *The House of Commons in the Twentieth Century*, Clarendon Press, 1979, give a historical account. But both are rather dry. Parliament comes to life in the sparkling diaries and reminiscences of the journalist Henry Lucy in five books: *A Diary of the Unionist Parliament, 1895–1900*, J. W. Arrowsmith, 1901; *The Balfourian Parliament, 1900–1905*, Hodder & Stoughton, 1906; *Later Peeps at Parliament Taken from Behind the Speaker's Chair*, George Newnes, 1904; *Memories of Eight Parliaments*, William Heinemann, 1908; and *Lords and Commoners*, T. Fisher Unwin, 1921.

The House of Lords is brilliantly dissected in Andrew Adonis, *Making Aristocracy Work: The Peerage and the Political System in Britain, 1884–1914*, Clarendon Press, 1993. Ramsay Muir, *Peers and Bureaucrats: Two Problems of English Government*, Constable, 1910, is also useful. Corinne Comstock

Weston, *The House of Lords and Ideological Politics: Lord Salisbury's Referendal Theory and the Conservative Party, 1846–1922*, American Philosophical Society, 1995, provides a valuable account of a theory which hit the buffers in 1909 when the peers rejected the People's Budget.

The chapter on the Cabinet in John Morley's biography of *Walpole*, Macmillan, 1889, received the imprimatur of Gladstone and is a good guide to how late Victorians understood it. Ivor Jennings, *Cabinet Government*, 2nd edition, Cambridge University Press, 1951, is a classic work. John P. Mackintosh, *The British Cabinet*, 3rd edition, Stevens, 1977, is also valuable, although his view that there has been a progressive evolution towards prime ministerial government in the twentieth century seems to me mistaken.

There are two good histories of local government. A classic work by Josef Redlich and Francis W. Hirst, first published in 1903, has been edited by Bryan Keith-Lucas as *History of Local Government in England*, Macmillan, 1958. J. A. Chandler, *Explaining Local Government: Local Government in Britain since 1800*, Manchester University Press, 2013, is a good general history. Patricia Hollis, *Ladies Elect: Women in English Local Government, 1865–1914*, Clarendon Press, 1987, is a fascinating account of how women used their influence in local government before they secured the parliamentary vote. Finally, J. G. Bulpitt, *Territory and Power in the United Kingdom: An Interpretation*, Manchester University Press, 1983, is an important theoretical discussion distinguishing between the 'high' politics of the centre – primarily foreign affairs and defence – and the 'low' politics of social policy which, until much later in the twentieth century, could be left to local authorities.

On Scotland, there are three standard works. Two are by I. G. C. Hutchison, *A Political History of Scotland 1832–1924: Parties, Elections and Issues*, John Donald, 1986, and *Scottish Politics in the Twentieth Century*, Macmillan, 2000. The third is Richard J. Finlay, *A Partnership for Good? Scottish Politics and the Union since 1880*, John Donald, 1997.

On Wales, the classic by Kenneth O. Morgan, *Wales in British Politics, 1868–1922*, 3rd edition, University of Wales Press, 1991, still stands supreme.

Ireland has attracted a vast literature. There are four excellent general histories: F. S. L. Lyons, *Ireland Since the Famine*, revised edition, Fontana, 1973; R. F. Foster, *Modern Ireland, 1600–1972*, Allen Lane, 1988; Paul Bew, *Ireland: The Politics of Enmity: 1789–2006*, Oxford University Press, 2007; and Alvin Jackson, *Ireland, 1798–1998: War, Peace and Beyond*, Wiley-Blackwell, 2010. Alvin Jackson has also written two outstanding general works, *Home Rule: An Irish History, 1800–2000*, Oxford University Press, 2003, and a book seeking to discover why the Scottish Union succeeded while the Irish did not, *The Two Unions: Ireland, Scotland and the Survival of the United Kingdom*,

Oxford University Press, 2012. There are also two modern books of essays of great value: W. E. Vaughan, ed., *A New History of Ireland, vol. VI: Ireland Under the Union, II; 1870–1921*, Clarendon Press, 1996; and Richard Bourke and Ian McBride, eds, *The Princeton History of Modern Ireland*, Princeton University Press, 2016.

Two good general short introductions to Irish history in relation to Britain are Patrick O'Farrell, *Ireland's English Question: Anglo-Irish Relations, 1534–1970*, Batsford, 1971, and Oliver MacDonagh, *Ireland: The Union and its Aftermath*, University College Dublin Press, 2003. Nicholas Mansergh, *The Irish Question 1840–1921*, 3rd edition, Allen & Unwin, 1975, is a penetrating discussion of attitudes towards Ireland. Finally, there is a sparkling book of essays on English and Irish stereotypes by R. F. Foster, *Paddy and Mr Punch: Connections in Irish and English History*, Allen Lane, 1993.

There are two valuable books showing how Ireland was governed during this period. Eunan O'Halpin, *The Decline of the Union: British Government in Ireland, 1892–1920*, Gill & Macmillan, 1987, and Lawrence McBride, *The Greening of Dublin Castle: The Transformation of Bureaucratic and Judicial Personnel in Ireland, 1892–1922*, Catholic University of America Press, 1991.

THE EMPIRE

The empire has attracted a vast literature, much of it distorted by ideological preconceptions. The essays in C. S. Goldman, ed., *The Empire and the Century*, first published in 1905 but reprinted by Routledge/Thoemmes Press in a new edition edited by Ewen Green in 1998, show how it appeared to contemporaries. Two good introductions are Bernard Porter, *The Lion's Share: A History of British Imperialism, 1850 to the Present*, the latest edition of which was published by Routledge in 2020, and Ronald Hyam, *Britain's Imperial Century, 1815–1914: A Study of Empire and Expansion*, Palgrave Macmillan, 2002.

Three volumes of *The Oxford History of the British Empire*, whose general editor is William Roger Louis, provide useful surveys, though they are not exciting to read: *The Nineteenth Century*, edited by Andrew Porter, Oxford University Press, 2001; *The Twentieth Century*, edited by Judith Brown; and *Historiography*, edited by Robin Winks.

Ronald Robinson and John Gallagher with Alice Denny, *Africa and the Victorians: The Official Mind of Imperialism*, Macmillan, 1961, is a classic interpretation, much criticised but never refuted. It should be supplemented by G. N. Uzoigwe, *Britain and the Conquest of Africa: The Age of Salisbury*, University of Michigan Press, 1974. Two magisterial volumes by John

Darwin, *The Empire Project: The Rise and Fall of the British World-System, 1830–1970*, Cambridge University Press, 2009, and *Unfinished Empire: The Global Expansion of Britain*, Allen Lane, 2012, offer a magnificent interpretation. Two older volumes which remain of great value are A. P. Thornton, *The Imperial Idea and its Enemies: A Study in British Power*, Macmillan, 1959, and Max Beloff, *Imperial Sunset: Britain's Liberal Empire, 1897–1921*, Methuen, 1969.

The transformation of empire into Commonwealth is best analysed by Nicholas Mansergh in the first volume of the second edition of *The Commonwealth Experience: The Durham Report to the Anglo-Irish Treaty*, Macmillan, 1982.

Useful interpretative works and books of essays are A. P. Thornton, *For the File on Empire: Essays and Reviews*, Macmillan, 1968; Ronald Hyam, *Understanding the British Empire*, Cambridge University Press, 2010; Bernard Porter, *Empire Ways: Aspects of British Imperialism* and *British Imperial: What the Empire Wasn't*, both published by I. B. Tauris in 2016. Bernard Porter, *Critics of Empire: British Radicals and the Imperial Challenge*, published by I. B. Tauris in 2007, shows that many critics of empire shared the assumptions of the imperialists.

Finally, Alan Sandison, *The Wheel of Empire: A Study of the Imperial Idea in Some Late Nineteenth and Early Twentieth-Century Fiction*, Macmillan, 1967, provides a fascinating account of how the empire was understood by novelists, while Rudyard Kipling's *Kim* is a must for anyone wishing to understand British attitudes towards India.

PARTY HISTORIES

The best general histories of the Conservative Party are John Ramsden, *An Appetite for Power: A History of the Conservative Party since 1830*, Harper-Collins, 1998, and Stuart Ball, *The Conservative Party and British Politics, 1902–1951*, Longman, 1995. Also of value is A. J. Davies, *We, the Nation: The Conservative Party and the Pursuit of Power*, Little, Brown, 1995. The essays in Stuart Ball and Anthony Seldon, eds, *Conservative Century: The Conservative Party since 1900*, Oxford University Press, 1994, cover all aspects of Conservative organisation and policy. Important also are two books by E. H. H. Green, *Ideologies of Conservatism: Conservative Political Ideas in the Twentieth Century*, Oxford University Press, 2004, and *The Crisis of Conservatism: The Politics, Economics and Ideology of the Conservative Party, 1880–1914*, Routledge, 1995. *The Crawford Papers: The Journals of David Lindsay, Twenty-Seventh Earl of Crawford and Tenth Earl of Balcarres, 1871–1940, during the years*

1892 to 1940, edited by John Vincent, Manchester University Press, 1984, are vital for understanding Unionist attitudes during this period. The Earl of Crawford, before succeeding to his title, had been Conservative Chief Whip in the Commons between 1911 and 1913.

The relevant volumes of the *Longman History of the Conservative Party* tend to concentrate on organisation rather than policy. They are Richard Shannon, *The Age of Salisbury 1881–1902: Unionism and Empire*, Longman, 1996, and John Ramsden, *The Age of Balfour and Baldwin, 1902–1940*, Longman, 1978.

On the Liberals, the standard history is David Dutton, *A History of the Liberal Party since 1900*, Palgrave Macmillan, 2013. But the *Liberal Magazine* is a wonderful first-hand source, giving excerpts from contemporary speeches and newspapers and illuminating the whole history of the period as well as the history of the Liberal Party. Two volumes of diaries give the inside flavour of Liberal politics during this period. Trevor Wilson, ed., *The Political Diaries of C. P. Scott, 1911–1928*, Collins, 1970, is very good on feeling amongst radical Liberals during the later period of Liberal government. Scott, editor of the *Manchester Guardian*, as *The Guardian* was then known, was particularly close to Lloyd George and sought to act as his conscience. Edward David has edited, to good effect, the very revealing diaries of a minor minister in the Asquith government, *Inside Asquith's Cabinet: From the Diaries of Charles Hobhouse*, John Murray, 1977.

A massive amount has been written on the Labour Party. Three good general histories are A. J. Davies, *To Build a New Jerusalem: The British Labour Movement from the 1890s to the 1990s*, Michael Joseph, 1992; Martin Pugh, *Speak for Britain! A New History of the Labour Party*, Vintage Digital, 2010; and Andrew Thorpe, *A History of the Labour Party*, Palgrave Macmillan, 2015. There are two valuable edited books of essays commemorating the centenary of the party in 2000, Brian Brivati and Richard Heffernan, eds, *The Labour Party: A Centenary History*, Macmillan, 2000, and Duncan Tanner, Pat Thane and Nick Tiratsoo, eds, *Labour's First Century*, Cambridge University Press, 2000.

A book by a German Social Democrat, which although describing the interwar Labour Party, casts a fascinating light on the ethos of the party: Egon Wertheimer, *Portrait of the Labour Party*, G. P. Putnam's Sons, 1929.

The relevant chapters of Robert McKenzie, *British Political Parties: The Distribution of Power within the Conservative and Labour Parties*, second edition, Heinemann, 1964, still remain of great value. But this book does not deal with the Liberal Party and, to my mind, underestimates the significance of popular pressures in the Conservative Party. Chapters 2 and 3 on 'The

Plutocratic Age' and 'The Challenge of Labour' in Michael Pinto-Duschinsky, *British Political Finance, 1830–1980*, American Enterprise Institute for Public Policy Research, 1981, contain a wealth of detail on the political parties, including the sale of honours.

On the Irish Party, F. S. L. Lyons, *The Irish Parliamentary Party, 1890–1910*, Faber & Faber, 1951, remains the standard work.

BIOGRAPHIES AND AUTOBIOGRAPHIES

Edward VII forbade an official life of Queen Victoria, and there is no really satisfactory biography. The standard work on her political influence is Frank Hardie, *The Political Influence of Queen Victoria, 1861–1901*, Oxford University Press, 1935, to be supplemented by his later *Political Influence of the British Monarchy, 1868–1952*, Batsford, 1970. Arthur Ponsonby's biography of his father, *Henry Ponsonby, Queen Victoria's Private Secretary: His Life from His Letters*, Macmillan, 1942, is also revealing.

There are, by contrast, many lives of Edward VII. The official life is by Sidney Lee, in two volumes of which the second covers the reign. Probably the best modern biography is by Jane Ridley, *Bertie: A Life of Edward VII*, Chatto & Windus, 2012. Other modern biographies are by Philip Magnus, *King Edward the Seventh*, John Murray, 1964; Giles St Aubyn, *Edward VII: Prince and King*, Collins, 1979, of particular value as containing excerpts from the papers of the king's private secretary, Sir Francis, later Lord Knollys; and Simon Heffer, *Power and Place: The Political Consequences of King Edward VII*, Weidenfeld & Nicolson, 1998.

There are three fine biographies of George V, the official one by Harold Nicolson, *King George the Fifth: His Life and Reign* [1952], Pan Books, 1967; Kenneth Rose, *King George V*, Weidenfeld & Nicolson, 1983; and Jane Ridley, *George V: Never a Dull Moment*, Chatto & Windus, 2021, informed by recent scholarship.

Parts of Vernon Bogdanor, *The Monarchy and the Constitution*, Clarendon Press, 1995, are relevant to this period.

A good entry into the voluminous biographical material on politicians is to read essays composed at the time. A. G. Gardiner, a Liberal journalist of the period, wrote three perceptive volumes of essays: *Prophets, Priests and Kings*, Alston Rivers, 1908; *Pillars of Society*, James Nisbet & Co., 1913; and *Portraits and Portents*, Harper & Brothers, 1926.

In 2006, Haus published a series of volumes on *The 20 British Prime Ministers of the 20th Century*, edited by Francis Beckett. Sadly, most are humdrum, but the exception is an excellent biography of *Balfour* by E. H. H. Green.

An earlier volume, *British Prime Ministers in the Twentieth Century, vol. 1: Balfour to Chamberlain*, edited by John P. Mackintosh, Weidenfeld & Nicolson, 1977, is of much greater value, providing perceptive essays on Balfour by Peter Fraser, Campbell-Bannerman by José F. Harris and Cameron Hazlehurst, and Asquith by Cameron Hazlehurst.

Roy Jenkins produces some acute vignettes in his collection of essays on *The Chancellors*, Macmillan, 1998, while R. F. V. Heuston's more substantial chapters in his *Lives of the Lord Chancellors, 1885–1940*, Clarendon Press, 1964, cast light not only on the three Lord Chancellors of the period – Halsbury, Loreburn and Haldane – but on much else also.

Lord Salisbury's official biography was written by his daughter, Lady Gwendolen Cecil. Unfortunately, she never completed the volume dealing with the years after 1895, but Andrew Roberts, *Salisbury: Victorian Titan*, Weidenfeld & Nicolson, 1999, is a masterly account. E. D. Steele, *Lord Salisbury: A Political Biography*, UCL Press, 1999, is also valuable, more perhaps on domestic affairs than on foreign policy. A. L. Kennedy, *Salisbury, 1830–1903: Portrait of a Statesman*, John Murray, 1953, is still worth consulting. There are important essays in Lord Blake and Hugh Cecil, eds, *Salisbury: The Man and his Policies*, Macmillan, 1987.

There are two good biographies of the Duke of Devonshire. The official biography by Bernard Holland, *The Life of Spencer Compton, Eighth Duke of Devonshire*, Longmans, Green & Co., 1911, has been superseded by Patrick Jackson, *The Last of the Whigs: A Political Biography of Lord Hartington, later Eighth Duke of Devonshire (1833–1908)*, Associated University Presses, 1994.

There are numerous biographies of Balfour, none wholly satisfactory. The best to my mind remains that of his niece Blanche E. C. Dugdale in two volumes, *Arthur James Balfour, First Earl of Balfour, 1848–1905*, and *Arthur James Balfour, First Earl of Balfour, 1906–1930*, Hutchinson, 1936, which contain fascinating excerpts from his conversation. Other worthwhile biographies are by Sydney Zebel, *Balfour: A Political Biography*, Cambridge University Press, 1973; Max Egremont, *Balfour: A Life of Arthur James Balfour*, Collins, 1980; Ruddock F. Mackay, *Balfour: Intellectual Statesman*, Oxford University Press, 1985; and R. J. Q. Adams, *Balfour: The Last Grandee*, John Murray, 2007. Denis Judd, *Balfour and the British Empire: A Study in Imperial Evolution, 1874–1932*, Macmillan, 1968, is also useful.

Two specialised studies are Catherine B. Shannon, *Arthur J. Balfour and Ireland, 1874–1922*, Catholic University of American Press, 1988, and Jason Tomes, *Balfour and Foreign Policy: The International Thought of a Conservative Statesman*, Cambridge University Press, 1997.

There are even more biographies of Joseph Chamberlain. The official biography was undertaken by J. L. Garvin, editor of *The Observer*, and continued by the Conservative politician Julian Amery. The relevant volumes of *The Life of Joseph Chamberlain* are J. L. Garvin, vol. 3, *1895–1900: Empire and World Policy*, Macmillan, 1934; Julian Amery, vol. 4, *1901–1903: At the Height of His Power*, Macmillan, 1951; and Julian Amery, vols 5 and 6, *1901–1968: Joseph Chamberlain and the Tariff Reform Campaign*, Macmillan, 1969. The biography is hagiographical but contains an enormous amount of original material and the volumes by Amery are exciting to read. Of other biographies, the best are probably Richard Jay, *Joseph Chamberlain: A Political Study*, Clarendon Press, 1981, and Michael Balfour, *Britain and Joseph Chamberlain*, Allen & Unwin, 1985, interpreting Chamberlain as the first great moderniser of British politics. Peter T. Marsh, *Joseph Chamberlain: Entrepreneur in Politics*, Yale University Press, 1994, draws out the effects of his career in business on his political approach. Peter Fraser, *Joseph Chamberlain: Radicalism and Empire, 1868–1914*, Cassell, 1966, is idiosyncratic but thought-provoking, while Enoch Powell, *Joseph Chamberlain*, Thames & Hudson, 1977, is characteristically eccentric but also characteristically stimulating. Charles W. Boyd, ed., *Mr Chamberlain's Speeches*, Constable, 1914, show what Chamberlain actually said rather than what commentators claimed that he had said.

Lady Victoria Hicks Beach, *Life of Sir Michael Hicks Beach (Earl St Aldwyn)*, Macmillan, 1932, in two volumes, contains a great deal of valuable original material.

There is no really good life of Milner covering this period. The best source is Cecil Headlam, *The Milner Papers, vol. 2, South Africa 1899–1905*, Cassell, 1933.

There are two biographies of Lansdowne, both more valuable for the original material they contain than analysis: Lord Newton, *Lord Lansdowne: A Biography*, Macmillan, 1929, and Simon Kerry, *Lansdowne: The Last Great Whig*, Unicorn, 2017.

The official biography of Austen Chamberlain is by Sir Charles Petrie, *The Life and Letters of the Right Hon. Sir Austen Chamberlain*, in two volumes, Cassell, 1939 and 1940. It contains a good deal of original material but is otherwise unrevealing. David Dutton, *Austen Chamberlain: Gentleman in Politics*, Ross Anderson, 1985, is better but still not quite what is needed. Chamberlain himself wrote reminiscences, *Down the Years*, Cassell, 1935, which contain some biographical scraps about his colleagues, but *Politics from Inside: An Epistolary Chronicle, 1906–1914*, Cassell, 1936, consisting of letters to his stepmother, Joe's third wife, is one of the most revealing sources that we have on Unionist politics during the period.

Sir Charles Petrie also wrote a biography of Austen's rival, *Walter Long and His Times*, Hutchinson, 1936, while Long himself wrote *Memories*, Hutchinson, 1923. Neither are particularly revealing and the best source on Long is a Bristol University PhD thesis completed in 1984, by Richard Murphy, 'Walter Long and the Conservative Party 1905–1912'.

Bonar Law received a great classic biography, never superseded, by Robert Blake, *The Unknown Prime Minister: The Life and Times of Andrew Bonar Law, 1858–1923*, Eyre & Spottiswoode, 1955, which is particularly good on constitutional issues. R. J. Q. Adams, *Bonar Law*, John Murray, 1999, adds little.

There are two modern biographies of Rosebery: Robert Rhodes James, *Rosebery: A Biography of Archibald Philip, Fifth Earl of Rosebery*, Weidenfeld & Nicolson, 1963, shows great insight and is by no means superseded by Leo McKinstry, *Rosebery: Statesman in Turmoil*, John Murray, 2005.

There are also two biographies of Rosebery's rival, Harcourt: the official biography, A. G. Gardiner, *The Life of Sir William Harcourt*, Constable, 1923, and Patrick Jackson, *Harcourt and Son: A Political Biography of Sir William Harcourt, 1827–1904*, Fairleigh Dickinson University Press, 2004; and two biographies of Campbell-Bannerman, who superseded them both, the official biography by J. A. Spender, *The Life of the Right Hon. Sir Henry Campbell-Bannerman, GCB*, Hodder & Stoughton, 1923, and John Wilson, *CB: A Life of Sir Henry Campbell-Bannerman*, Constable, 1973. Having been underestimated for much of his political career, perhaps Campbell-Bannerman is now in danger of being overestimated. The same seems also true of Attlee, the Prime Minister he most resembles.

Of the three major biographies of Asquith, the official one by J. A. Spender and his son, Cyril Asquith, *Life of Herbert Henry Asquith, Lord Oxford and Asquith*, Hutchinson, 1932, is probably the best and is particularly acute on constitutional issues. Roy Jenkins, *Asquith*, Collins, 1964, is a little too adulatory. Stephen Koss, *Asquith*, Allen Lane, 1976, adds some material from modern research. Asquith himself wrote various books of reminiscences in old age when short of cash: *Fifty Years of Parliament*, Cassell, 1926, and *Memories and Reflections*, Cassell, 1928, both in two volumes. He also wrote a book on *The Genesis of the War*, Cassell, 1923. But by far the best source on Asquith for the years after 1912 until the end of his premiership in 1916 are the voluminous letters to his confidante Venetia Stanley in Michael and Eleanor Brock, eds, *H. H. Asquith Letters to Venetia Stanley*, Oxford University Press, 1982. These letters are particularly good on Ulster and on the outbreak of war in 1914.

T. G. Otte's magnificent biography of Grey, *Statesman of Europe: A Life of Sir Edward Grey*, Allen Lane, 2020, is so near to definitive as to make everything else on Grey redundant. But there is still something to be gained from Keith Robbins, *Sir Edward Grey: A Biography of Lord Grey of Fallodon*, Cassell, 1971. The two volumes of Grey's own memoirs, *Twenty-Five Years, 1892–1916*, Hodder & Stoughton, 1925, reveal a man of great integrity striving desperately to preserve the peace.

Of the many biographies of Haldane, Stephen Koss, *Lord Haldane: Scapegoat for Liberalism*, Columbia University Press, 1969, is probably the best. The most recent biography by John Campbell, *Haldane: The Forgotten Statesman Who Shaped Britain and Canada*, Hurst & Co., 2020, is far too hagiographical. The subtitle is absurd in the light of the inadequacies of the army in 1914. Other biographies are Sir Frederick Maurice, *Haldane, 1856–1915: The Life of Viscount Haldane of Cloan*, Faber, 1937, in two volumes, and Dudley Sommer, *Haldane of Cloan: His Life and Times, 1856–1928*, Allen & Unwin, 1960. E. M. Spiers, *Haldane: An Army Reformer*, Edinburgh University Press, 1980, is important. Haldane himself wrote a valuable *Autobiography*, Hodder & Stoughton, 1929.

C. F. G. Masterman: A Biography by his widow Lucy [1939], Frank Cass, 1968, is very revealing on Liberal attitudes before 1914 from the vantage point of a junior minister in the Asquith government.

There are a vast number of biographies of Lloyd George. But none have quite succeeded in capturing that elusive personality. There is a good short biography by Martin Pugh, *Lloyd George*, Longman, 1988. Of longer biographies, probably the best is Bentley B. Gilbert, *David Lloyd George: A Political Life*, vol. 1, *The Architect of Change, 1863–1912*, Batsford, 1987, and vol. 2, *The Organiser of Victory, 1912–1916*, Batsford, 1992. The multi-volume biography by John Grigg, though beautifully written and with much interesting material, is weakened by insufficient understanding of its subject's Welsh background and is too hagiographical. Three volumes deal with this period: *The Young Lloyd George*, Eyre Methuen, 1973; *The People's Champion, 1902–1911*, Eyre Methuen, 1978; and *From Peace to War, 1912–1916*, Eyre Methuen, 1985. Don M. Cregier, *Bounder from Wales: Lloyd George's Career Before the First World War*, University of Missouri Press, 1976, contains much of interest. Peter Rowland, *Lloyd George*, Barrie & Jenkins, 1975, gives the facts but little else. Michael Fry, *Lloyd George and Foreign Policy: The Education of a Statesman, 1890–1916*, McGill-Queen's University Press, 1977, is valuable on a theme perhaps still insufficiently investigated. Lloyd George's own *War Memoirs*, published by Ivor Nicholson & Watson in 1933, are unreliable and should be treated with great caution. Chris Wrigley, *David Lloyd George and the British Labour Movement: Peace and War*, Harvester, 1976, is of great importance.

There are even more biographies of Churchill than of Lloyd George. Two of the best base themselves on the archives: Martin Gilbert, the official biographer, *Churchill: A Life*, Heinemann, 1991, and Norman Rose, *Churchill: An Unruly Life*, Simon & Schuster, 1994. But an even better introduction in some ways is a book based entirely on secondary sources, Roy Jenkins, *Churchill*, Macmillan, 2001. Jenkins is particularly good on Churchill's career before 1914, and he understands as so many biographers do not the practical constraints of political life.

The second volume of the official biography of Churchill, which is in eight volumes, was written by Winston's son, Randolph Churchill, *Young Statesman: Winston S. Churchill 1901–1914*, Heinemann, 1967, and it, together with the three accompanying *Companion* volumes, are a vital source for the period. Paul Addison, *Churchill on the Home Front, 1900–1955*, Jonathan Cape, 1992, is one of the few books to do justice to Churchill's achievements in domestic policy. Robert Rhodes James, *Churchill: A Study in Failure, 1900–1939*, Weidenfeld & Nicolson, 1970, remains of great interest. But the subtitle is misleading. What Rhodes James seeks to do is to show, not that Churchill failed, but why, despite his great abilities, he was so widely distrusted. Rhodes James has also edited the *Complete Speeches, 1897–1963*, in eight volumes, Chelsea House, 1974. Churchill's own autobiography, *My Early Life 1874–1908*, Thornton Butterworth, 1930, sparkles, and the first volume of his book on the First World Year, *The World Crisis, 1911–1918*, Thornton Butterworth, 1923, is full of insights.

The best biography of *Keir Hardie: Radical and Socialist*, is by Kenneth O. Morgan and was published by Weidenfeld & Nicolson in 1975. There is a superb biography of *Ramsay MacDonald* by David Marquand, Jonathan Cape, 1977, which shows that without him, the Labour Party might well not have survived until 1914, let alone replaced the Liberals. Philip Snowden wrote a revealing *Autobiography, vol. 1, 1864–1919*, Ivor Nicholson & Watson, 1934, and there is an efficient biography by Colin Cross, *Philip Snowden*, Barrie & Rockliff, 1966, the best that can be done for a politician who left no papers. Henderson also left no papers. He too has attracted a number of workmanlike biographies, the best of which are probably F. M. Leventhal, *Arthur Henderson*, Manchester University Press, 1989, and Chris Wrigley, *Arthur Henderson*, GPC Books, 1990. But the most acute analysis is undoubtedly R. I. McKibbin, 'Arthur Henderson as Labour Leader', in the *International Review of Social History*, 1978.

There are a number of biographies of John Redmond, the Irish leader. The first, by Denis Gwynn, *The Life of John Redmond*, Harrap, 1932, contains a great deal of original material. Paul Bew, *John Redmond*, Dundalgan

Press, 1996, is a good introduction. Joseph P. Finnan, *John Redmond and Irish Unity, 1912–1918*, Syracuse University Press, 2004, is an important specialised study. The best modern scholarly study is by Dermot Meleady in two volumes, *Redmond the Parnellite*, Cork University Press, 2008, and *John Redmond: The National Leader*, Merrion, 2013. The biography of Redmond's chief lieutenant by F. S. L. Lyons, *John Dillon: A Biography*, Routledge & Kegan Paul, 1968, is also of great value.

Of a number of biographies of Carson, A. T. Q. Stewart, *Edward Carson*, Gill, 1981, is the best introduction. The standard biography, now showing its age, is by H. Montgomery Hyde, *Carson: The Life of Sir Edward Carson, Lord Carson of Duncairn*, Heinemann, 1953.

But by far the most perceptive book on the two opposing leaders is by Alvin Jackson, *Judging Redmond and Carson*, Royal Irish Academy, 2018, showing that the Nationalist and the Unionist had more in common than might be suspected. The book benefits also from magnificent illustrations.

Of non-party people, the autobiography of Lord Beveridge, *Power and Influence*, Hodder & Stoughton, 1953, is surprisingly lively and revealing for someone often regarded as a dry bureaucrat. José Harris, *Beveridge: A Biography*, 2nd edition, Clarendon Press, 1997, is competent but rather dull.

SPECIFIC PERIODS AND TOPICS

The standard account of Unionist policy during the years 1895–1902 is Peter Marsh, *The Discipline of Popular Government: Lord Salisbury's Domestic Statecraft, 1881–1902*, Harvester Press, 1978. Both Robert McKenzie and Allan Silver, *Angels in Marble: Working Class Conservatives in Urban England*, Heinemann, 1968, and Martin Pugh, *The Tories and the People: 1880–1935*, Blackwell, 1985, primarily a history of the Primrose League, are of value for understanding the nature of mass support for the Conservatives. J. A. S. Grenville, *Lord Salisbury and Foreign Policy: The Close of the Nineteenth Century*, Athlone Press, 1970, and Lillian M. Penson, 'The Principles and Methods of Lord Salisbury's Foreign Policy', *Cambridge Historical Journal*, 1935, are standard works on Salisbury's foreign policy.

On wider foreign policy, A. J. P. Taylor, *The Struggle for Mastery in Europe, 1848–1918*, Clarendon Press, 1954, is a classic work, much criticised but never superseded. It is full of epigrammatic sentences to stimulate thought, even if sometimes to disagreement. Sneh Mahajan, *British Foreign Policy 1874–1914: The Role of India*, Routledge, 2002, is good on the significance of India. The first chapter of Michael Howard, *The Continental Commitment: The Dilemma of British Defence Policy in the Era of Two World Wars*, Maurice Temple

Smith, 1972, is a brilliant account of Britain's strategic dilemmas. Gordon Craig, *Germany 1866–1945*, Clarendon Press, 1978, is a standard work, giving the background to German foreign policy, while on Austria, A. J. P. Taylor, *The Habsburg Monarchy, 1809–1918: A History of the Austrian Empire and Austria–Hungary*, Hamish Hamilton, 1948, is a sparkling demolition of its pretensions.

F. R. Bridge and Roger Bullen, *The Great Powers and the European States System, 1814–1914*, 2nd edition, Pearson Longman, 2005, gives a good account of the working of the international system.

On relations with the United States, Kathleen Burk, *The Lion and the Eagle: The Interaction of the British and American Empires 1783–1972*, Bloomsbury, 2018, is a good introduction. T. G. Otte on *The China Question: Great Power Rivalry and British Isolation, 1894–1905*, Oxford University Press, 2007, is definitive, while G. N. Sanderson, *England, Europe and the Upper Nile, 1882–1899: A Study in the Partition of Africa*, Edinburgh University Press, 1965, provides the background to the Fashoda incident.

On the Jameson Raid, Robert Blake's 'The Jameson Raid and "The Missing Telegrams"' in Hugh Lloyd-Jones, Valerie Pearl and Blair Worden, eds, *History and Imagination: Essays in Honour of H. R. Trevor-Roper*, Duckworth, 1981, is the best short guide. Jeffrey Butler, *The Liberal Party and the Jameson Raid*, Clarendon Press, 1968, ranges wider than its title might suggest and is full of insight into the party politics of the time.

Of books on the Boer War, Thomas Pakenham, *The Boer War*, Weidenfeld & Nicolson, 1979, has become the standard account. It is beautifully written but to my mind tends to exonerate the Boers and is too harsh towards Milner and Chamberlain. Of a large number of other books on the war, perhaps the fairest is A. N. Porter, *The Origins of the South African War: Joseph Chamberlain and the Diplomacy of Imperialism, 1895–1899*, Manchester University Press, 1980. Peter Warwick, *Black People and the South African War, 1899–1902*, Cambridge University Press, 1983, analyses an aspect of the war too often forgotten, while S. B. Spies, *Methods of Barbarism? Roberts and Kitchener and Civilians in the Boer Republics, January 1900–May 1902*, Human & Rousseau, 1977, analyses the controversy over the concentration camps. Arthur Davey, *The British Pro-Boers 1877–1902*, Tafelberg, 1978, discusses opponents of the war.

On the Anglo-Japanese Alliances, the standard works are by Ian Nish, *The Anglo-Japanese Alliance: The Diplomacy of Two Island Empires, 1894–1907*, 2nd edition, Bloomsbury, 1985, and *Alliance in Decline: A Study of Anglo-Japanese Relations, 1908–23*, Bloomsbury, 1972.

Liberal problems after 1895 are analysed in Peter Stansky, *Ambitions and*

Strategies: The Struggle for the Leadership of the Liberal Party in the 1890s, Clarendon Press, 1964. H. C. G. Matthew, *The Liberal Imperialists: The Ideas and Politics of a Post-Gladstonian Elite*, Oxford University Press, 1973, analyses primarily organisational matters but gives no explanation of what the Liberal Imperialists were actually trying to do. Liberal views at the time can be discovered in Hilaire Belloc and others, *Essays in Liberalism by Six Oxford Men*, Cassell, 1897; Francis Hirst, Gilbert Murray and J. L. Hammond, *Liberalism and the Empire: Three Essays*, R. B. Johnson, 1900 – available in a 1998 edition by Routledge/Thoemmes Press with an introduction by Peter Cain; and Herbert Samuel, *Liberalism: An Attempt to State the Principles and Proposals of Contemporary Liberalism in England*, Grant Richards, 1902. Further material is available in biographies of the leaders, Rosebery, Harcourt and Campbell-Bannerman.

On the Labour Party during this period, the standard histories remain Henry Pelling, *The Origins of the Labour Party, 1880–1900*, 2nd edition, Clarendon Press, 1965; Frank Bealey and Henry Pelling, *Labour and Politics, 1900–1906: A History of the Labour Representation Committee*, Macmillan, 1958; and Philip P. Poirier, *The Advent of the Labour Party*, George Allen & Unwin, 1958, which covers much the same ground. Henry Pelling, *Popular Politics and Society in Late Victorian Britain*, Macmillan, 1968, is a masterly collection of essays primarily on the relationship between popular attitudes and the Labour Party. There is a truly superb history of the Independent Labour Party by David Howell, *British Workers and the Independent Labour Party, 1888–1906*, Manchester University Press, 1983, and a good account of the Fabians, A. M. McBriar, *Fabian Socialism and English Politics, 1884–1918*, Cambridge University Press, 1962, which torpedoes many of their exaggerated claims.

The first volume of the standard *History of the British Trade Unions* is edited by Hugh Clegg, Alan Fox and A. F. Thompson. It covers the years 1889 to 1910 and was published by Clarendon Press in 1964; the second volume, covering the years 1911 to 1933 is by Clegg alone and was published by Clarendon Press in 1985. Both volumes are crushingly dull. There is a good shorter *History of British Trade Unionism* by Henry Pelling, the latest edition of which was published by Palgrave Macmillan in 1992. Roy Gregory, *The Miners and British Politics, 1906–1914*, Oxford University Press, 1968, shows how and why the miners came to affiliate to the Labour Party. There is an important article by Norman McCord, 'Taff Vale Revisited', in *History*, 1993, while Keith Ewing, *Trade Unions, the Labour Party and the Law*, Edinburgh University Press, 1982, contains a good analysis of the *Osborne* judgment. Osborne's defence of his position is also well worth reading in two short books: *My Case: The Causes and Effects of the Osborne Judgment*, Eveleigh Nash, 1910, and *Sane Trade Unionism*, Collins, 1913. Finally, Robert Currie, *Industrial Politics*, Clarendon Press, 1979, challenges traditional stereotypes by arguing that the trade unions, far from being radical bodies promoting change, were actually rather conservative organisations constraining it. O. Kahn-Freund, 'Labour Law' in Morris Ginsberg, ed., *Law and Opinion in England in the Twentieth Century*, Stevens, 1959, is of fundamental importance for understanding the attitude of trade unions to the state.

On the 1902 Education Act, Neil Daglish, *Education Policy-Making in England and Wales: The Crucible Years, 1895–1911*, Woburn Press, 1996, is the best source, but an older book, G. A. N. Lowndes, *The Silent Social Revolution: An Account of the Expansion of Public Education in England and Wales, 1895–1935*, Oxford University Press, 1937, remains useful. On the sectarian squabbles, G. T. I. Machin, *Politics and the Churches in Great Britain, 1869–1921*, Clarendon Press, 1987, discusses the Church of England, D. W. Bebbington, *The Nonconformist Conscience: Chapel and Politics, 1870–1914*, George Allen & Unwin, 1982, the Nonconformists.

On the national efficiency movement, Bernard Semmel, *Imperialism and Social Reform: English Social-Imperial Thought, 1895–1914*, Allen & Unwin, 1960, and G. R. Searle, *The Quest for National Efficiency: A Study in British Politics and Political Thought, 1899–1914*, Blackwell, 1971, are full of insight.

The standard account of tariff reform is Alan Sykes, *Tariff Reform in British Politics, 1903–1913*, Clarendon Press, 1979. Anthony Howe, *Free Trade and Liberal England, 1846–1946*, Clarendon Press, 1997, explains the tenacious hold of free trade. So does Frank Trentmann, *Free Trade Nation: Commerce, Consumption and Civil Society in Modern Britain*, Oxford University Press, 2008. Alfred Gollin, *Balfour's Burden: Arthur Balfour and Imperial Preference*, Anthony Blond, 1965, glories in Balfour's political skills – skills which in the end turned to dust. Richard A. Rempel, *Unionists Divided: Arthur Balfour, Joseph Chamberlain and the Unionist Free Traders*, David and Charles, 1972, explains why the Unionist free traders failed.

There are two good books on Jewish immigration: John Garrard, *The English and Immigration: A Comparative Study of the Jewish Influx, 1880–1910*, Oxford University Press, 1971, and Bernard Gainer, *The Alien Invasion: The Origins of the Aliens Act of 1905*, Heinemann, 1972.

On the Anglo-French entente, the standard work is George Monger, *The End of Isolation: British Foreign Policy, 1900–1907*, Nelson, 1963. On the convention with Russia, Keith Neilson, *Britain and the Last Tsar: British Policy and Russia, 1894–1917*, Oxford University Press, 1995, is a work of great distinction.

The New Liberalism is discussed by Peter Weiler, *The New Liberalism: Liberal Social Theory in Great Britain, 1889–1914*, Garland, 1982, while Peter Clarke, *Liberals and Social Democrats*, Cambridge University Press, 1978, is a brilliant account of convergence between the two streams of thought. A. K. Russell, *Liberal Landslide: The General Election of 1906*, David and Charles, 1973, analyses the Liberal victory. But a pamphlet by M. Craton and H. W. McCready, 'The Great Liberal Revival, 1903–1906', Hansard Society, 1966, is also very valuable in explaining it.

The two volumes of Peter Rowland, *The Last Liberal Governments – The Promised Land, 1905–1910*, Barrie & Rockliff, 1968, and *Unfinished Business, 1911–1914*, Barrie & Jenkins, 1971 – describe what happened without explaining much. Ian Packer, *Liberal Government and Politics, 1905–15*, Palgrave Macmillan, 2006, is better.

H. G. Wells's novel *The New Machiavelli*, published in 1911, well conveys the political atmosphere of the period.

J. R. Hay, *The Origins of the Liberal Welfare Reforms 1906–1914*, Macmillan, 1975, is a good analytical introduction. But John Cooper, *The British Welfare Revolution, 1906–1914*, Bloomsbury, 2017, is now the best general book on this subject. An older book, Bentley B. Gilbert, *The Evolution of National Insurance in Great Britain: The Origins of the Welfare State*, Michael Joseph, 1966, remains of great value. H. V. Emy, *Liberals, Radicals and Social Politics, 1892–1914*, Cambridge University Press, 1973, is worth reading though the central arguments are not always clear. Two of the essays in David Gladstone, ed., *Before Beveridge: Welfare Before the Welfare State*, Institute of Economic Affairs, 1999 – by José Harris, on political thought and the welfare state, and Noel Whiteside, on the Lloyd George health insurance scheme – are important. On pensions, the best account is Pat Thane, *Old Age in English History: Past Experiences, Present Issues*, Oxford University Press, 2000. José Harris, *Unemployment and Politics: A Study in English Social Policy, 1886–1914*, Clarendon Press, 1972, explains Unionist and Liberal approaches. A bird's eye view by a civil servant, W. J. Braithwaite, *Lloyd George's Ambulance Wagon: Being the Memoirs of William J. Braithwaite*, Methuen, 1957, casts light not only on health insurance but also on Lloyd George's methods, some of them not very admirable.

Bruce K. Murray, *The People's Budget 1909/10: Lloyd George and Liberal Politics*, Clarendon Press, 1980, is a standard account of the Budget controversy. A much older book, Roy Jenkins, *Mr Balfour's Poodle: An Account of the Struggle between the House of Lords and the Government of Mr Asquith*, Heinemann, 1954, provides a solid and lively account of the crisis. Neal Blewett, *The Peers, the Parties and the People: The General Elections of 1910*,

Macmillan, 1972, looks at the crisis in a wider electoral context. There are two valuable contemporary articles on the significance of the 1910 elections: S. Rosenbaum, 'The General Election of January 1910, and the Bearing of the Results on Some Problems of Representation', *Journal of the Royal Statistical Society*, May 1910, and J. A. Hobson, 'The General Election: A Sociological Interpretation', *Sociological Review*, 1910.

David Dutton, *'His Majesty's Loyal Opposition': The Unionist Party in Opposition, 1905–1915*, Liverpool University Press, 1992, gives a workmanlike account of the Unionists during this period. Gregory D. Phillips, *The Diehards: Aristocratic Society and Politics in Edwardian England*, Harvard University Press, 1979, shows that the backwoodsmen were less irrational than is often thought.

The collection of essays edited by K. D. Brown, *The First Labour Party 1906–1914*, Croom Helm, 1985, show how feeble the Labour Party was in these years and how lucky it was to survive at all. But an alternative view is given in Ross McKibbin, *The Evolution of the Labour Party, 1910–1924*, Oxford University Press, 1974.

John D. Fair, *British Interparty Conferences: A Study of the Procedure of Conciliation in British Politics, 1867–1921*, Clarendon Press, 1980, handles a neglected subject with great skill. It is particularly important on the Constitutional Conference of 1910. Robert J. Scally, *The Origins of the Lloyd George Coalition: The Politics of Social-Imperialism, 1900–1918*, Princeton University Press, 1975, argues that Lloyd George's coalition proposals of 1910 prefigure his coalition government of 1916–22, though he presses his argument rather too hard.

On labour unrest, the chapter by Henry Pelling, 'The Labour Unrest, 1911–14', in his *Popular Politics and Society in Late Victorian Britain*, Macmillan, 1968, is a good introduction, dispelling many myths. George Askwith, *Industrial Problems and Disputes*, John Murray, 1920, gives the view of the government's chief industrial arbitrator.

On the suffragettes, the best introduction is Constance Rover, *Women's Suffrage and Party Politics in Britain, 1866–1914*, Routledge & Kegan Paul, 1967. The best modern analysis is in Sandra Holton, *Feminism and Democracy: Women's Suffrage and Reform Politics in Britain, 1900–1918*, Cambridge University Press, 1986. Martin Pugh, *The March of the Women: A Revisionist Analysis of the Campaign for Women's Suffrage, 1866–1914*, Oxford University Press, 2000, is important. Leslie Parker Hume, *The National Union of Women's Suffrage Societies 1897–1914*, Garland, 1982, and Andrew Rosen, *Rise Up, Women! The Militant Campaign of the Women's Social and Political Union, 1903–1914*, Routledge & Kegan Paul, 1974, analyse the two leading movements campaigning for the vote. Brian Harrison, *Separate Spheres: The Opposition to Women's Suffrage in Britain*, Croom Helm, 1978, discusses the opponents. David Morgan, *Suffragists and Liberals: The Politics of Woman Suffrage in England*, Basil Blackwell, 1975, analyses the problems which the suffragettes created for the Liberal government. The autobiography of Millicent Garrett Fawcett, *What I Remember*, G. P. Putnam's Sons, 1925, conveys the atmosphere of the moderate side of the campaign.

On the issue of the land, Ian Packer, *Lloyd George, Liberalism and the Land: The Land Issue and Party Politics in England, 1906–1914*, Boydell Press, 2001, is a good introduction. But Avner Offer, *Property and Politics 1870–1914: Landownership, Law, Ideology and Urban Development in England*, Cambridge University Press, 1981, is a brilliant interpretation.

Frances Donaldson, *The Marconi Scandal*, Rupert Hart-Davis, 1962, reveals a great deal on the politics of the period.

On Ireland, Ronan Fanning, *Fatal Path: British Government and Irish Revolution, 1910–1922*, Faber, 2013, is the most recent analysis. Nicholas Mansergh, *The Unresolved Question: The Anglo-Irish Settlement and its Undoing, 1912–1972*, Yale University Press, 1991, is a profound examination of the issues. Paul Bew, *Ideology and the Irish Question: Ulster Unionism and Irish Nationalism, 1912–1916*, Clarendon Press, 1994, analyses the ideological background.

Patricia Jalland, *The Liberals and Ireland: The Ulster Question in British Politics to 1914*, Harvester Press, 1980, is highly critical of Asquith. The conference papers in Gabriel Doherty, ed., *The Home Rule Crisis 1912–14*, Mercier Press, 2014, cast the light of modern scholarship on the crisis. James Doherty in *Irish Liberty, British Democracy: The Third Home Rule Crisis, 1909–14*, Cork University Press, 2019, argues, implausibly in my view, that there was considerable grassroots Liberal support for Home Rule.

A great deal has been written on the Ulster Unionists. A. T. Q. Stewart, *The Ulster Crisis: Resistance to Home Rule*, Faber, 1967, provides a narrative. The second volume of Patrick Buckland, *Irish Unionism: Ulster Unionism and the Origins of Northern Ireland, 1886–1922*, Gill and Macmillan, 1973, describes Unionist attitudes. Alvin Jackson, *The Ulster Party: Irish Unionists in the House of Commons, 1884–1911*, Clarendon Press, 1989, analyses Unionist parliamentary activities. A. T. Q. Stewart, *The Narrow Ground: Roots of Conflict in Ulster, 1609–1909*, Faber, 1977, and David W. Miller, *Queen's Rebels: Ulster Loyalism in Historical Perspective*, University College of Dublin Press, 1978, analyse in considerable depth the background to Ulster Unionism.

The Curragh crisis is examined by James Fergusson, *The Curragh Incident*, Faber, 1964, and Ian F. W. Beckett, *The Army and the Curragh Incident*, Bodley Head, 1986.

Partition is analysed in Denis Gwynn, *The History of Partition, 1912–1925*,

Browne and Nolan, 1950, and Michael Laffan, *The Partition of Ireland, 1911–1925*, Dublin Historical Association, 1983.

Cameron Hazlehurst, *Politicians at War, July 1914 to May 1915*, Jonathan Cape, 1971, seeks to make sense of Liberal manoeuvrings on the eve of war.

On pre-war foreign policy, Samuel R. Williamson Jr, *The Politics of Grand Strategy: Britain and France Prepare for War, 1904–1914*, Harvard University Press, 1969, remains the best general account. F. H. Hinsley, ed., *British Foreign Policy under Sir Edward Grey*, Cambridge University Press, 1977, is also important. Chapter 4 of A. J. P. Taylor, *The Trouble Makers: Dissent over Foreign Policy, 1792–1939*, Hamish Hamilton, 1957, on the radical dissenters, sparkles.

On the annexation of Bosnia, Bernadotte E. Schmitt, *The Annexation of Bosnia, 1908–1909*, Cambridge University Press, 1937, remains the standard work, as does E. C. Helmreich, *The Diplomacy of the Balkan Wars, 1912–13*, Harvard University Press, 1938. R. J. Crampton, *The Hollow Detente: Anglo-German Relations in the Balkans, 1911–14*, Prior, 1979, shows why cooperation between the two powers broke down.

There is, of course, a massive literature on the origins of the First World War. The background is admirably analysed in Paul Kennedy, *The Rise of Anglo-German Antagonism, 1860–1914*, Allen & Unwin, 1980. The first chapters of Hew Strachan, *The First World War: Volume 1, To Arms*, Oxford University Press, 2001, present the clearest narrative of what led to war. Zara Steiner and Keith Neilson, *Britain and the Origins of the First World War*, Palgrave Macmillan, 2003, analyse British policy.

The essays in R. J. W. Evans and H. Pogge von Strandmann, eds, *The Coming of the First World War*, Clarendon Press, 1988, analyse origins from the point of view of the various countries involved. John Zametica, *Folly and Malice: The Habsburg Empire, the Balkans and the Start of World War One*, Shepheard-Walwyn, 2017, highlights the Serb point of view.

Of general books, Christopher Clark, *The Sleepwalkers: How Europe Went to War in 1914*, Allen Lane, 2012, has been very influential. Its analysis reflects a view of the war first put forward by Lloyd George in his *War Memoirs*. As I argue in this book, I believe this interpretation to be radically mistaken.

By far the best book on the origins of the war, in my view, is T. G. Otte, *July Crisis: The World's Descent into War, Summer 1914*, Cambridge University Press, 2014, even though it seems to me too kind to the Germans, particularly Bethmann Hollweg, and too harsh to the Serbs.

After the war, an American historian, Bernadotte E. Schmitt, interviewed many of those in leading positions in 1914, including Grey. The fascinating results are to be found in *Interviewing the Authors of the War*, Chicago Literary Club, 1930.

ACKNOWLEDGEMENTS

Earlier drafts of this book have been scrutinised to its immense benefit by a number of kind friends and colleagues – Richard Aldous, William Beinart, Paul Bew, Nigel Biggar, Robert Blackburn, Gareth Cadwallader, John Carolan, John Cooper, Andrew Gailey, Alvin Jackson, Harshan Kumarasingham, Malcolm Murfett, Nancy Neville, Nick Owen, Clare Robertson, Anthony Teasdale, Pat Thane and Noel Whiteside. I owe a particular debt to my friend Tom Otte, doyen of diplomatic historians, who, as well as reading the whole text with great care, has encouraged and inspired me at every stage. I am grateful also to Paul Bogdanor for his comments and Hew Strachan for wise advice. All have saved me from errors and misinterpretations. But I have not always followed their advice, and any mistakes that remain are entirely my responsibility.

I am grateful also to the incomparable London Library without which this book could not have been written.

I am also deeply grateful to Ella Boardman of Biteback for scrutinising an earlier draft with meticulous care. She has saved me from many mistakes. And also to Olivia Beattie, my co-editor, for much good advice. I should also like to thank Martin Brown for providing the maps.

But my greatest debt is to Sonia, my wife, who has read the whole book in draft, and not only provided many valuable comments but encouraged and sustained me throughout. It is to her that this book is dedicated.

INDEX